# Health Care Facilities Handbook

## SIXTH EDITION

### EDITED BY

### Thomas W. Gardner, P.E.

With the complete text of the 1999 edition of NFPA 99,
*Standard for Health Care Facilities*

**National Fire Protection Association**
**Quincy, Massachusetts**

Product Manager: Pam Powell
Project Editor: Mary Strother
Text Processing: Louise Grant
Composition: Modern Graphics
Art Coordinator: Nancy Maria
Illustrations: Todd K. Bowman and George Nichols
Cover Design: Groppi Advertising Design
Manufacturing Buyer: Ellen Glisker
Printer: R. R. Donnelley

**Notice Concerning Liability:** Publication of this handbook is for the purpose of circulating information and opinion among those concerned for fire and electrical safety and related subjects. While every effort has been made to achieve a work of high quality, neither the NFPA nor the contributors to this handbook guarantee the accuracy or completeness of or assume any liability in connection with the information and opinions contained in this handbook. The NFPA and the contributors shall in no event be liable for any personal injury, property, or other damages of any nature whatsoever, whether special, indirect, consequential, or compensatory, directly or indirectly resulting from the publication, use of, or reliance upon this handbook. This handbook is published with the understanding that the NFPA and the contributors to this handbook are supplying information and opinion but are not attempting to render engineering or other professional services. If such services are required, the assistance of an appropriate professional should be sought.

**Notice Concerning Code Interpretations:** This sixth edition of the *Health Care Facilities Handbook* is based on the 1999 edition of NFPA 99, *Standard for Health Care Facilities*. All NFPA codes, standards, recommended practices, and guides are developed in accordance with the published procedures of the NFPA technical committees comprised of volunteers drawn from a broad array of relevant interests. The handbook contains the complete text of NFPA 99 and any applicable Formal Interpretations issued by the Association. These documents are accompanied by explanatory commentary and other supplementary materials.
The commentary and supplementary materials in this handbook are not a part of the Standard and do not constitute Formal Interpretations of the NFPA (which can be obtained only through requests processed by the responsible technical committees in accordance with the published procedures of the NFPA). The commentary and supplementary materials, therefore, solely reflect the personal opinions of the editor or other contributors and do not necessarily represent the official position of the NFPA or its technical committees.

NFPA No.: 99HB99
ISBN: 0-87765-442-5
Library of Congress Card Catalog No.: 99-074079

Printed in the United States of America
03     02     01                5     4     3

# Contents

# Foreword

NFPA 99, *Standard for Health Care Facilities*, is the result of integrating twelve documents developed by the Health Care Facilities Correlating Committee (formerly the Committee on Hospitals) over a period of 40 years. However, it is not the only document applicable to health care facilities; there are some 50 other NFPA documents that either address, in whole or in part, health care facilities or can be used by them.

In categorizing fire protection for health care facilities, two general divisions can be identified.

**Facility Fire Protection Features.** Those features built into or around a structure to minimize hazards, such as hydrants, types of structural protection, length of exit travel distances, and detection and extinguishing systems. They generally do not require human intervention to provide safety.

**Operational Fire Protection.** Those practices intended to minimize fire hazards once the health care facility is occupied, such as safe use of inhalation anesthetics, safe use of electricity, safe practices in laboratories, emergency electrical power, and emergency planning. These definitely rely on human intervention.

Some items (such as portable extinguishers, manual pull stations, and performance criteria for grounding systems), of course, could fit into both divisions. Generally, NFPA 99 is concerned with operational fire protection for the many activities occurring in hospitals, ambulatory health care centers, clinics, medical and dental offices, nursing homes, and limited care facilities. This includes provisions for patient care areas (e.g., wards, intensive care units, operating suites, hyperbaric and hypobaric facilities), certain laboratories, several facilitywide systems, and overall emergency planning for a facility in the event of an emergency (fire or otherwise) that interrupts the delivery of patient care.

The effort to combine these twelve health care facility documents began in late 1979 at the suggestion of Marvin J. Fischer, then Chairman of the Health Care Facilities Correlating Committee and Vice-President for Facilities Planning and Engineering Services, Brookdale Hospital Medical Center, Brooklyn, New York. It was his firm belief that combining these individual documents into one cohesive document would benefit health care personnel and patients, as well as designers, builders, and enforcing authorities. The correlating committee agreed, but to assure itself that those affected by the change concurred, it solicited comments on the idea in 1981. With overwhelming support, the committee proceeded with the first step: publication of a compilation of the latest editions of each of the documents into one bound volume in January 1982. This compilation was designated NFPA 99, *Health Care Facilities Code*.

The 1984 edition of NFPA 99 was the next step in the process: integration of the previous individual documents into one new document following the NFPA Manual of Style (all definitions in one chapter; requirements in the main body of the text; recommendations in the appendixes). The 1987 edition of NFPA 99 completed this integration process by restructuring text into a form that placed nonfacility-specific requirements in one portion and facility-specific requirements into another portion. (See Section 1-6 in Chapter 1 for details.) The creation of a handbook on NFPA 99 was a natural extension of the document once the combining process started. With so much material in one document, assistance, in the form of commentary, seemed the best method for sharing some of the history of this material as well as providing additional information and guidance in applying the standard to present conditions.

Codes and standards by themselves can be difficult to understand for those not involved in their development; however, it is not practical to include everything involving the requirements that have been adopted (e.g., the reasons behind requirements, the pros and cons, the voting, the striving for consensus, the research, the discussion). Appendix material can help. Of late, rationales are being stressed. Handbooks present another vehicle for helping readers to better understand the requirements and recommendations of a document.

It is the hope of the editor that this sixth edition of the *Health Care Facilities Handbook* continues to add to the resources on health care fire safety and is another useful adjunct for all those involved in protecting health care facilities from fire and associated hazards.

# About the Editor

Thomas W. Gardner, P.E., is currently principal in charge of the Atlanta area office of the consulting firm of Gage-Babcock & Associates, Inc., where his specialties include life safety analysis, code consultation, fire resistance, fire modeling, JCAHO Statements of Condition, and system design. He has designed automatic sprinkler, standpipe, fire pump, foam fire protection, clean agent fire protection, and fire detection/alarm systems. Mr. Gardner has been employed at Gage-Babcock & Associates since 1989.

One of his primary functions is staff consultant representing the American Health Care Association. In that capacity, he provides on-call fire protection consulting to AHCA members, investigates fire losses, and represents AHCA in all fire protection matters involving the NFPA and the model code organizations.

In addition to his work in health care fire safety, Mr. Gardner has been project manager/engineer for fire protection and life safety projects for a variety of public and private clients ranging from high-rise hotels and office buildings, waste water treatment plants, the National Archives II building, the VAMC Des Moines, the National Defense University (home of the National War College), and the U.S. Capitol complex. Prior to joining Gage-Babcock & Associates, he was with the U.S. Fire Administration and Grinnell Fire Protection Systems.

He is a member of the National Fire Protection Association's Technical Correlating Committee on Health Care Facilities and of the Technical Committee on Board and Care Facilities of the *Life Safety Code*. Mr. Gardner serves on the Executive Board of the NFPA Health Care Section (HCS), is vice chair of the HCS Codes and Standards Review Committee, and chair of the HCS Outreach Committee.

Mr. Gardner received his B.S. in general science from Fordham University in 1980 before earning a B.S. in fire protection engineering from the University of Maryland in 1986. He is a registered professional engineer in Maryland, Ohio, and Virginia. He is a full member in the Society of Fire Protection Engineers (SFPE), chairperson of their Engineering Education Committee, and past president of the SFPE Chesapeake chapter.

In 1975, he joined the volunteer fire service and has been a member of three fire departments. Mr. Gardner was a volunteer fire marshal in Hyattsville, MD, and is a former captain and member of the Manassas (VA) Volunteer Fire Company.

Mr. Gardner has lectured on health care fire safety at NFPA meetings, AHCA conventions, the Tennessee Health Care Association, and the New Hampshire Health Care Association. He has authored journal articles for *Fire Technology, Consulting Specifying Engineer, Provider,* and *Facility Care.*

# Acknowledgments

This handbook, the sixth edition and the first by this editor, is the result of substantial contributions by many talented and committed people. I am grateful to many colleagues who provided support and assistance. I am particularly indebted to Richard P. Bielen, chief systems and applications engineer at NFPA, who served as interim staff liaison to the Technical Committee on Health Care Facilities while this book was being prepared. Rich reviewed the entire manuscript, offering valuable comments and suggestions. The earlier work of Burton R. Klein, my predecessor as editor, is also gratefully acknowledged.

A number of experts from the field of health care facilities fire safety participated in preparing commentary. These valued members of the technical team included the following people:

Mark Allen, Beacon Medical Products, Charlotte, NC

David Brittain, Provac, Massillon, OH

Daniel Chisholm, Motor and Generator Institute, Winter Park, FL

Dale Dumbleton, American Medical Gas Institute, Metairie, LA

Douglas Erickson, Advanced Technologies Group, Inc., Lombard, IL

Peter Esherick, Patient Instrumentation Corporation, Schencksville, PA

Dr. Gerald Hoeltge, Cleveland Clinic Foundation, Cleveland, OH

Burton R. Klein, Burton R. Klein Associates, Newtonville, MA

David Mohile, Medical Engineering Services, Inc., Leesburg, VA

Hugh O. Nash, Jr., Nash Lipsey Burch LLC, Nashville, TN

Russell Phillips, Russell Phillips & Associates, Inc., Rochester, NY

Robert Solomon, National Fire Protection Association, Quincy, MA

Wilbur T. "Tom" Workman, Workman Hyperbaric Services, San Antonio, TX

A number of NFPA staff members were key to the production of this handbook. These include project editor Mary Strother, compositor Louise Grant, and art coordinator Nancy Maria. Craig Kampmier who joined the NFPA staff as senior fire protection specialist–health care towards the end of the handbook development process was involved from his first week on the job. The Editor is most grateful to product manager Pam Powell for her assistance, knowledge, perseverance, and friendship that kept this project on track.

The Editor is grateful to Rob Swift who provided his photography expertise and equipment to enhance the text with graphics. Prince William Health Systems and specifically George Siebert, safety director, assisted by providing access to their hospital where a number of photographs were taken.

The Editor is also grateful to Gage-Babcock & Associates, Inc., for the confidence and encouragement in my career and this project.

I must mention two others who operated behind the scenes. My brother, Dr. Allen R. Gardner, assisted me on numerous occasions when I needed to understand more about the medical procedures/equipment discussed in the standard allowing me to better describe the intended fire protection. And, of course, my wife Laura who supported me in this effort from the beginning.

Thomas W. Gardner

# PART 1

# NFPA 99, *Health Care Facilities,* and Commentary

Part 1 of this handbook includes the complete text and illustrations of the 1999 edition of NFPA 99, *Standard for Health Care Facilities.* The text and illustrations from the standard are printed in black, and they are the official requirements of NFPA 99. Line drawings and photographs from the standard are labeled "Figures."

Paragraphs that begin with the letter *A* are extracted from Appendix A of the standard. Although printed in black ink, this nonmandatory material is purely explanatory in nature. For ease of use, Appendix A material immediately follows the text paragraph to which it refers in this handbook.

Part 1 also includes Formal Interpretations on NFPA 99. These apply to previous and subsequent editions for which the requirements remain substantially unchanged. Formal Interpretations are not part of the official standard and are printed in shaded gray boxes.

In addition to standard text, appendixes, and Formal Interpretations, Part 1 includes commentary that provides the history and other background information for specific paragraphs in the standard. This insightful commentary takes the reader behind the scenes, into the reasons underlying the requirements. The commentary also guides the reader through the complex history of NFPA 99 and the twelve other NFPA standards that became part of it over the course of 40 years.

To readily identify commentary material, commentary text, captions, and tables are all printed in blue. So that the reader can easily distinguish between required illustrations from the standard and illustrations for the commentary, line drawings and photographs in the commentary are labeled "Exhibits." The distinction between figures in the standard and exhibits in the commentary is new for the sixth edition of the *Health Care Facilities Handbook.*

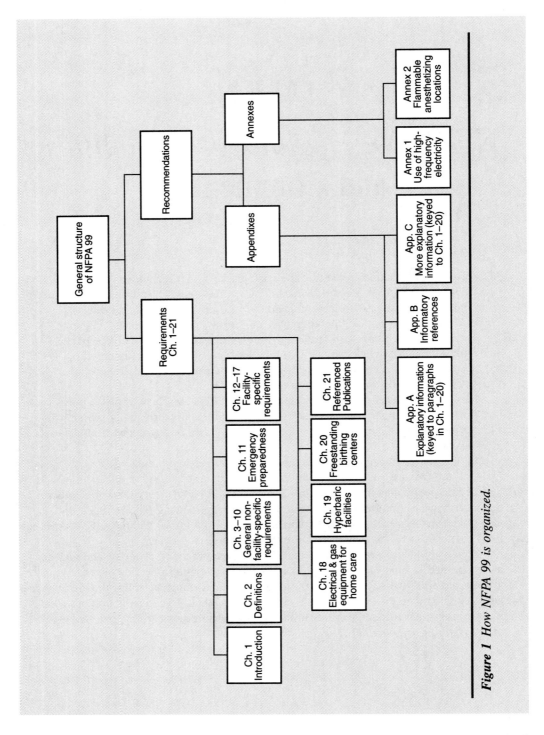

**Figure 1** *How NFPA 99 is organized.*

For the first time, this handbook also includes supplements. Part 2 is devoted to supplements, which explore, in more detail than the commentary, the background of four selected topics related to NFPA 99.

NFPA 99 is the result of integrating twelve documents develcped by the Health Care Facilities Correlating Committee (and its predecessor, the Committee on Hospitals) over a period of more than 40 years. The effort to combine those other documents into a stand-alone code began in 1979 at the suggestion of Marvin J. Fischer, who then chaired the Health Care Facilities Correlating Committee. The correlating committee solicited input and found overwhelming support for the idea of creating one cohesive document.

The first step, taken in 1982, was to compile the latest editions of relevant documents into one bound volume, designated as NFPA 99, *Health Care Facilities Code*. The 1984 edition integrated the individual documents into one new document that followed the *NFPA Manual of Style* (e.g., all definitions in one chapter, requirements in the main body of the text, and recommendations in appendixes). By the 1987 edition, restructured text placed nonfacility-specific requirements in one portion and facility-specific requirements in another portion. This restructuring completed the integration process.

In addition to NFPA 99, some fifty other NFPA documents address the fire safety needs of heath care facilities.

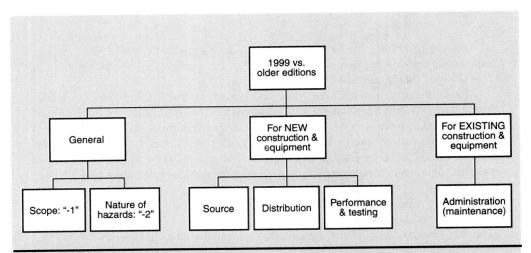

**Figure 2** *Existing vs. new requirements in Chapters 3 through 11 of NFPA 99-1999.*

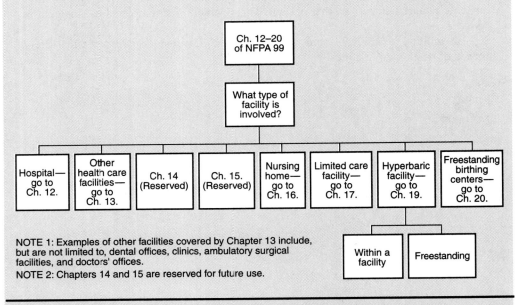

NOTE 1: Examples of other facilities covered by Chapter 13 include, but are not limited to, dental offices, clinics, ambulatory surgical facilities, and doctors' offices.
NOTE 2: Chapters 14 and 15 are reserved for future use.

**Figure 3** *Finding a requirement in a health care facility.*

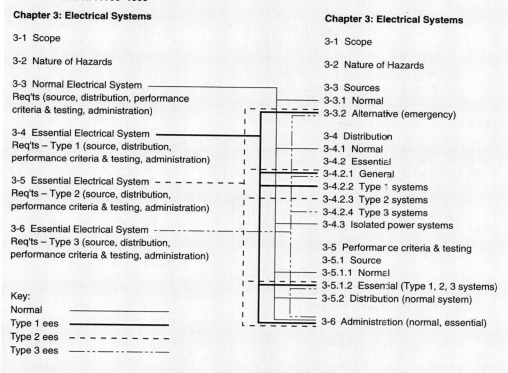

**Relocation of Requirements in Chapter 3**

**NFPA 99–1996 and NFPA 99–1999**

**Chapter 3: Electrical Systems**

3-1  Scope

3-2  Nature of Hazards

3-3  Normal Electrical System Req'ts (source, distribution, performance criteria & testing, administration)

3-4  Essential Electrical System Req'ts – Type 1 (source, distribution, performance criteria & testing, administration)

3-5  Essential Electrical System Req'ts – Type 2 (source, distribution, performance criteria & testing, administration)

3-6  Essential Electrical System Req'ts – Type 3 (source, distribution, performance criteria & testing, administration)

Key:
Normal
Type 1 ees
Type 2 ees
Type 3 ees

**NFPA 99–1993**

**Chapter 3: Electrical Systems**

3-1  Scope

3-2  Nature of Hazards

3-3  Sources
3-3.1  Normal
3-3.2  Alternative (emergency)

3-4  Distribution
3-4.1  Normal
3-4.2  Essential
3-4.2.1  General
3-4.2.2  Type 1 systems
3-4.2.3  Type 2 systems
3-4.2.4  Type 3 systems
3-4.3  Isolated power systems

3-5  Performance criteria & testing
3-5.1  Source
3-5.1.1  Normal
3-5.1.2  Essential (Type 1, 2, 3 systems)
3-5.2  Distribution (normal system)

3-6  Administration (normal, essential)

**Figure 4** *Relocation of requirements in Chapter 3.*

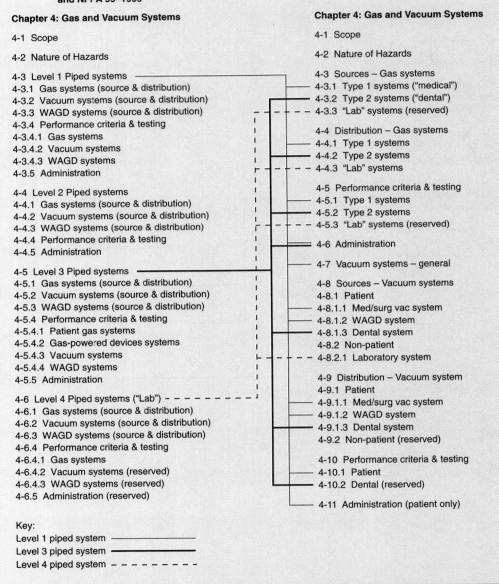

**Relocation of Requirements in Chapter 4**

| NFPA 99–1996 and NFPA 99–1999 | NFPA 99–1993 |
|---|---|
| **Chapter 4: Gas and Vacuum Systems** | **Chapter 4: Gas and Vacuum Systems** |

NFPA 99–1996
and NFPA 99–1999

**Chapter 4: Gas and Vacuum Systems**

4-1 Scope

4-2 Nature of Hazards

4-3 Level 1 Piped systems
4-3.1 Gas systems (source & distribution)
4-3.2 Vacuum systems (source & distribution)
4-3.3 WAGD systems (source & distribution)
4-3.4 Performance criteria & testing
4-3.4.1 Gas systems
4-3.4.2 Vacuum systems
4-3.4.3 WAGD systems
4-3.5 Administration

4-4 Level 2 Piped systems
4-4.1 Gas systems (source & distribution)
4-4.2 Vacuum systems (source & distribution)
4-4.3 WAGD systems (source & distribution)
4-4.4 Performance criteria & testing
4-4.5 Administration

4-5 Level 3 Piped systems
4-5.1 Gas systems (source & distribution)
4-5.2 Vacuum systems (source & distribution)
4-5.3 WAGD systems (source & distribution)
4-5.4 Performance criteria & testing
4-5.4.1 Patient gas systems
4-5.4.2 Gas-powered devices systems
4-5.4.3 Vacuum systems
4-5.4.4 WAGD systems
4-5.5 Administration

4-6 Level 4 Piped systems ("Lab")
4-6.1 Gas systems (source & distribution)
4-6.2 Vacuum systems (source & distribution)
4-6.3 WAGD systems (source & distribution)
4-6.4 Performance criteria & testing
4-6.4.1 Gas systems
4-6.4.2 Vacuum systems (reserved)
4-6.4.3 WAGD systems (reserved)
4-6.5 Administration (reserved)

NFPA 99–1993

**Chapter 4: Gas and Vacuum Systems**

4-1 Scope

4-2 Nature of Hazards

4-3 Sources – Gas systems
4-3.1 Type 1 systems ("medical")
4-3.2 Type 2 systems ("dental")
4-3.3 "Lab" systems (reserved)

4-4 Distribution – Gas systems
4-4.1 Type 1 systems
4-4.2 Type 2 systems
4-4.3 "Lab" systems

4-5 Performance criteria & testing
4-5.1 Type 1 systems
4-5.2 Type 2 systems
4-5.3 "Lab" systems (reserved)

4-6 Administration

4-7 Vacuum systems – general

4-8 Sources – Vacuum systems
4-8.1 Patient
4-8.1.1 Med/surg vac system
4-8.1.2 WAGD system
4-8.1.3 Dental system
4-8.2 Non-patient
4-8.2.1 Laboratory system

4-9 Distribution – Vacuum system
4-9.1 Patient
4-9.1.1 Med/surg vac system
4-9.1.2 WAGD system
4-9.1.3 Dental system
4-9.2 Non-patient (reserved)

4-10 Performance criteria & testing
4-10.1 Patient
4-10.2 Dental (reserved)

4-11 Administration (patient only)

Key:
Level 1 piped system ──────────
Level 3 piped system ━━━━━━━
Level 4 piped system – – – – – – – –

*Figure 5* *Relocation of requirements in Chapter 4.*

# CHAPTER 1

# Introduction

*Overview.* The following commentary provides the reader with a general background of NFPA 99 that reviews the physical organization of this NFPA 99 document, what former documents contributed to it, and how it came to be the standard it is today. It is important to review this history before detailing the specifics of Chapter 1. Users of NFPA 99 who know and understand this general background will find that their ability to apply, interpret, and review the standard is greatly increased.

*Extracted Text.* "Extracted text," identified by a dagger (†), is text from another NFPA document. Chapter 3 includes commentary on the development of the scope of Article 517 of NFPA 70, *National Electrical Code®*. That article includes much of the text from NFPA 76A, *Standard on Essential Electrical Systems*, which is now part of Chapter 3 of NFPA 99. (NFPA 76A no longer exists as an individual document.) The Health Care Facilities technical committees are responsible for establishing the criteria for performance, maintenance, and testing of, among other things, electrical systems and electrical appliances. Panel 17 of the *National Electrical Code* Committee, responsible for Article 517 of NFPA 70, establishes the requirements for electrical construction and installation requirements based on such performance criteria.

*Use of the Term Reserved.* The use of the term *reserved* in NFPA 99 does not indicate either the omission or imminent inclusion of text. Reserved sections were created in 1985, when a Subcommittee on Restructuring was analyzing ways of organizing the material included in NFPA 99–1984. The subcommittee chose to establish a matrix of function versus location. When this method was put into practice in 1987, the text of NFPA 99–1984 was rearranged to fit the new matrix. As this was done, some of the boxes in the matrix were found to have no text. The subcommittee then decided to retain the empty boxes so that the form of the new structure could be seen and that the numbering between chapters would be consistent. New text for these boxes may be added whenever the committee responsible for that material feels text is warranted or when public proposals recommending text are received. In either instance, all proposals for new text have to go through the full NFPA adoption procedures before being incorporated.

*Delineation Between New vs. Existing.* Chapters 3 through 10 are all similarly structured, with a delineation between requirements for new facilities and equipment and requirements for existing facilities and equipment. Each of these chapters has one section for each system discussed that includes the following:

1. Scope
2. Nature of hazards
3. Source requirements
4. Distribution requirements
5. Performance criteria and testing requirements
6. Administration requirements

Sections 3 through 5 of these requirements apply to new facilities and equipment. Section 6 applies to existing facilities and equipment.

*Integration of Individual Health Care Facility Requirements.* Combining twelve individual health care facilities documents has been an evolving process. As individually developed documents, all covered some aspect of health care fire safety. However, these individual documents did not readily translate into one integrated standard. The 1987 edition of NFPA 99 integrated all previous documents and created a structure that was intended to meet current and future needs. Although the 1990 and 1993 editions included technical changes, the basic structure of the document was not disturbed.

The 1996 edition made some significant changes to the structures of Chapters 3 and 4, although the overall structure established in 1987 remained undisturbed. All requirements for a particular type or level of system (be it electrical, gas, or vacuum) have been grouped into one section within a chapter. For example, all source, distribution, and performance criteria and testing for Type 1 essential electrical systems have been placed in Section 3-3 (previously, this information was included in several sections). This change continues in this 1999 edition, which makes it easier and quicker for users of the document to find the information they need.

*Responding to Changing Needs.* The health care facilities project itself is a product of changing needs in the health care field. In 1917, NFPA formed a committee to address the use of gases. In the 1930s, the problem of explosions in operating rooms due to changes in the way anesthesia was administered began to occur with alarming frequency. The Committee on Gases investigated the problem and developed recommendations for the safe use of anesthetic gases. In the 1940s other problems involving electricity and equipment in hospital operating rooms became evident, and a separate Committee on Hospital Operating Rooms was established to address these situations.

Over the years, standards and guidelines for other aspects of hospital activities involving fire and explosion hazards (including electric shock and emergency electric power) were established. To reflect this more inclusive approach, the name of the committee was changed once more. This newly named Committee on Hospitals included standing subcommittees on anesthetizing agents, respiratory therapy, laboratories, essential electrical systems, safe use of electricity, medical-surgical vacuum systems, safe use of high-frequency electricity, disaster planning, and hyperbaric/hypobaric facilities.

In 1975 the breadth of the subcommittees had become so extensive that the role of the Committee on Hospitals shifted again, and its function became that of correlating the diverse activities of the eight subcommittees under it. Thus, the Health Care Facilities Correlating Committee (formerly the Committee on Hospitals) came into existence, and the subcommittees were elevated to technical committees.

In 1985 the correlating committee realized that to be more effective it would have to be able to make technical changes in the documents under its responsibility. Since, under NFPA procedures, correlating committees cannot make such technical changes, the correlating committee petitioned the Standards Council to discharge the correlating committee and technical committees under it and establish a new, balanced technical committee, with standing subcommittees under it. These subcommittees were not to be simply the previous technical committees; rather, they were to reflect the restructuring of NFPA 99.

In the early 1990s the NFPA Standards Council restudied the way committees were operating and established two structures for committees. The Technical Committee on Health Care Facilities reviewed the results and petitioned the Council to have the project restructured within this framework. A new Technical Correlating Committee on Health Care Facilities was established to supervise the efforts of the technical committees. A new Technical Committee on Administration was also created to handle issues that were beyond the scopes of the other technical committees. Most recently, the Technical Correlating Committee combined the Technical Committee on Anesthesia Services and the Technical Committee on Gas Equipment because of similarities in their activities. The Technical Committee on Gas Delivery Equipment now replaces the two.

The 1987 edition of NFPA 99 introduced several major changes in addition to the restructuring of the document including the following: Material on hypobaric facilities was separated into a new document (NFPA 99B), because these facilities are no longer used for medical purposes; material on the home use of respiratory therapy (Appendix F in the 1984 edition of NFPA 99) was deleted entirely because the committee felt that a simplified brochure was a better way to get this safety information to patients; and the text of NFPA 56F–1983, *Standard on Nonflammable Medical Gas Systems,* was incorporated into Chapter 4. (NFPA 56F no longer exists as an individual document; Responsibility for this document was transferred by the Standards Council in October 1985 from the Technical Committee on Industrial and Medical Gases to the Technical Committee on Health Care Facilities.)

Numerous technical changes were made throughout the 1990 edition of NFPA

99 while the 1993 edition incorporated more technical changes as well as structural changes to make the document more user-friendly. These structural changes included clearly separating requirements from recommendations by placing all "guidance" related to text into Notes or into Appendix A of the document. In addition, flowcharts were added to help explain how NFPA 99 is structured and how requirements are found. Technical changes included the following: Adding requirements in Chapter 12 and recommendations in Annex 2 to further prevent or minimize fires in operating rooms; making major changes to requirements in Chapter 4 for installing, testing, and maintaining nonflammable medical piped gas systems; adding new sections on dental compressed air and dental vacuum requirements in Chapter 4; changing leakage current limits of patient-care-related electrical appliances to correlate more closely with an international document on the subject; revising laboratory requirements to correlate more closely with NFPA 45, *Standard on Fire Protection for Laboratories Using Chemicals;* changing essential electrical system requirements in ambulatory health care clinics and medical/dental offices; and extensively revising hyperbaric chamber requirements (see Chapter 19).

For the 1996 edition structural changes to Chapters 3 and 4, as previously noted, were made to make it easier to find requirements in these chapters. In 1996 technical changes included the following: relocating all requirements on flammable anesthetics and anesthetizing locations to a then new Annex 2 in the back of the document; adding Chapter 11 with requirements on emergency preparedness (and thus replacing a previous annex with recommendations on this subject); adding Chapter 18 on home health care since more patients are being discharged from health care facilities with gas- and electric-powered devices; and revising load testing criteria for emergency generators by referencing NFPA 110, *Standard for Emergency and Standby Power Systems,* which has new requirements for such testing.

In this 1999 edition the major structural change was to delete in its entirety the text of Chapter 13, formerly "Ambulatory Health Care Center Requirements," and replace it with requirements that apply to health care facilities other than hospitals, nursing homes, or limited care facilities. The committee made this change to Chapter 13 in concert with deleting in their entirety Chapter 14, formerly "Clinic Requirements," and Chapter 15, formerly "Medical and Dental Office Requirements." The purpose of this major change was to move away from chapters that based the required protection upon a "label" or designation given to a building, because such a classification does not always provide a true description of what health care is being provided to patients in the structure.

The committee was aware that authorities having jurisdiction are having problems interpreting the appropriate applications because current definitions of some facilities were not accurate. For 1999, the committee felt that several chapters could be combined into this new "other" health care facility chapter and made a technical change to all chapters where the level of risk to the patient (based upon life support) would determine the level (or complexity) of the systems (electrical, gas, vacuum, etc.) required in the facility.

## 1-1  Scope

The scope of this document is to establish criteria to minimize the hazards of fire, explosion, and electricity in health care facilities providing services to human beings. These criteria include performance, maintenance, testing, and safe practices for facilities, material, equipment, and appliances and include other hazards associated with the primary hazards.

This scope reflects the scopes of the twelve original individual documents from which NFPA 99 was created in 1984.

The scope was modified in the 1996 edition to reflect the committee's intent that NFPA 99 cover facilities treating only human beings. While freestanding veterinary facilities present many of the same hazards as hospitals, the committee believes facilities treating animals should be addressed in a separate document. (It should be noted that veterinary laboratories located within health care facilities are included and addressed in NFPA 99.)

## 1-2*  Application

This document shall apply to all health care facilities. Construction and equipment requirements shall be applied only to new construction and new equipment, except as modified in individual chapters. Only the altered, renovated, or modernized portion of an existing system or individual component shall be required to meet the installation and equipment requirements stated in this standard. If the alteration, renovation, or modernization adversely impacts existing performance requirements of a system or component, additional upgrading shall be required.

Chapters 12 through 18 specify the conditions under which the requirements of Chapters 3 through 11 shall apply in Chapters 12 through 18.

In NFPA 99 and most other standards, requirements are not intended to be applied retroactively. They apply only to new equipment and construction. Existing facilities should be considered individually. This is not meant, however, to authorize or condone clearly hazardous conditions (i.e., those presenting a distinct hazard to life). Minimum requirements for existing equipment and construction are specifically and clearly indicated in many instances in the document. (See also commentary at the beginning of this chapter on the subject of new vs. existing.) See Exhibit 1.1.

A revision in 1996 (see new sentence 2 beginning "Construction and equipment . . . " in paragraph 1 of Section 1-2) further clarifies intent with regard to new construction or equipment being added onto existing construction or equipment.

The intent of paragraph 2 of Section 1-2 is to clearly indicate how Chapters 3 through 11 are linked to Chapters 12 through 18 as a result of the structure of NFPA 99 created in 1987.

**Exhibit 1.1** *One of the almost 7000 hospitals in the United States, which are among the many types of facilities covered by NFPA 99, Standard for Health Care Facilities.* (Courtesy Rob Swift and Prince William Health Systems.)

**A-1-2 Organization of This Document.** Beginning with the 1987 edition, the organization of NFPA 99 reflected an attempt to make the document completely integrated and cohesive. Having been originally developed from 12 previously independent documents, the 1987 edition of NFPA 99 restructured all the existing text in the following way:

Chapter 1 is an introductory chapter.

Chapter 2 lists all definitions.

Chapters 3 through 11 contain requirements but do not state where they are applicable.

This organization of the document reflects the change in structure since 1996 of Chapters 3 and 4, wherein all requirements (source, distribution, performance criteria, and testing) for a particular type or level of system are now within one section (e.g., Section 3-3 contains all the requirements for a Type 1 essential electrical system; Section 4-5 contains all the requirements for a Level 1 piped gas or vacuum system).

Chapters 12 through 18 are "facility" chapters listing requirements from Chapters 3 through 11 that are applicable to specific facilities. These chapters also contain any additional requirements specific to that facility.

Chapter 19 contains safety requirements for hyperbaric facilities (whether freestanding or part of a larger facility).

Chapter 20 contains safety requirements for freestanding birthing centers.

Chapter 21 lists required references made in Chapters 1 through 20.

Appendix A contains nonmandatory information keyed to the text of Chapters 1 through 20 (e.g., A-5-4.2 is explanatory information on 5-4.2).

Appendix B lists informatory references.

Appendix C contains more explanatory information on Chapters 1 through 20, though not keyed to specific text (numbering is such that the first number after the letter C indicates the chapter to which material is related, e.g., Appendix C-7 contains information related to Chapter 7).

Finally, two annexes contain guidance on the following subjects: the use of high-frequency electricity (Annex 1) and flammable anesthetizing location criteria (Annex 2).

As a result of this restructuring, a reader interested in learning, for example, what the electrical system requirements are for a hospital would begin by first turning to Chapter 12 ("Hospital Requirements"), then to 12-3.3 ("Electrical System Requirements"). Similarly, electrical system requirements for a nursing home would be found by first turning to Chapter 16 ("Nursing Home Requirements"), then to 16-3.3 ("Electrical System Requirements").

General chapters have been organized in the following manner:

—1 Scope

—2 Nature of Hazards

—3 Type/Level 1

—4 Type/Level 2

—5 Type/Level 3

Each type/level is, in turn, organized in the following manner: source, distribution, performance criteria and testing, and administration.

The major topics considered in each facility chapter (12 through 18) under "General Requirements" (e.g., Sections 12-3, 13-3, etc.) are arranged in the following order (for consistency within the order of the general chapters):

.3 Electrical Systems

.4 Gas and Vacuum Systems

.5 Environmental Systems

.6 Materials

.7 Electrical Equipment

.8 Gas Equipment

The 1987 edition completed the original goal of combining the 12 previously individual documents under the jurisdiction of the former Correlating Committee on Health Care Facilities, now Technical Correlating Committee on Health Care Facilities. Cross-referencing to the previous individual documents was possible but would have been complicated because of the major difference between the structure of the previous individual documents and the structure of the 1987 edition of NFPA 99.

The numbers for the topics listed in Chapters 12 through 18 correspond directly with the numbers for the topics covered in Chapters 3 through 8.

## 1-3 Intended Use

This document is intended for use by those persons involved in the design, construction, inspection, and operation of health care facilities and in the design, manufacture, and testing of appliances and equipment used in patient care areas of health care facilities.

It should not be construed by persons involved in the activities listed that the material in NFPA 99 is required per se. Required use will depend on whether and by whom the document is adopted for use. This includes governmental as well as nongovernmental agencies or companies.

The subcommittee that restructured NFPA 99 for the 1987 edition took the diversity of the document's wide audience into consideration and tried to meet the needs of each. For example, requirements for systems, requirements for the major types of health care facilities, and requirements for manufacturers have all been addressed and placed separately.

## 1-4 Discretionary Powers of Authority Having Jurisdiction

The authority having jurisdiction for the enforcement of this document shall be permitted to grant exceptions to its requirements.

Nothing in this document is intended to prevent the use of systems, methods, or devices of equivalent or superior quality, strength, fire resistance, effectiveness, durability, and safety to those prescribed by this document, providing the following:

(a) Technical documentation is submitted to the authority having jurisdiction to demonstrate equivalency
(b) The system, method, or device is approved for the intended purpose.

While authorities having jurisdiction can adopt and enforce voluntary standards that they consider appropriate (e.g., adopt and enforce requirements as written; issue waivers to specific facilities not meeting certain requirements; adopt a document but change certain requirements), this section, which was previously in three of the twelve health care facilities documents, has been retained and extended to apply to the entire standard as a reminder to authorities that they can grant exemptions.

The second paragraph of Section 1-4 adds the concept of equivalency to the previous permission of allowing enforcing authorities (governmental and nongovernmental) to grant exceptions to requirements. This wording on equivalency is almost verbatim from 1-6.1 of the 1997 edition of NFPA *101*®, *Life Safety Code*®. [1] The authority having jurisdiction determines whether a submitter's "equivalency" is indeed equivalent.

## 1-5 Interpretations

The National Fire Protection Association does not approve, inspect, or certify any installation, procedure, equipment, or material. In determining the acceptability of installations, procedures, or material, the authority having jurisdiction may base acceptance on compliance with this document. To promote uniformity of interpretation and application of its standards, NFPA has established interpretation procedures. These procedures are outlined on the inside front cover of this document. Refer to Section 5 of the NFPA *Regulations Governing Committee Projects* for complete details.

## 1-6 Metric Units

While it is common practice for medical appliances to have metric units on their dials, gauges, and controls, many components of systems within the scope of this document, which are manufactured and used in the U.S., employ nonmetric dimensions. Since these dimensions (such as nominal pipe sizes) are not established by the National Fire Protection Association, the now Technical Correlating Committee on Health Care Facilities cannot independently change them. Accordingly, this document uses dimensions that are presently in common use by the building trades in the U.S. Conversion factors to metric units are included in C-4.5.

## 1-7 Effective Date

The effective date of application of any provision of this document is not determined by the National Fire Protection Association. All questions related to applicability shall be directed to the authority having jurisdiction.

## 1-8 Preface

This document's genesis was a series of explosions in operating rooms during surgery in the 1930s. The problem was traced to static discharges of sufficient energy to ignite the flammable anesthetic agents being used. A series of recommendations to mitigate the hazard were then promulgated. In addition, a Committee on Hospitals was established with responsibility to periodically review and revise recommendations.

Since then, the concerns of this Committee have grown to encompass many other fire and fire-related hazards related to the delivery of health care services. The Committee was also allowed to enlarge its scope to include all health care facilities.

The major concerns of the Committee are those hazards associated with operating a health care facility, treating patients, and operating laboratories. This includes the electrical system (both normal and emergency power), gas systems (both positive and negative pressure), medical equipment (both electrical and gas powered), environmental conditions peculiar to health care facilities operation, and the management of a facility in the event of disasters (e.g., fire, chemical spill) that disrupt normal patient care.

The Committee and its Subcommittees (now Technical Correlating Committee on Health Care Facilities and its Technical Committees) originally developed separate documents as hazards were identified. NFPA 99 is the result of a proposal to combine, organize, and integrate into one document all the material contained in the individual documents. The intent was, and still is, to provide as useful a document as possible to its many and varied users.

### Reference Cited in Commentary

1. NFPA *101®, Life Safety Code®,* 1997 edition.

# CHAPTER 2

# Definitions

Secretary's Note: The letters in parentheses at the end of each definition refer to the Technical Committee responsible for defining the term. The key to identifying responsibility follows:

(ADM): Technical Committee on Administration

(DIS): Technical Committee on Health Care Emergency Preparedness and Disaster Planning

(EE): Technical Committee on Electrical Equipment

(ES): Technical Committee on Electrical Systems

(GDE): Technical Committee on Gas Delivery Equipment

(HHF): Technical Committee on Hyperbaric and Hypobaric Facilities

(LAB): Technical Committee on Laboratories

(PIP): Technical Committee on Piping Systems

For the purposes of this document, the following definitions apply as indicated.

This list of committees reflects the restructuring of the Health Care Facilities project in 1994, the creation of a Technical Committee on Administration in 1995, and the combining of the Technical Committees on Anesthesia Services and Gas Equipment into the Technical Committee on Gas Delivery Equipment in 1996.

In 1996 all requirements and recommendations on flammable inhalation anesthetics were transferred to a newly created Annex 2, "Flammable Anesthetizing Locations." Due to this text transfer, references in Chapters 1 through 20, and in Appendixes A, B, and C, are only to nonflammable inhalation anesthetics, including anesthetizing locations.

## 2-1 Official NFPA Definitions

**Approved.*** Acceptable to the authority having jurisdiction.

**A-2-1 Approved.** The National Fire Protection Association does not approve, inspect, or certify any installations, procedures, equipment, or materials; nor does it approve or evaluate testing laboratories. In determining the acceptability of installations, procedures, equipment, or materials, the authority having jurisdiction may base acceptance on compliance with NFPA or other appropriate standards. In the absence of such standards, said authority may require evidence of proper installation, procedure, or use. The authority having jurisdiction may also refer to the listings or labeling practices of an organization that is concerned with product evaluations and is thus in a position to determine compliance with appropriate standards for the current production of listed items.

**Authority Having Jurisdiction.*** The organization, office, or individual responsible for approving equipment, an installation, or a procedure.

**A-2-1 Authority Having Jurisdiction.** The phrase "authority having jurisdiction" is used in NFPA documents in a broad manner, since jurisdictions and approval agencies vary, as do their responsibilities. Where public safety is primary, the authority having jurisdiction may be a federal, state, local, or other regional department or individual such as a fire chief; fire marshal; chief of a fire prevention bureau, labor department, or health department; building official; electrical inspector; or others having statutory authority. For insurance purposes, an insurance inspection department, rating bureau, or other insurance company representative may be the authority having jurisdiction. In many circumstances, the property owner or his or her designated agent assumes the role of the authority having jurisdiction; at government installations, the commanding officer or departmental official may be the authority having jurisdiction.

> As pointed out in A-2-1, even a health care facility can be the enforcing authority. Such authority, however, is possible only in the absence of any governmental regulations. To be sure, a facility can enforce more stringent requirements than the government, but this authority may not always be successful.
>
> For an interesting discussion on this aspect of authority and enforcement of codes and standards, see "Electricity, Safety and the Patient." [1]

**Code.*** A standard that is an extensive compilation of provisions on a broad subject matter or that is suitable for adoption into law independently of other codes and standards.

**A-2-1 Code.** The decision to designate a standard as a "code" is based on such factors as the size and scope of the document, its intended use and form of adoption, and whether it contains substantial enforcement and administrative provisions.

**Guide.** A document that is advisory or informative in nature and that contains only nonmandatory provisions. A guide may contain mandatory statements such as when a guide can be used, but the document as a whole is not suitable for adoption into law.

**Labeled.** Equipment or materials to which has been attached a label, symbol, or other identifying mark of an organization that is acceptable to the authority having jurisdiction and concerned with product evaluation, that maintains periodic inspection of production of labeled equipment or materials, and by whose labeling the manufacturer indicates compliance with appropriate standards or performance in a specified manner.

**Listed.*** Equipment, materials, or services included in a list published by an organization that is acceptable to the authority having jurisdiction and concerned with evaluation of products or services, that maintains periodic inspection of production of listed equipment or materials or periodic evaluation of services, and whose listing states that either the equipment, material, or service meets identified standards or has been tested and found suitable for a specified purpose.

**A-2-1 Listed.** The means for identifying listed equipment may vary for each organization concerned with product evaluation; some organizations do not recognize equipment as listed unless it is also labeled. The authority having jurisdiction should utilize the system employed by the listing organization to identify a listed product.

**Shall.** Indicates a mandatory requirement.

**Should.** Indicates a recommendation or that which is advised but not required.

**Standard.** A document, the main text of which contains only mandatory provisions using the word "shall" to indicate requirements and which is in a form generally suitable for mandatory reference by another standard or code or for adoption into law. Nonmandatory provisions shall be located in an appendix, footnote, or fine-print note and are not to be considered a part of the requirements of a standard.

## 2-2 Definitions of Terms Used in the Standard

**ACFM.** Actual cubic feet per minute. The unit used to express the measure of the volume of gas flowing at operating temperature and pressure, as distinct from the volume of a gas flowing at standard temperature and pressure (*see definition of SCFM*). (PIP)

The term *actual cubic feet per minute* (ACFM), as used in NFPA 99 for hyperbaric chambers, indicates the amount of air used for ventilation at the pressure and temperature used in the chamber. In contrast, the term *standard cubic feet per minute* (SCFM) is understood as air at atmospheric pressure at sea level. (See commentary in this chapter under the term *SCFM*.)

**Adiabatic Heating.** The temperature rise of a gas caused only by its compression. (HHF)

> In general thermodynamic terms, adiabatic heating refers to an energy exchange process in which there is no external gain or loss of heat energy. As used in this standard, it refers to the special case of the rapid compression of a gas in which the mechanical energy input serves to raise the temperature of the gas, as in a compressor. An example of adiabatic heating is the rise in temperature of the environment within a hyperbaric chamber during rapid compression.

**Aerosol.** An intimate mixture of a liquid or a solid in a gas; the liquid or solid, called the dispersed phase, is uniformly distributed in a finely divided state throughout the gas, which is the continuous phase or dispersing medium. (GE)

> Previous editions of the standard contained a definition of *air, oil-free, dry (air for testing)* immediately after the definition of *aerosol*. At one time, this type of air was used for pressure-testing purposes and could be confused with medical air (see definition of *medical compressed air*). The use of dry, oil-free air for testing nonflammable medical gas pipelines was eliminated in 1993, and only dry, oil-free nitrogen is to be used. Because such air was no longer permitted for testing purposes, the definition was deleted to avoid confusion on the part of the installer.

**Alarm System, Area.** A warning system that provides visible and audible signals for the monitoring of medical gas and vacuum systems serving a specific area, consisting of alarm panel(s) and associated actuating device(s). (PIP)

> Sometimes called *zone alarm* or mistakenly referred to as local alarm, typical applications for this alarm type are found in 4-3.1.2.2(c).

**Alarm System, Level III.** An area alarm system for patient nonflammable medical gases system, typically oxygen, nitrous oxide, and medical air in dental care facilities and medical care facilities. (PIP)

> This definition, new in the 1996 edition, refers to a specific type of alarm commonly used in a small office–based medical gas system, such as in a dental office. Requirements for a Level 3 alarm system are found in 4-5.1.2.8.

**Alarm System, Local.** A warning system that provides visible and audible signals for the monitoring functions of medical gas and vacuum system source equipment at the equipment site. (PIP)

> This alarm is commonly found on the control panel of air or vacuum equipment. Typical applications for this alarm type can be found in 4-3.1.2.1(d).

**Alarm System, Master.** A warning system that provides visible and audible signals for the monitoring of medical gas and vacuum sources and systems, consisting of alarm panel(s) and associated actuating device(s). (PIP)

> Typical applications for this alarm type can be found in 4-3.1.2.2(b). The definitions of area, local, and master alarms have been included because the terms were being misinterpreted.

**Alternate Power Source.** One or more generator sets, or battery systems where permitted, intended to provide power during the interruption of the normal electrical service; or the public utility electrical service intended to provide power during interruption of service normally provided by the generating facilities on the premises. (ES)

**Ambulatory Health Care Facility.** A building or part thereof used to provide services or treatment to four or more patients at the same time and meeting the provisions of either (a) or (b) below:

(a) Those facilities that provide, on an outpatient basis, treatment for patients that would render them incapable of taking action for self-preservation under emergency conditions without assistance from others, such as hemodialysis units or freestanding emergency medical units

(b) Those facilities that provide, on an outpatient basis, surgical treatment requiring general anesthesia. (ADM)

> For this 1999 edition, this term was revised from *ambulatory health care center* to *ambulatory health care facility* and the definition was modified slightly to correlate with the change made in NFPA *101, Life Safety Code.* [2] The NFPA 99 Technical Committee on Administration worked with the Committee on Safety to Life, which is responsible for NFPA *101,* to revise this term, and other health care related terms used in both documents, to reflect the appropriate level of risk of each. With the changes in medicine that have taken place, the former definitions for such facilities no longer fully corresponded with what takes place in them. (See Exhibit 2.1.)
>
> The specific requirements for Ambulatory Health Care Facilities are still located in Chapter 13, but the title of that chapter has been changed from "Ambulatory Health Care Center Requirements" (1996 edition) to "'Other' Health Care Center Facilities" (1999 edition).

**Ampacity.** Current-carrying capacity of electric conductors expressed in amperes. (ES)

**Anesthetic.** As used in this standard, applies to any inhalation agent used to produce relative analgesia or general anesthesia. (AS)

> Note the reference to inhalation as part of the definition.

**Exhibit 2.1** *A hospital facility, one of the many kinds of health care facilities defined in Chapter 2.* (Courtesy of Rob Swift and Prince William Hospital.)

**Anesthetizing Location.*** Any area of a facility that has been designated to be used for the administration of nonflammable inhalation anesthetic agents in the course of examination or treatment, including the use of such agents for relative analgesia *(see definition of Relative Analgesia).* (GDE)

**A-2-2 Anesthetizing Location.** For guidance on flammable anesthetizing locations, see Annex 2.

> This term is defined in a way to avoid the prior interpretation that a health care facility is considered an *anesthetizing location.* The key word is "designated." An area must be designated by the administrative body as an anesthetizing location before the requirements of 12-4.1 are applicable.
>
> It is necessary for a facility to designate certain areas as anesthetizing locations so that it is clear to all which requirements are applicable to these particular locations within the facility. Regular administration of inhalation anesthetics in a location not administratively designated for such practice could have serious consequences.
>
> This definition refers to areas where general anesthesia (i.e., inhalation anesthetics) is administered, not areas where only local anesthetics are administered.
>
> In 1996 the reference to flammable inhalation anesthetics was deleted. Since then, requirements for anesthetizing locations that use flammable inhalation anesthetics are located in Annex 2, "Flammable Anesthetizing Locations." Over the last few decades, the use of flammable inhalation anesthetics in the United States has dropped to a point where they are, essentially, no longer used. The committee responsible for anesthesia safety received a proposal for the 1996 edition to eliminate all references to flammable anesthetics. The committee decided to retain the require-

ments in a then newly created annex, since flammable anesthetics are used in some countries outside the United States. These requirements also serve as a reminder of all the precautions that need to be taken if flammable anesthetics were to some day be reintroduced into the surgical operating arena.

**Anoxia.** A state of markedly inadequate oxygenation of the tissues and blood, of more marked degree than hypoxia. (HHF)

**Appliance.** Electrical equipment, generally other than industrial, normally built in standardized sizes or types, which is installed or connected as a unit to perform one or more functions. (EE)

The definition used in this document agrees with that listed in NFPA 70, *National Electrical Code.*® [3]

The definition here encompasses many kinds of electrical end-use devices, from cord-connected devices such as a monitor to hard-wired devices such as a whirlpool bath or an X-ray machine. Larger physical plant equipment, such as pumps, air conditioners, and elevators, is generally not included. The way in which the device is used needs to be considered in determining the applicability of the provisions of this standard.

**Applicator.*** A means of applying high-frequency energy to a patient other than by an electrically conductive connection. (EE)

**A-2-2 Applicator.** In the given sense, an applicator is not an electrode since it does not use a conductive connection to the patient in order to function. A radio frequency "horn" of a diathermy machine is a typical applicator.

Other types of applicators that use electrode or magnetic fields are coils for inductive heating and capacitors for dielectric heating. High-frequency ultrasonic waves are also used for therapeutic heating, but they are not electromagnetic radiation.

**Area of Administration.** Any point within a room within 15 ft (4.3 m) of oxygen equipment or an enclosure containing or intended to contain an oxygen-enriched atmosphere. (GDE)

**Atmosphere.*** The pressure exerted by, and gaseous composition of, an environment. (HHF)

**A-2-2 Atmosphere.** As employed in this standard, atmosphere can refer to the environment within or outside of a hyperbaric facility. When used as a measure of pressure, atmosphere is expressed as a fraction of standard air pressure [14.7 psi (101.4 kPa)]. *(See Appendix C-3, Pressure Table, Column 1 of NFPA 99B.)*

The term *atmosphere* has two distinct meanings. Its general meaning is the space occupied by gases surrounding a particular region. This is usually air at a particular pressure and temperature. The term has another technical meaning, that of a unit of pressure. This meaning is used extensively in Chapter 19, "Hyperbaric Facilities." It is usually obvious from the text which meaning is pertinent.

**Atmosphere, Absolute (ATA).** *(See definition of Atmosphere.)* Two ATA = two atmospheres. (HHF)

> Understanding the concept of atmospheres absolute is important in hyperbaric chamber operations. An atmosphere of pressure is equal to 33 ft of seawater (FSW), 14.7 pounds per square inch (psi), or 101.4 kilo-Pascals (kPa). Though a chamber may be pressurized to an internal pressure of two atmospheres (29.4 psi or 66 FSW), a person exposed to that pressure environment responds physiologically to a pressure equivalent of three atmospheres absolute. Normal atmospheric pressure of one atmosphere or 14.7 psi must be taken into account and added to the actual chamber atmosphere.

**Atmosphere, Ambient.** The pressure and composition of the environment surrounding a chamber. (HHF)

> The Committee on Hyperbaric and Hypobaric Facilities (responsible for this definition) considered it important to be precise in describing the various atmospheres associated with hyperbaric operation (i.e., ambient and chamber). The term *composition* replaced *concentration,* because composition includes concentration and is more technically correct in describing the atmosphere surrounding the chamber.

**Atmosphere, Chamber.** The environment inside a chamber. (HHF)

**Atmosphere of Increased Burning Rate.*** Any atmosphere containing a percentage of oxygen or oxygen and nitrous oxide greater than the quotient of 23.45 divided by the square root of the total pressure in atmospheres, that is,

$$\frac{23.45}{\sqrt{TP_{atmos}}}$$

where $TP_{atmos}$ = total pressure in atmospheres. (HHF)

**A-2-2 Atmosphere of Increased Burning Rate.** The degree of fire hazard of an oxygen-enriched atmosphere varies with the concentration of oxygen and diluent gas and the total pressure. The definition contained in the current edition of NFPA 53, *Recommended Practice on Materials, Equipment, and Systems Used in Oxygen-Enriched Atmospheres,* and in editions of NFPA 56D, *Standard for Hyperbaric Facilities,* prior to 1982, did not necessarily reflect the increased fire hazard of hyperbaric and hypobaric atmospheres.

The definition of atmosphere of increased burning rate in Chapter 19 and in NFPA 99B, *Standard for Hypobaric Facilities,* defines an oxygen-enriched atmosphere with an increased fire hazard, as it relates to the increased burning rate of material in the atmosphere. It is based upon a 1.2 cm/sec burning rate (at 23.5 percent oxygen at 1 atmosphere absolute) as described in Figure A-2-2(a) from Technical Memorandum UCRI-721, *Chamber Fire Safety,* T. C. Schmidt, V. A. Dorr, and R. W. Hamilton, Jr., Ocean Systems Inc. Research and Development Laboratory, Tarrytown, NY 01591. *[See Figure A-2-2(a).]*

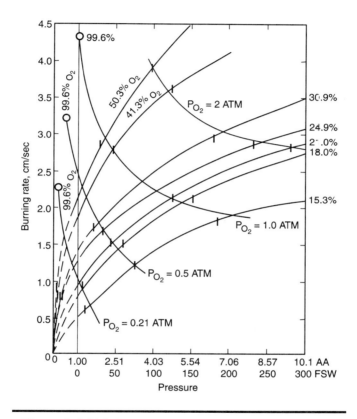

***Figure A-2-2(a)*** *Burning rates of filter paper strips at an angle of 45 degrees in $N_2$–$O_2$ mixtures.*

NOTE: Figure A-2-2(a) from Figure 4, Technical Memorandum UCRI-721, *Chamber Fire Safety*, T. C. Schmidt, V. A. Dorr, and R. W. Hamilton, Jr., Ocean Systems, Inc. Research and Development Laboratory, Tarrytown, NY 10591. Work carried out under U.S. Office of Naval Research, Washington, DC, Contract No. N00014-67-A-0214-0013. (From Cook, G. A., Meierer, R. E., Shields, B. M. *Screening of Flame-Resistant Materials and Comparison of Helium with Nitrogen for Use in Diving Atmospheres.* First summary report under ONR Contract No. 0014-66-C-0149. Tonawanda, NY: Union Carbide, 31 March 1967. DDC No. AD-651583.)

The definition accounts for the special atmospheres now in use by military, nonmilitary, and private sector operators of such chambers. It is based on actual test data under hyperbaric and hypobaric conditions.

Earlier editions of this standard addressed only the definition of *oxygen-enriched environments*. In the strictest sense of that definition, all hyperbaric chambers operated in such an enriched environment as soon as the chamber door or hatch was closed and the chamber pressurized. This definition did not accurately reflect the environmental conditions found in the majority of hyperbaric chambers in which the percent of oxygen concentration was maintained at 23.5 percent or below. The definition of *atmosphere of increased burning rate* was added to more correctly reflect adherence of oxygen concentrations at levels below 23.5 percent. Virtually all modern hyperbaric chamber operations routinely monitor interior chamber oxygen levels and increase chamber ventilation rates as levels approach 23.5 percent. If oxygen levels cannot be maintained below this maximum, then all hyperbaric chamber operations should be terminated. The current definition of increased burning rates reflects the fact that if a fire should occur, the rate of burning will be faster due to the increased partial pressure of oxygen found in a hyperbaric environment.

In Figure A-2-2(a):

ATM  =  atmospheres

AA  =  atmospheres absolute

FSW  =  feet of seawater

**Automatic.** Self-acting, operating by its own mechanism when actuated by some impersonal influence as, for example, a change in current, voltage, pressure, temperature, or mechanical configuration. (ES)

**Bends.** Decompression sickness; caisson worker's disease. *(See C-19.1.3.4.2.)* (HHF)

The term *bends* is commonly used to describe decompression sickness. Decompression sickness is a complex phenomenon that presents a variety of symptoms depending on the severity of the case. There are two general classifications: Type I (Mild)—pain only (usually associated with joint pain and skin manifestations); and Type II (Severe)—cerebral, spinal cord, vestibular, or cardiopulmonary injury. Though decompression sickness is usually associated with diving or hyperbaric operations, it is also possible to experience the bends from unprotected exposure to altitudes in excess of 18,000 ft (5486 m).

**Branch Circuit.** The circuit conductors between the final overcurrent device protecting the circuit and the outlet(s). (ES)

This definition conforms to that in NFPA 70, *National Electrical Code.* [3] It refers to the wiring and does not include the overcurrent device or the outlet.

**Branch Line.** See definition of Piping.

**Bulk Systems:**

*Bulk Nitrous Oxide System.* An assembly of equipment as described in the definition of bulk oxygen system that has a storage capacity of more than 3200 lb (1452 kg) [approximately 28,000 ft³ (793 m³) (NTP)] of nitrous oxide. (PIP)

*Bulk Oxygen System.* * An assembly of equipment such as oxygen storage containers, pressure regulators, pressure relief devices, vaporizers, manifolds, and interconnecting piping that has a storage capacity of more than 20,000 ft³ (566 m³) of oxygen (NTP) including unconnected reserves on hand at the site. The bulk oxygen system terminates at the point where oxygen at service pressure first enters the supply line. (PIP)

**A-2-2 Bulk Oxygen System.** The oxygen containers can be stationary or movable, and the oxygen can be stored as gas or liquid.

**Cannula, Nasal.** Device consisting of two short tubes to be inserted into the nostrils to administer oxygen or other therapeutic gases. (GDE)

The definition of this term was added to distinguish nasal cannula from nasal catheter, which is a slightly different apparatus for administering oxygen.

**Catheter, Nasal.** A flexible tube for insertion through the nose into the nasopharynx to administer oxygen or other therapeutic gases. (GDE)

**Clinic.** A health care facility where patients are seen on an ambulatory basis, but where surgery involving general anesthesia is not performed. (ADM)

In 1986, when the Restructuring Subcommittee was developing a new structure for NFPA 99, it first listed the many types of health care facilities and then analyzed the differences among the fire, explosion, and electrical hazards that existed within each of them, as covered by NFPA 99. Those facilities that had the same hazards were grouped together. Clinics were determined to be sufficiently different to warrant being a separate chapter (Chapter 14). In this 1999 edition, the text in former Chapter 14 has been deleted and the chapter is now reserved for future use. Requirements for clinics are now found in Chapter 13, "'Other' Health Care Center Facilities."

**Cold Room.** A refrigerated area large enough for personnel to enter. (LAB)

**Combustible.** A substance that if ignited will react with oxygen and burn. (GDE)

**Combustible Liquid.** See definition of Liquid and C-10.2.1. (LAB)

The definition used is from NFPA 30, *Flammable and Combustible Liquids Code.* [4]

**Combustion.*** A chemical process (such as oxidation) accompanied by the rapid evolution of heat and light. (AS)

See Exhibit 2.2.

**A-2-2 Combustion.** Combustion is not limited to a chemical reaction always involving oxygen. Certain metals, such as calcium and aluminum, will burn in nitrogen; nitrous oxide will support the combustion of phosphorus and carbon; and so on. However, this document deals with the more common process of fuels burning in air.

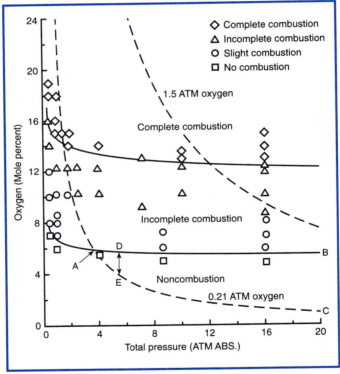

**Exhibit 2.2** *Three combustion zones for vertical paper strips in N₂–O₂ mixtures.* (From Figure 7, Technical Memorandum UCRI-721, *Chamber Fire Safety,* T. C. Schmidt, V. A. Dorr, and R. W. Hamilton, Jr., Ocean Systems, Inc. Research and Development Laboratory, Tarrytown, NY 10591.)

**Combustion Products.** The gases, volatilized liquids and solids, particulate matter, and ash generated by combustion. (GDE)

This is also referred to as products of combustion in other documents. See Section 6-2 for a discussion of the toxicological hazards of combustion products that result from materials subjected to fire. With the increased use of synthetic and plastic materials, the need for protection against the associated hazards grows. Research on the subject is continuing.

**Container.** A low-pressure, vacuum-insulated vessel containing gases in liquid form. (GDE)

This term is used in Chapter 8 specifically to refer to oxygen containers and is now widely accepted for this type of application. The term *cylinder* is reserved for high-pressure application.

**Critical Branch.** A subsystem of the emergency system consisting of feeders and branch circuits supplying energy to task illumination, special power circuits, and selected receptacles serving areas and functions related to patient care and that are connected to alternate power sources by one or more transfer switches during interruption of normal power source. (ES)

A high degree of selectivity should be used when choosing loads to be connected to the critical branch because this branch provides electric power to areas and equipment involved in the most critical patient care functions.

**Critical Care Area.** See definition of Patient Care Area.

**Critical Equipment.** That equipment essential to the safety of the occupants of the facility. (HHF)

**Critical System.** A system of feeders and branch circuits in nursing homes and custodial care facilities arranged for connection to the alternate power source to restore service to certain critical receptacles, task illumination, and equipment. (ES)

This term is used primarily in long-term facilities where life support systems are not normally used (see 3-5.2.2 on Type 2 essential electrical system distribution requirements). The critical system picks up those loads that allow the institution to maintain operational continuity.

**Cylinder.** A supply tank containing high-pressure gases or gas mixtures at pressures that can be in excess of 2000 psig (13.8 kPa gauge). (GDE)

See commentary under the definition of *container.*

**Decompression Sickness.** A syndrome due to evolved gas in the tissues resulting from a reduction in ambient pressure. (HHF)

Decompression sickness is a condition that develops when a person experiences a rapid reduction of pressure in his or her surrounding environment. For example, a scuba diver who ascends too rapidly from depth without giving the body sufficient time to off-gas additional amounts of nitrogen that have saturated the body's tissues will develop decompression sickness. This condition is due to the elevated partial pressure of nitrogen in the breathing medium. This evolution of inert gas produces a varying degree of symptoms based on the severity of the formation of inert gas "bubbles" in the bloodstream or tissues and their location in the body. Once bubbles have formed at depth, they respond to Boyle's law and increase in volume as the surrounding pressure is reduced. This condition is also possible from exposure to altitudes in excess of 18,000 ft (5486 m). As an example, the occupants of an aircraft flying at an altitude of 35,000 ft (10,668 m) that suddenly loses cabin pressurization would be rapidly exposed to an altitude above 18,000 ft (5486 m) and their risk of developing decompression sickness would be increased. (See the commentary after the definition of the term *bends* for additional information.)

**Detonation.** An exothermic reaction wherein the reaction propagates through the unreacted material at a rate exceeding the velocity of sound, hence the explosive noise. (GDE)

**Direct Electrical Pathway to the Heart.\*** An externalized conductive pathway, insulated except at its ends, one end of which is in direct contact with heart muscle while the other is outside the body and is accessible for inadvertent or intentional contact with grounded objects or energized, ground-referenced sources. (EE)

**A-2-2 Direct Electrical Pathway to the Heart.** Electrodes, such as those used for pacing the heart, and catheters filled with conductive fluids are examples of direct electrical pathways to the heart.

**Disaster.\*** Within the context of this document, a disaster is defined as any unusual occurrence or unforeseen situation that seriously overtaxes or threatens to seriously overtax the routine capabilities of a health care facility.

This definition was expanded in this 1999 edition to broaden the instances of when an event could be considered a disaster.

**A-2-2 Disaster.** A disaster can be either an event that causes or threatens to cause physical damage and injury to facility personnel or patients within the facility, or an event that requires expansion of facilities to receive and care for a large number of casualties resulting from a disaster that produces no damage or injury to the health care facility and staff, or a combination thereof.

Such a situation creates the need for emergency expansion of facilities, as well as operation of this expanded facility in an unfamiliar environment. Under this definition, the recognition of a disaster situation will vary greatly from one facility to another and from time to time in any given facility. Such recognition and concomitant activation of the Health Care Emergency Preparedness Plan is dependent upon mutual aid agreements, facility type, geographic location, bed capacity, bed occupancy at a given time, staff size, staff experience with disaster situations, and other factors. For example, the routine workload of the emergency department of a large metropolitan general hospital would constitute a disaster, requiring activation of the Health Care Emergency Preparedness Plan, were this same workload to be suddenly applied to a small community hospital. (DIS)

*Causes.* Disasters have a variety of causes, all of which should be considered in effective emergency preparedness planning. Among the most common are natural disasters such as earthquakes, hurricanes, tornadoes, and floods; mass food poisoning; industrial accidents involving explosion or environmental release of toxic chemicals; transportation accidents involving crashes of trains, planes, or automobiles with resulting mass casualties; civil disturbances; building fires; extensive or prolonged utility failure; collapse of buildings or other occupied structures; and toxic smogs in urban areas. Arson attempts and bomb threats have been made on health care facilities and should therefore be considered. Potential admission to the facility of high profile persons should be addressed. While the last does not involve mass casualties or the potential of mass casualties, the degree of disruption of normal routine will be sufficient to qualify it as a disasterlike situation.

NOTE: Disaster plans should reflect a facility's location from internal and external disasters. As an example, areas subject to frequent wildland fires should invoke countermeasures for smoke management and air quality maintenance.

This definition was introduced in the 1996 edition and reflects the change that transferred the *recommendations* on emergency preparedness that previously made up Annex 1 into a then newly created Chapter 11 consisting of *requirements.*

Disasters, as noted, can come in many forms that vary in intensity and impact health care facilities differently. A disaster can be an event that occurs within the facility and threatens patients or personnel, such as a fire or power outage. Utility failures, geological events, and incidents involving mass casualties are examples of disasters that occur externally but that can also impact the health care facility. Terrorism is another form of external disaster that can place demands on a health care facility. While facilities themselves are generally not targeted, they are expected to provide medical attention and other services when other facilities are attacked.

A *health care facility* disaster is, thus, any event that creates a volume of victims that will require a facility to institute special procedures and resources, such as altering staffing patterns and health care service. Additional information and communications systems will need to be instituted, and the overall activities of the facility will need to be adjusted to the different demands of providing services to injured victims.

Generically, a disaster is any situation that overwhelms or threatens the normal operational mode of an agency, complex, or system, including political subdivisions and their various arms.

Administratively, the president of the United States may declare the existence of a "disaster" in any affected locality after (1) the event has occurred; (2) the governor of the affected state has requested the declaration; and (3) the Federal Emergency Management Agency (FEMA) has made an evaluation that supports the request. This sequence is legally required before a presidential declaration is allowed.

However, in response to the enormous destruction and lengthy interruptions caused by Hurricane Andrew, the federal government has accelerated and simplified these procedures and continues to look at other ways to further streamline the process.

**D.I.S.S. Connector.** A threaded medical gas connector complying with the CGA Pamphlet V-5, *Diameter Index Safety System—Non-Interchangeable Low Pressure Connections for Medical Gas Applications.* (PIP)

> This type of connector has been referenced in Chapter 4 but was never formally defined until the 1996 edition.
> The D.I.S.S. standard is an internationally accepted standard for noninterchangeable, threaded, gas-specific connections. It is limited to applications under 200 psi (1380 kPa) (see also 8-3.1.3). The higher pressure applications utilize a Pin-Index Safety System [see 8-3.1.2 and A-8-5.1.2.1(b)].

**Double-Insulated Appliances.** Appliances having an insulation system comprising both basic insulation necessary for the functioning of the appliance and for basic protection against electric shock and supplementary insulation. The supplementary insulation is independent insulation provided in addition to the basic insulation to ensure protection against electric shock in case of failure of the basic insulation. (EE)

> This definition is in general agreement with other, non-NFPA documents that define the term. Supplementary insulation cannot be just any insulation. It must meet appropriate specifications set up by testing laboratories. Providing supplementary insulation can become complex when there are items such as controls, connectors, and motor shafts that penetrate to the interior of the device. CAUTION: A simple coat of epoxy paint does not constitute supplementary insulation.

**Electrical Life Support Equipment.** Electrically powered equipment whose continuous operation is necessary to maintain a patient's life. (ES)

> The way in which this term is defined and used in NFPA 99 is intended to ensure that electrical equipment requiring continuous electrical power for patient care will be operational if normal electric power is interrupted. (See 12-3.3.2, 13-3.3.2, etc.)
> In some instances, the location of some equipment can have a bearing on whether it fits this term and definition. For example, a dialysis machine in a hospital would fall within the definition of this term while one in an outpatient clinic probably would not.

**Electrode.** An electrically conductive connection to a patient. Some electrodes of interest are: (EE)

In the purest sense, an electrode is the terminal where electrical energy is transferred from a device to the patient or vice versa. An electrode, however, must be connected to a cable for the transfer to occur.

*Active Electrode.* An electrode intended to generate a surgical effect at its point of application to the patient. (EE)

*Bipolar Electrode.* An electrode consisting of adjacent contacts (e.g., the two legs of a forceps) such that the high-frequency current passes between the pair of contacts generating the surgical effect. (EE)

*Dispersive Electrode.* An electrode intended to complete the electrical path between patient and appliance and at which no surgical effect is intended. It is often called the "indifferent electrode," the "return electrode," the "patient plate," or the "neutral electrode." (EE)

The term used by the International Electrotechnical Commission for this type of electrode is *neutral electrode.* However, the use of this term is not intended to imply that it is related to the neutral conductor of the power supply system. The term *neutral electrode* is not used extensively in the United States because of this possible confusion.

**Emergency Preparedness.** The act of developing procedures and plans to create effective preparedness, mitigation, response, and recovery during a disaster affecting a health care facility. (DIS)

This new definition of *emergency preparedness* was added to this 1999 edition and reflects the intent of the committee that *emergency preparedness* is a total program of responding to disasters. The term was used in older editions but was not defined.

**Emergency System.** A system of circuits and equipment intended to supply alternate power to a limited number of prescribed functions vital to the protection of life and safety. (ES)

Previously, the definition for this term included a time limit for the restoration of power. The time limit was deleted in the 1996 edition because it constituted performance criteria, not a definition of the term. [See commentary on 3-4.2.1.4(d) for a discussion on restoration time.]

**Equipment Grounding Bus.** A grounding terminal bus in the feeder circuit of the branch circuit distribution panel that serves a particular area. (EE)

This bus should provide a common connection point for all the equipment grounding conductors in a given patient area. One equipment grounding bus might serve several patient locations fed from the same branch-circuit distribution panel. It is not intended that an additional grounding bus be installed if an appropriate bus is already present.

**Equipment System.** A system of circuits and equipment arranged for automatic or manual connection to the alternate power source and that serves primarily three-phase power equipment. (ES)

> Often, this system serves heavy equipment that is three-phase powered, such as pumps and fans. This type of equipment is necessary for the operation of the facility, but a brief interruption in service can be tolerated without serious consequences. Rapid transfer of these heavy loads to the alternate power source could cause large surges and further disrupt the system.

**Essential Electrical System.** A system comprised of alternate sources of power and all connected distribution systems and ancillary equipment, designed to ensure continuity of electrical power to designated areas and functions of a health care facility during disruption of normal power sources, and also to minimize disruption within the internal wiring system. (ES)

**Evacuation—Waste Gas.** See definition of Waste Anesthetic Gas Disposal.

> This definition was added in the 1996 edition to properly define the systems used for waste gas evacuation.

**Exposed Conductive Surfaces.** Those surfaces that are capable of carrying electric current and that are unprotected, uninsulated, unenclosed, or unguarded, permitting personal contact. (EE)

**Failure.\*** An incident that increases the hazard to personnel or patients or that affects the safe functioning of electric appliances or devices. (EE)

**A-2-2 Failure.** It includes failure of a component, loss of normal protective paths such as grounding, and short circuits or faults between energized conductors and the chassis.

**Fault Current.** A current in an accidental connection between an energized and a grounded or other conductive element resulting from a failure of insulation, spacing, or containment of conductors. (ES)

**Feeder.** All circuit conductors between the service equipment or the source of a separately derived system and the final branch-circuit overcurrent device. (ES)

> This definition is similar to that in NFPA 70, *National Electrical Code.* [3] (See NFPA 70 for definitions of the specific terms used.)

**Flame Resistant.\*** The property of a material that passes the small-scale test in NFPA 701, *Standard Methods of Fire Tests for Flame-Resistant Textiles and Films.* (HHF)

**A-2-2 Flame Resistant.** A source of ignition alternate to the gas burner specified in NFPA 701, *Standard Methods of Fire Tests for Flame Resistant Textiles and Films,* could be required for this test if it is to be performed in 100 percent oxygen at several atmospheres pressure.

This criterion applies to finishes and materials within hyperbaric and hypobaric chambers that must be flame resistant. For criteria concerning interior finishes, see 19-2.2.3. The supplementary appendix information is intended to ensure compatibility of results for hyperbaric conditions. The term *flame retardant* was deleted prior to this 1999 edition because it is no longer used.

**Flammable.\*** An adjective describing easy ignition, intense burning, and rapid rate of flame spread during combustion. It is also used as a noun to mean a flammable substance. (GDE)

**A-2-2 Flammable.** Many substances nonflammable in air become flammable if the oxygen content of the gaseous medium is increased above 0.235 ATA.

This definition expands on the definition of flammable that is based on a normal atmosphere and includes information peculiar to hyperbaric operation. See commentary under the definition of *oxygen-enriched atmosphere* for an explanation of how the value of 0.235 came to be used. See also the definition of *nonflammable*.

**Flammable Gas.** Any substance that exists in the gaseous state at normal atmospheric temperature and pressure and is capable of being ignited and burned when mixed with proper proportion of air, oxygen, or other oxidizers. (From NFPA 326, *Standard Procedures for the Safe Entry of Underground Storage Tanks.*)

The definition of *flammable gas* was revised in this 1999 edition to that used in NFPA 326, *Standard for the Safeguarding of Tanks and Containers for Entry, Cleaning, or Repair* [5], because the Technical Committee on Gas Delivery Equipment considered this definition to have the broadest applicability of the four currently used in NFPA documents.

**Flammable Liquid.** See definition of Liquid and C-10.2.1. (LAB)

The definition is from NFPA 30, *Flammable and Combustible Liquids Code.* [4]

**Flash Point.** The minimum temperature at which a liquid gives off vapor in sufficient concentration to form an ignitible mixture with air near the surface of the liquid within the vessel, as specified by appropriate test procedures and apparatus. *(See C-10.2.2.)* (LAB)

**Flow-Control Valve.** A valve, usually a needle valve, that precisely controls flow of gas. (GDE)

**Flowmeter.** A device for measuring volumetric flow rates of gases and liquids. (GDE)

It should be noted that some flowmeters can indicate mean flow rates, in addition to the volumetric flow rate, of a substance being measured.

**Flowmeter, Pressure Compensated.** A flowmeter indicating accurate flow of gas whether the gas is discharged into ambient pressure or into a system at nonambient pressure. (GDE)

**Frequency.*** The number of oscillations, per unit time, of a particular current or voltage waveform. The unit of frequency is the hertz. (EE)

**A-2-2 Frequency.** Formerly the unit of frequency was cycles per second, a terminology no longer preferred. The waveform can consist of components having many different frequencies, in which case it is called a complex or nonsinusoidal waveform.

**Fume Hood.*** An enclosure designed to draw air inward by means of mechanical ventilation. This definition does not include canopy hoods or recirculation laminar-flow biological-safety cabinets that are not designed for use with flammable materials. (LAB)

**A-2-2 Fume Hood.** Laboratory fume hoods prevent toxic, flammable, or noxious vapors from entering the laboratory, present a physical barrier from chemical reactions, and serve to contain accidental spills.

**General Care Area.** See definition of Patient Care Area.

**Governing Body.*** The person or persons who have the overall legal responsibility for the operation of a health care facility. (ADM)

**A-2-2 Governing Body.** See the *Accreditation Manual for Hospitals, Joint Commission on Accreditation of Healthcare Organizations,* Chicago, 1989.

**Ground-Fault Circuit Interrupter.** A device whose function is to interrupt the electric circuit to the load when a fault current to ground exceeds some predetermined value that is less than that required to operate the overcurrent protective device of the supply circuit. (ES)

**Grounding.** See definition of Grounding System.

The issue of grounding in health care facilities has been controversial. Grounding is a means of providing a low-resistance pathway to ground (the point of relative voltage) for metal parts of appliances not intended to carry currents. If a fault should occur within the appliance that induces a voltage between these parts and ground, current would flow through the grounding means rather than some higher-resistance path, such as a person touching the metal part. A method for providing that low-resistance path has evolved in the form of a third conductor in the power cord of appliances and a third conductor in the building circuit wiring. Thus, a continuous low-resistance path is created between the non-current-carrying metal parts of appliances and earth ground (see Exhibit 2.3).

Questions regarding the reliability of the third conductor method of grounding intensified in the health care community when the number of electrical appliances used in health care began to increase in the late 1960s. Instead of one or two electrical devices involved in any procedure, six or more might be attached to a patient. Some believed that this increase in electrical devices created a need for even more grounding mechanisms while others insisted that better quality and

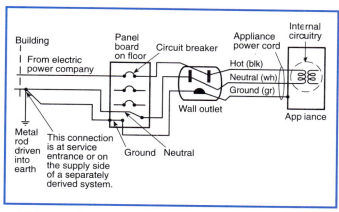

**Exhibit 2.3** *Grounding.*

maintenance of existing grounding methods was adequate. One method of grounding tried was equipotential grounding systems, but the concept proved to be too restrictive. By listing only performance criteria, the methods used to reach required performance levels were left to the discretion of equipment designers. (See 3-3.3.2.1.)

Grounding is a concern because most electrical power systems are grounded; that is, a conductor is physically connected to earth. This grounding is not relevant to the operation of the electrical appliance as long as the voltage difference between the two power conductors is the operating voltage of the appliance. However, grounding (and identifying) one conductor has long been established as a safety measure so that events such as lightning or transformer faults will not raise both conductors to a high voltage level in relation to the physical earth.

Although this safety measure solved one problem, it created another hazard. Many conductors found in a building (e.g., structural steel, plumbing) are physically connected to the earth, an arrangement that effectively makes them electrically connected to one side of the power line. In addition, a person could be connected to earth via his body capacitance even without a direct conductive connection to a grounded object. Thus, the possibility exists that everyone is connected to one power conductor and all that is needed is one accidental connection to the other power conductor to experience a shock.

It can be argued that it would be safer not to have either conductor grounded. For example, for a wiring system of limited size, such as an isolated power system in an operating room, ungrounded systems can be practical. However, capacitive coupling and other problems in large systems, such as a system for an entire building, would defeat the objective of an isolated power system.

**Grounding System.*** A system of conductors that provides a low-impedance return path for leakage and fault currents. (ES)

**A-2-2 Grounding System.** It coordinates with, but can be locally more extensive than, the grounding system described in Article 250 of NFPA 70, *National Electrical Code.*

**Hazard Current.** For a given set of connections in an isolated power system, the total current that would flow through a low impedance if it were connected between either isolated conductor and ground. The various hazard currents are as follows: (ES)

*Fault Hazard Current.* The hazard current of a given isolated power system with all devices connected except the line isolation monitor.

*Monitor Hazard Current.* The hazard current of the line isolation monitor alone.

*Total Hazard Current.* The hazard current of a given isolated system with all devices, including the line isolation monitor, connected. (ES)

> Hazard currents are not currents that actually flow under normal conditions. Rather, they are currents that are predicted to be able to flow under certain circumstances (i.e., with one line solidly grounded). This is not to say that there is no leakage current under normal conditions, but this leakage current will always be less than the actual hazard current.

**Hazardous Chemical.*** A chemical with one or more of the following hazard ratings as defined in NFPA 704, *Standard System for the Identification of the Hazards of Materials for Emergency Response:* Health—2, 3, or 4; Flammability—2, 3, or 4; Reactivity—2, 3, or 4. *(See C-10.2.3.)* (LAB)

**A-2-2 Hazardous Chemical.** For hazard ratings of many chemicals, see NFPA 49, *Hazardous Chemicals Data*, and NFPA 325, *Guide to Fire Hazard Properties of Flammable Liquids, Gases, and Volatile Solids*, both available in NFPA's *Fire Protection Guide to Hazardous Materials.*

**Health Care Facilities.** Buildings or portions of buildings in which medical, dental, psychiatric, nursing, obstetrical, or surgical care are provided. Health care facilities include, but are not limited to, hospitals, nursing homes, limited care facilities, clinics, medical and dental offices, and ambulatory care centers, whether permanent or movable. (ADM)

> This definition is consistent with that in NFPA *101, Life Safety Code.* [2] Note that for the purposes of NFPA 99 a portion of a building can be considered a health care facility. However, only that portion is considered a health care facility, not the entire building.

**Hood, Oxygen.** A device encapsulating a patient's head and used for a purpose similar to that of a mask. *(See definition of Mask.)* (HHF)

> The oxygen hood was developed for those patients unable to breathe oxygen in a hyperbaric chamber through a more traditional mask. It might be used, for example, by patients who are undergoing mandibular reconstruction surgery and are unable

to be fitted with an oronasal mask. The clear, flexible hood either is attached to a rubber neck dam/ring assembly or is taped to the patient's skin to help prevent oxygen leaks into the chamber environment. Hood inflation is maintained with a delicate balance of supply (100 percent oxygen) and exhaust. The hood assembly is the most commonly used oxygen delivery device in Class A clinical hyperbaric medicine chambers.

**Hospital-Based.** In the interpretation and application of this document, physically connected to a hospital. (GDE)

Stand-alone "daytime" health care facilities that include inhalation anesthetizing locations can readily be classified as ambulatory health care facilities. Those ambulatory care facilities located adjacent to, or forming a portion of, a hospital are more difficult to classify. The former Committee on Anesthetizing Agents (now part of the Committee on Gas Delivery Equipment) extensively debated the best and most practical method of determining whether a specific anesthetizing location would be governed by the requirements for hospital facilities or the requirements for ambulatory health care facilities. The definition of *hospital-based* reflects the conclusion that if an ambulatory health care facility that has an anesthetizing location is "physically connected" to a hospital, there is a reasonable chance that inpatients from the hospital will be operated on in the ambulatory care facility. For purposes of Chapter 13 and anesthetizing locations, "physically connected" means that a patient can be wheeled directly from the inpatient portion of the facility to the ambulatory health care facility without going outside or leaving the hospital premises. The concern of the Technical Committee on Gas Delivery Equipment was whether a hospital would be able to easily accommodate an overflow of its inpatient surgical patients through the use of operating rooms in the ambulatory health care facility.

**Hospital Facility.** A building or part thereof used for the medical, psychiatric, obstetrical, or surgical care, on a 24-hour basis, of four or more inpatients. *Hospital*, wherever used in this standard, includes general hospitals, mental hospitals, tuberculosis hospitals, children's hospitals, and any such facilities providing inpatient care. (ADM)

The definition of *hospital facility* is consistent with that in other NFPA documents, such as NFPA *101, Life Safety Code.* [2] It was revised in 1996 to conform to the *NFPA Style Manual.*

**Humidifier.** A device used for adding water vapor to inspired gas. (GDE)

**Hyperbaric.** Pressures above atmospheric pressure. (HHF)

**Hyperbaric Oxygenation.** The application of pure oxygen or an oxygen-enriched gaseous mixture to a subject at elevated pressure. (HHF)

This term is also known as *HBO*. Hyperbaric oxygen creates a more favorable oxygen diffusion gradient by providing increased tissue oxygen levels that are dissolved in the blood's plasma. The Undersea and Hyperbaric Medical Society defines HBO as "breathing 100 percent oxygen while pressurized in a hyperbaric chamber." HBO is routinely used to treat a variety of nonhealing wound conditions such as diabetic ulcers, failing skin flaps, and osteoradionecrosis of the mandible. It should be noted that 100 percent oxygen is never administered at gauge pressures greater than 66 FSW (29.4 psi or 3 ATA). If this cardinal rule is violated, the person breathing oxygen at this pressure (or greater) will experience oxygen toxicity, a condition similar to a grand mal seizure.

**Hypobaric.** Pressures below atmospheric pressure. (HHF)

**Hypoxia.** A state of inadequate oxygenation of the blood and tissue. (HHF)

**Immediate Restoration of Service.** Automatic restoration of operation with an interruption of not more than 10 seconds. (ES)

The immediate restoration does provide for a brief interruption of power for 10 seconds. If a particular appliance or procedure cannot tolerate even this brief interruption, a method of bridging or eliminating this 10-second period might need to be provided through the use of an uninterrupted power supply (UPS).

**Impedance.*** Impedance is the ratio of the voltage drop across a circuit element to the current flowing through the same circuit element. The unit of impedance is the ohm. (EE)

**A-2-2 Impedance.** The circuit element can consist of any combination of resistance, capacitance, or inductance.

Impedance is frequency-dependent and is stated at some frequency and in ohms. The symbol for impedance is the letter *Z*. Resistance, also measured in ohms, is only one element of an impedance but is not frequency-dependent. The elements of impedance caused by inductance and capacitance are called reactance. Reactance is also measured in ohms. The symbol for reactance is the letter *X*.

**Incident Command System (ICS).** The combination of facilities, equipment, personnel, procedures, and communications operating within a common organizational structure with responsibility for the management of assigned resources to effectively accomplish stated objectives pertaining to an incident described as *incident command system* in this document. (From NFPA 1600, *Recommended Practice for Disaster Management*.)

In the 1996 edition the term *incident management system* was added when a then new Chapter 11, with requirements on emergency preparedness, replaced a previous annex with information and recommendations on the subject. For this 1999 edition, the term *incident management system* (which was formerly defined but not used) has been deleted and replaced with the term *incident command system*. The term is defined here in coordination with the definition that appears in NFPA 1600, *Recommended Practice for Disaster Management*. [6] The committee responsible for this text believes health care facilities need to use this method of managing disasters in order to function more efficiently in conjunction with the fire service, which also uses this method in its operations. The use of this term also complies with the NFPA Standards Council directive to correlate terms used in more than one document.

**Intermittent Positive-Pressure Breathing (IPPB).** Ventilation of the lungs by application of intermittent positive pressure to the airway. (GDE)

**Intrinsically Safe.\*** As applied to equipment and wiring, equipment and wiring that are incapable of releasing sufficient electrical energy under normal or abnormal conditions to cause ignition of a specific hazardous atmospheric mixture. (HHF)

**A-2-2 Intrinsically Safe.** Abnormal conditions can include accidental damage to any part of the equipment or wiring, insulation or other failure of electrical components, application of overvoltage, adjustment and maintenance operations, and other similar conditions.

It is very difficult to obtain medical equipment (monitors, etc.) that has been certified as intrinsically safe for operation in the hyperbaric environment.

**Isolated Patient Lead.** A patient lead whose impedance to ground or to a power line is sufficiently high that connecting the lead to ground, or to either conductor of the power line, results in current flow below a hazardous limit in the lead. (EE)

The development of isolated patient leads is a direct result of the discovery, and testing, that very low levels of leakage currents in leads could be disruptive to the heart (see commentary on the definition of *leakage current*). Conversely, a nonisolated patient lead either is in direct electrical connection with the ground wire or does not have sufficient impedance to keep current flows in the leads below a hazardous limit.

The concept of an isolated patient lead does not relate only to the physical wire that is connected to the patient but to the wire as it is assembled to the appliance.

**Isolated Power System.\*** A system comprising an isolating transformer or its equivalent, a line isolation monitor, and its ungrounded circuit conductors. (ES)

**A-2-2 Isolated Power System.** See NFPA 70, *National Electrical Code*.

When the problem of explosions in operating rooms was first addressed in the 1940s, an *isolated power system* (IPS) was one of the techniques utilized to reduce the occurrence of sparks in the operating room. (A spark of sufficient energy is able to cause an explosion when flammable gases are present.) With the development of nonflammable anesthetics, however, the necessity of continuing to adhere to requirements developed for use with flammable anesthetics began to be questioned. The major issue in this regard was over the requirements for IPSs in nonflammable anesthetizing locations. (Note: The requirement for IPSs in flammable anesthetizing locations has never been an issue.)

The case for deleting requirements for IPSs formally began in 1977 during the revision of the 1973 edition of NFPA 56A, *Standard for Inhalation Anesthetics.* Comments were submitted in the fall of 1977 recommending deletion of mandatory requirements for IPSs in nonflammable anesthetizing locations. The then Committee on Anesthetic Agents rejected the comments. The issue, however, was raised at the 1978 NFPA Annual Meeting and an amendment approving the deletion of the requirements for IPSs was passed by the NFPA members present. Under the NFPA regulations governing committee projects, however, amendments to committee reports must be upheld by a two-thirds vote of the committee. This two-thirds majority was not reached and the association's amendment was rejected. The American Hospital Association appealed the committee action to the Standards Council. The Council directed the committee to meet and vote on the matter again. The Committee carried out this directive and reached the same conclusion. The matter was then appealed to the NFPA Board of Directors, who directed the committee to address the issue yet again.

The committee met for two days in February 1980 and extensively discussed the necessity of ungrounded electrical systems in anesthetizing locations. What emerged was a listing of four conditions in anesthetizing locations that the committee believed were sufficiently hazardous to warrant the installation of an ungrounded electrical system. These four conditions consisted of the following:

(1) The possibility that wet conditions, including standing fluids, on the floor existed.
(2) Three or more line-operated electrical devices were to be normally connected to the patient.
(3) Invasive procedures that could not be safely terminated immediately were to be carried out.
(4) Flammable anesthetics were to be used.

These conditions were added to NFPA 56A-1978, in the form of a Tentative Interim Amendment (TIA).

For the 1984 edition of NFPA 99, this TIA was proposed for incorporation into the standard (all TIAs become automatic proposals for the next edition of a document). However, proposals recommending that IPSs be required only in flammable anesthetizing locations were again received.

The following is a brief summary of the arguments put forth by proponents and opponents of IPSs in nonflammable anesthetizing locations.

Arguments for continuing to require IPSs in nonflammable anesthetizing locations included the following:

(a) Surgical techniques and procedures are involving more and more electrically powered devices; patient safety mandates uninterrupted power as much as is reasonably possible. An IPS allows the continued safe use of an appliance that has suffered a single fault, that is, a short circuit between a power conductor and the parts of the appliance. With a conventional system, the circuit breaker would open if such a fault occurred.

(b) The environment of the anesthetizing location, with the proliferation of electrical devices and the creation of wet environments due to frequent spillage of biological and other fluids onto gowns and floors, increases the electrocution hazard.

(c) Not all health care facilities have adequately trained their staff personnel to conduct preventive maintenance for modern diagnostic and therapeutic equipment now used in anesthetizing locations.

(d) IPSs sharply limit the maximum ground-seeking current that can flow through any conductor, including a human.

(e) IPSs are passive systems; they do not depend on activation to provide protection. Alternative measures [(i.e., ground-fault circuit interrupters (CFCIs)] included in NFPA 70, *National Electrical Code* [3], are not considered appropriate for anesthetizing locations.

(f) Nuisance alarms have been eliminated with the elevation of the alarm level of hazard current from 2 milliamperes to 5 milliamperes. The increased alarm level also allows the use of larger transformers so that the problem of overloading is ameliorated.

(g) The lack of published incident reports cannot be construed to mean that no electric shocks have occurred. The litigious climate prevalent in the United States today, particularly involving medical practitioners, discourages the reporting of incidents.

(h) Equipment in anesthetizing locations can be assembled and disassembled several times a day, thus subjecting it to frequent handling and abuse (unlike equipment in other patient care areas where this type of usage is not common).

(i) The cost of installing IPS during new construction is a minimal fraction of the total cost of constructing an anesthetizing location.

Arguments for eliminating the requirement for IPSs in nonflammable anesthetizing locations included the following:

(a) Adequate margins of safety against the hazards of fire, explosion, and electric shock can be achieved in nonflammable anesthetizing locations utilizing a conventional grounded system.

(b) The risk of accidental electric shock with conventional grounded systems is already so small that it is difficult to justify the additional cost of IPSs.

(c) Circuit breakers opening as a result of overloading the IPS is one of the more common causes of the loss of electric power in anesthetizing locations. (Note: This does not relate to the sizing of the isolation transformer but to the number and amperages of devices connected to each circuit on the IPS.)

(d) A portion of new anesthetizing locations do not have IPSs, and their record of incidents is little or no different from those anesthetizing locations with IPSs.

(e) Helpless, comatose, or unresponsive patients are also found in other areas of a health care facility, and IPSs are not required in these areas.

(f) Deleting this requirement does not prohibit those who desire IPSs from installing them.

(g) A primary hazard for which IPSs provide protection is a line-to-ground fault; however, this fault is now rare because of changes in equipment design.

The committee again rejected proposals to eliminate IPSs in nonflammable anesthetizing locations. At the 1983 NFPA Fall Meeting, amendments were once again passed deleting mandatory requirements for IPSs in nonflammable anesthetizing locations (the amendments permitted a grounded system). This time the committee reached a simple majority in support of the association's amendments but not the two-thirds majority required to accept them. A complaint was filed with the Standards Council recommending acceptance of the association amendments. New arguments for the complaint included the following:

(a) Several enforcement authorities had eliminated the mandatory requirement for IPSs in nonflammable anesthetizing locations.

(b) A majority of NFPA's Health Care Section, a majority of NFPA members, and a majority of the committee should not be ignored.

(c) The four criteria for installing IPSs, as listed in a TIA developed for NFPA 56A–1978, still essentially required IPSs in nonflammable anesthetizing locations.

The council heard three additional arguments at a hearing. First, with the combination of all twelve health care facilities documents into one document, the issue should have fallen under the jurisdiction of the then Committee on Safe Use of Electricity in Patient Care Areas of Health Care Facilities, and not the then Committee on Anesthetic Agents. Second, the Committee on Safe Use of Electricity in Patient Care Areas of Health Care Facilities developed electrical requirements for wet locations that were consistent with the requirements established by the Committee on Anesthetic Agents concerning anesthetizing locations. And third, ambulatory care facilities that performed only nonmajor procedures, but where general anesthesia was still administered, were not required to install IPSs in their facilities.

Under NFPA Regulations Governing Committee Projects, the Standards Council reviews all material related to the processing and adopting of a document and issues (or does not issue) a document based on this material. The council, in this case, voted to issue NFPA 99–1984 with the incorporation of the amendments that deleted the mandatory requirement for IPSs in nonflammable anesthetizing locations. In addition, the council recommended that the committee process, in the form of a footnote, a Tentative Interim Amendment, which does not include requirements, strongly recommending the installation of IPSs since all parties at the council hearing acknowledged that these systems do provide an added level of electrical safety for patients and staff.

A subsequent appeal of the Standards Council's decision was filed with the NFPA Board of Directors. While the board noted that the council's recommendation for a TIA was inappropriate, the council's action was upheld.

The issue of IPSs in anesthetizing locations was resolved—at least procedurally.

Permitting (for anesthesia purposes) a grounded electrical system in nonflammable anesthetizing locations, however, soon created another set of questions concerning requirements for wet locations.

An additional level of electrical safety is required in wet locations per NFPA 99. This safety is to be achieved essentially by either GFCIs or an IPS (depending on whether power interruption could be tolerated). When all anesthetizing locations were required to have IPSs, it was not necessary to determine whether an anesthetizing location was also a wet location, because the required level of safety was already provided. However, with the change in 1984, a new question had to be answered for each nonflammable anesthetizing location: Was it a wet location?

This question was extensively discussed for the 1987 edition of NFPA 99 by three subcommittees (Anesthesia Services, Electrical Equipment, and Electrical Systems) and by the then Technical Committee on Health Care Facilities. It was noted that during some surgical procedures, operating rooms remained "dry" (e.g., eye surgery, dermatological surgery), while during other procedures, extensive use or spillage of liquids or fluids made conditions very "wet" (e.g., cystoscopy, certain bowel procedures, cardiothoracic surgery). The definition of *wet location* was reviewed, and some changes were proposed, including a suggested list of "wet" and "dry" nonflammable anesthetizing locations. The Technical Committee on Health Care Facilities, the committee responsible for coordinating recommendations from all the subcommittees under it, could not agree on what changes should be made, in the form of either requirements or recommendations. Instead, an informatory note proposed by the former Technical Committee on Anesthetizing Agents was approved [in the 1996 edition of NFPA 99, all notes were moved to Appendix A; see A-12-4.1.2.6(a)]. This note called the reader's attention to the fact that wet location provisions could be applied to some anesthetizing locations because anesthetizing locations were patient care areas. No other changes (with regard to isolated power systems, electrical requirements for nonflammable anesthetizing locations, or the definition of *wet location*) were made. It is still the responsibility of the individual health care facility to decide which, if any, anesthetizing locations should be considered wet locations.

For the 1990 edition of NFPA 99, the subject of isolated power system requirements was again reviewed, this time by an ad hoc subcommittee appointed by the chairman of the then Technical Committee on Health Care Facilities. The major recommendation, and subsequent change, was a modification to the definition of *wet location.* (See commentary under the definition of *wet location.*)

The 1990s have seen a proliferation of outpatient surgery facilities and the number of arthroscopic procedures performed by orthopedic surgeons. Arthroscopic procedures are chief among those procedures that produce "standing fluids on the floor or drenching of the work area" (see definition of *wet location*). Since these arthroscopic procedures are done both on an inpatient and outpatient basis, where the possible interruption of power by GFCI receptacles cannot be tolerated, it is not safe to assume that these "minor surgeries" are not candidates for isolated power systems.

For a discussion on the need for maintaining continuity of power, see commentary under 3-2.4.2.

**Isolation Transformer.** A transformer of the multiple-winding type, with the primary and secondary windings physically separated, that inductively couples its ungrounded secondary winding to the grounded feeder system that energizes its primary winding. (ES)

Isolation transformers change a grounded electrical system to an ungrounded electrical system (see Exhibit 2.4) and provide an added level of protection against hazardous electric current flow for certain electrical faults within appliances.

Thus, the connection to ground of one conductor of the electrical power system is eliminated (see commentary under the definition of *grounding*), and two gross faults, rather than one, are required in order to cause a severe shock.

Where interruption of electrical power cannot be tolerated, a further advantage of an isolation transformer is that certain first faults within a device (e.g., line-to-ground) will not interrupt the flow of electricity to that device. This feature is especially important in areas such as operating rooms. A fault in a grounded electrical system, such as the phase (hot) conductor touching the chassis of a properly grounded

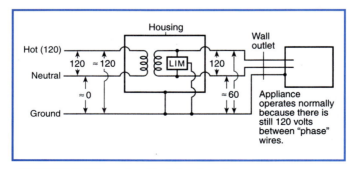

**Exhibit 2.4** *Schematic of isolation transformer.*

appliance, would create a short circuit and trip (open) either the appliance's overcurrent protector or the branch circuit breaker, removing power from the appliance or from all the appliances on that breaker. Such a fault in an ungrounded (isolated) electrical system would remove only one layer of protection, reducing the system to the equivalent of a conventionally grounded system but allowing the device to continue to be used if absolutely essential. A monitoring device (i.e., a line isolation monitor) can warn that a fault has occurred, and the fault can be identified without electrical power being interrupted. (Note: A line-to-line fault will trip a circuit breaker whether the appliance is operating from an IPS or from a grounded system.)

This added level of protection applies to gross macroshock effects (in the milliampere and ampere levels of current). It does not apply to microshock effects (in the microampere levels of current) because electrical systems usually have large enough capacitive couplings at these low current levels to negate the isolating effects of an isolation transformer.

Isolation transformers are built in various sizes. The units used in anesthetizing locations, for example, range up to 25 kVA. It is therefore necessary to know the approximate number of devices expected to be used and their power ratings when installing isolation transformer(s) in these locations. Otherwise, the transformer's circuit breaker overcurrent protection will sense too much current being drawn and will trip and cut off power to all devices connected to the circuit breaker.

When an isolation transformer is installed in a health care facility, it must be in conjunction with a line isolation monitor (LIM). (See the definition of *line isolation monitor.*) LIMs provide visual and audible indications of current flow between the output wires of the isolation transformer and ground as a result of coupling (resistive or capacitive). The LIM will alarm when this current passes above some preset value (now set at 5 milliamperes maximum).

**Laboratory.*** A building, space, room, or group of rooms intended to serve activities involving procedures for investigation, diagnosis, or treatment in which flammable, combustible, or oxidizing materials are to be used. (LAB)

**A-2-2 Laboratory.** These laboratories are not intended to include isolated frozen section laboratories; areas in which oxygen is administered; blood donor rooms in which flammable, combustible, or otherwise hazardous materials normally used in laboratory procedures are not present; and clinical service areas not using hazardous materials.

Diagnostic and/or therapeutic areas of health care facilities are often referred to as laboratories. For the purposes of this document, however, only those areas with the hazards indicated in the definition are considered laboratories. Note that a laboratory is not facility-dependent. Application of requirements are contained in Chapters 12 through 17.

Isolated frozen section laboratories are included in this definition if they use flammable liquids. They are not included if they do not use flammable liquids.

The phrase "located in any part of a health care facility and" was deleted for the 1993 edition of NFPA 99. The concept of a clinical laboratory is not facility-dependent. The committee was concerned that retention of the phrase "health care facility" within the definition might imply that NFPA 45, *Standard on Fire Protection for Laboratories Using Chemicals* [7], did not apply to clinical laboratories. NFPA 45 is the primary reference document for construction requirements, and it applies to all health care laboratories that store or use flammable or combustible liquids in quantity. NFPA 45 should be consulted for details concerning those volumes that determine applicability. (See the discussion after A-10-1.)

In this 1999 edition, the former second sentence of the definition was moved to Appendix A because the committee felt that this sentence, serving only to clarify intent, is not a proper part of the definition.

**Laboratory Work Area.\*** A room or space for testing, analysis, research, instruction, or similar activities that involve the use of chemicals. (LAB)

For this 1999 edition, the word *research* was added to the definition of the term *laboratory work area* to correlate the definition with that in NFPA 45, *Standard on Fire Protection for Laboratories Using Chemicals.* The note contained in the previous edition stating that "the work area might or might not be enclosed" was deleted because the definition was complete without this information.

**A-2-2 Laboratory Work Area.** See NFPA 45, *Standard on Fire Protection for Laboratories Using Chemicals.*

**Leakage Current.** Any current, including capacitively coupled current, not intended to be applied to a patient, that is conveyed from exposed metal parts of an appliance to ground or to other accessible parts of an appliance. (EE)

Leakage current is electric current as governed by Ohm's law:

$$I = \frac{V}{Z}$$

where:

$I$ = current

$V$ = voltage

$Z$ = impedance of the circuit (see definition of *impedance*)

There must be some driving force (voltage) and a closed circuit before current flows. Leakage current is a name given only to those particular currents meeting the preceding definition, and it is peculiar only in that part of the circuit that may be a capacitive coupling or a faulty resistive insulation. A human being may form part of the circuit (though not an intended part) and thus permit the flow of electric current. See A-9-2.1.13.4(c) for an extensive discussion on the leakage current limits contained in Chapters 7 and 9.

Leakage current became a growing concern in the health care community in the 1960s when cardiovascular medicine and surgery began invading the heart with electrical and electromechanical probes. Researchers discovered that the heart's pumping action could be interrupted with rather small levels of current—particularly at the power distribution frequency of 60 Hz current. Various factors contributed to the actual value required to fibrillate a specific heart, including the condition and temperature of the heart; the number and types of drugs being administered; the location and value of the electrical contact on or in the heart; and the variability and shape of the current waveform. The design, application, and maintenance of electromedical equipment in health care facilities were dramatically altered by this unintended current, an inevitable by-product of electrical equipment, and the relatively low levels of current that could be disruptive or lethal. [8]

For further details of the effects of currents, see A-3-2.2.2 and A-9-2.1.13.4(c).

**Level 3 Compressed Air System.\***  A system of component parts, including, but not limited to, air compressor, motor, receiver, controls, filters, dryers, valves and piping, that delivers compressed air <160 psig (1100 kPa) to power devices (hand pieces, syringe, cleaning devices, etc.) as a power source. (PIP)

**A-2-2 Level 3 Compressed Air System.** The system does not produce air to meet the medical requirements of medical air and is not intended to be used for air life support devices.

The need to provide a definition for a Level 3 compressed air system (provided for the first time in the 1996 edition) resulted from the way in which the term *dental compressed air* was defined and interpreted in the 1993 edition. That 1993 definition originated because all dental installations were being required to meet the quality of air requirements for medical compressed air. This definition of *dental compressed air* was subsequently seen as overly restrictive and not a proper identification of other applications that were possible. It was also not the intent of the committee to require compressed air used for powering dynamic devices and air-drying of teeth to meet the higher standard of medical compressed air. The current definition expands the potential applications of compressed air systems that meet the definition. Requirements in Chapter 4 have also been rewritten to be consistent with this new term and to ensure a more suitable and reliable quality of air.

In addition, the committee has developed piped gas system criteria, within Level 3 systems, for compressed air for patients for nonbreathing purposes (see 4-5.1.1.3) and compressed gas for gas-powered devices (see 4-5.1.1.4). The distribution criteria for these two sources are the same. (See Section 4-5 for all the requirements for Level 3 systems.)

Where a facility uses compressed air for breathing support, such as relative anesthesia (conscious sedation), it is the intent of the committee to require the compressed air quality to meet the higher standards of medical compressed air.

The application of Level 3 compressed air systems can be found by reviewing Chapters 12 through 17.

**Life Safety Branch.** A subsystem of the emergency system consisting of feeders and branch circuits, meeting the requirements of Article 700 of NFPA 70, *National Electrical Code*, and intended to provide adequate power needs to ensure safety to patients and personnel, and that is automatically connected to alternate power sources during interruption of the normal power source. (ES)

**Limited Care Facility.** A building or part thereof used on a 24-hour basis for the housing of four or more persons who are incapable of self-preservation because of age, physical limitation due to accident or illness, or mental limitations such as mental retardation/developmental disability, mental illness, or chemical dependency. (ADM)

> The term *health care facility* was added in the 1988 edition of NFPA *101, Life Safety Code* [2], and replaced *custodial care facility* and *supervisory care facility* with respect to life safety criteria.
> NFPA 99 followed suit in the 1990 edition for correlation purposes. Chapter 17, "Limited Care Facilities," replaced previous chapters, on custodial care and supervisory care facilities. Most of the specifics have been eliminated, and the criterion for classifying a facility is based on the ability of occupants (i.e., whether they are capable of self-preservation in an emergency that threatens the normal operation of the facility).
> See commentary under the definition of *ambulatory health care facility* for discussion on changes made regarding the definitions of various types of health care facilities.

**Limited-Combustible Material.*** A material (as defined in NFPA 220, *Standard on Types of Building Construction*) not complying with the definition of noncombustible material that, in the form in which it is used, has a potential heat value not exceeding 3500 Btu/lb (8141 kJ/kg) and complies with one of the following paragraphs (a) or (b). Materials subject to increase in combustibility or flame-spread rating beyond the limits herein established through the effects of age, moisture, or other atmospheric condition are considered combustible.

(a) Materials having a structural base of noncombustible material, with a surfacing not exceeding a thickness of $^1/_8$ in. (3.2 mm) and having a flame-spread rating not greater than 50

(b) Materials, in the form and thickness used, other than as described in (a), having neither a flame-spread rating greater than 25 nor evidence of continued progressive combustion and of such composition that surfaces that would be exposed by cutting through the material on any plane would have neither a flame-spread rating greater than 25 nor evidence of continued progressive combustion (PIP)

**A-2-2 Limited-Combustible Material.** See NFPA 259, *Standard Test Method for Potential Heat of Building Materials.*

**Line Isolation Monitor.** A test instrument designed to continually check the balanced and unbalanced impedance from each line of an isolated circuit to ground and equipped with a built-in test circuit to exercise the alarm without adding to the leakage current hazard. (ES)

> The function of a line isolation monitor is to check the hazard current from an isolated circuit to ground. Note that the hazard current is a predicted current, not one that is actually present.
>     This definition is in concert with that in NFPA 70, *National Electrical Code.* [3]

**Liquid.** Any material that has a fluidity greater than that of 300 penetration asphalt when tested in accordance with ASTM D5, *Test for Penetration of Bituminous Materials.* When not otherwise identified, the term *liquid* includes both flammable and combustible liquids. *(See C-10.2.1.)* (LAB)

**mA.** Milliampere.

**Manifold.** A device for connecting the outlets of one or more gas cylinders to the central piping system for that specific gas. (PIP)

**Manufactured Assembly.*** A factory-assembled product designed for aesthetics or convenience that contains medical gas or vacuum outlets, piping, or other devices related to medical gases. (PIP)

**A-2-2 Manufactured Assembly.** Examples are headwalls, columns, ceiling columns, ceiling hung pendants, movable track systems, and so on.

> This definition was added in 1996 to reflect the addition of specific requirements for these potentially large and complex subcomponents of a medical gas system that are assembled in a factory and integrated into the medical gas system on site.
>     There was some confusion as to whether these assemblies were an extension of the "piped system" or a separate "device" that plugged into the piped system. The committee responded by not only adding a definition for the term *manufactured assembly* but also establishing criteria for these units. The quantity and complexity of the piping that manufactured assemblies may contain can significantly affect the final testing, operation, and integrity of the complete system. It is the committee's intent to ensure that the integrity of the piping, as established by NFPA 99, does not diminish between the wall and the appliance interface because of the use of a "manufactured assembly" that creates a similar wall-like interface. [See 4-2.2 and 4-3.1.2.2(e).]

**Mask.** A device that fits over the mouth and nose (oronasal) or nose (nasal), used to administer gases to a patient. (GDE)

**Medical Air.*** For purposes of this standard, medical air is air that

(a) Is supplied from cylinders, bulk containers, medical air compressors, or has been reconstituted from oxygen USP and nitrogen NF, and

(b) Complies with the following:

    1. Medical Air USP

    2. Total hydrocarbons

        liquid                    nondetectable

        gaseous              <25 ppm

    3. Pressure dew point at 50 psig    <39°F (4°C)

    4. Permanent particulates        5 mg/m$^3$ at normal atmospheric pressure of particulate at 1 micron size or greater (PIP)

**A-2-2 Medical Air.** Air supplied from on-site compressor and associated air treatment systems (as opposed to medical air USP supplied in cylinders) that complies with the specified limits is considered medical air. Hydrocarbon carryover from the compressor into the pipeline distribution system could be detrimental to the safety of the end user and to the integrity of the piping system. Mixing of air and oxygen is a common clinical practice, and the hazards of fire are increased if the air is thus contaminated. Compliance with these limits is thus considered important to fire and patient safety. The quality of local ambient air should be determined prior to its selection for compressors and air treatment equipment.

> The "quality of air" may seem to be a subject that is outside the scope of this document and perhaps even that of NFPA. But the topic was brought before the former Medical Gas Application Panel (now incorporated into the Technical Committee on Piping Systems) by several panel members in 1984. At issue was the problem of oil and water introduced into piped air systems by compressors. Oil poses a fire hazard if the air is blended with oxygen for respiratory support, in addition to affecting patient medical treatment. To address the problem, the panel decided to list a set of criteria for medical air (i.e., air quality) that would define requirements and list performance criteria for compressor manufacturers.
>
> These limiting characteristics for medical air recommendations in the 1987 edition of NFPA 99 were derived from several documents and reflected the air quality standards available to the then Subcommittee on Nonflammable Medical Piped Gas Systems at the time. During deliberations for the 1990 edition of NFPA 99, the United States Pharmacopia (USP) revised its monograph for Compressed Air/USP to include air "packaged" in a "low pressure collecting tank." In the opinion of the subcommittee, however, the USP did not address specific safety and contamination problems unique to the production of medical air within a health care facility (e.g., some compressor failures can introduce oil into the airstream).

Thus, the subcommittee chose to retain limits for particulates, hydrocarbons, and dew point and to include only a reference to USP.

For 1993, the subcommittee reviewed the issue again at the direction of the Standards Council because of complaints on the issue. As a result, the definition was further limited, to address only safety issues specifically of concern to health care facilities. Dew point criteria and alarm set point can be found in 4-3.1.2.2(d)2. [See commentary on dew point under 4-3.1.2.1(b)3e.]

It should be noted that NFPA 99 does not require compressors to supply specification Grade D air. NFPA 99 also does not require the quality of outside, local air to meet Grade D air. This is outside the scope of the committee.

Air treatment systems for medical air compressor systems are not required by this standard because ambient air, taken from a location free from auto exhausts or other sources of pollution, is normally well within the limits required by Compressed Air/USP and the preceding definition. Compressors that comply with the definition of *medical air compressor* will not add contamination to the airstream and thus do not often require air treatment. (Liquid ring air compressors, it should be noted, use water to compress air, and the quality of the water source is of concern because of its effect on the air being compressed.)

Air quality does vary from place to place and from day to day and could in a few areas exceed the contaminant limits of USP air for unacceptably long periods. Variation can only be determined through knowledge of local conditions and air quality testing at the intake. A local office of the U.S. Environmental Protection Agency might be able to provide data on local conditions.

Where the quality of the intake air is unreliable, specific air treatment devices may be desirable. Where installed, these devices need to be monitored and maintained. Such devices add considerably to the purchase price and maintenance of the air system, but their use can offset even greater costs with respect to the effects of untreated air on the patient and the piped air system.

**Medical Air Compressor.** A compressor that is designed to exclude oil from the air stream and compression chamber and that does not under normal operating conditions or any single fault add any toxic or flammable contaminants to the compressed air. (PIP)

After adoption of the 1990 edition of NFPA 99, the NFPA Standards Council directed the then Technical Committee on Health Care Facilities to review the definition of *medical air compressor* because of unresolved controversy during the revision process. Although compressors can be designed to deliver the quality of air required for medical compressed air purposes, factors such as the inherent design of the compressor and the way it is maintained will influence the extent oil or other contaminants are injected into the medical compressed air line during a compressor failure.

For the 1993 edition, the then Subcommittee on Nonflammable Medical Piped Gas Systems believed that the most beneficial way to preclude extensive controls and sensors was to address this issue in the compressor design. The subcommittee (now the Technical Committee on Piping Systems) replaced the previous term, *oil-free air compressor,* with a new generic term, *medical air compressor,* and defined it in terms of performance criteria for the various types of compressors that could be used. The approach taken was to require more safeguards when the possibility of oil and other contaminants entering the piping system was greater.

The revised term and definition reflects the critical importance of excluding toxic and potentially damaging elements from the medical air both for the safety of equipment, where pure oxygen is commonly added to the air, and the safety of patients, who will often breathe the air without other filtration or purification. (See the definition for *medical air.*)

Appropriate limitations and safety devices are listed in Chapter 4 for each accepted technology.

**mV.**  Millivolt.

**Nebulizer.**  A device used for producing an aerosol of water and/or medication within inspired gas supply. (GDE)

**Negative Pressure.**  Pressure less than atmospheric. (GDE)

This definition can apply to air within the body as well as that in the surrounding environment.

**Nitrogen.**  An element that, at atmospheric temperatures and pressures, exists as a clear, colorless, and tasteless gas; it comprises approximately four-fifths of the earth's atmosphere. (GDE)

**Nitrogen Narcosis.**  A condition resembling alcoholic inebriation, which results from breathing nitrogen in the air under significant pressure. *(See C-19.1.3.2.2.)* (HHF)

Nitrogen, present in air in a concentration of almost 80 percent and under pressure, causes this condition.

When breathing air at increased pressures (either scuba or hyperbaric chamber air), the partial pressure of nitrogen increases accordingly. At depths greater than 100 FSW (partial pressure of nitrogen >2400 mm Hg), nitrogen narcosis becomes more prevalent. Symptoms include euphoria, fatigue, idea fixation, laughter, inability to reason normally, loss of fine movement, loss of judgment, overconfidence, and near-term memory impairment. In any diving operation, this condition can be fatal if not recognized. Routine hyperbaric chamber operations have virtually eliminated nitrogen narcosis as a hazard.

**Nitrogen, Oil-Free, Dry (Nitrogen for Brazing and Testing).**  Nitrogen complying, at a minimum, with nitrogen NF. (PIP)

This gas is used for pipe joining and pressure-testing purposes (see 4-3.4.1.2). In this 1999 edition, Grade M as specified in CGA, Inc.'s *Pamphlet G-10.1* [9] was deleted in favor of Grade NF as the nitrogen acceptable for use in pipes that will have medical application.

This gas is required to be oil-free because it is used in piped oxygen lines where particles of oil can be a fire hazard, as well as a hazard to patients.

Prior to the 1993 edition of NFPA 99, oil-free, dry air was permitted. In reviewing the hazards, it was decided to permit only oil-free, dry nitrogen to eliminate any presence of oxygen when testing pipelines.

**Nitrous Oxide.** An inorganic compound, one of the oxides of nitrogen. It exists as a gas at atmospheric pressure and temperature, possesses a sweetish smell, and is capable of inducing the first and second stages of anesthesia when inhaled. The oxygen in the compound will be released under conditions of combustion, creating an oxygen-enriched atmosphere. (GDE)

**Noncombustible (Hyperbaric).** Within the context of Chapter 19, "Hyperbaric Facilities," an adjective describing a substance that will not burn in 95 ± 5 percent oxygen at pressures up to 3 ATA (44.1 psia). (HHF)

A distinction between noncombustibility in hyperbaric chambers and in hypobaric chambers is made to reflect the different atmospheric conditions that exist inside these chambers and the conditions under which substances are considered noncombustible in each.

While 100 percent is normally the percentage used, 95 percent ± 5 percent is considered acceptable because of limitations on measuring techniques. [See definition of *noncombustible (hypobaric).*]

**Noncombustible (Hypobaric).** Within the context of NFPA 99B, *Standard for Hypobaric Facilities*, an adjective describing a substance that will not burn in 95 ± 5 percent oxygen at pressures of 760 mm Hg. (HHF)

**Noncombustible Material.** A material (as defined in NFPA 220, *Standard on Types of Building Construction*) that, in the form in which it is used and under the conditions anticipated, will not ignite, burn, support combustion, or release flammable vapors when subjected to fire or heat. Materials reported as noncombustible, when tested in accordance with ASTM E 136, *Standard Test Method for Behavior of Materials in a Vertical Tube Furnace at 750°C*, are considered noncombustible materials. (PIP)

**Nonflammable.** An adjective describing a substance that will not burn under the conditions set forth in the definition of flame resistant. (HHF)

**Nonflammable Anesthetic Agent.*** Refers to those inhalation agents that, because of their vapor pressure at 98.6°F (37°C) and at atmospheric pressure, cannot attain flammable concentrations when mixed with air, oxygen, or mixtures of oxygen and nitrous oxide. (GDE)

The list of nonflammable anesthetic agents is representative, not inclusive. Research is continuing into the development of other improved agents.

Any anesthetic agent that does not meet the definition of a nonflammable anesthetic agent is to be considered flammable because of its inherent properties or the manner in which it is used.

**A-2-2 Nonflammable Anesthetic Agent.** It is possible to halogenate a compound and render it partially or totally nonflammable by the substitution of one or more halogens (e.g., fluorine, chlorine, bromine) for hydrogen. Thus halothane ($CF_3CHClBr$) is almost completely halogenated and is nonflammable. Methoxyflurane ($CHF_2CCl_2OCH_3$) is partially halogenated and is nonflammable in conditions encountered during clinical anesthesia (if it is heated, its vapor concentration will increase enough to burn). Fluroxene ($CF_3CH_2OCHCH_2$) is halogenated even less; it is flammable in concentrations of 4 percent or greater.

The following agents are considered flammable during conditions of clinical use in anesthesia:

(a)  Cyclopropane
(b)  Divinyl ether
(c)  Ethyl chloride
(d)  Ethylene
(e)  Ethyl ether

The following agent is flammable during use in clinical anesthesia in higher concentrations:

(a)  Fluroxene

NOTE: Because fluroxene is flammable under certain conditions of use, it is listed as a flammable agent. Concentrations required for induction of anesthesia generally exceed 4 percent and are flammable. Maintenance of fluroxene anesthesia can be accomplished with concentrations of less than 4 percent, however.

The following agents are nonflammable during conditions of use in clinical anesthesia:

(a)  Chloroform
(b)  Halothane
(c)  Methoxyflurane
(d)  Nitrous oxide
(e)  Trichloroethylene
(f)  Enflurane

**Nonflammable Medical Gas System.**  A system of piped oxygen, nitrous oxide, compressed air, or other nonflammable medical gases. *(See Chapter 4, Gas and Vacuum Systems.)* (PIP)

**Nursing Home.**  A building or part thereof used for the housing and nursing care, on a 24-hour basis, of four or more persons who, because of mental or physical incapacity, might be unable to provide for their own needs and safety without the assistance of another person.

*Nursing home*, wherever used in this document, includes nursing and convalescent homes, skilled nursing facilities, intermediate care facilities, and infirmaries in homes for the aged. (ADM)

**Office Practice, Medical/Dental.**\* A building or part thereof in which the following occur:

(a) Examinations and minor treatments/procedures are performed under the continuous supervision of a medical/dental professional.
(b) Only sedation or local anesthesia is involved and treatment or procedures do not render the patient incapable of self-preservation under emergency conditions.
(c) Overnight stays for patients or 24-hour operation are not provided. (ADM)

**A-2-2 Office Practice, Medical/Dental.** Examples include dental office/ clinic, medical office/clinic, immediate care facility, and podiatry office.

This type of health care facility was not defined until the 1996 edition. The committee's intent was to clarify the requirements governing these offices. In this 1999 edition, the text in former Chapter 15 has been deleted and the chapter is now reserved for future use. Requirements for *office practice, medical/dental* are now found in Chapter 13.

**Operating Supply.** The portion of the supply system that normally supplies the piping systems. The operating supply consists of a primary supply or a primary and secondary supply. (PIP)

*Primary Supply.* That portion of the equipment that is actually supplying the system.

*Secondary Supply.* When existing, a supply that automatically supplies the system when the primary supply becomes exhausted. This is a normal operating procedure of the equipment. (PIP)

The term *secondary supply* should not be confused with the term *reserve supply.* A secondary supply will, in the course of normal operation, be brought on-line once the *primary supply* has dropped below the amount or pressure required for normal operation. A reserve supply is used only in the event of the failure of both the primary and secondary supplies. (See the definition of *reserve supply.*)

**Oxidizing Gas.** A gas that supports combustion. Oxygen and nitrous oxide are examples of oxidizing gases. There are many others, including halogens. (HHF)

**Oxygen.**\* An element that, at atmospheric temperatures and pressures, exists as a colorless, odorless, tasteless gas. (GDE)

*Oxygen, Gaseous.* A colorless, odorless, and tasteless gas; also, the physical state of the element at atmospheric temperature and pressure.

*Oxygen, Liquid.*\* Exists at cryogenic temperature, approximately $-300°F$ ($-184.4°C$) at atmospheric pressure. It retains all of the properties of gaseous oxygen, but, in addition, when allowed to warm to room temperature at atmospheric pressure, it will evaporate and expand to fill a volume 860 times its liquid volume.

**A-2-2 Oxygen.** Its outstanding property is its ability to sustain life and to support combustion. Although oxygen is nonflammable, materials that burn in air will burn much more vigorously and create higher temperatures in oxygen or in oxygen-enriched atmospheres.

**Oxygen Delivery Equipment.** Any device used to transport and deliver an oxygen-enriched atmosphere to a patient. If an enclosure such as a mask, hood, incubator, canopy, or tent is used to contain the oxygen-enriched atmosphere, then that enclosure is considered to be oxygen delivery equipment. (GDE)

**Oxygen-Enriched Atmosphere.** For the purpose of this standard, and only for the purpose of this standard, an atmosphere in which the concentration of oxygen exceeds 23.5 percent by volume. (HHF)

> The normal percentage of oxygen in air is 20.9 percent, commonly expressed as 21 percent. The value of 23.5 percent reflects an error factor of $\pm 2.5$ percent. Such a margin of error is necessary because of the imprecision of gas measurement devices and the practicality of reconstituting air from gaseous nitrogen and oxygen. Hyperbaric chambers located in areas of potential atmospheric pollution cannot be pressurized with air drawn from the ambient atmosphere. Such chambers are supplied by "air" prepared by mixing one volume of oxygen with four volumes of nitrogen. It is impractical to reconstitute large volumes of air with tolerances closer than 21 percent $\pm$ 2.5 percent.
>
> The Committee on Hyperbaric and Hypobaric Facilities, responsible for this definition in NFPA 99, did not intend to imply that the use of compressed air cylinders in normal atmospheric areas (i.e., outside hyperbaric chambers) would create an oxygen-enriched atmosphere. The compressed air expands as it leaves the cylinder, drops to normal atmospheric pressure, and is not oxygen-enriched.
>
> This definition varies slightly from the one appearing in NFPA 53, *Recommended Practice on Materials, Equipment, and Systems Used in Oxygen-Enriched Atmospheres.* [10] The committee preferred to limit the scope of the definition to the way the term is used throughout NFPA 99. The definition is independent of the atmospheric pressure of the area and is based solely on the percentage of oxygen. In defining the term, the committee took into consideration the issue of environments, such as a hyperbaric chamber, where the atmospheric pressure can vary. Under normal atmospheric conditions, oxygen concentrations above 23.5 percent will increase the fire hazard level. Different atmospheric conditions (e.g., pressure) or the presence of gaseous diluents, however, can actually increase or decrease the fire hazard level even if, by definition, an *oxygen-enriched atmosphere* exists. An oxygen-enriched atmosphere in and of itself does not always mean an increased fire hazard exists.

**A-2-2 Oxygen, Liquid.** If spilled, the liquid can cause frostbite on contact with skin.

**Oxygen Index.** The minimum concentration of oxygen, expressed as percent by volume, in a mixture of oxygen and nitrogen that will just support combustion of a material under conditions of ASTM D 2863, *Method for Measuring the Minimum Oxygen Concentration to Support Candle-like Combustion of Plastics (Oxygen Index).* (HHF)

**Oxygen Toxicity (Hyperbaric).** Physical impairment resulting from breathing gaseous mixtures containing oxygen-enriched atmospheres at elevated partial pressures for extended periods of time. Under the pressures and times of exposure normally encountered in hyperbaric treatments, toxicity is a direct function of concentration and time of exposure. *(See Appendix C-19.1.3.2.3.)* (HHF)

> There are two types of oxygen toxicity: pulmonary (Smith–Lorraine effect) and central nervous system (Paul Bert effect). Prolonged breathing of 60 percent to 100 percent oxygen for long periods of time can produce serious lung damage. Effects range from minor lung irritation to a pneumonia-like condition. Central nervous system oxygen toxicity occurs more rapidly than pulmonary toxicity and produces seizure activity similar to epileptic convulsions. Breathing 100 percent oxygen at 60 FSW for 30 continuous minutes will produce seizure activity in approximately 2 percent of the population. Neither pulmonary nor central nervous system oxygen toxicity is a problem in routine hyperbaric chamber operations due to well-established safety practices.

**Patient Bed Location.** The location of a patient sleeping bed, or the bed or procedure table of a critical care area. (ES)

> This definition, codified in 1993, confirms the standard's intent that the general locations of examination and procedure tables in critical patient care areas (e.g., operating and delivery), as well as in recovery areas and the immediate area surrounding patient sleeping beds, are intended to be considered patient bed locations. This is an important distinction because NFPA 70 (Sections 517-83 and 517-84) and NFPA 99 [3-3.2.1.2(a)1] stipulate the number of normal and critical branch circuits and receptacles required at general care and critical care patient bed locations. NFPA 99 now requires a normal receptacle at each critical care patient bed location so that a critical branch distribution system failure (i.e., transfer switch) will not black out the entire critical patient care area.

**Patient Care Area.** Any portion of a health care facility wherein patients are intended to be examined or treated.

**A-2-2 Patient Care Area.** Business offices, corridors, lounges, day rooms, dining rooms, or similar areas typically are not classified as patient care areas.

**(a)\* General Care Areas.** General care areas are patient bedrooms, examining rooms, treatment rooms, clinics, and similar areas in which it is intended that the patient will come in contact with ordinary appliances such as a nurse-call system, electric beds, examining lamps, telephones, and entertainment devices.

**A-2-2(a) Patient Care Area—General Care Areas.** In such areas, patients could be connected to patient-care-related electrical appliances (such as heating pads, electrocardiographs, drainage pumps, monitors, otoscopes, ophthalmoscopes, intravenous lines, etc.).

**(b) Critical Care Areas.** Critical care areas are those special care units in which patients are intended to be subjected to invasive procedures and connected to line-operated, patient-care-related electrical appliances. Examples of critical care areas include intensive care units, coronary care units, angiography laboratories, cardiac catheterization laboratories, delivery rooms, operating rooms, postanesthesia recovery rooms, and emergency rooms. (EE)

> This definition was enhanced by the committee in this 1999 edition to emphasize the need for area alarms in recovery and emergency rooms as required by 4-3.1.2.2. The committee also made editorial changes to clarify examples of such areas by placing them in a separate sentence.

**Patient-Care-Related Electrical Appliance.** An electrical appliance that is intended to be used for diagnostic, therapeutic, or monitoring purposes in a patient care vicinity. (EE)

**Patient Care Vicinity.** A space, within a location intended for the examination and treatment of patients, extending 6 ft (1.8 m) beyond the normal location of the bed, chair, table, treadmill, or other device that supports the patient during examination and treatment. A patient care vicinity extends vertically to 7 ft 6 in. (2.3 m) above the floor. (EE)

> The previously used term *patient vicinity* was considered vague. The term *patient care vicinity* more accurately conveys the intended meaning of places where patients are actually cared for.
>
> A *patient care vicinity* is an area within a room and does not extend through barriers such as walls, partitions, or floors. It is a fixed area that does not move with a patient through corridors, hallways, or waiting rooms.
>
> The dimensions of a patient care vicinity are based on the possible reach of the patient or the reach of an attendant who might be touching the bed with one hand and touching a piece of apparatus with the other. The dimensions include a small safety factor in the event of unforeseen circumstances. Vertically, the dimension provides for the use of an IV pole, orthopedic frames, or similar vertically mounted attachments. Dimensional limits were established so that in large rooms it would not be necessary to treat the entire room as the patient care vicinity. See Exhibit 2.5 (a)–(c).
>
> Like many code provisions, this definition provides a definable baseline for applying safety regulations. Such a baseline prevents requirements that are too restrictive (e.g., the whole hospital should be considered a patient care vicinity) and those that are too lenient (e.g., no need to designate any patient care vicinities).

**Patient Equipment Grounding Point.** A jack or terminal that serves as the collection point for redundant grounding of electric appliances serving a patient care vicinity or for grounding other items in order to eliminate electromagnetic interference problems. (EE)

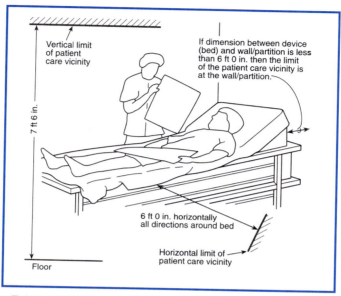

**Exhibit 2.5(a)** *A patient bed, one of the many kinds of patient care vicinities.*

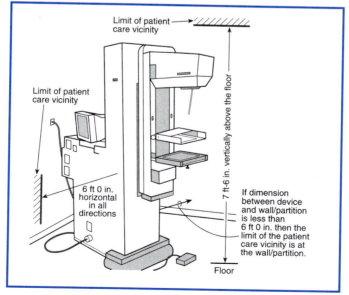

**Exhibit 2.5(b)** *A mammography machine, one of the many kinds of patient care areas.*

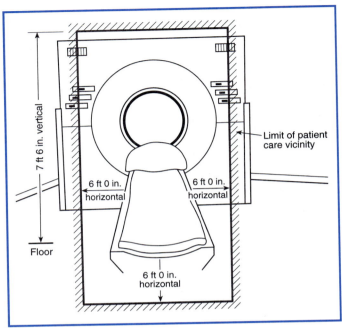

*Exhibit 2.5(c)* An MRI (magnetic resonance imaging) unit, one of the many kinds of patient care apparatuus.

The reference to electromagnetic interference was considered necessary by the Committee on Electrical Equipment because it is a recognized problem, and proper grounding will reduce its effects.

**Patient Lead.*** Any deliberate electrical connection that can carry current between an appliance and a patient. It is not intended to include adventitious or casual contacts such as a push button, bed surface, lamp, hand-held appliance, etc. (EE)

**A-2-2 Patient Lead.** This can be a surface contact (e.g., an ECG electrode); an invasive connection (e.g., implanted wire or catheter); or an incidental long-term connection (e.g., conductive tubing).

Also see definition of *Isolated Patient Lead.*

**Piped Distribution System.** A system that consists of a central supply system (manifold, bulk, or compressors) with control equipment and piping extending to points in the facility where nonflammable medical gases are required, with suitable station outlet valves at each use point. (PIP)

This term is also often applied to vacuum systems, even though that system flows to, rather than away from, the source.

**Piping.** The tubing or conduit of the system. There are three general classes of piping, as follows: (PIP)

*Main Lines.* Those parts of the system that connect the source (pumps, receivers, etc.) to the risers or branches, or both.

*Risers.* The vertical pipes connecting the system main line(s) with the branch lines on the various levels of the facility.

*Branch (Lateral) Lines.* Those sections or portions of the piping system that serve a room or group of rooms on the same story of the facility. (PIP)

These definitions now apply to both positive-pressure gas systems and negative-pressure vacuum systems because the layouts of the distribution systems of each are similar.

**Plug (Attachment Plug, Cap).** A device that, by insertion in a receptacle, establishes connection between the conductors of the attached flexible cord and the conductors connected permanently to the receptacle. (EE)

**Positive-Negative Pressure Breathing.** Ventilation of the lungs by the application of intermittent positive-negative pressure to the airway. (GDE)

**Positive Pressure.** Pressure greater than ambient atmospheric. (GDE)

**Pressure, Absolute.** The total pressure in a system with reference to zero pressure. (HHF)

**Pressure, Ambient.** Refers to total pressure of the environment referenced. (HHF)

**Pressure, Gauge.** Refers to total pressure above (or below) atmospheric. (HHF)

**Pressure, High.** A pressure exceeding 200 psig (1.38 kPa gauge) (215 psia). (GDE)

**Pressure, Partial.*** The pressure, in absolute units, exerted by a particular gas in a gas mixture. (The pressure contributed by other gases in the mixture is ignored.) (HHF)

**A-2-2 Pressure, Partial.** For example, oxygen is one of the constituents of air; the partial pressure of oxygen in standard air, at a standard air pressure of 14.7 psia, is 3.06 psia or 0.208 ATA or 158 mm Hg.

Dalton's law states, "In a mixture of gases the pressure exerted by each gas is the same as it would exert if it alone occupied the same volume; and the total pressure is the sum of the partial pressures of the component gases." This is an important gas law that should be understood. The effect of a component gas (such as carbon dioxide) could be insignificant at normal ambient pressure but extremely hazardous under hyperbaric conditions. For example, if 2 percent carbon dioxide exists at a chamber pressure of 5 ATA (132 FSW), it would have the same physiological effect as 10 percent breathed at sea level. Elevated partial pressures of carbon dioxide are thought to reduce one's tolerance to central nervous system oxygen toxicity.

**Pressure-Reducing Regulator.** A device that automatically reduces gas under high pressure to a usable lower working pressure. In hospitals, the term *regulator* is frequently used to describe a regulator that incorporates a flow-measuring device. (GDE)

**Pressure, Working.*** A pressure not exceeding 200 psig (11.6 kg/cm$^2$). (GDE)

**A-2-2 Pressure, Working.** A pipeline working pressure of 50 to 55 psig (2.9 to 3.2 kg/cm$^2$) is conventional because medical gas equipment is generally designed and calibrated for use at this pressure.

**Psia.** Pounds per square inch absolute, a unit of pressure measurement with zero pressure as the base or reference pressure. (HHF)

**Psig.** Pounds per square inch gauge, a unit of pressure measurement with atmospheric pressure as the base or reference pressure (under standard conditions, 0 psig is equivalent to 14.7 psia). (HHF)

See commentary under the definition of *atmosphere, absolute.*

**Quiet Ground.** A system of grounding conductors, insulated from portions of the conventional grounding of the power system, that interconnects the grounds of electric appliances for the purpose of improving immunity to electromagnetic noise. (ES)

**Reactance.** The component of impedance contributed by inductance or capacitance. The unit of reactance is the ohm. (EE)

See commentary under the definition of *impedance.*

**Reactive Material.** A material that, by itself, is readily capable of detonation, explosive decomposition, or explosive reaction at normal or elevated temperatures and pressures. *(See C-10-2.3.3.1 for definitions of Reactivity 3 and Reactivity 4.)* (LAB)

**Reference Grounding Point.** A terminal bus that is the equipment grounding bus, or an extension of the equipment grounding bus, and is a convenient collection point for installed grounding wires or other bonding wires where used. (EE)

**Refrigerating Equipment.** Any mechanically operated equipment used for storing, below normal ambient temperature, hazardous materials having flammability ratings of 3 or 4. It includes refrigerators, freezers, and similar equipment. (LAB)

**Relative Analgesia.** A state of sedation and partial block of pain perception produced in a patient by the inhalation of concentrations of nitrous oxide insufficient to produce loss of consciousness (conscious sedation). (GDE)

In addition to procedures performed in hospital locations, conscious sedation is frequently used in dental procedures.

**Remote.*** A use point and/or the gas system storage is considered remote if it cannot be accessed directly by walking from the front door of the treatment facility through to the use point or storage area without walking out through another exit. A remote use point is considered a separate single treatment facility. (PIP)

**A-2-2 Remote.** A gas storage supply system can be remote from the single treatment facility, but all use points must be contiguous within the facility. *[See Figure A-2-2(b).]*

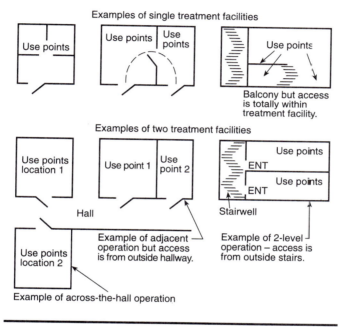

*Figure A-2-2(b) Examples of treatment facilities.*

Note that remoteness is not a matter of distance; rather, it is based on whether one must use an exit to go from the use point treatment facility to the storage area.

**Reserve Supply.** Where existing, that portion of the supply equipment that automatically supplies the system in the event of failure of the operating supply. The reserve supply only functions in an emergency and not as a normal operating procedure. (PIP)

Reserve supply should not be confused with secondary supply. (See the definition of *secondary supply,* which is defined within the definition of *operating supply.*)

**Safety Can.** An approved container, of not more than 5-gal (18.9-L) capacity, having a spring-closing lid and spout cover and so designed that it will safely relieve internal pressure when subjected to fire exposure. (LAB)

The definition for safety can is taken from NFPA 30, *Flammable and Combustible Liquids Code.* [4]

**Scavenging—Waste Gas.** See definition of Waste Anesthetic Gas Disposal.

**SCFM.** Standard cubic feet per minute. The unit used to express the measure of the volume of a gas flowing at standard conditions—a temperature of 68°F (20°C) and a pressure of 1 atmosphere (29.92 in. of Hg). (PIP)

*The SCFM is a standard reference. In an actual gas flow situation, the gas flow rate will be different as pressure and temperature change.*

*In connection with patient suction therapy and Level 1 vacuum systems, SCFM is the volume of air drawn into the vacuum system through patient drainage and aspiration equipment, the ambient room air, or both.*

**Selected Receptacles.** A minimal number of receptacles selected by the governing body of a facility as necessary to provide essential patient care and facility services during loss of normal power. (ES)

*While no specific number of receptacles is listed in Chapter 3, the Committee on Electrical Systems has emphasized the need to be judicious in selecting only the minimum number of receptacles for connection to the essential electrical system. While it can be argued that any electrical receptacle might be needed in an emergency, prudent selection, based on need and past experience, is to be used.*

*The committee has emphasized that limiting the number of receptacles on the essential electrical system limits the load on generator sets. The administration (or its duly appointed representatives) of a facility is responsible for determining the number and location of receptacles on the essential electrical system.*

*Readers are reminded that not every receptacle is to be wired to the essential electrical system. It is the intent of the committee that the entire facility not be placed on the essential electrical system.*

**Self-Extinguishing.** A characteristic of a material such that once the source of ignition is removed, the flame is quickly extinguished without the fuel or oxidizer being exhausted. (HHF)

**Semipermanent Connection.** A noninterchangeable gas connection, usually a D.I.S.S. connector, that is intended to be detached only for service and is not the point at which the user makes connections or disconnections. (PIP)

*This term was added in 1996 to address a practice commonly associated with the term manufactured assemblies, defined in this chapter.*

*The copper pipelines to these assemblies are commonly terminated with an outlet (typically a D.I.S.S. connector) that is hidden behind or within the manufac-*

tured assembly. The connection between this pipeline outlet and the outlets where the user makes connections (termed the *terminal*) is commonly made using flexible tubing (typically rubber hoses). Because these hoses and outlets are hidden, the flexible connections and outlets are accessible to maintenance personnel only when the manufactured assembly is disassembled.

This practice has created two distinct hazards. First, manufacturers are encouraging the installation of multiple station outlets to allow for convenient future connections. These station outlets are frequently not tested and certified, increasing the possibility of a latent cross connection that would be discovered only after the outlet is activated, which could be long after the system is in service. The second hazard results from the flexible assembly and connection hidden in the manufactured assembly. A leak or rupture would allow the development of an oxygen-enriched atmosphere that could have very serious consequences in a fire incident. [See 4-3.1.2.2(e) for requirements designed to mitigate these hazards.]

**Service Inlet.** The pneumatic terminus of a piped vacuum system that does not serve a critical Level 1 vacuum system. (PIP)

This term and the term *service outlet* were considered necessary by the committee to distinguish between an inlet for a Level 3 vacuum system and an inlet for a more critical level of patients, such as for a Level 1 vacuum system.

**Service Outlet.** The pneumatic terminus of a piped gas system that does not serve critical, continuous duty, nonflammable medical life support type gases such as oxygen, nitrous oxide, or medical air. (PIP)

**Single Treatment Facility.*** A diagnostic or treatment complex under a single management comprising a number of use points but confined to a single contiguous grouping of use points, that is, does not involve widely separated locations or separate distinct practices. For the purposes of this standard, a single treatment facility will be on a single level or one in which a person travels to a second level totally from within the confines of the treatment area. One-, two-, or three-level complexes in which entry to other use points is achieved through an outer foyer or hall entry are not considered single treatment facilities. (PIP)

**A-2-2  Single Treatment Facility.** The definition of single treatment facility was established to take into consideration principally single-level installations or those of a practice that could be two-level, but are reached by open stairs within the confines of the single treatment facility.

**Site of Intentional Expulsion.*** All points within 1 ft (0.3 m) of a point at which an oxygen-enriched atmosphere is intentionally vented to the atmosphere. For example, for a patient receiving oxygen via a nasal cannula or face mask, the site of expulsion normally surrounds the mask or cannula; for a patient receiving oxygen while enclosed in a canopy or incubator, the site of intentional expulsion normally surrounds the openings to the canopy or incubator;

for a patient receiving oxygen while on a ventilator, the site of intentional expulsion normally surrounds the venting port on the ventilator. (GE)

**A-2-2 Site of Intentional Expulsion.** This definition addresses the site of intended expulsion. Actual expulsion can occur at other sites remote from the intended site due to disconnections, leaks, or rupture of gas conduits and connections. Vigilance on the part of the patient care team is essential to ensure system integrity.

The material under A-2-2 is to call attention to the unexpected type of failure, such as from equipment, and the unintentional type of failure, such as from human error. Any resulting hazards should be addressed without delay. (See Exhibit 2.6.)

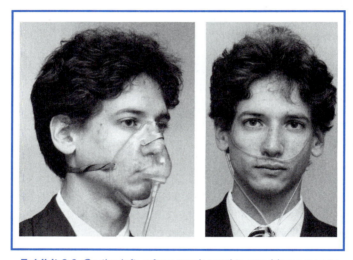

**Exhibit 2.6** On the left, a face mask used to provide oxygen to a patient. The site of intentional expulsion is 1 ft (0.3 m) away from any point on the face mask. On the right, a nasal cannula used to provide oxygen to a patient. The site of intentional expulsion is 1 ft (0.3 m) around nostrils.

The term *site of intentional expulsion* refers to intentional expulsion within the facility and does not refer to expulsion (exhaust) to the outside environment (as in building exhaust systems).

See also commentary under 7-6.2.3.1 and 9-2.1.9.3.

**Station Inlet.** An inlet point in a Type I medical-surgical piped vacuum distribution system at which the user makes connections and disconnections. (PIP)

This term distinguishes between the end connector of Level 1 piped vacuum systems and the end connector of Level 1 piped gas systems.

**Station Outlet.** An outlet point in a piped medical gas distribution system at which the user makes connections and disconnections. (PIP)

**Surface-Mounted Medical Gas Rail Systems.\*** A surface-mounted gasdelivery system intended to provide ready access for two or more gases through a common delivery system to provide multiple gas station outlet locations within a single patient room or critical care area. (PIP)

**A-2-2 Surface-Mounted Medical Gas Rail Systems.** It is the intent that surface-mounted medical gas rail systems would be permitted in individual patient rooms but would not be allowed to go directly through room walls to adjacent patient rooms. However, it is the intent to allow surface-mounted medical gas rails to be used in a given critical care area where there can be a partition separating certain patient care functions, essentially leaving the system within the given critical care area. As an example, two adjacent patient rooms outside of a critical care unit would not be permitted to have a surface-mounted medical gas rail interconnect between the two rooms through the wall. However, in a nursery where there might be one or two segregated areas for isolation, a medical gas rail system supplying more than one isolation room, but within the nursery area, would be permitted to be interconnected with the nursery system.

> A *surface-mounted medical gas rail system* (SMMGRS) is intended to service one given patient care area without penetrating any normal room wall enclosures. For example, two adjoining rooms could have rail systems connected in series from one source. The interconnection between the rooms is intended to be a section of the piping distribution system, not the rail itself.
>
> It is the intent of the committee that, where two adjoining areas in a room are separated with a partition that is not floor-to-ceiling, the SMMGRS could be continuous within the room enclosure.

**Task Illumination.** Provisions for the minimum lighting required to carry out necessary tasks in the areas described in Chapter 3, including safe access to supplies and equipment and access to exits. (ES)

**Terminal.\*** The end of a flexible hose or tubing used in a manufactured assembly where the user is intended to make connection and disconnection. (PIP)

**A-2-2 Terminal.** Terminals are constructed to comply with 4-3.1.2.4.

**Tube, Endotracheal.\*** A tube for insertion through the mouth or nose into the upper portion of the trachea (windpipe). (GDE)

**A-2-2 Tube, Endotracheal.** An endotracheal tube can be equipped with an inflatable cuff.

**Tube, Tracheotomy.\*** A curved tube for insertion into the trachea (windpipe) below the larynx (voice box) during the performance of an appropriate operative procedure (tracheotomy). (GDE)

**A-2-2 Tube, Tracheotomy.** A tracheotomy tube may be equipped with an inflatable cuff.

**Unattended Laboratory Operation.** A laboratory procedure or operation at which there is no person present who is knowledgeable regarding the operation and emergency shutdown procedures. Absence for even short periods without coverage by a knowledgeable person constitutes an unattended laboratory operation. (LAB)

> The slight difference between this definition and the one found in NFPA 45, *Standard on Fire Protection for Laboratories Using Chemicals* [7], reflects the feeling of the Committee on Laboratories that absence of personnel for even short periods constitutes unattended laboratory operation.

**Use Point.** A room, or area within a room, where medical gases are dispensed to a single patient for medical purposes. A use point is permitted to be comprised of a number of station outlets of different gases. (PIP)

**Utility Center (J box).*** The control enclosure for all services used. (PIP)

**A-2-2 Utility Center (J box).** Typically includes electrical receptacle(s), compressed air, nitrogen, vacuum, and water.

> This definition was added in 1996 to identify the enclosure that is found in typical Level 3 systems.

**Vacuum System—Level 1.** A system consisting of central-vacuum-producing equipment with pressure and operating controls, shutoff valves, alarm warning systems, gauges, and a network of piping extending to and terminating with suitable station inlets at locations where patient suction could be required. (PIP)

> This system, as the name implies, is what was formerly referred to as a *medical-surgical vacuum system*. It was renamed *vacuum system—Level 1* for the 1996 edition of NFPA 99 as a result of the restructuring of Chapter 4. This system is dedicated for patient suctioning and is not intended for other purposes. Use for waste anesthetic gas disposal is not recommended. (See 4-3.3 and its commentary for information on precautions.)
>
> Chapters 12 through 17 list the "level" of vacuum systems required for various health care facilities.

**Vacuum System—Level 3.*** A vacuum system, either a wet or dry piping system, designed to remove liquid, air-gas, and solids from the treated area. (PIP)

**A-2-2 Vacuum System—Level 3.** The system is not intended for Level 1 vacuum applications. A wet piping system is designed to accommodate liquid, air-gas, and solids through the service inlet. A dry piping system is designed to accommodate air-gas only through the service inlet. [Liquid(s) and solid(s) are trapped before entering the service inlet.]

**WAGD Interface.\*** A device provided on the anesthesia gas machine that connects the WAGD network to the patient breathing circuit. (PIP)

**A-2-2 WAGD Interface.** Interfaces are provided with overpressure, underpressure, overflow, and underflow compensation to ensure the breathing circuit is isolated from the WAGD system.

**Waste Anesthetic Gas Disposal (WAGD).** The process of capturing and carrying away gases vented from the patient breathing circuit during the normal operation of gas anesthetic equipment. (PIP)

WAGD is often termed *scavenging* or *evacuation.* WAGD, however, is technically correct and descriptive and is less susceptible to misinterpretation. Scavenging and evacuation have other medical uses and are sometimes confused with WAGD. For further information on WAGD, see commentary under 4-3.3.

**Wet Location.** A patient care area that is normally subject to wet conditions while patients are present. This includes standing fluids on the floor or drenching of the work area, either of which condition is intimate to the patient or staff. Routine housekeeping procedures and incidental spillage of liquids do not define a wet location. (ADM)

Wet locations are limited to areas where there are long-term significant amounts of water. Many patient areas become wet due to such things as washing, incontinence, or hot packs, but these areas are not considered wet locations for the purpose of this document.

This term appears in Chapter 2 because the definition, originally developed for hospitals, was deemed applicable to all health care facilities.

Extensive review and debate of this definition for the 1990 edition by three health care facilities committees, as well as from public proposals, resulted in the following modifications:

(1) "Standing water on the floor" was changed to "standing fluids on the floor" because water was not the only fluid liable to cause a hazard.

(2) "Routine dousing and drenching" was changed to just "drenching" because of confusion over how much "routine dousing" could create a wet condition; the fact that "routine drenching" could be misinterpreted; and because the phrase *routine housekeeping procedures* is used in the third sentence and could cause confusion with respect to the term *routine.*

(3) The addition of references to patients and staff was made because, without the presence of these individuals, there was no hazard.

(4) Mention of fluids on the floor and drenching of the work area was moved to a separate sentence to clarify that these are just two examples of what constitutes a wet condition. Definitions generally do not include examples because it could be misconstrued that these are the only conditions satisfying the definition of the term.

## References Cited in Commentary

1. J. Bruner and P. Leonard, "Electricity, Safety and the Patient" (Chicago: Year Book Medical Publishers, 1989), pp. 249–251. (Reprinted 1996, by authors, c/o Box 617, Groton, MA 01450.)
2. NFPA *101®, Life Safety Code®*, 1997 edition.
3. NFPA 70, *National Electrical Code®*, 1999 edition.
4. NFPA 30, *Flammable and Combustible Liquids Code,* 1996 edition.
5. NFPA 326, *Standard for the Safeguarding of Tanks and Containers for Entry, Cleaning, or Repair,* 1999 edition.
6. NFPA 1600, *Recommended Practice for Disaster Management,* 1995 edition.
7. NFPA 45, *Standard on Fire Protection for Laboratories Using Chemicals,* 1996 edition.
8. J. Bruner and P. Leonard, "Electricity, Safety and the Patient" (Chicago: Year Book Medical Publishers, 1989), pp. 68–70. (Reprinted 1996, by authors, c/o Box 617, Groton, MA 01450.)
9. Compressed Gas Association, Inc., 1725 Jefferson Davis Highway, Arlington, VA 22202, *Commodity Specification for Nitrogen,* CGA G-10.1, fifth edition, 1997.
10. NFPA 53, *Recommended Practice on Materials, Equipment, and Systems Used in Oxygen-Enriched Atmospheres,* 1999 edition.

# CHAPTER 3

# Electrical Systems

Chapter 3 was restructured for 1996 to make it easier to find requirements for the different types of essential electrical systems listed in this chapter. All the requirements for a particular system are now grouped into one section; for example, Section 3-4 covers requirements for Type 1 essential electrical systems. The way to determine which type of essential electrical system is required for a particular facility, however, has not changed; that is, Chapters 12 through 17 need to be reviewed.

This chapter deals with hazards caused by electrical systems in health care facilities. The material has been developed over many years by committees concerned with the reliability and continuity of the power supply to crucial equipment and systems and the risk of fires, explosions, electrical shock, and electrocution that might be caused by faults in the electrical system.

The material in this chapter that relates to the generation and distribution of emergency power was originally included in NFPA 76 (later NFPA 76A), the first health-care-related standard concerned solely with electrical supply and distribution problems. That standard contained information concerned with the designation of areas and equipment in health care facilities where an alternate source of electric power is necessary; the identification of emergency and equipment systems for these areas and equipment; and a method of generating electricity in lieu of the normal supply from electric utility companies. NFPA 76 required electric generators to be able to supply sufficient power to meet the load of the emergency circuits for a period of time. However, since many nonambulatory patients must remain in a health care facility during most emergencies *(the defend-in-place concept),* the length of time for emergency electric power to be able to function was left to individual health care facilities to determine. (NFPA *101, Life Safety Code* [1], contains minimum time requirements related to lighting being available for exiting a building in the event of an emergency.)

Originally, NFPA 76 addressed only hospitals; however, it was expanded over the years to include every type of health care facility. (Veterinary facilities, were not considered health care facilities were thus excluded.)

The chairman of the former Hospital Committee received frequent complaints in the 1960s about compliance with NFPA 76. Following the great Northeast power blackout in 1965, complaints ceased and it became standard procedure to provide emergency electric power appropriate to the needs of a facility.

In the late 1970s NFPA was queried about emergency power generation in other types of facilities. Until then, only health care facilities had a standard on the subject. This need led to the development of NFPA 110, *Standard for Emergency and Standby Power Systems* [2], a generic standard containing performance requirements for alternate electrical power sources that are applicable for any installation. As a consequence, some of the text in Chapter 3 of NFPA 99 fell under the scope of the committee responsible for NFPA 110. This text is identified by a dagger (†) and is considered extracted text under an NFPA policy governing text from one NFPA document that is used in another NFPA document.

Extracted text results when one NFPA document prints text that appears in another NFPA document instead of merely referencing that other document. It can be considered a direct quotation. It is necessary to specifically identify the edition any extracted text originates from because all NFPA documents are subject to revision at maximum intervals of five years.

Text that has been extracted is outside the scope of the committee that has chosen to excerpt it. Identifying such text with a dagger is a sign that the material is not to be changed during the revision process of the document where the text is extracted.

The NFPA Standards Council developed an Extract Policy in 1983 after many years of differences that developed between text in Article 517 (Health Care Facilities) of NFPA 70, *National Electrical Code* [3], and three health care documents (NFPA 56A, 76A, and 76B) covering inhalation anesthetics, essential electrical systems, and safe use of electricity (all of which became part of NFPA 99). (By the mid 1970s, much of the text in Article 517 had originated with these three documents.) After scopes of responsibilities were developed for Panel 17 (the committee responsible for Article 517) and the Health Care Facilities Committees, it became a matter of identifying which material in each committee's document(s) came from the others' document(s). The Health Care Facilities Committees removed the few paragraphs that fell within the scope of Panel 17. All other *National Electrical Code* [3] requirements in NFPA 99 are by reference only. The National Electrical Code Committee normally does not reference other documents within NFPA 70. Thus, Article 517 in NFPA 70 had many paragraphs identified as "extracted text."

As already noted, a similar situation occurred with NFPA 99 when NFPA 110, *Standard for Emergency and Standby Power Systems* [2], was first adopted by NFPA in 1985. Prior to that time, no other NFPA document covered requirements for generator sets used for emergency power. With the adoption of NFPA 110, some requirements for generators in NFPA 99 became "extracted" requirements (i.e., those requirements relative to safety and operating characteristics, as well as installation and maintenance practices). In 1990 further text was identified as extracted from NFPA 110.

All of the preceding commentary is informational only, since extracted text does not mean any more or less because it is extracted from another document. For users of this document, identification means only that some or all of the text in a particular paragraph actually comes from another NFPA document.

The material in this chapter that relates to protection against electric shock, fire, and explosion comes primarily from NFPA 56A and NFPA 76B, both of which dealt with the construction and maintenance of safe electrical systems prior to their incorporation into NFPA 99.

These documents were mainly concerned with (1) designating locations within the health care facility where patients are at abnormal risk of electric shock; (2) minimizing potential fault currents and leakage currents that could cause burns, arcs, or electric shock; (3) installing and maintaining appropriate grounding systems; and (4) establishing testing protocols and frequencies intended to identify deterioration or compromise of safety features.

All requirements and recommendations on *flammable* inhalation anesthetics were moved to a new Annex 2, "Flammable Anesthetizing Locations," in 1996. References in Chapters 1 through 20, and in Appendixes A, B, and C, are to *nonflammable* inhalation anesthetics only. This includes anesthetizing locations.

# 3-1* Scope

**A-3-1 Application of Requirements.** The application of requirements contained in this chapter for specific types of health care facilities can be found in Chapters 12 through 18.

Sections of Chapter 3 identified by a dagger (†) include text extracted from NFPA 110, *Standard for Emergency and Standby Power Systems*, 1996 edition. Requests for interpretations or revisions of the extracted text will be referred to the Technical Committee on Emergency Power Supplies.

Although complete compliance with this chapter is desirable, variations in existing health care facilities should be considered acceptable in instances where wiring arrangements are in accordance with prior editions of this document or afford an equivalent degree of performance and reliability. Such variations could occur, particularly with certain wiring in separate or common raceways, with certain functions connected to one or another system or branch, or with certain provisions for automatically or manually delayed restoration of power from the alternate (emergency) source of power.

**3-1.1** This chapter covers the performance, maintenance, and testing of electrical systems (both normal and essential) used within health care facilities.

This chapter does not apply to all medical facilities or all situations. Those responsible for a particular medical facility, or for an individual patient care function within a medical facility, are urged to evaluate the application of this chapter in relation to their particular situation. If additional electrical supply features are installed, installation is to be done in a manner consistent with the details and philosophy of this chapter.

This chapter is to be used in conjunction with NFPA 70, *National Electrical Code* [3], particularly Article 517, which addresses health care facilities.

**3-1.2** Specific requirements for wiring and installation on equipment are covered in NFPA 70, *National Electrical Code*.

**3-1.3** Requirements for illumination and identification of means of egress in health care facilities are covered in NFPA *101,® Life Safety Code.®* The alternate source of emergency power for illumination and identification of means of egress shall be the essential electrical system.

**3-1.4** This chapter does not cover the requirements for fire protection signaling systems except that the alternate source of power shall be the essential electrical system.

For requirements for signaling systems, see NFPA *101, Life Safety Code* [1], and NFPA 72, *National Fire Alarm Code®* [4].

**3-1.5** This chapter does not cover the requirements for fire pumps except that the alternate source of power shall be permitted to be the essential electrical system.

For requirements for fire pumps, see NFPA 20, *Standard for the Installation of Stationary Pumps for Fire Protection* [5].

**3-1.6** Requirements for the installation of stationary engines and gas turbines are covered in NFPA 37, *Standard for the Installation and Use of Stationary Combustion Engines and Gas Turbines.*

## 3-2* Nature of Hazards

The hazards attendant to the use of electricity include electrical shock, thermal injury, and interruption of power. *(For further information see A-3-2.)*

**A-3-2 Nature of Hazards.** The major concern in this chapter is electric shock resulting from degradation or some type of failure within normally safe electrical appliances or the facility's electrical distribution system. The defect could be in the wiring, in a component, or the result of deteriorating insulation. The failure could be caused by mechanical abuse or by improper use of the equipment.

Hospital service presents unusually severe environmental stress to equipment, similar to hard industrial use. Appliances are frequently subjected to large mechanical stresses in the course of being transported around the facility. Patients and staff, particularly those in operating rooms, critical care areas, clinical laboratories, and some physical therapy areas, are frequently surrounded by exposed, electrically grounded conductive surfaces that increase the risk of serious injury in the event of certain types of electrical failure.

Electricity passing through the body can stimulate excitable tissue, causing pain, involuntary muscle contractions, convulsions, or ventricular fibrillation. Also, electricity can cause tissue necrosis due to heat, chemical imbalance, or arcing. The effect of electricity depends upon the applied voltage, the magnitude of the current, the duration of application, whether the current is direct or alternating, the frequency of the current, and the size and location of the electrodes at which the current enters and leaves the body. The conductivity and dielectric strength of the skin is often a factor in determining the outcome of contact with electrified conductors.

Electrocution resulting from contact with equipment connected to ordinary branch circuit (i.e., less than 250 V at about 60 Hz) is usually a consequence of sustained ventricular fibrillation. When applied directly to the heart voltages of less than 100 mV RMS, 60 Hz can cause sustained ventricular fibrillation and death.

As already noted, the hazards addressed in this chapter and Chapter 7 relate primarily to electrical shock, power continuity, and fire. While these are important in any occupancy, the unique circumstances that are encountered in hospitals and other health care facilities require special consideration. Consequently, Chapter 3 goes into considerable detail regarding compliance with the requirements particular to health care facilities.

### 3-2.1  Fire and Explosions.

Electrical systems can be subject to the occurrence of electrical fires. Grounding systems, overcurrent protective devices, and other subjects discussed in this standard could be intended for fire prevention as well as other purposes. This aspect of electrical systems is the primary focus of other NFPA standards and will not be emphasized herein.

### 3-2.2  Shock.

**3-2.2.1  General.**  See A-3-2.

**3-2.2.2\*  Control.**  Control of electric shock hazard requires the limitation of electric current that might flow in an electric circuit involving the patient's body and is accomplished through a variety of alternative approaches covered in A-3-2.2.2.

**A-3-2.2.2**  *Shock Prevention.*  Since electric shock results from the effect of an electric current flowing through a part of the human body, three conditions should be satisfied simultaneously before a patient or staff member can be shocked. *[See Figure A-3-2.2.2(a).]* There should be:

(a)  One part of the body in contact with a conductive surface (Point 1)
(b)  A different part of the same body in contact with a second conductive surface (Point 2)

(c) A voltage source that will drive current through the body between those two points of contact (Point 3)

In the general case, six or seven independent and separable factors should combine simultaneously to satisfy these three conditions. *[See Figure A-3-2.2.2(b).]*

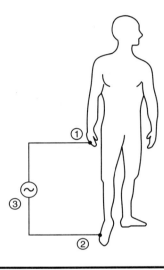

**Figure A-3-2.2.2(a)**  *The three basic conditions required to produce an electric shock.*

Several separate factors should be analyzed when evaluating a potential electric shock hazard. The following numbers refer to points in Figure A-3-2.2.2(b):

1. The likelihood that a piece of line-powered equipment will be within reach of the patient

2. The possibility of direct exposure of a "live" 110-V conductor through a damaged line cord or attachment plug. The likelihood that the equipment will have exposed metal parts that through some reasonably credible accident could become "live"

3. The likelihood that equipment is accidentally damaged or malfunctions in some way and the metal becomes "live," that is, electrified

4. The likelihood of the exposed metal parts not being grounded or accidentally becoming ungrounded

5. The likelihood that the patient (or staff member or visitor) will make good contact with this exposed, potentially live surface

6. The likelihood that a second exposed conductive surface that is, or that could through a reasonably credible event become, grounded is also within reach

7. The likelihood that the patient (or member of staff, or visitor) will make good contact with this grounded, or potentially grounded, surface

8. The probability that the resultant current flow will be sufficient to cause an injury

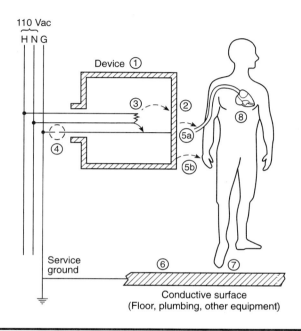

*Figure A-3-2.2.2(b)  General factors that should be considered when analyzing electrical safety.*

The chance of a patient actually sustaining an electric shock is a product of the likelihood that each of the above events will occur. If the likelihood of occurrence of any one event is very close to zero, then the risk of electric shock will be very close to zero. Put another way, six or seven links in a chain need to be intact in order for a shock to be sustained. If any one link can be made extremely weak, by design or operating procedure, the chance of receiving a shock will be minimal.

Working to minimize the occurrence of one factor (i.e., one safety factor) can achieve one "layer of protection." A second layer of protection is achieved by working to make the chance of occurrence of a second factor in the overall chain also very close to zero. However, extending this process to minimize the occurrence of all factors can lead to overdesign, overspecification, and less than cost-effective utilization of resources to control any problem.

Consider briefly each of the component factors. First, more could be done operationally to ensure that the minimum amount of line-powered equipment is within reach of the patient. Second, equipment that does not have a significant amount of exposed metal is to be preferred.

Third, the staff should be instructed to report all obviously damaged equipment, even if it is still functional. Fourth, all grounding circuits should be tested frequently. Fifth, minimize the amount of grounded metal that is within reach of the patient. Avoid when possible attaching any grounded leads directly to the patient. Do not deliberately ground any metal part, such as a curtain rail or a metal cabinet, that cannot become accidentally "live." Insulate the patient from ground as much as possible.

In consideration of these objectives, four basic principles can be examined to avoid electric shock:

(a)  Shock prevention by insulation and enclosure
(b)  Shock prevention by grounding
(c)  Shock prevention by device design
(d)  Shock prevention through user procedures

*Shock Prevention by Insulation and Enclosure.* Physical provisions should be made to prevent personal hazardous contact between energized conductors or between an energized conductor and ground.

(a) Noninsulated current-carrying conductors, which could produce hazardous currents, should be protected from contact through suitable enclosure.

(b) Energized conductors, which could produce hazardous currents when not in protective enclosures, should be insulated by materials suitable to the voltage and environment.

In order to minimize the probability of completing a hazardous circuit, exposed conductive surfaces not likely to be energized from internal sources should not be intentionally grounded. Insulated covering of such surfaces is desirable.

NOTE 1: Past measures recommended by earlier editions of NFPA standards and other standards associated with equipotential grounding and bonding of "dead metal" served to increase the likelihood that a patient or staff member would complete an undesirable pathway for electric shock.

NOTE 2: This principle does not intend to mandate construction of an insulated environment, but rather to avoid intentional grounding of otherwise dead metal surfaces.

*Shock Prevention by Grounding.* A grounding system for fault currents should be supplied for two reasons: to minimize the fraction of the fault current that might flow through an individual during the fault condition and to operate overcurrent devices in order to minimize the possibility of damage and fire. This grounding system should also be utilized to provide a safe path for leakage currents.

(a) Unless doubly insulated, each line-powered electrical appliance within the patient care vicinity should have a grounding wire, which normally carries the leakage current directly to ground, in the same power cable as the energized conductors.

(b) Each receptacle for line-powered electrical appliances should provide a low-impedance grounding connection and path.

*Shock Prevention by Device Design.* Leakage current should be minimized. New device designs should not intentionally provide a low-impedance path at 60 Hz from patient to ground.

*Shock Prevention Through User Procedures.*

*General:* A total electrical safety program incorporates the best features of design, manufacture, inspection, maintenance, and operation. The design should be such that limited departures from ideal conditions of maintenance and use will not cause unreasonable risks.

Where existing equipment that does not meet new-equipment requirements is to be used, such use is permissible if procedures of use and maintenance can establish an equivalent level of safety.

User procedures should include the following:

(a) Establishing a policy to prohibit the connection of nonisolated input equipment to externalized intracardiac electrodes
(b) Establishing user educational and training programs
(c) Establishing a testing and routine maintenance program

### 3-2.3 Thermal.

(Reserved)

### 3-2.4 Interruption of Power.

This section provides the rationale of why requirements for emergency power specific to health care facilities are so essential. A reliable supply of electricity, consistent with the needs of the medical procedures and activities performed in each health care facility, is required. In addition to contributing to general fire protection and life safety, electricity is essential for vital functions unique to health care facilities, such as special lighting, monitoring systems, and electromedical appliances. A failure of the normal electrical supply at one time or another is virtually unavoidable. Public utility sources and on-premises power generation sources are subject to interruption. This chapter provides standardized guidance for providing and maintaining an adequate portion of the total electrical system in the event of an interruption of normal electrical power. It does not guarantee that a total loss of electricity will not occur or that vital functions will not be left without a supply of electricity, although the track record for health care facilities with respect to emergency power has been excellent over the past two decades.

It will be emphasized several times in this handbook that it was never the intent of the committee responsible for developing emergency power criteria that a facility place its entire electrical load on the essential electrical system. Only selected items were to be wired so that, in the event of a loss of normal power, these items would be connected to the emergency generator and continue to function.

For a discussion on the need to maintain power, see commentary under 3-2.4.2.

It is worth stressing that emergency generators will not be activated by some electrical failure within a facility (e.g., a GFCI trips, a branch circuit breaker trips, or a cable is cut). Supplying electricity from generators will not correct the failure (i.e., electricity will only go as far as the point of interruption). Activation of emergency electric generator(s) is only to occur in the event of a failure of the normal power source to the main switchgear (i.e., ahead of the point where the normal power source is supplying power to the main distribution center).

**3-2.4.1 General.** Medical and nursing sciences are becoming progressively more dependent on electrical apparatus for the preservation of life of hospitalized patients. For example, year by year more cardiac operations are performed, in some of which the patient's life depends on artificial circulation of the blood. In other operations, life is sustained by means of electrical impulses that stimulate and regulate heart action. In still others, suction developed by electrical means is routinely relied on to remove body fluids and mucus that might otherwise cause suffocation. In another sense, lighting is needed in strategic areas in order that precise procedures can be carried out, and power is needed to safeguard such vital services as refrigerated stores held in tissue, bone, and blood banks.

Interruption of normal electrical service in health care facilities can be caused by catastrophes such as storms, floods, fires, earthquakes, or explosions; by failures of the systems supplying electrical power; or by incidents within the facility. For all such situations, electrical systems should be planned to limit internal disruption and to provide for continuity of vital services at all times. Outages might be corrected in seconds or might require hours for correction. This indicates that the system or protection needs to be designed to cope with the longest probable outage.

Selecting vital areas and functions considered to be essential, designing safeguards to ensure continuity in these circuits, and maintaining the electrical and mechanical components of such essential services so that they will work when called on are complex problems that warrant standardized guidance for regulating agencies, governing boards, and administrators of health care facilities and architects and engineers concerned with their construction. Such guidance is offered in this chapter.

This chapter is predicated on the basic principle of achieving dependability. It is intended to recognize the different degrees of reliability that can result from varying approaches to electrical design. Therefore, its requirements have been developed to allow the designer the flexibility needed to achieve a reliable electrical system.

**3-2.4.2 Need to Maintain Power.** Interruption of the supply of electric power in a facility can be a hazard. Implementation of the requirements of this chapter serves to maintain the required level of continuity and quality of electrical power for patient care electrical appliances.

In Chapter 2, under the definition of *isolated power system*, extensive commentary is included on the history of these systems as used in anesthetizing locations and as related to electrical and personnel safety. Under 3-4.2.1.4(d), there is additional commentary discussing how 10 seconds became the limit within which the restoration of electric power is to occur in the event of the loss of normal power to a health care facility.

The phrase *continuity of power* is a bit of a misnomer. It can have several meanings, depending on the context in which it is used. For some, it refers to the supply of electric power to a facility and the presence of some mechanism that is used to switch to a second source of power in the event the first source is interrupted (either the source itself stops supplying power or the wires carrying the power to a facility are accidentally or intentionally cut). For others, this phrase refers to equipment that allows electric power to continue to flow to a particular device even though one of several types of electrical faults has occurred that would normally stop the flow of electricity within the device. It is necessary to know or ascertain whether the term is intended to refer to the incoming electric power to a facility or the electric power being supplied to a specific device.

For the purposes of NFPA and this document, the phrase *continuity of power* falls within the context of the overall fire or electrical safety of people and property. While other concerns, such as the interruption of medical procedures or the efficacy of an appliance, are related, NFPA does not have the authority to make judgments or set standards in these other areas.

In the early 1960s, when the then Committee on Hospitals began to address the issue of emergency power, the question of how long facilities could tolerate loss of power until emergency power came on-line was discussed. A brief period of time (up to 10 seconds) was considered acceptable in view of the technology of the day and the medicine/surgery being practiced. Today, some in medicine do not want or cannot accept any loss of power. They contend that a loss of power for even a fraction of a second, or even just a power surge, can be damaging because of medicine's reliance on computers and the type of procedures performed. Loss of power would mean a shutdown of the computer and reprogramming or resetting after restoration of power. Since computers are now used (either alone or as part of a device) to store data as well as to control pumps, and so forth, this recycling could be detrimental to the patient if it occurs in the middle of a critical surgical procedure. Some medical procedures, such as neuro-microsurgery or cardiac bypass surgery, involve very intricate movements. A sudden loss of light could be harmful to the patient.

Others in medicine do not think that this 10-second downtime is serious enough to warrant the installation of equipment to eliminate this interval of no power. They feel that physicians are quite able to continue to take care of patients while there is a short, temporary loss of power. The important points here are "short" and "temporary." (Note: An electrical feeder fault within a facility will not allow power from any source to flow beyond the fault. It will also mean no power to all devices downstream from the fault, irrespective of a system that allows power to continue to flow to appliances for certain appliance faults.)

The debate over isolated power systems (IPSs) in anesthetizing locations includes the issue of continuous power because of the way IPSs function. In a grounded electrical system, an electrical fault either trips the equipment's internal fuse or trips a branch circuit breaker. IPSs react to certain electrical faults by activating an alarm while allowing power to continue to flow to equipment. An IPS, however, is not a source of power, like a generator set that actually provides power. The original intended use of isolated power systems was to provide electrical and personnel safety in the presence of flammable anesthetics. It was not to allow appliances to continue operating in the event of certain electrical faults within the appliance. However, the use of flammable anesthetics has practically stopped, and more and more electrical appliances are being used and relied on in anesthetizing locations, a fact that needs to be evaluated in terms of electrical and personnel safety.

Health care facilities need to be certain of their electrical needs and dependency and of the length of time, if any, power outage in various areas can be tolerated.

## 3-2.5* RF Interference.

(Reserved)

**A-3-2.5** See Annex 1, "The Safe Use of High-Frequency Electricity in Health Care Facilities," at the end of this document for recommendations.

## 3-3 Electrical System Requirements

### 3-3.1 Sources.

Each appliance of a hospital requiring electrical line power for operation shall be supported by power sources and distribution systems that provide power adequate for each service.

**3-3.1.1 Power/Utility Company.** (Reserved)

**3-3.1.2 On-Site Generator Set.** (Reserved)

### 3-3.2 Distribution.

### 3-3.2.1 General.

**3-3.2.1.1 Electrical Installation.** Installation shall be in accordance with NFPA 70, *National Electrical Code.*

**3-3.2.1.2 All Patient Care Areas.** *(See Chapter 2 for definition of Patient Care Area.)*

(a)* *Wiring, Regular Voltage.*

**A-3-3.2.1.2(a) Wiring, Regular Voltage.**
*Integrity of Insulation on Conductors.* At the time of installation, steps should be taken to ensure that the insulation on each conductor intended to be energized, or on quiet grounds, has not been damaged in the process of installation. When disconnected and unenergized the resistance should be at least 20 megohms when measured with an ohmmeter having an open-circuit test voltage of at least 500 V dc.

*Accessibility of Overcurrent Protection Devices.* Consideration should be given to providing reasonable accessibility to branch-circuit switching and overcurrent protection devices by the hospital staff in the patient care area. Consideration should also be given to providing labels at each receptacle and on installed equipment as to the location and identity of the distribution panel serving that power outlet or equipment, especially where the location or identity might not be readily apparent.

1.*  *Circuits.* Branch circuits serving a given patient bed location shall be fed from not more than one normal branch circuit distribution panel. When required, branch circuits serving a given patient bed location shall be permitted to be fed from more than one emergency branch circuit distribution panel.

        Critical care areas shall be served by circuits from (1) critical branch panel(s) served from a single automatic transfer switch and (2) a minimum of one circuit served by the normal power distribution system or by a system originating from a second critical branch transfer switch.

*Exception: Branch circuits serving only special-purpose outlets or receptacles (e.g., portable X-ray receptacles) need not conform to the requirements of this section.*

Circuits from more than one critical branch panel are allowed for those facilities that desire increased reliability at patient bed locations. It is not mandatory, however, to provide service from more than one critical branch panel. Since 1987, NFPA 70, *National Electrical Code* [3], has required at least one normal branch circuit for every critical care area patient bed location. NFPA 99 also requires a normal circuit, having correlated in 1993 with NFPA 70. The intent of this section is to provide a receptacle and a source of power that will remain in service in the event of a failure of the critical branch distribution system (e.g., a transfer switch failure). NFPA 99 permits the installation of a circuit fed from a second (or additional) critical branch transfer switch in lieu of the normal circuit. (See Exhibit 3.1.)

        In 1993 the term *patient bed location* replaced the term *patient vicinity* for defining a portion of a patient care area for electric wiring purposes. (See commentary under definition of *patient bed location*.)

**A-3-3.2.1.2(a)1** *Circuits.* The requirement that branch circuits be fed from not more than one distribution panel was introduced for several reasons. A general principle is to minimize possible potential differences between the grounding pins of receptacles in one area by bringing the grounding conductors to a common point. A specific reason is to simplify maintenance by making it easier to find the source for the receptacles in a room. This is particularly a problem in hospitals where emergency conditions might require rapid restoration of power.

A requirement to have only one phase of power in a patient vicinity was used for a short period by some designers based on the false premise that it would prevent faults involving 208 V from occurring. This practice was not widely adopted for several of the following reasons:

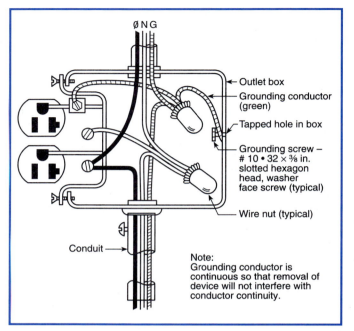

**Exhibit 3.1** *Typical method of wiring a receptacle to meet criteria of 3-3.2.1.2(a)2.*

(a) Occurrence of the fault addressed is extremely unlikely. It would require a double fault (loss of ground in the appliance plus 110 V coming in contact with the chassis) on two different appliances, in addition to the patient needing to touch both appliances simultaneously.

(b) If one phase of power dropped out, most of the power to that patient vicinity could be lost.

(c) Since at least one circuit to a patient vicinity has to be on an emergency circuit, single phasing a room would be more difficult and costly because of the correlation and extra wiring that would be necessary.

This chapter does not contain criteria requiring this wiring configuration.

2. *Grounding.*

(a) Grounding Circuitry Integrity. Grounding circuits and conductors in patient care areas shall be installed in such a way that the continuity of other parts of those circuits cannot be interrupted nor the resistance raised above an acceptable level by the installation, removal, or replacement of any installed equipment, including power receptacles.

(b)* Reliability of Grounding. In all patient care areas the reliability of an installed grounding circuit to a power receptacle shall be at least equivalent to that provided by an electrically continuous copper conductor of appropriate ampacity run from the receptacle to a grounding bus in the distribution panel. The grounding conductor shall conform to NFPA 70, *National Electrical Code.*

*Exception: Existing construction that does not use a separate grounding conductor shall be permitted to continue in use provided that it meets the performance requirements in 3-3.3.2, Grounding System in Patient Care Areas.*

Where metal receptacle boxes are used, the performance of the connection between the receptacle grounding terminal and the metal box shall be equivalent to the performance provided by copper wire no smaller than No. 12 AWG.

Acceptable grounding limits are listed in 3-3.3.2.

**A-3-3.2.1.2(a)2b** *Reliability of Grounding.* This requirement is usually met by appropriate mounting hardware, and not by wire jumpers.

The appendix material is included to avoid misinterpretation concerning the use of wire jumpers, as well as to avoid specifying a particular method to meet requirements for grounding.

3.* *Grounding Interconnects.* In patient care areas supplied by the normal distribution system and any branch of the essential electrical system, the grounding system of the normal distribution system and that of the essential electrical system shall be interconnected.

**A-3-3.2.1.2(a)3** *Grounding Interconnects.* The requirement for grounding interconnection between the normal and essential power systems follows the principle of minimizing possible potential differences between the grounding pins of receptacles in one area by bringing the grounding conductors to a common point.

Since the wiring for the normal electric power system and the essential electric power system are installed in separate conduits, it may be possible to have widely separated grounds. This section emphasizes that the grounding of both systems needs to be connected together locally to avoid potential differences between local grounds.

4. *Circuit Protection.*

a.* The main and downstream ground-fault protective devices (where required) shall be coordinated as required in 3-3.2.1.5.

**A-3-3.2.1.2(a)4a** *Circuit Protection.* Within the constraints of the equipment provided, consideration should be given to coordinating circuit breakers, fuses, and other overcurrent protective devices so that power interruption in that part of the circuit that precedes the interrupting device closest to a fault is not likely to occur.

It is difficult, if not impossible, to provide coordination (selectivity) for circuit breakers for high-level fault currents within the instantaneous trip ranges of two circuit breakers connected in series. Likewise, it is not always possible to achieve 100 percent coordination between two fuses or a fuse and circuit breaker. Still, designers should strive to achieve coordination where overcurrent protective devices serve emergency system loads and where nonselective tripping will needlessly interrupt circuits to critical care areas and life support systems.

    b.* If used, ground-fault circuit interrupters (GFCIs) shall be approved for the purpose.

**A-3-3.2.1.2(a)4b** Listed Class A ground-fault circuit interrupters trip when a fault current to ground is 6 mA or more.

  5. *Wiring in Anesthetizing Locations.*

    a. Wiring. Installed wiring shall be in metal raceway or shall be as required in NFPA 70, *National Electrical Code*, Sections 517-60 through 517-63.

    b. Raceway. Such distribution systems shall be run in metal raceways along with a green grounding wire sized no smaller than the energized conductors.

    c. Grounding to Raceways. Each device connected to the distribution system shall be effectively grounded to the metal raceway at the device.

This requirement is not applicable to double-insulated appliances, because these appliances do not have a grounding pin on their plugs.

    d. Installation. Methods of installation shall conform to Articles 250 and 517 of NFPA 70, *National Electrical Code*.

    e. Battery-Powered Emergency Lighting Units. One or more battery-powered emergency lighting units shall be provided in accordance with NFPA 70, *National Electrical Code*, Section 700-12(e).

In the 1993 edition of NFPA 99, operating rooms were required to have some general-purpose lighting connected to the normal electrical system or to have battery-powered lighting to provide at least 1½ hours of lighting in accordance with NFPA 70, Section 700-12(e). This requirement was changed in the 1996 edition of NFPA 99 to continue to be in accordance with Section 700-12(e) of NFPA 70, *National Electrical Code* [3].

    The committee feels that batteries provide several benefits. First, they provide some lighting during the standby generator start-up period (generally less than

10 seconds). Second, batteries provide backup for the generator in case of generator failure. Third, batteries provide backup for internal facility failure (i.e., transfer switch or circuit breakers on the load side of transfer switches), even when the outside utility source is not interrupted. It should be noted, however, that providing normal system circuits, as well as batteries, for selected operating room lighting provides additional protection for the internal facility failure already mentioned. (See Exhibit 3.2.)

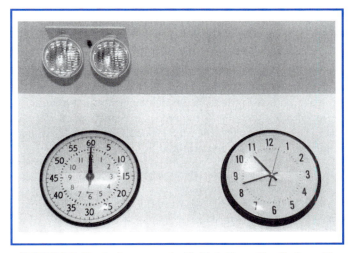

**Exhibit 3.2** *Two battery-operated lights in the ceiling that provide constant lighting in the operating room during the 10 seconds (maximum) between loss of normal power and restoration by emergency power, or when the emergency power system fails, or when power is interrupted within the facility that would not be restored by switching to emergency power.*

(b)  *Wiring, Low-Voltage.*

1.  Fixed systems of 30 V (dc or ac rms) or less shall be ungrounded, and the insulation between each ungrounded conductor and the primary circuit, which is supplied from a conventionally grounded distribution system, shall provide the same protection as required for the primary voltage.

*Exception: A grounded low-voltage system shall be permitted provided that load currents are not carried in the grounding conductors.*

It should not be inferred that low-voltage wiring has to be insulated the same way as 120-V wiring. Only insulation of low-voltage wiring on the transformer is required to be provided with protection equivalent to that of higher-voltage wiring.

2.  Wiring for low-voltage control systems and nonemergency communications and signaling systems shall not be required to be installed in metal raceways in anesthetizing locations.

    This paragraph is intended to eliminate confusion as to whether low-voltage systems are required to be installed in metal raceways in anesthetizing locations.

    (c) *Switches, Anesthetizing Locations.* Switches controlling ungrounded circuits within or partially within an inhalation anesthetizing location shall have a disconnecting pole for each conductor.

    (d) *Receptacles.*

1.* *Types of Receptacles.* Each power receptacle shall provide at least one separate, highly dependable grounding pole capable of maintaining low-contact resistance with its mating plug despite electrical and mechanical abuse. Special receptacles (such as four-pole units providing an extra pole for redundant grounding or ground continuity monitoring; or locking-type receptacles; or, where required for reduction of electrical noise on the grounding circuit, receptacles in which the grounding terminals are purposely insulated from the receptacle yoke) shall be permitted.

    For criteria on receptacles in patient care areas (new construction only), see Section 517-18 in NFPA 70, *National Electrical Code* [3]. For receptacle requirements in anesthetizing locations, see 3-3.2.1.2(d)4 in NFPA 99. For discussion on hospital-grade receptacles, see commentary under A-3-3.2.1.2(d)1.

**A-3-3.2.1.2(d)1** *Types of Receptacles.* It is best, if possible, to employ only one type of receptacle (standard three-prong type) for as many receptacles being served by the same line voltage to avoid the inability to connect life-support equipment in emergencies. The straight-blade, three-prong receptacle is now permitted in all locations in a hospital. Previously, special receptacles were specified in operating room locations and have caused compatibility problems.

    In the past, installers used only those receptacles listed as "hospital grade" because they were the only ones considered highly dependable. These receptacles generally had a green dot stamped on the face of the receptacle to indicate they were hospital grade and listed by testing laboratories. Today, there are a variety of high-grade commercial receptacles that adequately meet the intent of these criteria. To distinguish poor-quality receptacles from higher-quality, specification-grade receptacles, federal specification grade receptacles now have an identifier on the face of the receptacle. Hospital personnel need to ensure that only receptacles of appropriate quality are installed in patient care areas.

    Some facilities have been able to reduce the cost impact of the generally higher-priced, hospital-grade receptacles by purchasing large quantities or through group purchases.

2. *Minimum Number of Receptacles.* The number of receptacles shall be determined by the intended use of the patient care area. There shall be sufficient receptacles located so as to avoid the need for extension cords or multiple outlet adapters.

   a. Receptacles for Patient Bed Locations in General Care Areas. Each patient bed location shall be provided with a minimum of four receptacles.

   b. Receptacles for Patient Bed Locations in Critical Care Areas. Each patient bed location shall be provided with a minimum of six receptacles.

*Exception No. 1: Receptacles shall not be required in bathrooms or toilet rooms.*
*Exception No. 2: Receptacles shall not be required in areas where medical requirements mandate otherwise; for example, certain psychiatric, pediatric, or hydrotherapy areas.*

It is stressed that the number of receptacles specified is a minimum number. Additional receptacles should be considered if clinical considerations warrant them. The receptacles referred to are single receptacles. This clarification is necessary because six receptacles can consist of six single receptacles, three duplex receptacles, or some combination of single and duplex receptacles totaling six.

　　For circuit rating requirements, readers should review Section 210-3 in NFPA 70, *National Electrical Code* [3].

3. *Polarity of Receptacles.* Each receptacle shall be wired in accordance with NFPA 70, *National Electrical Code*, to ensure correct polarity.

4. *Anesthetizing Location Receptacles.* Receptacles for use in anesthetizing locations shall be listed for the use. In anesthetizing locations of new and existing construction having receptacles on isolated and grounded power, all receptacles shall be identified as to whether they are on isolated or grounded power.

Receptacles used in anesthetizing locations are to be *listed* as defined in Section 2-1. Receptacles listed as hospital grade would be acceptable. [See 3-3.2.1.2(d)1 and 9-2.1.2.1.]

　　The usual type of receptacle installed in a health care facility, one that accepts a plug with two flat, straight blades and a U-shaped pin, would be acceptable anywhere in nonflammable anesthetizing locations if the receptacle were listed.

　　The second sentence on isolated grounded power is included because it is not prohibited to have both isolated and grounded power circuits in an area that is not required to have isolated power. Properly labeling receptacles will at least tell staff and maintenance personnel which receptacles are on isolated power and which are not. If isolated and grounded power circuits are present in an operating room, equipment should preferably be plugged into all the ungrounded power circuits first.

5. *Receptacles and Amperage.* Receptacles for use with 250-V, 50-A, and 60-A ac service shall be designed for use in anesthetizing locations and shall be so designed that the 60-A receptacle will accept either the 50-A or the 60-A plug. Fifty-ampere receptacles

shall be designed so as not to accept the 60-A attachment plug. These receptacles shall be of the two-pole, three-wire design with the third contact connecting to the (green or green with yellow stripe) grounding wire of the electric system.

6. *Other Services Receptacles.* Receptacles provided for other services having different voltages, frequencies, or types on the same premises shall be of such design that attachment plugs and caps used in such receptacles cannot be connected to circuits of a different voltage, frequency, or type, but shall be interchangeable within each classification and rating required for two-wire, 125-V, single-phase ac service.

(e)* *Special Grounding.*

**A-3-3.2.1.2(e)** Care should be taken in specifying such a quiet grounding system since the grounding impedance is controlled only by the grounding wires and does not benefit from any conduit or building structure in parallel with it.

Quiet grounds are special grounding systems for reducing electrical noise and interference in communication or instrumentation systems. They might be needed when there is nearby high-power transmission equipment or when noise-sensitive equipment, such as a computer, is used. This section recognizes that such quiet grounds may be used and that they may be of peculiar design. This section also points out that the signal protection design must not compromise the electrical safety protection.

1. *Use of Quiet Grounds.* A quiet ground, if used, shall not defeat the purposes of the safety features of the grounding systems detailed herein.

These terminals or jacks can be of assistance in some locations (such as in older buildings with questionable grounds) or when unusual electrical noise is present. However, a properly constructed power system with a grounding conductor and electrical appliances with good third-wire ground connections are normally adequate for grounding purposes, as well as for eliminating interference on most physiological monitors.

2. *Patient Equipment Grounding Point.* A patient equipment grounding point comprising one or more grounding terminals or jacks shall be permitted in an accessible location in the patient care vicinity.

3.* *Special Grounding in Patient Care Areas.* In addition to the grounding required to meet the performance requirements of 3-3.3.2, additional grounding shall be permitted where special circumstances so dictate. *(See A-3-2, Nature of Hazards.)*

**A-3-3.2.1.2(e)3** Special grounding methods could be required in patient vicinities immediately adjacent to rooms containing high-power or high-frequency equipment that causes electrical interference with monitors or other electromedical devices. In extreme cases, electromagnetic induction can cause the voltage limits of 3-3.3.2 to be exceeded.

Electromagnetic interference problems can be due to a variety of causes, some simple, others complex. Such problems are best solved one at a time. In some locations, grounding of stretchers, examining tables, or bed frames will be helpful. Where necessary, a patient equipment grounding point should be installed. This can usually be accomplished even after completion of construction by installing a receptacle faceplate fitted with grounding posts. Special grounding wires should not be used unless they are found to be essential for a particular location because they can interfere with patient care procedures or present trip hazards.

> Eliminating electrical interference can be difficult due to the fact that the interference can be generated by various mechanisms: conducted (or power line), radiated, or coupled (via magnetic fields). It is often easier to locate and remove the source of the interference than it is to protect the appliance being disturbed. In any event, simple solutions, such as relocating the appliance, should be tried before expensive ones, such as the installation of special grounding or shielding.

(f) *Wet Locations.*

1.* Wet location patient care areas shall be provided with special protection against electric shock. This special protection shall be provided by a power distribution system that inherently limits the possible ground-fault current due to a first fault to a low value, without interrupting the power supply; or by a power distribution system in which the power supply is interrupted if the ground-fault current does, in fact, exceed a value of 6 mA.

**A-3-3.2.1.2(f)1** Moisture can reduce the contact resistance of the body, and electrical insulation is more subject to failure.

*Exception No. 1: Patient beds, toilets, bidets, and wash basins shall not be required to be considered wet locations.*

*Exception No. 2: In existing construction, the requirements of 3-3.2.1.2(f)1 are not required when written inspection procedure, acceptable to the authority having jurisdiction, is continuously enforced by a designated individual at the hospital, to indicate that equipment-grounding conductors for 120-V, single-phase, 15- and 20-A receptacles, equipment connected by cord and plug, and fixed electrical equipment are installed and maintained in accordance with NFPA 70, National Electrical Code, and applicable performance requirements of this chapter. The procedure shall include electrical continuity tests of all required equipment, grounding conductors, and their connections. These tests shall be conducted as follows.*

*Fixed receptacles, equipment connected by cord and plug, and fixed electrical equipment shall be tested:*

a. *When first installed*
b. *Where there is evidence of damage*
c. *After any repairs, or*
d. *At intervals not exceeding 6 months*

While 3-3.2.1.2(f)1 does not state where IPSs or GFCIs are required, it was observed at a January 1984 hearing before the NFPA Standards Council that this requirement can be applied to operating rooms because many meet the definition of *wet location* as listed in Chapter 2. It thus becomes necessary for a facility to determine which type of procedures will normally take place in each operating room and which special protection against electric shock has to be provided if wet procedures are likely to be performed.

See also related commentary under the definitions of *isolated power system* and *wet location* in Chapter 2.

Note that it is left to the user to determine the method of protection used in a particular location.

Exception No. 2 has been retained by the committee in the event a local jurisdiction enforces new construction requirements on existing construction as well. Requirements in each edition of NFPA 99 apply only to new construction, equipment, systems, and so forth, built or approved *after the effective date* of that edition, unless specifically noted otherwise. (See Section 1-2.)

2. The use of an isolated power system (IPS) shall be permitted as a protective means capable of limiting ground fault current without power interruption. When installed, such a power system shall conform to the requirements of 3-3.2.2.
3. Where power interruption under first fault condition (line-to-ground fault) is tolerable, the use of a ground-fault circuit interrupter (GFCI) shall be permitted as the protective means that monitors the actual ground fault current and interrupts the power when that current exceeds 6 mA.

The phrase *first fault condition* is included to clarify the conditions under which GFCIs would be permitted in wet locations.

(g) *Isolated Power.* An isolated power system shall not be required to be installed in any patient care area except as specified in 3-3.2.1.2(f). The system shall be permitted to be installed, however, and, when installed, shall conform to the performance requirements specified in 3-3.2.2.

See commentary under the definition of *isolated power system* in Chapter 2 for an explanation of the need for isolated power.

**3-3.2.1.3 Laboratories.** Power outlets shall be installed in accordance with NCCLS Standard ASI-5, *Power Requirements for Clinical Laboratory Instruments and for Laboratory Power Sources.* Outlets with two to four receptacles, or an equivalent power strip, shall be installed every 1.6 to 3.3 ft (0.5 to 1.0 m) in instrument usage areas, and either installation is to be at least 3.15 in. (8 cm) above the countertop.

Reference is made to the National Committee for Clinical Laboratory Standards (NCCLS) [6] document because of its growing use in the clinical laboratory field.

The document is intended to promote the safe installation and operation of electric equipment through the installation of an adequate number of properly located outlets that eliminate the need for extension cords, cube taps, or other makeshift arrangements. In many existing laboratories, circuits and outlets are inadequate to serve the multitude of modern, line-operated instruments now in common use.

The receptacles referred to in this section do not supersede any receptacles that should be installed in accordance with the requirements of NFPA 70, *National Electrical Code* [3], nor do they refer to receptacles necessary for "everyday" purposes, such as vacuuming. It would not be a good practice for maintenance personnel, for example, to have to reach across laboratory countertops, where experiments are being performed, to plug in a drill.

**3-3.2.1.4  Other Nonpatient Areas.** (Reserved)

**3-3.2.1.5  Ground-Fault Protection.**  When ground-fault protection is provided for operation of the service or feeder disconnecting means, an additional step of ground-fault protection shall be provided in the next level of feeder downstream toward the load. Ground-fault protection for operation of the service and feeder disconnecting means shall be fully selective such that the downstream device and not the upstream device shall open for downstream ground faults. The additional step of ground-fault protection shall not be required where the service or feeder disconnecting means does not serve patient care areas or equipment intended to support life, such as clinical air compressors and vacuum pumps. When equipment ground-fault protection is first installed, each level shall be performance tested to ensure compliance with the above.

> Paragraph 3-3.2.1.5 provides performance criteria for ground-fault protection, a subject first addressed by NFPA in 1975 in NFPA 70, *National Electrical Code.* [3] It reflects the committee's intent that ground-fault protection be installed in health care facilities to prevent tripping of the main or feeder ground-fault protection where it might needlessly interrupt power to patient care areas or to life-support equipment, such as clinical air compressors or clinical vacuum pumps.

**3-3.2.2*  Isolated Power Systems.**

> The performance, maintenance, and testing criteria for isolated power systems are listed in 3-3.3.4.
> For the use of isolated power systems in wet locations, see 3-3.2.1.2(f).

**A-3-3.2.2**  *Isolated Power.*  Patient protection is provided primarily by an adequate grounding system. The ungrounded secondary of the isolation transformer reduces the cross-sectional area of grounding conductors necessary to protect the patient against voltage resulting from fault current by reducing the maximum current in case of a single probable fault in the grounding system. The line isolation monitor is used to provide warning when a single fault occurs. Excessive current in the grounding conductors will not result in a hazard to the patient unless a second fault occurs. If the current in the grounding system does not exceed 10 milliamperes, even under fault conditions, the voltage across 9.84 ft (3 m) of No. 12 AWG wire will not exceed 0.2 millivolt, and the voltage across 9.84 ft (3 m) of No. 18 AWG grounding conductor in a flexible cord will not exceed 0.8 millivolt. Allowing 0.1 millivolt across each connector, the voltage between two pieces of patient-connected equipment will not exceed 2 millivolts.

The reference grounding point is intended to ensure that all electrically conductive surfaces of the building structure, which could receive heavy fault currents from ordinary (grounded) circuits, are grounded in a manner to bypass these heavy currents from the operating room.

### 3-3.2.2.1 Isolation Transformer.

(a) The isolation transformer shall be approved for the purpose.

(b) The primary winding shall be connected to a power source so that it is not energized with more than 600 V (nominal). The neutral of the primary winding shall be grounded in an approved manner. If an electrostatic shield is present, it shall be connected to the reference grounding point.

This value of 600 V allows three-phase transformers to supply single-phase power to the same anesthetizing location (correlating with changes in 2-6.3.3 and 2-6.3.4 in Annex 2, "Flammable Anesthetizing Locations"). There is no requirement for two transformers to isolate circuits in those rooms where three-phase power is needed.

(c) Wiring of isolated power systems shall be in accordance with Section 517-62 of NFPA 70, *National Electrical Code.*

Since the 1984 edition of NFPA 70, *National Electrical Code* [3], Article 517 has allowed three-phase, three-wire systems, with up to 600 V across the secondary of the transformer.

### 3-3.2.2.2 Impedance of Isolated Wiring.

(a)* The impedance (capacitive and resistive) to ground of either conductor of an isolated system shall exceed 200,000 ohms when installed. The installation at this point shall include receptacles but is not required to include lighting fixtures or components of fixtures. This value shall be determined by energizing the system and connecting a low-impedance ac milliammeter (0 to 1 mA scale) between the reference grounding point and either conductor in sequence. This test shall be permitted to be performed with the line isolation monitor *(see 3-3.2.2.3)* connected, provided the connection between the line isolation monitor and the reference grounding point is open at the time of the test. After the test is made, the milliammeter shall be removed and the grounding connection of the line isolation monitor shall be restored. When the installation is completed, including permanently connected fixtures, the reading of the meter on the line isolation monitor, which corresponds to the unloaded line condition, shall be made. This meter reading shall be recorded as a reference for subsequent line-impedance evaluation.

This test shall be conducted with no phase conductors grounded.

In March 1980 a Formal Interpretation was issued stating that the measurement technique suggested in A-3-3.3.2.3 for grounding systems was acceptable here as well. The committee did point out in using this configuration that the test in 3-3.2.2.2(a) was not to be conducted unless the connection between the line isolation monitor and the reference ground point was open at the time of the test.

Note that to determine impedance of isolated power wiring, it is necessary to convert the meter reading (in milliamperes) to line impedance (in ohms).

---

**Formal Interpretation 78-1**

Reference: 3-3.2.2.2(a) of NFPA 99-1996

*Question:* Is the measurement technique as outlined in Appendix A-3-3.3.2.3 acceptable for use in 3-3.2.2.2(a)?

*Answer:* Yes.

*Comment:* The text in 3-3.2.2.2(a) is a determination of the integrity of the isolation from ground of the two power conductors. The test in 3-3.3.2.3 is a determination of the integrity of the grounding system. As noted in the text, the test in 3-3.2.2.2(a) is not to be conducted unless the connection between the line isolation monitor and reference grounding point is open at the time of the test.

*Issue Edition:* 1978 of NFPA 56A

*Reference:* 3-3.3.1

*Date:* March 1980

---

**A-3-3.2.2.2(a)** It is desirable to limit the size of the isolation transformer to 10 kVA or less and to use conductor insulation with low leakage to meet the impedance requirements. Keeping branch circuits short and using insulation with a dielectric constant less than 3.5 and insulation resistance constant greater than 6100 megohmmeters (20,000 megohm-ft) at 60°F (16°C) reduces leakage from line to ground.

To correct milliammeter reading to line impedance:

$$\text{Line impedance (in ohms)} = \frac{V \times 1000}{I}$$

where $V$ = isolated power system voltage and $I$ = milliammeter reading made during impedance test.

(b) An approved capacitance suppressor shall be permitted to be used to improve the impedance of the permanently installed isolated system; however, the resistive impedance to ground of each isolated conductor of the system shall be at least 1 megohm prior to the connection of the suppression equipment. Capacitance suppressors shall be installed so as to prevent inadvertent disconnection during normal use.

### 3-3.2.2.3 Line Isolation Monitor.

See Exhibit 3.3.

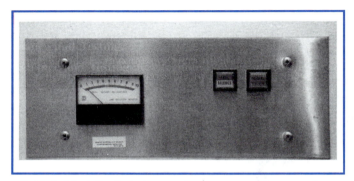

**Exhibit 3.3** *A line isolation monitor in an operating room that has an analog display. Digital displays are in widespread use as well.*

(a)* In addition to the usual control and protective devices, each isolated power system shall be provided with an approved continually operating line isolation monitor that indicates possible leakage or fault currents from either isolated conductor to ground.

**A-3-3.2.2.3(a)** Protection for the patient is provided primarily by a grounding system. The ungrounded secondary of the isolation transformer reduces the maximum current in the grounding system in case of a single fault between either isolated power conductor and ground. The line isolation monitor provides warning when a single fault occurs, or when excessively low impedance to ground develops, which might expose the patient to an unsafe condition should an additional fault occur. Excessive current in the grounding conductors will not result from a first fault. A hazard exists if a second fault occurs before the first fault is cleared.

(b) The monitor shall be designed such that a green signal lamp, conspicuously visible to persons in the anesthetizing location, remains lighted when the system is adequately isolated from ground; and an adjacent red signal lamp and an audible warning signal (remote if desired) shall be energized when the total hazard current (consisting of possible resistive and capacitive leakage currents) from either isolated conductor to ground reaches a threshold value of 5.0 mA under normal line voltage conditions. The line isolation monitor shall not alarm for a fault hazard current of less than 3.7 mA.

The alarm threshold value was raised from 2.0 mA to 5.0 mA in 1978 to account for the increased number of appliances that were being used during operations. It is now not uncommon in major procedures to have more than 20 electrically powered devices functioning.

Note that 5.0 mA is a maximum threshold value.

The committee did not feel that this change increased the risk to patient or staff. While 5.0 mA will produce tingling, it is still well below the 100 mA to 150 mA required to induce ventricular fibrillation from external, arm-to-arm contact with a power source.

Note that the hazard current value (5.0 mA) is the important factor and is not to be exceeded, regardless of the voltage, impedance, and so forth, of the system.

(c) The line isolation monitor shall have sufficient internal impedance such that, when properly connected to the isolated system, the maximum internal current that will flow through the line isolation monitor, when any point of the isolated system is grounded, shall be 1 mA.

*Exception:\* The line isolation monitor is permitted to be of the low-impedance type such that the current through the line isolation monitor, when any point of the isolated system is grounded, will not exceed twice the alarm threshold value for a period not exceeding 5 msec.*

Prior to the 1970s, the usual method of monitoring isolated systems was by high-impedance monitors. A radically different approach that used low-impedance technology was developed in the early 1970s. The exception, formally included in the 1984 edition of NFPA 99, reflects this advancement in technology.

High-impedance technology uses line isolation monitors (LIMs) that are in parallel with any fault impedance contributing to hazard current. Low-impedance technology uses line isolation monitors that are in series with any fault impedance. However, the time that the low-impedance LIMs are actually in series is very short (one cycle or less; 0.0167 seconds or less).

**A-3-3.2.2.3(c), Exception.** It is desirable to reduce this monitor hazard current provided this reduction results in an increased "not alarm" threshold value for the fault hazard current.

(d)* An ammeter connected to indicate the total hazard current of the system (contribution of the fault hazard current plus monitor hazard current) shall be mounted in a plainly visible place on the line isolation monitor with the "alarm on" (total hazard current = 5.0 mA) zone at approximately the center of the scale. It is desirable to locate the ammeter such that it is conspicuously visible to persons in the anesthetizing location.

**A-3-3.2.2.3(d)** The line isolation monitor may be a composite unit, with a sensing section cabled to a separate display panel section, on which the alarm and test functions are located, if the two sections are within the same electric enclosure.

Until 1970 former NFPA 56A (now part of NFPA 99) required only a red/green signal system with an audible alarm to indicate when the fault hazard current threshold had been exceeded. In 1970 the use of an ammeter was added to measure more precisely changes in the value of the fault hazard current. This provided more control since devices that significantly increased the current could be spotted or changes in the baseline current level could be seen.

At the time this requirement was written in 1970, only analog ammeters were generally available. The phrase "at approximately the center of the scale" should not be construed to exclude the digital-type meters that are available today. It can be argued that the midpoint of a 0 to 9 unit scale of a digital meter is between 4 and 5. Since the alarm threshold is now up to 5.0 mA, this meets the intent of alarming at approximately the center of the scale.

(e) Means shall be provided for shutting off the audible alarm while leaving the red warning lamp activated. When the fault is corrected and the green signal lamp is reactivated, the audible alarm silencing circuit shall reset automatically, or an audible or distinctive visual signal shall indicate that the audible alarm is silenced.

(f) A reliable test switch shall be mounted on the line isolation monitor to test its capability to operate (i.e., cause the alarms to operate and the meter to indicate in the "alarm on" zone). This switch shall transfer the grounding connection of the line isolation monitor from the reference grounding point to a test impedance arrangement connected across the isolated line; the test impedance(s) shall be of the appropriate magnitude to produce a meter reading corresponding to the rated total hazard current at the nominal line voltage, or to a lesser alarm hazard current if the line isolation monitor is so rated. The operation of this switch shall break the grounding connection of the line isolation monitor to the reference grounding point before transferring this grounding connector to the test impedance(s), so that making this test will not add to the hazard of a system in actual use, nor will the test include the effect of the line to ground stray impedance of the system. The test switch shall be of a self-restoring type.

This paragraph applies only to a switch used for testing. The actual values of alarming are set by 3-3.2.2.3(b) and 3-3.2.2.3(d). The Committee on Electrical Systems intends to review the subject of an acceptable current range for the test switch for the next edition of NFPA 99.

(g) The line isolation monitor shall not generate energy of sufficient amplitude and/or frequency, as measured by a physiological monitor with a gain of at least $10^4$ with a source impedance of 1000 ohms connected to the balanced differential input of the monitor, to create interference or artifact on human physiological signals. The output voltage from the amplifier shall not exceed 30 mV when the gain is $10^4$. The 1000 ohms impedance shall be connected to the ends of typical unshielded electrode leads (which are a normal part of the cable assembly furnished with physiological monitors). A 60-Hz notch filter shall be used to reduce ambient interference (as is typical in physiological monitor design).

Interference on physiological monitors can be caused from a variety of reasons including dried-out patient electrodes or a faulty patient cable; the location of the building with respect to transmitting antennas; or the line isolation monitor. This is possible particularly with some older models of LIMs because of the design of switching circuitry. The preceding performance test is included because of reports received over the years of interference from LIMs.

**3-3.2.2.4 Identification of Conductors for Isolated (Ungrounded) Systems.** The isolated conductors shall be identified in accordance with Section 517-160(a)(5) of NFPA 70, *National Electrical Code*.

## 3-3.3 Performance Criteria and Testing.

**3-3.3.1** (Reserved)

**3-3.3.2 Grounding System in Patient Care Areas.**

**3-3.3.2.1\* Grounding System Testing.** The effectiveness of the grounding system shall be determined by voltage measurements and impedance measurements.

Both voltage and impedance measurements are required because they check two different possible hazards.

Voltage measurement is a check to determine that there is no inadvertent connection or coupling that would raise the potential of the object being tested with respect to other parts of the grounding system. A problem would exist if conductive parts of the building structure became connected to ground but at points remote from the local power system grounds.

Impedance measurement is a check to verify that there is indeed a common grounding path for the power system within a patient vicinity.

**A-3-3.3.2.1** *Grounding System Testing.* In a conventional grounded power distribution system, one of the line conductors is deliberately grounded, usually at some distribution panel or the service entrance. This grounded conductor is identified as the neutral conductor. The other line conductor (or conductors) is (are) the high side of the line. The loads to be served by this distribution system are fed by the high and neutral conductors.

In addition to the high and neutral conductors, a grounding conductor is provided. One end is connected to the neutral at the point where the neutral is grounded, and the other end leads out to the connected loads. For purposes here, the load connection point will be considered to be a convenience receptacle, with the grounding conductor terminating at the grounding terminal of that receptacle.

This grounding conductor can be a separate wire running from the receptacle back to the remote grounding connection (where it joins the neutral conductor). If that separate conductor does not make any intermediate ground contacts between the receptacle and the remote ground, then the impedance of the connection between the receptacle and the remote ground is primarily the resistance of the grounding conductor itself and is, therefore, predictable.

If, however, the receptacle is also interconnected with the remote ground point by metallic conduit or other metallic building structures, the impedance of the circuit between receptacle and remote ground is not easily predictable, nor is it easy to measure accurately, although one can be sure that the impedance will be less than that of the grounding wire itself because of the additional parallel paths.

Fortunately, as will become apparent in the following paragraphs, the absolute value of the apparent impedance between the grounding contact of an outlet and the remote ground point need not be known or measured with great accuracy.

Ideally, and under no-fault conditions, the grounding system described earlier is supposed to be carrying no current at all. If that were true, then no voltage differences would be found between exposed conductive surfaces of any electrical appliances that were grounded to the grounding contacts of the receptacles that powered them. Similarly, there would be no voltage differences between these appliances and any other exposed metal surface that was also interconnected with the grounding system, provided that no currents were flowing in that interconnection.

Ideal conditions, however, do not prevail, and even when there are no "faults" within an appliance, residual "leakage" current does flow in the grounding conductor of each of the appliances, producing a voltage difference between the chassis of that appliance and the grounding contact of the receptacle that feeds it. Furthermore, this current can produce voltage differences among other appliances plugged into various receptacles on the system.

Fortunately, these leakage currents are small, and for reasonably low grounding-circuit impedances, the resulting voltage differences are entirely negligible.

If, however, a breakdown of insulation between the high side of the line and the chassis of an appliance should occur, the leakage condition becomes a fault condition, the magnitude of which is limited by the nature of the breakdown or, in the case of a dead short circuit in the appliance, the magnitude of the fault current is limited only by the residual resistance of the appliance power cord conductors and that of the power distribution system.

In the event of such a short circuit, the impedance of the grounding circuit, as measured between the grounding contact of the receptacle that feeds the defective appliance and the remote ground point where the neutral and grounding conductors are joined, should be so small that a large enough fault current will flow to ensure a rapid breaking of the circuit by the overcurrent protective device that serves that receptacle.

For a 20-A branch circuit, a fault current of 40 or more amperes would be required to ensure a rapid opening of the branch-circuit overcurrent-protective device. This corresponds to a circuit impedance of 3 ohms or less, of which the grounding system should contribute 1 ohm or less.

During the time this large fault current flows in the grounding system, the chassis of the defective appliance is raised many volts above other grounded surfaces in the same vicinity. The hazard represented by this condition is minimized by the fact that it exists for only a short time, and unless a patient simultaneously contacts both the defective appliance and some other grounded surface during this short time interval, there is no hazard. Further-more, the magnitude of an applied voltage required to produce a serious shock hazard increases as its duration decreases, so the rapidity with which the circuit is interrupted helps reduce shock hazard even if such a patient contact should occur.

If, however, the defect in the appliance is not such as to cause an immediate circuit interruption, then the effect of this intermediate level of fault current on the voltages appearing on various exposed conductive surfaces in the patient care vicinity should be considered.

Since all of this fault current flows in the grounding conductor of the defective appliance's power cord, the first effect is to raise the potential of this appliance above that of the receptacle that feeds it by an amount proportional to the power cord grounding conductor resistance. This resistance is required to be less than 0.15 ohm, so fault currents of 20 A or less, which will not trip the branch-circuit overcurrent-protective device, will raise the potential of the defective appliance above the grounding contact of its supply receptacle by only 3 V or less. This value is not hazardous for casual contacts.

The fault current that enters the grounding system at the grounding contact of any receptacle in the patient care vicinity could affect the potential at the grounding contacts of all the other receptacles, and, more importantly, it could produce significant voltage differences between them and other grounded surfaces, such as exposed piping and building structures.

If one grounded point is picked as a reference (a plumbing fixture in or near the patient care vicinity, for example), and then the voltage difference is measured between that reference and the grounding contact of a receptacle, produced by driving some known current into that contact, a direct measure of the effectiveness of the grounding system within the patient care vicinity is obtained. The "figure of merit" can be stated as so many volts per ampere of fault current. The ratio volts per ampere is, of course, impedance; but since the exact path taken by the fault current is not known, and since the way in which the reference point is interconnected with the grounding system is not known, it cannot be stated that this value is the impedance between the receptacle and some specific point, such as the joining of the neutral and grounding conductors. But it can be stated that this measured value of "effective impedance" is indicative of the effectiveness with which the grounding system minimizes voltage differences between supposedly grounded objects in the patient care vicinity that are produced by ground faults in appliances used in that vicinity. This impedance, which characterizes the ability of the grounding system to maintain nearly equipotential conditions within the patient care vicinity, is of prime importance in assessing shock hazard; but this impedance is not necessarily the same as the impedance between receptacle and remote ground point, which controls the magnitude of the short-circuit current involved in tripping the branch-circuit overcurrent-protective device.

Fault currents on the grounding system can also come from neutral-to-ground faults, which permit some current to flow in the neutral and some in the ground. This type of fault is often the cause of interference on EEG and ECG equipment. It is often not recognized easily because, except for 60-Hz interference, the equipment works perfectly properly. It is most easily found by causing a substantial change in the line-to-line load and noting changes in the ground-to-reference voltage.

A neutral-to-ground fault, as noted in the last paragraph of the appendix text, is not a common occurrence. When it does occur, it can be difficult to locate (it may not even be in the patient care area). The only visible manifestation is 60-Hz interference on ECG and EEG equipment. A shock hazard is possible, but very improbable. A neutral-to-ground fault is more a diagnostic safety problem.

(a) *New Construction.* The effectiveness of the grounding system shall be evaluated before acceptance.

*Exception No. 1: Small, wall-mounted conductive surfaces, not likely to become energized, such as surface-mounted towel and soap dispensers, mirrors, and so forth, need not be intentionally grounded or tested.*

*Exception No. 2: Large, metal conductive surfaces not likely to become energized, such as windows, door frames, and drains, need not be intentionally grounded or periodically tested.*

The fine distinction between Exception No. 1 and Exception No. 2 ("tested" and "periodically tested") should be noted. The committee responsible for this chapter was concerned that large metal conductive surfaces be tested at least once to ensure that such surfaces were not inadvertently carrying excessive potentials. No further testing need be done after this initial check. However, if major changes are made and there is concern whether conditions have changed, it is wise to conduct another test.

(b)* Whenever the electrical system has been altered or replaced, that portion of the system shall be tested.

The distinction between new and existing construction is a practical one. It is not possible to test existing construction before acceptance. However, if significant modifications are made to an existing structure so that the electrical system under construction is essentially new, it is prudent to test that portion as if it were new.

With the exception of the "reference to altered or replaced" in 3-3.3.2.1(b), all references to testing existing grounding systems were deleted for the 1996 edition. The committee believes that the effectiveness of grounding does not significantly change with the aging of a system that has not been altered or repaired. It is the committee's opinion that the recommendation found in previous editions to test the system annually is not appropriate. Testing of parts of the grounding system that have been altered or replaced is still required.

**A-3-3.3.2.1(b)** The grounding system (reference ground and conduit) is to be tested as an integral system. Lifting of grounds from receptacles and fixed equipment is not required or recommended for the performance of this test.

This appendix material clarifies how the system is to be tested. It is also not intended that testing be performed only if an entire electrical system is replaced. Whatever portion is repaired, replaced, or altered should be tested. If only one receptacle is replaced, then only that one receptacle need be tested.

**3-3.3.2.2 Reference Point.** The voltage and impedance measurements shall be taken with respect to a reference point. The reference point shall be one of the following:

(a) A reference grounding point *(see Chapter 2, Definitions)*

(b) A grounding point, in or near the room under test, that is electrically remote from receptacles, for example, an all-metal cold-water pipe

(c) The grounding contact of a receptacle that is powered from a different branch circuit from the receptacle under test

> This section is included in NFPA 99 so that more consistent voltage and impedance measurements will be taken. For subparagraph (b), plastic piping, while electrically remote, would not be acceptable.

**3-3.3.2.3\* Voltage Measurements.** The voltage measurements shall be made under no-fault conditions between a reference point and exposed fixed electrical equipment with conductive surfaces in a patient care vicinity. The voltage measurements shall be made with an accuracy of ±20 percent.

*Exception:\* Faceplates of wiring devices.*

> This text lists performance criteria only. The wiring methodology used to achieve the performance levels in the next several sections is left to the discretion of designers. The method used to install the wiring, however, needs to be in accordance with NFPA 70, *National Electrical Code* [3]. There may also be other authorities (governmental and nongovernmental) that have other requirements that must be met.
>
> The 20 mV value in 3-3.3.2.6 reports from various sources. This limit is reasonably attainable and provides a reasonable margin of safety.
>
> For 1996 the requirement to measure "exposed surfaces" was revised to specify just "exposed fixed electrical equipment with conductive surfaces in the patient vicinity." The committee considered this type of equipment the only type likely to become energized.
>
> Drs. Whaler, Steimer, and MacIntosh [7], in experiments on human reaction to electrical stimulus, found it was the amount of current that flowed that was critical (i.e., it was the current that induced the ventricular fibrillation). Thus, while the measurement in 3-3.3.2.6 is given in terms of a maximum voltage (20 mV) across a specified resistance (1000 ohms), the concern is the amount of current ($I = V/R$) that will flow under this condition. This fact is particularly important when measuring in the microampere range.

**A-3-3.3.2.3** *Grounding and Voltage and Leakage Current Measurement Circuits.* Effective grounding to safely handle both fault and leakage currents requires following the requirements of both Chapter 3 of NFPA 99 and Article 250 of NFPA 70, *National Electrical Code*, having good workmanship, and using some techniques that are not in these documents.

The performance of the grounding system is made effective through the existence of the green grounding wire, the metal raceway, and all of the other building metal. Measurements have shown that it is the metal raceway and building steel that provide most of the effective grounding path of less than 10 milliohms at the receptacle, including plug-to-receptacle imped-ance. The green grounding wire becomes a backup, not a primary grounding path performer.

Good practice calls for each receptacle to have a good jumper grounding connection to the metal raceway at the receptacle location in addition to having the green grounding wire connecting these points to the grounding bus in the distribution panel. Good workmanship includes seeing that these grounding connections are tight at each receptacle and that all metal raceway joints are secure and tight.

The voltage difference measurements listed in 3-3.3.2.3 in connection with power distribu-tion grounding systems should ideally be made with an oscilloscope or spectrum analyzer in order to observe and measure components of leakage current and voltage differences at all frequencies.

For routine testing, such instruments could be inconvenient. An alternative is to use a metering system that weighs the contribution to the meter reading of the various components of the signal being measured in accordance with their probable physiological effect.

A meter specifically designed for this purpose would have an impedance of approximately 1000 ohms, and a frequency characteristic that was flat to 1 kHz, dropped at the rate of 20 decibels per decade to 100 kHz, and then remained flat to 1 MHz or higher. This frequency response characteristic could be achieved by proper design of the internal circuits of the ampli-fier that probably precedes the indicating instrument or by appropriate choice of a feedback network around the amplifier. These details are, of course, left to the instrument designer.

If a meter specifically designed for these measurements is not available, a general-purpose laboratory millivoltmeter can be adapted for the purpose by adding a frequency-response-shaping network ahead of the meter. One such suggested network is shown in Figure A-3-3.3.2.3(a).

The circuit shown in Figure A-3-3.3.2.3(a) is especially applicable to measurements of leakage current, where the current being measured is derived from a circuit whose source imped-ance is high compared to 1000 ohms. Under these conditions, the voltage developed across the millivoltmeter will be proportional to the impedance of the network. The network impedance will be 1000 ohms at low frequencies and 10 ohms at high frequencies, and the transition between these two values will occur in the frequency range between 1 kHz and 100 kHz.

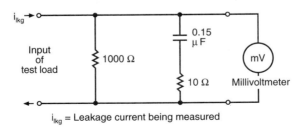

$i_{lkg}$ = Leakage current being measured

*Figure A-3-3.3.2.3(a)* *Circuit used to measure leakage current with high source impedance.*

The basic low-frequency sensitivity will be 1 millivolt (mV) of meter reading for each 1 milliampere (mA) of leakage current.

The millivoltmeter's own input impedance needs to be very large compared to 1000 ohms (100 kilohms), and the meter should have a flat frequency response to well beyond 100 kHz. (If the meter impedance is lower than 100 kilohms, then the 1000-ohm resistor can be raised to a higher value, such that the impedance of that resistor in parallel with the meter will still be 1000 ohms.)

The circuit in Figure A-3-3.3.2.3(a) can be used for the voltage difference measurements required in Section 3-5, but, because the source impedance will be very low compared to 1000 ohms, the frequency response of the measurement system will remain flat. If any high-frequency components, produced, for example, by pickup from nearby radio frequency transmitters, appear on the circuit being measured, then they will not be attenuated and the meter reading will be higher than it should be.

For meter readings below any prescribed limits, this possible error is of no consequence. For borderline cases it could be significant. To avoid this uncertainty when making voltage-difference measurements, a slightly more elaborate version of a frequency-response-shaping network is given in Figure A-3-3.3.2.3(b).

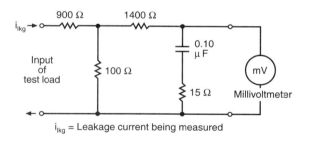

**Figure A-3-3.3.2.3(b)** *Circuit used to measure leakage current with low source impedance.*

Here the source being measured is separated from the frequency-response-shaping network by the combination of the 900-ohm and 100-ohm resistors. The frequency response characteristic is now independent of the circuit being tested.

This independence is achieved, however, at a loss in signal delivered to the millivoltmeter. The basic low-frequency sensitivity of this metering circuit is 1 millivolt of meter reading for 10 microamperes of leakage current or, on a voltage basis, 1 millivolt (mV) of meter reading for 10 millivolts (mV) at the input terminals of the network.

The millivoltmeter should have an input impedance of 150 kilohms and a frequency response flat to well beyond 100 kHz.

For either of the suggested networks, the resistors and capacitors should be mounted in a metal container close to the millivoltmeter to avoid stray pickup by the leads going to the meter.

**A-3-3.3.2.3, Exception.** The reference point can be the reference grounding point or the grounding contact of a convenient receptacle.

**3-3.3.2.4\* Impedance Measurements.** The impedance measurement shall be made with an accuracy of ±20 percent.

*For New Construction.* The impedance measurement shall be made between the reference point and the grounding contact of 10 percent of all receptacles in each patient care vicinity. The impedance measurement shall be the ratio of voltage developed (either 60 Hz or dc) between the point under test and the reference point to the current applied between these two points.

**A-3-3.3.2.4** It is not the intent that each receptacle be tested. It is intended that compliance be demonstrated through random testing. The 10 percent random testing should include a mixture of both normal and emergency receptacles.

Requirements for impedance testing of receptacles were reduced in 1996 to 10 percent of the receptacles located in the *patient care vicinity*. Paragraph 3-3.3.3 covers other testing of all receptacles in the patient care area that extends beyond the patient care vicinity.

The reason for this reduction to 10 percent of receptacles stems from the NFPA 70, *National Electrical Code,* requirement for multiple pathways to ground (grounding conductor and metallic conduit), which reduces the probability of ineffective grounding systems.

The deletion in 1996 of testing requirements for existing construction [former subparagraph (b)] is in concert with the deletion of voltage measurement requirements for existing construction.

In this 1999 edition, the text has been modified to express the intent that at least one receptacle be tested in each patient care vicinity that is roughly 6 ft (1.8 m) in all directions around the normal location of the bed, chair, table, treadmill, or other device that supports the patient during examination and treatment. Paragraph 3-3.3.2.4 includes a recommendation that, in the process of random testing of patient vicinities, both normal and emergency receptacles be tested. This does not imply that within each patient care vicinity it is necessary to test both a normal and emergency receptacle. For example, during the random testing an emergency receptacle might be tested at one patient care vicinity and a normal receptacle tested at another.

**3-3.3.2.5 Test Equipment.** Electrical safety test instruments shall be tested periodically, but not less than annually, for acceptable performance.

(a) Voltage measurements specified in 3-3.3.2.3 shall be made with an instrument having an input resistance of 1000 ohms ± 10 percent at frequencies of 1000 Hz or less.

(b) The voltage across the terminals (or between any terminal and ground) of resistance-measuring instruments used in occupied patient care areas shall not exceed 500 mV rms or 1.4 dc or peak to peak.

Research is still being conducted on the question of how best to measure and verify the integrity of building wiring systems. The high-current test has been found to temporarily weld poor connections together. The low-current test will not detect a connection point that is only barely making a connection. One test apparatus, included as an example in the 1984 edition of NFPA 99, could even harm users or self-destruct under some fault conditions; the example was later deleted to preclude problems.

Rather than include any recommendations on tester configuration, only instrument input resistance and maximum rms, dc, or peak-to-peak voltage across terminals for resistance-measuring instruments have been specified.

Whatever test instrument(s) are used, it is essential for accuracy of measurements that these instruments be checked to verify that they are functioning within their listed specifications. They should also be periodically checked to ensure they are operating safely.

### 3-3.3.2.6 Criteria for Acceptability for New Construction.

(a) Voltage limit shall be 20 mV.

(b) Impedance limit shall be 0.1 ohm.

*Exception: For quiet ground systems, the limit shall be 0.2 ohm.*

### 3-3.3.3 Receptacle Testing in Patient Care Areas.

This testing is to be performed on all new receptacles in patient care areas. Section 3-3.3 covers performance criteria and testing for new systems and equipment.

The continuity of all the grounding circuits may be verified by the impedance test of 3-3.3.2.4. However, physical integrity and polarity tests should be performed before the continuity test.

(a) The physical integrity of each receptacle shall be confirmed by visual inspection.

(b) The continuity of the grounding circuit in each electrical receptacle shall be verified.

(c) Correct polarity of the hot and neutral connections in each electrical receptacle shall be confirmed.

(d) The retention force of the grounding blade of each electrical receptacle (except locking-type receptacles) shall be not less than 115 g (4 oz).

Four ounces is considered a reasonable safety factor by the former Technical Committee on Safe Use of Electricity in Patient Care Areas for deciding when it is time to replace a receptacle. A low tension value means the ground pin of the attachment plug of the appliance is not making good contact with the grounding blade in the receptacle, thereby defeating the purpose of providing a low-impedance path to ground for the green ground wire of the appliance.

### 3-3.3.4 Isolated Power Systems.

See commentary under 3-3.2.2 regarding where isolated power systems are to be installed.

**3-3.3.4.1 Patient Care Areas.** If installed, the isolated power system shall be tested in accordance with 3-3.3.4.2.

**3-3.3.4.2 Line Isolation Monitor Tests.** The proper functioning of each line isolation monitor (LIM) circuit shall be ensured by the following:

(a) The LIM circuit shall be tested after installation, and prior to being placed in service, by successively grounding each line of the energized distribution system through a resistor of 200 × V ohms, where V = measured line voltage. The visual and audible alarms *[see 3-3.2.2.3(b)]* shall be activated.

(b) The LIM circuit shall be tested at intervals of not more than 1 month by actuating the LIM test switch *[see 3-3.2.2.3(f)]*. For a LIM circuit with automated self-test and self-calibration capabilities, this test shall be performed at intervals of not more than 12 months. Actuation of the test switch shall activate both visual and audible alarm indicators.

(c) After any repair or renovation to an electrical distribution system and at intervals of not more than 6 months, the LIM circuit shall be tested in accordance with paragraph (a) above and only when the circuit is not otherwise in use. For a LIM circuit with automated self-test and self-calibration capabilities, this test shall be performed at intervals of not more than 12 months.

## 3-3.4* Administration of Electrical System.

**A-3-3.4** Administration is in conjunction with 3-3.4.2, Distribution.

### 3-3.4.1 Source.

### 3-3.4.2 Distribution.

### 3-3.4.2.1* Responsibilities of Governing Body.

**A-3-3.4.2.1** See Sections 12-2, 13-2, and so forth, for responsibilities within specific facilities.

### 3-3.4.2.2 Policies. (Reserved)

### 3-3.4.2.3 Maintenance and Testing of Electrical System.

(a) *Testing Interval for Receptacles in Patient Care Areas.*

1. Testing shall be performed after initial installation, replacement, or servicing of the device.

2. Additional testing shall be performed at intervals defined by documented performance data.

*Exception:  Receptacles not listed as hospital-grade shall be tested at intervals not exceeding 12 months.*

> Previously specified intervals for testing were deleted for the 1996 edition. This change was based in part on previous text that allowed longer or shorter intervals of testing "if documentation could justify changing the interval." The result is reflected in subparagraph 2. It should be noted, however, that all receptacles in patient care areas are to be tested when testing is conducted.
>
> The exception does specify testing intervals for those receptacles not listed as hospital grade.

### 3-3.4.3 Recordkeeping.

**3-3.4.3.1\* General.** A record shall be maintained of the tests required by this chapter and associated repairs or modification. At a minimum, this record shall contain the date, the rooms or areas tested, and an indication of which items have met or have failed to meet the performance requirements of this chapter.

**A-3-3.4.3.1** While several approaches to documentation exist in hospitals, the minimum acceptable documentation should convey what was tested, when it was tested, and whether it performed successfully. Adopting a system of exception reporting can be the most efficient form of recordkeeping for routine rechecks of equipment or systems and thereby minimize technicians' time in recording the value of each measurement taken. For example, once a test protocol is established, which simply means testing the equipment or system consistent with this chapter, the only item (value) that needs to be recorded is what failure or what deviation from the requirements of the chapter was detected when a corrective action (repair) was undertaken. This approach can serve to eliminate, for example, the need to keep individual room sheets to record measured results on each receptacle or to record measurement values of all types of leakage current tests.

> The format of the documentation is left to the discretion and thus the responsibility of the facility. However, it is advisable to consult with inspection agencies, insurance companies, and other authorities for any recommended formats.

**3-3.4.3.2 Isolated Power System (Where Installed).** A permanent record shall be kept of the results of each of the tests.

> If an isolated power system (IPS) alarms, the source of the alarm needs to be investigated and corrected. For IPSs in operating rooms, immediate correction may be difficult if an operation is in progress. Immediately following the procedure, an investigation should be conducted and the results recorded with other tests.

**3-3.4.4 Information and Warning Signs.** (Reserved)

# 3-4 Essential Electrical System Requirements—Type 1

## 3-4.1 Sources (Type 1 EES).

The following paragraphs apply to situations in which the normal power source is a public utility and the alternate source is on-site generation. The exceptions apply to situations in which normal power is provided by on-site generation. It should be clearly noted that there must always be at least two independent power sources, and at least one of them must be located on-site. In certain situations the power source(s) defined as "normal" and "alternate" could change, and even be reversed, under different modes of operation.

The normal source should be made as reliable as possible, as dictated by local conditions. When the normal source is a public utility, the greatest reliability and continuity are provided by a properly protected network fed by multiple independent services. The next highest reliability level comes from multiple independent services with local automatic switching. This chapter does not require multiple services or network or switching arrangements because of widely varying local conditions and the limited availability of multiple services at certain locations.

With the low but probable occurrence of occasional blackouts from accidents, failures, or natural causes, multiple public utility services cannot be considered absolutely reliable and thus cannot be used as the alternate source in lieu of on-site generation.

When the normal source is on-site generation, it is suggested that its reliability be designed and maintained to at least equal that of any available public utility.

### 3-4.1.1 On-Site Generator Set.

Nothing in this section precludes the use of coolants for heat recovery purposes. See Exhibits 3.4 and 3.5.

**3-4.1.1.1\* Design Considerations.** Dual sources of normal power shall be considered. Such dual sources of normal power shall not constitute an alternate source of power as described in this chapter.

**A-3-4.1.1.1** *Design Considerations.*

(a) *Connection to Dual Source of Normal Power.* For the greatest assurance of continuity of electrical service, the normal source should consist of two separate full-capacity services, each independent of the other. Such services should be selected and installed with full recognition of local hazards of interruption, such as icing and flooding.

**Exhibit 3.4** *An example of an emergency generator for a large medical facility. This engine generates 250 kW of power.*

**Exhibit 3.5** *A 550-kW emergency generator. Note batteries at base of engine.*

Where more than one full-capacity service is installed, they should be connected in such a manner that one will pick up the load automatically upon loss of the other, and so arranged that the load of the emergency and equipment systems will be transferred to the alternate source (generator set) only when both utility services are deenergized, unless this arrangement is impractical and waived by the authority having jurisdiction. Such services should be interlocked in such a manner as to prevent paralleling of utility services on either primary or secondary voltage levels.

NOTE: In any installation where it is possible to parallel utility supply circuits, for example, to prevent interruption of service when switching from one utility source to another, it is imperative to consult the power companies affected as to problems of synchronization.

Facilities whose normal source of power is supplied by two or more separate central-station-fed services (dual sources of normal power) experience greater reliability than those with only a single feed.

(b) *Installation of Generator Sets.* For additional material on diesel engines, see *Diesel Engines for Use with Generators to Supply Emergency and Short Term Electric Power*, National Research Council Publication, 1132 *(see Appendix B).*

These measures cannot completely eliminate power interruptions within a facility. A facility can be affected by external incidents or failures beyond its control.

Essential electrical systems have to be designed as complete systems. They are not simply generators and transfer switches appended to normal distribution wiring. The horsepower for the engine, generator set overload, the number and rating of transfer switch(es), and placement and setting of overcurrent protective devices are just some of the design factors that have to be considered when designing the essential electrical system. The overall goal when designing the system should be to provide reliable power for fire protection, life safety, and medical functions.

Internal ground faults have, historically, caused destruction of electrical distribution equipment and power outages within facilities. This chapter attempts to mitigate the effects of such outages and to some degree to minimize their occurrence by requiring segregated distribution systems with multiple transfer switches. Internal ground faults are a major exposure that must be considered in the design of electrical systems. The proper engineering technique for coping with the ground fault problem is to divide, limit, and segregate the electrical system and its components. No single component or system can be functionally designed to be massive enough to withstand the sudden, extremely large currents that may be imposed when a major ground fault occurs.

This chapter does not require the application of all available technology and techniques that can be used for essential electrical systems. The optimum combination of realistic reliability, economics, and allowance for human factors is stressed in the design of an essential electrical system. Additional technology and techniques not mentioned in this chapter can and should be applied to individual facilities.

Provisions for the maintenance of main switchgear and supply feeders should be considered when establishing distribution details of the normal and essential electrical systems. Such maintenance is greatly simplified when the main switchgear can be deenergized while essential electrical systems are fed from the alternate source.

Distribution system arrangements shall be designed to minimize interruptions to the electrical systems due to internal failures by the use of adequately rated equipment. Among the factors to be considered are the following:

(a) *Abnormal currents.* Current-sensing devices, phase and ground, shall be selected to minimize the extent of interruption to the electrical system due to abnormal current caused by overload and/ or short circuits.

A single incoming power line, a single generator set, or a single transfer switch is allowed under certain conditions (see 3-4.2.2.1 and 3-5.2.2.1). However, this setup requires that everything has to function when needed. The Committee on Electrical Systems intends that a greater safety margin than this exist for a system supplying essential electricity when the normal power source is interrupted. Factors such as redundancy and separation of circuits need to considered when designing the essential electrical system.

(b) Abnormal voltages such as single phasing of three-phase utilization equipment, switching and/or lightning surges, voltage reductions, and so forth
(c) Capability of achieving the fastest possible restoration of any given circuit(s) after clearing a fault
(d) Effects of future changes, such as increased loading and/or supply capacity
(e) Stability and power capability of the prime mover during and after abnormal conditions
(f)* Sequence reconnection of loads to avoid large current inrushes that trip overcurrent devices or overload the generator(s)

**A-3-4.1.1.1(f)** Careful consideration should be given to the location of the spaces housing the components of the essential electrical system to minimize interruptions caused by natural forces common to the area (e.g., storms, floods, or earthquakes, or hazards created by adjoining structures or activities). Consideration should also be given to the possible interruption of normal electrical services resulting from similar causes as well as possible disruption of normal electrical service due to internal wiring and equipment failures.

Consideration should be given to the physical separation of the main feeders of the essential electrical system from the normal wiring of the facility to prevent possible simultaneous destruction as a result of a local catastrophe.

In selecting electrical distribution arrangements and components for the essential electrical system, high priority should be given to achieving maximum continuity of the electrical supply to the load. Higher consideration should be given to achieving maximum reliability of the alternate power source and its feeders rather than protection of such equipment, provided the protection is not required to prevent a greater threat to human life such as fire, explosion, electrocution, and so forth, than would be caused by the lack of essential electrical supply.

(g) Bypass arrangements to permit testing and maintenance of system components that could not otherwise be maintained without disruption of important hospital functions

The issue of making mandatory the use of bypass-isolation switches for automatic transfer switches has been addressed repeatedly over the years. The use of these switches has never been made a requirement because of their significant cost. Facilities considering installing this type of transfer switch need to carefully evaluate the cost/benefit ratio.

Bypass-isolation switches are, however, very useful for properly maintaining automatic transfer switches, and information describing their installation (if they are used) is included in 3-4.2.1.7.

(h) Effects of any harmonic currents on neutral conductors and equipment

Harmonic currents are not necessarily abnormal currents, but they can overheat conductors and equipment. This tendency to overheat is particularly great in "shared" neutral conductors.

(i) Generator load shed circuits designed for the purpose of load reduction or for load priority systems shall not shed life safety branch loads, critical branch loads serving critical care areas, medical air compressors, medical surgical vacuum pumps, fuel pumps, jockey pumps, or other generator accessories.

Generators operating in parallel on a common synchronizing bus often have load priority/ load shed circuits that shed load upon loss of one or more generators. It is a common practice to shed the equipment system load first upon loss of one or more generators. Generally, this reduction in load will keep the remaining generators from "cascading" so that generators remain on-line in order to support the remaining emergency system loads. The designer must be sure that highly critical loads, such as medical air compressors and medical-surgical vacuum pumps, are not shed when shedding the equipment system loads. It is advisable to place medical air compressors, medical-surgical vacuum pumps, fuel pumps, jockey pumps, and generator accessories on a separate equipment branch transfer switch that is not shed upon the loss of one or more generators. It should also be noted that 3-4.2.2.3(c) permits central suction and compressed air systems serving medical and surgical functions to be placed on the critical branch.

With regard to multiple generator systems, it is the intent of the committee to prohibit shedding of highly critical loads upon loss of one or more of the generators. It is sometimes necessary, however, to shed some emergency system loads in general patient care areas in order to maintain emergency system service in critical patient care areas. For this reason, in this 1999 edition, the words "emergency system loads" were replaced with the words "critical branch loads serving critical care areas." For example, a system with three generators on a common synchronizing bus might shed some equipment system loads upon loss of one generator and shed critical branch loads serving general patient care areas upon loss of the second generator. The system could not, however, shed the loads listed in 3-4.1.1.1(i) under any circumstances. In our example these loads would be served by the remaining on-line generator.

See also 3-4.1.1.5 regarding load shedding when multiple generator sets are installed.

**3-4.1.1.2** Essential electrical systems shall have a minimum of two independent sources of power: a normal source generally supplying the entire electrical system and one or more alternate sources for use when the normal source is interrupted.

It is not the intent of the committee responsible for this chapter that dual sources of normal power be used in lieu of an alternate power source. At least one source of power has to be on-site.

**3-4.1.1.3** The alternate source of power shall be a generator(s) driven by some form of prime mover(s) and located on the premises.

*Exception: Where the normal source consists of generating units on the premises, the alternate source shall be either another generating set or an external utility service.*

Even with the exception, it should be noted that at least one source of power (normal or alternate) must be on-site.

"Located on the premises" refers to property encompassing the facility, not to several noncontiguous pieces of property. For an unusual situation, see the following Formal Interpretation.

---

**Formal Interpretation 84-2**

Reference: 3-4.1.1.3 in NFPA 99-1996

*Question:* Is it the intent of 3-4.1.1.3 to allow a group of adjacent hospitals, which have a contractual agreement relative to the acquisition of electric power, to use the same generating units for their normal electric power source, and an external utility service as the alternate power source?

*Answer:* Yes.

Note: Each hospital otherwise meets the requirements for an essential electrical system as outlined in Chapter 3 of NFPA 99.

*(continues)*

---

*Issue Edition:* 1984 of NFPA 99

*Reference:* 8-2.1.1.2, Exception 1

*Date:* March 1986

This Formal Interpretation was issued in 1986 and was concerned with the exception and how it related to a group of adjacent hospitals that had a contractual agreement relative to the acquisition of electric power. The exception states that an external utility service can be the alternate power source if the facility has a generator on-site. In this instance a limited group of adjacent facilities had developed their own electric delivery system in lieu of each facility having their own generator. Because of this restricted access, and because each hospital otherwise met the requirements for an essential electrical system, the former Subcommittee on Electrical Systems (now Committee on Electrical Systems) felt that this arrangement met the intent of the exception and that an external utility service could serve as the alternate power source in this specific situation.

There are no restrictions in NFPA 99 regarding where a generator set can be located on the premises. Location depends on the number of buildings involved, climatic conditions, the noise levels that can be tolerated, ease of maintenance, ease of accessibility under adverse conditions, safety from flooding and numerous other factors. In light of several recent fires in a large teaching hospital that disrupted emergency generators and emergency wiring, it is clear that the protection of generators, transfer switching, and the running of power lines in the vicinity of the generator need to be carefully studied. Reasonable scenarios, including smoky conditions, sabotage, and accidental or deliberate explosions (e.g., the World Trade Center incident in 1994) should be examined.

**3-4.1.1.4 General.** Generator sets installed as an alternate source of power for essential electrical systems shall be designed to meet the requirements of such service.

(a) Type I and Type II essential electrical system power sources shall be classified as Type 10, Class X, Level 1 generator sets per NFPA 110, *Standard for Emergency and Standby Power Systems*.

(b) Type III essential electrical system power sources shall be classified as Type 10, Class X, Level 2 generator sets per NFPA 110, *Standard for Emergency and Standby Power Systems*.

While many of the requirements for general-purpose generator sets are set forth in NFPA 110, *Standard for Emergency and Standby Power Systems* [2], utility or general-purpose generators are not acceptable in health care facilities if they do not also meet the requirements listed in this chapter. These criteria (in NFPA 99) were originally developed for the generator portion of the essential electrical system to ensure the generators are reliable enough for the special needs of health care facilities.

Type 1, Type 2, and Type 3 "essential electrical systems" are referenced for applicability in Chapters 12 through 17 (e.g., see 12-3.3.2, 13-3.3.2, etc.). Type 10, as well as Class X and Level 1, "generator sets" have meaning in NFPA 110. Note that the terms *type, class,* and *level* are designators only and do not have definitions.

### 3-4.1.1.5 Uses for Essential Electrical System.

(a) The generating equipment used shall be either reserved exclusively for such service or normally used for other purposes of (1) peak demand control, (2) internal voltage control, (3) load relief for the external utility, or (4) cogeneration. If normally used for other purposes listed above, two or more sets shall be installed, such that the maximum actual demand likely to be produced by the connected load of the emergency system as well as medical air compressors, medical-surgical vacuum pumps, electrically operated fire pumps, jockey pumps, fuel pumps, and generator accessories shall be met with the largest single generator set out-of-service. Load shed circuits, if provided, shall not shed the above equipment upon loss of the largest single generator set.

*Exception: A single generator set that operates the essential electrical system shall be permitted to be part of the system supplying the "other purposes" as listed above, provided any such use will not decrease the mean period between service overhauls to less than three years.*

(b) Any loads served by the generating equipment not permitted in 3-4.2 to be on the essential electrical system shall be served by their own transfer switch(es) such that these loads (1) shall not be transferred onto the generating equipment if the transfer will overload the generating equipment, and (2) shall be shed upon a generating equipment overload. It shall not constitute "other purposes" as described in 3-4.1.1.5(a).

The words "demand and all other performance requirements of the essential electrical system" in the 1993 edition were replaced in the 1996 edition with the words "demand likely to be produced by the connected load of the emergency system as well as medical air compressors, medical-surgical vacuum pumps, electrically operated fire pumps, jockey pumps, fuel pumps, and generator accessories." The new wording is less restrictive and permits the use of multiple generator systems without needlessly oversizing the generating equipment to provide the redundant capacity that would have been required for the entire "essential electrical system." The new wording also ensures that highly critical equipment (i.e., medical air compressors) will remain on-line with a single generator out of service.

Users should carefully consider the risks involved when using a single emergency generator for peak shaving, load control, cogeneration, or other uses not specifically related to providing standby power. Even though there may be three years between overhauls, facilities with only one emergency generator will require a temporary generator during the overhaul period.

For the 1999 edition of NFPA 99, the text was revised to eliminate confusion created (in the 1996 edition) by placing the reference to peak demand control, internal voltage control, load relief external utility, and cogeneration in an exception. The "other purposes" mentioned under 3-4.1.1.5(a) includes all of the applications formally listed in the exception, whether a single generator or multiple generator installation is used.

The words "not permitted in 3-4.2 to be on the essential electrical system" are intended to differentiate the "additional" and "selected" loads that are permitted to be connected to the critical branch and/or equipment system (for effective facility operation) from larger blocks of load that might be served by the generating equipment at the user's discretion. For example, 3-4.2 permits selected equipment intended for patient care or for effective operation of the facility to be served by the critical branch and/or the equipment system. Selected offices, conference rooms, or public areas might have lighting and receptacles connected to the critical branch or equipment system to assist in emergencies or simply to better operate the facility during emergencies (i.e., triage or command center during natural disasters). On the other hand, an entire nonessential wing, gymnasium, or day-care center would be required to be connected to the generating equipment using a separate "nonessential" transfer switch. While the 1996 wording still leaves the authority having jurisdiction some discretion, it should help clarify the difference between "additional and/or selective" uses described in 3-4.2 and discretionary uses involving entire wings or buildings.

This new allowance could aid in exercising generator sets. The load they add might be helpful in meeting the load criteria that are stated in NFPA 110 [2] and are required by reference in 3-4.4.1.1(b)1 in NFPA 99.

### 3-4.1.1.6† Work Space or Room.

The specific size of the space or room for the generator set has been deliberately left undefined because of differences at each facility. However, separation of service transformers from generator sets has been included in the interest of safety (i.e., an incident affecting the service transformer might also damage the generator set if it were in the same area).

(a) Energy converters shall be located in a separate service room dedicated to the generating equipment, separated from the remainder of the building by fire separations having a minimum 2-hour fire rating, or located in an adequate enclosure outside the building capable of preventing the entrance of snow or rain and resisting maximum wind velocity required by the local building code. Rooms for such equipment shall not be shared with other equipment or electrical service equipment that is not a part of the essential electrical system. [110:5-2.4]

(b) The generating equipment shall be installed in a location that will permit ready accessibility and adequate [minimum of 30 in. (76 cm)] working space around the unit for inspection, repair, maintenance, cleaning, or replacement. [110:5-2.4]

**3-4.1.1.7\* Capacity and Rating.** The generator set(s) shall have sufficient capacity and proper rating to meet the maximum actual demand likely to be produced by the connected load of the essential electrical system(s) at any one time.

This section was modified in 1996 to further emphasize the standard's intent that generators be sized for the actual demand rather than the connected load. If the design engineer does not have experience with health care facilities or access to health care facility load data, Section 517-30(d) of NFPA 70, *National Electrical Code* [3], permits sizing for connected load or by means of the calculations described in Article 220 of NFPA 70. It is important to point out that sizing generators for connected load (or using the Article 220 calculations) can result in grossly oversizing generators, in which case actual demands are so small that the generator cannot be exercised with sufficient building load to ensure reliable operation. (Refer to 6-4.2 of NFPA 110, *Standard for Emergency and Standby Power Systems* [2], for testing requirements for Level 1 generators.)

NFPA 110-1996 is consistent with Article 517 of NFPA 70 and with NFPA 99. It simply says, "The energy converters shall have sufficient capacity and response to pick up and carry the load and to stabilize frequency and voltage within the time specified in 2-3.1 after loss of normal power."

Wording in Section 700-5(a) of NFPA 70 has been interpreted to mean that the emergency system is to be sized for all connected, but noncoincident, loads. However, when this wording was originally adopted in NFPA 70-1984, the intent was to imply that both noncoincident loading and diversity of loading can be taken into consideration when sizing for emergency systems. This was intended to correlate with NFPA 70-1984 Article 517 language that stated, "The essential electrical system shall have adequate capacity to meet the demand for the operation of all functions and equipment to be served by each branch." The language in NFPA 110, NFPA 99, and NFPA 70, Article 517, should take precedence over NFPA 70, Article 700, because the former specifically address health care facilities. It should also be noted that standby generators in health care facilities serve both the equipment system and the emergency system and that the emergency system consists of the life safety branch and the critical branch. While the life safety branch is similar to the emergency system of a non-healthcare facility (consisting of egress lighting, exit lights, life safety circuits, etc.), the equipment system and the critical branch are quite different. A considerable amount of diversity can be exercised in sizing the generator for equipment system and the critical branch loads.

Paragraph 3-4.1.1.1(i) clearly permits load shed circuits for multiple generator systems. These circuits are permitted to shed loads as required upon loss of one or more generators to prevent "cascading" (the loss of additional generators as the result of overloading). With single and multiple generator installations, load shed circuits, lockout circuits, and non-coincident loads (i.e., summer/winter) can and should be considered when determining the maximum expected system demand.

**A-3-4.1.1.7** *Capacity and Rating.* It is the intent of this section to mandate generator sizing based upon actual demand likely to be produced by the connected load of the essential electrical system(s) at any one time. It is not the intent of this section that generator sizing be based upon connected load or feeder calculation procedures described in NFPA 70, *National Electrical Code*. Demand calculations should be based upon prudent demand factors and historical data.

**3-4.1.1.8†  Load Pickup.** The generator set(s) shall have sufficient capacity to pick up the load and meet the minimum frequency and voltage stability requirements of the emergency system within 10 seconds after loss of normal power. [110: 3-4.1]

> Voltage and frequency stability of the alternate power source is necessary before connection to the load (i.e., the wiring system) in order to prevent damage to such items as voltage-sensitive equipment and fluorescent lighting. The operation of transfer switches is usually delayed until the voltage and frequency from the generator system are within specified limits. While this standard calls for such stability in a maximum of 10 seconds from the time normal power is lost, transfer to an alternate power source can be accomplished whenever stability of the alternate power source is achieved (even if less than 10 seconds). Ten seconds can seem like an eternity in critical areas such as operating rooms. (See also commentary under 3-4.4.1.3.)

**3-4.1.1.9†  Maintenance of Temperature.** Provisions shall be made to maintain the generator room at not less than 50°F (10°C) or the engine water-jacket temperature at not less than 90°F (32°C). [110: 3-3.1, 5-7.6]

> Experience has shown that generators required for essential electrical systems may not start, pick up, or maintain their connected load unless the temperatures listed in 3-4.1.1.9 are maintained.
> The temperatures listed are in concert with those in NFPA 110 since this is extracted text from NFPA 110, *Standard for Emergency and Standby Power Systems* [2].

**3-4.1.1.10†  Ventilating Air.** Provision shall be made to provide adequate air for cooling and to replenish engine combustion air. [110: 5-7.2, 5-7.4]

> Recent incidents suggest that serious consideration should be given to protecting the air supply for the generator set from fire and smoke. Smoke entering the generator air intake has caused generators to shut down.

**3-4.1.1.11  Cranking Batteries.** Internal combustion engine cranking batteries shall meet the battery requirements of NFPA 110, *Standard for Emergency and Standby Power Systems*.

for 2 hours. However, the committee responsible for emergency power in NFPA 99 believes that health care facilities should be alerted when their on-site liquid fuel supply for the essential electrical system is down to a 3-hour operating supply. This is an instance when the specific is more stringent than the general.

**3-4.1.1.15†  Alarm Annunciator.** A remote annunciator, storage battery powered, shall be provided to operate outside of the generating room in a location readily observed by operating personnel at a regular work station *(see NFPA 70, National Electrical Code, Section 700-12)*.

The annunciator shall indicate alarm conditions of the emergency or auxiliary power source as follows:

(a)  Individual visual signals shall indicate the following:

1.  When the emergency or auxiliary power source is operating to supply power to load

2.  When the battery charger is malfunctioning

(b)  Individual visual signals plus a common audible signal to warn of an engine-generator alarm condition shall indicate the following:

1.  Low lubricating oil pressure

2.  Low water temperature (below those required in 3-4.1.1.9)

3.  Excessive water temperature

4.  Low fuel—when the main fuel storage tank contains less than a 3-hour operating supply

5.  Overcrank (failed to start)

6.  Overspeed

Where a regular work station will be unattended periodically, an audible and visual derangement signal, appropriately labeled, shall be established at a continuously monitored location. This derangement signal shall activate when any of the conditions in 3-4.1.1.15(a) and (b) occur, but need not display these conditions individually. [110: 3-5.5.2]

For requirement (a)1, the usual practice is to provide a visual signal indicating that the generator is producing voltage.

For requirements (b)1 and (b)3, the audible/visual signal is generally a pre-shutdown type, providing a warning before shutdown actually occurs. It is not intended that two lights be provided at the alarm annunciator, one for warning (pre-shutdown) and one at shutdown. An annunciator remote from the generating room is useful only if it indicates impending problems.

An annunciator is normally located in one location near the generator(s). A derangement signal, if necessary, is in another location where continuous monitoring (i.e., 24 hours a day) is possible.

**3-4.1.4 Battery.** Battery systems shall meet all requirements of Article 700 of NFPA 70, *National Electrical Code.*

**3-4.1.5 Separate Utility.** (Reserved)

## 3-4.2* Distribution (Type 1 EES).

The paragraph covers the type of essential electrical system that should be installed, taking into consideration the medical procedures that will be carried out in the facility.

It was not the intent of the committee that developed the requirements for essential electrical systems that the entire facility have power restored if normal power were lost. Only specific portions are to be connected to the essential electrical system.

**A-3-4.2** *Distribution (Type 1 EES).* It should be emphasized that the type of system selected and its area and type of coverage should be appropriate to the medical procedures being performed in the facility. For example, a battery-operated emergency light that switches "on" when normal power is interrupted and an alternate source of power for suction equipment, along with the immediate availability of some portable hand-held lighting, would be advisable where oral and maxillofacial surgery (e.g., extraction of impacted teeth) is performed. On the other hand, in dental offices where simple extraction, restorative, prosthetic, or hygienic procedures are performed, only remote corridor lighting for purposes of egress would be sufficient. Emergency power for equipment would not be necessary. As with oral surgery locations, a surgical clinic requiring use of life support or emergency devices such as suction machines, ventilators, cauterizers, or defibrillators would require both emergency light and power.

### 3-4.2.1 General.

**3-4.2.1.1†** Electrical characteristics of the transfer switches shall be suitable for the operation of all functions and equipment they are intended to supply. [110: 4-1.1]

**3-4.2.1.2† Switch Rating.** The rating of the transfer switches shall be adequate for switching all classes of loads to be served and for withstanding the effects of available fault currents without contact welding. [110: 4-2.1]

For requirements on the capacity of switches, refer to Article 517 of NFPA 70, *National Electrical Code* [3].

### 3-4.2.1.3 Automatic Transfer Switch Classification. Each automatic transfer switch shall be approved for emergency electrical service *(see NFPA 70, National Electrical Code, Section 700-3)* as a complete assembly.

**3-4.2.1.4† Automatic Transfer Switch Features.** [110: 4-2.4]

(a) *General.* Automatic transfer switches shall be electrically operated and mechanically held. The transfer switch shall transfer and retransfer the load automatically.

The term *momentary interruption* indicates the time taken for the transfer switch to move from alternate source contacts to normal source contacts.

Note that consideration has been made for the condition where normal power is available but the alternate source has failed.

The exception takes into consideration the bypassing of manual delays for situations other than a failure of the alternate source (e.g., large motor loads). See Exhibit 3.6.

**Exhibit 3.6** *Detail of transfer switch cabinet for the life safety and critical branches of the essential electrical system.*

*Exception: It shall be permitted to program the transfer switch (1) for a manually initiated retransfer to the normal source, or (2) for an automatic intentional "off" delay, or (3) for an in-phase monitor relay or similar automatic delay method, so as to provide for a planned momentary interruption of the load. If used, this arrangement shall be provided with a bypass feature to permit automatic retransfer in the event that the alternate source fails and the normal source is available.*

(b) *Interlocking.* Reliable mechanical interlocking, or an approved alternate method, shall be inherent in the design of transfer switches to prevent the unintended interconnection of the normal and alternate sources of power, or any two separate sources of power.

This paragraph makes it clear that cogeneration of electrical power is not prohibited. (In this context, cogeneration is the concurrent production of electricity, by a generator source on the health care facility's premises, that will be used to augment electricity supplied by the utility company.) Such an operation must be accomplished very deliberately and in coordination with the local utility company.

The inadvertent interconnection of the normal and alternate sources of power, or of any two separate sources of power, is likely to cause major damage to an electrical system, as well as place personnel in danger. Components will probably be destroyed and require replacement or major repair, resulting in great expense and disruption to the facility.

The interlocking feature of the transfer switch must be reliable and fail-safe.

Available interlocking schemes vary from simple mechanical means to complex combinations of mechanical, electrical, and electronic means. It is recommended that all interlocking include a reliable stand-alone mechanical means that is completely independent of all electrical and electronic means. Those considering alternate methods are advised to give due recognition to the NFPA definition of *approved.* It should also be noted that 3-4.2.1.4(a) requires automatic transfer switches to be electrically operated and mechanically held.

Paralleling of generators is also not prohibited, provided proper safeguards such as automatic load shedding and wiring so arranged as to prevent backfeedings are used. Closed transition transfer is not prohibited, as well. However, the requirements for reliable interlocking included in this paragraph have to be met.

(c)* *Voltage Sensing.* Voltage sensing devices shall be provided to monitor all ungrounded lines of the normal source of power.

**A-3-4.2.1.4(c)** *Voltage Sensing.* Consideration should be given to monitoring all ungrounded lines of the alternate source of power when conditions warrant.

Monitoring only the ungrounded lines is considered satisfactory for essential electrical system purposes.

(d) *Time Delay on Starting of Alternate Power Source.* A time delay device shall be provided to delay starting of the alternate source generator. The timer is intended to prevent nuisance starting of the alternate source generator with subsequent load transfer in the event of harmless momentary power dips and interruptions of the normal source. The time range shall be short enough so that the generator can start and be on the line within 10 seconds of the onset of failure.

It is the intent of this chapter that essential electrical systems be powered by the alternate source within 10 seconds of failure of the normal source. ("Failure" can be thought of as a drop in voltage below a pre-established minimum for a specified length of time.) The 10-second value was set by the committee as the shortest practical time that could be accomplished and accepted while also considering technical and economic realities.

The 10-second value takes into consideration the following intervals: (1) a time delay on commanding the starting of the alternate power source, considered to be an on-site generator set; plus (2) the time for the generator set to start, attain operating voltage and frequency, and be capable of generating the required power; plus (3) time for operation of the transfer switches; plus (4) a design-safety interval factor.

Interval (1) is considered to be about 2 seconds, with a range from about 1 second to 3 seconds. The actual time is the result of setting of a field-adjustable timer to meet local needs. The timer starts when normal supply voltage is sensed to have dropped to less than the predetermined value, which is also selected to meet local needs.

Interval (2) is considered to be about 5 seconds, with a range from about 3 seconds to 6 seconds. It is a function of the generator set, its controls, and its loading. The interval is actually 0 second when the alternate source is an external utility service. (See 3-4.1.1.3 for instances in which an external utility may be an approved alternate source.)

Interval (3) is considered to be a fraction of a second. It is a function of the characteristics of the transfer switches. Time delays may be imposed upon interval (3) as part of an individual design to prevent loading the generator too rapidly.

Interval (4), used in establishing the 10-second value of the chapter, is about 3 seconds.

The committee considers the 10-second value to be reasonably attainable on a national and facilitywide basis. It is not based on the established needs of any fire protection, life safety, or medical function.

For equipment that cannot tolerate a loss of even a cycle of power (e.g., computer-driven equipment) or for procedures where a 10-second power outage cannot be tolerated, the use of uninterrupted power supplies (UPS) have to be considered. (For further discussion on this issue, see commentary under 3-2.4.2.)

(e) *Time Delay on Transfer to Alternate Power.* An adjustable time delay device shall be provided for those transfer switches requiring "delayed-automatic" operation. The time delay shall commence when proper alternate source voltage and frequency are achieved. The delay device shall prevent transfer to the alternate power source until after expiration of the preset delay.

(f)* *Time Delay on Retransfer to Normal Power.* An adjustable timer with a bypass shall be provided to delay retransfer from the alternate source of power to the normal. This timer will permit the normal source to stabilize before retransfer to the load and help to avoid unnecessary power interruptions. The bypass shall operate similarly to the bypass in 3-4.2.1.4(a).

**A-3-4.2.1.4(f)** *Time Delay on Retransfer to Normal Power.* It is recommended that the timer be set for 30 minutes *[see A-3-4.4.1.1(b)1]*. Consideration should also be given to an unloaded engine running time after retransfer to permit the engine to cool down before shutdown.

The 30-minute setting for the running of the generator is recommended, even if normal power is restored within 30 minutes and transfer switches return to their normal settings. This setting is recommended so the generator set will be lubricated adequately and acids and carbons burned out. The 30 minutes, if for a real run, could also be an acceptable substitute for one of the tests described in 3-4.4.1.1.

It should also be noted that an unloaded engine-running timer is recommended. Owners should consult manufacturers' recommendations for optimum run times, cooldown periods, and so forth.

(g)* *Test Switch.* A test switch shall be provided on each automatic transfer switch that will simulate a normal power source failure to the switch.

**A-3-4.2.1.4(g)** *Test Switch.* To maximize system reliability, it is good engineering practice to locate transfer switches as close as possible to the load that they serve. When transfer switches are installed in remote, infrequently accessed locations, it could be desirable to provide an annunciator at the operating engineer's facility to permit monitoring by a local control station.

Test switches permit appropriate testing of individual components and the entire essential electrical system without requiring interruption of the normal source.

The appendix recommendation can be considered a more efficient and cost-saving method for testing components.

(h)* *Indication of Switch Position.* Two pilot lights, properly identified, shall be provided to indicate the transfer switch position.

**A-3-4.2.1.4(h)** *Indication of Switch Position.* To maximize system reliability, it is good engineering practice to locate transfer switches as close as possible to the load that they serve. Where transfer switches are installed in remote, infrequently accessed locations, it might be desirable to provide an annunciator at the operating engineer's facility to permit visual indication of transfer switch positions by local indication.

One pilot light indicates that the switch is in the normal power position, and the other pilot light indicates that the switch is in the alternate power position. They not only indicate the transfer switch position to the system operator, but they can be useful in troubleshooting operational problems.

The commentary under A-3-4.2.1.4(g) is appropriate here as well.

(i) *Manual Control of Switch.* A means for the safe manual operation of the automatic transfer switch shall be provided.

**Formal Interpretation 77-1**

Reference: 3-4.2.1.4(i) of NFPA 99-1996

*Question:* Is it the intent of 3-4.2.1.4(i) to recommend (i.e., not make mandatory) that the manual operation of an automatic transfer switch be effected externally (i.e., without opening the switch's enclosure) as is recommended for the manual operation of nonautomatic switches [see 3-4.2.1.6(a)]?

*Answer:* Yes.

*Issue Edition:* 1977 of NFPA 76A

*Reference:* 8-2.2.4.9

*Date:* September 1978

Manual control is required so that operational problems of automatic transfer switches can be resolved or corrected. Manual control can be accomplished by direct manual means, electrical remote manual means, or both. Many operating personnel prefer the positive advantages of direct manual means.

This requirement has been included to safeguard those operating personnel who might place themselves at risk or injury or worse in attempting to troubleshoot malfunctions that have left patients in a facility without electrical power.

No guidelines have been included with respect to how switching might be accomplished. The committee concluded that no guidelines could be suggested without impinging on the design of some manufacturer's products. An appendix item to 3-4.2.1.6(a) was also deleted because the term *external operation* could not be satisfactorily defined.

(j) *Time Delay on Engine Shutdown.* A time delay of 5 minutes minimum to allow engine cooldown shall be provided for unloaded running of the alternate power source generator set prior to shutdown.

*Exception: Time delay need not be provided on small (15 kW or less) aircooled prime movers or if included with the engine control panel. [110: 4-2.4.8]*

(k)* *Motor Load Transfer.* Provisions shall be included to reduce excessive currents resulting from motor load transfer if such currents can damage essential electrical system equipment or cause nuisance tripping of essential electrical system overcurrent protective devices. [110: 4-2.4.12]

**A-3-4.2.1.4(k)**† Automatic transfer switches can be provided with accessory controls that provide a signal to operate remote motor controls that disconnect motors prior to transfer, and to reconnect them after transfer when the residual voltage has been substantially reduced. Another method is to provide in-phase monitors within the automatic transfer switch to prevent retransfer to the normal source until both sources are nearly synchronized. A third method is to use a programmed neutral position transfer switch. [110: A-4-2.4.12]

(l) *Isolation of Neutral Conductors.* Provisions shall be included for ensuring proper continuity, transfer, and isolation of the normal and the alternate power source neutral conductors whenever they are separately grounded, if needed, to achieve proper ground-fault sensing. *[See NFPA 70, National Electrical Code, Section 230-95(b).]* [110: 4-2.4.13]

**3-4.2.1.5 Nonautomatic Transfer Device Classification.** Nonautomatic transfer devices shall be approved for emergency electrical service *(see NFPA 70, National Electrical Code, Section 700-3).*

**3-4.2.1.6† Nonautomatic Transfer Device Features.** [110: 4-2.5]

(a) *General.* Switching devices shall be mechanically held. Operation shall be by direct manual or electrical remote manual control. Electrically operated switches shall derive their control power from the source to which the load is being transferred. A means for safe manual operation shall be provided.

(b) *Interlocking.* Reliable mechanical interlocking, or an approved alternate method, shall be inherent in the design in order to prevent the unintended interconnection of the normal and alternate sources of power, or of any two separate sources of power.

As in 3-4.2.1.4(b), this paragraph was changed to make it clear that cogeneration of electrical power is not prohibited. [See commentary under 3-4.2.1.4(b) on the subject of cogeneration.]

(c) *Indication of Switch Position.* Pilot lights, properly identified, shall be provided to indicate the switch position.

**3-4.2.1.7† Bypass-Isolation Switches.** [110: 4-4.1] Bypass-isolation switches shall be permitted for bypassing and isolating the transfer switch. If installed, they shall be in accordance with the following:

(a) *Bypass-Isolation Switch Rating.* The bypass-isolation switch shall have a continuous current rating and withstand current rating compatible with that of the associated transfer switch.

(b) *Bypass-Isolation Switch Classification.* Each bypass-isolation switch shall be listed for emergency electrical service as a completely factory-assembled and tested apparatus. *(See NFPA 70, National Electrical Code, Section 700-3.)*

(c)* *Operation.* With the transfer switch isolated or disconnected or both, means shall be provided so the bypass-isolation switch can function as an independent nonautomatic transfer switch and allow the load to be connected to either power source. Reconnection of the transfer switch shall be possible with a load interruption no greater than the maximum time in seconds by the type of essential electrical system.

Note that bypass-isolation switching is not mandated.
Bypass-isolation switches do eliminate system downtime when normal transfer

switches need maintenance, as well as provide an alternate method of transfer in the event normal transfer switches are damaged.

**A-3-4.2.1.7(c)†** Consideration should be given to the effect that load interruption could have on the load during maintenance and service of the transfer switch. [110: A-4-4.4]

## 3-4.2.2 Specific Requirements.

The use of the term *Type 1* is simply for identification purposes. In Chapters 12 through 17, the type of essential electrical system (1, 2, or 3) for a particular health care facility (hospital, nursing home, etc.) is stipulated. See Chapter 1, text and commentary, for a complete explanation of how NFPA 99 is structured and how it is to be used.

**3-4.2.2.1\* General.** Type I essential electrical systems are comprised of two separate systems capable of supplying a limited amount of lighting and power service, which is considered essential for life safety and effective facility operation during the time the normal electrical service is interrupted for any reason. These two systems are the emergency system and the equipment system.

The emergency system shall be limited to circuits essential to life safety and critical patient care. These are designated the life safety branch and the critical branch.

The equipment system shall supply major electrical equipment necessary for patient care and basic Type I operation.

Both systems shall be arranged for connection, within time limits specified in this chapter, to an alternate source of power following a loss of the normal source.

The number of transfer switches to be used shall be based upon reliability, design, and load considerations. Each branch of the emergency system and each equipment system shall have one or more transfer switches. One transfer switch shall be permitted to serve one or more branches or systems in a facility with a maximum demand on the essential electrical system of 150 kVA (120 kW).

This 1999 edition was amended to clarify the committee's long established intent that a typical type 2 system will have a minimum of two automatic transfer switches (emergency system and critical system) unless the maximum demand is determined to be less than 150 kVA (120 kW).

**A-3-4.2.2.1** *Separation of Wiring on Emergency System in Type 1 Systems.* In new construction, careful consideration should be given to the benefits of multiple transfer switches. However, selection of the number and configuration of transfer switches and associated switchgear is to be made with consideration given to the tradeoffs among reliability, transfer switch and generator load characteristics, maintainability, and cost.

In principle, Chapter 3 is designed to seek security of electrical function by protection against both internal disruption and the loss of primary power sources. In keeping therewith, Chapter 3 aims to limit the security deterioration that could occur when poorly maintained and heavy-current-consuming items are connected to the same feeders that supply critical patient care functions.

For greater protection, such segregation of suspect and critical connections is best carried out throughout the length of a feeder system, preferably including the transfer device. This practice gives rise to the phrase protected feeder.

While Chapter 3 must leave details of wiring and overcurrent protection to engineering judgment, in view of wide variations of conditions, the Committee on Electrical Systems' consensus is that feeders serving anesthetizing locations, special nursing care units, and special treatment areas, where continuity of care is vital to life, should be given security through the segregation of protected feeders and that, to the greatest extent practical, feeders should connect to the alternate source of power by means of separate transfer devices.

As a further protection against internal disruption, it is also recommended that, when practical, critical areas served by the essential electrical system have some portion of lighting and receptacles connected to feeders supplied by the general system.

The concept of separate systems, and thus separate transfer switches, dates back to the late 1960s. The intent of separate systems is to have a limited number of areas and functions on the essential electrical system and, with various systems having their own transfer switches, to provide the maximum protection for each.

After much discussion and various proposals, two major systems evolved: the emergency system and the equipment system.

The emergency system was, in turn, subdivided into the following two branches:

(a) The *life safety branch,* to which only exit lights, corridor lights, and alarm and activating devices are connected. These are related to life safety and are primarily intended to announce emergencies and to provide sufficient lighting and directions for exiting. There are very few receptacles on this branch, thus reducing the chances of the branch's being electrically violated and not operating in an emergency.

(b) The *critical branch,* to which single-phase loads (e.g., receptacles, task illumination) are connected to maintain essential medical care in patient care areas.

The *equipment system* is intended to maintain essential support services such as fans, pumps, and elevators.

Restoration of power to loads on the *emergency system* is to be automatic and should occur *within 10 seconds*. Restoration of power to loads on the *equipment system* does *not* have to be automatic, nor must it occur within 10 seconds; it can be time-delayed or manually operated. (See 3-4.2.2.3.)

The committee responsible for this chapter has reaffirmed its position that in new facilities the wiring for the emergency system and the equipment system be kept separate from each other and from the remainder of electrical circuits supplying normal electric power to the various parts of a facility. The major reason given for this separation was concern for reliability. It is, therefore, not acceptable to have panel boards with both normal and essential circuits on them (see NFPA 70, *National Electrical Code,* Article 517).

A Formal Interpretation was issued in July 1979 concerning an inquiry about whether a single overcurrent protective device (OPD) on the generator to the distribution board was permissible or whether a minimum of two OPDs was necessary: one for the emergency system and one for the equipment system. The Interpretation Committee believed that one feeder (and, thus, one OPD at the generator) was permitted to serve a distribution board, which in turn distributed power via transfer switches, and so on. It was noted that a single feeder is often used when the generator is remote from the distribution board. A parallel set of feeders was considered unnecessary and costly. No significant differences in safety or reliability were noted in using just one feeder.

---

**Formal Interpretation 77-2**

Reference: 3-4.2.2.1 of NFPA 99-1996

*Question:* Is it the intent of the Committee that 3-4.2.2.1 permit one feeder, protected by an overcurrent device at the generator, to serve a distribution board where the power is distributed through the necessary transfer switch or switches and branches or systems?

*Answer:* Yes.

*Issue Edition:* 1977 of NFPA 76A

*Reference:* 4-1

*Date:* July 1979

---

### 3-4.2.2.2 Emergency System.

The division of the emergency system (for Type 1 essential electrical systems) into two branches is for identification purposes. The life safety branch [see 3-4.2.2.2(b)] provides power only to those functions or warning systems, such as alarm systems, exit signs, lighting of means of egress, and communication systems, necessary for safely leaving any building in an emergency. The critical branch [see 3-4.2.2.2(c)] includes those functions that maintain essential patient services, because health care facility fire response is designed around a defend-in-place concept. Evacuation of the building occurs only when absolutely necessary. Paragraph 3-4.2.2.3 includes those functions that do not have to be restored within 10 seconds, because their rapid restoration is not critical. In addition, they might overload the alternate power source if they were to come on-line within the 10 seconds specified for the emergency system.

Of recent concern is whether a smoke-control or stair-pressurization system should be connected to the emergency system or to the equipment system. The Committee on Electrical Systems has not stated specifically whether such systems belong on any branch of the emergency system (e.g., is it necessary to restore power to these systems in 10 seconds?). Because of the increased use of such systems, it is expected that they will be addressed in a future edition of NFPA 99.

Task illumination does not necessarily mean that all lighting in a location need be connected to the essential electrical system. The lights that are connected will depend on the activities in the particular area.

(a) *General.* Those functions of patient care depending on lighting or appliances that are permitted to be connected to the emergency system are divided into two mandatory branches, described in 3-4.2.2.2(b) and (c).

Previously, NFPA 99 was unclear as to the method for serving generator accessories. The location of the new text makes it clear that if these items are served by a transfer switch, they are to be connected to an emergency system transfer switch that restores power in 10 seconds. This text gives the hospital design engineer some latitude in making this connection. Accessories can be supplied from a life safety branch transfer switch, a critical branch transfer switch, or, in some cases, directly off the standby generator. For example, a remote radiator may be fed directly from the standby generator by means of a relay that "picks up" when the generator output reaches nominal voltage.

†All ac-powered support and accessory equipment necessary to the operation of the EPS shall be supplied from the load side of the automatic transfer switch(es), or the output terminals of the EPS, ahead of the main EPS overcurrent protection, as necessary, to ensure continuity of the EPSS operation and performance. (NFPA 110: 5-12.5)

(b) *Life Safety Branch.* The life safety branch of the emergency system shall supply power for the following lighting, receptacles, and equipment:

1. Illumination of means of egress as required in NFPA *101,® Life Safety Code®*

Chapter 5 of NFPA *101, Life Safety Code* [1], lists where and how much illumination is required for means of egress.

Given the critical and urgent need for electricity in a fire emergency—for example, lighting when exiting and emergency instructions—the issue of whether there should be a backup to the backup is now debated. Is emergency power from a generator enough of a guarantee that lighting and power to other critical items will be restored, or should there be redundancy, such as automatic battery-charged lighting, in addition to a power generator? (The bombing of the World Trade Center in New York City, where stairwells went dark when the emergency generators shutdown from lack of cooling water, unfortunately brought this point to the forefront.) Given the maintenance associated with individual battery units, plus the number that would be required for some buildings (such as a 15-story hospital complex), there are just two situations involving lighting in NFPA 99 where a "backup to the backup" is required [see 3-4.2.2.2(b)5 and 3-3.2.1.2(a)5e], but there are no prohibitions against doing it either. When NFPA 76 was being developed, this issue was extensively debated. There has been no recent argument presented that has changed the committee's position on the subject. The committee will, of course, continue to review and study proposals addressing the subject.

2. Exit signs and exit direction signs required in NFPA *101, Life Safety Code*

3. Alarm and alerting systems including the following:

   a. Fire alarms

   This includes any type of fire alarm, whether for one area, one function, or the entire facility. These alarm and alerting systems may, under certain conditions, include interfaces with an engineered smoke-control system.

   b. Alarms required for systems used for the piping of nonflammable medical gases as specified in Chapter 4, "Gas and Vacuum Systems"

4.* Hospital communication systems, where used for issuing instruction during emergency conditions

**A-3-4.2.2.2(b)(4)** Departmental installations such as digital dialing systems used for intradepartmental communications could have impaired use during a failure of electrical service to the area. In the event of such failure, those systems that have lighted selector buttons in the base of the telephone instrument or in the desk units known as "director sets" will be out of service to the extent that the lights will not function and that the buzzer used to indicate incoming calls will be silenced. The lack of electrical energy will not prevent the use of telephones for outgoing calls, but incoming calls will not be signaled, nor will intercommunicating calls be signaled. This communication failure should be taken into consideration in planning essential electrical systems.

5. Task illumination, battery charger for emergency battery-powered lighting unit(s), and selected receptacles at the generator set location

   This recommendation ensures that there will always be lighting in the generator set area when normal power is interrupted or when emergency power fails. This system will be very important when trying to determine the cause of a generator set's not starting in a *real* emergency and is an example of the necessity of a "backup to the backup" because of the critical need for lighting.

6. Elevator cab lighting, control, communication, and signal systems

   Item 6 was added to the life safety branch in 1984 because of concern for persons who might be in elevators when normal power was interrupted and because these functions, in a real sense, provide a means of egress for these persons. Although power for elevator movement might be restored on a delayed or manual basis, it could be a very stressful wait for those in the elevators. The committee felt that restoring lights and communication within 10 seconds would reduce the possibility of panic.

7. Automatically operated doors used for building egress.

No function other than those listed above in items 1 through 7 shall be connected to the life safety branch.

This text, concerning automatically operated doors, was removed from 3-4.2.2.3 and added to 3-4.2.2.2 in 1999 because the committee believes that this requirement is related to life safety and that service needs to be restored in 10 seconds. The general public is not generally familiar with the manual operation of automatic doors under emergency conditions.

*Exception: The auxiliary functions of fire alarm combination systems complying with NFPA 72, National Fire Alarm Code, shall be permitted to be connected to the life safety branch.*

In a fire or other emergency, electricity is automatically interrupted to any hold-open devices (generally via any fire alarm signal) so that smoke and fire doors that are being held open will close and stay closed until manually reset. However, if a smoke or fire door requires an electrical motor in order to close, then that motor needs to be connected to the most reliable branch of the essential electrical system, that is, to the life safety branch. In this way, the door will close should normal power be lost and a fire alarm signal indicate an emergency (e.g., a smoke detector activates). (See Exhibit 3.7.)

If electromechanical locks for security (egress) doors of psychiatric wards unlock on loss of power, then the 120 V to the locks can be placed on the critical branch. However, if such doors require power to unlock and the locks are not connected to a battery system, then the 120 V to the locks would have to be placed on the life safety branch.

The exception was added in 1990 to account for new fire alarm systems that are integrated with voice paging, door unlocking, door release, and so on. The exception allows one system to be installed rather than two separate systems.

(c)* *Critical Branch.* The critical branch of the emergency system shall supply power for task illumination, fixed equipment, selected receptacles, and selected power circuits serving the following areas and functions related to patient care. It shall be permitted to subdivide the critical branch into two or more branches.

*Task illumination* will vary depending on the activity in a given area in an operating room. Sufficient lighting to maintain patient care would mean that all surgical lights are to be connected to the essential electrical system. In a general ward, it might be sufficient to connect just one overhead light in the room to the essential electrical system. A pediatric ward would require lighting to be restored everywhere youngsters

**Exhibit 3.7**  *A corridor door being held open by electric magnets. Magnets will deenergize upon interruption of electricity (e.g., from fire alarm activation, from loss of normal electric power), and doors will close. Doors have to be manually reset open when fire alarm is reset or power is restored.*

are allowed to go. Task illumination does not mean restoring power to lighting used for nonessential purposes or for activities that can be temporarily postponed.

**A-3-4.2.2.2(c)**  *Critical Branch.*  It is recommended that facility authorities give consideration to providing and properly maintaining automatic battery-powered lighting units or systems to provide minimal task illumination in operating rooms, delivery rooms, and certain special-procedure radiology rooms where the loss of lighting due to failure of the essential electrical system could cause severe and immediate danger to a patient undergoing surgery or an invasive radiographic procedure.

Because it is possible for both the normal and essential electrical power to be interrupted (e.g., an explosion, a fire involving transfer switches), the committee responsible for Chapter 3 added a requirement for the 1996 edition of NFPA 99 that anesthetizing locations have battery-powered emergency lighting units. [See 3-3.2.1.2(a)5e.] That requirement is not in Section 3-4 because it is not part of the essential electrical system.

1. Critical care areas that utilize anesthetizing gases, task illumination, selected receptacles, and fixed equipment

   These requirements were altered in 1984 to reflect changes in the requirements for isolated power systems (IPSs) in anesthetizing locations. The committee wanted to ensure that receptacles, task illumination, and fixed equipment in anesthetizing locations were on the essential electrical system whether IPSs were present or not.

   Debate has been considerable on whether *all* circuits in anesthetizing locations should be on the critical branch or whether, like other patient care areas, only *selected* or *special* circuits should be on the critical branch of the essential electrical system, with the rest connected to the normal electrical distribution system. Proponents of having both normal and essential circuits in an operating room argue that this requirement will increase reliability and that having all circuits on the essential electrical system subjects anesthetizing locations to a 100 percent loss of power if a transfer switch fails.

   In 1993 discussion expanded to consider the issue of the administration of anesthetizing gases (since MRI and CAT scan equipment includes the ability to administer such gases). After much debate, this section was revised to address "critical care areas" (which include anesthetizing locations) and requires that only "selected receptacles" need to be on the critical branch of the emergency system. The latter change is related to a change made in 3-3.2.1.2(a)1 regarding where circuits feeding a room or area can originate. The change from "all receptacles" to "selected receptacles" in 3-4.2.2.2(c)1 was made to permit the installation of a minimum of one normal circuit [and receptacle(s)] as required by 3-3.2.1.2(a)1. Remember that the definition of *patient bed location* includes procedure tables in critical care areas.

   Because this change allows selected receptacles in operating rooms to be on normal circuits (like other patient care areas), it is important that emergency-powered receptacles in operating rooms be clearly marked and/or readily distinguishable (e.g., color-coded) from those on the normal system. In the event of a failure of one of these systems (normal or emergency), personnel may have to quickly switch equipment to different receptacles.

2. The isolated power systems in special environments

   This reference to isolated power systems is not to be interpreted as meaning that this chapter requires the provision of such systems. Rather, it is the intent of the Committee on Electrical Systems that the electrical receptacles on isolated power systems in special environments be served from the critical branch, enabling power to be restored in 10 seconds to all receptacles on the isolated power system.

   Special environments are those areas, determined by the facility, where restoration of electricity (via the facility's essential electrical system) is critical for quality patient care.

3.  Patient care areas—task illumination and selected receptacles in the following:

    a.  Infant nurseries
    b.  Medication preparation areas
    c.  Pharmacy dispensing areas
    d.  Selected acute nursing areas
    e.  Psychiatric bed areas (omit receptacles)
    f.  Ward treatment rooms
    g.  Nurses' stations (unless adequately lighted by corridor luminaires)

4.  Additional specialized patient care task illumination and receptacles, where needed
5.  Nurse call systems
6.  Blood, bone, and tissue banks

    See Exhibit 3.8

**Exhibit 3.8** *Blood bank refrigerators, which have alarms that sound if the temperature inside any refrigerator changes more than 4°F (−15.5°C) (whether from power loss or equipment failure or door being left ajar). [See 3-4.2.2.2(c)6.]*

7.* Telephone equipment rooms and closets

**A-3-4.2.2.2(c)(7)** Departmental installations such as digital dialing systems used for intradepartmental communications could have impaired use during a failure of electrical service to the area. In the event of such failure, those systems that have lighted selector buttons in the base of the telephone instrument or in the desk units known as "director sets" will be out of service to the extent that the lights will not function and that the buzzer used to indicate incoming calls will be silenced. The lack of electrical energy will not prevent the use of telephones for outgoing calls, but incoming calls will not be signaled, nor will intercommunicating calls be signaled. This communication failure should be taken into consideration in planning essential electrical systems.

8. Task illumination, selected receptacles, and selected power circuits for the following:

   a. General care beds (at least one duplex receptacle per patient bedroom)
   b. Angiographic labs
   c. Cardiac catheterization labs

*See commentary after 3-4.2.2.2(c)9 on "mobile" cardiac catheterization labs.*

   d. Coronary care units
   e. Hemodialysis rooms or areas

*Hemodialysis areas are included on the emergency system of Type 1 essential electrical systems because of the condition of patients generally seen in the facilities that require Type 1 systems. In freestanding clinics, patients are usually not in immediate danger and can be handcranked off this device without ac power.*

   f. Emergency room treatment areas (selected)
   g. Human physiology labs
   h. Intensive care units
   i. Postoperative recovery rooms (selected)

9. Additional task illumination, receptacles, and selected power circuits needed for effective facility operation. Single-phase fractional horsepower motors shall be permitted to be connected to the critical branch.

*Item 9 should not be construed as an open-ended option to include anything on the critical branch. Only essential items should be included. However, whatever is determined to be "needed for effective facility operation" has to be known and included during the design of the essential electrical system so the generator is not overloaded. [See 3-4.4.1.1(b).] In addition to lighting, receptacles, and certain pieces of equipment needed for effective hospital operation, selected areas, such as administrative offices, conference rooms, waiting rooms, and public areas, are permitted to be connected to the critical branch to ensure effective hospital operation and to provide for patient care (i.e., triage) during emergencies and natural disasters. It is not the intent of the standard that large administrative suites, gymnasiums, day-care centers, and the like be permitted to be connected to the critical branch under this section. For large nonessential areas, see 3-4.1.1.5.*

   *For a discussion of task illumination, see commentary under 3-4.2.2.2.*

   *Exhaust fan motors were added to the critical branch for practicality. These motors are sometimes located at the end of a wing, making it costly to link up with* three-phase motors of the equipment system, which could be on the roof. The committee responsible for emergency power requirements did not feel that these small exhaust motors added significantly to the critical branch load. The 1996 edition permits other single-phase motors to be connected to the critical system if they are required for effective facility operation.

NFPA 99 does not currently address "mobile" patient labs such as mobile cardiac catheterization labs, mobile MRI units, and mobile CAT scanners. These labs are "housed" in tractor trailers and "connected" to a facility's utility supply (electricity, water, medical gases, etc.) by an umbilical cord. In light of no explicit requirements concerning mobile patient labs, one should assume for NFPA 99 purposes that when these mobile labs are connected to a facility via the utility umbilical cord, they should be treated like any other patient care area within the confines of the facility. For example, the electric power for task illumination and selected power circuits of mobile cardiac catheterization labs connected to the facility are to be connected to the essential electrical system in accordance with 3-4.2.2.2(c)8c.

### 3-4.2.2.3 Equipment System.

Some of the equipment in this section can initially draw heavy currents or be a large electrical load for the generator set (e.g., chillers, air-conditioner systems). This does not mean that a second generator set is required. It does mean that the timing of restoring power to such loads needs to be considered when the essential electrical system is being designed.

(a) *General.* The equipment system shall be connected to equipment described in 3-4.2.2.3(c)through (e).

(b) *Connection to Alternate Power Source.* The equipment system shall be installed and connected to the alternate power source, such that equipment described in 3-4.2.2.3(d) is automatically restored to operation at appropriate time lag intervals following the energizing of the emergency system. Its arrangement shall also provide for the subsequent connection of equipment described in 3-4.2.2.3(e) by either delayed-automatic or manual operation.

The absence of specific time lag intervals is deliberate. These intervals are dependent on the facility and its activities and on the technical judgment of those designing the essential electrical system.

(c) *AC Equipment for Nondelayed Automatic Connection.* Generator accessories, including but not limited to, the transfer fuel pump, electrically operated louvers, and other generator accessories essential for generator operation, shall be arranged for automatic connection to the alternate power source.

If everything on the essential electrical system were restored at the same time, the generator could be overloaded, even though it might be capable of carrying the total load if it were restored over a period of time.

(d)* *Equipment for Delayed-Automatic Connection.* The following equipment shall be arranged for delayed-automatic connection to the alternate power source:

**A-3-4.2.2.3(d)** The equipment in 3-4.2.2.3(d)1 through 3 can be arranged for sequential delayed-automatic connection to the alternate power source to prevent overloading the generator where engineering studies indicates that it is necessary.

1. Central suction systems serving medical and surgical functions, including controls. It shall be permitted to place such suction systems on the critical branch.

   Central suction systems are permitted to be connected to the critical branch for two reasons. First, power may be required to be restored within 10 seconds depending on the medical/ surgery application, the load on the compressor, the storage capability of the compressor's receiver, and other considerations. Second, standby systems utilizing multiple generators often have load shed circuits, and the equipment system is often shed upon loss of one or more generators. Because of the highly critical nature of some central suction systems, the facility designer may prefer to place these systems on the critical branch or to provide a separate equipment branch transfer switch that is not affected by the load shed circuit.

2. Sump pumps and other equipment required to operate for the safety of major apparatus, including associated control systems and alarms
3. Compressed air systems serving medical and surgical functions, including controls. It shall be permitted to place such air systems on the critical branch.

   This section was changed in 1996 to permit medical and surgical compressed air systems to be served by the critical branch instead of the equipment system. The reasons for this allowance are the same as those listed under the commentary for 3-4.2.2.3(c)1 for central suction (vacuum) systems serving medical and surgical functions.

4. Smoke control and stair pressurization systems
5. Kitchen hood supply and/or exhaust systems, if required to operate during a fire in or under the hood

   Subparagraphs 4 and 5 were added in 1993 as a result of a public proposal where it was argued that fans are generally shut down in an emergency to prevent the spread of smoke. These particular fans can be used in providing smoke control.

(e) *Equipment for Delayed-Automatic or Manual Connection.* The following equipment shall be arranged for either delayed-automatic or manual connection to the alternate power source *[also see A-3-4.2.2.3(d)]:*

1. Heating equipment to provide heating for operating, delivery, labor, recovery, intensive care, coronary care, nurseries, infection/isolation rooms, emergency treatment spaces, and general patient rooms, and pressure maintenance (jockey or make-up) pump(s) for water-based fire protection systems

   This exception dates from the early 1960s during the development of an emergency power standard. It was added strictly for economic reasons—to save costs on the system. In the early 1970s it became, by coincidence, an energy conservation measure. It is also an aid to facilities that use electric heat throughout because, in an emergency, only selected rooms would have to be heated if the facility met this exception.

*Exception:\* Heating of general patient rooms during disruption of the normal source shall not be required under any of the following conditions:*

   *a. The outside design temperature is higher than +20°F (−6.7°C), or*

   *b. The outside design temperature is lower than +20°F (−6.7°C) and a selected room(s) is provided for the needs of all confined patients [then only such room(s) need be heated], or*

   *c. The facility is served by a dual source of normal power as described in 3-3.2.1.1.*

**A-3-4.2.2.3(e)1, Exception.** The outside design temperature is based on the 97½ percent design value as shown in Chapter 24 of the ASHRAE *Handbook of Fundamentals.*

2. Elevator(s) selected to provide service to patient, surgical, obstetrical, and ground floors during interruption of normal power *[For elevator cab lighting, control, and signal system requirements, see 3-4.2.2.2(b)(6).]*
   In instances where interruption of normal power would result in other elevators stopping between floors, throw-over facilities shall be provided to allow the temporary operation of any elevator for the release of patients or other persons who are confined between floors.
3. Supply, return, and exhaust ventilating systems for surgical and obstetrical delivery suites, intensive care, coronary care, nurseries, and emergency treatment spaces.

   It should be observed that no distinction is made between clinical and nonclinical exhaust fans for laboratory fume hoods. All such exhaust fans are to be connected to the equipment system of the essential electrical system. The purpose of this requirement is to prevent backfeeding of air between those laboratories that were connected and those that were not.

4.  Supply, return, and exhaust ventilating systems for airborne infectious/isolation rooms, protective environment rooms, exhaust fans for laboratory fume hoods, nuclear medicine areas where radioactive material is used, ethylene oxide evacuation and anesthesia evacuation. Where delayed automatic connection is not appropriate, such ventilation systems shall be permitted to be placed on the critical branch.

> With the types of infectious diseases being treated in acute care environments, and the need to maintain an environment as free of indoor air quality problems as possible, the mechanical ventilation systems serving these areas cannot be on a manual connection to the emergency power supply system. A significant delay of service cannot be tolerated without potentially disastrous results. Facilities should have the flexibility to add these ventilation systems to the critical branch if they deem it necessary.

5.  Hyperbaric facilities
6.  Hypobaric facilities
7.  Autoclaving equipment shall be permitted to be arranged for either automatic or manual connection to the alternate source.
8.  Controls for equipment listed in 3-4.2.2.3.
9.* Other selected equipment shall be permitted to be served by the equipment system.

> As previously noted, item 9 should not be construed as a carte blanche allowance for anything to be connected to the equipment system. Each item should be reviewed as to its effect on patient safety should power to the item be interrupted for an extended period of time.

**A-3-4.2.2.3(e)(9)**  Consideration should be given to selected equipment in kitchens, laundries, and radiology rooms and to selected central refrigeration.

It is desirable that, where heavy interruption currents can be anticipated, the transfer load be reduced by the use of multiple transfer devices. Elevator feeders, for instance, might be less hazardous to electrical continuity if they are fed through an individual transfer device.

### 3-4.2.2.4 Wiring Requirements.

(a)* *Separation from Other Circuits.* The life safety branch and critical branch of the emergency system shall be kept entirely independent of all other wiring and equipment.

> In 1977 the committee responsible for essential electrical systems reaffirmed its position that the wiring for the normal power and the essential electrical system be separated. It considered this to be the only way to ensure against simultaneous damage to both systems. This position has not changed.
>
> For requirements on the installation of wires, see Sections 517-44 and 700-9(b) in NFPA 70, *National Electrical Code.*

**A-3-4.2.2.4(a)**  See NFPA 70, *National Electrical Code*, for installation requirements.

(b) *Receptacles.*

1.  The number of receptacles on a single branch circuit for areas described in 3-4.2.2.2(c)(8) shall be minimized to limit the effects of a branch circuit outage. Branch circuit overcurrent devices shall be readily accessible to nursing and other authorized personnel.

    The intention of the Committee on Electrical Systems here is to limit the number of receptacles on a branch circuit (in this instance, essential electrical systems' circuits) to minimize power outages of these circuits caused by overloading. It is considered poor practice to design systems in a manner such that a faulty piece of equipment connected to a circuit could, by opening its branch circuit protective device, cause other essential equipment to become inoperative. Outages of these circuits can be life-threatening because of the condition of patients and their dependency on the electrical equipment being used for their care (these electrical devices are functioning in a life-support capacity). Nursing personnel are specifically identified since they are always in a patient care area and need to be able to reset circuit breakers if assistance is not readily available.

2.*  The cover plates for the electrical receptacles or the electrical receptacles themselves supplied from the emergency system shall have a distinctive color or marking so as to be readily identifiable.

    It is very important that *all* facility personnel know what the different colors signify so that in an emergency they will know which necessary (essential) devices to plug into those outlets on the essential electrical system.

    It is prudent to plug life-support devices into receptacles on essential electrical circuits so that these devices will be repowered automatically within 10 seconds when normal power is interrupted.

    It should be noted that the use of a distinctive color or marking is acceptable. The color chosen should be very obvious and not similar to any other color used. A marking (such as an *E* or the letters *EMER*) should not be easily removable by such things as cleaning fluids.

    If it is necessary to remove receptacles during repairs or renovations, extra care needs to be exercised not to mix up cover plates.

**A-3-4.2.2.4(b)2**  If color is used to identify these receptacles, the same color should be used throughout the facility.

(c) *Switches.* Switches installed in the lighting circuits connected to the essential electrical system shall comply with Article 700, Section E, of NFPA 70, *National Electrical Code*.

(d) *Mechanical Protection of the Emergency System.* The wiring of the emergency system shall be mechanically protected by raceways, as defined in NFPA 70, *National Electrical Code*.

*Exception No. 1: Flexible power cords of appliances or other utilization equipment connected to the emergency system shall not be required to be enclosed in raceways.*

*Exception No. 2: Secondary circuits of transformer-powered communication or signaling systems shall not be required to be enclosed in raceways unless otherwise specified by Chapters 7 or 8 of NFPA 70, National Electrical Code.*

Wiring for with Type 1 essential electrical systems is required in raceways because of the high percentage of nonambulatory patients found in facilities requiring this type of system. (For an example, see 12-3.3.2 in Chapter 12, "Hospital Requirements.") Patients in these facilities can or might be anesthetized, comatose, in traction, or connected to electrical life-support equipment. As such, the former Technical Committee on Essential Electrical Systems (now Committee on Electrical Systems) considered these facilities to need the greatest mechanical protection for electrical wiring since evacuation (or even movement) was the action least desired. Accordingly, the essential electrical systems in these facilities are provided with the most protection.

From this it should not be construed that the patients in facilities with Type 2 or Type 3 essential electrical systems are considered any less important. It means only that it is easier, in general, to move these patients in an emergency, if only horizontally to another portion of the building.

For the definition of "Raceway" and the type allowed, see Article 100 in NFPA 70, *National Electrical Code.* [3] For reader reference, Type AC cable is listed as a cable, not as a raceway.

Exception No. 1, while obvious, was added because there were questions as to whether portable (cord-connected) equipment became part of the essential electrical system when connected to it.

Exception No. 2 was not considered to diminish reliability. NFPA 70 should be reviewed regarding when enclosure in raceways is required.

## 3-4.3 Performance Criteria and Testing (Type 1 EES).

**3-4.3.1 Source.** The branches of the emergency system shall be installed and connected to the alternate power source specified in 3-4.1.1.2 and 3-4.1.1.3 so that all functions specified herein for the emergency system shall be automatically restored to operation within 10 seconds after interruption of the normal source.

See commentary on 3-4.2.1.4(d) regarding how the 10-second criteria were selected.

This 10-second clock does not simply note, for example, that there has been a drop in voltage from 120 V ac to 118 V ac. The clock starts when the normal source has dropped to a pre-established level and has remained there for a specified period of time. After 10 seconds have elapsed, the generator is required to accept the electrical load. (See 3-4.3.2.1 or 3-5.3.2.1.)

This chapter requires one level of redundancy for sources of power but does not require redundancy for transfer switches or distribution wiring. (The battery-powered light now required in anesthetizing locations is considered a "backup to the backup" just for that area but is not part of the essential electrical "system.") It is left to each facility to make its own determinations concerning the possible simultaneous failure of the normal and alternate source of power and possible failures of transfer switches or distribution wiring and what to do in this event. Such determinations, however, are not required by this chapter.

### 3-4.3.2 Transfer Switches.

**3-4.3.2.1** The essential electrical system shall be served by the normal power source except when the normal power source is interrupted or drops below a predetermined voltage level. Settings of the sensors shall be determined by careful study of the voltage requirements of the load.

**3-4.3.2.2** Failure of the normal source shall automatically start the alternate source generator after a short delay *[see 3-4.2.1.4(d)]*. When the alternate power source has attained a voltage and frequency that satisfies minimum operating requirements of the essential electrical system, the load shall be connected automatically to the alternate power source.

Paragraph 3-4.3.2.1 defines what constitutes a loss of normal power. When this failure occurs, the generator starts. However, transfer of loads does not occur until after the alternate power source has attained minimum operating requirements for loads. This is ensured through requirements of the transfer switch. [See 3-4.2.1.4(a).]

**3-4.3.2.3** Upon connection of the alternate power source, the loads comprising the emergency system shall be automatically reenergized. The load comprising the equipment system shall be connected either automatically after a time delay *[see 3-4.2.1.4(e)]* or nonautomatically and in such a sequential manner as not to overload the generator.

**3-4.3.2.4** When the normal power source is restored, and after a time delay *[see 3-4.2.1.4(f)]*, the automatic transfer switches shall disconnect the alternate source of power and connect the loads to the normal power source. The alternate power source generator set shall continue to run unloaded for a preset time delay *[see 3-4.2.1.4(j)]*.

Paragraph 3-4.2.1.4(j) sets criteria for time delay on engine shutdown.

**3-4.3.2.5** If the emergency power source fails and the normal power source has been restored, retransfer to the normal source of power shall be immediate, bypassing the retransfer delay timer.

**3-4.3.2.6** If the emergency power source fails during a test, provisions shall be made to immediately retransfer to the normal source.

In most testing schemes, a failure, such as a loss of normal power, has to be simulated. If the alternate power source fails during the test, however, nothing will happen to restore the normal power source, because normal power was shut down to simulate the failure. This paragraph requires a facility to be able to retransfer to normal power if this situation develops.

**3-4.3.2.7** Nonautomatic transfer switching devices shall be restored to the normal power source as soon as possible after the return of the normal source or at the discretion of the operator.

## 3-4.4 Administration (Type 1 EES).

### 3-4.4.1 Maintenance and Testing of Essential Electrical System.

### 3-4.4.1.1 Maintenance and Testing of Alternate Power Source and Transfer Switches.

(a) *Maintenance of Alternate Power Source.* The generator set or other alternate power source and associated equipment, including all appurtenant parts, shall be so maintained as to be capable of supplying service within the shortest time practicable and within the 10-second interval specified in 3-4.1.1.8 and 3-4.3.1. Maintenance shall be performed in accordance with NFPA 110, *Standard for Emergency and Standby Power Systems,* Chapter 6.

This paragraph sets the performance goal that the maintenance program for the alternate power source should be designed to achieve. The alternate power source is expected to provide power within 10 seconds of interruption of the normal source. (Again, the 10-second restoration criterion is for the *emergency system* of the essential electrical system. The *equipment system* of the essential electrical system can have power restored subsequent to that for the emergency system.) The specific test and maintenance activities for the alternate power source are those of 3-4.4.1.1. These are not to be considered as a complete maintenance program, however. They are only minimum elements. Each facility is expected to prepare a maintenance program that will meet the performance goal of 3-4.4.1.1. Appendix C-3.2 contains suggested elements for consideration in preparing such a program. Paragraph 3-4.4.2 requires documentation of the implementation of the program.

(b) *Inspection and Testing.*

In recognition of the hospital facility manager's need to schedule testing around the medical needs of the facility, some latitude is permitted in terms of the timing of the test. The new wording allows the facility manager to schedule the testing to provide minimum disruption of facility operation.

1.*   *Test Criteria.* Generator sets shall be tested twelve (12) times a year with testing intervals between not less than 20 days or exceeding 40 days. Generator sets serving emergency and equipment systems shall be in accordance with NFPA 110, *Standard for Emergency and Standby Power Systems*, Chapter 6.

The requirements of this section have been reviewed and debated extensively over the past decade. Energy conservation, optimum generator equipment test intervals, actual loading versus simulated loading, and the effect on patient safety and equipment have been among the major topics under scrutiny. There is universal agreement that the generator set and the essential electrical system need to be tested periodically to be reasonably certain that they will function in an actual emergency. Differences exist, however, as to how often and under what conditions this testing should be conducted. The actual running time of the engine must be long enough to ensure that engine parts are properly lubricated; however, this must be balanced by a test load large enough to ensure acids and carbon are purged by the operating temperature of the engine. Thus, two basic parameters, load and operating temperature, are listed in 6-4.2 of NFPA 110, *Standard for Emergency and Standby Power Systems* [2], with 30 minutes an absolute minimum running time.

For 1996 there was, again, extensive debate within the Committee on Electrical Systems and the Committee on Emergency Power Supplies regarding which amount of testing would be adequate enough to provide reasonable assurance that the engine (prime mover) would operate when needed in an emergency. The monthly testing was still seen as necessary, as was the minimum of 30 minutes. It was the *load* on the engine that created the most debate. A major indicator that insufficient loading is occurring is *wetstacking,* a condition that can cause serious engine problems. Additional load testing of an engine that has exhibited wetstacking has been included in the 1996 edition of NFPA 110.

NFPA 110 is referenced here, rather than showing extracted text, in order to ensure that the two documents will never be in conflict on the issue, even when NFPA 110 revises requirements.

If, as is the case in many instances, a large generator in relation to the load is installed (e.g., to account for the largest motor connected to the essential electrical system), the operating temperature of the generator might not be reached in 30 minutes. This factor should be considered when testing the generator.

A note was added in 1987 as a reminder that knowledge of what is actually connected to the essential electrical system will prevent a generator overload. A periodic review of the load on the essential electrical system is suggested. That note was revised for 1993 to add the words "demand likely to be produced by" to avoid implying that generators are required to be sized for connected load, which is not the intent. In this 1999 edition, this information is contained in paragraph 2 of A-3-4.4.1.1(b)1.

**A-3-4.4.1.1(b)1 Test Interval.** When indications such as the issuance of storm warnings indicate that power outages might be likely, good practice recommends the warming up of generator sets by a regular exercise period. Operation of generator sets for short intervals should be avoided, particularly with compression ignition engines, since it is harmful to the engines.

Records of changes to the essential electrical system should be maintained so that the actual demand likely to be produced by the connected load will be within the available capacity.

2. *Test Conditions.* The scheduled test under load conditions shall include a complete simulated cold start and appropriate automatic and manual transfer of all essential electrical system loads.

Testing procedures might range from manually disconnecting power to the power sensors on transfer switches to manually opening the main incoming feeder breakers. It is very important that each test method be fully understood by all staff through appropriate notification and that the consequences of each method (if something fails to function) be weighed carefully. A procedure for returning to the normal power source should also be established in the event a failure occurred during testing.

There is a false assumption that disconnecting a facility's mains is the best method of testing the standby generator(s) and essential electrical system. One has to always consider the possibility that failure of the disconnecting means or some other unexpected contingency might make it difficult or impossible to restore normal power. It is probably better to initiate engine start by interrupting power just ahead of the transfer switch(es) on an alternating or rotating basis in order to make sure each transfer switch has an intact engine start circuit.

3. *Test Personnel.* The scheduled tests shall be conducted by competent personnel. The tests are needed to keep the machines ready to function and, in addition, serve to detect causes of malfunction and to train personnel in operating procedures.

Training programs should take into consideration the requirements of local, state, and federal authorities. Some authorities having jurisdiction might have regulations or have certification criteria for "generator mechanics." The Occupational Safety and Health Administration (OSHA) mandates training in such areas as electrical safety, personal protective equipment, and hazard communication. Relevance to emergency generators should be determined.

### 3-4.4.1.2 Maintenance and Testing of Circuitry.

Power failures are generally associated with failures on the electric utility system. However, many power failures, especially in large facilities, are known to occur within the health care facility. A significant number of these internal power failures occur because of circuit breaker failure. Therefore, circuit breakers should be inspected regularly and tested periodically.

In 1996 the requirement was revised to allow a facility to use its discretion in determining the appropriate interval for exercising these components. Annual inspection is required, but annual operation of the breaker is no longer mandatory. Some facilities may want to operate breakers periodically based on the facility's particular needs. Other useful maintenance techniques include the following:

(a) *Infrared Testing.* Some facilities choose to conduct infrared testing only if there is evidence of heating. Others prefer to conduct infrared testing every three years to five years.

(b) *High-Current Testing.* Generally this test is done with varying levels of current while recording trip times. This calibration exercise verifies that the breaker is tripping in reasonable accordance with the manufacturer's time–current curve. If the test set is capable of producing sufficiently high current levels, the breaker's interrupting rating can also be verified. This type of test and calibration can be expensive, so the user could prefer to test only selected main and distribution breakers on an as-needed basis.

Another time-marker in the life-cycle maintenance schedule should occur following retransfer back to normal power source. An inspection of circuit breakers feeding each transfer switch should be made to ascertain that circuit breakers did not open after the alternate power source was removed from the breaker and normal power.

(a)* *Circuit Breakers.* Main and feeder circuit breakers shall be inspected annually and a program for periodically exercising the components shall be established according to manufacturer's recommendations.

**A-3-4.4.1.2(a)** Main and feeder circuit breakers should be periodically tested under simulated overload trip conditions to ensure reliability *(see C-3.2).*

(b) *Insulation Resistance.* The resistance readings of main feeder insulation shall be taken prior to acceptance and whenever damage is suspected.

Taking resistance measurements on a periodic basis has been found to be unnecessary and disruptive of facility activities (it can require shutdown of the entire system). Thus, resistance testing is required only at the times listed.

Knowledge of initial resistance readings or of past resistance readings when feeders not tested initially were functioning normally is needed to diagnose certain actual failures or detect certain incipient failures of electrical feeders. The readings are to be recorded and available in the maintenance record. (See 3-4.4.2.)

**3-4.4.1.3 Maintenance of Batteries.** Storage batteries used in connection with essential electrical systems shall be inspected at intervals of not more than 7 days and shall be maintained in full compliance with manufacturer's specifications. Defective batteries shall be repaired or replaced immediately upon discovery of defects (see NFPA 70, *National Electrical Code*, Section 700-4).

Nonfunctioning starting batteries or malfunction of the starting/charging system itself are the most common reasons for the emergency power source to fail to come on-line. The lack of proper maintenance is usually the cause for these failures.

Spare charged starting batteries for engine generator sets are a prudent investment to provide flexibility to maintenance personnel in taking emergency starting actions when generators do not start. These batteries should be connected to the charger and isolated from the main set. Such spare batteries, however, are not required by this chapter.

For further guidance on maintenance of batteries, see 6-3.6 of NFPA 110, *Standard for Emergency and Standby Power Systems.* [2]

Battery-powered lights are required in selected areas, such as anesthetizing locations and rooms housing generator sets. When installed, they are intended to provide lighting (1) during the maximum 10-second interval permitted between loss of normal power and the switch to emergency power and (2) in the event of simultaneous failure of the alternate source and normal source. When installed, it is suggested that adequate attention be given to the proper maintenance of these required battery systems and any other battery systems. See Exhibit 3.9.

**Exhibit 3.9** *Detail of batteries used for starting an engine used for emergency power purposes. Note the clean contacts. Poor battery maintenance is cited by authorities having jurisdiction as the major reason for generators' failing to start.*

**3-4.4.2 Recordkeeping.** A written record of inspection, performance, exercising period, and repairs shall be regularly maintained and available for inspection by the authority having jurisdiction.

Use of computers to store records of inspections, maintenance, and other information should be acceptable if such data can readily be made available for inspectors. If this method is used, a backup hard copy of data is highly recommended.

The practice of "trending" (i.e., reviewing data gathered over a period of time) is a valuable tool in the science of preventive maintenance. It should be used throughout this process. Computer spreadsheets can aid significantly in this endeavor.

## 3-5  Essential Electrical System Requirements—Type 2

### 3-5.1  Sources (Type 2 EES).

The requirements for sources for Type 2 essential electrical systems shall conform to those listed in 3-4.1.

### 3-5.2  Distribution (Type 2 EES).

**3-5.2.1  General.** The distribution requirements for Type 2 essential electrical systems shall conform to those listed in 3-4.2.1.

### 3-5.2.2  Specific Requirements.

**3-5.2.2.1\*  General.** Type 2 essential electrical systems are comprised of two separate systems capable of supplying a limited amount of lighting and power service, which is considered essential for the protection of life and safety and effective operation of the institution during the time normal electrical service is interrupted for any reason. These two separate systems are the emergency system and the critical system.

The number of transfer switches to be used shall be based upon reliability, design, and load considerations. Each branch of the emergency system and each critical system shall have one or more transfer switches. One transfer switch shall be permitted to serve one or more branches or systems in a facility with a maximum demand on the essential electrical system of 150 kVA (120 kW).

> The 1999 edition was amended to clarify the committee's long established intent that a typical Type 2 system will have a minimum of two automatic transfer switches (emergency system and critical system) unless the maximum demand is determined to be less than 150 kVA (120 kW).

**A-3-5.2.2.1** *Separation of Wiring on Emergency System in Type 2 Systems.* In principle, Chapter 3 is designed to seek security of electrical function by protection against both internal disruption and the loss of primary power sources. In keeping therewith, Chapter 3 aims to limit the security deterioration that could occur when poorly maintained and heavy-current-consuming items are connected to the same feeders that supply critical patient care functions.

For greater protection, such segregation of suspect and critical connections is best carried out throughout the length of a feeder system, preferably including the transfer device. This practice gives rise to the phrase protected feeder.

While Chapter 3 must leave details of wiring and overcurrent protection to engineering judgment, in view of wide variations of conditions, the Committee on Electrical Systems consensus is that feeders serving anesthetizing locations, special nursing care units, and special treatment areas, where continuity of care is vital to life, should be given security through the segregation of protected feeders and that, to the greatest extent practical, feeders should connect to the alternate source of power by means of separate transfer devices.

As a further protection against internal disruption, it is also recommended that, when practical, critical areas served by the essential electrical system have some portion of lighting and receptacles connected to feeders supplied by the general system.

**3-5.2.2.2 Emergency System.** The emergency system shall supply power for the following lighting, receptacles, and equipment:

(a)     Illumination of means of egress as required in NFPA *101, Life Safety Code*
(b)     Exit signs and exit directional signs required in NFPA *101, Life Safety Code*
(c)     Alarm and alerting systems, including the following:

1. Fire alarms

As in 3-4.2.2.2(b)3.a, all fire alarms are to be connected to the essential electrical system.

2. Alarms required for systems used for the piping of nonflammable medical gases as specified in Chapter 4, "Gas and Vacuum Systems"

(d)*   Communication systems, where used for issuing instructions during emergency conditions

**A-3-5.2.2.2(d)** Departmental installations such as digital dialing systems used for intradepartmental communications could have impaired use during a failure of electrical service to the area. In the event of such failure, those systems that have lighted selector buttons in the base of the telephone instrument or in the desk units known as "director sets" will be out of service to the extent that the lights will not function and that the buzzer used to indicate incoming calls will be silenced. The lack of electrical energy will not prevent the use of telephones for outgoing calls, but incoming calls will not be signaled, nor will intercommunicating calls be signaled. This communication failure should be taken into consideration in planning essential electrical systems.

See commentary at beginning of 3-4.2.2.2 for an explanation of why only those functions listed for the life safety branch of Type 1 essential electrical systems, equivalent to the emergency system of Type 2 essential electrical systems, are to be placed on such circuits.

(e) Sufficient lighting in dining and recreation areas to provide illumination to exit ways of 5 footcandles minimum
(f) Task illumination and selected receptacles at the generator set location
(g) Elevator cab lighting, control, communication, and signal systems

See commentary under 3-4.2.2.2(b)6; the reason for inclusion of elevators is the same.

No function other than those listed above in items (a) through (g) shall be connected to the emergency system.

See commentary at beginning of 3-4.2.2.2 for an explanation of why only those functions listed for the life safety branch of Type 1 essential electrical systems, equivalent to the emergency system of Type 2 essential electrical systems, are to be placed on such circuits.

### 3-5.2.3.1  Critical System.

(a) *General.* The critical system shall be so installed and connected to the alternate power source that equipment listed in 3-5.2.2.3(b) shall be automatically restored to operation at appropriate time-lag intervals following the restoration of the emergency system to operation. Its arrangement shall also provide for the additional connection of equipment listed in 3-5.2.2.3(c) by either delayed-automatic or manual operation.

(b) *Delayed-Automatic Connections to Critical System.* The following equipment shall be connected to the critical system and be arranged for delayed-automatic connection to the alternate power source:

1. Patient care areas—task illumination and selected receptacles in the following:

   a. Medication preparation areas
   b. Pharmacy dispensing areas
   c. Nurses' stations (unless adequately lighted by corridor luminaires)

2. Supply, return, and exhaust ventilating systems for airborne infectious isolation rooms
3. Sump pumps and other equipment required to operate for the safety of major apparatus and associated control systems and alarms
4. Smoke control and stair pressurization systems

   See commentary under 3-4.2.2.3(d)5.

5. Kitchen hood supply and/or exhaust systems, if required to operate during a fire in or under the hood

(c)* *Delayed-Automatic or Manual Connections to Critical System.* The following equipment shall be connected to the critical system and be arranged for either delayed-automatic or manual connection to the alternate power source:

**A-3-5.2.2.3(c)** *Equipment for Automatic or Manual Connection.* Other selected equipment can be served by the critical system.

NOTE: Consideration should be given to selected equipment in kitchens and laundries, and to selected central refrigeration.

It is desirable that, where heavy interruption currents can be anticipated, the transfer load be reduced by the use of multiple transfer devices. Elevator feeders, for instance, might be less hazardous to electrical continuity if they are fed through an individual transfer device.

1. *Heating Equipment to Provide Heating for General Patient Rooms.* Heating of general

patient rooms during disruption of the normal source shall not be required under any of the following conditions:

a.* The outside design temperature is higher than $+20°F$ ($-6.7°C$), or

**A-3-5.2.2.3(c)1a** The outside design temperature is based on the 97½ percent design value as shown in Chapter 24 of the ASHRAE *Handbook of Fundamentals*.

b. The outside design temperature is lower than $+20°F$ ($-6.7°C$) and, where a selected room(s) is provided for the needs of all confined patients, then only such room(s) need be heated, or

c. The facility is served by a dual source of normal power as described in 3-4.1.1.1.

The same rationale as for the exception to 3-4.2.2.3(e)1, on the heating of general patient rooms, applies here as well—to reduce energy needs by the moving and grouping of patients as is practical.

2. *Elevator Service.* In instances where interruptions of power would result in elevators stopping between floors, throw-over facilities shall be provided to allow the temporary operation of any elevator for the release of passengers. *[For elevator cab lighting, control, and signal system requirements, see 3-5.2.2.2(g).]*

(d) *Optional Connections to the Critical System.* Additional illumination, receptacles, and equipment shall be permitted to be connected only to the critical system.

**3-5.2.3.2 Wiring Requirements.**

(a)* *Separation from Other Circuits.* The emergency system shall be kept entirely independent of all other wiring and equipment.

**A-3-5.2.2.4(a)** See NFPA 70, *National Electrical Code*, for installation requirements.

(b)* *Receptacles.* The cover plates for the electrical receptacles or the electrical receptacles themselves supplied from the emergency system shall have a distinctive color or marking so as to be readily identifiable.

**A-3-5.2.2.4(b)** If color is used to identify these receptacles, the same color should be used throughout the facility.

## 3-5.3 Performance Criteria and Testing (Type 2 EES).

**3-5.3.1 Source.** The emergency system shall be installed and connected to the alternate source of power specified in 3-4.1.1.2 and 3-4.1.1.3 so that all functions specified herein for the emergency system will be automatically restored to operation within 10 seconds after interruption of the normal source.

The commentary under 3-4.3.1 applies here as well.

**3-5.3.2 Transfer Switches.**

**3-5.3.2.1** The essential electrical system shall be served by the normal power source except when the normal power source is interrupted or drops below a predetermined voltage level. Settings of the sensors shall be determined by careful study of the voltage requirements of the load.

**3-5.3.2.2** Failure of the normal source shall automatically start the alternate source generator, after a short delay *[see 3-4.2.1.4(d)]*. When the alternate power source has attained a voltage and frequency that satisfies minimum operating requirements of the essential electrical system, the load shall be connected automatically to the alternate power source.

†All ac-powered support and accessory equipment necessary to the operation of the EPS shall be supplied from the load side of the automatic transfer switch(es), or the output terminals of the EPS, ahead of the main EPS overcurrent protection, as necessary, to ensure continuity of the EPSS operation and performance. (NFPA 110: 5-12.5)

> Previously, NFPA 99 was unclear regarding the method for serving generator accessories. This text gives the hospital design engineer some latitude in making this connection. Accessories can be supplied from a transfer switch or, in some cases, directly off the standby generator. For example, a remote radiator can be supplied directly from the standby generator by means of a relay that "picks up" when the generator output reaches nominal voltage.

**3-5.3.2.3** Upon connection of the alternate power source, the loads comprising the emergency system shall be automatically reenergized. The loads comprising the critical system shall be connected either automatically after a time delay *[see 3-4.2.1.4(e)]* or nonautomatically and in such a sequential manner as not to overload the generator.

**3-5.3.2.4** When the normal power source is restored, and after a time delay *[see 3-4.2.1.4(f)]*, the automatic transfer switches shall disconnect the alternate source of power and connect the loads to the normal power source. The alternate power source generator set shall continue to run unloaded for a preset time delay *[see 3-4.2.1.4(j)]*.

> Paragraph 3-4.2.1.4(j) sets criteria for time delay on engine shutdown.

**3-5.3.2.5** If the emergency power source fails and the normal power source has been restored, retransfer to the normal source of power shall be immediate, bypassing the retransfer delay timer.

**3-5.3.2.6** If the emergency power source fails during a test, provisions shall be made to immediately retransfer to the normal source.

**3-5.3.2.7** Nonautomatic transfer switching devices shall be restored to the normal power source as soon as possible after the return of the normal source or at the discretion of the operator.

## 3-5.4 Administration (Type 2 EES).

### 3-5.4.1 Maintenance and Testing of Essential Electrical System.

#### 3-5.4.1.1 Maintenance and Testing of Alternate Power Source and Transfer Switches.

(a) *Maintenance of Alternate Power Source.* The generator set or other alternate power source and associated equipment, including all appurtenant parts, shall be so maintained as to be capable of supplying service within the shortest time practicable and within the 10-second interval specified in 3-4.1.1.8 and 3-5.3.1.

(b) *Inspection and Testing.* Generator sets shall be inspected and tested in accordance with 3-4.4.1.1(b).

#### 3-5.4.1.2 Maintenance and Testing of Circuitry. Circuitry shall be maintained and tested in accordance with 3-4.4.1.2.

#### 3-5.4.1.3 Maintenance of Batteries. Batteries shall be maintained in accordance with 3-4.4.1.3.

### 3-5.4.2 Recordkeeping. A written record of inspection, performance, exercising period, and repairs shall be regularly maintained and available for inspection by the authority having jurisdiction.

# 3-6 Essential Electrical System Requirements—Type 3

## 3-6.1 Sources (Type 3 EES).

The alternate source of power for the system shall be specifically designed for this purpose and shall be either a generator, battery system, or self-contained battery integral with the equipment.

**3-6.1.1** Generators shall conform to 3-4.1.1.

**3-6.1.2** Battery systems shall conform to 3-4.1.2.

## 3-6.2 Distribution (Type 3 EES).

**3-6.2.1 General.** The distribution requirements for Type 3 essential electrical systems shall conform to those listed in 3-4.2.1.

### 3-6.2.2 Specific Requirements.

**3-6.2.2.1 General.** Type 3 essential electrical systems are comprised of a system capable of supplying a limited amount of lighting and power service that is considered essential for life safety and orderly cessation of procedure during the time normal electrical service is interrupted for any reason.

**3-6.2.2.2 Connection to the Essential Electrical System.** The system shall supply power for task illumination that is related to the safety of life and that is necessary for the safe cessation of procedures in progress.

### 3-6.2.2.3 Wiring Requirements.

(a) *General.* The design, arrangement, and installation of the system shall be in accordance with NFPA 70, *National Electrical Code*.

(b)* *Receptacles.* The cover plates for the electrical receptacles or the electrical receptacles themselves supplied from the emergency system shall have a distinctive color or marking so as to be readily identifiable.

**A-3-6.2.2.3(b)** If color is used to identify these receptacles, the same color should be used throughout the facility.

## 3-6.3 Performance Criteria and Testing (Type 3 EES).

### 3-6.3.1 Source.

**3-6.3.1.1** The emergency system shall have an alternate source of power separate and independent from the normal source that will be effective for a minimum of 1½ hours after loss of the normal source.

The 1½-hour requirement is consistent with the minimum requirements of NFPA *101, Life Safety Code.* [1] However, readers are reminded that 1½ hours might not be sufficient for some medical procedures.

**3-6.3.1.2** The emergency system shall be so arranged that, in the event of failure of normal power source, the alternate source of power shall be automatically connected to the load within 10 seconds.

See commentary on 3-4.2.1.4(d) for an explanation of how the 10-second criterion was selected.

### 3-6.3.2 Transfer Switches with Engine Generator Sets.

The number of transfer switches for a Type 3 essential electrical system is not suggested in this section because the number is dependent on the load, and so forth. (For the number of transfer switches in Type 1 or Type 2 systems with the maximum demand on the essential electrical system, see 3-4.2.2.1 or 3-5.2.2.1, respectively.)

**3-6.3.2.1** The operation of the equipment shall be arranged such that the load will be served by the normal source except when the normal source is interrupted, or when the voltage drops below the setting of the voltage sensing device. The settings of the voltage sensing relays shall be determined by careful study of the voltage requirements of the load.

**3-6.3.2.2** When the normal source is restored, and after a time delay *[see 3-4.2.1.4(f)]*, the automatic transfer switch shall disconnect the alternate source of power and connect the loads to the normal power source.

**3-6.3.2.3** If the alternate power source fails and the normal power source has been restored, retransfer to the normal source of power shall be immediate.

**3-6.3.3 Transfer Switches with Battery System.**

**3-6.3.3.1** Failure of the normal source shall automatically transfer the load to the battery system.

**3-6.3.3.2** Retransfer to the normal source shall be automatic upon restoration of the normal source.

## 3-6.4  Administration (Type 3 EES).

**3-6.4.1 Maintenance and Testing.**

**3-6.4.1.1 Maintenance and Testing of Alternate Power Source and Transfer Switches.**

(a) *Maintenance of Alternate Power Source.* The generator set or other alternate power source and associated equipment, including all appurtenant parts, shall be so maintained as to be capable of supplying service within the shortest time practicable and within the 10-second interval specified in 3-4.1.1.8 and 3-6.3.1.

(b) *Inspection and Testing.* Generator sets shall be inspected and tested in accordance with 3-4.4.1.1(b).

(c) *Stored Energy Power Source.* Maintenance and testing of stored emergency power supply systems shall be in accordance with NFPA 111, *Standard on Stored Electrical Energy Emergency and Standby Power Systems,* Section 6-1 through 6-4.5.

**3-6.4.1.2 Maintenance and Testing Circuitry.** Circuitry shall be maintained and tested in accordance with 3-4.4.1.2.

**3-6.4.1.3 Maintenance of Batteries.** Batteries shall be maintained in accordance with 3-4.4.1.3.

**3-6.4.2 Recordkeeping.** A written record of inspection, performance, exercising period, and repairs shall be regularly maintained and available for inspection by the authority having jurisdiction.

### References Cited in Commentary

1. NFPA *101®, Life Safety Code®,* 1997 edition.
2. NFPA 110, *Standard for Emergency and Standby Power Systems,* 1999 edition.
3. NFPA 70, *National Electrical Code®,* 1999 edition.
4. NFPA 72, *National Fire Alarm Code®,* 1999 edition.
5. NFPA 20, *Standard for the Installation of Stationary Pumps for Fire Protection,* 1999 edition.
6. NCCLS Standard ASI-5, *Power Requirements for Clinical Laboratory Instruments and for Laboratory Power Sources.*

7. Whaler, Steimer, and MacIntosh.
8. NFPA 37, *Standard for the Installation and Use of Stationary Combustion Engine and Gas Turbines,* 1998 edition.

# CHAPTER 4

# Gas and Vacuum Systems

For the 1999 edition of NFPA 99, *Standard for Health Care Facilities,* the subject of the "level of risk" to patients from the use of piped gas and vacuum systems was extensively reviewed by the Technical Committee on Piping Systems. Since this concept was first included in Chapter 4 of the 1996 edition of NFPA 99, there have been a considerable number of questions (and some confusion) regarding the supplanting of the term *type* with the term *level* to categorize various systems.

Answering these concerns involves reviewing not only the requirements of Chapter 4, but also the structure and intent of Chapters 3 to 11 (nonfacility-specific requirements) and their relationship to Chapters 12 to 19 (facility-specific requirements).

Chapter 4, "Gas and Vacuum Systems," categorizes piped gas and vacuum systems by the level of risk to patients, with Level 1 systems the most reliable and complex because patients being served by this system will be at the greatest risk should the system fail (i.e., patients being served by this system are the most dependent on this system's functioning properly). Level 2 systems are a step down from Level 1 systems; Level 3 systems are another step down; and Level 4 systems are another step down. This does not mean that Level 4 systems are marginal systems; rather, the needs of patients (if any) are not as critical as the other three systems.

The current structure of NFPA 99 provides requirements from Chapters 3 to 11 for the various facilities listed in Chapters 12 to 19. (Chapters 12 to 17 can also add specific requirements for special locations.) It is in these chapters (Chapters 12 to 19) that a particular level of piped gas and vacuum systems from Chapter 4 is specified for the various facilities listed. The particular system selected is based on the level of risk to which patients would be exposed should the system fail or not function properly. The name on the front door of the facility is not the determiner of which system is installed.

As an example, Chapter 12, "Hospitals," lists—that is, requires—a Level 1 piped gas system (see 12-3.4.1). The Technical Committee responsible for piped gas system requirements believes that the condition of patients in this category of facility requires this level of system. Note also the exception included in this section; this exception was included because in portions of the facility a completely separate piped gas system could be installed that would not serve patients who required a Level 1 system.

Chapter 4 in this 1999 edition of NFPA 99 has requirements for a Level 2 piped gas and vacuum system. (In the 1996 edition of NFPA 99, this level was "Reserved." The Technical Committee determined that there was a group of patients whose level of risk was not quite as serious as those for whom a Level 1 system was necessary but whose level of risk was greater than those served by a Level 3 system.

The Technical Committee responsible for piping systems also noted the inability of new forms of delivery of health care to fit into the scheme developed in the mid-1980s for Chapters 13 to 15. The definition of the terms for *ambulatory health care center, clinic, and medical/dental office,* and the requirements for the level of piped gas and vacuum systems of each, did not mesh with the level of care and treatment being provided by these new facilities. After much debate, the text of Chapters 13 to 15 was deleted and a new Chapter 13 developed. This chapter covers all the health care facilities not covered by Chapters 12 ("Hospitals"), Chapter 16 ("Nursing Homes"), and Chapter 17 ("Limited Care Facilities"). The definitions and requirements for these three categories of facilities were (and still are) workable.

New Chapter 13 reflects the intent of the Technical Committee on Piping Systems that the piped gas and vacuum system installed be appropriate for the level of risk to which a patient was exposed; that is, the greater the risks if the system failed, the greater the number of safety features to be included.

Finally, with the creation of a new Chapter 13, it was necessary, for correlation purposes, for the Technical Committee on Piping Systems to review requirements for piped gas and vacuum systems in Chapters 12, 16, and 17. Some changes were made, resulting in 12-3.4, 16-3.4, and 17-3.4.

Natural gas, hydrogen, and acetylene are flammable gases, so they are not included under the requirements for piped nonflammable medical gases for Level 1, Level 2 or Level 3 systems. However, they are permitted in Level 4 systems (i.e., those used in laboratories).

Readers should be aware that requirements for piped gas systems are different from requirements for piped vacuum systems. While both systems utilize networks of pipes, alarms, valves, and terminals, specifics, such as direction of flow and type of piping allowed, are quite different.

Often, these two systems are installed simultaneously. In these instances, care should be taken to ensure correct operation, particularly to prevent cross-connection and ensure correct placement of alarms.

Readers are reminded that the requirements in Chapter 4 are applicable only to new installation, unless specifically noted otherwise. (See Section 1-2 in Chapter 1.)

Readers should review Chapter 8 for requirements for freestanding cylinders that are not associated with piped gas systems, including their storage and transfilling.

## 4-1* Scope

**A-4-1** *Application of Requirements.* The application of requirements contained in this chapter for specific types of health care facilities can be found in Chapters 12 through 18.

Gases covered include, but are not limited to, oxygen, nitrogen, nitrous oxide, air, carbon dioxide, natural gas, ethylene oxide, hydrogen, helium, and acetylene.

Section 4-3 covers Level 1 piped gas, vacuum and waste anesthetic gas disposal (WAGD) systems; Section 4-4 covers Level 2 piped gas, vacuum and WAGD systems; Section 4-5 covers Level 3 piped gas, vacuum and WAGD (also referred to as scavenging) systems; Section 4-6 covers Level 4 piped gas and vacuum systems.

**4-1.1*** This chapter covers the performance, maintenance, installation, and testing of (1) nonflammable medical gas systems with operating pressures below 300 psig (2068 kPa), (2) flammable and nonflammable laboratory gas systems, (3) vacuum systems used within healthcare facilities, (4) waste anesthetic gas disposal (WAGD) systems, and (5) manufactured assemblies that are intended for connection to the medical gas, vacuum, or WAGD systems.

NFPA 99 includes requirements for the installation, maintenance, and performance of waste anesthetic gas disposal (WAGD). Changing the scope of the document highlights this additional set of requirements.

The 300-psig (2068-kPa) operating pressure range recognizes the growing need for facilities to be able to combine physical plant safety with the clinical safety and convenience of centrally supplied medical gas systems to drive application devices that operate above 200 psig (1380 kPa) (e.g., new devices for bone surgery).

System operation was previously limited to a 200-psig (1380-kPa) working pressure because of existing standard station outlet design. The use of the higher operating pressure requires not only the same safeguards for systems operating at pressures below 200 psig (1380 kPa), but also some additional safeguards, including the selection of piping material, the safe working size of piping, and the need to use specialized station outlets capable of operating at up to 300 psig (2068 kPa). This change, first addressed in the 1993 edition of NFPA 99, was further modified for 1996 as a result of field experience.

With the introduction of mobile systems, such as CAT scanners, MRI systems, and lithotripter units, questions have been raised as to whether, or how, the requirements of fixed building systems, such as medical piped gas and vacuum systems, are applicable to mobile systems. Some facilities provide controlled exterior temporary utility connections, though with more safety measures. This new condition is not addressed as yet in Chapter 4, but is under review for the next edition.

**A-4-1.1** Operation of piped medical gas systems at pressures in excess of 200 psig (1380 kPa) involves certain restrictions because of the limitations in materials. *(See 4-3.1.2.7.)*

**4-1.2** Wherever the term medical gas occurs in this chapter, the provisions shall apply to all patient gas systems. Wherever the name of a specific gas occurs, the provision applies only to that gas.

**4-1.3** This chapter does not apply to portable compressed gas systems.

**4-1.4** An existing system that is not in strict compliance with the provisions of this standard shall be permitted to be continued in use as long as the authority having jurisdiction has determined that such use does not constitute a distinct hazard to life.

This provision was added in the 1996 edition in response to inquiries on the applicability of requirements in subsequent (new) editions of the standard to existing installations. It is not intended that a facility modify an existing piped gas or vacuum system each time a new edition of NFPA 99 is published. Although this subject is covered in Chapter 1, many persons do not refer back to it. Its inclusion here is intended to permit users and enforcers to clearly ascertain whether an existing installation needs to be revised to conform to later additions of the standard.

## 4-2 Nature of Hazards

### 4-2.1* Gas Systems.

**A-4-2.1** See Section 8-2.

The requirements for the installation of medical piped gas systems are the result of the fire and patient-safety hazards posed by such systems and the then Committee on Gases being given the responsibility to address them (see following commentary, in addition to Section 8-2). Other types of codes (e.g., life safety) could affect these systems and should be consulted as necessary.

The subject of piped gas systems and their hazards was first brought before the then NFPA Committee on Gases in 1932. Some of the concerns raised at the time included the following:

(a) Piped systems were beginning to carry oxidizing gases throughout a building via a network of pipes. Although these types of gases don't burn, they do support and intensify the burning of combustibles that are already burning. (Note: Initially, there were no restrictions on flammable anesthetic gases, but in 1950 their piping was prohibited, thereby eliminating one possible source of explosions and fire.)

(b) A large quantity of gas in cylinders was being concentrated/stored in one area.

(c) There was the possibility of buildup of potentially hazardous gas concentrations if the pipes leaked.

(d) Patient safety would be in jeopardy should there be either a mix-up of gases at the supply site or from some interruption in the piping system, a cross-connection of piping, or an actual loss of gas.

These concerns remain relevant, even today.

With respect to piped medical air, on-site compressors connected to a piping distribution are now used more often than cylinders of compressed air to provide medical grade air to patients. Failure of a compressor(s) can create fire and electrical hazards. Maintenance of these systems has become very important.

The use of piped gas systems has become almost universal. If these systems are installed in accordance with, or are not tested to, NFPA 99, patient safety can be jeopardized.

## 4-2.2*  Vacuum Systems.

There are potential fire and explosion hazards associated with medical gas central piping systems and medical-surgical vacuum systems. The various components are usually not independent isolated components, but are parts of a larger system dedicated to total patient care and safety.

Many of these components are covered by existing standards to minimize the fire, explosive, and patient safety hazard. With the increased use of vacuum systems, the potential for mistaken interconnection with oxidizing gases, for ingestion of flammable anesthetic gases, and for undercapacity requiring extended overheated operation all present potential hazards or compound other hazardous conditions that should be properly addressed. While the potential for these problems exists, the former Subcommittee on Vacuum Systems and Equipment was unaware of the actual occurrence of any significant fire-related hazards with vacuum systems.

There are also potential hazards to patients in the unplanned shutdown or failure of the systems secondary to a fire and/or the inability of the system to provide adequate levels of performance under normal or emergency situations. There is also the potential for mistaken interconnection with pressurized nonflammable medical gas systems described in Sections 4-3 through 4-6.

**A-4-2.2**  Section 4-3 covers requirements for Level 1 piped gas and vacuum systems; Section 4-4 covers Level 2 piped gas and vacuum systems; Section 4-5 covers Level 3 piped gas and vacuum systems; and Section 4-6 covers Level 4 piped gas and vacuum systems.

In the early 1970s a number of guidelines were developed by various gas manufacturers, equipment suppliers, industry associations, and engineering publications on the subject of "medical-surgical vacuum systems." Few of these guidelines were based on any broad-based documented performance data, and each differed significantly from the other on the requirements for such systems. Few were universally accepted by designers, user institutions, and enforcing agency inspectors because there was no consistency in adequate systems design; no appropriate warning systems; and no appropriate interface with other NFPA standards without misinterpretation.

Because a standard for piped gases already existed (NFPA 56F, *Standard for Nonflammable Medical Gas Systems,* which is now incorporated into NFPA 99), the development of a document on medical-surgical vacuum systems was considered appropriate. (One of the leading proponents of this NFPA project was the Compressed Gas Association [CGA].) A committee, separate from the Technical Committee on Industrial and Medical Gases that developed NFPA 56F, was established by NFPA to deal with the unique mechanics, physics, and requirements of medical vacuum systems. The new committee was placed within the Health Care Facilities Project because it did not involve the convenience of gases under positive pressure.

At the initial meetings of the committee in 1971, to which clinical and industry members were invited, it became apparent that there was insufficient data to substantiate most of the sizing methods then available. The consensus of the committee was that it should not begin the development of a new document unless basic use criteria were established and confirming test surveys were carried out.

Basic testing was done to determine the degree of vacuum, volume flow (displacement), and so forth, required to operate various equipment used for procedures such as blood removal, tracheal suction, gastric suction, and thoracic suction. The original data were developed with the CGA and various institutional members present. In general, the committee found that as vacuum increased, the actual displacement curve became flat. A 15-in. Hg factor was ideal; a 12-in. Hg was a minimally acceptable value. At 15 in. Hg vacuum, the displacement curve flattened out.

Flow requirements were also determined for situations when a catheter was left open. Airflow is considerably higher with a catheter or suction tip open to the atmosphere than when it is inserted in body fluids. It was demonstrated that 0.25 SCFM was required when the catheter was occluded and that 1.5 SCFM was displaced when the suction tip or catheter was left in an open condition. An open catheter or suction tip running continuously is considered poor suctioning technique in that it reduces the degree of vacuum in the entire system in general, as well as specifically at station inlets in the same or adjacent rooms. This technique is discouraged. [See 4-3.5.6.1(d).]

The basic sizing criteria developed by the committee was based on the following four major elements:

(a) Documented testing on representative pieces of ancillary clinical equipment to determine capabilities and the level of vacuum required to evacuate body fluids and air to simulate outlets improperly or unintentionally left open.
(b) Realistic vacuum levels as established by clinical input.
(c) Establishment of a minimum number of vacuum terminals for various locations and use based on empirical input from medical professionals.
(d) Empirical development of simultaneous use curves that reflect the fact that as a hospital's size (and the number of vacuum terminals) increases, the percentage of utilization of individual terminals decreases.

Test surveys, to confirm the accuracy of the basic criteria, were conducted by representatives of the American Society for Hospital Engineering and the Compressed Gas Association.

The former Subcommittee on Medical-Surgical Vacuum Systems, in combination with the American Society for Hospital Engineering and the Compressed Gas Association, collected sizable data from 1975 through 1980 in an attempt to make the document produced, designated NFPA 56K, as accurate as possible. It represented a database significantly beyond that used in other previously promulgated methods. Data from 67 hospitals were used to confirm and verify the sizing criteria (data from other hospitals surveyed were considered invalid for a variety of reasons). The 67 data points were not used to formulate the sizing criteria; rather, they were used to verify and confirm the basic criteria. The 67 data points had an actual consumption of approximately 34 percent of the NFPA 56K design-rated flow and 17 percent of total source capacity. When considering open terminals, actual consumption was 48 percent of the sizing criteria and 24 percent of the total source capacity. The committee chose not to reduce the design criteria, based on the number of hospitals surveyed.

The surveys also raised the question of whether to design a vacuum system for bed occupancy rather than total bed count. The answer was the latter, for if a hospital had a 34 percent occupancy, the vacuum requirements would be more than one-third of the requirements at 100 percent occupancy. Looking at the diversity factors, the flow requirement may be only slightly higher for full occupancy.

The committee considered it appropriate to observe testing of various manufacturers' devices because the document would affect such manufacturers and because such testing provided worst-case volume displacements and degree of vacuum necessary for various suction-therapy devices. These maximum displacements and levels of vacuum were used as a prime base for the calculations in this chapter, although the displacements are used in less than 50 percent of patient suction applications and in less than 10 percent of suctioning time for maximum open aspiration. (Note: The last are always momentary applications.) By using this worst-case measurement as a prime base, considerable excess safety margin has been incorporated into the requirements that follow.

The testing of the five manufacturers' devices that had the highest in-use displacements was considered a good representation for such purposes and was the basis for these requirements.

When NFPA 56K was incorporated into NFPA 99 in 1984, the committee responsible for NFPA 56K voted to change the document from a recommended practice to a standard. This was accomplished for those portions of NFPA 56K for which a consensus on minimum quantitative requirements was reached. Those portions in which criteria were still only recommended were retained as recommendations in the form of notes or appendix material in NFPA 99.

This 1996 edition of NFPA 99 and the revisions to vacuum system requirements were the result of a long, evolved process. NFPA initially emphasized the differences between piped vacuum and piped gases through two separate standards and separate committees. That emphasis continued within NFPA 99 until 1994, when the two subcommittees were merged into the Technical Committee on Piping Systems. The 1996 edition of NFPA 99 was the first edition to recognize the normal practice of designing, installing, and commissioning these systems simultaneously by organizing Chapter 4 to emphasize the similarities between these two systems.

For more history on the development of these vacuum system requirements, see C-4.6.

### 4-2.3 Manufactured Assemblies.

Specific hazards associated with manufactured assemblies are the same as those listed in 4-2.2 as well as additional hazards resulting from improper assembly, separation and leakage resulting from hidden semi-permanent connections, improper connection resulting in cross-connection, and blockage and flow problems resulting from damage to hoses, etc.

The need to establish requirements for manufactured assemblies was recognized by the committee during the 1996 revision cycle. Without defined requirements, it is not possible to maintain the high quality of safety that is prescribed for piped gas systems if the total system requirements are not extended to include the many different manufactured assemblies being installed today.

Manufactured assemblies are deemed to require the same system integrity as the remainder of the piped system.

### 4-2.4 Waste Anesthetic Gas Disposal (WAGD) Systems.

There are potential fire and explosion hazards associated with the gases that are removed from the anesthesia machine by the WAGD system. These gases typically include oxygen, nitrous oxide, and halogenated anesthetics. There are also potential hazards to patients and staff resulting from exposure to these gases or from improper interface between the very low pressures in the breathing circuit and the high vacuum present in some WAGD systems. There is also the hazard of interconnection between the WAGD system and the other medical gas systems, and especially the medical surgical vacuum system.

# 4-3 Level 1 Piped Systems

## 4-3.1 Piped Gas Systems (Source and Distribution)—Level 1.
### 4-3.1.1* Source—Level 1.

The term *level* is used for designation and reference purposes only. (Prior to the 1996 edition of NFPA, piped gas systems were categorized by the term *type.*) Chapters 12 through 18 state the applicability of a particular level of patient piped gas system. See 12-3.4.1, 13-3.4.1, 14-3.4.1, and so on, for the level of system required for hospitals, ambulatory health care centers, and other health care facilities.

**A-4-3.1.1** For bulk oxygen systems, see NFPA 50, *Standard for Bulk Oxygen Systems at Consumer Sites.*

NFPA 50 is not the only standard applicable for bulk oxygen systems. NFPA 99, as an example, covers alarms and their testing for all medical gas systems, including those whose sources are bulk systems.

**4-3.1.1.1 Cylinder and Container Management.** Cylinders in service and in storage shall be individually secured and located to prevent falling or being knocked over.

(a)* Cylinders or supply containers shall be constructed, tested, and maintained in accordance with the U.S. Department of Transportation specifications and regulations.

The U.S. Department of Transportation (DOT) regulations for the manufacture and requalification of compressed gas cylinders provide for reasonably safe and economical cylinders. These regulations are thus referenced to avoid redundancy. Cylinders complying with DOT regulations are also considered safe for the storage of gases in health care facilities.

**A-4-3.1.1.1(a)** Regulations of the U.S. Department of Transportation (formerly U.S. Interstate Commerce Commission) outline specifications for transportation of explosives and dangerous articles (*Code of Federal Regulations*, Title 49, Parts 171–190). In Canada, the regulations of the Canadian Transport Commission, Union Station, Ottawa, Ontario, apply.

(b) Cylinder contents shall be identified by attached labels or stencils naming the components and giving their proportions. Labels and stencils shall be lettered in accordance with CGA Pamphlet C-4, *Standard Method of Marking Portable Compressed Gas Containers to Identify the Material Contained.*

(c) Contents of cylinders and containers shall be identified by reading the labels prior to use. Labels shall not be defaced, altered, or removed.

### 4-3.1.1.2 Storage Requirements (Location, Construction, Arrangement).

The 1996 edition suggested that any amount of compressed medical gas should be stored in a room or cabinet specifically designed for that purpose. The authority having jurisdiction's decision to remove cylinders from the bedside, nurses' station, utility rooms, and so forth is reflected in this 1999 text. However, all cylinders must be secured to prevent falling.

Storage requirements for cylinders used in connection with piped gas systems have been organized in all of the following ways:

(a)  Nonflammable gases (any quantity; in-storage, connected, or both)
(b)  Additional requirements for nonflammable gases greater than 3000 ft$^3$ (85 m$^3$)
(c)  Additional requirements for nonflammable gases less than 3000 ft$^3$ (85 m$^3$)

(Text on flammable inhalation agents has been moved to Annex 2, "Flammable Anesthetizing Locations.")

Storage requirements for freestanding cylinders and containers (i.e., those not in the room where the manifold for a piped system is installed) are now listed in 8-3.1.11.

(a)* *Nonflammable Gases (Any Quantity; In-Storage, Connected, or Both)*

**A-4-3.1.1.2(a)**  This includes oxidizing gases.

1.   Sources of heat in storage locations shall be protected or located so that cylinders or compressed gases shall not be heated to the activation point of integral safety devices. In no case shall the temperature of the cylinders exceed 130°F (54°C). Care shall be exercised when handling cylinders that have been exposed to freezing temperatures or containers that contain cryogenic liquids to prevent injury to the skin.
2.*  Enclosures shall be provided for supply systems cylinder storage or manifold locations for oxidizing agents such as oxygen and nitrous oxide. Such enclosures shall be constructed of an assembly of building materials with a fire-resistive rating of at least 1 hour and shall not communicate directly with anesthetizing locations. Other nonflammable (inert) medical gases may be stored in the enclosure. [Flammable gases shall not be stored with oxidizing agents.] Storage of full or empty cylinders is permitted. Such enclosures shall serve no other purpose.

The intent of sentence 4 in subparagraph (a)2 is for flammable gases to be stored separately from oxidizing gases. It is acceptable for inert gases to be stored with oxidizing or flammable gases. (See Exhibit 4.1.)

**A-4-3.1.1.2(a)2**  Conductive flooring is not required in cylinder storage locations that are not a part of a surgical or obstetrical suite.

Conductive flooring is not required for those cylinder storage locations or manifold enclosures used only for nonflammable medical gases *(see 2-6.5 of Annex 2).*

**Exhibit 4.1** *Medical gas cylinders stored in a wire mesh enclosure in a loading dock area.*

3. Provisions shall be made for racks or fastenings to protect cylinders from accidental damage or dislocation.
4. The electric installation in storage locations or manifold enclosures for nonflammable medical gases shall comply with the standards of NFPA 70, *National Electrical Code*, for ordinary locations. Electric wall fixtures, switches, and receptacles shall be installed in fixed locations not less than 152 cm (5 ft) above the floor as a precaution against their physical damage.
5. Storage locations for oxygen and nitrous oxide shall be kept free of flammable materials *[see also 4-3.1.1.2(a)7]*.

   Although nonflammable compressed gases are to be kept separated from volatile liquids and flammable gases, oxygen and nitrous oxide gas cylinders can be stored together.

6. Cylinders containing compressed gases and containers for volatile liquids shall be kept away from radiators, steam piping, and like sources of heat.
7. Combustible materials, such as paper, cardboard, plastics, and fabrics, shall not be stored or kept near supply system cylinders or manifolds containing oxygen or nitrous oxide. Racks for cylinder storage shall be permitted to be of wooden construction. Wrappers shall be removed prior to storage.

   Wooden storage racks are permitted as a result of a Formal Interpretation by the former Technical Committee on Anesthetizing Agents in July 1976. The committee incorporated the allowance during the revision for the 1978 edition of NFPA 56A, *Standard on the Use of Inhalation Anesthetics*. It was pointed out that such racks were economical, convenient, and not proven to be a hazard over the test of time. (Note: This is the only exception with respect to combustible materials within gas cylinder storage rooms.)

*Exception: Shipping crates or storage cartons for cylinders.*

8. When cylinder valve protection caps are supplied, they shall be secured tightly in place unless the cylinder is connected for use.

   If a cylinder that does not have a cylinder valve protection cap falls, the cylinder valve could snap off. Depending on cylinder size, quantity of gas within the cylinder, and the orifice size at the break, the cylinder could be propelled rapidly and/or violently about after it landed on the floor.

9. Containers shall not be stored in a tightly closed space such as a closet *[see 8-2.1.2.3(c)]*.

   Note that this restriction applies only to containers (i.e., low-pressure vessels) because this type of storage vessel continuously vents small amounts of gaseous oxygen vapor to prevent overpressurization of the container.

10. *Location of Supply Systems.*

    A fire in a room that contained both cylinders and compressors could damage intake pipes, causing the compressors to then spread products of combustion throughout the piping distribution system. In turn, a fire from a compressor could damage cylinders or cylinder valves, providing more gases for combustion.

    These dangers emphasize the requirement that nothing is to be placed in a supply system storage location except the cylinders and containers of nonflammable gases.

    There is no prohibition against medical air compressors and vacuum pumps being in the same room as air handlers, chillers, or gas hot water heaters. The reason for this, in part, is the requirement for air compressor intakes and vacuum pump exhausts to be located outdoors.

    a. Except as permitted by 4-3.1.1.2(a)10c, supply systems for medical gases or mixtures of these gases having total capacities (connected and in storage) not exceeding the quantities specified in 4-3.1.1.2(b)1 and 2 shall be located outdoors in an enclosure used only for this purpose or in a room or enclosure used only for this purpose situated within a building used for other purposes.

    b. Storage facilities that are outside, but adjacent to a building wall, shall be in accordance with NFPA 50, *Standard for Bulk Oxygen Systems at Consumer Sites*.

    This requirement addresses the safety concerns created by an outdoor cylinder or container storage-facility (i.e., one not enclosed in a 1-hour fire-rated enclosure) located near windows.

   c. Locations for supply systems shall not be used for storage purposes other than for containers of nonflammable gases. Storage of full or empty containers shall be permitted. Other nonflammable medical gas supply systems or storage locations shall be permitted to be in the same location with oxygen or nitrous oxide or both. However, care shall be taken to provide adequate ventilation to dissipate such other gases in order to prevent the development of oxygen-deficient atmospheres in the event of functioning of cylinder or manifold pressure-relief devices.
   d. Air compressors and vacuum pumps shall be located separately from cylinder patient gas systems or cylinder storage enclosures. Air compressors shall be installed in a designated mechanical equipment area, adequately ventilated and with required services.

Prior to the 1996 edition, this requirement was only directly applicable to *medical* air compressors and vacuum pumps. It was revised in 1996 to apply to any compressor or vacuum system covered in Chapter 4, that is, Level 1, Level 2, Level 3, or Level 4.

11. *Construction and Arrangement of Supply System Locations.*

   a. Walls, floors, ceilings, roofs, doors, interior finish, shelves, racks, and supports of and in the locations cited in 4-3.1.1.2(a)10a shall be constructed of noncombustible or limited-combustible materials.
   b. Locations for supply systems for oxygen, nitrous oxide, or mixtures of these gases shall not communicate with anesthetizing locations or storage locations for flammable anesthetizing agents.
   c. Enclosures for supply systems shall be provided with doors or gates that can be locked.

Although there is no requirement that storage rooms for gases be locked, they need to be "secured" if the public has access. In light of reported thefts of nitrous oxide cylinders for substance-abuse purposes, and to prevent unauthorized persons (including small children) from creating a hazard or harming themselves, some means of limiting access to storage rooms is prudent.

   d. Ordinary electrical wall fixtures in supply rooms shall be installed in fixed locations not less than 5 ft (1.5 m) above the floor to avoid physical damage.
   e. Where enclosures (interior or exterior) for supply systems are located near sources of heat, such as furnaces, incinerators, or boiler rooms, they shall be of construction that protects cylinders from reaching temperatures exceeding 130°F (54°C). Open electrical conductors and transformers shall not be located in close proximity to enclosures. Such enclosures shall not be located adjacent to storage tanks for flammable or combustible liquids.
   f. Smoking shall be prohibited in supply system enclosures
   g. Heating shall be by steam, hot water, or other indirect means. Cylinder temperatures shall not exceed 130°F (54°C).

Indirect heating means that the "source" of the heat is "outside" the room. Only the resulting heat (in the form of warm air, hot water pipes, steam pipes) will pass into the room.

(b) *Additional Storage Requirements for Nonflammable Gases Greater Than 3000 ft³ (85 m³).*

Prior to the 1993 edition of this standard, the dividing line for requirements of storage systems was 2000 ft³ (57 m³). This limit was based on the use of four oxygen and two nitrous oxide cylinders of "G" size. The limit of 2000 ft³ (57 m³) was increased to 3000 ft³ (85 m³) to reflect current practice, with appropriate safety, of using larger "H" size cylinders. The committee has received no reports of hazards using this size cylinder.

1. Oxygen supply systems or storage locations having a total capacity of more than 20,000 ft³ (566 m³) (NTP), including unconnected reserves on hand at the site, shall comply with NFPA 50, *Standard for Bulk Oxygen Systems at Consumer Sites.*

   NFPA 50, *Standard for Bulk Oxygen Systems at Consumer Sites* [1], requires bulk systems to be located either outside or in a building used only for that purpose. Because this paragraph requires locations storing more than 20,000 ft³ (566 m³) of oxygen to comply with NFPA 50, the maximum amount of oxygen that can be stored inside a health care facility is 20,000 ft³ (566 m³).

   As noted previously, there are portions of Chapter 4 of NFPA 99 that are also applicable to bulk oxygen systems. (See commentary under 4-3.1.1.)

2. Nitrous oxide supply systems or storage locations having a total capacity of 3200 lb (1452 kg) [28,000 ft³ (793 m³) (NTP)] or more, including unconnected reserves on hand at the site, shall comply with CGA Pamphlet G-8.1, *Standard for the Installation of Nitrous Oxide Systems at Consumer Sites.*
3. The walls, floors, and ceilings of locations for supply systems of more than 3000 ft³ (85 m³) total capacity (connected and in storage) separating the supply system location from other occupancies in a building shall have a fire resistance rating of at least 1 hour. This shall also apply to a common wall or walls of a supply system location attached to a building having other occupancy.
4. Locations for supply systems of more than 3000 ft³ (85 m³) total capacity (connected and in storage) shall be vented to the outside by a dedicated mechanical ventilation system or by natural venting. If natural venting is used, the vent opening or openings shall be a minimum of 72 in.² (0.05 m²) in total free area.

   Venting systems for gas storage locations should not be interconnected with other facility air-handling systems.

(c) *Storage Requirements for Nonflammable Gases Less Than 3000 ft³ (85 m³).* Doors to such locations shall be provided with louvered openings having a minimum of

72 in.$^2$ (0.05 m$^2$) in total free area. Where the location of the supply system door opens onto an exit access corridor, louvered openings shall not be used, and the requirements of 4-3.1.1.2(b) 3 and 4 and the dedicated mechanical ventilation system required in 4-3.1.1.2(b)4 shall be complied with.

> When a manifold or other bulk storage room opens onto an exit access corridor, it could be dangerous to have excess nonflammable gases dumping into this corridor when it is being used as an exit from a fire or other emergency. The change to this paragraph mandates the use of dedicated mechanical ventilation. This ventilation would be in operation 24 hours a day and would remove any gases vented from the tanks or other storage containers directly to the outside of the facility. Before this 1999 edition, the standard allowed louvered vents in the doors under other circumstances. These louvered vents would occasionally exist in doors that led into exit access corridors.
>
> Venting is deemed necessary regardless of the amount of gas stored because a closed room presents the possibility of creating an increased combustion-supporting atmosphere from a leaking cylinder. Storage of liquid oxygen in containers in a closed room would be extremely hazardous because containers continually vent a small amount of gas to the atmosphere.
>
> The requirements for storage locations that have openings onto exit access corridors were modified in 1996 to correlate with NFPA *101, Life Safety Code.* [2]

### 4-3.1.1.3 Material—Oxygen Compatibility.

(a)* Oxygen system components, including, but not limited to, containers, valves, valve seats, lubricants, fittings, gaskets, and interconnecting equipment including hoses, shall have adequate compatibility with oxygen under the conditions of temperature and pressure to which the components may be exposed in the containment and use of oxygen. Easily ignitible materials shall be avoided unless they are parts of equipment or systems that are approved, listed, or proved suitable by tests or by past experience.

A-4-3.1.1.3(a) Compatibility involves both combustibility and ease of ignition. Materials that burn in air will burn violently in pure oxygen at normal pressure and explosively in pressurized oxygen. Also, many materials that do not burn in air will do so in pure oxygen, particularly under pressure. Metals for containers and piping must be carefully selected, depending on service conditions. The various steels are acceptable for many applications, but some service conditions can call for other materials (usually copper or its alloys) because of their greater resistance to ignition and lower rate of combustion.

Similarly, materials that can be ignited in air have lower ignition energies in oxygen. Many such materials can be ignited by friction at a valve seat or stem packing or by adiabatic compression produced when oxygen at high pressure is rapidly introduced into a system initially at low pressure.

(b) The provisions of 4-3.1.1.3(a) also apply to nitrous oxide, oxygen-nitrous oxide mixtures, and to other medical gas mixtures containing more than 23.5 percent oxygen.

(c)  Manufactured assemblies in which are intended to be piped nitrous oxide or oxygen shall be (1) constructed of metal, or (2) tested to pass a minimum 200 flame spread rating and 200 smoke developed index in accordance with NFPA 255, *Standard Method of Test of Surface Burning Characteristics of Building Materials*, or, if constructed of polymers (plastic, fiberglass, etc.), a rating of 94 VO or better.

> These requirements for the construction of manufactured assemblies take into consideration the possibility that an oxygen-enriched atmosphere can be created inside the assembly should there be a leak or rupture inside the enclosure. The guidance listed is not sufficient by itself to prevent all problems should a fire occur. Additional fire safety measures should be considered for areas where these assemblies are installed.

**4-3.1.1.4  Gas Central Supply Systems.**  The central supply system shall be a system of cylinders and necessary supply equipment assembled as described in either 4-3.1.1.5 or 4-3.1.1.6, or a bulk supply system *(see 4-3.1.1.7)*, which can be of the permanently installed type or the trailer type. The medical air source, in addition to the preceding, shall be permitted to be two or more compressors that deliver medical air and that comply with 4-3.1.1.2(a)10b, 4-3.1.1.2(b)2, and 4-3.1.1.9.

> Backfeeding is a way of pressurizing a piped gas system through a station outlet and is opposite to the normal way of pressurizing a system. It is sometimes done when the supply source is interrupted or portions of the system need to shut down. This is a very poor practice. Station outlets were designed for flow in an outward direction. Outlets are also designed for certain pressures, such as 50 psig (345 kPa) for air and oxygen and approximately 200 psig (1379 kPa) for nitrogen. Backfeeding from a cylinder could mean a pressure up to 2000 psig (13,793 kPa) could suddenly appear at the outlet. Backfeeding should not be done except under certain circumstances such as planned temporary shutdowns.

**4-3.1.1.5\*  Cylinder Systems Without Reserve Supply.**  *(See Figure 4-3.1.1.5.)*

**A-4-3.1.1.5**  See C-4.1 and C-4.2.

(a)  A cylinder manifold shall have two banks (or units) of cylinders that alternately supply the piping system, each bank having a pressure regulator and cylinders connected to a common header. Each bank shall contain a minimum of two cylinders or at least an average day's supply unless normal delivery schedules require a greater supply. When the content of the primary bank is unable to supply the system, the secondary bank shall automatically operate to supply the system. An actuating switch shall be connected to the master signal panels to indicate when, or just before, the changeover to the secondary bank occurs.

(b)  A check valve shall be installed between each cylinder lead and the manifold header to prevent the loss of gas from the manifolded cylinders in the event the pressure relief device on an individual cylinder functions or a cylinder lead (pigtail) fails. The check valve shall be of a material suitable for the gases and pressures involved.

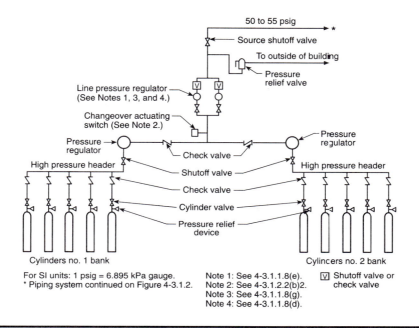

**Figure 4-3.1.1.5** *Typical cylinder supply system without reserve supply (schematic). Supply systems with different arrangements of valves and regulators are permissible if they provide equivalent safeguards. (Level 1 Gas Systems)*

A check valve is needed for situations when the pressure relief valve on a cylinder functions or a cylinder lead fails in order to prevent backfeeding from one cylinder to another. (See Exhibit 4.2.)

**4-3.1.1.6\* Cylinder Supply Systems with Reserve Supply.** *(See Figure 4-3.1.1.6.)*

**A-4-3.1.1.6** See C-4.1 and C-4.2.

(a)  A cylinder supply system with reserve supply shall consist of:

1. A primary supply, which supplies the piping system.
2. A secondary supply, which shall operate automatically when the primary supply is unable to supply the system. An actuating switch shall be connected to the master signal panels to indicate when, or just before, the changeover to the secondary bank occurs.
3. A reserve supply, which shall operate automatically in the event that both the primary and secondary supplies are unable to supply the system. An actuating switch shall be connected to the master signal panels to indicate when, or just before, the reserve begins to supply the piping system.

***Exhibit 4.2*** *Cylinder manifold source for a nitrous oxide piped gas system.*

(b)* The reserve supply shall consist of three or more manifolded high-pressure cylinders connected as required under 4-3.1.1.8(b), and either shall be equipped with check valves as required in 4-3.1.1.5(b) or shall be provided with an actuating switch that shall operate the master signals when the reserve supply drops to one day's supply.

The reserve supply, as noted, consists of high-pressure gas cylinders, as opposed to low-pressure cryogenic containers. Containers are not used as reserve supplies in these types of systems because they can loose approximately 3 percent per day in boil-off and might not contain enough, or any, gas when needed (i.e., when the main or primary supply is depleted).

**A-4-3.1.1.6(b)** See C-4.1 and C-4.2.

(c)* A cryogenic liquid storage vessel shall be installed either as indicated in Figure 4-3.1.1.6, or as indicated in Figure 4-3.1.1.5 with the addition of a reserve supply connected as shown in Figure 4-3.1.1.6.

**A-4-3.1.1.6(c)** See C-4.1 and C-4.2.

(d) When cryogenic liquid storage vessels are designed to prevent the loss of the gas produced by the evaporation of the cryogenic liquid in the secondary supply, they shall be designed so that the gas produced shall pass through the line pressure regulator before entering the piped distribution system.

(e) Cryogenic liquid storage vessels shall be constructed to withstand high pressure [2200 psig (15.2 MPa gauge)] or shall be provided with suitable pressure relief devices upstream of the control unit.

(f) Cylinder supply systems designed in accordance with 4-3.1.1.6 do not require check valves between each cylinder lead and the manifold header on the primary and secondary supplies.

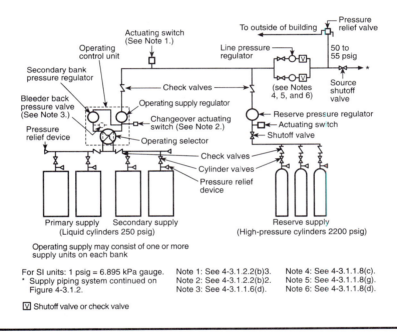

**Figure 4-3.1.1.6** *Typical cylinder supply system with reserve supply (schematic). Supply systems with different arrangements of valves and regulators are permissible if they provide equivalent safeguards. (Level 1 Gas Systems)*

**4-3.1.1.7\* Bulk Medical Gas Systems.** *(See Figure 4-3.1.1.7.)*

As noted in the commentary under 4-3.1.1, portions of Chapter 4 of NFPA 99 are relevant for bulk medical gas systems.

The selection of the type of bulk system a facility will use is made based on economics and convenience. The decision will particularly affect the master alarms. Users are cautioned to observe the different alarm requirements for each bulk system type listed here.

The requirements of NFPA 50 for bulk supply systems are an important aspect of a medical facility's piped gas system. Highlighting NFPA 54, *National Fuel Gas Code* [3], will hopefully send the reader and code official to NFPA 54 for information on the installation, testing, and performance of bulk supplies of medical gases. The need to properly maintain the tank farm is as important as the need to maintain the piped gas system. Many instances affecting patient care have occurred as a result of an improperly maintained bulk system or the improper liquefied gas being placed into the bulk vessel.

**A-4-3.1.1.7** See C-4.1 and C-4.2 and NFPA 50, *Standard for Bulk Oxygen Systems at Consumer Sites.*

The bulk supply system should be installed on a site that has been prepared to meet the requirements of NFPA 50, *Standard for Bulk Oxygen Systems at Consumer Sites*, or CGA Pamphlet G-8.1, *Standard for the Installation of Nitrous Oxide Systems at Consumer Sites*. Storage unit(s), reserve, pressure regulation, and signal actuating switch(es) are components of the supply system. Shutoff valves, piping from the site, and electric wiring from a signal switch(es) to the master signal panels are components of the piping system.

The bulk supply system is normally installed on the site by the owner of this system. It is the responsibility of the owner or the organization responsible for the operation and maintenance of the bulk supply system to ensure that all components of the supply system—main supply, reserve supply, supply system signal actuating switch(es), and delivery pressure regulation equipment—function properly before the system is put in service.

(a) The bulk system shall consist of two sources of supply, one of which shall be a reserve supply for use only in an emergency. An actuating switch shall be connected to the master signal panels to indicate when, or just before, the reserve begins to supply the system. There are two types of bulk supply systems:

1. The alternating type with two or more units alternately supplying the piping system. When the primary supply is unable to supply the bulk system, the secondary supply automatically becomes the primary supply and a new secondary supply, not the reserve supply, is connected when or before this changeover takes place. An actuating switch shall be connected to the master signal panels to indicate when, or just before, the changeover occurs.
2. The continuous type with one or more units continuously supplying the piping system while another unit remains as the reserve supply and operates only in case of an emergency.

(b) The secondary supply and the reserve supply referred to in 4-3.1.1.7(a) shall each contain at least an average day's supply and shall consist of the following:

See Exhibit 4.3.

1. Three or more manifolded high-pressure cylinders connected as required under 4-3.1.1.5(a) and 4-3.1.1.8(b), and provided with an actuating switch, which shall operate

***Exhibit 4.3*** *Storage tanks, holding bulk supplies of liquid oxygen, which are usually found in health care facilities. The smaller tank acts as a reserve supply. Note the security fencing and the signs prohibiting smoking in the vicinity.*

the master alarm signal when the reserve supply is reduced to one day's average supply; or

2. A cryogenic liquid storage unit used as the reserve for a bulk supply system provided with an actuating switch that shall operate the master alarm signal when the contents of the reserve are reduced to one day's average supply, and another actuating switch that shall operate the master alarm signal if the gas pressure available in the reserve unit is reduced below the pressure required to function properly. It shall also be designed to prevent the loss of gas produced by the evaporation of the cryogenic liquid in the reserve and so that the gas produced shall pass through a line pressure regulator before entering the piped distribution system.

A cryogenic system is allowed as a reserve supply, but only if it is connected to the master alarm panel as indicated. Cryogenic systems continually boil off gas, so it is critical that their status be monitored. While evaporating gas may be channeled into the piping system, its loss means that much less will remain in the container for use when the primary supply is depleted.

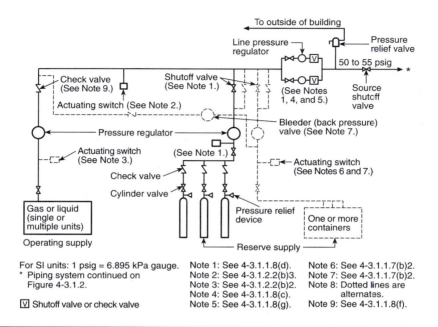

For SI units: 1 psig = 6.895 kPa gauge.
* Piping system continued on
Figure 4-3.1.2.

Ⅴ Shutoff valve or check valve

Note 1: See 4-3.1.1.8(d).
Note 2: See 4-3.1.2.2(b)3.
Note 3: See 4-3.1.2.2(b)2.
Note 4: See 4-3.1.1.8(c).
Note 5: See 4-3.1.1.8(g).

Note 6: See 4-3.1.1.7(b)2.
Note 7: See 4-3.1.1.7(b)2.
Note 8: Dotted lines are
alternates.
Note 9: See 4-3.1.1.8(f).

*Figure 4-3.1.1.7* *Typical bulk supply system (schematic). Bulk supply systems with different arrangements of valves, regulators, and gas supply units are permissible if they provide equivalent safeguards. The reserve supply shown in dotted lines indicates the arrangements outlined in 4-3.1.1.7(b)2 or 3. (Level 1 Gas Systems)*

**4-3.1.1.8\* General Requirements for Gas Central Supply Systems.** Piped oxygen and medical air shall not be piped to, or used for, any purpose except for use in patient care applications.

> The 1999 edition includes all gas systems that could produce an asphyxiating environment during a relieving scenario (e.g., nitrogen, argon, carbon dioxide). A release of an asphyxiating gas in an enclosed area could be hazardous to persons inside or around the immediate area. All gases, except medical air, should be vented to the outside to prevent this occurrence.

**A-4-3.1.1.8** This should include fueling torches, blowing down or drying any equipment such as lab equipment, endoscopy or other scopes, or any other purposes. Also prohibited is using the oxygen or medical air to raise, lower, or otherwise operate booms or other devices in ORs or other areas.

(a) *Cylinders.* Cylinders shall be designed, constructed, tested, and maintained in accordance with 4-3.1.1.1(a). Cylinders in service shall be adequately secured. Cylinders in storage shall be secured and located to prevent them from falling or being knocked over.

(b) *Manifolds.* Manifolds shall be of substantial construction and of a design and materials suitable for the gases and pressures involved. Mechanical means shall be provided to ensure the connection of cylinders containing the proper gas to the manifold. Cylinder valve outlets and manifold or regulator inlet connections shall comply with the CGA Pamphlet V-1, *Standard for Compressed Gas Cylinder Valve Outlet and Inlet Connections* (ANSI B57.1, CGA B96). When any nonflammable medical gases or gas mixtures are to be piped, care shall be taken to ensure noninterchangeability of cylinders or equipment. Manifolds shall be obtained from and installed under the supervision of a manufacturer or supplier familiar with proper practices for their construction and use.

(c) *Pressure Regulation.* Pressure-regulating equipment shall be installed in the supply main upstream of the final line-pressure relief valve *[see 4-3.1.1.8(e)]*. Where multiple piping systems for the same gas at different operating pressures are required, separate pressure-regulating equipment, relief valves, and source shutoff valves shall be provided for each pressure.

Sentence 2 recognizes that there are numerous piped gas systems that use the same gas sources or manifolds but have varying operating system distribution pressure requirements. The committee believes that the overall safety of a system operating at several different pressures should be equal to that of a system at a single operating pressure. Each section within an operating system that operates at a different pressure should be independent of other section(s).

(d) *Shutoff Valves.* A manually operated shutoff valve shall be installed upstream of each pressure regulator, and a shutoff valve or a check valve shall be installed downstream.

For criteria of shutoff valves for the distribution portion of a piped gas system, see 4-3.1.2.3.

(e) *Pressure Relief Valves.* Each central supply system shall have a pressure relief valve set at 50 percent above normal line pressure, installed downstream of the pressure regulator and upstream of any shutoff valve. This pressure relief valve shall be permitted to be set at a higher pressure, provided another pressure relief valve set at 50 percent above normal line pressure is installed in the main supply line. All pressure relief valves shall close automatically when excess pressure has been released. Pressure relief valves set at 50 percent above normal line pressure shall be vented to the outside from all gas systems, except medical air, or if the total capacity of the supply system is in excess of 3000 ft³ (85 m³) of gas. Pressure relief valves shall be of brass or bronze and specially designed for the gas service involved.

1. The pressure relief valve downstream of the line pressure regulator in nitrogen systems used to provide power for gas-driven medical tools or instruments, and for other systems that vary from the normal 50- to 55-psig (340- to 380-kPa gauge) line pressure (for example, systems supplying medical gases to hyperbaric chambers), shall be set at 50 percent above line pressure.

The location of the pressure relief valve in relation to shutoff valves is important. There should be no shutoff valve positioned in a location that would allow pressure to build up in the supply portion of a system if the shutoff valve were closed.

(f) *Check Valves.* Supply systems complying with 4-3.1.1.6 or 4-3.1.1.7 *(see Figures 4-3.1.1.6 and 4-3.1.1.7)* shall have a check valve in the primary supply main, upstream of the point of intersection with the secondary or reserve supply main.

(g) *Final Line Regulators.* Final line regulators shall be duplexed with suitable valving to permit service to the regulators without completely shutting down the gas piping system.

This requirement, added in 1990, originally allowed regulators for all new central supply systems to be either duplexed or placed in a three-valve bypass arrangement. This requirement was altered in 1996 to require a full bypass arrangement to prevent pressures of possibly 150 psig to 300 psig (1034 kPa to 2069 kPa) or more from entering the distribution pipeline. These pressures could readily damage pressure switches, station outlets, and so forth not designed for such pressures.

Bypasses are intended to facilitate serviceability while a system remains in operation and can be arranged in a variety of ways to facilitate this objective. The committee considers regulators particularly likely to require service, the reason for mandating bypass requirements.

(h) *Emergency Oxygen Supply Connection.* Where the cryogenic oxygen supply is located outside of the building served, there shall be incorporated in the piping system and inlet for connecting a temporary auxiliary source of supply for emergency or maintenance situations. The inlet shall be located on the exterior of the building served and shall be physically protected to prevent tampering and unauthorized access. It shall be labeled "EMERGENCY LOW PRESSURE GASEOUS OXYGEN INLET." This connection shall be installed downstream of the shutoff valve on the main supply line *[see 4-3.1.2.3(b)]* and be suitably controlled with the necessary valves to allow emergency supply of oxygen and isolation of the piping to the normal source of supply. It shall have one check valve in the main line between the main line shutoff valve and the tee'd connection and one check valve between the tee'd connection and the emergency supply shutoff valve. *[See Figure 4-3.1.1.8(h) and Figure 4-3.1.2.]*

Placing the relief valve downstream instead of upstream of the check valve on the emergency fill line better protects the patient if someone overpressured the emergency low-pressure oxygen connection. In the present location, if someone realized the error of overpressuring the patient side of the check valve, this pressure would be greater than the pressure between the emergency connection at the box and the check valve located on the emergency low-pressure oxygen connection. The relief valve would no longer protect the patient.

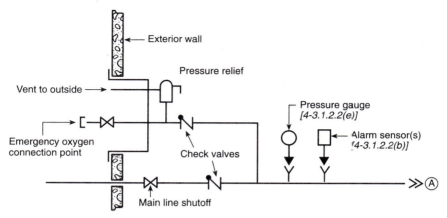

**Figure 4-3.1.1.8(h)** *Emergency oxygen supply connection.*

1. The emergency oxygen supply connection piping assembly shall be provided with a pressure relief valve of adequate size to protect the downstream piping system and related equipment from exposure to pressures in excess of 50 percent higher than normal pipeline pressure.
2. The inlet shall be female NPT, sized for 100 percent of the system demand at the emergency source gas pressure.

The purpose of this connection is to allow the facility to be supplied from a temporary source of oxygen while repairs to or the replacement of an outdoor oxygen supply source is completed. The connection should be sufficiently remote from the supply source to allow this temporary connection without impeding the work that is being done on the bulk system. It would be inappropriate, therefore, to locate the connection within the enclosure around the source supply or in any area where access to the supply source would be compromised while using the connection.

The connection should be located in an area that will remain accessible in any weather. It would be unsuitable, for example, to require a temporary source vehicle to have to traverse a lawn or snow drifts to supply the facility in an emergency.

Prior to the 1993 edition, no specific fitting-type connection was identified. This resulted in a number of different, and potentially hazardous, practices that were reported to the committee (e.g., a high-pressure connection to a low-pressure line). For 1996 the committee received numerous requests to define the type of connector at the emergency connection of the connector. The committee considered that identifying the capacity was a more appropriate manor of defining the requirement. (See Exhibit 4.4.)

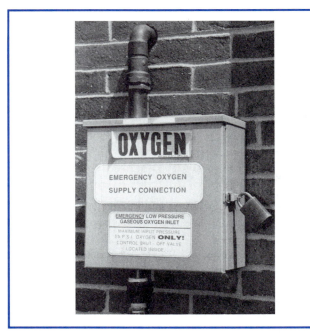

***Exhibit 4.4*** *An emergency oxygen supply inlet used in case of failure of the normal source.*

3. The emergency oxygen supply connection shall be located on the main building where it is accessible by emergency supply vehicle at all times in all weather conditions. The connection shall not be mounted on or at the main oxygen supply source.

**4-3.1.1.9 Medical Air Compressor Supply Systems.** See Figure 4-3.1.1.9.

Figure 4-3.1.1.9 has been extensively revised for the 1999 edition. Previously, facilities, designers, and manufacturers were compelled to design their systems exactly as shown, that is, compressors-receiver, dryers-filters, and so forth. Since NFPA does not intend to restrict technology or design, the previous diagram constituted a potential for misapplication of NFPA 99. The new diagram allows for other sequences of equipment as long as the net result is that medical air meets the requirements of NFPA 99.

The redesign of the diagram is intended to reflect the various subsystems that comprise a medical air plant. The diagram includes only the elements mentioned in the text, but otherwise it is intentionally devoid of further detail regarding organization, order, or technology. Specific design detail is left to the manufacturer and facility owner.

Critical to use of this diagram are the specific references included in each

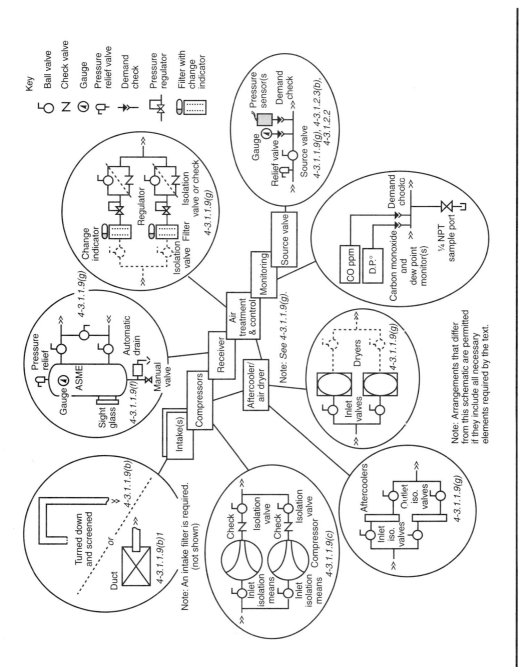

***Figure 4-3.1.1.9*** *Typical duplex medical air compressor system (schematic). (Level 1 Gas Systems)*

blowup detail and especially the note that reads: "Arrangements which differ from this schematic are permitted if they include all necessary elements required by the text." The user is cautioned to refer to the text first and to use the diagram only to illuminate the text.

(The requirements in this section are written to assist in the construction of a system capable of producing *medical air* in a wide range of situations. The following requirements were developed within the framework of the definition of *medical air,* as defined in Chapter 2. A clear comprehension of the definition of this term is beneficial for understanding the requirements of this section.)

This section applies to compressed air systems that will be used to distribute medical compressed air throughout a facility and that are intended or expected to provide air for direct patient purposes. Special, limited systems would not necessarily fall within this intent. However, any such system should be totally separate and noninterconnectable to the medical air system. If that system were intended for the driving of dynamic devices with medical applications, such as dental drills, the requirements of Level 3 compressed air (see 4-5.1.1.3) would be applicable.

Design criteria for equipment components of the medical air compressor system are addressed as they relate to the safety of the system. Efficacy criteria are not within the scope of the committee.

The number of individual devices and the accompanying risk of the failure of a single device rendering the entire medical air supply system unusable have been considered since the 1990 edition of NFPA 99. This problem has been addressed through provisions for duplexing or bypassing each important element (device) in the system. Should any device fail, the system could be kept in operation while that element was serviced or replaced. The 1996 edition limited the earlier allowance for "three valve bypasses" in certain instances and required full bypass arrangements for more sensitive devices, such as regulators and filters. The decision to duplex or use a bypass arrangement should be based on the degree of importance of the device to the effective operation of the system. For example, if the receiver were removed from the system, the compressor might short-cycle, causing some compressors to be partially or even totally damaged.

The term *oil-free compressor* was eliminated in the 1993 edition of NFPA 99. In its place a set of criteria for a *medical air compressor* was developed that, under a single component failure, would not introduce contaminants into the medical compressed air chamber or supply lines. (See commentary in Chapter 2 under the terms *medical air compressor* and *medical air* for further discussion.)

See Exhibits 4.5, 4.6, and 4.7.

(a)* *General.* The medical air compressor shall take its source from the outside atmosphere and shall not add contaminants in the form of particulate matter, odor, or other gases. It shall be connected only to the medical air piping distribution system and shall not be used for any other purpose.

***Exhibit 4.5*** *A medical compressed air source. Compressors are in the foreground of this unit, the receiver is in the middle, and dryers are in the background.*

***Exhibit 4.6*** *Twin-tower desiccant dryer and refrigerated noncycling dryer installed near medical air compressor. The desiccant unit is the facility's primary dryer with the refrigerated unit used when the desiccant is being serviced.*

**Exhibit 4.7** *Main shutoff valves and filters for a medical compressed air system.*

The medical air compressor is also not to be used for air-driven patient therapy devices such as air cushion mattresses, for cleaning or blowing down scopes either before or after use of sterilizers, for laboratory or pneumatic temperature controllers, or for other nonpatient functions. The use of the medical air compressor to power pneumatically driven arms, booms, pendants, or columns is also inappropriate.

**A-4-3.1.1.9(a)** It is the intent that the medical air piping distribution system support only the intended need for breathable air for such items as IPPB and long-term respiratory assistance needs, anesthesia machines, and so forth. The system is not intended to be used to provide engineering, maintenance, and equipment needs for general hospital support use. It is the intent that the life safety nature of the medical air be protected by a system dedicated solely for its specific use. The medical air distribution system could also supply air-driven instruments that exhaust into the pharynx. This might be a dental or other surgical device.

As a compressed air supply source, a medical air compressor should not be used to supply air for other purposes because such use could increase service interruptions, reduce service life, and introduce additional opportunities for contamination.

(b) *Compressor Intake.* Except as provided in 4-3.1.1.9(b)1, the intake to medical air compressors shall be located outdoors above roof level a minimum distance of 10 ft (3 m) from any door, window, exhaust, other intake, or opening in the building, and a minimum distance of 20 ft (6 m) above the ground. Intakes shall be turned down and screened or otherwise be protected against the entry of vermin or water, with screening that shall be fabricated or composed of a noncorrosive material such as stainless steel or other suitable material. Compressor intake piping shall be of materials approved for vacuum piping under

4-3.2.2.2(a) that will not add contaminants in the form of particulate matter, odor, or other gases. *(See C-4.2.6.)*

1. If a source is available that is equal to or better than outside air (air already filtered for use in operating room ventilating systems, for example), it shall be permitted to be used for the medical air compressors. This alternate source of supply air must be available on a continuous 24-hour-per-day, 7-day-per-week basis. Ventilating systems having fans with motors or drive belts located in the air stream shall not be used as a source of medical air intake.
2. The compressor air intake shall be located where no contamination from engine exhausts, fuel storage vents, vacuum system discharges, particulate matter, or odor of any type is anticipated.

Air intakes for separate compressors shall be permitted to be joined together to one common intake, provided such intake is appropriately sized. Where this is done, open inlet piping to a compressor removed for service shall be isolated by manual or check valve, blind flange, or tube cap to prevent backflow.

No decision will have greater impact on the ongoing quality of medical air than the location of the intake. Location is a decision unique to each site, and the dimensions cited should be considered as the starting point in a detailed site investigation. The occurrences of contaminated air are frequently found to be associated with intake placement close to, or downwind of, vacuum exhausts, WAGD exhausts, laboratory or sanitary vents, HVAC exhausts, loading docks, and other sources of polluted air.

If a building has a series of stepped (staggered) roofs, the best location for the intake becomes more complicated to determine. Meeting all the requirements of this section does not necessarily mean locating the intake above the highest roof. Factors such as the size of each roof, the nearest doors and windows, and other equipment on the roof all influence the final location(s). Criteria on the type of screening that is permissible were added in 1993 to protect patient safety. Note that the screening has to be noncorrosive.

The piping material from the intake to the compressor was specified for the first time in the 1996 edition as a result of numerous inquiries received by the committee concerning whether the compressor intake piping had to be high temperature brazed, similar to the pressurized portion of the gas piping system. The choice of materials also suitable for vacuum service reflects the need for materials that are durable and will not corrode, but also recognizes the low-pressure nature of an air intake. The allowance of stainless steel permits an occasional but acceptable practice. The actual selection of material should be made taking into consideration the type of compressor and the economic advantages of available materials.

It is advisable to conduct periodic tests to verify that the alternative source [subparagraph (b)1] is equal to or better than the ambient source and that it remains that way. Conditions can change, causing the source of air to become unacceptable.

The air characteristics to be tested can be determined by reference to the definition of *medical air* and a review of local air quality records.

The committee now requires alternative sources of air to be available 24 hours per day. This means such sources need to be maintained at all times. Many air-handling systems that might be used as a source of air are shut off during nonpeak times, thus lowering the quality and quantity of air within the system.

A major concern of the committee is that of air taken from air ventilating systems that have motors and bearing systems in the air duct. On failure, these systems can generate noxious vapors that would be taken in by the compressor.

Running a common intake for several compressors is often done when intakes would have to be piped considerable distances. When it is done, care must be taken to size the intake and intake filter(s) appropriately. In addition, isolation means are necessary to prevent room air from being drawn into the operating compressor(s) when other compressors are removed from service. If proper isolation or valving at compressors is not installed, equipment can be damaged and pipelines contaminated.

(c) *Multiple Compressors.* Two or more compressors shall be installed that serve this system alternately or simultaneously on demand. The compressor(s) shall be sized to serve peak demand with the largest compressor out of service. Each compressor shall have an automatic means to prevent backflow through off-cycle units and a shut-off valve to isolate it from the centrally piped system and other compressors for maintenance or repair without loss of pressure in the system.

The design principle is for any single compressor to be able to be removed from service for maintenance or replacement, without compromising the ability of the remaining compressor(s) to meet the demand. The actual sizing of the medical compressed air system requires a detailed engineering review, along with a knowledge of this standard (e.g., see 4-5.1.3.3 for individual station outlet gas flow test requirements).

Because repair and maintenance are a normal part of system operation, each compressor must be valved both automatically and with a manual shutoff valve. The use of the compressor outlet valve as the "automatic means" described here is considered bad engineering practice.

(d) *Electrical Power and Control.*

1. *Backup Operation.* A device shall be provided to automatically activate the additional compressor(s) if the unit in operation is incapable of adequately maintaining pressure. A signal indicating that the reserve compressor is running shall operate a local audio and visual alarm and serve to activate remote master alarms.
2. *Alternation.* Compressors shall be provided with automatic or manual alternation to allow division of operating time. If automatic alternation of compressors is not provided, the facility shall arrange a proper schedule for manual alternation.

The reserve compressor alarm (sometimes referred to as a "lag in use" alarm) warns of the activation of the off-duty compressor. This condition could indicate the following: (1) failure of the on-duty compressor; (2) inadequate capacity in the on-duty compressor; or (3) a controls failure or some other unusual event. All of these conditions are important and need to be checked.

3. *Motor Controls.* Each compressor shall be provided with a dedicated disconnect switch, motor starting device, and overload protection. The disconnect switches shall be installed in the electrical circuit ahead of each motor starter. Where compressor systems having two or more compressors employ a control transformer or other voltage control power device, at least two such devices shall be provided. Control circuits shall be arranged in such a manner that the shutdown of one compressor does not interrupt the operation of another compressor.

4. *Electrical Power.* Electrical equipment and wiring shall conform to the requirements of NFPA 70, *National Electrical Code.* Emergency electrical service for the compressors shall conform to the requirements of the essential electrical system as described in Chapter 3 of this document.

(e) *Monitors and Alarms.*

1. The medical air compressor shall be designed to prevent the introduction of contaminants or liquid into the pipeline by:

   a.   Elimination of oil anywhere in the compressor, or
   b.*  Separation of the oil-containing section from the compression chamber by at least two seals that create an area open to atmosphere that allows direct and unobstructed visual inspection of the interconnecting shaft for confirmation by the facility operators of proper seal operation without disassembly of the compressor. The vent and inspection opening(s) shall each be no smaller than 1.5 shaft diameters in size.

   This type of compressor can provide a visual indication of the failure of the critical seals between the oil-lubricated crankcase and the compression chamber, but the seal must be easily seen. The provision for an opening of 1.5 shaft diameters is intended to ensure that the visual inspection required in 4-3.1.1.9(i)2 can be effectively performed.

**A-4-3.1.1.9(e)1b**  Examples of 4-3.1.1.9(e)1a are liquid ring and permanently sealed bearing compressors.

An example of 4-3.1.1.9(e)1b is an extended head compressor with an atmospheric vent between the compression chamber and the crankcase.

2. Air compressors shall meet the criteria in 4-3.1.1.9(a) to be used for medical air service and shall be alarmed appropriately for conditions that may affect air quality during use or in the event of failure, including: water carryover, material wear or decomposition, or oil or hydrocarbon carryover.

3. Ambient temperature range for air-cooled equipment shall be as recommended by the manufacturer.

4. The use of a liquid ring air compressor, as defined in 4-3.1.1.9(e)1 under medical air compressor—type (a), shall require separate compressor sensors that shut down that compressor when the water exceeds the design level in the separator and activate a local alarm. In addition, a high water level in the receiver shall activate an alarm that shuts down the liquid ring compressor system and activates the local alarm. Service water and seal water shall be as recommended by the manufacturer.

*The technical committee changed type 1 to type a and type 2 to type b in 4-3.1.1.9(e)4, 5, 6, and 4-3.1.1.9(h)2.*

5. The use of permanently lubricated sealed bearing compressors, as defined in 4-3.1.1.9(e)1a under medical air compressor—type (a), shall require monitoring of the air temperature at the immediate outlet of each cylinder with a "high temperature" switch that shuts down the compressor and activates both master and local alarms. If the air compressor has water-cooled heads, a high-water-level switch in the receiver shall activate both master and local alarms and shut down the system. The temperature switch setting shall be as recommended by the manufacturer.

6. The use of a medical air compressor, as defined in 4-3.1.1.9(e)1 under medical air compressor—type (b), shall monitor air temperature at the immediate outlet of each cylinder with a "high temperature" switch that shuts down the compressor and activates both the master and local alarms. If the air compressor has water-cooled heads, a high water-level switch in the receiver shall activate both master and local alarms and shut down the system. The compressor shall contain coalescing filters with an "element change indicator" and a charcoal filter with colormetric hydrocarbon indicator.

*In developing the criteria for medical air compressor operation and single component failure, the committee recognized that modes of failure vary among the different types of compressor designs. The requirements of this chapter were made specific to the design type of compressor. (See Section 1-4 on the issue of equivalency.)*

(f) *Receivers.* The receiver shall be equipped with a pressure relief valve, automatic drain, sight glass, and pressure gauge and shall have the capacity to ensure practical on-off operation. The receiver shall comply with Section VIII, Unfired Pressure Vessels, of the ASME *Boiler and Pressure Vessel Code* and shall be corrosion resistant. Piping within compressor systems upstream of the source shutoff valve shall comply with 4-3.1.2.7 and 4-3.1.2.8 except that stainless steel shall be permitted to be used as a piping material.

*A sight glass enables visual inspection of automatic drains to see whether they are operating properly.*

*It should be noted that piping between compressors and source shutoff valves requires the same integrity as the rest of the piping system. This integrity criteria were extended to piping within the entire compressor package for 1996. [For piping requirements for compressor intake, see 4-3.1.1.9(b).]*

Criteria for receivers are covered in the ASME *Boiler and Pressure Vessel Code*. [4]

(g)* *Accessories.* Compressor systems for medical air shall be equipped with intake filter-mufflers of the dry type, aftercoolers or air dryers, or both, line filter(s) appropriate for the intake air conditions and compressor type, pressure regulators, and a pressure relief valve set at 50 percent above nominal line pressure to ensure the delivery of medical air *(see definition of Medical Air in Section 2-2).*

The medical air receiver shall be provided with a three-valve bypass to permit service to this device without shutting down the medical air system.

Dryer systems shall be, at a minimum, duplexed and valved to permit isolation of individual components to allow for maintenance or repair in the event of failure, while still continuing to adequately treat the flow of air. Under normal operation, only one dryer shall be open to airflow with the other dryer valved off. Each dryer system shall be designed to provide air at a maximum dew point of 35°F (1.7°C) at the peak calculated demand of the system. *[See 4-3.1.2.2(b)3g.]* System design shall preclude formation of liquid water in the air line.

Aftercoolers, where required, shall be duplexed and provided with individual condensate traps. The receiver shall not be used as an aftercooler or aftercooler trap.

Where more than two devices are provided, the peak calculated demand shall be met with the largest single unit out of service.

Final line filters located upstream of the final line regulators shall be duplexed with appropriate valves to permit service to these devices without shutting down the medical air system. Each of the filters shall be sized for 100 percent of the system peak calculated demand at design conditions and shall be rated for a minimum of 98 percent efficiency at 1 micron. These filters shall be equipped with a continuous visual indicator showing the status of the filter element life.

All final line regulators shall be multiplexed with isolating valves to permit service to the regulator without completely shutting down the gas piping system. Each of the regulators shall be sized for 100 percent of the system peak calculated demand at design condition.

Requirements for medical air compressor systems were extensively revised in 1990 as a result of field reports of problems involving reliability and maintenance.

Because the maintaining of a +35°F (1.7°C) pressure dew point (PDP) criterion is important, it requires a continually functional dryer. Redundancy of this component was added in 1990 to ensure this criterion was met. [See commentary under 4-3.1.2.1(d)2 for a discussion of dew point requirements and why each dryer system is to be designed to provide air at a maximum dew point of 35°F (1.7°C) PDP at peak demand.] Local conditions and the actual utilization of the dryer should dictate the dryer used to prevent the problem of liquid water forming in the lines. Location of dryers is dependent on the type of technology used. Figure 4-3.1.1.9 is typical but not the only configuration. It is required that dryers, like other source equipment, be placed ahead of final filters and regulators.

More duplexing of items that are part of the compressor source system was added in 1993. This included aftercoolers (where required) and final line filters and regulators. Duplexing of compressor components allows maintenance to be performed without necessitating a shutdown of the entire system.

Dryers have optimum operating characteristics, which are dependent on the type of medical air compressor used, the operating pressure range of the medical compressors, and the discharge temperature of compressors. Selection for optimum efficiency will thus vary from system to system.

Duplexed air filters (98 percent efficient at 1 micron or greater) are required as part of the piped air system. This quality of filter and filters of even better quality are readily available. Selection of filters should be based on the characteristics of the compressor, probable intake conditions, and other considerations that affect the quality of the air leaving source equipment.

Filters of any type require periodic replacement, maintenance, or both. To facilitate this, filters must be duplexed. Final line filters require a visual indicator to ensure proper maintenance of these filters.

The practice of operating the pipeline system at higher pressures with remote air line regulators is not permitted. The medical air is to be piped throughout the facility at 50 psig ( +5/-0) (345 kPa) . The piping system needs to be designed adequately to accommodate this pressure at the far reaches of the facility.

Finally, while it is important to provide valves around regulators and filters to permit their servicing, piping unions should also be used to permit easier removal of these items should they need replacement.

*Air-Treatment Systems.* Air-treatment systems do what their name implies. They are composed of air compressors, receiver(s), and any additional arrangements of dryers and filtration equipment required to deliver the desired quality of medical air. They also include controls, sensors, and alarms to ensure a continued supply of the desired quality of air.

Air-treatment systems for medical air compressor systems are not mandated by this standard because ambient air, taken from a location free from auto exhausts or other sources of pollution, can be well within the limits required by NFPA 99. Compressors that comply with the definition and requirements of *medical air compressor* (see definition in Chapter 2) are designed not to add contamination to the airstream and thus do not require air treatment.

Air quality can vary from place to place and day to day and can in a few areas exceed the contaminant limits for air set by this standard for unacceptably long periods. This can only be determined through knowledge of local conditions and air quality testing at the intake. Testing of these conditions could be necessary on a regular basis.

Where the quality of the intake air is unreliable, specific air-treatment devices can be desirable. Where installed, these devices must be monitored and alarmed. Such devices do require increased frequency of maintenance of the air system, but their use should be reviewed in light of what untreated air can do to the piped air system. See Exhibits 4.8 and 4.9.

**A-4-3.1.1.9(g)** The utilization of an air-treatment system is the joint responsibility of the system designer, hospital clinical and engineering staffs, and the authority having jurisdiction. Different types of compressors have characteristics that affect the selection of the type of air-treatment system. Some air-treatment systems impose an additional load upon the compressors that must be accounted for in the sizing of the system (usable capacity). The compressor duty cycle must be chosen in accordance with the manufacturer's recommendation.

The type of air compressor and air condition at the intake will govern the type of filter provided for the air compressor supply system. All filters should be examined quarterly for the presence of liquids or excessive particulates and replaced according to the manufacturer's instructions.

(h)* *Dryers, Filters, and Regulators.* Dryers, filters, and regulators shall be provided with isolating valves upstream and downstream to allow service to the component without shutting down the system. *[See Figures 4-3.1.1.9(h)1 and 4-3.1.1.9(h)2.]*

Redundancy of critical components to compensate for potential failure has always been an important underlying principle in medical gas and vacuum systems designed to meet NFPA 99. Successive revisions have expanded the principle of redundancy to include components that could require service in the ordinary course of operation and would require shutting down the system. Through all these revisions, a single principle has emerged—single fault. The single fault principle provides that no single failure should be able to render the system inoperable.

This principle is significant. Without it, NFPA 99 would quickly begin to stack redundancy on top of redundancy, attempting to compensate for any combination of failures (if A fails and B fails . . .), which is beyond the intent of a minimum safe standard.

Such an eventuality had emerged in the arrangement shown in Figure 4-3.1.1.9 for air system components, where previous editions of NFPA 99 illustrated separate four valve bypass for each component. While undoubtedly a convenient arrangement, it far exceeded the single fault principle. The change to 4-3.1.1.9(h) and Figure 4-3.1.1.9 explicitly permit a single fault arrangement or the more elaborate multiple valve arrangement.

To ensure the continued maintenance of medical compressed air, the appropriate monitors for each type of compressor were defined, consistent with the single component failure and the available monitoring technology. These controls had appeared as recommendations in the appendix prior to the 1993 edition of NFPA 99, but they were considered essential by the committee and moved to the requirement portion of NFPA 99 for the 1993 edition.

In the 1996 edition, this section was extensively rewritten for clarity, but rela-

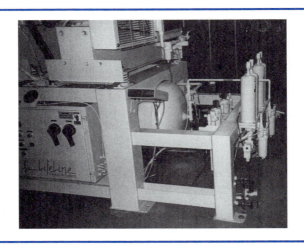

**Exhibit 4.8** *Medical air compressor system showing control panel, sight glass for receiver tank, two twin-tower desiccant dryer packages, dual filter banks, and dew point analyzer. These more compact desiccant dryers have been well received by facilities due to their smaller size and ability to be prepiped by the manufacturer.*

**Exhibit 4.9** *A portion of the piping around a medical air compressor system. Note the dual air line regulators with valves and unions permitting repairs. Also note the dew point analyzer, the cabon monoxide analyzer, the test port, the sensor chamber for the analyzers, and the source valve.*

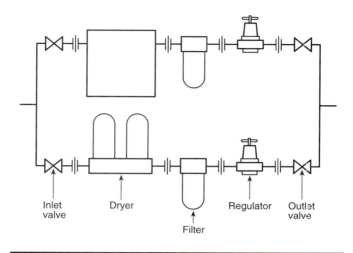

**Figure 4-3.1.1.9(h)1** *Dryers, filters, regulators—configuration 1.*

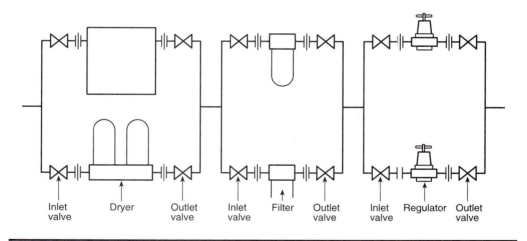

**Figure 4-3.1.1.9(h)2** *Dryers, filters, regulators—configuration 2.*

tively few new requirements were added. It has been made clear that required local alarms can be individually displayed locally but drawn to the master alarms as a group. Typically, this signal might read "Medical Air System Fault" [see 4-3.1.2.2(b)3f] and would cause a technician to examine the compressor to determine which of several advisory alarms had been activated. Only problems that are potentially serious, such as dew point, still require their own signal connected to the master alarm panel.

Readers are referred to the commentary under 4-3.1.2.2(b)3g on the development of criteria for dew point monitoring.

It is important to note the requirement for a local alarm. Most commonly, this requirement will be met on the medical air compressor controls, but in the case where a facility has multiple medical air compressor and vacuum pump sets, the standard would permit a single local alarm in a central location to monitor all the individual units or a local alarm panel at each location.

**A-4-3.1.1.9(h)** Two sequences are equally acceptable. The components may be sequenced: Inlet Valve - Dryer - Filter - Regulator - Outlet Valve OR they may be sequenced Inlet Valve - Dryer - Outlet Valve - Inlet Valve - Filter - Outlet Valve - Inlet Valve - Regulator - Outlet Valve.

(i)* *Medical Air Quality.* The monitoring of air quality downstream of the regulators and upstream of the piping system, as well as the monitoring system response, shall be as follows for each compressor installation.

1.  For compressors that eliminate oil anywhere in the compressor [4-3.1.1.9(e)1a], such as liquid ring and permanently sealed bearing compressors, monitoring shall consist of, but not be limited to, dew point and carbon monoxide. These parameters shall be monitored on a continuous basis.
2.* For compressors that have separation of the oil-containing section from the compression chamber by an area open to atmosphere, which allows continuous visual inspection of the interconnecting shaft [4-3.1.1.9(e)1b], such as extended head compressors with an atmospheric vent between the compression chamber and the crankcase, monitoring shall consist of, but not be limited to, dew point, carbon monoxide, gaseous hydrocarbons, and liquid hydrocarbons. Dew point, carbon monoxide, and liquid hydrocarbons shall be monitored on a continuous basis, and gaseous hydrocarbons shall be monitored on a quarterly basis.

Liquid hydrocarbons shall be monitored by pigment indicators or other type of instrument permanently installed downstream of each compressor (type b) and shall be inspected and documented daily.

**A-4-3.1.1.9(i)** One method for a decision on the quality of the medical air is the following:

1.  Test at the intake and at the sample connection valve.
2.* If the two purities agree within the limits of accuracy of the test, the compressor system can be accepted.
3.  If the air is found to exceed the values in the definition of Medical Compressed Air in Section 2-2, the facility can elect to install purification apparatus for the contaminants in question.

**A-4-3.1.1.9(i)2**  Other functions can be added at the request of the facility, such as low water pressure, etc.

3.  For all compressor types, dew point shall be alarmed in the machine room and at each of the two master alarm panels indicated in 4-3.1.2.2(a)1b.

Carbon monoxide shall be alarmed on the local alarm panel located in the machine room.

A ¼-in. NPT valved sample port shall be provided immediately downstream of the final line pressure regulators and upstream of the source shutoff valve to allow for sampling of the medical air.

A local alarm panel shall be mounted in the machine room in an area of responsible observation. This panel shall alarm, as a minimum, the following functions:

a.  Backup compressor operating
b.  High water level in receiver
c.  High water level in separator (if so equipped)
d.  High discharge air temperature (if so equipped)
e.  High carbon monoxide level

At least ONE signal from the local alarm shall be connected to the two master alarm panels [4-3.1.2.2(b)2] to indicate that a problem is present with the source equipment.

If the above signals are incorporated into the main control panel of the machinery, it shall still be required to bring one signal from the machine room to each of the master alarm panels indicating that a problem is present.

If there is more than one compressor for the facility, or if the compressors are in different locations in the facility, it shall be required to either have a local alarm panel that combines all the signals from all the machinery, or have a local alarm panel at each machinery site.

The paragraph refers only to air compressors. Hence, references to vacuum pump systems were deleted for the 1999 edition.

(j) *Antivibration on Considerations.* If required by equipment dynamics or location, antivibration mountings, in accordance with the manufacturer's recommendations, shall be installed under components, and flexible couplings shall interconnect the air compressor units, the receiver, intake lines, and the supply line from the storage receiver.

Not all systems require antivibration mountings. Determination should be made by knowledgeable persons. Consideration needs to be given to seismic requirements as well.

(k) *Different Pressures.* Where medical air piping systems at different operating pressures are required, the piping shall separate after the filters but shall be provided with separate line regulators, dew point monitors, relief valves, and source shutoff valves.

(l) *Component Material.* Components such as compressors, aftercoolers, and dryers shall be permitted to be made of materials suitable for the service.

The construction materials for components of the medical air compressor system are permitted to be of a variety of materials. This is an exception to the general rule outlined in 4-3.1.1.9(f). This allowance recognizes that making components from the same materials can be prohibitively expensive and, in some cases, impractical. Therefore, the committee has allowed the manufacturer to select materials for components such as the compressor, aftercoolers, receiver, regulators, filters, and dryers.

**4-3.1.2  Distribution—Level 1 (Manifold, Piping, Valving/Controls, Outlets/ Terminals, Alarms).** See Figure 4-3.1.2.

**4-3.1.2.1  General Requirements.**

The entire alarm section of Level 1 systems was rewritten for the 1996 edition to clarify requirements and to incorporate technical changes, including the following:

(a) A sound level requirement for alarm panels set at 80 dB measured at 3 ft (1 m)

(b) Addressing the possibility of an alarm lamp failure without any indication to facility staff

(c) The supervision of alarms to indicate whether their sensor wiring is cut or becomes disconnected

(d) The addition of "demand check fittings" on sensors to facilitate removal for testing or service

(e) A specific reference to NFPA 70, *National Electrical Code* [5], requiring raceways or conduit to protect sensor wiring

These additions were made to reflect general practice today and to improve the reliability of alarm panels and systems.

See Exhibit 4.10.

The 1983 edition of NFPA 56F (which was incorporated into NFPA 99 in 1987) did not restrict manufacturers in the way pipes were to be cleaned. If a manufacturer complied with the requirements of former 4-3.1.2.3(a), an inspection of pipes might be all that was necessary. If the manufacturer had not followed requirements, then washing and appropriate cleaning on the job site was permitted.

Requirements for the cleaning of piping used for oxygen service were added in the 1987 edition of NFPA 99 to clarify when manufacturer-cleaned piping was acceptable. CGA Pamphlet G-4.1 [6] covers such items as the selection of the type of cleaning process to be used, precleaning, steam or hot water cleaning, caustic cleaning, acid cleaning, solvent washing, vapor degreasing, mechanical cleaning, inspection/quality control procedures, and packaging procedures (to keep cleaned pipe clean). The CGA document allows the use of cleaning solvents that are prohibited when cleaning is accomplished on the job site because the entire CGA G-4.1 [6]

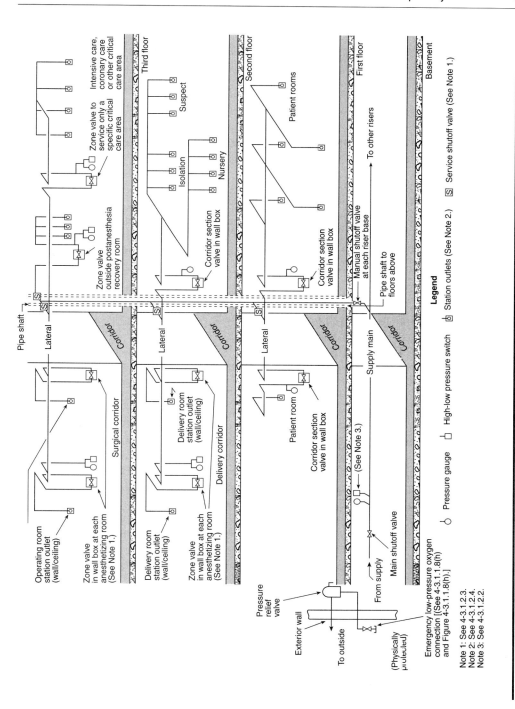

***Figure 4-3.1.2*** *Location of valves, pressure switches, and piping for medical gas systems (schematic). (Level 1 Gas Systems)*

**Exhibit 4.10** *Typical pressure gauge and sensor for monitoring pressure inside piped gas system. Gas specific demand checks are now required.*

manufacturing process is a very controlled process. In addition, the time lapse from manufacturer cleaning to use at the job site will allow any residual vapors to evaporate and not cause a problem.

The use of trichloroethylene on-site was banned in the 1990 edition of NFPA 99. This restriction was imposed because controlling and disposing of trichloroethylene at the job site can be a considerable hazard. In addition, residuals of trichloroethylene cannot be easily removed and can present a distinct hazard to patients and to personnel who are installing piping.

All on-site cleaning of new piping construction was banned in the 1993 edition, with the exception of cleaning necessary to prepare the immediate joint area for brazing. Suppliers and contractors will need to protect material that has previously been cleaned for oxygen service during delivery to, and storage on, the job site (e.g., caps should not be removed from the ends of pipes until the piping is ready for installation and brazing; caps should be removed one at a time).

Piping that has been cleaned and labeled "oxy" or "oxygen" indicates that it has been cleaned in such a manner as to be suitable for the piping of oxygen. It also means that the piping is suitable for use with any other nonflammable medical gas. The requirement for manufacturer-cleaned piping for all nonflammable medical piped gas systems to be suitable for oxygen eliminates the possibility that some manufacturer-cleaned piping will be suitable for some nonflammable gases but not others and helps to ensure the correct piping is installed. [See 4-3.1.2.1(b).]

The referencing and use of ASTM B 819 [7] tubing [see 4-3.1.2.7(c)] permits on-site recleaning only in certain instances as noted. No other cleaning is allowed on-site.

(a) *Oxygen Compatibility.* Components in nonflammable medical gas systems shall be of materials that are suitable for oxygen service. *(See 4-3.1.1.3, Material—Oxygen Compatibility.)* Pipe (tube), fittings, valves, and other components shall have been thoroughly cleaned internally to remove oil, grease, and other readily oxidizable materials, as if for oxygen service.

(b) *Cleanliness.* Materials that have been cleaned for use in medical gas piping systems shall be plugged, capped, or otherwise sealed until installed. Particular care shall be taken in the storage and handling of such material to maintain its clean condition. Immediately before final assembly, such material shall be visually examined internally for contamination. Material that has become contaminated and is no longer suitable for oxygen service shall not be installed.

(c) *On-Site Recleaning.* On-site recleaning of the interior surfaces of tubes, valves, fittings, and other components shall be limited to recleaning surfaces in the immediate vicinity of the joints that have become contaminated prior to brazing. Such surfaces shall be cleaned by washing in a clean, hot water/alkaline solution, such as sodium carbonate or trisodium phosphate (1 lb to 3 gal of potable water). Interior surfaces shall be thoroughly scrubbed and rinsed with clean, hot potable water.

### 4-3.1.2.2 Gas Warning Systems.

(a)* *General.*

Computers are increasingly being used as collection points and transaction logs for building information. In some cases, computers have been seen as substitutes for the alarm panels required in 4-3.1.2.2(b). The former Subcommittee on Nonflammable Medical Piped Gas Systems (now part of the Committee on Piping Systems) does not consider such computer systems substitutes for alarm panels meeting the intent of 4-3.1.2.2(b)2. The enormous number of alarms and conditions computer systems can monitor can also overshadow the significance of any one individual alarm, even very important ones such as those for medical gas systems.

**A-4-3.1.2.2(a)**  See C-4.2.

1. All local, master, and area alarm panels used for medical gas systems shall provide the following:

   a. Separate visual indicators for each condition monitored
   b. Cancelable audible indication of an alarm condition. The audible indicator shall produce a minimum of 80 dBA measured at 3 ft (1 m). A second indicated condition occurring while the alarm is silenced shall reinitiate the audible signal
   c. A means to visually indicate a lamp or LED failure

2. Local, master, and area alarms shall indicate visually and audibly if

   a. The monitored condition occurs
   b. The wiring to the sensor or switch is disconnected

3. Each local, master, and area alarm panel shall be labeled for its area of surveillance (e.g., $O_2$, vacuum, medical air), etc., and room(s) served. Each indicator shall be separately labeled indicating the condition monitored.

   With the 1999 edition, the technical committee standardized color, pressure, and labeling of all medical gas outlets, valves, and pipelines. Previous references to CGA documents would entail purchasing another code document. Table 4-3.1.2.4 includes requirements for all typical gases, including medical, laboratory, and regular air.

4. Where multiple panels are intended to indicate the same condition(s):

   a. At least one panel shall be connected directly to the sensor(s) or switch(es).
   b. Both master alarms required by 4-3.1.2.2(b)2 shall be connected by dedicated wiring directly to the sensor(s) or switch(es).
   c. Other panels shall be permitted to be connected through indirect means such as data transmission lines provided that such indirect means are fully supervised and failure of such indirect transmissions is indicated at all panels so connected.

5. Local, master, and area alarms shall be powered from the life safety branch of the emergency system as described in Chapter 3, "Electrical Systems."

6. All pressure switches, pressure gauges, and pressure-sensing devices downstream of the source valve shall be provided with a gas specific demand check fitting to facilitate servicing, testing, or replacement.

   The requirement for demand check fittings on gauges, sensors, and so forth was new to the 1996 edition. Although added to the text, the demand checks were not illustrated on the drawings. Demand checks were added for the 1999 edition. At the same time, the drawing was revised to more accurately show the emergency oxygen inlet. This drawing has been separated from 4-3.1.2 for clarity.

   Demand checks serve a useful purpose for allowing sensors, gauges, and other devices with which they serve (such as alarm panels) to be conveniently detached from the pipeline for servicing, testing, or replacement. Without these checks, many tests required by NFPA 99 become impractical. The requirement that all demand checks be gas specific was also added. However, it is recognized that there are other places where demand checks are not required to perform these operations, and therefore the expense of the checks is not warranted.

   The need for gas-specific demand checks stems from the requirement that alarms be tested on a routine basis (a prime reason for the original demand check requirement). Because the sensors are detached from the lines periodically, it was possible to install the sensors on the wrong lines when reattaching them. Gas-specific connectors reduce this risk.

7. The responsible authority of the facility shall ensure that all labeling of alarms, where room numbers or designations are used, is accurate and up-to-date.

8. All wiring from switch or sensors shall be supervised or protected as required by Section 517-30(c)(3) of NFPA 70, *National Electrical Code,* for emergency system circuits.

9. A centralized computer (e.g., a building management system) shall not substitute for any required medical gas alarm panel, but shall be permitted to be used to supplement the medical gas alarm system.

   (b) *Master Alarms.*

1. A master alarm system shall be provided to monitor the operation and condition of the source of supply, the reserve (if any), and the pressure of the main lines of all medical gas piping systems.

   The basic intent of this section is to provide continuous observation of the master alarm signal panel by personnel who, upon hearing the alarm, know what to do. (Exhibit 4.11 shows a typical master alarm panel.) It was, and still is, assumed by the committee responsible for this material that one alarm signal panel would be located in an engineering department. This is a reasonable assumption.

   It is not necessary to have two separate sensor systems. One sensor is adequate as long as the output signal is connected to two separately located warning panels (i.e., signal output can be wired in parallel).

*Exhibit 4.11 Master alarm panel mounted in the engineering offices of a hospital. This panel, which is available in a variety of sizes, has the ability to report up to 24 impulses.*

2. The master alarm system shall consist of two or more alarm panels located in two separate locations. One panel shall be located in the principal working area of the individual responsible for the maintenance of the medical gas piping systems and one or more panels shall be located to assure continuous surveillance during the working hours of the facility (e.g., the telephone switchboard, security office, or other continuously staffed location).

3. Each master alarm panel shall include visual indicators for each of the following conditions:

   a.* A separate indicator shall be provided for all systems supplied by a manifold or an alternating-type bulk system that has as part of its normal operation a changeover from one portion of the operating supply to another portion. It shall indicate when, or just before, this changeover occurs.

**A-4-3.1.2.2(b)3a**  See C-4.1 and C-4.2.

   b.* Where a manifold or bulk supply consists of one or more units that continuously supply the piping system while another unit remains as the reserve supply and operates only in case of an emergency, it shall be indicated separately for each system when, or just before, this changeover occurs.

**A-4-3.1.2.2(b)3b**  See C-4.1 and C-4.2.

   c.* Where check valves are not provided for each cylinder lead of the reserve supply for a manifold or bulk supply system, it shall be indicated separately for each system when the reserve supply is reduced to one average day's supply. If check valves are provided in each cylinder lead, this signal is not required.

The lack of a check valve for the individual leads from cylinders is a potentially dangerous situation because it limits reserve supply capabilities. Should a leak in one cylinder occur or one cylinder be depleted, the other cylinder(s) could backflow into the leaking or depleted cylinder. The intended reserve capacity of the system would thus be degraded and, with total reserve capacity unknown, shutdown could occur prematurely (i.e., there would be an alarm only when the entire system was low, not when the main supply was low). When check valves are in place in each reserve line, this possibility is eliminated.

**A-4-3.1.2.2(b)3c**  See C-4.1 and C-4.2.

This signal will be present only if the reserve supply consists of high-pressure cylinders that do not have check valves in the cylinder leads or is provided by a second bulk liquid storage unit.

   d. When a cryogenic liquid storage unit is used as a reserve for a bulk supply system, it shall be indicated separately for each system when the contents of the reserve is reduced to one average day's supply and when the gas pressure available in the reserve unit is reduced below the pressure required to function properly.

This paragraph, added in 1993, coincides with the requirements listed in 4-3.1.2.2(b)3e.

e.* It shall be indicated separately for each medical gas piping system when the pressure in the main line increases 20 percent or decreases 20 percent from the normal operating pressure. The actuating switch for these signals shall be installed in the main line immediately downstream (on the piping distributing side) of the main line shutoff valve or the source valve if the main line shutoff valve is not required.

One actuating switch (signal) would be acceptable if it indicated whether pressure was increasing and decreasing. A signal that just indicated pressure was changing would not be helpful. Thus sentence one of the text includes the phrase "increases . . . or decreases . . . ."

Increases or decreases in the pressure in the pipeline can be caused by depletion of the gas supply and regulator(s) failing. By monitoring pressure changes, these alarms can prevent a minor problem from becoming a major incident.

Starting with the 1996 edition, the main line shutoff valve could be eliminated if the source of equipment were within the facility. If the main line is eliminated, the actuating switch for these signals shall be installed immediately downstream (on the piping distribution side) of the source shutoff valve. Supply systems remote from the facility (such as oxygen bulk supplies) would still require both a source valve and a main valve just inside the facility. The pressure switch in this instance would be just downstream of the main valve where it first enters the facility or building.

**A-4-3.1.2.2(b)3e** See C-4.1.

f. Each of the individual alarms required in 4-3.1.2.2(d)1 shall be indicated. This shall be either by a separate indicator for each condition monitored or with a single indicator labeled "Medical Air System Fault" or similar wording and that indicates when any of the conditions monitored occurs.

g. A separate indicator shall be provided for dew point per 4-3.1.2.2(d)2.

The alarm specified in this paragraph will apply to the dew point monitor for all systems and to any air-treatment system where installed. These alarms will be echoed at the master alarm panel [see 4-3.1.2.1(b)1].

Because many facilities now use desiccant-type dryers, which can provide dew points in the $-40°F$ to $-100°F$ ($-40°C$ to $-73°C$) range, it is important to remember that the dew point alarm system provided with these systems will need to be capable of monitoring a value that low. Dew point monitors that read out "below range" are not appropriate.

The 1987 edition of NFPA 99 included a requirement that the dew point of piped medical compressed air systems be monitored. That edition, however, only suggested a recommended value in a table in the appendix. After considering several proposed limits, the former Subcommittee on Nonflammable Medical Piped Gas Systems agreed to a value for the 1990 edition and included the value as a requirement in Chapter 4 of NFPA 99.

This dew point criterion represents the nominal performance of a refrigerated dryer [35°F (1.7°C), with 4 Fahrenheit degrees added to allow for individual variation in systems]. The latter is used for the alarm set point. The committee recognizes that to attain this dew point, the system should be designed for best performance and therefore separately notes in 4-3.1.1.9(g) that the design dew point should be 35°F (1.7°C) PDP. This should not burden the system or damage downstream equipment.

The question of the pressure at which dew point is to be expressed was decided by reference to the preferred location of the sensor, which is immediately downstream of the pressure regulators and filters. [See 4-3.1.1.9(h).] This location should see system pressure, so it was agreed by the committee to express dew point at system pressure (39°F at 50 psig is equivalent to 4°F at 0 psig). [See also 4-3.4.1.3(j).]

In 1993 the wording mandating "pressure dew point" was an attempt to provide one standard for dew point readings. While it is relatively easy to convert Celsius to Fahrenheit, it is seldom easy to convert atmospheric dew point readings to pressure dew point readings. It is the intent of the committee to set a maximum for the dew point of the medical air within the pipeline at pressure, and not after it is expanded and expelled into the room.

The pressure dew point reading is to be taken at pipeline operating pressure [50 psig (345 kPa)] downstream of the air line regulator, and not at compressor operating pressures that go up and down with operation of the compressor. For instance, many compressors energize at 75 psig (517 kPa) and turn off at 95 psig (695 kPa). Pressure dew points at these pressures would be lower than the dew point of the medical air downstream of the regulator at 50 psig (345 kPa).

The basic intent of setting a dew point is the preclusion of liquid water forming in the pipes. Users are advised that the minimum dew point that will prevent water from forming in pipes will vary from system to system.

Chapter 4 uses the term *dew point* frequently. The following is offered for those readers not familiar with the term.

In a compressed air system, the temperature at which water vapor begins to condense into liquid is called the dew point. In a health care facility setting, dryers are used to remove moisture from an airstream. Although there are several different types of dryers, all are designed to remove the water in a medical air stream below the +39°F (4°C) pressure dew point (PDP) alarm point called for in NFPA 99.

As an example, merely because the air has been dried to a dew point of +30°F (−1°C) PDP does not mean that the air will necessarily feel cold, as this is only the temperature to which the air has been treated. For example, if air dried to a dew point of +35°F (−1.6°C) PDP is blown into a room where the temperature of the ambient air is +70°F (21°C), the expelled air will not give up any moisture. However, if the same treated air is expelled into a room where the ambient air is only +20°F (−6.6°C), water will be expelled because the ambient temperature is below the temperature to which the air has been treated.

For another example, a dryer is drying the air only to a dew point of +60°F

(15.5°C) PDP. The pipeline distributing this air has been installed inside the facility, but on an exterior wall that has not been adequately insulated. The pipeline is exposed to temperatures of +35°F to +40°F (1.6°C–4.4°C) inside this wall. It is quite possible that water will form as the air passes through this colder area and be expelled out patient outlets.

Refrigerated, noncycling dryers are standard in many health care facilities in the United States. Unfortunately, unless these dryers are sized properly and have a fairly constant flow through them, they cannot adequately treat an air stream and provide continuous dew point readings of +35°F (−1.6°C) PDP, as called for in Chapter 4.

Regenerative dryers employ an adsorptive chemical desiccant that attracts and holds moisture on its surface. These units have two towers, one that collects moisture while the other is dried of moisture that it has collected. A timing circuit reverses the rolls of the towers after a pre-set time, and dry air is used to drive collected moisture off of the chemical. These dryers are capable of discharging air at a constant dewpoint of 0°F PDP to −100°F (−17.8°C to 37.8°C) PDP, regardless of flow through the system.

(c) *Area Alarms.*

1. Area alarms shall be provided for each medical gas piping system supplying anesthetizing locations and other vital life support and critical care areas such as postanaesthesia recovery, intensive care units, coronary care units.
2. Area alarm panels shall be located at the nurses' station or other location that will provide for responsible surveillance.

An area alarm panel for a piped Level 1 gas system is not required at all nurses' stations. Only those areas listed in 4-3.1.2.2(c)1 require one because the alarm panel must be in a constantly staffed area so the alarm can be heard. The areas listed in 4-3.1.2.1(c)1 meet this criterion.

When multiple alarms are installed at a common nurses' station and the alarms monitor separate areas controlled by distinct zone valves, the alarms should be labeled for the specific areas they control.

The proper location for an area alarm is inside the room or area being monitored by the alarm panel, near the nurses' station. It should not be mounted out in the hall near the zone valve box assembly because it cannot be continuously monitored in this area.

The proper location for area alarms in intensive care nurseries, which typically have no nurses' station, is on a common wall visible to several nurses at all times. It is also permitted to install more than one alarm panel in intensive care nurseries that have only one large zone for an entire area but are divided into several "pods." This would ensure that staff is warned about gas delivery problems even if no incubators near the alarm panel were currently in use. See Exhibit 4.12.

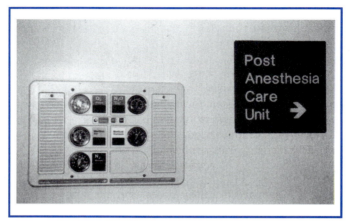

**Exhibit 4.12** *An area alarm panel for the operating room and signage to the post-anesthesia recovery unit.*

3.* Area alarms shall indicate if the pressure in the local line increases 20 percent or decreases 20 percent from normal line pressure.

**A-4-3.1.2.2(c)3** See C-4.1.

4.* Actuating switches or sensors for critical care areas shall be placed in the individual line supplying each such specific area. No valve, other than valves located in areas accessible only to authorized personnel, shall intervene between the sensor or switch and the outlets intended to be monitored by the alarm.

The requirements for the location of actuating switches differ between anesthetizing locations and vital life support and critical care units. Exhibit 4.13 illustrates the different applications.

Requirements are different due to the inherently closer supervision of patients by staff in anesthetizing locations and to the provision of emergency supplies of critical gases on anesthesia machines.

According to 4-3.1.2.3(j), the service shutoff valve shall be upstream of this actuating switch where the lateral branches off the riser, not after the actuating switch as indicated in 4-3.1.2.2(c)4. The service valve is a maintenance valve only and is located immediately where the lateral line(s) branches off the riser. All zone valve and alarm sensor locations are to be downstream of the service valve. The alarm pickup points for an anesthetizing area, then, should be downstream of the locked service valve location in the line supplying the anesthetizing area, but prior to any of the individual room shutoff valves.

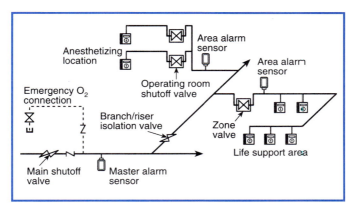

**Exhibit 4.13** *The different locations for activating switches of a piped gas system.*

**A-4-3.1.2.2(c)4** This signal is intended to provide immediate warning for loss of, or increase in, system pressure for each individual vital life support and critical care area.

5.* Actuating switches or sensors for anesthetizing areas shall be placed in the individual line supplying each such specific area with the individual room shutoff valve being the only one between the actuating switch and the outlets.

**A-4-3.1.2.2(c)5** This signal is intended to provide immediate warning for loss of, or increase in, system pressure for all anesthetizing locations supplied from a single branch line—not for each individual operating or delivery room.

(d) *Local Alarms.*

Alarms are sometimes placed in each anesthetizing location. This arrangement exceeds the requirements of NFPA 99 and is thus permitted. The user who wishes to implement such a system is advised to consider the requirements and limitations for additional master alarms at multiple locations per 4-3.1.2.2(b).

The placement of an alarm panel inside each operating room does not remove the requirement for an area alarm panel at the OR nurses' control desk. The purpose of this panel at the OR control desk is to allow staff to alert all the operating rooms at once should there be a supply problem with the medical gases requiring use of machine-mounted portable tanks. Many times alarms inside operating rooms have been silenced without some corrective action taken, or alarm panels have not been maintained.

The term *local alarm* was defined in 1993, but very little criteria for these alarms were included in Chapter 4. For the 1996 edition, the committee established requirements and placed them in this section.

A local alarm panel is to be mounted in an area of responsible observation.

The panel would alarm, as a minimum, for the conditions listed in (a) through (c). This would include, but is not limited to, the following:

(a) Lag compressor operating
(b) High water level in receiver
(c) High water level in separators (if so equipped)
(d) High discharge air temp (if so equipped)
(e) Carbon monoxide level high
(f) Lag vacuum pump operating

In accordance with 4-3.1.2.2(d), a signal from the local alarm is to be connected to the two master alarm panels to indicate when any local alarm has been activated because of a source equipment problem. The dew point alarm is to be connected both locally and at each of the two master alarm panels per 4-3.1.1.9(i)3.

The net result is master alarm coverage for all local alarm functions without having to connect all individual signals directly to the master locations.

1. An indicator shall be provided for each of the individual alarms required in 4-3.1.1.9 at the air compressor site. These indicators shall comply with 4-3.1.2.2(a)1, 2, and 3 and shall be grouped together in a single location (e.g., in an alarm panel or with the system controls).
2. Dew point for medical air shall be monitored and alarmed per 4-3.1.1.9(i) to indicate a line pressure dew point above 39°F (3.9°C).
3. Carbon monoxide for medical air shall be monitored and alarmed per 4-3.1.1.9(i) to indicate a level above 10 ppm.

(e) *Pressure Gauges for Gases.* The scale range of positive pressure analog gauges shall be such that the normal reading falls within the middle 50 percent of the scale. The scale range of digital gauges shall be not more than two times the working pressure. The rated accuracy of pressure gauges used for testing shall be one percent (full scale) or better at the point of reading. Pressure gauges shall be in compliance with ANSI/ASME B-40.1, *Gauges, Pressure Indicating Dial-Type, Elastic Elements.*

1.* A pressure gauge shall be installed in the main line adjacent to the actuating switch required in 4-3.1.2.2(b)3e. It shall be appropriately labeled and shall be readily visible from a standing position.

**A-4-3.1.2.2(e)1** See C-4.2.

2.* An appropriately identified pressure gauge, connected to the line being monitored, shall be installed at each area alarm panel location. It shall be appropriately labeled and shall be readily visible from a standing position.

**A-4-3.1.2.2(e)2** See C-4.2.

**4-3.1.2.3 Gas Shutoff Valves.** Shutoff valves accessible to other than authorized personnel shall be installed in valve boxes with frangible or removable windows large enough to permit manual operation of valves.

*Exception: Shutoff valves for use in certain areas, such as psychiatric or pediatric, shall be permitted to be secured to prevent inappropriate access.*

> Shutoff valves in boxes (zone valve box assemblies) have for years been required to be readily accessible in an emergency. This has not been practical, however, in areas such as such as pediatric or psychiatric wards.
>
> For the 1996 edition, the exception to 4-3.1.2.3 permitted emergency shutoff valves in certain areas to be secured so that patients would not have access to them. While this exception put a greater burden on staff, the committee felt that staff who work in these areas could be trained to know how to use these valves in an emergency.
>
> Typical modifications to secure valves in these locations can include a lockable valve box door with only staff having the key; removable handles that are kept at the nurses' station; and the shutoff valves installed inside a locked area such as the nurses' station or the drug storage area in the unit.
>
> Shutoff valves placed in a locked room would need to be relocated should the type of patients in that area change. Therefore, consideration should be given to using a standard location for the valves, and removing handles or installing a lockable door as the safety feature.

(a) *Source Valve.* A shutoff valve shall be placed at the immediate outlet of the source of supply to permit the entire source of supply, including all accessory devices (such as air dryers, final line regulators, etc.), to be isolated from the piping system. The source valve shall be located in the immediate vicinity of the source equipment. It shall be labeled "SOURCE VALVE FOR THE (SOURCE NAME)."

> The provision for a source valve was made to eliminate an anomaly in the requirements for piped gas systems created when the leak testing in 4-3.4.1.2(b) was done with the main line shutoff valve closed. This situation allowed a system to be tested without testing the piping between the valve and the source equipment. As this line could run substantial distances, a distinct hazard existed. The provision for a source valve is intended to eliminate this anomaly.
>
> In the 1996 edition, the source valve was permitted to substitute for the main line shutoff valve if both would normally be located inside the building. (Exhibit 4.14 illustrates a shutoff valve.) This is commonly the case with a medical air compressor system or can happen with a manifold room in the basement. This eliminates the wasteful installation of a source valve and a main line valve inches apart (as has been reported to committee members).

(b) *Main Valve.* The main supply line shall be provided with a shutoff valve. The valve shall be located to permit access by authorized personnel only (e.g., by locating in a ceiling or behind a locked access door). The main supply line valve shall be located downstream of the source valve and outside of the source room, enclosure, or where the main line first enters the building. This valve shall be identified. A main line valve shall not be required where the source shutoff valve is accessible from within the building.

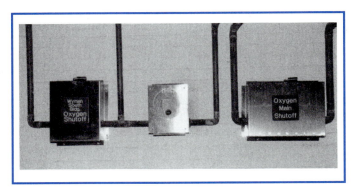

***Exhibit 4.14*** *The main oxygen shutoff valve in a hospital.*

(c) *Riser Valve.* Each riser supplied from the main line shall be provided with a shutoff valve adjacent to the riser connection. Riser valves shall remain accessible and shall not be obstructed.

> This valve allows one riser to be shut down without having to shut down the entire piped gas distribution system (e.g., for repairs, modifications). In addition, during new construction, a shutoff valve at the base of each riser will allow isolation and testing of the system in increments.
>
> While ball valves at the base of risers have been required for many years, a change in the 1996 edition mandated that these valves not be blocked from access. Committee members have frequently observed riser valves visually obscured or access blocked by other service ducts or piping. Since the riser valves are not just a construction valve but allow a facility more flexibility with future work or additions to the medical gas pipeline systems, these valves should always be accessible only to service personnel.

(d) *Zone Valve.* Station outlets shall not be supplied directly from a riser unless a manual shutoff valve located in the same story is installed between the riser and the outlet with a wall intervening between the valve and the outlet *(see Figure 4-3.1.2).* This valve shall be readily operable from a standing position in the corridor on the same floor it serves. Each lateral branch line serving patient rooms shall be provided with a shutoff valve that controls the flow of medical gas to the patient rooms. Zone valves shall be so arranged that shutting off the supply of medical gas to one zone will not affect the supply of medical gas to the rest of the system. A pressure gauge shall be provided downstream of each zone valve.

> The purpose of requiring a "wall" between the valves and outlets is to allow someone to shut off the flow of gas to a fire scene without being directly exposed to the fire and any products of combustion. This wording has been included in this portion of requirements since 1974. For the 1996 edition, the criterion for a "corridor

wall" was revised to a "wall" to correlate with newer editions of NFPA *101, Life Safety Code.* [2]

A zone valve box assembly is permitted to be installed at the nurses' station of a patient area as long as patient rooms have walls and doors, for example, an intensive care unit that has rooms with walls and doors. An emergency suite, however, might only have curtains separating cubicles from the nurses' station. In this case, the nurses' station is not an acceptable location for the valve box.

Also, while it has been a requirement since 1977 that new piped gas systems have a gauge in, or near, the alarm panel location [see 4-3.1.2.1(e)], and gauges downstream of lateral branch line shutoff valves (zone valve box assemblies), this standard does not mandate installing new gauges, valves, zone valve box assemblies with gauges, or alarm panels in existing systems. A renovation project may make their installation possible, depending on the extent of the project.

During both the new construction of medical gas systems and the renovation of existing medical gas systems, systems should not be installed that would allow one of the following conditions to exist:

(a) Tie-ins made downstream from an existing zone valve and a second set of zone valves installed. This creates a condition whereby zone valves are installed in series.

(b) Zone valves and piping installed in such a manner that a zone valve controls piping in more than one zone.

The preceding conditions compromise both fire safety and patient care because closure of a single set of valves would create undesirable effects.

(e) *Service Valves.* Service shutoff valves shall be placed where the lateral branches off of the riser prior to any zone valve box assembly on that branch. Only one valve shall be required for each branch off of a riser regardless of how many zone valve boxes are installed on that lateral. These valves shall be installed to allow a facility to make changes in piping in individual areas without shutting down an entire riser or facility.

(f) *In-Line Valves.* In-line shutoff valves intended for use to isolate piping for maintenance or modification shall be located in a secure area, be latched or locked open, and be identified in accordance with 4-3.5.4.2.

In-line shutoff valves are recommended to enhance servicing capabilities while minimizing disruption to patient care. However, such shutoff valves are not required, nor were they intended, for every station outlet.

As an example, in an intensive care unit with 20 beds arranged in a U-shaped pattern, the normal practice is to have one set of valves in a box with the gas feeding from one end of the U to the other. This is a problem if one oxygen outlet at a bedside in the middle of the unit has to be replaced—oxygen for the entire unit would have to be shut down. An alternate solution would be to pipe the gas in a complete loop, or O, and install a few service valves in the piping in the ceiling.

When one bed has to be worked on, only two valves would have to be closed, isolating a couple of beds.

Another example of an area where in-line shutoff valves would be helpful is the intensive care nursery. In most arrangements, the isolettes are grouped in pods or along walls. Valving to isolate groups of these beds would prevent disrupting the flow of gases to all of the beds.

It should also be noted that these service valves are to be located behind ceiling tiles, or inside casework, and should not be readily accessible in an emergency (i.e., " . . . in a secure area . . . or locked open . . ."). This will preclude the need to install multiple alarm panels.

(g) *Shutoff Valves.* Shutoff valves provided for the connection of future piping shall be located in a secure area, and be latched or locked closed. Downstream piping shall be closed with a brazed cap with tubing allowance for removal and rebrazing.

(h) *Shutoff Valves (New or Replacement).* New or replacement pipeline shutoff valves shall be of a quarter-turn ball type manufactured with extensions for brazing, and with an indicating handle and shall be of metallic construction. Valves shall be the three-piece type with full-size ports.

The pipeline shutoff valve has become the standard type of valve used in medical gas systems. It allows for the quick shutoff of gas, which is highly desirable in an emergency such as a fire. The addition of "extensions" in 1996 is to eliminate the need to dissemble valves for brazing. The requirement that new valves be three-piece construction helps for maintenance purposes.

Note that this requirement, like other sections of 4-3.1, applies to new construction or repairs. It is not the intent of the committee that existing, properly functioning equipment be replaced.

(i) *Shutoff Valves (Manual).* Manual shutoff valves in boxes shall be installed where they are visible and accessible at all times. The boxes shall not be installed behind normally open or normally closed doors, or otherwise hidden from plain view.

It has always been the intent of the committee that zone valve box assemblies be readily accessible and visible at all times. These valve boxes, for example, should not be installed behind doors that will be normally open or held open or next to doors that will be opened in an emergency, because such valve boxes may be hidden as patients are removed from a fire scene. Further, if floor actuating switches are used, doors will not close if someone is standing on the switch. This could make it difficult to shut off the gases in the affected area if the valve box is behind the opened door. (See Exhibit 4.15.)

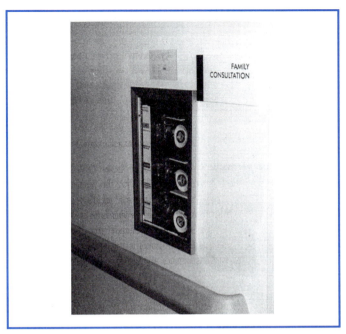

**Exhibit 4.15** *A typical zone valve box assembly in a unit of the facility. Note there is a sign permanently affixed to the wall showing what room is controlled by these valves.*

(j) *Shutoff Valves (Service).* Service shutoff valves shall be placed where the lateral branches off of the riser prior to any zone valve box assembly on that branch. Only one valve shall be required for each branch off of a riser regardless of how many zone valve boxes are installed on that lateral. These valves shall be installed to allow a facility to make changes in piping in individual areas without shutting down an entire riser or facility.

These valves shall be installed in a locked chase or shall be located in a secure area, latched open and identified in accordance with 4-3.5.4.2.

Service shutoff valves reduce the number of valves and areas affected when only one floor of a multistory building requires shutdown for maintenance or other reasons.

Service shutoff valves are to be located immediately off the riser *prior* to any zone valves installed on that lateral. With such valves installed at the origin of the lateral branch, even if that lateral branch leads to four or five separate zone valve sets, it is easier to plan the temporary shutdown of those four or five zones rather than an entire facility.

These valves are to be held in the open position and either in a locked chase or locked open at all times.

All such valves should have labels indicating gas and area controlled.

(k) Medical gases shall not be installed in the same zone valve box assembly with flammable gases.

(l) Anesthetizing locations and other vital life-support and critical areas, such as postanesthesia recovery, intensive care units, and coronary care units, shall be supplied directly from the riser without intervening valves except as provided in 4-3.1.2.3(f), 4-3.1.2.3(m), or 4-3.1.2.3(n).

(m) A shutoff valve shall be located immediately outside each vital life-support or critical care area in each medical gas line, and located so as to be readily accessible in an emergency. Valves shall be protected and marked in accordance with 4-3.5.4.2.

All gas-delivery columns, hose reels, ceiling tracks, control panels, pendants, booms, alarm panels, or other special installations shall be located downstream of this valve.

Freestanding birthing centers and birthing centers in hospitals present some difficulty in terms of whether they meet the criteria of vital life support or critical areas. Generally, birthing centers are used when no problems are evident or anticipated. If a medical complication develops (e.g., the onset of fetal distress), the patient is immediately transferred either to a nearby hospital in the case of a freestanding birthing center or, if the birthing center is in a hospital, to a nearby delivery room equipped to handle such complications. In the instance where there is no capability to handle complications, the group of birthing rooms would not be considered in the same category as critical care areas, and so forth, and would not be required to have individual gas shutoff valves to each room. However, if one particular birthing room is equipped to handle complications and is capable of providing life-support measures, that birthing room would be required to have gas shutoff valves to the room. It is thus necessary to review the level of care that will be provided in each and every birthing room in a facility.

(n) A shutoff valve shall be located outside each anesthetizing location in each medical gas line, so located as to be readily accessible at all times for use in an emergency. These valves shall be so arranged that shutting off the supply of gas to any one operating room or anesthetizing location will not affect the others. Valves shall be of an approved type, mounted on a pedestal or otherwise properly safeguarded against physical damage, and marked in accordance with 4-3.5.4.2.

One way to meet the prohibition of a shutoff valve between the zone valve and riser valve for anesthetizing locations, but install an end valve for the extension of a piped gas system [see 4-3.1.2.4(f)], is to use a secured (locking) feature for the end valve. After an extension is made, this valve is secured open, with access restricted to authorized personnel. In essence, the valve is considered to not be there for ordinary or emergency shutoff purposes. However, it must be labeled in accordance with 4-3.5.4.2 because such valves do control gas to patients.

It should be noted that 4-3.1.2.13 contains additional requirements and does not supersede 4-3.1.2.3. To meet the requirements of both paragraphs, the method just described or an equivalent method can be used.

---

**Formal Interpretation 90-1**

Reference: 4-3.1.2.2(d)4

*Background:* Paragraph 4-3.1.2.2(b)6 permits in-line shutoff valves for maintenance and future expansion provided that such valves are in a secure area or are locked open. Paragraph 4-3.1.2.2(d)4 requires anesthetizing locations and other life support areas to be supplied directly from risers without intervening valves except for readily accessible valves outside each area.

*Question:* Does 4-3.1.2.2(d)4 supersede 4-3.1.2.2(b)6?

*Answer:* No.
Issue Edition: 1990
Reference: 4-4.1.3.1
Issue Date: September 4, 1991
Effective Date: September 24, 1991

---

Locating a shutoff valve outside each anesthetizing location is required for the following emergency and maintenance purposes:

(a) The outside location provides better control.
(b) Staff outside an operating room, in addition to those inside, would be able to shut off the gas supplies if required or necessary.

*Outside* is intended to mean near the OR door that leads to a central core, such as where nursing stations are located. It does not mean a rear door through which equipment might be brought, nor a side door where a common scrub room might be located.

If there is more than one operating room in the anesthetizing location, each room is to have an independent shutoff valve.

This wording does not preclude a facility from installing an additional shutoff valve inside an operating room.

### 4-3.1.2.4 Station Outlets.

The use of station outlets for purposes other than medical gas is not condoned. Air station outlets designed for patient use, for example, should not be used for equipment blowdown, cleaning, and so forth. Because these applications are nonmedical, the gas supply should originate from a source other than the medical air source.

Minimum flow characteristics for station outlets [see 4-3.4.1.3(h)] were established by the committee in 1993 and apply to the installation of new piped gas systems only. The committee did not believe it was realistic to establish requirements retroactively for existing station outlets.

When installing gas station outlets, it is a good practice to consider the space directly over the outlets as well as the distance between the outlets. Because oxygen and vacuum therapy equipment frequently have a height of 7 in. (0.18 m) or more, installing outlets directly under overbed lights or under cabinets could cause the outlets to be useless.

Similarly, many suction canisters in use today are at least 7 in. (0.18 m) or more in diameter. Thus, if oxygen, vacuum, and air are specified at a patient bed location, the best installation sequence would be oxygen–air–vacuum. This would allow the vacuum outlet and equipment to be on the end, not cramped between other equipment.

Another point to consider is the number of outlets installed at each patient bed location. For instance, it is usually better, and less expensive, to provide two separate oxygen outlets rather than to install a "twinning" device that plugs into one outlet and provides two outlets.

The reuse of old medical gas outlets in renovation projects because be avoided since manufacturers make improvements in flow characteristics in newer style outlets. In addition, because used outlets generally require extensive cleaning and refurbishing, with new O-rings and other seals, the cost of a new outlet will most likely be comparable.

See Exhibits 4.16 and 4.17.

For the convenience of the user, Table 4-3.1.2.4 brings into one place several important bits of information, previously found in several different locations, including the 1988 Compressed Gas Association Standard CGA-9, *Standard Color-Marking of Compressed Gas Cylinders Intended for Medical Use* [8], which was incorporated by reference.

**Exhibit 4.16** *Typical gas outlet/vacuum inlet configuration in an operating room.*

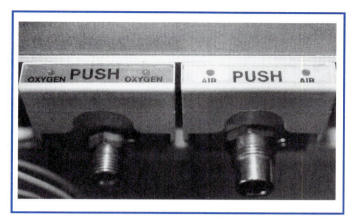

*Exhibit 4.17* Station outlets at the head end of a patient bed in a manufactured assembly. Note that the oxygen outlet is mechanically different from the medical air outlet. This is to prevent mix-up in gases when hoses are connected to outlets.

In this table, each medical gas and vacuum system is assigned a shorthand designation, color scheme, and standard operating pressure range. The table is intended to be a general guideline, not to precisely set requirements. Note that there is no precise definition for any color. See Exhibit 4.18.

(a)* Each station outlet for medical gases, whether threaded or noninterchangeable quick-coupler, shall be gas-specific and shall consist of a primary and a secondary valve (or assembly). The secondary valve (or unit) shall close automatically to stop the flow of medical gas when the primary valve (or unit) is removed. Each outlet shall be legibly identified with the name or chemical symbol of the gas contained. Where chemical symbols are used, they shall be in accordance with CGA Pamphlet P-2, *Characteristics and Safe Handling of Medical Gases. (See Table 4-3.1.2.4.)*

**A-4-3.1.2.4(a)**  See 4-3.1.2.7(c) and 4-3.1.2.11 for additional requirements for tubes used in systems at nonstandard pressures.

The purpose of the automatic secondary check valve is to shut off the flow of gas when the primary valve is removed for servicing.

(b) Threaded outlets shall be noninterchangeable connections complying with CGA Pamphlet V-5, *Diameter-Index Safety System—Non-Interchangeable Low Pressure Connections for Medical Gas Applications.*

(c) Each station outlet, including those mounted in columns, hose reels, ceiling tracks, or other special installations, shall be designed so that parts or components that are required to be gas-specific for compliance with 4-3.1.2.4(a) cannot be interchanged between station outlets for different gases.

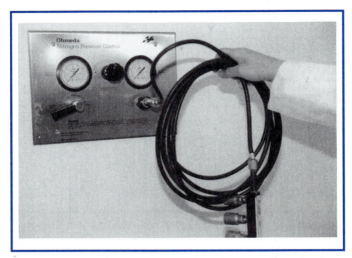

**Exhibit 4.18** *Control panel in an operating room for a piped nitrogen system used to power pneumatic devices, such as high-speed drills. [See 4-3.1.2.4 if operating pressure is above 160 psig (1103 kPa).]*

1. The use of common parts such as springs, O-rings, fasteners, seals, and shutoff poppets shall be permitted.

   (d) Station outlets in patient rooms shall be located at an appropriate height above the floor to prevent physical damage to equipment attached to the outlet. They shall be permitted to be recessed or otherwise protected from damage.

   (e) When multiple wall outlets are installed, including those for vacuum, there must be sufficient spacing between outlets to permit the simultaneous use of adjacent outlets with any of the various types of therapy equipment.

   (f) Pressure gauges and manometers for medical gas piping systems shall be cleaned and degreased.

   (g) Outlets intended for the connection of manufactured assemblies shall be D.I.S.S. connectors.

**4-3.1.2.5 Surface-Mounted Medical Gas Rail Systems.**

This section codifies the technology of a surface-mounted extension of the traditional piped system, which was introduced in the mid-1980s. It does have limitations and restrictions, as noted in the commentary and in both Section 2-2 and A-2-2 under the term *surface-mounted medical gas rail systems.*

Caution is necessary when deciding the number of additional station outlets that will be added to a system by the installation of a surface-mounted medical gas

*Table 4-3.1.2.4 Standard Designation Colors and Operating Pressures for Level 1 Gas and Vacuum Systems*

| Gas Service | Abbreviated Name | Colors (Background/Text) | Standard Pressure |
|---|---|---|---|
| Medical air | | Yellow/black | 50 psig $+5/-0$ |
| | | | 345 kPa $+35/-0$ |
| Carbon dioxide | $CO_2$ | Grey/black or grey/white | 50 psig $+5/-0$ |
| | | | 345 kPa $+35/-0$ |
| Helium | He | Brown/white | 50 psig $+5/-0$ |
| | | | 345 kPa $+35/-0$ |
| Nitrogen | $N_2$ or $HPN_2$ | Black/white | 160 psig $+25/-0$ |
| | | | 1145 kPa $+173/-0$ |
| Nitrous oxide | $N_2O$ | Blue/white | 50 psig $+5/-0$ |
| | | | 345 kPa $+35/-0$ |
| Oxygen | $O_2$ | Green/white or white/green | 50 psig $+5/-0$ |
| | | | 345 kPa $+35/-0$ |
| Oxygen/carbon dioxide mixtures | $O_2/CO_2$ $n\%$ ($n$ is % of $CO_2$) | Green/white | 50 psig $+5/-0$ |
| | | | 345 kPa $+35/-0$ |
| Medical-surgical vacuum | | White/black | 15 in.Hg to 30 in.Hg |
| | | | 380 mmHg to 760 mmHg |
| Waste anaesthetic gas disposal | WAGD | Violet/white | Varies with system type |
| Other mixtures | Gas A %/Gas B % | Colors as above; major gas for background/ minor gas for text | None |
| Nonmedical air | | Yellow & white diagonal stripe/black | None |
| Nonmedical vacuum | | White & black diagonal stripe/black boxed | None |
| Laboratory air | | Yellow and white checkerboard/black | None |
| Laboratory vacuum | | White and black checkerboard/black boxed | None |

rail system. It is akin to the use of electrical extension cords where, if too many appliances are connected, the fuse or circuit breaker for the branch circuit will trip. In this situation, the gas flow rate could be appreciably affected.

(a) Listed or approved surface-mounted medical gas rail systems shall be permitted to be installed where multiple use of medical gases and vacuum at a single patient location are required or anticipated. The surface-mounted medical gas rail system shall be made of material as identified in 4-3.1.2.7(a) or a material exhibiting the mechanical, thermal, and sealing integrity of a brazed joint complying with 4-3.1.2.12. Individual gas channel sizes shall be in conformity with good engineering practice for proper delivery of maximum volumes specified. The ends of the surface-mounted medical gas rails shall not be used for station outlets.

(b) Medical gas rails shall be permitted only where entirely visible in the room. Medical gas rails shall not pass into or through walls, partitions, and so forth.

(c) Station outlet locations for future expansion that are capped shall not be readily removable via screwdriver, pliers, wrench, and so forth, but shall require a special tool to remove them when expansion is undertaken.

(d) Openings in surface-mounted medical gas rail systems for station outlet assemblies or station outlet plug caps shall be gas-specific.

(e) All fittings used for internal and external connection of surface-mounted medical gas rail systems shall be made especially for brazed connection, or shall be assembled with screw-thread-type brass fittings with bronze- or copper-brazing-type fittings.

(f)* Connections of surface-mounted medical gas rail systems to piping systems of dissimilar metals shall require plating of the connecting components to prevent interaction between dissimilar metals.

**A-4-3.1.2.5(f)** Typical plating would be nickel plating over copper or brass per Federal Specification QQ-N290, Class I, Type 7.

It should be noted that there is no reference to a specific type of metal that can be used. Material that is specified in 4-3.1.2.7(c) or material that is equivalent in mechanical, thermal, and sealing integrity to that of a brazed joint can be used. [Note: This equivalency must be determined under actual operating conditions since the melting point of some materials—e.g., for basic aluminum—it is below 1000°F (538°C). However, with appropriate design consideration, aluminum alloys can be selected with melting points above 1000°F (538°C). The 1000°F criterion results from brazing having to meet ANSI/AWS Standard A5.8., *Specification for Brazing Filler Metal.*] The committee is aware that some authorities are restricting aluminum medical gas rails from installations on the basis of the melting point of pure aluminum and are not considering the melting point of the specific aluminum alloy being used.

It is a general industry practice to use fittings compatible with both metals if the metal used for the medical gas rail system is dissimilar to that of the piping system to which it is connected.

The use of performance criteria (in lieu of specifications) was a deliberate action on the part of the Medical-Gas Application Panel and the Technical Committee on Industrial and Medical Gases, which originally proposed this section as a Tentative Interim Amendment to NFPA 56F-1983. The criterion was made as performance-oriented as possible to allow suppliers freedom of design. Compliance will thus have to be determined by a testing laboratory acceptable to the authority having jurisdiction.

The use of the term *patient location* was very deliberate so as not to exclude any new type of patient treatment configuration that might be developed and eventually lend itself to this type of system.

It should also be noted that a rail system can serve only one (single) patient location. A separate rail system must be installed for each patient location. It cannot penetrate a normal wall enclosure (floor to ceiling). For further discussion on this point, see commentary under the definition of *surface-mounted medical gas rail systems* in Chapter 2 and commentary on manufactured assemblies under 4-3.1.2.6.

(g) The installation of the surface-mounted medical gas rail system shall be tested per 4-3.4.1.

### 4-3.1.2.6 Manufactured Assemblies.

This section on manufactured assemblies was new to the 1996 edition. The entire question of manufactured assemblies—modular headwalls, ceiling columns, booms, pedestals, and horizontal trunking systems—was previously left to the discretion of users and manufacturers with only general guidance in NFPA 99. A variety of problems, however, were reported to the committee as a result of the way these products are installed and applied. The committee recognized these issues and included this section to provide safety guidance for these "subsections" of a medical gas system.

Traditionally, the pipeline would be considered to end at the station outlet where the copper tubing terminated. In manufactured assemblies, several station outlets could be placed along the length of the assembly, ostensibly for "future convenience." The manufactured assembly is then placed over the station outlets, usually with a panel that can be removed for access to the outlets.

Attached to some of the station outlets are flexible connectors (usually rubber hoses) connected to a remote terminal point where the user will actually make connections and disconnections. This user outlet (defined as a *terminal*) forms an extension of the pipeline, but which in practice is permanent. Hoses and station outlets are hidden behind or within the manufactured assembly.

Hiding the station outlets and using flexible hoses present hazards relative to the operation of a safe medical gas and vacuum system. Some of these hazards are outlined below.

(a) Hidden station outlets are problematic for testing and certification. Unless the testing agency is made aware of their presence and these items are left accessible, it is easy to overlook them during the test process.

(b) Flexible connectors and, particularly, rubber hoses are far less fire resistant than copper pipe. Use of these items significantly increases risks to patients and staff should a fire occur within or near the assembly. Hiding them behind a panel, where their physical condition cannot be readily inspected, particularly for any deterioration, greatly increases the risk of a rupture.

(c) The number of connections and outlets from the pipeline that are enclosed inside the manufactured assembly greatly increases the risk of small leaks that can occur with any connection or seal. There is significant risk of developing an oxygen-enriched atmosphere behind the panel. This would greatly increase the speed with which a fire in the vicinity would spread.

(d) The use of standard station outlets in series with the terminal is known to create a significant flow restriction. This in turn risks inadequate flow of gas in some clinical situations.

Although these risks are very real and of great concern, manufactured assemblies have been used with success for decades and are integral to the creation and management of an efficient clinical environment. The committee's objective was to address these concerns without reducing operational effectiveness.

(a) Manufactured assemblies employing flexible hoses or tubing shall be as follows:

1. Be attached to the medical gas pipelines using semi-permanent connections to station outlets (inlets). Where the station outlets (inlets) are not fully and immediately accessible (i.e., can be manipulated without necessitating removal of panels, doors, etc.), the station outlets (inlets) shall additionally comply with 4-3.1.2.4(g) and shall be permitted to consist of only a primary check, omitting the secondary check required in 4-3.1.2.4(a). The station outlet (inlet) shall be permanently attached to the pipeline.
2. Use hoses and flexible connectors complying with 4-3.1.2.9(h) and having a flame spread rating of 200 in accordance with NFPA 255, *Standard Method of Test of Surface Burning Characteristics of Building Materials*, except that these shall be permitted to be concealed inside the manufactured assembly provided the hoses and connectors can be accessed for replacement or repair.
3. Be provided with a terminal complying with 4-3.1.2.4(a), (c), (d), and (e) at the point where the user makes connections and disconnections.
4. Be internally cleaned and delivered to the installation site in compliance with 4-3.1.2.1.
5. Shall require testing of flexible hoses and tubing in accordance with 4-3.4.1.3(a) and (e) upon removal, replacement, or addition.

(b) Manufactured assemblies employing copper tubing and intended for direct brazed connection to the pipeline shall be as follows:

1. Comply with 4-3.1.2.7(a), (b), (c), (e), (f), (g), and (i)
2. Be provided with a station outlet (inlet) at the point where the user makes connections and disconnections
3. Be assembled and delivered to the installation site in compliance with 4-3.1.2.1, 4-3.1.2.8, and 4-3.1.2.10

**4-3.1.2.7 Piping Materials.** The provisions of this section apply to field-installed piping for the distribution of medical piped gases.

Requirements for piping penetrating walls inside a building are covered in NFPA *101, Life Safety Code.* [2]

Readers are reminded that 4-3.1.2.10 applies to distribution requirements for Level 1 piped gas systems. Distribution requirements for Level 3 piped gas systems can be found in 4-5.1.2.10.

(a) Tubes, valves, fittings, station outlets, and other piping components in medical gas systems shall have been cleaned for oxygen service prior to installation.

On-site cleaning of new piping prior to installation is prohibited because of the inability to properly prepare piping for oxygen service at the installation site. This major change in installation requirements began with the 1993 edition of NFPA 99 and reflects the environmental hazards of using phosphates and other regulated chemicals.

(b) Piping for nonflammable medical gas systems shall be suitable for oxygen service in accordance with 4-3.1.2.1. Each length of tube shall be permanently labeled and delivered plugged or capped. Fittings, valves, and other devices shall be sealed and marked. The installer shall furnish documentation certifying that all installed piping materials comply with the requirements of this paragraph.

(c) Piping shall be ASTM B 819 specification hard drawn seamless medical gas tubing; ASTM B 819 tubing is identified by the markings "OXY," "MED," "OXY/MED," "OXY/ ACR," or "ACR/MED" in green (Type K) or blue (Type L). Main and branches shall be not less than ½ in. nominal size. Factory-installed tube on station outlets extending no further than 8 in. from the outlet body shall be permitted to be ⅜ in. O.D. (¼ in. nominal) size. Connections to gauges and alarm switches and runouts to alarm panels shall be permitted to be ¼ in. O.D. (⅛ in. nominal) size.

In this 1999 edition, previous references to a minimum inside diameter were removed, because copper tube that meets ASTM B 819, *Standard Specification for Seamless Copper Tube for Medical Gas Systems* [7], already exceeds these requirements.

*Exception: For systems operated at pressures between 200 and 300 psig (1380 and 2070 kPa, respectively), ASTM B 819, Type K copper shall be used.*

The American Society for Testing and Materials (ASTM) has developed a standard for materials that are available cleaned and marked for oxygen service.

It should be noted that any of the piping listed is acceptable for Level 1 piped gas systems operating at 50 psig ($+5/-0$) (345 kPa). It should also be noted that all piping for Level 1 piped gas systems has to be "hard-drawn." Part of the reason for requiring hard-drawn piping is that soft tubing kinks very easily, and kinking causes restriction of flow. The ¼-in. hard K tubing extension that comes installed from the manufacturer of the outlets is acceptable because its prime purpose is to move the closest point of brazing away from the internal components of the outlets. All connections to this tubing must be ½ in. or greater, and since the standard in the industry is already ½-in. drops for positive-pressure gases such as oxygen, air, nitrogen, and nitrous oxide, and ¾-in. drops for vacuum and evacuation, this should not be a problem.

Level 3 patient piped gas systems also require hard-drawn medical gas tubing, except for a certain size of soft copper tubing that has been prepared for oxygen service according to 1985 Pamphlet CGA-4.1, *Cleaning Equipment for Oxygen Service* [6]. (See 21-1.2.6.) Tubing for Level 3 piped gas systems used for gas-powered devices has different requirements. (See 4-5.1.3.1.)

Galvanized steel is not permitted for piped gas systems because the plating on this type of pipe can flake off under pressure and flow. These pieces of zinc could then flow through piping and block orifices of station outlets.

A limitation on piping material for use in systems where the operating pressure is between 200 psig and 300 psig (1380 kPa and 2068 kPa) was added in 1993. (See 4-3.1.2.4.)

For additional piping requirements between the medical air compressor and the source shutoff valve, see 4-3.1.1.9(b), (f), and (k).

(d)  Where seismic construction is required by the building code, piping shall be properly braced.

With health care facilities needing to perform in adverse conditions such as an earthquake, it is imperative that medical gas piping be properly braced for seismic incidents. This paragraph highlights the need for many requirements for seismic bracing found in the model building codes.

The revision of the wording in this paragraph in this 1999 edition reflects an attempt to harmonize the requirements of NFPA 99 with the *National Electrical Code*, NFPA 70. [5]

(e)*  Except as provided under 4-3.1.2.7(g) and (h), joints in copper tubes shall be brazed using capillary fittings complying with ANSI B16.22, *Wrought Copper and Copper Alloy Solder-Joint Pressure Fittings*, or brazing fittings complying with MSS SP-73, *Brazing Joints for Wrought and Cast Copper Alloy Solder Joint Pressure Fittings*. Cast fittings shall not be used for brazed joints.

**A-4-3.1.2.7(e)**  A distinction is made between deep-socket solder-joint fittings (ANSI B16.22) and those having shallow sockets for brazing (MSS SP-73). The use of shallow-socket brazing fittings improves the quality of the brazement without decreasing its strength, particularly in larger sizes which are difficult to heat. See Table A-4-3.1.2.7(e) for socket depths conforming to MSS SP-73. The installer can use MSS SP-73 fittings (if available) or have the sockets on ANSI B16.22 fittings cut down to MSS depths. Where shallow-socket fittings are used for the medical gas piping, care should be taken to avoid their use in other piping systems where joints may be soldered instead of brazed.

See also C-4.2.

See 4-3.1.2.11 for additional requirements for shutoff valves used in systems at nonstandard pressures.

*Table A-4-3.1.2.7(e)  Socket Depths for MSS SP-73 Brazing Fittings*

| Tube Size | | Socket Depth | |
|---|---|---|---|
| ¼ in. | ( ⅜ in. OD) | 0.17 in. | (³⁄₁₆ in.) |
| ⅜ in. | ( ½ in. OD) | 0.20 in. | (¹³⁄₆₄ in.) |
| ½ in. | ( ⅝ in. OD) | 0.22 in. | (⁷⁄₃₂ in.) |
| ¾ in. | ( ⅞ in. OD) | 0.25 in. | (¼ in.) |
| 1 in. | (1⅛ in. OD) | 0.28 in. | (⁹⁄₃₂ in.) |
| 1¼ in. | (1⅜ in. OD) | 0.31 in. | (⁵⁄₁₆ in.) |
| 1½ in. | (1⅝ in. OD) | 0.34 in. | (¹¹⁄₃₂ in.) |
| 2 in. | (2⅛ in. OD) | 0.40 in. | (¹³⁄₃₂ in.) |
| 2½ in. | (2⅝ in. OD) | 0.47 in. | (¹⁵⁄₃₂ in.) |
| 3 in. | (3⅛ in. OD) | 0.53 in. | (¹⁷⁄₃₂ in.) |
| 4 in. | (4⅛ in. OD) | 0.64 in. | (⁴¹⁄₆₄ in.) |
| 5 in. | (5⅛ in. OD) | 0.73 in. | (⁴⁷⁄₆₄ in.) |
| 6 in. | (6⅛ in. OD) | 0.83 in. | (⁵³⁄₆₄ in.) |

(f) Valves, fittings, and other piping components shall be cleaned for oxygen service by the manufacturer in accordance with CGA Pamphlet G-4.1, *Cleaning Equipment for Oxygen Service*, except that fittings shall be permitted to be cleaned by a supplier or agency other than the manufacturer.

(g) Joints in medical gas tube shall be brazed except that memory-metal couplings having temperature and pressure ratings not less than that of a brazed joint shall be permitted. Flared and compression-type connections shall be prohibited throughout the piping system, including connections to station outlets, alarm devices, and other components. Unions shall not be permitted in the distribution pipeline system.

See commentary under 4-3.2.2.2(g) for a description of one type of fitting that meets the criteria of memory-metal couplings.

This section was extensively revised for the 1996 edition. The committee clarified the issues of unions (not allowed in the distribution system) and threaded connections (allowed for certain pieces of equipment because it is an accepted industry practice and acceptable in medical gas systems for the devices listed).

*Exception: Threaded connections for air compressor sets and devices such as manifolds, pressure regulators, relief valves, pressure switches, and pressure gauges.*

(h) Listed or approved metallic gas tube fittings that, when made up, provide a permanent joint having the mechanical, thermal, and sealing integrity of a brazed joint shall be permitted to be used in lieu of brazed joints.

(i) Turns, offsets, and other changes in direction in piping shall be made with fittings complying with 4-3.1.2.7(e).

**4-3.1.2.8 Pipe Joints.**

Changes made in 1987 with regard to joining pipes were the result of problems reported to the former Medical Gas Application Panel of the Committee on Industrial and Medical Gases. (Responsibility for that panel, which is now part of the Committee on Piping Systems, was transferred to the Health Care Facilities Project). The way pipes are joined reflects committee concern that piping remain intact during a fire and withstand some degree of physical shaking and impact. Problems over the years have included mechanically weak joints and overheated piping and fittings. Changes to address problems have included all of the following:

(a) Reference to a specific American Welding Society (AWS) standard
(b) Reference to the inclusion of a phosphorous element in the brazing alloy
(c) Continuous purging of the pipe with an inert gas (e.g., nitrogen) while brazing

The change to ANSI/AWS 5.8 [8] was made to reference a national standard requiring the melting point of the brazing alloy to be a minimum of 1000°F (538°C). [This temperature criteria had been required by the committee for over 40 years, but no reference to a standard to achieve it had been included.] Reference to a specific type of brazing alloy was deleted to avoid prohibiting new technology.

(a)* *Threaded Joints.*

**A-4-3.1.2.8(a)** Where threaded joints are tinned, soft solder should be used. If sealing compound is used, it should be applied sparingly so that excess sealant is not forced inside the system.

1. Threaded joints in medical gas distribution piping shall be limited to the connection of pressure gauges, alarm pressure switches, and similar devices.
2. Threads on pipe and fittings shall be tapered pipe threads complying with ANSI B1.20.1, *Pipe Threads, General Purpose.*
3. Threaded joints in piping systems shall be made up with polytetrafluoroethylene (such as Teflon®) tape or other thread sealant suitable for oxygen service. Sealants shall be applied to the male threads only.

(b)* *Brazed Joints.*

This requirement (on the use of fittings) was added in 1990 to make it clear that fittings are required whenever pipes are joined. It had always been assumed by the committee that this was being done, and the requirement clarified the committee's position.

In 1996 the use of brazing fittings (short socket fittings) for making joints was added to the types of fittings allowed.

**A-4-3.1.2.8(b)**  All brazed joints should have a brazing alloy exhibiting a melting temperature in excess of 1000°F (538°C) to retain the integrity of the piping system in the event of fire exposure.

1.  Brazed tube joints shall be the socket type. Filler metals shall bond with and be metallurgically compatible with the base metals being joined. Flux shall not be used except where permitted under 4-3.1.2.8(b)1b. Brazing filler metals shall comply with ANSI/AWS A5.8, *Specification for Brazing Filler Metal*, except that filler metals having compositions not conforming to the exact ANSI/AWS A5.8 classifications shall be permitted when used according to the manufacturer's instructions.

    a.  Copper-to-copper joints shall be brazed using a copper-phosphorus or copper-phosphorus-silver brazing filler metal (BCuP series) without flux.

    The copper-phosphorus and copper-phosphorus-silver (BCuP series) brazing filler metal is designed to be used with like metals only. The phosphorus within the (BCuP series) brazing rod acts as the flux. On dissimilar metals, a flux must be applied to wet the tube and fitting, as well as to stop oxidation caused by the heat of the torch.

    b.  Dissimilar metals, such as copper and bronze or brass, shall be brazed using an appropriate flux with a silver (BAg series) brazing filler metal.

2.  Joints to be brazed in place shall be accessible for proper preparation, assembly, heating, filler application, cooling, cleaning, and inspection.
3.  Tube ends shall be cut square using a sharp tubing cutter to avoid deforming the tube. The cutting wheel shall be free from grease, oil, or other lubricant not suitable for oxygen service. The cut ends of tube and pipe shall be deburred with a sharp, clean deburring tool, taking care to prevent chips from entering the tube or pipe.
4.  The surfaces to be brazed shall be mechanically cleaned using a clean stainless steel wire brush or equivalent. The use of steel wool shall be prohibited due to the possible presence of oil. Mechanical cleaning shall not result in grooving of the surfaces to be joined. After mechanical cleaning, the surfaces shall be wiped using a clean, lintfree white cloth. During this cleaning, care shall be taken to avoid contamination of the "cleaned for oxygen" internal surfaces of the tube and components. Joints shall be recleaned if contaminated prior to brazing. Joints shall be brazed within 1 hour of being cleaned.
5.  Where dissimilar metals, such as copper and bronze or brass, are being brazed, flux shall be applied sparingly to minimize contamination of the inside of the tube with flux. The flux shall be applied and worked over the surfaces to be brazed using a stiff stainless steel bristle brush to ensure adequate coverage and wetting of the surfaces with flux. Where possible, short sections of copper tube shall be brazed to the noncopper component

and the interior of the subassembly shall be cleaned of flux prior to installation in the piping system. Flux-coated brazing rods shall be permitted to be used in lieu of the application of flux to the surfaces to be joined on tube ¾ in. nominal size and smaller.

6.   Tube ends shall be inserted fully into the socket of the fitting. Where flux is permitted, the joint shall be heated slowly until the flux has liquefied. Once this has occurred, or where flux is not used, the joint shall be heated quickly to the brazing temperature, taking care not to overheat the joint. Techniques for heating the joint, applying the brazing filler metal, and making horizontal, vertical, and large-diameter joints shall be as stated in sections on "Applying Heat and Brazing" and "Horizontal and Vertical Joints" in the chapter on "Joining and Bending" in the CDA *Copper Tube Handbook*.

7.*   **While being brazed, joints shall be continuously purged with oil-free dry nitrogen to prevent the formation of copper oxide on the inside surface of the joint. The flow of purge gas shall be maintained until the joint is cool to the touch.**

**A-4-3.1.2.8(b)7** The intent is to provide an oxygen-free atmosphere within the tubing and to prevent the formation of copper oxide scale during brazing. This is accomplished by filling the piping with a low-volume flow of low-pressure inert gas.

Note that oil-free dry air and carbon dioxide are no longer permitted. Industrial-grade carbon dioxide, in particular, has oil contaminants that cannot be cleaned out after brazing pipes.

*Exception: A final connection to an existing pipeline shall be permitted to be made without the use of a nitrogen purge. After final connection, the affected downstream portions of the pipeline shall be tested in accordance with 4-3.4.1.3(i) with the gas of system designation.*

New piped gas systems have to be purged with nitrogen during installation. When connecting to the piping of an existing system, however, purging with nitrogen is not recommended for several reasons. The primary reason for a nitrogen purge is to prevent the formation of copper oxide scale. If the final connection is made without nitrogen, only a small amount of scale that can easily be blown out during final purging and analysis will be formed.

Another reason not to use nitrogen for a final connection to an existing system is that if a ball valve is not present for isolation, it is possible to fill up an entire pipeline with nitrogen during a tie-in procedure. It would then be necessary to blow down all outlets in a facility to be sure that the nitrogen is removed from the system. If a ball valve is present but has a defective seal, it is also possible to contaminate the existing piping system with nitrogen.

The exception was modified for the 1996 edition with the addition of the reminder that the affected portion needs to be tested just like any new or modified portion of a system.

8.   During and after installation, openings in the piping system shall be kept capped or plugged to avoid unnecessary loss of purge gas while brazing and to prevent debris or

other contaminants from entering the system, except that during brazing, a discharge opening shall be provided on the opposite side of the joint from where the purge gas is being introduced. During brazing, the purge gas flow rate shall be maintained at a level that will not produce a positive pressure in the piping system. After brazing, the discharge opening shall be plugged or capped to prevent contamination of the inside of the tube.

9.  After brazing, the outside of all joints shall be cleaned by washing with water and a stainless steel wire brush to remove any residue and permit clear visual inspection of the joint. Where flux has been permitted, hot water shall be used.

10. Each brazed joint shall be visually examined after cleaning of the outside of the joint. The following conditions shall be considered unacceptable:

    a.  Flux or flux residue
    b.  Excessive oxidation of the join
    c.  Presence of unmelted filler metal
    d.  Failure of the filler metal to be clearly visible all the way around the joint at the interface between the socket and the tube
    e.  Cracks in the tube or componen
    f.  Cracks in the braze filler metal
    g.  Failure of the joint to hold the test pressure under 4-3.4.1.2(c)

    Visual inspection is to be done after brazing, using only a cloth to wipe the brazed joint clean. The purpose of visual inspection is to see whether brazement has flowed properly. If it has not flowed properly or there is a bridge brazement at the joint, it is indicative that penetration is questionable and workmanship is shoddy.

    The visual inspection is not intended to establish the exact degree of penetration. Penetration is established by the procedures used in the brazing process. Those procedures are intended to achieve adequate penetration. The visual inspection is by "sight only," as the name implies.

    The subsequent leak and pressure tests (see 4-3.4.1.2) demonstrate, among other things, that the degree of penetration is adequate for the installation. Actual quantitative degree of penetration is not defined.

11. Brazed joints that are found to be defective under 4-3.1.2.8(b)10, conditions a, c, d, f, or g, shall be permitted to be repaired, except that no joint shall be repaired more than once. Brazed joints that are found to be defective under 4-3.1.2.8(b)10, conditions b and e, shall be replaced.

    Normally, the failure of a brazed joint is caused either by lack of heat or the overheating of a joint. The alloy of silver and copper separates within the joint when overheated. The temperature needed to remelt the alloy is approximately 1800°F (968°C), which is much higher than the original melting temperature of the alloy of 1200–1500°F (649–815°C). The melting temperature of copper is approximately 1975°F (1065°C). The temperature needed to repair the bad joint is close to the melting temperature of the copper tubing. As a result, the copper tubing could melt when a brazed joint is being repaired or become soft (annealed). If the repaired joint is moved, raised, or stepped on during additional work in the area, for example, the repaired joint has a high probability of leaking. Consequently, the repair compromises the integrity of the medical gas system.

This requirement addresses the issue of how much repairing of a joint is reasonable and possible. Repeated repair of a joint would potentially contaminate the cleanliness of the pipe. Also, the probability of achieving an acceptable joint deteriorates with each attempted repair. Further attempted repair could, in fact, compromise the integrity of the medical gas system.

### 4-3.1.2.9 Piping Installation

(a) Piping systems shall be designed and sized to deliver the required flow rates at the utilization pressures.

(b) Piping shall be supported from the building structure in accordance with MSS Standard Practice SP-69, *Piping Hangers and Supports—Selection and Application*. Hangers and supports shall comply with MSS Standard Practice SP-58, *Pipe Hangers and Supports— Materials, Design and Manufacture*. Hangers for copper tube shall have a copper finish. In potentially damp locations, copper tube hangers or supports shall be plastic-coated or otherwise insulated from the tube. Maximum support spacing shall be as follows:

| | |
|---|---|
| ¼ in. (.635 cm) nominal | 5 ft (1.52 m) |
| ⅜ in. (.953 cm) nominal | 6 ft (1.83 m) |
| ½ in. (1.27 cm) nominal | 6 ft (1.83 m) |
| ¾ in. (1.91 cm) nominal | 7 ft (2.13 m) |
| 1 in. (2.54 cm) nominal | 8 ft (2.44 m) |
| 1¼ in. (3.175 cm) nominal | 9 ft (2.74 m) |
| 1½ in. (3.81 cm) nominal and larger | 10 ft (3.05 m) |
| Vertical risers, all sizes | Every floor, but not to exceed 15 ft (4.57 m) |

The reference to piping being supported directly from the building structure is to preclude the use of duct work or other piping for support.

(c) Piping shall be protected against freezing, corrosion, and physical damage. Buried piping outside of buildings shall be installed below the local level of frost penetration. Buried piping that will be subject to surface loads shall be buried at a sufficient depth to protect the piping from excessive stresses. The minimum backfilled cover above the top of buried piping outside of buildings shall be 36 in. (91.4 cm), except that the minimum cover shall be permitted to be reduced to 18 in. (45.7 cm) where physical damage to the piping is not likely to occur. Trenches shall be excavated so that the pipe has a firm, substantially continuous bearing on the bottom of the trench.

Underground piping shall be installed in a continuous enclosure to protect the pipe from damage during backfilling. The enclosure shall be split or otherwise provide access at the joints during visual inspection and leak testing. Backfill shall be clean and compacted so as to protect and uniformly support the piping. A continuous tape or marker placed immediately above the enclosure shall clearly identify the pipeline by specific name. In addition, a continuous warning means shall be provided above the pipeline at approximately one-half the depth of bury. Where underground piping is installed through a wall sleeve, the ends of the sleeve shall be sealed to prevent the entrance of ground water. Piping underground within buildings or embedded in concrete floors or walls shall be installed in a continuous conduit.

Buried piping cannot be placed directly into poured concrete. It must be installed within a conduit so that it will not be affected by the weight or the settling of the concrete.

The depth of burying depends on such factors as the climatic conditions of the region, the type of traffic anticipated, and the routing of the piping.

The installation of buried piping outside of buildings is covered, but the installation of piping within or under slabs within the building is not covered. There is a need for a continuous conduit to eliminate the possibility of a medical gas pipe or joint leak under or within the concrete floor or concrete wall.

(d) Medical gas risers shall be permitted to be installed in pipe shafts if protected from physical damage, effects of excessive heat, corrosion, or contact with oil.

The committee is unaware of problems when gas piping is placed in the same riser shafts with other utilities, such as water and electricity, as long as protection, such as from damage, heat, corrosion, and oil, is provided. The phrase *shall be permitted* is used, however, because the committee did not want to require placing pipes in shafts.

(e) Piping shall not be installed in kitchens or electrical switchgear rooms.

(f) Medical gas piping shall be permitted to be located in the same service trench or tunnel with fuel gas lines, fuel oil lines, electrical lines, steam lines, and similar utilities provided that the space is ventilated (naturally or mechanically) and the ambient temperature around the medical gas piping is limited to 130°F (54°C) maximum. Medical gas piping shall not be located where subject to contact with oil, including flooding in the case of a major oil leak.

(g) Piping exposed in corridors and other areas where subject to physical damage from the movement of carts, stretchers, portable equipment, or vehicles shall be suitably protected.

(h) Hoses and flexible connectors, both metallic and nonmetallic, shall be no longer than necessary and shall not penetrate or be concealed in walls, floors, ceilings, or partitions. Flexible connectors, metallic or nonmetallic, shall have a minimum burst pressure of 1000 psig (6900 kPa gauge).

This requirement includes permanently installed flexible hosing that terminates in a station outlet. Such hosing is considered an integral part of the piped gas distribution system.

Prior to the 1987 edition of NFPA 99, former NFPA 56F (now incorporated into NFPA 99) did not cover extension hoses (hoses not permanently connected). These flexible hoses connected to the piping system, however, transport gas like regular rigid piping and present the same hazards as rigid metal pipe. Therefore, the former Subcommittee on Nonflammable Medical Piped Gas Systems developed minimum performance criteria for these items.

Because such hoses are subject to movement and wear, some means of visually inspecting the hoses on a periodic basis was appropriate. With the 1993 edition of NFPA 99, the use of flexible hoses was restricted to exposed areas where the hoses can be inspected and maintained. Thus, hoses cannot be concealed inside walls.

Previously, this paragraph referenced 4-3.1.2.2(a)9 for metallic connectors. Because the scope of this paragraph is hoses, the reference to connectors was deleted in the 1999 edition.

(i) Where a system originally used or constructed for use at one pressure and for a gas is converted for operation at another pressure or for another gas, all provisions of 4-3.1.2.1, 4-3.1.2.4, 4-3.1.2.8, 4-3.1.2.10, 4-3.1.2.12, 4-3.4.1, and the Exception to 4-3.1.2.7(c) shall apply as if the system were new. **Vacuum systems shall never be converted for use as gas systems.**

The last sentence, prohibiting the converting of a vacuum pipeline into a gas pipeline, might seem obvious, but the committee wishes to stress that the contamination to which a pipeline is exposed when it is used for vacuum precludes it from *ever* being used for carrying gas.

**4-3.1.2.10\*  Installation Requirements.**

This section, extensively revised in 1993, applies to all gas piping systems, regardless of operating pressure(s). For systems that operate at nonstandard pressures, additional requirements are listed in 4-3.1.2.11.

**A-4-3.1.2.10** The responsible authority of the facility should ensure that procedures are established to provide for the testing, maintenance, and operation of nonflammable medical gas piping systems.

(a) *Equipment and Component Installation.*

1. The installation of individual components shall be made in accordance with the instructions of the manufacturer. Such instructions shall include directions and information deemed by the manufacturer to be adequate for attaining proper installation, testing,

maintenance, and operation of the medical gas systems. These instructions shall be left with the owner.

2. The installation shall be made by qualified, competent technicians experienced in making such installations. *(See 4-3.1.2.12 for brazer performance.)*

3. Brazing shall be performed by individuals who are qualified under the provisions of 4-3.1.2.12.

(b) Health care organization personnel shall be permitted to install piping systems if all the requirements of Section 4-3 are met during installation.

(c) The installer of medical gas piping and equipment shall maintain on-the-job site documentation regarding the qualification of brazing procedures and individual brazers per 4-3.1.2.12 prior to installation.

(d) Two or more medical gas piping systems shall not be interconnected for testing or for any other reason. Leak testing shall be accomplished by separately charging and testing the individual piping system.

This requirement addresses the potential problem created if a temporary connection for pressure testing is not removed. The resultant cross-connection could be hazardous.

The intent of this paragraph is to prohibit this interconnection even on a temporary basis. Each piping system is to be tested separately.

It should also be noted that the provisions of 4-3.4.1.2(b) and 4-3.4.2.2 state that nitrogen is the only acceptable test medium for pressure testing.

**4-3.1.2.11 Systems Having Nonstandard Operating Pressures.** The following requirements apply to gas piping systems having an operating pressure other than the standard 50 to 55 psig (345 to 380 kPa) [or 160 psig (1103 kPa) for nitrogen], and are in addition to the minimum requirements listed in 4-3.1.2.3 through 4-3.1.2.9.

The recognition of operating pressures other than 50 psig (345 kPa) was first included with the adoption of the 1993 edition. In doing so, it required that testing of these systems be evaluated separately. This section addresses the safety hazards of all components and materials appropriate to their operational use.

It should be noted that the installation requirements of 4-3.1.10 and the testing requirements of 4-3.4.1 are applicable to these systems, except as noted.

(a) Pipelines, shutoff valves, and station outlets in systems having nonstandard operating pressures shall be labeled for gas name and operating pressure.

(b) Where operating pressures are 200 to 300 psig (1380 to 2068 kPa), the following applies:

1. Only Type K medical gas tube (ASTM B819) shall be used.
2. Brazing procedures and brazers shall be qualified as required under 4-3.1.2.12.

(c) Station outlets in systems having nonstandard operating pressures shall meet the following additional requirements:

1. Be gas-specific
2. Be pressure-specific where a single gas is piped at more than one operating pressure [e.g., a station outlet for oxygen, 80 psig (550 kPa) shall not accept an adapter for oxygen, 50 psig (345 kPa)]
3. If operated at a pressure above 80 psig (550 kPa) but below 200 psig (1380 kPa), be either DISS style or comply with 4-3.1.2.4
4. If operated at a pressure between 200 and 300 psig (1380 to 2068 kPa), the station outlet shall be so designed as to prevent the removal of the adapter until the pressure has been relieved, to prevent the adapter injuring the user or others when removed from the outlet.
5. Be labeled for the gas name and operating pressure [e.g., nitrogen, 250 psig (1725 kPa)]

(d) *Testing.* When systems operated at different pressures are installed, each pipeline shall be tested separately.

**4-3.1.2.12  Qualification of Brazing Procedures and Brazer Performance.** Brazing procedures and brazer performance shall be qualified in accordance with either Section IX, Welding and Brazing Qualifications, of the ASME *Boiler and Pressure Vessel Code*, or AWS B2.2, *Standard for Brazing Procedure and Performance Qualifications*, both as modified below.

The former Subcommittee on Nonflammable Medical Piped Gas Systems (now part of the Committee on Piping Systems) was made aware in 1991 of an increasing trend toward requiring some degree of qualification of brazing procedures. To complicate the situation, differing qualification standards were being generated and employed in various localities. For the 1993 edition, the committee defined a qualification standard by referencing portions of standards from other national organizations. At the same time, it defined the procedures to permit and recognize an equivalent qualifying procedure.

The inclusion of permissible language in 1996 was to strengthen the paragraph that allowed noncertified personnel to perform medical gas system installation and testing. The 1996 edition required only individuals working on medical gas systems to have the necessary qualifications. Determining whether the individual was qualified was left to the building owner or authority having jurisdiction, based on criteria provided in the document. The technical committee does not wish to prohibit personnel employed by a medical facility from installing and modifying medical gas systems. [(See 4-3.1.2.10.3(b).] In-house personnel with appropriate qualifications can work on medical gas systems and be within the requirements on NFPA 99.

(a) Brazers shall be qualified by visual examination of the test coupon followed by sectioning except that a tension test shall be permitted to be substituted for sectioning. Where tension tests are used for brazer qualification, they shall be performed in accordance with ASME IX.

This portion of Chapter 4 covers requirements for qualifying a brazer. It is not the field test for determining the integrity of brazed joints in a piped gas or vacuum system, which is covered under 4-3.4, Performance Criteria and Testing—Level 1 (Gas, Vacuum, WAGD).

The 1993 edition of NFPA 99 listed only "tension testing" as the test method for brazers. It was pointed out in several proposals to the committee during the revision for the 1996 edition that the text was being misinterpreted by some persons and that there were other tests that would adequately indicate whether a brazer had made a joint having tensile strength equal to or greater than that of a tube or fitting. These tests are sectioning and macroetching tests and are considered acceptable in lieu of a tension test. [Concern over this issue was so high during 1994 that a Tentative Interim Amendment was issued in early 1995 addressing it. That TIA subsequently became the basis for the change made to this paragraph.]

(b) The Brazing Procedure Specification shall address cleaning, joint clearance, overlap, internal purge gas, purge gas flow rate, and filler metal.

(c) The Brazing Procedure Qualification Record and the Record of Brazer Performance Qualification shall document filler metal used, cleaning, joint clearance, overlap, internal purge gas and flow rate used during brazing of the test coupon, and no internal oxidation exhibited on the completed test coupon.

(d) Brazing procedures qualified by a technically competent group or agency are permitted under the following conditions:

1. The Brazing Procedure Specification and the Procedure Qualification Record shall meet the requirements of this standard.
2. The employer shall obtain a copy of both the Brazing Procedure Specification and the supporting qualification records from the group or agency and shall sign and date these records, thereby accepting responsibility for the qualifications that were performed by the group or agency.
3. The employer shall qualify at least one brazer following each Brazing Procedure Specification used.

(e) An employer shall be permitted to accept Brazer Qualification Records of a previous employer under the following conditions:

1. The brazer shall have been qualified following the same or an equivalent procedure as that which he/she will use for the new employer.
2. The new employer shall obtain a copy of the record of Brazer Performance Qualification tests from the previous employer and shall sign and date these records, thereby accepting responsibility for the qualifications performed by the previous employer.

(f) Performance qualification of brazers shall remain in effect indefinitely unless the brazer does not braze with the qualified procedure for a period exceeding 12 months, or there is a specific reason to question the ability of the brazer.

**4-3.1.2.13 Labeling.** The gas content of medical gas piping shall be readily identifiable by appropriate labeling with the name and pressure of the gas contained. Such labeling shall be by means of metal tags, stenciling, stamping, or adhesive markers, in a manner that is not readily removable. Labeling shall appear on the piping at intervals of not more than 20 ft (6 m) and at least once in each room and each story traversed by the piping system. Where supplementary color identification of piping is used, it shall be in accordance with the gases and colors indicated in CGA Pamphlet C-9, *Standard Color-Marking of Compressed Gas Cylinders Intended for Medical Use.* Only those systems operating at nonstandard pressures shall be labeled with the name of the gas and the operating pressure.

> The inadvertent mixing of gases or the mislabeling of gas station outlets can create a gas that is injurious to patients and staff.
>
> There are several reasons that color coding is not the primary method for identifying piping. Some people may be color-blind and therefore not be able to distinguish color correctly. Color-coding also means that people must be relied on to accurately remember a color-code scheme. Forgetting the color-code could be hazardous to patients and staff.

**4-3.1.2.14  Identification.**

(a) *Piping.* Pipe labeling shall include the name or chemical symbol for the system gas and its operating pressure. Piping shall be identified by stenciling or adhesive markers as follows:

1. At intervals of not more that 20 ft (6 m)
2. At least once in or above every room
3. On both sides of partitions penetrated by the piping
4. At least once in every story height traversed by risers

(b) *Shutoff Valves.* Shutoff valves shall be identified as to the following:

1. The particular medical gas or vacuum system
2. A caution to not close or open the valve except in an emergency
3. The rooms or areas served

(c) *Station Outlets and Inlets.* Station outlets and inlets shall be identified as to the specific medical gas or vacuum provided.

**4-3.1.2.15 Documentation.** The installer of medical gas piping and equipment shall furnish documentation certifying the following prior to installation:

(a) The qualification of brazing procedures per 4-3.1.2.12
(b) The qualification of individual brazers per 4-3.1.2.12
(c) That pipe (tube), fittings, valves, and other pipeline components are cleaned for oxygen service and are marked and sealed per 4-3.1.2.1

## 4-3.2 Piped Vacuum Systems (Source and Distribution)—Level 1.

### 4-3.2.1 Source (Vacuum Pumps)—Level 1.

The order of this material is consistent with the material contained in 4-3.1.1.9 on compressors for medical air.

**4-3.2.1.1 Multiple Pumps.** Two or more pumps shall be installed that serve this system alternately or simultaneously on demand. The pump(s) shall be sized to serve peak demand with the largest pump out of service. Each pump shall have an automatic means to prevent backflow through off-cycle units and a shutoff valve to isolate it from the centrally piped system and other pumps for maintenance or repair without loss of vacuum in the system.

See C-4.3.4.

**4-3.2.1.2 Backup Operation.** A device shall be provided to automatically activate the additional pump(s) if the unit in operation is incapable of adequately maintaining vacuum. A local audible and visual alarm, with a single signal reported to the master alarm, shall be provided to indicate when the reserve or off-duty pump is in operation.

Previous guidelines recommended that each of the two vacuum pumps provide 75 percent of the calculated system demand. Later, 100 percent backup operation was considered necessary by the committee because this system is felt to be a critical hospital utility. For the 1996 edition, text was modified to require only that pumps be sized so that the system would still be operational with the largest pump out of service. This was a more realistic design configuration.

The committee is still cognizant that failure or shutdown of pump(s) (causing reduction or loss of vacuum) can be injurious or fatal to patients. Vacuum systems in health care facilities (in particular those systems that are used in surgery and for respiratory therapy) are true life-saving, life-support systems.

The requirements of 4-3.2.1.3 and 4-3.2.1.4, in particular, ensure against unplanned vacuum loss.

Exhibit 4.19 illustrates a triplex vacuum pump, and Exhibit 4.20 illustrates a vertical mount duplex vacuum pump.

This signal is intended to notify maintenance personnel that a piece of normally standby equipment is operating. This usually indicates a system malfunction that should be investigated.

See commentary under 4-3.1.1.9(c) on the subject of reserve compressor(s) for a piped medical compressed air system.

**4-3.2.1.3 Alternation.** Pumps shall be provided with automatic or manual alternation to allow division of operating time. If automatic alternation of pumps is not provided, the facility shall arrange a proper schedule for manual alternation.

Alternation of pumps (automatically or manually) is required because it allows even wear on both pumps, thereby extending the life of the pumps and reducing the

*Exhibit 4.19* A triplex vacuum pump setup for a piped medical vacuum system, including control panel.

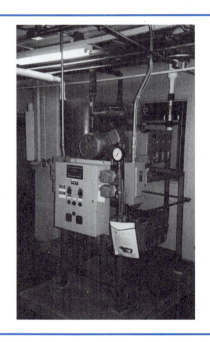

*Exhibit 4.20* A vertical mount duplex vacuum pump system with control panel and receiver. The pump is an oil-flooded rotary vane unit.

probability of system failure at any given time. Most automatic alternators incorporate the automatic operation of the second pump in the event of failure or overdemand on the pump in use. Whether pump alternation is automatic or manual, activation of the nonoperating pump must be automatic in the event of operating pump failure or overload. Additionally, the pump is to be sized at the stopping point of the operating range so the stop setting can be reached on intermitten: operation.

**4-3.2.1.4 Motor Controls.** Each pump shall be provided with a dedicated disconnect switch, motor starting device, and overload protection. The disconnect switches shall be installed in the electrical circuit ahead of each motor starter. Where vacuum pump units having two or more pumps employ a control transformer or other voltage-reducing control power device, at least two such devices shall be provided. Control circuits shall be arranged in such a manner that the shutdown of one pump does not interrupt the operation of another pump.

**4-3.2.1.5 Electrical Power.** Electrical equipment and wiring shall conform to the requirements of NFPA 70, *National Electrical Code*. Emergency electrical service for the pumps shall conform to the requirements of the essential electrical system as described in Chapter 3 of this document.

> For 1996 electrical requirements were extensively revised so that the system will continue to function if power to one pump fails or the circuitry to one pump is interrupted.

**4-3.2.1.6 Receivers (Tanks).** Receiver(s) shall be installed. Receivers shall comply with Section VIII, Unfired Pressure Vessels, of the ASME *Boiler and Pressure Vessel Code* and shall meet the standing pressure tests of 4-3.4.2 of this chapter, and full vacuum of 29.92 in. of mercury. A suitable method shall be provided for drainage so that substances that might accumulate can be drained from the receiver(s) [tank(s)]. The method shall provide means to drain and service the receiver without interrupting the vacuum system.

> Prior to 1996 receivers were optional depending on pump cycling. With the 1996 edition, receivers are now required. This reflects both good engineering and manufacturing practice, as well as current field practice.
>
> Since the receiver is part of the vacuum piping system, it too has to be metallic. The ASME *Boiler and Pressure Vessel Code* [4] is considered appropriate for the subject of vacuum receivers.

**4-3.2.1.7 Piping.** Piping between vacuum pump(s), discharge(s), receiver(s), and the vacuum main line valve shall be in accordance with 4-3.2.2.2(a) except that steel pipe shall be permitted to be either black or galvanized.

> The subject of source piping for vacuum systems was first addressed in 1990 because it was not clear what type of piping was intended to be used between these items. For the 1996 revision, the committee received and accepted proposals that piping

material be the same as that permitted for the distribution portion of the system, with the exception as noted.

**4-3.2.1.8 Noise and Vibration.** Provision shall be made to minimize the transmission of noise and vibration created by the central vacuum source beyond the space in which the equipment is located. Flexible coupling shall be installed in the piping to and from the equipment. Flexible couplings shall be rated for temperature, and pressure or vacuum, at the point of installation.

Flexible couplings were made a requirement in 1996 because some form of vibration reduction is now generally installed.

**4-3.2.1.9 Exhausts.** The exhaust from vacuum pumps shall be discharged outdoors in a manner that will minimize the hazards of noise and contamination to the hospital and its environment. The exhaust shall be located remote from any door, window, air intake, or other openings in buildings with particular attention given to separate levels for intake and discharge. Care shall also be exercised to avoid discharge locations contraindicated by prevailing winds, adjacent buildings, topography, and other influences. Outdoor exhausts shall be protected against the entry of insects, vermin, debris, and precipitation. Exhaust lines shall be sized to minimize back pressure. Discharge piping shall be free of dips or loops that might trap condensate or oil. If such discharge piping is unavoidable, a trapped drip leg shall be installed to keep the piping free of fluid buildup. Discharge of pumps utilizing a common exhaust pipe shall be fitted with a check valve, a manual valve, or arranged to permit capping of the active pipe when removing or servicing a pump.

The discharging of exhausts to the outside is intended because the discharge from patient drainage is always contaminated. Such discharge can carry infectious organisms that should never be discharged within a building.

Manifolding of exhausts represents considerable savings if the distances of pipe runs are great. However, adequate ability to isolate each pump is necessary when manifolding exhausts. This requires shutoff valves on both the inlet side of each pump and the exhaust side. In addition, discharge velocities need to be known for pumps so that adequately sized piping is used. Otherwise, constriction of flow or backflow might occur.

There are no requirements relative to the material for the exhaust system because the exhaust system is not part of the therapeutic portion of the vacuum system. However, a facility still needs to be concerned about proper exhausting because of the presence of contaminants and fire, life safety, and structural hazards from the material used.

A proposal received, and accepted, for the 1996 edition pointed out that drip leg(s) are not always necessary, depending on the way exhaust piping is run. Thus, the installation of drip legs is now "as required" by the manufacturer or designer.

**4-3.2.1.10 Typical Vacuum Source.** A schematic of a typical Level 1 vacuum source is shown in Figure 4-3.2.1.10.

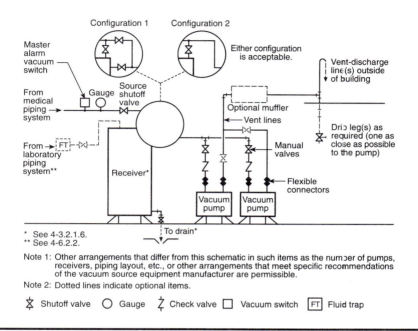

*Figure 4-3.2.1.10  Typical Level 1 vacuum source.*

The locations of the switch and the gauge have been clarified to locate them on the pipeline systems side of the source/main line valve(s). In the 1996 edition, the pressure switch and pressure gauge were shown on the incorrect side of the source valve. (The error was only in the diagram; the text was correct.) For this 1999 edition, the technical committee correctly relocated both items to the hospital side of the source valve.

When selecting a method of isolating a pump for servicing, consideration should be given to the damage that can be caused to some equipment when operating against a closed valve. In Figure 4-3.2.1.10 the various ways servicing and draining the receiver can be accomplished are illustrated through configurations 1 and 2.

### 4-3.2.2 Distribution (Piping, Valving/Controls, Station Inlets, Alarms)—Level 1.

**4-3.2.2.1 General.** The locations and number of vacuum system station inlets in a system shall be determined by consultation with medical and facility staff having knowledge of the requirements for, and the utilization of, vacuum in each space or patient location.

**4-3.2.2.2  Vacuum System Piping Network.**

(a) *Vacuum Network Piping.* Piping shall be corrosion-resistant metal such as seamless copper water tube (ASTM B 88, Types K, L, M), copper ACR tube (ASTM B 280), copper medical gas tube (ASTM B 819), stainless steel tube, or galvanized steel pipe [1½ in. minimum size] (ASTM A 53). Pipe threads shall comply with ANSI B1.20.1, *Pipe Threads, General Purpose.* Copper tube shall be hard drawn temper except that annealed tube shall be permitted underground. Joints in copper tube shall be soldered or brazed. Joints in stainless steel tube shall be brazed or welded. Joints in galvanized steel pipe shall be threaded or flanged. Soldering shall be performed in accordance with ASTM B 828, *Making Capillary Joints by Soldering of Copper and Copper Alloy Tube and Fittings.* Solder metal (ASTM B 32) shall contain less than 0.2 percent lead. Brazing shall be in accordance with 4-3.1.2.8(b) except that nitrogen purging while brazing shall not be required.

> Corrosion-resistant metal piping has always been recommended because of its strength, resistance to damage and collapse, and resistance to mechanical and fire damage. These criteria are crucial for life-support systems. The former Subcommittee on Vacuum Systems and Equipment studied the issue of piping material very carefully and concluded that there were no valid engineering reasons to exclude noncopper, metal piping in vacuum systems.
>
> In addition, the experience of most committee members indicated that copper piping for vacuum systems is usually marked sufficiently to preclude its being mistaken for medical gas pipelines and that adhering to criteria on inspection (see 4-3.2.2.2 and 4-3.4.2.2) can and does reveal any mistakes.
>
> The use of plastic pipe was considered during the early development phase on the subject of medical-surgical vacuum systems but was not accepted because of the fire hazard imposed by plastics. Concern was for the potential of localized failure of plastic pipes due to heat generated by confined fires. This could cause the vacuum system to be breached more easily than if metal piping were used. There was also concern for toxic and/or noxious fumes from plastic pipe in the event of a fire. Future changes in technology could ultimately alter this position but until then, only corrosion-resistant metal piping is acceptable.

(b) *Marking.* If copper vacuum piping is installed along with any medical gas piping, either the vacuum piping or the medical gas piping shall, prior to installation, be prominently labeled or otherwise identified to preclude using materials or installation procedures in the medical gas system that are not suitable for oxygen service. If medical gas tube (ASTM B 819) with brazed joints is used for the vacuum piping, such special marking shall not be required, provided that the vacuum piping installation meets all requirements for medical gas piping, including the prohibition of flux on copper-to-copper joints and the use of a nitrogen purge while brazing.

> Copper-to-copper joints do not require a flux because the BCuP series rod has phosphorus in the alloy that acts as the flux for these joints.

(c) *Minimum Sizes.* Mains and branches shall be not less than ⅞ in. O.D. (¾ in. nominal) size. Drops to individual vacuum inlets shall be not less than ⅝ in. O.D. (½ in. nominal) size (0.500 in. minimum inside diameter), except that the tube attached immediately to the station inlet body and not extending more than 8 in. (20.3 cm) from the station inlet shall be permitted to be½ in. O.D. (⅜ in. nominal) size (0.400 in. minimum inside diameter). Connections to gauges and alarm switches and runouts to alarm panels shall be permitted to be ¼ in. O.D. (⅛ in. nominal) size.

(d) *Support.* Piping shall be supported from the building structure in accordance with MSS Standard Practice SP-69, *Piping Hangers and Supports—Selection and Application.* Hangers and supports shall comply with MSS Standard Practice SP-58, *Pipe Hangers and Supports—Materials, Design, and Manufacture.* Hangers for copper tube shall have a copper finish. In potentially damp locations, copper tube hangers or supports shall be plastic-coated or otherwise insulated from the tube. Maximum support spacing shall be as follows:

| | |
|---|---|
| ¼ in. (.635 cm) nominal | 5 ft (1.52 m) |
| ⅜ in. (.953 cm) nominal | 6 ft (1.83 m) |
| ½ in. (1.27 cm) nominal | 6 ft (1.83 m) |
| ¾ in. (1.91 cm) nominal | 7 ft (2.13 m) |
| 1 in. (2.54 cm) nominal | 8 ft (2.44 m) |
| 1¼ in. (3.175 cm) nominal | 9 ft (2.74 m) |
| 1½ in. (3.81 cm) nominal and larger | 10 ft (3.05 m) |
| Vertical risers, all sizes | Every floor, but not to exceed 15 ft (4.57 m) |

(e) *Copper Tube Fittings.* Fittings for joining copper tube shall be pressure-rated copper, brass, or bronze made especially for brazing or soldering, except as provided in 4-3.2.2.2(f) and (g). Fittings shall be wrought or cast, except that cast fittings shall not be brazed.

(f) *Mechanically Formed Branch Connections.* The use of drilled and extruded tee-branch connections to copper mains and branches shall be permitted. Such connections shall be made in accordance with the tool manufacturer's instructions and the joint shall be brazed.

The method, demonstrated to the former Subcommittee on Vacuum Systems, involves the use of a special drill that first drills a hole in a pipe and then forms out a portion of the pipe, creating a fitting from the pipe itself. It has been considered acceptable only for piping used for vacuum systems and is not acceptable for piped gas systems.

(g) *Shape-Memory Couplings.* Memory-metal couplings providing joints equivalent to a soldered or brazed joint shall be permitted.

This type of fitting is radically different from those requiring the use of a hot flame and solder (brazing) to form a seal at each end of the fitting joining two pipes. Metallic shape memory fittings are made of a special alloy that contracts upon heating (e.g., if kept very cold, contraction occurs upon exposure to ambient temperatures). Thus, fittings are kept in liquid nitrogen until ready for use. When fittings are removed from the super-cold nitrogen, the installer has about 30 seconds to slip half the fitting over the end of one of the joining pipes and place the other pipe into the other half of the fitting. The fitting, since it is now exposed to a warmer temperature, will contract, creating a permanent and very tight seal. No flame or solder is required.

(h) *Unions.* Unions, flare nuts, and similar straight-threaded connections shall be permitted only in exposed locations and shall not be concealed in walls or ceilings.

(i) *Protection.* Piping exposed in corridors and other areas where subject to physical damage from the movement of carts, stretchers, portable equipment, or vehicles shall be suitably protected. Piping embedded in concrete floors or walls shall be installed in a continuous conduit.

(j) *Underground Piping.* Piping shall be protected against freezing, corrosion, and physical damage. Buried piping outside of buildings shall be installed below the local level of frost penetration. Buried piping that will be subject to surface loads shall be buried at a sufficient depth to protect the piping from excessive stresses. The minimum backfilled cover above the top of buried piping outside of buildings shall be 36 in. (91.4 cm), except that the minimum cover shall be permitted to be reduced to 18 in. (45.7 cm) where physical damage to the piping is not likely to occur. Trenches shall be excavated so that the pipe has a firm, substantially continuous bearing on the bottom of the trench. Underground piping shall be installed in a continuous enclosure to protect the pipe from damage while backfilling. The enclosure shall be split or otherwise provide access at the joints during visual inspection and leak testing.

Backfill shall be clean and compacted so as to protect and uniformly support the piping. A continuous tape or marker placed immediately above the enclosure shall clearly identify the pipeline by specific name. In addition, a continuous warning means shall be provided above the pipeline at approximately one-half the depth of bury. Where underground piping is installed through a wall sleeve, the ends of the sleeve shall be sealed to prevent the entrance of ground water. Piping under ground within buildings or embedded in concrete floors or walls shall be installed in a continuous conduit.

(k) *Penetrations.* Where piping penetrates fire barriers such as walls, partitions, or ceiling/floor assemblies having required fire resistance ratings, the penetration shall be protected in accordance with the requirements of NFPA *101, Life Safety Code*, and the applicable building codes.

(l) *Conversion.* Vacuum piping systems shall not be converted for use as a pressurized gas system.

**4-3.2.2.3 Vacuum System Valve Boxes.** Valve boxes shall be permanently labeled in substance as follows:

> CAUTION: MEDICAL-SURGICAL VACUUM VALVE
> DO NOT CLOSE EXCEPT IN EMERGENCY
> THIS VALVE CONTROLS VACUUM TO . . . .

## 4-3.2.2.4 Vacuum System Valves Not in Boxes.

All shutoff valves that are not in labeled boxes, such as in the main line, risers, or above suspended ceilings, shall be identified by means of durable tags, nameplates, or labels in substance as follows:

> **CAUTION:** MEDICAL-SURGICAL VACUUM VALVE
> DO NOT CLOSE EXCEPT IN EMERGENCY
> THIS VALVE CONTROLS VACUUM TO. . . .

**4-3.2.2.5 Vacuum System Station Inlets.** Each station inlet for vacuum shall be legibly labeled in substance as follows:

> **SUCTION**

or

> **VACUUM**

or, if used,

> **WASTE ANESTHETIC GAS DISPOSAL**

### 4-3.2.2.6 Vacuum System Shutoff Valves.

(a) *General.* Shutoff valves shall be provided to isolate appropriate sections or portions of the piping system for maintenance, repair, or planned future expansion need, and to facilitate periodic testing. All valves, other than those in valve boxes, shall be located in a secure area accessible to authorized personnel only, or be locked or latched open (or closed).

Shutoff valves are necessary, but are subject to accidental and deliberate tampering if placed in an area that is not controlled. Adequate securing of their accessibility is vital for patient safety.

(b) *Valve Types.* Shutoff valves shall be metallic and of a type that will create no greater flow restriction than the piping to which they are connected.

Valves are to be made of metal because they are an integral part of the piping system and should meet the same standards as the piping.

(c) *Source Shutoff Valve.* A shutoff valve shall be installed immediately upstream (on the terminal or inlet side) of the receiver tank in the vicinity of the source equipment.

(d) *Main Line Valve.* The main supply line shall be provided with a shutoff valve where the main line first enters the building. A main line valve shall not be required if the source valve is accessible from within the building.

(e) *Riser Valves.* Shutoff valves shall be provided at the base of vertical risers servicing more than one floor.

(f) *Service Valves.* A shutoff valve shall be provided on each floor between the riser and the first station inlet to allow for maintenance and periodic testing without serious disruption of service. In single-story facilities, a shutoff valve shall be installed between the main line and the first terminal of each branch line.

With a requirement that a shutoff valve be placed on each floor, it is prohibited to have shutoff valves control station inlets on different floors.

(g) *Zone Valve.* A shutoff valve shall be located immediately outside of each vital life-support, critical care, or anesthetizing location in each vacuum line, and located as to be readily accessible in an emergency or for maintenance of the terminals or piping within the individual zone served.

(h) *Valve Boxes.* Shutoff valves accessible to other than authorized personnel shall be installed in valve boxes with frangible or removable windows large enough to permit manual operation of valves.

While subparagraph (h) is only a declaratory type of requirement (relative to placing shutoff valves, other than those restricted to authorized personnel, in boxes), the rest of 4-3.2.2.6 clearly requires shutoff valves throughout a Level 1 vacuum system. For an explanation of the exception to this subparagraph, see the commentary on the exception to 4-3.1.2.3.

The requirements for shutoff valves for vacuum systems in anesthetizing locations were modified in 1995. See 4-1.2.3(n).

*Exception: Shutoff valves for use in certain areas, such as psychiatric or pediatric, shall be permitted to be secured to prevent inappropriate access.*

(i) New or replacement valves shall be of a quarter-turn shutoff type with an indicating handle (i.e., ball or butterfly valve).

### 4-3.2.2.7 Vacuum System Station Inlets.

For the 1996 edition of NFPA 99, the Committee on Piping Systems deleted all requirements regarding the number of station inlets in a particular room or area because it is not within the scope of the committee. In addition, other organizations have published recommendations as noted in C-4.8.

The term *station inlet* was decided upon in 1990 to describe the end terminal of a vacuum system. The term *inlet* is considered the most technically accurate with respect to function. It was chosen by the former Subcommittee on Vacuum Systems after much discussion because the vacuum system inlets were being confused with positive-pressure medical piped gas system station outlets. See Exhibit 4.21.

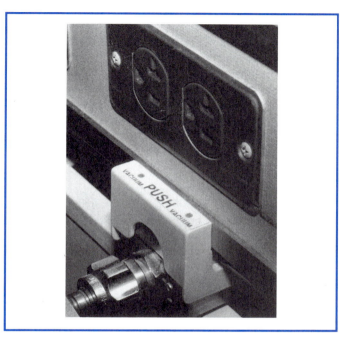

***Exhibit 4.21*** *A typical vacuum station inlet with a device connected to it. The receptacle and cover plate above the inlet are red, indicating that it is wired to the essential electrical system.*

(a) *General.* Each station inlet for vacuum shall be equipped with a valve mechanism of a type not interchangeable with other systems (e.g., oxygen, compressed air) and either a threaded connection or a quick coupler.

(b) *Threaded Connections.* Valves with threaded connections shall conform to the Diameter-Index Safety System as described in the CGA Pamphlet V-5.

(c) *Secondary Check Valves.* Vacuum station inlets shall not incorporate a secondary check valve.

(d) *Physical Protection.* Station inlets shall be located so as to avoid physical damage to the valve or attached equipment.

(e) *Physical Spacing.* Careful consideration shall be given to provide adequate spacing between the station inlets and adjacent medical gas outlets.

(f) *Removable Assemblies.* Components of the vacuum station inlet necessary to the maintenance of vacuum specificity shall be legibly marked to identify VACUUM or SUCTION system. Components not specific to vacuum shall not be required to be marked.

(g) *Manufactured Assemblies.* Inlets intended for the connection of manufactured assemblies shall be D.I.S.S. connectors.

### 4-3.2.2.8 Master Alarm System for Vacuum Systems.

Suction therapy is truly life-supporting. Patients receiving suction therapy are generally in serious condition, nonambulatory, and incapable of self-preservation. Failure of suction therapy can be injurious and life threatening. Thus, the proper functioning of alarms to indicate a failure or shutdown of a Level 1 vacuum system is most essential. Warning systems were nonexistent or conflicting in some of the design guidelines prior to the development of the following alarm system requirements beginning in the late 1970s. Requiring such systems was part of the rationale for the development of NFPA 56K (now part of NFPA 99).

(a) *General.* To ensure continuous responsible observation, the master alarm signal panels shall be located in two separate warning locations, wired in parallel to a single sensor to indicate when the vacuum in the main line drops below the level required in 4-3.4.2.2(c)4b. Audible and noncancellable visual signals shall be installed in the office or principal working area of the individual responsible for the maintenance of the vacuum system and, to ensure continuous surveillance, at the telephone switchboard, the security office, or other continuously staffed locations.

This section was revised in 1996 to be consistent with that for piped gas systems because alarms for both systems are often installed at the same time, and the critical nature of the alarms is similar for both systems.

(b) *Actuator Switch.* The actuator (vacuum switch) for the master alarm shall be connected to the main line immediately upstream (on the terminal or inlet side) of the source valve (the main line valve, if so equipped).

(c) *Alarm Panels.* The master alarm signal panel(s) required in 4-3.2.2.8(a) (each with visual and audible signal) shall be actuated by the vacuum switch described in 4-3.2.2.8(b).

(d) *Panel Labels.* The master alarm signal panel(s) shall be appropriately labeled.

(e)* *Combined Alarm Signals.* The vacuum alarm signal shall serve only the medical-surgical vacuum system.

**A-4-3.2.2.8(e)** The master alarm signal panel for the vacuum system can be combined with other alarm signals for other facility systems, such as oxygen, emergency electrical power, or fire alarms, provided that the function of this alarm signal is clearly distinguished from the others by labeling as described in 4-3.2.2.8(d).

See Table 4-3.4.1.4 for list of master alarm signals. See 4-3.1 and Chapter 3.

This paragraph was introduced in 1990. It recognizes the growing utilization of computers, while also noting the necessity of maintaining existing safety requirements when a new technology, such as computers, is used. The paragraph was revised in 1996 to reflect the change in 4-3.2.2.8(a) that requires two separate master alarm panels.

(f)* *Alarm System Power.* The master alarm signal system shall be energized by the essential electrical system described in 4-3.2.1.5.

**A-4-3.2.2.8(f)** See also Chapter 3.

(g) *Connection to Centralized Computers.* The connection of the master alarm system to a centralized computer (e.g., a building management system) shall be permitted. The computer shall not constitute one of the two master alarm panels required.

**4-3.2.2.9 Area Alarm Systems for Vacuum Systems.**

(a)* *General.* Area alarms shall be provided for anesthetizing locations and critical care areas. Warning signals shall be provided for all medical-surgical vacuum piping systems supplying these areas to indicate if the vacuum decreases from the normal operating range.

**A-4-3.2.2.9(a)** For additional information concerning alarms for central medical-gas piping systems, refer to Sections 4-3 and 4-4.

(b) *Visual and Audible Signals.* The vacuum area alarm system shall incorporate both cancellable audible and noncancellable visual signals that are activated by actuators (vacuum switches) connected to the vacuum line serving each specific area.

(c) *Alarm Panels.* The visual and audible signal panels shall be installed at nurses' stations or other suitable locations in the areas described in 4-3.2.2.9(a) and be appropriately labeled.

(d)* *Actuating Switches.* The actuating switch for anesthetizing locations shall be in the specific line supplying the operating or delivery room suites, with the individual room shutoff valve being the only one between the actuating switch and the room inlets.

The area alarm actuating switch for each vital life support and critical care unit shall be in the specific line serving that area. No shutoff valve shall be installed between the actuating switch and the inlets.

This section was revised for the 1996 edition to be consistent with that for piped gas systems for both anesthetizing locations and life support/critical areas. Confusion in applying previous requirements that were different and opposite to piped gas systems had previously been reported to the committee.

**A-4-3.2.2.9(d)** This signal is intended to provide immediate warning for loss of, or increase in, system pressure for each individual vital life support and critical care area.

This signal is intended to provide immediate warning for loss of, or increase in, system pressure for all anesthetizing locations supplied from a single branch line—not for each individual operating or delivery room.

(e) *Actuating Switch Settings.* Actuating (vacuum switches) for the area alarm signals shall be set to activate their respective warning signals (visual and audible) at and below 12 in. Hg of vacuum.

Only low-vacuum alarming is stipulated because the upper limit can vary depending on system design.

It should also be noted that the high alarm setting and vacuum are not related to the operating level of pumps.

A minor but important editorial change was made in 1996 that revised text from "below 12 in." to "at and below 12 in." This clarifies the level at which the alarm is to be activated.

(f)* *Electrical Power.* The area alarm signal system shall be energized by the essential electrical system described in 4-3.2.1.5.

**A-4-3.2.2.9(f)**  See also Chapter 3.

**4-3.2.2.10  Vacuum System Gauges.**

(a) *Main-Line Gauge.* A vacuum gauge shall be provided in the main vacuum line adjacent to the actuator (vacuum switch) for the master alarms, with this gauge located immediately upstream (on the terminal or inlet side) terminal or inlet of the source valve (the main line valve, if so equipped). Those with "normal range" display shall indicate normal only between 12 and 19 in. Hg (vacuum).

(b) *Area Gauge.* Vacuum gauges shall be located at each area vacuum alarm signal location, with this gauge connected upstream (on the terminal or inlet side) of any valve controlling that area. Those with "normal range" display shall indicate normal only between 12 and 19 in. Hg (vacuum).

Gauges, particularly area gauges, should be checked regularly and, if necessary, calibrated to ensure optimum vacuum for patient therapy.

Because the degree of vacuum available constantly changes within an optimum preset range, gauges are not to require manual activation to determine the condition of the system. [See also A-4-3.2.2.10(c).]

(c)* *Vacuum Gauge Identification.* All permanently installed vacuum gauges and manometers for the vacuum system shall be continuous reading, manufactured expressly for vacuum, and labeled: VACUUM.

**A-4-3.2.2.10(c)**  Vacuum gauges should have an indicated range of 0 in. to 30 in. Hg (vacuum).

Vacuum gauges can be part of shutoff valves in boxes, or incorporated in a unit with gauges for the central medical gas piping systems described in Sections 4-3 through 4-5.

**4-3.2.2.11  Installation of Vacuum System Piping.**

(a) *General.* The provisions of this section shall apply to field-installed piping for vacuum systems.

(b) *Materials and Joints.* Piping materials and joining methods shall be in accordance with 4-3.2.2.2.

While reference is made to 4-3.2.2.2, it should be noted that soldering of piping for vacuum systems is permitted. Technically, there is no justification for silver brazing vacuum system piping because a vacuum system cannot leak its contents and cause a hazard, even in the event of a fire that causes vacuum lines to leak (i.e., the system is under negative pressure compared to the atmosphere). A melting point not less than 450°F (232°C) was extensively discussed in the 1980s, and considered adequate for joint integrity, structural consideration, and general safety by the committee responsible for vacuum systems. Conversely, oxidizing gases (e.g., oxygen, nitrous oxide, compressed air) are gases under 3.5 atmospheres pressure within a piped gas system and can leak into the atmosphere. Therefore, these systems require tubing, such as copper tubing, that cannot ignite in 100 percent oxidizing gases as opposed to ferrous metals that can ignite in such an atmosphere and cause hazards. These piped gas systems also require higher-temperature brazing at joints [not less than 1000°F (538°C)] to reduce the probability of leaking and/or breaking joints in the event of a nearby fire.

The committee also recognized the possibility of a mix-up in new construction when piped vacuum and gas systems can be installed simultaneously and adjacent to each other. Thus, the suggestion that all pipes meet gas system requirements when installed simultaneously to prevent a possible mix-up.

Given the critical nature of these systems, inspection of joints before walls, ceiling, and so forth, are closed in, in accordance with 4-3.2.2.11(f), is considered essential.

(c) *Open Ends.* Care shall be taken to maintain the interior of the piping system free of debris or other foreign matter. Pipe, tube, and fittings shall be inspected visually prior to installation. During installation, open ends of piping shall be temporarily sealed.

(d) *Flux.* Where flux is used for soldered or brazed joints, it shall be used sparingly to avoid excess flux inside of the finished joint.

(e) *Cleaning.* After soldering or brazing, the outside of all joints shall be cleaned by washing with water and a stainless steel brush to remove any residue and permit clear visual inspection of the joint. If flux has been used, joints shall be washed with hot water.

(f) *Visual Inspection.* Each soldered or brazed joint shall be visually examined after cleaning of the outside of the joint. The following conditions shall be considered unacceptable:

1. Flux or flux residue
2. Excessive oxidation of the joint
3. Presence of unmelted solder or braze filler metal
4. Cracks in the tube or component
5. Failure of the solder or braze filler metal to be clearly visible all the way around the joint at the interface between the socket and the tube
6. Cracks in the solder or braze filler metal
7. Failure of the joint to hold the test pressure under 4-3.4.2.2(b)2

(g) *Repairs.* Soldered or brazed joints that are found to be defective under 4-3.2.2.11(f)1, 3, 4, 6, or 7 shall be permitted to be repaired, except that no joint shall be repaired more than twice. Joints that are found to be defective under 4-3.2.2.11(f)2 or 5 shall be replaced.

(h) *Piping Identification.* Vacuum piping shall be readily identified by appropriate labeling, such as MEDICAL-SURGICAL VACUUM, or MED/SURG VAC. Labeling shall be by means of stamped metal tags, stenciling, or printed adhesive markers, and shall not be readily removable. Labels shall be spaced at intervals of not more than 20 ft (6.1 m), except that at least one label shall be visible in or above each room or area. Flow arrows (if used) shall point from the station inlets toward the receiver or pump.

## 4-3.3 Waste Anesthetic Gas Disposal (WAGD) Systems (Source and Distribution)—Level 1.

The 1996 edition expanded the options available for implementation of WAGD and for the first time explicitly included requirements for a variety of different WAGD methods. The decision of which method to use is best made based on clinical preferences and practice, economics, and safety. Along with the inclusion of three alternative methods, a certain minimum level of operating safety was added, including for the first time alarms and redundant WAGD producers.

The committee added these requirements to recognize the variety of existing WAGD implementations and to permit all known viable methods while providing the user with baseline safety criteria.

In 1980 the term *waste anesthetic gas evacuation* (WAGE) was agreed upon by the former Committee on Medical-Surgical Vacuum Systems to describe the collection (by scavengers) and disposal (by a disposal system) of waste anesthetic gases that can be present in the surgical area. For the 1984 edition of NFPA 99, the term *evacuation* was changed to *disposal* because ANSI Z79.11-1982, *Anesthetic Equipment-Scavenging Systems for Excess Anesthetic Gases* [10], used the term *disposal* as opposed to *evacuation*. Because that document was developed in coordination with international standards organizations, the NFPA committee responsible for vacuum system requirements in NFPA 99 followed suit.

WAGD is sometimes called *scavenging*. It is preferable, however, to use the term *scavenging* in connection with the equipment used between the anesthesia machine and inlet of a disposal system rather than with the function itself. [See also commentary on waste anesthetic gases under 4-3.3.1.3(a).]

See Exhibit 4.22

### 4-3.3.1 Source—Level 1.

**4-3.3.1.1\* General.** WAGD systems shall be designed and implemented after consultation with the medical staff having knowledge of the requirements to determine the type of system, number and placement of terminals, and other required safety and operating devices.

**A-4-3.3.1.1** A functioning WAGD system will permit the facility to comply with occupational safety requirements by preventing the accumulation of waste anesthetic gases in the work environment.

***Exhibit 4.22*** *Scavenging device mounted on the side of an anesthesia setup that connects to the waste anesthetic gas disposal system in an operating room.*

WAGD using the HVAC (heating, ventilation, and air conditioning) are not within the scope of this chapter.

Some facilities have dedicated WAGD systems and dedicated medical-surgical vacuum systems. Indiscriminate connection of waste gas removal devices to the medical-surgical vacuum system, and vice versa, can cause system malfunctions and can jeopardize patient safety.

Techniques for scavenging waste anesthetic gases include disposal into an existing medical-surgical vacuum system or into the return-exhaust of the air-handling system for the room. Until recent years, operating room air was not recirculated. Today, if recirculation of air is practiced, disposal of waste anesthetic gases into the room exhaust system might not seem appropriate. To counter this situation, dilution of any flammable gases can reduce concentrations well below their limit of flammability. Nonflammable gases, for which no level of toxicity to attending personnel has been established, would also be diluted to the vanishing point. Questions surrounding waste anesthetic gas disposal and its safety are still very much in debate by experts in the field.

### 4-3.3.1.2  Dedicated WAGD Vacuum Producers.

(a) The WAGD source shall consist of multiple vacuum producers (vacuum pumps, blowers, fans, etc.) that alternately or simultaneously on demand serve the WAGD system.

(b) Producers used exclusively for WAGD use shall be designed of materials, and shall use lubricants where needed, that are inert in the presence of oxygen, nitrous oxide, and halogenated anesthetics.

Due to the possible presence of a concentration of gases that are strong oxidizers in a dedicated WAGD vacuum system, it is imperative that a vacuum producer use a sealant, such as water (in liquid ring pumps), or perfluorinatedpolyether (PFPE) (synthetic) oil (in oil-sealed pumps) and PFPE grease (in oil-less pumps), that will not react with explosive force when the sealant come in contact with these oxidizers.

(c) WAGD plants shall comply with 4-3.2.1.1 through 4-3.2.1.5.

(d) The WAGD vacuum producer shall be located to comply with 4-3.2.1.8.

(e) The exhaust for the WAGD system shall comply with 4-3.2.1.9.

### 4-3.3.1.3  Medical-Surgical Vacuum Source used for WAGD.

A medical-surgical vacuum refers to the application of suction therapy directly to the patient. WAGD is an environmental control system and a ventilation function used for the protection of operating room staff. Because WAGD directly connects with the patient breathing circuit, its proper design, installation, and functioning is a matter of importance to patient safety.

The committee responsible for Chapter 4, recognizing that anesthetizing areas should provide staff protection from pollution by anesthetizing gases, recommends that WAGD systems be used.

On the basis of flow, a properly implemented WAGD system would not add significantly to a medical-surgical vacuum system (MSVS). This was found in surveys by the former Committee on Medical-Surgical Vacuum Systems (now Sub-committee on Vacuum Systems and Equipment) and confirmed in ANSI Z79.11-1982, *Standard for Anesthetic Equipment-Scavenging Systems for Excess Anesthetic Gases* [10]. The maximum volume flowing into a properly implemented WAGD from a single patient is less than 0.54 SCFM, which is worst-case displacement/momentary demand [maximum 5 seconds or 0.045 standard $ft^3$ (1.27 L)] during oxygen flush or because of occluded scavenging equipment (as noted in Table A1 in ANSI Z79.11). Normal operational displacement is less than 0.35 SCFM (see C-4.6, point 3).

The committee considers implementation of WAGD through connection into a medical-surgical vacuum system (MSVS), however, as undesirable for the following reasons:

(a)  ANSI Z79.11-1982 [10] states that the maximum safe negative pressure for the patient "shall not exceed 0.5 cm $H_2O$ (0.01446847 in Hg)." This is a very low vacuum level compared to the minimum 12 in. Hg of vacuum in the MSVS.

(b) The standard alarm systems and monitoring gauges required for MSVS cannot be used in a WAGD system. WAGD requires switches, sensors, and gauges appropriate for the very low vacuum levels encountered and, in some implementations, can require the use of flow in place of pressure as an operating indicator.

(c) Nonrecirculating ventilation systems, dedicated blower systems, and passive systems (ambient differential) have all been demonstrated to be effective for WAGD. The intent of ANSI Z79.11-1982 [10] that the pressure of a scavenging system approximate ambient pressure in normal use can be met by these system, but not by an MSVS system.

(d) Some of the valving and piping material acceptable for use in an MSVS is not acceptable for WAGD. This includes components made of some elastomers (many anesthetic agents can cause O-rings made of these materials to swell) and aluminum, brass, magnesium, tin, and lead (halothane and other fluorinated agents can attack these unalloyed metals in the presence of water vapor).

(e) The International Standards Organization (ISO) and the British Standards Institute oppose using an MSVS for WAGD. Both organizations concur with 0.5 cm $H_2O$ as the maximum safe negative pressure for patients.

For further information, see the following:

"Potential Pulmonary Barotrauma When Venting Anesthesia Gases to Suction," Sharrock and Leith, *Anesthesiology* 46, 1977.

"Waste Anesthetic Gases in Operating Room Air," J. H. Lecky, M.D., *Journal of ASA,* 1980.

*"Gas Scavenging—WAGD," L. D. Bridenbaugh, M.D., Clinical Engineering Series,* Academic Press, 1981.

(a) *Uses.* A medical-surgical vacuum source complying with this standard shall be permitted to be used for WAGD.

(b)* *Explosion Hazard.* Flammable anesthetic or other flammable vapors shall be diluted below the lower flammable limit prior to disposal into the medical-surgical vacuum system.

**A-4-3.3.1.3(b)** For further information, see A-5-4.1 (re: ANSI Z79.11), and C-12.1.3.1 on flammable anesthetic agents.

Flammable and nonflammable gases are known to be incompatible with some seals and piping used in medical-surgical vacuum systems. If waste anesthetic gas disposal is to be included as part of the medical-surgical vacuum system, it should be recognized that this activity might cause deterioration of the vacuum system. The station inlet performance tests outlined in 4-3.5.6.1(c) are extremely important in maintaining the integrity of the medical-surgical vacuum system, and they should be made at more frequent intervals if waste anesthetic gas disposal is included in the vacuum system.

Nurse anesthetist schools and anesthesiology residency programs have not taught flammable anesthetics administration since 1982. In addition, it was reported to the former Subcommittee on Vacuum Systems (now part of the Committee on Piping Systems) that the use of flammable anesthetics was encountered in only three locations out of 1500 in JCAH surveys conducted in 1982. Of late, the use of flammable anesthetics in the United States has essentially ceased.

The committee is concerned, however, that the emergency use of flammable anesthetics can contribute additional and unnecessary hazards if a medical-surgical vacuum system is used for WAGD. This paragraph has remained to draw attention to the potential hazard of a medical-surgical vacuum system used for WAGD when flammable anesthetics are used.

### 4-3.3.1.4 Venturi-Driven WAGD.

(a) Where a venturi within the station inlet is used to produce WAGD vacuum, the venturi shall not be user adjustable (i.e., shall require the use of special tools).

(b) Venturi WAGD shall be produced using air or an inert drive gas.

(c) Drive air for venturi WAGD shall not come from the medical air system.

### 4-3.3.2 Distribution—Level 1.

### 4-3.3.2.1 WAGD Distribution Network.

(a) *Inlets.* WAGD networks shall provide a WAGD inlet at each anesthetizing location.

(b) *Distribution Network.* WAGD distribution networks shall be constructed of corrosion-resistant materials appropriate for use with oxygen, nitrous oxide, and halogenated anesthetics in the concentrations encountered in the anesthetic breathing circuit.

(c) *Distribution Network Support.* WAGD distribution networks shall be supported directly from the building structure by pipe hooks, straps, bands, or hangers suitable for the size and weight of the network material. Supports shall be placed to ensure that support is provided at the joints, and placed at intervals which ensure adequate support for the size and weight of the network material.

(d) *Devices.* The distribution network shall be provided with balancing valves, dampers, or other devices necessary to balance the flows and pressures through the network to those required by the WAGD interfaces in use with the facility's gas anesthetic machines.

### 4-3.3.2.2 WAGD Valves and Dampers.

(a) *Valves.* WAGD valves or dampers shall be provided where necessary for system balance or convenience of maintenance. Where valves are provided, they shall be labeled by means of durable tags, nameplates, or labels:

**CAUTION:** WASTE ANESTHETIC GAS DISPOSAL VALVE
DO NOT CLOSE EXCEPT FOR SERVICE
THIS VALVE CONTROLS WAGD TO . . . .

(b) *Dampers.* (Reserved)

**4-3.3.2.3 WAGD Inlets.**

(a) WAGD inlets shall be provided in all locations where nitrous oxide or halogenated anesthetic agents are likely to be administered.

The locations where WAGD inlets must be installed is a very complex issue in a health care environment where the nature of anesthesia is changing rapidly. At one time, most general anesthesia involved gaseous anesthetics; now much general anesthesia is injected. As a result, almost any site in the hospital could be an anesthetizing location, thereby greatly complicating the question of where to place WAGD inlets.

The change to 4-3.2.2.3(a) in 1999 addresses this issue at least in part by allowing the designer to define an anesthetizing location for the purpose of WAGD as a site where nitrous oxide or halogenated anesthetic will be administered. While it is understood that there are other instances for installing a WAGD inlet (e.g., use of portable supplies of nitric oxide), these are the major waste gases of widespread concern today.

(b) Each station inlet for WAGD shall be of a type appropriate for the flow and vacuum level required by the WAGD interfaces in use with the facility's gas anesthetic machines. They shall be located to avoid physical damage to the inlet. If the inlet can be disassembled for service, each component shall be legibly marked "WAGD" or similar. WAGD inlets shall be not interchangeable with other systems, including medical-surgical vacuum.

**4-3.3.2.4 WAGD Alarms.**

(a) Alarms or other automatic mechanisms shall be provided to inform the user that the WAGD system is operational.

**4-3.3.2.5 WAGD System Distribution Network Installation.**

(a) *Assembly.* The WAGD network shall be assembled using such materials and methods as will assure the network is free of leaks under operating vacuum levels.

(b) *Labeling.* The WAGD network shall be identified by appropriate labeling such as WASTE ANESTHETIC GAS DISPOSAL. Such labeling shall be by means of metal tags, stenciling, stamping, or adhesive markers in a manner that is not readily removable. Labeling shall appear on the network at intervals of not more than 20 ft (6.1 m) and at least once in or above each room and each story traversed by the piping. Arrows (where used) shall point from the terminal to the vacuum producer.

## 4-3.4 Performance Criteria and Testing—Level 1 (Gas, Vacuum, WAGD).

Prior to the 1993 edition, testing requirements were located in several parts of Chapter 4. In the 1993 edition, all testing was consolidated to make the document more user-friendly. For the 1996 edition, all requirements for Level 1 piped gas and vacuum systems were placed in Section 4-3.

The testing specified in 4-3.4 is based, in part, on the U.S. Department of Veterans Affairs Test Protocol.

Because there are currently no national certification or registration programs for installers, inspectors, or testers of nonflammable medical piped gas systems, a facility should research and check the references of any persons or companies being considered to perform these tasks. A check with local and/or state authorities on any relevant regulations can prove useful in this regard. (See also commentary under 4-3.4.1.1.) There may be local or state requirements mandating a permit before a piping system can be installed. Some states have begun referencing all or portions of NFPA 99 in this regard. Some states are requiring compliance with American Society of Sanitary Engineers/ANSI Standard 6000 [11] as a minimum for installers of medical gas systems.

### 4-3.4.1 Piped Gas Systems—Level 1.

**4-3.4.1.1\* General.** Inspection and testing shall be performed on all new piped gas systems, additions, renovations, temporary installations, or repaired systems, to assure the facility, by a documented procedure, that all applicable provisions of this document have been adhered to and system integrity has been achieved or maintained.

This inspection and testing shall include all components of the system or portions thereof including, but not limited to, gas bulk source(s), manifolds, compressed air source systems (e.g., compressors, dryers, filters, regulators), source alarms and monitoring safeguards, master alarms, pipelines, isolation valves, area alarms, zone valves, and station inlets (vacuum) and outlets (pressure gases).

All systems that are breached and components that are subject to additions, renovations, or replacement (e.g., new gas sources-bulk, manifolds, compressors, dryers, alarms) shall be inspected and appropriately tested.

Systems shall be deemed breached at the point of pipeline intrusion by physical separation or by system component removal, replacement, or addition. The breached portions of the systems subject to inspection and testing shall be confined to only the specific altered zone and components in the immediate zone or area that is located upstream for vacuum systems and downstream for pressure gases at the point or area of intrusion.

The inspection and testing reports shall be verified and a certificate and submitted directly to the party that contracted for the testing. That party shall then submit the report through channels to the responsible authority and any others that are required. These reports shall contain detailed listings of all findings and results.

The responsible facility authority shall review these inspection and testing records prior to the use of all systems. This responsible facility authority shall ensure that all findings and results of the inspection and testing have been successfully completed, and all documentation pertaining thereto shall be maintained on-site within the facility.

Before piping systems are initially put into use, the health care facility authority shall be responsible for ascertaining that the gas delivered at the outlet is that shown on the outlet label and that the proper connecting fittings are checked against their labels. This can be accomplished by accepting the results of 4-3.4.1.3, System Verification.

Manufactured assemblies shall, prior to arrival at the installation site, be pretested to comply with 4-3.4.1.2(a) through 4-3.4.1.2(e), except that 4-3.4.1.2(c) shall be permitted to be performed by any leak testing method that will assure a pressure decay of less than 1 percent in 24 hours. The manufacturer shall provide documentation attesting to the performance and successful completion of these tests.

The reference in paragraph 2 to bulk source(s) should not be interpreted to include the testing as required by NFPA 50, *Standard for Bulk Oxygen Systems at Consumer Sites* [1]. It refers only to the testing of bulk supply signals that are connected to the master alarm panels [see 4-3.4.1.4(a)5] and to testing of the bulk oxygen system when it interfaces with the piped distribution system.

The committee responsible for this text has frequently been asked to define what portions of a system must be tested and what tests must be conducted after the system is breached. For the 1993 edition, this question was addressed with the expanded text in 4-3.4.1.1. For the 1996 edition, further changes were made to paragraphs 2 through 5 to reflect the committee's intent. The following examples are provided as guidance in attempting to answer some of these questions:

- If an oxygen outlet were added to a 50-room zone, and the entire zone was drained of oxygen and refilled with nitrogen for the work, then the entire zone would need to be retested prior to returning the system to normal operation and the connection of patients.
- If a five-story riser were shut down for a tie-in on the second floor, and nitrogen was not used for the tie-in, it should be necessary only to check the closest outlets upstream and downstream of the tie-in for particulate and concentration and to check on the furthermost outlet for concentration. (These steps are in addition to whatever tests are necessary for the new section itself prior to tie-in.)

Note that test reports are to be certified. (See paragraphs 1 and 5.) However, NFPA does not certify persons who install or test medical gas systems, nor does it review or approve any test reports issued as a result of testing or inspecting of such systems. This verification, however, does need to be done by qualified, competent persons.

Paragraph 5 was modified for the 1996 edition. Test reports are now to be sent directly to the party contracting for the testing; that party will, in turn, distribute copies to necessary authorities, insurers, and other parties requiring a copy of the report. This change reflects the difficulty at times of determining who the authority(-ies) having jurisdiction is for a particular installation and the additional parties that need to receive a copy of the report. The contracting party should be in a better position to know this than the testing (verification) company.

Note the addition of a new subparagraph (a) on the subject of manufactured assemblies, and the order of testing that applies.

**A-4-3.4.1.1** See also NFPA 50, *Standard for Bulk Oxygen Systems at Consumer Sites.*

**4-3.4.1.2 Installer Performance Testing.** The following tests shall be conducted by the installer or representative prior to those tests listed in 4-3.4.1.3, System Verification. Test gas shall be oil-free, dry nitrogen.

Where manufactured assemblies are to be installed, tests required under this section shall be performed at all station outlets after completion of the pipeline and after installation of any manufactured assemblies employing copper tubing but prior to installation of any manufactured assemblies employing flexible hoses or tubing.

> A new exception to the system verification portion of NFPA 99 was added prior to 4-3.4.1.3(a). This exception acknowledges that it might not be practical to use nitrogen as the test gas in all instances. For example, if a small amount of oxygen, air, or vacuum outlets are added to an existing in-use zone, the existing zone valve might be of older design and might leak nitrogen back across the seals into the oxygen system during pressure testing procedures. Also it would be inappropriate to pressurize the existing zone to 150 psig (1034 kPa) for the leak test. Because the exception to 4-3.1.2.8(b)(7) already permits tie-in work to be made with source gas at source gas pressure [50 psig (345 kPa) oxygen, for instance, for an oxygen tie-in], it was considered appropriate to permit small project(s), with the permission of the authority having jurisdiction, to be installed and tested with source gases at source pressure. Obviously, it is still very important to perform the leak test at source gas pressure, the blowdown for particulate, and the concentration test. This eliminates the facility having to do a major shutdown and risk lateral or main line contamination due to older valves.
>
> As an example, a facility could renovate several rooms in a zone, perform all the installer testing as necessary using nitrogen prior to tying into the rest of the zone. The verifier could perform all necessary testing using the source gas (oxygen, air, etc.) or vacuum. This approach would minimize downtime and risk for the facility, as well as keep cost nominal for a small project.
>
> Beginning in the 1993 edition, system testing was divided into those tests to be conducted by the installer prior to the final verification tests (4-3.4.1.2) and those tests to be conducted by a technically qualified party experienced in testing piped gas systems and verifying the installation (4-3.4.1.3).
>
> Fatalities have occurred due to cross-connection of gases. It is absolutely essential to verify that labeling of outlets and the delivered gas are the same. The tests listed in this section have been developed, among other reasons, for that purpose. Other methods acceptable to the authority having jurisdiction can be used for testing for cross-connections. (See Section 1-4.)
>
> The sequence previously listed for installer testing of medical gas systems would have required the installer to install, remove, and then reinstall medical gas faceplates. For the 1996 edition, the order was modified to a normal sequence of events in the installation and preliminary testing of a medical gas pipeline. A blowdown of pipelines is now to be done before an initial pressure test. The revised

sequence is more practical, will save considerable time, and will lessen the possibility of damage to outlet components.

(a) *Blow Down.* After installation of the piping, but before installation of the station outlets and other medical gas system components (e.g., pressure-actuating switches for alarms, manifolds, pressure gauges, or pressure relief valves), the line shall be blown clear by means of oil-free, dry nitrogen *(see Section 2-2, Definitions).*

(b)* *Initial Pressure Test.* Before attachment of system compcnents (e.g., pressure-actuating switches for alarms, manifolds, pressure gauges, or pressure relief valves), but after installation of the station outlets, with test caps (if supplied) in place (e.g., rough-in assembly), each section of the piping system shall be subjected to a test pressure of 1.5 times the working pressure [minimum 150 psig (1 MPa gauge)] with oil-free, dry nitrogen *(see Section 2-2, Definitions).* This test pressure shall be maintained until each joint has been examined for leakage by means of soapy water or other equally effective means of leak detection safe for use with oxygen. The source shutoff valve shall be closed. Leaks, if any, shall be located, repaired, and retested in accordance with this paragraph.

> Pressure testing is conducted as a means to find leaks. It is important to locate leaks, particularly those that can create an oxygen-enriched atmosphere, because such atmospheres reduce the temperature at which items can be ignited, as well as enhance the burning of those combustibles that have ignited.
>
> Leaks not only represent an additional fire hazard, they are also considered by many to pose significant health risks. Excessive exposure of staff to gases such as nitrous oxide have reportedly been linked to diseases. Financially, leaks represent waste of limited resources.
>
> It is also very important that the leak-testing solution be spec_fically approved for oxygen service. Solutions approved for "compressed gas" are not necessarily approved for "oxygen service." This holds true even for a medical air pipeline. It is better to use ordinary soapy water than to use a solution that is not approved for oxygen service.

**A-4-3.4.1.2(b)**  This is intended to test those stages of construction that might not be accessible at a later time.

(c) *Cross-Connection Test.*

1. It shall be determined that no cross-connection of piping systems exists. All medical gas systems shall be reduced to atmospheric pressure. All sources of test gas shall be disconnected from all of the medical gas systems with the exception of the one system to be checked. This system shall be pressurized with oil-free nitrogen *(see Section 2-2, Definitions)* to 50 psig (350 kPa gauge). With appropriate adapters matching outlet labels, each individual station outlet of all medical gas systems installed shall be checked to determine that test gas is being dispensed only from the outlets of the medical gas system being tested.

a. The source of test gas shall be disconnected and the system tested shall be reduced to atmospheric pressure. Each additional piping system shall then be tested in accordance with 4-3.4.1.2(e)1.

b. Where a medical vacuum piping system is installed, the cross-connection testing shall include that piped vacuum system with all medical gas piping systems.

c. All medical-surgical vacuum systems shall be in operation so that these vacuum systems are tested at the same time the medical gas systems are tested.

d. Each station outlet shall be identified by label (and color marking, if used).

Note that, as with piping, color marking of station outlets is secondary to labeling.

2. The presence and correctness of labeling required by this standard for all components (e.g., station outlets, shutoff valves, and signal panels) shall be verified.

(d) *Piping Purge Test.* In order to remove particulate matter in the pipelines, a heavy, intermittent purging of the pipeline shall be done. The appropriate adapter shall be obtained, and a high-flow purge shall be put on each outlet. The outlet shall be allowed to flow fully until the purge produces no discoloration in a white cloth.

The pulse purge test required in 4-3.4.1.2(d) has been found to effectively break up material in the pipeline, such as copper oxide scale and other by-products of fabrication, and transport it to the outlet being purged.

This purge is to be conducted into a clean, white cloth loosely held over the adapter. For purposes of this test, the adapter used must be an adapter only, and not have a flowmeter or other flow-restricting device. These types of adapters are generally available directly from the manufacturers. Some facilities might retain some as well.

An appropriate adapter is necessary to prevent damage to the O-rings from screwdrivers, pencils, nails, tubing, or other miscellaneous items used to open the outlet and let gas out. As an example, when the proper adapter is used, the O-rings cannot unseat themselves under high purge. Plastic poppets and other outlet components can also be damaged if the appropriate adapter is not used.

(e)* *Standing Pressure Test.* After testing of each individual medical gas system in accordance with 4-3.4.1.2(b), the completely assembled station outlets and all other medical gas system components (e.g., pressure-actuating switches for alarms, manifolds, pressure gauges, or pressure relief valves) shall be installed, and all piping systems shall be subjected to a 24-hour standing pressure test at 20 percent above the normal operating line pressure. The test gas shall be oil-free, dry nitrogen *(see Section 2-2, Definitions)*. The source shutoff valve shall be closed.

A-4-3.4.1.2(e)  This is the final pressure test of the completely installed system and is intended to locate any leaks that would be more likely to occur at lower pressure, for example, leaks in station outlet valve seals.

The value of 20 percent above normal operating pressure permits testing without damage to other system components and without activation of any installed pressure relief valves.

During installation (see 4-3.1.2.3) and during the testing phase, only oil-free, dry nitrogen is permitted to be used for systems designed after February 1993. Other gases, including air, can potentially contaminate the line before it is put into service.

1. After the piping system is filled with test gas, the supply valve and all outlets shall be closed and the source of test gas disconnected. The piping system shall remain leak-free for 24 hours. When making the standing pressure test, the only allowable pressure changes during the 24-hour test period shall be those caused by variations in the ambient temperature around the piping system. Such changes shall be permitted to be checked by means of the following pressure-temperature relationship: the calculated final absolute pressure (absolute pressure is gauge pressure plus 14.7 psig if gauge is calibrated in psig) equals the initial absolute pressure times the final absolute temperature (absolute temperature is temperature reading plus 460°F if thermometer is calibrated in Fahrenheit degrees), divided by the initial absolute temperature.

$$\left( P_f = \frac{P_i \times T_f}{T_i} \right)$$

2. Leaks, if any, shall be located, repaired, and retested in accordance with 4-3.4.1.2(e).

**4-3.4.1.3 System Verification.** The following tests shall be performed after those listed in 4-3.4.1.2, Installer Performance Testing. The test gas shall be oil-free, dry nitrogen.

This testing shall be conducted by a party technically competent and experienced in the field of medical gas pipeline testing. Such testing shall be performed by a party other than the installing contractor.

When systems have been installed by in-house personnel, testing shall be permitted by personnel of that organization who meet the requirements of 4-3.4.1.

All tests required under 4-3.4.1.3 shall be performed after installation of any manufactured assemblies employing flexible hoses or tubing. Where there are multiple possible connection points for terminals, each possible position shall be tested independently.

When a health care organization has highly trained personnel and proper testing equipment, medical gas system testing can be performed by in-house personnel, rather than by an outside agency. Regardless of who conducts the testing, the same methods required by NFPA 99 must be followed. Necessary reports must be generated and submitted to the manager in charge of the project. If for some reason the system does not test out properly, corrective actions must be taken and system reverification performed.

If in-house personnel perform the testing, they (rather than a hired third party) are responsible for the proper operation of the medical gas system.

As an option the addition at the end of the second paragraph of "Who shall be independent of the equipment supplier, installer, or manufacturer" could help avoid any conflict of interest.

It is the intent of the committee that testing for this portion be conducted by a responsible, technically competent individual(s). However, that individual(s) does not need to be a third party. If the facility has technically competent staff, they can perform the test. The only limitation is that the installing contractor is expressly prohibited from performing these tests.

As noted in the commentary for 4-3.4.1.1, NFPA does not certify verifiers. Chapter 4 of NFPA 99 does not, as yet, list qualifications for verifiers, other than as noted in paragraph 2 of 4-3.4.1.3. (See commentary under 4-3.4.1.1 for further discussion on this subject.)

Portions of the testing required in 4-3.4.1.1(a)–(k) are based on the U.S. Department of Veterans Affairs Test Protocol.

*Exception: Where permitted by the authority having jurisdiction, for small projects affecting a limited number of areas where the use of nitrogen is impractical, the source gas shall be permitted to be used for the tests listed in 4-3.4.1.3(a)1, (c)1, (d)2, and paragraph 2 of (e).*

(a) *Cross-Connection Test.* After closing of walls and completion of requirements of 4-3.4.1.2, it shall be determined that no cross-connection of piping systems exists by either of the following methods:

1.  All medical gas systems shall be reduced to atmospheric pressure. All sources of test gas from all of the medical gas systems, with the exception of the one system to be checked, shall be disconnected. This system shall be pressurized with oil-free, dry nitrogen *(see Section 2-2, Definitions)* to 50 psig (350 kPa gauge). With appropriate adapters matching outlet labels, each individual station outlet of all medical gas systems installed shall be checked to determine that test gas is being dispensed only from the outlets of the medical gas system being tested.

    a.  The source of test gas shall be disconnected and the system tested reduced to atmospheric pressure. Proceed to test each additional piping system in accordance with 4-3.4.1.3(a)1.
    b.  Where a medical vacuum piping system is installed, the cross-connection testing shall include that piped vacuum system with all medical gas piping systems.

2.  An alternate method of testing to ensure that no cross-connections to other piping systems exists follows:

    a.  Reduce the pressure in all medical gas systems to atmospheric.
    b.  Increase the test gas pressure in all medical gas piping systems to the values indicated in Table 4-3.4.1.3(a)2. Simultaneously maintain these nominal pressures throughout the test.

Pressures in Table 4-3.4.1.3(a)2 are for testing purposes only and are not reflective of operating pressures.

*Table 4-3.4.1.3(a)2  Alternate Test Pressures*

| Medical Gas | Pressure | |
|---|---|---|
| | psig | kPa gauge |
| Gas mixtures | 20 | 140 |
| Nitrogen | 30 | 210 |
| Nitrous oxide | 40 | 280 |
| Oxygen | 50 | 350 |
| Compressed air | 60 | 420 |

Note: Systems at nonstandard pressures shall be tested at a pressure at least
10 psi (69 kPa) greater or less than any other system.

The intent of the table is to reinforce the pressure differential requirement.
Sequences and pressures other than those listed can be substituted.

It is also necessary to use a gauge that can accurately differentiate pressure.
For example, a gauge that reads only in 10-psig (69 kPa) markings would not be
sufficient when the pressure differential is only 5 psig (35 kPa).

c. Any medical-surgical vacuum systems shall be in operation so that these vacuum
systems are tested at the same time the medical gas systems are tested.

d. Following the adjustment of pressures in accordance with 4-3.4.1.3(a)2b and c, each
station outlet for each medical gas system shall be tested using the gas-specific
connection for each system with a pressure (vacuum) gauge attached. Each pressure
gauge used in performing this test shall be calibrated with the line pressure regulator
gauge used to provide the source pressure.

e. Each station outlet shall be identified by label (and color marking, if used), and the
pressure indicated on the test gauge shall be that listed in 4-3.4.1.3(a)2b for the
system being tested.

Note that as with piping, color marking of station outlets is secondary to labeling.

(b) *Valve Test.* Valves installed in each medical gas piping system shall be tested to
verify proper operation and rooms or areas of control. Records shall be made listing the
rooms or areas controlled by each valve for each gas. The information shall be utilized to
assist and verify the proper labeling of the valves.

(c) *Outlet Flow Test.* All outlets shall be tested for flow.

The flow specification applies to new installations designed, installed, or approved
after February 1993 when these criteria were first included in NFPA 99. The committee has not attempted to define a requirement for systems already installed.

1. *General.* These flow tests shall be performed at the station outlet or terminal where the user makes connections and disconnections. Tests shall be performed with the use of oil-free, dry nitrogen or with the gas of system designation.
2. Oxygen, nitrous oxide, and air outlets shall deliver 3.5 SCFM with a pressure drop of no more than 5 psig (35 kPa), and static pressure of 50 psig (349 kPa).
3. Nitrogen outlets shall deliver 5.0 SCFM with a pressure drop of no more than 5 psig and static pressure of 160 psig (1118 kPa).

(d) *Alarm Testing.*

1.* *General.* All warning systems for each medical gas piping system shall be tested to ensure that all components function properly prior to placing the piping system in service. Permanent records of these tests shall be maintained.

Warning systems that are part of an addition to an existing piping system shall be tested prior to the connection of the new piping to the existing system.

**A-4-3.4.1.3(d)1** See C-4.1.

2. *Warning Systems.* Tests of warning systems for new installations (initial tests) shall be performed after the cross-connection testing [4-3.4.1.3(a)], but before the purging and verifying [4-3.4.1.3(e)]. Initial tests of warning systems that can be included in an addition or extension to an existing piping system shall be completed before connection of the addition to the existing system. Test gases for the initial tests shall be oil-free, dry nitrogen or gas of system designation.

3. *Master Alarm Systems.*

   a. The master alarm system tests shall be performed for each of the nonflammable medical gas piping systems. Permanent records of these tests shall be maintained with those required under 4-3.5.3.
   b. The audible and noncancellable visual signals of 4-3.1.2.2(a)1b shall indicate if the pressure in the main line increases or decreases 20 percent from the normal operating pressure.

4. *Area Alarm Systems.* The warning signals for all medical gas piping systems supplying anesthetizing locations and other vital life-support and critical care areas, such as post-anesthesia recovery, intensive care units, coronary care units, and so forth, shall indicate if the pressure in the piping system increases or decreases 20 percent from the normal operating pressure. *[See 4-3.1.2.2(c)3.]*

(e) *Piping Purge Test.* In order to remove any traces of particulate matter deposited in the pipelines as a result of construction, a heavy, intermittent purging of the pipeline shall be done. The appropriate adapter shall be obtained from the facility or manufacturer, and high purge rates of at least 225 L/min (8 cfm) shall be put on each outlet. After the purge is started, it shall be rapidly interrupted several times until the purge produces no discoloration in a white cloth loosely held over the adapter during the purge. In order to avoid possible damage to the outlet and its components, this test shall not be conducted using any implement other than the proper adapter.

For each positive-pressure gas system, the cleanliness of the piping system shall be verified. A minimum of 35 ft$^3$ (1000 L) of gas shall be filtered through a clean, white 0.45-micron filter at a minimum flowrate of 3.5 SCFM (100 L/min). Twenty-five percent of the zones shall be tested at the outlet most remote from the source. The filter shall accrue no more than 0.1 mg of matter from any outlet. If any outlet fails this test, the most remote outlet in every zone shall be tested. The test shall be performed with the use of oil-free, dry nitrogen.

(f) *Piping Purity Test.* For each positive-pressure system, the purity of the piping system shall be verified. The test shall be for dew point, total hydrocarbons (as methane), and halogenated hydrocarbons, and compared with the source gas. This test shall be performed at the outlet most remote from the source. The two tests shall in no case exceed variation as specified in Table 4-3.4.1.3(f). The test shall be performed with the use of oil-free, dry nitrogen gas.

*Table 4-3.4.1.3(f)  Maximum Allowable Variation Table*

| | |
|---|---|
| Dew point | 5°C @ 50 psig |
| Total hydrocarbons as methane | 1 ppm |
| Halogenated hydrocarbons | 2 ppm |

The committee was alerted in 1991 to the potential hazard that exists if a test is not conducted to determine that no hydrocarbon residuals exist in the gas piping system before it is pressurized with nitrogen. This potential hazard is present in each branch line of the pipeline.

This is not a test of the purity of the service gas; rather, it is a test for purity of the piping system *before* it is put into service with the service gas. The test is to be conducted with oil-free, dry nitrogen, as noted, without source gases or air compressors connected. The test is also a comparative one, with the requirement being the value between the measurement at the source and most remote outlet [i.e., the values listed in Table 4-3.4.1.3(f)].

A test for dew point variation is included, in addition to the two hydrocarbon tests, because a differential value greater than 41°F (5°C) would indicate moisture exists in the pipeline.

A requirement for dew point testing has been included in NFPA 99 since 1987, although it was not codified in a testing section until 1990. Despite this, many new installations are completed and commissioned without conducting what is considered a basic test. Since 1993, both the pipeline itself [4-3.4.1.3(f)] and delivered medical compressed air [4-3.4.1.3(j)] have been subject to a dew point test, with results included in the final testing report.

Facilities that do not, as yet, have dew point analyzers installed would benefit from this testing, because it frequently uncovers problems with equipment already in operation.

(g)* *Final Tie-in Test.* Prior to the connection of any work or any extension or addition to an existing piping system, the tests in 4-3.4.1.3(a) through 4-3.4.1.3(f) shall be successfully performed. After connection to the existing system and before use of the addition for patient care, the tests in 4-3.4.1.3(h) through 4-3.4.1.3(j) shall be completed. Permanent records of these tests shall be maintained in accordance with 4-3.5.3.

The final connection between the addition and existing system shall be leak-tested with the gas of system designation at the normal operating pressure. This pressure shall be maintained until each joint has been examined for leakage by means of soapy water or other equally effective means of leak detection safe for use with oxygen.

**A-4-3.4.1.3(g)** This leak test uses the source gas and the system pressure for which the system is designed in order to avoid contaminating the existing system.

This again reinforces that labeling is the primary means of identification, as opposed to color-coding, and that accuracy of labeling needs to be ensured.

(h) *Operational Pressure Test.*

It is the intent of the Committee on Piping Systems to establish minimum pressure requirements for various gases. Ranges other than those listed could be necessary.

1. *General.* These flow tests shall be performed at the station outlet (inlet) or terminal where the user makes connections and disconnections.
2. Piping systems, with the exception of nitrogen systems, shall maintain pressure at 50 +5/−0 psig (345 +35/−0 kPa gauge) at all station outlets at the maximum flow rate in 4-3.4.1.3(h)5.
3. A nitrogen system shall be capable of delivering at least 160 psig (1103 kPa gauge) to all outlets at flow in 4-3.4.1.3(h)7.
4. Piping systems that vary from the normal pressures in 4-3.4.1.3(h)2 and 3 shall be capable of delivering flows and pressures consistent with their intended use.
5. Oxygen, nitrous oxide, and air outlets shall deliver 3.5 SCFM with a pressure drop of no more than 5 psig (35 kPa) and static pressure of 50 psig (345 kPa).
6. Oxygen and air outlet serving critical care areas shall permit a transient flow rate of 6.0 SCFM for 3 seconds.
7. Nitrogen outlets shall deliver 5.0 SCFM with a pressure drop of no more than 5 psig (35 kPa) and static pressure of 160 psig (1103 kPa).

(i) *Medical Gases Concentration Test.* After purging each system with the gas of system designation, the following shall be performed:

1. Each pressure gas source and outlet shall be analyzed for concentration of gas, by volume.
2. Analysis shall be with instruments designed to measure the specific gas dispensed.

3. Allowable concentrations shall be within the following:

| | |
|---|---|
| Oxygen | 99 plus percent oxygen |
| Nitrous oxide | 99 plus percent nitrous oxide |
| Nitrogen | Less than 1 percent oxygen or 99 plus percent nitrogen |
| Medical air | 19.5 percent to 23.5 percent oxygen |
| Other gases | Concentration as specified by their labeling ±1 percent, unless otherwise specified |

An oxygen analyzer should be used for oxygen, medical air. A nitrous oxide analyzer should be used for analysis of the amount of nitrous oxide. An oxygen analyzer can also be used to determine the absence of nitrogen by having a reading of less than 1 percent oxygen. However, because nitrous oxide is an inhaled gas, the true concentration must be determined so that the verifier is able to assure that all the test gas (nitrogen) is out of the nitrous oxide line.

(j) *Medical Air Purity Test (Compressor System)*. The medical air source shall be analyzed for concentration of contaminants by volume. Sample(s) shall be taken for the air system test at a sample point as specified in 4-3.1.1.9(j)3. The test results shall not exceed the following parameters:

| | |
|---|---|
| Dew point | 39°F (4°C) @ 50 psig |
| Carbon monoxide | 10 ppm |
| Carbon dioxide—air | 500 ppm |
| Gaseous hydrocarbons—air | 25 ppm (as methane) |
| Halogenated hydrocarbons—air | 2 ppm |

These are tests of medical compressed air for those parameters that can affect the safety of the system. Piping purity testing is covered under 4-3.4.1.3(f).
For a discussion on dew point monitoring, see commentary under 4-3.1.2.1(b)3g.

(k) *Labeling*. The presence and correctness of labeling required by this standard for all components (e.g., station outlets, shutoff valves, and signal panels) shall be verified.

**4-3.4.1.4 Source Equipment Verification.** Source equipment verification shall be performed following the installation of the interconnecting pipelines, accessories, and source equipment. The pressure test shall be performed downstream of the compressor isolation valve and upstream of pipeline regulators at the highest system operating pressure for 2 hours, with no more than a 10 percent pressure drop. *(See Table 4-3.4.1.4.)*

Table 4-3.4.1.4, revised in this 1999 edition, is intended to draw all alarm requirements into a central location for ease of reference and use. Unlike the earlier versions, the revised table does not repeat requirements from the text but refers the user to the appropriate reference. The table now includes all alarms (including master, area, and local alarms).

(a) *Gas Supply Sources.*

1. The system apparatus shall be tested for proper function, including the changeover from one cylinder bank to the other and the actuation of the changeover signal, before the system is put into service.
2. The system apparatus shall be tested for proper function, including the changeover from primary to secondary supply (with its changeover signal) and the operation of the reserve (with its reserve in use signal), before the system is put into service.
3. If the system has an actuating switch and signal to monitor the contents of the reserve, its function shall be tested before the system is put into service. If a system uses a liquid source for the reserve, the "Reserve Pressure Low" shall be tested.
4. If the system has an actuating switch and signal to monitor the pressure of the reserve unit, its function shall be tested before the system is put into service.
5. The bulk supply signal and the master signal panel installations shall be arranged with the owner or the organization responsible for the operation and maintenance of the supply system for the testing of the bulk supply signals to ensure proper identification and activation of the master signal panels to be sure the facility can monitor the status of that supply system. These tests shall also be conducted when changing storage units.
6. For master alarm systems, the manufacturer's operating instructions shall be followed, or the assistance of the owner or the organization responsible for the operation and maintenance of the bulk supply system shall be requested for the following tests.
   a. Pressurize the piping system and connect the electric power to the signal panels.
   b. Check the main-line pressure gauge *[see 4-3.1.2.1(e)1]* to ascertain that it indicates the desired pressure *[see 4-3.4.1.3(h)]* and is properly labeled. Check the alarm signal panels to ensure that they indicate normal operation and that none of the warning signals are activated.
   c. Check required alarmed functions of the supply and reserve to ascertain that the proper signal is indicated and properly labeled.

(b) *Medical Air Compressor.*

1. The proper functioning of the medical air system shall be tested before it is put into service. This shall include the purity test for air quality, and the test of the alarm sensors after calibration and setup per the manufacturer's instructions and automatic switchover as outlined in 4-3.1.1.9(d)2.
2. The following tests shall be conducted at the sample point of the medical air system.
   a. The operation of the system control sensors, such as dew point, air temperature, and all other air-quality monitoring sensors and controls, shall be checked for proper operation and function before the system is put into service.
   b. The quality of medical air as delivered by the compressor air supply shall be verified after installation of new components prior to use by patients. The test shall be

performed a minimum of 24 hours after continuous running of the machinery, at a sample port downstream of the pressure regulator and upstream of the piping system as defined in Figure 4-3.1.1.9. A demand of approximately 25 percent of the rated compressor capacity shall be created to cause the compressors to cycle on and off continuously and the dryers to operate for the 24-hour period.

This requirement clarifies that the compressor must be run continuously under at least a 25 percent load for 24 hours before testing.

The modification made for the 1996 edition intended to clarify that air quality testing of a new compressor is to be performed after the system is in operation for *at least* 24 hours.

Previously, the document gave the impression that testing was to be done initially and then after 24 hours. This was clarified to clearly indicate that in order to properly assess the operation of the air treatment plant, the system is to be *in operation for at least 24 hours* **and** with a load of at least 25 percent of the rated load of the system for the 24 hours. This test method will cause the equipment involved (e.g., compressors, dryers, regulators) to cycle for at least 24 hours and will permit the air treatment equipment to reach its full capacity for drying.

## 4-3.4.2 Piped Vacuum Systems—Level 1.

### 4-3.4.2.1 Performance.

(a)* *Minimum Vacuum and Operating Range.* The vacuum pumps and collection piping shall be capable of maintaining a vacuum of 12 in. of mercury (Hg) at the station inlet farthest away from the central vacuum source when the calculated demand for the hospital is drawn in the system.

**A-4-3.4.2.1(a)** See C-4.3 for examples.

During the development of NFPA 56K (now part of NFPA 99), the committee responsible for this text pointed out that the operating range criteria of 15 in. to 19 in. (38 cm to 48 cm) at the receiver was a suggestion based on a medical-user requirement for the safest and most effective suctioning procedures. The recommendation was not related to pump design or size. Any pump that could maintain the minimum vacuum requirement (12 in. Hg) was satisfactory.

Reference to ACFM was deleted because it is always changing. The capacity of vacuum pumps is based on SCFM, calculated for the total of Group A and Group B station inlets in the system. (See revised chart in C-4.4.)

All calculated demands are given in SCFM for pipe and equipment sizing. A system designer should verify that the equipment selected is rated in SCFM at the operating vacuum range selected, not in ACFM at the operating vacuum range.

(b)* *Overall System Pressure-Drop Criteria.* Tube sizes shall be in conformity with good engineering practice for delivery of maximum design volumes.

*Table 4-3.4.1.4 Monitoring Requirements for Required Alarm Signals (Level 1 Systems)*

**Master Signals from Sources**

**Master Alarm Signals**

| | Manifold w/o Reserve | Manifold w/ Reserve | Cryogenic Bulk w/Cryo Reserve | Cryogenic Bulk w/Cyl Reserve | Air Via | Air Via | Air Via Liquid Ring | Vacuum Pump |
|---|---|---|---|---|---|---|---|---|
| Changeover | 4-3.1.1.5(a) | 4-3.1.1.6(a)2 | 4-3.1.1.7(a)1 | 4-3.1.1.7(b)2 | | | | |
| Liquid level low | | | 4-3.1.1.7(a) | 4-3.1.1.7(a) | | | | |
| Reserve in use | | 4-3.1.1.6(a)3 | 4-3.1.1.7(a) | 4-3.1.1.7(a) | | | | |
| Reserve level low | | | 4-3.1.1.7(b)2 | | | | | |
| Reserve pressure low | | | 4-3.1.1.7(b)2 | 4-3.1.1.6(b) | | | | |
| Dew point high | | | | | 4-3.1.1.9(d)1 | 4-3.1.1.9(d)1 | 4-3.1.1.9(e)1 | |
| Local alarm | | | | | 4-3.1.1.9(e)1 4-3.1.1.9(h) | 4-3.1.1.9(e)1 4-3.1.1.9(h) | 4-3.1.1.9(h) | 4-3.2.1.2 |

**Master Signals from Pipeline**

| | |
|---|---|
| High line pressure | 4-3.1.2.2(b)3e |
| Low line pressure | 4-3.1.2.2(b)3e |
| Low vacuum | 4-3.2.2.8(a) |

**Area Alarm Signals**

| | |
|---|---|
| High line pressure (for each gas piped to area) | 4-3.1.2.2(c)3 |
| Low line pressure (for each gas piped to area) | 4-3.1.2.2(c)3 |
| Low vacuum (if piped) | 4-3.2.2.9(e) |
| WAGD (if piped) | 4-3.3.2.4 |

**Local Alarm Signals**

| | |
|---|---|
| High water in receiver | 4-3.1.1.9(e) |
| Carbon monoxide high | 4-3.1.1.9(i)3 |
| Backup compressor in operation | 4-3.1.1.9(d) |
| Backup vacuum pump in operation | 4-3.2.1.2 |
| High water in separator (if so equipped) | 4-3.1.1.9(e)4 |
| High discharge air temperature (if so equipped) | 4-3.1.1.9(e)6 |

**A-4-3.4.2.1(b)** It is recommended that vacuum pressure loss, from source to farthest station inlet, when the calculated demand is drawn on the vacuum system, be limited to 3 in. Hg.

In developing system pressure drop criteria, the former Subcommittee on Vacuum Systems and Equipment (now part of the Committee on Piping Systems) decided that 3 in. Hg was as restrictive a criterion as was necessary and it was included as a recommendation. This value, while only a recommendation, is indicative of adequate pipe sizing and no undue restrictions in mains and risers. [The terminal performance tests of 4-3.4.2.1(c) will reveal to what degree, if any, the smaller lines to each individual station inlet are obstructed.]

A negative pressure loss (i.e., the vacuum level "drops") to a level below the low point of the normal operating range in a section of the vacuum system could indicate that piping in that section is restricted or too small or that pipe runs are too extensive. Increasing section capacity can be achieved by removal of any possible restrictions, the installation of parallel piping with the affected branch line, or the setting of a higher operating range. A higher operating range will increase operating and equipment costs. This should be taken into consideration when determining whether a higher range or additional parallel piping will be used to add to section capacity.

A negative pressure drop below the minimum required degree of vacuum at the vacuum receiver (tank) or in the main line (assuming all vacuum pumps are running continuously and pipes are sized properly) could indicate a need for greater displacement capacity downstream (i.e., toward the pumps) of the vacuum system main-line valve or could indicate restrictions upstream of the pumps.

Under these circumstances, the vacuum main-line valve, receiver, check valves, and pump inlets should be checked. If they are found to be restricting flow, corrective action should be taken.

If the vacuum main-line valve, receiver, check valves, and pump inlets are clear and a low degree of vacuum continues, a check for leaks should be performed. If leaks are discovered, they should be properly sealed.

If no normalities continue to be found but a low degree of vacuum still persists, the vacuum source displacement could be inadequate due to limited pump capacity. This can be corrected, and the minimum required vacuum at the farthest point in the system per 4-3.4.2.2(c)4b maintained by adding more additional vacuum pump capacity (e.g., such as by triplexing an existing duplex set).

(c)* *Minimum Flow and Pressure Requirements at Vacuum Station Inlets.* Piping shall be sized such that 3 SCFM can be evacuated through any one station inlet without reducing vacuum pressure below 12 in. Hg at an adjacent station inlet.

The intent of wording is to remind readers that flow and vacuum requirements are applicable throughout the vacuum system and not just at one terminal (i.e., any one station inlet. . .).

It should not be assumed that a maximum system pressure drop under design flow conditions is 3 in. Hg. The 3 SCFM flow is only a measurement at one terminal when comparing vacuum pressure at an adjacent terminal. (See commentary under the definition of *SCFM* in Chapter 2 for a discussion on this term.)

The flow rate of 3 SCFM is representative of a vacuum terminal with none of the normal ancillary equipment attached (i.e., vacuum regulator, suction trap bottle, connecting tubing, and suction tip). This equipment has a restrictive effect on airflow. In fact, tests indicate that the flow of 3 SCFM is about twice the maximum flow through a terminal connected to the normal ancillary equipment. The 3-SCFM flow would probably occur only during a worse-case test of an unrestricted terminal. (Past documentation of the committee responsible for vacuum system safety criteria showed that one testing company, over a 5-year period, found thousands of terminals not operating properly.)

The 12-in. Hg minimum vacuum level was selected in consultation with clinical staff on the committee and in coordination with the use of the ancillary vacuum equipment. Normal bronchial or thoracic suction is performed under intermittent operation, requiring a low degree of vacuum and a slightly higher volume displacement. In general, the committee found that as vacuum increased, the actual displacement curve for fluids became flat. A 15-in. Hg vacuum was ideal; a 12-in. Hg vacuum was a minimal accepted value; and at a 14-in. to 16-in. Hg vacuum, the liquid displacement curve flattened out.

The use of an artificially high vacuum results in the potential for tissue damage at the catheter tip.

Leaks in the vacuum system result in low-vacuum, high-volume flow. The need to go to higher vacuum levels to achieve a 12-in. Hg vacuum could be the result of poor use practices, such as the improper sealing of suction fittings due to little or no maintenance, or of an artificially increased demand load caused by suction left open and running when not in use.

**A-4-3.4.2.1(c)** This is not a criterion for pump sizing purposes. See C-4.3 for pump sizing recommendations.

**4-3.4.2.2 Testing.**

The testing criteria and sequencing were revised in 1996 to be consistent with that for Level 1 piped gas systems.

(a) *General*. Inspection and testing of medical vacuum systems shall be in accordance with 4-3.4.1.1.

(b) *Installer Performance Testing*. The following tests shall be conducted by the installer or his/her representative prior to those tests listed in 4-3.4.2.2(c), System Verification. The test gas shall be oil-free, dry nitrogen.

A change in the installer-performed testing sequence was made again for this 1999 edition to correct a problem. The technical committee has now removed any mention of when the walls are to be closed up in the sequence of testing. While the initial blowdown test should always be done with the walls open to permit removal of blockages, many installers also prefer to do their cross-connection testing with the walls exposed to allow correction of cross lines to be repaired. Otherwise, the walls would need to be open for the 150-psig (1034-kPa) pressure test to soap all the joints, install the walls for cross-connection work to permit using the proper adapters on the installed outlets, remove the walls for repairs for any cross-connections, and so forth.

Care should be exercised during the cross-connection test that the outlets are not damaged by using the wrong types of adapters to activate them. If the outlets are temporarily installed for the cross-connection test, the connections should be kept clean and intact if removed afterward.

The technical committee wishes to reinforce that the initial pressure test is not a timed test; the pipeline is kept pressurized only until it is checked for leaks (however long that takes). The standing pressure test is the timed test.

1. *Blow Down.* After installation of the piping network, but before installation of vacuum inlets and other vacuum system components, all lines shall be blown clear using oil-free, dry nitrogen.
2. *Initial Pressure Test.* Before the vacuum source, vacuum inlets, alarm switches, and gauges are connected to the vacuum network piping, the vacuum network piping shall be subjected to a test pressure of not less than 150 psig (1034 kPa gauge) by means of oil-free, dry nitrogen. This test pressure shall be maintained until each joint has been examined for leakage by use of soapy water or other suitable means. All leaks shall be repaired and the section retested.
3. *Cross-Connection Test (Initial).* It shall be determined that no cross-connections exist between the vacuum system and any medical gas system. Vacuum systems shall be tested at the same time as medical gas systems, as described in 4-3.4.1.2(c).
4.* *Standing Pressure Test.* After the vacuum inlets are connected to the vacuum network piping, but before the vacuum source, alarm switches, and gauges are connected, the vacuum network piping shall be subjected to a test pressure of not less than 60 psig (413 kPa gauge) by means of oil-free, dry nitrogen. After allowance for temperature variation, the pressure at the end of 24 hours shall be within 5 psig (345 kPa gauge) of the initial pressure. Corrective action shall be taken if this performance is not verified. After completion of the test, corrections, and reverification if necessary, the system shall be connected to the vacuum pumps, receiver(s) [tanks(s)], alarm actuators (vacuum switches), and gauges.

The test pressure value is to be "not less than 60 psig (413 kPa gauge)" to avoid damage to vacuum station inlets not designed to withstand the previous recommendation of 150 psig (1034 kPa) (i.e., vacuum lines normally operate between approximately 12-in. and 20-in. Hg vacuum).

**A-4-3.4.2.2(b)4** For information on how to correct pressure for temperature changes, see Section 4-3.

> The committee felt it essential to ensure that only vacuum use points are connected to the Level 1 vacuum system. Cross-connection with a Level 1 gas system would artificially load the medical-surgical vacuum system during normal operation and prevent the system from achieving design vacuum and flow performance. It would also present a distinct safety problem in the event of a fire (oxygen and nitrous oxide enhance and accelerate combustion). Therefore, the cross-connection test listed here is the same as for piped gas systems.
>
> A final vacuum test, as part of a system verification procedure, is considered essential to ensure that all components of the system are functioning properly when connected together. An example (which is a *recommendation* and *not* a requirement or an endorsement) given in the appendix before this 1999 edition was of a vacuum level loss of 1.5 in. Hg in 1 hour, with a beginning vacuum in excess of 12 in. Hg. See explanatory note at A-4-3.4.2.2(c)2.

(c) *System Verification.* The following tests shall be performed after those listed in 4-3.4.2.2(b), Installer Performance Testing. The test gas shall be oil-free, dry nitrogen.

This testing shall be conducted by a party technically competent and experienced in the field of medical vacuum pipeline testing, and independent of the installer.

> System verification, added for 1996, is in concert with the verification procedures for Level 1 piped gas systems.

1.  *Cross-Connection Test (Final).* After walls have been closed and the requirements of 4-3.4.2.2(b) have been completed, it shall be determined that no cross-connections exist between the vacuum system and any medical gas system, using one of the methods described in 4-3.4.1.3(a).
2.* *Vacuum Test.* After the vacuum piping has been connected to the vacuum pumps, receiver(s) [tank(s)], vacuum gauges, and vacuum alarm switches, a vacuum test shall be performed on the entire system.

> The reference to the vacuum level loss for the purpose of determining acceptable leakage was removed. The leakage rate in a vacuum system is specifically dependent on volume. The standard engineering equation for determining the leakage rate is PV/T (pressure times volume over time). A vacuum system could have an in-leakage that results in a loss of 1.5 in. Hg in 1 hour in a large hospital piping network and could be considered "tight." The identical in-leakage in a small facility, such as a surgery center, with very little piping volume, could be considered "leaky." Furthermore, the initial vacuum level needs to be in excess of 17 in. Hg to allow for a constant in-leakage that permits the 1.5 in. Hg vacuum loss that this test requires. This is because in-leakage is constant above about 15 in. Hg; below that vacuum level, it changes.

A final vacuum test, as part of a system verification procedure, is considered essential to ensure that all components of the system are functioning properly when connected together. The example (a recommendation and not a requirement or an endorsement) given in the appendix needs to be tempered by the number of installed terminals. For example, a 1.5-in. Hg drop in 1 hour for a system of 500 installed terminals represents a less serious problem than the same leakage for a system of 50 installed terminals, which would warrant an investigation of the leak sources.

**A-4-3.4.2.2(c)2** An acceptable method of testing is by means of shutting down portions of the system using the shutoff valves described in 4-3.2.2.6 to determine the capability of that portion to maintain a vacuum.

3. *Valve Test.* Valves installed in vacuum systems shall be tested to verify proper operation and rooms or areas of control. Records shall be made listing the rooms or areas controlled by each valve. The information shall be utilized to assist and verify the proper labeling of the valves.

4. *Alarm Test.*

   a. *General.* Alarms for vacuum systems shall be tested to ensure that all components function properly prior to the piping system being placed into service. Permanent records of these tests shall be maintained. Alarms that are part of an addition to an existing vacuum system shall be tested prior to connection of the new piping to the existing system.

   b. *Alarm Criteria.* Unless otherwise indicated, vacuum system alarms shall indicate if the vacuum in the piping system drops to 12 in. Hg and below.

   Medical personnel on the committee requested that alarms activate when the vacuum level dropped below the minimum value of 12 in. Hg. Below 12-in. Hg vacuum, the rate and volume of fluid removal (particularly in areas such as surgery and critical care units) is too low for optimum patient care. Less than 12 in. Hg is considered unsatisfactory for the removal of heavy mucus, loose tissue particles, coagulated blood, and so forth. [See additional commentary on this subject under 4-3.4.2.1(c).] However, since this 12-in. Hg value is a performance criterion, the value at which the alarm sensor is set is not specified. The designer determines which setting is necessary to meet a minimum of 12-in. Hg vacuum.

5. *Source Equipment Verification.* The proper functioning of the vacuum source system shall be tested before it is put into service.

**4-3.4.3 Waste Anesthetic Gas Disposal System—Level 1.**

**4-3.4.3.1** WAGD distribution networks shall be sized to deliver vacuum at a pressure and flow appropriate to the WAGD interfaces in use with the facility's gas anesthetic machines.

**4-3.4.3.2** WAGD systems shall be included in all cross-connection testing per 4-3.4.2.2(b)4.

**4-3.4.3.3** Vacuum and flow at each terminal inlet shall be as required by the WAGD interfaces in use with the facility's gas anesthetic machines. The network shall be sized, and the vacuum producer selected, to provide this level of vacuum and flow simultaneously at all terminal inlets when all inlets are in use.

**4-3.4.3.4** Where required, the network shall be adjusted or balanced prior to the commencing of testing or as part of the testing process.

**4-3.4.3.5** Testing shall be performed as appropriate to ensure that each inlet is capable of providing vacuum and flow. At a minimum, the following tests shall be performed:

(a) Start the vacuum producer and assure it is operating correctly.

(b) Open one inlet per room, and test with the adjacent inlet open, taking into consideration that the adjacent inlet might be in another room.

**4-3.4.3.6** Venturi drive systems shall follow the requirements of 4-3.4.1 except 4-3.4.1.3(f) and 4-3.4.1.3(i) and (j).

## 4-3.5 Administration—Level 1.

**4-3.5.1 Responsibility of Governing Body.** (Reserved)

**4-3.5.2 Gas System Policies—Level 1.**

For policies on cylinders and containers (e.g., transferring, transfilling) that are freestanding and not associated with a piped gas system, see Chapter 8, "Gas Equipment."

**4-3.5.2.1 Gases in Cylinders and Liquefied Gases in Containers—Level 1.**

NFPA has produced a film on this subject entitled "Safe Handling of Medical Gases" (VC-4). [12] The film illustrates the hazards associated with gases, how cylinders should be handled, how piped systems work, and emergency measures to take in the event of an incident involving medical gases.

(a)* *Handling of Gases.* Administrative authorities shall provide regulations to ensure that standards for safe practice in the specifications for cylinders; marking of cylinders, regulators, and valves; and cylinder connections have been met by vendors of cylinders containing compressed gases supplied to the facility.

**A-4-3.5.2.1(a)** *Safe Practice for Cylinders Containing Compressed Gases. Specifications for Cylinders.* All cylinders containing compressed gases, such as anesthetic gases, oxygen, or other gases used for medicinal purposes, whether these gases are flammable or not, should comply with the specifications and be maintained in accordance with regulations of the U.S. Department of Transportation.

(b) *Special Precautions—Oxygen Cylinders and Manifolds.* Great care shall be exercised in handling oxygen to prevent contact of oxygen under pressure with oils, greases, organic lubricants, rubber, or other materials of an organic nature. The following regulations, based on those of the CGA Pamphlet G-4, *Oxygen*, shall be observed:

1. Oil, grease, or readily flammable materials shall never be permitted to come in contact with oxygen cylinders, valves, regulators, gauges, or fittings.
2. Regulators, fittings, or gauges shall never be lubricated with oil or any other flammable substance.
3. Oxygen cylinders or apparatus shall never be handled with oily or greasy hands, gloves, or rags.
4. Particles of dust and dirt shall be cleared from cylinder valve openings by slightly opening and closing the valve before applying any fitting to the cylinder.
5. The high-pressure valve on the oxygen cylinder shall be opened before bringing the apparatus to the patient or the patient to the apparatus.
6. The cylinder valve shall be opened slowly, with the face of the gauge on the regulator pointed away from all persons.
7. An oxygen cylinder shall never be draped with any materials such as hospital gowns, masks, or caps.
8. Oxygen fittings, valves, regulators, or gauges shall never be used for any service other than that of oxygen.
9. Gases of any type shall never be mixed in an oxygen cylinder or any other cylinder.
10. Oxygen shall always be dispensed from a cylinder through a pressure regulator.
11. Regulators that are in need of repair or cylinders having valves that do not operate properly shall never be used.
12. Oxygen equipment that is defective shall not be used until it has been repaired by competent personnel. If competent in-house repairs cannot be made, such equipment shall be repaired by the manufacturer or his or her authorized agent; or it shall be replaced.
13. Oxygen cylinders shall be protected from abnormal mechanical shock, which is liable to damage the cylinder, valve, or safety device. Such cylinders shall not be stored near elevators, gangways, or in locations where heavy moving objects will strike them or fall on them.
14. Cylinder-valve protection caps, where provided, shall be kept in place and be hand tightened, except when cylinders are in use or connected for use.

    These caps can protect the valve in case the cylinder topples over. [See commentary on 4-3.1.1.2(a)8 for the potential hazard of a broken cylinder valve.]

15. Cylinders shall be protected from the tampering of unauthorized individuals.
16. Valves shall be closed on all empty cylinders in storage.
17. Oxygen shall be referred to by its proper name, *oxygen*, not *air*. Liquid oxygen shall be referred to by its proper name, not *liquid air*.
18. Oxygen shall never be used as a substitute for compressed air.
19. Cylinders or cylinder valves shall not be repaired, painted, or altered.

20. Safety relief devices in valves or cylinders shall never be tampered with. Sparks and flame shall be kept away from cylinders; a torch flame shall never be permitted under any circumstances to come in contact with cylinder valves or safety devices. Valve outlets clogged with ice shall be thawed with warm—not boiling—water.

21. The markings stamped on cylinders shall not be tampered with. It is against federal statutes to change these markings without written authority from the Bureau of Explosives.

22. Markings used for the identification of contents of cylinders shall not be defaced or removed, including decals, tags, stenciled marks, and upper half of shipping tag.

23. The owner of the cylinder shall be notified if any condition has occurred that might permit any foreign substance to enter a cylinder or valve, giving details and cylinder number.

24. Even if they are considered to be empty, cylinders shall never be used as rollers, supports, or for any purpose other than that for which they are intended by the supplier.

25. When small-size (A, B, D, or E) cylinders are in use, they shall be attached to a cylinder stand or to therapy apparatus of sufficient size to render the entire assembly stable. Individual cylinder storage associated with patient care areas are not required to be stored in enclosures.

26. Cylinders and containers shall not be dropped, dragged, or rolled.

27. Freestanding cylinders shall be properly chained or supported in a proper cylinder stand or cart.

    Many carts are commercially available that hold a cylinder in such a manner as to make tipping them over very difficult.

28. Cylinders shall not be chained to portable or movable apparatus such as beds and oxygen tents.

    Cylinders are to be well secured to a wall, rack, or nonmovable structure while in use to prevent them from being knocked over.

29.* Cylinders shall not be supported by, and neither cylinders nor containers shall be placed in proximity of, radiators, steam pipes, or heat ducts.

**A-4-3.5.2.1(b)29** Cylinder and container temperatures greater than 125°F (52°C) can result in excessive pressure increase. Pressure-relief devices are sensitive to temperature and pressure. When relief devices actuate, contents are discharged.

30. Very cold cylinders or containers shall be handled with care to avoid injury.

31. Cylinders and containers shall not be handled with hands, gloves, or other materials contaminated with oil or grease.

    (c) *Making Cylinder and Container Connections.*

1.* Wrenches used to connect respiratory therapy equipment shall be manufactured of steel or other suitable material of adequate strength.

**A-4-3.5.2.1(c)1** Use of so-called nonsparking wrenches and tools is not necessary.

2. Cylinder valves shall be opened and connected in accordance with the following procedure:

   a. Make certain that apparatus and cylinder valve connections and cylinder wrenches are free of foreign materials.
   b. Turn the cylinder valve outlet away from personnel. Stand to the side—not in front and not in back. Before connecting the apparatus to cylinder valve, momentarily open cylinder valve to eliminate dust.
   c. Make connection of apparatus to cylinder valve. Tighten connection nut securely with an appropriate wrench *[see 4-3.5.2.1(c)1].*
   d. Release the low-pressure adjustment screw of the regulator completely.
   e. Slowly open cylinder valve to full open position.
   f. Slowly turn in the low-pressure adjustment screw on the regulator until the proper working pressure is obtained.
   g. Open the valve to the utilization apparatus.

3. Connections for containers shall be made in accordance with the container manufacturer's operating instructions.

   (d) *Care of Safety Mechanisms.*

1. Personnel using cylinders and containers and other equipment covered in this chapter shall be familiar with the Pin-Index Safety System *(see 8-3.1.2)* and the Diameter-Index Safety System *(see 8-3.1.3),* both designed to prevent utilization of the wrong gas.
2. Safety relief mechanisms, noninterchangeable connectors, and other safety features shall not be removed, altered, or replaced.

   (e) *Laboratory Gases.*

1.* *Use of Gases.* Gases shall be handled and used with care and with knowledge of their hazardous properties, both individually and in combination with other materials with which they can come in contact. *(See NFPA 49, Hazardous Chemicals Data, and NFPA 491, Guide to Hazardous Chemical Reactions.)*

**A-4-3.5.2.1(e)1** *Handling of Gas Containers.* The precautions outlined in CGA Pamphlet P-1, *Safe Handling of Compressed Gases,* and Pamphlet P-2, *Characteristics and Safe Handling of Medical Gases,* should be observed. *(See Appendix B.)* These publications cover such items as moving and storage of cylinders, labeling, withdrawing of cylinder contents, and handling of leaking cylinders. Cryogenic fluids are to be used only in containers designed for the purpose, such as a double-walled thermos bottle.

Caps are to be replaced promptly after each use to prevent the solidification of atmospheric water vapor in the pouring neck, which otherwise could convert a safe cylinder into a potential bomb.

Protective clothing and eye shields should be used to prevent burns from issuing gases or spilled liquids. Effects of flammable and oxidizing properties are intense and demand special fire protection measures and handling. Inadvertent saturation of clothing by oxygen or spills on asphalt flooring, for example, require prompt and accurate corrective measures. Ample ventilation is needed to prevent hazardous concentrations, for example, of nitrogen, which could cause asphyxiation. For routine cooling operations, liquid air or oxygen should never be used as substitutes for liquid nitrogen.

2. *Cylinders.* In a laboratory, gas cylinders being held for prompt use shall not exceed 2 days' working needs, except as permitted in 4-6.1.1.1. Cylinders shall be in racks or secured in position.

   The requirement takes into consideration weekday as well as weekend operations.

3. *Working Supplies.* The aggregate accumulation of cylinders at any one working station shall not exceed one extra cylinder for each cylinder actually connected for use. All cylinders shall be secured in a rack or secured in an upright position.

### 4-3.5.2.2 Storage of Cylinders and Containers—Level 1.

(a)* Facility authorities, in consultation with medical staff and other trained personnel, shall provide and enforce regulations for the storage and handling of cylinders and containers of oxygen and nitrous oxide in storage rooms of approved construction, and for the safe handling of these agents in anesthetizing locations. Storage locations for flammable inhalation anesthetic agents, established in any operating or delivery suite, shall be limited by space allocation and regulation to not more than a 48-hour normal requirement for any such suite. In storage locations, cylinders shall be properly secured in racks or adequately fastened. No cylinders containing oxygen or nitrous oxide, other than those connected to anesthetic apparatus, shall be kept or stored in anesthetizing locations.

**A-4-3.5.2.2(a)** Electric wiring and equipment in storage rooms for oxygen and nitrous oxide are not required to be explosionproof.

(b) *Nonflammable Gases.*

1. Storage shall be planned so that cylinders can be used in the order in which they are received from the supplier.
2. If stored within the same enclosure, empty cylinders shall be segregated from full cylinders. Empty cylinders shall be marked to avoid confusion and delay if a full cylinder is needed hurriedly.
3. Cylinders stored in the open shall be protected against extremes of weather and from the ground beneath to prevent rusting. During winter, cylinders stored in the open shall be protected against accumulations of ice or snow. In summer, cylinders stored in the open shall be screened against continuous exposure to direct rays of the sun in those localities where extreme temperatures prevail.

### 4-3.5.2.3 Patient Gas Systems—Level 1.

(a)* Piping systems shall not be used for the distribution of flammable anesthetic gases.

**A-4-3.5.2.3(a)** These requirements do not restrict the distribution of helium or other inert gases through piping systems.

The level of the medical piped gas system applicable to a specific type of facility is listed in Chapters 12 through 18.

(b) Nonflammable medical gas systems used to supply gases for respiratory therapy shall be installed in accordance with 4-3.1 of this chapter.

(c) Maintenance programs in accordance with the manufacturers' recommendations shall be established for the medical air compressor supply system as connected in each individual installation.

(d)* The responsible authority of the facility shall establish procedures to ensure that all signal warnings are promptly evaluated and that all necessary measures are taken to reestablish the proper functions of the medical gas system.

**A-4-3.5.2.3(d)** Activation of any of the warning signals should immediately be reported to the department of the facility responsible for the medical gas piping system involved. If the medical gas is supplied from a bulk supply system, the owner or the organization responsible for the operation and maintenance of that system, usually the supplier, should also be notified. As much detail as possible should be provided.

This paragraph, originally only a recommendation covering medical air, reflects the concern of the committee for the importance of piped gas systems and the need for some backup capabilities if the main piped system stopped for whatever reasons.

(e) Piping systems for gases shall not be used as a grounding electrode.

(f) The facility shall have the capability and organization to implement a plan to cope with a complete loss of any medical gas system.

(g) A periodic testing procedure for nonflammable medical gas and related alarm systems shall be implemented.

This testing is usually the responsibility of a maintenance or engineering department either directly or through outside contractors. However, it should involve the respiratory therapy service as well.

No minimum intervals for the testing of existing systems are recommended in this document because of the vast differences in use and the subsequent wear and tear on systems. Material in C-4.2 is only a recommendation, not a required program for existing systems.

**Caution:** Proper performance of some of these tests requires isolation of the piped gas system. These tests are to be conducted only if no patients are being served by that portion of the system.

(h) The test specified in 4-3.4.1.3(i) shall be conducted on the downstream portions of the medical gas piping system whenever a system is breached or whenever modifications are made or maintenance performed.

> The only test required after an oxygen (pure or mixed) or medical compressed air portion of an existing piped medical gas system is repaired is an analysis test to ensure that no cross-connection of gases has been created. (Note: This is in addition to the "installation" tests required for any new piping.) This may seem unnecessary when replacing a broken outlet or zone valve, for example, but it is very important to document that the correct gas is flowing out of a labeled outlet. There can be no compromise in patient safety with respect to gases that will be inhaled by patients.
>
> More elaborate testing than that listed is available. Performance of additional tests is at the discretion of the facility's owner.
>
> For a modified portion of an existing system, the extent of testing will depend on how much of the existing system is able to be isolated and unaffected by the work or modifications on the new portion.
>
> Once verification and analysis have been conducted on the modified portion of a system, it does not have to be repeated until the system is again breached or modified.
>
> (For recommendations on maintenance of a piped gas system, see C-4.2.)

(i)* Periodic retesting of audible and visual alarm indicators shall be performed to determine that they are functioning properly, and records of the test shall be maintained until the next test.

**A-4-3.5.2.3(i)** See C-4.2.

**4-3.5.3\* Gas Systems Recordkeeping—Level 1.** Prior to the use of any medical gas piping system for patient care, the responsible authority of the facility shall ensure that all tests required in 4-3.4.1 have been successfully conducted and permanent records of the test maintained in the facility files.

**A-4-3.5.3** All testing should be completed before putting a new piping system, or an addition to an existing system, into service. Test procedures and the results of all tests should be made part of the permanent records of the facility of which the piping system forms a part. They should show the room and area designations, dates of the tests, and name(s) of persons conducting the tests.

**4-3.5.4 Gas Systems Information and Warning Signs—Level 1.**

**4-3.5.4.1** The gas content of medical gas piping systems shall be readily identifiable by appropriate labeling with the name and pressure of the gas contained. Such labeling shall be by means of metal tags, stenciling, stamping, or adhesive markers, in a manner that is not readily removable. Labeling shall appear on the piping at intervals of not more than 20 ft (6 m) and at least once in each room and each story traversed by the piping system.

Where supplementary color identification of piping is used, it shall be in accordance with the gases and colors indicated in CGA Pamphlet C-9, *Standard Color-Marking of Compressed Gas Cylinders Intended for Medical Use.* Only those systems operating at nonstandard pressures shall be labeled with the name of the gas and the operating pressure.

Color-coding is never to be used alone; it is supplementary to labeling. The name of the contents in the cylinder or container must be spelled out due to the possibility of color blindness and to prevent having to rely on memory. Exhibits 4.23, 4.24, and 4.25 show sample labeling.

**Exhibit 4.23** *Example of an existing gas piping system labeled with the name of the gas and the direction of its flow. New systems will be required to have labels indicating the pressure level of the gas in the pipe, if other than standard pressure, as well as the gas name and flow direction.*

**4-3.5.4.2** The shutoff valves described in 4-3.1.2.3, 4-3.1.2.3(m), and 4-3.1.2.3(n) shall be labeled to reflect the rooms that are controlled by such valves. Labeling shall be kept current from initial construction through acceptance. Valves shall be labeled in substance as follows:

> **CAUTION:** (NAME OF MEDICAL GAS) VALVE
> DO NOT CLOSE EXCEPT IN EMERGENCY
> THIS VALVE CONTROLS SUPPLY TO . . . .

**4-3.5.4.3** Pressure gauges and manometers for medical gas piping systems shall be identified: (NAME OF GAS) USE NO OIL!

***Exhibit 4.24*** *Labeled medical gas and vacuum piping above ceiling panel.*

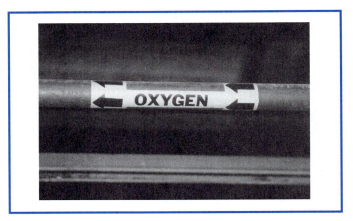

***Exhibit 4.25*** *Labels on pipes that are part of a piped gas or vacuum system.*

## 4-3.5.5 Gas System Transport and Delivery—Level 1.

**4-3.5.5.1** Personnel concerned with use and transport of equipment shall be trained in proper handling of cylinders, containers, hand trucks, supports, and valve protection caps.

Training in the safe handling and use of cylinders and related items should take place during orientation. Patient, staff, and visitor safety can be compromised if personnel do not receive training first.

**4-3.5.5.2\*** Large cylinders (exceeding size E) and containers larger than 100 lb (45.4 kg) weight shall be transported on a proper hand truck or cart complying with 8-5.2.

**A-4-3.5.5.2** Section 4-3 covers requirements for Level 1 piped gas and vacuum systems; Section 4-4 covers Level 2 piped gas and vacuum systems; Section 4-5 covers Level 3 piped gas and vacuum systems; and Section 4-6 covers Level 4 piped gas and vacuum systems.

**4-3.5.6 Vacuum System Policies—Level 1.**

**4-3.5.6.1 Patient Vacuum Systems.**

(a)* *Maintenance.* The facility shall establish routine preventive maintenance programs applicable to both the vacuum piping system and to the secondary equipment attached to vacuum station inlets to ensure the continued good performance of the entire vacuum system.

The specific hazard(s) involved will vary among facilities, as will the precautions required.

**A-4-3.5.6.1(a)** Vacuum systems from station inlets to the exhaust discharge should be considered contaminated unless proven otherwise. Methods exist to disinfect the system or portions thereof.

Clogging of regulators, for example, with lint, debris, or dried body fluids, reduces vacuum system performance.

System leaks can degrade performance and compromise the quality of patient care due to a reduced degree of vacuum in branches and lines to individual terminal inlets.

The intervals for such tests have been left to the judgment of the staff of the facility because usage and wear and tear on systems can vary markedly among facilities.

(b) *Leakage Tests.* The facility shall perform periodic tests for detecting leaks in the system in accordance with 4-3.4.2.2.

(c)* *Station Inlet Performance Tests.* Station inlet terminal performance, as required in 4-3.4.2.1(c), shall be tested on a regular preventive maintenance schedule as determined by the facility maintenance staff. The test shall be based on flow of free air (SCFM) into a station inlet while simultaneously checking the vacuum level.

**A-4-3.5.6.1(c)** The test can be conducted using (1) a rotometer or other flow-measuring device and (2) a vacuum gauge, both devices being fitted with the appropriate station inlet connector.

The test procedure will be to measure the flow with the station inlet wide open while simultaneously measuring the vacuum level at an adjacent wall station inlet or other station inlet on the same branch line.

It is recognized that this criterion might not be met by some existing systems. It is the responsibility of facility personnel, based on past experience and use, to determine the acceptable alternate performance criterion for their system(s).

(d)* *Instruction of Staff.* The facility shall instruct its personnel in the proper uses of the vacuum system in order to eliminate practices that reduce the system's effectiveness, such as leaving suction tips and catheters open when not actually aspirating, and using equipment arrangements that are improperly trapped or are untrapped.

**A-4-3.5.6.1(d)** Suction collection bottles that are used as part of patient treatment equipment should be equipped with an overflow shutoff device to prevent carryover of fluids into equipment of the piping system. It is recommended that a separate vacuum trap with shutoff be used between the suction collection bottle and the vacuum system station inlet.

> As with Level 1 piped gas systems, a plan and set of procedures should be developed for coping with the complete loss of vacuum for Level 1 piped vacuum systems. Staff should be instructed on the procedures.
>    The loss of vacuum of Level 1 piped vacuum systems can seriously affect patient care and safety. An emergency plan should consider how vacuum can rapidly be restored to those patients most dependent on it. Piped vacuum systems (like compressed medical air systems that use compressors) are completely dependent on electricity to function. Thus, one major factor to include in any plan is the electricity sources to the vacuum pumps (i.e., Is the normal source reliable? Is the vacuum system connected to the essential electrical system in the event of loss of normal electric power?).

(e) *Contamination.* Liquid or debris shall not be introduced into the medical-surgical vacuum system for disposal.

(f) *Nonmedical Use.* The medical-surgical vacuum system shall not be used for vacuum steam condensate return or other nonmedical or nonsurgical applications.

(g) *Modifications.* Whenever the medical-surgical vacuum system is breached, the tests of 4-3.4.2 shall be conducted on any new or modified portion of the system.

**4-3.5.7  Vacuum System Recordkeeping—Level 1.** Upon completion of the tests described in 4-3.4.2.2, a written record of the performance of these tests shall be maintained in the permanent records of the facility.

**4-3.5.8  Vacuum System Information and Warning Signs—Level 1.**

**4-3.5.8.1  Piping Distribution System.** The piping distribution system shall conform to 4-3.2.2.3 and 4-3.2.2.4.

**4-3.5.8.2  Gauge Identification.** Gauge identification shall conform to 4-3.2.2.10(c).

**4-3.5.9  WAGD System Policies—Level 1.**

**4-3.5.9.1  Maintenance.** The facility shall establish routine preventative maintenance programs applicable to the WAGD system.

**4-3.5.9.2  Performance Tests.** The facility shall establish routine testing programs to assure that the WAGD system performs as required in 4-3.4.3.

## 4-4  Level 2 Piped Systems

### 4-4.1  Piped Gas Systems (Source and Distribution).

Level 2 piped gas systems shall conform to the requirements for Level 1 piped gas systems.

*Exception No. 1: Medical air compressors shall be permitted to be simplex.*

*Exception No. 2: Dryers, aftercoolers, filters, and regulators, as listed in 4-3.1.1.9(g), shall be permitted to be simplex.*

*Exception No. 3: A single alarm panel, as described in 4-3.1.2.2(b)2 shall be mounted in an area of continuous surveillance while the facility is in operation.*

*Exception No. 4: One alarm panel that complies with 4-3.1.2.2(b)3a, b, c, and d, and with 4-3.1.2.2(c)2 and 5, shall be permitted.*

*Exception No. 5: Pressure switches shall be mounted at the source with a pressure gauge or readout located at the master alarm panel.*

### 4-4.2  Piped Vacuum Systems (Source and Distribution).

Level 2 piped vacuum systems shall conform to the requirements for Level 1 piped vacuum systems.

*Exception: Medical vacuum pumps shall be permitted to be simplex.*

### 4-4.3  Piped WAGD Systems (Source and Distribution).

Level 2 piped WAGD systems shall conform to the requirements for Level 1 piped WAGD systems.

*Exception: Medical WAGD pumps shall be permitted to be simplex.*

### 4-4.4  Performance Criteria and Testing.

**4-4.4.1  Piped Gas Systems—Level 2.** The performance and testing criteria for Level 2 piped gas systems shall conform to the requirements for Level 1 piped gas systems.

**4-4.4.2  Piped Vacuum Systems— Level 2.** The performance and testing criteria for Level 2 piped vacuum systems shall conform to the requirements for Level 1 piped vacuum systems.

**4-4.4.3  Piped WAGD Systems— Level 2.** The performance and testing criteria for Level 2 piped WAGD systems shall conform to the requirements for Level 1 piped WAGD systems.

### 4-4.5 Administration—Level 2.

**4-4.5.1 Responsibility of Governing Body.** (Reserved)

**4-4.5.2 Piped Gas Systems Policies—Level 2.** The policies for Level 2 piped gas systems shall conform to the requirements for Level 1 piped gas systems.

**4-4.5.3 Piped Vacuum Systems— Level 2.** The policies for Level 2 piped vacuum systems shall conform to the requirements for Level 1 piped vacuum systems.

**4-4.5.4 Piped WAGD Systems— Level 2.** The policies for Level 2 piped WAGD systems shall conform to the requirements for Level 1 piped WAGD systems.

## 4-5 Level 3 Piped Systems

For an explanation of the term *Level 3,* see commentary under 4-3.1.1.

Material on Level 3 patient piped gas systems comes from Chapter 6 of NFPA 56F, *Standard for Nonflammable Medical Gas Systems,* which was incorporated into NFPA 99 in 1987.

Designers, manufacturers, suppliers, installers, enforcers, and dentists began working in concert in the early 1980s to draft operating specifications to meet general office practice piping systems. The concurrent development of medical compressed air requirements only intensified the effort because piped dental systems, with no other safety standard specifically designated for them, were suddenly being made to conform to the medical compressed air quality standard. This was not the intent of the committee.

To address this situation, a limited number of changes to the then Type 2 system requirements were made for the 1993 edition of NFPA 99. Concurrently, the chairman of the Committee on Piping Systems appointed a task force consisting of representatives from the American Dental Association, the United States Air Force Dental Facilities Command, manufacturers, and OSHA. Their effort was solidified for the 1996 edition with committee proposals that replaced Type 2 systems with Level 3 systems applying to any office practice piping system. [For piped gas systems in Level 3 systems, some restrictions are stipulated, such as a maximum capacity of 3000 ft$^3$; see 4-5.5.2.3(a) for details.]

The definition of *single treatment facility* was revised in conjunction with clarifications to the scope of Level 3 piped gas systems in response to problems reported to the committee with the material (e.g., When were Level 3 systems permitted and when were Level 1 systems required?). Application is now based only on storage volume and not the number of use points. Chapters 12 through 18 indicate where Level 3 systems are permitted. (See 12-3.4.1, 13-3.4.1, 14-3.4.1, etc.)

## 4-5.1 Piped Gas Systems (Source and Distribution)—Level 3.

### 4-5.1.1 Source—Level 3.

**4-5.1.1.1** Cylinders in service and in storage shall be individually secured and located to prevent falling or being knocked over.

(a) Cylinders or supply containers shall be constructed, tested, and maintained in accordance with the U.S. Department of Transportation specifications and regulations.

(b) Cylinder contents shall be identified by attached labels or stencils naming the components and giving their proportions. Labels and stencils shall be lettered in accordance with CGA Pamphlet C-4, *Standard Method of Marking Portable Compressed Gas Containers to Identify the Material Contained.*

(c) Contents of cylinders and containers shall be identified by reading the labels prior to use. Labels shall not be defaced, altered, or removed.

### 4-5.1.1.2* Storage Requirements (Location, Construction, Arrangement).

**A-4-5.1.1.2** When the storage/supply enclosure is remote from the single treatment facility, it should be locked for security reasons to prevent tampering. Access should be only via authorized staff or fire department. When the enclosure is within the single treatment facility, it is left to the discretion of the single treatment facility management as to whether greater benefit is achieved by immediate access or by security. An enclosure with direct access from a public hallway should be locked. If the door to the enclosure opens onto an exit access corridor, see 4-5.1.1.2. *(See Figure A-4-5.1.1.2.)*

> Reference to door enclosure requirements is included as a reminder that the door requirements for Level 3 gas systems also must comply with NFPA *101, Life Safety Code* [2], when the doors to such storage locations open onto an exit access corridor.
> Curious young patients and the accumulation of combustible clutter in storage areas are two situations when restricting access is necessary.

(a) Enclosures for supply systems shall be provided with doors or gates. If the enclosure is outside and/or remote from the single treatment facility, it shall be kept locked. If the storage area is within the single treatment facility (i.e., is not remote), it shall be permitted to be locked.

(b) *Nonflammable Gases (3000 ft³ or less; In-Storage, Connected, or both).*

1. Doors to such locations shall be provided with louvered openings having a minimum of 72 in.² (0.05 m²) in total free area. Where the location of the supply system door opens onto an exit access corridor, louvered openings shall not be used, and a dedicated mechanical ventilation system or by natural venting of a minimum of 72 in.² (0.05 m²) shall be used.
2. Sources of heat in storage locations shall be protected or located so that cylinders or compressed gases shall not be heated to the activation point of integral safety devices. In no case shall the temperature of the cylinders exceed 130°F (54°C). Care shall be

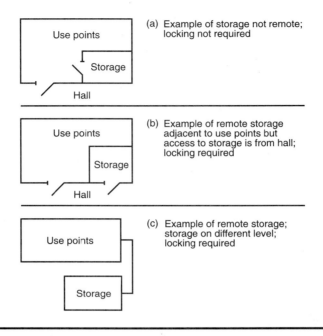

*Figure A-4-5.1.1.2  Examples of storage/supply enclosures.*

exercised when handling cylinders that have been exposed to freezing temperatures or containers that contain cryogenic liquids to prevent injury to the skin.

3. Enclosures shall be provided for supply systems, cylinder storage or manifold locations for oxidizing agents such as oxygen and nitrous oxide. Such enclosures shall be constructed of an assembly of building materials with a fire-resistive rating of at least 1 hour and shall not communicate directly with anesthetizing locations. Other nonflammable (inert) medical gases shall be permitted to be stored in the enclosure. Flammable gases shall not be stored with oxidizing agents. Storage of full or empty cylinders is permitted. Such enclosures shall serve no other purpose.

4. The electric installation in storage locations or manifold enclosures for nonflammable medical gases shall comply with the standards of NFPA 70, *National Electrical Code,* for ordinary locations. Electric wall fixtures, switches, and receptacles shall be installed in fixed locations not less than 5 ft (152 cm) above the floor as a precaution against their physical damage.

5. Storage locations for oxygen and nitrous oxide shall be kept free of flammable materials *[see also 4-5.1.1.2(b)7].*

6. Cylinders containing compressed gases and containers for volatile liquids shall be kept away from radiators, steam piping, and like sources of heat.

7. Combustible materials, such as paper, cardboard, plastics, and fabrics, shall not be stored or kept near supply system cylinders or manifolds containing oxygen or nitrous oxide.

Racks for cylinder storage shall be permitted to be of wooden construction. Wrappers shall be removed prior to storage.

*Exception: Shipping crates or storage cartons for cylinders.*

8. When cylinder valve protection caps are supplied, they shall be secured tightly in place unless the cylinder is connected for use.

9. Containers shall not be stored in a tightly closed space such as a closet *[see 8-2..2.3(c)]*.

10. *Location of Supply Systems.*

    a. Storage facilities that are outside, but adjacent to a building wall, shall be located such that the distance to any window of the adjacent building is greater than 25 ft (7.6 m).
    b. Locations for supply systems shall not be used for storage purposes other than for containers of nonflammable gases. Storage of full or empty containers shall be permitted. Other nonflammable medical gas supply systems or storage locations shall be permitted to be in the same location with oxygen or nitrous oxide or both. However, care shall be taken to provide adequate ventilation to dissipate such other gases in order to prevent the development of oxygen-deficient atmospheres in the event of functioning of cylinder or manifold pressure-relief devices.
    c. Air compressors and vacuum pumps shall be located separately from cylinder patient gas systems or cylinder storage enclosures. Air compressors shall be installed in a designated mechanical equipment area, adequately ventilated and with required services.

11. *Construction and Arrangement of Supply System Locations.*

    a. Locations for supply systems for oxygen, nitrous oxide, or mixtures of these gases shall not communicate with anesthetizing locations or storage locations for flammable anesthetizing agents.
    b. Where enclosures (interior or exterior) for supply systems are located near sources of heat, such as furnaces, incinerators, or boiler rooms, they shall be of construction that protects cylinders from reaching temperatures exceeding 130°F (54°C). Open electrical conductors and transformers shall not be located in close proximity to enclosures. Such enclosures shall not be located adjacent to storage tanks for flammable or combustible liquids.
    c. Smoking shall be prohibited in supply system enclosures.
    d. Heating shall be by steam, hot water, or other indirect means. Cylinder temperatures shall not exceed 130°F (54°C).

**4-5.1.1.3\* Level 3 Patient Gas Supply Systems.** *(See Figure 4-5.1.1.3.)* Compressed air shall be provided by a Level 3 compressed air system as defined in Chapter 2.

**A-4-5.1.1.3** Level 3 compressed air and nitrogen gas systems are used primarily to drive gas-powered power devices. Similar applications are in podiatry and plastic surgery. Examples of these are air used to drive turbine-powered drills and air used to dry teeth and gums. Some dental hand pieces have an internal self-contained air return system, while other hand pieces discharge air into the atmosphere. Some discharge a mixture of air and water. Nitrogen is often piped as an alternate or reserve supply to the compressor system.

The application of dental compressed air is not used for life-support purposes such as respirators, IPPB machines, analgesia, anesthesia, and so forth. Air discharged into the oral cavity is incidental and not a primary source of air to sustain life. However, if there is a coincident use of dental air for providing respiratory support, the requirements of dental air will be superseded by those of the respiratory support, and the compressed air system must produce the higher-quality medical compressed air as defined in Chapter 2. This could affect the selection of a compressor.

A dental compressed air system should not be used to provide power for an air-powered evacuation system without specific attention paid to the discharge of the evacuated gases and liquids. An open discharge of evacuated gases into the general environment of an operatory could compromise the quality of breathing air in the treatment facility. Air discharge should be vented to the outside of the building through a dedicated vent.

An air power evacuation system might require significant quantities of air to operate. Manufacturers' recommendations should be followed regarding proper sizing of the air compressor. Inadequate sizing can result in overheating, premature compressor failures, and inadequate operating pressures and flows.

Reports received by members of the former Subcommittee on Nonflammable Medical Piped Gas Systems (now part of the Committee on Piping Systems) indicated that Level 1 gas system requirements were being applied to Level 3 gas systems, particularly dental air systems for dental offices. As a result, beginning in 1989 the committee considered proposals and detailed technical information from the dental industry, clinical representatives, and others on the development of requirements for Level 3 gas systems. The material generated was incorporated into the 1993 edition of NFPA 99.

For the 1996 edition of NFPA 99, the Committee on Piping Systems made further changes, dividing source requirements into two categories: (1) those supplying air that will be blown inside the oral cavity or that will be used for an air power evacuation system (4-5.1.1.3), and (2) those driving gas-powered devices, such as high-speed turbine dental drills (4-5.1.1.4).

If Level 3 compressed air and Level 1 compressed air are to be used in the same facility (such as an oral surgery suite) and from the same compressor supply system, the requirements of Level 1 air will supersede those of Level 3 compressed air.

An air power evacuation system could require significant quantities of air to operate. Manufacturers' recommendations should be followed regarding proper sizing of the air compressor. Inadequate sizing can result in overheating, premature compressor failures, and inadequate operating pressures and flows.

(a) Level 3 compressed air shall be permitted to be used to power air-powered devices for evacuation only if the exhaust of the evacuation device is a closed vent to the outside of the building.

> The committee is concerned that Level 3 compressed air may be used inappropriately to power a waste anesthetic gas scavenging system (WAGS) that would discharge indiscriminately into the facility (e.g., in a dental office). The committee, recognizing that there are many ways to accomplish scavenging in the practice of dentistry and oral surgery, cautions that the discharge must be appropriately vented to the outside when Level 3 compressed air is used as the power source.

(b) Equipment shall be obtained from and be installed under the supervision of a manufacturer(s) or supplier(s) familiar with proper practices for its construction and use. Maintenance programs, in accordance with the recommendations of manufacturer(s), shall be established for the dental air compressor supply system as connected in each individual installation.

> This paragraph was added in 1993 to address reports that systems were being procured and installed from suppliers not appropriately knowledgeable about dental systems. The resulting poor or faulty systems exposed patients to unnecessary risks.

(c)\* The compressor system shall be permitted to be a single, duplex, or multicompressor system.

**A-4-5.1.1.3(c)** Compressed-air quality can be compromised and expected life of system components can be shortened if an undersized system is installed. Manufacturers' recommendations should be followed regarding proper sizing of the air compressor(s).

(d) Each system installation shall include appropriate disconnect switch(es), motor-starting device(s), and motor overload protection device(s). For single, duplex, or multicompressor systems, a means for activation/deactivation of each individual compressor shall be provided by the supplier or contractor. When multiple compressors are used, alternation of units, and a means to activate the additional unit(s) should the in-service unit(s) be incapable of maintaining adequate pressure, shall be provided. Manual or automatic switchover shall be permitted.

(e)\* Level 3 compressed air systems shall be equipped with intake filter-muffler(s) of the dry type; receiver(s); shutoff valves; air dryer(s); in-line final particulate filters rated at 5 microns, 98 percent efficiency, with filter status indicator; and downstream pressure regulator(s) to ensure the delivery of compressed air with a maximum allowable 0.05 ppm liquid oil and 40 percent relative humidity at operating pressure and temperature.

The air intake shall be from outside the building when practical or shall be located within a room where no chemical-based material is stored or used.

The compressor air intake shall be located where no contamination from vacuum system discharges or particulate matter is anticipated. The compressor air intake shall be taken from a space other than an operatory and other than the room or space in which there is an open or semi-open discharge from a Level 3 vacuum system. *[See 4-5.1.1.3.]*

**A-4-5.1.1.3(e)**  The environmental air source for the compressor inlet should take into consideration possible contamination by particulates, concentrations of biological waste contaminants, ozone from nearby brush-type electric motors, and exhaust fumes from engines.

Air taken from an outside atmosphere could cause harmful condensation problems in the compressor. Long runs of inlet tube should also be avoided as it will degrade compressor performance. The compressor manufacturer's recommendations should be followed regarding appropriate pipe size to prevent possible degradation of system performance.

A dental air compressor and dental vacuum system can be in the same equipment room as long as the inlet for the dental air compressor does not draw air from a room or space containing an open discharge for the dental vacuum system.

Atmospheric air in an operatory can have traces of mercury vapor and other contaminants. A compressor inlet location that would draw its supply directly from an operatory should be avoided.

> Care should be taken not to install the intake for the Level 3 air system in the same room as an open vacuum discharge. Committee members have received verbal reports of actual installations that are configured this way and believes this practice must be avoided as specified in A-4-5.1.1.3(e).
>
> When Level 3 compressed air intakes are located outside, care should be exercised to avoid contamination, obstruction, and/or water condensation. In selecting an inside intake location, any area where analgesia gases could be present is to be avoided.
>
> Caution is recommended to ensure that the inlet source for the compressor is located to obtain the cleanest possible air. Compressors located in garage locations could potentially introduce carbon monoxide (CO) into the compressed air system. In addition, inlets taking air from operatories are not permitted because the operatory area can be contaminated with germs, bacteria, and so forth, from the oral cavities of other patients.

(f)  The system shall be equipped with a pressure relief valve, pressure gauge, and receiver with drain plug or a manual drain or an automatic drain. Receiver(s) shall have the capacity to ensure practical on/off operation of the compressor(s). Receiver(s) shall comply with Section VIII, Unfired Pressure Vessels, of the ASME *Boiler and Pressure Vessel Code*.

(g)*  An appropriate moisture indicator shall be provided. The moisture indicator shall be located in the active airstream prior to or after the receiver but upstream of any system pressure regulators.

The moisture indicator shall indicate if the relative humidity of the compressed air exceeds 40 percent at line pressure and temperature.

**A-4-5.1.1.3(g)**  A color dew point monitor downstream of the receiver indicating the quality of air coming into the receiver is desirable.

A color dew point monitor in the main treatment facility is appropriate to help the staff promptly identify when the system is being degraded with air of dew point higher than is acceptable.

The design of the color monitor should be such that the normal tolerance of variations will limit the maximum moisture at 39°F at 100 psig (3.9°C at 690 kPa) at activation.

One type of indicator is a moisture-indicating color disk that changes color when moisture reaches a preset value. When this occurs, service and/or maintenance is necessary.

(h)  An oil indicator sensor per 4-5.1.1.3(e) shall be located downstream of the receiver as shown in Figures 4-5.1.1.3 and 4-5.1.1.4. The oil indication device shall be capable of measuring an oil concentration of 0.05 ppm with an accuracy of ±0.03 ppm in compressed air at 80 to 100 psig (552 to 689 kPa).

(i)  The service outlet shall not be interchangeable with the medical air station outlet.

The intent here is to make it impossible for any quick-connect adapter that is used for dental compressed air with pressures between 0 psig to 100+ psig (0 kPa to 690+ kPa) to be mistakenly, or unknowingly, connected to an analgesia machine intended to provide regulated 50-psig (345-kPa) medical compressed air. If medical compressed air is desired, it should be available only through a standard station outlet complying with this chapter. Conversely, dental compressed air connects should not have to incorporate the double check valves required of standard station outlets for medical compressed air.

**4-5.1.1.4  Level 3 Gas-Powered Devices Supply Systems.**  See Figure 4-5.1.1.4.

See commentary under 4-5.1.1.3 regarding the two different Level 3 supply systems addressed in these paragraphs.

(a)*  The nitrogen operating pressure shall be designed for operating pressures below 160 psig (1103 kPa) for consideration as Level 3.

This requirement was added in the 1996 edition for two reasons. A Level 3 system is intended to be a very simple, uncomplicated system. A nitrogen system higher than 160 psig (1103 kPa) is a special high-pressure operation that is beyond the intent of a Level 3 installation. In addition, most Level 3 system air compressors that operate with a nitrogen backup will stall out at pressures above 160 psig. This requirement will prevent damage to compressors.

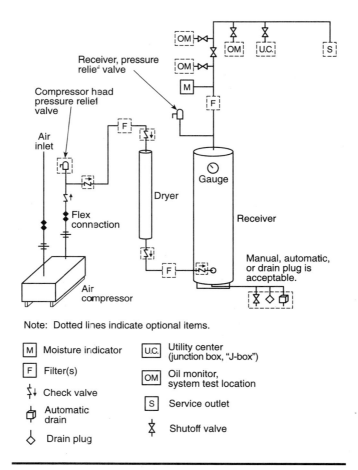

*Figure 4-5.1.1.3  Level 3 patient gas system (typical).*

**A-4-5.1.1.4(a)**  If nitrogen is used as a backup supply to a compressed gas system, the nitrogen operating pressure should be regulated so as not to exceed the operating pressure of the Level III compressed air system.

(b)  Supply systems providing nitrogen gas to power devices shall use nitrogen oil-free, dry as defined in Chapter 2.

(c)  Level 3 nitrogen systems shall either have regulator(s) mounted on the individual cylinder(s) or the cylinder(s) can be connected to a manifold via pigtail and pressure regulated at the manifold. The cylinder(s) shall be individually secured to prevent falling.

(d)*  The nitrogen cylinder gas supply shall be permitted to be independent of the 3000 ft$^3$ (85 m$^3$) consideration for Level 3 patient nonflammable medical gases classification.

Nitrogen gas cylinder storage in compressor rooms and also in the same storage area with nonflammable medical gases shall be permitted.

**A-4-5.1.1.4(d)** The ft$^3$ (or m$^3$) of stored nitrogen gas is not restricted.

(e) Cylinder storage shall avoid direct heating from steam, hot water, or other indirect means. Cylinder temperatures shall not exceed 130°F (54°C).

(f) The nitrogen gas supply system shall be a system of cylinders and necessary supply equipment assembled with that which will permit alternately supplying the required supply gas. When the content of one primary cylinder is unable to supply the normal operating pressures, the secondary cylinder(s) shall be activated manually. Automatic switchover shall be permitted.

(g) Where nitrogen gas is used as a backup for a Level 3 compressed air system, a check valve and shutoff valve shall be located in each supply line prior to the "T" connection to the main line. *[See Figure 4-5.1.1.4.]*

**4-5.1.2 Distribution for Patients—Level 3 (Manifold, Piping, Valving/Controls, Outlets/Terminals, Alarms).**

Readers should note the differences in distribution requirements for Level 3 piped gas systems for patients (4-5.1.2) and those distribution requirements for Level 3 piped gas systems for gas-powered devices (4-5.1.3).

**4-5.1.2.1** Mechanical means shall be provided to ensure the connection of cylinders containing the proper gas to the piping system. Cylinder valve outlets for nonflammable gases and gas mixtures for medical purposes shall comply with CGA Pamphlet V-1, *Standard for Compressed Gas Cylinder Valve Outlet and Inlet Connections* (ANSI B57.1; CSA B96).

**4-5.1.2.2** Threaded connections between the regulators and the piping system shall comply with CGA Pamphlet V-5, *Diameter-Index Safety System*.

**4-5.1.2.3** Flexible connectors of other than all-metal construction used to connect outlets of pressure regulators to fixed piping shall not exceed 5 ft (1.5 m) in length and shall not penetrate walls, floors, ceilings, or partitions. Flexible connectors shall comply with the provisions of 4-5.1.2.2.

**4-5.1.2.4** A shutoff valve or check valve shall be installed downstream of each pressure regulator.

**4-5.1.2.5** A pressure relief valve set at 50 percent above normal line pressure shall be installed downstream of the shutoff or check valve required in 4-5.1.2.4. Pressure relief valves shall be of brass or bronze and designed for oxygen service.

**4-5.1.2.6\*** Supply systems supplying a single treatment facility as outlined in 4-5.5.2.3(a)3 shall contain as a minimum the following:

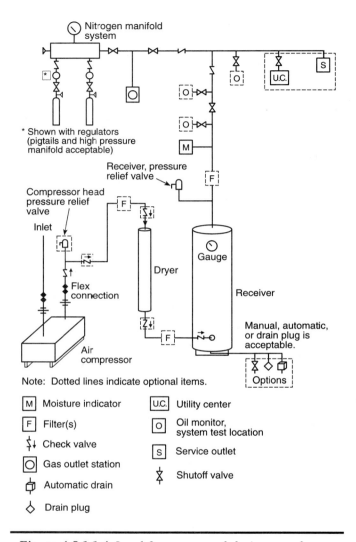

Note: Dotted lines indicate optional items.

| | | | |
|---|---|---|---|
| M | Moisture indicator | U.C. | Utility center |
| F | Filter(s) | O | Oil monitor, system test location |
| ⇅ | Check valve | S | Service outlet |
| O | Gas outlet station | ⋈ | Shutoff valve |
| ⊡ | Automatic drain | | |
| ◇ | Drain plug | | |

**Figure 4-5.1.1.4** *Level 3 gas-powered devices supply system.*

(a) Two cylinders of oxygen and two cylinders of nitrous oxide (if used) if storage is remote, or two cylinders of oxygen and one cylinder of nitrous oxide (if used) if storage is not remote.

(b) The cylinders for each gas service shall be manifolded so that the cylinders can alternately supply the piping system. Each bank shall contain at least an average day's supply.

When the content of the primary bank is unable to supply the system, the secondary bank shall be capable of being manually switched to supply the system. Automatic switchover shall be permitted.

(c) When the supply system is remote, the switchover shall be automatic.

**A-4-5.1.2.6** If the supply system is within the confines of a single treatment facility, a simple manual transfer is permissible. Only high/low pressure alarms are required. The gases are to be manifolded so a quick manual transfer is possible without life-threatening consequences.

However, if the supply system is remote, a prompt transfer of gases becomes more difficult. It could require transcending one or more flights of stairs and/or going to a remote location on the same floor. Under these situations an automatic system is required.

**4-5.1.2.7\*** Supply systems supplying two single treatment facilities as outlined in 4-5.5.2.3(a)4 shall contain as a minimum:

(a) Two cylinders of oxygen and two cylinders of nitrous oxide (if used).

(b) The cylinders for each gas service shall be manifolded so that the cylinders can alternately supply the piping system. Each bank shall contain at least an average day's supply. When the content of the primary bank is unable to supply the piping system, the secondary bank shall automatically operate to supply the piping system.

**A-4-5.1.2.7** The installation of a supply serving more than one single treatment facility creates by its very nature a remote location relative to the other facility. Because more than one practice could be involved, the transfer of oxygen and nitrous oxide gases is to be automatically achieved.

**4-5.1.2.8 Warning Systems for Gases.**

(a) An automatic pressure switch, which will actuate a visual and audible alarm when the line pressure drops below or increases above normal line pressure, shall be connected to each main supply line within a single treatment facility. *[See 4-5.4.1.3(f).]* The automatic pressure switch shall be installed downstream of any main supply line shutoff valve that may be required by the provisions of 4-5.1.2.11(b)2 and 3.

(b) A warning system as required in 4-5.1.2.8(a) shall be installed in each single treatment facility served by the supply system. The warning system shall be comprised of an audible and noncancellable visual signal and shall be installed to be heard and seen at a continuously attended location during the time of operation of the facility.

(c) A warning system as outlined in 4-5.1.2.8(b) shall be installed to indicate whenever automatic changeover occurs or is about to occur. The signal shall remain uncancellable until the reserve supply bank has been replenished. The sensor alarm shall be independent of the sensor actuator of 4-5.1.2.8(a). When two treatment facilities are served by a common supply system, the automatic changeover alarm shall indicate in both facilities.

(d) A signal shall be indicated separately for each medical gas piping system when the pressure in the main line increases 20 percent or decreases 20 percent from the normal operating pressure. The actuating switch for these signals shall be installed in the main line immediately downstream (on the piping distribution side) of the main line shutoff valve or the source valve if the main line shutoff valve is not required. *(See C-4.1.)*

(e) A pressure gauge shall be installed in the main line adjacent to the actuating switch. It shall be appropriately labeled and be readily visible from a standing position. *(See C-4.5.)*

### 4-5.1.2.9 Pressure Gauges for Gas Systems.

(a) Pressure gauges and manometers for medical gas piping systems shall be cleaned for oxygen service.

(b) Pressure gauges and manometers for medical piping systems shall be identified:

(NAME OF GAS) USE NO OIL!

### 4-5.1.2.10* Gas Piping

**A-4-5.1.2.10** One of the major concerns is the cross-connection of piping systems of different gases. The problem of cross-connection of oxygen and other gases such as nitrous oxide, air, and nitrogen can readily be recognized/prevented by the use of different sizes of tubing. It is recommended that piping and manifolds for oxygen service be of a different size than the piping intended for other gas services. The piping for other than oxygen can be of a smaller size. Generally, oxygen is installed in ½-in. O.D. tube size and other gases with ⅜-in. O.D. tube size.

(a) *Gas Piping.* The provisions of this section apply to field-installed piping for the distribution of nonflammable medical piped gases.

The soft copper tubing listed in the exception is permitted only in Level 3 system installations. The committee was made aware that Level 3 installations often have the piping buried in a poured concrete floor. Rigid tubing and brazed connectors are impractical in these situations. The material listed in ASTM B 88 [13] (Type K or Type L) first became available cleaned for oxygen service at the time of the revision to the 1993 edition. Only sizes up to ½ in. diameter were considered appropriate for the exception.

If piping is buried in a poured concrete floor, it must still be protected in accordance with 4-3.1.2.2(a)11.

1. Tubes, valves, fittings, station outlets, and other piping components in medical gas systems shall have been cleaned for oxygen service prior to installation.
2. Piping for nonflammable medical gas systems shall be suitable for oxygen service in accordance with 4-5.1.2.10(a)3. Each length of tube shall be permanently labeled and delivered plugged or capped. Fittings, valves, and other devices shall be sealed and marked. The installer shall furnish documentation certifying that all installed piping materials comply with the requirements of this paragraph.
3. Piping shall be ASTM B 819 specification hard drawn seamless medical gas tubing; ASTM B 819 tubing is identified by the markings "OXY," "MED," "OXY/MED,"

"OXY/ACR," or "ACR/MED" in green (Type K) or blue (Type L). Main and branches shall be not less than ½ in. nominal size. Factory-installed tube on station outlets extending no farther than 8 in. from the outlet body shall be permitted to be ⅜ in. O.D. (¼ in. nominal) size. Connection to gauges and alarm switches and runouts to alarm panels shall be permitted to be ¼ in. O.D. (⅛ in. nominal) size.

*Exception: For systems operated at pressures between 200 and 300 psig (1380 and 2070 kPa, respectively), ASTM B 819, Type K copper shall be used.*

Copper tube shall, wherever possible, be installed overhead or below floor level. Only where the installation requires installing in a slab, exceptions below are permitted to apply:

a. Annealed (soft temper) ASTM B 88 (Type K or L) copper tube that has been prepared for oxygen service according to CGA Pamphlet G-4.1, *Cleaning Equipment for Oxygen Service,* shall be permitted to be used up to ½ in. O.D. (⅜ in. nominal) size.
b. The tube shall be installed in conduit sufficiently large to accept the following gases (if used): $O_2$, $N_2O$, $N_2$, MA, DA, Level 3 vacuum.
c. The pipe shall be a continuous run from entry to exit of the conduit. PVC conduit shall be permitted for Level 3 vacuum only.
d. All station outlets (inlets) shall be permitted to be completed after the slab is complete.
e. All tests shall be completed per 4-5.4.1.2.

4. Except as provided under 4-5.1.2.10(a)8 and 9, joints in copper tubes shall be brazed using capillary fittings complying with ANSI B16.22, *Wrought Copper and Copper Alloy Solder-Joint Pressure Fittings,* or brazing fittings complying with MSS SP-73, *Brazing Joints for Wrought and Cast Copper Alloy Solder Joint Pressure Fittings.* Cast fittings shall not be used for brazed joints.

*Exception: Flared connections shall be permitted where exposed at station outlets and manifold connections.*

5. Valves, fittings, and other piping components shall be cleaned for oxygen service by the manufacturer in accordance with CGA Pamphlet G-4.1, *Cleaning Equipment for Oxygen Service,* except that fittings shall be permitted to be cleaned by a supplier or agency other than the manufacturer.
6. Piping systems shall be designed and sized to deliver the required flow rates at the utilization pressures.
7. Piping shall be supported from the building structure in accordance with MSS Standard Practice SP-69, *Piping Hangers and Supports Selection and Application.* Hangers and supports shall comply with MSS Standard Practice SP-58, *Pipe Hangers and Supports Materials, Design and Manufacture.* Hangers for copper tube shall have a copper finish. In potentially damp locations, copper tube hangers or supports shall be plastic-coated or otherwise insulated from the tube. Maximum support spacing shall be as follows:

| | |
|---|---|
| ¼ in. (.635 cm) nominal | 5 ft (1.52 m) |
| ⅜ in. (.953 cm) nominal | 6 ft (1.83 m) |
| ½ in. (1.27 cm) nominal | 6 ft (1.83 m) |
| ¾ in. (1.91 cm) nominal | 7 ft (2.13 m) |
| 1 in. (2.54 cm) nominal | 8 ft (2.44 m) |
| 1¼ in. (3.175 cm) nominal | 9 ft (2.74 m) |
| 1½ in. (3.81 cm) nominal and larger | 10 ft (3.05 m) |
| Vertical risers, all sizes | Every floor, but not to exceed 15 ft (4.57 m) |

8. Joints in medical gas tube shall be brazed except that memory-metal couplings having temperature and pressure ratings not less than that of a brazed joint shall be permitted. Compression-type connections shall be prohibited throughout the piping system, including connections to station outlets, alarm devices, and other components. Unions shall not be permitted in the distribution pipeline system.

*Exception: Threaded connections for air compressor sets and devices such as manifolds, pressure regulators, relief valves, pressure switches, and pressure gauges.*

9. Listed or approved metallic gas tube fittings that, when made up, provide a permanent joint having the mechanical, thermal, and sealing integrity of a brazed joint shall be permitted to be used in lieu of brazed joints.
10. Turns, offsets, and other changes in direction in piping shall be made with fittings complying with 4-5.1.2.10(a)4.
11. Piping shall be protected against freezing, corrosion, and physical damage. Buried piping outside of buildings shall be installed below the local level of frost penetration. Buried piping that will be subject to surface loads shall be buried at a sufficient depth to protect the piping from excessive stresses. The minimum backfilled cover above the top of buried piping outside of buildings shall be 36 in. (91.4 cm), except that the minimum cover shall be permitted to be reduced to 18 in. (45.7 cm) where physical damage to the piping is not likely to occur. Trenches shall be excavated so that the pipe has a firm, substantially continuous bearing on the bottom of the trench. Underground piping shall be installed in a continuous enclosure to protect the pipe from damage while backfilling. The enclosure shall be split or otherwise provide access at the joints during visual inspection and leak testing. Backfill shall be clean and compacted so as to protect and uniformly support the piping. A continuous tape or marker placed immediately above the enclosure shall clearly identify the pipeline by specific name. In addition, a continuous warning means shall be provided above the pipeline at approximately one-half the depth of bury. Where underground piping is installed through a wall sleeve, the ends of the sleeve shall be sealed to prevent the entrance of ground water. Piping underground within buildings or imbedded in concrete floors or walls shall be installed in a continuous conduit.
12. Medical gas risers shall be permitted to be installed in pipe shafts if protected from physical damage, effects of excessive heat, corrosion, or contact with oil.

13. Piping shall not be installed in kitchens or electrical switchgear rooms.

14. Medical gas piping shall be permitted to be located in the same service trench or tunnel with fuel gas lines, fuel oil lines, electrical lines, steam lines, and similar utilities provided that the space is ventilated (naturally or mechanically) and the ambient temperature around the medical gas piping is limited to 130°F (54°C) maximum. Medical gas piping shall not be located where subject to contact with oil, including flooding in the case of a major oil leak.

15. Piping exposed in corridors and other areas where subject to physical damage from the movement of carts, stretchers, portable equipment, or vehicles shall be suitably protected.

16. Where a system originally used or constructed for use at one pressure and for a gas is converted for operation at another pressure or for another gas, all provisions of 4-5.1.2.12, 4-5.1.2.10(b), 4-5.4, and the exception to 4-5.1.2.10(a)3 shall apply as if the system were new. Vacuum systems shall never be converted for use as gas systems.

(b) *Brazed Joints.*

1. Brazed tube joints shall be the socket type. Filler metals shall bond with and be metallurgically compatible with the base metals being joined. Flux shall not be used except where permitted under 4-5.1.2.10(b)1b. Brazing filler metals shall comply with ANSI/AWS A5.8, *Specification for Brazing Filler Metal,* except that filler metals having compositions not conforming to the exact ANSI/AWS A5.8 classifications shall be permitted when used according to the manufacturer's instructions.

   a. Copper-to-copper joints shall be brazed using a copper-phosphorus or copper-phosphorous-silver brazing filler metal (BCuP series) without flux.

   b. Dissimilar metals, such as copper and bronze or brass, shall be brazed using an appropriate flux with a silver (BAg series) brazing filler metal.

2. Joints to be brazed in place shall be accessible for proper preparation, assembly, heating, filler application, cooling, cleaning, and inspection.

3. Tube ends shall be cut square using a sharp tubing cutter to avoid deforming the tube. The cutting wheel shall be free from grease, oil, or other lubricant not suitable for oxygen service. The cut ends of tube and pipe shall be deburred with a sharp, clean deburring tool, taking care to prevent chips from entering the tube or pipe.

4. The surfaces to be brazed shall be mechanically cleaned using a clean stainless steel wire brush or equivalent. The use of steel wool shall be prohibited due to the possible presence of oil.

Mechanical cleaning shall not result in grooving of the surfaces to be joined. After mechanical cleaning, the surfaces shall be wiped using a clean, lint-free white cloth. During this cleaning, care shall be taken to avoid contamination of the cleaned item for oxygen internal surfaces of the tube and components. Joints shall be recleaned if contaminated prior to brazing. Joints shall be brazed within 1 hour of being cleaned.

5.  Where dissimilar metals, such as copper and bronze or brass, are being brazed, flux shall be applied sparingly to minimize contamination of the inside of the tube with flux. The flux shall be applied and worked over the surfaces to be brazed using a stiff stainless steel bristle brush to ensure adequate coverage and wetting of the surfaces with flux. Where possible, short sections of copper tube shall be brazed to the noncopper component and the interior of the subassembly shall be cleaned of flux prior to installation in the piping system. Flux-coated brazing rods shall be permitted to be used in lieu of the application of flux to the surfaces to be joined on tube ¾ in. nominal size and smaller.

6.  Tube ends shall be inserted fully into the socket of the fitting. Where flux is permitted, the joint shall be heated slowly until the flux has liquefied. Once this has occurred, or where flux is not used, the joint shall be heated quickly to the brazing temperature, taking care not to overheat the joint. Techniques for heating the joint, applying the brazing filler metal, and making horizontal, vertical, and large-diameter joints shall be as stated in sections on "Applying Heat and Brazing" and "Horizontal and Vertical Joints" in the chapter on "Joining and Bending" in the CDA *Copper Tube Handbook.*

7.* While being brazed, joints shall be continuously purged with oil-free dry nitrogen to prevent the formation of copper oxide on the inside surface of the joint. The flow of purge gas shall be maintained until the joint is cool to the touch.

**A-4-5.1.2.10(b)7** The intent is to provide an oxygen-free atmosphere within the tubing and to prevent the formation of copper oxide scale during brazing. This is accomplished by filling the piping with a low-volume flow of low-pressure inert gas.

*Exception: A final connection to an existing pipeline shall be permitted to be made without the use of a nitrogen purge. After final connection, the affected downstream portions of the pipeline shall be tested in accordance with 4-5.4.1.3 with the gas of system designation.*

8.  During and after installation, openings in the piping system shall be kept capped or plugged to avoid unnecessary loss of purge gas while brazing and to prevent debris or other contaminants from entering the system; except that during brazing, a discharge opening shall be provided on the opposite side of the joint from where the purge gas is being introduced. During brazing, the purge gas flow rate shall be maintained at a level that will not produce a positive pressure in the piping system. After brazing, the discharge opening shall be plugged or capped to prevent contamination of the inside of the tube.

9.  After brazing, the outside of all joints shall be cleaned by washing with water and a stainless steel wire brush to remove any residue and permit clear visual inspection of the joint. Where flux has been permitted, hot water shall be used.

10. Each brazed joint shall be visually examined after cleaning of the outside of the joint. The following conditions shall be considered unacceptable:

    a.  Flux or flux residue
    b.  Excessive oxidation of the joint
    c.  Presence of unmelted filler metal

d. Failure of the filler metal to be clearly visible all the way around the joint at the interface between the socket and the tube

e. Cracks in the tube or component

f. Cracks in the braze filler metal

g. Failure of the joint to hold the test pressure under 4-5.4.1.2

11. Brazed joints that are found to be defective under 4-5.1.2.10(b)10 conditions a, c, d, f, or g, shall be permitted to be repaired, except that no joint shall be repaired more than once. Brazed joints that are found to be defective under 4-5.1.2.10(b)10, conditions b and e, shall be replaced.

(c)* *Threaded Joints.*

**A-4-5.1.2.10(c)** Where threaded joints are tinned, soft solder should be used. If sealing compound is used, it should be applied sparingly so that excess sealant is not forced inside the system.

1. Threaded joints in medical gas distribution piping shall be limited to the connection of pressure gauges, alarm pressure switches, and similar devices.

2. Threads on pipe and fittings shall be tapered pipe threads complying with ANSI B1.20.1, *Pipe Threads, General Purpose.*

3. Threaded joints in piping systems shall be made up with polytetrafluoroethylene (such as Teflon®) tape or other thread sealant suitable for oxygen service. Sealants shall be applied to the male threads only.

(d) *Manufactured Equipment and Component Installation.*

1. The installation of individual components shall be made in accordance with the instructions of the manufacturer. Such instructions shall include directions and information deemed by the manufacturer to be adequate for attaining proper installation, testing, maintenance, and operation of the medical gas systems. These instructions shall be left with the owner

2. The installation shall be made by qualified, competent technicians experienced in making such installations.

(e) *Prohibited Interconnections.* Two or more medical gas piping systems shall not be interconnected for testing or for any other reason. Leak testing shall be accomplished by separately charging and testing the individual piping system.

(f)* *Fittings.* Fittings shall be manufactured from metallic corrosion-resistant materials suitable for the system pressures [not to exceed 160 psig (1103 kPa)].

**A-4-5.1.2.10(f)** Acceptable materials are wrought copper, brass, or bronze.

(g) *Connectors and Joints.* Connectors and joints shall be brazed or threaded NPT.

(h) *General Requirements.*

1. *Oxygen Compatibility.* Components in nonflammable medical gas systems shall be of materials that are suitable for oxygen service. *(See 4-3.1.1.3, Material—Oxygen Compati-*

*bility.)* Pipe (tube), fittings, valves, and other components shall have been thoroughly cleaned internally to remove oil, grease, and other readily oxidizable materials, as if for oxygen service.

2. *Cleanliness.* Materials that have been cleaned for use in medical gas piping systems shall be plugged, capped, or otherwise sealed until installed. Particular care shall be taken in the storage and handling of such material to maintain its clean condition. Immediately before final assembly, such material shall be visually examined internally for contamination. Material that has become contaminated and is no longer suitable for oxygen service shall not be installed.

3. *On-Site Cleaning.* On-site cleaning of the interior surfaces of tubes, valves, fittings, and other components shall be limited to recleaning surfaces in the immediate vicinity of the joints that have become contaminated prior to brazing. Such surfaces shall be cleaned by washing in a clean, hot water/alkaline solution, such as sodium carbonate or trisodium phosphate (1 lb to 3 gal of potable water). Interior surfaces shall be thoroughly scrubbed and rinsed with clean, hot potable water.

**4-5.1.2.11  Gas Shutoff Valves.**

Prior to 1996 edition, this section listed requirements only for emergency valves. The committee recognized the need to address non-emergency shutoff valves [see subsection (a)] given that such valves are needed for maintenance, isolating problems, repairs, and so forth.

(a) *Non-Emergency Shutoff Valves.* Systems operating at varying operating pressures from 0-200 psig (1380 kPa), and not operating at a constant regulated 50 psig (345 kPa), shall have a manual shutoff valve within the facility between the source and all service outlets.

(b) *Emergency Shutoff Valves.*

Note that emergency shutoff valves are to be located in the use point locations. This is in addition to those that are required at the supply source.

1.* Where the central supply is remote from the medical gas system use points, the main supply line shall be provided with a shutoff valve so located in the single treatment facility as to be accessible from use-point locations in an emergency.

**A-4-5.1.2.11(b)1** Should a fire occur at night or when the facility is not in use, fire fighters should not be confronted with a potential pressurized gas source that could feed the fire and cause extensive damage and risk of life. Good economics also dictate that when the system is not in use, the leakage of gas through hoses, couplings, etc., can be minimized if the system is shut off and portable equipment disconnected. *(See Figure A-4-5.1.2.11(b)1.)*

2. Where the supply is remote from a single treatment facility, the main supply line shall be provided with a shutoff valve so located in the single treatment facility as to be accessible from use-point locations in an emergency. Such valves shall be labeled to

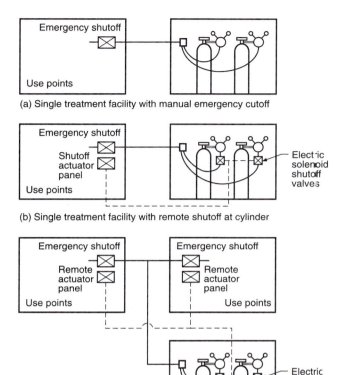

(a) Single treatment facility with manual emergency cutoff

(b) Single treatment facility with remote shutoff at cylinder

(c) Two single treatment facilities require individual emergency shutoff valves even with remote actuator shutoff at supply.

**Figure A-4-5.1.2.11(b)1**  *Shutoff valves.*

indicate the gas controlled and shall shut off only the gas to that single treatment facility. A remotely activated shutoff at the supply cylinder shall not be used for emergency shutoff. For clinical purposes, such a remote actuator shall not fail-closed in the event of a loss of electric power. If remote actuators are the type that fail-open, it shall be mandatory that cylinder shutoff valves be closed whenever the system is not in use. *[See 4-5.5.2.3(f).]*

It was always the committee's intent that the solenoid valves be located on the cylinders (as required in sentence 3). This was the basis for the development of former Type II, now Level 3, systems. This is further illustrated by Figure A-4-5.1.2.11(b)1.

The last two sentences (on remote actuators and cylinder shutoff valves) are included to address the following: (1) new shutoff valve technology that does not change state when electric power supplied to them is interrupted, and (2) fire hazards and shutoff valves when a facility is not in use. In facilities, such as freestanding dental or medical offices that are generally not supervised 24-hours per day, it is a serious hazard to leave systems pressurized without supervision. In the event of a fire and hose break, nothing would prevent high-pressure oxygen from accelerating the fire and adding problems to fire-fighting operations.

3. Where the central supply system supplies two single treatment facilities, each facility shall be provided with a shutoff valve so located in each treatment facility as to be accessible from the use-point locations in an emergency. Such valves shall be labeled to indicate the gas controlled and shall shut off only the gas to that single treatment facility. A remotely activated shutoff at the supply manifold shall not be used for emergency shutoff valves for dual treatment facility installations. For clinical purposes, such a remote actuator shall not fail-closed in the event of a loss of electric power. If remote actuators are the type that fail-open, it shall be mandatory that cylinder shutoff valves be closed whenever the system is not in use. *[See 4-5.5.2.3(f).]*

See commentary under 4-5.1.2.11(b)2 with respect to the last two sentences on remote actuators.

4. Each riser supplied from the main line shall be provided with a shutoff valve adjacent to the riser connection. Riser valves shall remain accessible and shall not be obstructed.

**4-5.1.2.12 Gas Station Outlets.** See C-4.2.

(a)* Station outlets shall be located at an appropriate height above the floor to prevent physical damage to equipment attached to the outlet.

Floor mounts for Level 3 gas systems shall not be recessed and shall be permitted to be mounted in or on the dental junction box, when mounted to the floor.

**A-4-5.1.2.12(a)** Station outlets can be recessed or otherwise protected from damage.

(b) Station outlets shall be located to avoid physical damage to the valve and attached equipment.

(c)* Each station outlet for medical gases, whether threaded or noninterchangeable quick-coupler, shall be gas-specific and shall consist of a primary and a secondary valve (or assembly). The secondary valve (or unit) shall close automatically to stop the flow of medical gas when the primary valve (or unit) is removed. Each outlet shall be legibly identified with the name or chemical symbol of the gas contained. Where chemical symbols are used, they shall be in accordance with the CGA Pamphlet P-2, *Characteristics and Safe Handling of Medical Gases.* Where supplementary color identification is used, it shall be in accordance with CGA Pamphlet C-9, *Standard Color-Marking of Compressed Gas Cylinders Intended for Medical Use. (See Table 4-5.1.2.12.)*

**A-4-5.1.2.12(c)** See 4-3.1.2.7(c) and 4-3.1.2.11 for additional requirements for tubes used in systems at nonstandard pressures.

The purpose of the automatic secondary check valve is to shut off the flow of gas when the primary valve is removed for servicing.

(d) Threaded outlets shall be noninterchangeable connections complying with CGA Pamphlet V-5, *Diameter-Index Safety System Q Non-Interchangeable Low Pressure Connections for Medical Gas Applications.*

(e) Each station outlet, including those mounted in columns, hose reels, ceiling tracks, or other special installations, shall be designed so that parts or components that are required to be gas-specific for compliance with 4-5.1.2.12(c) cannot be interchanged between station outlets for different gases.

1. The use of common parts such as springs, O-rings, fasteners, seals, and shutoff poppets shall be permitted.

(f) When multiple wall outlets are installed, including those for vacuum, there must be sufficient spacing between outlets to permit the simultaneous use of adjacent outlets with any of the various types of required equipment.

(g) Outlets intended for the connection of manufactured assemblies shall be D.I.S.S. connectors, or noninterchangeable gas-specific, semi-permanent connectors.

**4-5.1.3 Distribution for Gas-Powered Devices—Level 3.**

**4-5.1.3.1** The provisions of this section apply to field-installed piping for the distribution of gases to power devices.

(a) Piping shall be Type K or L copper (hard drawn or annealed) or brass (schedule 40 or 80). If Level 3 system dynamic gas piping is installed simultaneously with other patient gas piping systems, either the Level 3 system piping shall be labeled or otherwise identified prior to installation in order to preclude inadvertent inclusion in a nonflammable medical gas piping system, or the Level 3 system piping shall be cleaned and degreased in accordance with 4-5.4.1.

(b)* Fittings shall be manufactured from corrosion-resistant materials suitable for the system pressures [not to exceed 160 psig (1103 kPa)].

**A-4-5.1.3.1(b)** Acceptable materials are wrought copper, brass, or bronze.

(c) Connectors and joints shall be brazed, or threaded NPT.

(d) Piping shall be supported from the building structure in accordance with MSS Standard Practice SP-69, *Piping Hangers and Supports—Selection and Application.* Hangers and supports shall comply with MSS Standard Practice SP-58, *Pipe Hangers and Support—Materials, Design and Manufacture.*

(e) Piping shall be protected against freezing, corrosion, and physical damage. Buried piping outside of buildings shall be installed below the local level of frost penetration. Buried piping that will be subject to surface loads shall be buried at a sufficient depth to protect

*Table 4-5.1.2.12 Standard Designation Colors and Operating Pressures for Level 3 Gas and Vacuum Systems*

| Gas Service | Abbreviated Name | Colors (Background/Text) | Standard Pressure |
|---|---|---|---|
| Medical air | MedAir | Yellow/black | 50 psig +5/−0 |
| | | | 345 kPa +35/−0 |
| Carbon dioxide | $CO_2$ | Grey/black or grey/white | 50 psig +5/−0 |
| | | | 345 kPa +35/−0 |
| Helium | He | Brown/white | 50 psig +5/−0 |
| | | | 345 kPa +35/−0 |
| Nitrogen | $N_2$ or $HPN_2$ | Black/white | 160 psig +25/−0 |
| | | | 1145 kPa +173/−0 |
| Nitrous oxide | $N_2O$ | Blue/white | 50 psig +5/−0 |
| | | | 345 kPa +35/−0 |
| Oxygen | $O_2$ | Green/white or white/green | 50 psig +5/−0 |
| | | | 345 kPa +35/−0 |
| Oxygen/carbon dioxide mixtures | $O_2/CO_2$ $n\%$ ($n$ is % of $CO_2$) | Green/white | 50 psig +5/−0 |
| | | | 345 kPa +35/−0 |
| Medical-surgical vacuum | MedVac | White/black | 15 in. Hg to 30 in. Hg |
| | | | 380 mmHg to 760 mmHg |
| Waste anaesthetic gas disposal | WAGD | Violet/white | Varies with system type |
| Other mixtures | Gas A %/Gas B % | Colors as above; major gas for background/ minor gas for text | None |
| Dental air | — | Yellow & white diagonal stripe/black | None |
| Dental vacuum | — | White & black diagonal stripe/black | None |
| Laboratory air | LabAir | Yellow and white checkerboard/black | None |
| Laboratory vacuum | LabVac | White and black checkerboard/black boxed | None |

Note: Colors used should approximate standard colors such as process green for oxygen green or process blue for nitrous oxide blue.

the piping from excessive stresses. The minimum backfilled cover above the top of buried piping outside of buildings shall be 36 in. (91.4 cm), except that the minimum cover shall be permitted to be reduced to 18 in. (45.7 cm) where physical damage to the piping is not likely to occur. Trenches shall be excavated so that the pipe has a firm, substantially continuous bearing on the bottom of the trench. Underground piping shall be installed in a continuous enclosure to protect the pipe from damage while backfilling. The enclosure shall be split or otherwise provide access at the joints during visual inspection and leak testing. Backfill shall be clean and compacted so as to protect and uniformly support the piping. A continuous tape or marker placed immediately above the enclosure shall clearly identify the pipeline by specific name. In addition, a continuous warning means shall be provided above the pipeline at approximately one-half the depth of bury. Where underground piping is installed through a wall sleeve, the ends of the sleeve shall be sealed to prevent the entrance of ground water. Piping underground within buildings or imbedded in concrete floors or walls shall be installed in a continuous conduit.

(f) Gas piping shall be permitted to be located in the same-service trench or tunnel with fuel gas lines, fuel oil lines, electrical lines, steam lines, and similar utilities provided that the space is ventilated (naturally or mechanically) and the ambient temperature around the medical gas piping is limited to 130°F (54°C) maximum. Gas piping shall not be located where subject to contact with oil, including flooding in the case of a major oil leak.

(g) Piping exposed in corridors and other areas where subject to physical damage from the movement of carts, stretchers, portable equipment, or vehicles shall be suitably protected.

(h) Hoses and flexible connectors, both metallic and nonmetallic, shall be no longer than necessary and shall not penetrate or be concealed in walls, floors, ceilings, or partitions. Flexible connectors, metallic or nonmetallic, shall have a minimum burst pressure of 1000 psig (6900 kPa gauge). *[See 4-3.1.2.9(h).]*

### 4-5.1.3.2 Gas Shutoff Valves.

(a) Emergency gas shutoff valves shall not be required. Shutoff valves for isolation of a duplex system operation components shall be provided as recommended by the manufacturer.

(b) Where nitrogen gas is used as a backup for a Level 3 compressed air system, a check valve and shutoff valve shall be located in each supply line prior to the tee connection in the main line. *[See Figure 4-5.1.1.4.]*

### 4-5.1.3.3 Service Outlets.

(a) Outlets from Level 3 piping systems shall be either a shutoff valve with a threaded female pipe connect, or a quick-connect fitting with a single check valve.

(b) Service outlets shall be located to avoid physical damage.

### 4-5.1.3.4 Alarms.

(a) Gases used to power devices, such as in a compressed air or nitrogen system, as well as Level 3 vacuum systems, shall not be required to have an alarm system.

## 4-5.2 Piped Vacuum Systems (Source and Distribution)—Level 3.

### 4-5.2.1* Source—Level 3.

The subject of Type II (dental) vacuum systems was first introduced in the 1993 edition to address nonhospital-based dental facilities because no guidance for systems of this size existed. (The only criteria developed by NFPA had been on medical-surgical vacuum systems and were not entirely appropriate for dental facilities.) Of particular concern were installations that had both a compressor(s) and vacuum pump(s) in the same room without proper installation of intake and exhaust pipes, respectively.

In 1996 Type II vacuum systems were replaced with Level 3 piped vacuum systems, and the subject underwent extensive revision, in large measure as a result of input from the dental community. Readers are again reminded that the requirements for the 1996 edition still apply to new systems or renovated portions of existing systems. (See Section 1-4.)

**A-4-5.2.1** Level III vacuum systems can be used for dental, podiatry, and medical care facilities. See definition of Vacuum Systems—Level III in Chapter 2.

**4-5.2.1.1** Service inlets shall be either a shutoff valve with a threaded female pipe connector, or a quick-connect fitting with a single check valve.

**4-5.2.1.2** Level 3 vacuum pumps shall be suitable for the intended purpose. Wet vacuum piping system shall have a liquid/air separator in the system. *[See Figures 4-5.2.1.2(a) through (d).]*

Equipment shall be obtained from and be installed under the supervision of a manufacturer(s) or supplier(s) familiar with proper practices for its construction and use. Maintenance programs, in accordance with the recommendations of manufacturer(s), shall be established for the dental air compressor supply system as connected in each individual installation.

**4-5.2.1.3** Liquids from a Level 3 vacuum system, per 4-5.2.2, shall be directly connected to the sanitary drainage system through an appropriately trapped and vented drain. *[See Figures 4-5.2.1.3(a) and (b).]*

The Committee on Piping Systems is aware that many different types of drainage systems were being used and that some, in fact, permitted airborne contaminants to be improperly contained. The 1996 edition addressed this issue by requiring a trapped and vented drain to prevent airborne contaminant from reentering the air around a trap.

**4-5.2.1.4\*** The gas discharge from a Level 3 vacuum system shall be piped to the outside. The gas shall be discharged outdoors in a manner that will minimize the hazards of noise and contamination to the facility and to the environment.

**A-4-5.2.1.4** Improper design will permit gas pressure to build up in the ventilation system and might blow the trap liquid seals.

**4-5.2.1.5** The exhaust shall be located remote from any door, window, air intake, or other openings in the building with particular attention given to separate levels of intake or discharge.

Care shall also be exercised to avoid discharge locations contraindicated by prevailing winds, adjacent buildings, topography, and other influences.

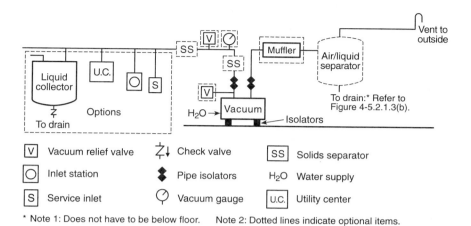

*Figure 4-5.2.1.2(a)* Typical Level 3 wet or dry piping system with single vacuum pump source.

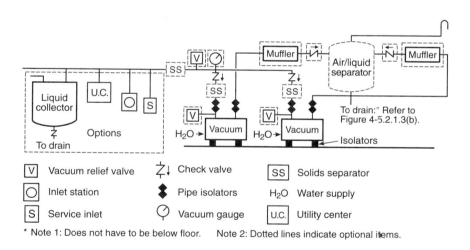

*Figure 4-5.2.1.2(b)* Typical Level 3 wet or dry piping system with duplex vacuum source.

**4-5.2.1.6** Exhaust to the outdoors shall be protected against the entry of insects, vermin, debris, and precipitation. Exhaust lines shall be sized to minimize back pressure.

**4-5.2.1.7** Discharge of the vacuum systems utilizing common exhaust pipes shall be fitted with a check valve, a manual valve, or arranged to permit capping of the active pipe when removing and servicing a vacuum pump or components.

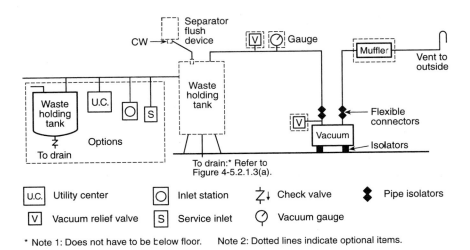

**Figure 4-5.2.1.2(c)** *Typical Level 3 wet or dry piping system with single vacuum source.*

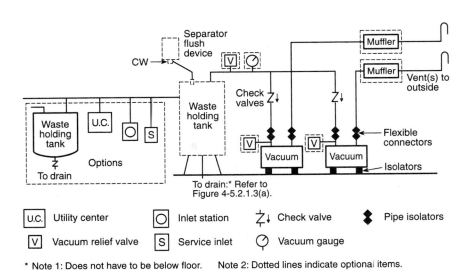

**Figure 4-5.2.1.2(d)** *Typical Level 3 wet or dry piping system with duplex vacuum source.*

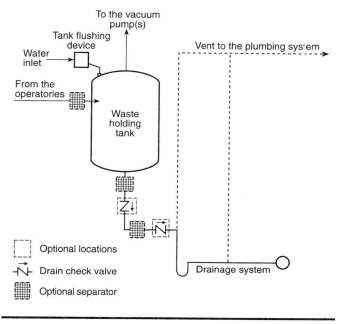

*Figure 4-5.2.1.3(a)* *Drainage from a gravity-drained, liquid collector tank.*

**4-5.2.1.8\*** Vacuum exhaust from separate pumps shall follow the manufacturer's recommendations.

**A-4-5.2.1.8** Care should be taken to ensure the dual exhaust systems do not develop excessive back pressure when using a common exhaust line.

**4-5.2.2 Distribution—Level 3.**

**4-5.2.2.1** Piping materials shall be corrosion-resistant material having a smooth interior surface. Piping shall be sized according to the manufacturer's recommendations. All piping shall be provided with adequate and accessible clean-out facilities on mains and branches and shall be accessible for inspections, maintenance, and replacement.

**4-5.2.2.2** Nonflammable waste gases shall be permitted to be disposed of through a Level 3 vacuum system provided that its inclusion in the system does not affect the overall performance of the other parts of the vacuum system.

**4-5.2.2.3** Piping materials shall be PVC schedule 40, copper or other corrosion-resistant material. Piping shall be sized in accordance with the manufacturer's recommendations. All piping shall be provided with adequate and accessible "cleanouts" per the manufacturer's or design engineers' specifications.

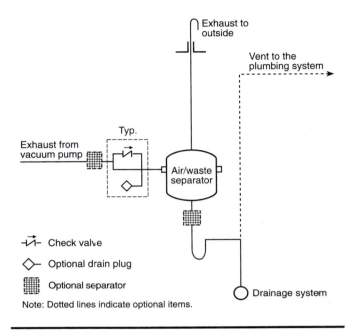

*Figure 4-5.2.1.3(b)* *Drainage from a positive discharge vacuum pump through an air/liquid separator.*

It is the intent of the committee that all piping be provided with adequate and accessible clean-out facilities on the mains and the branches. It is also the intent that these clean-out facilities be accessible for inspection, maintenance, and replacement. While it is impractical to have buried piping accessible for inspection, the clean-outs must be accessible.

**4-5.2.2.4** All piping shall have smooth interior walls to avoid debris buildup.

**4-5.2.2.5** Piping shall be sloped a minimum of ¼ in. per 10 ft (0.65 cm per 30 m) toward the vacuum pump or a single location before the vacuum pump. Systems shall be free of local low sections that can collect liquids or debris. Pipe hangers shall be used per the manufacturer's recommendations.

**4-5.2.2.6** Where any other vacuum systems or piping systems are used, pipe shall be labeled as to type and gas/vacuum being used.

**4-5.2.2.7** Level 3 vacuum systems shall not be required to have an alarm system.

## 4-5.3 Piped WAGD Systems—Level 3.

**4-5.3.1 Source—Level 3.** (Reserved)

**4-5.3.2 Distribution—Level 3.** (Reserved)

## 4-5.4 Performance Criteria and Testing—Level 3 (Gas, Vacuum, WAGD).

There are four subsections addressing performance criteria and testing for Level 3 systems:

4-5.4.1, Piped Patient Gas Systems

4-5.4.2, Piped Gas-Powered Devices Gas Systems

4-5.4.3, Piped Vacuum Systems

4-5.4.4, Piped WAGD Systems

### 4-5.4.1 Piped Patient Gas Systems—Level 3.

This section was completely revised for the 1996 edition to correlate more closely with the testing for Level 1 piped gas systems (4-3.4.1). Many of the hazards associated with piping for Level 1 systems are also present for Level 3 systems.

**4-5.4.1.1 General.** Inspection and testing shall be performed on all new piped gas systems (including oxygen, nitrous oxide, nitrogen, Level 3 compressed air and Level 3 vacuum), additions, renovations, or repaired systems to assure the facility that all applicable provisions of this document have been adhered to and all system integrity has been achieved or maintained.

This inspection and testing shall include all components of the system or portions thereof including, but not limited to, cylinder room equipment, compressed air source systems, vacuum system, alarms, pipelines, shutoff valves, station outlets, and terminal service outlets/inlets.

An existing system that is not in strict compliance with the provisions of this standard shall be permitted to be continued in use as long as the authority having jurisdiction has determined that such use does not constitute a distinct hazard to life.

All systems that are breached and components that are subject to additions, renovations, or replacement shall be appropriately tested.

Systems shall be deemed breached at the point of pipeline intrusion by physical separation or by system component removal, replacement, or addition. The breached portions of the systems subject to inspection and testing shall be all the new and existing components in the immediate zone or area that is located upstream for vacuum systems and downstream for pressure gases at the point or area of intrusion.

The responsible facility authority shall review all inspection and testing prior to the use of all systems covered by this document. The responsible authority shall ensure that all findings and results of the inspection and testing have been completed and all documentation pertaining thereto shall be maintained on-site, within the facility.

**4-5.4.1.2 Piping Integrity Test.** The following test shall be conducted by the installer, representative of the supplier, or representative of the manufacturer. The test gas shall be oil-free, dry nitrogen.

(a) *Blowdown.* After installation of the piping, the terminal outlets, or station outlets, and all brazing of joints, but before installation of other components (e.g., pressure-actuating switches for alarms, manifolds, pressure gauges, or pressure relief valves), the line shall be blown clear by means of oil-free, dry nitrogen *(see Section 2-2, Definitions).*

(b) *Initial Pressure Test.* Before attachment of system components (e.g., pressure activating switches for alarms, manifolds, pressure gauges, or pressure relief valves), but after installation of the station outlets, with test caps (if supplied) in place (e.g., rough-in assembly), and before closing of the walls, each section of the piping system shall be subjected to a test pressure of 1.5 times the working pressure [minimum 150 psig (1 MPa gauge)] with oil-free, dry nitrogen.

1.  The test pressure shall be maintained until each joint has been examined for leakage by means of soapy water or other equally effective means of leak detection safe for use with oxygen. Leaks, if any, shall be located, repaired, and retested in accordance with this paragraph.
2.  The source shutoff valve shall then be closed. The test shall remain static for a period of 24 hours with a maximum allowable pressure loss of 5 psig (35 kPa). Leaks, if any, shall be located, repaired, and retested in accordance with this paragraph.

(c) *Piping Purge.* In order to remove particulate matter in the pipelines, a heavy, intermittent purging of the pipeline shall be done. The appropriate adapter shall be obtained, and a high-flow purge shall be put on each outlet. The outlet shall be allowed to flow fully until the purge produces no discoloration in a white cloth. Piping shall be capped after testing.

(d) No further brazing to the piping system shall be permitted after the tests in this section have been completed. Additional assembly shall be limited to installing the manifold and operating components of the system.

**4-5.4.1.3 System Verification and Final Testing.** The following test shall be performed after those listed in 4-5.4.1.2. This testing shall be conducted by a party technically competent and experienced in the field of Level 3 medical gas, Level 3 compressed air, and Level 3 vacuum systems and testing.

(a) All systems shall be activated with the intended "use gas" (i.e., oxygen, nitrous oxide, etc.) at the normal operating pressure [50 psig (345 kPa)]. The source shutoff valve shall then be closed. The test shall remain static for a period of 24 hours with a maximum allowable pressure loss of 5 psig (35 kPa). Leaks, if any, shall be located, repaired, and retested in accordance with this paragraph.

(b) After walls have been closed in, and all brazing fabrication completed, completion of the system shall be made. Manifolds, regulators, hoses, alarms, compressors, vacuum pumps, and all accessories to the system shall be assembled before final testing.

(c) *Static Pressure Test.* The pressure test below shall be conducted at normal operating pressure. The test gas shall be the intended service gas. The test shall remain static for a period of 24 hours with a maximum allowable pressure loss of 5 psig (35 kPa). Leaks, if any, shall be located, repaired, and retested in accordance with this paragraph.

After testing of each individual medical gas system in accordance with 4-5.4.1.2(b), the completely assembled station outlets and all other gas system components (e.g., pressure-actuating switches for alarms, manifolds, pressure gauges, or pressure relief valves) shall be subjected to a 24-hour standing pressure test at normal operating line pressure. The source shutoff valve shall be closed.

After the piping system is filled with gas, the supply valve and all outlets shall be closed and the source of gas disconnect. The piping system shall remain leak-free for 24 hours. When making the standing pressure test, the only allowable pressure changes during the 24-hour test period shall be those caused by variations in the ambient temperature around the piping system. Such changes shall be permitted to be checked by means of the following pressure--temperature relationship: the calculated final absolute pressure (absolute pressure is gauge pressure plus 14.7 psig if gauge is calibrated in psig) equals the initial absolute pressure times the final absolute temperature (absolute temperature is temperature reading plus 460°F if thermometer is calibrated in Fahrenheit degrees, divided by the initial absolute temperature.

$$\left( P_f = \frac{P_i \times T_f}{T_i} \right)$$

(d) *Pressure Relief Test.* Each gas pressure relief valve in the piping system shall be tested to ensure the pressure relief valves actuate at less than 50 percent over pressure from their maximum operating pressure. The pressure relief valve specified in 4-5.1.2.5 shall close automatically when the excess pressure has been released.

(e) *Cross Connection Test.* The oxygen system only shall be activated and all other gases shall be at zero (0) psig (0 kPa). All service outlets including vacuum shall be tested using appropriate secondary connectors. Only oxygen shall flow from the oxygen station outlet and all other outlets shall have no gas flow. The oxygen outlet shall be purged until a white cloth does not show any particulate or discoloration.

1. The test of 4-5.4.1.3(e) shall be repeated for each gas and vacuum piping system.

(f) *Alarm Testing for Gas Systems.* The automatic pressure switch connected to each main supply line within a single treatment facility shall actuate a visual and audible alarm when the line pressure drops approximately 20 percent below or increases approximately 20 percent above normal line pressure. All functions shall be tested. *(See 4-5.1.2.8.)*

The intent of the committee is to reference a percentage above and below the operating pressure of gas, irrespective of the actual operating pressure.

(g)* *Additional Test of Secondary Equipment.* Testing also shall be conducted on the piping system with the intended secondary equipment to make sure the safety alarms and provisions of the secondary equipment are verified. The instructions of the manufacturer or supplier of secondary equipment shall be followed for any additional recommended tests of the piping and or secondary equipment.

**A-4-5.4.1.3(g)** This will ensure that the required pressure and flow meet the secondary equipment manufacturer's requirements.

**4-5.4.2 Piped Gas-Powered Devices Gas Systems—Level 3.**

**4-5.4.2.1** Level 3 piping systems shall be static pressure tested to 150 psig (1034 kPa) or 150 percent of maximum pressure, whichever is greater, for 24 hours. The pressure loss shall not exceed a 5 psig (35 kPa) drop in pressure. This test shall be conducted after all service outlets are installed and before the compressor system is connected.

**4-5.4.2.2** After a system has been installed, other performance testing shall be conducted as recommended by the manufacturer.

**4-5.4.2.3** Records of all tests shall be maintained in the facility.

**4-5.4.3 Piped Vacuum Systems—Level 3.**

**4-5.4.3.1** The piping system shall be pressurized to 15 psig (103 kPa).

**4-5.4.3.2** The system shall maintain the static pressure for a minimum of 24 hours. The pressure drop shall not exceed 5 psig (35 kPa).

**4-5.4.3.3** The test shall be performed before the vacuum pump is installed.

**4-5.4.3.4** All recorded test information shall be retained at the facility.

**4-5.4.4 Piped WAGD Systems—Level 3.** (Reserved)

**4-5.5 Administration—Level 3.**

**4-5.5.1 Responsibility of Governing Body.** (Reserved)

**4-5.5.2 Gas System Policies—Level 3.**

**4-5.5.2.1** Policies for gases in cylinders and liquefied gases in containers for Level 3 piped gas systems.

(a)* *Handling of Gases.* Administrative authorities shall provide regulations to ensure that standards for safe practice in the specification for cylinders; marking of cylinders, regulators, and valves; and cylinder connections have been met by vendors of cylinders containing compressed gases supplied to the facility.

**A-4-5.5.2.1(a)** *Safe Practice for Cylinders Containing Compressed Gases. Specifications for Cylinders.* All cylinders containing compressed gases, such as anesthetic gases, oxygen, or other gases used for medicinal purposes, whether these gases are flammable or not, should comply with the specifications and be maintained in accordance with regulations of the U.S. Department of Transportation.

(b) *Special Precautions—Oxygen Cylinders and Manifolds.* Great care shall be exercised in handling oxygen to prevent contact of oxygen under pressure with oils, greases, organic lubricants, rubber, or other materials of an organic nature. The following regulations, based on those of the CGA Pamphlet G-4, *Oxygen,* shall be observed:

1. Oil, grease, or readily flammable materials shall never be permitted to come in contact with oxygen cylinders, valves, regulators, gauges, or fittings.
2. Regulators, fittings, or gauges shall never be lubricated with oil or any other flammable substance.
3. Oxygen cylinders or apparatus shall never be handled with oily or greasy hands, gloves, or rags.
4. Particles of dust and dirt shall be cleared from cylinder valve openings by slightly opening and closing the valve before applying any fitting to the cylinder.
5. The high-pressure valve on the oxygen cylinder shall be opened before bringing the apparatus to the patient or the patient to the apparatus.
6. The cylinder valve shall be opened slowly, with the face of the gauge on the regulator pointed away from all persons.
7. An oxygen cylinder shall never be draped with any materials such as hospital gowns, masks, or caps.
8. Oxygen fittings, valves, regulators, or gauges shall never be used for any service other than that of oxygen.
9. Gases of any type shall never be mixed in an oxygen cylinder or any other cylinder.
10. Oxygen shall always be dispensed from a cylinder through a pressure regulator.
11. Regulators that are in need of repair or cylinders having valves that do not operate properly shall never be used.
12. Oxygen equipment that is defective shall not be used until it has been repaired by competent personnel. If competent in-house repairs cannot be made, such equipment shall be repaired by the manufacturer or his or her authorized agent; or it shall be replaced.
13. Oxygen cylinders shall be protected from abnormal mechanical shock, which is liable to damage the cylinder, valve, or safety device. Such cylinders shall not be stored near elevators, gangways, or in locations where heavy moving objects will strike them or fall on them.
14. Cylinder-valve protection caps, where provided, shall be kept in place and be hand tightened, except when cylinders are in use or connected for use.
15. Cylinders shall be protected from the tampering of unauthorized individuals.
16. Valves shall be closed on all empty cylinders in storage.
17. Oxygen shall be referred to by its proper name, *oxygen*, not *air*. Liquid oxygen shall be referred to by its proper name, not *liquid air*.
18. Oxygen shall never be used as a substitute for compressed air.
19. Cylinders or cylinder valves shall not be repaired, painted, or altered.
20. Safety relief devices in valves or cylinders shall never be tampered with. Sparks and flame shall be kept away from cylinders; a torch flame shall never be permitted under any circumstances to come in contact with cylinder valves or safety devices. Valve outlets clogged with ice shall be thawed with warm—not boiling—water.
21. The markings stamped on cylinders shall not be tampered with. It is against federal statutes to change these markings without written authority from the Bureau of Explosives.

22. Markings used for the identification of contents of cylinders shall not be defaced or removed, including decals, tags, stenciled marks, and upper half of shipping tag.
23. The owner of the cylinder shall be notified of any condition has occurred that might permit any foreign substance to enter a cylinder or valve, giving details and cylinder number.
24. Even if they are considered to be empty, cylinders shall never be used as rollers, supports, or for any purpose other than that for which they are intended by the supplier.
25. When small-size (A, B, D, or E) cylinders are in use, they shall be attached to a cylinder stand or to therapy apparatus of sufficient size to render the entire assembly stable. Individual cylinder storage associated with patient care areas are not required to be stored in enclosures.

New language in this 1999 edition permits what has been a standard work practice on patient-occupied floors: the use of small oxygen cylinders without the need to store them in an approved manner. For decades, the health care community has struggled with how to meet the previous requirement [4-3.5.2.2(a) in the 1996 standard] and efficiently provide patient care. Small E cylinders and an occasional H cylinder are placed in and around patient care units to supplement the piped gas system. The small cylinders are mainly used while transporting patients around the facility. Many authorities having jurisdiction have insisted that even these small cylinders be stored in an approved storage cabinet or properly protected room, thereby removing them from the patient care vicinity and reducing the effectiveness of having them available for patient use in an emergency or during transport.

26. Cylinders and containers shall not be dropped, dragged, or rolled.
27. Freestanding cylinders shall be properly chained or supported in a proper cylinder stand or cart and comply with 4-5.1.1.1.
28. Cylinders shall not be chained to portable or movable apparatus such as mobile carts, cabinets, or dental units.
29.* Cylinders shall not be supported by, and neither cylinders nor containers shall be placed in proximity of, radiators, steam pipes, or heat ducts.

**A-4-5.5.2.1(b)29** Cylinder and container temperatures greater than 125°F (52°C) can result in excessive pressure increase. Pressure-relief devices are sensitive to temperature and pressure. When relief devices actuate, contents are discharged.

30. Very cold cylinders or containers shall be handled with care to avoid injury.
31. Cylinders and containers shall not be handled with hands, gloves, or other materials contaminated with oil or grease.

   (c) *Making Cylinder and Container Connections.*

1.* Wrenches used to connect Level 3 system equipment shall be manufactured of steel or other suitable material of adequate strength.

**A-4-5.5.2.1(c)(1)** Use of so-called nonsparking wrenches and tools is not necessary.

2. Cylinder valves shall be opened and connected in accordance with the following procedure:

   a. Make certain that apparatus and cylinder valve connections and cylinder wrenches are free of foreign materials.
   b. Turn the cylinder valve outlet away from personnel. Stand to the side, not in front and not in back. Before connecting the apparatus to cylinder valve, momentarily open cylinder valve to eliminate dust.
   c. Make connection of apparatus to cylinder valve. Tighten connection nut securely with an appropriate wrench *[see 4-5.5.2.1(c)1]*.
   d. Release the low-pressure adjustment screw of the regulator completely if adjustable style regulator, consult with instructions if a preset style regulator.
   e. Slowly open cylinder valve to full open position.
   f. Slowly turn in the low-pressure adjustment screw on the regulator until the proper working pressure is obtained. *[See 4-5.5.2.1(c)1d.]*
   g. Open the valve to the utilization apparatus or system.

3. Connections for containers shall be made in accordance with the container manufacturer's operating instructions.

   (d) *Care of Safety Mechanisms.*

1. Personnel using cylinders and containers and other equipment covered in this chapter shall be familiar with the Pin-Index Safety System *(see 8-3.1.2)* and the Diameter-Index Safety System *(see 8-3.1.3)*, both designed to prevent utilization of the wrong gas.
2. Safety relief mechanisms, noninterchangeable connectors, and other safety features shall not be removed, altered, or replaced.

   (e) *Laboratory Gases.*

1. *Use of Gases.* Gases shall be handled and used with care and with knowledge of their hazardous properties, both individually and in combination with other materials with which they can come in contact. *(See NFPA 49, Hazardous Chemicals Data, and NFPA 491, Manual of Hazardous Chemical Reactions.)*

**4-5.5.2.2 Storage of Cylinders and Containers Level 3.**

   (a) Facility authorities, in consultation with facility staff and other trained personnel, shall provide and enforce regulations for the storage and handling of cylinders and containers of oxygen and nitrous oxide in storage rooms of approved construction, and for the safe handling of these agents in treatment locations.

   (b) *Nonflammable Gases.*

1. Storage shall be planned so that cylinders can be used in the order in which they are received from the supplier.

2. If stored within the same enclosure, empty cylinders shall be segregated from full cylinders. Empty cylinders shall be marked to avoid confusion and delay if a full cylinder is needed hurriedly.

### 4-5.5.2.3 Patient Gas Systems—Level 3.

See Chapters 12 through 18 (12-3.4.1, 13-3.4.1, and so on) to learn which level of gas system is applicable in each type of health care facility.

(a)* Level 3 nonflammable medical gas systems cover installations that:

1. Have not more than 3000 ft$^3$ (85 m$^3$) total capacity of all gases (excluding nitrogen and medical air in cylinder for powered devices) connected and in storage at one time, except that the total capacity of all gases shall be permitted to be increased to 5000 ft$^3$ (143 m$^3$) excluding nitrogen and medical air for powered devices) if oxygen is used in a DOT Specification 4L (liquid) cylinder, and
2. Have a listed pressure regulator directly connected to each cylinder, and
3. Supply only a single treatment facility and also as a minimum comply with the specific requirements of 4-5.1.2.6, or
4. Supply a maximum of two adjoining single treatment facilities and also as a minimum comply with the specific requirements of 4-5.1.2.7.

**A-4-5.5.2.3(a)** It is the intent to provide a simple, safe piping system for small facilities. Although the number of use points could be a consideration, it was felt that actual gas use is a more accurate indicator of complexity. Applications involving a storage in excess of 3000 ft$^3$ (85 m$^3$) would have a complexity warranting installation in accordance with the provisions of Level I patient gas distribution systems.

Although the principal intent is to provide simple installations for single treatment facilities, numerous applications exist where a remote use point creates essentially a second treatment facility or where the supply system might be shared by another health care professional such as another dentist, podiatrist, oral surgeon, or general medicine practioner. The addition of another treatment facility requires incremental safety precautions.

A maximum of two single treatment facilities also approximates the limit with which a 3000 ft$^3$ (85 m$^3$) supply system can provide [5000 ft$^3$ (143 m$^3$) when liquid oxygen is used].

It is acknowledged that older user analgesia equipment has offered a nitrous oxide lockout device that requires a minimum of 3 L/min oxygen flow. However, a reasonable percentage of older equipment without this safety feature is in daily use. The storage and piping system is based upon the potential use, either initially or subsequently, of one of the older style analgesia equipment in one of the single treatment facilities.

The quantity of 3000 ft$^3$ (85 m$^3$), or 5000 ft$^3$ (143 m$^3$) if liquid oxygen storage, is to be taken as the total combined storage of gases if there is more than one supply system in the single treatment facility.

(b) *Material Oxygen Compatibility.*

1.\* Oxygen system components including, but not limited to, containers, valves, valve seats, lubricants, fittings, gaskets, and interconnecting equipment including hoses, shall have adequate compatibility with oxygen under the conditions of temperature and pressure to which the components may be exposed in the containment and use of oxygen. Easily ignitable materials shall be avoided unless they are parts of equipment or systems that are approved, listed, or proved suitable by tests or by past experience.

The volume of gas in storage was increased from 2000 ft$^3$ to 3000 ft$^3$ (57 m$^3$ to 85 m$^3$) with the 1993 edition of NFPA 99 to allow the use of H cylinders instead of G-type cylinders. [See commentary on 4-3.1.1.2(b) for further discussion on this change.]

**A-4-5.5.2.3(b)1** Compatibility involves both combustibility and ease of ignition. Materials that burn in air will burn violently in pure oxygen at normal pressure and explosively in pressurized oxygen. Also, many materials that do not burn in air will do so in pure oxygen, particularly under pressure. Metals for containers and piping must be carefully selected, depending on service conditions. The various steels are acceptable for many applications, but some service conditions can call for other materials (usually copper or its alloys) because of their greater resistance to ignition and lower rate of combustion.

Similarly, materials that can be ignited in air have lower ignition energies in oxygen. Many such materials can be ignited by friction at a valve seat or stem packing or by adiabatic compression produced when oxygen at high pressure is rapidly introduced into a system initially at low pressure.

2. The provisions of 4-5.5.2.3(b)1 also apply to nitrous oxide, oxygen–nitrous oxide mixtures, and to other medical gas mixtures containing more than 23.5 percent oxygen.
3. Manufactured assemblies in which are intended to be piped nitrous oxide or oxygen shall be (a) constructed of metal, or (b) tested to pass a minimum 200 flame spread rating and 200 smoke developed index in accordance with NFPA 255, *Standard Method of Test of Surface Burning Characteristics of Building Materials,* or, if constructed of polymers (plastic, fiberglass, etc.), a rating of 94 VO or better.

(c) Maintenance programs in accordance with the manufacturer's recommendations shall be established for the medical air compressor supply system as connected in each individual installation.

(d) Medical gas systems not specifically provided for in 4-5.5.2.3(a), such as systems within a hospital served by a central supply system, or systems serving three or more treatment facilities, as might be found in a medical or dental office building, shall comply in all respects with Level 1 systems.

(e) Equipment shall be obtained from and be installed under the supervision of a manufacturer or supplier familiar with proper practices for its construction and use.

(f) Every facility shall establish a procedure for manually turning off the gas supply at the cylinder valves at the end of the work day, or when the facility is not in use. No other method such as Emergency Shutoff Valves or remote actuators [4-5.1.2.11(b)] shall be used to turn off the gas supply.

**4-5.5.3 Gas System Recordkeeping—Level 3.** (Reserved)

**4-5.5.4 Gas System Information and Warning Signs—Level 3.** The shutoff valves of 4-5.1.2.11 shall be labeled to indicate the gas controlled and to indicate that they are to be closed only in an emergency.

**4-5.5.5** Policies for gas system transport and delivery (Level 3) shall comply with the following.

**4-5.5.5.1** Personnel concerned with use and transport of equipment shall be trained in proper handling of cylinders, containers, hand trucks, supports, and valve protection caps.

**4-5.5.5.2** Large cylinders (exceeding size E) and containers larger than 100 lb (45.4 kg) weight shall be transported on a proper hand truck or cart complying with 8-5.2.

**4-5.5.6 Vacuum System Policies—Level 3.** (Reserved)

**4-5.5.7 Vacuum System Recordkeeping—Level 3.** (Reserved)

**4-5.5.8 Vacuum System Information and Warning Signs—Level 3.** (Reserved)

**4-5.5.9 WAGD System Policies—Level 3.** (Reserved)

# 4-6 Level 4 Piped Systems

## 4-6.1 Piped Gas Systems (Source and Distribution)—Level 4.

### 4-6.1.1 Source—Level 4.

**4-6.1.1.1** When a laboratory is intended to be routinely and frequently operated with flammable gases supplied from a manifold compressed system, the containers shall either:

(a) Be in a separate room having a fire-resistance classification of at least 1 hour and be ventilated in accordance with 4-3.1.1.2, or
(b) Be located outside of the building and connected to the laboratory equipment by a permanently installed piping system.

*Exception: Wherever the volume and nature of the gas, in the judgment of the laboratory safety officer or other authority having jurisdiction, do not offer a hazard, the requirement for the remote locations of the cylinder shall be permitted to be waived.*

There may be local ordinances on this issue of flammable gas cylinders inside occupied buildings. They should be investigated as well

**4-6.1.1.2** When a laboratory is intended to be routinely and frequently operated with nonflammable gases supplied from a manifold compressed system:

(a) The manifold within the laboratory shall consist of not more than six cylinders,
(b) Manifolds larger than six cylinders shall conform to 4-6.1.1.1, and
(c) Cylinders shall be secured in position.

Six cylinders was considered a reasonable breakpoint by the committee. While the gases involved are nonflammable, the committee felt that the quantity stored inside a laboratory working area should not be open-ended.

**4-6.1.1.3** A pressure-reducing valve shall be connected to each gas cylinder and adjusted to a setting to limit pressure in the piping system at the minimum required gas pressure.

**4-6.1.1.4** Pressure regulators shall be compatible with the gas for which they are used.

**4-6.1.1.5** Piping systems shall not be used for gases other than those for which they are designed and identified.

*Exception: If a system is to be converted for use with a gas other than that for which it was originally installed, it shall be inspected for suitability for the proposed gas; purged with an inert gas (such as nitrogen); cleaned when oil, grease, or other readily oxidizable materials are present; and pressure tested in accordance with the appropriate piping standard. Each outlet of such a system shall be identified by chemical name and specifically converted for use with the successor gas.*

**4-6.1.2  Distribution—Level 4.**

**4-6.1.2.1\*** Piping systems for fuel gases, such as manufactured gas, natural gas, and LP-Gas, shall comply with NFPA 54, *National Fuel Gas Code*, and NFPA 58, *Liquefied Petroleum Gas Code*.

**A-4-6.1.2.1  Piping Systems.** Piping systems supplying medical gases to patients should be reserved exclusively for that purpose so as to protect the patients from administration of gas other than that intended for their use. Therefore laboratory gas piping systems should not be used to pipe gas for use by hospital patients. This warning is also intended to apply to piping systems intended to supply gas to patients within a laboratory facility. Such a system should not be used to supply laboratory equipment other than that directly involved with the patient procedure.

**4-6.1.2.2** Piping systems for gaseous hydrogen shall comply with NFPA 50A, *Standard for Gaseous Hydrogen Systems at Consumer Sites*.

**4-6.1.2.3** Piping systems for nonflammable gases shall comply with Level 1 gas systems as specified in this chapter.

**4-6.1.2.4** Piping systems for acetylene shall comply with NFPA 51, *Standard for the Design and Installation of Oxygen-Fuel Gas Systems for Welding, Cutting, and Allied Processes*.

**4-6.1.2.5** Supply and discharge terminals of piping systems shall be legibly and permanently marked at both ends with the name of the gas piping, after testing, to establish their content and continuity.

## 4-6.2 Piped Vacuum Systems—Level 4.

**4-6.2.1 Source.** (Reserved)

**4-6.2.2\* Distribution.** Where only one set of vacuum pumps is available for a combined medical-surgical vacuum system and an analysis, research, or teaching laboratory vacuum system, such laboratories shall be connected separate from the medical-surgical system directly to the receiver tank through its own isolation valve and fluid trap located at the receiver. Between the isolation valve and fluid trap, a scrubber shall be permitted to be installed.

**A-4-6.2.2** Any laboratory (such as for analysis, research, or teaching) in a hospital that is used for purposes other than direct support of patient therapy should preferably have its own self-supporting vacuum system, independent of the medical-surgical vacuum system. A small laboratory in patient care areas used in direct support of patient therapy should not be required to be connected directly to the receiver or have fluid traps, scrubbers, and so forth, separate from the rest of the medical-surgical vacuum system.

> A separate vacuum system for nonpatient purposes is recommended for several reasons. Laboratories often require different levels, operating ranges, and displacements of vacuum from those for patient care areas. These differences, including usage rates, make planning difficult, particularly if coordination of the laboratory system with the patient system is included. Laboratory systems are also much more likely to aspirate vapors, fumes, and/or liquids of unusual nature, including exotic chemicals that could contaminate the patient vacuum system and damage pumps and other components of the system.
>
> If a separate laboratory vacuum source (receiver tank) is not possible, laboratory piping needs to be connected directly into the receiver tank(s), as already noted. [This allowance for one source is not permitted for piped medical air systems (see 4-3.1.1.9).] For 1993 requirements were revised by requiring a separate isolation valve and fluid trap for the laboratory piping system to prevent material suctioned from laboratories from getting into the patient vacuum system. Scrubbers are needed only when waste products are extremely hazardous.

## 4-6.3 Piped WAGD Systems—Level 4.

(Reserved)

## 4-6.4 Performance Criteria and Testing—Level 4 (Gas, Vacuum, WAGD).

**4-6.4.1 Piped Gas Systems—Level 4.** Piped gas systems (Level 4) shall be tested in accordance with 4-3.4.1.

**4-6.4.2 Piped Vacuum Systems—Level 4.** (Reserved)

**4-6.4.3 WAGD Systems—Level 4.** (Reserved)

## 4-6.5 Administration—Level 4.

(Reserved)

### References Cited in Commentary

1. NFPA 50, *Standard for Bulk Oxygen Systems at Consumer Sites,* 1999.
2. NFPA *101®, Life Safety Code®,* 1997 edition.
3. NFPA 54, *National Fuel Gas Code,* 1999 edition.
4. ASME *Boiler and Pressure Vessel Code*, Section VIII, Unfired Pressure Vessels, 1990.
5. NFPA 70, *National Electrical Code®,* 1999 edition.
6. CGA-4.1, Compressed Gas Association Standard, *Cleaning Equipment for Oxygen Service,* 1985.
7. ASTM B 819, *Standard Specification for Seamless Copper Tube for Medical Gas Systems,* 1992.
8. CGA-9, *Standard Color-Marking of Compressed Gas Cylinders Intended for Medical Use,* 1988.
9. ANSI/AWS A5.8, *Specification for Brazing Filler Metal,* 1989.
10. ANSI Z.79.11, *Standard for Anesthetic Equipment-Scavenging Systems for Excess Anesthetic Gases,* 1982.
11. American Society of Sanitary Engineers/ANSI Standard 6000.
12. NFPA film, "Safe Handling of Medical Gases," VC-4.
13. ASTM B 88, *Specification of Seamless Copper Water Tube,* 1992.

# CHAPTER 5

# Environmental Systems

Laboratory air-conditioning systems should be designed to conserve energy by recirculating the air. If a separate air-conditioning system serves the clinical laboratory, however, it may recirculate a reasonable percentage of the air removed by the air-conditioning system instead of exhausting 100 percent to the outdoors. The system should be designed so it can be switched to 100 percent exhaust in the case of a large chemical spill or similar accident.

It should be recognized that most clinical laboratory tests are now done by machine processors using dry chemicals with reactions occurring in the solid phase. As a result, fewer solvents are being used, and fewer hydrocarbon fuels are present. This technology has reduced the hazard level in laboratories, particularly the amount of products of combustion that would be released in a fire. This, in turn, reflects the amount of toxic air that would be subject to circulation.

(Note: In this commentary, air conditioning means conditioning the air by heating, cooling, or filtering.)

## 5-1* Scope

This chapter covers the performance, maintenance, and testing of the environmental systems used within health care facilities.

**A-5-1** *Application of Requirements.* The application of requirements contained in this chapter for specific types of health care facilities can be found in Chapters 12 through 18.

## 5-2* Nature of Hazards

**A-5-2** See Sections 3-2 and 8-2 for information on hazards.

## 5-3 Source

Air exhausted from laboratory areas shall not be recirculated to other parts of the facility.

## 5-4* Distribution

**A-5-4** For additional distribution requirements, see NFPA 90A, *Standard for the Installation of Air Conditioning and Ventilating Systems*, and NFPA 90B, *Standard for the Installation of Warm Air Heating and Air Conditioning Systems*.

### 5-4.1* Ventilation—Anesthetizing Locations.

The anesthetizing locations referred to in this section are only those using nonflammable inhalation anesthetics. (See Exhibit 5.1.) Ventilation requirements for flammable anesthetizing locations were moved to Annex 2 in the 1996 edition.

This section addresses smoke control in anesthetizing locations, not fire control. Fire control measures are addressed in Chapters 3, 4, and 12, as well as in other documents such as NFPA *101, Life Safety Code.* [1]

Activities such as surgery, the use of inhalation anesthetics, and the presence of an unconscious or immobile patient added challenges to smoke control and fire response in anesthetizing locations.

See also commentary under 5-4.1.3.

**Exhibit 5.1** *An air handler unit for the anesthetizing location of a hospital. Note the duct-type smoke detector near the center of the photograph.*

**A-5-4.1** Mechanical ventilation is required as a means of diluting flammable gases and maintaining the proper humidity. It is also the most effective and aseptic method of maintaining a uniform humidity within the area.

*General.* Anesthetizing locations used solely for the induction of anesthesia need only be ventilated at a rate sufficient to maintain the proper humidity.

The dilution of flammable and nonflammable gases is most effectively accomplished by 100 percent fresh air (100 percent exhaust) through nonrecirculating air-conditioning systems. Now, however, some codes and standards allow recirculating air-conditioning systems in anesthetizing locations. This reduces the gas-purging effect and increases the possibility of elevated gas concentrations. Care should be taken to ensure that effective scavenging of the gases is available (and used) in these locations.

Anesthetizing locations in which clinical procedures are performed, such as operating rooms, delivery rooms, and certain treatment rooms, require special ventilation as described below. This special ventilation serves not only to maintain humidity but also to reduce the hazard of infection, which is accomplished by dilution and removal of airborne microbial contamination and dilution of flammable gases. It also contributes to odor control and comfort of personnel.

The Committee on Anesthesia Services recognizes that a hazard can be created by the chronic exposure of anesthesia and other operating room personnel to low concentrations of vapors or commonly employed volatile liquid inhalation anesthetic agents. For further information, see the following publications:

(a) Cohen, E. N., et al. Anesthesia, pregnancy and miscarriage; A study of operating room nurses and anesthetists. *Anesthesiology* 35:343, 1971.
(b) Whitcher, C. E., et al. Chronic exposure to anesthetic gas in the operating room. *Anesthesiology* 35:348, 1971.
(c) Yanagida, H., et al. Nitrous oxide content in the operating suite. *Anesth. and Analg.* 53:347, 1974.
(d) Frey, R., et al. How strong is the influence of chronic exposure to inhalation anesthetics on personnel working in operating theatres? W.F.S.A. *Newsletter* No. 10, June 1974.

*The Health Hazard*

(a) Cohen, E. N., et al. Occupational disease among operating room personnel—a national study. *Anesthesiology* 41:321-340, 1974.
(b) Spence, A. A., et al. Occupational hazards for operating room-based physicians. *JAMA* 238:955-959, 1977.
(c) Cohen, E. N., et al. A survey of anesthetic health hazards among dentists. J. *Am. Dent. Assoc.* 90:1291-1296, 1975.

(d) Greene, N., Report on American Cancer Society study of causes of death amongst anesthetists. Annual Meeting, American Society of Anesthesiologists, New Orleans, Louisiana, 18 October 1977.

(e) Hazleton Laboratories America, Inc. Final Reports, CDC-99-74-46, National Institute for Occupational Safety and Health, 1014 Broadway, Cincinnati, Ohio. Long-term inhalation reproductive and teratogenic toxicity evaluation of nitrous oxide plus halothane. 14 November 1975. Cytogenic evaluation of spermatogonial cells in the rat following long-term inhalation exposure to nitrous oxide plus halothane. 17 November 1976.

(f) Chang, W. C., et al. Ultrastructural changes in the nervous system after chronic exposure to halothane. *Exp. Neurol.* 45:209-219, 1974.

(g) Quimby, K. L., et al. Behavioral consequences in rats from chronic exposure to 10 ppm halothane during early development. *Anesth. and Analg.* 54:628-633, 1975.

(h) Kripke, B. J., et al. Testicular reaction to prolonged exposure to nitrous oxide. *Anesthesiology* 44:104-113, 1976.

(i) Fink, B. R., ed. *Toxicity of Anesthetics.* Part Four, "Teratogenic Effects." Baltimore, Williams & Wilkins Co., 308-323, 1968.

(j) Bruce, D. L., et al. Trace anesthetic effects on perceptual, cognitive and motor skills. *Anesthesiology* 40:453-458, 1973.

(k) Bruce, D. L., and Bach, M. J. Psychological studies of human performance as affected by traces of enflurane and nitrous oxide. *Anesthesiology* 42:194-196, 1975.

(l) Smith, G., and Shirley, A. W. Failure to demonstrate effects of low concentrations of nitrous oxide and halothane on psychomotor performance. *Br. J. Anaesth.* 48:274, 1976.

(m) Davison, L. A., et al. Psychological effects of halothane and isoflurane anesthesia. *Anesthesiology* 43:313-324, 1975.

(n) Walts, L. F., et al. Critique: Occupational disease among operating room personnel. *Anesthesiology* 42:608-611, 1975.

(o) Cohen, E. W., and Brown, B. W. Comment on the critique. *Anesthesiology* 42:765-766, 1975.

(p) Fink, B. R., and Cullen, B. F. Anesthetic pollution: What is happening to us? *Anesthesiology* 45:79-83, 1976.

(q) Lecky, J. H. Chronic exposure to anesthetic trace levels. *Complications in Anesthesia*, edited by L. H. Cooperman and F. K. Orkin. J. B. Lippincott Co., Phila.

*Reduction and Control Methods*

(a) Pisiali, R. L., et al. Distribution of waste anesthetic gases in the operating room air. *Anesthesiology* 45:487-494, 1976.

(b) Whitcher, C. E., et al. Control of occupational exposure to nitrous oxide in the dental operatory. J. *Am. Dent. Assoc.* 95:763-766, 1977.

(c) Muravchick, S. Scavenging enflurance from extracorporeal pump oxygenators. *Anesthesiology* 47:468-471, 1977.

(d) Whitcher, C. E., et al. Development and evaluation of methods for the elimination of waste anesthetic gases and vapors in hospitals. HEW Publication No. (NIOSH) 75-137, GPO stock no. 1733-0071. Supt. of Documents, Govt. Print. Off., 1975.

(e) Whitcher, C. E., et al. Control of occupational exposure to $N_2O$ in the dental operatory. HEW Publication No. (NIOSH) 77-171. Cincinnati, U.S. Department of Health, Education and Welfare, Public Health Services Center for Disease Control, National Institute for Occupational Safety and Health.

(f) Lecky, J. H., et al. In-house manual for the control of anesthetic gas contamination in the operating room. University of Pennsylvania Hospital publication.

(g) Lecky, J. H. The mechanical aspects of anesthetic pollution control. *Anesth. and Analg.* 56:769, 1977.

*Dealing with Personnel*

Lecky, J. H. Notice to employees on the potential health hazards associated with occupational exposure to anesthetics. University of Pennsylvania Hospital publication.

*NIOSH—OSHA*

Criteria for a recommended standard: Occupation exposure to waste anesthetic gases and vapors. HEW Publication No. (NIOSH) 77-140. Cincinnati, U.S. Department of Health, Education and Welfare, Public Health Service Center for Disease Control, National Institute for Occupational Safety and Health.

*ANSI Z79*

American National Standards Institute, Committee Z79, SC-4 *Anesthesia Gas Scavenging Devices and Disposal Systems*, J. H. Lecky, M.D., Chairman, ANSI/Z79.11-1982.

A prudent course of action pending further data on this topic lies in the installation of a gas scavenging system for use when inhalation anesthetic techniques are employed with gas flows in excess of metabolic and anesthetic requirements. Care must be taken in the selection and application of any such system to a gas anesthesia apparatus or anesthesia ventilator to avoid exposing the breathing circuit to any pressure less than atmospheric, and also to avoid the dumping of any flammable vapors into a central suction system not designed for such operation.

These are only some of the hazards associated with using the medical-surgical vacuum system for waste anesthetic gas disposal (WAGD).

For further information on waste anesthetic gas disposal (scavenging), see commentary under Section 2-2 and 4-3.3.

*Operating Rooms, Delivery Rooms, and Special Procedure Rooms.* Ventilation air should be supplied from several outlets located on the ceiling or high on the walls of the location. Air should be exhausted by several inlets located near the floor on opposite walls. The air distribution pattern should move air down and through the location with a minimum of draft to the floor for exhaust.

Studies indicate that an air change rate equivalent to 25 room volumes of air per hour dilutes bacteria dispersed into the room by human activity. When properly filtered, 80 percent can be recirculated with no more microbial contamination than 100 percent outdoor air filtered in the same manner. *(See ASHRAE Handbook on HVAC Applications, Chapter 7, "Table on Pressure Relationships and Ventilation of Certain Hospital Areas.")* A positive air pressure relative to the air pressure of adjoining areas should be maintained in the anesthetizing location. This is accomplished by supplying more air to the location than is exhausted from it. Such pressurization will eliminate the infiltration of contaminated air around perimeter openings of door closures or other wall openings during clinical procedures.

Ventilation systems should incorporate air filters with an efficiency of not less than 90 percent when tested in accordance with ASHRAE Standard 52-76, *Method of Testing Air Cleaning Devices Used in General Ventilation for Removing Particulate Matter.* (Summarized in ASHRAE *Handbook*—Chapter 10, Equipment.)

*Humidity Control.* The ventilation system must incorporate humidity equipment and controls to maintain a relative humidity of at least 50 percent or as provided in 5-4.2.1. Although the high level of humidity is not sufficiently reliable for complete dissipation of electrostatic charges, this humidity does reduce the hazard of electrostatic spark discharges under many conditions. The control of airborne bacteria is facilitated in this range of humidity.

> The classic reference on bacteria growth and infection versus humidity level is Dunklin and Puck, "Lethal Effect of Relative Humidity on Airborne Bacteria." [2] Another good reference is McDade and Hall, "Survival of *Staphylococcus aureus* in the Environment." [3] A third noteworthy article is Sonneland, "Does Operating Room Modernization Affect Incident of Infection?" [4]

*Temperature.* The temperature to be maintained in operating rooms should be chosen on the basis of the well-being of the patient and operating teams. It is recommended that the equipment provide for a room temperature in a range of 20°C (68°F) to 24°C (75°F) with controls for selecting any desired temperature within this range.

**5-4.1.1\*** The mechanical ventilation system supplying anesthetizing locations shall have the capability of controlling the relative humidity at a level of 35 percent or greater.

> The committee responsible for this material believes that maintaining a minimum level of humidity should be the major concern for nonflammable anesthetizing locations. Higher values of humidity can be used, if desired.

**A-5-4.1.1** Advantages claimed for humidity include avoidance of hypothermia in patients, especially during long operative procedures; the fact that floating particulate matter increases in conditions of low relative humidity; and the fact that the incidence of wound infections can be minimized following procedures performed in those operating rooms in which the relative humidity is maintained at the level of 50 to 55 percent.

**5-4.1.2** Supply and exhaust systems for windowless anesthetizing locations shall be arranged to automatically vent smoke and products of combustion.

**5-4.1.3** Ventilating systems for anesthetizing locations shall be provided that automatically (a) prevent recirculation of smoke originating within the surgical suite and (b) prevent the circulation of smoke entering the system intake, without in either case interfering with the exhaust function of the system.

Requirements for ventilation are now stated in terms of the desired performance rather than the particular type of damper or sensing mechanism to be used. This is in concert with the general move toward more performance-based codes and standards.

See Chapter 5 of the 1996 edition of NFPA 72, *National Fire Alarm Code*®[5], for types of detection for sensing smoke.

The stated performance criteria are applicable for most system configurations. However, there are situations and system types, such as a recirculating system, not envisioned by the committee, that may require a shutdown of the air-handling system for an anesthetizing location so as not to jeopardize the safety of staff required to stay in the operating room during a fire. (Note: this procedure was necessary in a March 1989 fire that occurred in a Michigan hospital.)

For the purpose of this discussion, the anesthetizing location is a suite of operating rooms (ORs) that is part of a facility. It can occupy a portion of a floor or a whole floor. An OR's air-conditioning (AC) system is usually designed to be a separate and unique system for that suite. Properly maintained, the AC system, in turn, maintains a positive pressure in the entire suite with respect to other occupancies adjacent to the suite on that floor. Within the ORs, individual operating rooms are maintained at a positive pressure to the spaces surrounding them by the AC system.

Some AC systems are designed to provide 100 percent fresh air (i.e., none of the exhaust air is circulated back to the ORs). Other AC systems are designed to recirculate a large percentage of the exhaust air back into the ORs. If a fire occurs outside the OR, either of the two types of AC systems will keep smoke out of the OR. A more difficult situation arises when the fire is in the sterile core of the suite but still not in an operating room. In this situation, the noncirculating AC system will minimize the intrusion of smoke from the fire into the operating rooms themselves. AC systems designed to recirculate air can be designed to switch to 100 percent exhaust during this fire condition. The most difficult fire condition is a fire in an individual operating room. Here, design criteria require that the room be positively pressurized with respect to the adjacent spaces. Unless the supply air to the involved operating room is shut down, the smoke generated by the fire will leak to adjacent spaces. If the supply air cannot be individually controlled for each operating room, the entire supply air system may have to be shut down while the exhaust air system is kept running to keep the smoke from the fire inside the involved room from spreading into adjacent rooms.

Shutdown of the exhaust portion of an AC system or the entire AC system may be necessary to prevent smoke from being drawn into a particular room or rooms in an anesthetizing location [i.e., to comply with (b) in 5-4.1.3, ". . .prevent the circulation of smoke entering the system intake . . .," but not the criteria of ". . .without . . .interfering with the exhaust function of the system"].

It should be noted that 5-4.1.3 does not mandate a completely separate smoke control system. Smoke removal is required, but the method is left to the designers of such systems.

**5-4.1.4** The electric supply to the ventilating system shall be served by the equipment system of the essential electrical system specified in Chapter 3, "Electrical Systems."

**5-4.1.5** Window-type temperature regulating units (air conditioners) are permitted to be installed in exterior windows or exterior walls of anesthetizing locations *(see also 2-3.4 and 2-3.5 in Annex 2)*. Where such units are employed, the provisions of 5-4.1.1 shall be met.

**5-4.1.6** Systems that capture or dispose of waste anesthetic gases, if installed, shall prevent their reentry into the facility. *(See 4-3.3.2 for further requirements on WAGD systems.)*

The 1996 revision increased the variety of methods that can be used to dispose of waste anesthetic gases to the outside of a facility. In this 1999 edition, a reference to 4-3.3.2 was added to remind the user about the requirements of alarm systems, ductwork, labeling, and so on.

"Scavenging apparatus" (as they are commonly referred to) do not actually exhaust waste anesthetic gases to the outside of the facility. Instead, they collect and contain waste anesthetic gases as part of a waste anesthetic gas disposal (WAGD) system that then exhausts the collected gases to the outside of the facility.

## 5-4.2 Ventilation—Laboratories.

General requirements for the design and construction of ventilation systems (duct work and equipment) are covered in NFPA 90A, *Standard for the Installation of Air Conditioning and Ventilating Systems.* [6] Requirements in this section are specific for ventilation systems in laboratories.

A previous document, designated NFPA 56C (now incorporated into NFPA 99), included the restriction that only preset or barometric dampers could be installed in exhaust ducts serving fume hoods. That restriction was removed by Association action in November 1980. Those favoring the allowance of any type of damper design cite the reasonably reliable hardware now available and energy conservation opportunities as evidence in support of lifting the restriction. Others argue that the lack of reliable control of the exhaust capacity at each hood, the hostile environment around dampers inside the ductwork, and the inadequate maintenance that is generally given to dampers substantiate a restriction to preset dampers only and a separate fan for each hood. At present this chapter does not address this subject or the subject of multiple fume hoods connected to a single exhaust.

Systems with multiple hoods on a single exhaust, with automatic, motorized dampers, or with both should be monitored for proper ventilation at each hood immediately prior to its use. Hoods used more or less continuously can have an airflow indicator or a visual/audible alarm installed to warn operators and others in the area if the airflow drops below a safe level. Sensing equipment is now available that is not located in the exhaust stream and that provides an alarm. With the proper attention to details, this equipment can be maintained.

The use, inspection, and maintenance of ventilation systems in the laboratory should be coordinated among all areas involved. Whenever any cycling of fans or ventilation systems is instituted or energy management programs are employed, the impact of the positive/negative pressure differentials of laboratories and other sensitive areas needs to be accounted for in the system programming. Where pressure differentials are required, ventilation systems should be provided with overrides and imbalance alarms connected to an attended location. Direct measurement of pressure differential is seldom reliable because the quality of general construction for most laboratories is simply not "tight" enough, or "leakproof" enough, to produce a reasonably measurable differential pressure from the difference between ventilation air supplied and exhausted. However, equipment is available to reliably measure and display the ventilation air quantities, supplied and exhausted, to demonstrate the correct "negativeness" (or "positiveness") of laboratory spaces.

**5-4.2.1\*** Laboratories provided with mechanical ventilation throughout or employing fume hoods as a fixed part of the exhaust system shall have the air supply and exhaust balanced to provide a negative pressure with respect to surrounding hospital occupancies.

*Exception: Laboratories for procedures requiring maximum protection against contamination and not involving infectious or noxious materials are permitted to be arranged for slight positive pressure when the safety of the arrangement is affirmed by a responsible laboratory official.*

**A-5-4.2.1 Ventilation Design.** Prevalent practice when laboratories are provided with supply and exhaust ventilation is to design the fume hood exhaust as an integral part of the balanced ventilating system, so that the fume hood exhaust is in constant operation.

In general, the use of fume hoods for fixed parts of the exhaust system is a poor practice that should be avoided. For energy conservation, and if variable-volume fume hood exhaust controls are employed, the use of fume hoods as a fixed part of the ventilation system should also be avoided. Variable-volume control of the primary laboratory ventilating system to offset variable hood exhaust quantities, while simultaneously maintaining the required relative pressure between the laboratory and its adjacent areas, can introduce complexities that make controls difficult to set and maintain reliably. This is particularly true if pneumatic controls are used. Other means are available to maintain fume hood exhaust flows at variable, but desired, levels when hood sashes are moved. Electronic and direct digital control equipment is readily available to solve this problem.

**5-4.2.2** Exit corridors shall not be used as plenums to supply or exhaust air from laboratory areas.

This requirement refers to exit access corridors. It does not apply to circulation corridors within the laboratory.

**5-4.2.3\*** Exhaust systems for laboratory ventilation shall be arranged with motors and fans located at the discharge end of the systems, and with the exhaust air discharged above the roof in such a manner that it will not be drawn into any air intake or blown into windows.

**A-5-4.2.3** The discharge side of fume hood exhaust fans is under positive pressure and often leaks toxic fumes into the surrounding environment; therefore, all fume hood exhaust fans should be installed outdoors, and not inside penthouses or other mechanical equipment enclosures that have to be frequented by maintenance and service personnel.

A Formal Interpretation was issued in March 1980 after what was formerly the Committee on Laboratories received a question regarding the meaning of the term *roof.* Since the term was not defined in the glossary of NFPA 56C (now incorporated into NFPA 99), the Interpretation Committee considered it the intent of the technical committee that the term have the following meaning (as defined in *Webster's Third New International Dictionary*): "The outside cover of a building or structure including the roofing and all the materials and construction necessary to maintain the cover upon its walls or other support."

The requirement for discharge "above the roof" was extensively discussed by the then Committee on Laboratories during the revision of the 1980 edition of NFPA 56C. Public comments noting some difficulty in meeting this requirement had been received. The committee responded that the requirement applied to new construction only and reflected good engineering design practice. In essence, any other location for discharge included too many variables to reasonably ensure the safety of laboratory or other personnel (e.g., wind pressure on a side of a building would defeat side wall fans; erection of a new building adjacent to a laboratory could eliminate the clear area around the side of a building).

The committee noted that even with above-the-roof discharge, cases have been reported where exhaust fumes were drawn in through air intake ducts of nearby, higher buildings.

The appendix information calls attention to the problem of the accumulation of fume hood exhausts from the discharge side of fume hood exhaust fans. Maintenance personnel, who may not be aware of the hazard, can ingest the toxic substances the fume hood removed from human contact in the first place.

**Formal Interpretation 73-1**

*Reference:* 5-4.2.3

*Question:* Was it the intent of the Committee that the term "roof" in 5-4.2.3 have that meaning as defined in *Webster's Third International Dictionary* (since the term was not defined in Chapter 2): The outside cover of a building or structure including the roofing and all the materials and construction necessary to maintain the cover upon its walls or other support?

*Answer:* Yes.

*Issue Edition:* 1973 of NFPA 56C
*Reference:* 3-3.4.6
*Date:* March 1980

## 5-4.3 Hood—Laboratories.

Another source of information on fume hoods can be found in A-6-3 through A-7-2 and F-1.3 and F-1.9 of the 1996 edition of NFPA 45, *Standard on Fire Protection for Laboratories Using Chemicals.* [7]

Fume hoods are very susceptible to ventilation fluctuations that can lead to a range of hazards depending on the process or activity taking place within the hood. The installation of hoods in areas of minimum traffic or air turbulence, the construction specifications for the hood and any associated utilities and shutoffs, warning signs and emergency directions and procedures, and periodic tests and inspections for performance need to be taken into account within the facility safety and/or hazard surveillance program. (See Exhibit 5.2.)

Where hood operation involves hazardous or flammable materials, an alarm that is audible and visible should signal any lack of proper hood operation.

**5-4.3.1\*** Fume hood and biological safety cabinet requirements shall comply with NFPA 45, *Standard on Fire Protection for Laboratories Using Chemicals.*

**A-5-4.3.1** Biological safety cabinets (BSC) that are vented to the outside share some characteristics with chemical fume hoods. The interiors of each are at negative pressure with respect to the ambient environment. BSC are not intended to be used for protection from exothermic or potentially explosive chemical reactions. *[See HHS Publication No. (CDC) 93-8395, Biosafety in Microbiological and Biomedical Laboratories, for a description of BSC and their ventilating requirements.]*

For the reasons cited in A-5-4.3.1, the hazards of biological safety cabinets were added to those for fume hoods in the 1996 edition.

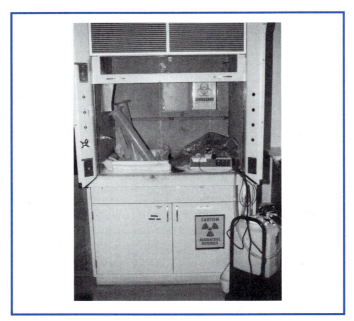

**Exhibit 5.2**  *Typical laboratory fume hood with the access window partially open.*

**5-4.3.2** Fume hoods shall be located in areas of minimum air turbulence, away from doors and windows, and in a manner that will not impede access to egress.

**5-4.3.3\*** Fume hoods intended for use with radioactive isotopes shall be constructed of stainless steel or other material suitable for the particular exposure.

**A-5-4.3.3** See NFPA 801, *Standard for Fire Protection for Facilities Handling Radioactive Materials*, for related information.

**5-4.3.4\*** Fume hood ventilating controls shall be so arranged that shutting off the ventilation of one fume hood will not reduce the exhaust capacity or create an imbalance between exhaust and supply for any other hood connected to the same system.

The operation of these controls shall be tested annually by a qualified person who shall certify the result of the test.

> When fume hoods are shut off, their airflow reverses. This reversal is cause for concern about the air from the hood that is allowed to enter the room. The flow reversal that occurs from an individual hood with a fan that serves just that hood is not as serious a concern as the flow reversal that occurs when a fume hood is ganged with other fume hoods onto one fan. In this situation, when the fan is shut off, the contents of the exhaust from one hood can accidentally discharge into the laboratory space of another area through the fume hood located in that area.

Reliable sensors can detect this condition when the fume hood fan is turned on, but there are no sensors available to detect the condition when the fan is shut off. Serious thought should be given to the consequences of ganging fume hood exhausts together. In general, this practice of ganging fume hoods should be avoided.

The second paragraph was added for several reasons. Fume hood ventilating controls today are complex and require an understanding of air movement to balance properly. Improper balance and operation of these controls can create hazardous fire conditions and endanger personnel. For example, an inadequate exhaust can trap flammable gases and cause them to ignite in the presence of an ignition source such as a Bunsen burner, or it might create a back draft of toxic fumes. An annual check is a reasonable interval of time to ensure adequate operation and reveal any significant drifts in settings.

The stipulation that the person be "qualified" was considered necessary to ensure that only competent persons worked on these systems. Many health care facilities have staff members who are quite competent in inspecting and testing fume hood controls. This paragraph is intended to allow the utilization of these persons in lieu of contracting these services from an outside source.

**A-5-4.3.4** The qualified person can be a staff member of the facility.

**5-4.3.5** Fume hoods shall be so designed that the face velocity ventilation is adequate to prevent the backflow of contaminants into the room, especially in the presence of cross drafts or the rapid movements of an operator working at the face of the hood.

**5-4.3.6** Shutoff valves for services, including gas, air, vacuum, and electricity, shall be outside of the hood enclosure in a location where they will be readily accessible in the event of fire in the hood. The location of such shutoffs shall be legibly lettered in a related location on the exterior of the hood.

## 5-5 Performance Criteria and Testing

(Reserved)

## 5-6 Administration

### 5-6.1 Anesthetizing Locations.

**5-6.1.1** Ventilating and humidifying equipment for anesthetizing locations shall be kept in operable condition and be continually operating during surgical procedures *(see A-5-4.1)*.

**5-6.1.2** All gas storage locations or manifold enclosures shall be routinely inspected to ensure that the ventilation requirements stated in 4-3.1.1.2(b) and 4-3.1.1.2(c) are not obstructed.

## 5-6.2* Laboratories.

Warning signs describing the nature of any hazardous effluent content shall be posted at fume hoods' discharge points, access points, and filter locations.

**A-5-6.2** Warning signs should include, or reference, information on hazards, and on the changing, handling, and disposal of filters.

### References Cited in Commentary

1. NFPA *101*®, *Life Safety Code*®, 1997 edition.
2. Dunklin and Puck, "Lethal Effect of Relative Humidity on Airborne Bacteria," *Journal of Experimental Medicine,* vol. 87, pp. 87–101, 1988. (the classic reference on bacteria growth and infection versus humidity level)
3. McDade and Hall, "Survival of *Staphylococcus aureus* in the Environment," *American Journal of Hygiene,* vol. 28, pp. 330–337, 1963.
4. Sonneland, "Does Operating Room Modernization Affect Incident of Infection?" *Hospital Topics,* vol. 44, pp. 149–151, June 1966.
5. NFPA 72, *National Fuel Alarm Code*®, 1999 edition.
6. NFPA 90A, *Standard for the Installation of Air Conditioning and Ventilating Systems,* 1999 edition.
7. NFPA 45, *Standard on Fire Protection for Laboratories Using Chemicals,* 1996 edition.

# CHAPTER 6

# Materials

This subject is included because of past fires involving combustibles that have been reported. Of most concern are those fires occurring inside operating rooms because of the nature of the activities there and the limitations on the types of fire responses possible.

To date, the committees of the Health Care Facilities Project have not been able to develop criteria on the materials themselves. Instead, the emphasis has been on training and preventive measures [as was done in 1993 in Chapters 7 and 12, and former Annex 2 (now Annex 1)].

A task group is currently studying the hazards of combustibles used in operating rooms. Ideas from the public are most welcomed and appreciated.

NFPA *101, Life Safety Code* [1], provides some criteria on furnishings, bedding, and decorations in health care facilities. Refer to 12-7.5 and 13-7.5 in the 1997 edition of that code.

## 6-1* Scope

This chapter covers the hazards associated with the use of flammable and combustible materials used within health care facilities.

**A-6-1** *Application of Requirements.* The application of requirements contained in this chapter for specific types of health care facilities can be found in Chapters 12 through 18.

## 6-2 Nature of Hazards

### 6-2.1 Flammability.

(Reserved)

### 6-2.2  Combustible Loading.

**6-2.2.1  Flammable Agents.** Facility administrative authorities, in consultation with the medical staff and others with training and expertise, shall determine the adequacy of storage space for disinfecting agents and medicaments *(see NFPA 30, Flammable and Combustible Liquids Code and NFPA 45, Standard on Fire Protection for Laboratories Using Chemicals, for storage cabinet requirements)* and shall provide and enforce regulations for the storage and handling of containers of such agents. Said regulations also shall provide for the periodic inspection and maintenance of said storage locations.

> This material, previously located in Chapter 4, is the beginning of the committees' efforts to address combustible loading in health care facilities. Developing guidance for this subject is difficult because the problem is not easy to identify or to quantify. The committees welcome any input from readers on this topic.

**6-2.2.2  Flammable Materials.**  (Reserved)

> The committee added this new reserved section for the 1999 edition. Materials, such as surgical drapes, tracheal tubes, gauze sponges, waste products, and so forth, that can burn when exposed to ignition sources, can be hazardous, especially in the presence of an oxygen-enriched atmosphere. This section on flammable materials was added to call attention to the subject and will be addressed by the Task Group on Combustibles. (See Exhibit 6.1.)

*Exhibit 6.1  A typical hospital supply closet containing many combustibles. (Courtesy of Rob Swift and Prince William Health Systems.)*

### 6-2.3 Toxicity of Products of Combustion.

Many substances, when subjected to a fire, undergo a chemical change resulting in a new toxic product. This is especially true of many plastic substances. Many highly toxic combustion products can cause sudden unconsciousness, cardiovascular collapse, and severe injury or death, even though the person injured is relatively remote from the fire. These combustion products have been found to cause injury after passing through halls, ventilating systems, and even electrical conduit.

### 6-2.4 Chemical Burns.

(Reserved)

### 6-2.5 Safety.

(Reserved)

### 6-2.6 Radioactivity.

(Reserved)

## 6-3 Source

(Reserved)

## 6-4 Distribution

(Reserved)

## 6-5 Performance Criteria and Testing

(Reserved)

## 6-6 Administration

(Reserved)

### Reference Cited in Commentary

1. NFPA *101®, Life Safety Code®,* 1997 edition.

# CHAPTER 7

# Electrical Equipment

In the late 1960s, many health care professionals became concerned with the problem of microampere range electric currents causing ventricular fibrillation. This occurs when a conductive pathway carrying these small currents flows within or adjacent to the chambers of the heart. Such pathways include cardiac monitoring leads or catheters containing ionizable fluids. The problems associated with the use of these devices, plus the continuous increase in the number of devices used for one patient (both direct contact and ancillary) led to the concept behind *electrically susceptible patient location* and *electrically susceptible patient.* (These terms are no longer used because they are misleading. All living organisms are affected by electricity that is imposed on them.)

An NFPA committee was established in the late 1960s to address the subject of patient electrical safety. The document that resulted, NFPA 76B, *Safe Use of Electricity in Patient Care Areas of Health Care Facilities,* was adopted first as a manual in 1971 and then as a tentative standard in 1973. After several major revisions, it was adopted as a full standard in 1980. In 1984 it was one of twelve health care documents combined to form NFPA 99.

There have been significant improvements in equipment design and utilization practices since the subject of electric currents and ventricular fibrillation was first addressed. Despite these advances, however, hazards still remain.

Originally, NFPA 76B covered performance criteria for the electrical wiring systems in hospitals and the design, maintenance, and safe use of portable and fixed line-powered electrical appliances in hospitals. In 1984 NFPA 76B became Chapter 9 of NFPA 99. When NFPA 99 was restructured in 1987, wiring provisions were incorporated into the requirements for electrical systems in Chapter 3, appliance provisions for health care facilities were placed in Chapter 7, and manufacturer provisions were placed in Chapter 9.

Concern about electrical safety in the health care community increased as physicians and surgeons began to probe below the surface of the skin. Probing the surface and inside of the heart revealed that the organ was very sensitive to any electrical current impressed upon it. Although experiments on human response to external electrical stimuli had been conducted in the 1700s by Benjamin Franklin and others before him, electrical contacts in the cardiac region did not become common until the early 1960s. By the mid-1960s, there were reports of patients going into ventricular fibrillation during catherization procedures for no apparent reason. Resultant research showed that small electrical currents (at levels well below the perceptible sensation threshold) could cause fibrillation. Insurance mortality statistics for noncatheterized electrical accidents seemed to support the same conclusion. Efforts began on the medical, engineering, manufacturing, and maintenance fronts to reduce the likelihood that electrical current could accidentally find its way through patients and health care personnel to cause cardiac and other electrical disruptive problems.

The initial reaction of the health care community and subsequent media coverage brought much attention to the problem. Improvements in equipment design and a better understanding of the hazards, however, brought the matter into better perspective. Thus, NFPA 76B reflected a general consensus of reasonable measures to take to improve electrical safety in patient care areas of hospitals.

There has been much discussion on whether there is a need for a document separate from the *National Electrical Code* to cover the subject of the safe use of electricity in health care facilities. There appears to be little question that most of this subject is well outside the responsibilities of electrical inspection authorities. The issue extends beyond the installation of the wiring system and includes manufacturing criteria and operational practices. While other organizations may have addressed portions of this subject, a document that ties all facets of the problem together is vital to all builders, inspectors, operators, engineers, and practitioners involved in the use of electricity in health care facilities. This chapter and Chapter 3 provide a link between the requirements of the electrical equipment and the electrical system in a health care facility. Similarly, this chapter and Chapter 9 are linked because both proper design and proper operation are required for the safe utilization of equipment. The developers of NFPA 76B were very much aware of these relationships, which remain even after NFPA 76B was incorporated into NFPA 99. Electrical safety is addressed as a system phenomenon, which allows flexibility in achieving a reasonable level of safety in health care facilities.

As noted in Chapter 5, in the 1996 edition, all of the requirements and recommendations on *flammable* inhalation anesthetics were transferred to a new Annex 2, "Flammable Anesthetizing Locations." Because of this transfer of text, references in Chapters 1 through 20 and in Appendixes A, B, and C are only to *nonflammable* inhalation anesthetics, including anesthetizing locations.

# 7-1* Scope

The scope of this chapter has been questioned many times because of its similarity to other NFPA and non-NFPA documents, particularly NFPA 70, *National Electrical Code*. [1] The scope of the committee responsible for the material in this chapter was reviewed in 1979 by the Standards Council, particularly in relation to a new scope for Panel 17 of the National Electrical Code Committee. While no changes in the scope of the committee were made, the distinction between the two documents was clarified. The Health Care Facilities technical committees are responsible for the criteria for performance, maintenance, and testing of, among other things, electrical systems and electrical appliances. Panel 17, responsible for Article 517 of NFPA 70, is responsible for electrical construction and installation requirements based on such performance criteria.

While it could be argued that it is easier to place all factors relating to health care fire safety in one document, the Standards Council chose to divide responsibilities in the aforementioned way for several reasons. First, the division is a practical one. Electrical installation requirements are largely the same in all occupancies. Electrical inspectors, contractors, and others concerned with installation are familiar with the *National Electrical Code*. [1] Although Article 517 contains special requirements peculiar to health care facilities, these requirements are similar to general provisions. While designers need some general knowledge of installation requirements for wiring, they are primarily concerned with equipment interaction with users to achieve safe design and use. A second compelling reason for this division of responsibilities is the problems that would exist in coordination and correlation if separate installation documents were developed for different occupancies. It has thus been a long-established policy that electrical installation requirements for all occupancies be contained in the *National Electrical Code*. [1]

As noted in the prologue to this chapter, the scope of the original document on safe use of electricity, NFPA 76B, was not limited to electrical appliances per se. Rather, the multifaceted aspects of electricity and its associated hazards were covered. With the restructuring of NFPA 99 in 1987, requirements for electrical wiring systems were moved to Chapter 3. The scopes of Chapter 7 (covering electrical appliance use and maintenance) and Chapter 9 (covering requirements for manufacturers) are not at odds with the *Federal Medical Devices Amendment Act of 1976* [2], which governs medical devices. This chapter sets up minimum performance criteria for appliances. The Food and Drug Administration (assigned to implement the Medical Devices Amendment Act) can use this voluntary document for its purposes if it wishes, just as other agencies or organizations use NFPA documents.

While this chapter does not require formal approval or listing of appliances, it does indicate that authorities having jurisdiction might do so. Users should consult appropriate authorities on this matter.

**A-7-1** *Application of Requirements.* The application of requirements contained in this chapter for specific types of health care facilities can be found in Chapters 12 through 18.

This chapter originated from a concern about electrical safety in the hospital. It resulted in NFPA 76B-1980, *Safe Use of Electricity in Patient Care Areas of Hospitals* (incorporated into NFPA 99 in 1984).

This chapter states the basic electrical safety performance criteria for patient care areas to be followed by personnel. Chapter 9 provides performance criteria for manufacturers of appliances. Chapter 3 provides performance criteria for the installation implementation requirements contained in Article 517, NFPA 70, *National Electrical Code.* The purpose of these chapters is the practical safeguarding of patients and staff from the hazards arising from the use of electricity in medical diagnosis and therapy.

The material in this appendix, as it relates to electrical safety *(see A-3-1 and A-7-1),* interprets some of the basic criteria by presenting different methodologies and alternative procedures to achieve the level of safety defined by the criteria.

**7-1.1** This chapter covers the performance, maintenance, and testing of electrical equipment used within health care facilities.

**7-1.2** Although an appliance that yields erroneous data or functions poorly can be dangerous, quality and assurance of full appliance performance is not covered except as it relates to direct electrical or fire injury to patients or personnel.

**7-1.3** This chapter does not require formal approval or listing of any appliance.

**7-1.4** Experimental or research apparatus built to order or under development shall be used under qualified supervision and shall have a degree of safety equivalent to that described herein or have a degree of safety that has been deemed acceptable by the facility.

## 7-2* Nature of Hazards

**A-7-2** Section 7-2 is intended to be informational. See also Section 3-2 for related electrical hazards.

### 7-2.1* Fire and Explosion.

Transmission of electricity generates heat. The normal operating temperature of a device is a function of material and design. Equipment or wiring faults can cause abnormal temperature increases. These abnormal temperatures can cause fire and explosions. Use of oxygen or other oxidizing agents lowers ignition temperatures. Normal operating temperatures of equipment not designed for use in oxygen-enriched atmospheres can cause fires if used in oxygen-enriched atmospheres.

**A-7-2.1** See 8-2.1.2.4(c) for other fire ignition hazards.

## 7-2.2 Electrical Shock.

### 7-2.2.1 Elimination of Shock Hazards.

**7-2.2.1.1** Personnel are cautioned to be aware of the hazards presented by defective or improperly employed electrical equipment *(see 7-2.2.2)* and to avoid the use of defective electrical equipment *(see 7-6.2.2.4).*

> Training covering electrical hazards and safe practices should be conducted to make personnel sensitive to this problem. This training should occur during orientation and should be periodically reviewed.

**7-2.2.1.2** Adequate grounding for electrical equipment is an important safeguard against fire and electric shock *(see 3-3.3.2 and 7-5.1.2.2).*

**7-2.2.2\* Effects of Moisture.** Moisture, in the form of liquids, vapors, or mists, can degrade insulation to the point where fire, equipment malfunction, and electric shock hazard become a threat. Moisture can enter equipment as a result of defective seals, leaks, or inadvertent spillage. Vessels containing liquids should not be placed on electrical equipment.

**A-7-2.2.2** See 3-3.2.1.2(f), Wet Locations.

## 7-2.3 Burns.

**7-2.3.1 Heated Surfaces.** Sustained skin contact with surfaces of equipment that have temperatures in excess of 107°F (42°C) can cause burns. Caution is required when exposing patients to warmed surfaces, particularly when they are helpless.

**7-2.3.2\*** High-frequency electromagnetic fields, particularly those from electrosurgical generators and from lasers, are used to intentionally destroy tissue. Inadvertent burns, or ignition of combustible materials, is a hazard.

**A-7-2.3.2** See Annex 1, "The Safe Use of High-Frequency Electricity in Health Care Facilities."

## 7-2.4 Interruption of Power.

(Reserved)

> Even brief interruptions of power can cause some equipment to malfunction, particularly appliances with computer components, such as physiological monitoring systems. Readers are referred to essential electrical system requirements described in Chapter 3, which allow a switchover time of up to 10 seconds. If an appliance cannot tolerate even this brief interruption, special power provisions could need to be arranged.
>
> In 1993 requirements for the manufacturers of patient-care-related electrical

appliances were added that ensure new appliances will not malfunction because of brief interruptions of power (as might occur when normal power is interrupted and then restored by the essential electrical system). Older equipment may not be designed to meet this new criterion, and health care personnel should be aware of potential hazards with these older appliances, particularly those with computer components. (See 9-2.1.6.5.)

### 7-2.5* RF Interference.

*Radio frequency interference* (RFI) and *electromagnetic interference* (EMI) refer to electromagnetic radiation that comes from outside sources. This radiation can affect the proper operation of medical devices. Sources of RFI and EMI can be a radio station transmitting tower, portable telephones, electric power lines, or even other medical devices. A related term, *electromagnetic compatibility (EMC),* denotes the ability of a device to function properly in the presence of disturbing electromagnetic fields.

Some cellular telephones, because of their operating characteristics, have been shown to activate the alarm signals of smoke and heat detectors and to interfere with the operation of medical equipment. Facilities that experience these problems should contact the manufacturers of the suspect phones to learn how to mitigate the problem.

The increasing proliferation of electrical devices in health care facilities, along with their increased sophistication (making them more prone to gross and subtle failures), demands heightened awareness of these potential hazards. Specific recommendations and requirements for ameliorating the problems of RFI and EMI are being studied by many agencies.

**A-7-2.5** See Annex 1, "The Safe Use of High-Frequency Electricity in Health Care Facilities."

### 7-2.6 Mechanical Injury.

(Reserved)

---

## 7-3 Source

### 7-3.1* Electrical System.

**A-7-3.1** See Chapter 3.

### 7-3.2 Battery.

(Reserved)

# 7-4 Distribution

(Reserved)

# 7-5 Performance Criteria and Testing

## 7-5.1 Patient-Care-Related Electrical Appliances and Equipment.

*Readers are reminded of the structure of NFPA 99, and that 7-5.1 applies only to patient-care-related electrical appliances.* Exhibit 7.1 is an example of a patient-care-related electrical appliance.

Requirements for patient-care-related electrical appliances used in flammable anesthetizing locations (formerly 7-5.1.1.2 through 7-5.1.1.5 and 7-5.1.2.5 through 7-5.1.2.7 in the 1993 edition) were transferred to Annex 2, which covers such locations, in the 1996 edition.

Requirements for low-voltage appliances can be found in 9-2.1.10. Installation requirements for such appliances can be found in NFPA 70, *National Electrical Code* [1], Section 517-64.

### 7-5.1.1 Permanently Connected (Fixed).

**7-5.1.1.1 Grounding of Appliances.** Patient-connected electric appliances shall be grounded to the equipment grounding bus in the distribution panel by an insulated grounding conductor run with the power conductors.

### 7-5.1.2 Cord- and Plug-Connected (Portable).

**7-5.1.2.1 General.** All patient-care-related electrical equipment supplied by a flexible cord and plug, carrying 20 V or more, shall meet the requirements of 7-5.1.2.

**7-5.1.2.2 Grounding of Appliances.** All cord-connected electrically powered appliances used in the patient care vicinity shall be provided with a three-wire power cord and a three-pin grounding-type plug.

*Exception: Double-insulated appliances shall be permitted to have two conductor cords.*

During revision for the 1984 edition of NFPA 99, the committee responsible for this chapter received several proposals recommending that patient-care-related appliances enclosed in plastic cases, but not technically double insulated, be permitted in patient care vicinities. The committee did not accept these recommendations and stated that the present minimum level of safety (i.e., grounded or double insulated) was necessary within the patient care vicinity. Appliances not meeting either of these requirements are acceptable outside the patient care vicinity.

Double-insulated appliances are not merely appliances with some nonconductive coating around a metal chassis. Double insulation involves deliberate efforts to

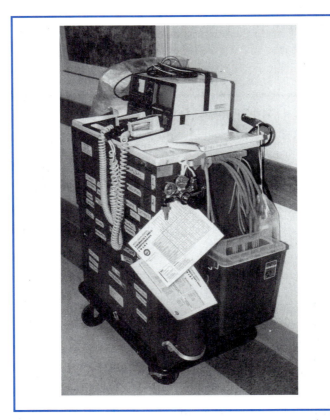

**Exhibit 7.1** *Typical emergency cart. These carts are strategically placed throughout patient care areas in the event a patient suddenly goes into cardiac arrest.*

prevent non-current-carrying conductive components from becoming energized and accessible to contact by persons using the appliance. One type of double-insulated appliance has a normal insulation plus a second layer of insulation in case the normal one fails or is breached. Another type uses a single insulation, which is much heavier than normal combined with other protective measures. What ever method is used, appliances qualifying as double insulated require special testing or examination by qualified personnel (see also commentary in Chapter 2 on the definition of *double-insulated appliances*). Note that the requirement and the exception do not specify listing of appliances. (See 7-1.4.)

The problem of electromagnetic interference should be considered in relation to sensitive monitoring equipment that may be double insulated. The operation of equipment in various locations at various times may be necessary to learn of any problems.

Another recent concern involves appliances that operate from low-voltage power supplies. If these power supplies are the three-wire, grounded configuration type but have only a two-wire isolated output, does the case of the appliance necessarily have to be grounded? The answer is that if the output of the power supply is truly isolated (i.e., meets the electrical safety requirements for isolated leads), the case does not have to be grounded.

**7-5.1.2.3 Attachment Plugs.** Attachment plugs installed by the facility shall meet the requirements of 9-2.1.2.1.

**7-5.1.2.4 Power Cords.** Power cords installed by the facility shall meet the requirements of 9-2.1.2.2.

Facilities should be aware that replacing, lengthening, or shortening the power cord supplied by the manufacturer could affect the device's warranty and any listing. The manufacturer or distributor should be contacted before modifications are made to any part of a device.

**7-5.1.2.5 Line Voltage Equipment—Anesthetizing Locations.** Flexible cord for portable lamps or portable electric appliances operating at more than 12 V between conductors, intended for use in anesthetizing locations, shall be continuous and without switches from the appliance to the attachment plug and of a type designated for extra-hard usage in accordance with Section 501-11 of NFPA 70, *National Electrical Code*. Cords shall be protected at the entrance to equipment by a suitable insulating grommet. The flexible cord shall be of sufficient length to reach any position in which the portable device is to be used, and the attachment plug shall be inserted only in a fixed, approved receptacle. For correct use and maintenance of adapters, the provisions of 7-6.2.1.5 shall apply.

The former 7-5.1.2.5(a) was deleted for this 1999 edition because the committee felt that it was overly restrictive to require a storage device for the flexible power cord on all portable equipment.

The phrase "shall be continuous and without switches from the appliance to the attachment plug" in the first sentence has been interpreted by the former Committee on Anesthetizing Agents (now part of the Technical Committee on Gas Delivery Equipment) to mean that extension cords are not permitted in any type of anesthetizing location (flammable or nonflammable). Comments by the Interpretation Committee at the time noted that the original requirement prohibiting the use of extension cords related to the vicinity around flammable gases where arcs or sparks could cause explosions (e.g., where an appliance mated with a receptacle). Some of the reasons that were noted for continuing the prohibition in all anesthetizing locations included the following:

(a) The possibility of mechanical damage to the cord connector from lying on the floor

(b) The possibility of short circuits resulting from spilled fluids and liquids typically found in operating rooms

(c) The possibility of short circuits resulting from the lack of controllability over inventory (typical for extension cords)

(d) The unreliability inherent in the introduction of additional connectors into a circuit

(e) The probability of using a cord or connectors of inadequate ampacity

(f) The probability of incorrect polarization

(g) The compromise of overcurrent protection caused by the introduction of increased grounding wire resistance

(h) The probability that a prohibited extension cord might subsequently be used in the presence of flammable anesthetics

The last sentence on adapters was added when it was pointed out to the committee that such adapters may be necessary in unusual situations. Regular use of such adapters is not the intent of the committee, as seen by Exception Nos. 2 and 3 that follow. (See 7-6.2.1.5 or further requirements for such unusual circumstances.)

For this 1999 edition, one sentence and the former Exception Nos. 2 and 3 in the 1996 edition were deleted because the committee determined that they were redundant with provisions in 7-5.1.2.2 and 7-5.1.3.2.

*Exception No. 1: Foot-treadle-operated controllers are permitted in any anesthetizing location if appended to portable electric appliances in an approved manner. Foot-treadle-operated controllers and their connector shall be splashproof.*

*Exception No. 2: Two or more power receptacles supplied by a flexible cord are permitted to be used to supply power to plug-connected components of a movable equipment assembly that is rack-, table-, or pedestal-mounted provided:*

*(a) The receptacles are an integral part of the equipment assembly, permanently attached; and*

*(b)\* The sum of the ampacity of all appliances connected to the receptacles shall not exceed 75 percent of the ampacity of the flexible cord supplying the receptacles; and*

**A-7-5.1.2.5 Exception No. 2(b)** Whole-body hyperthermia/hypothermia units should be powered from a separate branch circuit.

*(c) The ampacity of the flexible cord is suitable and in accordance with the current edition of NFPA 70, National Electrical Code; and*

*(d)\* The electrical and mechanical integrity of the assembly is regularly verified and documented through an ongoing maintenance program.*

**A-7-5.1.2.5 Exception No. 2(d)** See 3-3.2.1.2(d)4 for criteria of receptacles.

*Exception No. 3: Overhead power receptacles are permitted to be supplied by a flexible cord (ceiling drop) that is connected at a ceiling-mounted junction box either:*

*(a) Permanently; or*

*(b)\* Utilizing a locking-type plug cap and receptacle combination, or other method of retention. In either connection mode, suitable strain relief shall be provided.*

**A-7-5.1.2.5 Exception No. 3(b)** The disconnection means is permitted only to facilitate replacement; as such, ceiling drop cords may not be disconnected for alternative usage. See 3-3.2.1.2(d)4 for criteria of receptacles.

Overhead receptacles are one method of decreasing the number of electrical cords on the floor. Exhibit 7.2 is an example of an overhead receptacle. Electrical cords on floors are subject to more abuse than those plugged into an overhead receptacle.

The requirement of a locking-type receptacle applies only at the ceiling-mounted junction box. The receptacles at the bottom of the drop cord can be a normal straight blade type.

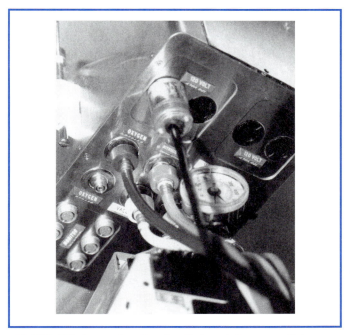

**Exhibit 7.2** *An overhead station that contains gas outlets, vacuum inlets, and electrical receptacles. Note that receptacles and plugs are of the twist-lock type because plugs hang vertically down, supporting the weight of the cord from receptacles.*

**7-5.1.2.6 Adapters and Extension Cords.** Adapters and extension cords shall meet the following requirements:

(a)    Attachment plugs shall meet the requirements of 9-2.1.2.1.
(b)*    Power cords shall be adequate for the application to avoid overload (i.e , 16 AWG or greater) and shall meet the requirements of 9-2.1.2.2.

**A-7-5.1.2.6(b)** For policy on the use of extension cords, see 7-6.2.1.5.

This section was added in 1990 to reflect the original intent of the committee to include requirements for both extension cords and adapters.

**7-5.1.3 Testing Requirements (Fixed and Portable).**
**7-5.1.3.1 Physical Integrity.** The physical integrity of the power cord and attachment plug and cord-strain relief shall be confirmed by visual inspection or other appropriate tests.

Verification of the integrity of the power cord, its conductors and insulation, and of the power plug, with particular attention to the condition of the grounding means, can prevent the possible introduction or utilization of an unsafe appliance in the clinical area.

A visual inspection before an appliance is used can often identify physical deteriorations.

**7-5.1.3.2\* Resistance.** The resistance between the appliance chassis, or any exposed conductive surface of the appliance, and the ground pin of the attachment plug shall be measured. The resistance shall be less than 0.50 ohm. The cord shall be flexed at its connection to the attachment plug or connector and at its connection to the strain relief on the chassis during the resistance measurement. This measurement shall apply only to appliances that are used in the patient care vicinity. *(See A-7-5.1.3.2 for suggested test methods.)*

*Exception: The requirement does not apply to escutcheons or nameplates, small screws, and so forth, that are unlikely to become energized.*

For appliances that use a battery charger, the measurement should be made to the ground pin of the charger with the battery charger not connected to the ac power supply.

The maximum resistance allowed for an appliance used within a patient care area of a facility has been the subject of some debate. The value required of manufacturers has long been accepted as 0.15 ohm and is based on the total resistance of 15 ft (4.6 m) of No. 18 wire, the contact resistance at connectors, and a safety factor. This value of 0.15 ohm is listed in 9-2.1.13.2.

Manufacturer requirements were moved into a separate chapter of former NFPA 76B in 1980 because the committee recognized that there could be differences between hospital and manufacturer requirements. One of these differences was the value of the resistance of the ground wire. In the 1980 edition of NFPA 76B, the value was the same for both hospitals and manufacturers: 0.15 ohm. However, for the 1984 edition of NFPA 99 (when NFPA 76B was incorporated), public proposals were submitted to raise the measured value for hospitals to 0.50 ohm. Some of the major reasons given for this proposed increase included the inaccuracy of measuring devices and the lack of data showing the existence of safety hazards at values greater than 0.15 ohm.

While a single measurement or series of measurements below 0.50 ohm are acceptable, readings that increase each time measurements are made are a telltale sign of deterioration that could indicate incipient problems or failure. It should be remembered that power cords and connections can be subject to severe abuse.

**A-7-5.1.3.2** There are several methods for measuring ground-wire resistance accurately. Three examples are described below:

(a) *Two-Wire Resistance Technique.* A known current is fed through the unknown resistance. A high-input-impedance voltmeter measures the voltage drop across the resistance and R is calculated as V/I. This technique measures the lead resistance in series with the unknown resistance. When the unknown resistance is a ground wire (less than 0.15 ohm), the lead resistance is appreciable. This is accounted for by shorting the lead wires together and "zeroing" the voltmeter. The actual resistance in effect subtracts out the lead wire resistance. In order for this technique to be reasonably accurate for measuring ground wires, an active high-impedance millivoltmeter must be used.

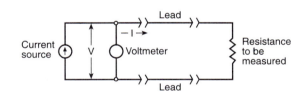

*Figure A-7-5.1.3.2(a)*  *Two-wire resistance technique.*

(b) *Four-Wire Resistance Technique.* This technique is very similar to the two-wire resistance technique. The difference is that the known current is fed to the resistance to be measured through a pair of leads separate from the pair of leads to the voltmeter. The voltmeter is measuring the true voltage across the resistance to be measured regardless of the resistance of the measuring leads. This method eliminates the need for zeroing out the measuring lead resistance.

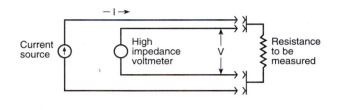

*Figure A-7-5.1.3.2(b)* *Four-wire resistance technique.*

(c) *AC Current Method.* This technique utilizes a step-down transformer of known voltage output to feed current through the ground wire and measure the current that flows. The impedance of the ground wire is then calculated by Ohm's Law.

NOTE: The internal impedance of the measuring circuit must be established with the test leads shorted. This value needs to be subtracted from the test measurement.

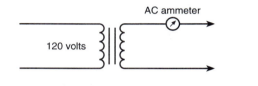

*Figure A-7-5.1.3.2(c)* *AC current method.*

**7-5.1.3.3\* Leakage Current Tests—General.** The following requirements shall apply to all tests.

> The test equipment requirements outlined in this section were revised in 1984 to improve the equipment's ability to account for frequency weighting to low-impedance sources. Paragraph A-7-5.1.3.3 was added to the 1984 edition of NFPA 99 to explain how frequency weighting is achieved. The network shown in Figure A-7-5.1.3.3 is consistent with international documents on the subject.
> The frequency range for testing was also modified in 1984 from "essentially dc" to "dc" because the committee's intent was to make measurements from dc to 1 kHz.

**A-7-5.1.3.3** *Leakage Current Measurements.* For complex leakage current waveforms, a single reading from an appropriate metering system can represent the physiologically effective value of the composite waveform, provided that the contribution of each component to the total reading is weighted in accordance with 7-5.1.3.3 or 9-2.1.13.3.

This "weighting" can be achieved by a frequency-response-shaping network that precedes a flat-response meter, or by a meter whose own frequency response characteristic matches 7-5.1.3.3 or 9-2.1.13.3.

If the required performance is obtained by a meter with integral response shaping properties, then that meter should have a constant input resistance of 1000 ohms. (A high-input-impedance meter can be used by shunting a 1000-ohm resistor across the meter's input terminals.)

If, however, the required frequency response is obtained by a network that precedes an otherwise flat-response meter, then the input impedance of the network should be 1000 ohms ± 10 percent, over the frequency range from 0 to 1 MHz, and the frequency response of the network-meter combination should be substantially independent of the impedance of the signal source.

For maximum chassis leakage current allowed (i.e., 300 microamperes) below 1 KHz, this network will yield the limiting current of 10 mA above 30 KHz.

A suggested input network is shown in Figure A-7-5.1.3.3.

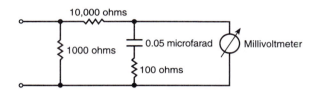

**Figure A-7-5.1.3.3** *Leakage current measurements (1.0 millivolt meter reading corresponds to input current of 1.0 microampere).*

This suggested network will give a proportional response up to 100 kHz. However, it is cautioned that the use of this network-meter combination was originally designed when the chassis leakage current limit was 100 microamperes to conform to a maximum leakage current limit of 10 mA per 7-5.1.3.3(c). For higher frequency values, this network-meter circuit is usable only to 30 kHz in order to meet the 10-mA limitation.

The 10-mA limitation addresses thermal safety, not shock hazard.

In 1980, when manufacturer requirements were placed in a separate chapter of NFPA 76B, *Safe Use of Electricity in Patient Care Areas of Hospitals* (incorporated into NFPA 99 in 1984), some tests for manufacturers were not included. One test for hospitals was also inadvertently not included. The tests next described are now in the same sequence as those for manufacturers in 9-2.1:

(a) Chassis
    1. Permanently wired
    2. Cord-connected
(b) Patient leads
    1. Lead-to-ground (nonisolated input)
    2. Lead-to-ground (isolated input)
    3. Isolated test (isolated input)

  4. Between leads (nonisolated input)
  5. Between leads (isolated input)

The values for leakage currents reflect exhaustive discussion of studies conducted on humans and dogs, actual measurements during cardiac surgery, and manufacturing capabilities. For further information, see A-9-2.1.13.4(c).

(a) *Resistance Test.* The resistance tests of 7-5.1.3.2 shall be conducted before undertaking any leakage current measurements.

It is important to first verify that the appliance is properly grounded because operator safety and test results can otherwise be affected. Exhibit 7.3 is an example of an electrical safety tester.

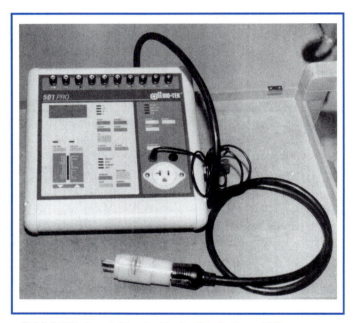

**Exhibit 7.3** *A portable electrical safety tester, which measures, among other things, leakage current of devices, wiring polarity, and receptacle integrity.*

(b) *Techniques of Measurement.* Each test shall be performed with the appropriate connection to a properly grounded ac power system at nominal voltage of the equipment.

The last phrase (". . . at nominal voltage of the equipment") was added to clarify that leakage currents are to be measured and met at the usual operating voltage of equipment.

(c)* *Frequency of Leakage Current.* The leakage current limits stated in 7-5.1.3.4, 7-5.1.3.5, and 7-5.1.3.6 shall be rms values for dc and sinusoidal waveforms up to 1 kHz. For frequencies above 1 kHz, the leakage current limits shall be the values given in 7-5.1.3.4, 7-5.1.3.5, and 7-5.1.3.6 multiplied by the frequency, in kHz, up to a maximum of 10 mA.

**A-7-5.1.3.3(c)** The limits for nonsinusoidal periodic, modulated, and transient waveforms remain to be determined.

For complex leakage-current waveforms, a single reading from an appropriate metering system can represent the physiologically effective value of the composite waveform, provided that the contribution of each component to the total reading is weighted in accordance with 7-5.1.3.3(c). This weighting can be achieved by a frequency-response-shaping network that precedes a flat-response meter, or by a meter whose own frequency-response characteristic matches 7-5.1.3.3(c).

(d) *Leakage Current in Relation to Polarity.* Leakage current measurements shall be made with the polarity of the power line normal, with the power switch of the appliance in the position shown in Table 7-5.1.3.3(d), and with all operating controls in the position to cause maximum leakage current readings.

*Table 7-5.1.3.3(d)*

| Par. No. | Power Switch Setting | |
| --- | --- | --- |
| | **On and Off** | **On** |
| 7-5.1.3.4 | X | |
| 7-5.1.3.5 | X | |
| 7-5.1.3.6(a) | | X |
| 7-5.1.3.6(b) | | X |
| 7-5.1.3.6(c) | X | |
| 7-5.1.3.6(d) | | X |
| 7-5.1.3.6(e) | | X |

Leakage current is to be measured using power that is supplied directly from the normal electrical distribution, not from power supplied from an isolation transformer. Otherwise, incorrect values will result because neither power conductor would be tied to ground.

**7-5.1.3.4 Chassis Leakage Current, Fixed Equipment.** Permanently wired appliances in the patient care vicinity shall be tested prior to installation while the equipment is temporarily insulated from ground. The leakage current from frame to ground of permanently wired appliances installed in general or critical patient care areas shall not exceed 5.0 mA with all grounds lifted.

After installation, it may not be easy to disconnect ground(s) or temporarily insulate an appliance from ground. It is also very unlikely that the grounding will be disturbed after being permanently wired. Permanently wired appliances can thus be considered a part of a building's wiring system after installation. This is the reason the tests conducted after installation are different from those conducted during installation. [See 7-6.2.1.2(b) Exception No. 4.]

### 7-5.1.3.5 Chassis Leakage Current, Portable Equipment.

(a) The leakage current for cord-connected appliances shall be measured. The limit shall be 300 microamperes. Figure 7-5.1.3.5 shows one method of performing this test.

If multiple devices are connected together and one power cord supplies power, the leakage current shall be measured as an assembly.

When multiple devices are connected together and more than one power cord supplies power, the devices shall be separated into groups according to their power supply cord and the leakage current shall be measured independently for each group as an assembly.

*Exception No. 1: Where existing or special equipment (such as mobile X-ray machines) exhibits chassis leakage current between 300 and 500 microamperes, this condition does not represent a hazard to the patient as long as the grounding connection is intact. Such equipment shall be permitted to be kept in service provided a documented maintenance schedule is established to ensure the integrity of the grounding connection. A three-month interval is a nominal period. Depending on the intensity of the use of the appliance and prior test data, the hospital shall be permitted to establish a protocol with shortened or lengthened time intervals.*

*Exception No. 2: Where existing equipment exceeds 500 microamperes, methods to reduce leakage current, such as the addition of small isolation transformers to that device, or methods that provide equivalent safety by adding redundant equipment ground are permissible.*

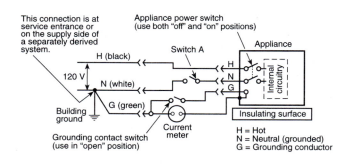

**Figure 7-5.1.3.5** *Test circuit for measuring chassis leakage current.*

For many years, the limit for chassis leakage current of patient-care-related appliances in the United States was 100 microamperes under all circumstances (e.g., ground open, reversed polarity). For the 1990 edition, the former Committee on Health Care Facilities received proposals to raise the limit to 500 microamperes with the ground open. The primary rationale behind this proposed increase was the fact that the 500-microampere limit had been the value specified in the international standard, IEC (International Electrotechnical Commission) 60601-1, *Medical Electrical Equipment* [3], for years. IEC 60601-1 had been used in European countries for more than 10 years and was widely accepted in many other countries.

This proposal prompted considerable debate among members of the then Subcommittee on Electrical Equipment and the Technical Committee on Health Care Facilities.

Those in favor of raising the limit to 500 microamperes argued that the European experience with a 500-microampere limit had not proven to be hazardous and that there were important economic reasons for harmony in standards. They also argued that the IEC had sound epidemiological evidence for setting its limit at 500 microamperes under single-fault conditions, which included an open ground. The 100-microampere limit in NFPA 99 also included two exceptions that allowed existing equipment with up to 250 microamperes and existing or special equipment with up to 500 microamperes to be used if certain precautions and maintenance were performed (e.g., ensuring the integrity of the appliance's ground).

Opponents of this proposal argued that there was sound experimental evidence supporting the U.S. 100-microampere limit in the first place and that later data have not changed that rationale. The U.S. limit included a safety factor greater than the IEC limit. They also pointed out that the patient environment had become much more complex over the past decade, with patients connected to multiple devices becoming the norm. Also, the IEC concept of a *single fault* differed from U.S. criteria. For an explanation of the rationale for the 100-microampere limit in greater detail, see A-9-2.1.13.4(c).

Both sides debated the relative probabilities of a device's ground opening and the chassis leakage current finding its way into the heart of a patient to cause injury. There was much discussion concerning whether the quantity of instrumentation in the rest of the world was as great as in the United States and, therefore, whether non-U.S. experiences with the higher value were even relevant in the United States.

The NFPA Standards Council (via a complaint over Association action) voted to return the proposal to committee, thereby retaining the 100-microampere limit for the 1990 edition of NFPA 99. The issue was appealed to the NFPA Board of Directors, which sustained the decision of the Standards Council.

The debate both within the United States and between the United States and IEC continued over this criterion for chassis leakage current limit, however. The then Subcommittee on Electrical Equipment again reviewed this issue extensively during the revision for the 1993 edition. A public forum was held in the summer of 1991. The subcommittee arrived at the consensus that a 300-microampere limit was a reasonable compromise between increments in safety and increments in cost. It also provided a level of harmonization with IEC 60601-1. [3]

The second paragraph of text that deals with multiple appliances was added during the revision of the 1984 edition of NFPA 99. For rack-mounted or cart-mounted appliances with one power cord, the leakage current is the sum from each appliance. It is this sum that will pass through a person should the ground of the power cord be broken and the person touch the chassis of the cart or rack and some ground. (See also commentary under 9-2.1.3.8.)

Paragraph 3 of the text was added to the 1990 edition to further clarify how measurements were to be made when several power cords were involved in the assembly, as with some computer systems. Because of interconnections, grounding may still be intact if one power cord loses ground and multiple power cords are used.

(b) Measurements shall be made with the appliance ground broken in two modes of appliance operation: power plug connected normally and with the appliance both on and off (if equipped with an on/off switch). When the appliance has fixed redundant grounding (e.g., permanently fastened to the grounding system), the chassis leakage current test shall be conducted with the redundant grounding intact. Test shall be made with Switch A in Figure 7-5.1.3.5 closed.

It may seem unproductive to measure the leakage current with the redundant ground intact, because redundant grounding presents a dead short across the meter input that causes the measured leakage current to read zero. The Committee on Electrical Equipment believes, however, that the leakage current measurement should still be made as a check that the redundant grounding is indeed in place. Because redundant grounding is used only in potentially hazardous circumstances, it is worthwhile to check its presence.

The polarity-reversal test done by users (facilities) was eliminated when former NFPA 76B was adopted in 1980. Manufacturers were, and still are, required to test appliances in both the normal and reversed polarity modes. Because manufacturers conducted both tests, the probability of a problem occurring when received by the end user was perceived to be low, the result being the relaxation of testing requirements for the end user.

### 7-5.1.3.6  Lead Leakage Current Tests and Limits, Portable Equipment.

See 7-5.1.3.3 for general requirements governing the conducting of leakage current tests.

(a)* *Lead to Ground (Nonisolated Input).* The leakage current between all patient leads connected together and ground shall be measured with the power plug connected normally and the device on. Figure 7-5.1.3.6(a) is an example of an acceptable test configuration. The leakage current shall not exceed 100 microamperes for ground wire open and closed.

**A-7-5.1.3.6(a)** Although the chassis leakage current value is 300 microamperes, patient lead leakage current limit for nonisolated input has been intentionally limited to 100 microamperes.

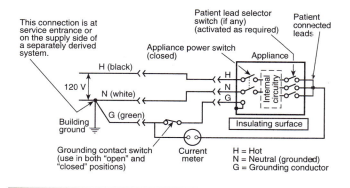

***Figure 7-5.1.3.6(a)*** *Test circuit for measuring leakage current between patient leads and ground (nonisolated).*

This decision is in recognition of the need for a greater level of electrical safety for those portions of devices that make direct electrical patient connection.

The committee added this appendix material to this 1999 edition because of questions on the apparent inconsistency between chassis leakage current limit and lead leakage values for nonisolated inputs.

(b) *Lead to Ground (Isolated Input).* The leakage current between each patient lead and ground for an appliance with isolated leads shall be measured with the power plug connected normally and the device on. Figure 7-5.1.3.6(b) is an example of an acceptable test configuration. The leakage current shall not exceed 10 microamperes with the ground intact and 50 microamperes with the ground open.

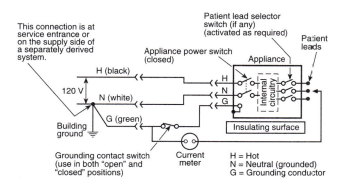

***Figure 7-5.1.3.6(b)*** *Test circuit for measuring leakage current between patient leads and ground (isolated).*

For the 1990 edition of NFPA 99, the limit for the lead leakage current in 7-5.1.3.6(b) was changed from 10 microamperes under all conditions to 50 microamperes with the ground open. This change was made to be consistent with the requirements of the International Electrotechnical Commission Standard IEC 60601-1. [3] The 50-microampere value has been the standard in much of the world for years.

(c) *Isolation Test (Isolated Input).* The current driven into the leads of an appliance that has isolated leads, when an external power source at line voltage and frequency is applied between each lead and ground, shall be measured in accordance with Figure 7-5.1.3.6(c). The leakage current shall not exceed 50 microamperes in each case. The test is made with the appliance's normal patient cables.

Suitable safety precautions (such as including a resistance in series to limit the current, insulation of the meter, and a momentary switch) shall be taken to protect the operator.

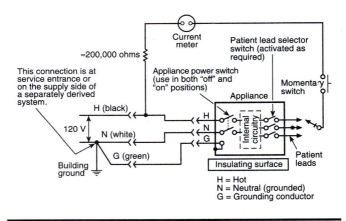

*Figure 7-5.1.3.6(c)* *Test circuit for measuring the electrical isolation of isolated patient leads.*

In appliances without a power cord or with ungrounded, exposed conductive surfaces, measurements shall be made with the exposed conductive surfaces temporarily grounded. If there is no exposed conductive surface, measurement shall be made with a simulated surface, as described in 9-2.1.13.4(b), Appliances with No Exposed Conductive Surfaces, that is also temporarily grounded.

Only isolated patient leads shall be connected to intracardiac catheters or electrodes.

The limit for this sink current—that is, the current driven by an external source into the isolated patient leads—was increased from 20 microamperes to 50 microamperes in the 1993 edition of NFPA 99. This was done because experience showed that there was limited hazard at this level. The limit is now in harmony with international standards.

The cautionary language of the second paragraph was added to the 1984 edition because the hazard associated with this test is present wherever it is accomplished. (The cautionary note had previously been included only in manufacturer requirements.)

(d) *Between Leads (Nonisolated Input).* The leakage current between any one lead (not ground) and each other lead shall be measured. Figure 7-5.1.3.6(d)/(e) is an example of an acceptable test configuration. The leakage current shall not exceed 50 microamperes for the ground wire open and closed.

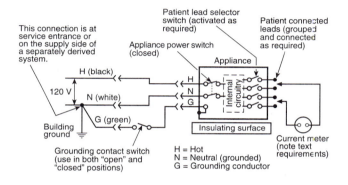

***Figure 7-5.1.3.6(d)/(e)*** *Test circuit for measuring leakage current between patient leads (nonisolated and isolated).*

(e) *Between Leads (Isolated Input).* The leakage current between any one lead (not ground) and each other lead shall be measured. Figure 7-5.1.3.6(d)/(e) is an example of an acceptable test configuration. The leakage current shall not exceed 10 microamperes with the ground intact and 50 microamperes with the ground open.

For the 1990 edition of NFPA 99, the leakage current limit, when measured with the ground wire open, was changed from 10 microamperes to 50 microamperes. For details of this significant change, see commentary under 7-5.1.3.6(b).

## 7-5.2 Nonpatient Electrical Appliances and Equipment.

The only criteria developed for nonpatient electrical appliances and equipment by the Committee on Electrical Equipment are for those nonpatient appliances used in patient care areas and laboratories. These are situations in which problems have been reported or that present unusual electrical risks to staff or patients. No criteria have been developed thus far for office equipment, maintenance equipment, and so forth.

Users should also realize that manufacturers of nonmedical devices that happen to be used in patient care areas are within their rights to advise purchasers that their device is not a medical device if they (the manufacturer) make no claims, written or otherwise, about their device's acceptability for use in a medical application.

**7-5.2.1 Permanently Connected (Fixed).** (Reserved)

**7-5.2.2 Cord- and Plug-Connected (Portable).**

**7-5.2.2.1 Patient Care Area.** The leakage current for facility-owned appliances (e.g., housekeeping or maintenance appliances) that are used in a patient care vicinity and are likely to contact the patient shall be measured. The leakage current shall be less than 500 microamperes. Tests shall be made with Switch A in Figure 7-5.1.3.5 in the open position for two-wire equipment that is not double-insulated.

Household or office appliances not commonly equipped with grounding conductors in their power cords shall be permitted provided they are not located within the patient care vicinity. For example, electric typewriters, pencil sharpeners, and clocks at nurses' stations, or electric clocks or TVs that are normally outside the patient care vicinity but might be in a patient's room, shall not be required to have grounding conductors in their power cords.

Requirements, as well as commentary, relative to appliances not owned by a facility are covered in 7-6.2.1.10. In this 1999 edition, the last sentence to the first paragraph was added to correlate with a correction made in 9-2.1.13.4(a).

**7-5.2.2.2\* Laboratory.**

Previously, this material was applicable only to electrical equipment used in hazardous areas of laboratories. Several proposals have been submitted to the Committee on Laboratories (responsible for the material on electrical hazards of laboratory equipment) regarding the complete deletion of this paragraph.

In 1996, this material, previously in Section 7-6, was moved and revised to apply to all new electrical equipment in laboratories. The committee believes all electrical equipment needs to meet a minimum level of safety. Text was also revised in 1996 to clarify that the current edition of NFPA 45, *Standard on Fire Protection for Laboratories Using Chemicals* [4], is the lead document on this subject.

**A-7-5.2.2.2** As a guideline, 500 microamperes is recommended as the maximum allowable leakage current limit for laboratory equipment.

This appendix material was added in 1990 for guidance only. Laboratories generally contain a wide variety of instruments, some cord connected and some permanently wired. A single limit of 500 microamperes would not be appropriate in all instances. The 500-microamperes limit might be appropriate for most cord-connected instruments, but the limits of 7-5.1.3.4 might be more appropriate for fixed equipment.

(a) Portable equipment intended for laboratory use shall be grounded or otherwise arranged with an approved method to protect personnel against shock.

(b) All electrical heating equipment to be used for laboratory procedures shall be equipped with overtemperature-limit controls so arranged that thermostatic failure will not result in hazardous temperatures. When such equipment is intended for use with flammable or combustible liquids, its electrical components shall be explosionproof, intrinsically safe, or ventilated in a manner that will prevent accumulation of flammable atmospheres under normal conditions of operation.

(c) Heating equipment equipped with fans shall be arranged with an interlock arranged to disconnect the heating elements when the fan is inoperative, unless the fan is not essential to safe operation.

(d)* Electrical equipment intended for use in laboratories shall meet the requirements of NFPA 45, *Standard for Laboratories Using Chemicals*.

**A-7-5.2.2.2(d)** Electrical equipment has been a frequent source of ignition of flammable concentrations of gases and vapors when combustible and flammable liquids and gases have been used in or near equipment not designed or safe for such use. While general and special ventilation will usually prevent the accumulation of flammable concentrations of gases and vapors in health care laboratories, the hazards should be recognized. Recommended practice is to evaluate at least annually what combustible and flammable liquids and gases are being used in the laboratory, what electrical equipment is exposed to flammable vapors and gases routinely or under reasonably foreseeable circumstances, whether special listed and labeled electrical equipment is available and justified, or whether equivalent safety can be provided more economically and practically by ventilation or quantity limitations.

As an educational measure in laboratories that have many personnel and electrical devices and that handle combustible or flammable liquids in containers larger than 1.69 oz (50 ml), electrical equipment not listed or labeled for use in hazardous atmospheres should be marked with precautionary signs or labels with a legend such as:

May ignite flammable vapors or gases. Not safe for use with exposed organic liquids with flash point temperatures below 100°F (37.8°C) (or the temperature of the high-limit cutoff if the equipment is designed for heating, e.g., oil bath or hot plate).

# 7-6 Administration

## 7-6.1 Responsibilities of Governing Body.

(Reserved)

## 7-6.2 Policies.

### 7-6.2.1 General.

**7-6.2.1.1** Medical and surgical electrical instrumentation and monitoring devices, as well as all electric appliances used for the care and entertainment of the patient, purchased or otherwise acquired for use by the facility (e.g., leased, donated, constructed on-site, loaned, etc.), shall meet the safety performance criteria of 9-2.1, Patient-Care-Related Electrical Appliances, in Chapter 9, "Manufacturer Requirements."

The reference to Chapter 9 is included for information on manufacturer requirements. Users are not required to meet manufacturer requirements. User tests are those specified in this chapter.

### 7-6.2.1.2 Testing Intervals.

(a) The facility shall establish policies and protocols for the type of test and intervals of testing for each appliance.

(b) All appliances used in patient care areas shall be tested in accordance with 7-5.1.3 or 7-5.2.2.1 before being put into service for the first time and after repair or modification. Patient-care-related electrical appliances shall be retested at intervals determined by their normal location or area of normal use, but not exceeding the intervals listed below:

General care areas—12 months

Critical care areas—6 months

Wet locations—6 months

*Exception No. 1: The testing intervals listed are intended to be nominal values, and facilities shall be permitted to adopt a protocol using either longer or shorter intervals provided that there is a documented justification based on previous safety testing records for the equipment in question, unusually light or heavy utilization, or similar considerations.*

*Exception No. 2: Facility-owned household or other appliances that are used in the patient care vicinity, but that are not intended to contact the patient, shall be tested at intervals deemed appropriate by the facility. Some equipment in this category requires only an infrequent visual inspection. The facility shall be permitted to structure a testing protocol and frequency for some equipment that might be more limited than that prescribed in 7-5.1.3.*

*Exception No. 3: The tests specified in 7-5.1.3.6, Lead Leakage Current Tests and Limits, Portable Equipment, shall be required only for incoming inspections and following repairs and modifications that might have compromised the patient lead leakage current.*

The establishment of testing intervals is intended to eliminate the possibility of utilizing unsafe devices in patient care areas. Justification for interval periods may be based on the device's design, manufacturing guidelines, application or life-support function, age, performance history and institutional experiences with similar devices, and risk level (i.e., the type of hazard to be prevented).

Exception No. 3 was included to clarify that these tests should not be conducted routinely. The isolation test, in fact, can be hazardous and can damage nonisolated patient equipment if not performed by knowledgeable persons. The percentage of existing appliances failing the test (i.e., those not working at all), aside from those whose failure was readily apparent, was so low that requiring the test on a periodic basis was not considered productive.

*Exception No. 4:\* After the installation of fixed equipment, it shall be tested periodically in accordance with 3-3.3.2.3, and meet the following criteria:*

*(a) 500 mV for general care areas*
*(b) 40 mV for critical care areas*

**A-7-6.2.1.2b, Exception No. 4.** The 500-mV limit is based on physiological values. Since the actual voltages normally measured in modern construction are usually less than 10 mV with nominal construction, voltages exceeding 20 mV might indicate a deteriorating condition and should be investigated.

The 40-mV limit is based on physiological values. Since the actual voltages normally measured in modern construction are usually less than 10 mV with nominal construction, voltages exceeding 20 mV might indicate a deteriorating condition and should be investigated.

This text was moved here from Chapter 3 because it applies to electrical equipment, not the electrical system.

**7-6.2.1.3 Protection of Patients with Direct Electrical Pathways to the Heart.** Only equipment that is specifically designed for the purpose, that is, provided with suitable isolated patient leads or connections *(see 9-2.1.12, Direct Electrical Pathways to the Heart),* shall be connected directly to electrically conductive pathways to a patient's heart. Such electrically conductive pathways include intracardiac electrodes such as implanted pacemaker leads and guide wires. The facility shall have a policy that prohibits the use of external cardiac pacemakers and pacing leads with external terminals that are not properly protected from potentially hazardous contact with conductive surfaces.

This text was moved here from Chapter 3 because it applies to electrical equipment, not the electrical system.

**7-6.2.1.4 Controls.** Electrical appliance controls (such as bed, pillow speakers, television, and nurse-call controls) that do not meet the minimum requirements of 9-2.1, Patient-Care-Related Electrical Appliances, shall be mounted so that they cannot be taken into the bed.

*Exception: Existing low-voltage controls used in general patient-care areas.*

**7-6.2.1.5 Adapters and Extension Cords.** Adapters and extension cords shall be permitted to be used. The wiring shall be tested for physical integrity, polarity, and continuity of grounding at the time of assembly and periodically thereafter. Adapters and extension cords shall meet the requirements of 7-5.1.2.6.

*Exception: Three-to-two-prong adapters shall not be permitted.*

The scope of this section was changed in 1990 to include extension cords, in addition to adapters, as this was the original intent of the former Committee on Safe Use of Electricity in Patient Care Areas.

Conducting periodic performance verification of adapters and extension cords as part of the equipment control program will be effective only if all adapters and extension cords are properly identified. Each adapter or extension cord introduced into patient care areas needs to be so labeled to facilitate its identification and subjection to periodic testings.

Caution is advised in the use of extension cords. They are intended to be temporary and are not intended to replace an adequate number of receptacles. Extension cords, in their original concept, were meant as a one-for-one extension of an appliance cord when the cord did not reach (easily or otherwise) a receptacle. They, in essence, extended the receptacle beyond the wall. Over time, extension cords were also expanded to allow more than one appliance to be plugged into them. This is when trouble began. With more than a one-for-one capability, the original wall receptacle could now support more electrical loading than was originally intended or designed. Overloading can lead to overheating and fires. As such, adequate branches (and receptacles) should be added to meet anticipated electrical loads in an area. Extension cords are not to be substituted as a means to correct this problem.

Text was revised in 1996 to clearly indicate that the use of three-to-two adapters is prohibited and to eliminate reference to distinctive plugs. Distinctive plugs can have appropriate extension cords. Reference was also added to 7-5.1.2.6, which mandates high-quality construction for adapters and extension cords.

**7-6.2.1.6\*  Appliances Intended to Deliver Electrical Energy.** Electrical-energy-delivering appliances shall conform to the leakage, grounding, and other requirements of this chapter when powered but not delivering energy.

**A-7-6.2.1.6** When delivering energy, such appliances may deviate from these requirements only to the extent essential for their intended clinical function.

Appliances that intentionally or that can inadvertently apply electrical energy to the patient or to components in contact with the patient require special safety considerations.

Since there is a wide range of power levels, output frequencies, and purposes of appliances that apply electricity directly to patients or to patient-connected devices, it is not feasible to cite them in detail.

This requirement was previously included only in the manufacturer portion of NFPA 99 but is now included here because of its applicability to health care facility personnel conducting leakage current tests.

Although it is primarily the responsibility of the manufacturer to design safe power-delivering equipment, facility personnel are responsible for ensuring that the equipment functions properly and is used correctly. This responsibility is particularly important where repairs are made by facility personnel.

**7-6.2.1.7  Specification of Conditions of Purchase.** The procurement authority shall include in its purchasing documents any appropriate requirements or conditions specifically related to the facility's use of the appliance, including, but not restricted to, the following:

(a)  The type of appliance listing or certification required, if any
(b)  The delivery of manufacturer's test data, where pertinent
(c)  Special conditions of use (such as in anesthetizing or other locations with special hazards)
(d)  Unusual environmental conditions (such as high humidity, moisture, salt spray, etc.), and
(e)*  The type of electric power system (i.e., grounded or isolated) intended to energize the appliance, the nature of the overcurrent devices, the use of auxiliary emergency power, and so forth, when pertinent

**A-7-6.2.1.7(e)**  The facility might wish to reference compliance with this chapter and Chapter 9 on its purchasing document.

Specific documents addressing, among other issues, items (a) through (e) of 7-6.2.1.7 are used by some hospitals. The document is attached to all purchase requisitions issued for electrically powered patient care appliances. Over the years, this policy has helped control the introduction of items with compliance deficiencies and has ensured the hospital future access to replacement parts and product safety enhancements.

**7-6.2.1.8*  Manuals for Appliances.**  Purchase specifications shall require the vendor to supply suitable manuals for operators or users upon delivery of the appliance. The manuals shall include installation and operating instructions, inspection and testing procedures, and maintenance details. *[See 9-2.1.8.1(m).]*

The requirements here and the recommendations in A-7-6.2.1.8 can be incorporated into a condition-of-purchase document. (See 7-6.2.1.7.) In addition, the user can request that the vendor provide all safety-related enhancements for the duration of the life of the device.

**A-7-6.2.1.8**  Consideration should be given to requiring the vendor to sell parts to the individual or group designated by the hospital to service the equipment following the warranty period.

**7-6.2.1.9  System Demonstration.**  Any system consisting of several electric appliances shall be demonstrated as a complete system, after installation, by the vendor designated to assume system responsibility, and prior to acceptance of the system by the facility. The vendor shall demonstrate the operation of the system and provide appropriate initial instruction to operators and maintenance personnel.

*Exception: Facilities that assemble their own systems.*

A facility should consider expanding the demonstration into a training program if many staff members will be using the system or if the system is very complex. It might even be necessary to periodically repeat the demonstration or program.

**7-6.2.1.10 Electrical Equipment Systems.** Purchase contracts for electrical equipment systems, such as nurse call and signaling, that consist of interconnected elements, shall require that the elements be listed to function together, that the manufacturers provide appropriate documentation for such interconnection, and that the systems be installed by personnel qualified to do such installations.

> The committee added this new section in the 1999 edition because of the increase in medical electrical equipment being used in the form of interconnected elements. This equipment can be obtained from a variety of manufacturers and installed by anyone. For patient safety, these systems must function as a whole. If the entire process has not been coordinated, patient safety can be compromised.

**7-6.2.1.11 Appliances Not Provided by the Facility.** Policies shall be established for the control of appliances not supplied by the facility.

> Specific policies will depend on the facility's resources and staff, but some type of control over this group of appliances is essential for both patient and staff safety as well as legal liability purposes.
>
> Some of the questions that should be asked when dealing with appliances that have not been supplied by the facility include the following: Is the appliance a medical device or does the manufacturer make no claims as to its design or use as a medical device? Is the device to be used by the facility staff on the patient? Is the appliance owned by the patient and to be used only by the patient?
>
> One possible policy is to subject all equipment that is brought into the facility for use to an incoming inspection as if the equipment were owned by the facility. These inspections would be made for all equipment (whether owned by a patient or staff member) brought into the facility. Periodic checks should be made to ascertain whether the equipment still within the facility continues to meet requirements or whether it has been damaged.

**7-6.2.2 Servicing and Maintenance of Equipment.**

**7-6.2.2.1** Service manuals, instructions, and procedures provided by the manufacturer shall be used in the maintenance of equipment.

**7-6.2.2.2** A scheduled preventive maintenance program shall be followed.

**7-6.2.2.3** Areas designated for the servicing of oxygen equipment shall be clean, free of oil and grease, and not used for the repair of other equipment.

**7-6.2.2.4** Defective electrical apparatus shall be tagged and repaired or discarded.

**7-6.2.2.5** Administrative vigilance shall be exercised to monitor the use of appliances and portable electrical equipment, such as drills, that can cause electrical interference during operative procedures.

> This paragraph was revised in 1996 to reflect both the fact that flammable inhalation anesthetics are no longer used in the United States and that there is an increased

concern over certain electrical devices interfering with the proper operation of other electrical devices.

### 7-6.2.3 During Surgery.

**7-6.2.3.1** Active electrodes or other applicators of electrosurgical devices shall be properly secured, as recommended by the manufacturer of the device, when not in active use. This includes, but is not limited to, electrosurgical devices, surgical lasers, electrocautery, and fiberoptics.

These provisions were introduced for the 1993 edition to reduce the risk of fire ignited by appliances that generate high energy. It is recognized that appliances such as electrosurgical units and lasers intentionally deliver energy at levels high enough to ignite flammable materials in the operating field. This may be further exacerbated by oxygen or nitrous oxide concentrations leaking from the ventilation system or by the presence of flammable liquids such as isopropyl alcohol. Research into the development of nonflammable drapes has been ongoing for many years, but a solution has yet to be found that is economical, maintains appropriate levels of fire safety and sterility, is convenient, and is safe for the environment.

Fire safety in the operating room requires a continuing training program for all operating room staff on the hazards of high-energy surgical devices.

**7-6.2.3.2** The cable that provides power from the electrosurgical generator to the active electrode shall be disconnected from the generator when contamination occurs.

The increasing use of multiple electrosurgical units during a procedure, and the automatic action capabilities of these units, has heightened the danger of the inadvertent activation of electrosurgical units. The common practice of dropping a contaminated electrode and allowing it to dangle in, or beside, the drapes has been implicated in several operating room fires.

### 7-6.2.4 During Administration of Respiratory Therapy.

**7-6.2.4.1\*** Electrical equipment used within the site of intentional expulsion shall have no hot surfaces. When only the remote control or signal leads of a device are to be used in the site of intentional expulsion, only the control or signal leads shall be required to comply with this section.

**A-7-6.2.4.1** For further information, see manufacturer requirements for equipment used within the site of intentional expulsion in 9-2.1.9.3.

*Exception: Small (less than 2 W), hermetically sealed heating elements such as light bulbs.*

For the 1987 edition of NFPA 99, the concept of the term *site of administration* was replaced by the term *site of intentional expulsion*. The earlier term had been established when NFPA 56B, *Standard for Respiratory Therapy,* was developed in the 1960s. The new term was a way of creating an easily identifiable and enforceable boundary [e.g., 1 ft (30 cm) around vents or expulsion points of oxygen-delivery equipment] where no electrical equipment was to be brought unless it was listed for use in an oxygen-enriched atmosphere. This 1-ft (30-cm) boundary was a conservative value. It was known, and has since been measured in a controlled study, that any escaping oxygen is quickly diluted into the atmosphere, and that oxygen concentrations return to normal levels at approximately 2 in. to 5 in. (5 cm to 13 cm).

The new term was incorporated into NFPA 99 through a proposal that redefined the hazardous area to just that area where oxygen or an oxygen-enriched atmosphere was deliberately vented to the atmosphere. (For examples of this concept, refer to the definition of *site of intentional expulsion* in Chapter 2.) The proposal reflected a 1986 hospital study on the number and type of incidents reported over the years and the current practices in hospitals. However, while the hazardous area is now smaller and more reflective of where higher-than-normal oxygen levels will occur, it does not negate all the other precautions that need to be observed when oxygen is being administered (e.g., no smoking in the room).

The requirements in this section are intended for users within health care facilities. Manufacturer requirements are more complex and are listed in 9-2.1.9.3.

**7-6.2.4.2\*** Electrical equipment used within oxygen delivery equipment shall be listed for use in oxygen-enriched atmospheres, or sold with the intent to be used in oxygen-enriched atmospheres.

Paragraphs 7-6.2.4.1 and 7-6.2.4.2 reflect a major change made in 1987 regarding the extent of area considered hazardous when oxygen is administered for respiratory therapy purposes. (See commentary under 7-6.2.4.1 and under the definition of *site of intentional expulsion* in Chapter 2 for a description of this change.)

For changes in manufacturer criteria associated with this change, see 9-2.1.9.3.

**A-7-6.2.4.2** For further information, see manufacturer requirements for equipment used in oxygen delivery equipment in 9-2.1.

The use of electrical equipment in spaces where there is a high oxygen content is a matter of concern because of the fire hazard. It is particularly a problem where the oxygen is "pure," that is, 80–90 percent, because materials not very flammable in ordinary air become extremely flammable in pure oxygen.

In medical practice, particularly in surgery, patients are often given supplemental oxygen, via respirator, anesthesia machines, and so forth. Such supplements may range from room air to 100 percent oxygen. Clearly, different levels of protection are needed.

This standard addresses the problem by defining three elements of the situation:

(a) *Kind of Air.* An Oxygen-Enriched Atmosphere (OEA) is air that ranges from slightly enriched (23.5 percent rather than 21 percent) to total oxygen (100 percent).

(b) *Kind of Apparatus.* Oxygen Delivery Equipment (ODE) is a device to deliver an OEA to a patient.

(c) *Kind of Space.* A Site of Intentional Expulsion (SIE) is a small volume where oxygen that has been delivered to the patient is discharged to the ambient air.

When an OEA is within an ODE, it is much more likely to have a high concentration of oxygen. Paragraph 9-2.1.9.3 therefore advises manufacturers, and 7-6.2.4.2 advises users, of precautions to take to reduce the fire hazard. Paragraph 9-2.1.9.3 lists four ways of attacking the problem. Note that an OEA can be created not only in a ventilator or oxygen tubing, but also in an oxygen tent or incubator. Special precautions should be taken.

At the other extreme of hazard is a space in the open air, the SIE. This space is defined as within 12 in. (30.5 cm) of the exhaust port, because, in most instances, dilution to ambient levels occurs within a few inches of the port; 12 in. (30.5 cm) provides an adequate safety factor. Paragraph 9-2.1.9.3 provides guidance to minimize this hazard by requiring that only those parts of the apparatus that are intended to be within the SIE are of concern. Even these, such as nurse call buttons, leads, and so forth, do not necessarily need to be listed for use in OEA because they usually conform to provisions of subparagraph (d), that is, they do not have hot surfaces and they meet the requirements of Figures 9-2.1.9.3(a) through (f).

The intent of 7-6.2.4.2 is to advise users to specify appliances that meet higher requirements where the hazard is higher, but not to overspecify where the hazard is minimal. Thus, as they are ordinarily used, nurse call buttons, pillow speakers, and so forth, do not need to be listed for use in oxygen-enriched atmospheres.

Note, however, that these requirements apply only to the intended use. The user should exercise vigilance to guard against an unintended use or an accidental failure, which can vastly increase the hazard.

The use of small device appendages, such as nurse call buttons and pillow speakers, in oxygen-enriched atmospheres has been the subject of heated debates in the health care community. Because the use of such appendages has been so widespread and the administration of supplemental oxygen ever increasing, a reasonable compromise on their use was needed.

The Committee on Electrical Equipment was aware that, while the text of 7-6.2.4.2 was technically correct, it was difficult for most users to fully comprehend. To clarify the issue, the lengthy appendix guidance in A-7-6.2.4.2 was added in 1996. It should be read not as an explicit recommendation, but as an educational exercise to aid the user to better understand the problem and the intended use of these appendages.

**7-6.2.4.3\*** When high-energy-delivering probes (such as defibrillator paddles) or other electrical devices that do not comply with 7-6.2.4.1 are deemed essential to the care of an individual patient and must be used within a site of administration or within oxygen delivery equipment, they shall be used with extreme caution.

**A-7-6.2.4.3** Where possible, combustible materials such as hair, fabric, and paper should be removed from the vicinity of where the energy is delivered. Water-soluble surgical jelly has been shown to dramatically reduce the combustibility of these materials.

Some of these types of devices will need to be used in emergencies such as cardiac arrest. As noted, extreme caution is to be exercised if oxygen is also being used.

### 7-6.2.5 Laboratory.

The use, inspection, and maintenance of electrical equipment and appliances used in laboratories need to be coordinated among all areas responsible for the equipment and appliances. Typically, the electrical safety, preventive maintenance, and hazard surveillance programs are all involved in laboratory electrical safety.

It is a good practice to include all aspects of electrical safety within the laboratory (equipment, wiring, maintenance, and testing) and to review them in conjunction with the facility-wide safety program to determine whether they conform to the requirements of the authority having jurisdiction.

**7-6.2.5.1\*** The laboratory shall establish policies and protocols for the type of test and intervals of testing for each appliance.

**A-7-6.2.5.1** One reason for requiring testing of all electrical equipment used in the laboratory is to provide minimum assurance against electrical macroshock hazards.

Because a document covering the electrical safety of laboratory equipment does not currently exist, the committee responsible for laboratory requirements considers it reasonable that electrical equipment intended for use in laboratories be tested for electrical safety. As noted in A-7-6.2.5.2, a study of incidents showed which devices were most involved with laboratory fires.

A *recommended* chassis leakage current limit is included in A-7-5.2.2.2.

**7-6.2.5.2\*** The physical integrity of the power cord and attachment plug and cord strain-relief shall be confirmed at least annually by visual inspection and other appropriate tests.

**A-7-6.2.5.2** Most laboratory fires involve biomedical or other electronic equipment failures. The most common ignition factors are short circuits or ground faults. Electrical wire or cable insulation is the material most likely to first ignite in a clinical laboratory fire. (Reference: Hoeltge, G.A., Miller, A., Klein, B.R., Hamlin, W.B., Accidental fires in clinical laboratories, *Arch Pathol Lab Med*, vol. 1, no. 17:1200-1204, 1993.)

Laboratories in many instances use combustible and flammable liquids and gases with or near electrical equipment that is not designed or safe for such use. Because electrical equipment has been a frequent source of ignition for such vapors and gases, a periodic assessment of the following is recommended:

(a) The types of combustible and flammable liquids and gases being used in the laboratory

(b)  The types of electrical equipment being exposed to flammable vapors and gases (either routinely or likely)

(c)  Whether special listed or labeled electrical equipment is available or justified

(d)  Whether equivalent safety can be provided more economically and practicably by ventilation or quantity limitations

Precautionary signs and labels should be used as appropriate.

## 7-6.3 Recordkeeping.

### 7-6.3.1 Patient Care Appliances.

**7-6.3.1.1 Instruction Manuals.** A permanent file of instruction and maintenance manuals as described in 9-2.1.8.1 shall be maintained and be accessible. It shall preferably be in the custody of the engineering group responsible for the maintenance of the appliance. Duplicate instruction manuals shall be available to the user. Any safety labels and condensed operating instructions on an appliance shall be maintained in readable condition.

**7-6.3.1.2\* Documentation.** A record shall be maintained of the tests required by this chapter and associated repairs or modifications. At a minimum, this record shall contain the date, unique identification of the equipment tested, and an indication of which items have met or have failed to meet the performance requirements of this section.

**A-7-6.3.1.2** While several approaches to documentation exist in hospitals, the minimum acceptable documentation should convey what was tested, when it was tested, and whether it performed successfully. Adopting a system of exception reporting can be the most efficient form of recordkeeping for routine rechecks of equipment or systems and thereby minimize technicians' time in recording the value of each measurement taken. For example, once a test protocol is established, which simply means testing the equipment or system consistent with this chapter, the only item (value) that needs to be recorded is what failure or what deviation from the requirements of the chapter was detected when a corrective action (repair) was undertaken. This approach can serve to eliminate, for example, the need to keep individual room sheets to record measured results on each receptacle or to record measurement values of all types of leakage current tests.

**7-6.3.1.3 Test Logs.** A log of test results and repairs shall be maintained and kept for an appropriate time.

## 7-6.4 Use.

(Reserved)

## 7-6.5 Qualification and Training of Personnel.

**7-6.5.1** Personnel concerned with the application and maintenance of electric appliances, including physicians, nurses, nurse aids, engineers, technicians, and orderlies, shall be cognizant of the risks associated with their use. To achieve this end, the hospital shall provide appropriate programs of continuing education for its personnel.

This program shall include periodic review of manufacturers' safety guidelines and usage requirements for electrosurgical units and similar appliances.

Continuing education programs are extremely important in hazard prevention. Although all professional personnel should be involved in ongoing training, it is especially important for engineers and technicians who install, repair, maintain, and evaluate medical appliances and systems.

**7-6.5.2** Personnel involved in the use of energy-delivering devices, including, but not limited to, electrosurgical units, surgical lasers, electrocauterizers, and fiberoptics, shall receive periodic training in fire suppression.

This paragraph was added in 1993 as a result of several serious fires in operating rooms. (See commentary under 7-6.2.3.1 for discussion on this topic.)

**7-6.5.3** Equipment shall be serviced by qualified personnel only.

Complying with this standard through the servicing and testing of medical appliances can eliminate hazardous conditions. The committee responsible for the material in this chapter believes that only qualified professionals can determine compliance with this standard's requirements. Due to the complexity of the hospital environment and the interdisciplinary training and background required to perform such tasks appropriately, safety technology for patient care appliances should be provided only by trained professionals.

### References Cited in Commentary

1. NFPA 70, *National Electrical Code®*, 1999 edition.
2. Federal Medical Devices Amendment Act of 1976 (PL 94-295).
3. International Electrotechnical Commission Standard (IEC) 60601-1 (1988-12), *Medical Electrical Equipment — Part 1: General Requirements for Safety.*
4. NFPA 45, *Standard on Fire Protection for Laboratories Using Chemicals,* 1996 edition.

# CHAPTER 8

# Gas Equipment

Fires in and around oxygen tents and other respiratory therapy apparatus, such as heated humidifiers, have occasionally occurred over the years. While the frequency of these fires was not great, they were often fatal, especially to those patients in oxygen tents. Recognizing that respiratory therapy equipment and treatment posed a significant hazard, especially in the presence of oxygen-enriched atmospheres, the late Dr. Carl Walter, then Chairman of the Hospitals Committee, appointed a subcommittee in 1964 to develop a safety standard for respiratory therapy. The result, NFPA 56B, *Standard for Respiratory Therapy,* was adopted as a tentative standard in 1966 and officially adopted two years later. The document addressed the many sources of respiratory therapy and the hazards associated with the use of respiratory equipment, especially when oxygen-enriched atmospheres were utilized. (See Chapter 2 for the definition of *oxygen-enriched atmosphere.*)

Since the oxygen-enriched atmosphere is usually an essential component of respiratory therapy, the prevention of fires revolves around the elimination of any sources of ignition and flammable substances within this atmosphere. A study revealed that the most likely causes of fires in oxygen tents were attempts by patients to smoke and sparking toys given to children in pediatric wards. Precautions relating to these hazards were incorporated into the standard.

The requirements of NFPA 56B (now divided between Chapters 4 and 8 of NFPA 99) are recognized and used by respiratory therapists and other hospital and fire safety personnel. Adherence to these requirements (both voluntarily and administratively) has drastically reduced the number of fires in and around respiratory therapy equipment.

In the 1996 edition, requirements and recommendations on *flammable* inhalation anesthetics were transferred to the then new Annex 2, "Flammable Anesthetizing Locations." Because of this text transfer, references in Chapters 1 through 20, and in

Appendixes A, B, and C, are only to the use of *nonflammable* inhalation anesthetics, including anesthetizing locations.

## 8-1* Scope

**A-8-1** *Application of Requirements.* The application of requirements contained in this chapter for specific types of health care facilities can be found in Chapters 12 through 18.

**8-1.1** This chapter covers the performance, maintenance, and testing of gas equipment used within health care facilities.

While this chapter is intended for use by respiratory therapists and other personnel in health care facilities, the guidance offered can also be used in the home care setting. The increased use of oxygen as a singular therapy, such as for the treatment of chronic obstructive pulmonary disease or in conjunction with other therapies like mechanical ventilation has increased the risk of oxygen-fed fires occurring in the home. Combined with the fact that the home environment is filled with potential sources of ignition — that in health care facilities have been restricted or eliminated altogether — the risks involved in home respiratory care are significant indeed. For example, up to half of patients on home oxygen admit to smoking, according to a Johns Hopkins University Study [1] cited by the American Association for Respiratory Care.

The use of membrane or pressure swing adsorber-type oxygen concentrators has increased dramatically in the past several years as a means of providing oxygen therapy in the home and in some health care facilities (primarily nursing homes). These devices produce high concentrations of oxygen, though at much lower flows than those possible from either high-pressure cylinder/regulator combinations or portable liquid reservoirs. Often the concentrator is located in one part of the patient's living quarters with long tubing to allow freedom of movement. This tubing is often run across the floor. If the tubing is severed, elevated concentrations of oxygen would be released at that point. Should this occur near a source of ignition, such as an electric motor or a pilot on a gas stove, a fire can result. (See Exhibit 8.1.)

**8-1.2*** This chapter applies to the use of nonflammable medical gases, vapors, and aerosols, and the equipment required for their administration, at normal atmospheric pressure.

The phrase *at normal atmospheric pressure* can cause confusion. Some equipment, such as IPPB machines, ventilators, and resuscitation equipment, functions internally at pressures above normal (room) atmospheric pressure, but the devices themselves are employed in a normal atmospheric pressure environment. This environment differs from the inside of a hyperbaric chamber in which a total environment above normal atmospheric pressure is created. (See 8-1.4.)

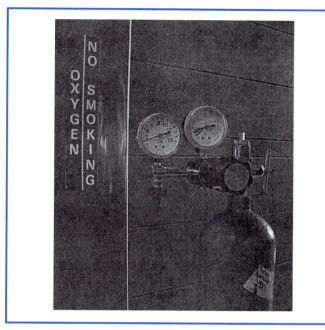

**Exhibit 8.1** *The presence of medical gases such as oxygen, a major consideration in health care fire safety. (Courtesy of Rob Swift and Prince William Health Systems.)*

**A-8-1.2** Respiratory therapy is an allied health specialty employed with medical direction in the treatment, management, control, diagnostic evaluation, and care of patients with deficiencies and abnormalities of the cardiopulmonary system.[1]

Respiratory therapy includes the therapeutic use of the following: medical gases and administration apparatus, environmental control systems, humidification, aerosols, medications, ventilatory support, broncho-pulmonary drainage, pulmonary rehabilitation, cardiopulmonary resuscitation, and airway management.[2]

There is a continual need for human diligence in the establishment and maintenance of safe practices for respiratory therapy. It is essential for personnel having responsibility for respiratory therapy to establish and enforce appropriate programs to fulfill provisions of this chapter.

It is the responsibility of the administrative and professional staff of a hospital, or safety director if one is appointed, to adopt and enforce appropriate regulations for a hospital. In other health care facilities, responsibility could be assigned to a safety director or other responsible person, who is, in turn, responsible to the administration.

[1]Courtesy of the American Association for Respiratory Therapy, 1720 Regal Row, Dallas, TX 75235.
[2]Ibid.

In institutions having a respiratory therapy service, it is recommended that this service be directly responsible for the administration of this chapter. Hazards can be mitigated only when there is continual recognition and understanding.

In 1999 the American Association for Respiratory Care estimated that there are 92,000 respiratory therapy practitioners in the United States. These practitioners can be instrumental in applying the requirements established in this chapter for health care facilities. (See Exhibit 8.2.)

*Exhibit 8.2* Respiratory therapy practitioners implementing requirements for safe use of gas equipment. (Courtesy of American Association for Respiratory Care.)

With increases in medical knowledge and advances in science and technology, the list of uses given in paragraph 2 of A-8-1.2 will be subject to additions, changes, or both.

**8-1.3** When used in this chapter, the term *oxygen* is intended to mean 100 percent oxygen as well as mixtures of oxygen and air.

This should not be confused with the air around us, which contains 21 percent oxygen under normal conditions.

**8-1.4\*** This chapter does not apply to special atmospheres, such as those encountered in hyperbaric chambers.

**A-8-1.4** See Chapter 19, "Hyperbaric Facilities."

# 8-2* Nature of Hazards

**A-8-2** See 7-2.2.2 for electrical hazards associated with gas equipment.

## 8-2.1 Fire and Explosions.

For further discussion on the issue of fires and explosions, see commentary under 12-4.1.2.10.

### 8-2.1.1 Inhalation Anesthetizing Locations.

**8-2.1.1.1** Oxygen and nitrous oxide, the gases normally used for relative analgesia and as components of general anesthesia, are strong oxidizing gases and individually or as a mixture support combustion quite readily.

Nitrous oxide will, in fact, support combustion in the absence of oxygen.

**8-2.1.1.2** Inhalation gases or vapors introduce fire, chemical, mechanical, and electrical hazards that are all interrelated. Any mixture of inhalation gases will support combustion. In an oxygen-enriched atmosphere, materials that are flammable and combustible in air ignite more easily and burn more vigorously. The materials that could be found on or near patients include hair oils, oil-based lubricants, skin lotions, clothing, linens, paper, rubber, alcohols, acetone, and some plastics.

Even a patient's body hair can be considered a combustible if the right circumstances and a high enough concentration of oxygen exist. For example, in an environment in which 100 percent oxygen escapes from a hand resuscitator and envelopes the patient's torso, a cardiac defibrillator can cause a spark if adequate contact gel is not used. If such a spark occurs while the oxygen is in use as just described, the patient's body hair could ignite.

**8-2.1.1.3** A hazard exists if any of the components of an oxygen or nitrous oxide supply system become contaminated with oil or grease.

Contamination need not be in large amounts or visible to the naked eye. At the pressures released inside regulators [>2000 psi (>14,480 kPa)] and with 100 percent oxygen, minute amounts of contaminant can cause the regulator to either catch fire or explode.

**8-2.1.1.4\*** Sources of ignition can include open flames, burning tobacco, electric heating coils, defective electrical equipment, and adiabatic heating of gases.

**A-8-2.1.1.4** Sudden compression or recompression of a gas to high pressure can generate large increase in temperature [up to 2000°F (1093°C)] that can ignite any organic material present, including grease. *(See also NFPA 53, Recommended Practice on Materials, Equipment, and Systems Used in Oxygen-Enriched Atmospheres.)*

Temperatures hot enough to melt some plastics used in respiratory care equipment do not normally seem dangerous. These same temperatures become extremely dangerous in an oxygen-enriched atmosphere because, instead of melting the plastics, such temperatures are sufficient to cause ignition of these materials.

**8-2.1.1.5** A hazard exists if either oxygen or nitrous oxide leaks into a closed space, creating an oxygen-enriched atmosphere.

**8-2.1.1.6** A hazard exists if improper components are employed to connect equipment containing pressurized oxygen or nitrous oxide.

### 8-2.1.2 During Respiratory Therapy Administration.

**8-2.1.2.1** The occurrence of a fire requires the presence of combustible or flammable materials, an atmosphere of oxygen or other oxidizing agents, and a source of ignition. Combustible materials can be unavoidably present when oxygen is being administered, but flammable liquids and gases and ignition sources are avoidable.

Any mixture of breathing gases used in respiratory therapy will support combustion. In an oxygen-enriched atmosphere, materials that are combustible and flammable in air ignite more easily and burn more vigorously. Materials not normally considered to be combustible may be so in an oxygen-enriched atmosphere.

**8-2.1.2.2** Combustible materials that could be found near patients who are to receive respiratory therapy include hair oils, oil-based lubricants, skin lotions, facial tissues, clothing, bed linen, tent canopies, rubber and plastic articles, gas-supply and suction tubing, ether, alcohols, and acetone.

It has become rare to find anesthetics such as cyclopropane and ether at the bedsides of patients on respiratory therapy or under any medical care. Because cyclopropane is no longer available commercially in the United States, the reference to it was dropped for this 1999 edition. Ether has been included in the requirements to draw attention to the possibility that flammable gases may be moved near patients (though it is very unlikely).

**8-2.1.2.3** A particular hazard exists when oxygen equipment becomes contaminated with oil, grease, or other combustible materials. Such contaminants will ignite readily and burn more rapidly in the presence of high oxygen concentrations and make it easier to ignite less combustible materials with which they come in contact.

An oxygen-enriched atmosphere normally exists in an oxygen tent, croup tent, incubator, and similar devices when supplemental oxygen is being employed in them. These devices are designed to maintain a concentration of oxygen higher than that found in the atmosphere.

Oxygen-enriched atmospheres can exist in the immediate vicinity of all oxygen administration equipment. *(See definition of Site of Intentional Expulsion in Section 2-2.)*

The transfer of liquid oxygen from one container to another container can create an oxygen-enriched atmosphere within the vicinity of the containers.

If oxygen is supplied by a container that stores the oxygen as a liquid, there will be a small amount of oxygen vented into the vicinity of the container after a period of nonuse of the equipment. Larger amounts of oxygen will be vented if the container is accidentally tipped over or placed on its side. This venting may create an oxygen-enriched atmosphere if the container is stored in a confined space *[see 4-3.1.1.2(a)9]*.

The hazard involves oxygen equipment at any pressure. Previously, reference had been to high-pressure oxygen equipment.

**8-2.1.2.4** Sources of ignition include not only the usual ones in ordinary atmospheres, but others that become significant hazards in oxygen-enriched atmospheres *(see 8-2.1.2.1)* such as the following:

(a) Open flames, burning tobacco, and electric radiant heaters are sources of ignition.

Lighted cigarettes, cigars, and pipes are the most common sources of ignition where respiratory therapy is administered. Smoking regulations should be developed to eliminate the introduction of these ignition sources into the area of administration. (See Chapter 2 for the definition of *area of administration* and 8-6.2.1 for requirements on elimination of sources of ignition.) Other sources of ignition such as alcohol and acetone, however, are generally still present at the bedside and used in conjunction with other respiratory care procedures, for example, removal of tape residue from a patient's face postextubation.

(b) The discharge of a cardiac defibrillator can serve as a source of ignition.

Such occurrences have been documented by committee members. In many of these instances, the rush of activities surrounding the patient resulted in a mask or cannula being removed from the patient without the oxygen supply to it being shut off. Flash fires developed when defibrillators were discharged.

(c) Arcing and excessive temperatures in electrical equipment are sources of ignition. Electrically powered oxygen apparatus and electrical equipment intended for use in an oxygen-enriched atmosphere are sources of ignition if electrical defects are present.

Electrically powered coagulation and cutting devices with energy levels of 10 W to 400 W are common open-spark sources in or near oxygen-enriched atmospheres. (For further details, see Annex 1, "The Safe Use of High-Frequency Electricity in Health Care Facilities.")
    An electrical safety inspection program should be instituted to detect problems before equipment deteriorates to the point that it can cause ignition.

(d) Electrical equipment not conforming to the requirements of 7-6.2.4.1, which can include, but is not limited to, electric razors, electric bed controls, hair dryers, remote television controls, and telephone handsets, can create a source of ignition if introduced into an oxygen-enriched atmosphere *(see 7-6.2.4.1).*

(e) A static discharge having an energy content that can be generated under normal conditions in respiratory therapy will not constitute an ignition source as long as easily ignited substances (such as alcohols, acetone, oils, greases, or lotions) are not present.

> A study by R. J. Plano [2] confirmed that blankets and sheets do not present a fire hazard from static sparks inside an oxygen tent. Therefore, there is an even lower hazard when oxygen is administered by cannula.
>
> Static discharge is not the same condition as that of spark-generating toys, which are a definite hazard inside oxygen tents.
>
> Reference to substances such as ether and cyclopropane were deleted because they are no longer used in the United States as inhalation anesthetics.

(f) Rapid opening of cylinder valves can cause sudden increase in downstream gas pressure and temperature caused by the adiabatic heat of recompression with consequent ignition of combustible materials in contact with the hot gas downstream, including the valve seat.

> Extreme caution should be taken when opening cylinder valves. Valves should be opened slowly because of the phenomenon of adiabatic heating. There should also be a policy to ensure that valves and regulators are kept free from contaminants.

## 8-2.2 Toxicity.

### 8-2.2.1 During Respiratory Therapy Administration.

**8-2.2.1.1** Chemical hazards can be associated with the presence of residual sterilant in high-pressure equipment.

**8-2.2.1.2** Some breathing mixtures can decompose in contact with hot surfaces and produce toxic or flammable substances *(see 8-6.2).*

**8-2.2.1.3** Smoldering combustion of flammable substances can occur with the production of significant amounts of toxic gases and fumes.

## 8-2.3 Safety (Mechanical Injury; Cross-Connection, and So Forth).

**8-2.3.1 Inhalation Anesthetizing Locations.** A large amount of energy is stored in a cylinder of compressed gas. If the valve of a cylinder is struck (or strikes something else) hard enough to break off the valve, the contents of the cylinder could be discharged with sufficient force to impart dangerous reactive movement to the cylinder.

### 8-2.3.2 During Respiratory Therapy Administration.

**8-2.3.2.1 Mechanical Hazards.** Cylinders and containers can be heavy and bulky and can cause personal injury or property damage (including to the cylinder or container) if improperly handled. In cold climates, cylinders or containers stored outdoors or in unheated ventilated rooms can become extremely cold *[see 4-3.5.2.1(b)30 and 4-3.5.2.1(b)31]*. A hazardous situation could develop if these cylinders or containers are heated *[see 4-3.5.2.1(b)29]*.

Cylinders and containers should never be left standing without some type of physical support such as a stand, a cart, or being strapped to a wall. (See 4-3.5.5.) A high-pressure, gas-filled cylinder can create mechanical hazards if there is a sudden, uncontrollable release of its contents (e.g., from falling over and cracking open).

**8-2.3.2.2** Improper maintenance, handling, or assembly of equipment can result in personal injury, property damage, or fire.

**8-2.3.2.3** A hazardous condition exists if cylinders or containers are improperly located so that they can become overheated or tipped over. If a container is tipped over or placed on its side, liquid oxygen could be spilled. The liquid can cause frostbite on contact with skin.

Placing high-pressure cylinders near heat sources such as radiators or stoves can cause the pressure to increase beyond the cylinder's pressure relief limit, resulting in uncontrolled venting. This situation is particularly dangerous if the heat source is also a source of ignition, such as a stove.

Small liquid containers, such as those used to provide metered oxygen therapy via mask or cannula in the home, or the larger reservoirs used to refill therapeutic devices present other significant hazards beyond those of frostbite from the approximately $-300°F$ ($-184°C$) liquid. Liquid oxygen expands 860 times in the transition from liquid to the gaseous state. Therefore, what seems to be a small leak or spill can, in fact, release a significant quantity of 100 percent oxygen into the area around the container. In addition, liquid oxygen can cause certain greases or oils to ignite spontaneously if they should come in contact with each other. All types of lotions, hair care products, lubricants, and oils should be kept away from any liquid oxygen reservoirs.

**8-2.3.2.4** A hazardous condition exists if there is improper labeling of cylinders or containers or inattention to the manufacturer's label or instructions.

All cylinders and containers should be checked for color coding, labeling, attached labeling, and proper Pin-Index Safety System or Diameter-Index Safety System fitting before being placed in service. Exhibit 8.3 is an example of a label on an oxygen cylinder. If there is any doubt about the contents of a cylinder or container, a sample of the contents should be analyzed. (See 8-6.4.1.6 for requirements on labeling.)

**8-2.3.2.5** A hazardous condition exists if care is not exercised in making slip-on and other interchangeable connections when setting up equipment.

**Exhibit 8.3** *Sample labeling on an oxygen cylinder in a health care facility. (Courtesy of Rob Swift and Prince William Health Systems.)*

**8-2.3.2.6** Safety features, including relief devices, valves, and connections, are provided in equipment and gas supply systems. Altering or circumventing these safety features by means of adapters creates a hazardous condition.

**8-2.3.2.7 Extreme danger to life and property can result when compressed gases are mixed or transferred from one cylinder to another.**

> The boldface type of 8-2.3.2.7 emphasizes the committee's concerns regarding transfilling gases between cylinders or mixing gases. The unpredictability of the results of these activities justifies this concern. (The term *transfilling,* as used in 8-6.2.5.1, applies only to the transfer of gaseous oxygen or oxygen-containing mixtures at high pressure.) See 8-6.2.5.1 regarding conditions under which transfilling is allowed. Mixing of compressed gases is never allowed. A cross-connection can be considered a mixing of gases and presents the same hazard as mixing of compressed gases (never allowed).

**8-2.3.2.8** A hazardous condition exists if devices, such as fixed or adjustable orifices and metering valves, are directly connected to cylinders or systems without a pressure-reducing regulator.

**8-2.3.2.9** Hazardous conditions are created when pressure-reducing regulators or gauges are defective.

## 8-2.4* Electric Shock.

(Reserved)

**A-8-2.4** See 7-2.2 for additional information.

# 8-3 Source

## 8-3.1 Cylinders and Containers.

**8-3.1.1** Cylinders and containers shall comply with 4-3.1.1.1(a).

**8-3.1.2** Cylinder valve outlet connections shall conform to CGA V-1. *Standard for Compressed Gas Cylinder Valve Outlet and Inlet Connections* (ANSI B57.1) (includes Pin-Index Safety System for medical gases). *[See 4-3.1.1.1(a).]*

See A-8-5.1.2.1(b) for more information on the Pin-Index Safety System.

**8-3.1.3** When low-pressure threaded connections are employed, they shall be in accordance with the Compressed Gas Association standard for noninterchangeable, low-pressure connections for medical gases, air, and suction, CGA Pamphlet V-5, *Diameter-Index Safety System*.

See Section 2-2 under the definition of *D.I.S.S. connector* for more information on the Diameter Index Safety System.

**8-3.1.4** Low-pressure quick-coupler connections shall be noninterchangeable between gas services.

**8-3.1.5** Regulators and gauges intended for use in high-pressure service shall be listed for such service.

**8-3.1.6** Pressure-reducing regulators shall be used on high-pressure cylinders to reduce the pressure to working pressures.

**8-3.1.7** Approved regulators or other gas-flow control devices shall be used to reduce the cylinder pressure of every cylinder used for medical purposes. All such devices shall have connections so designed that they attach only to cylinders of gas for which they are designated.

**8-3.1.8\*** Equipment that will permit the intermixing of different gases, either through defects in the mechanism or through error in manipulation in any portion of the high-pressure side of any system in which these gases might flow, shall not be used for coupling cylinders containing compressed gases.

**A-8-3.1.8** It is particularly important that the intermixing of oxidizing and flammable gases under pressure be scrupulously avoided. Such mixing may result in a violent explosion.

See text and commentary for 8-2.3.2.7 concerning this hazard. See 8-6.2.5.1 regarding the subject of transfilling.

**8-3.1.9** Cylinder valve outlet connections for oxygen shall be Connection No. 540 as described in CGA V-1, *Standard for Compressed Gas Cylinder Valve Outlet and Inlet Connections* (ANSI B57.1).

**8-3.1.10** Cylinder valve outlet connections for nitrous oxide shall be Connection No. 326 as described in CGA V-1, *Standard for Compressed Gas Cylinder Valve Outlet and Inlet Connections* (ANSI B57.1).

**8-3.1.11  Storage Requirements.**

The storage criteria for cylinders or containers are the same, whether they are for anesthetizing, respiratory therapy, or laboratory use.

This section also serves as a reminder that cylinders and containers need to be stored properly. Proper storage, for example, is in a room dedicated for such a purpose, not, for instance, in a corner of a nurse's station. Note, however, that a cylinder placed next to a patient's bed, with the intention that it will be used within a short time, would not be considered as being in storage. The cylinder would, of course, have to be secured in such a way that it could not tip over (e.g., chained to a wall).

This section was completely revised in 1996 for a variety of reasons. Previously, requirements in Chapter 8 for the storage of freestanding cylinders and containers simply referenced those requirements in Chapter 4 for storage rooms for piped gas systems. This is still the case for freestanding cylinders and containers totaling more than 3000 ft$^3$ (85 m$^3$). The text in 8-3.1.11.2 was created for situations where the total volume of gases was less than 3000 ft$^3$ (85 m$^3$). The committee responsible for this text accepted the argument that significantly lower hazards exist when the volume of gases involved is less than 3000 ft$^3$ (85 m$^3$). It was also pointed out that the storage requirements in Chapter 4 took into consideration not only the cylinders and containers within the room, but also the piping distribution system connected to the manifold(s) in the room.

It should be noted that rooms storing liquefied gases in volumes even less than 3000 ft$^3$ (85 m$^3$) have to meet additional ventilation requirements because they vent gas continually.

**8-3.1.11.1** Storage for nonflammable gases greater than 3000 ft$^3$ (85 m$^3$) shall comply with 4-3.1.1.2 and 4-3.5.2.2.

**8-3.1.11.2** Storage for nonflammable gases less than 3000 ft$^3$ (85 m$^3$).

(a) Storage locations shall be outdoors in an enclosure or within an enclosed interior space of noncombustible or limited-combustible construction, with doors (or gates outdoors) that can be secured against unauthorized entry.

(b) Oxidizing gases, such as oxygen and nitrous oxide, shall not be stored with any flammable gas, liquid, or vapor.

(c) Oxidizing gases such as oxygen and nitrous oxide shall be separated from combustibles or incompatible materials by either:

1. A minimum distance of 20 ft (6.1 m), or
2. A minimum distance of 5 ft (1.5 m) if the entire storage location is protected by an automatic sprinkler system designed in accordance with NFPA 13, *Standard for the Installation of Sprinkler Systems,* or
3. An enclosed cabinet of noncombustible construction having a minimum fire protection rating of one-half hour for cylinder storage. An approved flammable liquid storage cabinet shall be permitted to be used for cylinder storage.

(d) Liquefied gas container storage shall comply with 4-3.1.1.2(b)4.

(e) Cylinder and container storage locations shall meet 4-3.1.1.2(a)11e with respect to temperature limitations.

(f) Electrical fixtures in storage locations shall meet 4-3.1.1.2(a)11d.

(g) Cylinder protection from mechanical shock shall meet 4-3.5.2.1(b)13.

(h) Cylinder or container restraint shall meet 4-3.5.2.1(b)27.

(i) Smoking, open flames, electric heating elements, and other sources of ignition shall be prohibited within storage locations and within 20 ft (6.1 m) of outside storage locations.

(j) Cylinder valve protection caps shall meet 4-3.5.2.1(b)14.

**8-3.1.11.3 Signs.** A precautionary sign, readable from a distance of 5 ft (1.5 m), shall be conspicuously displayed on each door or gate of the storage room or enclosure. The sign shall include the following wording as a minimum:

**CAUTION**
OXIDIZING GAS(ES) STORED WITHIN
NO SMOKING

In this new 1999 edition, the technical committee added this requirement for signage to warn facility staff and others of the presence of such gases. The contents of such rooms and enclosures present a significant fire hazard.

## 8-3.2 Generators.

(Reserved)

# 8-4 Distribution

(Reserved)

# 8-5  Performance Criteria and Testing

## 8-5.1  Patient-Care-Related Gas Equipment.

### 8-5.1.1  Fixed. (Reserved)

### 8-5.1.2  Portable.

### 8-5.1.2.1*  Anesthetic Apparatus.

**A-8-5.1.2.1** If the sole source of supply of nonflammable medical gases, such as nitrous oxide and oxygen, is a system of cylinders attached directly to and supported by the device (such as a gas anesthesia apparatus) used to administer these gases, it is recommended that two cylinders of each gas be attached to the administering device.

(a)  Anesthetic apparatus shall be subject to approval by the authority having jurisdiction.

(b)*  Each yoke on anesthetic apparatus constructed to permit attachment of small cylinders equipped with flush-type valves shall have two pins installed as specified in CGA V-1 (Pin-Index Safety System) (ANSI B57.1).

**A-8-5.1.2.1(b)**  *Pin-Index Safety System.* The Pin-Index Safety System consists of a combination of two pins projecting from the yoke assembly of the apparatus and so positioned as to fit into matching holes drilled into the cylinder valves. It is intended to provide against the possibility of error in attaching the flush-type valves, with which gas cylinders and other sources of gas supply are equipped, to gas apparatus having yoke connections.

(c)  After any adjustment or repair involving use of tools, or any modification of the gas piping supply connections or the pneumatic power supply connections for the anesthesia ventilator, or other pneumatically powered device if one is present, and before use on patients, the gas anesthesia apparatus shall be tested at the final common path to the patient to determine that oxygen and only oxygen is delivered from the oxygen flowmeters and the oxygen flush valve if any. Interventions requiring such testing shall include, but not be limited to, the following:

1. Alteration of pipeline hoses or fittings
2. Alteration of internal piping
3. Adjustment of selector switches or flush valves
4. Replacement or repair of flowmeters or bobbins

Before the gas anesthesia apparatus is returned to service, each fitting and connection shall be checked to verify its proper indexing to the respective gas service involved.

An oxygen analyzer, or a similar device, known to be accurate at 0 percent, 21 percent, and 100 percent oxygen, is a suitable test instrument *(see C-12.2).*

(d)*  Yoke-type connections between anesthesia apparatus and flush-type cylinder valves (commonly used with anesthetic gas cylinders) shall be Connection No. 860 in accordance with CGA V-1, *Compressed Gas Cylinder Valve Outlet and Inlet Connections* (ANSI B57.1).

**A-8-5.1.2.1(d)**  Fabrication specifications are contained in CGA Pamphlet V-1 (ANSI B57.1), *Compressed Gas Cylinder Valve Outlet and Inlet Connections*. Connection No. 860 shown in that document illustrates the system. Connection Nos. 870 (Oxygen, Medical), 880 (Oxygen-Carbon Dioxide Mixture), 890 (Oxygen-Helium Mixture), 900 (Ethylene), 910 (Nitrous Oxide), 920 (Cyclopropane), 930 (Helium), and 940 (Carbon Dioxide) are for specific medical gases and gas mixtures and utilize the basic dimensions of Connection 860.

**8-5.1.2.2  Apparatus for Administering Respiratory Therapy.**

(a)  Oxygen tent circulation/conditioning apparatus, pressure breathing apparatus, and other equipment intended to rest on the floor shall be equipped with a base designed to render the entire assembly stable during storage, transport, and use. If casters are used, they shall conform to Class C of U.S. Government Commercial Standard 223-59, *Casters, Wheels, and Glides for Hospital Equipment*.

(b)  Oxygen tent canopies having flexible components shall be fabricated of materials having a maximum burning rate classification of "slow burning." Oxygen enclosures of rigid materials shall be fabricated of noncombustible materials.

(c)  Equipment supplied from cylinders or containers shall be designed and constructed for service at full cylinder or container pressure or constructed for use or equipped with pressure-reducing regulators.

(d)  Humidification or reservoir jars containing liquid to be dispersed into a gas stream shall be made of clear, transparent material, impervious to contained solutions and medications, and shall permit observation of the liquid level and consistency.

The use of devices prefilled with sterile water is common in hospitals today. These devices meet the requirements of this section because they are clear and allow observation of the liquid level.

(e)  Humidifiers and nebulizers shall be equipped with provisions for overpressure relief or alarm if the flow becomes obstructed.

Alarms can be easily tested by briefly occluding the outlet port to see whether pop-off occurs.

(f)  Humidifiers and nebulizers shall be incapable of tipping or shall be mounted so that any tipping or alteration from the vertical shall not interfere with function or accuracy.

## 8-5.2  Nonpatient Gas Equipment.

### 8-5.2.1  Carts and Hand Trucks.

**8-5.2.1.1  Construction.**  Carts and hand trucks for cylinders and containers shall be constructed for the intended purpose and shall be self-supporting. They shall be provided with appropriate chains or stays to retain cylinders or containers in place.

**8-5.2.1.2 Use.** Carts and hand trucks that are intended to be used in anesthetizing locations or cylinder and container storage rooms communicating with anesthetizing locations shall comply with the appropriate provisions of 12-4.1.

**8-5.2.2 Gas Equipment — Laboratory.** Gas appliances shall be of an approved design and installed in accordance with NFPA 54, *National Fuel Gas Code*. Shutoff valves shall be legibly marked to identify the material they control.

# 8-6 Administration

## 8-6.1 Responsibility of Governing Body.

(Reserved)

## 8-6.2 Policies.

The hazard of an oxygen-enriched atmosphere does not exist when oxygen is only supplied to a room through piping but is not used. It is when the oxygen is actually being administered that the precautions (policies) in 8-6.2 need to be taken.

The attachment of a flowmeter to a station outlet would not automatically require the precautionary measures listed in this section, provided the flowmeter is in the "off" mode. However, once a device is connected to the flowmeter, the measures listed would need to be followed.

### 8-6.2.1 Elimination of Sources of Ignition.

It is very important that visitors be informed of a facility's policies so as not to jeopardize the safety of patients, other visitors, and staff.

**8-6.2.1.1** Smoking materials (matches, cigarettes, lighters, lighter fluid, tobacco in any form) shall be removed from patients receiving respiratory therapy and from the area of administration.

A policy on smoking should be developed for the entire facility to avoid confusion and to generally reduce the hazard from smoking.

**8-6.2.1.2\*** No sources of open flame, including candles, shall be permitted in the area of administration.

**A-8-6.2.1.2** Patients and hospital personnel in the area of administration should be advised of respiratory therapy hazards and regulations.

Visitors should be cautioned of these hazards through the prominent posting of signs *(see 8-6.4.2)*.

**8-6.2.1.3\*** Sparking toys shall not be permitted in any patient care area.

Young children cannot be expected to understand the hazards associated with the administration of respiratory therapy. It is incumbent upon respiratory therapy personnel and other staff to explain these hazards and what measures are necessary to prevent accidents/incidents.

**A-8-6.2.1.3** Such toys have been associated with fire incidents in health care facilities.

A suggested text for precautionary signs for oxygen tent canopies and oxygen hoods used in pediatric nursing units is:

**CAUTION:** OXYGEN IN USE
ONLY TOYS APPROVED BY
NURSES MAY BE GIVEN TO CHILD

**8-6.2.1.4** Nonmedical appliances that have hot surfaces or sparking mechanisms shall not be permitted within oxygen delivery equipment or within the sight of intentional expulsion.

The committee added this text in the 1999 edition to be consistent with expected oxygen-enriched atmospheres in oxygen delivery equipment or within the site of intentional expulsion, as well as to be consistent with 7-6.2.4.1.

**8-6.2.2 Misuse of Flammable Substances.**

Note that in 8-6.2.2.1 through 8-6.2.2.3, restrictions on the use of flammable substances in oxygen-enriched atmospheres are not related to the amount of substance used (either momentarily or over a period of time), but simply to their use.

**8-6.2.2.1** Flammable or combustible aerosols or vapors, such as alcohol, shall not be administered in oxygen-enriched atmospheres as outlined in 8-2.1.2.3(a).

An alcohol/oxygen mixture vapor may be necessary in the treatment of pulmonary disorders. Reference to 8-2.1.2.3(a) is included to indicate that such vapors are prohibited in oxygen tents and other oxygen-enriched environments but not when used for masks or nasal catheters.

**8-6.2.2.2** Oil, grease, or other flammable substances shall not be used on/in oxygen equipment.

In this 1999 edition the word *contaminants* was replaced with *substances* because contaminants could imply that they (contaminants) were intentionally being used. The phrase *on/in* replaced *with* to reinforce the intent that the paragraph refers to equipment and not patients.

**8-6.2.2.3** Flammable and combustible liquids shall not be permitted within the site of intentional expulsion.

To combat the drying effects of oxygen on the skin around the face when oxygen is administered by cannula or mask or to treat diaper rash on babies in croup tents, only water-based lubricants are to be used.

### 8-6.2.3 Prevention of Chemical Breakdown. (Reserved)

This section was reserved for the 1996 edition because the hazards previously addressed were those associated with flammable inhalation anesthetics. For a discussion of flammable inhalation anesthetics, see Annex 2, "Flammable Anesthetizing Locations."

### 8-6.2.4 Servicing and Maintenance of Equipment.

**8-6.2.4.1** Defective equipment shall be immediately removed from service.

**8-6.2.4.2** Defective electrical apparatus shall not be used.

**8-6.2.4.3** Areas designated for the servicing of oxygen equipment shall be clean, free of oil and grease, and not used for the repair of other equipment.

**8-6.2.4.4** Service manuals, instructions, and procedures provided by the manufacturer shall be used in the maintenance of equipment.

**8-6.2.4.5** A scheduled preventive maintenance program shall be followed.

### 8-6.2.5 Gases in Cylinders and Liquefied Gases in Containers.

This section, previously in Chapter 4, was moved here because it applies to freestanding cylinders and containers.

### 8-6.2.5.1 Transfilling Cylinders.

(a) Mixing of compressed gases in cylinders shall be prohibited.

Here, the term *mixing* is intended to mean the combining of two *different* gases. The combining of two different cylinders with the *same* gas is called *transfilling*. The mixing of some types of gases can cause an explosion.

This mixing should not be confused with the administration of various combinations of gases during surgery or respiratory therapy. This activity is the result of much research on combinations that do not create a hazard.

(b) Transfer of gaseous oxygen from one cylinder to another shall be in accordance with CGA Pamphlet P-2.5, *Transfilling of High Pressure Gaseous Oxygen to Be Used for Respiration*. Transfer of any gases from one cylinder to another in patient care areas of health care facilities shall be prohibited.

There is much concern over transfilling cylinders containing gas under high pressure within health care facilities. While adherence to CGA Pamphlet P-2.5 [3] will minimize hazards, there is the question of whether the procedures outlined in the CGA document will be followed. Transfilling places a heavy burden of responsibility on health care facilities.

For the 1987 edition of NFPA 99, arguments for and against transfilling within health care facilities were weighed by four committees in the Health Care Facilities Project. Those favoring the prohibition of transfilling in health care facilities cited the lack of assurance that the provisions of the CGA document would be followed all the time. The then Technical Committee on Health Care Facilities, taking into consideration that the CGA document, if followed, did provide a reasonable level of safety for transfilling, allowed transfilling, but restricted it to non-patient-care areas. This location restriction reflects a concern for patient, staff, and visitor safety. It should be noted that transfilling is allowed only for oxygen since procedures for other gases used in the medical environment have not yet been developed.

**8-6.2.5.2 Transferring Liquid Oxygen.** Transferring of liquid oxygen from one container to another shall be accomplished at a location specifically designated for the transferring that is as follows:

(a) Separated from any portion of a facility wherein patients are housed, examined, or treated by a separation of a fire barrier of 1-hour fire-resistive construction; and

(b) The area is mechanically ventilated, is sprinklered, and has ceramic or concrete flooring; and

(c) The area is posted with signs indicating that transferring is occurring, and that smoking in the immediate area is not permitted.

Despite the fact that transfilling small liquid oxygen containers at a patient's bedside had been prohibited, the committee responsible for this text was aware that the practice was continuing in many health care facilities. As a response, the committee, in 1990, prescribed that transfilling be done "remote from patient care areas." Since even this criterion has raised questions, the committee revised the wording again in 1996 to clarify where, and under what conditions, such transfilling is to be accomplished if it is done on health care facility property.

CGA Pamphlet P-2.6 [4] outlines specific procedures to be followed when transferring liquid oxygen from one container to another.

CGA Pamphlet P-2.7 [5] is a relatively new document that complements CGA Pamphlet P-2.6 [4] and was developed specifically for health care facilities.

Transferring shall be accomplished utilizing equipment designed to comply with the performance requirements and producers of CGA Pamphlet P-2.6, *Transfilling of Low-Pressure Liquid Oxygen to Be Used for Respiration*, and adhering to those procedures.

The use and operation of small portable liquid oxygen systems shall comply with the requirements of CGA Pamphlet P-2.7, *Guide for the Safe Storage, Handling and Use of Portable Liquid Oxygen Systems in Health Care Facilities*.

**8-6.2.6 Ambulatory Patients.** Ambulatory patients on oxygen therapy, whether in or out of a health care facility, shall be permitted free access to all areas that prohibit smoking and that have no open flames.

> The use of portable oxygen systems has grown dramatically in the United States. The former Subcommittee on Gas Equipment (now incorporated into the Committee on Gas Delivery Equipment) felt it appropriate to address the subject in this paragraph on ambulatory patients because administration of oxygen is usually initiated in medical facilities.
>
> Although the scope of the Health Care Facility Project generally limits it to the confines of health care facilities, the former subcommittee felt that the allowances and restrictions afforded to patients receiving oxygen therapy inside a health care facility should be accorded and followed by persons outside the facility. This provision places some responsibilities on both the users and owners of establishments. The user needs to be aware of the environment he or she is entering and whether or not a "no open flame" policy exists. Owners need to enforce whatever policy is established for designated areas. Appropriate signs warning that oxygen may be in use or directing oxygen users where they can safely sit should be posted. Ensuring the safety of all persons in an area or room may be further compounded if a language barrier exists.
>
> There are many people who mistakenly still believe that oxygen is a flammable or explosive gas. This provision is intended to show that the use of oxygen is safe when reasonable precautions are taken.
>
> See Chapter 18 for further safety requirements for the home environment.

## 8-6.3 Recordkeeping.

(Reserved)

## 8-6.4 Use (Including Information and Warning Signs).

### 8-6.4.1 Labeling.

**8-6.4.1.1** Equipment listed for use in oxygen-enriched atmospheres shall be so labeled.

**8-6.4.1.2** Oxygen-metering equipment and pressure-reducing regulators shall be conspicuously labeled:

OXYGEN — USE NO OIL

**8-6.4.1.3** Flowmeters, pressure-reducing regulators, and oxygen-dispensing apparatus shall be clearly and permanently labeled, designating the gas or mixture of gases for which they are intended. Apparatus whose calibration or function is dependent on gas density shall be labeled as to the proper supply gas pressure (psig/kPa) for which it is intended.

**8-6.4.1.4\*** Canopies or enclosures intended to contain patients shall be labeled with the information that oxygen is in use and that precautions related to the hazard shall be observed.

The labels shall be located on the enclosure interior in a position to be read by the patient and on two or more opposing sides of the enclosure exterior.

*Exception: In health care facilities where smoking is prohibited and signs are prominently (strategically) placed at all major entrances, secondary signs with no-smoking language are not required. The nonsmoking policies shall be strictly enforced.*

See commentary under A-8-6.4.2 for information on signs located in smokefree facilities.

**A-8-6.4.1.4** A suggested minimum text for labels is given in Figure A-8-6.4.1.4.

CAUTION
OXYGEN IN USE
KEEP FLAMES AWAY
NO SMOKING

NO ELECTRICAL APPLIANCES

**Figure A-8-6.4.1.4** *Suggested minimum text for canopy or enclosure labels.*

**8-6.4.1.5** Oxygen-metering equipment, pressure-reducing regulators, humidifiers, and nebulizers shall be labeled with the name of the manufacturer or supplier.

**8-6.4.1.6** Cylinders and containers shall be labeled in accordance with ANSI/ CGA C-4, *Standard Method of Marking Portable Compressed Gas Containers to Identify the Material Contained*. Color coding shall not be utilized as a primary method of determining cylinder or container content.

See commentary under 8-2.3.2.4 for further information.

**8-6.4.1.7** All labeling shall be durable and withstand cleansing or disinfection.

**8-6.4.2\* Signs.** Precautionary signs, readable from a distance of 5 ft (1.5 m), shall be conspicuously displayed wherever supplemental oxygen is in use, and in aisles and walkways leading to that area. They shall be attached to adjacent doorways or to building walls or be supported by other appropriate means.

*Exception: In health care facilities where smoking is prohibited and signs are prominently (strategically) placed at all major entrances, secondary signs with no-smoking language are not required. The nonsmoking policies shall be strictly enforced.*

**A-8-6.4.2** Precautionary signs should be at least 8 in. × 11 in. (21 cm × 28 cm) in size. Any material that can burn in air will burn more rapidly in the presence of oxygen.

Special signs and additional precautionary measures should be employed whenever foreign languages present a communication problem. *(See Figure A-8-6.4.2.)*

**CAUTION**
**OXYGEN IN USE**
**NO SMOKING**

**NO OPEN FLAMES**

*Figure A-8-6.4.2 A suggested minimum text for precautionary signs.*

Any material that can burn in air will burn more rapidly in the presence of oxygen. No electrical equipment is allowed within an oxygen enclosure or within 5 ft (1.5 m) of it.

It is incumbent upon staff to learn whether a language barrier exists and to provide material in the appropriate language. This can normally be determined at the time of admission.

Signs with bright, clear letters, such as red letters on a white background, should be used.

Caution signs are necessary, even in facilities where smoking has been banned or restricted to certain locations. While NFPA 99 requires smokefree health care facilities to post appropriate signs only at major entrances to meet the signage requirement (through exception), a facility is also required to strictly enforce non-smoking policies. With numerous signs prominently displaying a facility's smokefree policy, and good enforcement of this policy, the committee believes the level of protection discussed here will be sufficient to prevent smoking-related fire hazards.

### 8-6.4.3 Transportation, Storage, and Use of Equipment.

**8-6.4.3.1** Flow-control valves on administering equipment shall be closed prior to connection and when not in use.

Releasing the pressure on the gauge by the flow control valve, while the cylinder is not in use, will extend the life of the gauge itself.

**8-6.4.3.2** Apparatus shall not be stored or transported with liquid agents in reservoirs.

**8-6.4.3.3** Care shall be observed in attaching connections from gas services to equipment and from equipment to patients.

Accepted procedures should always be followed when making attachments.

**8-6.4.3.4** Fixed or adjustable orifice mechanisms, metering valves, regulators, and gauges shall not be connected directly to high-pressure cylinders unless specifically listed for such use and provided with appropriate safety devices.

**8-6.4.3.5** Nasal respiratory therapy catheters shall be color coded green. Verification of proper connection to oxygen therapy equipment is necessary to prevent accidental attachment to gastric or intestinal catheters.

Today, the use of nasal catheters is extremely rare, but they are still employed, especially in centers that treat persons with chronic lung disease. This requirement is to be observed in areas where nasal catheters are used.

## 8-6.5  Qualification and Training of Personnel.

Equipment shall be serviced by qualified personnel only.

### References Cited in Commentary

1. Johns Hopkins University Study (cited by the American Association for Respiratory Care), 1720 Regal Row, Dallas, TX 75235.
2. R. J. Plano, *Modern Hospital,* vol. 95, no. 3, Sept. 1960.
3. CGA Pamphlet P-2.5, *Transfilling of High-Pressure Gaseous Oxygen to Be Used for Respiration,* 1987 edition.
4. CGA Pamphlet P-2.6, *Transfilling of Low-Pressure Liquid Oxygen to Be Used for Respiration,* 1983 edition.
5. CGA Pamphlet P-2.7, *Guide for the Safe Storage, Handling, and Use of Portable Liquid Oxygen Systems in Health Care Facilities,* 1994 edition.

# CHAPTER 9

# Manufacturer Requirements

The contemporary health care facility is filled with a myriad of sophisticated manufactured equipment. In many cases, the safety of such equipment has major consequences for the well-being of patients and staff alike.

Chapter 9 addresses safety requirements for manufactured equipment used in health care facilities. At present, the chapter is devoted exclusively to electrical appliances that are related to patient care. However, the chapter reserves sections for possible future requirements for nonpatient electrical equipment, for gas equipment, and for materials.

## 9-1* Scope

This chapter covers the performance, maintenance, and testing, with regard to safety, required of manufacturers of equipment used within health care facilities.

**A-9-1** *Application of Requirements.* The application of requirements contained in this chapter for specific types of health care facilities can be found in Chapters 12 through 18.

## 9-2 Electrical Equipment

### 9-2.1* Patient-Care-Related Electrical Appliances.

**A-9-2.1** It is the intent that 9-2.1 should not be used by authorities having jurisdiction over health care facilities to limit health care facilities' purchases to patient-care-related electrical appliances meeting these requirements. Rather, it is the intent to encourage equipment manufacturers to conduct the specified tests in order to ensure state-of-the-art electrical safety in their patient-care-related electrical appliances. Similarly, it is not the intent of the Technical Committee to require health care facilities to conduct tests using these manufacturer requirements to verify that their patient-care-related electrical appliances are in conformance with the requirements of this chapter. In this respect, it is the intent of the Committee that health care facilities perform only those tests specified in 7-5.1.

The requirements in this section were originally developed for inclusion in the 1980 edition of NFPA 76B, *Standard for Safe Use of Electricity in Patient Care Areas of Hospitals.* As in Chapters 3 through 8, this chapter does not specify where these requirements are applicable. Instead, its application is determined by references in Chapters 12 through 18, specific references in other chapters (as is the case in Chapter 7), or by a facility or an authority choosing to enforce these requirements.

### 9-2.1.1 Mechanical Construction.

**9-2.1.1.1 Separation of Patient Circuits.** Patient-connected circuits within an appliance shall be sufficiently separated or insulated from all other circuits within the appliance to prevent accidental contact with hazardous voltages or currents.

**9-2.1.1.2 Mechanical Stability.** The appliance shall be mechanically stable in the position of normal use. If the appliance is intended for use in an anesthetizing location, 12-4.1 applies.

### 9-2.1.2 Electrical Requirements—Appliances Equipped with Power Cords.

### 9-2.1.2.1 Attachment Plugs.

(a)* *General.* Attachment plugs listed for the purpose shall be used on all cord-connected appliances.

**A-9-2.1.2.1(a)** Hospital grade listing is acceptable but not required.

In the past, health care facility appliances were frequently provided with molded or other light-duty plugs that are appropriate for household use but not for the severe conditions that can exist in hospitals. Because of the construction specifications of these light-duty plugs, it was possible that the ground connection inside these plugs (between the wire and the pin) could break and not be evident because the device would still be able to function. Hazards such as these led to the development of heavy-duty plugs that could withstand hospital abuse. These plugs were labeled hospital grade and were appropriately marked. (The term *hospital grade* was used because the heaviest use of appliances occurred in hospitals.)

Users outside hospital facilities have been attracted to these improved plugs, and manufacturers are now providing heavy-duty plugs that are equivalent to, but not labeled as, hospital grade. See Exhibit 9.1 for an example of a heavy-duty electrical plug. These heavy-duty plugs are sometimes less expensive than hospital grade plugs. It is the intent of this section to allow the use of such heavy-duty plugs.

Household or other light-duty plugs, such as molded rubber plugs that secure the grounding pin only by rubber, are not acceptable.

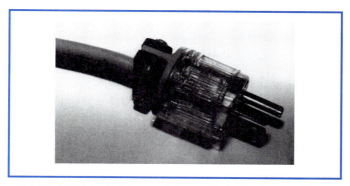

**Exhibit 9.1** *A typical heavy-duty electrical plug for portable equipment. The high-impact casing, along with a power cord that is also heavy-duty, prevents accidental damage or disconnection. The see-through cover of this model allows for quick plug inspection.*

(b)* *Construction and Use.* The plug (cap) shall be a two-pole, three-wire grounding type.

By making the green ground wire longer than the phase conductors and the grounding prong on the plug longer than the phase prongs, the phase conductors will disengage first. This order of disengagement is desired by the committee because it keeps the equipment grounded until after the phase wires prongs have disengaged.

It is the intent of the committee responsible for this text that twisted wires not be tinned. This position is based on experience and reports, such as in *Health Devices* [1], that indicate more occurrences of loosening connections with tinned, twisted wires than with untinned, twisted wires. No controlled studies on this issue have been conducted of late, however.

Aluminum wire should be used only with plugs specifically designed for such wire.

**A-9-2.1.2.1(b)** See ANSI C73.11, C73.12, C73.45, and C73.46; and Sections 410-56, 410-57, and 410-58 of NFPA 70, *National Electrical Code*.

*Exception No. 1: Appliances used in special locations or for special purposes, equipped with plugs approved for the location [e.g., 3-3.2.1.2(d)].*

*Exception No. 2: If the power cord of an appliance does not require and does not contain a grounding conductor, it shall not be fitted with a grounding-type plug [see 9-2.1.2.2(e), Cords without Grounding Conductors].*

*Exception No. 3: Appliances supplied by other than 120-V single-phase systems shall use the grounding-type plug (cap) appropriate for the particular power system (e.g., ANSI C73.16, C73.17, C73.18, C73.28, C73.83, C73.84, C73.86, C73.87, C73.88, C73.89, C73.90, C73.91, C73.92, C73.94, and C73.95).*

The grounding prong shall be constructed so that it cannot be easily broken. The grounding prong of the plug shall be the first to be connected to and the last to be disconnected from the receptacle. If screw terminals are used, the stranded conductor shall be twisted to prevent stray strands, but the bundle shall not be tinned after twisting. If the conductor is not twisted, it shall be attached by an approved terminal lug. The power cord conductors shall be arranged so that the conductors are not under tension in the plug. The grounding conductor shall be the last one to disconnect when a failure of the plug's strain relief allows the energized conductors to be disrupted.

(c) *Strain Relief.* Strain relief shall be provided. The strain relief shall not cause thinning of the conductor insulation. The strain relief of replaceable plugs shall be capable of being disassembled. Plugs are permitted to be integrally molded onto the cord jacket if the design is listed for the purpose.

(d) *Testing.* The wiring of each cord assembly shall be tested for continuity and polarity at the time of manufacture, when assembled into an appliance, and when repaired.

**9-2.1.2.2 Power Cords.**

(a)* *Material and Gauge.* The flexible cord, including the grounding conductor, shall be of a type suitable for the particular application, listed for use at a voltage equal to or greater than the rated power line voltage of the appliance, and have an ampacity, as given in Table 400-5(A) of NFPA 70, *National Electrical Code,* equal to or greater than the current rating of the device.

"Hard Service" (SO, ST, or STO) or "Junior Hard Service" (SJO, SJT, or SJTO) or equivalent listed flexible cord shall be used *(see Table 400-4 of NFPA 70, National Electrical Code)* except where an appliance with a cord of another designation has been listed for the purpose.

**A-9-2.1.2.2(a)** "Hard Service" cord is preferable where the cord may be subject to mechanical abuse. A cord length of 10 ft (3.1 m) is recommended for general locations, and 18 ft (5.5 m) for operating rooms, but can be of a different length if designed for a specific location.

(b) *Grounding Conductor.* Each electric appliance shall be provided with a grounding conductor in its power cord. The grounding conductor shall be no smaller than No. 18 AWG. The grounding conductor of cords longer than 15 ft (4.6 m) shall be no smaller than No. 16 AWG. Grounding conductors shall meet the resistance requirements of 9-2.1.13.2, Grounding Circuit Continuity.

*Exception: A grounding conductor in the power cord need not be provided for listed double-insulated appliances, but such a grounding conductor shall be permitted to be used to ground exposed conductive surfaces (see 9-2.1.3.2, Grounding of Exposed Conductive Surfaces).*

(c) *Separable Cord Sets.* A separable power cord set shall be permitted to be used if it can be shown that an accidental disconnection is unlikely or not hazardous. Separable power cord sets shall be designed so that the grounding conductor is the first to be connected and the last to be disconnected. Cord-set plugs and receptacles at the appliance shall be polarized in accordance with ANSI C73.13 and C73.17.

Appliances with separable cord sets shall meet the grounding-wire-resistance requirements of 9-2.1.13.2, Grounding Circuit Continuity—Measurement of Resistance, when the cord set is connected to the appliance. Both the cord set and the means of connection to the appliance shall be listed for the purpose.

See cautionary note in commentary to 9-2.1.4.2.

(d) *Connection to Circuit and Color Codes.* Power cords, regardless of whether intended for use on grounded or isolated power systems, shall be connected in accordance with the conventions of a grounded system. *(See Sections 200-2 through 200-10 of NFPA 70, National Electrical Code.)*

The circuit conductors in the cord shall be connected to the plug and the wiring in the appliance so that any of the following devices, when used in the primary circuit, are connected to the ungrounded conductor: the center contact of an Edison base lampholder; a solitary fuseholder; a single-pole, overcurrent-protective device; and any other single-pole, current-interrupting device. *[See Exception No. 2 to Section 210-5(b) of NFPA 70, National Electrical Code.]*

*Exception: If a second fuseholder or other overcurrent-protective device is provided in the appliance, it shall be permitted to be placed in the grounded side of the line.*

The exception correlates with other U.S. and international documents.

(e) *Cords Without Grounding Conductors.* If the power cord of an appliance does not require and does not contain a grounding conductor, it shall not be fitted with a grounding-type plug.

(f) *Testing.* The wiring of each cord assembly shall be tested for continuity and polarity at the time of manufacture, when assembled into an appliance, and when repaired.

(g) *Cord Strain Relief.* Cord strain relief shall be provided at the attachment of the power cord to the appliance so that mechanical stress, either pull, twist, or bend, is not transmitted to internal connections. If the strain relief is molded onto the cord, it shall be bonded to the jacket and shall be of compatible material.

(h)* *Storage.*

**A-9-2.1.2.2(h)**  See 7-5.1.2.5(a).

**9-2.1.3 Wiring Within Appliances Equipped with Power Cords.**

**9-2.1.3.1  Protection of Wiring in Appliances.** Within the appliance, the power conductors of the cord and the associated primary wiring (other than the grounding conductor) shall be mounted and dressed to minimize the likelihood of accidental electrical contact with the frame or exposed conductive parts of the appliance.

**9-2.1.3.2*  Grounding of Exposed Conductive Surfaces.** All exposed conductive surfaces of an electric appliance likely to become energized from internal sources shall be bonded together to provide electric continuity with the connection to the grounding conductor.

**A-9-2.1.3.2** Size and location are the main criteria used in determining what is not likely to become energized and thus exempted from the bonding and grounding requirements. Items such as screws, nameplates, hinges, metal trim, handles, and other hardware are unlikely to become energized because of their size. If they are sufficiently isolated from internal sources they need not be grounded.

Also, it is unnecessary for exposed conductive surfaces to be grounded separately with individual or looped grounding wires if, by reliable contact or connection with other grounded metal portions (frame), these surfaces can maintain ground.

**9-2.1.3.3  Connection to Permit Replacement.** The connection of the power cord to the appliance shall permit ready replacement of the cord except where the power cord is not intended to be replaced by the user.

**9-2.1.3.4  Connection of the Grounding Conductor.** The grounding conductor shall be connected to the exposed metal or frame of the appliance by a terminal or bolt so that a reliable electrical connection is always maintained. The connection shall be arranged so that it will not be broken during electrical or mechanical repair of the appliance, except during replacement of the power cord.

The power cord shall be arranged so that the grounding conductor is the last to disconnect when a failure of the strain relief at the appliance allows the cord to be pulled free. When a grounding conductor is not required and is not provided, the appliance shall be visibly labeled to indicate that fact.

**9-2.1.3.5  Connections with Grounding Conductor.** Any component, such as a filter or test circuit, within an appliance that intentionally reduces the impedance between the energized conductors and the grounding conductor shall be in operation when the leakage current tests specified in 9-2.1.13.4, Leakage Current from Appliance to Ground, are performed.

**9-2.1.3.6*  Overcurrent Protection.** An overcurrent protective device shall be permitted to be placed in the attachment plug, in the power cord, or in the main body of the appliance.

The overcurrent protective device shall precede any other components within the appliance, including the primary power-control switch.

**A-9-2.1.3.6** It is recommended that a listed overcurrent protective device be used in the power input circuit of all appliances.

The former Committee on Safe Use of Electricity in Patient Care Areas of Health Care Facilities (now the Committee on Electrical Equipment) intended that overcurrent devices be permitted but not required. The appendix text, however, indicates the committee's desire that such protection should be provided. If overcurrent protection is included, the requirements of this section are to be followed.

Overcurrent protection within an appliance is a way of protecting the appliance itself and other appliances on the same branch circuit. The overcurrent protector will open when a fault within an appliance causes current to flow in excess of the overcurrent protector's rating. Since an appliance's overcurrent protection rating should be less than the rating of the branch circuit breaker, the branch circuit breaker will not open if a fault occurs in the appliance. While only appliances are directly protected in this way, the loss of one appliance can be significant to patients relying on the continuous operation of medical electrical appliances.

*Exception: Listed insulated terminal blocks or strips, listed connecting devices, and RFI filters for use on power systems shall be permitted to precede the overcurrent device (see 9-2.1.3.5).*

This requirement shall not preclude the use of overcurrent protective devices within the appliance. The power-control switch and overcurrent protective device shall be permitted to be combined into one component provided it is identified to indicate the combined function.

**9-2.1.3.7 Primary Power-Control Switch.** When a primary power-control switch is provided on an appliance, it shall interrupt all primary power conductors, including the neutral conductor. The grounding conductor shall not be interrupted by the switch.

*Exception: When the primary power wiring of an appliance is polarized so as to ensure the proper connection of its neutral conductor to the electric distribution system of the building, that neutral conductor need not be interrupted by a primary power-control switch.*

The former Committee on Safe Use of Electricity in Patient Care Areas of Health Care Facilities (now the Committee on Electrical Equipment) recognized the hazards associated with in-line switches (e.g., they are more easily damaged than a switch mounted on the chassis of a device), but the committee noted that there were circumstances when in-line switches were the preferred way to control power. A portable lamp, for example, whose location would make it inconvenient to use an on/off switch on the lamp base would be allowed an in-line switch. As a result, the committee allowed their use, but only under the conditions specified.

An in-line switch shall be permitted in a primary power cord only if the switch is listed with the appliance with which it is intended to be used.

**9-2.1.3.8 Rack- or Cart-Mounted Equipment.** Each appliance mounted in an equipment rack or cart, when rated by the manufacturer as a stand-alone appliance, shall independently meet the requirements of 9-2.1.13.

When multiple appliances, as designated by the manufacturer, are mounted together in a cart or rack, and one power cord supplies power, the cart or rack shall meet the requirements of 9-2.1.13.

The requirements of the first paragraph were revised in 1984 to include provisions for stand-alone appliances that could be included in a rack or cart. Requiring a rack or cart with one power cord to meet the requirements of this chapter (see paragraph 2) takes into consideration the fact that all the leakage current passes through the one main power cord. If the ground in this main power cord is broken, all the leakage current could pass through a person touching any one of the appliances mounted on the cart or rack. The committee felt that, because of this cumulative effect, the entire system should be treated as one appliance and adhere to the requirements of this chapter as one appliance.

### 9-2.1.4 Connectors and Connections to Devices.

**9-2.1.4.1 Indexing of Receptacles for Patient Leads.** Receptacles on appliances shall be designed and constructed so that those contacts that deliver electric current in a way and of a magnitude greater than 500 microamperes, when measured in accordance with 9-2.1.13.5(a), (b), (d), and (e), are female and indexed. Receptacles and plugs shall be polarized if improper orientation can create a hazard.

It is not the committee's intention to dictate appliance design; however, it is recommended that careful study be given to connector selection. Inputs of multimodality monitoring equipment should be distinctive in order to avoid situations where, for example, an ECG signal could be confused with a pressure signal, resulting in improper signals and probable patient injury. In particular, great care should be exercised to clearly differentiate leads that deliver energy, such as powering pressure transducers, from those that only receive signals.

**9-2.1.4.2\* Distinctive Receptacles for Patient Leads.** Where reversal or misconnection of patient leads to an appliance might constitute a hazard (for example: reversal of active and dispersive electrodes of electrosurgical machines), distinctive, noninterchangeable connections shall be employed.

**A-9-2.1.4.2** The purpose of these requirements is to prevent interchanging connectors in any manner that permits the inadvertent delivery of a hazardous current to a patient.

Through appropriate design, patient leads should not be able to be connected to power receptacles.

### 9-2.1.4.3 Patient Lead Connections.

(a) *Lead Termination.* The connector, distal to the patient, on a patient lead shall be constructed so that the connector cannot be inserted to make contact with the live parts of a power receptacle or to engage any part of the appliance that can introduce a risk of electric shock, fire, or personal injury.

(b) *Isolated Patient Lead.* The appliance connector of an isolated patient lead shall be constructed so that, when not inserted properly in the appliance, the end of the conductor of the lead cannot contact a surface that might be grounded.

This section was added in 1996 to expand on the requirements in 9-2.1.4.1 and 9-2.1.4.2. Patient monitoring leads are being more widely used in health care facilities at patients' bedsides. The same patient leads can also be used in the home where they are often applied by less-experienced persons more likely to make a mistake in their utilization.

Some older models of patient leads use simple blade terminals as connectors to the appliance. These models can also be inserted into power line receptacles or extension cords. In one reported case, the color-coded ECG cables (white/black/green) were confused with the power line conductors (also white/black/green). Connection to the power line in this manner can be fatal, particularly to very young patients and nonresponsive patients. Although the incident level of such accidents appears to be low, the problem is still a very serious one due to the hazard level involved. New appliances are now being made with changes in the design of patient terminals. (See Exhibit 9.2.) A permanent adaptor is available for the leads of existing appliances.

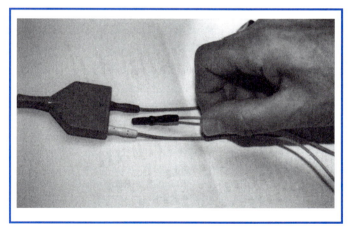

**Exhibit 9.2** *ECG leads, which have a special end configuration to prevent the lead from being accidentally inserted into a standard power outlet.*

**9-2.1.5\* Line Voltage Variations and Transients—General.** All appliances shall be capable of operating within line voltage variations that conform with ANSI C84.1, *Voltage Ratings: Electric Power Systems and Equipment.*

**A-9-2.1.5** The design of an appliance intended for life support should minimize the effects on performance of transient, line voltage variations, or other electrical interference. The design of all appliances should minimize the production of line variations and transients.

> Appliances, particularly those with digital terminal ports and controls, should be hardened (i.e., made electromagnetically compatible) to resist the effects of power line transients and other electromagnetic interference (EMI) and to limit their effects as sources of EMI.
>
>    For a further discussion of this subject, see commentary under 7-2.5.

**9-2.1.6  General Design and Manufacturing Requirements.**

**9-2.1.6.1  Thermal Standards.**  Electric appliances not designed to supply heat to the patient, and operated within reach of a nonambulatory patient, shall not have exposed surface temperatures in excess of 122°F (50°C). Surfaces maintained in contact with the skin of patients and not intended to supply heat shall not be hotter than 104°F (40°C).

**9-2.1.6.2  Toxic Materials.**  Surfaces that contact patients shall be free of materials that commonly cause toxic reactions. Coatings used on these surfaces shall conform to ANSI Z66.1, *Specifications for Paints and Coatings Accessible to Children to Minimize Dry Film Toxicity.*

**9-2.1.6.3*  Chemical Agents.**  Electric appliances containing hazardous chemicals shall be designed to facilitate the replenishment of these chemicals without spillage to protect the patient, the operating personnel, and the safety features of the appliance from such chemicals.

**A-9-2.1.6.3**  Preference should be given to the use of replaceable sealed canisters of chemicals.

**9-2.1.6.4  Electromagnetic Compatibility.**  All appliances shall be designed so that they are capable of operating in a radio frequency electromagnetic environment where limits are established by IEC 60601-1-2.

> This requirement was added by the Committee on Electrical Equipment to this new 1999 edition. The problem of electromagnetic compatibility and electromagnetic interference are of rapidly increasing concern in health care facilities. This results from the expanding use of electrical devices in general, and those using information processing components in particular. Such devices are inherently more subject to disturbance by electrical energy of low amplitude and over wide frequency ranges. Such disturbances can cause improper operation, give erroneous diagnostic data, deliver improper therapy, and possibly lead to electric hazards.
>
>    At the time the committee wrote this part of the document, there was no national or international consensus on what limits manufacturers should use in the design of devices to operate in electromagnetic environments. In the 1998 Fall Meeting Report on Proposals, the committee expressed the hope that such consensus may be reached in the near future.

### 9-2.1.6.5  Operation with Essential Electrical System.

(a) *General.* Equipment (fixed or appliances) shall be designed to operate normally when energized by a standby power source that conforms to the requirements of Chapter 3.

(b) *Power Transfer.* Following transfer of power between the normal power system and the essential electrical system, a patient-care-related appliance shall resume function in the mode of operation that existed prior to the transfer.

*Exception: If the appliance cannot maintain its mode of operation in the event of a power transfer, it shall default to a nonhazardous status and clearly indicate by audible or visible signals that its mode of operation has changed.*

(c) *Programmable Appliances.* Deenergization of the power supply of a programmable appliance shall not result in the loss or change of any part of the program or data required for normal operation.

*Exception No. 1:  This requirement does not apply to computers and programmable appliances that are not directly related to patient care.*

*Exception No. 2:  Patient-care-related appliances that could suffer loss of program or vital data shall default to a start-up status and clearly indicate by audible or visual signals that its program or data has been altered or lost.*

With the use of appliances that contain digital and computer components come additional concerns about power supply problems. Pre-computer-age appliances rarely were sensitive to brief interruptions of power, such as those that could occur during the testing or use of the essential electrical system. Computer hardware and software, however, can be extremely sensitive to even the briefest interruptions of power.

This material, added in 1993, does not provide design information but is intended to alert the manufacturers of patient-care-related electrical appliances of the nature of this problem. It establishes performance requirements for new appliances and requires that appliances be designed to default to a safe condition and provide a warning(s) if they cannot be designed to be unaffected by power interruption.

Facilities should ensure that existing appliances whose operating characteristics are affected by loss of power do not become unsafe or give erroneous signals or data in the event of a power interruption.

For further information and guidance on this subject, see commentary under 7-2.5 and 9-2.1.5.

### 9-2.1.7  Fire and Explosion Hazards.

**9-2.1.7.1  Materials and Supplies.** Materials used in the construction of, and supplies for, electric appliances shall be noncombustible or flame retardant and impermeable to liquids and gases to the extent practicable; or the materials used in the construction of, and supplies for, electric appliances shall not ignite from internal heating or arcing resulting from any and all possible fault conditions. This includes spillage of liquids such as water and intravenous solutions onto the appliance.

*Exception: Materials used in the construction and operation of electric appliances shall be permitted to be combustible when it is essential to their intended function.*

**9-2.1.7.2\* Oxygen-Enriched Atmospheres.** Electric appliances employing oxygen, or that are intended to be used in oxygen-enriched atmospheres, shall comply with the appropriate provisions of Chapter 8, "Gas Equipment," and Chapter 19, "Hyperbaric Facilities," in addition to all applicable provisions of this chapter.

**A-9-2.1.7.2** See also NFPA 53, *Recommended Practice on Materials, Equipment, and Systems Used in Oxygen-Enriched Atmospheres.*

**9-2.1.7.3 Inhalation Anesthetizing Locations.** Electric appliances used in inhalation anesthetizing locations shall comply with the provisions of Chapter 7, "Electrical Equipment," and 12-4.1, in addition to all applicable provisions of this chapter.

**9-2.1.8 Instruction Manuals and Labels.**

**9-2.1.8.1 Manuals.** The manufacturer of the appliance shall furnish operator's, maintenance, and repair manuals with all units. These manuals shall include operating instructions, maintenance details, and testing procedures.

The manuals shall include the following where applicable:

(a) Illustrations that show location of controls
(b) Explanation of the function of each control
(c) Illustrations of proper connection to the patient and other equipment
(d) Step-by-step procedures for proper use of the appliance
(e) Safety considerations in application and in servicing
(f) Difficulties that might be encountered, and care to be taken if the appliance is used on a patient simultaneously with other electric appliances
(g) Schematics, wiring diagrams, mechanical layouts, parts lists, and other pertinent data for the appliance as shipped
(h) Functional description of the circuit
(i) Electrical supply requirements (volts, frequency, amperes, and watts), heat dissipation, weight, dimensions, output current, output voltage, and other pertinent data
(j) The limits of electrical supply variations—performance specifications of the appliance shall be given for the applicable limits of electrical supply variations.
(k) Technical performance specifications including design levels of leakage current
(l) Instructions for unpacking (readily available upon opening), inspecting, installing, adjusting, and aligning
(m) Comprehensive preventive and corrective maintenance and repair procedures

Where appropriate, the information itemized shall be permitted to be supplied in the form of a separate operating manual and a separate maintenance manual, except that the separate maintenance manual shall also include essentially all the information included in the operating manual.

> These requirements would be satisfied with a manufacturer providing at least one complete set of manuals. For any additional sets, either complete or just the operator or service portion, the purchaser would have to discuss his or her needs with the manufacturer. Additional charges could be involved.
>
> A complete manual set should be kept in the location where the equipment is maintained. A copy of an operator's manual should be kept with the appliance.

**9-2.1.8.2 Operating Instructions on Appliances.** Condensed operating instructions shall be visibly and permanently attached to, or displayed on, any appliance that is intended to be used in emergency situations and that could result in injury or death to the operator or patient if improperly used.

**9-2.1.8.3 Labeling.** The manufacturer shall furnish, for all appliances, labels that are readily visible and legible and that remain so after being in service for the expected life of the appliance under hospital service and cleaning conditions. Controls and indicators shall be labeled to indicate their function. When appropriate, appliances shall be labeled with precautionary statements. All appliances shall be labeled with model numbers, date of manufacture, manufacturer's name, and the electrical ratings including voltage, frequency, current, and/or wattage of the device. Date of manufacture shall be permitted to be a code, if its interpretation is provided to the user. Appliances shall be labeled to indicate if they (1) are listed for use as medical equipment and (2) have isolated patient leads. Appliances intended for use in anesthetizing locations shall be labeled in an approved manner. *(See 12-4.1.)*

> Adequate and appropriate labeling is necessary to reduce the chances of misuse. Appliances are not required to be listed by 9-2.1 (formerly part of NFPA 76B, *Standard for the Safe Use of Electricity in Patient Care Areas of Hospitals*), but if they are, they should be so labeled. Government agencies, such as the U.S. Food and Drug Administration, might have additional regulatory requirements for labeling.

**9-2.1.9 Additional Requirements for Special Appliances.**

**9-2.1.9.1 Signal Transmission Between Appliances.**

(a)* *General.* Signal transmission lines from an appliance in a patient location to remote appliances shall employ a signal transmission system designed to prevent hazardous current flowing in the grounding interconnection of the appliances.

**A-9-2.1.9.1(a)** This can be accomplished by using a signal transmission system that is isolated from ground or presents a high impedance to ground; that employs a common signal grounding wire between appliances served from the same reference grounding point; that employs an additional grounding path between the common signal grounding wire and reference grounding point in the patient vicinity; or by other means intended to reduce potential differences in the patient care vicinity due to grounding currents to a safe level.

This appendix material outlines several possible methods of preventing hazardous current levels. There may be others that could be acceptable.

(b) *Outdoor Signal Transmission.* Outdoor signal transmission lines from appliances attached to patients shall be equipped with surge protection appropriate to the type of transmission line used. Such appliances or signal transmission lines shall be designed to prevent a hazard to the patient from exposure of the lines to lightning, power contact, power induction, rise in ground potential, radio interference, and so forth.

### 9-2.1.9.2 Appliances Intended to Deliver Electrical Energy.

(a)* *Conditions for Meeting Safety Requirements.* Electrical-energy-delivering appliances shall conform to the leakage, grounding, and other requirements of this chapter when powered but not delivering energy.

**A-9-2.1.9.2(a)** When delivering energy, such appliances can deviate from these requirements only to the extent essential for their intended clinical function. Appliances that intentionally or that could inadvertently apply electrical energy to the patient or to components in contact with the patient require special safety considerations. Since there is a wide range of power levels, output frequencies, and purposes of appliances that apply electricity directly to patients or to patient-connected devices, it is not feasible to cite them in detail.

(b) *Specific Requirements by Type of Device.*

1.* *Electrically Powered Transducers.* Exposed metal parts of these devices shall be considered electrodes and meet the applicable requirements of 9-2.1.13, Manufacturers' Tests for Safety of Patient-Care-Related Electrical Appliances. Connectors shall be designed to prevent inadvertent interchange of leads if interchange could constitute a hazard to the patient or operator.

**A-9-2.1.9.2(b)1** Electrically powered transducers include pressure transducers, flowmeters, endoscopes, and so forth. The electrical energy is not intended to be applied to the patient but to a device that contacts the patient.

The intent here is to prohibit interconnections that could cause a shock hazard, not necessarily to prohibit all interconnections. It is good design practice to minimize interconnections to prevent signal interference, but this subject falls outside the scope of the committee responsible for this chapter. (See Exhibit 9.2.)

2.* *Patient Impedance Measuring Devices.* For a particular application, the combination of frequency and current levels shall limit the applied current to the minimum necessary to achieve the medical purposes, but not to exceed the limits given in 9-2.1.13.5, Lead Leakage Current Tests and Limits.

**A-9-2.1.9.2(b)2** Assessment of physiologic functions by electric impedance measurements usually requires direct contact with the patient and injection of electric current.

*Exception: The limits given in 9-2.1.13.5 shall be permitted to be exceeded if essential for the intended clinical function.*

> This exception was added by the committee for this new 1999 edition because there are instances when the applied current necessary for impedance measurement must exceed lead leakage current limits in order to successfully measure impedance.

3.* *Electrotherapeutic Devices.* Appliances that require specific pulse forms or high power levels shall be designed to protect the operator and attendant personnel from accidental electric shock.

**A-9-2.1.9.2(b)3** Electrotherapeutic devices include devices for electrosleep, electroanesthesia, and electroshock.

4.* *Electrosurgery.* Electrosurgical devices shall meet the requirements of 9-2.1.9.2(a), Conditions for Meeting Safety Requirements.

**A-9-2.1.9.2(b)4** See Annex 1, "The Use of High-Frequency Electricity in Health Care Facilities," for information on electrosurgical devices.

Electrosurgery uses high levels of continuous or pulsed radio frequency power. It presents some unique hazards. It generates sparks with the attendant ignition hazard. It generates radio frequency interference that could obstruct monitoring. It can cause burns at inadvertent ground return paths if its return circuit is inadequate. Demodulation products could contain components that cause fibrillation or stimulation. DC monitoring currents can cause chemical burns. Capacitive or inductive coupling may occur.

> This appendix material calls attention to the possibility of an electrosurgical unit not being isolated at 60-Hz current. For more guidance on this subject, see Annex 1, "The Safe Use of High-Frequency Electricity in Health Care Facilities."

*Electrosurgery.* Electrosurgical unit output circuits are commonly designated as isolated or ground-referenced on the basis of their isolation at their operating (RF) frequency. No assumption about isolation at 60 Hz should be made unless the device is specifically labeled as having an "isolated patient circuit (60 Hz)," in which case the device is to conform to the requirements of 9-2.1.13.5(c), Isolation Test.

5.* *Cardiac Defibrillation.* Cardiac defibrillators shall be designed to protect the operator and attendant personnel from accidental electric shock.

**A-9-2.1.9.2(b)5** Cardiac defibrillation applies high-voltage, short-duration pulses to the patient.

> Exhibit 9.3 is an example of an appliance that is intended to deliver high power to a patient.

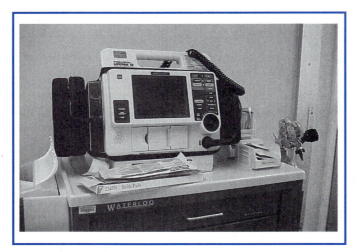

**Exhibit 9.3**  *A defibrillator unit, an example of an electronic device whose output is high-energy electricity that is applied directly into the patient's body. (Courtesy of Rob Swift and Prince William Health Systems.)*

**9-2.1.9.3  Electrical Equipment in Oxygen-Enriched Atmospheres.**  Appliances or part(s) of an appliance or system (e.g., pillow speaker, remote control, pulse oxymeter probe) to be used in the site of intentional expulsion shall comply with the requirements of this section. Those parts of an appliance or system not within oxygen delivery equipment, or not intended to be used in the site of intentional expulsion, shall not be required to comply with this section. Electrically powered equipment intended to be used within oxygen delivery equipment shall comply with (a), (b), (c) or (d) as listed below.

> This paragraph was revised in 1996 to clarify the parts of an appliance that need to conform to the requirements of this section (i.e., that portion of a patient-care-related electrical appliance within the site of intentional expulsion).
>
> Also, it should be noted that this section provides four alternative methods, any one of which can be used to satisfy the requirement allowing the use of a device in an oxygen-enriched atmosphere.

(a) Listed for use in oxygen-enriched atmospheres.

(b) Sealed so as to prevent an oxygen-enriched atmosphere from reaching electrical components. The sealing material shall be of the type that will still seal even after repeated exposure to water, oxygen, mechanical vibration, and heating from the external circuitry.

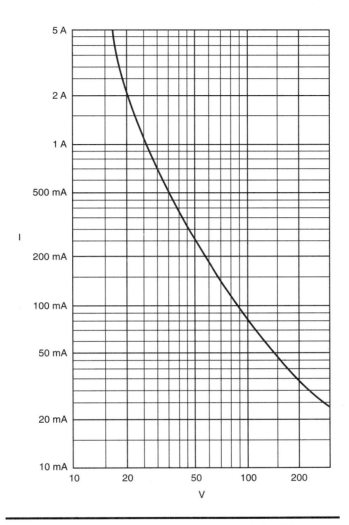

*Figure 9-2.1.9.3(a)* *Resistance circuits (L < 1 mH).*
*Minimum igniting currents, applicable to all circuits*
*containing cadmium, zinc, or magnesium.*

(c)  Ventilated so as to limit the oxygen concentration surrounding electrical components to below 23.5 percent by volume.

(d)  Both of the following:

1.  No hot surfaces over 573°F (300°C).

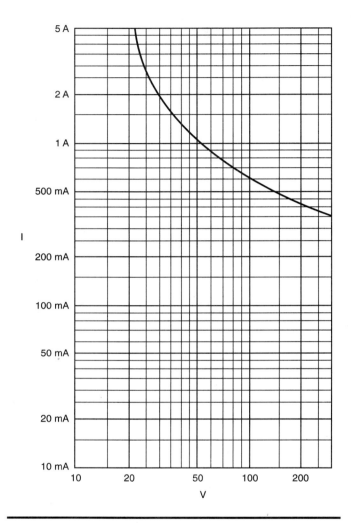

***Figure 9-2.1.9.3(b)*** *Resistance circuits (L < 1 mH).*
*Minimum igniting currents, applicable to circuits where*
*cadmium, zinc, or magnesium can be excluded.*

*Exception: Small (less than 2-W) hermetically sealed heating elements such as light bulbs.*

2. No exposed switching or sparking points of electrical energy that fall to the right of the
   curve for the appropriate type of circuit contained in Figures 9-2.1.9.3(a) through (f).
   The dc (or peak ac) open-circuit voltage and short-circuit current shall be used.

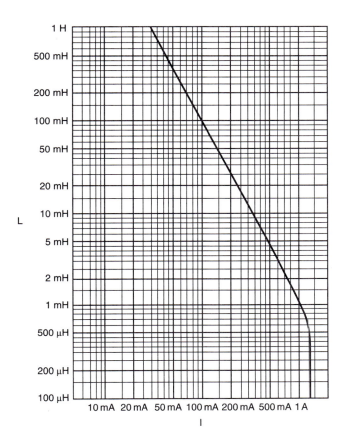

***Figure 9-2.1.9.3(c)*** *Inductance circuits (L > 1 mH).*
*Minimum igniting currents at 24 V, applicable to all circuits*
*containing cadmium, zinc, or magnesium.*

Before the 1987 edition of NFPA 99, only equipment complying with 9-2.1.9.3(a) (i.e., equipment listed for use in oxygen-enriched atmospheres) was considered acceptable for use within the site of administration [i.e., 1 ft (0.31 m) around oxygen-delivery equipment]. For the 1987 edition of NFPA 99, *site of administration* was replaced by the concept of the *site of intentional expulsion* (see commentary in Chapter 2 under this term and in 7-6.2.4.1). This reduced the area considered hazardous to 1 ft (0.31 m) from the vent(s) where oxygen-enriched air was "expelled" (or vented) from equipment. In addition, the former Subcommittee on Gas Equipment (now Committee on Gas Delivery Equipment) approved the allowance of four other safety measures for electrically powered oxygen delivery equipment (for 1993, this number was reduced to three measures). (See 7-6.2.4 for further criteria for users of electrical equipment within the site of intentional expulsion and of electrical equipment used within oxygen delivery equipment.)

The curves in Figures 9-2.1.9.3(a) through (f) are the curves for methane atmospheres and are from former NFPA 493, *Standard for Intrinsically Safe Apparatus*. (NFPA 493 was withdrawn as an NFPA standard and cannot be referenced in other NFPA documents.) However, the committee believes that the information contained in these graphics is still relevant. The committee decided to utilize these well-documented graphs after extensive research [2] concluded that under worst-case conditions the ignition energy necessary to ignite dry cotton lint was somewhat greater than the minimum energy necessary to ignite methane atmospheres.

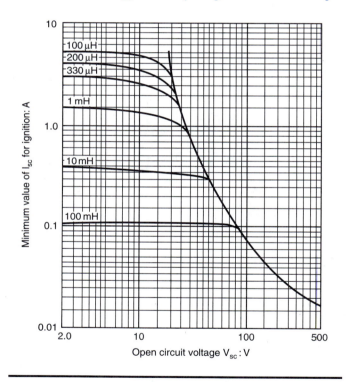

*Figure 9-2.1.9.3(d)  Inductance circuits (L > 1 mH).*
*Minimum igniting currents for various voltages, applicable to all circuits containing cadmium, zinc, or magnesium.*

**9-2.1.10 Low-Voltage Appliances and Appliances Not Connected to the Electric Power Distribution System.**

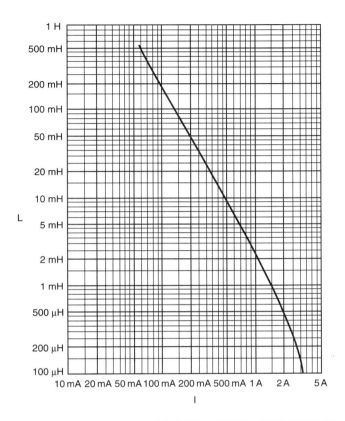

***Figure 9-2.1.9.3(e)*** *Inductance circuits (L > 1 mH).*
*Minimum igniting currents at 24 V, applicable only to circuits*
*where cadmium, zinc, or magnesium can be excluded.*

**9-2.1.10.1 General.** Appliances and instruments operating from batteries or their equivalent or from an external source of low voltage or that are not connected to the electric power distribution system shall conform to all applicable requirements of 9-2.1, Patient-Care-Related Electrical Appliances. This shall include communication, signaling, entertainment, remote-control, and low-energy power systems.

*Exception: Telephones.*

**9-2.1.10.2 Rechargeable Appliances.** Battery-operated appliances that are rechargeable while in use shall meet all the requirements of 9-2.1.13.3, Leakage Current Tests, for line-operated appliances.

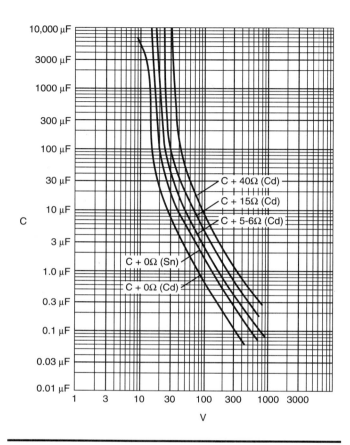

***Figure 9-2.1.9.3(f)*** *Capacitance circuits minimum ignition voltages. The curves correspond to values of current-limiting resistance as indicated. The curve marked Sn is applicable only where cadmium, zinc, or magnesium can be excluded.*

**9-2.1.10.3 Low-Voltage Connectors.** Attachment plugs used on low-voltage circuits shall have distinctive configurations that do not permit interchangeable connection with circuits of other voltages.

**9-2.1.10.4 Isolation of Low-Voltage Circuits.** Circuits of 30 V (dc or ac rms) or less shall be electrically isolated from the power distribution system. Grounded low-voltage circuits shall be permitted provided that load currents are not carried in the grounding conductor.

**9-2.1.11 Cardiac Monitors and Electrocardiographs.** Monitoring of cardiac activity is crucial to effective defibrillation. Design of electrocardiographs, cardiac monitors, or blood-pressure monitors intended for use on patients in critical care shall include protection against equipment damage during defibrillation of the patient.

**9-2.1.12\*  Direct Electrical Pathways to the Heart.**  The requirements of this section shall apply only to manufacturers except where specifically noted.

**A-9-2.1.12**  This section is concerned with the patient who has either of two types of direct electrical connections to the heart. The obvious and most hazardous conductor comprises a wire in contact with the heart muscle. This can be a pacemaker electrode, a guide wire, or a transthoracic or implanted electrode. The second type of conductor is a liquid column contained within a nonconductive catheter with the internal end in the heart.

> In the appendix material, "transthoracic" refers to electrodes that enter the heart through the chest wall.
>
> A direct electrical pathway to the heart is not established by a simple invasive procedure to a peripheral vessel. The end of the electrical probe or liquid-filled conductor inside the body must come in contact with the heart to establish a direct electrical pathway to it.
>
> Although this section is intended primarily to guide manufacturers in the design of safe equipment, health care facility personnel also need to be aware of these design requirements so that they are not compromised. Some of the requirements listed apply specifically to facility operating personnel but were placed in this section because of their relationship to manufacturers' requirements. Listing requirements for both allows facility personnel to appreciate the totality of the problem. A close relationship needs to be maintained between manufacturers and users in order to meet the requirements of this critical area of electrical safety.

**9-2.1.12.1  Cardiac Electrodes.**

(a) *General.* Appliances that have isolated patient leads shall be labeled as having isolated patient leads in accordance with 9-2.1.13.5, Lead Leakage Current Tests and Limits.

(b)\* *Insulation of Cardiac Leads.* Pacemaker leads and other wires intended for insertion into the heart, together with their adapters and connections to appliances, shall be insulated except for their sensing or stimulation areas.

**A-9-2.1.12.1(b)**  The user is required to have a policy to protect pacing leads with external terminals from potentially hazardous contact with conductive surfaces (*see 7-6.2.1.3, Protection of Patients with Direct Electrical Pathways to the Heart*).

*Exception No. 1: Metal stylets or guide wires temporarily introduced into a vein or artery for purposes of positioning a catheter need not be insulated. When such guide wires are inside the heart, the operator shall exercise extreme care to ensure safe use. When used in conjunction with electrical devices (e.g., positioning catheters by use of ECG recordings), the guide wire shall be insulated as required above.*

*Exception No. 2: Insulated wires designed to be introduced through a surgical needle, or other special wires where it is not practicable to maintain insulation, shall not be required to maintain insulation during introduction or manipulation. At such times the operator shall take appropriate safeguards.*

(c) *Safety Requirements for Cardiac Electrodes.* The electrode catheter, fitting, and associated appliance, when assembled, shall meet the applicable requirements of 9-2.1.13.5, Lead Leakage Current Tests and Limits, for isolated patient leads.

(d) *Insulation of Pacemaker Connections.* Uninsulated or open-type connectors shall not be used for external cardiac pacemaker terminals.

## 9-2.1.12.2 Liquid-Filled Catheters.

(a)* *Cardiac Catheter System.* Any conductive element of a liquid catheter system that can come in contact with the liquid column shall be insulated from ground or electric energy sources.

**A-9-2.1.12.2(a)** A liquid catheter system can consist of the catheter itself, pressure transducers, electronic appliances, and associated accessories.

(b) *Nonconductive Cardiac Catheters.* A nonconductive catheter containing a conductive liquid, when connected to its appropriate system, shall meet the applicable requirements of 9-2.1.13.5, Lead Leakage Current Tests and Limits, for isolated patient leads, with the patient end of the liquid-filled catheter considered to be an electrode.

(c) *Conductive Cardiac Catheters.* If the liquid column is contained in a catheter made of conductive material having an electrical conductivity approximating that of blood, the system shall not require connection to an isolated patient lead. Conductive catheters shall be appropriately identified.

**9-2.1.12.3\* Angiographic Catheters.** Appliances used to inject contrast media into the heart or major vessels shall meet the same safety requirements as other liquid-filled catheter systems.

**A-9-2.1.12.3** Although contrast injectors are not intended to apply electrical energy to the patient, they could deliver current from the power source and also could generate transient voltages large enough to be hazardous.

The committee has noted that the contrast medium, not the injector, is the major hazard. The injector, however, should be designed to reduce the hazard.

**9-2.1.13 Manufacturers' Tests for Safety of Patient-Care-Related Electrical Appliances.**
**9-2.1.13.1 General.** This section describes tests by manufacturers for the safe operation of an appliance. The tests in this subsection are in addition to the design requirements of the entire section 9-2.1, Patient-Care-Related Electrical Appliances. The appliance manufacturer shall perform the testing adequate to ensure that each finished appliance will meet the specified test limits of this section.

*Exception: Tests that are potentially destructive need only be performed by the manufacturer to ensure design compliance for new appliances.*

It is not necessary for manufacturers to perform all of these tests. Only those tests necessary to ensure that appliances meet the requirements of this section need to be performed.

**9-2.1.13.2 Grounding Circuit Continuity—Measurement of Resistance.** The resistance between the appliance chassis, or any exposed conductive surface of the appliance, and the ground pin of the attachment plug shall be measured. The resistance shall be less than 0.15 ohm. The cord shall be flexed at its connection to the attachment plug or connector, and at its connection to the strain relief on the chassis during the resistance measurement.

If there is no grounding conductor (as is the case in most listed double-insulated appliances), this test cannot be performed. However, if there is a grounding conductor, even if unnecessary, the test should be conducted. This will avoid a possible misunderstanding on the part of the user concerning the significance of the grounding.

**9-2.1.13.3\* Leakage Current Tests.**

**A-9-2.1.13.3** For complex leakage current waveforms, a single reading from an appropriate metering system can represent the physiologically effective value of the composite waveform, provided that the contribution of each component to the total reading is weighted in accordance with 7-5.1.3.3 or 9-2.1.13.3.

This "weighting" can be achieved by a frequency-response-shaping network that precedes a flat-response meter, or by a meter whose own frequency response characteristic matches 7-5.1.3.3 or 9-2.1.13.3.

If the required performance is obtained by a meter with integral response shaping properties, then that meter should have a constant input resistance of 1000 ohms. (A high-input-impedance meter can be used by shunting a 1000-ohm resistor across the meter's input terminals.)

If, however, the required frequency response is obtained by a network that precedes an otherwise flat-response meter, then the input impedance of the network should be 1000 ohms $\pm$ 10 percent, over the frequency range from 0 to 1 MHz, and the frequency response of the network-meter combination should be substantially independent of the impedance of the signal source.

For maximum chassis leakage current allowed (i.e., 300 microamperes) below 1 kHz, this network will yield the limiting current of 10 mA above 30 kHz.

A suggested input network is shown in Figure A-7-5.1.3.3.

These currents usually derive from the line power by resistive paths, or capacitive or inductive coupling. However, they also include currents from other sources generated within the appliance and are measured by the tests described in this chapter.

These leakage current limits are based on acute events, for example, sensation, duration tetany, or ventricular fibrillation. Appliance design should aim to reduce such current as much as possible. In properly grounded appliances, maximum chassis leakage current is in the grounding conductor and not through the patient.

These tests are not known to be adequate where currents (such as dc or high frequency) are introduced into the patient for long periods and where low-level effects must be considered. *(See also A-7-5.1.3.3.)*

> This suggested network will give a proportional response up to 100 kHz. However, it is cautioned that the use of this network–meter combination was originally designed when the chassis leakage current limit was 100 mA to conform to a maximum leakage current limit of 10 mA per 7-5.1.3.3.(c). For higher frequency values, this network–meter circuit is usable only to 30 kHz in order to meet the 10-mA limitation.
>
> The 10-mA limitation addresses thermal safety, not shock hazard.
>
> When manufacturer requirements were placed in a separate chapter of NFPA 76B, *Standard for the Safe Use of Electricity in Patient Care Areas of Hospitals,* some tests for manufacturers were not included. One test for hospitals was also inadvertently not included. The following tests are now in the same sequence as those for manufacturers in 9-2.1:
>
> (a) Chassis
> 1. Permanently wired
> 2. Cord-connected
> (b) Patient leads
> 1. Lead-to-ground (nonisolated input)
> 2. Lead-to-ground (isolated input)
> 3. Isolated test (isolated input)
> 4. Between leads (nonisolated input)
> 5. Between leads (isolated input)
>
> The values for leakage currents reflect exhaustive discussion of studies conducted on humans and dogs, actual measurements during cardiac surgery, and manufacturing capabilities. For further information, see A-9-2.1.13.4(c).

(a) *Techniques of Measurement.* Each test shall be performed with the appropriate connection to a properly grounded ac power system.

(b)* *Frequency of Leakage Current.* The leakage current limits stated in 9-2.1.13.4, Leakage Current from Appliance to Ground, and 9-2.1.13.5, Lead Leakage Current Tests and Limits, shall be rms values for dc and sinusoidal waveforms up to 1 kHz. For frequencies above 1 kHz, the leakage current limits shall be the values given in 9-2.1.13.4 and 9-2.1.13.5 multiplied by the frequency, in kHz, up to a maximum of 10 mA.

This "weighting" can be achieved by a frequency-response-shaping network that precedes a flat response meter, or by a meter whose own frequency response characteristic matches 9-2.1.13.3(b).

**A-9-2.1.13.3(b)** The limits for nonsinusoidal periodic, modulated, and transient waveforms remain to be determined.

For complex leakage current waveforms, a single reading from an appropriate metering system can represent the physiologically effective value of the composite waveform, provided that the contribution of each component to the total reading is weighted in accordance with 9-2.1.13.3(b).

For the reason behind a maximum value of 10 mA, see commentary following A-7-5.1.3.3.

(c) *Leakage Current in Relation to Polarity.* Leakage current measurements shall be made with the polarity of the power line normal and reversed, with the power switch of the appliance "on" and "off," and with all operating controls in the positions to cause maximum leakage current readings. The leakage current limits in 9-2.1.13.4 and 9-2.1.13.5 shall not be exceeded under any of these conditions.

Material on manufacturer leakage current testing was reorganized and made congruent with facility testing procedures. (See also commentary on 7-5.1.3.3.) Leakage current is to be measured from power supplied directly from the normal electrical distribution, not from power being supplied from an isolation transformer. Incorrect values will result otherwise.

## 9-2.1.13.4 Leakage Current from Appliance to Ground.

(a) *Test Methods.* The current shall be measured from the exposed conductive surfaces of the appliance to ground with all grounding conductors open at the end nearest the power receptacle. The appliance shall not be grounded by any other means. The current meter shall be inserted between the exposed conductive surfaces and ground. This test shall be made under the conditions of 9-2.1.13.3. This test is illustrated in Figure 9-2.1.13.4(a).

Figure 9-2.1.13.4(a) reflects a better way to measure leakage current, that is, by connecting a probe to exposed conductive surfaces.

The equipment addressed in this section and in 7-5.2.2.1 deals with non-patient care appliances that will be used in the patient care vicinity. These types of appliances are not intended to contact the patient, but the possibility exists that they could do so.

(b) *Appliances with No Exposed Conductive Surfaces.* When the appliance has no exposed conductive surface, one shall be simulated by placing a 3.9 in. by 7.8 in. (10 cm by 20 cm) bare metal foil in intimate contact with the exposed surface. This shall be considered the "exposed metal surface" of the appliance and all appropriate tests shall be performed to the foil.

The dimensions of the metal foil are considered to approximate the surface area of a hand touching an appliance. Hence, the leakage current measured here is a capacity-

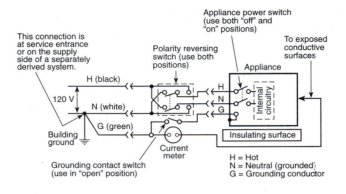

*Figure 9-2.1.13.4(a)* Test circuit for measuring leakage current from exposed conductive surfaces.

coupled area measurement instead of a point measurement. The committee felt this was a reasonable test for manufacturers to conduct for such appliances. It is a particularly pertinent test when appliances are covered with an insulating film but are not listed as double insulated.

(c)* *Chassis Leakage Current Limits.*

1. *Cord-Connected Appliances.* Cord-connected appliances that are intended for use in the patient care vicinity shall not exceed 300 microamperes of chassis leakage current as measured in 9-2.1.13.4(a), Test Methods.
2. *Permanently Wired Equipment.* Permanently wired equipment installed in the patient care vicinity shall not have leakage current from the frame to ground in excess of 5.0 mA. The leakage current shall be measured prior to installation by the installer and verified and accepted by the facility. This measurement shall be made in accordance with 9-2.1.13.4(a) while the equipment is temporarily insulated from ground.

**A-9-2.1.13.4(c)**  The chassis leakage current limits given in 9-2.1.13.4(c) and in other sections, combined with the grounding wire requirements, are based on a concept of two layers of protection. Either the limited leakage current or an intact grounding system will provide protection. However, it is generally agreed that not only with medical equipment but also with conventional appliances, there should be two levels of protection. This means that both safeguards will have to fail before the subject is at hazard.

For general application (household appliances) the leakage current limit is generally set at 500 microamperes at 60 Hz. The limit of 500 microamperes is based on the work of Dalziel and others which indicates that different individuals in the general population will exhibit responses to electrical shock at differing levels. A small percentage, perhaps 5 percent, will react to a current level of 500 microamperes with an involuntary movement that could trigger a secondary accident. Some individuals are sensitive to an electric shock sensation as low as 100 microamperes. A reasonable compromise seems to be to set the limit at 500 for the general public. It should be noted that in 7-5.2.2.1, this is the limit for household-type appliances.

*References:*

Dalziel, C. F., and Lee, W. R., Reevaluation of lethal, electric currents effects of electricity on man. *Transactions on Industry and General Applications.* Vol. IGA-4, No. 5, September/October 1968.

Roy, O. A., Park, G. R., and Scott, J. R., Intracardiac catheter fibrillation thresholds as a function of duration of 60 Hz current and electrode area. *IEEE Trans. Biomed. Eng.* BME 24:430-435, 1977.

Roy, O. A., and Scott, J. R., 60 Hz ventricular fibrillation and pump failure thresholds versus electrode area. *IEEE Trans. Biomed. Eng.* BME 23:45-48, 1976.

Watson, A. B., Wright, J. S., and Loughman, J., Electrical thresholds for ventricular fibrillation in man. *Med. J. Australia* 1:1179-1181, 1973.

Weinberg, D. I., et al., Electric shock hazards in cardiac catheterization. *Elec. Eng.* 82:30-35, 1963.

For equipment in the patient care vicinity it seems reasonable to reduce this limit to 300 microamperes, because of the special circumstances involved in hospitals. Some of these factors are as follow:

(a) Some patients could be wet or have some other low-impedance connection to the ground. For this reason the assumption usually made for the general public that they are moderately insulated from ground is not valid.
(b) Patients are sick, tend to be unresponsive, tend to be obtunded, and might not be able to perform the evasive maneuvers that an alert adult would perform when experiencing an electrical shock.
(c) The nature of the patient's illness could exacerbate the response to electric shock.
(d) Hospital patients are increasingly in close proximity to more and more electrical equipment.
(e) Hospital equipment is subject to industrial-type abuse. It is handled roughly, is sometimes wet, and sometimes not properly maintained. All of this increases the probability of deterioration and consequent increase in leakage.
(f) The economics of the problem has been considered. The medical appliance industry has responded to the requirement for 300 microamperes maximum leakage by designing equipment within that limit. It has been shown to be feasible and not unduly uneconomical. In the few cases where, for technical reasons, it is impractical to reach these limits, other solutions are available.

It should be emphasized that the reduced leakage current limit is not based on clear technical evidence but represents considered opinion. Therefore, if a particular appliance has a leakage current somewhat above 300 microamperes, it is not implied that it is dangerously unsafe. It does indicate that such an appliance should be examined to determine whether there is a reason for the higher leakage. If the leakage cannot be reduced, it can be compensated for by more-intensive preventive maintenance to ensure that the grounding conductor is intact.

For the 1993 edition of NFPA 99, the chassis leakage current limit was raised to 300 microamperes because experience indicated that the safety factor originally used could be reduced without compromising patient safety.

It should be further noted that the shock hazards produced by these current levels apply to external contacts, that is, body surface ECG lead or a skin contact with the chassis of an appliance. These current values do not apply to intracardiac leads. For such leads the hazard is not startle, involuntary muscular motion, or "let-go." It is frank fibrillation of the heart, and is caused at levels a factor of 1000 below those necessary to cause fibrillation by external contacts. It is impractical to provide protection to the patient who has an intracardiac lead by means of the control of chassis leakage current, isolated power systems, ground fault interrupter circuits, or other similar external devices. Protection for such patients can be achieved only by the protection of the intracardiac lead. This is discussed in 9-2.1.12, Direct Electrical Pathways to the Heart. For such patients the limit of such leads has been placed at 10 microamperes with the ground intact (i.e., under normal conditions). Again there is a safety factor involved. The lower limit of hazardous currents seems to be about 100 microamperes at 60 Hz. A safety factor of 10 has been established because of most of the reasons above, and because of the following:

(a) Patients with intracardiac leads are usually ones whose hearts are already in jeopardy.
(b) Such patients usually have even more electrical equipment near them than does the average patient.
(c) It has been shown to be economically quite feasible to maintain such leads at a limit of 10 microamperes with the ground intact (i.e., under normal conditions).

The material in 9-2.1 is applicable only to manufacturers of patient-care-related electrical appliances.

The former Committee on Safe Use of Electricity in Patient Care Areas of Health Care Facilities (now the Committee on Electrical Equipment) rejected the concept of subdividing these types of appliances into two categories: appliances likely to contact the patient and appliances not likely to contact the patient. The committee noted that it was also not its intent to have two categories of patient-care-related electrical appliances because all cord-connected patient-care-related electrical appliances in a patient care vicinity are likely to contact patients. The committee modified the previous title of 9-2.1.13.4(c)1 to reflect that the limit applied to all cord-connected patient-care-related electrical appliances.

Chassis leakage current limits were extensively debated by the Health Care Facilities Committees during the revisions for the 1990 and 1993 editions of NFPA 99. For the 1990 edition, proposals to raise the limit to 500 microamperes were presented. Consensus for this value could not be reached and the value remained at 100 microamperes. For the 1993 edition, there were proposals again to raise the limit and after much debate, the value was raised to 300 microamperes. (For discussion on this issue, see commentary following 7-5.1.3.5.)

The reference to "facility" in 9-2.1.13.4(c)2 of the main text is made because that paragraph requires both the manufacturer and the facility to participate in the test.

### 9-2.1.13.5  Lead Leakage Current Tests and Limits.

See the commentary under the exception to 9-2.1.9.2(b)2.

(a) *Lead to Ground (Nonisolated Input).* The lead leakage current to ground shall be measured under the conditions of 9-2.1.13.3, Leakage Current Tests. The test shall be made between each patient lead and ground and between the combined patient leads and ground. The test shall be made with the patient leads active (e.g., in the case of a multilead instrument, the lead selector switch shall be advanced through all operating positions). Each measurement shall be performed with the grounding conductors both opened and closed. For this purpose the grounding conductor shall be interrupted at the plug end of the appliance cord. Figure 9-2.1.13.5(a) is an example of an acceptable test configuration. The leakage current shall not exceed 100 microamperes.

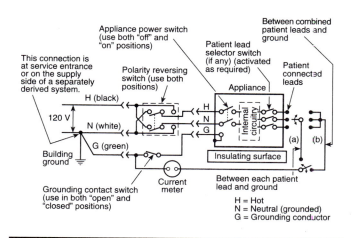

***Figure 9-2.1.13.5(a)*** *Test circuit for measuring leakage current between patient leads and ground (nonisolated).*

While the organization of lead leakage current tests for manufacturers and health care facilities has been made congruent (see commentary on 7-5.1.3.6), the test and value for the lead-to-ground test for nonisolated inputs have been made more exacting for manufacturers than for users (i.e., health care facilities).

For health care facilities, this lead test is to be conducted with the patient leads combined (connected together). For manufacturers, this test is to be conducted between each patient lead and ground and between combined patient leads and ground. Making both individual and combined measurements is technically more accurate in the instance of active driven leads, because the current would be only in the driven leads. Otherwise, their contribution of leakage current could be shunted off through another lead when measured in the combined configuration, and an accurate meter reading would not be taken. Requiring both tests brings this requirement into conformity with the Association for Advancement of Medical Instrumentation and its document *Safe Current Limits.* [3]

The former Committee on Safe Use of Electricity in Patient Care Areas of Health Care Facilities (now the Committee on Electrical Equipment) did not feel that health care facilities needed to be this exacting in their measurements when conducting the lead-to-ground test for nonisolated inputs.

In 1996 the leakage current limit was raised from 50 microamperes to 100 microamperes. This change is consistent with international standards such as IEC 60601-1. [4]

(b) *Lead to Ground (Isolated Input).* The leakage current to ground between each patient lead and ground shall be measured under the conditions of 9-2.1.13.3, Leakage Current Tests. The test shall be made with the patient leads active (e.g., in the case of a multilead instrument, the lead selector switch shall be advanced through all operating positions). Each measurement shall be performed with the grounding conductors both opened and closed. For this purpose the grounding conductor shall be interrupted at the plug end of the appliance cord. Figure 9-2.1.13.5(b) is an example of an acceptable test configuration. The leakage current shall not exceed 10 microamperes with the ground intact and 50 microamperes with the ground open.

The leakage current limit was raised in 1990 to conform with the IEC 60601-1 document. [4]

(c) *Isolation Test (Isolated Input).* The isolation between each patient lead and ground for an appliance that has been labeled as having isolated patient leads shall be measured by observing the current produced by applying an external source of power-line frequency and voltage between the lead and ground while the leads are approximately 8 in. (20 cm) from a grounded conductive surface. Similarly, the isolation at the apparatus terminals to the patient cables shall be measured. Figure 9-2.1.13.5(c) is an example of an acceptable test configuration. At the patient end of the leads, the leakage current shall not exceed

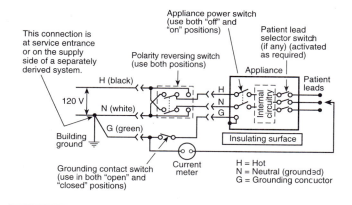

**Figure 9-2.1.13.5(b)**  *Test circuit for measuring leakage current between patient leads and ground (isolated).*

50 microamperes and at the apparatus terminals, 25 microamperes. Only appliances meeting this requirement shall be permitted to be identified as having isolated patient leads.

Suitable safety precautions (such as including a resistance in series to limit the current, insulation of the meter, and a momentary switch) shall be taken to protect the operator. In appliances without a power cord or with ungrounded, exposed conductive surfaces, measurements shall be made with the exposed conductive surfaces temporarily grounded. If there is no exposed conductive surface, measurement shall be made with a simulated surface, as described in 9-2.1.13.4(b), Appliances with No Exposed Conductive Surfaces, which is also temporarily grounded.

In 1996 the leakage current limit was raised to conform with international standards such as IEC 60601-1. [4]

(d) *Between Leads (Nonisolated Input).* The current between any pair of leads or any single lead and all others shall be measured under the conditions of 9-2.1.13.3, Leakage Current Tests. Each measurement shall be performed with the grounding conductors both opened and closed. For this purpose the grounding conductor shall be interrupted at the plug end of the appliance cord. Figure 9-2.1.13.5(d)/(e) is an example of an acceptable test configuration. The leakage current shall not exceed 50 microamperes.

*Exception: Measuring leakage current between any single lead and all other leads need only be performed to assure the approval agency of design compliance.*

(e) *Between Leads (Isolated Input).* The current between any pair of leads or any single lead and all others shall be measured under the conditions of 9-2.1.13.3, Leakage Current Tests. Each measurement shall be performed with the grounding conductors both opened and closed. For this purpose the grounding conductor shall be interrupted at the plug end of

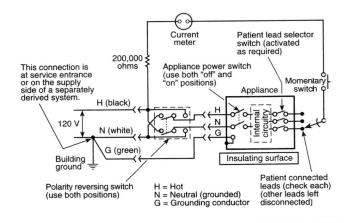

**Figure 9-2.1.13.5(c)** *Test circuit for measuring the electrical isolation of isolated patient leads.*

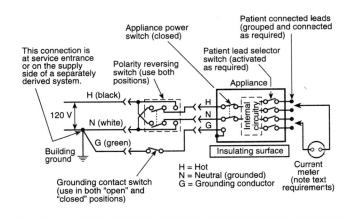

**Figure 9-2.1.13.5(d)/(e)** *Test circuit for measuring leakage current between patient leads (nonisolated and isolated).*

the appliance cord. Figure 9-2.1.13.5(d)/(e) is an example of an acceptable test configuration. The leakage current shall not exceed 10 microamperes with the ground intact and 50 microamperes with the ground open.

*Exception: Measuring leakage current between any single lead and all other leads need only be performed to ensure the approval agency of design compliance.*

As with the two testing configurations in 9-2.1.13.5(a), the purpose of the change requiring manufacturers to measure leakage current both with and without patient leads is for accuracy and to ensure that the maximum value at apparatus terminals is safe as well as consistent among manufacturers. This requirement makes the test conform with other U.S. documents. Again, health care facilities need to make this measurement only with the patient cable connected.

In 1990 the leakage current limit was changed to be in concert with international standards such as IEC 60601-1. [4]

## 9-2.2 Nonpatient Electrical Equipment.

(Reserved)

## 9-3 Gas Equipment

(Reserved)

## 9-4 Material

(Reserved)

### References Cited in Commentary

1. *Health Devices,* 4:75, vol. 4, no. 75, 1975.
2. Lipschultz, *Medical Instrumentation,* Association for Advancement of Medical Instrumentation, 3330 Washington Blvd., Suite 400, Arlington, VA 22201-4598.
3. *Safe Current Limits,* Association for the Advancement of Medical Instrumentation, 3330 Washington Blvd., Suite 400, Arlington, VA 22201-4598.
4. (IEC) International Electrotechnical Commission Standard 60601-1 (1988-12), *Medical Electrical Equipment—Part 1: General Requirements for Safety.*

# CHAPTER 10

# Laboratories

In 1966 the Subcommittee on Hospital Laboratories was created out of the Committee on Hospitals. This subcommittee was charged with developing a standard that would address the hazards associated with the operation of laboratories within health care facilities. Despite the fact that clinical laboratories usually contained flammable and combustible gases, solvents, and solids at the time, there were no fire safety requirements for the safe use of such chemicals in laboratories.

Of particular concern to the subcommittee were the construction criteria for hospital laboratories. Laboratories were often placed close to patient care areas for convenient access to patients requiring tests and for efficient transmission of laboratory results to nursing units on patient floors. This proximity to patient care areas posed a serious fire exposure hazard to patients.

In 1968 the subcommittee proposed a manual on the subject. NFPA 56CM, which was adopted as a full standard in 1973 (NFPA 56C). Included in the document were safety precautions for the storage and handling of flammable and combustible substances and requirements for the posting of hazard symbols, as detailed in NFPA 704, *Standard System for the Identification of the Hazards of Materials for Emergency Response* [1]. The requirement for the use of this system of signage was removed in 1998, however, and made effective with the 1999 edition. (See 10-8.2.1.)

In 1975 NFPA 45, *Standard on Fire Protection for Laboratories Using Chemicals* [2], was adopted. It became apparent at that time, and later when NFPA 56C was incorporated in NFPA 99, that the scopes of the two documents needed to be clearly delineated to avoid any overlapping of requirements. With the advice of the Standards Council, any potential for conflict was resolved with the adoption of certain ground rules that would govern the development of NFPA 99 and NFPA 45. NFPA 45 would detail the construction requirements that apply to any laboratory, including health care laboratories, where flammable or combustible liquids are stored or used in quantity. NFPA 99 would focus on the additional fire prevention and protection practices relevant to health care occupancies. Distinguishing between these two primary standards increases in importance as laboratories providing in-patient care move out of hospitals and as freestanding laboratories expand their scope of services.

Over the years, the requirements for laboratories in health care facilities have undergone continual refinement. The adoption and enforcement of the provisions contained herein have virtually eliminated hospital and other health care facility laboratories as a source of danger to patients and laboratory personnel. Property damage, however, remains a serious issue. Based on 1992 through 1996 averages, NFPA estimates that just under 100 fires reported to U.S. local fire departments occur in laboratories of health care facilities each year. These fires cause an estimated three non-fatal injuries and $420,000 in direct property damage per year. (These national estimates are based on fire department data from NFPA's annual survey of fire experience and the U.S. Fire Administration's National Fire Incident Reporting System.)

## 10-1* Scope

Most clinical laboratories use ignitible liquids, and many store flammable gases. This, along with the presence of considerable quantities of medical supplies and paper documents, contributes to the ignition fuel load. Any of the multiple items of electrical equipment in use can become an ignition source under the right conditions. Laboratory employees need to be aware of these hazards, know how best to prevent fire, and know how to prevent fire emergencies.

Patients incapable of self-preservation can occasionally be found in some clinical laboratories that are in or adjacent to patient care areas. The scope of this chapter was defined primarily as for the protection of these patients.

In 1980 all references to nonflammable gases were deleted from NFPA 56C. In addition, requirements for liquefied gases were also deleted because they are generally not used in clinical laboratories. However, in 1984 (when NFPA 56C was incorporated into NFPA 99), guidance on nonflammable piped gas systems was added in the interest of safety for laboratory personnel.

**A-10-1 Application of Requirements.** The application of requirements contained in this chapter for specific types of health care facilities can be found in Chapters 12 through 18.

*Table on Using NFPA Documents for Laboratories in Health Care Facilities.* The following are some considerations in determining which document (NFPA 99 or 45) should be consulted first when designing or operating a laboratory in a health care facility (i.e., those laboratories under the jurisdiction of a health care facility as defined in Chapter 2 of NFPA 99). In addition, the following paragraphs should be reviewed in conjunction with this table:

1-1.1 in NFPA 45-1996, *Standard on Fire Protection for Laboratories Using Chemicals* and Sections 1-1 and 10-1 in NFPA 99-1999

Table A-10-1 was added in 1993 to help users of NFPA 45 and 99 determine which document was applicable to a particular laboratory. Patients "incapable of self-preservation" include bedridden, hospitalized patients. It also includes nonhospitalized patients undergoing general anesthesia and patients under deep conscious sedation. For example, a clinical laboratory located within a hospital building and in a regular patient area would use NFPA 99 as its primary standard. An independent, freestanding clinical laboratory would refer directly to NFPA 45.

The more difficult decision regarding applicability concerns the degree of separation of a hospital laboratory from areas of direct patient care. Most hospital laboratories that are completely detached from their inpatient facility or that are separated from it by 2-hour construction should use NFPA 45. Paragraph 12-1.2.2 of NFPA *101, Life Safety Code* [3], permits such services to be classified as business occupancies. Exceptions to this basic rule would be the presence of nonambulatory patients visiting the laboratory for phlebotomy and anesthetized patients brought to the laboratory for special studies. In such exceptional cases, NFPA 99 would be the primary document even for freestanding clinical labs.

*Table A-10-1*

| Location of Laboratory | Primary Reference Document |
|---|---|
| 1. Laboratory in bldg. with inpatients | 99 |
| 2. Laboratory in bldg. with outpatients incapable of self-preservation | 99 |
| 3. Laboratory in a bldg. with outpatients capable of self-preservation | 45 |

**10-1.1\*** This chapter establishes criteria to minimize the hazards of fire and explosions in laboratories, as defined in Chapter 2.

This section is not intended to cover hazards resulting from the misuse of chemicals, radioactive materials, or biological materials that will not result in fires or explosions. Although it deals primarily with hazards related to fires and explosions, many of the requirements to protect against fire or explosion, such as those for hood exhaust systems, also serve to protect persons from exposure to nonfire health hazards of these materials.

The omission of any standards for protection from radiation, from infectious organisms, or from genetically active agents is not intended to minimize the seriousness of such hazards. Laboratory personnel need to be aware of all the other types of hazards to be contained. By meeting with local fire authorities and providing appropriate signs, the laboratory's leadership can apprise fire responders of all the types of potential exposure that might be encountered in responding to an incident in the laboratory. Paragraph 10-8.2.2 was added in 1999 to underscore this goal.

Requirements and recommendations of other organizations and agencies should be reviewed and integrated with the requirements of this chapter to be sure that fire safety preparations and environmental, chemical, and biological safety precautions do not interfere with one another. As safety training programs in laboratory fire prevention and preparedness are developed, introduction to applicable fire codes can be integrated with other regulatory requirements.

**A-10-1.1** Before a hazardous chemical is ordered, controls should be established to ensure that adequate facilities and procedures are available for receiving, storing, using, and disposing of the material. Information sources include the following:

NFPA 49, *Hazardous Chemicals Data*

NFPA 325, *Guide to Fire Hazard Properties of Flammable Liquids, Gases, and Volatile Solids*

NFPA 491, *Guide to Hazardous Chemical Reactions*

NOTE: NFPA 49 and NFPA 325 are available in the NFPA publication *Fire Protection Guide to Hazardous Materials*, 12th edition, 1997.

Class IA and IB flammable liquids in glass containers larger than the 1-qt (0.91-L) size should be transported in suitable containers of sufficient size to hold the contents of the glass containers.

Another source of information on hazardous chemicals is the material safety data sheets (MSDSs) provided by manufacturers for the chemicals they produce.

Because of the nature of health care facility laboratory work, engineering and work-practice controls have been developed for use by all laboratories. While construction and equipment requirements are applicable to new laboratories (per Section 1-2), safe work practices with respect to laboratory activities always apply.

## 10-1.2 Interface with Existing Codes and Standards.

**10-1.2.1\*** NFPA 45, *Standard on Fire Protection for Laboratories Using Chemicals*, is the basic NFPA standard for laboratories that covers the construction, ventilation systems, and related fire protection of all laboratories in all facilities. However, this chapter (Chapter 10) has more stringent requirements for laboratories located in health care facilities. Where interface with existing NFPA or other consensus codes and standards occurs, reference is made to the appropriate source in the text.

**A-10-1.2.1** While NFPA 45 provides basic requirements and guidance for laboratory design, fire separation and sprinkler requirements are more stringent for laboratories in health care facilities. In addition, NFPA 99 has more stringent and realistic limitations of quantities of flammable liquids in laboratories, requires hood discharge above the roof, allows valves on emergency water supplies, encourages laboratory safety program activities, and recommends placement of flammable gas cylinders outside of the laboratory.

**10-1.2.2** Where necessary, due to the special nature of laboratories, codes and standards are supplemented in this text so as to apply more specifically to buildings or portions of buildings devoted to laboratory usage.

## 10-2 Nature of Hazards

This portion of Chapter 10 has been continually revised over the years to include such items as fire loss prevention procedures and fire exit drill requirements.

Laboratories using large quantities of materials that could cause explosions should be particularly observant of the safety procedures in the following paragraphs, in addition to any other practices required by enforcing authorities.

The development of a manual may be helpful for identifying, listing, and implementing safety procedures for laboratory emergencies. A manual is also useful for documentation and review of procedures and as an orientation tool for new employees.

### 10-2.1 Fire Loss Prevention.

#### 10-2.1.1 Hazard Assessment.

**10-2.1.1.1** An evaluation shall be made of hazards that may be encountered during laboratory operations before such operations are begun. The evaluation shall include hazards associated with the properties of the chemicals used, hazards associated with the operation of the equipment, and hazards associated with the nature of the proposed reactions (e.g., evolution of acid vapors or flammable gases).

The utilization of NFPA 49, *Hazardous Chemicals Data* [4], and NFPA 704, *Standard System for the Identification of the Hazards of Materials for Emergency Response* [1], can greatly assist in evaluating the hazard potential of flammable and combustible liquids in a laboratory.

Manufacturers' material safety data sheets, prepared according to the General Industry Standards of the Occupational Safety and Health Administration of U.S. Department of Labor, are also important sources of this information on flammable and combustible liquids. MSDSs may be the only available source of information for purchased mixtures and proprietary formulations.

**10-2.1.1.2** Periodic reviews of laboratory operations and procedures shall be conducted with special attention given to any change in materials, operations, or personnel.

Whenever new laboratory processes are introduced, the impact on fire protection and preparedness needs to be considered. Any safety considerations should be part of the written standard operating procedures for the laboratory. Most authorities recommend that these written procedures be reviewed and updated annually.

**10-2.1.1.3*** Unattended operations and automatic laboratory equipment shall be provided with periodic surveillance or with automatic monitoring devices to detect and report abnormal operation.

Periodic checks on unattended operations and automatic laboratory equipment can be performed by security personnel on their normal rounds, support service personnel (housekeeping, transport, etc.), or supervisors or other laboratory personnel in adjacent or nearby laboratories. The operation of such equipment can also be monitored electronically at a remote location. The person(s) responsible for the operation of the equipment should inform personnel performing the periodic inspections what constitutes abnormal operation, how often the equipment needs to be checked, and what actions should be taken if something abnormal is observed (e.g., an emergency shutdown switch/sequence, an emergency phone number). Detailed instructions should be posted near the equipment, and the specifics of such checks should be included in the training of off-shift personnel who frequent the laboratory area. These instructions should display the date on which they were last revised, and a regular schedule for review and revision should be in place. This is especially important for tissue processors, which are characteristically operated unattended at night and combine heat and combustible solvents. (See also 10-4.2.1.) The importance of safety checks cannot be overstated.

The committee added A-10-2.1.1.3 in the 1996 edition to emphasize the value of a final check of operating equipment before the laboratory is left unattended.

**A-10-2.1.1.3** A safety check of the health care facility laboratory by designated laboratory personnel should be made prior to leaving the facility unattended.

**10-2.1.1.4** When chemicals and reagents are ordered, steps shall be taken to determine the hazards and to transmit that information to those who will receive, store, use, or dispose of the chemicals.

NFPA 49, *Hazardous Chemicals Data* [4], and NFPA 704, *Standard System for the Identification of the Hazards of Materials for Emergency Response* [1], are intended for the benefit of fire fighters who are entering a hazardous zone and can also identify hazards to laboratory personnel who receive, store, use, or dispose of hazardous chemicals. Material safety data sheets are also good sources for this information.

**10-2.1.2 Fire Prevention Procedures.** Fire prevention procedures shall be established in accordance with Section 10-8.

> An important editorial change was introduced to the 1999 edition when the words "in accordance with Section 10-8" were added. The processes for maintaining the laboratory's fire protection and prevention program are to be a structured activity within the laboratory's comprehensive safety program.

**10-2.1.3 Emergency Procedures.**

**10-2.1.3.1** Procedures for laboratory emergencies shall be developed. Such procedures shall include alarm actuation, evacuation, and equipment shutdown procedures, and provisions for control of emergencies that could occur in the laboratory, including specific detailed plans for control operations by an emergency control group within the organization or a public fire department.

> The emergency procedures for a laboratory should be custom designed to address the specific hazards common to that location. Most laboratories, however, need to consider alternative plans for evening, weekend, or holiday operation when fewer staff are present and for emergency conditions (severe weather, civil disorders, etc.) when staff resources might be altered. Persons who will be responding to emergencies should review the laboratory's emergency procedures for clarity and specific understanding of all plans. Emergency procedures should be written and reviewed with all employees at regular intervals.

**10-2.1.3.2** Emergency procedures shall be established for controlling chemical spills.

> A chemical spill procedure and spill kit should be readily available to personnel who receive, store, use, and dispose of hazardous chemicals. Kits containing neutralizers, absorbents, cleanup tools (scoops, brushes, boxes, or bags), and personal protective items (goggles, aprons, gloves) can be purchased or assembled by knowledgeable laboratory personnel. Potential users of any spill kit should be provided with written procedures and training in its use.
>
> The type of spill kit selected should be appropriate for the chemical hazards present in an area. For example, some chemicals, such as hydrofluoric acid and mercury, require a special spill kit.

**10-2.1.3.3\*** Emergency procedures shall be established for extinguishing clothing fires.

> See cautions in A-10-2.1.3.3 regarding the use of fire blankets.

**A-10-2.1.3.3** Laboratory personnel should be thoroughly indoctrinated in procedures to follow in cases of clothing fires. The single most important instruction, one that should be stressed until it becomes second nature to all personnel, is to immediately drop to the floor and roll. All personnel should recognize that, in case of ignition of another person's clothing, they should immediately knock that person to the floor and roll that person around to smother the flames. Too often a person will panic if his or her clothing ignites and will run, resulting in more severe, often fatal burn injuries.

It should be emphasized that safety showers or fire blankets are of secondary importance. They should be used only when immediately at hand. It should also be recognized that rolling on the floor not only smothers the fire, but also helps to keep flames out of the victim's face and reduce inhalation of smoke.

Improper use of fire blankets can increase the severity of smoke and fire injuries if the blanket funnels smoke towards the face or if the blanket is not removed after the flames have been extinguished.

One method for extinguishing clothing fires is the "Stop, Drop, and Roll" procedure recommended by NFPA. As noted in the appendix material, it should be an automatic reflex reaction.

NFPA 99 does not require that fire blankets as depicted in Exhibit 10.1 be installed in the laboratory, but fire blankets can be a very effective means of extinguishing a clothing fire. If used improperly, however, they can also contribute to

**Exhibit 10.1** *A well-organized safety area in the laboratory, including a fire blanket in a metal sleeve, as well as a portable fire extinguisher, a safety procedure reminder sign, and an egress map indicating the nearest exits.*

the degree of injury. For example, if used while the victim is in a standing position, a blanket can act as a chimney that delivers hot gases directly to the face and respiratory tract. Instructions for emergency action to extinguish clothing fires in a laboratory should emphasize the following:

(a) If your clothes catch fire, stop immediately where you are, drop to the ground, roll over and over and back and forth, covering your face and mouth with your hands; this action will prevent flames from burning your face and smoke from entering your lungs. Roll over and over for a long time until the flames are extinguished. Cool the burn with cool water for 10–15 minutes. Call for help.

(b) If you are using a fire blanket on a person whose clothing is on fire, take the blanket to the victim. Slide the blanket across the victim *from head toward feet* (pushing flames and toxic gases away from the face) to smother flames. Remove all smoldering clothing immediately (do not allow blanket to trap heat from remaining smoldering clothing). Note: Fire blankets can be particularly harmful when synthetic fabrics are involved. They can increase the amount and severity of burns. Thus, *once fire is extinguished, blankets should be immediately removed.*

### 10-2.1.4 Orientation and Training.

Orientation and training are particularly important for new personnel so that they can become familiar with specific procedures and features of a laboratory. Frequent in-service safety training programs can reinforce safety information to new staff and provide a valuable review to existing staff.

Laboratory safety policies, procedures, and emergency plans should be coordinated with institution-wide emergency plans to avoid conflict and contradiction in an emergency.

**10-2.1.4.1** New laboratory personnel shall be taught general safety practices for the laboratory and specific safety practices for the equipment and procedures they will use.

**10-2.1.4.2** Continuing safety education and supervision shall be provided, incidents shall be reviewed monthly, and procedures shall be reviewed annually.

**10-2.1.4.3\*** Fire exit drills shall be conducted at least quarterly. Drills shall be so arranged that each person shall be included at least annually.

This section implements exit drills for laboratories as specified in 13-7.1.2 of NFPA *101, Life Safety Code*. [3] Drills can be announced or unannounced, and an appropriate exit drill can involve only a subset of the entire laboratory staff at a time. One should be mindful of the working hours of employees who may be on the premises only at night or on weekends. The committee's intent is that each laboratory employee be included in at least one drill over the course of a year.

**A-10-2.1.4.3** Interruption of essential services is not required.

## 10-3 Structure

This section and Section 10-5 reflect current practices and correlate with requirements of NFPA *101, Life Safety Code* [3] (e.g., exit access travel distance, openings in corridor barriers, fire protection features).

### 10-3.1* Construction and Arrangement.

**A-10-3.1** The types of construction are defined in NFPA 220, *Standard on Types of Building Construction.* Also, for a discussion of fire-resistive construction and fire resistance of building materials and construction assemblies, see the NFPA *Fire Protection Handbook.* For information on the fire resistance, installation, and maintenance of fire doors, see NFPA 80, *Standard for Fire Doors, Fire Windows, and Smoke-Control Door Assemblies.*

**10-3.1.1*** Construction of laboratories shall comply with the requirements of NFPA 45, *Standard on Fire Protection for Laboratories Using Chemicals*, and NFPA *101, Life Safety Code*, and with the following additional requirements. Health care laboratories shall be separated from surrounding health care areas and from exit corridors by fire-resistive construction with a minimum rating of 1 hour, and all openings protected by ¾-hour-rated assemblies.

The level of fire separation for laboratories is based on each laboratory's working supply of flammable or combustible liquids. The total amount of flammable or combustible liquids and the type of storage will determine whether a laboratory is classified as an ordinary or severe hazard. Quantities in excess of those identified in 10-7.2.2 are considered severe hazards.

For ordinary hazard laboratories either a 1-hour fire separation with at least C-labeled 45-minute-rated doors, or a smoketight room (equal to 30-minute walls and 20-minute doors for existing construction, 1-hour walls in new construction) protected by an automatic fire extinguishing system is required. For severe hazard laboratories either a 2-hour fire separation with at least B-labeled 1½-hour-rated doors or a 1-hour fire separation with at least a C-labeled 45-minute-rated door and an automatic fire suppression system is required. See Table 10.1.

Appropriate exceptions are identified. In 1996, the phrase "by the authority having jurisdiction" was added in Exception No. 1 to clarify intent regarding who classifies the hazard level of laboratories.

Refer to Chapters 12 and 13 of NFPA *101, Life Safety Code* [3], for applicable requirements. Any automatic release device can hold open a door to a hazardous area if the device deactivates upon activation of a manual fire alarm system, a local smoke detector, or a complete fire detection or extinguishing system.

**A-10-3.1.1** NFPA 45 provides basic requirements and guidance for laboratory design, but fire separation and sprinkler requirements are more stringent for laboratories in health care facilities. In addition, NFPA 99 requires hood discharge above the roof, allows valves on

*Table 10.1 Separation Requirements*

| Ordinary Hazard | Severe Hazard |
|---|---|
| <10 gal flammable liquids or <60 gal flammable liquids stored in a flammable liquids cabinet | >10 gal flammable liquids or >60 gal flammable liquids stored in a flammable liquids cabinet |
| *requires:* | *requires:* |
| 1-hour separation with C-labeled 45-minute doors | 2-hour separation with B-labeled 1½-hour doors |
| *or:* | *or:* |
| smoketight room with automatic fire extinguishing system | 1-hour separation with C-labeled 45-minute doors and an automatic fire extinguishing system |

emergency water supplies, and has other specific requirements based on the unique nature of facilities for care of patients who might be incapable of self-preservation.

*Exception No. 1: Laboratories that are protected by automatic extinguishing systems and that are not classified by the authority having jurisdiction as a severe hazard are not required to be separated. (See A-10-5.1 for one method of calculating the hazard fire severity.)*

*Exception No. 2: Any opening in a laboratory corridor barrier shall be permitted to be held open only by an automatic release device complying with the applicable requirements in NFPA 101, Life Safety Code.*

**10-3.1.2** Interior finish in laboratories and means of egress shall comply with the applicable sections of NFPA *101, Life Safety Code.*

## 10-3.2 Exit Details.

Requirements in 10-3.2 correlate with those of Chapters 12 and 13 in NFPA *101, Life Safety Code* [3], for health care facilities.

**10-3.2.1\*** Any room arranged for laboratory work that has an area in excess of 1000 ft$^2$ (92.9 m$^2$) shall have at least two exit access doors remote from each other, one of which shall open directly onto a means of egress.

A second means of access to an exit shall be provided for any laboratory work areas in which hazards exist as defined in 3-4.1 of NFPA 45, *Standard on Fire Protection for Laboratories Using Chemicals.*

Exit access door requirements were revised in 1980 to make them less restrictive while still providing an equivalent degree of safety (e.g., one door could open to another room, assuming 1-hour fire-resistive construction, etc., separated the two areas). Note that at least one door is required to open onto a means of egress.

Laboratory areas smaller than 1000 ft² (92.9 m²) also need a second means of egress if the hazard potential warrants it, as defined in 3-4.1 of NFPA 45, *Standard on Fire Protection for Laboratories Using Chemicals* [2].

**A-10-3.2.1** A door to an adjoining laboratory work area is considered to be a second access to an exit.

**10-3.2.2** Travel distance between any point in a laboratory unit and an exit access door shall not exceed 75 ft (22.9 m).

This requirement was added in 1984 to emphasize the importance of not creating tenuous situations in laboratories. These requirements are somewhat more restrictive than specified in 12-2.6 and 13-2.6 of NFPA *101, Life Safety Code* [3].

**10-3.2.3** Exit access doors from laboratories shall meet the requirements of NFPA *101, Life Safety Code*.

**10-3.2.4** Laboratory corridors constituting access to an exit shall meet the requirements of NFPA *101, Life Safety Code*. Corridors shall be maintained clear and unobstructed at all times.

Pre-1987 editions of NFPA 99 for laboratory requirements specified corridor widths in excess of those contained in NFPA *101, Life Safety Code* [3]. With the 1987 edition of NFPA 99, the then Subcommittee on Laboratories (responsible for Chapter 10 in NFPA 99) deferred all corridor requirements to NFPA *101* (sentence one of 10-3.2.4). It should be noted that the width of corridors that constitute access to an exit will vary depending on the occupancy classification of a laboratory per NFPA *101* (e.g., if properly separated from the rest of a health care facility, the laboratory is classified as business/industrial; if the laboratory is not separated, it is classified as health care). If the laboratory will be used by patients on litters or beds, the requirement of 10-3.2.5 takes precedence.

Sentence two of 10-3.2.4 reflects experience that while a corridor can be built to NFPA *101* criteria, the effective width of corridors can be narrowed by the placement of objects in the corridors (e.g., water coolers, boxes, chairs, temporary equipment). (Sections 12-2.3 and 13-2.3 of NFPA *101, Life Safety Code* [3], detail the requirements for health care occupancies.)

**10-3.2.5** Laboratory corridors, used for the transporting of patients in beds or litters, and constituting access to an exit, shall be not less than 96 in. (243.8 cm) in clear and unobstructed width.

This section takes into consideration those laboratory corridors (or portions therein) that constitute an access to an exit and through which patients in beds or litters might be wheeled. This section applies only to laboratories performing in vivo procedures requiring patients to be transported into the laboratory for the test or procedure. This requirement, it should be noted, is applicable only to new construction. The 96-in. (243.8-cm) value takes into consideration the need to be able to turn a bed around in the corridor and for beds to be able to pass each other. This is the same value as in NFPA *101, Life Safety Code* [3], for patient areas in new health care occupancies.

NFPA 99 is currently silent on the subject of laboratory corridor width for existing construction.

### 10-3.3 Exhaust Air.

Exhaust air shall conform to Section 5-3.

### 10-3.4* Ventilation.

Ventilation shall comply with 5-4.2 and with the requirements of NFPA 45, *Standard on Fire Protection for Laboratories Using Chemicals.*

**A-10-3.4** Subsection 5-4.3 gives ventilation requirements that are specific for laboratories in health care facilities and are in addition to the basic laboratory ventilation requirements contained in Chapter 6 of NFPA 45.

### 10-3.5 Fume Hoods.

Fume hoods shall conform to 5-4.3 and 5-6.2.

## 10-4 Equipment

For general safety requirements for electrical appliances used in laboratories, see Chapter 7.

### 10-4.1 General.

Laboratory apparatus shall comply with the requirements of NFPA 45, *Standard on Fire Protection for Laboratories Using Chemicals.*

### 10-4.2 Equipment Employing Liquids.

**10-4.2.1*** Tissue processors and similar automatic equipment that release ignitible (flammable or combustible) vapors into the ambient workspace shall be operated at least 5 ft (1.52 m) from the storage of combustible materials, unless separated by 1-hour fire-resistive construction.

C-10.1 describes four tissue processor fires that were fueled by combustible reagents in containers stored below the processor. The intent of 10-4.2.1 is to isolate equipment capable of igniting such reagents during unattended periods of operation. Although a flammable safety cabinet less than 5 ft (1.52 m) away could satisfy the 1-hour construction requirement, great care should be exercised in the location of combustible reagent storage near equipment intended to be operated in an unattended mode.

This section applies only to equipment that operates on an open system principle. (Newer equipment operates on a closed-system basis.)

Distillation apparatus for the recycling and reuse of xylenes and alcohols is increasingly prevalent among clinical laboratories. This equipment is characteristically designed to be a closed system, but such systems qualify as "similar automatic equipment" if they release combustible vapors. C-10.1 describes an example of a fire incident that began in a xylene distillation apparatus.

**A-10-4.2.1** Tissue processors that operate as a closed system contain ignitible vapor hazards within the processor and thus do not pose a hazard requiring a 5-ft (1.52-m) separation.

**10-4.2.2\*** Unattended laboratory operations employing flammable or combustible reagents shall be conducted in an area equipped with an automatic fire extinguishing system.

Paragraph 10-2.1.1.3 contains the general requirements for unattended operation and automatic laboratory equipment. Paragraph 10-4.2.2 contains requirements specifically for those unattended operations or equipment that employs flammable or combustible reagents. It is based on committee knowledge of actual fires involving unattended experiments where no automatic fire protection was present.

Routine operations performed by tissue processors, solvent recovery stills, and other automated equipment increase the possibility of fire due to the repetitive nature of the process and the casual attitude that can accompany routine operations. The committee believes special attention needs to be directed toward the design and installation of the automatic fire detection and extinguishing equipment specifically intended for such unattended operation.

Laboratory occupancies in health care facilities often contain very expensive equipment that could be destroyed or become extremely hazardous if exposed to an accidental discharge from a sprinkler system. One design consideration to eliminate any possibility of an accidental discharge from a sprinkler system is through the installation of a preaction system. This type of system is defined in NFPA 13, *Standard for the Installation of Sprinkler Systems* [5], as "a sprinkler system employing automatic sprinklers attached to a piping system containing air that may or may not be under pressure, with a supplemental fire detection system installed in the same areas as the sprinklers. Actuation of the fire detection system opens a valve that permits water to flow into the sprinkler piping system and to be discharged from any sprinklers that may be open." Thus, no water needs to be within the sprinkler stationed over special equipment. It is only when the fire detection system senses fire or heat that water is released into the sprinkler piping system.

**A-10-4.2.2** One method of safeguarding unattended processes is to place the equipment in a pan large enough to contain any spilled materials, preferably within a fume hood protected by some form of automatic fire extinguishment or detection.

# 10-5* Fire Protection

**A-10-5** Examination of laboratory fire records demonstrates the extra vulnerability of premises with substantial amounts of combustible contents. The use of noncombustible shelving, benches, and furniture will reduce production of smoke and damage to facilities, with substantial savings where expensive laboratory equipment is present, even in sprinklered areas.

Self-contained breathing apparatus should be considered for equipping personnel for rescue operations in areas with special fire hazards. Training is required for effective use of such equipment. It is desirable to coordinate equipment and training with local fire department personnel.

**10-5.1*** Automatic fire extinguishing protection shall be provided in all laboratories, including associated storage rooms, where

(a) Laboratories are not separated from surrounding areas by at least 1-hour fire-resistive construction with door openings protected by Class C self-closing fire doors, and employ quantities of flammable, combustible, or hazardous materials less than that which would be considered severe.

(b) Laboratories are not separated from surrounding areas by at least 2-hour fire-resistive construction with door openings protected by Class B self-closing doors, and employ quantities of flammable, combustible, or hazardous materials considered severe.

**A-10-5.1** Where there is a need to reduce equipment damage and facilitate return to service, consideration should be given to an approved gaseous agent total flooding system in laboratories.

The hazard level of a laboratory is considered severe if quantities of flammable, combustible, or hazardous materials are present that are capable of sustaining a fire condition of sufficient magnitude to breach a 1-hour fire separation.

To determine the combustible content or heat potential of flammable or combustible materials capable of breaching or penetrating a 1-hour-rated fire separation, one method is included in the 14th edition of the NFPA *Fire Protection Handbook*, where formulas and tables for calculating the equivalence of time versus fire severity are given. Specific reference is made to Section 6, Chapter 8, Confinement of Fire and Smoke in Buildings, and Table 6-8A. Heat of combustion (Btu/lb) for materials common to laboratories can be found in Section 3, Chapter 11, Fire Hazard of Materials — Tables and Charts, of the handbook. Specific reference is made to Table 3-11B, Table 3-11G, Table 3-11H, and Table 3-11L.

NOTE 1: The weights of combustible contents in Table 6-8A are those of ordinary combustible materials taken at 8000 Btu/ lb. For converting other than ordinary combustibles to pounds per square foot (psf), divide the total Btu value by 8000/Btu/lb.

NOTE 2: In the 17th edition of the NFPA *Fire Protection Handbook*, see Section 6, Chapter 6, Table 6-6A; and Appendix A, respectively.

The above, it should be noted, is only one of several methods for calculating the hazard level of a laboratory with regard to combustibles breaching a 1-hour fire separation.

The following chart can be used as a guide in making the above determination:

| | Hazard | |
| Wall Rating | Not Severe | Severe |
|---|---|---|
| Less than 1-hour | Automatic fire extinguishing system required | Not allowed |
| 1-hour | No automatic fire extinguishing system required | Automatic fire extinguishing system required |
| 2-hour | No automatic fire extinguishing system required | No automatic fire extinguishing system required |

Requirements for automatic fire extinguishing protection were substantially revised for the 1980 edition of former NFPA 56C (now essentially Chapter 10 of NFPA 99). Instead of requiring their installation in all laboratories, the criteria were identified that determine the need for such systems. The criteria for separation and containment were based on the quantity and degree of hazard. The subject of automatic fire extinguishing systems strictly with respect to separation requirements can be found in 10-3.1.1 (see commentary on 10-3.1.1 for further information).

In 1980, while the above requirements were being proposed, arguments were submitted that suggested that an appropriate number of portable fire extinguishers were adequate for fire protection instead of an automatic extinguishing system. The committee pointed out that laboratories are not always staffed and that an automatic system was required only when the fuel load was anticipated to exceed the fire rating of the enclosure.

To help determine how the hazard level could be calculated, the committee included one method in the appendix, as shown in A-10-5.1, that could be used for making the calculation.

The chart was added in 1984 to eliminated confusion about the requirements of 10-5.1. It was the intent of the committee that laboratories employing hazardous material less than severe, and not separated by a 1-hour-rated wall, have an automatic fire extinguishing system.

A note formerly below 10-5.1(b) and now included in the text of the appendix calls attention to the fact that there are types of extinguishing systems other than water that should be reviewed for use in such areas as computer rooms (which may or may not be sprinklered). In 1996 the committee replaced the specific reference to Halon 1301, with "an approved gaseous agent total flooding system." Halon 1301 is gradually being eliminated from clinical laboratory applications and elsewhere because of its negative impact on the environment.

**10-5.2** Automatic fire extinguishment and fire detection systems, where required, shall be connected to the facility fire alarm system and shall be arranged to immediately sound an alarm.

This paragraph would be applicable only if an automatic fire detection and extinguishing system were installed.

If a laboratory is excluded by one of the criteria in 10-5.1, no connection to a facility sprinkler system would be required; however, a review of appropriate fire/smoke detectors connected to the facility fire alarm system should be made.

**10-5.3** Portable fire extinguishers suitable for the particular hazards shall be located so that they will be readily available to personnel in accordance with NFPA 10, *Standard for Portable Fire Extinguishers*. Clinical laboratories that typically employ quantities of flammable, combustible, or hazardous materials less than that which would be considered severe shall be classified as ordinary hazard per NFPA 10 for purposes of extinguisher placement.

In addition to the selection, distribution, inspection, maintenance. and recharging of portable fire extinguishers as specified in NFPA 10, *Standard for Portable Fire Extinguishers* [6], Section 31-4 of NFPA *101, Life Safety Code* [3], sets forth operational plans and staff responsibilities in a fire emergency. It includes provisions within the fire plan for fire extinguishment. This familiarity with selection, extinguishing characteristics, and the location, operation, and use of fire extinguishers should be incorporated into new employee orientation, periodic retraining, and instruction on fire exit drills.

Considerations such as minimizing damage to equipment, specimens, or records contained in the laboratory could warrant the installation of such alternatives to water extinguishing systems as a gaseous agent total flooding system.

The second sentence, added in 1996 on the advice of the Technical Correlating Committee on Health Care Facilities, is intended to make clear the placement of portable fire extinguishers in relation to the amount of hazardous material.

See Exhibit 10.2 for an example of a fire extinguisher cabinet.

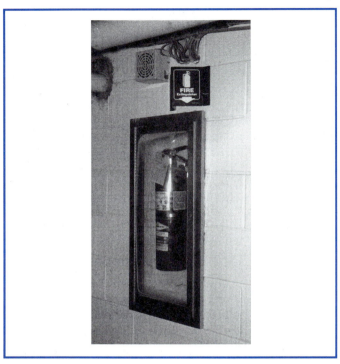

*Exhibit 10.2* A typical fire extinguisher cabinet with door. The curved Plexiglas® increases extinguisher visibility while protecting the unit from damage.

## 10-6* Emergency Shower

Where the eyes or body of any person can be exposed to injurious corrosive materials, suitable fixed facilities for quick drenching or flushing of the eyes and body shall be provided within the work area for immediate emergency use. Fixed eye baths shall be designed and installed to avoid injurious water pressure.

If shutoff valves or stops are installed in the branch line leading to safety drenching equipment, the valves shall be OS and Y (outside stem and yoke), labeled for identification, and sealed in the open position. The installation of wall-mounted portable eye-wash stations shall not preclude the adherence to the provisions of this section.

OS and Y–type valves were selected because of their reliability and the ease in determining whether they are open or closed. Other types could be used if it is demonstrated that they are equivalent in character and performance. (See paragraph

2 in Section 1-4 regarding the subject of *equivalency.*) An example of an OS and Y valve is shown in Exhibit 10.3.

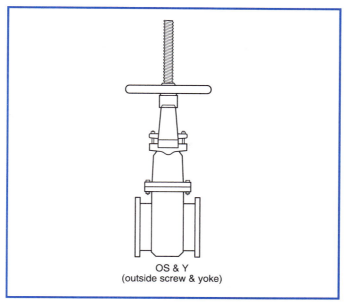

OS & Y
(outside screw & yoke)

**Exhibit 10.3**  *An outside screw and yoke sprinkler system water control valve.*

**A-10-6** *Protective Devices.* Showers should be controlled by a nonautomatic shutoff device. Although a self-closing shower valve (favored by most designers) would minimize flooding of the building if, for example, the shower were maliciously activated, it does not afford maximum help to the injured user. Since a person would have to use one hand to keep the valve open, efforts to remove clothing or wipe away offending materials would be greatly hampered.

Although emergency showers are rarely used, their use when necessary can mean the difference between superficial burns and serious disfigurement, or loss of life. In some cases where such showers have not been activated for long periods, they have been found inoperative. It is essential that emergency showers be provided and tested from time to time to determine that their valves are in good operating condition. Advance planning needs to be made to handle the water that will flow in a test.

Floor drains in areas of hospitals and other health care facilities are likely to dry out if the floors are not wet-mopped regularly, and dry traps can permit passage of gases, vapors, odors, and vermin. Since a floor drain will be of great value if a safety shower is used, resulting in the release of several hundred gallons of water, it is recommended that floor drains be filled with water regularly, or in new construction that some plumbing be provided to fill the traps manually, automatically, or incidentally by plumbing design.

Previous editions stated that floor drains were "not recommended" because they tended to dry out and permit entry of noxious gases into the laboratory. The committee reviewed the subject in 1993 and added a paragraph to this appendix material recommending floor drains be installed (and maintained) because of the overriding value of such drains in cleaning up after a drenching shower.

See Exhibits 10.4 and 10.5(a) and (b) for photographs of one safety shower and two types of eyewash units.

Another consideration is to be sure that all holes in floor slabs that have not been sealed around pipes to prevent the passage of smoke be so sealed, and in a manner that will prevent water from flowing to lower floors from the discharge of an emergency shower or sprinkler head.

Shower heads on flexible water lines at sink locations can be useful for eye flush and skin or clothing spills. (See 10-8.1.4 for inspection procedures.)

Shutoff valves for showers allow repair, replacement, and testing without necessitating the shutdown of an entire sprinkler system.

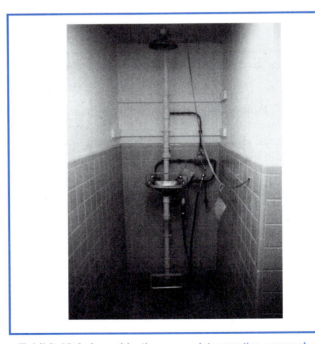

**Exhibit 10.4** *A combination one-point operation eyewash and shower. Eye and body contamination with chemical or body fluid substances can be flushed.*

**Exhibit 10.5(a)** *A conventional one-point operation plumbed eyewash, with signage to ensure location visibility from any area within the acceptable travel distance, and an inspection tag.*

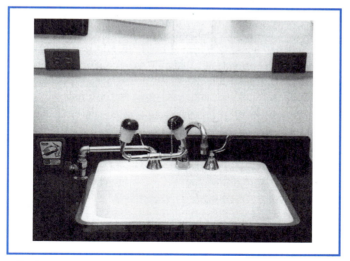

**Exhibit 10.5(b)** *This one-point operation swing-out eyewash combines accessibility, space, and utility considerations.*

Wall-mounted portable eyewash stations do not contain an adequate supply of water for the 15-minute flushing recommended by chemical manufacturers.

## 10-7 Flammable and Combustible Liquids

The material in this section correlates with NFPA 30, *Flammable and Combustible Liquids Code* [7], which contains general requirements for such liquids. Unless otherwise noted, the term *liquids* in Section 10-7 refers to flammable or combustible liquids.

### 10-7.1 General.

Flammable and combustible liquids shall be handled and used with care and with knowledge of their hazardous properties, both individually and in combination with other materials with which they can come in contact.

### 10-7.2* Storage and Use.

**A-10-7.2** *Storage and Use of Flammable Liquids.* Plastic containers are sometimes used to avoid breakage problems posed by glass containers or contamination problems with metal containers. Plastic containers need to be chosen with particular attention to their compatibility with the liquid to be contained. For example, polyethylene containers are generally unsuitable for aldehydes, ketones, esters, higher molecular-weight alcohols, benzene, toluene, various oils, silicone fluids, and halogenated hydrocarbons. In addition to labeling containers for identification of contents, it is important to label plastic containers for identification of their constituent materials to avoid misuse.

In some cases, listed or labeled stainless steel or tin-lined safety containers offer a solution to contamination problems.

**10-7.2.1*** Flammable and combustible liquids shall be used from and stored in approved containers in accordance with NFPA 30, *Flammable and Combustible Liquids Code*, and NFPA 45, *Standard on Fire Protection for Laboratories Using Chemicals*. Storage cabinets for flammable and combustible liquids shall be constructed in accordance with Section 4-3 of NFPA 30, *Flammable and Combustible Liquids Code*.

To determine the maximum size container for a flammable or combustible liquid, the liquid's hazard classification must be known. The hazard classification can be determined by first reviewing NFPA 325, *Fire Hazard Properties of Flammable Liquids, Gases, and Volatile Solids* [8]. The maximum size container can be determined from Table 4-2.3 in NFPA 30, *Flammable and Combustible Liquids Code* [7], for maximum allowed size. Storage cabinets for flammable and combustible liquids are to be constructed in accordance with Section 4-3 of NFPA 30, *Flammable and Combustible Liquids Code* [7]. Such a storage cabinet, fabricated from sheet metal, is shown in Exhibit 10.6.

The committee added the last sentence to the 1999 edition to emphasize the intent that the cabinet's construction be consistent with NFPA 30.

**Exhibit 10.6** *Laboratory flammable liquids cabinet with necessary and appropriate warning signs.*

**A-10-7.2.1**† Table A-10-7.2.1 is a portion of Table 4-2.3 in NFPA 30, *Flammable and Combustible Liquids Code*. NFPA 45 provides more specific guidance for use of flammable and combustible liquids in laboratories, in addition to basic requirements set forth in NFPA 30.

**10-7.2.2\*** Established laboratory practices shall limit working supplies of flammable or combustible liquids. The total volume of Class I, II, and IIIA liquids outside of approved storage cabinets and safety cans shall not exceed 1 gal (3.78 L) per 100 ft$^2$ (9.23 m$^2$). The total volume of Class I, II, and IIIA liquids, including those contained in approved storage cabinets and safety cans, shall not exceed 2 gal (7.57 L) per 100 ft$^2$ (9.23 m$^2$). No flammable

*Table A-10-7.2.1 Maximum Allowable Size of Containers and Portable Tanks*

| Container Type | Flammable Liquids | | | Combustible Liquids | |
| --- | --- | --- | --- | --- | --- |
| | **Class 1A** | **Class 1B** | **Class 1C** | **Class II** | **Class III** |
| Glass | 1 pt | 1 qt | 1 gal | 1 gal | 5 gal |
| Metal (other than DOT drums) or approved plastic | 1 gal | 5 gal | 5 gal | 5 gal | 5 gal |
| Safety cans | 2 gal | 5 gal | 5 gal | 5 gal | 5 gal |

For SI Units: 1 pt = 0.49 L; 1 qt = 0.95 L; 1 gal = 3.8 L.

or combustible liquid shall be stored or transferred from one vessel to another in any exit corridor or passageway leading to an exit. At least one approved flammable or combustible liquid storage room shall be available within any health care facility regularly maintaining a reserve storage capacity in excess of 300 gal (1135.5 L). Quantities of flammable and combustible liquids for disposal shall be included in the total inventory.

*Exception: Very small laboratory work areas acceptable to the authority having jurisdiction.*

Paragraph 10-7.2.2 was extensively revised in 1980 to clarify how much flammable or combustible liquid was permitted outside of storage cabinets per 5000 ft² (461 m²) of laboratory area and how much could be stored in a laboratory per 5000 ft² (461 m²).

In 1993 the basis for hazard assessment was changed from "per 5000 sq ft" to "per 100 sq ft." This change was worded to parallel the method of hazard assessment used by NFPA 45, *Standard on Fire Protection for Laboratories Using Chemicals.* [2] The new ordinary level of hazard, which had been <10 gal per 5000 ft² (461 m²) outside of a safety cabinet or <60 gal per 5000 ft² (461 m²) within approved cabinetry or safety cans, became 1 gal (3.78 L) and 2 gal (7.57 L) per 100 ft² (9.23 m), respectively.

The new values were not arithmetically equivalent to the old. The change was precipitated by ambiguity in the former wording: Should a laboratory smaller than 5000 ft² (461 m²) use the 10 gal/60 gal (38 L/228 L) limit or should it prorate those amounts proportional to its size? A Formal Interpretation (84-1) on this subject was issued in 1984. The former Technical Committee on Laboratories in Health Care Facilities reviewed the matter and noted that it was their intent that the 10-gal (38-L) limit be applied to any laboratory up to 5000 ft² (461 m²) (i.e., there was no proportioning just because a laboratory was smaller). This meant that unnecessarily large amounts of ignitible liquids might have been found stored within very small labs. With the 1993 edition of NFPA 99, that Formal Interpretation became moot. Proportioning is now implied in the standard.

The then Subcommittee on Laboratories in Health Care Facilities recognized that a few very small laboratories might have a need to store quantities larger than those listed. The exception was inserted for those laboratories. In any case, the listed amounts specify maximum quantities. Laboratories should have on hand only the minimum amounts necessary for safe laboratory operation as noted in the appendix.

Depending on quantity and type, chemicals within a laboratory, particularly flammable liquids, can constitute a serious fire hazard. Careful consideration should be given to the quantities and reactive qualities of chemicals stored in a laboratory. A systematic review of chemical inventory by qualified laboratory personnel can aid in providing the most appropriate (safe) level of flammable storage within the laboratory.

Approved storage cabinets are described in Section 4-3, "Design Construction and Capacity of Storage Cabinets" of NFPA 30, *Flammable and Combustible Liquids Code.* [7] Approved cabinets can be of either metal (see Exhibit 10.7) or wood (see Exhibit 10.8), as long as the materials and construction techniques appropriate for each are followed. One advantage of wooden cabinets is that they often can be constructed locally or in-house and custom designed to fit into the space available, as opposed to trying to locate a manufactured cabinet to fit the desired space.

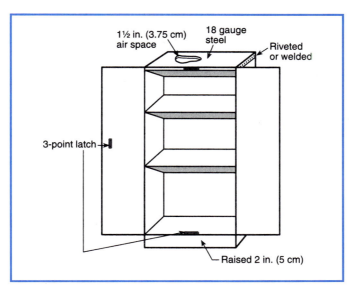

**Exhibit 10.7** *Metal cabinets whose construction is acceptable. (Source: NFPA 30 Handbook, 1996.)*

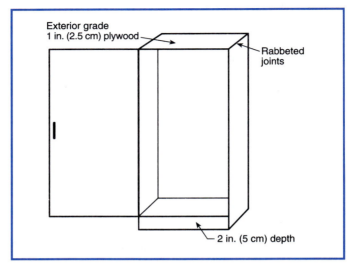

*Exhibit 10.8 Wooden cabinets whose construction is acceptable. Note that NFPA 30 does not require a three-point latch on the doors because wood does not tend to warp or distort when exposed to fire, as metal does. (Source: NFPA 30 Handbook, 1996.)*

**A-10-7.2.2** The goal is to keep the fuel load to a limit that is as low as is practicable. In no case should excessive amounts be stored. Constant effort needs to be exerted to prevent the overstocking of hazardous chemicals. The laboratory manager can help keep stocks at a safe level by encouraging small and more frequent requisitions, by developing a reliable stock inventory system, by assuring convenient and prompt deliveries from the central stock room, by selecting brands that are the most popular and not necessarily the cheapest, and by discouraging (except perhaps for large-scale research-type projects) the practice of purchasing the largest containers, including bulk supplies in 55-gal (208.2-L) drums.

**10-7.2.3** Venting of storage cabinets shall be permitted. Storage cabinets with approved flame arresters shall be permitted to be exhausted through a fume hood exhaust system. Construction of the venting duct within the laboratory shall be equal to the rating of the cabinet.

The venting criteria is included so that those laboratories that choose to vent would have safety guidelines. It should be noted, however, that venting is optional.

Some reasons for venting include preventing a buildup of positive pressure within cabinets and reducing the accumulation of fumes that pose a fire hazard.

**10-7.2.4** Flammable or combustible liquids shall not be positioned near Bunsen burners, ovens, hot pipes and valves, or other sources of heat, in corridors, or within exhaust canopies.

**10-7.2.5\*** Class I flammable liquids shall not be stored in ordinary refrigerators, freezers, or coolers. If Class I flammable liquids are stored under refrigeration (e.g., for analytical purposes), the storage devices shall be listed flammable materials storage refrigerators or refrigerators listed for Class I, Division 1, Group C locations. The outside doors of refrigerators shall be labeled to denote whether or not they are acceptable for storage of flammable liquids. If the refrigerator is not listed for the purpose, the warning shall be worded to prohibit all storage of flammable liquids.

There are hazards associated with the storage of ignitible liquids in any type of refrigerator (i.e., vapors can build up with no way to vent them). Alternative means for storage of such liquids exist, as noted in 10-7.2.1 and 10-7.2.3. This section, modified in 1993, applies only to Class I flammable liquids.

Modification of clinical lab refrigerators by health care personnel was tacitly condoned in the past; this is no longer the case. For refrigerators storing flammable material, the committee changed "approved" to "listed" to indicate its intent that such refrigerators are to be tested and listed by an organization acceptable to the authority having jurisdiction.

**A-10-7.2.5** *Walk-in Thermal-Controlled Boxes.* Procedures likely to result in toxic or flammable atmospheres should be discouraged within "walk-in" refrigerators or other types of temperature-controlled boxes. A warning sign such as the one indicated here should be posted on every box.

**DANGER:** NOT EXPLOSIONPROOF

NOT VENTILATED

GROUND ALL ELECTRICAL EQUIPMENT

DO NOT STORE DRY ICE

DO NOT SMOKE

New boxes should include at least the following features: a latch that can be released by a person inside the box when the door is locked from the outside; latch and door frames designed to allow actuation under all conditions of freezing; a floor with a nonconductive surface; neoprene matting to insulate up to 10,000 V; a view-window in the door; an independently circuited high-temperature thermostat and alarm (for warm boxes); vaporproof duplex electrical receptacles; an alarm that can be heard throughout the occupied work area and an alarm button at the inside door frame that will keep operating after actuation; conduits sealed (in cold boxes) in a manner to prevent accumulation of water vapor such as in the globe protectors of the light fixtures; and adjustable exhaust vent and air intake of at least 15 CFM for general ventilation, with provisions for installing a flexible hose and miniature canopy in a manner to provide local ventilation at a specific work site. As explosionproof laboratory apparatus becomes available, it should be substituted for less safe equipment used in enclosed thermal-control boxes.

*Non-Walk-in Refrigerators.* The use of domestic refrigerators for the storage of typical laboratory solvents presents a significant hazard to the laboratory work area. Refrigerator temperatures are almost universally higher than the flash points of the flammable liquids most often stored in them. In addition to vapor accumulation, a domestic refrigerator contains readily available ignition sources, such as thermostats, light switches, and heater strips, all within or exposing the refrigerated storage compartment. Furthermore, the compressor and its circuits are typically located at the bottom of the unit, where vapors from flammable liquid spills or leaks can easily accumulate.

Explosionproof refrigeration equipment is designed to protect against ignition of flammable vapors both inside and outside the refrigerated storage compartment. This type is intended and recommended for environments such as pilot plants or laboratory work areas where all electrical equipment is required to be explosionproof.

The design concepts of the flammable material storage refrigerators are based on the typical laboratory environment. The primary intent is to eliminate ignition of vapors inside the storage compartment from sources also within the compartment. In addition, flammable material storage refrigerators incorporate such design features as thresholds, self-closing latch doors, friction latches or magnetic door gaskets, and special methods for the inner shell. All of these features are intended to control or limit the loss potential should an exothermic reaction occur within the storage compartment. Finally, the compressor and its circuits and controls are often located at the top of the unit to further reduce the potential for ignition of floor-level vapors. In general, the design features of a commercially available flammable material storage refrigerator are such that they provide several safeguards not available through modification of domestic models.

Every laboratory refrigerator should be clearly labeled to indicate whether or not it is acceptable for storage of flammable materials. Internal laboratory procedures should ensure that laboratory refrigerators are being properly used. The following are examples of labels that can be used on laboratory refrigerators:

**DO NOT STORE FLAMMABLE SOLVENTS**
**in this refrigerator**

**NOTICE:** This is not an "explosionproof" refrigerator, but it has been designed to permit storage of materials producing flammable vapors. Containers should be **well stoppered or tightly closed.**

Safety standards and safe work practices are often not introduced until accidents begin to happen. Better, safer equipment is developed once the hazards present themselves. Such was the case with the storage of diethyl ether in the early 1970s. Laboratories often stored diethyl ether in the cold to retard vaporization and the formation of dangerous peroxides. The volatility of diethyl ether, a Class 1A liquid (as defined in NFPA 30, *Flammable and Combustible Liquids Code* [7]), was such that, even when refrigerated at a temperature range of 4°C to 6°C (39°F to 43°F), easily ignitible vapors could accumulate. Explosions would occur when electrical switches or lamps within conventional refrigerator cabinets ignited these vapors. These violent accidents led to the development of explosionproof refrigerators, which greatly reduced the risk that these flammable vapors would ignite. Some examples of design changes were the use of thermostats with sealed or externally mounted contact points and the absence of lights inside the refrigerator.

## 10-7.3 Transfer of Flammable or Combustible Liquids.

Transfer from bulk stock containers to smaller containers shall be made in storage rooms as described in NFPA 30, *Flammable and Combustible Liquids Code*, or within a fume hood having a face velocity of at least 100 ft (30.5 m) per minute.

## 10-7.4 Handling of Flammable and Combustible Liquids.

Procedures and policies for handling flammable and combustible liquids need to be incorporated into laboratory practices. They must also be monitored to ensure that they are in effect. General requirements for policies, procedures, and training are contained in 10-2.1.4.

Paragraph 10-7.4.1 is a refinement of previous guidelines on heating flammable and combustible liquids, using the flash point as the hazard criterion. This means that laboratory personnel must know the flash point of the type of liquid they are using. Paragraph 10-7.4.2 is a reaffirmation of the prohibition of open flames when heating any flammable or combustible liquid.

**10-7.4.1** Flammable liquids and combustible liquids with flash points lower than 200°F (93.3°C) (Class I, II, and IIIA liquids) shall be heated in hoods or with special local exhaust ventilation if the quantities exceed 10 ml, or if the liquid is heated to within 30°F (16.6°C) of the flash point of the liquid.

**10-7.4.2** Flammable or combustible liquids shall be heated with hot water, steam, or an electric mantle, depending upon their boiling points. Open flames shall not be employed.

## 10-7.5* Disposal of Hazardous Materials.

Disposal of hazardous materials shall be accomplished off the premises by a disposal specialist or at a safe location away from the health care facility by competent personnel using procedures established in concurrence with the authority having jurisdiction.

Disposal is possible by any disposal specialist or by whatever procedures are acceptable to the authority having jurisdiction.

**A-10-7.5** *Disposal of Hazardous Materials.* Because disposal techniques for various hazardous materials produced in hospital research involve complicated problems, they cannot be adequately discussed herein. Such materials include the toxic product of mixing sodium cyanide and acids in the drain system; nuisance or alarming odors such as produced by mercaptans or lutidine; violently water-reactive solids or liquids like phosphoric anhydride and thionyl chloride; potential explosives like picric acid; strong oxidizers like perchloric acid; and radioactive, pathogenic, corrosive, or potentially harmful wastes, such as television picture tubes, syringes, and aerosol cans.

Many chemicals can be disposed of at the bench through the ingenuity of the chemist, such as the reacting of small quantities of potassium with tertiary butyl alcohol.

Flammable and combustible liquids that are miscible with water in all proportions may be flushed down a drain within a laboratory room in quantities not exceeding 1 pt (0.45 L), thoroughly mixed with at least 3 gal (11.4 L) of cold water. This precaution for minimizing flammable vapor concentrations in building drains could be unacceptable to pollution-control authorities.

Vaporization should not be used for routine disposal of liquids.

Drain lines and traps from laboratory benches, safety showers, hood floors, mechanical equipment rooms, storage rooms, and so forth, should have water added at regular intervals to assure that traps will not be the source of flammable or toxic vapor release. Where self-priming traps are provided, an annual inspection for proper operation should be made. Addition of mineral oil or similar liquids is sometimes used to reduce evaporation of water from traps.

Federal regulations (i.e., those of the U.S. Environmental Protection Agency) and state regulations should be reviewed with regard to the way hazardous material is to be disposed. This applies to gases, liquids, and solids.

## 10-8* Maintenance and Inspection

**A-10-8** Comprehensive discussions of the goals and procedures to provide safe working conditions in clinical laboratories are available from the National Committee for Clinical Laboratory Standards. *(See B-1.2.6.)*

### 10-8.1 Procedures.

The laboratory safety program should be part of, and coordinated with, the facili-tywide safety program. The integration of fire protection with biohazard protection and radiation safety is important for the success of the program. Such a laboratory safety program should help define the specific fire prevention and preparedness process as directed in 10-2.1.2. Preventive maintenance programs and electrical safety tests and inspections are to encompass appropriate laboratory equipment.

**10-8.1.1** For adequate laboratory safety, careful maintenance and watchfulness are impera-tive.

**10-8.1.2\*** A safety officer shall be appointed to supervise safe practices in the laboratory. Responsibilities shall include ensuring that the equipment and preparation for fire fighting are appropriate for the special fire hazards present. These responsibilities shall be in addition to surveillance of hazards attendant to caustics, corrosives, compressed gases, electrical installations, and other hazards indigenous to laboratories in health care facilities. This individual shall also supervise the periodic education of laboratory personnel, including new employee orientation, in the nature of combustible and flammable liquids and gases, first-aid fire fighting, and the use of protective equipment and shall review unsafe conditions observed or reported.

**A-10-8.1.2** This individual may be the safety officer for the health care facility or can be a specifically designated laboratory safety officer.

The Subcommittee on Laboratories broadened the responsibilities for the laboratory safety officer because it believes all hazards associated with clinical laboratories and their functioning should be under the purview of the laboratory safety officer. The provisions of A-10-8.1.2 help ensure that the most qualified individual is appointed.

Large laboratories may require the expertise and resources of a safety committee. The responsibilities of the safety officer may be delegated among the members of such a committee. Committees composed of workers of different job classifications and levels of training often are the best way to determine the employees' need to know about fire protection and prevention practices. Discussions in such committees should include review of incidents, accidents, drills, and procedures with the goal of reducing the level of hazards.

**10-8.1.3\*** Operations and equipment related to safe operations and practices, including such items as ventilating provisions, fire protection apparatus, periodical flushing of sinks, emergency showers and eye-wash units, shelf stocks and storage of flammable and combustible materials, and caustic and corrosive liquids shall be reviewed at appropriate, regular intervals. A system of prompt reporting of defective equipment and its prompt repair shall be instituted, and periodic inspections shall be made of all electrical and gas equipment. The laboratory safety officer shall prepare and supervise the proper completion of a safety checklist that can be preserved for record.

**A-10-8.1.3** Regulations should be adopted for routine housekeeping and laboratory cleanup practices.

The laboratory safety officer should make periodic inspections of the laboratory premises to determine that electric cords in use are of adequate conductor size with safe insulation and that circuits are not overloaded through the use of multiple taps.

Several good laboratory safety checklists are available, such as the one developed by the College of American Pathologists Inspection and Accreditation Program (*see Appendix B*). The laboratory safety officer could augment or modify one of these for his or her own facility if he or she so wished.

The list is not considered exhaustive. Another good source for a safety checklist is the National Committee for Clinical Laboratory Standards.

Hazards particular to each laboratory should be evaluated to determine frequency of inspection.

**10-8.1.4** Periodic safety inspection shall include the testing of all emergency showers, eye baths, and other emergency equipment.

Periodic safety inspections can be conducted by the laboratory safety officer or incorporated into other safety programs.

**10-8.1.5*** A system for disposing of hazardous chemicals and combustible trash shall be established and regularly maintained. Disposal of chemical wastes shall be in accordance with good safety practices and environmental standards.

The reference to environmental standards reflects the committee's concern for safety and environmental protection when disposing of hazardous chemicals.

**A-10-8.1.5** Information sources for safe handling, storage, and emergency response to spills or fires in hazardous materials include NFPA 49, *Hazardous Chemicals Data*.

## 10-8.2 Identification of Hazards.

**10-8.2.1*** All doors leading to laboratories in health-related facilities shall be marked with signage indicating the fire hazards of materials when significant quantities, as defined below, are intended to be used within the area. For signage purposes, ''significant quantities'' in an area shall include any of the following:

(a) Hazardous materials in glass containers that are 1 gal (4.4 L) in size or larger
(b) Compressed gases or cryogenic liquids in containers that are greater than 5 in. (12.7 cm) in diameter and 15 in. (48 cm) in length
(c) Dry hazardous chemicals in containers in excess of 5 lb (2.2.7 kg)
(d) Aggregate quantities of hazardous materials exceeding 200 lb (91 kg), or flammable liquids exceeding 10 gal (44.4 L)

Previous editions of NFPA 99 specified the use of NFPA 704, *Standard System for the Identification of the Hazards of Materials for Emergency Response*. [1] In the 1999 edition, the committee removed specific reference to NFPA 704 from the text of the standard. However, the intent and essential characteristics of an acceptable signage system were retained.

The signage on entry ways or safety cabinetry should reflect the presence of ''significant quantities'' of fuel to avoid the overuse and overreaction to labeling. The definition of significant quantities, which was introduced into the standard in 1993, has been clarified in the 1999 edition.

**A-10-8.2.1** The identification system of NFPA 704, *Standard System for the Identification of the Hazards of Materials for Emergency Response*, can be used on doors leading to laboratories as well as on doors of approved flammable liquid storage cabinetry and on doors of refrigerators. *(See C-10.2.3.)*

Unlike a research or academic chemistry laboratory where a simple signage system is difficult to apply, the quantity and variety of ignitible liquids in clinical laboratories is characteristically modest. The Committee on Laboratories continues to recommend the use of NFPA 704, *Standard System for the Identification of the Hazards of Materials for Emergency Response* [1], on doors leading to laboratories and on cabinets because of its widespread recognition by the fire service. In those facilities that choose to use NFPA 704, laboratory personnel should be familiar with the symbol as well. A summary of this signage system is reproduced in C-10.2.3.

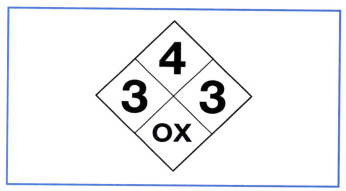

**Exhibit 10.9** *The NFPA 704 Diamond System for labeling (e.g., chemicals).*

Exhibit 10.9 is a replica of the "NFPA 704 diamond." Numbers used range from 0 to 4, with 4 being the most hazardous (e.g., a "4" in the flammability box means extremely flammable; a "0" in the flammability box means "will not burn.") Several color arrangements are allowed.

(a) The background of each square is the colored listed, and numbers are some contrasting color (e.g., black, white).
(b) The background is white, and the color of numbers corresponds to color assigned for hazard.

Any special hazards are indicated by the use of a symbol, for example,

W̶ means avoid the use of water because of an unusual reactivity to water

**OX** means materials possess oxidizing properties

☢ means materials possess radioactivity hazards.

**10-8.2.2\*** All doors leading to laboratories, laboratory work areas, and laboratory storage areas, shall be identified with signs to warn emergency response personnel of unusual or severe hazards that are not directly related to the fire hazards of contents.

This section was added to the 1999 edition to emphasize the laboratory's responsibility to alert emergency personnel concerning significant environmental hazards other than those directly relevant to fire control. The wording or symbols used will be immediately recognizable to those approaching the laboratory in response to a fire emergency.

**A-10-8.2.2** Examples of severe or unusual hazards that might require signage include, but are not limited to, biohazards, radioactive chemicals, carcinogens, mutagens, teratogens, and high energy lasers.

**10-8.2.3** It shall be the responsibility of the laboratory safety officer to ensure periodically that the signage properly indicates the nature of the materials being used within the identified space.

Other laboratory staff are urged to become familiar with this ID system as well.

**10-8.2.4** It shall be the duty of the senior person responsible for activities in respective laboratory areas to inform the laboratory safety officer of changes in protocol and procedures that involve variations in the fire and associated hazards of materials used in individual spaces.

Laboratory personnel and facilitywide disaster planners need to coordinate closely to ensure that hazards related to laboratories are identified and properly addressed in the facility's disaster plans. (See also Chapter 11.)

# 10-9  Transfer of Gases

**10-9.1** Transfer of gaseous oxygen shall be in accordance with 8-6.2.5.1(b).

For background on this allowance, see commentary under 4-6.2.1.5(b).

**10-9.2** Transfer of all other gases from one cylinder to another within the laboratory shall be prohibited.

**10-9.3** Transfer of liquid oxygen shall be in accordance with 8-6.2.5.2.

# 10-10  Laboratory Gas Cylinder Storage for Non-Piped Use

Section 10-10 refers only to *non-piped* gases, that is, freestanding cylinders and containers. Specifications for piped systems (including those for laboratories) remain in Chapter 4 (refer to 12-3.4, 13-3.4, etc., for piping system requirements that are applicable to a laboratory in a hospital or "other" health care facility).

## 10-10.1 Cylinder and Container Management.

Requirements shall be in accordance with 4-3.1.1.1.

## 10-10.2 Storage Requirements (Location, Construction, Arrangement; Any Quantity; Flammable and Nonflammable Gases).

**10-10.2.1** Storage shall be in cylinders complying with 4-3.1.1.1.

**10-10.2.2** Flammable gas cylinder storage for a laboratory, if inside any health care facility, shall be in a separate room or enclosure reserved exclusively for that purpose, having a fire-resistance classification of at least 2 hours, and ventilated in accordance with 2-6.5 of Annex 2.

*Exception: Except as permitted in 4-6.1.1.1.*

Cylinders in storage shall be kept in racks or secured in position.

This section applies to the storage of individual flammable gas cylinders. Requirements for a storage area used to connect cylinders for a manifold system are listed in 4-6.1.1.1 of Chapter 4.

The 2-hour requirement in this section has been used in order to be consistent with federal regulations and NFPA *101, Life Safety Code.* [3]

The following recommendations for ventilation within the room or enclosure where flammable gas cylinders are stored should be considered. There should be eight air changes per hour, air should be ceiling supplied and floor exhausted (with physical separation between each as great as possible), and exhaust should be discharged to the exterior. While a gravity or mechanical ventilation system is allowed, a mechanical one will require additional electrical safety and emergency power requirements. (See Chapter 3 for emergency power requirements.)

Flammable and oxidizing gases are not to be stored or utilized in a common room in any type of health care facility.

**10-10.2.3** Rooms or enclosures for storage of cylinders shall be well ventilated. Electrical equipment in flammable-gas storage areas shall comply with NFPA 70, *National Electrical Code*, for Class I, Division 2 locations.

While sentence one of 10-10.2.3 applies to all storage locations, specific requirements for flammable gas cylinder storage rooms in laboratories are identified in 10-10.2.2.

**10-10.2.4** Enclosures for storage of nonflammable gases shall have at least 1-hour fire-resistive construction, in accordance with 4-3.1.1.2(a).

Note that this section addresses the subject of storage of only nonflammable gas cylinders. A fire resistance rated separation is required between flammable and nonflammable gases. In addition, the storage of flammable and nonflammable gases in the same enclosure is prohibited.

**10-10.3**  The total quantity and size of cylinders containing oxygen, flammable gas, liquefied flammable gas, and gas with Health Hazard Ratings of 3 or 4 shall comply with Table 8-1 of NFPA 45, *Standard on Fire Protection for Laboratories Using Chemicals*. The number of reserve cylinders within general laboratory work areas shall not exceed one week's working supply.

### References Cited In Commentary

1. NFPA 704, *Standard System for the Identification of Hazards of Materials for Emergency Response,* 1996 edition.
2. NFPA 45, *Standard on Fire Protection for Laboratories Using Chemicals,* 1996 edition.
3. NFPA *101®, Life Safety Code®,* 1997 edition.
4. NFPA 49, *Hazardous Chemical Data,* 1994 (available in NFPA's *Fire Protection Guide to Hazardous Materials,* 1997).
5. NFPA 13, *Standard for Installation of Sprinkler Systems,* 1999 edition.
6. NFPA 10, *Standard for Portable Fire Extinguishers,* 1998 edition.
7. NFPA 30, *Flammable and Combustible Liquids Code,* 1996 edition.
8. NFPA 325, *Fire Hazard Properties of Flammable Liquids, Gases, and Volatile Solids,* 1994 (available in NFPA's *Fire Protection Guide to Hazardous Materials,* 1997).

# CHAPTER 11

# Health Care Emergency Preparedness

For this 1999 edition, the term *emergency preparedness* was substantially (but not universally) substituted for the term *disaster* because in the past NFPA 99 used multiple terms to describe one issue and this created confusion. The committee noted a distinct difference between *disaster* as an event or occurrence and *emergency preparedness* as a term that best describes preparation for the many situations that might require a health care facility to manage an incident. *Emergency preparedness* is also a term most easily identified by the other agencies that will interface with a health care facility during an incident.

NFPA 3M, *Manual on Hospital Emergency Preparedness,* which is now the basis of Chapter 11 (which first appeared in the 1996 edition of NFPA 99), grew out of the need to provide guidance for meeting the requirements for fire drills as contained in NFPA *101, Life Safety Code* [1]. A detailed plan of action was needed for the various emergencies that could occur in hospitals because of the difficulty in readily evacuating patients. These included both internal emergencies (such as fires within the hospital) and external ones (such as natural disasters), which could impact the hospital in terms of a large number of injured being brought to the facility for treatment or the hospital having to be evacuated because of toxic fumes or damage.

When the Health Care Facilities Committee initially established a committee in 1968 to study this situation, only hospital emergency preparedness was addressed. In 1975 other health care facilities were included because it was recognized that these facilities faced the same emergencies as hospitals. In addition, the emergency plans of these facilities might involve coordination with other health care facilities. For example, a small nursing home could coordinate its emergency plan with a nearby hospital.

In 1992 NFPA established a separate project on Disaster Management. The committee was charged with developing a document to cover disaster planning as a whole. That document, designated NFPA 1600, *Recommended Practice for Disaster Management* [2], and this chapter are intended to be mutually supportive and compatible and to lead to more attention to the subject of emergency preparedness (as appropriate) in all NFPA documents.

This chapter essentially codifies what many health care facilities are already practicing with regard to emergency preparedness, notably the incorporation of an incident command (or management) system.

## 11-1* Scope

This chapter establishes minimum criteria for health care facility emergency preparedness management in the development of a program for effective disaster preparedness, mitigation, response, and recovery.

In this 1999 edition, the term *disaster management* has been replaced with *emergency preparedness* to keep the text consistent with committee action on other portions of the document. The committee is of the opinion that there are two parts of a properly implemented plan: the emergency preparedness plan and disaster planning.

**A-11-1** Since no single model of a disaster plan is feasible for every health care facility, this chapter is intended to provide criteria in the preparation and implementation of an individual plan. The principles involved are universally applicable; the implementation needs to be tailored to the specific facility.

Every health care facility should have a plan of action for the various emergencies that can affect the facility. The plan should also mesh with the plans of surrounding and supporting installations and agencies.

Each health care facility should also have a management plan that is compatible to and will mesh with the responding emergency agencies. It should be noted that this plan should be designed to respond to any emergency situation, unlike the previous plan of responding to either internal or external emergency situations and not considering coordination with responding emergency agencies.

## 11-2 Purpose

The purpose of this chapter is to provide those with the responsibility for disaster management planning in health care facilities with a framework to assess, mitigate, prepare for, respond to, and recover from disasters. This chapter is intended to aid in meeting requirements for having an emergency preparedness management plan.

A health care facility's responsibility to its community during a disaster is not simply one of moral commitment or mission. Its responsibility also stems from regulatory standards and insurance considerations to preserve the facility's resources.

One of the greatest threats to the smooth operation of a health care facility in an emergency is the presence of the "it can't happen here" syndrome. This attitude underscores the need for a heightened awareness of possible hazards, even those so remote physically (e.g., a brush fire in an urban area) as to escape initial appraisal by planners. Either the events themselves or their side effects should be considered for the problems they could impose on the facility.

An emergency preparedness plan is intended to aid the persons charged with responsibility for designing and implementing emergency preparedness management at each health care facility. The procedure is to establish a planning process that is realistic and can be implemented prior to or during any emergency situation. This is the framework that is essential for a disaster management plan.

## 11-3* Applicability

This chapter is applicable to any health care facility that is intended to provide medical treatment to the victims of a disaster.

**A-11-3** Such facilities include, but are not limited to, hospitals, clinics, convalescent or nursing homes, and first-aid stations (disaster receiving stations). Such facilities could be formally designated by a government authority as disaster treatment centers. Such facilities would not normally include doctors' or dentists' offices, medical laboratories, or school nurseries, unless such facilities are used for treatment of disaster victims.

Any facility that cares for large numbers of people, such as hospitals (all types), long-term care facilities (all types), and large clinics, and that provides medical care during a disaster is within the scope of this standard. During a disaster the staffing, supplies, communications, and medical care services will be drastically altered. These changes should be planned for in every emergency preparedness plan to make the necessary transition(s) as seamless as possible. See Exhibit 11.1 for an example of changing the use of a trauma room during a disaster.

## 11-4 Responsibilities

### 11-4.1* Authority Having Jurisdiction (AHJ).

The AHJ shall be cognizant of the requirements of a health care facility with respect to its uniqueness for continued operation of the facility in an emergency.

**A-11-4.1** In time of disaster all persons are subject to certain constraints or authorities not present during normal circumstances. All disaster plans written by a health care facility

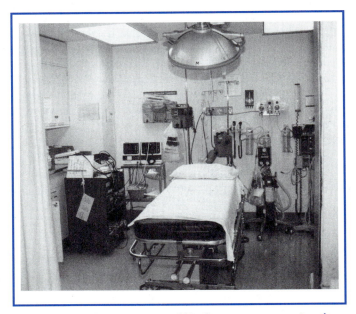

**Exhibit 11.1** *A trauma room within the emergency center of a hospital. It could serve as another/backup operating room during a disaster.*

should be reviewed and coordinated with such authorities so as to prevent confusion. Such authorities include, but are not limited to, civil authorities (such as a fire department, police department, public health department, or emergency medical service councils), and civil defense or military authorities.

Further, an authority having jurisdiction can impose upon the senior management of the facility the responsibility for participating in a community disaster plan.

Nongovernment authorities (such as a facility's insurance carrier) could also require the facility to participate in community emergency preparedness plans.

## 11-4.2 Senior Management.

It shall be the responsibility of the senior management to provide its staff with plans necessary to respond to a disaster or an emergency. Senior management shall appoint an emergency preparedness committee, as appropriate, with the authority for writing, implementing, exercising, and evaluating the emergency preparedness plan.

Senior management at a health care facility is responsible for ensuring that their facility can function during any emergency situation. Their responsibility includes developing the emergency plan, implementing the plan, and educating and training the staff, as well as evaluating the plan to ensure it can be implemented and will work properly. (See Supplement 3, "Conducting Emergency Drills at Health Care Facilities.") Senior management might want to review the emergency preparedness plan not only for its functional capabilities but also to ensure that it does not conflict with other rules, regulations, and practices. If a conflict does occur, there should be an authorized transitional plan so that the emergency preparedness plan can be activated.

## 11-4.3* Emergency Preparedness Committee.

The emergency preparedness committee shall have the responsibility for the overall disaster planning and emergency preparedness within the facility, under the supervision of designated leadership.

The emergency preparedness committee shall model the emergency preparedness plan on the incident command system (ICS) in coordination with local emergency response agencies.

**A-11-4.3** *Emergency Preparedness Planning Committee.* The incident command system (ICS) is a system having an identified chain of command that adapts to any emergency event. ICS establishes common terminology and training for incident management. This allows emergency responders from hospitals and all involved organizations to respond to an incident and be familiar with the management concepts and terminology of other responders. It also facilitates the request and processing of mutual aid requests.

A widely accepted structure of an ICS is illustrated in Figure A-11-4.3.

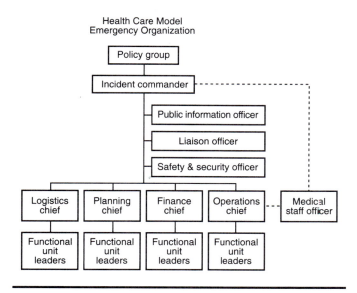

**Figure A-11-4.3** *Health care model emergency organization.*

A policy group consists of senior managers constituted to provide decisions related to items or incident decisions not in the disaster plan.

The command staff consists of the incident commander and support staff. This support staff consists of the public information officer, liaison officer, and safety officer.

In addition to the command staff, there are four sections, each with a section chief responding directly to the incident commander: plans section, logistics section, operations section, and finance section.

Due to the nature of a health care facility, one deviation from the traditional ICS is made to show a line of medical control. Note the advisory position of the "medical staff officer."

> This committee is responsible for the development of the emergency preparedness plan. This process includes realistic planning for emergencies that could occur within the facility as well as emergency situations that could bring an influx of patients to the facility. Planning might also include any situation for which the facility would send staff members to the emergency site. See Exhibit 11.2 for an emergency preparedness planning development process flow chart.
>
> The last paragraph of A-11-4.3 establishes the use of the incident command system (ICS). Although this concept may seem foreign to many health care facilities, most facilities have the basic components of ICS in place. With little change, the facility can make the transition to this new emergency preparedness management system. See NFPA 1561, *Standard on Fire Department Incident Management System,* for more information on the ICS.[3]
>
> All roles and responsibilities need to also be delineated in written form so they can be studied, incorporated into training programs, and then rehearsed, drilled, and evaluated for effectiveness.

## 11-5 General Requirements

> The emergency preparedness plan should be designed so that it establishes a line of authority within the facility. It is important that this authority structure be established on all three shifts. The person declaring the emergency can be from an outside agency; however, a senior person within the facility must also have the authority to initiate the emergency preparedness plan. If an emergency situation takes place in the facility, a decision must be made to initiate the plan without delay.
>
> The plan should not depend on any special individual or group for implementation. The people on duty at the time of the disaster should be capable of implementing it. Overall coordination, which must be developed and rehearsed regularly, is critical. Local and state emergency response services, working along with the medical, nursing, and administrative services of a health care facility, can provide all the components required for victims of a disaster.
>
> An emergency preparedness plan should also reflect a facility's location in

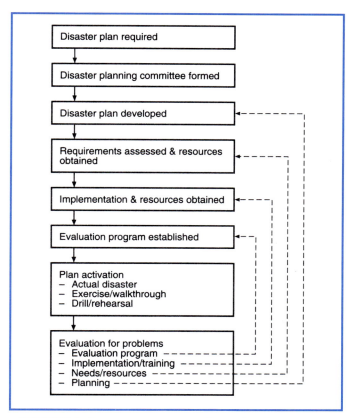

**Exhibit 11.2** *An emergency preparedness planning development process.*

relation to potential disasters. As an example, areas subject to frequent wildland fires should invoke countermeasures for smoke management and air quality maintenance.

Situations outside the facility can cause the plan to go into effect by any of several authorities having jurisdiction.

Unlike the decision to implement the emergency preparedness plan for a situation within the facility, the plan cannot be terminated, in most cases, without the coordination and approval of the authority having jurisdiction, that is, the fire chief, government officials, or other civil authorities.

**11-5.1\*** When a facility declares itself in a disaster mode, or when the authority having jurisdiction (AHJ) declares a state of disaster exists, the disaster plan shall be activated.

Planning shall be based on realistic conceptual events and operating capacity thresholds that necessitate activation of the plan.

**A-11-5.1** Hazard identification and risk assessment should determine whether the following types of hazards are applicable:

(a) Natural disasters
(b) Technological/industrial disasters
(c) Civil/political disasters.

For further information on disaster management, see NFPA 1600, *Recommended Practice for Disaster Management.*

Every health care facility should anticipate the types of emergencies likely to occur and what its role might be in such emergencies. A plan taking into account as many eventualities as are reasonably probable should be developed (e.g., an aircraft crash plan should be developed if a major airport is close by). Plans should be based on the strengths of the resources available. Only by matching disaster potentials with resources can the emergency preparedness plan provide maximum benefit to the community.

**11-5.2\*** The decision to activate the emergency preparedness plan shall be made by the authority designated within the plan, in accordance with the facility's activation criteria. The decision to terminate shall be made by the designated authority in coordination with the authority having jurisdiction and other civil or military authorities involved.

**A-11-5.2** *Planning.* By basing the planning of health care emergency preparedness on realistic conceptual events, the plan reflects those issues or events that are predictable for the environment the organization operates in. Thus, such conceptual planning should focus on issues, such as severe weather typical in that locale; situations that may occur due to close proximity of industrial or transportation complexes; or earthquake possibilities due to local seismic activity. Planning for these events should also focus on the capacity of the health care organization to provide services in such an emergency. Capacity thresholds are different for all facilities, but have to do with issues such as the availability of emergency departments, operating suites and operating beds, as well as logistical response and facility utilities. There is no way to plan for all possible emergencies, but by focusing on logical conceptual events and operating capacity thresholds, the health care organization can develop realistic plans as well as guidelines for staff to activate those plans.

This appendix information was added in 1999 because the Committee on Disaster Planning felt that guidance should be provided on determining the basis of the plan. Specifically it should be based on realistic conceptual events and operating capacity.

**11-5.3** The emergency preparedness plan, as a minimum, shall include the following.

In addition to developing the emergency preparedness plan, a mechanism for periodic updating and distribution needs to be established.
An emergency plan of each department needs to be a subset of the facility's

overall plan. A department should not have a plan that is totally independent of the rest of the facility.

It is worth emphasizing that each facility needs to develop an emergency preparedness plan best-suited to its needs, its activities, and its capabilities. (See also Supplement 3, "Conducting Emergency Drills at Health Care Facilities.")

**11-5.3.1\*  Identification of Emergency Response Personnel.** All personnel designated or involved in the emergency preparedness plan of the health care facility shall be supplied with a means of identification, which shall be worn at all times in a visible location. Specific means of identification for incident command system (ICS) personnel shall be provided, such as vests, baseball caps or hard hats.

See Exhibit 11.3 for an example of emergency protocol procedures intended to be affixed to an ID badge.

**Exhibit 11.3** *The emergency protocol procedures for fire and emergency response, as well as accidental exposure to biohazards, which are printed on the front and back of a red plastic card, affixed to all ID card badge holders. All employees and volunteers wear an ID badge.*

**A-11-5.3.1**  Where feasible, photo identifications or other means to assure positive identification should be used.

Visitor and crowd control create the problem of distinguishing staff from visitors. Such identification should be issued to all facility personnel, including volunteer personnel who might be utilized in disaster functions.

NOTE:  Care should be taken to assure that identification cards are recalled whenever personnel terminate association with the health care facility.

Members of the news media should be asked to wear some means of identification, such as the press card, on their outside garments so that they are readily identifiable by security guards controlling access to the facility or certain areas therein. Clergy also will frequently accompany casualties or arrive later for visitations and require some means of identification.

Some consideration should be given to a method for identifying critical staff who could be called to the facility during an emergency but arrive without proper identification. Key medical personnel have been known to respond to facilities only to be denied entry because they did not bring the necessary identification. A phone contact to key organizations to confirm identity can eliminate potential problems.

Any person not familiar with the plan or the facility will be a detriment to the operation of the plan. It is important that a form of identification be established for the emergency situation and that it be different from the normal identification worn daily by the staff.

The facility should have a specific plan for accrediting the large number of visitors who may seek access into the facility during an emergency. The facility may very well be operating under uncertain and possibly dangerous conditions, and staff will need to be flexible but firm in handling each situation.

A plan should also include a way of keeping track of visitors so that the incident commander will be able to account for everyone during relocation.

Beeper systems in use before a disaster can serve as a framework for establishing access lists.

**11-5.3.2\*  Continuity of Essential Building Systems.**  When designated by the emergency preparedness management plan to provide continuous service in a disaster or emergency, health care facilities shall establish contingency plans for the continuity of essential building systems, as applicable:

**A-11-5.3.2**  For essential building systems, consideration should be given to the installation of exterior building connectors to allow for the attachment of portable emergency utility modules.

Water storage systems should be inventoried and protected to the greatest extent possible.

During an emergency within the facility or outside the facility, several essential building services must be continued, or the patients will have to be evacuated. It is important that, for these services, the facility have contingency plans that are part of the overall emergency preparedness plan. Many vendors in the surrounding areas can provide these services. It is up to the facility to make the necessary arrangements and provide hookups for these systems to be used.

It should be noted that several types of water are used in health care facilities. These include potable (drinking water), fire protection water, and water used by sanitation and building environmental control systems. See Exhibit 11.4 for an example of a fire pump used to supply water for sprinkler and standpipe systems. A plan should be in place to separate the potable water from the system water. System water can be pumped in from a number of sources. Potable water can be distributed in bottles or cans.

**Exhibit 11.4** *Fire pumps used in a hospital. Key staff members need to know how these function.*

(a)* Electricity

**A-11-5.3.2(a)** See Sections 3-4, 3-5, and 3-6 for types of essential electrical systems for health care facilities.

(b)  Water
(c)  Ventilation
(d)  Fire protection systems
(e)  Fuel sources
(f)  Medical gas and vacuum systems (if applicable)
(g)* Communication systems

**A-11-5.3.2(g)** *Telecommunication Systems.* Emergency internal and external communication systems should be established to facilitate communication with security forces and other authorities having jurisdiction as well as internal patient care and service units in the event normal communication methods are rendered inoperative.

The basic form of communication in a disaster is the telephone system. As part of the contingency plan to maintain communication, a plan for restoring telephone systems or using alternate systems is necessary. Typically, the first line of internal defense for a system outage is strategically placed power-failure telephones that are designed to continue to function in the event of system failure. Plans for external outages and load control should include the use of pay phones that have first priority status in external system restoration.

Contingency plans should also contain strategies for the use of radio-frequency communications to supplement land-line usage. The plan should include a means to distribute and use two-way radio communication throughout the facility. A plan for the incorporation and use of amateur radio operators should also be considered.

It should be recognized that single-channel radio communication is less desirable than telephone system restoration due to the limited number of messages that can be managed. Cellular telephones, although useful in some disaster situations, should not be considered a contingency having high reliability due to their vulnerability to load control schemes of telephone companies.

> An increase in telephone traffic can almost always be expected in a disaster. A means of expanding telephone service quickly and efficiently needs to be included in any plan. Pre-arranged unlisted telephone numbers can be of crucial importance.
>
> Installation of pay telephones should be considered in more than just the traditional places, such as a lobby. At least one telephone should be located near, or even in, the disaster control center(s).
>
> Cellular phones should not be considered because of load control.
>
> One of the best methods for communication within the facility during a disaster is through a messenger system. This need became apparent during the response to the bombing of the Murah Federal Office Building in Oklahoma City. In this incident, rescuers from different agencies didn't have a common radio channel. The use of normal and cellular telephone service was lost because these systems became quickly overloaded (between use by rescuers and the general public who were calling in associated emergencies from the bomb blast). Messengers or "runners" were the most effective means for any agency to communicate with another.
>
> Many amateur radio clubs are willing to provide communications services during emergencies. These clubs can set up operations and can provide contact with resources outside the facility and disaster area.

**11-5.3.3\*  Staff Management.** Planning shall include the alerting and managing of all staff and employees in a disaster, as well as consideration of (1) housing, (2) transportation of staff and staff family, and (3) critical incident staff stress debriefing.

**A-11-5.3.3** Management of staff and employees allows for the best and most effective use of the entity's human resources during disaster operations. Consideration should be given to both personnel on-hand and those that can be alerted. Specifically, staff management includes the following:

(a) Assignment of roles and responsibilities
(b) Method for identifying human resource needs to include status of families
(c) Method for recalling personnel and augmenting staff
(d) Management of space (housing, day care, etc.)
(e) Management of staff transportation
(f) Critical incident stress debriefing (Many case histories show that not only victims but also rescuers and treatment/ handler staff bear serious emotional or even mental scars from their traumatic experiences. Emergency room and ambulance staff can also benefit from such help when stress has been acute.)

Staff management and high staff morale is essential for any emergency preparedness plan to work. Staff assignments should be clear and concise. It is important that any staff that is placed in a position of authority understand the position, the hazards that exist, and the chain of command they are to follow.

The well-being of the staff is also essential. Hours worked, rest, sleeping accommodations, and nourishment are necessary to maintain the proper well-being of the staff. Of most concern to the staff are their families and what is going on outside the facility. News from the outside should be distributed as part of the public information officer's responsibilities.

Depending on the type of emergency, there needs to be contingency plans for staff transportation to and from the facility. Inclement weather could require four-wheel drive vehicles to transport the staff. The public information officer should have a script in place to request this type of service through the news media. Any plan should include pickup and drop-off points, weather updates, and fuel provisions as appropriate.

The subject of stress debriefing of staff [subparagraph (f)] was first addressed in the 1990 edition of NFPA 99 because of the growing awareness that traumatic incidents can affect staff and their ability to maintain patient care. This problem is often not recognized until a staff member collapses or a serious misjudgment occurs. Senior management should be mindful of this potential problem because it can occur at any level. Some of this stress can be acute and might affect staff members throughout the rest of their lives unless dealt with immediately. Making staff aware of this potential problem is now understood to be another important factor that needs to be addressed in emergency preparedness planning.

An article on staff behavior and stress can be found in *FIRE, The Journal of the Fire Protection Profession*.[4]

**11-5.3.4\*  Patient Management.** Plans shall include provisions for management of patients, particularly with respect to clinical and administrative issues.

**A-11-5.3.4** The plans should focus also on modification or discontinuation of nonessential patient services, control of patient information, and admission/discharge and transfer of patients. Emergency transfer plans need to consider the proper handling of patient personal property and medical records that will accompany the patient as well as assurance of continuity of quality care. Evaluation of space, patient transport resources, and a process to ensure patient location information should be included.

The sooner triage can be instituted, the higher the chances are of saving more victims.

Besides the normal patient medical management, medical control through the senior medical officer could require that patients be discharged or transferred to other facilities. Once the evaluation of space (patient bed number) is completed, the chief medical officer can require that patients who are not critical be discharged to make room for patients coming from the outside. If the facility is impacted by an emergency situation within the facility, patients can be sent to other receiving facilities. It is important that the emergency preparedness plan take into account patient charts, nursing notes, and other information that is pertinent to the well-being of patients. Patients should always have the same quality of care no matter what facility they are in.

Special transportation for neonatal care patients, cardiac or critical care patients, and other similar cases should be part of the emergency preparedness plan. See Exhibit 11.5 for an example of specialized transportation for patients.

A receiving area or areas should be set up for incoming patients. These areas could have separate locations, depending on the severity of the patients' medical condition. Exhibit 11.6 shows an information panel that includes the hospital's emergency procedures.

*Exhibit 11.5* *A helicopter used to transport patients from accident scenes or other emergencies, requiring regional coordination for optimal effectiveness. (Photo by Mark C. Ide. Courtesy of Life Flight, University of Massachusetts Medical Center, Worcester, MA)*

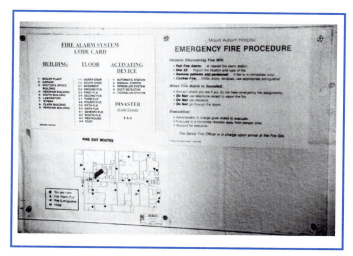

**Exhibit 11.6** *An information panel that includes the hospital's emergency procedures, codes, and a "you are here" map showing floor plan and nearest exits.*

**11-5.3.5\* Logistics.** Contingency planning for disasters shall include as a minimum stockpiling or ensuring immediate or at least uninterrupted access to critical materials such as the following:

(a) Pharmaceuticals
(b) Medical supplies
(c) Food supplies
(d) Linen supplies
(e) Industrial and potable (drinking) waters

**A-11-5.3.5** *Logistics.* It will be essential to assess these kinds of resources currently available within the health care facility itself, and within the local community as a whole. Community sources identification can be effectively performed by the local disaster council, through the cooperation of local hospitals individually or collectively through local hospital associations, nursing homes, clinics, and other outpatient facilities, retail pharmacies, wholesale drug suppliers, ambulance services, and local medical/surgical suppliers and their warehouses.

Knowing the location and amount of in-house and locally available medical and other supply sources, a given health care facility could then desire to stockpile such additional critical material and supplies as could be needed to effectively cope with the disaster situation. Stockpiling of emergency preparedness supplies in carts should be considered as they facilitate stock rotation of outdated supplies, provide a locally secured environment, and are easily relocated to alternate site locations both within and outside the facility.

**11-5.3.6\* Security.** Security plans shall be developed that address facility access, crowd control, security staff needs, and traffic control.

Allowing the general public access to an operational area during a disaster makes it very difficult for health care providers to administer patient care. It also creates an unsafe condition for everyone. Access control plays an important part of any emergency situation. During the planning stages, the security officer should establish which resources are available both within the facility and with outside agencies.

Disaster situations are also a prime time for the violation of recognized safety practices. Staff will be tempted to lift objects and people without sufficient help, which can result in musculo-skeletal injuries. Hygiene practices are apt to be foregone, resulting in a potential for a variety of exposures. Equipment might clutter walkways, posing trip hazards. Exit/egress paths and other emergency equipment might become blocked and inaccessible. These, along with a multitude of other safety violations, need to be evaluated by a dedicated individual who will ensure that staff, patients, and visitors are afforded appropriate protection.

**A-11-5.3.6** *Security and Traffic Control.* Facilities should formally coordinate their security needs during a disaster with local law enforcement agencies. This action could be necessary as a means to supplement the facility security capabilities, or to provide all security needs when the facility lacks its own internal security forces.

The health care institution will find it necessary to share its disaster plans with local law enforcement agencies, or better still involve them in the process of planning for security support during disasters. The information should at least include availability of parking for staff, patients, and visitors, and normal vehicular, emergency vehicular, and pedestrian traffic flow patterns in and around the facility. The extent of the security and traffic control problems for any given health care facility will depend upon its geographical location, physical arrangement, availability of visitor parking areas, number of entrances, and so forth.

(a) *Crowd Control.* Visitors can be expected to increase in number with the severity of the disaster. They should not be allowed to disrupt the disaster functioning of the facility. Ideally, a visitor's reception center should be established away from the main facility itself, particularly in major disasters. Volunteer personnel such as Red Cross, Explorer Scouts, or other helpers can be utilized as liaisons between the visitors and the health care facility itself. Normal visiting hours on nursing units should be suspended where possible.

Language barriers can make even the best disaster plans ineffectual. Valuable time can be lost trying to convey emergency directions or procedures to those who speak languages other than the one predominantly spoken in the facility. Signs in the languages that are often heard in the halls of a facility can help. (See also NFPA 170, *Standard for Fire Safety Symbols* [5], for symbols that are widely used in the United States.)

(b) *Vehicular Traffic Control.* Arrangement for vehicular traffic control into and on the facility premises should be made in the disaster planning period. It will be necessary to direct ambulances and other emergency vehicles carrying casualties to triage areas or the emergency room entrance, and to direct incoming and outgoing vehicles carrying people, supplies, and equipment. Charts showing traffic flow and indicating entrances to be used, evacuation routes to be followed, and so forth, should be prepared and included in the Health Care Disaster Plan. Parking arrangements should not be overlooked.

Traffic control is essential during any emergency situation, whether patients are being transported to another facility or are being brought to the facility. One traffic control plan assigns facility security officers to handle the internal security operations and the local police department or other government agency to control the traffic patterns outside the facility. As with evacuation routes, traffic control patterns, both internal and external, should be preplanned and made part of the master emergency preparedness plan.

If health care facility personnel are utilized for traffic control, basic instructions are essential. Orange traffic vests or some other suitable form of identification also should be provided to signify their authority and to provide a measure of personal safety (i.e., so they are more easily seen).

(c) *Internal Security and Traffic Control.* Internal security and traffic control are best conducted by facility trained personnel, that is, regular health care facility security forces, with reinforcements as necessary. Additional assistance from the local law enforcement agencies should be coordinated in the disaster planning phase. Upon activation of the Health Care Disaster Plan, security guards should be stationed at all unlocked entrances and exits, as necessary. Entrance to the facility should be restricted to personnel bearing staff identification cards and to casualties. In the case of major access corridors between key areas of the facility, pedestrian traffic should be restricted to one side of the corridor, keeping one side of the corridor free for movement of casualties. Traffic flow charts for internal traffic should also be prepared in the planning phase, as is the case with external traffic control.

Some facilities have no security forces because they have no need for them on a regular basis. Such facilities have to consider how security services can be quickly put into action in an emergency.

To minimize security requirements during disaster conditions, points of access and egress to buildings should be minimized (being careful not to create a dangerous situation in terms of emergency egress from the facility). All staff and employees can be required to enter and leave the facility through easily controlled points marked with signs hung on doors directing people to active entrances and exits.

It should be noted that the request for military support and the invoking of martial rule are mutually exclusive. Military support could be necessary in some situations because of the capability or manpower it can provide to an area.

Health care facilities are better prepared to handle victims than they are to handle the concerned families and friends of the victims. A professional and efficient program for visitor control during the disaster will be significant in how the overall program actually performs and, quite importantly, how it is later perceived by the public. Identifying visitors with special badges, listing the names of visitors and the patients they are seeing, and being prompt, courteous, and considerate in the handling of information and requests are all important factors in the visitor center.

It is good practice to have a first-aid cart at the visitor control center for treating visitors' medical problems resulting from the anxiety and shock of the emergency situation.

Visitors might also have to accompany injured family members for a variety of reasons including language barriers. Staff should not try to enforce normal rules that might ordinarily exclude visitors from certain areas or procedures if this situation exists.

### 11-5.3.7* Public Affairs.

**A-11-5.3.7** *News Media.* Because of the intense public interest in disaster casualties, news media representatives should be given as much consideration as the situation will permit. Ideally, news media personnel should be provided with a reception area, with access to telephone communication and, if possible, an expediter who, though not permitted to act as spokesman for news releases, could provide other assistance to these individuals. News media personnel should not be allowed into the health care facility without proper identification. To alert off-duty health care staff and for reassuring the public, use of broadcast media should be planned. Media representatives should have access to telephone communications. Media representatives should be requested to wear some means of identification for security purposes.

All health care facility personnel should be advised on handling media requests, especially during emergency preparedness implementation. Preplanning with media personnel can ease the strain of dealing with requests under trying circumstances.

Under the scope of the incident command officer (ICO), one person serves as the public information officer (PIO). This person should be in direct contact with the incident commander to communicate with the news media. In the emergency preparedness planning phase, this person should determine where the news media will be staged (and the media's level of access to the facility), issue press credentials, and handle all news releases from the ICO.

The PIO should also notify the media of staff recall and where the staff should report. A person from the PIO staff should monitor radio and television transmissions to determine whether the information is correct and keep the PIO briefed on any breaking news so the staff can be informed.

It is important to issue press releases at a scheduled time. If the press does not get the information on a timely basis, they may report inaccurate information or enter the disaster scene.

**11-5.3.7.1** Health care facilities shall have a designated media spokesperson to facilitate news releases.

**11-5.3.7.2** An area shall be designated where media representatives can be assembled, where they will not interfere with the operations of the health care facility.

**11-5.3.8  Staff Education.**  Each health care facility shall implement an educational program. This program shall include an overview of the components of the emergency preparedness plan and concepts of the Incident Command System. Education concerning the staff's specific duties and responsibilities shall be conducted upon reporting to their assigned departments or position.

General overview education of the Emergency Preparedness Plan and the Incident Command System shall be conducted at the time of hire. Department/staff specific education shall be conducted upon reporting to their assignments or position and annually thereafter.

> For additional guidance (education) for staff, see commentary under A-11-5.3.7 on media response.
>
> After the emergency preparedness plan has been formulated, each staff member should attend an educational session explaining the overall scope of the plan. The educational programs, which should be broken down by department, should include specific information pertaining to the responsibilities of individual staff members during the emergency.
>
> It is important that this education take place for all full-time and part-time employees and volunteers. Employees under contract or agency personnel (e.g., temporary nursing agency personnel) should also know what is expected in an emergency. See Exhibit 11.7.

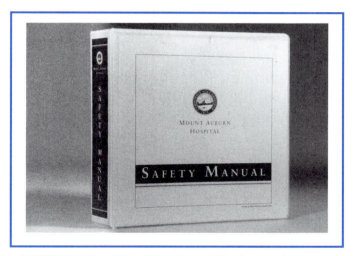

*Exhibit 11.7  A safety training manual. Employees at some facilities receive safety training as part of their orientation. All aspects of safety training are contained in a safety manual that was prepared by a safety committee.*

**11-5.3.9\*  Drills.**  Each organizational entity shall implement one or more specific responses of the emergency preparedness plan at least semi-annually. At least one semi-annual drill shall rehearse mass casualty response for health care facilities with emergency services, disaster receiving stations, or both.

**A-11-5.3.9** Experiences show the importance of drills to rehearse the implementation of all elements of a specific response including the entity's role in the community, space management, staff management, and patient management activities.

To consider an exercise a drill, the following aspects are typically incorporated and documented: a general overview of the scenario, activation of the disaster plan, evaluation of all involved participants/departments, a critique session following the drill, and any identified follow-up training to correct or improve any deficiencies.

> The rehearsal of an emergency preparedness plan should be as realistic a test of that plan as possible. Preparation for the rehearsal should involve the following: training, walk-through familiarizations, and discussions after the walk-through to resolve questions or problems. Exhibits 11.8 and 11.9 show some of the equipment with which facility staff should be familiar.

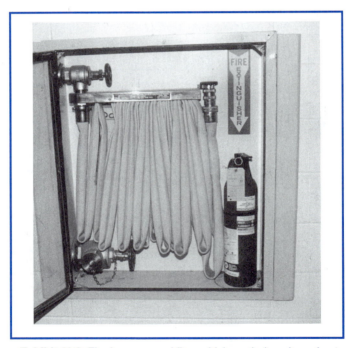

*Exhibit 11.8* Fire hose assemblies, which are being phased out because fire departments cannot rely on their being maintained properly for use in an emergency (the fire hose valves should be maintained so fire departments can connect their "standpipe pack" hose for suppression or "mop-up" operations). As reasons for dropping these familiar units, facilities have cited poor hose conditions, possible vandalism damage that makes the unit unreliable, and the risk of injury when hoses are used by untrained personnel.

***Exhibit 11.9*** *A hospital's fire alarm annunciator panel, located at each outside entrance to the facility.*

It would be very helpful to involve as many outside agencies that might respond to a real emergency as possible. Simulation of patient management and movement is also helpful in evaluating the emergency preparedness plan; it should not, however, involve actual patients.

During a simulation, volunteers who have been made to look like victims and counseled on typical behavior for specific injury types can provide a level of realism for all staff, particularly those who may not have dealt with the trauma of viewing, transporting, or attending to an injured victim. During the rehearsal, staff members can discover whether they will be able to handle the duties expected of them.

All parts of the emergency preparedness plan should be tested, including media and visitors' functions, as well as security and traffic control.

Non-JCAHO accredited hospitals and other types of health care facilities should conduct disaster drills at least annually, unless enforcement authorities direct them to do so more frequently.

It cannot be stressed enough that emergency preparedness plans should not only be developed in coordination with local fire and disaster management agencies, but they should also be rehearsed in coordination with these same groups. Plans cannot be developed in isolation.

**11-5.3.10\*  Operational Recovery.**  Plans shall reflect measures needed to restore operational capability to pre-disaster levels. Fiscal aspects shall be considered because of restoral costs and possible cash flow losses associated with the disruption.

**A-11-5.3.10** Recovery measures could involve a simple repositioning of staff, equipment, supplies, and information services; or recovery could demand extensive cleanup and repair. It can, under certain circumstances, present an opportunity to evaluate long-range ideas concerning modifications to the facility. Filing of loss claims might require special approaches.

*Finance.* Health care facilities should have access to cash or negotiable instruments to procure immediately needed supplies.

> The subject of recovery planning was first addressed in 1984 because studies showed that a emergency preparedness plan must include not only actions to deal with a disaster *while* it is occurring, but also steps to take *after* the crisis stage has passed and a facility begins to return to a normal state of operation.
>
> Recovery can be as simple as cleaning up one area of the facility or as complicated as finding suitable buildings, supplies, and equipment to continue some services until the facility is back in normal operation. Recovery can involve long-range planning for both financial and architectural efforts. A key element is computer software backup and data backup. Because most health care facilities are computerized, arrangements for data storage should be made off premises. In addition, should the emergency impair the computer network, arrangements should be made to find equivalent systems that will run the software and access the data.
>
> Arrangements should also be made to secure financing for supplies that will be needed immediately. Good record keeping is a must for claims reporting. Correspondence with the facility insurance agent or insurance company should be started as soon as the emergency has been mitigated. Supplies could be required for internal and external disasters.
>
> A very good article on recovery planning was written by W. E. Rogers, Director of Risk Management at Conemaugh Valley Memorial Hospital, Johnstown, Pennsylvania [6]. While it discusses only fire recovery planning, it can be applied to other types of disasters as well. The article is still timely.

### References Cited in Commentary

1. NFPA *101®*, *Life Safety Code®*, 1997 edition.
2. NFPA 1600, *Recommended Practice for Disaster Management*, 1995 edition.
3. NFPA 1561, *Standard on Fire Department Incident Management System*, 1995 edition.
4. *FIRE, The Journal of the Fire Protection Profession*, Lipshultz and Klein, "A Behavioral Approach to Managing Disaster Related Risks," Vol. 82, No. 1018, April 1990, p. 28, FMJ International Publications, Surrey, England.
5. NFPA 170, *Standard for Fire Safety Symbols*, 1999 edition.
6. W. E. Rogers, "Fire Recovery Planning in Health Care Institutions," NFPA *Fire Journal*, March 1982.

# CHAPTER 12

# Hospital Requirements

Electrical hazards, so much a concern in the 1970s, have decreased significantly in recent years. Exhibit 12.1 is one example of a hospital fire involving medical equipment. The reduction in hazards came about through the improved design and quality of electrical appliances. The development of sophisticated, but ever-smaller, circuitry has made it no longer necessary for a patient to be deliberately grounded in order to obtain noisefree signals. Successive levels of isolation have also separated the patient from accidental exposure to line voltage. The universal installation of grounding receptacles has profoundly reduced the danger of electric shock from domestic appliances and cord-connected devices in the hospital. With recognition that the hospital environment was hostile and abusive to equipment, industrial-grade fittings and cables became the rule for connectors and power cords, respectively. Exhibit 12.2 is one example of such improved equipment. However, these items are the weakest link in the safety chain, and they require regular inspection, testing, and repair when needed. The measures to establish electrical "safety" were straightforward, inexpensive, and effective.

Although electrical hazards have certainly decreased, they have not been eliminated. Scattered fatalities due to electricity have occurred in recent decades. All of these incidents, however, have involved children and were caused by an inattentive or untrained attendant. Training and verification of qualifications remain a vital part of any electrical safety program.

As noted in Chapter 1, Chapters 12 through 18 and Chapter 20 are "facility" chapters listing requirements from Chapters 3 through 11 that are applicable to specific facilities. Chapter 12 lists requirements that are specific for hospital facilities. The definition of *hospital facility* appears in Chapter 2.

**Exhibit 12.1**  *A Petersburg, Virginia, hospital, where five patients died in a 1994 fire. The fire, which involved smoking materials and an air flotation mattress, was fed by oxygen released from the piped oxygen distribution system.*

**Exhibit 12.2**  *A hospital-grade receptacle, identified by a green dot on its face. (Courtesy of Pass and Seymour/Legrand)*

# 12-1 Scope

This chapter addresses safety requirements of hospitals.

# 12-2 General Responsibilities

**12-2.1** As used in this chapter, the term *hospital* (except where it obviously refers to the physical structure) shall mean the entity and that portion of its internal governing structure that has the responsibility for the elements of hospital operation covered by this chapter, including building design, purchasing specifications, inspection procedures, maintenance schedules, and training programs affecting such use.

**12-2.2** It is understood that the individuals who are responsible will vary from one hospital to another, although in most cases the hospital's administration exercises the concomitant authority. It is further recognized that fulfillment of this responsibility frequently occurs by means of delegating appropriate authority to staff, consultants, architects, engineers, and others.

**12-2.3** To achieve the performance criteria of Chapters 1 through 11, the governing body of the hospital shall be permitted to assign responsibility to appropriate hospital personnel, consultants, architects, engineers, or others.

**12-2.4** The hospital shall ensure that policies are established and maintained that permit the attending physician to satisfy the emergency needs of any patient that could supersede the requirements of this chapter. Each such special use shall be clearly documented and reviewed to attempt to have future similar needs met within the requirements of this chapter.

## 12-2.5 Electricity.

It shall be the responsibility of the hospital to provide an environment that is reasonably safe from the shock and burn hazards attendant with the use of electricity in patient care areas.

The hospital shall establish policies and procedures related to the safe use of electric appliances.

Each hospital shall be permitted to select a specific electrical safety program that is appropriate to its particular needs.

The physical protection afforded by the installation of an electrical distribution system that meets the requirements of this chapter and the purchase of properly constructed and tested appliances shall be augmented by having designated departments of the facility assume responsibility for the continued functioning of the electrical distribution system (Chapter 3) and the inspection, testing, and maintenance of electrical appliances (Chapter 7).

The hospital shall adopt regulations and practices concerning the use of electric appliances and shall establish programs for the training of physicians, nurses, and other personnel who might be involved in the procurement, application, use, inspection, testing, and maintenance of electrical appliances for the care of patients.

## 12-2.6 Patient Care Areas.

Areas of a hospital in which patient care is administered are classified as general care areas or critical care areas, either of which is permitted to be classified as a wet location. The governing body of the facility shall designate the following areas in accordance with the type of patient care anticipated and with the following definitions of the area classification. *(See definition of Patient Care Area in Chapter 2.)*

(a) *General Care Area.* See definition in Chapter 2.
(b) *Critical Care Area.* See definition in Chapter 2.
(c) *Wet Location.* See definition in Chapter 2.

Patient care areas are categorized as general care and critical care. Patients in different areas may be at different levels of risk of electrical exposure. Distinct requirements for each category of patient care area are necessary.

It is important to note that the governing body of the facility is responsible for the designation of these areas. This can and should be done in consultation with medical staff and engineering staff, taking into consideration the conditions and practices of the facility. While this places responsibility on the facility, it also provides the facility with an opportunity to safeguard its own operations, rather than leaving the designations to an outside agency.

Variations in patient care area categorization within facilities can be expected. For example, general surgical recovery rooms may have conditions quite different from eye surgery recovery rooms.

The terms *general care area, critical care area,* and *wet location* originally appeared in Chapter 12 because they were developed for NFPA 76B, *Electricity in Patient Care Areas of Health Care Facilities.* NFPA 76B applied only to hospitals. In the 1987 edition of NFPA 99, the term *patient care area* was defined in Chapter 2 because previously there had been no definition of the term provided in text. Also for the 1987 edition, the definition of *wet location* was considered sufficiently generic to warrant applicability throughout the document (i.e., in all types of health care facilities) and was moved to Chapter 2. In the 1993 edition of NFPA 99, the terms *general care area* and *critical care area* were also seen to be applicable beyond just hospital environs.

For the 1990 edition of NFPA 99, a review of wet locations was made by an ad hoc subcommittee of the Technical Committee on Health Care Facilities. Many differences of opinion existed (and continue to exist) on just what constitutes a wet location. In addition to modifying the definition of this term, the subcommittee pointed out that the two terms *patient care areas* and *wet locations* are not mutually exclusive. Patient care areas may be wet locations, but a wet location is not necessarily a patient care area.

See commentary in Chapter 2 under *wet location* for an explanation of the term and for background on the controversy surrounding this definition.

Electrical requirements for wet locations are listed in 3-3.2.1.2(f). Further commentary on wet locations and anesthetizing locations is also included under 12-4.1.2.6(a).

### 12-2.7 Anesthesia.

It shall be the responsibility of the governing body of the hospital to designate anesthetizing locations.

### 12-2.8 Laboratories.

The governing boards of hospitals shall have the responsibility of protecting the facilities (for patient care and clinical investigation) and the personnel employed therein.

## 12-3 General Requirements

This "-3" section is arranged in the same sequence as in Chapters 1 through 8. Subsections "-3.1" and "-3.2" are reserved because Chapters 1 and 2 apply to the entire document and there are no requirements in those chapters that are specific only to Chapter 12. Chapters 3 through 8 contain general requirements and Chapters 12 through 18 and Chapter 20 reference these chapters or portions therein. Thus, 12-3.3 references electrical system requirements from Chapter 3 that are applicable to hospitals, 12-3.4 references gas and vacuum system requirements from Chapter 4 that are applicable to hospitals, and so forth.

### 12-3.1 (Reserved)

### 12-3.2 (Reserved)

### 12-3.3 Electrical System Requirements.

**12-3.3.1** The electrical distribution system for patient care areas shall conform to the requirements in Chapter 3, "Electrical Systems."

These requirements apply to new construction. Existing installations need not be modified, provided that they meet the operational safety requirements in 3-3.3.2 and 3-3.3.3.

**12-3.3.2** The essential electrical distribution system shall conform to a Type 1 system, as described in Chapter 3, "Electrical Systems."

Hospitals shall be permitted to serve the essential electrical system needs of contiguous or same-site facilities with the generating equipment of the hospital.

Exhibit 12.3 shows a hospital bed setup with essential electrical receptacles.

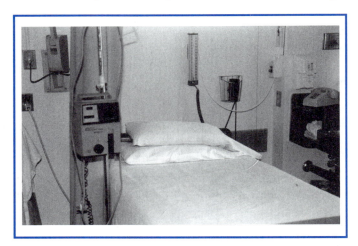

**Exhibit 12.3** *Typical general care bed setup. Note the receptacle and cover plate at the far left; they are red. This identifies the receptacle as being wired to the essential electrical system.*

### 12-3.4 Gas and Vacuum System Requirements.

This section has been completely revised for 1999 to reflect the committee's effort to have the level of risk to the patient (based on life support) determine the level (or complexity) of the systems (electrical, gas, vacuum, etc.) required in the facility.

**12-3.4.1** If installed, patient gas systems shall conform to Level 1 gas systems of Chapter 4.

**12-3.4.2** If installed, a Level 3 patient gas system of Chapter 4 shall be permitted when not served by the hospital's central patient gas systems.

**12-3.4.3** If installed, patient vacuum systems shall conform to Level 1 vacuum systems of Chapter 4.

**12-3.4.4** If installed, a Level 3 patient vacuum system of Chapter 4 shall be permitted when not served by the hospital's central patient vacuum system.

**12-3.4.5** If installed, patient WAGD systems shall conform to Level 1 WAGD systems of Chapter 4.

**12-3.4.6** If installed, laboratory gas systems shall conform to Level 4 gas systems of Chapter 4.

**12-3.4.7** If installed, laboratory vacuum systems shall conform to Level 4 vacuum systems of Chapter 4.

Exhibit 12.4 shows the extensive amount of electronic equipment and medical gas/vacuum outlets in a patient care area.

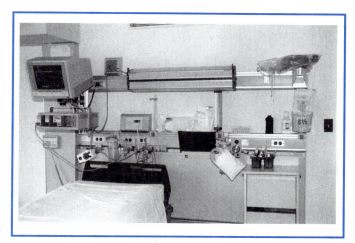

**Exhibit 12.4** *The range of electronic equipment and medical gas and vacuum system outlets used in a typical intensive care patient unit. Note the on/off switch at far right has a red cover plate, indicating that it is wired to the essential electrical system.*

## 12-3.5* Environmental System Requirements.

(Reserved)

**A-12-3.5** See 12-4.1 and 12-4.2 for requirements for anesthetizing locations and laboratories, respectively.

## 12-3.6 Material Requirements.

(Reserved)

## 12-3.7 Electrical Equipment Requirements.

**12-3.7.1\* Patient Care Areas.** Electrical appliances shall conform to Chapter 7.

**A-12-3.7.1** The requirements of Chapter 7 apply to all electrical appliances. Chapter 7 requirements and procedures are intended to be implemented by the hospital to evaluate existing equipment or to evaluate new equipment as part of routine incoming inspection procedures for all appliances in patient care areas. *(See 7-5.1 and 7-5.2.2.1.)*

**12-3.7.2\* Laboratories.** Equipment shall conform to the nonpatient electrical equipment requirements in Chapter 7.

**A-12-3.7.2** See 7-5.2.2.2 for performance criteria; see 7-6.2.5 for policies.

## 12-3.8 Gas Equipment Requirements.

**12-3.8.1 Patient.** Equipment shall conform to the patient equipment requirements in Chapter 8, "Gas Equipment."

**12-3.8.2 Nonpatient.** Equipment shall conform to the nonpatient equipment requirements in Chapter 8, "Gas Equipment."

**12-3.9** (Reserved)

**12-3.10** (Reserved)

**12-3.11** Hospitals shall comply with the provisions of Chapter 11 for disaster planning, as appropriate.

# 12-4\* Specific Area Requirements

**A-12-4** This is in addition to any applicable requirements in Section 12-3.

This appendix material is an important reminder that stresses the structure of NFPA 99 and how requirements are to be applied for each type of facility in Chapters 12 through 18 and Chapter 20. As an example, Section 12-3 lists requirements that are applicable to all hospitals. Section 12-4 lists additional requirements for specific areas within hospitals (e.g., 12-4.1 covers anesthetizing locations; 12-4.2 covers laboratories). It should be clearly understood that the requirements of Section 12-4 cannot be considered alone, but must be applied in conjunction with the requirements of Section 12-3. Section 12-4 requirements can be considered supplemental to any of the general requirements listed in Section 12-3.

## 12-4.1 Anesthetizing Locations.

The first health-care-related document produced by the NFPA, *Anesthetic Gases and Oxygen in Hospitals,* was published in 1934 and was originally the responsibility of the Committee on Gases. This document covered piping and storage of medical gases and oxygen chambers (the latter resembling a room within a room, with oxygen being pumped into the inner room).

A separate Committee on Hospitals was established in the late 1930s to address only the use of flammable anesthetics in operating rooms. It published a guideline in 1941 and a Recommended Practice in 1944, designated NFPA 56. Over the years, the name of this publication has changed a number of times. In 1962 it became the *Standard on the Use of Flammable Anesthetics* and, in 1970, the *Standard on the Use of Inhalation Anesthetics* because of the introduction of nonflammable anesthetics.

During the initial development of fire and explosion precautions for hospital operating suites, it became apparent that one of the principal sources of the ignition of flammable anesthetic gases was static electricity. Through efforts of the Bureau of Mines, and especially Dr. George Thomas, an anesthesiologist and one of the earliest advocates of fire safety in the hospital operating suite, studies were conducted to determine the cause of static electricity in operating suites and methods for mitigating this hazard. As a result of these studies, a number of precautions were incorporated into the very first editions of NFPA 56 (from 1944 and afterward). These precautions applied not only to permanently installed equipment and fixtures, but also to supplies, personnel attire, and personal safety practices used in the operating room. These precautions included all of the following:

1. Installation of conductive flooring
2. Maintenance of a relative humidity of 50 percent to 55 percent
3. Elimination of garments and drapes made from synthetic fibers
4. Use of conductive and antistatic materials
5. Compliance with Class 1, Group C requirements for suction, pressure, or insufflation (for tonsillectomy) equipment and for other portable equipment
6. Compliance with Class 1, Group C requirements for receptacles and switches in hazardous locations
7. Use of conductive shoes or conductive shoe covers and the testing of their efficacy before personnel entered flammable anesthetizing locations
8. Use of isolation transformers to supply ungrounded electric power, along with ground contact indicators (today line isolation monitors are used), to detect whether the ungrounded power was being compromised

See Exhibits 12.5 and 12.6 for examples of hospital isolated power system equipment.

As a result of the promulgation, adoption, and enforcement of these provisions, the incidence of fires and explosions in operating rooms fell drastically. While there has never been a retrospective study to evaluate the effects of the original safety requirements for operating rooms, adherence to these principles has made operating room personnel more cognizant of dangers. See Exhibit 12.7 for a typical operating room setup.

In 1956 a totally nonflammable inhalation anesthetic agent, halothane, was introduced into anesthesiology. In subsequent years, a number of other nonflammable, polyhalogenated anesthetic agents were also introduced. Because many anesthesiologists and anesthetists recognized the dangers of fires and explosions from flammable anesthetics and electrosurgery, the use of nonflammable agents became widespread and the administration of cyclopropane and diethyl ether declined.

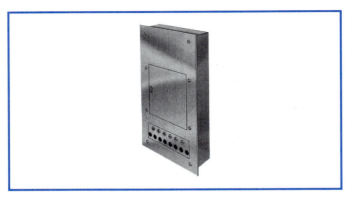

**Exhibit 12.5** *An example of a hospital isolated power system with built-in isolation transformer, line isolation monitor, and grounded busbar. (Courtesy of Square D Co.)*

At the recommendation of William Dornette, M.D., the then chairman of the Sectional Committee on Flammable Anesthetics, provisions for the use of nonflammable anesthetics were incorporated into NFPA 56, and the concepts of the *nonflammable anesthetizing location* and the *mixed facility* were included in the 1970 edition. That edition (designated NFPA 56A) recognized for the first time those operating suites in which flammable agents were no longer employed. If no flammable agents were employed in the hospital, each of the operating rooms became a nonflammable anesthetizing location. In those hospitals where some anesthetizing locations were designated for the use of flammable anesthetics and other locations designated for the use of nonflammable anesthetics only, the term *mixed facility* was applied.

In 1972 under the guidance of Dr. Dornette, NFPA 56A was completely reorganized and provisions for flammable and nonflammable anesthetizing locations and mixed facilities were placed into separate chapters. This structure was maintained when the document was incorporated into NFPA 99 as Chapter 3. In the 1987 edition of NFPA 99, much of that material became 12-4.1. Specific anesthetizing location requirements appear in NFPA 99 when they are different from requirements for patient care areas. (See the organizational information in A-12-4.)

By the mid-1970s, medical training programs in the United States were no longer teaching the use of flammable anesthetics. As a result, the number of operating room personnel familiar with the handling and use of flammable agents continually decreased. The committee, however, has not relaxed requirements that apply to flammable agents because flammable agents are still used in other parts of the world. For the 1996 edition of NFPA 99, all requirements for flammable inhalation anesthetics were grouped together and placed in Annex 2, "Flammable Anesthetizing Locations." This was intended to make it easier for those facilities still using

**Exhibit 12.6** *Line isolation monitor (top) for use with isolated power systems, remote indicator alarm (middle), and multiple annunciator panel (bottom) which can monitor several operating rooms from a central location, such as a nurses' station. (Courtesy of Square D Co.)*

flammable anesthetics to review the additional precautions necessary for using this type of anesthetic.

With the firm acceptance of the concept of the nonflammable anesthetizing location and the abandonment of the use of flammable anesthetics in a significant number of American hospitals, efforts were made by various members of the former Technical Committee on Anesthetizing Agents to modify the requirements for *isolated power*. (The requirement for isolated power had been retained for nonflammable anesthetizing locations.) Other members of the committee, however, pointed to the frequent spillage of biological and other fluids, the increasing use of electrical

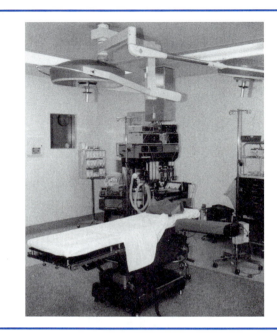

**Exhibit 12.7** *A typical operating room setup. The use of a dozen electronic devices is not uncommon in today's procedures.*

equipment in operating rooms, and the ready access to opportunities for grounding of personnel as serious hazards for electrical shock. In 1984 changes were made that allowed the relaxation of some of these requirements, and provisions now allow for the elimination of isolated power under certain circumstances. (See 12-4.1.2.6.)

Before the concept of nonflammable anesthetizing locations, the maintenance of a relative humidity of 50 percent to 55 percent was mandatory because of the significant role humidity plays in reducing static electricity. With the advent of nonflammable anesthetizing locations, the maintenance of relative humidity in this range was no longer necessary strictly to prevent explosions. Hospital engineers also pointed out that it was very costly to maintain relative humidity in this range during winter, when the outside temperature could be very low and the amount of water vapor contained in the ambient air is minimal. As a result, requirements for humidity control in nonflammable anesthetizing locations were dropped for the 1978 edition of NFPA 56A. There was extensive discussion on this subject for the 1984 edition of NFPA 99 and a range of humidity control was established. In 1990 a further change was made wherein only a minimum level is stated. (See 5-4.1.)

Although the use of flammable anesthetic agents has virtually ceased, *other flammable agents,* such as alcohol, flammable prepping agents, and bone cement, can still be found in anesthetizing locations. These flammable agents, combined with a large combustible load in the operating room and the use of oxidizing agents (oxygen and nitrous oxide), have not as yet been fully addressed by committees within the Health Care Facilities project. In addition, the extensive use of electrosurgical units, which create a combination of sparks and small flames, also is a matter of concern. (See further commentary on this subject under 12-4.1.2.10.)

While there are no restrictions on the *types of fabric* that can be worn by personnel or used for draping patients in nonflammable anesthetizing locations, institutions should be sure that such materials are not highly combustible. The increased use of flammable liquids, the presence of oxygen, and sparks and small flames caused by cautery and electrosurgical devices pose a problem should a fire involving these materials occur. (Oxygen, while not a flammable gas, greatly enhances combustion once it has begun.)

The resistance value of *conductive flooring still in use in nonflammable anesthetizing locations* can be allowed to rise in value since it would then resemble the resistance value of regular flooring. The concern here is that conductive floors will become too conductive and thus pose an electric shock hazard. The static discharge problem is not an issue in nonflammable anesthetizing locations, so a rise in the resistance of the floor is not of concern.

There are various options with regard to conductive flooring still in use in nonflammable anesthetizing locations. The floor can be checked to ensure the resistance of the floor is rising (or at least not falling below required values), it can be physically removed, or the floor can be covered in some manner. As a result of data from the American Hospital Association indicating that conductive flooring generally only rises in value, the testing of conductive floors in nonflammable anesthetizing locations needs to be carried out only once.

In the event a floor reading drops below 10,000 ohms, remedial action needs to be taken. (While the text of 12-4.1.4.4 in the 1993 edition of NFPA 99 stated only that readings were to be taken monthly when they fall below 10,000 ohms, the last part of the sentence, ". . .until the flooring again exceeds 10,000 ohms resistance," clearly implied that some remedial action is to be taken by the facility.) When readings again exceed 10,000 ohms, testing needs to be carried out only as indicated. (From a use perspective, the 10,000-ohm lower limit is a moot point because it is almost routine in major surgical procedures for floors to become covered with fluids and thus be rendered highly conductive. Testing, however, is to be conducted when flooring is dry and clean.)

### 12-4.1.1 General.

**12-4.1.1.1 Scope.** The purpose of this section is to establish performance and maintenance criteria for anesthetizing locations and for equipment and facilities ancillary thereto in order to safeguard patients and health care personnel from fire, explosion, electrical, and related hazards associated with the administration of inhalation anesthetics.

This section applies to all anesthetizing locations and related storage areas within hospitals in which inhalation anesthetics are administered.

This section is intended to provide requirements to protect against explosions or fires, electric shock, mechanical injury from compressed gases or compressed gas cylinders, or anoxia from erroneous gas connections and similar hazards, without unduly limiting the activities of the surgeon or anesthesiologist. This principle, without minimizing any of the aforementioned dangers, recognizes that the physicians shall be guided by all the hazards to life that are inherent to surgical procedures carried out in anesthetizing locations.

This section does not cover animal operative facilities unless the animal operative facility is integral to a hospital.

The provisions of this section do not apply to the manufacture, storage, transportation, or handling of inhalation anesthetics prior to delivery to the consuming health care facility. They do not apply to any use other than in an anesthetizing location and related storage areas.

**12-4.1.1.2 Purpose.** This section contains the requirements for administration and maintenance that shall be followed as an adjunct to physical precautions specified in 12-4.1.2.

**12-4.1.1.3\* Recognition of Hazards and Responsibility.**

**A-12-4.1.1.3** In determining whether existing construction or equipment does or does not constitute a hazard to life, due consideration should be given to the record of incidents or accidents of the facility in question and whether equipment used in the facility is subject to documented preventive maintenance. Absence of incidents and accidents, and the existence of a well-documented preventive maintenance program covering all electrical equipment used in anesthetizing locations in the facility, indicates that minimal hazard to life exists.

For example, isolated power systems would not be required in existing anesthetizing locations in health care facilities meeting the above criteria.

It was the intent of the Subcommittee on Anesthesia Services (now incorporated into the Committee on Gas Delivery Equipment) that changes to future editions of this section be applied judiciously to existing facilities (similar to NFPA *101, Life Safety Code* [1], which specifically differentiates between new and existing occupancies).

The appendix material is a further clarification with respect to the specific issue of existing anesthetizing locations that do not have isolated power systems. It was originally drafted as a Tentative Interim Amendment in 1980.

It should be noted again that a patient care area that is designated as a wet location would require an added level of electrical protection. [See A-12-4.1.2.6(a) and commentary under 12.4.1.2.6(a).]

(a) The hazards involved in the use of inhalation anesthetic agents can be successfully mitigated only when all of the areas of hazard are fully recognized by all personnel, and when the physical protection provided is complete and is augmented by attention to detail by all personnel of administration and maintenance having any responsibility for the functioning of anesthetizing locations. Since 12-4.1.1 and 12-4.1.2 are expected to be used as a text by those responsible for the mitigation of associated hazards, the requirements set forth herein are frequently accompanied by explanatory text.

(b) Responsibility for the maintenance of safe conditions and practices in anesthetizing locations falls mutually upon the governing body of the hospital, all physicians using the anesthetizing locations, the administration of the hospital, and those responsible for hospital licensing, accrediting, or other approval programs.

(c) Inasmuch as the ultimate responsibility for the care and safety of patients in a hospital belongs to the governing board of the hospital, that body, in its responsibility for enforcement of requirements contained in this chapter, shall determine that adequate regulations with respect to anesthesia practices and conduct in anesthetizing locations have been adopted by the medical staff of the hospital and that adequate regulations for inspection and maintenance are in use by the administrative, nursing, and ancillary personnel of the hospital.

(d) By virtue of its responsibility for the professional conduct of members of the medical staff of the hospital, the organized medical staff shall adopt regulations with respect to the use of inhalation anesthetic agents and to the prevention of electric shock and burns *(see C-12.3)* and through its formal organization shall ascertain that these regulations are regularly adhered to.

(e) In meeting its responsibilities for safe practices in anesthetizing locations, the hospital administration shall adopt or correlate regulations and standard operating procedures to ensure that both the physical qualities and the operating maintenance methods pertaining to anesthetizing locations meet the standards set in this chapter. The controls adopted shall cover the conduct of professional personnel in anesthetizing locations, periodic inspection to ensure the proper grounding of dead metal *(see 3-3.3.2),* and inspection of all electrical equipment, including testing of line isolation monitors.

### 12-4.1.1.4 Rules and Regulations.

(a) Hospital authorities and professional staff shall jointly consider and agree upon necessary rules and regulations for the control of personnel concerned with anesthetizing locations. Upon adoption, rules and regulations shall be prominently posted in the operating room suite. Positive measures are necessary to acquaint all personnel with the rules and regulations established and to ensure enforcement.

(b) The hazard symbols contained in NFPA 704, *Standard System for the Identification of the Hazards of Materials for Emergency Response*, shall be employed throughout the hospital, as appropriate. Such use is particularly important in the operating suite and in gas and volatile liquid storage facilities.

NFPA 704 provides a simple method for identifying an area's level of hazard. Fire departments are familiar with NFPA 704, *Standard System for the Identification of the Hazards of Materials for Emergency Response* [2], and can quickly interpret the coding used in the document and take appropriate measures when extinguishing a fire in that area. Once an area's level of hazard has been identified, the area should be checked periodically to determine whether the assigned coding is still applicable. For further details on the "704 diamond," see commentary under 10-8.2.1.

### 12-4.1.2 Requirements for ALL Anesthetizing Locations.

**12-4.1.2.1 Ventilation.** Ventilation of anesthetizing locations shall conform to 5-4.1 and 5-6.1.

### 12-4.1.2.2 Germicides.

(a) Medicaments, including those dispersed as aerosols, can be used in anesthetizing locations for germicidal purposes, for affixing plastic surgical drape materials, for preparation of wound dressing, or for other purposes.

(b) Liquid germicides used in anesthetizing locations, whenever the use of cautery or electrosurgery is contemplated, shall be nonflammable.

(c)* Whenever flammable aerosols are employed, sufficient time shall be allowed to elapse between deposition and application of drapes to permit complete evaporation and dissipation of any flammable vehicle remaining.

**A-12-4.1.2.2(c)** Some tinctures and solutions of disinfecting agents can be flammable, and can be used improperly during surgical procedures. Tipping containers, accidental spillage, and the pouring of excessive amounts of such flammable agents on patients expose them to injury in the event of accidental ignition of the flammable solvent.

Users should note that there are differences between subparagraphs (b) and (c) (specifically the form of the germicide). The committee responsible for this requirement has repeated its concern about the use of flammable liquid germicides when cautery or electrosurgery is contemplated. Occasional operating room fires involving these two elements have been reported.

Such documented incidents include "Fire following use of electrocautery during emergency percutaneous transtracheal ventilation." [3] (It is a widely held belief that most incidents are never reported in the literature. They are documented but not reported or written up for publication.)

Incidents involving isopropyl alcohol, acetone, and iodine demonstrate why these liquid flammable germicides are not to be used when procedures involving cautery or electrosurgery will be performed. While these products are claimed to be fast-drying, they are most likely only fast-drying in air. If the product should drip down the side of a patient, it can become trapped. If it is not exposed to air, it may not dry during surgery. Combustion is likely if the electrosurgical device emits a spark near the wet area.

With the ban on the use of fluorocarbons as propellants (liquid Freon® had been a popular skin degreasing agent), manufacturers of aerosol products have had to seek alternative agents, some of which can be highly flammable (e.g., isobutane, propane). Nitrous oxide, an oxidizing agent that is equal to oxygen in supporting combustion, is also employed as a propellant. With the commercial disappearance of the old, quite inexpensive Freons, care must be taken that they are not replaced by flammable degreasing agents in the operating room. All modern liquid anesthetic agents are nonflammable and potent degreasers, but they are also expensive.

**12-4.1.2.3 Smoking and Open Flames.** Smoking and open flames shall be prohibited in all anesthetizing locations.

**12-4.1.2.4 Electrical Safeguards.**

See introductory commentary under chapter heading on the subject of electrical hazards.

(a) Physical safeguards built into the anesthetizing locations or storage areas will not provide protection unless safe practices are followed and good maintenance is provided.

(b) Scheduled inspections and written reports shall be maintained.

(c) Rules to require prompt replacement of defective electrical equipment shall be adopted and rigidly enforced.

(d) Personnel working in anesthetizing locations shall be instructed in these electrical safeguards.

(e) All electrical equipment used in inhalation anesthetizing locations and areas ancillary thereto, or in other areas using conductive floors constructed in accordance with this section, shall be periodically tested for electrical safety. *(See C-12.1.2.1.2.)*

(f) Members of the professional staff shall be required to submit for inspection and approval any special equipment they wish to introduce into anesthetizing locations. Such equipment shall meet the requirements for the protection against electric shock as given in Chapter 7 *(see 7-5.1.1.1).*

From a safety perspective, it is very important that electrical and mechanical appliances be tested before they are used on patients.

(g) Line-powered equipment that introduces current to the patient's body shall have the output circuit isolated from ground to ensure against an unintentional return circuit through the patient.

*Exception: Equipment whose output circuit is grounded or ground-referenced shall be permitted, provided that the design provides equivalent safety to an isolated output.*

This exception was added to the 1978 edition of NFPA 56A (now part of NFPA 99) because new designs of electrosurgical units "ground-referenced" patients, but limited current that could flow through a patient via the designated return electrode to a nonhazardous level.

### 12-4.1.2.5 Electric Connections and Testing.

(a) Administrative authorities shall ascertain that electric maintenance personnel are completely familiar with the function and proper operation of ungrounded electric circuits required by 2-6.3.2 in Annex 2. The significance of the signal lamps and audible alarms installed to indicate accidental grounds shall be explained to all personnel affected. A permanent sign shall be installed close to the position of the signal lamps to indicate their significance. Circuits in the panel boxes shall be clearly labeled, distinguishing between grounded and ungrounded, emergency and normal circuits, so that immediate recognition is possible.

(b) Extension cords shall not be connected to lighting fixtures in anesthetizing locations under any circumstances.

### 12-4.1.2.6 Electrical Systems.

See introductory commentary under chapter heading on the subject of electrical hazards.

(a)* A grounded electrical distribution system shall be permitted to be installed in anesthetizing locations.

**A-12-4.1.2.6(a)** If an anesthetizing location is a wet location, the provisions of 3-3.2.1.2(f) apply.

The appendix information on wet locations was added during the revision process for the 1987 edition of NFPA 99 to draw attention to the fact that the allowance of grounded electrical systems in nonflammable anesthetizing locations raised many other concerns. While a grounded electrical system could be permitted based on the use of nonflammable anesthetics, the degree of wetness needed to be considered because a wet location required an additional level of electrical safety than that required for an ordinary location.

Former NFPA 76B required an additional level of electrical safety in patient care areas designated as wet locations. (See Section 2-2 for a definition of *wet location.*) The level of safety essentially called for ground fault circuit interrupters (GFCIs) or isolated power systems (IPSs), depending on whether power interruption was tolerable. [See 3-3.2.1.2(f).] This requirement did not apply to nonflammable anesthetizing locations as long as IPSs were required in these locations (in accordance with former NFPA 56A). With the change in 1984 that permitted grounded electrical systems in nonflammable anesthetizing locations, these requirements for additional levels of safety in patient care areas became a matter of consideration given that nonflammable anesthetizing locations are patient care areas.

For the 1987 edition of NFPA 99, three subcommittees (Anesthetizing Services, Electrical Equipment, and Electrical Systems) and the then Technical Committee on Health Care Facilities reviewed the situation. Proposals and comments recommending reverting to the previous criteria requiring isolated power systems in all anesthetizing locations (some based on patient/staff electrical safety, others on the power-continuation issue) were considered. The only change that the Technical

Committee on Health Care Facilities could agree on was the addition of a note referring to wet location provisions [now located in A-3-3.2.1.2(f)1].

The Chairman of the Technical Committee on Health Care Facilities appointed an ad hoc subcommittee in 1987 to review the entire situation again and present recommendations to the technical committee. Requests for input from the public were also made. The ad hoc subcommittee met several times and made several recommendations to the technical committee. The major recommendation was a modification to the definition of *wet location*. (See commentary in Section 2-2 under *wet location*.)

For a discussion on the need to maintain power, see commentary under 3-2.4.2. For the types of electrical service allowed in nonflammable anesthetizing locations, refer to Article 517 of NFPA 70, *National Electrical Code*. [4] Three-phase, four-wire panel boards are not prohibited in nonflammable anesthetizing locations.

Because isolated power systems are not required under certain conditions in nonflammable anesthetizing locations, the issue of whether additional grounded circuits can be added in the rooms of facilities that already have isolated power installed arises. NFPA 99 does not prohibit such a practice, but this mixing of isolated and grounded electrical circuits in one room defeats the purpose of having only isolated power in a particular area. Matters were further complicated by a change in 1993 that allowed some ("selected") receptacles in an anesthetizing location to be on the essential electrical system. This matter should be given a thorough review before a decision concerning installation or rewiring is made.

**(b)** High-voltage wiring for X-ray equipment shall be effectively insulated from ground and adequately guarded against accidental contact.

**(c)** Approved permanently installed equipment shall be permitted to be supplied through a grounded single-phase or three-phase distribution system if installed in accordance with 2-6.3.3 of Annex 2.

This paragraph and 7-5.1.1.2 reflect previously made changes in former 12-4.1.3.3 and 12-4.1.3.4 (now 2-6.3.3 and 2-6.3.4 in Annex 2, "Flammable Anesthetizing Locations") that allowed three-phase grounded power in anesthetizing locations for certain permanently installed equipment. These revisions were originally prepared as a Tentative Interim Amendment to NFPA 56A-1978 (TIA 56A-78-2) when the problem of three-phase power was brought before the committee in early 1980. This paragraph does not apply to nonflammable anesthetizing locations with grounded electrical systems, although it does have applicability for those facilities that do install isolated power systems in nonflammable anesthetizing locations.

The former NFPA 56A allowed only X-ray equipment in anesthetizing locations to be supplied by a grounded electrical system. The change extended the allowance to all fixed equipment.

The reasoning behind this change was that fixed equipment would be bolted to structural metal and thus permanently grounded. It would also be grounded through rigid or flexible metallic conduit. In the event of an electrical fault within the equipment, the case of the equipment could not be raised to a potentially hazardous level for personnel who may be grounded.

Consistent with this reasoning, and recognizing the vulnerability of flexible cords, cord-connected attachments and accessories to fixed equipment are required (by former 12-4.1.3.3, now 2-6.3.3 in Annex 2, "Flammable Anesthetizing Locations") to operate at 24 V or less supplied by an isolating transformer or to be supplied by isolated power at line voltage.

Article 517 of NFPA 70, *National Electrical Code* [4], now permits nonmetallic conduit for circuits other than branch circuits serving patient care areas [see Section 517-30(c)(3), Exception No. 3, in NFPA 70]. With this change, 12-4.1.2.6(c) might merit reconsideration inasmuch as it is observed that some equipment (e.g., the electrically powered operating table) can be fixed only to studs set in concrete.

(d) An isolation transformer shall not serve more than one operating room except as provided in 12-4.1.2.6(e). For purposes of this section, anesthetic induction rooms are considered part of the operating room or rooms served by the induction rooms. If an induction room serves more than one operating room, the isolated circuits of the induction room shall be permitted to be supplied from the isolation transformer of any one of the operating rooms served by that induction room.

*Exception: In existing hospitals where one isolation transformer is serving more than one inhalation anesthetizing location, provided the system has been installed in accordance with previous editions of this section (formerly NFPA 56A) where such systems were permitted.*

While one transformer cannot serve more than one operating room in new facilities, there is no restriction on using more than one transformer in one operating room. The purpose of this exception is to reduce cumulative leakage current from tripping line isolation monitor alarms.

The exception is an example of the differentiation between requirements for new and existing anesthetizing locations. The exception reflects the fact that the requirement of 12-4.1.2.6(d) was only a recommendation until 1971. A Formal Interpretation in December 1977 clarified the issue of nonretroactive application. This clarification, however, was incorporated as an exception in the 1978 edition of NFPA 56A, which was then incorporated into NFPA 99.

---

**Formal Interpretation**

Reference: 12-4.1.2.6(d) in NFPA 99

*Background:* Paragraph 12-4.1.2.6(d) states that an isolation transformer in the isolated power system shall not serve more than one room (except for a special system intended to serve such things as portable X-ray units). This mandatory requirement was adopted in May 1971 after having been presented as a nonmandatory recommendation in the 1954 through 1970 editions of the document. An Official Interpretation published in the NFPA *Fire News* in 1958 confirmed that separate transformers for each room were recommended but not required at that time. Since 12-4.1.2.6(d) does not exempt isolated power systems installed prior to May 1971, one could imply that all such systems shall now have one or more separate isolation transformers for each room.

*Question:* Is it the intent of 12-4.1.2.6(d) to require one or more separate isolation transformers for each room of an anesthetizing location regardless of the date of installation?

*Answer:* No, provided the isolated power system and its associated isolation transformers meet the requirements of the edition of the standard in effect at the date of installation.

*Issue Edition:* 1973 of NFPA 56A

*Reference:* 3324

*Date:* December 1977

(e) Isolation transformers shall be permitted to serve single receptacles in several patient areas when the receptacles are reserved for supplying power to equipment requiring 150 V or higher (e.g., items such as portable X-ray units) and when the receptacles and mating plugs are not interchangeable with the receptacles on the local isolated power system.

This provision was included to avoid the necessity of having a 208-V or 240-V transformer in each room (in addition to any other isolation transformers for regularly used 120-V equipment) to supply high-voltage devices used only occasionally. In some installations, a push-button system is used to lock out all the circuits except those in the room where the high-voltage device will be used. This requirement ensures that only one high-voltage device is used at a time.

### 12-4.1.2.7 Gases.

(a) *Storage Locations or Manifold Enclosures for Oxygen and Nitrous Oxide.* The location and ventilation of storage rooms or manifold enclosures for oxygen and nitrous oxide shall comply with Chapters 4 and 5.

(b) *Nonflammable Medical Gas Piping Systems.* Oxygen and nitrous oxide manifolds and piping systems that supply anesthetizing locations shall comply with Chapter 4.

**12-4.1.2.8 Anesthetic Apparatus.** Anesthetic apparatus shall conform to the requirements in 8-5.1.2.1.

**12-4.1.2.9 Electrical Equipment.** See 12-3.7.1.

**12-4.1.2.10 Fire Loss Prevention.**

This section is one part of a multipart response to several fatal operating room fires that occurred in 1990 and to proposals submitted to the NFPA to address issues raised by them. This section addresses electrical appliances that are most likely to be ignition sources in anesthetizing locations. It is intended for operating room staff as well as those responsible for appliances used in operating rooms (e.g., biomedical engineers and technicians and risk managers).

Why are precautions and training necessary when flammable anesthetics are no longer used? A little history might help explain this apparent dichotomy.

Knowledge of the particulars might have been vague, but operating room personnel came to appreciate that the cyclopropane and ether used for anesthesia were highly flammable substances that might even explode if ignited when mixed with oxygen. Despite this awareness of the dangers involved with performing surgery, the electrosurgical unit (ESU) was, in fact, often employed while a flammable anesthetic was being administered to the patient. The ESU was, however, employed with circumspection and utilized only if there was no effective alternative, as in surgery on the brain.

In the 1970s flammable anesthetics were being phased out. Operating room fires that did not involve flammable anesthetics, however, were still being reported. Surgeons were regularly employing the ESU; in fact, knot tying to control "bleeders" had become an overnight antiquity. While the hazard of flammable anesthetics had been eliminated, the hazard of electricity had taken its place.

Then came a second event that would further aggravate the problem. The pulse oximeter (the oxygen-saturation monitor) became a resounding commercial success. By 1985 it had become a designated component of "the standard of care" and keeping the patient's oxygen saturation at 100 percent became commonplace. This new tool would come to be joined by still another influence that would have a multiplying effect. At the same time, performing outpatient surgery under local anesthesia, accompanied by sometimes heavy sedation, became a strong trend. Oxygen was administered by a loose-fitting mask, by nasal cannulae, or through a hose under the tented drapes. An oxygen-enriched atmosphere was being created under the drapes or (for facial or head surgery) even in the operating field. Because eyelashes or facial hair, along with dry gauze sponges, can readily be ignited even by a battery-operated cautery, it should have come as no surprise that flash fires occurred with increasing frequency. The number of these flash fires, however, was tiny relative to the number of operations performed. Just the right set of circumstances had to exist for an adverse event to occur, so the majority of hospital personnel were spared any first-hand appreciation of the fire risk.

The medical literature abounds with candid reports of fires associated with the ESU and, more recently, lasers. However, according to some anesthesiologists no reliable data exist concerning the actual incidence of operating room fires.

(a) *Hazard Assessment.*

1. An evaluation shall be made of hazards that could be encountered during surgical procedures. The evaluation shall include hazards associated with the properties of electric-

ity, hazards associated with the operation of surgical equipment, ard hazards associated with the nature of the environment.

2. Periodic reviews of surgical operations and procedures shall be conducted with special attention given to any change in materials, operations, or personnel.

(b) *Fire Prevention Procedures.* Fire prevention procedures shall be established.

(c) *Emergency Procedures.*

1. Procedures for operating room/surgical suite emergencies shall be developed. Such procedures shall include alarm actuation, evacuation, and equipment shutdown procedures, and provisions for control of emergencies that could occur in the operating room including specific detailed plans for control operations by an emergency control group within the organization or a public fire department.

2. Emergency procedures shall be established for controlling chemical spills.

3. Emergency procedures shall be established for extinguishing drapery, clothing, or equipment fires.

(d) *Orientation and Training.*

1. New operating room/surgical suite personnel, including physicians and surgeons, shall be taught general safety practices for the area and specific safety practices for the equipment and procedures they will use.

2. Continuing safety education and supervision shall be provided, incidents shall be reviewed monthly, and procedures shall be reviewed annually.

3. Fire exit drills shall be conducted periodically.

The former 12-4.1.3 (on flammable anesthetizing locations) was transferred to Annex 2, "Flammable Anesthetizing Locations," because the use of flammable inhalation anesthetics has virtually ceased in the United States. The text has been retained in an annex because NFPA 99 is known to be used in other countries where flammable inhalation anesthetics are still used.

The former 12-4.1.4 (on nonflammable anesthetizing locations) was deleted because the only remaining requirement peculiar to this type of anesthetizing location was that for conductive flooring that might still be in place from the time that flammable anesthetics were used. Testing of these floors was no longer considered necessary because any floor becomes conductive with routine cleaning. In addition, without proper maintenance, conductive floors have been observed over time to only increase in their resistance value.

## 12-4.2* Laboratories.

Laboratories in hospitals shall comply with the requirements of Chapter 10 as applicable and the requirements of NFPA 45, *Standard on Fire Protection for Laboratories Using Chemicals*, as applicable.

**A-12-4.2** NFPA 45, *Standard on Fire Protection for Laboratories Using Chemicals*, establishes basic requirements for all laboratories using chemicals, but important additional requirements are contained in Chapter 10 and in Chapters 4, 5, and 7.

> The reference to NFPA 45, *Standard on Fire Protection for Laboratories Using Chemicals [5],* is included to refer users of NFPA 99 to additional fire safety guidance for laboratories that is not included in this document.

### References Cited in Commentary

1. NFPA *101®, Life Safety Code®,* 1997 edition.
2. NFPA 704, *Standard System for the Identification of the Hazards of Materials for Emergency Response,* 1996 edition.
3. T. A. Bowdle, M. Glenn, H. Colston, and D. Eisele, "Fire following use of electrocautery during emergency percutaneous transtracheal ventilation," *Anesthesiology* 1987, 66: 697–698.
4. NFPA 70, *National Electrical Code®,* 1999 edition.
5. NFPA 45, *Standard on Fire Protection for Laboratories Using Chemicals,* 1996 edition.

# CHAPTER 13

# "Other" Health Care Facilities

In this new 1999 edition, the former Chapter 13, "Ambulatory Health Care Center Requirements," has been deleted in its entirety and replaced with requirements from Chapters 1 through 11 that apply to health care facilities other than hospitals, nursing homes, or limited care facilities. (Readers should review the commentary at the beginning of Chapter 12 to understand how this requirement structure is intended to be used for each type of health care facility discussed in Chapters 12 through 18 and Chapter 20.)

The committee made this change (in the 1999 edition) to Chapter 13 in concert with the deletion in their entirety of former Chapter 14, "Clinic Requirements," and former Chapter 15, "Medical and Dental Office Requirements." The purpose of this major change was to move away from chapters that based the required protection on a "label" or designation given to a building, because such a classification doesn't always provide a true description of what health care is being provided to patients in the structure. The committee was aware that authorities having jurisdiction were having problems in interpretation of the appropriate applications because current definitions of some facilities were not accurate.

The existing chapters for hospitals (Chapter 12), nursing homes (Chapter 16), and limited care facilities (Chapter 17) have been retained in the 1999 edition because the committee felt that these designations were indicative of the health care being provided to the patients. Although Chapter 2 still defines *ambulatory health care facility, clinic,* and *medical/dental office,* the level of health care being provided in such facilities is not well defined. For example, when ambulatory health care facilities were first conceived and operated in the mid-1960s, they were freestanding nonhospital-based buildings where, by today's standards, we would today consider relatively simple procedures were performed on an "outpatient" basis. Today, procedures are still performed on an outpatient basis, but the complexity of the type of procedures performed at ambulatory health care facilities has risen dramatically.

**539**

**Exhibit 13.1** *Increasingly complex procedures are performed in medical and dental offices. (Courtesy of Rob Swift and Prince William Health Systems.)*

Therefore, the committee felt that several chapters could be combined into this new "Other" health care facility chapter where the level of risk to the patient (based on life support) would determine the level (or complexity) of the systems (electrical, gas, vacuum, etc.) required in the facility. (See Exhibit 13.1.)

## 13-1 Scope

This chapter addresses safety requirements for facilities, or portions thereof, that provide diagnostic and treatment services to patients in health care facilities other than hospitals, nursing homes, or limited care facilities as defined in Chapter 2.

## 13-2 General Responsibilities

### 13-2.1 Laboratories.

The governing boards of these facilities shall have the responsibility of protecting the facilities (for patient care and clinical investigation) and the personnel employed therein.

# 13-3 General Requirements

See commentary under Section 12-3 for an explanation of how Section 13-3 is to be used.

**13-3.1** (Reserved)

**13-3.2** (Reserved)

## 13-3.3 Electrical System Requirements.

**13-3.3.1 Electrical Distribution System.** (Reserved)

**13-3.3.2 Essential Electrical Distribution System.** The essential electrical distribution system shall conform to a Type 3 system as described in Chapter 3.

Readers are reminded that the term *type* is used only as a designator. The term is, in actuality, defined by the criteria provided for each of the various types listed in Chapter 3 (e.g., for Type 1 essential electrical system requirements, see Section 3-4).

See commentary under 16-3.3.2 regarding the term *electrical life support equipment*.

**13-3.3.2.1** If electrical life support equipment is required, the essential electrical distribution system shall conform to a Type 1 system as described in Chapter 3.

**13-3.3.2.2** If critical care areas are present, the essential electrical distribution system shall conform to a Type 1 system as described in Chapter 3.

## 13-3.4 Gas and Vacuum System Requirements.

This section has been completely revised for the 1999 edition to reflect the committee's effort to have the level of risk to the patient (based upon life support) determine the level (or complexity) of the systems (electrical, gas, vacuum, etc.) required in the facility.

Readers are reminded that the term *Level* is used only as a designator. The term is, in actuality, defined by the criteria provided for each of the various Levels listed in Chapter 4 (e.g., for Level 1 gas and vacuum system requirements, see Section 4-3).

**13-3.4.1** If installed where patients are provided mechanical ventilation or assisted mechanical ventilation, patient gas systems shall conform to Level 1 piped gas systems of Chapter 4.

A single alarm panel, as described in 4-3.1.2.2(b)2, shall be mounted in an area of continuous surveillance while the facility is in operation.

**13-3.4.2** If installed where patients, due to medical, surgical, or diagnostic intervention, are dependent on the piped gas system, the patient gas system shall conform to Level 2 piped gas systems of Chapter 4.

**13-3.4.3** If installed where the patient population is not on critical life support equipment, the patient gas system shall conform to Level 3 piped gas systems of Chapter 4.

**13-3.4.4** If installed where patients are provided mechanical ventilation or assisted mechanical ventilation, patient vacuum systems shall conform to Level 1 piped vacuum systems of Chapter 4.

**13-3.4.5** If installed where patients, due to medical, surgical, or diagnostic intervention, are dependent on the piped vacuum system, the patient vacuum system shall conform to Level 2 piped vacuum systems of Chapter 4.

**13-3.4.6** If installed where the patient population is not on critical life support equipment, the patient vacuum system shall conform to Level 3 piped vacuum systems of Chapter 4.

**13-3.4.7** If installed, patient WAGD systems shall conform to Level 1 WAGD systems in Chapter 4.

**13-3.4.8** If installed, laboratory gas systems shall conform to Level 4 gas systems of Chapter 4.

**13-3.4.9** If installed, laboratory vacuum systems shall conform to Level 4 vacuum systems in Chapter 4.

## 13-3.5 Environmental Systems.

(Reserved)

## 13-3.6 Material Requirements.

(Reserved)

## 13-3.7 Electrical Equipment Requirements.

**13-3.7.1 Patient Care Areas.** If critical care areas are present, electrical appliances shall conform to Chapter 7.

**13-3.7.2 Laboratories.** Equipment shall conform to 7-5.2.2 and Section 7-6.

## 13-3.8 Gas Equipment Requirements—Patient.

Gas equipment shall conform to the patient equipment requirements in Chapter 8.

**13-3.9** (Reserved)

**13-3.10** (Reserved)

**13-3.11** Facilities covered by this chapter shall comply with the provisions of Chapter 11 for emergency preparedness planning, as appropriate.

# CHAPTER 14

# (Reserved)

In this new 1999 edition, the former Chapter 14, "Clinic Requirements," has been deleted in its entirety and reserved for future use. Readers should review the commentary at the beginning of Chapter 13 to understand the reorganization of requirements and the reservation of Chapter 14 for future use.

# CHAPTER 15

# (Reserved)

In this new 1999 edition, the former Chapter 15, "Medical and Dental Office Requirements," has been deleted in its entirety and reserved for future use. Readers should review the commentary at the beginning of Chapter 13 to understand the reorganization of requirements and the reservation of Chapter 15 for future use.

**CHAPTER 16**

# Nursing Home Requirements

This chapter lists requirements from Chapters 1 through 11 that apply to nursing homes. (Readers should review the commentary at the beginning of Chapter 12 to understand how this structuring of requirements is intended to be used for each type of health care facility discussed in Chapters 12 through 18 and Chapter 20.) The term *nursing home* is defined in Chapter 2.

Fire safety in nursing homes has improved dramatically over the past 30 years. Fire incident data from NFPA indicate that fire fatalities from multiple-death fires in nursing homes from 1966 to 1975 averaged 15.8 deaths per year. With the proper application of modern codes and standards, the nursing home fire safety record is a true success story. Fire fatalities from multiple-death fires in nursing homes from 1979 to 1998 dropped to an average of 1.3 deaths per year. [1] This is an impressive fire safety record for any sleeping-type occupancy. Exhibit 16.1 is one example of a "successful fire" resulting from an explosion in a nursing home. [2]

## 16-1 Scope

This chapter addresses safety requirements of nursing homes.

## 16-2 General Responsibilities

### 16-2.1 Laboratories.

The governing boards of nursing homes shall have the responsibility of protecting the facilities (for patient care and clinical investigation) and the personnel employed therein.

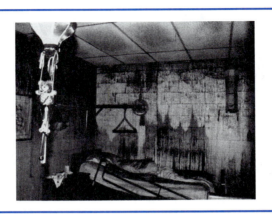

**Exhibit 16.1** *A Massachusetts 101-bed nursing home, where twenty-one sprinklers controlled a post-explosion fire in 1992. The facility was completely evacuated, and injuries to civilians and fire fighters were minor.*

## 16-3 General Requirements

See commentary under Section 12-3 for an explanation of how Section 16-3 is to be used.

**16-3.1** (Reserved)

**16-3.2** (Reserved)

### 16-3.3 Electrical System Requirements.

**16-3.3.1 Electrical Distribution System.** (Reserved)

**16-3.3.2** Essential electrical distribution systems shall conform to the Type 2 systems as described in Chapter 3.

*Exception: Any freestanding nursing home that:*

*(a) Maintains admitting and discharge policies that preclude the provision of care for any patient or resident who needs to be sustained by electrical life support equipment, and*

The term *electrical life support equipment* was adopted in 1984 to more accurately reflect the type of equipment that would require a generator set supplying ac power. Only if a device supports life and requires ac electricity to function is an essential electrical system required. (See definition of *electrical life support equipment* in Chapter 2.)

*(b) Offers no surgical treatment requiring general anesthesia, and*

*(c) Provides an automatic battery-powered system or equipment that will be effective for at least 1½ hours and is otherwise in accordance with NFPA 101, Life Safety Code, and NFPA 70, National Electrical Code, and that will be capable of supplying lighting of at least 1 ft-candle to exit lights, exit corridors, stairways, nursing stations, medication preparation areas, boiler rooms, and communication areas. This system must also supply power to operate all alarm systems.*

The length of time and light level are in agreement with Chapter 5 of NFPA *101, Life Safety Code.* [3]

While reference is made to battery-powered systems for supplying emergency power in subparagraph (c) of the exception, any suitable method of supplying electric power would be acceptable, provided the criterion of 1½ hours of electric power is met. It was not the intent of the former Technical Committee on Essential Electrical Systems that a battery-powered system had to be provided or was the only means by which emergency power could be provided. The exception simply allows a battery-powered system to be used under certain conditions. A regular emergency generator set system is acceptable. (The Subcommittee on Electrical Systems reaffirmed this by issuing a Formal Interpretation in May 1988, as well as by making several changes to this subparagraph during the revision for the 1990 edition of NFPA 99.) It should be noted that if a generator set is used, it must meet the applicable requirements for generator sets as listed in Chapter 3.

---

**Formal Interpretation 87-1**

Reference: 16-3.3.2, 17-3.3.2 in NFPA 99

*Question:* Is it the intent of 16-3.3.2 and 17-3.3.2 to allow the use of a generator set for supplying electric power for required lighting and alarms?

*Answer:* Yes.

*Comment:* The generator set must meet the applicable requirements for generator sets in Chapter 3.

*Issue Edition:* 1987

*Reference:* 16-3.3.2, 17-3.3.2

*Date:* May 1988

---

**16-3.3.2.1** Nursing homes that meet the requirement in the Exception to 16-3.3.2 shall be permitted to use a battery system or self-contained battery integral with equipment in lieu of the alternate power source required in 3-4.1.1.3.

## 16-3.4  Gas and Vacuum System Requirements.

This section has been completely revised for the 1999 edition to reflect the committee's effort to have the level of risk to the patient (based on life support) determine the level (or complexity) of the systems (electrical, gas, vacuum, etc.) required in the facility.

**16-3.4.1** If installed where patients are provided mechanical ventilation or assisted mechanical ventilation, patient gas systems shall conform to Level 1 piped gas systems of Chapter 4. A single alarm panel, as described in 4-3.1.2.2(b)1, shall be mounted in an area of continuous surveillance while the facility is in operation.

**16-3.4.2** If installed where patients, due to medical, surgical, or diagnostic intervention, are dependent on the piped gas system, the patient gas system shall conform to Level 2 piped gas systems of Chapter 4.

**16-3.4.3** If installed where the patient population is not on critical life support equipment, the patient gas system shall conform to Level 3 piped gas systems of Chapter 4.

**16-3.4.4** If installed where patients are provided mechanical ventilation or assisted mechanical ventilation, patient vacuum systems shall conform to Level 1 piped vacuum systems of Chapter 4.

**16-3.4.5** If installed where patients, due to medical, surgical, or diagnostic intervention, are dependent on the piped vacuum system, the patient vacuum system shall conform to Level 2 piped vacuum systems of Chapter 4.

**16-3.4.6** If installed where the patient population is not on critical life support equipment, the patient vacuum system shall conform to Level 3 piped vacuum systems of Chapter 4.

**16-3.4.7** If installed, patient WAGD systems shall conform to Level 1 WAGD systems in Chapter 4.

**16-3.4.8  Laboratory Gas Systems.** (Reserved)

**16-3.4.9  Laboratory Vacuum Systems.** (Reserved)

## 16-3.5  Environmental Systems.

(Reserved)

## 16-3.6  Material Requirements.

(Reserved)

### 16-3.7 Electrical Equipment Requirements.

**16-3.7.1 Patient Care Areas.** (Reserved)

**16-3.7.2 Laboratories.** Equipment shall conform to 7-5.2.2 and Section 7-6.

### 16-3.8 Gas Equipment Requirements.

**16-3.8.1 Patient.** Equipment shall conform to requirements for patient equipment in Chapter 8.

**16-3.9** (Reserved)

**16-3.10** (Reserved)

**16-3.11** Nursing homes shall comply with the provisions of Chapter 11 for emergency preparedness planning, as appropriate.

## 16-4* Specific Area Requirements

See commentary under Section 12-4 for an explanation of how Section 16-4 is to be used.

**A-16-4** This is in addition to other nursing home requirements listed in Section 16-3.

### 16-4.1 Laboratories.

Laboratories in nursing homes shall comply with the requirements of Chapter 10, as applicable.

### References Cited in Commentary

1. Analysis of NFPA fire incident data by Gage-Babcock & Associates, Inc., Fairfax, Virginia, 1998.
2. NFPA Fire Investigation Report, *Nursing Home Fire, Woburn, MA*, October 30, 1992.
3. NFPA *101®*, *Life Safety Code®*, 1997.

# Limited Care Facility Requirements

Chapter 17 lists requirements from Chapters 1 through 11 that apply to limited care facilities. (Readers should review the commentary at the beginning of Chapter 12 to understand how this structuring of requirements is intended to be used for each type of health care facility discussed in Chapters 12 through 18 and Chapter 20.) The term *limited care facility* is defined in Chapter 2.

*Limited care facility* was first defined by the Technical Committee on Safety to Life in the 1988 edition of NFPA *101, Life Safety Code.* [1] It replaced the terms *custodial care facility* and *supervisory care facility* for life safety purposes. The Technical Committee on Health Care Facilities reviewed NFPA 99 and voted to follow suit for operational safety purposes and correlate with the Safety to Life Committee.

## 17-1 Scope

This chapter covers safety requirements of limited care facilities.

## 17-2 General Responsibilities

### 17-2.1 Laboratories

The governing boards of limited care facilities shall have the responsibility of protecting the facilities (for patient care and clinical investigation) and the personnel employed therein.

## 17-3  General Requirements

See commentary under Section 12-3 for an explanation of how Section 17-3 is to be used.

**17-3.1**  (Reserved)

**17-3.2**  (Reserved)

### 17-3.3  Electrical System Requirements.

**17-3.3.1  Electrical Distribution System.**  (Reserved)

**17-3.3.2**  Essential electrical distribution systems shall conform to the Type 2 systems as described in Chapter 3.

*Exception: Any freestanding limited care facility that:*

*(a) Maintains admitting and discharge policies that preclude the provision of care for any patient or resident who needs to be sustained by electrical life support equipment, and*

See commentary under 16-3.3.2 Exception (a) regarding the term *electrical life support equipment.*

*(b) Offers no surgical treatment requiring general anesthesia, and*

See commentary under 16-3.3.2 Exception (c) regarding time requirements, light level, and the use of a regular generator set instead of a battery-powered system. (See also Formal Interpretation 87-1 after 16-3.3.2.)

*(c) Provides an automatic battery-powered system or equipment that will be effective for at least 1½ hours and is otherwise in accordance with NFPA 101, Life Safety Code, and NFPA 70, National Electrical Code, and that will be capable of supplying lighting of at least 1 ft-candle to exit lights, exit corridors, stairways, nursing stations, medication preparation areas, boiler rooms, and communication areas. This system must also supply power to operate all alarm systems.*

**17-3.3.2.1**  Limited care facilities that meet the requirements in the Exception to 17-3.3.2 shall be permitted to use a battery system or self-contained battery integral with equipment in lieu of the alternate power source required in 3-4.1.1.3.

### 17-3.4  Gas and Vacuum System Requirements.

This section has been completely revised for the 1999 edition to reflect the committee's effort to have the level of risk to the patient (based on life support) determine the level (or complexity) of the systems (electrical, gas, vacuum, etc.) required in the facility.

**17-3.4.1** If installed where patients are provided mechanical ventilation or assisted mechanical ventilation, patient gas systems shall conform to Level 1 piped gas systems of Chapter 4.

**17-3.4.2** If installed where patients, due to medical, surgical, or diagnostic intervention, are dependent on the piped gas system, the patient gas system shall conform to Level 2 piped gas systems of Chapter 4.

**17-3.4.3** If installed where the patient population is not on critical life support equipment, the patient gas system shall conform to Level 3 piped gas systems of Chapter 4.

**17-3.4.4** If installed where patients are provided mechanical ventilation or assisted mechanical ventilation, patient vacuum systems shall conform to Level 1 piped vacuum systems of Chapter 4.

**17-3.4.5** If installed where patients, due to medical, surgical, or diagnostic intervention, are dependent on the piped vacuum system, the patient vacuum system shall conform to Level 2 piped vacuum systems of Chapter 4.

**17-3.4.6** If installed where the patient population is not on critical life support equipment, the patient vacuum system shall conform to Level 3 piped vacuum systems of Chapter 4.

**17-3.4.7** If installed, patient WAGD systems shall conform to Level 1 WAGD systems in Chapter 4.

## 17-3.5 Environmental Systems.

(Reserved)

## 17-3.6 Material Requirements.

(Reserved)

## 17-3.7 Electrical Equipment Requirements.

**17-3.7.1 Patient Care Areas.** (Reserved)

**17-3.7.2 Laboratories.** Equipment shall conform to 7-5.2.2 and Section 7-6.

## 17-3.8 Gas Equipment Requirements.

(Reserved)

## 17-3.9 (Reserved)

## 17-3.10 (Reserved)

**17-3.11** Limited care facilities shall comply with the provisions of Chapter 11 for emergency preparedness planning, as appropriate.

# 17-4* Specific Area Requirements

See commentary under Section 12-4 for an explanation of how Section 17-4 is to be used.

**A-17-4** This is in addition to other limited care facility requirements listed in Section 17-3.

## 17-4.1 Laboratories.

Laboratories in limited care facilities shall comply with the requirements of Chapter 10, as applicable.

Laboratories in limited care facilities shall comply with the requirements of Chapter 10, as applicable.

### Reference Cited in Commentary

1. NFPA *101®*, *Life Safety Code®*, 1997 edition.

# CHAPTER 18

# Electrical and Gas Equipment for Home Care

This chapter, first introduced in the 1996 edition, provides another facet of safety in the use of medical appliances. It is not intended to imply that a home is a health care facility, but rather that the use of medical appliances in the home can pose the same hazards as in health care facilities and, therefore, appropriate safety requirements should apply.

The growing use of medical appliances in the home is being driven by two major forces. First, advances in technology have made many complex appliances easier to operate by nonmedical personnel. Second, the escalating cost of health care delivery has forced patients to leave hospitals while they still might need treatment requiring medical appliances. There is every indication that this trend toward home health care will continue to grow, and safety standards need to address this issue.

This chapter opens what will probably be a long debate on how best to establish requirements for the use of medical appliances in home health care that achieve safety levels equivalent to those in health care facilities. There were no changes to this chapter from the 1996 to the 1999 edition of the code.

## 18-1* Scope

This chapter addresses the requirements for the safe use of electrical and gas equipment used for medical treatment outside health care facilities.

**A-18-1** As part of the current decentralization of health care modalities, traditionally the province of hospitals, patients are being treated at home using electrical and gas appliances that, if used in a health care facility, would come under the purview of this standard.

## 18-2 (Reserved)

## 18-3 Equipment

**18-3.1** (Reserved)

**18-3.2** (Reserved)

**18-3.3** (Reserved)

**18-3.4** (Reserved)

**18-3.5** (Reserved)

**18-3.6** (Reserved)

### 18-3.7 Electrical Equipment.

Electrical equipment used in the home for health care shall conform to such requirements of Chapter 7 as applicable.

> A home is a significantly different environment from that of a hospital or other health care facility, and the demands on electrical equipment will vary. The electrical power system in a home can vary more than in a health care facility, placing more demand on equipment, or the amount of time the equipment is actually in use can be less than in a health care facility, creating less of a demand on equipment. Equipment should be designed and used to achieve an appropriate safety level.

### 18-3.8 Gas Equipment.

Gas equipment used in the home for health care shall conform to such requirements of Chapter 8 as applicable.

> See commentary under 18-3.7.

## 18-4 Administration

### 18-4.1 Responsibility.

It shall be the responsibility of the equipment supplier, which could be a hospital, an equipment rental company, or an equipment sales company, to:

(a) Appropriately instruct the equipment user to operate the equipment safely. This shall include written instructions, demonstrations, and periodic review of the use.

(b) Provide instruction on user maintenance of the equipment, provide supervision of the maintenance, and provide such higher level maintenance as is appropriate.

Because home care equipment will most likely be used by nonprofessional, relatively unskilled persons, safety is a shared responsibility. The term *supplier* can be a single entity (e.g., a hospital) or it can be a chain of entities (e.g., a doctor, a hospital, an equipment rental company, a service company). There should be a clear understanding of how these various parties share the legal and moral burdens of responsibility.

# CHAPTER 19

# Hyperbaric Facilities

For additional information on specific regulatory issues related to the safe operation of clinical hyperbaric medicine facilities, see Supplement 4, "Regulatory Issues Affecting the Safety of Clinical Hyperbaric Medicine Facilities."

## 19-1* Introduction and Scope

**A-19-1** During the past 20 years there has been a widespread interest in the use of oxygen at elevated environmental pressure to increase the partial pressure of oxygen in a patient's tissues in order to treat certain medical conditions or to prepare a patient for surgery. These techniques are also employed widely for the treatment of decompression sickness (e.g., bends, caisson worker's disease) and carbon monoxide poisoning.

Recently, however, the level of knowledge and expertise has increased so dramatically that the codes are in need of updating. By the end of 1988, there were 218 hyperbaric facilities in operation in the U.S. and Canada. These facilities supported hyperbaric medical treatments for 62,548 patients between 1971 and 1987. As these facilities provide therapy for disorders indicated for treatment, these numbers will continue to increase. As the number of facilities increases, the number of patients treated will also increase.

The use of hyperbaric oxygen continues to expand. As of this writing, more than 350 known facilities were practicing clinical hyperbaric medicine in the United States. Unsubstantiated reports indicate there may be over 500 such facilities. As the role of hyperbaric oxygen in wound healing continues to be validated, this number will grow. Industry representatives report annual growth rates on the order of 30 percent. Due to this rapid expansion, an accurate estimate of the total number of patients treated is not available at this time.

Such treatment involves placement of the patient, with or without attendants, in a hyperbaric chamber or pressure vessel, the pressure of which is raised above ambient pressure. In the course of the treatment, the patient breathes up to 100 percent oxygen.

The use of hyperbaric chambers to treat patients requires chamber operators, hyperbaric medical staff, and medical treatment facility personnel to understand the requirements necessary to maintain a safe environment both within the hyperbaric chamber and in the surrounding area. In most military or industrial applications, all personnel involved are normally healthy and capable of independent movement. However, in clinical hyperbaric treatment situations, this is usually not the case. Many patients in clinical situations will not be ambulatory and will require assistance during an emergency. In addition, most will not be familiar with related support equipment such as oxygen delivery systems and will require special care to ensure adherence to required safety procedures. Many of the requirements identified in this standard have been included to recognize this fact. Because of the unique situation this presents to first responders, emergency personnel are encouraged to work closely with local clinical hyperbaric facilities to develop realistic emergency training situations to serve as valuable learning tools should a real emergency develop.

In addition to being used for patient care, these chambers also are being employed for research purposes using experimental animals and, in some instances, humans.

The partial pressure of oxygen present in a gaseous mixture is the determinate factor of the amount of available oxygen. This pressure will rise if the volume percentage of oxygen present increases, or if the total pressure of a given gas mixture containing oxygen increases, or if both factors increase. Since the sole purpose of the hyperbaric technique of treatment is to raise the total pressure within the treatment chamber, an increased partial pressure of oxygen always is available during treatment unless positive means are taken to limit the oxygen content. In addition, the patient is often given an oxygen-enriched atmosphere to breathe.

During the past decade, the debate concerning the possible increase in the flammability of materials in regular air mixtures at higher pressures has intensified. Early studies of the flammability and ease of ignition of combustible materials in compressed air atmospheres suggested that there was a significant increase in both ease of ignition and flame spread. This belief culminated in the initial definition of *oxygen-enriched atmosphere* (in the first edition of NFPA 56D) as an atmosphere where the amount of oxygen exceeded 21 percent, the total pressure exceeded one atmosphere absolute, or both.

Subsequent studies suggested that regular air mixtures at higher pressures are not particularly hazardous and that only increased concentrations of oxygen lead to greater hazards. In Figure A-2-2(a) (see Chapter 2), the graph of the burning rate for filter paper versus pressure seems to indicate that this is not true; that is, as pressure increases, holding oxygen percent constant (21 percent line), the burning rate increases from about 0.85 cm/sec to about 2.9 cm/sec at 10.1 atmospheres. On this basis, either increased partial pressure of oxygen or increased percent oxygen will cause an increased risk and require special care.

There is continual need for human diligence in the establishment, operation, and maintenance of hyperbaric facilities. It is the responsibility of the chief administrator of the facility possessing the hyperbaric chamber to adopt and enforce appropriate regulations for hyperbaric facilities. In formulating and administering the program, full use should be made of technical personnel highly qualified in hyperbaric chamber operations and safety.

It is essential that personnel having responsibility for the hyperbaric facility establish and enforce appropriate programs to fulfill the provisions of this chapter.

Potential hazards can be controlled only when continually recognized and understood by all pertinent personnel.

With the growth of clinical hyperbaric medicine and the use of hyperbaric chambers has come a growing realization of the need for standardization of training and adherence to accepted safety practices. Until recently, there was no organized effort to ensure that hyperbaric chamber operators maintained minimum skill levels in hyperbaric chamber operations and demonstrated a basic understanding of the hazards involved.

In response to this need, the National Board of Diving and Hyperbaric Medicine Technology (NBDHMT) was created to provide a certification system for this basic level of understanding. Since its establishment in 1989, as of January 1999, 1207 hyperbaric technicians, nurses, and physicians have become board certified by examination. This represents a 48 percent increase from the number reported in the 1996 edition. Many of the more progressive clinical hyperbaric medicine programs in the country today require that all staff personnel be certified. As more program directors require their personnel to be certified, awareness of the risks associated with hyperbaric medicine will increase. Awareness, in turn, should help reduce the number of operator errors, which were the cause of the majority of hyperbaric chamber incidents over the past two decades, as cited by Sheffield and Desautels [1]. As an example, in 1996 a fatal Class B hyperbaric chamber accident resulted from a patient's having a chemically fueled pocket warmer on his person. When the oxygen penetrated the synthetic blanket he had taken into the chamber and then penetrated his clothing, the warmer ignited the chamber atmosphere, causing the chamber to explode and killing two people and injuring two others. This tragic accident might have been prevented if the chamber operator had conducted a safety search of the patient prior to chamber entry.

## 19-1.1 Purpose.

**19-1.1\*** The purpose of this chapter is to set forth minimum safeguards for the protection of patients or other subjects of, and personnel administering, hyperbaric therapy and experimental procedures. Its purpose is also to offer some guidance for rescue personnel who are not ordinarily involved in hyperbaric chamber operation, but who could become so involved in an emergency.

**A-19-1.1.1** Much is known about the safe application of hyperbaric medicine for the protection of hardware, personnel, and facilities. Nonetheless, as new medical instrumentation and engineering techniques are developed, new safety issues will continue to arise. Consequently, the Subcommittee on Hyperbaric and Hypobaric Facilities believes that this publication is needed for general guidance in areas of technological change and uncertainty as well as for firm requirements in areas where the technology is well understood and stable. Comments based on continuing experience are solicited so that this chapter can be revised from time to time.

> This is an open invitation to users and manufacturers to come before the committee with new information that can be incorporated into Chapter 19. This process worked extremely well for recent editions of the document, in that extensive new material has been added, out-of-date material removed, and many parts of the text changed. Technical committee members routinely encourage industry involvement in the dynamic process of standard development.

**19-1.1.2** Requirements cited in this section are minimum ones. Discretion on the part of chamber operators and others might dictate the establishment of more stringent regulations.

## 19-1.2 Scope.

**19-1.2.1\*** This chapter applies to hyperbaric chambers and associated facilities that are used, or intended to be used, for medical applications and experimental procedures at pressures from 0 psig to 100 psig (14.7 psia to 114.7 psia) (0 to 690 kPa gauge).

**A-19-1.2.1** This chapter does not apply to respiratory therapy employing oxygen-enriched atmospheres at ambient pressures. *(See Chapter 8, Gas Equipment.)*

> The critical concern here is the use of an enclosed space where the occupants must rely on the outside staff for life safety.
>
> Even if hyperbaric training chambers are used only occasionally for medical purposes, the requirements set forth in this chapter would be applicable because (1) fire protection and building construction requirements are intended to protect building occupants and the building itself; and (2) mistakes are more likely to occur in nonmedical (e.g., training) chambers when emergency circumstances mandate their immediate use for medical-related purposes.

**19-1.2.1.1** This chapter covers the recognition of and protection against hazards of an electrical, explosive, or implosive nature, as well as fire hazards.

> The very nature of hyperbaric operations lends itself to all of the preceding hazards, any of which could produce a fire. Although the electrical portion of the standard has

been relaxed during the past several revisions, hyperbaric operators must maintain stringent electrical safeguards. The risk of explosion of a device can be minimized by providing a nitrogen purge to the component that reduces the amount of available oxygen to support spark generation. Implosion can be minimized by providing ventilation ports for closed air spaces.

**19-1.2.1.2** Medical complications of hyperbaric procedures are discussed primarily to acquaint rescue personnel with these problems.

Medical complications of hyperbaric operations are generally rare. However, when complications are present, they usually involve a patient's inability to equalize pressure in closed air cavities, such as the middle ears or sinuses, on descent (pressurization). This inability to equalize pressure produces ear or sinus pain. Even more uncommon is the reaction termed *oxygen toxicity* caused by elevated partial pressures of oxygen. This condition is possible when 100 percent oxygen is breathed at depths greater than 60 ft (18.2 m) of seawater (FSW). It is also possible for some susceptible patients to experience this reaction at depths shallower than 60 FSW. Oxygen toxicity resembles a grand mal seizure and is effectively treated by reducing the partial pressure of inspired oxygen. These reactions, as well as detailed discussions on the physiological and medical aspects of hyperbaric oxygen therapy, are well documented in scientific literature. All operators are encouraged to develop an in-depth understanding of these areas. References can be obtained from organizations such as the Undersea and Hyperbaric Medical Society [2] and the American College of Hyperbaric Medicine [3]. (For more information, see references at the end of Chapter 19.)

**19-1.2.2\*** This chapter applies to both single- and multiple-patient-occupancy hyperbaric chambers, to animal chambers the size of which precludes human occupancy, and to those in which the chamber atmosphere contains an oxygen partial pressure greater than 0.21 atmosphere absolute (3.09 psia).

**A-19-1.2.2** Hazards differ significantly depending on the occupancy and chamber atmosphere. For this reason, chambers are classified *(see 19-1.4)* for the purpose of defining the hazards and setting forth the safeguards within the chapter.

## 19-1.3 Application of This Chapter.

Only the altered, renovated, or modernized portion of an existing system or individual component shall be required to meet the requirements of this chapter. It shall not require the alteration or replacement of existing construction or equipment. Existing construction or equipment shall be permitted to be continued in use when such use does not constitute a distinct hazard to life.

The new wording in this section of the 1999 edition was added to clarify the extent to which Chapter 19 applies to existing equipment and to bring it into closer conformance with the wording of Section 1-2, Application, regarding new construction.

## 19-1.4 Classification of Chambers.

**19-1.4.1 General.** Chambers shall be classified according to occupancy in order to establish appropriate minimum essentials in construction and operation.

**19-1.4.2\* Occupancy.**

(a) Class A—Human, multiple occupancy
(b) Class B—Human, single occupancy
(c) Class C—Animal, no human occupancy

**A-19-1.4.2** Chambers designed for animal experimentation but equipped for access of personnel to care for the animals are classified as Class A for the purpose of this chapter.

The concern is for the safety of any individual who may be required to enter the chamber (i.e., the enclosed space).

At the time this chapter was first developed as a standard (see Supplement 4, "Regulatory Issues Affecting the Safety of Clinical Hyperbaric Medicine Facilities"), the definitions of "Class A" versus "Class B" chambers were simple and clear-cut. Class A chambers were usually large multiplace (multi-occupancy) compressed air chambers, had the capability to lock people in and out under pressure, required extensive support and control systems, and were supported by a fairly large operating staff. By contrast, Class B chambers were typically small, single-place (single-occupancy) cylinders, frequently made mostly of clear acrylic for maximum visibility, pressurized with 100 percent oxygen, and movable. Because of their size and operational simplicity, the medical staff required to operate these chamber systems was (and generally remains) small. See Exhibits 19.1 and 19.2.

However, more recently, Class B chamber designs have begun to evolve and are becoming more sophisticated. Small chambers are now available with auxiliary personnel compartments to allow for a patient to be attended if necessary. Other manufacturers are now producing Class B chambers with large diameter acrylic tubes to improve the patient treatment environment and reduce patient apprehension that is sometimes associated with hyperbaric chamber treatment. Other manufacturers are producing Class B chambers that use compressed air instead of oxygen as the pressurization gas. In these chambers, the patient is given oxygen by an oronasal mask or oxygen head tent. As the growth of hyperbaric medicine continues, and new uses for hyperbaric oxygen are validated, there will no doubt be innovative engineering efforts to respond to this situation. It is clear that the features traditionally used for classifying hyperbaric chambers are becoming less distinct. The technical committee continues to evaluate the need for adopting new classification criteria. See Exhibits 19.3 and 19.4.

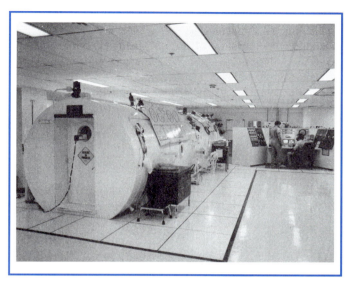

***Exhibit 19.1*** *Typical Class A hyperbaric chamber. (Courtesy of Jefferson C. Davis Wound Care and Hyperbaric Medicine Center, Methodist Hospital, San Antonio, TX)*

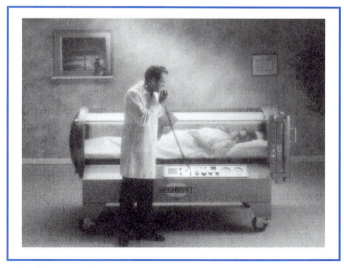

***Exhibit 19.2*** *Typical Class B hyperbaric chamber. (Courtesy of Sechrist Industries, Inc., Anaheim, CA)*

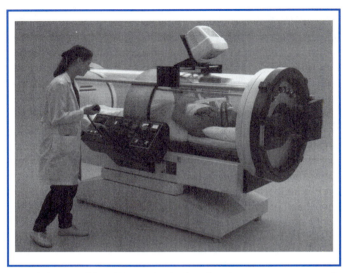

*Exhibit 19.3*   *Class B hyperbaric chamber that uses compressed air as pressurization gas. Oxygen is delivered to the patient via an oronasal mask or oxygen head tent. (Courtesy of Nth Systems, Inc., San Antonio, TX)*

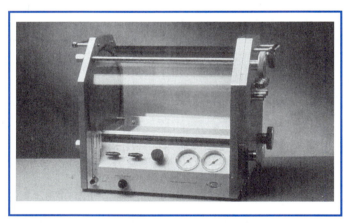

*Exhibit 19.4*   *Typical Class C hyperbaric chamber. (Courtesy of Sechrist Industries, Inc., Anaheim, CA)*

## 19-1.5 Nature of Hazards.

**19-1.5.1** This chapter for the use of hyperbaric facilities is intended to provide protection against fire, explosion, and other hazards without unduly limiting the activities of professional personnel involved in patient (in the case of hospitals) or other care. This principle, without minimizing the hazards, recognizes that professional personnel shall be guided by all of the hazards to life that are inherent in and around hyperbaric treatment procedures.

**19-1.5.2\*** Potential hazards involved in the design, construction, operation, and maintenance of hyperbaric facilities are formidable. For a discussion of these hazards, see the information in C-19.

**A-19-1.5.2** The navies of the world have established an enviable safety record in their use of hyperbaric facilities for deep-sea-diving research, training, and operations. A knowledge of this safety record should not lull hyperbaric personnel into a false sense of security, however. The potential hazards remain. Where civilian personnel — patients, experimental subjects, and chamber attendants — are involved, an appreciation of these hazards and their mitigation becomes even more important.

> Other military organizations have also maintained equally impressive hyperbaric chamber safety records. The United States Air Force is an excellent example. A primary reason for this success is a very aggressive initial and recurring training requirement. Operators are routinely exposed to hyperbaric chamber operations and practice a variety of emergency response procedures.
>
> Civilian medical facilities are urged to follow the military's lead by developing their own comprehensive training program and devoting the time necessary to conduct training. This is particularly important since medical facilities can house nonambulatory patients who may be completely unfamiliar with the chambers and their operational features. Training should include not only hazard recognition and prevention but emergency responses to accidents as well. Additionally, all medical treatment facilities are encouraged to develop a safety awareness program for all prospective patients. They too must understand the hyperbaric environment and its potential hazards.

## 19-2 Construction and Equipment

### 19-2.1 Housing for Hyperbaric Facilities.

**19-2.1.1** For Class A chambers located inside a building, the chamber(s) and all ancillary service equipment shall be protected by 2-hour fire-resistive-rated construction.

*Exception No. 1:\* Free-standing, dedicated buildings containing only a Class A chamber(s) and ancillary service equipment.*

**A-19-2.1.1, Exception No. 1.** For guidance on minimum construction requirements, depending on occupancy classification, see NFPA *101, Life Safety Code.*

*Exception No. 2: Chambers not contiguous to a health care facility, and either located in a mobile, vehicle-mounted facility or not permanently affixed to a foundation.*

This section was revised in 1996 to clarify the requirement for a 2-hour firewall for those facilities that were either freestanding or movable. Committee members believe that hyperbaric facilities that are not contiguous with another building do not pose an increased fire risk to that building and its occupants. Exception Nos. 1 and 2 were included to reflect this philosophy. More recently, questions have been asked that indicate confusion still exists with this particular exception — in particular, the issue of a chamber not being permanently affixed to a foundation, and whether Class B chambers, many of which are designed with casters for ease of relocation, fall under the exception. The current Exception No. 2 to 19-2.1.1 refers only to Class A chambers, not to Class B chambers. To reduce the ambiguity, the technical committee will consider this exception in greater detail for the 2002 edition of the standard.

**19-2.1.1.1\*** If there are connecting doors through such common walls of contiguity, they shall be at least B-label, 1½-hour fire doors.

**A-19-2.1.1.1** Characteristics of building construction housing hyperbaric chambers and ancillary facilities are no less important to safety from fire hazards than are the characteristics of the hyperbaric chambers themselves. It is conceivable that a fire emergency occurring immediately outside a chamber, given sufficient fuel, could seriously endanger the life or lives of those inside the chamber. Since the service facilities such as compressors, cooling equipment, reserve air supply, oxygen, and so forth, will in all probability be within the same building, these will also need protection while in themselves supplying life-maintaining service to those inside.

Prior to the 1996 edition, it was required that "all construction and finish materials be of noncombustible materials under standard atmospheric conditions." When the provisions of 19-2.1.1 were changed to require "2-hour fire-resistive-rated construction," that provision was no longer appropriate. It was also felt that it is virtually impossible (and impractical) to construct a room for hyperbaric application entirely of noncombustible materials.

**19-2.1.1.2** When used for hyperbaric procedures, the room or rooms housing the Class A or Class B chambers shall be for the exclusive use of the hyperbaric operation. Service equipment (e.g., compressors) shall be permitted to be located in multi-use spaces meeting the requirements of 19-2.1.1.

This requirement was revised in 1996 to clarify that the room or rooms housing either a Class A or Class B chamber need to be used solely for hyperbaric procedures when the system is operational. If the chamber system is nonfunctional (stored), then this requirement does not apply. The committee felt it is important not to allow hyperbaric treatment operations to take place in the immediate area where other medical procedures, such as critical care, are performed. Location of service equipment in other rooms is allowable as long as those rooms meet the requirements of 19-2.1.1.

**19-2.1.1.3** The supporting foundation for any chamber shall be sufficiently strong to support the chamber. Consideration shall be given to any added floor stresses that will be created during any on-site hydrostatic testing.

Hydrostatic testing is required after a Class A chamber has been relocated and installed. The purpose of this test is to ensure that the weld integrity has been maintained during shipment and installation. Hydrostatic testing is not normally required again unless major maintenance requiring through-hull penetrations or welding has been performed on the chamber. Class B chambers are not hydrostatically tested after relocation and installation.

**19-2.1.2** A hydraulically calculated automatic wet pipe sprinkler system meeting the requirements of NFPA 13, *Standard for the Installation of Sprinkler Systems*, shall be installed in the room housing a Class A chamber and in any ancillary equipment rooms.

*Exception: Class A chambers not contiguous to a health care facility, and either located in a mobile, vehicle-mounted facility or not permanently affixed to a foundation.*

This sprinkler system is intended to protect occupants in a Class A chamber from the effects of a fire outside the chamber. The system is also intended to protect equipment ancillary to the operation of the chamber, that is, equipment that is essential to the safety and evacuation of any occupants of the chamber.

The exception was added in 1996 because the committee felt that requiring sprinkler protection in mobile, vehicle-mounted facilities or those not permanently affixed to a foundation was not practical. See earlier commentary on the exception to 19-2.1.2.

**19-2.1.2.1\*** Chamber room sprinkler heads shall be an approved type equipped with fusible elements. The element temperature ratings shall be as low as possible, consistent with the requirements against false operation in NFPA 13.

**A-19-2.1.2.1** In addition to the functions of building protection, the chamber room sprinkler system should be designed to ensure a degree of protection to chamber operators and occupants who likely will not be able to immediately evacuate the premises in the event of a fire.

The purpose of this requirement is to protect operators and support equipment in the event of a fire *external* to the chamber and to ensure sufficient time to bring the chamber to normal atmosphere and evacuate the chamber occupants. These sprinklers are intended to protect the structure and to prevent a fire from spreading beyond the immediate area of the hyperbaric facility.

Inadvertent activation of sprinklers is extremely rare. NFPA 13, *Standard for the Installation of Sprinkler Systems* [4], contains requirements for sprinkler temperature ratings for given locations based on such factors as maximum localized temperatures. This paragraph stresses that sprinklers rated for the lowest possible temperature are to be used when protecting the chamber room itself.

The committee has noted that sprinkler systems for Class A chambers are intended to protect persons *within* the chamber from the effects of a fire *outside* the chamber, as well as to protect the building and persons in the building where the chamber is located.

This commentary serves as a caution to designers and installers of sprinkler systems as to the purpose of a chamber sprinkler system.

**19-2.1.3** The room or rooms housing Class B and C chambers shall be afforded sprinkler protection in accordance with 19-2.1.2.

*Exception: Chambers not contiguous to a health care facility, and either located in a mobile, vehicle-mounted facility or not permanently affixed to a foundation.*

This section was added in 1996 to address the fire hazards associated with both Class A and Class B chambers. Until the 1996 edition, a room housing a Class B or Class C chamber was not required to have sprinkler protection. Several Class B chamber mishaps in other countries brought attention to the need for all rooms housing a hyperbaric chamber of any class to be sprinkler protected. This sprinkler system is intended to protect the building and its occupants from a fire within the Class B chamber. Unfortunately, traditional thinking has been that it is not usually very helpful or feasible to install a sprinkler system inside a Class B chamber. Advances in fire detection and suppression technology might redirect this thinking in the near future. See 19-2.6 and earlier commentary on the exception to 19-2.1.2.

Chambers not contiguous to a health care facility are exempted from this requirement because they are separate from an occupied building and not readily connectable to a main sprinkler system. The exception in this section refers only to Class B and C chambers. As stated in the commentary for A-19-2.1.1, Exception No.1, questions that indicate confusion still exists with this particular exception have been asked. In particular, the issue of a chamber not being permanently affixed to a foundation, and whether Class B chambers, many of which are designed with casters for ease of relocation, fall under the exception. To reduce the ambiguity, the technical committee will consider this exception in greater detail for the 2002 edition of the standard.

## 19-2.2 Fabrication of the Hyperbaric Chamber.

**19-2.2.1\*** Chambers for human occupancy, and their supporting systems, shall be designed and fabricated to meet ANSI/ASME PVHO-1, *Safety Standard for Pressure Vessels for Human Occupancy*, by personnel qualified to fabricate vessels under such codes. The chamber shall be stamped in accordance with ANSI/ASME PVHO-1. As a minimum, animal chambers shall be designed, fabricated, and stamped to meet ANSI/ASME Section VIII, Division 1 code requirements.

> The change from PVHO-1a to PVHO-1 [5] was adopted to reflect the current ASME-PVHO document designation. The requirement for vessel stamping was added for ready visual reference for regulatory personnel to see that the vessel was designed, fabricated, and tested in accordance with ASME-PVHO requirements.

**A-19-2.2.1** Other chapters in NFPA 99 contain many requirements that could appear to relate to hyperbaric facilities but could be inappropriate. The requirements of other chapters in NFPA 99 should be applied to hyperbaric facilities only where specifically invoked by this chapter.

> Because this chapter applies only to new construction and equipment, the committee believes all new chambers that will be used for human occupancy should be designed and fabricated to the ANSI/ASME standard. PVHOs that do not meet the requirements of the ASME or equivalent standard are being fabricated in other countries and are subject to importation to this country.
>
> This section recognizes that the standards for animal chambers may not need to be as restrictive as those for human occupancy. Previously, no distinction was made because of a concern that there may be occasion for human occupancy in larger animal chambers. If animal chambers might have human occupancy at any time, they need to meet the appropriate standards for human occupancy chambers.
>
> This commentary cautions against using other portions of NFPA 99 without taking into consideration the relationship, if any, to safety in a hyperbaric environment.

**19-2.2.2** Class A chambers shall be equipped with a floor that is structurally capable of supporting equipment and personnel necessary for the operation of the chamber according to its expected purpose.

**19-2.2.2.1** The floor of Class A chambers shall be noncombustible.

**19-2.2.2.2** If the procedures to be carried out in the Class A hyperbaric chamber require antistatic flooring, the flooring shall be installed in accordance with the provisions of 12-4.1, Anesthetizing Locations.

> A conductive floor will eliminate the buildup of any static charge on occupants as they move about the chamber.

**19-2.2.2.3** If a bilge is installed, access to the bilge shall be provided for cleaning purposes. The floor overlaying the bilge shall be removable or, as an alternative, there shall be other suitable access for cleaning the bilge.

> Traditional Class A chambers are designed and constructed in such a manner that they contain a bilge. A bilge is created when level flooring or decking is secured

in the horizontal or upright cylinder to provide a level walking or treatment surface. Even with the new rectangular, post-tensioned concrete hyperbaric room construction recently demonstrated by the United States Air Force, a bilge to the false flooring that will be installed is probably necessary.

The buildup of dirt, dust, or liquids in a bilge cannot be tolerated in any hyperbaric operation due to the increased fire risk. The entire bilge area needs to be accessible to allow for routine cleaning.

**19-2.2.2.4** If the interior floor of a Class A chamber consists of removable floor (deck) plates, the plates shall be mechanically secured and electrically bonded to the chamber to ensure a positive electrical ground and to prevent movement of the plate, which could cause injury to personnel.

Providing a solid floor that is readily removable for cleaning purposes but retains the ability to provide antistatic bonding is difficult to achieve, but not impossible.

**19-2.2.3** The interior of Class A chambers shall be unfinished or treated with a finish that is inorganic-zinc-based or high-quality epoxy or equivalent, or that is flame resistant.

Finishes such as inorganic-zinc-based finishes are required because the referenced test methods listed under the definition of *flame resistant* are not applicable to the types of interior finishes generally used for the inside walls of hyperbaric chambers. Some finish is required for steel chambers to prevent rusting. The option of flame-resistant finishes is included because in the future there may be finishes that meet the flame-resistant criteria.

Because of the need for periodic cleaning of the interiors of chambers, steel surfaces cannot normally be left uncoated. However, any coatings used should provide maximum protection and minimum risk for the occupants in the event of fire.

**19-2.2.3.1** If the interior of a Class A chamber is treated (painted) with a finish listed above, the cure procedure and minimum duration for each coat of finish to off gas shall be in accordance with the manufacturers' application instructions and material safety data sheets.

The requirement to allow a minimum of 72 hours for off gassing was dropped in favor of relying on new paint technology and manufacturer recommendations for paint application and on information available in representative material safety data sheets.

**19-2.2.3.2\*** If sound-deadening materials are employed within a hyperbaric chamber, they shall be flame resistant as defined in Chapter 2, "Definitions."

**A-19-2.2.3.2** Many commercial sound-deadening materials that might be flame resistant are porous, and will absorb water from activation of the fire-suppression system and retain odor.

Metallic panels that contain a large quantity of small holes or are made of wire mesh and are installed about 1 in. (2.5 cm) away from the chamber wall can be used to form an acoustic baffle. These panels should be made from corrosive-resistant materials such as stainless steel or aluminum and can be painted in accordance with 19-2.2.3.

Although not prohibited, the use of aluminum within any chamber should be kept to a minimum because, under certain circumstances, aluminum will burn in an ambient atmosphere of air.

**19-2.2.4\*** A sufficient number of viewing ports and access ports for piping and monitoring and related leads shall be installed during initial fabrication of the chamber.

**A-19-2.2.4** Prudent design considerations suggest that at least 50 percent excess pass-through capacity be provided, for future use, given the difficulty of adding pass-throughs to the chamber after it is constructed and tested.

Chambers are designed and tested to meet code requirements when first constructed. Any construction to add ports or other openings in the chamber after it has already been in operation will require retesting of the pressure vessel, an expensive and disruptive process. Installing extra ports during the original construction will save both time and effort later. A recent mishap occurred after the metal door (hatch) of a Class A chamber had been replaced with a door made of acrylic to provide additional light and improve visibility into the inside of the chamber. When first pressurized after the modification, the replacement door failed. The resulting force generated by the failure dislodged the chamber from its fixed foundation, propelling it into the rear wall of the room. Proper design and testing could have prevented this mishap from occurring.

**19-2.2.4.1** Access ports in Class A chambers for monitoring and other electrical circuits shall be housed in enclosures that are weatherproof both inside and outside the chamber for protection in the event of sprinkler activation.

Weatherproofing enclosures allows for cleaning of the chamber and testing of the deluge fire suppression system without the risk of shorting electrical components.

**19-2.2.4.2** Viewports and penetrator plates shall be designed and fabricated according to ANSI/ASME PVHO-1, *Safety Standard for Pressure Vessels for Human Occupancy.*

It should be noted that the service life of acrylic viewports is currently 10 years from fabrication. Even if spare viewports have been in storage for longer than 10 years, they cannot be placed into hyperbaric service. The ASME-PVHO [5] is currently evaluating criteria to extend the service life of acrylic viewports installed in clinical hyperbaric systems and to differentiate between design life and service life for viewports.

## 19-2.3 Illumination.

**19-2.3.1** Unless designed for chamber use, sources of illumination shall be mounted outside the pressure chamber and arranged to shine through chamber ports or through chamber penetrators designed for fiberoptic or similar lighting.

The mounting of lighting outside the chamber substantially reduces the hazards that could occur should a lamp break. It is also easier to change and maintain externally mounted lamps.

**19-2.3.1.1** Lighting fixtures used in conjunction with viewports shall be designed so that temperature ratings for the viewport material given in ANSI/ASME PVHO-1 are not exceeded.

Where chambers are designed for lights to shine through the viewports, extreme caution must be taken ensure that the light source is positioned far enough away from the viewport to minimize viewport heating. Mishaps have occurred where the light source has been placed too close to the viewport, causing older glass viewports to catastrophically fail or acrylic viewports to become warped beyond safe use. The temperature rating of the viewport material is important when designing such lighting fixtures.

**19-2.3.1.2** Gasket material shall be of a type that permits the movement of thermal expansion and shall be suitable for the temperatures, pressures, and composition of gases involved. Gaskets of O-rings shall be confined to grooves or enclosures, which will prevent their being blown out or squeezed from the enclosures or compression flanges.

The requirement that gasketing material be noncombustible was removed in 1993 since the manufacturers of hyperbaric chambers indicated that it is presently impossible to design materials for hyperbaric chambers that are absolutely noncombustible.

**19-2.3.2** Lighting permanently installed inside the chamber and portable lighting for temporary use inside the chamber shall meet the requirements of 19-2.7.3.10.

In earlier editions, 19-2.3.2 through 19-2.3.4 contained the requirements that included temperature restrictions for electrical equipment and lighting whether installed inside or outside of the chamber. This wording now eliminates duplication and conflict with other portions of the standard, including that of 19-2.7.1.4 for locating ballasts outside of the chamber. Specification requirements for permanent and portable lighting for temporary use inside the chamber must meet the requirements of 19-2.7.3.10.

**19-2.3.3** Emergency lighting for the interior of the chamber shall be provided.

Wording for changed to clarify the technical committee's intent that lighting for the interior of the chamber should be connected to an appropriate essential electrical system to allow illumination during periods of main power outage and so forth. However, unless emergency treatment operations are being conducted during a power loss, chamber operations should be terminated if power cannot be readily restored.

## 19-2.4 Chamber Ventilation.

Criteria for ventilation rates are provided for Class A and B chambers. Paragraphs 19-2.4.1 through 19-2.4.3 pertain to Class A chambers while 19-2.4.4 through 19-2.4.4.1 apply to Class B chambers. Additionally, material previously found in 19-2.8.7 and its related subparagraphs was relocated to this section to separate the requirements for air production from monitoring requirements for clarification.

**19-2.4.1** Whenever the Class A chamber is used as an operating room, it shall be adequately ventilated and the air supply thereto conditioned according to the minimum requirements for temperature for hospital operating rooms as specified in 12-4.1, Anesthetizing Locations.

*Exception:* *Class A chambers that are not used in the capacity of an operating room shall maintain a temperature that is comfortable for the occupants [usually 75° ± 5°F (22° ± 2°C)]. The thermal control system should be designed to maintain the temperature below 85°F (29°C) during pressurization, if possible, and above 65°F (19°C) during depressurization, if possible.*

**A-19-2.4.1, Exception.** Section 12-4.1, Anesthetizing Locations, specifies a desirable temperature of 68°F (20°C). It is impractical to maintain such a temperature during pressurization, but efforts should be made in the design and operation of thermal control systems to maintain the temperature as close to 75°F (22°C) as possible. The air-handling system of all Class A chambers should be capable of maintaining relative humidity in the range of 50 to 70 percent during stable depth operations.

The exception is included because the temperature levels specified in 19-2.4.1 would be too cold for patients in nonoperating room conditions who are clad only in hospital gowns and robes.
Controlling humidity between 50 percent and 70 percent is recommended for static electricity control, patient comfort, and avoidance of prolonged exposure to both high and very low humidity, either of which can cause medical problems.

**19-2.4.1.1** The minimum ventilation rate for a Class A chamber shall be 3 actual cu ft (0.085 actual m³) per minute of air per chamber occupant not using a breathing mask overboard dump system that exhausts exhaled gases. The minimum threshold rate shall be 3 actual cu ft per minute (0.085 actual m³ per minute).

*Exception:* * *The ventilation rate requirements of this paragraph are waived when saturation operations are conducted in the chamber, provided that carbon dioxide removal and odor control are accomplished and that the monitoring requirements of 19-2.8.5.1 and 19-2.8.6 are met.*

**19-2.4.1.2** If inhalation anesthetic agents are being utilized (e.g., nitrous oxide, methoxyflurane, halothane), a closed anesthetic system with exhaled-gas scavenging and overboard dumping shall be employed.

Paragraph 19-2.4.1.2 requires a closed breathing circuit with scavenging of the gases. Flammable inhalation anesthetics should not be allowed to be used inside a chamber. (See 19-2.4.1.2.1.)

**19-2.4.1.2.1** Flammable inhalation anesthetics (i.e., cyclopropane, ethyl ether, ethylene, and ethyl chloride) shall not be employed.

**19-2.4.1.3** Provision shall be made for ventilation during nonpressurization of Class A chambers as well as during pressurization.

During all phases of chamber operation, including pressurization, maintenance of level pressure, and depressurization, a positive means of ventilation needs to be provided to manage levels of oxygen, carbon dioxide, and other gases to within prescribed limits and to provide for patient comfort (temperature, humidity, and odor control).

When a chamber is not expected to be used for an extended period of time, some form of powered ventilation should be provided to prevent stale conditions.

**19-2.4.1.4** Individual breathing apparatus shall be supplied for each occupant of a Class A chamber for use in case air in the chamber is fouled by combustion or otherwise. Each breathing apparatus shall be available for immediate use, and the breathing mixture shall be independent of chamber atmosphere. The breathing gas supply shall be sufficient for simultaneous use of all breathing apparatus. Such apparatus shall function at all pressures that can be encountered in the chamber. In the event of a fire within a chamber, provision shall be made to switch all breathing apparatus to an air supply that is independent of the chamber atmosphere.

Availability of an alternative source of air for the breathing of all chamber occupants will allow for an orderly decompression of the chamber should the interior chamber air be fouled by contaminants. The wording clearly indicates that the emergency breathing media be air and that it be independent of the main chamber air supply.

It is vital that all breathing devices for all occupants be capable of being switched to air in an emergency. The method of switching the breathing media during an emergency should be simple and require a minimum amount of time to activate.

**19-2.4.1.5** An alternative source for breathing air shall be available outside a Class A chamber for use by personnel in the event that the air in the vicinity of the chamber is fouled by smoke or other combustion products of fire.

> The *immediate* evacuation of patients and staff in the event of fire or smoke conditions might not be practical when operating a multiplace chamber. Alternative breathing air sources must be available for the chamber operator to use while he or she is continuing chamber operations to evacuate the chamber occupants. This alternative breathing air source can be designed into the chamber operator's console or be immediately available (portable, wall mount). Due to the variety of alternative breathing air sources available to meet this requirement, the technical committee does not intend for the application of special OSHA annual physical requirements, pulmonary function studies, and so forth, normally required for people who are subject to the routine use of self-contained breathing apparatus (SCBA).

**19-2.4.2\*** Sources of air for chamber atmospheres shall be such that toxic or flammable gases are not introduced. Compressor intakes shall be located so as to avoid air contaminated by exhaust from activities of vehicles, internal combustion engines, stationary engines, or building exhaust outlets.

**A-19-2.4.2** If intakes are located where it could be possible for maintenance to be conducted in the immediate vicinity, a warning sign should be posted.

> This section emphasizes the need to place the compressor intake in a location where the air it will be drawing in is not contaminated. The recent re-introduction of mobile-based hyperbaric systems requires special attention to ensure that the compressor intake is located away from potential sources of contamination.

**19-2.4.2.1** Positive efforts shall be undertaken to ensure that air for chamber atmosphere is not fouled by handling. This air supply shall be monitored as required in 19-2.8.7.

> Air-handling equipment (e.g., compressors) that uses oil must be monitored carefully to ensure that oil seals and oil removal devices are intact and working properly to provide an oilfree atmosphere in the chamber.

**19-2.4.2.2** The use of conventional oil-lubricated compressors shall be permitted provided they are fitted with air treatment packages designed to produce medical air, and they meet the monitoring requirements of 19-2.8.7. The air treatment packages shall include automatic safeguards.

> This section was relocated in the 1999 edition to 19-2.4.2.2 from 19-2.8.7 in the 1996 edition to better reflect the proper location to maintain continuity of the requirements. Also, this section supports the opinion of the technical committee that air compressor technology is now available to provide for a variety of cost-effective means to meet the requirements of this section.

**19-2.4.2.3** Air compressor installations shall consist of two or more individual compressors with capacities such that required system flow rates can be maintained on a continuous basis with any single compressor out of operation unless the exception to 19-2.7.2.3 is satisfied. Each compressor shall be supplied from separate electrical branch circuits.

The intent of this requirement (relocated here in the 1999 edition) is to ensure that chamber operations can proceed when necessary, such as the need to support a life- or limb-threatening emergency hyperbaric treatment. The technical committee supported giving operators more than one way to meet this requirement (capability can be met by either redundant compressors or stored air). The requirement that each compressor be powered from separate electrical branch circuits also supports the need to maintain emergency treatment capability. The terminology is consistent with *NEC* definitions. This section was relocated in 1999 from 19-2.8.7 in the 1996 edition to better reflect the proper location to maintain continuity of the requirements.

**19-2.4.2.4** Air compressor installations that supply medical air to piped gas systems as well as to hyperbaric facilities shall meet the requirements of 4-3.1.1.9 in Chapter 4 and the requirements of this chapter. Air compressor installations that are used exclusively for hyperbaric facilities shall meet the requirements of this chapter only.

Chapter 4 contains many requirements for redundancy, monitoring, and alarms that are not considered necessary for dedicated hyperbaric air plants. Hyperbaric air plants can be shut down for maintenance and repair and, consequently, are not considered to require the same levels of redundancy, monitoring, or alarms as hospital medical air compressor installations. In general, medical air systems cannot be shut down. The explicit exception is considered necessary by the technical committee to avoid unnecessary application of Chapter 4 requirements to air plants dedicated specifically to hyperbaric use. This section was relocated in this 1999 edition from 19-2.8.7 in the 1996 edition to maintain continuity of the requirements.

**19-2.4.3** Warming or cooling of the atmosphere within a Class A chamber shall be permitted by circulating the ambient air within the chamber over or past coils through which a constant flow of warm or cool water is circulated. Dehumidification shall be permitted through the use of cold coils; humidification, by the use of an air-powered water nebulizer. Suitable noncombustible packing and nonflammable lubricant shall be employed on the fan shaft.

**19-2.4.4 Ventilation of Class B Chambers.**

Traditionally, Class B chambers have been pressurized with 100 percent oxygen. This section was added in 1990 to recognize that Class B chambers might be pressurized with air. Class B chambers so pressurized need to meet the same ventilation criteria as Class A chambers. This edition further clarifies the technical committee's intent by changing the term *ventilation* to *pressurization*.

**19-2.4.4.1** Class B chambers, if pressurized with air, shall conform to the ventilation requirements of Class A chambers.

This change was adopted to require that all chambers, regardless of their classification, be capable of exchanging the pressurization gas during treatment operations to maintain comfort, odor control, oxygen, carbon dioxide buildup, and so forth.

## 19-2.5 Fire Protection in Class A Chambers.

This section contains minimum requirements for the design and construction of more cost-effective fire protection systems for hyperbaric chambers.

Note that it is a requirement that Class A chambers have both a handline system and a deluge system. However, although not mandatory, the deluge system can be automatic. If the deluge system is automatic, an automatic alarm with the capability of manual activation should be considered. This manual activation capability is important in Class A hyperbaric chambers used for medical purposes, particularly surgery, where the possibility of an automatic system activating during a surgical procedure can be hazardous. Operators who have used chambers in these circumstances indicate that handlines are usually adequate for fire suppression. However, the final design of the system is up to the local user and should be clearly outlined in the user design specification.

Some other concerns include the following:

(a) The capacity of the extinguishing system must be suitable for the particular chamber design. The application of a deluge system is dependent on a very quick, thorough soaking, but the soaking should be limited in duration to prevent possible flooding. Further, the deluge system must perform as specified across the pressure design range of the chamber. As noted, all electrical systems, except those that are intrinsically safe, must be disconnected to avoid potential for electric shock during the use of the fire extinguishing system.

(b) Testing of both the deluge system and the handline system should be done as indicated. A bypass system that will functionally test both of these systems is allowed as long as the bypass is a device that will normally be in the nonfunctioning position (i.e., a bypass that could be left in operation is not allowed). The purpose of this requirement is to prevent any possibility of the system being left in the test mode, thereby defeating the handline and/or the deluge system.

(c) All of the fire safety systems should be supplied with emergency power to ensure that in the event of power failure or power loss due to a fire, alarm systems, suppression systems, and other emergency systems that are part of the chamber will still function properly.

Note that this section does not require deluge systems in areas such as transfer locks. However, handline systems must be provided in every compartment of a multicompartment hyperbaric chamber.

**19-2.5.1 General Requirements.**

**19-2.5.1.1** A fire suppression system consisting of an independently supplied and operating handline and deluge system shall be installed in all Class A chambers.

> The technical committee believes strongly that there should not be a common source of potential failure that could render either system inoperable should that common component fail. This level of redundancy provides an extra margin of safety for the occupants of Class A chambers.

**19-2.5.1.2** Design of the fire suppression system shall be such that failure of components in either the handline or deluge system will not render the other system inoperative.

> This requirement recognizes that neither handlines nor the deluge system takes precedent over the other. This equal priority status reflects the fact that the gravity of the situation should dictate which system is primarily activated to extinguish the fire. It also reconfirms the intent of not having a common source of failure that would render either system inoperable.

**19-2.5.1.3** System design shall be such that activation of either the handline or the deluge system shall automatically cause the following:

(a) Visual and aural indication of activation shall occur at the chamber operator's console.
(b) All ungrounded electrical leads for power and lighting circuits contained inside the chamber shall be disconnected. Intrinsically safe circuits, including sound-powered communications, are not required to be disconnected.
(c) Emergency lighting *(see 19-2.3.3)* and communication, where used, shall be activated.

> Special activities conducted inside a chamber might dictate other actions to occur automatically and/or simultaneously.

**19-2.5.1.4\*** A fire alarm signaling device shall be provided at the chamber operator's control console for signaling the telephone operator or a suitable authority to activate the emergency fire/rescue network of the institution containing the hyperbaric facility.

**A-19-2.5.1.4** This requirement does not preclude the use of an alarm system affording direct fire department contact.

> A fire in a chamber or in the room housing the chamber requires immediate fire assistance. Chamber operators need to be able to signal for this assistance directly from the control console in either instance.

**19-2.5.1.5\*** Fire blankets and portable carbon dioxide extinguishers shall not be installed in or carried into the chamber.

**A-19-2.5.1.5** Experience has shown that fire blankets, portable carbon dioxide extinguishers, and other methodology intended to "snuff out" fires by excluding air are not effective in controlling fires in oxygen-enriched atmospheres. Valuable time can be lost in attempting to use such devices.

**19-2.5.1.6** Booster pumps, control circuitry, and other electrical equipment involved in fire suppression system operation shall be powered from a critical branch of the emergency electrical system as specified in 19-2.7.2.2(e).

**19-2.5.2 Deluge System Requirements.** A fixed water deluge extinguishing system shall be installed in all chamber compartments that are designed for manned operations. In chambers that consist of more than one chamber compartment (lock), the design of the deluge system shall ensure adequate operation when the chamber compartments are at different depths (pressures). The design shall also ensure the independent or simultaneous operation of deluge systems.

*Exception: Chamber compartments that are used strictly as personnel transfer compartments (locks), and for no other purposes, are not required to have a fixed deluge system.*

This paragraph and its exception clarify the issue of whether a deluge system is required in transfer locks. They also provide minimum performance criteria for deluge systems that are installed in multicompartment (lock) chambers where each chamber can be pressurized simultaneously to different depths. "Deluge System Requirements" was added as the section heading to facilitate ready reference to this section.

**19-2.5.2.1\*** Manual activation and deactivation deluge controls shall be located at the operator's console and in each chamber compartment (lock) containing a deluge system. Controls shall be designed to prevent unintended activation.

The committee believes that all manual deluge control stations need to have the capability to activate, as well as shut off, the deluge system.

As Class A chambers become larger and different design configurations are developed, it is important that multiple control stations be provided to ensure ready access by chamber occupants.

**A-19-2.5.2.1** More than one control station could be required in a compartment (lock) depending on its size.

**19-2.5.2.2** Water shall be delivered from the sprinkler heads as specified in 19-2.5.2.4 within 3 seconds of activation of any affiliated deluge control.

The time constraints for deluge system activation make clear what is required, particularly from a design point of view, to ensure sufficient response time to deal with a chamber fire. The wording in previous editions ("beginning not less than 3 seconds") was changed to clearly define the requirement that water be delivered to the sprinklers *within* 3 seconds.

**19-2.5.2.3\*** The number and positioning of sprinkler heads shall be sufficient to provide reasonably uniform spray coverage with vertical and horizontal (or near horizontal) jets. Average spray density at floor level shall be not less than 2 gpm/ft$^2$ (81.5 L/min/m$^2$) with no floor area larger than 1 m$^2$ receiving less than 1 gpm/ft$^2$ (40.75 L/min/m$^2$).

**A-19-2.5.2.3** Experience has shown that when water is discharged through conventional sprinkler heads into a hyperbaric atmosphere, the spray angle is reduced because of increased resistance to water droplet movement in the denser atmosphere. This is so even though the water pressure differential is maintained above chamber pressure. Therefore, it is necessary to compensate by increasing the number of sprinkler heads. It is recommended that spray coverage tests be conducted at maximum chamber pressure.

Some chamber configurations, such as small-diameter horizontal cylinders, could have a very tiny "floor," or even no floor at all. For horizontal cylinder chambers and spherical chambers, "floor level" should be taken to mean the level at ¼ diameter below the chamber centerline or actual "floor level," whichever gives the larger floor area.

This material provides guidance for determining the type, number, and placement of deluge sprinklers and recommends that tests be conducted at maximum chamber pressure. (However, some believe that deluge systems should be tested across the entire chamber pressure range, not just at maximum pressure.)

**19-2.5.2.4** There shall be sufficient water available in the deluge system to maintain the flow specified in 19-2.5.2.3 simultaneously in each chamber compartment (lock) containing the deluge system for 1 minute. The limit on maximum extinguishment duration shall be governed by the chamber capacity (bilge capacity also, if so equipped) and/or its drainage system.

**19-2.5.2.5** The deluge system shall have stored pressure to operate for at least 15 seconds without electrical branch power.

**19-2.5.3 Handline System Requirements.** A handline extinguishing system shall be installed in all chamber compartments (locks). At least two handlines shall be strategically located in treatment compartments (locks). At least one handline shall be located in each personnel transfer compartment (lock). If any chamber compartment (lock) is equipped with a bilge access panel, at least one handline shall be of sufficient length to allow use of the handline for fire suppression in the bilge area.

"Handline System Requirements" was added as the section heading to make the document easier to read and cross-reference.

**19-2.5.3.1** Handlines shall have a ½-in. minimum internal diameter and shall have a rated working pressure greater than the highest supply pressure of the supply system.

Specific minimum criteria for handlines are included because of the type of service to which they could be subjected.

**19-2.5.3.2** Each handline shall be activated by a manual, quick-opening, quarter-turn valve located within the compartment (lock). Hand-operated, spring-return to close valves at the discharge end of handlines shall be permitted.

Wording from earlier editions could be construed to mean that the only permissible control valve for a handline suppression system is a quarter-turn valve that can be found attached to the chamber shell some distance away from the end of the hose.

**19-2.5.3.3** Handlines shall be equipped with override valves placed in easily accessible locations outside the chamber.

The handline override valve should be located so that it can be controllable from the control console, but it need not necessarily be located at the console.

**19-2.5.3.4** The water supply for the handline system shall be designed to ensure a 50 psi (345 kPa) minimum water pressure above the maximum chamber pressure. The system shall be capable of supplying a minimum of 5 gpm (18.8 L/min) simultaneously to each of any two of the handlines at the maximum chamber pressure.

**19-2.5.4 Automatic Detection System Requirements.** Automatic fire detection systems are optional. Whether installed and used in an alarm function or in an automatic deluge activation function, they shall meet the requirements set forth below.

This wording reflects the committee's intent that automatic fire detection systems and automatic activation of a deluge system are optional. If installed, however, they need to meet the requirements listed. The section heading "Automatic Detection System Requirements" was added to make the document easier to read and cross-reference.

**19-2.5.4.1** Surveillance fire detectors responsive to the radiation from flame shall be employed. Type and arrangement of detectors shall be such as to respond within 1 second of flame origination.

**19-2.5.4.2\*** The number of detectors employed and their location shall be dependent on the sensitivity of each detector and the configuration of the spaces to be protected.

**A-19-2.5.4.2** Additional detectors are recommended to avoid "blind" areas if the chamber contains compartmentation.

**19-2.5.4.3** The system shall be powered from the critical branch of the emergency electrical system or shall have automatic battery back-up.

**19-2.5.4.4** If used to automatically activate the deluge system, the requirements for manual activation/deactivation in 19-2.5.2.1 and deluge system response time in 19-2.5.2.2 shall still apply.

**19-2.5.4.5** The system shall include self-monitoring functions for fault detection and appropriate fault alarms and indications.

**19-2.5.5 Testing Requirements.** The deluge and handline systems shall be functionally tested at least annually per 19-2.5.2.3 for deluge systems and 19-2.5.3.4 for handline systems. If a bypass system is used, it shall not remain in the test mode after completion of the test.

During initial construction, or whenever changes are made to the installed system, testing of spray coverage per 19-2.5.2.3 shall be performed at surface pressure, and at maximum operating pressure. The requirements of 19-2.5.2.3 shall be satisfied under both conditions. A detailed record of the test results shall be supplied to the authority having jurisdiction and the hyperbaric facility safety director.

> This paragraph establishes criteria for the annual testing of deluge and handline systems and for bypass circuitry. The committee believes testing in a bypass mode needs to be permitted to avoid interior deluging of the chamber.
>
> Historically, many Class A hyperbaric facilities have not conducted periodic testing or fire suppression system activation. In some cases, operators have even been surprised when they have needed to activate the system and found it did not work.
>
> The concept of a test bypass circuit is included to encourage designers to add this feature so operators will be more likely to conduct routine testing. Such a bypass allows all system components to be activated with the exception of the actual sprinklers. When this system is employed, it can be tested with no chamber preparation or cleanup required. However, criteria need to be included for safety purposes so that the deluge system does not remain in the bypass (test) mode.
>
> Earlier editions referred operators to 19-2.5.2.3 for deluge testing requirements. The requirements set forth in this paragraph are really design/performance requirements, not test requirements. A change was made in this 1999 edition to refer operators to 19-2.5.2.4, the proper paragraph for test requirements. Furthermore, the minimum spray pattern test defined in 19-2.5.2.3 defeated the objective of allowing a system bypass circuit to test the system without spraying the inside of the chamber.
>
> The section heading "Testing Requirements" was added to make the document easier to read and cross-reference.
>
> This section, new in the 1999 edition, was added to stress that changes made to the deluge system can affect the spray pattern and other criteria. Even though minimum test conditions (surface pressure and maximum pressure) are prescribed, testing is recommended across the entire pressure continuum of the chamber.
>
> The new requirement for test data documentation and reporting was added to maintain quality control in the maintenance of deluge fire suppression systems.

## 19-2.6 Fire Protection in Class B and C Chambers.

Class B and C chambers shall not be required to comply with 19-2.5, Fire Protection in Class A Chambers.

> Class B and Class C chambers are not required to comply with 19-2.5 because all chambers must be vented to the exterior of the building in which they are located,

and all new chambers must be fabricated to ASME/PVHO-1. [5] Also, operating procedures for Class B chambers allow ready removal and evacuation of a single patient from an area.

In addition, the sprinkler protection of 19-2.5, unfortunately, has not been proven effective in Class B or Class C chambers, particularly if the atmosphere is oxygen enriched.

While the space inside a Class B hyperbaric chamber if pressurized with 100 percent oxygen is considered a hazardous location, the room in which the chamber is located is not a hazardous location, particularly since exhausts are required to be vented to the exterior of the building. Thus, there is no requirement for a conductive floor, and so forth, in the room where this type of chamber is located. Prudence would suggest grounding the chamber if it is nonelectric.

## 19-2.7 Electrical Systems.

Because uncontrolled decompression can be life threatening, the systems supporting hyperbaric chambers are critical. Electrical service, needed to supply power and light for the critical portions of the chamber's control and life-support features, is to be powered by an emergency power system.

Paragraphs 19-2.7.1.1 through 19-2.7.1.6 attempt to ensure that the electrical equipment required for hyperbaric service is primarily located on the exterior of the chamber and that in the event of failure the equipment is accessible. In the event of fire within the chamber, equipment located outside the chamber will not be affected by the activation of the handline or the deluge systems in the chamber. Obviously, electric motors that are performing a function must be located within the chamber; however, it would not be expected that they be operational if the deluge system is activated.

### 19-2.7.1 General.

**19-2.7.1.1** The requirements of NFPA 70, *National Electrical Code*, or local electrical codes shall apply to electrical wiring and equipment in hyperbaric facilities within the scope of this chapter, except as such rules are modified in this section. Where unusual conditions exist in a specific facility, the authority having jurisdiction shall judge with respect to the application of specific rules.

While NFPA 70, *National Electrical Code* [6], is the governing document with respect to electrical wiring in general, the special requirements of hyperbaric facilities have to take precedence. The intent of 19-2.7 is to address those specialized requirements by referencing NFPA 70 as appropriate and to expand on those requirements as necessary.

**19-2.7.1.2** All hyperbaric chamber service equipment, switchboards, panels, or control consoles shall be located outside of, and in the vicinity of, the chamber.

**19-2.7.1.3** Console or module spaces containing both oxygen piping and electrical equipment shall be continuously ventilated or continuously monitored for excessive oxygen concentrations whenever the electrical equipment is energized.

Technology exists for remote monitoring that eliminates the need for routing gas lines (especially oxygen) into a control console. However, if the routing of such lines is necessary, then the interior of the console must be either continuously ventilated or monitored for oxygen buildup.

**19-2.7.1.4\*** For the fixed electrical installation, no circuit breakers, line fuses, motor controllers, relays, transformers, ballasts, lighting panels, or power panels shall be located inside of the chamber. If motors are to be located in the chamber, they shall meet the requirements of 19-2.7.3.9.

**A-19-2.7.1.4** It is recommended that system design be such that electric motors not be located inside the chamber.

**19-2.7.1.5** All electrical equipment connected to or used in conjunction with hyperbaric patients shall comply with the requirements of Chapter 7, "Electrical Equipment in Health Care Facilities," and with the applicable paragraphs of 19-2.7.3.

Intrinsically safe wiring is addressed in 19-2.7.3.

**19-2.7.1.6** In the event of activation of the room sprinkler system, electrical equipment shall be protected from sprinkler water to the maximal extent possible, but need not remain functional so long as manual means sufficient to safely decompress the chamber are provided.

Previous editions included slang terminology such as "terminate the dive." Such terminology has been replaced with the more technically correct phase "decompress the chamber."

## 19-2.7.2 Electrical Service.

**19-2.7.2.1** All hyperbaric facilities intended for human occupancy shall contain an electrical service that is supplied from two independent sources of electric power. For hyperbaric facilities located in a hospital, one power source shall be a prime-mover-driven generator set located on the premises of the facility. This service shall be designated as the Emergency System and shall meet the requirements of Chapter 3, "Electrical Systems," of this standard for hyperbaric systems based in health care facilities. Article 700, Emergency Systems, of NFPA 70, *National Electrical Code,* shall apply to hyperbaric systems located in facilities other than health care facilities.

As with the previous paragraphs, the effort here is to ensure that under any emergency condition there is appropriate electrical power to ensure that the life safety portions of the hyperbaric chamber continue to function, allowing the safe decompression of the system and the safe return of the staff and patients to the exterior of the chamber.

While NFPA 99 covers only health care facilities, the reference to Article 700 of NFPA 70 is included for those hyperbaric facilities in locations other than health care facilities.

**19-2.7.2.2** Electrical equipment associated with life support functions of hyperbaric facilities shall be connected to the critical branch of the emergency system; that is, such equipment shall have electrical power restored within 10 seconds of interruption of normal power. Such equipment shall include, but not necessarily be limited to:

(a) Electrical power outlets located within the chamber
(b) Chamber emergency lighting, whether internally or externally mounted
(c) Chamber intercommunications
(d) Alarm systems, including fire detectors
(e) Chamber fire suppression system equipment and controls. Booster pumps (if installed) shall be on separate branch circuits serving no other loads.
(f) Other electrical controls used for chamber pressurization and ventilation control
(g) A number of chamber room lights (either overhead or local) to ensure continued safe operation of the facility during a normal power outage

This paragraph primarily addresses the question of power outages in and around the chamber. In the event of a total power outage in the facility servicing the hyperbaric chamber, adequate electrical power should be provided to ensure the safe completion of any operations in progress and appropriate decompression of the system to allow the occupants to exit the chamber safely.

**19-2.7.2.3** Electric-motor-driven compressors and auxiliary electrical equipment normally located outside the chamber and used for chamber atmospheric control shall be connected to the equipment system *(see Chapter 3, Electrical Systems)* or the emergency system *(see NFPA 70, National Electrical Code, Article 700)*, as applicable. Such equipment shall be arranged for delayed-automatic or manual connection to the alternate power source so as to prevent excessive current draw on the system during restarting.

*Exception: When reserve air tanks or non-electric compressor(s) of sufficient capacity to maintain pressure and ventilation airflow within the chamber and supply air for the chamber pressurization are provided, the compressor(s) and auxiliary equipment need not have an alternate source of power.*

External systems that are critical to the environment of the chamber must have the capability to continue to function in the event of a power outage. The reference to delayed automatic or manual connection to the emergency power source is important when initial large-drawing loads, such as motors and compressors, are involved.

Again, the primary concern is for the safety of the chamber occupants.

The exception was reworded for the 1999 edition in recognition of the fact that many systems are designed to operate off of low-pressure instead of high-pressure air sources and to eliminate vague terms.

**19-2.7.2.4** Electrical control and alarm systems design shall be such that hazardous conditions (e.g., loss of chamber pressure control, deluge activation, spurious alarms) do not occur during power interruption or during power restoration.

This is an important system design consideration. Chamber operators and personnel might have more important matters to deal with during a power interruption than responding to false alarms or regaining control of chamber pressure.

**19-2.7.3 Wiring and Equipment Inside Chambers.** This paragraph and subparagraphs contain requirements for the safe use of electrical equipment in the hyperbaric, oxygen-enriched environment (OEA) of the Class A chamber. The following general rules shall be satisfied in the use of electrical devices and equipment:

(a) No equipment or equipment component installed in or used in the chamber shall present an explosion or implosion hazard under the conditions of hyperbaric use. All equipment shall be rated, or tested and documented, for intended hyperbaric conditions prior to use.

(b) Only the minimum amount of electrical equipment necessary for the safe operation of the chamber and for required patient care shall be permitted in the chamber. No portable equipment shall be permitted in the chamber which is not needed for the patient treatment at hand.

(c) Signs prohibiting the introduction of flammable liquids, gases, and other articles not permitted by this chapter, into the chamber shall be posted at the chamber entrance(s).

(d) The requirements under this section are intended to protect against the elevated fire risks known to exist in a pressurized air environment and shall not be construed as classifying the chamber interior as a Class I (as defined in NFPA 70, *National Electrical Code,* Article 500) hazardous location.

This entire section has been replaced for the 1999 edition. The chamber hazard classification as Class I was investigated with respect to the criteria of NFPA 497, *Recommended Practice for the Classification of Flammable Liquids, Gases, or Vapors and of Hazardous (Classified) Locations for Electrical Installations in Chemical Process Areas.* [7] Analysis of potential flammable gaseous contaminants, along with the history of over 25 years of experience in the hyperbaric industry since the adoption of the requirements, shows that there is negligible likelihood of a flammable or explosive gas mixture occurring in the chamber atmosphere. Potential hazard sources considered included hydrocarbon vapors from compressor lubricants, CO, gases via the compressor intake, and materials (isopropyl alcohol, hairsprays, etc.) brought into the chamber. At worst, the likelihood is no greater than it is in most unclassified areas. The electrical measures required for Class I locations have proven to be expensive to implement and impractical for many applications in the hyperbaric environment.

The new requirements in this section are an attempt to replace the Class I rules with rules that are designed to provide protection against the increased flammability and to lower ignition energies and temperatures of solid materials in an enclosed, air pressurized hyperbaric environment. Some of the new rules still use methods specified for Class I locations; therefore, it should be made clear to enforcement authorities that this does *not* imply that the chamber interior is specified as Class I. These new rules should make it easier for users to use limited types of medical devices for patient treatment while maintaining the necessary margin of safety in the Class A chamber environment. At the same time, it should be made very clear that *only* essential electrical equipment should be allowed in the chamber. The quantity of electrical devices has as much bearing on electrical safety as do the other safety measures required by this section. Users are cautioned not to take lightly altering medical devices for use in the hyperbaric environment. Unfortunately, most manufacturers of medical devices have not tested or certified their devices for use in the hyperbaric environment. If a specific device is to be used in the chamber, the user is recommended to seek certification from the manufacturer to do so. Local modifications should be kept to an *absolute* minimum. However, when necessary, all modifications and test results are to be documented.

*Exception: Where conformance with Class I, Division 1 requirements is specified in the following paragraphs, conformance with Class I, Division 2 requirements is permitted to be substituted if the limitations on the use in the chamber of alcohol and other agents that emit flammable vapors in the Exception to 19-3.1.5.2 are strictly observed and such restrictions are prominently posted.*

**19-2.7.3.1 Conductor Insulation.** All conductors inside the chamber shall be insulated with a material classified as flame resistant as defined in Chapter 2.

*Exception No. 1: Insulation on conductors that form an integral part of electrical equipment approved for use inside the chamber, including patient leads, need not meet the flame resistance classification.*

*Exception No. 2: Ground conductors inside of a conduit need not be insulated.*

This section was reworded in this edition to clarify the intent of the requirement and exception.

**19-2.7.3.2 Wiring Methods.** Fixed wiring shall be installed in threaded RMC or IMC conduit utilizing waterproof threaded metal joints, fittings, boxes, and enclosures. A continuous ground shall be maintained between all conductive surfaces enclosing electrical circuits and the chamber hull using approved grounding means. All threaded conduit shall be threaded with an NPT standard conduit cutting die that provides ¾-in. taper per ft (1.9 cm per every

0.3 m). Such conduit shall be made wrenchtight to prevent sparking when fault current flows through the conduit system.

> Although Class I, Division 1 and 2 requirements have been dropped in the 1999 edition, the technical committee felt that fixed wiring methods should still be stringent. The methods required in 19-2.7.3.2 will assure good grounding continuity of the wire and circuit enclosures (very important from the shock and fire prevention viewpoint) and will provide good physical protection of the circuit's suppression system. These requirements will also provide a level of safe containment against potential hazards from overheated or flaming wires. The relative expense of installing threaded RMC or IMC should also tend to discourage the "over-electrification" of the chamber interior.

*Exception No. 1: Wiring classified as intrinsically safe for any group location and installed in accordance with NFPA 70, National Electrical Code, Article 504, Intrinsically Safe Systems, shall be permitted using any of the methods suitable for ordinary locations.*

*Exception No. 2: Threaded, liquidtight flexible metal conduit installed in accordance with NFPA 70, Article 351, shall be permitted when protected from damage by suitable physical barriers such as equipment panels.*

**19-2.7.3.3 Drainage.** Means of draining fixed conduit and fixed equipment enclosures shall be provided.

> The references to sealing and Article 570 of NFPA 70 [6] were dropped in the 1999 edition. However, drainage is still important because of the fire suppression system and the need to wash the chamber interior periodically.

**19-2.7.3.4** Flexible cords used to connect portable utilization equipment to the fixed electrical supply circuit shall be of a type approved for extra-hard utilization in accordance with NFPA 70, *National Electrical Code,* Table 70-4, shall include a ground conductor, and shall otherwise meet the requirements of NFPA 70, Article 501-11.

*Exception: The normal cord supplied with the device shall be permitted when the portable device is rated at less than 2 A and the cord is securely positioned out of traffic and protected from physical abuse.*

> The exception has been added for the 1999 edition. The technical committee felt it was impractical to change the cords on all equipment. Electromedical equipment is manufactured to demanding standards and might very well lose its approval listing if modified. (See comment on 19-2.7.3.) The restrictions in this exception along with the requirements in 19-2.7.4.2 that the power supply circuit be ungrounded and monitored should provide adequate protection.

**19-2.7.3.5\* Receptacles.** Receptacles installed in the chamber shall be waterproof, of the type providing for connection to the grounding conductor of the flexible cord, and shall be supplied from isolated power circuits meeting the requirements of 19-2.7.4.2. The design of the receptacle shall be such that sparks cannot be discharged into the chamber environment when the plug is inserted or withdrawn under electrical load. One of the following shall be satisfied to protect against inadvertent withdrawal of the plug under electrical load:

(a) The receptacle-plug combination shall be of a locking type, or

(b) The receptacle shall carry a label warning against unplugging under load, and the power cord shall be secured and protected against trip hazards from the movement of personnel in the chamber.

> The requirements of this section have been completely revised for 1999. The combined protective measures adopted by the technical committee are felt to provide a reasonable level of safety, namely, no sparking in the chamber, prudent measures against disconnecting under electrical load, and the requirement for power switches for connected devices. The committee added subparagraph (b) in recognition that electromedical equipment is built to very strict standards and could lose its approval listing if cords or plugs are modified or replaced.

**A-19-2.7.3.5** It should be recognized that interruption of any powered circuit, even of very low voltage, could produce a spark sufficient to ignite a flammable agent.

**19-2.7.3.6\* Switches.** Switches in the fixed wiring installation shall be waterproof. Switch make and break contacts shall be housed in the electrical enclosure so that no sparks from arcing contacts can reach the chamber environment.

> As with other sections of 19-2.7, this section has also been revised from earlier editions. Because Class I hazardous area measures are not required, it was felt that the measures cited will ensure that the area of electrical activity (such as switch arcing, if present) is adequately isolated from possible flammable materials in the chamber.

**A-19-2.7.3.6** It is recommended that all control switching functions inside the chamber be accomplished using intrinsically safe circuits that control power and control circuits located outside of the chamber.

**19-2.7.3.7\* Temperature.** No electrical equipment installed or used in the chamber shall have an operating surface temperature in excess of 85°C (185°F).

> This section was reworded for 1999 to clarify the meaning and intent of the requirement. In making this change, the committee considered data from the 1994 edition of NFPA 53, *Recommended Practice on Materials, Equipment, and Systems Used in Oxygen-Enriched Atmospheres* [8], in which a table showed a minimum hot plate ignition temperature of 365°C (689°F) for cotton sheeting in 6 ATA air. (See Table 19-1.) The recommendation of a minimum temperature of 85°C (185°F) provides a good safety factor for fault conditions and protection of chamber occupants from burn hazards in close chamber quarters.

**Table 19.1 Minimum Hot Plate Ignition Temperatures of Six Combustible Materials in Oxygen-Nitrogen Mixtures at Various Total Pressures**

| Material | Oxidant | Ignition Temperature, °C | | | |
|---|---|---|---|---|---|
| | | Total Pressure, atmospheres | | | |
| | | 1 | 2 | 3 | 6 |
| Cotton | Air | 465 | 440(425)† | 385 | 365 |
| sheeting | 42% O$_2$, 58% N$_2$ | 390 | 370 | 355 | 344 |
| | 100% O$_2$ | 360 | 345 | 340 | 325 |
| Cotton | Air | 575 | 520(510) | 485(350) | 370(325) |
| sheeting | 42% O$_2$, 58% N$_2$ | 390(350) | 335 | 315 | 295 |
| treated* | 100% O$_2$ | 310 | — | 300 | 285 |
| Conductive | Air | 480 | 395 | 370 | 375 |
| rubber | 42% O$_2$, 58% N$_2$ | 430 | 365 | 350 | 350 |
| sheeting | 100% O$_2$ | 360 | — | 345 | 345 |
| Paper drapes | Air | 470 | 455 | 425 | 405 |
| | 42% O$_2$, 58% N$_2$ | 430 | — | 400 | 370 |
| | 100% O$_2$ | 410 | — | 365 | 340 |
| Nomex fabric | Air | >600 | >600 | >600 | 560 |
| | 42% O$_2$, 58% N$_2$ | 550 | 540 | 510 | 495 |
| | 100% O$_2$ | 520 | 505 | 490 | 470 |
| Polyvinyl | air | >600 | — | 495 | 490 |
| chloride | 42% O$_2$, 58% N$_2$ | 575 | — | 370 | 350 |
| sheet | 100% O$_2$ | 390 | — | 350 | 325 |

*Cotton sheeting treated with Du Pont X-12 fire retardant; amount of retardant equal to 12 percent of cotton specimen weight.

†Values in parentheses indicate temperature at which material glowed.

Source: From the 1994 edition of NFPA 53, *Recommended Practice on Materials, Equipment, and Systems Used in Oxygen-Enriched Atmospheres.*

**A-19-2.7.3.7** It is the intention of this paragraph that equipment used in the chamber be incapable of igniting, by heating, any material or fabric that could come into contact with the surface of the equipment.

**19-2.7.3.8** There shall be no exposed live electrical parts other than those that are intrinsically safe or that constitute patient monitoring leads which are part of electromedical equipment meeting the requirements of 19-2.7.3.12.

This section was expanded for this 1999 edition to identify that electromedical devices are built to standards (e.g., ANSI/AAMI ESI, *Safe Limits for Electromedical Apparatus* [9]; UL 544, *Medical and Dental Equipment* [10]; IEC 60513 TR3,

*Fundamental Aspects of Safety Standards for Medical Electrical Equipment* [11])
that are intended for patient safety, that limit currents in patient leads to very low
energies incapable of igniting materials or fabrics in the chamber, and so should
not need the added protection from intrinsically safe design.

**19-2.7.3.9** Motors shall meet the requirements of NFPA 70, *National Electrical Code,* Article
501-8(a)(1) for the chamber pressure and oxygen concentration, or shall be of the totally
enclosed types meeting NFPA 70, Article 501-8(a)(2) or (3).

Explosionproof motors that are tested and approved for Class 1, Division 1, Group
C locations at maximum chamber pressure and oxygen concentration would be
allowed, but such equipment is currently not commercially available. Purged or
inert gas-filled motors that automatically deenergize when the protective measure
fails also would be allowed.

**19-2.7.3.10\* Lighting.** Lighting installed or used inside the chamber shall meet the temperature requirements of this section and be rated for a pressure of $1\frac{1}{2}$ times the chamber working
pressure. Permanently installed fixtures shall be rated and approved for Class I (Division 1
or 2) classified areas, shall have lens guards installed, and shall be located away from areas
where they would experience physical damage from the normal movement of people and
equipment. Ballasts and other energy storage components that are part of the lighting circuit
shall be installed outside the chamber in accordance with 19-2.7.1.4. Portable fixtures intended
for spot illumination shall be shatterproof or otherwise protected from physical damage.

This change clarifies that currently available explosionproof fixtures will protect
the lighting elements for permanent lighting installations. Earlier requirements for
pressure, shatterproof, and ballast location are retained from previous editions.

**A-19-2.7.3.10** It is strongly recommended that high-intensity local task lighting be accomplished using through-hull fiber optic lights. Many high-intensity lights will not meet the
temperature requirements specified in this paragraph.

**19-2.7.3.11\* Low-Voltage, Low-Power Equipment.** Sensors, signaling, alarm, communication, and remote control equipment installed or used in the chamber for operation of the
chamber shall meet the following criteria:

(a) Equipment shall be isolated from mains power by design of the power supply circuit,
by opto-isolation, or by other electronic isolation means.

(b) Circuits such as headset cables, sensor leads, and so forth, not enclosed as required
in 19-2.7.3.2, shall be either part of approved intrinsically safe equipment, or limited by
circuit design to no more than 28 V and 0.5 A under normal or circuit fault conditions.

(c) Chamber speakers shall be of a design in which the electrical circuitry and wiring
is completely enclosed. Electrical rating shall not exceed 28 V rms and 25 W.

(d) Battery operated, portable intercom headset units shall meet the requirements of 19-2.7.3.12(d) for battery operated devices.

**A-19-2.7.3.11** The requirement for isolation from mains supply in (a) is not the same as the requirement in 19-2.7.4.2 that circuits supplying power to portable utilization equipment inside the chamber be isolated, monitored, and alarmed.

It is recommended that intrinsically safe sensors and controls be used whenever possible.

The technical committee felt strongly that if circuits (e.g., patient leads, intercom headset cords, etc.) could not be isolated by physical containment, then their current should be limited by fusing, intrinsically safe design, or other means to a level incapable of igniting materials in the chamber. Limited data available to the committee suggested that something on the order of 1 J would provide a conservative basis for fire protection from materials like paper and cotton fabric in a pressurized air environment. This would represent a very large spark in a contact break scenario in a low-voltage circuit.

Years of experience have shown that low-voltage circuits are a lesser threat than 120-V circuits. If bulk materials, such as electrical insulation, circuit boards, and so forth, used in electrical devices are considered as potential fire sources, then overheating from a fault condition would be a more likely cause of ignition than would be electrical spark discharge. Technical reference data indicated that the minimum ignition temperature of materials similar to those used in electrical equipment exceeds 490°C (914°F). Modern low-voltage, low-power electronic equipment that uses low-power-consuming circuit elements should not generate sufficient ignition temperatures even under fault conditions.

**19-2.7.3.12\* Patient Care Related Electrical Appliances.** Portable patient care related electrical appliances used in a chamber shall meet, as a minimum, the following electrical safety requirements:

(a) The appliance shall be designed and constructed in accordance with Chapter 9, "Manufacturer Requirements."
(b) The electrical and mechanical integrity of the appliance is verified and documented through an ongoing maintenance program as required in Chapter 7, "Electrical Equipment."
(c) The appliance shall conform to the requirements of 19-2.7.3(a) and 19-2.7.3.7.
(d) Appliances that utilize oxygen shall contain provisions to prevent oxygen accumulation in the electrical portions of the equipment under normal and abnormal conditions.

**A-19-2.7.3.12** These requirements are only the minimum requirements for electrical safety. There are many other safety concerns that should be addressed on a case by case basis. Meeting the requirements of this section does not indicate that proper device performance will occur in the hyperbaric environment, and that the device will be safe for use with patients.

Electromedical equipment used in contact with or near patients is required to meet stringent standards for leakage currents under various conditions and even under fault conditions. The requirements of Chapter 19 are put in force to maintain patient safety and prescribe maximum leakage currents (10 mA), which is well below that which could precipitate a fire in a Class A chamber. The administrative and maintenance procedures that are already in place should provide reasonable assurance that equipment is maintained in a safe operating condition.

The primary hazards that come from the use of batteries in the hyperbaric environment come from short circuiting the terminals, which in turn causes heat and spark generation, and from improper or faulty charging of rechargeable batteries that can generate excessive heat and off-gassing that can lead to pressure buildup within the battery. The requirement for battery enclosures should preclude the risk of short-circuiting, and prohibiting battery changing and charging in the chamber should eliminate a major battery hazard.

### 19-2.7.3.12.1 Battery-Operated Devices.

(a) Batteries shall be fully enclosed and secured within the equipment enclosure.
(b) Batteries shall be suitable for the chamber operating pressure, and be of a sealed type that does not off-gas during normal use.
(c) Batteries or battery-operated equipment shall not undergo charging while located in the chamber. Batteries shall not be changed on equipment located in the chamber.
(d) The equipment electrical rating shall not exceed 12 V and 48 W.

### 19-2.7.3.12.2 Cord-Connected Devices.

(a) All portable, cord-connected equipment shall have an on–off power switch.
(b) The equipment electrical rating shall not exceed 120 V and 2 A.

*Exception: Cord-connected devices not meeting the requirements of (b) shall be permitted if the electrical portions of the equipment are inert-gas purged.*

(c) The plug of cord-connected devices shall not be used to interrupt power to the device.

### 19-2.7.4 Grounding and Ground Fault Protection.

**19-2.7.4.1** The chamber shall be grounded according to the requirements of NFPA 70, *National Electrical Code,* Article 250, Grounding. Resistance between the chamber and ground point shall not exceed 1 ohm.

Chamber grounding is necessary for the following reasons:

(a) Electrical equipment is connected to it.
(b) It is necessary for the proper functioning of the isolated power system.
(c) Most intrinsically safe equipment requires a resistance to ground on the order of a few ohms or less.

**19-2.7.4.2** In health care facilities, electrical power circuits located within the chamber shall be supplied from an ungrounded electrical system equipped with a line isolation monitor with appropriate signal lamps and audible alarms. Such circuits shall meet the requirements of NFPA 70, Article 517-160, Isolated Power Systems, and 517-160(b), Line Isolation Monitor. Branch circuits shall not exceed 125 V or 15 A.

> Although this paragraph refers to chambers in health care facilities, the requirement applies to internal power circuits located in all chambers, regardless of the installation site. The voltage or amperage limits were added to the 1999 edition because the technical committee felt there should be restrictions on running large, portable electrical loads in the chamber. The limits set should meet the reasonable needs of any chamber operator for a power receptacle.

**19-2.7.4.3** Wiring located both inside and outside the chamber, which serves line level circuits and equipment located inside the chamber, shall meet the grounding and bonding requirements of NFPA 70, Article 501-16.

> This requirement for grounding and bonding is intended to ensure both of the following:
>
> (a) The equipment ground circuit for equipment used in the chamber is reliable given the hazard classification of chambers.
> (b) A reliable ground path is maintained for the proper functioning of the line isolation monitor of the isolated power system.

### 19-2.7.5  Wiring Outside the Chamber.

**19-2.7.5.1** Those electrical components that must remain functional for the safe termination of a dive following activation of the room sprinkler system shall be enclosed in waterproof housing.

> Previous requirements that all conduits outside chambers be rigid metal have been found to be overly restrictive. Waterproofing is considered sufficient.

**19-2.7.5.1.1** All associate conduits shall be waterproof and shall meet the requirements of NFPA 70, *National Electrical Code*. Such conduits shall be equipped with approved drains.

**19-2.7.5.2\*** All other electrical devices outside the chamber shall meet the requirements of NFPA 70.

**A-19-2.7.5.2** It is necessary that these circuits be protected from exposure to water from the room sprinkler system protecting the chamber housing in the event of a fire in the vicinity of the chamber while it is in operation.

**19-2.7.6 Additional Wiring and Equipment Requirements inside Class B Chambers.** The requirements in this section shall apply to Class B chambers whether they are pressurized with oxygen or with air.

The new sentence was added to the 1999 edition to clarify the restrictive environment for additional equipment inside Class B chambers regardless of the pressurization gas. The use of additional equipment inside Class B chambers is generally limited due to the fact that there is usually no inside medical attendant to control the equipment inside the chamber, there is no interior fire suppression system, and there is little room for extra equipment.

**19-2.7.6.1** Electrical equipment inside Class B chambers shall be restricted to communication functions and patient physiological monitoring leads. Circuits shall be designed to limit the electrical energy to wire leads into the chamber under normal or fault conditions to no more than 28 V and ½ W. Communication wires shall be protected from physical damage and from coming into contact with flammable materials in the chamber by appropriate barriers or conduit. Patient monitoring leads shall be part of approved electromedical apparatus meeting the requirements in 19-2.7.3.12.

The restriction for using regular line-powered equipment in Class B chambers is retained for the 1999 edition. The new material was added in recognition of the fact that what happens to a circuit during fault conditions is as important as how it responds in normal operating conditions. Additionally, protection of fixed wiring is important to prevent electrical faults. Patient leads, and so forth, must meet stringent requirements referenced in 19-2.7.3.12.

**19-2.7.6.2** Lighting inside the chamber shall be supplied from external sources.

A typical Class B chamber is constructed predominantly of clear acrylic so light transmission into the chamber is usually sufficient. However, there are Class B chamber designs that do not use clear acrylic pressure tubes as a major component of the pressure boundary. Users of these alternative Class B chamber designs are referred to 19.2.3.1 and its subparagraphs for guidance on the use of external light sources.

**19-2.7.6.3** No electrical circuit in a Class B chamber shall operate at a temperature exceeding 60°C (140°F).

The technical committee felt that is was important to address the fire safety factor for circuitry in Class B chambers. There is good data in Table 19.1 (Table 5-3.2.8 from NFPA 53, *Recommended Practice on Materials, Equipment, and Systems Used in Oxygen-Enriched Atmospheres* [8]) that shows a minimum hot plate ignition temperature of 300°C (572°F) for treated cotton sheeting in 3 ATA oxygen. The recommended 60°C (140°F) temperature was felt to provide a conservative safety margin. Patient burn safety in a restricted space was also a consideration in setting this limit.

## 19-2.8 Communications and Monitoring.

This section addresses only communication and monitoring. Section 19-2.7 addresses electrical wiring and equipment.

Ordinary communication equipment is generally not suitable for use within hyperbaric chambers because of potential sparking from switches or arcing from microphones. Unless measures are taken to control these possibilities, a fire can occur in the chamber. This section provides guidance for the mitigation of that hazard.

Prior to the 1993 edition of NFPA 99, communication equipment in hyperbaric chambers was required to be intrinsically safe and to operate on less than 5 V. The requirements for intrinsic safety were, and still are, valid, but the 5-V criterion was found to be unnecessary for intrinsically safe devices. Exceptions to this 5-V requirement were allowed in the 1984 edition after the National Aeronautics and Space Administration conducted fire tests with intrinsically safe microphones that operated at 28 V. This section incorporates this and other tests and experiences.

### 19-2.8.1 General.

**19-2.8.1.1** Detectors, sensors, transducers, and communications equipment located inside the chamber shall meet the requirements of 19-2.7.3.11. Wiring methods in the chamber shall meet the applicable requirements in 19-2.7.3.

Every effort has been made to place "electrical" requirements, such as electrical wiring, in their appropriate section (see 19-2.7) instead of in the communication section.

**19-2.8.1.2** Control equipment, power amplifiers, output transformers, and monitors associated with communications and monitoring equipment shall be installed outside the chamber or shall otherwise meet the requirements of 19-2.7.3.11.

The portions of control and/or monitoring equipment that draw large currents must be kept outside the chamber. The prohibition also covers monitoring displays with oscilloscopes because these systems might implode under the increased pressures created in hyperbaric chambers.

### 19-2.8.2* Intercommunications.

**A-19-2.8.2** Intercommunications equipment is mandatory for safe operation of a hyperbaric facility.

**19-2.8.2.1*** An intercommunication system shall connect all personnel compartments (locks), main compartments (locks), and the chamber operator's control console.

This paragraph clearly indicates that there is to be communication between all portions of the hyperbaric chamber and the chamber operator(s), including pass-through locks that may be only temporarily occupied. The recommendations for multichannel systems also allow for medical or chamber personnel to conduct private conversations that may be sensitive to patients or other occupants.

**A-19-2.8.2.1** It is recommended that multiple compartment (lock) Class A chambers be equipped with multiple channel systems, and that, in addition, a sound-powered telephone or surveillance microphone be furnished.

Class A chambers of the configuration described are capable of being used for operations where substantial decompression obligations can be incurred. A back-up communication system for these types of chambers is a long-standing design practice and is considered essential to overall facility safety.

**19-2.8.2.2** Oxygen mask microphones shall be approved intrinsically safe at the maximum proposed pressure and 95 ± 5 percent oxygen.

The standard allows the use of oxygen mask microphones that meet all these criteria. It is important to recognize that devices that prove safe in oxygen at atmospheric pressure could possibly be unsafe at hyperbaric chamber pressures. Therefore, any device that is to be used in a hyperbaric chamber must be tested for that particular use.

**19-2.8.3** Automatic fire detection equipment, when used, shall meet the applicable requirements in 19-2.7.3 and 19-2.5.4.

As indicated earlier, any fire detection equipment must meet the general standards for wiring in hyperbaric chambers, as delineated in 19-2.7.3.

**19-2.8.4 Combustible Gas Detection.**

The use of potentially flammable materials is strictly controlled in other parts of Chapter 19 (e.g., 19-2.4.1.2). An integral part of the exception to 19-3.1.5.2 is the monitoring of the concentration of combustible gases in the hyperbaric chamber by a suitable device.

Combustible gas monitoring, along with ventilation, is the most effective way of preventing a hazardous gas mixture from occurring inside the chamber when gases are used. The committee believes that the 10 percent *lower explosive limit (LEL)* alarm level will provide sufficient advance warning of a problem so that effective measures to prevent further buildup of gas concentrations to flammable concentration levels can be taken. The LEL for a given gas is essentially unchanged for an increase in atmospheric pressure.

**19-2.8.4.1** The chamber atmosphere shall be continuously monitored for combustible gas concentrations whenever any volatile agents *(see 19-2.4.1.2)* are used in the chamber. The monitor shall be set to provide audible and visual alarms at 10 percent lower explosion limit (LEL) for the particular gas used.

### 19-2.8.5  Oxygen Monitoring.

**19-2.8.5.1**  Oxygen levels shall be continuously monitored in any chamber in which nitrogen or other diluent gas is added to the chamber to reduce the volumetric concentration of oxygen in the atmosphere (saturation operations). Audible and visual alarms shall indicate unsafe low oxygen partial pressure in the chamber.

> In any chamber where the oxygen levels are possibly increasing because of the addition of oxygen, or where the levels are reducing in concentration because of the addition of other gases, the oxygen level should be monitored at all times to provide a warning in the event of unintended deviations from normal, desired levels.

**19-2.8.5.2**  Oxygen levels shall be continuously monitored in Class A chambers when breathing mixtures containing in excess of 21 percent oxygen by volume are being breathed by patients or attendants and/or any flammable agents are present in the chamber. Audible and visual alarms shall indicate volumetric oxygen concentrations in excess of 23.5 percent.

> Under no circumstances are Class A chambers to be operated with interior oxygen levels in excess of 23.5 percent. When measured oxygen levels approach 23.5 percent, chamber operators should increase chamber ventilation and inspect the components of the oxygen delivery system (regulator, breathing masks, oxygen hoods, etc.) for leaks. If leaks cannot be stopped and the increased ventilation rate does not bring the oxygen level to below 23.5 percent, chamber operations should be terminated.
>
> Another factor making the intrinsic safety approach workable (see 19-2.7.3) is that of keeping the oxygen concentration in the chamber from rising above that for normal air.
>
> It should be noted that when no flammable agents (in either liquid, gaseous, or solid form) are present inside the chamber, one of the four elements of the fire tetrahedron required for combustion, namely fuel, is absent. As a result, variations in oxygen concentration do not impact combustion taking place.

**19-2.8.6  Carbon Dioxide Monitoring.**  The chamber atmosphere shall be monitored during saturation operations whenever ventilation is not used *(see 19-2.4.1.1, Exception)* to ensure that carbon dioxide levels do not exceed safe levels.

> The requirement for carbon dioxide monitoring recognizes that in unventilated chambers, the $CO_2$ concentration could become dangerous without warning.
>
> Alarm levels are dependent on the specific situation, so they are not listed. They are left to the discretion of the chamber safety officer.

**19-2.8.7\* Chamber Gas Supply Monitoring.** The air supply of Class A and Class B chambers shall be sampled periodically for concentrations of carbon monoxide. The frequency of such monitoring shall depend on the location of the air intake relative to potential sources of contamination. Air supplied from oil-lubricated compressors capable of contaminating the compressor output due to wear or failure shall be continuously monitored for volatilized hydrocarbons as well as carbon monoxide at a location downstream from the oil filter when the compressors are running. As a minimum, the air supplied to Class A and B chambers shall meet the requirements for medical air as defined in Chapter 2.

> This requirement recognizes that there are two potential sources of contamination of the air supply to a hyperbaric chamber. The first is the ambient air itself. This can usually be expected to be relatively stable, but periodic testing will alert the chamber operators if conditions are changing. The other source of contamination can be the air-compression equipment. If oil-lubricated compressors are used, the potential for the failure of the seals or air purification system exists, even though devices can be inserted in the discharge line to filter the air. In the event of this type of failure, a rapid contamination of the air supply would be expected. For that reason, the use of oil-lubricated compressors is discouraged. However, if oil-lubricated compressors are used, they must be monitored to ensure that the air supply does not become contaminated.
>
> The title of 19-2.8.7 was changed for the 1999 edition in recognition that the requirements of this section cover more than just air; the section covers other gas supplies as well.

**A-19-2.8.7** It is recommended that air be sampled at the air intake location at times when the intake air is likely to have maximum impurities (e.g., when vehicles or stationary engines upwind of the intake are running).

Air supplied to chambers periodically pressured with pure oxygen could need to meet more stringent requirements with respect to air quality.

> Since the probability of contamination of the compressed air supply will vary from site to site, the chamber safety director should decide the frequency of sampling. For a location with a high probability of contamination [and this would include an air system using an oil-lubricated compressor(s)], continuous monitoring when the compressor(s) is running is recommended.
>
> If oil-lubricated compressors are used, the compressor output gas needs to be continuously monitored for volatized hydrocarbons and carbon monoxide. With proper maintenance procedures and state-of-the-art purification systems, modern oil-lubricated compressors have demonstrated their ability to produce compressed air that meets hyperbaric air quality standards. However, positive steps need to be taken to ensure that output air will not be contaminated as a result of any failure condition.
>
> For this edition, the technical committee clarified the minimum air quality standards without making reference to the specific grade of air.

**19-2.8.8\*** Electrical monitoring equipment used inside the chamber shall comply with the applicable requirements of 19-2.7.

**A-19-2.8.8** It is recommended that information about the status of an anesthetized or otherwise monitored patient be transmitted to the inside chamber attendants via the intercommunications system. As an alternative, the monitor indicators can be placed adjacent to a chamber viewport (or viewports) for direct observation by inside personnel.

**19-2.8.9** Closed-circuit TV monitoring of the chamber interior shall be employed for chamber operators who do not have direct visual contact of the chamber interior from their normal operating location.

Closed-circuit TV monitoring is a standard industry practice.

### 19-2.9 Other Equipment and Fixtures.

**19-2.9.1** All furniture permanently installed in the hyperbaric chamber shall be grounded.

**19-2.9.2** Exhaust from all classes of chambers shall be piped outside of the building, the point of exit being clear of all neighboring hazards and clear of possible reentry of exhaust gases into the building, and protected by a grille or fence of at least 2-ft (0.6-m) radius from the exhaust port. A protective grille or fence is not required when the exhaust is above the building height.

External exhaust requirements were extended to Class C chambers (thereby affecting all chambers) because potential health hazards exist as a result of the exhausts from all classes of chambers. For Class C chambers that are pressurized with 100 percent oxygen, the external exhaust requirement now reduces the fire risk associated with elevated oxygen concentrations building up in the room or rooms housing a Class C chamber.

**19-2.9.3** The supply piping for all air, oxygen or other breathing mixtures from certified commercially supplied flasks shall be provided with a particulate filter of at least 10 microns or finer. The filter shall meet the construction requirements of ANSI/ASME PVHO-1, and be located as close as practical to the source.

This section was added to the 1999 edition because the technical committee was informed that particulate matter was coming out of flasks that had been previously commercially certified. This requirement was added to help reduce the fire risk in piping systems.

## 19-3 Administration and Maintenance

### 19-3.1 General.

**19-3.1.1 Purpose.** Section 19-3 contains requirements for administration and maintenance that shall be followed as an adjunct to physical precautions specified in Section 19-2.

It cannot be stressed strongly enough that even the best systems in the world can be rendered unsafe if they are not checked regularly and maintained. Such checking and maintenance includes careful monitoring of written controls. such as written safety procedures, to ensure that they remain current. This practice is in addition to adherence to the controls themselves and to the regular inspection of the physical facility.

The National Board of Diving and Hyperbaric Medicine Technology now offers board certification in hyperbaric technology. This rigorous examination recognizes superior knowledge of all aspects of hyperbaric operations (hyperbaric physiology, medical treatment rationale and procedures, effects of pressure changes, hyperbaric safety and emergency procedures, hyperbaric operations, etc.). As more hyperbaric operators pursue certification, overall professional skill levels will increase. As the technical level increases, the quality of the administration, operation, and maintenance of hyperbaric facilities will improve.

**19-3.1.2 Recognition of Hazards.** The hazards involved in the use of hyperbaric facilities can be mitigated successfully only when all of the areas of hazard are fully recognized by all personnel and when the physical protection provided is complete and is augmented by attention to detail by all personnel of administration and maintenance having any responsibility for the functioning of the hyperbaric facility. The nature and degree of these hazards are outlined in Appendix C-19 of this document and shall be reviewed by the safety director. Since Section 19-3 is expected to be used as a text by those responsible for the mitigation of hazards of hyperbaric facilities, the requirements set forth herein are frequently accompanied by explanatory text.

**19-3.1.3 Responsibility.**

This section sets up a four-point safety check over the hyperbaric chamber and related support systems. The governing body of the institution where the chamber is housed must set a firm policy to ensure safe operation of the chamber. The management of the institution, in concert with the technical staff of the chamber, must develop procedures for the safe operation of the chamber. The technical operating staff then is responsible for the correct execution of the procedures. Finally, licensing and accrediting agencies must periodically review all three (policy, procedures, and compliance) to ensure the safety of patients and staff who use hyperbaric chambers. At present, more emphasis is needed from licensing and accrediting agencies to ensure compliance with applicable hyperbaric safety procedures and standards.

**19-3.1.3.1** Personnel having responsibility for the hyperbaric facility, and those responsible for licensing, accrediting, or approving institutions or other facilities in which hyperbaric installations are employed, shall establish and enforce appropriate programs to fulfill the provisions of this chapter.

In the interest of maintaining high levels of hyperbaric safety, accrediting agencies for health care organizations are encouraged to become more involved in the application of this standard.

**19-3.1.3.2\*** A safety director shall be designated in charge of all hyperbaric equipment. The safety director shall work closely with facility management personnel and the hyperbaric physician(s) to establish procedures for safe operation and maintenance of the hyperbaric facility. He or she shall make necessary recommendations for departmental safety policies and procedures. The safety director shall have the authority to restrict or remove any potentially hazardous supply or equipment items from the chamber.

Although it is not the intent of the technical committee to establish a specific job description for a safety director, the committee feels strongly that the safety director position is one of the most responsible in any hyperbaric facility. Note that a safety director is *required* for any hyperbaric facility, regardless of the type of chambers (Class A, B, or C) used in the facility.

**A-19-3.1.3.2** The complexity of hyperbaric chambers is such that one person should be designated chamber operator, such as one in a position of responsible authority. Before starting a hyperbaric run, this person should acknowledge, in writing, in an appropriate log, the purpose of the run or test, duties of all personnel involved, and a statement that he or she is satisfied with the condition of all equipment. Exceptions should be itemized in the statement.

Safety, operational, and maintenance criteria of other organizations are published, for example, the Undersea & Hyperbaric Medical Society Safety Committee documents and the Compressed Gas Association pamphlets, and should be reviewed by the safety director. The safety director should serve on the health care facility safety committee.

Guidance on how to set up a comprehensive hyperbaric safety program, recommended job descriptions and responsibilities for specific positions, minimum training and staffing requirements, and operational and maintenance procedures are readily available from organizations such as the Undersea and Hyperbaric Medical Society, trade associations, and so forth. Directors of hyperbaric facilities are strongly encouraged to work with the designated safety director to consider these guidelines in setting up an overall safety program tailored to the need of the specific facility.

Having the safety director serve on the medical facility safety committee recognizes the unique safety needs of a hyperbaric facility and helps establish the legitimate place of the hyperbaric safety program in the overall medical facility effort.

**19-3.1.3.3\*** The ultimate responsibility for the care and safety of patients (in the case of a hospital) and personnel (in any institution) is that of the governing board. Hence it is incumbent upon that body to insist that adequate rules and regulations with respect to practices and conduct in hyperbaric facilities, including qualifications and training of hyperbaric personnel, be adopted by the medical or administrative staff of the institution, and that adequate regulations for inspection and maintenance are in use by the administrative, maintenance, and ancillary (and in the case of a hospital, nursing and other professional) personnel.

> It is important to remember that, while members of the governing board might not personally write safety procedures, the board must ensure that they are written and followed. The requirement for the governing board to consider qualifications and training of hyperbaric personnel has been added to this edition. Guidance from professional organizations such as the Undersea and Hyperbaric Medical Society is available to assist in this matter. The governing board is also encouraged to support continuing medical education needs of hyperbaric technicians, especially in areas such as safety.

**A-19-3.1.3.3** It is recommended that training of hyperbaric chamber personnel be closely monitored, following the guidelines and publications of the Undersea & Hyperbaric Medical Society, Baromedical Nurses Association, and the National Board of Diving and Hyperbaric Medical Technology.

> There is a growing recognition of the need for national standards to define the minimum training requirements for hyperbaric personnel, regardless of their specialty. Certification in hyperbaric technology is validation that a person has attained a higher level of knowledge in various aspects of clinical hyperbaric medicine and technology. All hyperbaric staff are encouraged to pursue certification. Many facilities now require that their technical staff be certified, a trend that is expected to increase.
>
> The Undersea and Hyperbaric Medical Society, the National Board of Diving and Hyperbaric Technology, and the Baromedical Nurses Association maintain listings for courses that are available for initial training and continuing education.

**19-3.1.3.4** By virtue of its responsibility for the professional conduct of members of the medical staff of the health care facility, the organized medical staff shall adopt adequate regulations with respect to the use of hyperbaric facilities located in health care facilities *(see C-19.2 and C-19.3)* and through its formal organization shall ascertain that these regulations are regularly adhered to. The safety director shall be included in the planning phase of these regulations.

> The intent of this paragraph is to require the hyperbaric facility safety director to be involved with the medical staff to develop appropriate regulations for the safe and efficient operation of a hyperbaric facility.

**19-3.1.3.5\*** In meeting its responsibilities for safe practices in hyperbaric facilities, the administration of the facility shall adopt or correlate regulations and standard operating procedures to ensure that both the physical qualities and the operating maintenance methods pertaining to hyperbaric facilities meet the standards set in this chapter. The controls adopted shall cover the conduct of personnel in and around hyperbaric facilities and the apparel and footwear allowed. They shall cover periodic inspection of static-dissipating materials and of all electrical equipment, including testing of ground contact indicators. Electrical, monitoring, life support, protection, and ventilating arrangements in the hyperbaric chamber shall be inspected and tested regularly.

**A-19-3.1.3.5** In the case of a hyperbaric facility located in a hospital, hospital licensing and other approval bodies, in meeting their responsibilities to the public, should include in their inspections not only compliance with requirements for physical installations in hyperbaric facilities, but also compliance with the requirements set forth in Section 19-3 of this chapter.

> This section has been retained to underscore the importance of the leadership of the medical facility and the management of the hyperbaric facility itself working together to plan and implement the hyperbaric medicine program. The more widely known what the requirements for hyperbaric facility safety are, the more comprehensive the program will be. Also, administrators are more likely to support necessary hyperbaric requirements if they clearly understand the need.
>
> Accrediting agencies should be aware of the requirements for both facility installation and continued safe operation found in this standard and should survey for hyperbaric facility compliance.

### 19-3.1.4 Rules and Regulations.

**19-3.1.4.1\* General.** The administrative, technical, and professional staffs shall jointly consider and agree upon necessary rules and regulations for the control of personnel concerned with the use of hyperbaric facilities. Upon adoption, rules and regulations shall be prominently posted in and around the hyperbaric chamber. Positive measures are necessary to acquaint all personnel with the rules and regulations established and to assume enforcement. Training and discipline are mandatory.

**A-19-3.1.4.1** It is recommended that all personnel, including trainees and those involved in the operation and maintenance of hyperbaric facilities, and including professional personnel and (in the case of hospitals) others involved in the direct care of patients undergoing hyperbaric therapy, be familiar with this chapter. Personnel concerned should maintain proficiency in the matters of life and fire safety by periodic review of this chapter, as well as any other pertinent material.

> Prior to the 1999 edition, this section simply recommended that administrators, technical personnel, and medical personnel work together to establish specific rules and regulations for control of personnel. This edition now requires this joint planning.
>
> It must be stressed that merely writing emergency procedures is not enough. Procedures must be practiced regularly to ensure that chamber personnel will react quickly and appropriately when called upon.

**19-3.1.4.2** The medical director of hyperbaric medicine shall work with the safety/technical director to establish the minimum staff qualifications, experience, and compliment based on the number and type of hyperbaric chambers in use, their maximum treatment capacity, and the type of hyperbaric therapy normally provided.

This requirement, new to the 1999 edition, was added to make sure that the medical and safety/technical directors work closely together to determine the minimum staffing requirements and qualifications necessary to safely operate and maintain the hyperbaric facility. Factors such as the type and number of chambers, anticipated patient treatment load, potential medical severity of the patient(s), and so forth, should be considered in making this determination. Guidance from organizations such as the Undersea and Hyperbaric Medical Society, the American College of Hyperbaric Medicine, the Baromedical Nurses Association, the National Board of Diving and Hyperbaric Technology is available for review.

**19-3.1.4.3** All personnel, including those involved in maintenance and repair of the facility, shall become familiar with emergency equipment — its purposes, applications, operation, and limitations.

It is important to train *all* personnel involved, as it is impossible to know in advance who will be available in an emergency or what special conditions the actual emergency will impose on the facility and staff.

**19-3.1.4.4** Emergency procedures best suited to the needs of the individual facility shall be established. All personnel shall become thoroughly familiar with these procedures and the methods of implementing them. Individual circumstances dictate whether such familiarization can best be afforded through the medium of a procedure manual. Personnel shall be trained to safely decompress occupants when all powered equipment has been rendered inoperative.

These procedures have been upgraded in earlier editions from recommendations to requirements because they are critical to the prevention of a fire mishap and the quick response to a fire if one should occur.

In the past, most of the training for proper decompression was provided to operators of Class A chambers. However, there are Class B chambers capable of air pressurization that can subject occupants to decompression requirements. Accordingly, operators of these types of hyperbaric systems should be thoroughly trained in decompression procedures.

**19-3.1.4.5** A suggested outline for emergency action in the case of fire is contained in C-19.2.

**19-3.1.4.6*** Fire training drills shall be carried out at regular intervals.

**A-19-3.1.4.6** A calm reaction (without panic) to an emergency situation can be expected only if the above recommendations are familiar to and rehearsed by all concerned.

Operators of all classes of hyperbaric chambers are strongly encouraged to actively involve their local fire department in periodic fire emergency training sessions. Such collaborative efforts are vital to help orient nonhyperbaric specialists to the unique requirements of hyperbaric facilities.

**19-3.1.4.7** During chamber operations with occupant(s) in a chamber, the operator shall be physically present, and shall maintain visual or audible contact with the control panel or the chamber occupant(s).

Mishaps have occurred during chamber operations when the operator was not present. The technical committee feels strongly that the physical presence of a chamber operator should not be compromised. Clear visual and audible contact with chamber occupants is essential to maintaining safety.

### 19-3.1.5  General Requirements.

**19-3.1.5.1  Open Flames and Hot Objects.**  Smoking, open flames, hot objects, and ultraviolet sources, which would cause premature operation of flame detectors, when installed, shall be prohibited from hyperbaric facilities, both inside and outside, and in the immediate vicinity of the chamber. The immediate vicinity of the chamber is defined as the general surrounding area from which activation of the flame detector can occur.

**19-3.1.5.2  Flammable Gases and Liquids.**

(a) Flammable agents (including devices such as laboratory burners employing bottled or natural gas and cigarette lighters) shall be forbidden inside the chamber and from the proximity of the compressor intake.

*Exception: For Class A chambers, flammable agents used for patient care, such as alcohol swabs, parenteral alcohol-based pharmaceuticals, and topical creams, shall be permitted in the chamber if the following conditions are met:*

*1.  Such use is approved by the safety director, or other authority having jurisdiction.*

*2.\* The quantities of such agents are limited so that they are incapable of releasing sufficient flammable vapor into the chamber atmosphere to exceed the LEL for the material. A safety factor shall be included to account for the localized concentrations, stratification, and the absence of ventilation.*

**A-19-3.1.5.2(a), Exception No. 2.**  Allowable quantities for the exception can be determined from the chamber volume, flammable agent vapor density, and lower explosive limit (LEL). Experience has shown that increased pressure has little effect on LEL for a given flammable gas and oxygen concentration. A safety factor of 10 is recommended. Flammable liquids should be confined to nonbreakable, nonspill containers.

***Example of Limiting Quantity of Flammable Agent Substance: Isopropyl alcohol (2-propanol)***

LEL = 2%/vol. (irrespective of chamber pressure)

Vapor density: 2.1 relative to air

Liquid density: 786 g/L

Air density: 0.075 lb/ft$^3$ at STP

The limiting case occurs at the lowest ambient pressure, that is, 1 atmosphere:

$$\text{Alcohol vapor density at LEL} = 0.02 \times 2.1 \times 0.075$$
$$= 0.00315 \text{ lb/ft}^3$$
$$= 1.43 \text{ g/ft}^3$$

For a relatively small 500-ft$^3$ chamber, this implies:

$$1.43 \times 500 = 715 \text{ g alcohol vapor at LEL}$$

Using a safety factor of 10 to account for uneven vapor concentrations gives 71.5 g = 91 ml alcohol.

One could conclude that even 90 ml alcohol is more than would be needed for most any medical procedure. The above calculation also does not account for the mitigating effect of ventilation.

Many "inert" halogenated compounds have been found to act explosively in the presence of metals, even under normal atmospheric conditions, despite the fact that the halogen compound itself does not ignite in oxygen, or, in the case of solids such as polytetrafluoroethylene, is self-extinguishing. Apparently these materials are strong oxidizers whether as gases, liquids (solvents, greases), or solids (electrical insulation, fabric, or coatings). Some halogenated hydrocarbons that will not burn in the presence of low-pressure oxygen will ignite and continue to burn in high-pressure oxygen. Customarily, Class A chambers maintain internal oxygen concentration that does not exceed 23.5 percent.

Parts of this chapter deal with the elements required to be incorporated into the structure of the chamber to reduce the possibility of electrostatic spark discharges, which are a possible cause of ignition in hyperbaric atmospheres. The elimination of static charges is dependent on the vigilance of administrative activities in materials, purchase, maintenance supervision, and periodic inspection and testing. It cannot be emphasized too strongly that an incomplete chain of precautions generally will increase the electrostatic hazard. For example, conductive flooring can contribute to the hazard unless all personnel wear conductive shoes, all objects in the room are electrically continuous with the floor, and humidity is maintained.

*3. The oxygen monitoring requirement of 19-2.8.5.2 is observed.*

(b) No flammable liquids, gases, or vapors shall be permitted inside any Class B chamber.

Subparagraph (a) was extensively revised in 1993 because of some confusion as to whether and how much of certain flammable agents could be used inside a hyperbaric chamber.

Previously, the exception allowed the introduction of small quantities of flammable agents, such as alcohol swabs, after "approval by a board of competent authorities." The exception was extensively reworked during the 1993 revision to ensure that approvals are provided by the safety director rather than the vague term *board of competent authorities.* Carefully defined quantitative methods were provided to determine what a safe limit is for these materials.

The prohibition of *any* flammable liquid, gas, or vapor in Class B chambers [per subparagraph (b) added in 1996] is singled out due to the extreme hazard it presents in an oxygen-enriched environment. As a further preventive measure, all operators should aggressively prevent the introduction of static-producing materials in Class B chambers.

### 19-3.1.5.3 Personnel.

(a) The number of occupants of the chamber shall be kept to the minimum number necessary to carry out the procedure.

(b) Antistatic procedures as directed by the safety director shall be employed whenever atmospheres containing more than 23.5 percent oxygen by volume are used.

This requirement indicates that the primary responsibility for the special requirements of each chamber should be addressed by the safety director, who is familiar with the chamber use. It also means that operators of Class B chambers need to prevent static-producing materials in the chamber when oxygen levels exceed 23.5 percent.

(c) In Class A and Class B chambers with atmospheres containing more than 23.5 percent oxygen by volume, electrical grounding of the patient shall be ensured by the provision of a high-impedance conductive pathway in contact with the patients skin.

The intent of subparagraphs (b) and (c) is to minimize the buildup of static electricity in chambers, while at the same time allowing medical procedures to be carried out.

There are various methods of grounding the patient to the frame of the chamber. Conductive material that meets the conductivity requirements in Annex 2, "Flammable Anesthetizing Locations" would be acceptable. The main point is that patients must be grounded to prevent static electricity buildup.

In the 1996 edition, the technical committee changed the requirement for a "conductive strap" to a "conductive pathway" because the original requirement was considered too restrictive. Patients can be adequately grounded using other methods such as conductive mattress covers.

(d) Because of the possibility of percussion sparks, shoes having ferrous nails that make contact with the floor shall not be permitted to be worn in Class A chambers.

### 19-3.1.5.4 Textiles.

(a) Silk, wool, or synthetic textile materials shall not be permitted in Class A or Class B chambers unless the fabric meets the flame resistant requirements of 19-3.1.5.4(d).

These materials, unless treated, are strong producers of static electricity. This restriction includes Class B chambers because the same hazards exist in both chambers.

(b) Garments fabricated of 100 percent cotton or an antistatic blend of cotton and a polyester fabric shall be permitted in Class A chambers equipped with fire protection as specified in 19.2.5, and in Class B chambers.

This paragraph (revised in 1993 and again in 1996) lists specifically what types of fabrics are permissible inside a chamber. The permissibility includes Class A chambers that meet the fire protection requirements in 19-2.5. It is important that these changes be noted, and followed, by all chamber safety directors.

If antistatic blends of cotton and polyester fabric are used in Class B chambers, operators should periodically evaluate the fabric's continued ability to remain static free. If an antistatic condition cannot be ensured, the garment needs to be removed from hyperbaric service and clearly marked NOT FOR HYPERBARIC CHAMBER USE or some similar warning.

(c) Suture material, alloplastic devices, bacterial barriers, surgical dressings, and biologic interfaces of otherwise prohibited materials shall be permitted to be used at the discretion of the physician or surgeon in charge with the concurrence of the safety director. This permission shall be stated in writing for all prohibited materials employed *(see A-19-3.1.3.2).*

(d) Where flame resistance is specified, the fabric shall meet the requirements set forth for the small-scale test in NFPA 701, *Standard Methods of Fire Tests for Flame-Resistant Textiles and Films*, except that the test shall be performed in an atmosphere equivalent to the maximum oxygen concentration and pressure proposed for the chamber.

NFPA 701, *Standard Methods of Fire Tests for Flame Propagation of Textiles and Films* [12], neither considers nor addresses the hyperbaric environment. Thus, the exception clause is included to ensure that textiles remain flame resistant at the oxygen concentration and pressure to be experienced.

**19-3.1.5.5** All chamber personnel shall wear garments of the overall or jumpsuit type, completely covering all skin areas possible, and as tightfitting as possible.

**19-3.1.5.6\*** The use of flammable hair sprays, hair oils, and skin oils shall be forbidden for all chamber occupants-patients as well as personnel. Whenever possible, patients shall be stripped of all clothing, particularly if it is contaminated by dirt, grease, or solvents, and then reclothed as specified in 19-3.1.5.5. All cosmetics, lotions, and oils shall be removed from the patient's body and hair.

Patients should never be allowed to enter the chamber in regular clothing. Also, all clothing patients will wear inside the chamber should be inspected to ensure that no hazardous items such as cigarette lighters or liquid-fueled pocket warmers that could serve as an ignition source are taken into the chamber. Although it adds time and can require dedicated staff, the act of having patients change into approved clothing is one thing the operator has direct control over. Further, if the garments selected for use in the chamber have no pockets, it is more difficult for patients to take forbidden items into the chamber with them. Recent fatal accidents might have been prevented had this disciplined action been applied.

**A-19-3.1.5.6** It can be impractical to clothe some patients (depending upon their disease or the site of any operation) in such garments. Hospital gowns of flame-resistant textile should be employed in such a case.

**19-3.1.5.7** All other fabrics used in the chamber such as sheets, drapes, and blankets shall be of inherently flame-resistant materials.

The 1996 edition eliminated the statement "free hanging drapes shall be minimized" because it was felt by the committee to be unenforceable.

## 19-3.2 Equipment.

**19-3.2.1** All equipment used in the hyperbaric chamber shall comply with Section 19-2. This includes all electrical and mechanical equipment necessary for the operation and maintenance of the hyperbaric facility, as well as any medical devices and instruments used in the facility. Use of unapproved equipment shall be prohibited. *[See 19-3.1.5.4(c).]*

**19-3.2.1.1** Portable X-ray devices, electrocautery equipment, and other similar high-energy devices shall not be operated in the hyperbaric chamber unless approved by the safety director for such use. Photographic equipment employing photoflash, flood lamps, or similar equipment shall not remain in the hyperbaric chamber when the chamber is pressurized. Lasers shall not be used under any condition.

**19-3.2.1.2** Equipment known to be, or suspected of being, defective shall not be introduced into any hyperbaric chamber or used in conjunction with the operation of such chamber until repaired, tested, and accepted by qualified personnel and approved by the safety director *(see 19-3.1.3.2).*

**19-3.2.1.3** The use of paper shall be kept to an absolute minimum in hyperbaric chambers, and any paper brought into the chamber shall be stored in a closed metal container. Containers shall be emptied after each chamber operation.

The use of paper products in hyperbaric chambers is discouraged by the committee because of the fire hazard they present. Paper products include paper cups, towels, and tissues. If paper products need to be used, a minimal number should be brought inside the chamber, and they are to be stored in a closed metal container.

**19-3.2.1.4** No equipment shall be allowed in the chamber that does not meet the temperature requirements of NFPA 70, *National Electrical Code,* Article 500-3(a), (b), and (c).

Hyperbaric facility safety directors need to be vigilant that this requirement is not breached.

**19-3.2.2\*** Oxygen containers, valves, fittings, and interconnecting equipment shall be all metal to the extent possible. Valve seats, gaskets, hoses, and lubricants shall be selected carefully for oxygen compatibility under service conditions.

**A-19-3.2.2** Users should be aware that many items if ignited in pressurized oxygen-enriched atmospheres are not self-extinguishing. Iron alloys, aluminum, and stainless steel are, to various degrees, in that category as well as human skin, muscle, and fat, and plastic tubing such as polyvinyl chloride (Tygon). Testing for oxygen compatibility is very complicated. Very little data exist and many standards still have to be determined. Suppliers do not normally have facilities for testing their products in controlled atmospheres, especially high-pressure oxygen. Both static conditions and impact conditions are applicable. Self-ignition temperatures normally are unknown in special atmospheres.

**19-3.2.3** Equipment used inside the chamber requiring lubrication shall be lubricated with oxygen-compatible flame-resistant material.

*Exception: Factory-sealed antifriction bearings shall be permitted to be used with standard hydrocarbon lubricants in Class A chambers that do not employ atmospheres of increased oxygen concentration.*

The exception allows new, factory-sealed bearings under the conditions specified. As a result, rolling equipment that is ordinarily used in the hospital can be used in the hyperbaric chamber. The small amounts of hydrocarbons involved inside a sealed bearing system should not provide a major source of flammable material. If bearings begin to leak, they should be taken out of service immediately and either repaired or replaced.

**19-3.2.4** Equipment of cerium, magnesium, magnesium alloys, and similar manufacture shall be prohibited from the chamber interior. *(See also A-19-3.2.2.)*

The use of light metals inside hyperbaric chambers has always been prohibited. Many light metals are capable of burning in air. (Magnesium is particularly known for this property and is used for incendiary bombs.) Placement in a hyperbaric chamber where the atmospheric pressure (normal or oxygen-enriched) is elevated would only make it easier for such metals to burn. This restriction applies only to the use of such metals inside a chamber.

**19-3.2.5** Radiation equipment, whether infrared or roentgen ray, can make hyperbaric chambers even more hazardous. In the event that such equipment is introduced into a hyperbaric chamber, hydrocarbon detectors shall be installed. In the event that flammable gases are detected in excess of 1000 parts per million, such radiation equipment shall not be operated until the chamber atmosphere is cleared.

The monitoring of radiation equipment has always been required. Placement here was only a relocation of text.

## 19-3.3 Handling of Gases.

**19-3.3.1** The institution's administrative personnel shall ensure that rules and regulations are provided to ensure the safe handling of gases in the hyperbaric facility *(see 19-3.1.5.2 and C-19-1.1.3.2).*

**19-3.3.2** Oxygen and other gases shall not be introduced into the chamber in the liquid state.

> Gases in a liquid state are prohibited because liquid gases can boil off and quickly change the composition of the atmosphere in the chamber, creating a hazardous condition.

**19-3.3.3** Flammable gases shall not be used or stored in the chamber or in the hyperbaric facility.

**19-3.3.4\*** Quantities of oxygen stored in the chamber shall be kept to a minimum.

**A-19-3.3.4** Pressurized containers of gas can be introduced into the hyperbaric chamber, provided that the container and its contents are approved for such use by the safety director.

**19-3.3.5** Nonflammable gases shall be permitted to be piped into the hyperbaric facility. Shutoff valves accessible to facility personnel shall be provided for such piping at the point of entry to the room housing the chamber. Storage and handling of nonflammable gases shall meet the applicable requirements of Chapter 4, "Gas and Vacuum Systems," of this document and NFPA 50, *Standard for Bulk Oxygen Systems at Consumer Sites.*

## 19-3.4 Maintenance.

### 19-3.4.1 General.

**19-3.4.1.1** The hyperbaric safety director shall be ultimately responsible for ensuring that all valves, regulators, meters, and similar equipment used in the hyperbaric chamber are properly compensated for safe use under hyperbaric conditions and tested periodically. Pressure relief valves shall be tested and calibrated periodically.

> Most gas regulators depend on atmospheric pressure as a reference point to operate properly. No device of this type should ever be used in a chamber unless it has been properly examined by the hyperbaric safety director to ensure that its use is appropriate.

**19-3.4.1.2** The hyperbaric-safety director shall also be ultimately responsible for ensuring that all gas outlets in the chambers are properly labeled or stenciled in accordance with CGA C-4, *Standard Method of Marking Portable Compressed Gas Containers to Identify the Material Contained.*

**19-3.4.1.3** Before piping systems are initially put into use, it shall be ascertained that the gas delivered at the outlet is shown on the outlet label and that proper connecting fittings are checked against their labels, in accordance with Sections 4-3 through 4-6 in Chapter 4.

Although this requirement is rudimentary, accidents that have repeatedly occurred could have been avoided if this simple procedure had been conducted.

**19-3.4.1.4** The requirements set forth in Section 4-3 of Chapter 4 concerning the storage, location, and special precautions required for compressed gases shall be followed.

**19-3.4.1.5** Storage areas for hazardous materials shall not be located in the room *(see 19-2.1)* housing the hyperbaric chamber. Flammable gases, except as provided in 19-3.1.5.2, Exception No. 1, shall not be used or stored in the hyperbaric room.

The committee believes flammable gases should not be used or stored in hyperbaric facilities under any circumstances. [It does recognize the need for items such as alcohol swabs and has allowed their use (see 19-3.1.5.2), but only if approved by authorities knowledgeable of the hazards involved in hyperbaric operations.]

**19-3.4.1.6** All replacement parts and components shall conform to original design specification.

This short sentence is very important from the standpoint of technology, safety, and philosophy. Throughout this chapter, the need for careful design of chambers to ensure the utmost safety for all users has been stressed. After extended use, parts sustain wear and tear and damage or will fatigue and have to be replaced, repaired, or otherwise renewed. When replacing parts of a hyperbaric chamber, it is critical that the replacement parts conform to the standards in effect at the time of the original fabrication of the chamber. This ensures that the parts meet the requirements that were originally built into the chamber. Replacing carefully "spec'd parts" with "ordinary hardware" could severely compromise the safety of the equipment and personnel inside the chamber. This is not an excuse or ploy to create a monopoly for the original manufacturer of the equipment. The integrity of hyperbaric chambers requires chamber administrators to keep carefully written specifications for all parts of the chamber (and/or equipment) so that suitable (equivalent) replacement parts can be purchased.

**19-3.4.2 Maintenance Logs.**

**19-3.4.2.1** Installation, repairs, modifications of equipment, and so forth, related to a chamber shall be evaluated by engineering personnel, tested under pressure, and approved by the safety director. Logs of the various tests shall be maintained.

**19-3.4.2.2** Operating equipment logs shall be maintained by engineering personnel. They shall be signed before chamber operation by the person in charge *(see A-19-3.1.3.2)*.

**19-3.4.2.3** Operating equipment logs shall not be taken inside the chamber.

Careful attention to details, such as maintenance logs, is of immeasurable aid toward achieving and maintaining a safe environment.

## 19-3.5 Electrical Safeguards.

**19-3.5.1** Electrical equipment shall be installed and operated in accordance with 19-2.7.

**19-3.5.1.1** All electrical circuits shall be tested before chamber pressurization. This test shall include a ground fault check to verify that no conductors are grounded to the chamber, as well as a test of normal functioning *(see 19-2.7.2.3)*.

**19-3.5.1.2** In the event of fire, all nonessential electrical equipment within the chamber shall be deenergized insofar as possible before extinguishing the fire. Smoldering, burning electrical equipment shall be deenergized before extinguishing a localized fire involving only the equipment *(see 19-2.5)*.

Once electrical equipment is de-energized, a fire in a hyperbaric chamber becomes a simple Class A fire, readily extinguishable with water. (Note: The term Class A refers to a fire involving combustible materials, not the type of chamber involved.)

## 19-3.6 Electrostatic Safeguards.

### 19-3.6.1 Administration.

**19-3.6.1.1 General.** The elimination of static charges is dependent on the vigilance of administrative supervision of materials purchased, maintenance, and periodic inspection and testing.

**19-3.6.1.2 Textiles.** Textiles used or worn in the hyperbaric chamber shall conform to 19-3.1.5.4 through 19-3.1.5.7.

### 19-3.6.2 Maintenance.

**19-3.6.2.1 Conductive Floors.** For chambers containing conductive floors, the requirements of 2-6.3.8 in Annex 2, "Flammable Anesthetizing Locations," shall apply.

### 19-3.6.2.2 Furniture Used in the Chamber.

(a)* Periodic inspection shall be made of leg tips, tires, casters, or other conductive devices on furniture and equipment to ensure that they are maintained free of wax, lint, or other extraneous material that could insulate them and defeat the purpose for which they are used. Periodic inspection shall also be made to avoid transporting such materials from other areas to conductive floors. Metals capable of impact sparking shall not be allowed for casters or furniture leg tips.

**A-19-3.6.2.2(a)** Ferrous metals can cause such sparking, as can magnesium or magnesium alloys if contact is made with rusted steel.

(b) Casters shall not be lubricated with oils or other flammable materials. Lubricants shall be oxygen compatible and flame resistant.

(c) Wheelchairs and gurneys with bearings lubricated and sealed by the manufacturer shall be permitted in Class A chambers where conditions prescribed in 19-2.8.5 are met.

In previous editions, the present requirement of subparagraph (c) was included as a note. The technical committee felt the text important enough to include as a requirement within the body of the standard. The requirement for oxygen monitoring as specified in 19-2.8.5 is a prerequisite for the use of sealed bearings

**19-3.6.2.3 Conductive Accessories.** Conductive accessories, such as belting, rubber accessories, plastics, covers, and sheeting used inside the chamber, shall meet the conductivity and antistatic requirements of 2-6.3.8, Reduction in Electrostatic Hazard in Annex 2.

**19-3.6.3 Testing.** Conductive testing, if required, shall be in accordance with requirements in Annex 2, "Requirements for Flammable Anesthetizing Locations."

Inspection and testing is considered vital because of the deterioration of materials that occurs in oxygen-enriched atmospheres.

**19-3.6.3.1\*** Materials containing rubber shall be inspected regularly, especially at points of kinking.

Conductive rubber materials contain large amounts of carbon that can lessen their mechanical strength (particularly in oxygen-enriched atmospheres). They should be checked more frequently than ordinary rubber products to ensure their safe condition.

**A-19-3.6.3.1** Materials containing rubber deteriorate rapidly in oxygen-enriched atmospheres.

**19-3.6.4 Fire Protection Equipment.** Electrical switches, valves, and electrical monitoring equipment associated with fire detection and extinguishment shall be visually inspected before each chamber pressurization. Fire detection equipment shall be tested each week and full testing, including discharge of extinguishing media, conducted annually. Testing shall include activation of trouble circuits and signals.

**19-3.6.5 Housekeeping.** It is absolutely essential that all areas of, and components associated with, the hyperbaric chamber be kept meticulously free of grease, lint, dirt, and dust. A regular housekeeping program shall be implemented whether or not the facility is in regular use. The persons assigned to this task shall be thoroughly indoctrinated in the hazards to occupants under normal operation.

Accumulation of grease, lint, dirt, and dust is very undesirable from a sanitary viewpoint. In a hyperbaric chamber, however, there is the added concern that such accumulations within materials, objects, or equipment can introduce additional fire hazards because of the high degree of flammability resulting from the oxygen-enriched atmosphere inside the chamber.

## References Cited in Commentary

1. P. J. Sheffield, and D. A. Desantels, "Hyperbaric and Hypobaric Chamber Fires: A 73-year Analysis." *Undersea Hyper Med,* 1997, 24(3): 153–164.

2. Undersea and Hyperbaric Medical Society, 10531 Metropolitan Ave., Kensington, MD 20895; (301) 942-2980 (http://www.uhms.org).
3. American College of Hyperbaric Medicine, P.O. Box 25914–130, Houston, TX 77265; (713) 528-5931 (http://hyperbaricmedicine.org).
4. NFPA 13, *Standard for the Installation of Sprinkler Systems,* 1999 edition.
5. ANSI/ASME PVHO-1, *Safety Standard for Pressure Vessels for Human Occupancy.* American Society of Mechanical Engineers, 345 West 47th Street, New York, NY 10017.
6. NFPA 70, *National Electrical Code®,* 1999 edition.
7. NFPA 497, *Recommended Practice for the Classification of Flammable Liquids, Gases, or Vapors and of Hazardous (Classified) Locations for Electrical Installations in Chemical Process Areas,* 1997 edition.
8. NFPA 53, *Recommended Practice on Materials, Equipment, and Systems Used in Oxygen-Enriched Atmospheres,* 1994 edition.
9. ANSI, American National Standard Institute, 11 West 42nd St., New York, NY 10036; (212) 642-4900.
10. UL, Underwriters Laboratories, Inc., 333 Pfingsten Road, Northbrook, Il 60062; (847) 272-8800.
11. IEC, International Electrotechnical Commission (standards available from ANSI).
12. NFPA 701, *Standard Methods of Fire Tests for Flame Propagation of Textiles and Films,* 1999 edition.

## Additional References of Interest

Baromedical Nurses Association, P.O. Box 24113, Halethorpe, MD 21227; (410) 789-5690.

National Board of Diving and Hyperbaric Medicine Technology, 3052 General Collins Ave., New Orleans, LA 70114-6850; (504) 366-8871.

# CHAPTER 20

# Freestanding Birthing Centers

Chapter 20, "Freestanding Birthing Centers," is new to the 1999 edition of NFPA 99. The former Chapter 20, "Referenced Publications," is now Chapter 21.

The Technical Correlating Committee received a number of inquiries between 1995 and 1998 concerning freestanding birthing centers. Specifically questioned was whether they were or were not "health care facilities," and thus whether there were any requirements in NFPA 99 for them. The Technical Correlating Committee met with representatives of the National Association of Childbearing Centers during the revision cycle for the 1996 edition of NFPA 99, but took no action during that cycle.

After considerable discussion on these facilities, at an October 21, 1997, meeting, the Technical Correlating Committee now believes that if these facilities use (1) patient-care-related appliances, (2) gas-powered medical equipment, (3) perform procedures where the loss of electrical power would cause electrical incidents or patient injury, or (4) install piped medical gas or vacuum systems, then such facilities should comply with the requirements for such equipment or systems as do other types of health care facilities (i.e., Chapters 12–17).

## 20-1 Scope

This chapter addresses the requirements for the safe use of electrical and gas equipment, and for electrical, gas, and vacuum systems used for the delivery and care of infants in freestanding birthing centers.

## 20-2 General Responsibilities

(Reserved)

## 20-3 General Requirements

**20-3.1** (Reserved)

**20-3.2** (Reserved)

### 20-3.3 Electrical System Requirements.

Electrical systems used in freestanding birthing centers shall conform to such requirements of Chapter 3 as applicable.

### 20-3.4 Gas and Vacuum System Requirements.

Gas and vacuum systems used in freestanding birthing centers shall conform to such requirements of Chapter 4 as applicable.

**20-3.5** (Reserved)

**20-3.6** (Reserved)

### 20-3.7 Electrical Equipment Requirements.

Electrical equipment used in freestanding birthing centers shall conform to such requirements of Chapter 7 as applicable.

### 20-3.8 Gas Equipment Requirements.

Gas equipment used in freestanding birthing centers shall conform to such requirements of Chapter 8 as applicable.

# CHAPTER 21

# Referenced Publications

## 21-1 Referenced Publications

The following documents or portions thereof are referenced within this standard and shall be considered part of the requirements of this document. The edition indicated for each reference is the current edition as of the date of the NFPA issuance of this document.

### 21-1.1 NFPA Publications.

National Fire Protection Association, 1 Batterymarch Park, P.O. Box 9101, Quincy, MA 02269-9101.

NFPA 10, *Standard for Portable Fire Extinguishers*, 1998 edition.

NFPA 13, *Standard for the Installation of Sprinkler Systems*, 1996 edition.

NFPA 30, *Flammable and Combustible Liquids Code*, 1996 edition.

NFPA 37, *Standard for the Installation and Use of Stationary Combustion Engines and Gas Turbines*, 1998 edition.

NFPA 45, *Standard on Fire Protection for Laboratories Using Chemicals*, 1996 edition.

NFPA 50, *Standard for Bulk Oxygen Systems at Consumer Sites*, 1996 edition.

NFPA 51, *Standard for the Design and Installation of Oxygen-Fuel Gas Systems for Welding, Cutting, and Allied Processes*, 1997 edition.

NFPA 54, *National Fuel Gas Code*, 1996 edition.

NFPA 58, *Standard for the Storage and Handling of Liquefied Petroleum Gases*, 1998 edition.

NFPA 70, *National Electrical Code®*, 1999 edition.

NFPA 72, *National Fire Alarm Code*, 1996 edition.

NFPA 99B, *Standard for Hypobaric Facilities*, 1999 edition.

NFPA *101®*, *Life Safety Code®*, 1997 edition.

NFPA 110, *Standard for Emergency and Standby Power Systems*, 1999 edition.

NFPA 220, *Standard on Types of Building Construction*, 1995 edition.

NFPA 255, *Standard Method of Test of Surface Burning Characteristics of Building Materials*, 1996 edition.

NFPA 326, *Standard Procedures for the Safe Entry of Underground Storage Tanks*, 1993 edition.

NFPA 701, *Standard Methods of Fire Tests for Flame-Resistant Textiles and Films*, 1996 edition.

NFPA 704, *Standard System for the Identification of the Hazards of Materials for Emergency Response*, 1996 edition.

NFPA 1600, *Recommended Practice for Disaster Management*, 1995 edition.

## 21-1.2 Other Publications.

**21-1.2.1 ANSI Publications.** American National Standards Institute, Inc., 11 West 42nd Street, New York, NY 10036.

ANSI/ASME B-40.1-1991, *Gauges, Pressure Indicating Dial-Type, Elastic Elements.*

ANSI B120.1-1983, *Pipe Threads, General Purpose.*

ANSI B16.22-1989, *Wrought Copper and Copper Alloy Solder-Joint Pressure Fittings.*

ANSI B57.1 (See CGA V-1.)

ANSI C73-1973, *Plugs and Receptacles.*

ANSI C84.1-1989, *Voltage Ratings: Electric Power Systems and Equipment.*

ANSI C-4 (See CGA C-4).

ANSI G-7.1 (See CGA G-7.1).

ANSI Z66.1-1964 (R 1972), *Specifications for Paints and Coatings Accessible to Children to Minimize Dry Film Toxicity.*

**21-1.2.2 ASHRAE Publication.** American Society of Heating, Refrigerating and Air Conditioning Engineers, Inc., 1791 Tullie Circle, N.E., Atlanta, GA 30329.

ASHRAE *Handbook of Fundamentals*—1985, Chapter 24.

**21-1.2.3 ASME Publications.** American Society of Mechanical Engineers, 345 East 47th Street, New York, NY 10017.

ANSI/ASME PVHO-1-1990, *Safety Standard for Pressure Vessels for Human Occupancy.*

ASME *Boiler and Pressure Vessel Code* (1990).

**21-1.2.4 ASTM Publications.** American Society for Testing and Materials, 100 Barr Harbor Drive, West Conshohocken, PA 19428.

ASTM A 53-1994, *Standard Specification for Pipe, Steel, Black and Hot-Dipped, Zinc-coated, Welded and Seamless.*

ASTM B 32-1995, *Standard Specification for Solder Metal.*

ASTM B 88-1992, *Specification for Seamless Copper Water Tube.*

ASTM B 280-1992, *Specification for Seamless Copper Tubing for Air Conditioning and Refrigeration Field Service.*

ASTM B 819-1992, *Standard Specification for Seamless Copper Tube for Medical Gas Systems.*

ASTM B 828-1992, *Making Capillary Joints by Soldering of Copper and Copper Alloy Tube and Fittings.*

ASTM D 5-1986, *Test for Penetration of Bituminous Materials.*

ASTM D 2863-1991, *Method for Measuring the Minimum Oxygen Concentration to Support Candle-like Combustion of Plastics (Oxygen Index)* (ANSI D2863).

ASTM E 136-1982, *Standard Test Method for Behavior of Materials in a Vertical Tube Furnace at 750°C.*

**21-1.2.5 AWS Publications.** American Welding Society, Inc., 550 N.W. LeJeune Road, Miami, FL 33126.

ANSI/AWS A5.8-1989, *Specification for Brazing Filler Metal.*

AWS B2.2-1985, *Standard for Brazing Procedure and Performance Qualifications.*

**21-1.2.6 CGA Publications.** Compressed Gas Association, Inc., 1725 Jefferson Davis Highway, Arlington, VA 22202.

Pamphlet C-4-1990, *Standard Method of Marking Portable Compressed Gas Containers to Identify the Material Contained.*

Pamphlet C-9-1988, *Standard Color-Marking of Compressed Gas Cylinders Intended for Medical Use.*

Pamphlet G-4-1987, *Oxygen.*

Pamphlet G-4.1-1985, *Cleaning Equipment for Oxygen Service.*

Pamphlet G-7.1-1989, *Commodity Specification for Air* (ANSI Z86.1).

Pamphlet G-8.1-1990, *Standard for the Installation of Nitrous Oxide Systems at Consumer Sites.*

Pamphlet G-10.1-1991, *Commodity Specification for Nitrogen.*

Pamphlet P-2-1989, *Characteristics and Safe Handling of Medical Gases.*

Pamphlet P-2.5-1987, *Transfilling of High Pressure Gaseous Oxygen to Be Used for Respiration.*

Pamphlet P-2.6-1983, *Transfilling of Low-Pressure Liquid Oxygen to Be Used for Respiration.*

Pamphlet P-2.7-1994, *Guide for the Safe Storage, Handling and Use of Portable Liquid Oxygen Systems in Health Care Facilities.*

Pamphlet P-9-1980, *Inert Gases: Argon, Nitrogen and Helium.*

Pamphlet V-1-1987, *Standard for Compressed Gas Cylinder Valve Outlet and Inlet Connections* (ANSI B57.1).

Pamphlet V-5-1985, *Diameter-Index Safety System — Non-Interchangeable Low Pressure Connections for Medical Gas Applications.*

**21-1.2.7 Copper Development Association Publication.** Copper Development Assn., 260 Madison Avenue, 16th floor, New York, NY 10016.

*Copper Tube Handbook.*

**21-1.2.8 ISA Publication.** Instrument Society of America, P.O. Box 12277, Research Triangle Park, NC 27709.

RP 12.6-1987, *Installation of Intrinsically Safe Systems in Hazardous Locations.*

**21-1.2.9 MSS Publications.** Manufacturer's Standardization Society of the Valve and Fittings Industry, Inc., 127 Park Street NE, Vienna, VA 22180.

SP-58 (1988) *Pipe Hangers and Supports — Materials, Design, and Manufacture.*
SP-69 (1983) *Pipe Hangers and Supports — Selection and Application.*
SP-73 (1986) *Brazing Joints for Wrought and Cast Copper Alloy Solder Joint Pressure Fittings.*

**21-1.2.10 NCCLS Publication.** National Committee for Clinical Laboratory Standards, 940 West Valley Road, Suite 1400, Wayne, PA 19087-1898.

NCCLS ASI-5, *Power Requirements for Clinical Laboratory Instruments and for Laboratory Power Sources.*

**21-1.2.11 UL Publication.** Underwriters Laboratories Inc., 333 Pfingsten Road, Northbrook, IL 60062.

UL Subject 94-1991, *Burning Tests for Plastics.*

**21-1.2.12 U.S. Government Publication.**

**21-1.2.12.1** U.S. Dept. of Defense, Naval Publications & Form Center (NPFC 103), 5801 Tabor Avenue, Philadelphia, PA 19120.

MIL-Standard 104B, *Limit for Electrical Insulation Color.*

# APPENDIX A

# Explanatory Material

The material contained in Appendix A of this standard is not part of the requirements of the code but is included with the code for informational purposes only. For the convenience of readers, in this handbook the Appendix A material is interspersed among the language of Chapters 1 through 20 and, therefore, is not repeated here.

# APPENDIX B

# Referenced and Informatory Publications

## B-1 Referenced and Informatory Publications

The following documents or portions thereof are referenced within this standard for informational purposes only and thus are not considered part of the requirements of this document. The edition indicated for each reference is the current edition as of the date of the NFPA issuance of this document.

### B-1.1 NFPA Publications.

National Fire Protection Association, 1 Batterymarch Park, P.O. Box 9101, Quincy, MA 02269-9101.

NFPA 10, *Standard for Portable Fire Extinguishers*, 1998 edition.

NFPA 30, *Flammable and Combustible Liquids Code*, 1996 edition.

NFPA 45, *Standard on Fire Protection for Laboratories Using Chemicals*, 1996 edition.

NFPA 49, *Hazardous Chemicals Data*, 1994 edition. (No longer in print; appears in NFPA *Fire Protection Guide to Hazardous Materials,* 12th edition, 1997.)

NFPA 50, *Standard for Bulk Oxygen Systems at Consumer Sites*, 1996 edition.

NFPA 53, *Recommended Practice on Materials, Equipment, and Systems Used in Oxygen-Enriched Atmospheres*, 1999 edition.

NFPA 54, *National Fuel Gas Code*, 1996 edition.

NFPA 70, *National Electrical Code®*, 1999 edition.

NFPA 80, *Standard for Fire Doors, Fire Windows, and Smoke-Control Door Assemblies*, 1999 edition.

NFPA 90A, *Standard for the Installation of Air Conditioning and Ventilating Systems*, 1996 edition.

NFPA 90B, *Standard for the Installation of Warm Air Heating and Air Conditioning Systems*, 1996 edition.

NFPA 99B, *Standard for Hypobaric Facilities*, 1999 edition.

NFPA *101®, Life Safety Code®*, 1997 edition.

NFPA 220, *Standard on Types of Building Construction*, 1995 edition.

NFPA 259, *Standard Test Method for Potential Heat of Building Materials*, 1998 edition.

NFPA 325, *Guide to Fire Hazard Properties of Flammable Liquids, Gases, and Volatile Solids*, 1994 edition. (No longer in print; appears in NFPA *Fire Protection Guide to Hazardous Materials,* 12th edition, 1997.)

NFPA 491, *Guide to Hazardous Chemical Reactions*, 1997 edition.

NFPA 704, *Standard System for the Identification of the Hazards of Materials for Emergency Response*, 1996 edition.

NFPA 780, *Standard for the Installation of Lightning Protection Systems*, 1997 edition.

NFPA 801, *Standard for Fire Protection for Facilities Handling Radioactive Materials,* 1998 edition.

NFPA *Fire Protection Handbook*, 18th edition, 1997.

## B-1.2 Other Publications.

The following publications are available from the addresses listed.

**B-1.2.1 AATCC Publication.** American Association of Textile Chemists and Colorists, P.O. Box 886, Durham, NC 27701.

AATCC Test Method 76-1989, *Determination of the Electrical Resistivity of Fabrics*, included in 1962 Technical Manual (ANSI/AATCC 76).

**B-1.2.2 ASHE Publication.** American Society for Healthcare Engineering, One North Franklin, Chicago, IL 60606.

*Hospital Mutual Aid Evacuation Plan*, Februry 1977.

**B-1.2.3 ASHRAE Publications.** American Society of Heating, Refrigerating and Air Conditioning Engineers, Inc., 1791 Tullie Circle, NE, Atlanta, GA 30329.

*ASHRAE Guide and Data Book* (Annual).

*ASHRAE Handbook on HVAC Systems and Equipment*, 1992 (Chap. 10, Steam Systems, 1992).

ASHRAE *Handbook on HVAC Applications*, 1991 (Chap. 7, Health Care Facilities, 1995).

**B-1.2.4 ASME Publication.** American Society of Mechanical Engineers, United Engineering Center, 345 E. 47th Street, New York, NY 10017.

ASME *Boiler and Pressure Vessel Code*, Section IX, Welding and Brazing Qualifications, 1995.

**B-1.2.5 ASTM Publications.** American Society for Testing and Materials, 100 Barr Harbor Drive, West Conshohocken, PA 19428.

ASTM D 56-1993, *Test Method for Flash Point by Tag Closed Tester* (ANSI).

ASTM D 93-1994, *Test Methods for Flash Point by Pensky-Martens Closed Tester* (ANSI).

ASTM D 2240-1991, *Test Method for Rubber Property — Durometer Hardness.*
ASTM G 63-1992, *Guide for Evaluating Nonmetallic Materials for Oxygen Service.*
ASTM G 88-90, *Guide for Designing Systems for Oxygen Service.*
ASTM G 93-88, *Practice for Cleaning Methods for Material and Equipment Used in Oxygen-Enriched Environments.*
ASTM G 94-1992, *Guide for Evaluating Metals for Oxygen Service.*

**B-1.2.6 CGA Publications.** Compressed Gas Association, Inc., 1725 Jefferson Davis Highway, Arlington, VA 22202.

CGA Pamphlet E-10-1977, *Maintenance of Medical Gas and Vacuum Systems in Health Care Facilities* (draft).
CGA Pamphlet G-8.1-1990, *Standard for the Installation of Nitrous Oxide Systems at Consumer Sites.*
CGA Pamphlet P-1-1991, *Safe Handling of Compressed Gases*
CGA Pamphlet P-2-1989, *Characteristics of Safe Handling of Medical Gases*
CGA Pamphlet V-1-1994, *Compressed Gas Cylinder Valve Outlet and Inlet Connections* (ANSI B57.1)

**B-1.2.7 JCAHO Publication.** Joint Commission on the Accreditation of Healthcare Organizations, One Renaissance Blvd., Oakbrook Terrace, IL 60181.

*Accreditation Manual for Hospitals*, 1995.

**B-1.2.8 NCCLS Publication.** National Committee for Clinical Laboratory Standards, 940 West Valley Road, Suite 1400, Wayne, PA 19087-1898.

GP17-T, *Guidelines for Laboratory Safety.*
GP5-A, *Clinical Laboratory Waste Management.*
M29-T2, *Protection of Laboratory Workers from Infectious Disease Transmitted by Blood, Body Fluids, and Tissue.*

**B-1.2.9 Ocean Systems Publication.** Ocean Systems, Inc. Research and Development Laboratory, Tarrytown, NY 10591. Work carried out under U.S. Office of Naval Research, Washington, DC, Contract No. N00014-67- 0014-67-A-0214-0013

Technical Memorandum UCR1-721, *Chamber Fire Safety.*

**B-1.2.10 U.S. Government Publications.** U.S. Government Printing Office, Superintendent of Documents, Washington, DC 20402.

*Code of Federal Regulations*, Title 49.
*Federal Test Method Standard No. 101B, Method 4046.*
*Code of Federal Regulations*, Title 29, Part 1910, Subpart 1030, "Bloodborne Pathogens."
*Code of Federal Regulations*, Title 29, Part 910, Subpart 1910, "Occupational Exposures to Chemical Laboratories."
*Code of Federal Regulations*, Title 49, Parts 171 through 190 (U.S. Dept. of Transporta-

tion, Specifications for Transportation of Explosives & Dangerous Articles) (In Canada, the regulations of the Board of Transport Commissioners, Union Station, Ottawa, Canada, apply.)

Commercial Standard 223-59, *Casters, Wheels, and Glides for Hospital Equipment*

NRC Publication 1132, *Diesel Engines for Use with Generators to Supply Emergency and Short Term Electric Power*, (Also available as Order No. O.P.52870 from University Microfilms, P.O. Box 1366, Ann Arbor, MI 48106.)

**B-1.2.11 U.S. Pharmacopia Publication.** U.S. Pharmacopia, 12601 Twinbrook Parkway, Rockville, MD 20852.

USP *Standard for Compressed Air*, Document No. XXII/NFXVII.

# B-2 Published Articles on Fire Involving Respiratory Therapy Equipment, and Related Incidents.

Benson, D. M., and Wecht, C. H. Conflagration in an ambulance oxygen system. *Journal of Trauma*, vol. 15, no. 6:536-649, 1975.

Dillon, J. J. Cry fire! *Respiratory Care*, vol. 21, no. 11: 1139-1140, 1976.

Gjerde, G. E., and Kraemer, R. An oxygen therapy fire. *Respiratory Care*, vol. 25, no. 3 3:362-363, 1980.

Walter, C. W. Fire in an oxygen-powered respirator. *JAMA* 197:44-46, 1960.

Webre, D. E., Leon, R., and Larson, N.W. Case History; Fire in a nebulizer. *Anes. and Analg.* 52:843-848, 1973.

# B-3 Addresses of Some Other Organizations Publishing Standards or Guidelines.

American Industrial Hygiene Assoc., 475 Wolf Ledges Parkway, Akron, OH 44311.

American Conference of Governmental and Industrial Hygienists, P.O. Box 1937, Cincinnati, OH 45201.

College of American Pathologists, 325 Waukegan Road, Northfield, IL 60003.

Scientific Apparatus Makers Assoc., 1101 16th Street, NW, Washington, DC 20036.

# B-4 Addresses of Organizations and Agencies that Provide Health Care Emergency Preparedness Educational Material (Written or Audio-Visual) (Ref.: Chapter 11.)

**Publications**

This list represents the organizations that the committee was aware of at the time Chapter 11 was reviewed. It is neither an exhaustive list nor an endorsement of the materials mentioned.

National Fire Protection Association, 1 Batterymarch Park, P.O. Box 9101, Quincy, MA 02269-9101.

American Health Care Association, 1200 Fifteenth Street NW, Washington, DC 20005.

American Hospital Association, 840 North Lake Shore Drive, Chicago, IL 60611.

American Medical Association, 535 North Dearborn Street, Chicago, IL 60610.

American National Red Cross, National Headquarters, 17th & D Streets, NW, Washington, DC 20006.

American Nurses' Association, 10 Columbus Circle, New York, NY 10019.

Association of American Railroads, 1920 L Street NW, Washington, DC 20036.

Charles C. Thomas Publisher, 301-327 East Lawrence Avenue, Springfield, IL 60611.

Dun-Donnelley Publishing Corp., 666 Fifth Avenue, New York, NY 10019.

Federal Emergency Management Agency, Washington, DC 20472.

Florida Health Care Association, P.O. Box 1459, Tallahassee, FL 32302.

Helicopter Association International, 1635 Prince Street, Alexandria, VA 22314-2818.

International Association of Fire Chiefs, 4025 Fair Ridge Drive, Fairfax, VA 22033-2868.

Joint Commission on Accreditation of Healthcare Organizations (JCAHO), One Renaissance Blvd., Oakbrook Terrace, IL 60181.

Pan American Health Organization, 525 23rd Street NW, Washington, DC 20036 (Attn.: Editor, Disaster Preparedness in the Americas).

University of Delaware, Disaster Research Center (Publications), Newark, DE 19716.

U.S. Department of Transportation (available from Superintendent of Documents, U.S. Government Printing Office, Washington, DC 20402).

**Audio-visual material**

National Fire Protection Association, 1 Batterymarch Park, P.O. Box 9101, Quincy, MA 02269-9101.

Abbott Laboratories, Audio/Visual Services, 565 Fifth Avenue, New York, NY 10017.

Brose Productions, Inc., 10850 Riverside Drive, N. Hollywood, CA 91602.

Federal Emergency Management Agency, Office of Public Affairs, Washington, DC 20472.

Fire Prevention Through Films, Inc., P.O. Box 11, Newton Highlands, MA 02161.

General Services Administration, National Audiovisual Center, Reference Section, Washington, DC 20409.

Helicopter Association International, 1635 Prince Street, Alexandria, VA 22314-2818.

Pyramid, P.O. Box 1048, Santa Monica, CA 90406.

University of Illinois Medical Center, Circle Campus, Chicago, IL 60612.

# APPENDIX C

# Additional Explanatory Notes to Chapters 1–20

---

*This appendix is not a part of the requirements of this NFPA document but is included for informational purposes only.*

NOTE: Sections of Appendix C identified by a dagger (†) include text extracted from NFPA 30, *Flammable and Combustible Liquids Code*, and NFPA 704, *Standard System for the Identification of the Fire Hazards of Materials*. Requests for interpretations or revisions of the extracted text will be referred to the Technical Committee on General Storage of Flammable Liquids and the Technical Committee on Fire Hazards of Materials, respectively.

For more information on extracted text, see commentary at the beginning of Chapter 3.

---

## C-3 Additional Information on Chapter 3

Appendix C-3 consists of the following:

C-3.1 Typical Hospital Wiring Arrangement *(See Figure C-3.1.)*

C-3.2 Maintenance Guide for an Essential Electrical System

C-3.3 Suggested Format for Listing Functions to Be served by the Essential Electrical System in a Hospital

### C-3.1 Typical Hospital Wiring Arrangement.

### C-3.2 Maintenance Guide for an Essential Electrical System.

This generalized maintenance guide is provided to assist administrative, supervisory, and operating personnel in establishing and evaluating maintenance programs for emergency electric generating systems.

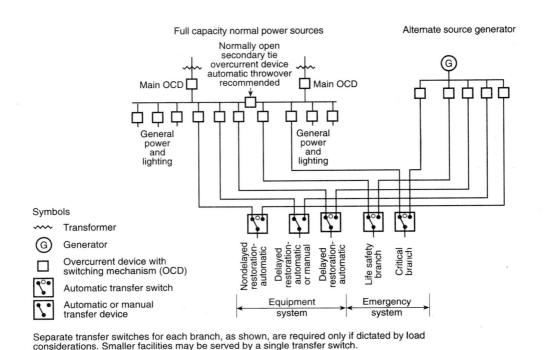

*Figure C-3.1 Typical hospital wiring arrangement.*

*Monthly:*

1. Testing of generator sets and transfer switches under load and operating temperature conditions at least every 30 days. A 30-minute exercise period is an absolute minimum, or the engine manufacturer's recommendations should be followed.
2. Permanently record all available instrument readings during the monthly test.
3. During the monthly test, check the following system or systems applicable to your installation:

Natural Gas or Liquid Petroleum Gas System:

   Operation of solenoids and regulators

   Condition of all hoses and pipes

   Fuel quantity

Gasoline Fuel System:

   Main tank fuel level

   Operation of system

Diesel Fuel System:

   Main tank fuel level

   Day tank fuel level

   Operation of fuel supply pump and controls

Turbine Prime Movers: Follow manufacturer's recommended maintenance procedure

Engine Cooling System:

   Coolant level

   Rust inhibitor in coolant

   Antifreeze in coolant (if applicable)

   Adequate cooling water to heat exchangers

   Adequate fresh air to engine and radiators

   Condition of fan and alternator belts

   Squeeze and check condition of hoses and connections

   Functioning of coolant heater (if installed)

Engine Lubricating System:

   Lubricating oil level

   Crankcase breather not restricted

   Appearance of lubricating oil

   Correct lubricating oil available to replenish or change

   Operation of lubricating oil heater (if installed)

   Oil pressure correct

Engine Electrical Starting System:

   Battery terminals clean and tight

   Add distilled water to maintain proper electrolyte level

   Battery charging rate

   Battery trickle charging circuit operating properly

   Spare batteries charged if provided

Engine Compressed Air Starting System:

   Air compressor operating properly

   Air compressor lubricating oil level

   Spare compressed air tanks full

   Main compressed air tanks full

   Drain water from compressed air tanks

Engine Exhaust System:

    Condensate trap drained

    No exhaust leaks

    Exhaust not restricted

    All connections tight

Transfer Switch:

    Inside clean and free of foreign matter

    No unusual sounds

    Terminals and connectors normal color

    Condition of all wiring insulation

    All covers tight

    Doors securely closed

General:

    Any unusual condition of vibration, deterioration, leakage, or high surface temperatures or noise

    Maintenance manuals, service log, basic service tools, jumpers, and supplies readily available

    Check and record the time intervals of the various increments of the automatic start-up and shutdown sequences

    Overall cleanliness of room

    No unnecessary items in room

4. After the monthly test:

Take prompt action to correct all improper conditions indicated during test.

Check that the standby system is set for automatic start and load transfer.

*Quarterly:*

1. On generator sets:

Engine Electrical Starting System:

    Check battery electrolyte specific gravity

    Check battery cap vents

Engine Lubricating System: Check lubricating oil (or have analyzed if part of an engineered lube oil program)

2. Fuel System:

Drain water from fuel filters (if applicable)

Drain water from day tank (if applicable)

Check fuel gauges and drain water from main fuel tanks

Inspect all main fuel tank vents

*Semiannually:*

1. On generator sets:

Engine Lubricating System:

Change oil filter (if sufficient hours)

Clean crankcase breather

Fuel System:

General inspection of all components

Change fuel filter

Change or clean air filter

Governor:

Check all linkages and ball joints

Check oil level (if applicable)

Observe for unusual oil leakage

Generator:

Check brush length and pressure

Check appearance of slip rings and clean if necessary

Blow out with clean, dry compressed air

Engine Safety Controls: Check operation of all engine-operating alarms and safety shutdown devices (generator not under load during this check)

*Annually:*

1. On generator sets:

Fuel System:

Diesel: Analyze fuel for condition (replace if required)

Gasoline: Replace fuel

Natural Gas or Liquefied Petroleum Gas: Examine all supply tanks, fittings, and lines

Lubricating Systems:

Change oil

Change oil filter

Replace carburetor air filter

Cooling System:

    Check condition and rod-out heat exchangers if necessary

    Change coolant on closed systems

    Clean exterior of all radiators

    Check all engine water pumps and circulating pumps

    Examine all duct work for looseness

    Clean and check motor-operated louvers

Exhaust System: Check condition of mufflers, exhaust lines, supports, and connections

Ignition System:

    Spark ignition engines

    Replace points and plugs

    Check ignition timing

    Check condition of all ignition leads

Generator:

    Clean generator windings

    Check generator bearings

    Measure and record resistance readings of generator windings using insulation tester (megger)

Engine Control:

    General cleaning

    Check appearance of all components

    Check meters

2. Transfer Switch: Inspect transfer switch and make repairs or replacements if indicated
3. On main switchgear and generator switchgear:

Operate every circuit breaker manually

Visually check bus bars, bracing, and feeder connections for cleanliness and signs of overheating

*Every Three Years:*

1. System Controls: Reevaluate the settings of the voltage sensing and time delay relays
2. Main Switchgear and Generator Switchgear:

Determine whether changes to the electrical supply system have been made that require a revision of the main circuit breaker, fuse, or current-limiting bus duct coordination.

Calibrate and load test main circuit breakers. Spot-check bus bar bolts and supports for tightness. Obtain and record insulation tester readings on bus bars and circuit breakers. Obtain and record insulation tester readings on internal distribution feeders.

*Periodically:*

1. Prime Mover Overhaul: Each prime mover should have a periodic overhaul in compliance with the manufacturer's recommendation or as conditions warrant.
2. Connected Load: Update the record of demand and connected load and check for potential overload.

### C-3.3 Suggested Format for Listing Functions to Be Served by the Essential Electrical System in a Hospital.

*Explanation.* It may be advantageous, in listing the specific functions for a given construction project or building review, to list them, at the outset, by geographical location within the project, in order to ensure comprehensive coverage. Every room or space should be reviewed for possible inclusion of the following:

(a) Lighting (partial or all)
(b) Receptacles (some or all)
(c) Permanently wired electrical apparatus

The format suggested herein is offered as a convenient tool, not only for identifying all functions to be served and their respective time intervals for being reenergized by the alternate electric source, but also for documenting other functions that were considered, discussed, and excluded as nonessential. This last column is considered worthy of attention. *(See Figure C-3.3.)* It may be that the hospital engineer or the reviewing authority will wish to keep on file a final copy of the list, which would be the basis for the electrical engineer's detailed engineering design.

Although this suggested format is intended for use by a hospital it may, with suitable changes, be useful for other health care facilities.

# C-4 Additional Information on Chapter 4

Appendix C-4 consists of the following:

C-4.1 Initial Testing of Nonflammable Medical Piped Gas Systems (Level 1 Systems)

C-4.2 Retesting and Maintenance of Nonflammable Medical Piped Gas Systems (Level 1 Systems)

C-4.3 Examples, Level 1 Vacuum System Sizing

C-4.4 Vacuum Flow Chart and Formulas

C-4.5 Metric Conversion Factors

C-4.6 Comments on Derivation of Design Parameters for Level 1 Vacuum Systems

C-4.7 Oxygen Service Related Documents

C-4.8 AIA Recommended Number of Station Outlets/Inlets

Essential Electrical Systems

Hospital _____    Date _____

| Room no. | Room name | Function served* | Emergency system | | Equipment system | | Non-essential |
|----------|-----------|------------------|-----------------|---------------|-----------------|----------------|---------------|
| | | | Life safety branch | Critical branch | Delayed auto.** | Delayed manual | |
| | | | | | | | |
| | | | | | | | |
| | | | | | | | |
| | | | | | | | |
| | | | | | | | |
| | | | | | | | |
| | | | | | | | |
| | | | | | | | |
| | | | | | | | |
| | | | | | | | |
| | | | | | | | |
| | | | | | | | |
| | | | | | | | |
| | | | | | | | |
| | | | | | | | |
| | | | | | | | |
| | | | | | | | |
| | | | | | | | |
| | | | | | | | |

\* Indicate precise lighting, receptacles, and/or equipment. Use a separate line for each function.

\*\* Indicate time interval.

*Figure C-3.3* *Essential electrical systems.*

## C-4.1 Initial Testing of Nonflammable Medical Piped Gas Systems (Level 1 Systems).

NOTE: Numbers in brackets refer to paragraphs in Chapter 4 of text.

Readers should note the following are only general recommendations. Specific required testing is listed in Section 4-3 of Chapter 4. It also should be noted that these recommendations apply to a Level 1 piped gas system, although portions may be applicable to a Level 3 piped gas system.

**C-4.1.1 [4-3.1.1.8(e)]** The pressure relief valve, set at 50 percent above normal line pressure, should be tested to assure proper function prior to use of the system for patient care.

**C-4.1.2  [4-3.1.1.9(f)]** The proper functioning of the safety valve, automatic drain, pressure gauge, and high-water-level sensor should be verified before the system is put into service.

**C-4.1.3 [4-3.1.2.2(b)3a] Changeover Warning Signal—Manifold or Alternating Bulk Supply—4-3.1.1.5(a), 4-3.1.1.6(a)2, and 4-3.1.1.7(a)1.**

1. Start a flow of gas from an outlet of the piping system.
2. Close the shutoff valve or cylinder valves on the number 1 bank (Figure 4-3.1.1.5), the primary supply of the manifold (Figure 4-3.1.1.6), or the primary unit of the alternating bulk supply to simulate its depletion. Changeover should be made to the number 2 bank, secondary supply, or the alternate bulk unit.
3. Check main-line pressure gauge to ensure maintenance of the desired pressure.
4. Check signal panels for activation of the proper changeover signal.
5. Silence the audible signal; visual signal should remain.
6. Open the valves closed in Step 2. Close the valve on the number 2 bank, secondary supply, or alternate bulk unit. When changeover back to original primary supply has occurred, reopen the valve. This will reinstate system to its original status.
7. Check signal panels for deactivation of warning signals.
8. Stop flow of gas from the piping system.

**C-4.1.4 [4-3.1.2.2(b)3d] Reserve-in-Use Warning Signal—4-3.1.1.6(a)3, 4-3.1.1.6(c), and 4-3.1.1.7(a).**

1. Start a flow of gas from the piping system.
2. Close the proper shutoff valves to simulate depletion of the operating supply. Reserve should begin to supply the piping system.
3. Check the main-line pressure gauge. Pressure should remain at the desired level.
4. Check the master signal panels to determine that the reserve-in-use signals have been activated.
5. Silence the audible signal. Visual signal should remain.
6. Open the shutoff valves closed in Step 2.
7. Check master signal panels for deactivation of the warning signals.
8. Stop the flow of gas from the piping system.

**C-4.1.5 [4-3.1.2.2(b)3d] Reserve Supply Low (Down to an average one-day supply)—4-3.1.1.6(b) and 4-3.1.1.7(b)1 and 2.**

*High-Pressure Cylinder Reserve.*

1. Start a flow of gas from the piping system.
2. Close all operating supply shutoff valves (to use pressure from the reserve).
3. Close the reserve supply shutoff valve or, if necessary, the reserve cylinder valves, depending on the exact location of the actuating switch (to reduce pressure on the actuating switch, simulating loss of reserve).
4. Open the operating supply valves closed in Step 2 (so that only the "reserve low" signal should be activated).
5. Check the master signal panels for activation of the proper signal.

6. Silence the audible signal. Visual signal should remain.
7. Open reserve supply valve or cylinder valves closed in Step 3.
8. Check master signal panels for deactivation of the warning signals.
9. Stop flow of gas from the piping system.

*Liquid Bulk Unit Reserve.* This type of reserve requires an actuating switch on the contents gauge and another actuating switch for the gas pressure being maintained in the reserve unit. Reduced contents or gas pressure in the reserve unit would indicate less than a day's supply in reserve.

Simulation of these conditions requires the assistance of the owner or the organization responsible for the operation and maintenance of the supply system as it will vary for different styles of storage units.

**C-4.1.6 [4-3.1.2.2(b)3e] High or Low Pressure in Piping System.** Initial test of the area alarms covered in 4-3.4.1.3(d)4 can be done at the same time.

1. Increase the pressure in the piping system to the high-pressure signal point (20 percent above normal pressure).
2. Check all master signal panels (and area signals) to ensure that the properly labeled warning signal is activated; also check main-line pressure gauge and area gauges to ensure their function.
3. Silence the audible signal. Visual signal should remain.
4. Reduce piping system pressure to the normal. A flow from the system is required to lower the pressure and permit readjustment of the line regulator.
5. Check all signal panels for deactivation of the signals.
6. Close main-line shutoff valve.
7. Continue the flow from the system until pressure is reduced to the low-pressure signal point (20 percent below normal).
8. Check all signal panels for activation of the properly labeled warning signal; also check main-line gauge and area pressure gauges to ensure their function.
9. Silence the audible signal. Visual signal should remain.
10. Open main-line shutoff valve.
11. Check main-line gauge for proper line pressure.
12. Check all signal panels for deactivation of warning signals.

**C-4.1.7 [4-3.1.2.2(c)1]** This signal should be initially tested at the time the tests of C-4.1.4 are performed.

## C-4.2 Retesting and Maintenance of Nonflammable Medical Piped Gas Systems (Level 1 Systems).

NOTE: Numbers in brackets refer to paragraphs in Chapter 4 of text.

**C-4.2.1 [4-3.1.1.5]** These systems should be checked daily to assure that proper pressure is maintained and that the changeover signal has not malfunctioned. Periodic retesting of the routine changeover signal is not necessary as it will normally be activated on a regular basis.

**C-4.2.2 [4-3.1.1.6]** These systems should be checked daily to assure that proper pressure is maintained and that the changeover signal has not malfunctioned. Periodic retesting of the routine changeover signal is not required. Annual retesting of the operation of the reserve and activation of the reserve-in-use signal should be performed.

**C-4.2.3 [4-3.1.1.6(b)]** If the system has an actuating switch and signal to monitor the contents of the reserve, it should be retested annually.

**C-4.2.4 [4-3.1.1.7]** Maintenance and periodic testing of the bulk system is the responsibility of the owner or the organization responsible for the operation and maintenance of that system. The staff of the facility should check the supply system daily to ensure that medical gas is ordered when the contents gauge drops to the reorder level designated by the supplier. Piping system pressure gauges and other gauges designated by the supplier should be checked regularly, and gradual variation, either increases or decreases, from the normal range should be reported to the supplier. These variations might indicate the need for corrective action.

Periodic testing of the master signal panel system, other than the routine changeover signal, should be performed. Request assistance from the supplier or detailed instruction if readjustment of bulk supply controls is necessary to complete these tests.

**C-4.2.5 [4-3.1.2.2(e)1]** The main-line pressure gauge should be checked daily to ensure the continued presence of the desired pressure. Variation, either increases or decreases, should be investigated and corrected.

**C-4.2.6 [4-3.1.1.9(b)]** Quarterly rechecking of the location of the air intake should be made to ensure that it continues to be a satisfactory source for medical compressed air.

> The quarterly check might include a physical inspection for accumulations of debris around the intake; an examination of the immediate area around the intake for new exhausts that could pollute air being drawn in or for any changes that might affect the air circulation in the area of the intake; and an examination of Environmental Protection Agency reports on air quality in the locality. If any of these examinations raise concerns about the air purity or quality, a more detailed purity examination should be conducted.

**C-4.2.7 [4-3.1.1.9(f)]** Proper functioning of the pressure gauge and high-water-level sensor should be checked at least annually. Check the receiver drain daily to determine if an excessive quantity of condensed water has accumulated in the receiver.

**C-4.2.8 [4-3.1.1.9(g)]** An important item required for operation of any medical compressed air supply system is a comprehensive preventive maintenance program. Worn parts on reciprocating compressors can cause high discharge temperatures resulting in an increase of contaminants in the discharge gas. Adsorber beds, if not changed at specified time intervals, can become saturated and lose their effectiveness. It is important that all components of the system be maintained in accordance with the manufacturers' recommendations. It is important that any instrumentation, including analytical equipment, be calibrated routinely and maintained in operating order. Proper functioning of the dew point sensor should be checked at least annually.

**C-4.2.9 [4-3.1.2.2(a)1]** When test buttons are provided with signal panels, activation of the audible and visual signals should be performed on a regular basis (monthly).

**C-4.2.10 [4-3.1.2.2(b)3a] Changeover Warning Signal—Manifold or Alternating Supply—4-3.1.1.5(a), 4-3.1.1.6(a)2, and 4-3.1.1.7(a)2.** As this is a routine signal that is activated and deactivated at frequent intervals, there is no need for retesting UNLESS it fails. If the reserve-in-use signal is activated because both units of the operating supply are depleted without the prior activation of the changeover signal, it should be repaired and retested.

**C-4.2.11 [4-3.1.2.2(b)3b] Reserve-In-Use Warning Signal—4-3.1.1.6(a)2 and 3.** All components of this warning signal system should be retested annually in accordance with Steps 2 through 7 of the procedure given in C-4.1.4. Audible and visual signals should be tested periodically during the year (monthly).

**C-4.2.12 [4-3.1.2.2(b)3d] Reserve Supply Low (Down to an average one-day supply)—4-3.1.1.6(b) and 4-3.1.1.7(b)2.** *High-Pressure Cylinder or Liquid Reserve.* All components of these signal warning systems should be retested annually in accordance with Steps 2 through 8 of the procedure given in C-4.1.5. If test buttons are provided, audible and visual signals should be periodically tested throughout the year (monthly).

**C-4.2.13 [4-3.1.2.2(d)]** The medical compressed air system alarms in 4-3.4.1.4(b)1 should be checked at least annually.

**C-4.2.14 [4-3.1.2.2(e)1]** This pressure gauge should be checked on a daily basis to ensure proper piping system pressure. A change, increase or decrease, if noted, can give evidence that maintenance is required on the line pressure regulator and could thus avoid a problem.

**C-4.2.15 [4-3.1.2.2(a)2]** This pressure gauge should be checked on a daily basis to ensure proper system pressure. A gradual change, increase or decrease, if noted, will give an indication of a developing problem that could be avoided by preventive maintenance.

**C-4.2.16 [4-3.4.1.3(d)]** Annual retesting of all components of warning systems, if it can be done without changing piping system line pressure, should be performed.

**C-4.2.17 [4-3.4.1.3(d)2]** If test buttons are provided, the retesting of audible and visual alarm indicators should be performed monthly.

**C-4.2.18 [4-3.1.2.3]** Shutoff valves should be periodically checked for external leakage by means of a test solution or other equally effective means of leak detection safe for use with oxygen.

**C-4.2.19 [4-3.1.2.4]** Station outlets should be periodically checked for leakage and flow. Instructions of the manufacturer should be followed in making this examination.

Flow rates for a given pressure can vary among systems due to the differences among manufacturers and among the various models of a manufacturer. The committee responsible for this material has not included a recommended value for existing systems. What is important, however, is the consistency of readings over a period of time after a facility has determined what the minimum acceptable flow rates are for the devices that it will be connecting to the system.

## C-4.3 Examples, Medical-Surgical Vacuum System Sizing.

These examples serve only to illustrate how sizing of medical-surgical vacuum systems should be approached.

The sizing recommendations that were in Appendix A were moved to Appendix C in the 1999 edition to make the information easier to use. Table C-4.3.4, with references to the A and B inlets, was removed from the 1996 edition of this standard, making the sizing equations unusable. The 1999 edition reintroduces that table, with this caveat: The reader should be aware that the table was originally published in 1980. Since that time, new applications for vacuum use that are not reflected in this table have developed. Appropriate caution should be applied in its use. Type A inlets are for the more critical uses (i.e., intensive care), while Type B inlets are for the less critical uses (i.e., patient rooms). Contrary to some thinking, applying all unfamiliar inlet uses to the A types can, in some cases, result in undersizing. Care should be taken to designate A and B inlets accurately.

NOTE: The following material is included in this appendix for the convenience of the many designers using the material. The user should be aware that the material has not been reexamined since its initial publication in 1980, and that appropriate caution should be applied in its use.

**C-4.3.1  Example 1.**  Vacuum Source Sizing Example. Calculate the required vacuum pump capacity to meet the demands of a hypothetical hospital with rooms and station inlets quantities described below:

Pump Sizing for 3 in. Hg

Piping Pressure Drop:

| | |
|---|---|
| Minimum allowable system vacuum | 12 in. Hg Vac. |
| Design pressure drop | 3 in. Hg Vac. |
| Minimum operating vacuum at receiver | 15 in. Hg Vac. |

**C-4.3.2  Example 2.**  Pipe Sizing Example (Not Related to Examples 1 and 3). See Figure C-4.3(a).

**C-4.3.3  Example 3.**  Pipe Sizing Example (Not Related to Examples 1 and 2). See Figure C-4.3(b).

To maintain the minimum operating vacuum at the receiver, typical control settings for

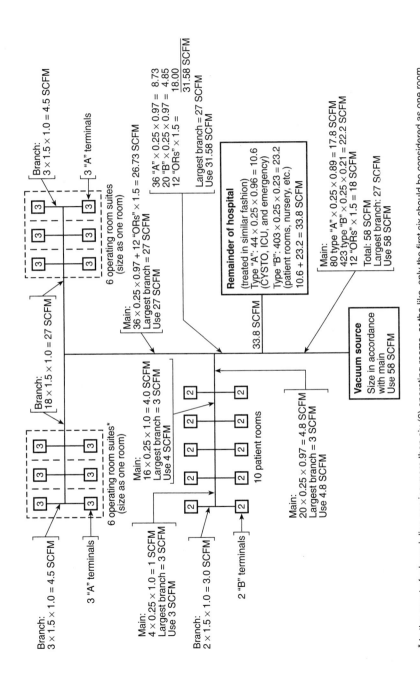

*Figure C-4.3(a) Typical branch and main sizing.*

* In the event of a branch line serving more than six (6) operating rooms, or the like, only the first six should be considered as one room. The branch sizing for the remaining rooms should use the same procedure as for other branch lines. See Figure C-4.3(b).

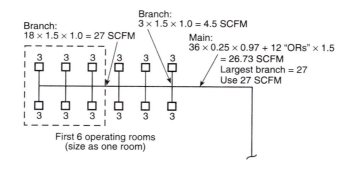

**Figure C-4.3(b)** *Sizing branch lines serving large operating suites*

a duplex vacuum pump installation might be as follows (assuming pumps are located at the receiver):

NOTE: Three-inch vacuum pressure loss used in the illustration can be varied to suit system design.

|  | Start | Stop |
|---|---|---|
| Lead Switch | 16 in. Hg Vac. | 19 in. Hg Vac. |
| Lag Switch | 15 in. Hg Vac. | 18 in. Hg Vac. |

### C-4.3.4 Recommended Vacuum Source Sizing.

The material in this appendix represents one of the most thoroughly researched methodologies for the sizing of vacuum systems. The original research is somewhat dated and the requirements should be used with some care and with attention to the unique requirements of the facility. Nevertheless, this method for sizing has proven effective and is widely used.

It is debated within the committee whether vacuum sizing is even within the scope of the standard. After much discussion during the 1999 revision cycle, it was agreed to retain the sizing method in the appendix, where it cannot be construed to be mandatory and is presented for informational purposes only.

*Unweighted System Demand.* Pump sizing is based upon first determining the total number of station inlets in each of Groups A and B. These totals, each multiplied by 0.25 SCFM, provide the two basic figures necessary to calculate total demand on the system.

*Percentage in Use Factor.* The two SCFM totals thus determined (one for each group) are multiplied by the appropriate "percent in use" factor as shown on the curves illustrated in Figure C-4-3.4, Simultaneous Use Curves.

*Total Weighted System Demand.* Adding these two calculated demand totals (for Groups A and B) and, in addition, allowing 1.5 SCFM for each operating room provides the total

*Table C-4.3.1(a) Hospital Parameters*

| Room Designation | Number of Rooms or Beds | Number of Station Inlets | Type/Usage |
|---|---|---|---|
| Operating Rooms | 6 | 18 | A |
| Cystoscopy Rooms | 2 | 6 | A |
| Delivery Rooms | 4 | 12 | A |
| Recovery Rooms | 13 | 39 | A |
| ICUs | 24 | 72 | A |
| Emergency Rooms | 10 | 10 | A |
| Emergency Rooms—Major Trauma | 2 | 6 | A |
| Patient Rooms | 385 | 385 | B |
| Nurseries | 30 | 30 | B |
| Treatment and Examination Rooms | 20 | 20 | B |
| Autopsy | 1 | 1 | B |
| Respiratory Care | 1 | 1 | B |
| Dialysis Unit | 4 | 2 | B |

*Table C-4.3.1(b) Calculations*

| Type of Room | No. of Station Inlets | SCFM | Use Factor* | Adjusted SCFM |
|---|---|---|---|---|
| Type A | 163 | $163 \times 0.25 = 41$ | 0.52 | 21 |
| Type B | 439 | $439 \times 0.25 = 110$ | 0.22 | 24 |
| Operating Rooms | 6 | $6 \times 1.5 = 9$ | 1.0 | 9 |
| | | | | 54** |

*Per Table C-4-3.4.

**Does not include waste anesthetic gas evacuation.

system demand and the required vacuum pump capacity. The pump should be selected to handle this flow or the maximum flow established for mains, whichever is higher.

*Summary.* The basic sizing formula is:

$$\text{Vacuum Pump Size (SCFM)} = N_A \times 0.25 \times \text{U.F.}_A + N_B \times 0.25 \times \text{U.F.}_B + N_{OR} \times 1.5$$

where:

$N_A$ = number of A-type terminals

$N_B$ = number of B-type terminals

$\text{U.F.}_A$ = use factor for A-type terminal total

$\text{U.F.}_B$ = use factor for B-type terminal total

$N_{OR}$ = number of operating rooms

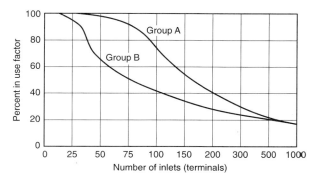

Note 1: If the medical-surgical vacuum system is to be used for the disposal of waste anesthetic gases, caution must be taken to ensure that the system is designed for the additional volume required. It is recommended that 4-3.3.1, Waste Anesthetic Gas Disposal, be consulted as well. It is essential that the design team consult with medical and hospital staff when determining the minimum number of station inlets.

Note 2: It should be understood that the percentage in use factors obtained from this figure represent an average hospital. Hospitals with heavier-than-average use can require higher use factors.

*Figure C-4.3.4  Simultaneous use curves.*

**C-4.3.4.1** Depending on anticipated vacuum system demand and utilization, as determined by consultation with the medical hospital staff, two or more centrally piped systems might be considered.

Where several adjacent buildings are each equipped with vacuum sets, installation of a valved, normally closed, cross-connection line should be considered to provide emergency backup and operating economy under low load conditions. The tube should be adequately sized. Consideration should also be given to the fact that, when the valve is open, continuous-duty operation of the single vacuum source can pose special design problems.

Consideration should be given to being able to interconnect two or more duplex pump systems.

**C-4.3.4.2** One method of indicating the reserved vacuum pump is in use is to activate the alarm from the vacuum switch that starts the reserve vacuum pump.

**C-4.3.4.3** Characteristics of the vacuum pump and volume of the piping system are considerations for proper receiver sizing.

**C-4.3.4.4** Vibration can possibly cause motor deterioration and premature piping failures. Excessive noise can interfere with trouble alarms being heard.

**C-4.3.4.5** Vacuum exhaust from separate pumps can be manifolded to a common exhaust line.

**C-4.3.4.6** See Table C-4.8 for recommended number of outlets and inlets for piped gas and vacuum systems, respectively. *(See Table C-4.3.4.)*

*Table C-4.3.4 Number of Vacuum Station Inlets without Waste Anesthetic Gas Disposal*

|  | Minimum Number of Station Inlets | Usage Group |
|---|---|---|
| Anesthetizing Locations |  |  |
| Operating room | 3/rm | A |
| Cystoscopy | 3/rm | A |
| Delivery | 3/rm | A |
| Special Procedures | 3/rm | A |
| Other Anesthetizing Locations | 3/rm | A |
| Acute Care Locations (Nonanesthetizing Locations) |  |  |
| Recovery Room | 3/bed | A |
| ICUs (Except Cardiac) | 3/bed | A |
| Special Procedures | 2/rm | A |
| Emergency Rooms | 1/bed | A |
| Emergency Rooms— Major Trauma | 3/bed | A |
| Cardiac ICU (CCU) | 2/bed | A |
| Catheterization Lab | 2/rm | B |
| Surgical Excision Rooms | 1/rm | B |
| Dialysis Unit | (1/2)/bed | B |
| Birthing Rooms | 2/rm | A |
| Subacute Care Areas (Nonanesthetizing Locations) |  |  |
| Nurseries | 1/bed | B |
| Patient Rooms | 1/bed | B |
| Exam and Treatment Rooms | 1/bed | B |
| Respiratory Care | Convenience |  |
| Other |  |  |
| Autopsy | 1/table | B |
| Central Supply | Convenience | B |
| Equipment Repair, Calibration, and Teaching | Convenience | B |

**C-4.3.4.7** For requirements for piping within the source portion of the vacuum system, see 4-3.2.1.7.

**C-4.3.4.8 Recommended Minimum Pipe Sizing.** *Branch and Riser Sizing.* Branch sizing should be on the basis of a flow into the system of 1.5 SCFM per station inlet served, commencing with the station inlet on the branch farthest from the vacuum source(s), until all of the station inlets in a room have been accommodated. Branch lines serving more than one room should be sized as mains in accordance with the paragraph below. Operating room suites, ICU suites, and the like, comprising several rooms, should be treated as one room. Risers should be sized in the same manner as branches.

 *Mains.* Sizing should be on the basis of 0.25 SCFM per station inlet served, as described in C-4.3, with the further provision that the size of any main line should not be less than the largest pipe in any branch served by that main. The flow rate to be handled at any point in the main should be computed on the number of A and B stations connected thereto, multiplied by 0.25 SCFM, the simultaneous use percentage plus the allowance of 1.5 SCFM per operating room, or the flow from the largest branch served, whichever is greater.

## C-4.4 Vacuum Flow Chart and Formulas.

Flow chart sizing is based on SCFM, not ACFM. As an example, 100 SCFM through a 3-in. Type L copper tube results in a pressure drop of 0.32 in. Hg/100 ft. However, 100 ACFM through the same 3-in. tube would result in a pressure drop of 0.1 in. Hg/100 ft.

NOTE: Pressure drops at other vacuum levels can be closely approximated by dividing the pressure drop found from the chart (for a given SCFM and pipe size) by the ratio:

$$\frac{30 - \text{new vacuum level}}{15}$$

Formulas for Calculating Pressure Drop
for Other Types and Sizes of Pipe

(Eq. 1) Darcy's Formula:

$$P = 0.01414f\left(\frac{L}{D}\right) \times \frac{\rho V^2}{2g}$$

where:

$P$ = pressure drop in. Hg abx.

$f$ = friction factor determined from Moody Diagram

$L$ = length of pipe, ft

$D$ = internal diameter of pipe, ft

$\rho$ = density of air at upstream pressure, lb/ft$^3$

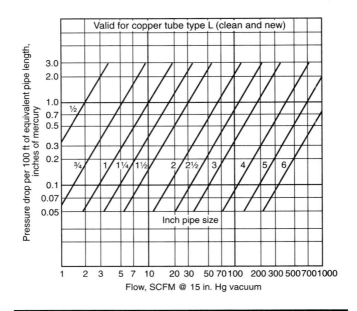

***Figure C-4.4*** *Vacuum flow chart.*

$V$ = velocity of air at upstream pressure, ft/sec

$g$ = gravitation constant, 32.2 ft/sec$^2$

For clean, new copper tube K, L, or M, the friction factor can be closely approximated by the following relation:

$$f = \frac{0.184}{(Re_N)^{0.2}} \qquad \text{(Eq. 2)}$$

where:

$Re_N$ = Reynold's number, $(\rho VD)/\mu$

$\mu$ = absolute (dynamic) viscosity, lb/(sec ft)

Friction factors of commercial steel pipe are higher.

## C-4.5 Metric Conversion Factors.

1 in. = 2.540 cm

1 ft = 30.48 cm

1 atm = 29.92 in. Hg = 760 mm Hg

$$1 \text{ lb/in.}^2 = 4.882 \text{ kg/m}^2$$
$$1 \text{ ft}^3/\text{min} = 28.32 \text{ L/min}$$

## C-4.6 Comments on Derivation of Design Parameters for Medical-Surgical Vacuum Systems.

While most vacuum system design parameters, such as pressure drop, are derived from the laws of physics, two very important items are almost entirely empirical. The number of vacuum station inlets needed for various types of rooms or functional areas of a health care facility and, second, the number of station inlets that are in simultaneous operation at any given time.

> This material was prepared by the former Committee on Medical-Surgical Vacuum systems (now part of the Committee on Piping Systems) to educate the reader as well as to provide some historical background.

The reasons for this empiricism are obvious. The number of station inlets needed for any particular room depends not only on the medical needs of the patients being treated, but also upon the location of those station inlets within each room and the individual characteristics of each vacuum device attached to the station inlets. The number of station inlets in simultaneous use (the diversity factor) depends not only on the type of medical facility involved but also, to some extent, on the geographical area that the facility serves.

The number of vacuum station inlets needed and the diversity factor determine the "load" on the vacuum system. This load is then used to determine the required vacuum pump capacity as well as the sizing of the piping between station inlets and pumps. One design approach would be to assume a "worst-case" situation (such as all installed station inlets are in simultaneous use). Another would be to assume a fixed diversity factor regardless of facility size.

All such arbitrary approaches can be criticized as being either unnecessarily expensive or resulting in inadequate systems. Clearly, design recommendations must be based upon the actual vacuum needs in "real-life" facilities. Given the obvious limitations of time and money, these recommendations can be based only on a survey of a fraction of the total number of health care facilities in existence at any one time.

In 1974, the then NFPA Sectional Committee on Medical-Surgical Vacuum Systems[1] examined representative samples of suction apparatus to determine the design requirements

---

[1]In 1974, the Sectional Committee was actually an ad hoc Subcommittee (formed in 1971) of the Committee on Hospitals. In 1975, it became a full Sectional Committee under the jurisdiction of the Correlating Committee on Health Care Facilities. In 1976, Sectional Committees were raised to Technical Committee level. In 1985, the Health Care Facilities Project was reorganized, with the Technical Committee on Medical-Surgical Vacuum Systems becoming the Standing Subcommittee on Vacuum Systems and Equipment. The responsibility for this topic now rests with the Technical Committee on Piping Systems.

(i.e., flow rates and vacuum) for the associated station inlets. "As-delivered" samples of the apparatus of five leading manufacturers, covering an estimated 90 percent of all equipment then in common use in the United States, were measured in the presence of Sectional Committee members at the engineering laboratories of one of the manufacturers. Field conditions were simulated by the use of saline solutions and whole-blood samples provided for this purpose by a member of the Sectional Committee. The flow rate given in 4-3.4.2.1(c) and minimum vacuum given in 4-3.4.2.1(a) are based on these measurements. Periodic review of these 1974 measurements indicated that they were still valid as of 1980.

In 1976, the Sectional Committee on Medical-Surgical Vacuum Systems examined the vacuum systems of nine hospitals to determine the types and locations of their vacuum station inlets, the number of station inlets in use throughout the day, and total demand on the vacuum source(s) as the various station inlets were used. These hospitals ranged in size from 100 beds to 1200 beds, and, in terms of the types of medical procedures performed and demands placed on their vacuum systems, were considered a fair representation of hospitals in the United States. Flow-rate and pressure-recording instruments were provided by one of the manufacturers. The original data was based on these measurements.

Between 1976 and 1977, the vacuum systems of approximately 20 additional hospitals were examined by one or more members of the Sectional Committee. Several of these systems were being examined because of malfunctions or inadequate performance. The others were new systems being designed and installed, or new extensions to existing systems. The information obtained from these hospitals was used to make minor corrections to original data.

The sampling of hospital vacuum systems was expanded in 1978. Whereas previous data were based upon short, 90-minute data observations, newer data were based upon one-week data acquisition. Although 13 hospital systems were studied, only 9 contained usable data. This information was later expanded in 1980 by data from 21 additional hospital systems. In total, data from 67 vacuum systems have been gathered by the CGA, industry members of the Technical Committee on Medical-Surgical Vacuum Systems, and by the American Society for Hospital Engineering. Hospital sizes varied from 40 to 1200 beds and constituted a broader representation than before.

The data from the 1978–1980 surveys (30) were analyzed using the existing 1978 formulae. All but eight systems fit the existing formulae. The important conclusions from an analysis indicated the following:

1. The number of operating rooms was found to be the single most important parameter affecting SCFM demand.
2. The total number of A-type and B-type terminals was the second most important parameter.
3. Whether the hospital used the central vacuum system for waste anesthetic gas disposal was not found to be statistically significant in this group of data.

The basic 1978 formulae were subsequently adjusted in 1980 to accommodate an additional 1.5 SCFM requirement for each operating room. The formulae were now found to have virtually 100 percent unanimity with all 67 data samples. Additionally, the formulae provide for a sizing that gives 2½ times the observed peak demand, a margin that should be enough for even the most conservative users.

Over the years several members of the Technical Committee on Medical-Surgical Vacuum Systems have planned, designed, and supervised the installation of a number of these systems using the procedures outlined in Chapter 4 and its associated Appendixes A-4 and C-4. These systems have continued to perform as intended.

### C-4.7 Oxygen Service Related Documents.

The following publications may be used for technical reference:

ASTM G63, *Guide for Evaluating Nonmetallic Materials for Oxygen Service.*

ASTM G88, *Guide for Designing Systems for Oxygen Service.*

ASTM G93, *Practice for Cleaning Methods for Material and Equipment Used in Oxygen-Enriched Environments.*

ASTM G94, *Guide for Evaluating Metals for Oxygen Service.*

### C-4.8 AIA Recommended Number of Station Outlets/Inlets.

See Table C-4.8.

## C-8 Additional Information on Chapter 8

Appendix C-8 consists of the following:

C-8.1 Medical Safeguards, Respiratory Therapy

C-8.2 Glossary of Respiratory Therapy Terminology

C-8.3 Suggested Fire Response, Respiratory Therapy

C-8.4 Typical Gas Cylinders

### C-8.1 Medical Safeguards, Respiratory Therapy.

#### C-8.1.1 General.

**C-8.1.1.1** Personnel setting up, operating, and maintaining respiratory therapy equipment, including suction apparatus, should familiarize themselves with the problems of the use of each individual unit.

**C-8.1.1.2** Respiratory therapy equipment should be stored and serviced in an area apart from that used for other functions. Preferably the respiratory therapy service should be supplied with its own workroom/ storeroom. Such a room or area may be divided into three sections—cleanup and sterilization, repair, and storage and reissue.

*Table C-4.8 Station Outlets/Inlets for Piped Oxygen, Vacuum, and Medical Air Systems (From AIA Minimum Construction Guidelines for Health Care Facilities)*

| Location | Oxygen Outlets | Vacuum Inlets | Medical Air Outlets |
|---|---|---|---|
| Patient Rooms (Medical and Surgical) | 1 (one outlet accessible to each bed) | 1 (one inlet accessible to each bed) | — |
| Examination/Treatment (Medical, Surgical, and Post-partum Care) | 1 | 1 | — |
| Isolation (Infectious and Protective) (Medical and Surgical) | 1 | 1 | — |
| Security Room (Medical, Surgical, and Postpartum) | 1 | 1 | — |
| Critical Care (General) | 2 | 3 | 1 |
| Isolation (Critical) | 2 | 3 | 1 |
| Coronary Critical Care | 2 | 2 | 1 |
| Pediatric Critical Care | 2 | 3 | 1 |
| Newborn Intensive Care | 3 | 3 | 3 |
| Newborn Nursery (Full-Term)[1] | 1 | 1 | 1 |
| Pediatric and Adolescent | 1 | 1 | 1 |
| Pediatric Nursery | 1 | 1 | 1 |
| Psychiatric Patient Rooms | — | — | — |
| Seclusion Treatment Room | — | — | — |
| General Operating Room | 2 | 3 | 1 |
| Cardio, Ortho, Neurological | 2 | 3 | — |
| Orthopedic Surgery | 2 | 3 | — |
| Surgical Cysto and Endo | 1 | 3 | — |
| Post-Anesthetic Care Unit | 1 | 3 | — |
| Anesthesia Workroom | 1 per workstation | — | 1 per workstation |
| Outpatient Recovery | 1 | 3 | — |
| Postpartum Bedroom | 1 | 1 | — |
| Caesarean/Delivery Room | 2 | 3 | — |
| Labor Room | 1 | 1 | 1 |
| Recovery Room | 1 | 3 | — |
| Labor/Delivery/Recovery (LDR) | 2 | 2 | — |
| Labor/Delivery/Recovery (LDRP) | 2 | 2 | — |
| Initial Emergency Management per bed | 1 | 1 | — |
| Triage Area (Definitive Emergency Care) | 1 | 1 | — |
| Definitive Emergency Care Exam/Treatment Rooms | 1 | 1 | 1 |
| Definitive Emergency Care Holding Area | 1 | 1 | — |
| Trauma/Cardiac Room(s) | 2 | 3 | 1 |
| Orthopedic and Cast Room | 1 | 1 | — |
| Cardiac Catheterization Lab | 1 | 2 | 2 |
| Autopsy Room | — | 1 per workstation | 1 per workstation |

[1] In facilities with newborn intensive care units, outlet requirements in a newborn nursery (full-term) could be reduced.

**C-8.1.1.3** Storage of respiratory therapy equipment should be systematic and segregated from areas of storage of other items of medical equipment. If drawers or cabinets are employed, proper labeling should be utilized to ensure ready availability of equipment.

**C-8.1.1.4** Personnel must be aware of the exact location of equipment in storage to facilitate emergency use.

**C-8.1.2 Handling of Equipment.** Proper procedures must be established for mechanical cleansing and sterilization of equipment coming in contact with patients or through which patients breathe. There must be no residual chemical deposits that might be toxic to the patient and no residual bacteria that might cause cross-infection.

**C-8.1.2.1** Mechanical cleansing and sterilization should be carried out after each patient application.

**C-8.1.2.2** Mechanical cleansing should be sufficiently thorough to remove blood, saliva, mucus, residual adhesive tape, and other debris.

**C-8.1.2.3** Use of improper combinations of medication in therapy equipment should be avoided.

**C-8.1.3 Tracheotomy and Endotracheal Tube Connection.**

**C-8.1.3.1** Pressure breathing apparatus can be connected directly to a tracheotomy or endotracheal tube. Connectors designed to afford a tight fit between breathing tubes of a pressure breathing apparatus and the tracheal tube should have an internal diameter at least as large as that of the tube.

**C-8.1.3.2** A tracheotomy collar should not obstruct movement of gas through the tracheotomy tube.

**C-8.1.3.3** To avoid reducing the effective lumen of tracheotomy tubes and interfering with movement of gas in and out of the lungs, suction tubes or other devices must not remain in the tracheotomy tubes.

> Suction catheters should be no larger than one-half the diameter of the lumen. The suction procedure should not last more than 15 seconds, and reoxygenation of the patient should occur before suctioning is repeated.

**C-8.1.4 Suction Equipment for Respiratory Care.**

**C-8.1.4.1** Equipment employed for patient suction includes the source of suction, the interconnecting tubing, and collection and trap bottles. The bottle used for collection can contain the trap. A trap is a mechanism preventing spillage of liquid contents into the source of suction if the bottle overfills.

**C-8.1.4.2** Suction equipment should be set up and applied only by qualified individuals.

**C-8.1.4.3** Sources of suction without pressure regulation should not be connected directly to a tube to be inserted into a body cavity for continuous suction. Regulation of suction pressure is not required for clearing of the oral cavity or removal of blood or other bodily fluids from open wounds.

> Sentence two was added because the kinds of body fluids present in oral cavities and open wounds affect vacuum regulators after short periods of time. In addition, rapid evacuation is often critical for these situations and vacuum regulators, by design, restrict suction.

**C-8.1.4.4** Suction regulators should be serviced by qualified individuals. Defective regulators should not be employed.

**C-8.1.4.5** Trap bottles should be fixed to the wall or other appropriate stationary object to prevent tipping and subsequent spillage of liquid contents into the source of suction.

**C-8.1.4.5.1** Trap bottles should be utilized between collection bottles and the source of suction to prevent spillage (*see C-8.1.4.1 and C-8.1.4.5*).

**C-8.1.4.5.2** Collection bottles should be placed below the site of suction drainage from the patient, thus allowing gravitational pull to aid rather than impede flow into the collection bottle.

**C-8.1.4.5.3** Collection bottles should be placed as close as practical to the patient to reduce the length of tubing required and to increase the efficiency of suction.

**C-8.1.4.5.4** The overflow-preventive mechanism of the trap bottle should be cleaned each time the bottle is emptied and should be tested periodically to ensure proper functioning.

**C-8.1.4.6** Suction tips or tubes with the largest practical internal diameter should be employed.

> The commentary on C-8.1.3.3 applies here as well.

**C-8.1.4.7** Tubing employed for connection of the various components of the suction system should possess an internal diameter of at least 0.25 in. (6.4 mm). The wall thickness of the tubing should be sufficient to prevent collapse during all conditions of use.

**C-8.1.4.8** Suction tubing employed in a hazardous location is to be electrically conductive.

## C-8.2 Glossary of Respiratory Therapy Terminology.

**Arrhythmia.** Irregularity of heartbeats.

**Asphyxia.** Suffocation from lack of oxygen and an accumulation of carbon dioxide.

**Aspiration.** Removal of accumulated mucus by suction.

**Bronchi.** The two primary divisions of the trachea.

**CPAP.** Continuous positive airway pressure.

**CPR.** Cardiopulmonary resuscitation.

**Croup Tent.** Equipment utilized to provide environmental control inside a canopy in relation to oxygen concentration, temperature, humidity, and filtered gas.

**Cyanosis.** A bluish discoloration of skin and mucus membranes due to excessive concentration of reduced hemoglobin in the blood.

**Defibrillate.** Use of electrical shock to synchronize heart activity.

**Diffusion.** Transfer of gases across the alveolar capillary membrane.

**EKG, ECG.** Electrocardiogram.

**Hemoglobin.** The chemical compound in red blood cells that carries oxygen.

**Hypoxia.** An abnormally decreased supply or concentration of oxygen.

**IMV.** Intermittent mandatory ventilation.

**IPPB.** Intermittent positive pressure breathing.

**PEEP.** Positive end expiratory pressure.

**Respiration.** The exchange by diffusion of gases between the alveoli, the blood, and the tissue.

**RLF.** A disease entity of the premature infant causing blindness.

> There is no reference to oxygen in the definition of *RLF* because there are questions in the medical community concerning the role oxygen plays in the production of RLF.

**Thorax.** The chest; the upper part of the trunk between the neck and the abdomen.

**Trachea.** The windpipe leading from the larynx to the bronchi.

**Ultrasonic Nebulizer.** A device that produces sound waves that are utilized to break up water into aerosol particles.

**Ventilation.** Movement of air into and out of the lungs.

**Ventilator.** Machine used to support or assist nonbreathing or inadequately breathing patient.

## C-8.3 Suggested Fire Response, Respiratory Therapy.

Suggested procedure in the event of fire involving respiratory therapy apparatus.

**C-8.3.1 General.** Fires in oxygen-enriched atmospheres spread rapidly, generate intense heat, and produce large volumes of heated and potentially toxic gases. Because of the immediate threat to patients and personnel, as well as the damage to equipment and possible spread to the structure of the building, it is important that all personnel be aware of the steps necessary to save life, to preserve limb, and, within reason, to extinguish or contain the fire.

### C-8.3.2 Steps to Take in Event of Fire.

**C-8.3.2.1** The following steps are recommended in the event of a fire, in the approximate order of importance:

(a) Remove the patient or patients immediately exposed from the site of the fire if their hair and clothing are not burning; if they are burning, extinguish the flames. *(See C-8.3.4 and C-8.3.5.)*

(b) Sound the fire alarm by whatever mode the hospital fire plan provides.

(c) Close off the supply of oxygen to the therapy apparatus involved if this step can be accomplished without injury to personnel. *(See C-8.3.3.)*

(d) Carry out any other steps specified in the fire plan of the hospital. For example:

1. Remove patients threatened by the fire
2. Close doors leading to the site of the fire
3. Attempt to extinguish or contain the fire *(See C-8.3.4.)*
4. Direct fire fighters to the site of the fire
5. Take whatever steps necessary to protect or evacuate patients in adjacent areas

### C-8.3.3 Closing Off of Oxygen Supply.

**C-8.3.3.1** In the event of a fire involving respiratory therapy equipment connected to an oxygen station outlet, the zone valve supplying that station is to be closed.

**C-8.3.3.1.1** All personnel are cautioned to be aware of the hazard of such a step to other patients receiving oxygen supplied through the same zone valve. Steps should be taken to minimize such hazards, realizing that closing the valve is of foremost importance.

**C-8.3.3.2** In the case of oxygen therapy apparatus supplied by a cylinder or container of oxygen, it is desirable to close the valve of the cylinder or container, provided that such closure can be accomplished without injury to personnel.

NOTE: Metallic components of regulators and valves can become exceedingly hot if exposed to flame. Personnel are cautioned not to use their bare hands to affect closure.

### C-8.3.4 Extinguishment or Containment of Fire.

**C-8.3.4.1** Fire originating in or involving respiratory therapy apparatus generally involves combustibles such as rubber, plastic, linen, blankets, and the like. Water or water-based extinguishing agents are most effective in such fires.

**C-8.3.4.1.1** Precautions should be observed if electrical equipment is adjacent to or involved in the fire, because of the danger of electrocution of personnel if streams of water contact live 115-V circuits.

**C-8.3.4.1.2** Before attempting to fight such a fire with water or a water-based extinguishing agent, such electrical apparatus should be disconnected from the supply outlet, or the supply circuit deenergized at the circuit panel.

**C-8.3.4.1.3** If such deenergization cannot be accomplished, water should not be employed. *(See C-8.3.4.2.)*

**C-8.3.4.2** Fires involving or adjacent to electrical equipment with live circuits can be fought with extinguishers suitable for Class C fires, in accordance with NFPA 10, *Standard for Portable Fire Extinguishers.*

NOTE: Chemical extinguishers are not effective against fires in oxygen-enriched atmospheres unless the source of oxygen is shut off. See C-8.3.3 for closing off oxygen supply.

### C-8.3.5 Protection of Patients and Personnel.

**C-8.3.5.1** Because of the intense heat generated, serious and even fatal burns of the skin or of the lungs from inhaling heated gases are possible sequelae to the oxygen-enriched-atmosphere fire. Thus, it is essential that patients be removed from the site of the fire whenever practical.

NOTE: Where a nonambulatory patient is connected to a burning piece of therapy equipment, it might be more practical as the initial step to remove the equipment and/or extinguish the fire than to remove the patient.

**C-8.3.5.2** The large quantities of noxious gases produced constitute a threat to life from asphyxia, beyond the thermal burn problem.

**C-8.3.5.2.1** Personnel are cautioned not to remain in the fire area after patients are evacuated if quantities of gaseous combustion products are present.

### C-8.3.6 Indoctrination of Personnel.

**C-8.3.6.1** It is highly desirable that personnel involved in the care of patients, including nurses, aides, ward secretaries, and physicians, irrespective of whether or not they are involved in respiratory therapy practices, be thoroughly indoctrinated in all aspects of fire safety, including the following:

(a) The location of zone valves of nonflammable medical gas systems where employed, and the station outlets controlled by each valve.

(b) The location of electrical service boxes, and the areas served thereby.

(c) The location of fire extinguishers, indications for their use, and techniques for their application.

(d) The recommended methods of evacuating patients, and routes by which such evacuation is accomplished most expeditiously. Reference should be made to the facility's fire plan.

(e) The steps involved in carrying out the fire plan of the hospital.

(f) The location of fire alarm boxes, or knowledge of other methods, for summoning the local fire department.

## C-8.4 Typical Gas Cylinders.

See Table C-12.5, Typical Gas Cylinders.

# C-10 Additional Information on Chapter 10

Appendix C-10 consists of the following:

C-10.1 Fire Incidents in Laboratories

C-10.2 Related Definitions, Laboratories

## C-10.1 Fire Incidents in Laboratories.

The following descriptions of laboratory fires are selected from previous editions of NFPA 99 and from the National Fire Incident Reporting System data base.

*Iowa, October 1980*

A hospital fire, originating in a second-floor pathology laboratory, occurred when electrical wires arced and ignited cloth towels placed under beakers. The beakers contained tissue samples, alcohol, and formaldehyde. The contents of the beakers caused the fire to spread to other larger containers of chemicals in the lab.

There was a 20- to 30-minute delay in detection of this fire because there was no automatic smoke detection equipment in the laboratory. Smoke detectors in the air ducts located in the hallways did operate when the smoke filtered out of the lab. There was no automatic sprinkler system.

No other specifics were reported as to the cause of the electrical arcing.

Direct property damage was estimated at $20,000.

*Pennsylvania, December 1980*

A small fire, of electrical nature, broke out in a hospital laboratory. The fire involved a condensate drip tray which was used to dissipate water from a refrigerator unit. The probable fire scenario was that a short circuit resulted from the aging rubber insulation of the cord. The unit is always left "on."

No direct property damage was reported for this fire. There were no automatic sprinklers in the lab area of the hospital. There were heat detectors in the area, but no smoke detectors. The fire generated large amounts of smoke.

*Rhode Island, October 1981*

A fire occurred in a blood bank/donor lab in a hospital. A patient was lying on one of three contour couches in the donor room giving blood. The technician pushed a button to raise the couch, then heard a pop, and saw flames and smoke coming from the couch. The technician tried unsuccessfully to extinguish the fire with a portable fire extinguisher.

A supervisor pulled the manual pull station and the fire department arrived within 3 minutes.

One civilian and one fire fighter were injured in the fire.

There was extensive smoke and soot damage in the area. Direct property damage was estimated at $12,000. The fire occurred in an unsprinklered building.

The cause of the fire was determined to be a short circuit in the wiring in the motor of the couch.

*New Jersey, April 1982*

A small hospital fire occurred in a processing laboratory where tissue samples are cut and mounted in metal or polypropylene cassettes and then run through a processor. In the processor, the mounted samples are dipped in a series of baths. The cassettes were stored in polystyrene cabinets.

The cause of the fire was undetermined. Damage was confined to a 6-ft$^2$ area in the corner of the tissue lab. The fronts of the cassette cabinets suffered partial melting and some cassettes had the paraffin melted. It was estimated that 80 percent of the specimen cassettes were intact and salvageable.

Total direct property damage was estimated at $70,000 and business interruption at $4,000.

A single sprinkler head operated and extinguished the fire. The waterflow alarm was received by the hospital switchboard and the municipal dispatching service.

*Massachusetts, April 1982*

A tissue laboratory in a hospital was the scene of a fire that resulted in $50,000 in direct property damage. An additional $50,000 was lost due to business interruption.

The tissue lab was located in the pathology area of the lab building and housed 11 tissue processing machines. Eight of the machines were used to dehydrate tissue samples in a xylene concentrated solution or an alcohol solution.

When a technician left the room at 5:15 p.m., all the machines were functioning properly. Twenty minutes later, a waterflow and smoke detection alarm was received at the command center with direct transmission to the fire department. Two sprinkler heads helped control the fire. The fire was extinguished by the fire department using a 1 ½-in. hand line from an interior standpipe. The fire was attributed to the jamming of one of the baskets of a processing machine as it was being moved from one carriage to another. The motor failed to shut down as it should have, overheated, and eventually ignited the flammable xylene and alcohol solutions.

*Tennessee, May 1984*

The overheating of xylene inside a distiller located in the hospital lab resulted in a fire. Apparently, the escaping flammable vapors were ignited by ordinary electrical equipment in the room. Prompt and effective automatic sprinkler activation helped minimize fire damage.

The fire occurred in a fourth floor histology lab. Among the contents of the lab were small xylene stills for reclaiming used solvent, and also tissue processing equipment. A technician had filled the distiller with xylene. Some time later, another person working in the area of the distiller noticed that an odor was coming from the unit and that the solution had a brown color to it. This employee left to find someone to inspect the distiller. This employee returned with another worker to find a grayish haze around the console. Just after leaving the room, the employees saw smoke coming from under the door. A "Code Red" was sounded and the lab was evacuated. The technician who originally was running the machine returned at the sound of the alarm and tried to turn off the instrument by crawling on the floor, but was unable to do so because of the smoke and smell of xylene.

Property loss was estimated at $150,000, and business interruption resulted in an additional $15,000.

*Florida, December 1985*

A fire broke out in a hospital pathology lab and resulted in $100,000 in property damage, and an additional $2,000 in business interruption. The pathology lab analyzes tissue samples from patients. These samples are preserved in an embedding center using paraffin as the preserving agent.

The cause of the fire was determined to be the failure of a thermostat that controls the temperature of the heating element that melts the paraffin in the tissue embedding center.

The fire damaged two tissue embedding centers, an ultrasonic cleaner, two light fixtures, a wood wall cabinet, as well as damaging the wall and ceiling. Microscopes, computer terminals, measuring equipment, and tissue slides and samples were among the items damaged by smoke and soot. The fire damage was confined to the lab.

An employee smelled smoke coming from the lab and noticed that the lab door was hot. A security guard was called immediately and pulled the alarm at a manual station in the hallway. The fire department extinguished the fire with dry chemicals and an inside hose stream located in the hallway. There were no heat or smoke detectors inside the pathology lab. The building was unsprinklered.

*New York, April 1988*

A hospital laboratory was the scene of a $250,000 fire. The fire started when a professor was sterilizing a pair of scissors using the "flaming" procedure. The "flaming" method involves dipping an item into alcohol and then burning off that alcohol with a Bunsen burner. The professor carried out the procedure once, then tried to do it a second time because he thought he had contaminated the scissors. During the second attempt, the alcohol he dipped the scissors into ignited because the scissors were still hot. The container of alcohol was dropped and the fire spread to nearby combustibles, including other flammable liquids.

A security guard noticed the fire and immediately pulled the alarm signaling the fire department and hospital fire brigade. The fire department responded promptly and extinguished the fire.

There were no automatic sprinklers in the fire area. Three civilians were injured in the fire.

*California, April 1989*

The thermostat of a low-temperature lab oven (incubator) malfunctioned, causing the oven to overheat. The unit heated to approximately 200 degrees overnight, causing a smoldering fire. An employee discovered the fire in the sixth-floor laboratory in the medical center when he arrived early to work. His first action was to shut off the incubator, after which he called the fire department.

Fire destroyed the contents of the incubator, and the incubator itself needed repairs due to exposure to dry powder agent. Smoke damage also occurred in the lab and hallway. Property damage was estimated at $1,000.

An alarm sounded after the fire department had used an extinguisher on the fire. The type of alarm was not reported.

*California, November 1989*

Four fire fighters were injured at a fire in a pathology lab at a multi-story hospital medical center when they were exposed to toxic chemical debris and human tissue. The fire originated in a stainless steel cabinet which had two glass-windowed doors. There were two pieces of equipment in the cabinet which were used to process tissue by dipping trays of tissues into a series of containers. The machines were about 20 years old.

The official cause of the fire was listed as a malfunctioning piece of electrically powered lab equipment igniting volatile flammable liquid. The exact point of failure could not be determined.

Automatic detection equipment was present and operated. There was no automatic sprinkler system present in the lab. Direct property loss was estimated at $325,000. No estimates were given for business interruption.

*Michigan, March 1981*

A building that housed various analytical research and development laboratories was the scene of a $60,000 fire. The laboratory involved in the fire was used essentially for liquid and gas chromatography.

The fire occurred when solvent leakage inside, or adjacent to, a liquid chromatograph ignited from an electrical source. Apparently, a small amount of solvent was spilled for up to 25 minutes and subsequently ignited. The fire burned through a plastic tube feeding a waste solvent container on a shelf. The spilled waste solvent intensified the fire. Liquid chromatography uses solvents of methanol and iso-octane.

An employee first heard a crackling and then saw flames at the base of the liquid chromatography instrument. Employees immediately attacked the fire with a dry chemical fire extinguisher. Also, two sprinkler heads operated, limiting the spread of fire within the laboratory. The fire department received a waterflow alarm, a manual fire alarm box, and several phone calls. Fire fighters found the fire nearly out on arrival because of sprinkler activation and consumption of the spilled liquid.

*Virginia, June 1981*

A small fire occurred in a laboratory that manufactures interferon. During this process, red and white blood cells are separated, and the white cells are placed in beakers with nutrients. A virus is introduced to the white cell cultures which then produce the interferon. A centrifuge is used to separate the interferon from the white cells. The process is carried out in a small refrigerated room isolated from other areas by insulated metal panel walls and ceiling.

In the early afternoon, an employee stabilized a magnetic stirring rod which had been banging the side of one of the glass beakers.

Minutes later, personnel noticed smoke and fire within the refrigerated room and immediately extinguished the fires with extinguishers. The fire department also was notified.

Alcohol spilling onto the electrical parts of the magnetic stirrer caused the fire. The spilling was caused by inadequate supervision of the magnetic stirrer.

The fire resulted in $235,000 in direct property damage and an additional $40,000 in business interruption. Metal walls and ceiling panels, some laboratory equipment, and an unknown quantity of interferon were destroyed or damaged in the fire.

There were no automatic detection or suppression systems in the building. There were manual pull stations and portable extinguishers.

*Tissue Processor Fire.* Operated 24 hours per day, but unattended from 11 p.m. to 7 a.m., a tissue processor was suspected of causing $200,000 damage because the incident occurred after 11 p.m. and there were no detectors or automatic extinguishing equipment in the laboratory. Flammable liquids in glass containers stored in an open shelf below the equipment contributed to the intensity of the fire.

Aside from damage to the laboratory, electrical cables in the corridor near the incident shorted and caused power to be interrupted in the hospital. Fire doors closed, but the fire alarm was not sounded.

*Hot Plate Fires.* Acetone, being poured at the sink in a patient treatment lab, was ignited by a nearby hot plate that had just been turned off. The technician dropped the container, which was metal and which, fortunately, fell in an upright position. The patient was safely evacuated, but the fire was intense enough to melt the sweated water pipe fittings of the window ventilator.

Petroleum ether caught fire while a chemist was pouring it in a fume hood from its large glass container—presumably ignited by a nearby hot plate that had recently been turned off. He dropped the glass container on the floor and ran from the room. The bottle broke; ignition caused enough pressure to blow open the lab escape hatch and slam the entrance door shut.

*Refrigerator Explosion.* Eighty ml of diazomethane dissolved in ether detonated in a domestic-type refrigerator. The door blew open, the frame bowed out, and the plastic lining ignited, causing a heavy blanket of soot to be deposited far down the adjoining corridor. *(See 10-7.2.5.)*

*Pressure Filter Fire.* At an eastern hospital pharmacy, a fire-conscious technician prepared for pressure filtering of 50 gal (220 L) of isopropyl alcohol by placing a towel on a table adjacent to the pump; in the event of fire he planned to smother flames of alcohol inadvertently spilled on his person. As he attempted to turn on the pump, the defective switch ignited alcohol on his hands. Instinctively, he reached for the towel as he had previously rehearsed in his mind but, in doing so, he tripped over the hose that was conducting alcohol by gravity from a large open kettle to the suction side of the pump. The hose slipped from its fittings, thereby dumping 50 gal (220 L) of the flaming solvent onto the floor. He escaped with minor injuries, but the pharmacy was destroyed.

(Many fires are intensified by an unfortunate sequence of minor unsafe practices that in themselves seem almost too insignificant to worry about.)

*Water Bath Fire.* When the thermostat on a water bath malfunctioned, the bath overheated, causing the acrylic lid to sag and contact the heater elements. A fire resulted. Heater equipment should always be protected by overtemperature shutoffs. (Based on *DuPont Safety News,* June 14, 1965.)

*Peroxide Explosion.* A distillation apparatus exploded within a lab fume hood. It was caused by the detonation of the residual peroxide. The drawn sash prevented injury, although the electric mantle was torn to shreds. The investigator was using "some isopropyl ether," which had been kept in a clear glass bottle. He allowed the distillation to continue to dryness.

Investigators should become more aware of the nature of ether peroxide formations. Dioxane and ethyl and isopropyl ethers are the most common offenders. Age, sunlight, air space above liquid, and clear glass containers help to create these explosive peroxides. Test frequently for peroxide; filter out peroxides through a column of 80 mesh Alorco activated alumina, as suggested by Dasler and Bauer, *Ind. Eng. Chem. Anal.,* Ed. 18, 52 (1964). Never leave distillations unattended.

## C-10.2  Related Definitions, Laboratories.

The following definitions are taken from other NFPA documents and are critical to the understanding of Chapter 10.

**C-10.2.1†** The following definitions are taken from NFPA 30, *Flammable and Combustible Liquids Code*:

(a) *Flammable Liquid.* A liquid having a closed cup flash point below 100°F (37.8°C) and having a vapor pressure not exceeding 40 psia (2068 mm Hg) at 100°F (37.8°C) shall be known as Class I liquid. Class I liquids shall be subdivided as follows:

1. Class IA shall include those having flash points below 73°F (22.8°C) and having a boiling point below 100°F (37.8°C).
2. Class IB shall include those having flash points below 73°F (22.8°C) and having a boiling point at or above 100°F (37.8°C).
3. Class IC shall include those having flash points at or above 73°F (22.8°C) and below 100°F (37.8°C).

(g) *Combustible Liquid.* A liquid having a closed cup flash point at or above 100°F (37.8°C). Combustible liquids shall be subdivided as follows:

1. Class II liquids shall include those having flash points at or above 100°F (37.8°C) and below 140°F (60°C).
2. Class IIIA liquids shall include those having flash points at or above 140°F (60°C) and below 200°F (93°C).
3. Class IIIB liquids shall include those having flash points at or above 200°F (93°C).

**C-10.2.2†** The following definition is also taken from NFPA 30, *Flammable and Combustible Liquids Code:*

(a) The flash point of a liquid having a viscosity less than 45 SUS at 100°F (37.8°C) and a flash point below 200°F (93.4°C) shall be determined in accordance with ASTM D 56-1982, *Standard Test Method for Flash Point by the Tag Closed Cup Tester.*

(b) The flash point of a liquid having a viscosity of 45 SUS or more at 100°F (37.8°C) or a flash point of 200°F (93.4°C) or higher shall be determined in accordance with ASTM D 93-1980, *Test Methods for Flash Point by the Pensky-Martens Closed Tester.*

**C-10.2.3** The following definitions are based on NFPA 704, *Standard System for the Identification of the Fire Hazards of Materials.*

**C-10.2.3.1 Health Hazard.** A health hazard is any property of a material that, either directly or indirectly, can cause injury or incapacitation, either temporary or permanent, from exposure by contact, inhalation, or ingestion.

**C-10.2.3.1.1 Degrees of Health Hazard.** 4—Materials that on very short exposure could cause death or major residual injury even though prompt medical treatment was given, including those that are too dangerous to be approached without specialized protective equipment. This degree should include the following:

(a) Materials that can penetrate ordinary rubber protective clothing

(b) Materials that under normal conditions or under fire conditions give off gases that are extremely hazardous (i.e., toxic or corrosive) through inhalation or through contact with or absorption through the skin

3—Materials that on short exposure could cause serious temporary or residual injury even though prompt medical treatment was given, including those requiring protection from all bodily contact. This degree should include the following:

(a) Materials giving off highly toxic combustion products

(b) Materials corrosive to living tissue or toxic by skin absorption

2—Materials that on intense or continued exposure could cause temporary incapacitation or possible residual injury unless prompt medical treatment was given, including those requiring use of respiratory protective equipment with independent air supply. This degree should include the following:

(a) Materials giving off toxic combustion products

(b) Materials giving off highly irritating combustion products

(c) Materials that either under normal conditions or under fire conditions give off toxic vapors lacking warning properties

1—Materials that on exposure would cause irritation but only minor residual injury even if no treatment is given, including those that require use of an approved canister-type gas mask. This degree should include the following:

(a) Materials that under fire conditions would give off irritating combustion products

(b) Materials that on the skin could cause irritation without destruction of tissue

0—Materials that on exposure under fire conditions would offer no hazard beyond that of ordinary combustible material

**C-10.2.3.2 Flammability Hazard.** Flammability describes the degree of susceptibility of materials to burning. The form or condition of the material, as well as its inherent properties, affects its flammability.

**C-10.2.3.2.1 Degree of Flammability Hazard.** 4—Materials that will rapidly or completely vaporize at atmospheric pressure and normal ambient temperature or that are readily dispersed in air and that will burn readily. This degree should include the following:

(a) Gases

(b) Cryogenic materials

(c) Any liquid or gaseous material that is a liquid while under pressure and having a flash point below 73°F (22.8°C) and having a boiling point below 100°F (37.8°C) (Class IA flammable liquids)

(d) Materials that on account of their physical form or environmental conditions can form explosive mixtures with air and that are readily dispersed in air, such as dusts of combustible solids and mists of flammable or combustible liquid droplets

3—Liquids and solids that can be ignited under almost all ambient temperature conditions. Materials in this degree produce hazardous atmospheres with air under almost all ambient temperatures or, though unaffected by ambient temperatures, are readily ignited under almost all conditions. This degree should include the following:

(a) Liquids having a flash point below 73°F (22.8°C) and having a boiling point at or above 100°F (37.8°C) and those liquids having a flash point at or above 73°F (22.8°C) and below 100°F (37.8°C) (Class IB and Class IC flammable liquids)

(b) Solid materials in the form of coarse dusts that may burn rapidly but that generally do not form explosive atmospheres with air

(c) Solid materials in a fibrous or shredded form that may burn rapidly and create flash fire hazards, such as cotton, sisal, and hemp

(d) Materials that burn with extreme rapidity, usually by reason of self-contained oxygen (e.g., dry nitrocellulose and many organic peroxides)

(e) Materials that ignite spontaneously when exposed to air

2—Materials that must be moderately heated or exposed to relatively high ambient temperatures before ignition can occur. Materials in this degree would not under normal conditions form hazardous atmospheres with air, but under high ambient temperatures or under moderate heating may release vapor in sufficient quantities to produce hazardous atmospheres with air. This degree should include the following:

(a) Liquids having a flash point above 100°F (37.8°C), but not exceeding 200°F (93.3°C)

(b) Solids and semisolids that readily give off flammable vapors

1—Materials that must be preheated before ignition can occur. Materials in this degree require considerable preheating, under all ambient temperature conditions, before ignition and combustion can occur. This degree should include the following:

(a) Materials that will burn in air when exposed to a temperature of 1500°F (816°C) for a period of 5 minutes or less

(b) Liquids, solids, and semisolids having a flash point above 200°F (93.3°C) (This degree includes most ordinary combustible materials.)

0—Materials that will not burn. This degree should include any material that will not burn in air when exposed to a temperature of 1500°F (816°C) for a period of 5 minutes.

**C-10.2.3.3 Reactivity (Instability) Hazards.** Reactivity describes the ability of a material to chemically react with other stable or unstable materials. For purposes of this hazard identification system, the other material is water, if reaction with water releases energy. Reactions with common materials other than water can release energy violently, but are beyond the scope of this identification system.

Unstable materials are those that, in the pure state or as commercially produced, will vigorously polymerize, decompose, or condense, become self-reactive, or undergo other violent chemical changes.

Stable materials are those that normally have the capacity to resist changes in their chemical composition, despite exposure to air, water, and heat encountered in fire emergencies.

**C-10.2.3.3.1 Degree of Reactivity (Instability) Hazard.** 4—Materials that in themselves are readily capable of detonation or of explosive decomposition or explosive reaction at normal temperatures and pressures. This degree should include materials that are sensitive to mechanical or localized thermal shock at normal temperatures and pressures.

3—Materials that in themselves are capable of detonation or of explosive decomposition or explosive reaction but that require a strong initiating source or that must be heated under confinement before initiation. This degree should include materials that are sensitive to thermal or mechanical shock at elevated temperatures and pressures or that react explosively with water without requiring heat or confinement.

2—Materials that in themselves are normally unstable and readily undergo violent chemical change but do not detonate. This degree should include materials that can undergo chemical change with rapid release of energy at normal temperatures and pressures or that can undergo violent chemical change at elevated temperatures and pressures. It should also include those materials that can react violently with water or that can form potentially explosive mixtures with water.

1—Materials that in themselves are normally stable, but that can become unstable at elevated temperatures and pressures or that may react with water with some release of energy, but not violently.

0—Materials that in themselves are normally stable, even under fire exposure conditions, and that are not reactive with water.

# C-11 Additional Information on Chapter 11

Appendix C-11 consists of the following:

C-11.1 General Considerations

C-11.2 Personnel Notification and Recall

C-11.3 Special Considerations and Protocols

## C-11.1 General Considerations.

The basic plan should be written broadly, providing general but concise coverage of disaster responsibilities and procedures for each facility department and providing detailed responsibilities and procedures for those functions not normally a part of regular routines, for example, operation of the disaster control center. Keyed to the basic plan, the departmental annexes of the plan then outline individual department responsibilities in greater detail. Finally, the disaster procedures for each function within each department are described in terms of actual instructions for individual staff members and employees. Individuals should never be mentioned by name in the plan; rather, responsibilities and procedures should be written in terms of job title. The health care occupancy chapters of NFPA *101, Life Safety Code*, are relevant for review and rehearsals.

## C-11.2 Personnel Notification and Recall.

Medical staff, key personnel, and other personnel needed will be notified and recalled as required. In order to relieve switchboard congestion, it is desirable to utilize a pyramidal system to recall individuals who are off duty or otherwise out of the facility. Under the pyramidal system, an individual who has been notified will notify two other individuals, who in turn will each notify two other individuals, and so on. A current copy of the notification and recall roster, with current home and on-call telephone numbers, will be maintained at the hospital switchboard at all times. In case the pyramidal system is to be utilized, each individual involved in the system must maintain a current copy of the roster at all times, in order that each knows whom they are to notify and the telephone numbers concerned. It is essential that key personnel rosters be kept current.

## C-11.3 Special Considerations and Protocols.

**C-11.3.1 Fire and Explosion.** In the event that the health care facility need not be completely evacuated immediately, the actions staff should take when they are alerted to a fire are detailed in Chapter 31 of NFPA *101, Life Safety Code*.

**C-11.3.2 Severe Storm.** The warning system operated by the National Oceanic and Atmospheric Administration will, in most cases, provide adequate time to permit the health care facility to take certain precautions, and if disaster appears inevitable, to activate the Health Care Disaster Plan in advance of the disaster event. Assuming evacuation is not feasible, some precautions include the following:

(a) Draw all shades and close all drapes as protection against shattering glass.
(b) Lower all patient beds to the low position, wherever possible.
(c) Place blankets on patients/residents.
(d) Close all doors and windows.

> The U.S. Weather Bureau, as a result of studies, no longer recommends that windows on a particular side of a building be kept open during severe windstorms.

(e) Bring indoors those lawn objects that could become missiles.
(f) Remove all articles from window ledges.
(g) Relocate patients/residents to windowless hallways or rooms.

**C-11.3.3 Evacuation.** Evacuation can be partial or total. It might involve moving from one story to another, one lateral section or wing to another, or moving out of the structure. Even partial evacuations can involve all categories of patients; where these are people who would not routinely be moved, extraordinary measures might be required to support life. It is also necessary to ensure movement of supplies in conjunction with any evacuation. Decisions to evacuate might be made as a result of internal problems or under menace of engulfing external threats. In all cases, the following considerations govern:

It should again be noted that, while movement (particularly evacuation to the outside) is the least desired action for a health care facility to take, it may be necessary in some disasters. A facility needs to be prepared for situations when total evacuation is necessary since it has occurred in the past in health care facilities.

(a) Move to pre-designated areas, whether in the facility, nearby, or in remote zones. Evacuation directives will normally indicate destinations.

NOTE: It is recommended to predesign a mutual aid evacuation plan with other health care facilities in the community. *(See B-1.2 for one document on the subject of health care community mutual aid and evacuation planning.)*

(b) Ensure movement of equipment, supplies, and medical records to accompany or meet patients and staff in the new location.

Patients on electrical life-support equipment require the most consideration when evacuating to a new location. Plans have to be made for both the physical needs of such patients during the move and the capabilities of the new location.

(c) Execute predetermined staffing plans. Some staff will accompany patients; others will rendezvous in the new location. Maintenance of shifts is more complex than normal, especially when (1) some hard-to-move patients stay behind in the threatened location, and (2) staff might be separated from their own relocated families.

(d) Protection of patients and staff (during and after movement) against the threatening environment must be provided.

(e) Planning must consider transportation arrangements and patient tracking.

An increase in certain activities, such as the production and transportation of toxic chemicals and the number of arson incidents, has increased the probability of evacuation of health care facilities in times of emergency involving these activities. Natural events such as hurricanes, tornadoes, and volcanic eruptions can also necessitate such action. The nuclear accident at the Three Mile Island Nuclear Plant in Pennsylvania and the eruption of Mount St. Helens required the temporary evacuation of hospitals in those areas.

For most incidents, facilities require only an internal patient relocation plan because of the defend-in-place concept for health care facilities. This concept considers facilities to be composed of many zones that can provide safe areas of refuge. However, facilities also should be prepared for outside relocation of patients if certain internal conditions, such as the interruption of both normal and emergency electrical power, or external events require it.

A well-organized relocation plan incorporates most components of an evacuation plan on a unit-by-unit or zone-by-zone basis as necessary. Should an evacuation be ordered, additional consideration needs to be given to the adequate care of patients once they have left the confines (and protection) of the facility. This would include providing shelter adjacent to the facility or transportation to another facility, the transferring of the patient's *medical records and any vital supplies,* and staff support for each patient.

**C-11.3.4 High Profile.** Admission of a high profile person to a health care facility in an emergency creates two sets of problems that might require partial activation of the Health Care Emergency Preparedness Plan. These problems are as follows:

**C-11.3.4.1 Security.** Provision of security forces in this situation will normally be a responsibility of the U.S. Secret Service or other governmental agency. However, activation of facility security forces might be required to prevent hordes of curious onlookers from entering facility work areas and interfering with routine facility functioning. Routine visiting privileges and routine visiting hours might need to be suspended in parts of the facility.

**C-11.3.4.2 Reception of News Media.** The news media reception plans will need to be activated. In this instance, additional communications to the news reception center will be required. Additional telephones and telephone lines can be installed on an emergency basis on request to the local telephone company. Such requests for additional telephone connections in the facility should, however, first be coordinated with the senior Secret Service officer or governmental representative accompanying the dignitary.

**C-11.3.5 Other Protocols as Deemed Desirable.** In addition to the above, there should follow a number of additional protocols for internal disasters, to be determined by the geographical location of the individual health care facility, for example, natural disasters, civil disturbance protocol, bomb threat protocol, hazardous material protocol, loss of central services (power, water, and gas).

**C-11.3.6 Activation of Emergency Utility Resources.** In the planning phase, backup utility resources will have been stockpiled and arrangements made for mutual aid when required. Such utilities include electrical power, water, and fuel. Through prior coordination with the local office of emergency preparedness or fire department, mobile generators and auxiliary pumps can be obtained in the internal disaster situation. Through these same sources arrangements could be made to supply water tank trucks. Obviously, such planning is in addition to routine planning, in which all health care facilities maintain emergency electrical power plants and, in those areas requiring central heating in winter, backup supplies of oil, coal, or gas. Priorities for use of available power (e.g., air circulation but not air conditioning) must be determined. Sanitation requirements can become overriding in prolonged disasters, and even an ordinary strike by garbage collectors can cause difficulties.

**C-11.3.7 Civil Disturbance.** Large-scale civil disturbances in recent years have shown that health care facilities and their personnel are not immune to the direct effects of human violence in such disturbances. Hospitals in large urban areas must make special provisions in their disaster plans to ensure the physical safety of their employees in transit from the hospital exit to and from a secure means of transportation to their homes. In extreme cases it might be necessary to house employees within the health care facility itself during such civil disturbances. Examples of direct attacks or sniping are extremely rare.

Another aspect of civil disturbances not to be overlooked in facility security planning is the possibility that a given health care facility might have to admit and treat large numbers of prisoners during such emergencies; however, security guards for such patients will normally be provided by the local police department.

Provisions for securing windowed areas on lower floors that could be subject to items being thrown from hostile crowds should be included in the civil disturbance plan. Items such as heavy window screens, guards, substantial drapes, or window shades can be considered as reasonable precautions.

**C-11.3.8 Bomb Threats.** The disaster potential inherent in the telephoned bomb threat warrants inclusion of this disaster contingency in the Health Care Emergency Preparedness Plan. Experience has shown that facility personnel must accompany police or military bomb demolition personnel in searching for the suspected bomb, since speed is of the essence and only individuals familiar with a given area can rapidly spot unfamiliar or suspicious objects or condition in the area. This is particularly true in health care facilities. The facility switchboard operator must be provided with a checklist to be kept available at all times, in order to obtain as much information as possible from the caller concerning location of the supposed bomb, time of detonation, and other essential data, which must be considered in deciding whether or not to evacuate all or part of the facility.

The response of police and fire authorities to bomb threats varies considerably from locality to locality. Knowing exactly what assistance local authorities provide will dictate the level of involvement of the health care facility in the response to the bomb threat. A facility's plans should reflect the requirements or suggestions of local authorities.

**C-11.3.9 Radioactive Contamination.** Disaster planning must consider the possibility of radioactive materials being released from nuclear reactors or transportation accidents, as well as from internal spills. These incidents could require that health care staff and patients be sheltered. Shelter areas can be selected in existing structures and should be planned for during the design of new facilities or additions. Similarly, plans must also consider radiation dose control and decontamination of victims or staff personnel and public safety in connection with nuclear accidents or incidents such as reactor excursions.

Radioactive contamination plans should consider both internal and external disasters. Transportation accidents involving radioactive materials can contaminate rescue workers as well as victims, and this possibility should be considered in the development of any contamination plan.

NFPA 801, *Standard for Fire Protection for Facilities Handling Radioactive Materials* [1], covers this subject, including a section specifically addressing hospital activities.

**C-11.3.10 Hazardous Materials.** There are at least three major sources of concern with regard to non-radioactive hazardous materials. The first is the possibility of a large spill or venting of hazardous materials near the facility; this is especially likely near major rail or truck shipping routes, near pipelines, or near heavy manufacturing plants. Second, every facility contains within its boundaries varying amounts of such materials, especially in the laboratory and custodial areas. A spill of a highly volatile chemical can quickly contaminate an entire structure by way of the air ducts. Finally, contaminated patients can pose a risk to staff, though on a more localized basis. Usually removal of their clothing will reduce the risk materially. In any case, staff must be prepared to seek advice on unknown hazards. This type of advice is not usually available from poison centers, but rather from a central referral, such as CHEMTREC, and its toll-free emergency information service number (800-424-9300).

> The reactions of health care facilities to an incident involving nonradioactive hazardous materials can range from localization and sealing off of contaminated areas or persons to the complete evacuation of the facility. Emergency preparedness plans need to consider both extremes.
>
> Regulatory laws and instructions that govern the response to threats from the use of hazardous materials have been adopted of late. Facilities need to be aware of any regulations governing use or shipment of hazardous materials.

**C-11.3.11 Volcanic Eruptions.** While most of the direct effects of a volcanic eruption are covered in other protocols for disasters (fire, explosion, etc.), it is necessary to make special provisions for functioning in areas of heavy to moderate ash fall. This hazard can exist hundreds of miles downwind from the eruption.

Volcanic "ash" is actually finely pulverized rock blown out of the volcano. Outside the area of direct damage, the ash varies from a fine powder to a coarse sand. General housekeeping measures can exclude much ash. It should be noted, however, that people move about freely during and after ash fall.

Ash fall presents four problems for health care facilities.

1. People require cleanup (brushing, vacuuming) before entering the building.
2. Electromechanical and automotive equipment and air-filtering systems require special care because of the highly abrasive and fine penetration nature of the ash.

> Ash penetration can even result in the short circuiting of devices' electrical systems.

3. Increased flow of patients with respiratory complaints can be expected.
4. Eye protection is required for people who must be out in the dust. (No contact lenses should be worn; goggles are suggested.) Dust masks are available. They are approved by the National Institute for Occupational Safety and Health (NIOSH), and are marked TC-21 plus other digits.

While the threat of volcanic eruptions is not as widespread as other potential disasters, incidents such as the 1980 eruption of Mount St. Helens in Washington demonstrate the need to address this subject.

Volcanoes of the Mount St. Helens type are present from Alaska to California, but the effects of major volcanic eruptions may not be confined to these areas. The entire northwest of the United States, as well as portions of Canada, experienced the effects of the Mount St. Helens eruption.

# C-12  Additional Information on Chapter 12

Appendix C-12 consists of the following:

C-12.1  Nature of Hazards, Anesthetizing Locations

C-12.2  Related Hazards and Safeguards, Anesthetizing Locations

C-12.3  Text of Suggested Signs and Posters for Inhalation Anesthetizing Locations

C-12.4  Suggested Procedures in Event of a Fire or Explosion, Anesthetizing Locations

C-12.5  Cylinder Table

## C-12.1  Nature of Hazards, Anesthetizing Locations.

**C-12.1.1  General.**  The environment of the modern operating room poses numerous hazards, even in those rooms in which flammable agents are prohibited.

**C-12.1.2  Hazards Present in All Anesthetizing Locations.**

**C-12.1.2.1  Electric Shock and Spark Hazards—High-Frequency Burn.**

**C-12.1.2.1.1**  When a human body becomes the connecting link between two points of an electric system that are at different electric potentials, the person is likely to suffer an electric shock or high-frequency burns. When there is a highly conductive pathway from outside the body to the heart or great vessels, small electric currents could cause ventricular fibrillation. If a conductive material bridges two points of an electric system that are different electric potentials, the contact is likely to create a spark or an arc and intense heating of one or more of the conductors involved.

**C-12.1.2.1.2**  Electric equipment that is defective or faulty grounded produces a definite shock hazard if connected to conventional grounded electric circuits and employed in the presence of purposely conductive flooring, as installed in corridors adjacent to operating rooms, or wet flooring as might be encountered in sterilizing or scrub rooms during use.

**C-12.1.2.1.3**  Improper use of the high-frequency electrosurgical unit, alone or in combination with certain items of medical monitoring equipment, can cause serious high-frequency burns to the patient or to personnel. *(See Annex 1, Safe Use of High-Frequency Electricity in Health Care Facilities.)*

### C-12.1.2.2 Toxicologic Hazards.

**C-12.1.2.2.1** The use of some modern nonflammable inhalation anesthetic agents with high-flow techniques and in the absence of venting of the exhaled gases to the atmosphere can create low-grade toxicity in personnel who work regularly in the operating room *(see A-5-4.1)*.

### C-12.1.2.3 Mechanical Hazards.

**C-12.1.2.3.1** A large amount of energy is stored in a cylinder of compressed gas. If the valve of a cylinder is struck (or strikes something else) hard enough to break off the valve, the contents of the cylinder can be discharged with sufficient force to impart dangerous reactive movement to the cylinder.

**C-12.1.2.3.2** A hazard exists when hospital personnel attempt to transfer the contents of one compressed gas cylinder into another.

### C-12.1.3 Hazards Related to the Use of Flammable Substances.

### C-12.1.3.1 Flammable Anesthetic Agents.

**C-12.1.3.1.1** The use of flammable anesthetic agents is attended by considerable fire and explosion risk because these agents form flammable mixtures with air, oxygen, or nitrous oxide. In many cases, these mixtures are violently explosive. Fatal accidents have resulted from explosions of such mixtures during anesthesia.

**C-12.1.3.1.2** The following inhalation agents are considered flammable during conditions of clinical use in anesthesia: cyclopropane, diethyl ether, ethyl chloride, and ethylene.

The flammability of a compound can be reduced by substitution of a halogen (fluorine, chlorine, or bromine) for hydrogen at one or more positions in the molecular structure. Several inhalational anesthetics are thus halogenated. Halogenated agents are not necessarily nonflammable under all conditions.

Conflicting reports in the literature as to flammability limits probably represent differences in experimental techniques. Both the nature of the source of ignition and the configuration of the test chamber are critical. Some agents can be ignited only under optimal conditions never duplicated in clinical anesthesia. In one study, ignition of chloroform in oxygen could be obtained only in a closed steel bomb with a fuse producing an ignition temperature of 2000°C to 3000°C (1093°F to 1649°F) and with a chloroform concentration of 20 percent to 25 percent.[1]

Trichloroethylene, used in concentrations higher than recommended, is flammable in oxygen and nitrous oxide. Methoxyflurane is nonflammable in concentrations obtainable at room temperature; however, a heated vaporizer can produce flammable mixtures.

Halothane, enflurane, and isoflurane are nonflammable under almost all conditions encountered in clinical anesthesia. High concentrations of nitrous oxide increase the range of flammability. Given laboratory conditions employing a closed tube, zero humidity, and sufficient ignition energy (far greater than that obtainable from incidental static electricity) it is possible to ignite a mixture of 4.75 percent halothane in 30 percent oxygen provided

---

[1]Brown, T. A. and Morris, G. The ignition risk with mixtures of oxygen and nitrous oxide with halothane. *Brit. J. Anaesth.* 38:164-173, 1966.

the balance of the atmosphere is nitrous oxide. If the oxygen concentration in a mixture with nitrous oxide is allowed to fall to 20 percent, 3.25 percent halothane is flammable. In these same nitrous oxide-oxygen atmospheres, the corresponding minimal flammable concentrations of enflurane are 5.75 percent and 4.25 percent, respectively, and of isofluorane, 7.0 percent and 5.25 percent.[1]

The fact that halothane has for years been widely employed without significant problems relating to flammability suggests that the data in the preceding paragraph are of more theoretical than practical concern.

**C-12.1.3.1.3** The use of closed rebreathing systems for the administration of flammable anesthetic agents normally tends to restrict the region likely to be hazardous. To secure a reasonable measure of protection, however, it has been found necessary to apply certain basic safeguards in any room in which these agents are used.

**C-12.1.3.2 Flammable Medicaments, Including Aerosol Products.**

**C-12.1.3.2.1** Medicaments, including those dispersed as aerosols, frequently are used in anesthetizing locations for germicidal purposes, for affixing plastic surgical drape materials, for preparation of wound dressings, or for other purposes.

**C-12.1.3.2.2** A particular hazard is created if cautery or high-frequency electrosurgical equipment is employed following use of a flammable medicament for preparation of the skin *(see C-12.1.3.2.1)*, since the liquid remaining on the skin or vapors pocketed within the surgical drapes can be ignited.

> See commentary under 12-4.1.2.2 in Chapter 12 for more discussion on the hazards associated with flammable medicaments, particularly in connection with electrosurgical units.

**C-12.1.3.3 Sources of Ignition.**

**C-12.1.3.3.1** Potential sources of ignition of flammable anesthetics in anesthetizing locations include the following:

(a) Fixed electric equipment
(b) Portable electric equipment
(c) Accumulation of static electricity
(d) Electrosurgical equipment and
(e) Open flames and heated objects above the ignition temperature of the flammable gases in use.

Other potential sources of ignition are percussion sparks, ignition of oxidizing and flammable gases from accidental mixing under pressure (8-3.1.8), and ignition from improper handling of oxygen cylinders [4-3.5.2.1(b)].

---

[1]Cruice, M. S. Lower explosion limits of three anesthetics in mixtures of oxygen and nitrous oxide. Hazards Research Corp. Report 3296 to Ohio Medical Products, Madison, Wisconsin, 5 March 1974.

The Technical Committee on Anesthesia Services is cognizant of suggestions that the detonation of ether peroxides formed by the oxidation of ether over a period of time can be a cause of explosions in anesthesia machines. Frequent emptying of the ether bottle and cleaning of the ether evaporator inside anesthetizing locations is a simple and desirable precaution.

Many types of hospital construction afford reasonable protection against lightning hazards. However, because of the storage and use of combustible anesthetic agents, the increased protection offered by the installation of lightning rods might be desirable for some types of buildings, particularly those of wood (frame) construction in outlying areas. Lightning protection, if installed, should conform to the requirements of NFPA 780, *Standard for the Installation of Lightning Protection Systems*.

**C-12.1.3.3.2** Experience indicates that the ignition of flammable mixtures by electrostatic spark is a great hazard. Electrostatic charges can accumulate on personnel and metallic equipment. Electrostatic charges can set up dangerous potential differences only when separated by materials that are electrically nonconducting. Such insulators act as barriers to the free movement of such charges, preventing the equalization of potential differences. A spark discharge can take place only when there is no other available path of greater conductivity by which this equalization can be effected. Such a spark can ignite a flammable mixture of gases.

**C-12.1.3.3.3** In many cases, the hazards of electric shock and electrostatic discharge coexist. Measures to mitigate one hazard might enhance the other, however. It is necessary, therefore, to weigh both hazards in recommending precautionary measures for either.

An example of this inverse relationship is a damp or highly humid environment where the electric shock hazard is increased but electrostatic discharge is decreased.

**C-12.1.3.3.4** An obvious and, hence, less frequent cause of the ignition of flammable anesthetic agents is by open flame or hot materials at or above the ignition temperature of the agents. The lowest ignition temperature in air of any of the anesthetic agents mentioned in C-12.1.3.1.2 is that of diethyl ether: 180°C (365°F). The most effective safeguard against this source of ignition is a constant vigilance on the part of the operating room personnel to prevent the introduction of sources of flames and hot objects into the anesthetizing locations *(see 12-4.1.2.3)*.

**C-12.1.4 Hazards That Can Be Present in Nonflammable Anesthetizing Locations.**

**C-12.1.4.1 Electrostatic Hazard.**

**C-12.1.4.1.1** Conductive flooring is not a requirement for nonflammable anesthetizing locations. The uncontrolled use of static-producing materials in such locations, however, can lead to the following:

(a) Electrostatic discharge through sensitive components of electronic equipment, causing equipment failure

(b) Inadvertent use of these materials in flammable anesthetizing locations where mixed facilities exist *(see definition of Mixed Facility in Chapter 2)*

(c) Impaired efficiency because of electrostatic clinging, or

(d) The involuntary movement of personnel subject to electrostatic discharges

**C-12.1.4.2 Hazard of Flammable Substances.**

**C-12.1.4.2.1** Nonflammable anesthetizing locations are neither designed nor equipped for the use of any flammable substances, be they inhalation anesthetic agents or medicaments containing benzene, acetone, or the like. A hazardous situation is created any time any such flammable substance is inadvertently or intentionally introduced into a nonflammable anesthetizing location *(see also C-12.1.3.2)*.

**C-12.1.5 Hazards That Can Be Present in Mixed Facilities.**

**C-12.1.5.1** Mixed facilities contain both flammable and nonflammable anesthetizing locations. Movable furniture, portable equipment, and conductive accessories intended for sole use in nonflammable anesthetizing locations might be introduced inadvertently into a flammable anesthetizing location, with the attendant dangers of ignition of flammable gas mixtures from electrical or electrostatic sparks.

**C-12.1.5.2** Personnel working in mixed facilities might not take the proper precautions in reference to wearing apparel and the use of conductive grounding devices when entering flammable anesthetizing locations.

**C-12.1.5.3** A particular hazard exists if regulations [*see C-12.3, Set (3)*] are not adopted, posted, and complied with or if the anesthetizing locations are not identified as noted in 2-6.4.5 in Annex 2.

## C-12.2 Related Hazards and Safeguards, Anesthetizing Locations.

**C-12.2.1 General.**

**C-12.2.1.1** The gas anesthesia apparatus and anesthetic ventilators constitute essential items (in most cases) for the administration of inhalation anesthesia. The safe use of these devices is predicated upon their cleanliness and proper function, as well as an understanding of their proper operation, maintenance, and repair.

**C-12.2.2 Selection of a Gas Anesthesia Apparatus.**

**C-12.2.2.1** The individual selecting a gas anesthesia apparatus, either for initial purchase or for application in a given case, should be certain that the apparatus is the proper one for the given application or applications and that it is in good repair. See C-12.2.3, Suggested Method for Ensuring Proper Delivery of Oxygen and Nitrous Oxide; C-12.2.4, Disposable Masks, Bags, Tubing, and Bellows; and C-12.2.5, Decontamination and Routine Cleaning of Reusable Items.

**C-12.2.3 Suggested Method for Ensuring Proper Delivery of Oxygen and Nitrous Oxide.**

**C-12.2.3.1** This method is recommended to prevent delivery of a gas different from that indicated by the flowmeters and to detect mixing of gases inside the machine that can result in delivery of dangerous gas mixtures to the patient. The following materials are needed:

(a) Three (3) ft (91.5 cm) of anesthesia delivery hose, and

(b) An accurate oxygen meter, analyzer, or detector [*see 8-5.1.2.1(c)*]. This device can be of the paramagnetic, platinum electrode, gas chromatographic, or mass spectrometer type.

**C-12.2.3.2** Detailed steps of a method of testing anesthesia machines to assure the absence of hazard due to crossed connections between oxygen and nitrous oxide follow.

**C-12.2.3.2.1 Premises.**

(a) It is reasonable to conclude that no hazardous cross-connections or cross-leakages are present if gas from the only source available is delivered by only those valves intended for that gas, and that no gas is delivered by those valves when their intended source is unavailable, but other sources are available.

(b) It is not necessary to know the composition of a gas in order to determine the extent of the circuit it supplies.

(c) The operation of the oxygen circuit is independent, but the operation of some or all of the other circuits might be at least partially dependent on the operability of the oxygen circuit, for example, fail-safe valves.

**C-12.2.3.2.2 Method.** All anesthesia machines have at least one source of oxygen. This can be a large cylinder, one or two small cylinders, or a pipeline supply. Some machines have two such sources, and a very few have all three. Each should be tested separately. Proceed as follows:

(a) Disconnect all gas sources and open all needle valves and flush valves until all gas has stopped flowing from the machine outlet. Then close all needle valves and flush valves. Be certain that all cylinder pressure gauges read zero. Connect an oxygen cylinder to an oxygen hanger yoke and open the cylinder valve. Pressure must rise in the corresponding oxygen pressure gauge only. Close the cylinder valve.

(b) Repeat Step (a) exactly for each oxygen hanger yoke, including any fed by high-pressure lines from large cylinders. Leave the cylinder in the last hanger yoke tested, with the cylinder valve open.

(c) Open in succession and leave open all the needle valves for gases other than oxygen. Briefly open any flush valve for a gas other than oxygen. No flow should occur at the machine outlet. An easy way to test for gas flow is to simply place the machine outlet tube in a glass of water and observe bubbling. Stand clear when flush valves are operated.

(d) Open and close in succession each of the oxygen needle valves, including any that provide an independent source of oxygen for vaporizers, and the oxygen flush valve. Flow should occur at the associated flowmeter or the machine outlet each time a valve is opened.

(e) If the machine is equipped for a pipeline oxygen supply, close the oxygen cylinder valve and open the oxygen flush valve. When gas stops flowing at the machine outlet, close the flush valve and all needle valves and connect the oxygen pipeline inlet to an oxygen pipeline outlet with the oxygen supply hose. Then repeat Steps (c) and (d).

(f) Since it is now established that oxygen is delivered to the oxygen needle and flush valves, and is not delivered to any other needle or flush valve, it remains to be determined that oxygen and oxygen alone is also available to perform any other function for which it is essential. A valve that shuts off the supply of any other gas to the appropriate needle valve in the event of oxygen supply pressure failure, commonly called a "fail-safe" valve, performs such a function. It should be tested as follows:

1. Disconnect the pipeline supply and open the oxygen flush valve until flow stops at the machine outlet, then close the flush valve. Install a cylinder of nitrous oxide in one hanger yoke, open the cylinder valve, and note the pressure on all cylinder pressure gauges. Only the nitrous oxide gauge should show any pressure.
2. Open in succession and leave open all the needle valves for gas other than nitrous oxide. Briefly open any flush valve for a gas other than nitrous oxide. No flow should occur at the machine outlet, nor at any flowmeter.

NOTE: An easy way to test for gas flow is to simply place the machine outlet tube in a glass of water and observe bubbling. Stand clear when flush valves are operated.

3. Open and close in succession each of the nitrous oxide needle valves and nitrous oxide flush valves. If any delivers flow, all should do so.
4. If neither the nitrous oxide needle valves nor the nitrous oxide flush valve delivers flow, open the oxygen cylinder valve and repeat Steps 2 and 3. Each nitrous oxide needle valve and flush valve should deliver flow to the machine outlet.
5. Close the nitrous oxide cylinder valve and open a nitrous oxide needle valve until all gas stops flowing, then remove the nitrous oxide cylinder and close the needle valve. Repeat Steps 1 through 4 using any other nitrous oxide yoke.
6. If the machine is equipped for a pipeline nitrous oxide supply, close the nitrous oxide cylinder valve and open a nitrous oxide needle valve until all gas stops flowing, then close all needle valves and flush valves. Connect the nitrous oxide pipeline inlet to a nitrous oxide pipeline outlet with the nitrous oxide supply hose. Then repeat Steps 2 through 4.

**C-12.2.4 Disposable Masks, Bags, Tubing, and Bellows.**

**C-12.2.4.1** It is well recognized that newer technologies often lead to the introduction of new equipment and techniques, which in turn might lead to new hazards, or the potentiation of old ones. For example, the use of disposable and nondistensible conductive accessories potentiate the hazards of excessive airway pressures. These components should be employed only when it is assured that system pressure cannot become excessive.

**C-12.2.4.1.1** Many plastic items are combustible. Most of these materials will emit toxic compounds when subjected to thermal decomposition. Special care must be exercised during storage, use, and disposal of these items in order to preclude accidental ignition. Due consideration must be given to on-site storage of trash prior to removal from the operating suite. The presence of these items on the hospital premises contributes significantly to the solid waste disposal problem facing the modern hospital.

**C-12.2.4.1.2** The Technical Committee on Gas Delivery Equipment recommends that purchasing policies of an institution, as well as the practices of individual physicians and nurses, take into consideration the multiple problems posed by plastic items, and limit purchases and use of them to those items deemed essential for the proper function of the institution.

**C-12.2.5 Decontamination and Routine Cleaning of Reusable Items.**

**C-12.2.5.1** Under certain circumstances, infectious organisms can be cultured from the breathing passages of ventilators, anesthesia valves, absorbers, tubing, bags, masks, and connectors. Some of these organisms can remain viable for many days. Although evidence that cross-infection from such sources can and does occur is very scanty, it is suggested that the user of such equipment consider implementation of one of the following methods. Mechanical cleansing with soap and water should precede sterilization. Alternative approaches to routine cleansing include the following:

(a) Mechanical cleansing with soap and water, followed by air drying in a stream of compressed air

(b) Mechanical cleansing with soap and water, followed by exposure to a preparation such as dialdehyde solution

(c) Mechanical cleansing with soap and water, followed by ethylene oxide, steam, or dry heat sterilization

**C-12.2.5.2** Following gross contamination, the step outlined in C-12.2.5.1(b) or C-12.2.5.1(c) should be employed.

NOTE 1: Whenever ethylene oxide or dialdehyde is used, care must be taken to ensure complete removal of residuals.

NOTE 2: Recommendations for cleansing and sterilization supplied by the manufacturer of the item of equipment should be followed.

**C-12.2.5.2.1** External contamination of the gas anesthesia apparatus, ventilator, and other equipment employed on and around the patient at least at weekly intervals, as well as immediately after use in an infectious case, is likewise recommended.

**C-12.3 Text of Suggested Signs and Posters for Inhalation Anesthetizing Locations.**

SET (1)
REGULATIONS FOR SAFE PRACTICE IN
NONFLAMMABLE ANESTHETIZING LOCATIONS

The following rules and regulations have been adopted by the medical staff and administration. NFPA 99-1999, subsection 12-4.1, Anesthetizing Locations, shall apply in all inhalation anesthetizing locations.

(Insert Date) (Insert Name of Hospital Authority)

The use or storage of any of the following flammable agents or germicides shall be prohibited from all operating rooms, delivery rooms, and other anesthetizing locations in this hospital.

By reason of their chemical composition, these agents present a hazard of fire or explosion:

cyclopropane    ethyl chloride

diethyl ether    ethylene

1. **Nonflammable Anesthetizing Location.**

   a. *Definition.* The term *nonflammable anesthetizing location* shall mean any anesthetizing location designated for the exclusive use of nonflammable anesthetizing agents.

2. **Equipment.**

   a. No electrical equipment except that judged by the Engineering Department of _____ Hospital as being in compliance with NFPA 99-1999, subsection 12-4.1, Anesthetizing Locations, shall be used in any anesthetizing location.

   b. When a physician wishes to use his or her personal electrical equipment, it shall first be inspected by the Engineering Department and, if judged to comply with NFPA 99-1999, subsection 12-4.1, Anesthetizing Locations, it shall be so labeled.

   c. Photographic lighting equipment shall be of the totally enclosed type or so constructed as to prevent the escape of sparks or hot metal particles.

3. **Personnel.** Smoking shall be limited to dressing rooms and lounges with doors leading to the corridor closed.

4. **Practice.**

   a. The use or storage of flammable anesthetic agents shall be expressly prohibited in a nonflammable anesthetizing location.

   b. If cautery, electrosurgery, or a hot or arcing device is to be used during an operation, flammable germicides or flammable fat solvents shall not be applied for preoperative preparation of the skin.

   c. A visual (lighted red lamp) or audible warning signal from the line isolation monitor serving an anesthetizing location indicates that the total hazard current has exceeded allowable limits. This suggests that one or more electrical devices is contributing an excessively low impedance to ground, which might constitute a fault that would expose the patient or hospital personnel to an unsafe condition should an additional fault occur. Briefly and sequentially unplugging the power cord of each electrical device in the location will usually cause the green lamp to light, showing that the system has been adequately isolated from ground, when the potentially defective device has been unplugged. The continuing use of such a device, so identified, should be questioned, but not necessarily abandoned. At the earliest opportunity the device should be inspected by the hospital engineer or other qualified personnel and, if necessary, repaired or replaced.

d. Transportation of patients while an inhalation anesthetic is being administered by means of a mobile anesthesia machine shall be prohibited, unless deemed essential for the benefit of the patient in the combined judgment of the surgeon and anesthesiologist.

e. If, in the combined judgment of the anesthesiologist responsible for the administering of the anesthetic and the surgeon performing the operation, the life of the patient would be jeopardized by not administering a flammable anesthetic agent, the following steps shall be taken:

1. Both surgeon and anesthesiologist involved in the case shall attest to the reason for administering a flammable anesthetic in a nonflammable anesthetizing location on the patient's record and in the operating room register.

2. The hazard of static sparks shall be reduced by electrically interconnecting the patient, operating room table, anesthesia gas machine, and anesthesiologist by wet sheets or other conductive materials. Conductive accessories shall be used for the electrically conductive pathways from the anesthesia gas machine to the patient.

3. If cautery, electrosurgery, or electrical equipment employing an open spark is to be used during an operation, flammable anesthetics shall not be used. Flammable germicides or flammable fat solvents shall not be applied for the preoperative preparation of the field.

5. **Enforcement.**

It shall be the responsibility of _____ (name) (an anesthesiologist or other qualified person appointed by the hospital authority to act in that capacity) to enforce the above regulations.

## C-12.4 Suggested Procedures in the Event of a Fire or Explosion, Anesthetizing Locations.

**C-12.4.1 General.** Fires in hospitals pose unique problems for hospital personnel, patients, and fire service personnel. Hospitals store and use relatively large quantities of flammable and combustible substances. Oxygen-enriched atmospheres are often employed in medical therapy and are utilized routinely during administration of anesthesia. The presence of flammable and combustible substances and oxygen-enriched atmospheres under the same roof with nonambulatory patients presents an extra-hazardous situation. All hospital personnel should understand the steps to take to save life, preserve limb, and contain smoke and/or limit fire until the fire department arrives. It is recommended that the procedures delineated herein, or similar ones, become a part of the fire safety regulations of every hospital.

**C-12.4.2  Steps to Take in the Event of a Fire or Explosion.**

**C-12.4.2.1** The following steps, listed in the approximate order of their importance, should be taken by all personnel, should fire occur. If an explosion occurs, and it is not followed by fire, follow the procedure outlined under C-12.4.2.2. If a fire follows an explosion, proceed as follows:

(a) Remove the immediately exposed patient or patients from the site of the fire, if their hair or clothing are not burning. If they are burning, extinguish the flames *(see C-12.4.4 and C-12.4.5)*.

(b) Sound the fire alarm by whatever mode the hospital fire plan provides.

NOTE: It is assumed that each hospital has a fire plan, prepared in consultation with representatives of the local fire department. In such a plan, immediate notification of the local fire department is essential.

(c) Close off the supply of oxygen, nitrous oxide, and air to any equipment involved, if this step can be accomplished without injury to personnel *(see C-12.4.3)*.

(d) Close doors to contain smoke and isolate fire.

(e) Remove patients threatened by the fire.

(f) Attempt to extinguish or contain the fire *(see C-12.4.4)*.

(g) Direct the fire fighters to the site of the fire.

(h) Take whatever steps are necessary to protect or evacuate patients in adjacent areas.

NOTE 1: In the event of a fire in an operating room while an operative procedure on an anesthetized patient is in progress, it might be necessary to extinguish the fire prior to removing the patient from the room.

NOTE 2: During an operation, it may be more hazardous to move patients than to attempt to extinguish or contain the fire. The attending physician must determine which step would present the lesser hazard—hurriedly terminating an operative procedure or continuing the procedure and exposing the members of the operating team and the patient to the hazards stemming from the fire.

**C-12.4.2.2** The following steps are recommended in the event of an explosion involving inhalation anesthesia apparatus.

(a) Disconnect the patient from the apparatus.

(b) Procure a new gas anesthesia apparatus and make every effort to save the life of the patient and prevent injury to the patient.

**C-12.4.2.3** It is essential that all equipment involved in a fire or explosion be preserved for examination by an authority attempting to determine the cause. Additionally, pertinent administrative data, including photographs, should be recorded. The report should state the following:

(a) Whether wearing apparel of all persons in the room at the time of the fire or explosion had to meet the requirements listed in Annex 2

(b) Whether portable equipment, low-voltage instruments, accessories, and furniture had to meet the requirements listed in Annex 2

(c) Whether the ventilating system was being operated in accordance with 5-4.2 of Chapter 5

**C-12.4.2.3.1** The area involved, with all involved items in place, should be closed off and secured for later examination by a responsible authority.

### C-12.4.3  Closing Off Oxygen, Nitrous Oxide, and Air Supply.

**C-12.4.3.1** In the event of a fire involving equipment connected to an oxygen, nitrous oxide, and air station outlet, the zone valve supplying that station is to be closed [*see C-12.4.6.1(a)*].

**C-12.4.3.1.1** Immediately, all patients receiving oxygen through the same zone valve must be supplied with individual oxygen cylinders.

NOTE:  Each gas line to an operating room should have an individual zone valve *(see Section 4-3 in Chapter 4, Gas and Vacuum Systems)*. Thus, closing of all valves to one room would not endanger patients in other rooms.

**C-12.4.3.2** If fire involves apparatus supplied by a cylinder of oxygen, it is desirable to close the cylinder valve, if this can be done without injuring personnel.

NOTE:  Metal components of regulators and valves can become excessively hot if exposed to flame. Personnel are cautioned not to use their bare hands to affect closure.

### C-12.4.4  Extinguishment or Containment of Fire.

The issue of fire extinguisher use inside operating rooms is very complicated because of the unusual environment during surgery when one person, the patient, is either unconscious or immobile, his or her internal body cavity is exposed, and sterile conditions need to be maintained. In addition, while staff is always present during surgery, they might not be able to respond to a fire immediately. Finally, the effects of extinguishers, including water-based extinguishers, can be adverse to the patient.

Portable halon extinguishers have been promoted, with some controversy, for use in operating rooms. Halon, however, has all but been completely phased out due to environmental concerns, and alternative "clean-agents" are continuing to be developed.

Contributing to the uncertainty of fire extinguisher use in operating rooms is the extensive use of oxygen and the resultant creation of an oxygen-enriched atmosphere. It has been suggested by some that it might be better to try to remove burning drapes from the patient before trying to use an extinguisher on the drapes.

NFPA *101, Life Safety Code* [2], and NFPA 10, *Standard for Portable Fire Extinguishers* [3], offer some general criteria for fire extinguisher placement. One of the best solutions for fighting fires in operating rooms is, of course, taking steps to *prevent* fire from occurring in the first place. Prevention involves reviewing the proper methods for procedures that can create hazards (e.g., the use of flammable liquids), as well as educating staff on the need to prevent incidents.

Periodic training involving all persons who work in operating rooms is essential. (See requirements and recommendations on the subjects of training and education in 7-6.5.1 and 12-4.1.2.10(d) in Chapters 7 and 12; and 1-3.8 and 1-5.2.5 in Annex 1.)

**C-12.4.4.1** Fire originating in or involving inhalation anesthesia apparatus generally involves combustibles such as rubber. Water or water-based extinguishing agents are most effective in such fires.

(a) Precautions should be taken if line-powered electrical equipment is adjacent to or involved in fire, because of the danger of electrocution of personnel if streams of water contact live circuits.

(b) Before attempting to fight fire with water or a water-based extinguishing agent, electrical apparatus should be disconnected from the supply outlet, or the supply circuit deenergized at the circuit panel.

(c) If such deenergization cannot be accomplished, water should not be employed *(see C-12.4.4.3)*.

**C-12.4.4.2** Fires involving, or adjacent to, electrical equipment with live circuits must be fought with extinguishers suitable for "Class C" fires in accordance with NFPA 10, *Standard for Portable Fire Extinguishers*.

**C-12.4.4.3** Fire extinguishers are classified according to the type of fire for which each is suited.

(a) Fires involving ordinary combustibles such as rubber, plastic, linen, wool, paper, and the like are called "Class A" fires. These can be fought with water or water-based extinguishing agents. Hose lines are suitable for this purpose. Portable extinguishers suitable for "Class A" fires are identified with the letter A contained in a (if colored) green triangle.

(b) "Class B" fires involve flammable liquids and should be fought only with an extinguisher identified by the letter B contained in a (if colored) red square.

(c) "Class C" fires involve electrical equipment and should be fought only with an extinguisher identified by the letter C contained in a (if colored) blue circle.

(d) Carbon dioxide and some dry chemical extinguishers are labeled for "Class B" and "Class C" fires. Some dry chemical units can be used for all three types *(see NFPA 10, Standard for Portable Fire Extinguishers, Appendix B)*.

**C-12.4.5 Protection of Patients and Personnel.**

**C-12.4.5.1** Serious and even fatal burns of the skin or lungs, from inhaling heated gases, are possible. Thus, it is essential that patients be removed from the scene of the fire whenever practical. Where an anesthetized patient is connected to a burning piece of equipment, it might be more practical as the initial step to remove the equipment and/ or extinguish the fire than to remove the patient.

**C-12.4.5.2** Noxious gases produced by fire constitute a threat to life from asphyxia, beyond the thermal burn problem.

Personnel are cautioned not to remain in the fire area after patients are evacuated, unless they are wearing proper emergency apparatus.

**C-12.4.6 Indoctrination of Personnel.**

**C-12.4.6.1** It is highly desirable that personnel involved in the care of patients, including nurses, aides, ward secretaries, and physicians, irrespective of whether they are involved in anesthesia practices, be thoroughly indoctrinated in all aspects of fire safety, including the following:

(a) The location of zone valves of nonflammable medical gas systems and the station outlets controlled by each valve

(b) The location of electrical service boxes and the areas served thereby

(c) The location and proper use of fire extinguishers *(see C-12.4.4)*

(d) The recommended methods and routes for evacuating patients *(see Chapter 11, Health Care Emergency Preparedness)*

(e) The steps involved in carrying out the fire plan of the hospital

(f) The location of fire alarm boxes, or knowledge of other methods for summoning the fire department

**C-12.4.6.2** To ensure that personnel are familiar with the procedures outlined above, regular instructive sessions and fire drills should be held.

**C-12.5 Cylinder Table.**

See Table C-12.5.

# C-13 Additional Information on Chapter 13

Appendix C-13 consists of the following:

C-13.1 Typical Gas Cylinders, Anesthetizing Locations

C-13.2 Text of Suggested Regulations, Anesthetizing Locations

### C-13.1 Typical Gas Cylinder Table, Anesthetizing Locations.

*(See Table C-12.5.)*

### C-13.2 Text of Suggested Regulations for Nonflammable Inhalation Anesthetizing Locations and Gas Storage Areas in Nonhospital-Based Ambulatory Care Facilities.

The following rules and regulations have been adopted. The requirements of subsection 12-4.1, Anesthetizing Locations, of NFPA 99-1999 shall apply to all anesthetizing locations and gas storage areas in this facility.

The use of any of the following flammable agents shall be prohibited from the premises. By reason of their chemical composition, these agents present a hazard of fire or explosion.

| | |
|---|---|
| cyclopropane | fluroxene |
| divinyl ether | ethyl chloride |
| ethyl ether | ethylene |

Smoking shall be limited to those areas of the premises not directly connected with the anesthetizing location or the location for storage of compressed gas cylinders.

Compressed gas cylinders shall be connected to the manifold, and otherwise handled and stored, as provided in Chapter 13 of NFPA 99-1999.

Defective electrical equipment shall not be used on the premises.

Gas pipeline alarm systems shall be monitored, and responsible personnel notified of any fall in pressure or alarm condition.

## C-19 Additional Information on Chapter 19

Appendix C-19 consists of the following:

C-19.1 Nature of Hazards

C-19.2 Suggested Procedures to Follow in Event of Fire in Class A Chambers

C-19.3 Suggested Procedures to Follow in Event of Fire in Class B Chambers

C-19.4 Pressure Table

### C-19.1 Nature of Hazards.

#### C-19.1.1 Fire and Explosion.

**C-19.1.1.1** The occurrence of a fire requires the presence of combustible or flammable materials, an atmosphere containing oxygen or other oxidizing agent(s), and heat or energy source of ignition.

NOTE: Certain substances such as acetylenic hydrocarbons can propagate flame in the absence of oxygen.

*Table C-12.5 Typical Medical Gas Cylinders, Volume and Weight of Available Contents.* All Volumes at 70°F (21.1°C).*

| Cylinder Style & Dimensions | Nominal Volume In.$^3$/Liter | Contents | Air | Carbon Dioxide | Cyclo-Propane | Helium | Nitrogen | Nitrous Oxide | Oxygen | Mixtures of Oxygen: Helium | Mixtures of Oxygen: $CO_2$ |
|---|---|---|---|---|---|---|---|---|---|---|---|
| **B** 3½ in. O.D. × 13 in. 8.89 × 33 cm | 87/1.43 | psig | | 838 | 75 | | | | 1900 | | |
| | | L | | 370 | 375 | | | | 200 | | |
| | | lb-oz | | 1-8 | 1-7¼ | | | | — | | |
| | | kg | | 0.68 | 0.66 | | | | — | | |
| **D** 4½ in. O.D. × 17 in. 10.8 × 43 cm | 176/2.88 | psig | 1900 | 838 | 75 | 1600 | 1900 | 745 | 1900 | ** | ** |
| | | L | 375 | 940 | 870 | 300 | 370 | 940 | 400 | 300 | 400 |
| | | lb-oz | — | 3-13 | 3-5½ | — | — | 3-13 | — | ** | ** |
| | | kg | — | 1.73 | 1.51 | — | — | 1.73 | — | ** | ** |
| **E** 4¼ in. O.D. × 26 in. 10.8 × 66 cm | 293/4.80 | psig | 1900 | 838 | | 1600 | 1900 | 745 | 1900 | ** | ** |
| | | L | 625 | 1590 | | 500 | 610 | 1590 | 660 | 500 | 660 |
| | | lb-oz | — | 6-7 | | — | — | 6-7 | — | ** | ** |
| | | kg | — | 2.92 | | — | — | 2.92 | — | ** | ** |
| **M** 7 in. O.D. × 43 in. 17.8 × 109 cm | 1337/21.9 | psig | 1900 | 838 | | 1600 | 2200 | 745 | 2200 | ** | ** |
| | | L | 2850 | 7570 | | 2260 | 3200 | 7570 | 3450 | 2260 | 3000 |
| | | lb-oz | — | 30-10 | | — | — | 30-10 | 122 ft$^3$ | ** | ** |
| | | kg | — | 13.9 | | — | — | 13.9 | — | ** | ** |
| **G** 8½ in. O.D. × 51 in. 21.6 × 130 cm | 2370/38.8 | psig | 1900 | 838 | | 1600 | | 745 | | ** | ** |
| | | L | 5050 | 12,300 | | 4000 | | 13,800 | | 4000 | 5330 |
| | | lb-oz | — | 50-0 | | — | | 56-0 | | ** | ** |
| | | kg | — | 22.7 | | — | | 25.4 | | ** | ** |
| **H or K** 9¼ in. O.D. × 51 in. 23.5 × 130 cm | 2660/43.6 | psig | 2200 | | | 2200 | 2200 | 745 | 2200† | | |
| | | L | 6550 | | | 6000 | 6400 | 15,800 | 6900 | | |
| | | lb-oz | — | | | — | — | 64 | 244 ft$^3$ | | |
| | | kg | — | | | — | — | 29.1 | | | |

NOTES:

*These are computed contents based on nominal cylinder volumes and rounded to no greater variance than ±1%.

**The pressure and weight of mixed gases will vary according to the composition of the mixture.

†275 ft$^3$/7800 L cylinders at 2490 psig are available upon request.

*This table reprinted with permission from the Compressed Gas Association, Inc.*

**C-19.1.1.2** Under hyperbaric conditions utilizing compressed air, the partial pressure of oxygen is increased. Leakage of oxygen into the atmosphere of the chamber (for example from improper application of respiratory therapy apparatus) can further increase markedly the oxygen partial pressure.

**C-19.1.1.2.1** The flammability or combustibility of materials generally increases as the partial pressure of oxygen increases, even when the percentage of oxygen in the gas mixture remains constant. Materials that are nonflammable or noncombustible under normal atmospheric conditions can become flammable or combustible under such circumstances.

**C-19.1.1.3 Sources of Fuel.**

**C-19.1.1.3.1** Materials that might not ignite in air at atmospheric pressure or require relatively high temperatures for their ignition but that burn vigorously in 100 percent oxygen include, but are not necessarily limited to, the following: tricresyl phosphate (lubricant); certain types of flame-resistant fabrics; silicone rubber; polyvinyl chloride; asbestos-containing paint; glass fiber-sheathed silicone rubber-insulated wire; polyvinyl chloride-insulated asbestos-covered wire and sheet; polyamides; epoxy compounds; and certain asbestos blankets.

NOTE: Flammable lubricants are used widely in equipment designed for conventional use, including shafts, gear boxes, pulleys and casters, and threaded joints, which are coupled and uncoupled.

> This list is for informational purposes only and does not necessarily reflect what can be practiced today in the United States (i.e., some materials are no longer allowed but might be in use in existing chambers).

**C-19.1.1.3.2** The flammability of certain volatile liquids and gases containing carbon and hydrogen is well known. Hazards and safeguards for their use in oxygen-enriched atmospheres at ambient pressure are well documented in subsection 12-4.1, Anesthetizing Locations, of NFPA 99. See also NFPA 325, *Guide to Fire Hazard Properties of Flammable Liquids, Gases, and Volatile Solids.*

NOTE: Repeated reference to subsection 12-4.1 is made throughout Chapter 19. These references do not imply, and should not be construed to mean, that flammable anesthetics can or should be employed in or around hyperbaric facilities.

**C-19.1.1.3.3** Human tissues will burn in an atmosphere of 100 percent oxygen. Body oils and fats, as well as hair, will burn readily under such circumstances.

**C-19.1.1.3.4** When a conventional loose cotton outergarment, such as scrub suits, dresses, and gowns employed in hospital operating suites, is ignited in an atmosphere of pure oxygen, the garment will become engulfed in flame rapidly and will be totally destroyed within 20 seconds or less.

**C-19.1.1.3.4.1** If such a garment is ignited in a compressed air atmosphere, the flame spread is increased. When oxygen concentration exceeds 23.5 percent at elevated total pressure, flame spread is much more rapid, and at 6 ATA, is comparable to 95 ± 5 percent at 1 ATA.

Flame spread in air (21 percent oxygen) is somewhat increased at 6 ATA, but not to the level of 95 ± 5 percent at 1 ATA.

**C-19.1.1.3.4.2** Combustible fabrics have tiny air spaces that become filled with oxygen when exposed to oxygen-enriched environments. Once removed to atmospheric air (e.g., room air outside the chamber), the fabric will burn, if ignited, almost as rapidly as if it were still in the oxygen environment. This hazard will remain until the oxygen trapped in the air spaces in the fabric has had time to diffuse out and be replaced by air.*

> Chamber personnel need to remain continuously alert to this phenomenon. If any clothing or similar fabric catches fire, corrective action must be instantaneous. Burning clothes should be removed from the body as quickly as possible.

**C-19.1.1.3.5** Oil-based or volatile cosmetics (facial creams, body oils, hair sprays, and the like) constitute a source of fuel that is highly flammable in an oxygen-enriched atmosphere.

**C-19.1.1.4 Sources of Ignition.**

**C-19.1.1.4.1** Sources of ignition that might be encountered in a hyperbaric chamber include, but are not necessarily limited to, the following: defective electrical equipment, including failure of high-voltage components of radiological or monitoring equipment; heated surfaces in broken vacuum tubes or broken lamps used for general illumination, spot illumination, or illumination of diagnostic instruments; the hot-wire cautery or high-frequency electrocautery; open or arcing switches, including motor switches; bare defibrillator paddles; overheated motors; and electrical thermostats.

**C-19.1.1.4.2** Sources of ignition that should not be encountered in a hyperbaric facility, but that might be introduced by inept practice, include the following: lighted matches or tobacco, static sparks from improper use of personal attire, electrical wiring not complying with 19-2.7 of Chapter 19, cigarette lighters, and any oil-contaminated materials that present a spontaneous heating hazard.

> Before a child enters a chamber for hyperbaric therapy, a thorough check should be done to ensure that the child does not bring any sparking-type toys into the chamber. The failure to conduct such a check reportedly resulted in a fatal fire in a Class B chamber.

**C-19.1.1.4.3** In oxygen-enriched atmospheres, the minimum energy necessary to ignite flammable or combustible materials is reduced in most instances below the energy required in atmospheres of ambient air.

**C-19.1.2 Mechanical Hazards.**

**C-19.1.2.1 General.**

**C-19.1.2.1.1** A large amount of potential energy is stored in even a small volume of compressed gas. In hyperbaric chambers of moderate or large size, the potential energy of the chamber's compressed atmosphere, if released suddenly, can produce devastating destruction to adjacent structures and personnel, as well as to structures and personnel remote from the site of the chamber. Such sudden release could result from failure of the vessel structure, its parts, or its piping.

**C-19.1.2.1.2** A particular hazard can be created if individuals attempt to drill, cut, or weld the vessel in a manner contrary to ASME *Boiler and Pressure Vessel Code.*

**C-19.1.2.2** The restriction on escape and the impedance to rescue and fire-fighting efforts posed by the chamber create a significant hazard to life in case of fire or other emergency.

**C-19.1.2.2.1** A particular hazard exists to chamber personnel in the event of a fire within the structure housing the chamber. Inability to escape from the chamber and loss of services of the chamber operator would pose serious threats to the lives of all occupants of the chamber.

**C-19.1.2.2.2** All personnel involved in hyperbaric chamber operation and therapy, including patients and family, must be made aware of the risks and hazards involved. Fire prevention is essential. Extinguishment of a fire within a Class B chamber is impossible. Extinguishment of a fire within a Class A chamber is only possible utilizing equipment already installed in such a chamber, and then often only by the efforts of the occupants of such a chamber or the chamber operator.

> Fire prevention measures in a Class B chamber are essential due to the elevated oxygen level within them and to the fact that the patient receiving therapy is the sole occupant of the chamber.

**C-19.1.2.3** The necessity for restricting viewing ports to small size limits the vision of chamber operators and other observers, reducing their effectiveness as safety monitors.

**C-19.1.2.4** Containers and enclosures can be subjected to collapse or rupture as a consequence of the changing pressures of the hyperbaric chamber. Items containing entrained gas include, but are not necessarily limited to, the following: ampuls, partially filled syringes, stoppered or capped bottles, cuffed endotrachael tubes, and pneumatic cushions employed for breathing masks or aids in positioning patients. The rupture of such containers having combustible or flammable liquids would also constitute a severe fire or explosion hazard.

**C-19.1.2.4.1** The sudden collapse of containers from high external pressures will result in adiabatic heating of the contents. Therefore the collapse of a container of flammable liquid would constitute a severe fire or explosion hazard both from heating and from a spill of the liquid. *(See 19-3.1.5.2 and C-19.1.1.3.2.)*

**C-19.1.2.5** Other mechanical hazards relate to the malfunction, disruption, or inoperativeness of many standard items when placed in service under pressurized atmospheres. Hazards that might be encountered in this regard are implosion of illuminating lamps and vacuum tubes; overloading of fans driving gas at higher density; and inaccurate operation of standard flowmeters, pressure gauges, and pressure-reducing regulators.

NOTE: Illuminating lamps or vacuum tubes, which implode, or overloaded fans, are sources of ignition.

### C-19.1.3 Pathophysiological, Medical, and Other Related Hazards.

**C-19.1.3.1** Exposure of pregnant chamber occupants to hyperbaric atmospheres might result in fetal risk.

> This warning was added to the 1996 edition to highlight recent research that suggests that there is potential risk to the fetus of any female who is (or might be) pregnant and exposed to the increased pressures in a hyperbaric chamber.

**C-19.1.3.2** Medical hazards that can be encountered routinely include compression problems, nitrogen narcosis, oxygen toxicity, and the direct effects of sudden pressure changes.

**C-19.1.3.2.1** Inability to equalize pressure differentials between nasopharynx (nose) and nasal sinuses or the middle ear can result in excruciating pain and might cause rupture of the eardrum or hemorrhage into the ear cavity or nasal sinus.

**C-19.1.3.2.2** The breathing of air (78 percent nitrogen) under significant pressures (as by chamber personnel breathing chamber atmosphere) can result in nitrogen narcosis, which resembles alcoholic inebriation. The degree of narcosis is directly related to the amount of pressurization. Nitrogen narcosis results in impairment of mental functions, loss of manual dexterity, and interference with alertness and ability to think clearly and act quickly and intelligently in an emergency.

**C-19.1.3.2.3** Oxygen toxicity can develop from breathing oxygen at partial pressures above 0.50 atmospheres absolute for a significant length of time. Oxygen toxicity can affect the lungs (pain in the chest, rapid shallow breathing, coughing), nervous system (impaired consciousness and convulsions), or other tissues and organs, or combinations thereof.

> The 1996 edition was revised to stipulate a level beyond which pulmonary oxygen toxicity is possible. Breathing oxygen at pressures less than 0.5 atmospheres for indefinite periods does not produce oxygen toxicity of the lungs or central nervous system.

**C-19.1.3.2.4** Direct effects of reduction in pressure can include inability to equalize pressures between the nasopharynx and sinuses or middle ear, expansion of gas pockets in the gastrointestinal tract, and expansion of trapped gas in the lungs.

**C-19.1.3.2.5** The presence of personnel within the cramped confines of the hyperbaric chamber in close proximity to grounded metallic structures on all sides creates a definite shock hazard if accidental contact is made with a live electrical conductor or a defective piece of electrical equipment. Such accidental contact also could be a source of ignition of flammable or combustible materials. *(See C-19.1.1.4.)*

**C-19.1.3.3** Medical hazards that are not ordinarily encountered during hyperbaric oxygen therapy, but that might arise during malfunction, fire, or other emergency conditions, include electric shock and fouling of the atmosphere of the chamber with oxygen, nitrous oxide, carbon dioxide, carbon monoxide, pyrolysis products from overheated materials, or the toxic products of combustion from any fire.

**C-19.1.3.3.1** Increased concentrations of carbon dioxide within the chamber, as might result from malfunction of the systems responsible for monitoring or removal thereof, can be toxic under increased pressures.

**C-19.1.3.3.2** The development of combustion products or gases evolved from heated nonmetallics within the closed space of the hyperbaric chamber can be extremely toxic to life because of the confining nature of the chamber and the increased hazards of breathing such products under elevated pressure.

NOTE: Extreme pressure rises have accompanied catastrophic fires in confined atmospheres. These pressures have driven hot, toxic gases into the lungs of victims as well as exceeding the structural limits of the vessel in at least one case.

**C-19.1.3.4** Physiological hazards include exposure to high noise levels and decompression sickness. Rapid release of pressurized gases can produce shock waves and loss of visibility.

**C-19.1.3.4.1** During hyperbaric therapy, and especially during compression, the noise level within the chamber becomes quite high. Such a level can be hazardous because it is distractive, interferes with communication, and can produce permanent sensory-neural deafness.

**C-19.1.3.4.2** Decompression sickness (bends, caisson worker's disease) results from the elution into the bloodstream or extravascular tissues of bubbles of inert gas (mainly nitrogen) that becomes dissolved in the blood and tissue fluids while breathing air at elevated pressures for a significant period of time.

NOTE: Rapid decompression of the chamber can occur if the pressure relief valve is damaged from exposure to a fire external to the chamber or from the venting of hot products of combustion from within the chamber.

**C-19.1.3.4.3** The use of decompression procedures will prevent immediate escape from the Class A chamber by occupants during emergency situations.

NOTE: These procedures are not followed if chamber occupants are exposed to a "no-decompression exposure" [compression to less than 2 atmospheres absolute (ATA) air], or when compressed to 2 ATA or higher pressures and breathing 100 percent oxygen.

The reader is reminded that 100 percent oxygen is never breathed at pressures greater than 66 FSW or 29.4 psig (202 kPa).

**C-19.1.3.4.4** The sudden release of gas, whether by rupture of a container or operation of a device such as used in fire fighting, will produce noise, possible shock waves, reduced or obscured visibility, and temperature changes. The initial effect might be to cool the air, but resulting pressure rises will cause adiabatic heating.

**C-19.1.3.5** In summary, the hazards of fire and related problems in hyperbaric systems are real. By the very nature of the hyperbaric atmosphere, increased partial pressures of oxygen are present routinely. Flammability and combustibility of materials are increased. Ignition energy is lowered. Both immediate escape and ready entry for rescue are impeded. Finally, attendants within the chamber, through effects of the elevated noise level and nitrogen pressure, might be unable to respond to emergencies quickly and accurately.

## C-19.2 Suggested Procedures to Follow in Event of Fire in Class A Chambers.

NOTE: The procedures contained in C-19.2 are adopted from those employed by the U.S. Air Force. These procedures are published herein only as a guide for those who are preparing procedures for their own hyperbaric facilities. Their publication herein is not to be construed as implying that they become a literal part of the standard procedure in any hyperbaric facility.

> The procedures listed in C-19.2.1 and C-19.2.2 reflect the latest emergency practices of the U.S. Air Force. The Committee on Hyperbaric and Hypobaric Facilities considered it appropriate to include such an example for the benefit of the user.

### C-19.2.1 Fire Inside Chamber.

*Inside Observer.*

(a) Advise outside.
(b) Don breathing air mask.
(c) Activate fire suppression system and/or hand-held hoses.

*Console Operator.*

(a) Maintain chamber depth.
(b) Activate the fire suppression system, if needed.
(c) Ensure breathing gas is compressed air.
(d) Notify the fire department by activating fire alarm station or telephone.
(e) Note time of fire and record progress of events.

*Hyperbaric Chamber (System) Technician (Outside).*

(a) Stand by with a fire extinguisher.
(b) Assist in unloading chamber occupants.

*Physician/Safety Monitor (Outside).*

(a) Direct operations and assist crew members wherever necessary.
(b) Terminate procedure as soon as possible.

*Other Personnel.*

(a) Stand by to evacuate chamber personnel.

### C-19.2.2 Fire Outside Chamber.

*Console Operator.*

(a) Notify the inside observer to stand by for emergency return to normal atmospheric pressure.
(b) Notify fire department by activating fire alarm station or telephone.
(c) Change chamber breathing gas to compressed air.
(d) Don fire mask.
(e) Note time of fire and record progress of events.

*Hyperbaric Chamber (System) Technician (Outside).*

(a) Ensure that compressor intake is drawing outside air.
(b) Man fire extinguisher.
(c) Help chamber operator to don fire mask.

*Physician/Safety Monitor (Outside).*

(a) Direct operations.
(b) Determine whether procedure should be terminated.

*Other Personnel.*

(a) Stand by to evacuate chamber personnel.

### C-19.3 Suggested Procedures to Follow in Event of Fire in Class B Chambers.

**C-19.3.1** For fires within facility not involving the chamber

(a) Turn off oxygen source.
(b) Decompress chamber.
(c) Remove patient and evacuate to safe area.

**C-19.3.2** For fire within chamber

(a) Turn off oxygen source.
(b) Decompress chamber.
(c) Remove patient.
(d) Sound fire alarm of facility.
(e) Evacuate area.
(f) Attempt to suppress fire, or close door and await arrival of fire service personnel.

Note 1 to Table C-19.4 clarifies that it is the percent of oxygen in the atmosphere that is of fire concern, not the partial pressure of oxygen.

*Table C-19.4 Pressure Table*

| Atmosphere Absolute (ATA) | mm Hg | psia | psig | Equivalent Depth in Ft Seawater | Equivalent Depth in M Seawater | mm Hg Oxygen Pressure of Compressed Air | mm Hg Oxygen Pressure of Oxygen-Enriched Air (23.5%) |
|---|---|---|---|---|---|---|---|
| 1 | 760 | 14.7 | 0 | 0 | 0 | 160 | 179 |
| 1.5 | 1140 | 22 | 7.35 | 16.5 | 5.07 | 240 | 268 |
| 2.0 | 1520 | 29.4 | 14.7 | 33.1 | 10.13 | 320 | 357 |
| 2.5 | 1900 | 36.7 | 22.0 | 49.7 | 15.20 | 400 | 447 |
| 3.0 | 2280 | 44.1 | 29.4 | 66.2 | 20.26 | 480 | 536 |
| 3.5 | 2660 | 51.4 | 36.7 | 82.7 | 25.33 | 560 | 625 |
| 4.0 | 3040 | 58.8 | 44.1 | 99.2 | 30.40 | 640 | 714 |
| 5.0 | 3800 | 73.5 | 58.8 | 132.3 | 40.53 | 800 | 893 |

NOTE 1: The oxygen percentage in the chamber environment, not the oxygen partial pressure, is of principal concern, as concentrations above 23.5 percent oxygen increase the rate of flame spread. Thirty percent oxygen in nitrogen at 1 ATA (228 mm Hg $pO_2$), increases burning rate. However, 6 percent oxygen in nitrogen will not support combustion, regardless of oxygen partial pressure (at 5 ATA, 6 percent oxygen gives 228 mm Hg $pO_2$).

NOTE 2: The Subcommittee on Hyperbaric and Hypobaric Facilities recommends that one unit of pressure mea surement be employed. Since a variety of different units are now in use, and since chamber operators have not settled upon one single unit, the above table includes the five units most commonly employed in chamber practice.

## References Cited in Commentary

1. NFPA 801, *Standard for Fire Protection for Facilities Handling Radioactive Materials,* 1998 edition.
2. NFPA *101®, Life Safety Code®,* 1997 edition.
3. NFPA 10, *Standard for Portable Fire Extinguishers,* 1998 edition.

# The Safe Use of High-Frequency Electricity in Health Care Facilities

*This annex is not a part of the requirements of this NFPA document but is included for informational purposes only.*

NOTE: Cross-references (of numbered paragraphs) refer to paragraphs within this annex unless otherwise noted.

The late Dr. Carl W. Walter, Chairman of what was the Committee on Hospitals in the 1960s, appointed a subcommittee to draft a document on the safe use of high-frequency medical devices. A document had been considered necessary for some time because high-frequency electrosurgery could and did cause injuries to patients and staff. The result was NFPA 76CM, *Safe Use of High-Frequency Electrical Equipment in Hospitals,* a manual that was adopted in 1970 and upgraded to a recommended practice in 1975.

This recommended practice, which became Appendix E in the 1984 edition of NFPA 99 and is now this Annex 1, is a valuable guide to the safe use of this energy and equipment and is highly recommended reading for anesthesiologists, anesthetists, operating room nurses, surgeons, and those who maintain and service high-frequency electrical equipment. Since high-frequency electrosurgery is often used in anesthetizing locations, readers should study this material in conjunction with 12-4.1, Anesthetizing Locations.

Although this annex contains recommendations and information, not requirements, users and manufacturers should note that these recommendations have generally been accepted as good practice for many years. While not intended to be incorporated into law, these recommendations have been referenced in litigation and have afforded valuable advice.

There is relatively little commentary on this annex, as compared to other chapters in NFPA 99, because the text itself incorporates a great deal of explanatory material.

## 1-1 Introduction

### 1-1.1 Purpose.

The purpose of this annex is to provide information and recommendations for the reduction of electrical and thermal hazards associated with the use of high-frequency electricity in health care facilities.

### 1-1.2 Scope.

This annex covers principles of design and use of electrical and electronic appliances generating high-frequency currents for medical treatment in hospitals, clinics, ambulatory care facilities, and dental offices, whether fixed or mobile.

*Exception No. 1: This annex does not cover communication equipment, resuscitation equipment (e.g., defibrillators), or physiological stimulators used for anesthesic, acupuncture, and so on.*

*Exception No. 2: This annex does not cover experimental or research apparatus built to order, or under development, provided such apparatus is used under qualified supervision and provided the builder demonstrates to the authority having jurisdiction that the apparatus has a degree of safety equivalent to that described herein.*

While this annex covers many of the principles of design and use, it does not cover all of them. Emphasis is on those features that relate to fire hazards.

### 1-1.3 Frequency Range.

For the purposes of this annex, high frequency is intended to mean any electrical energy generated in the radio-frequency range from approximately 100 kHz (100,000 cyc/sec) to microwave frequencies.

### 1-1.4 Intended Use.

This annex is intended for use by operating personnel practicing the electrical or the medical arts, as well as apparatus designers. It thus contains material of an informative nature as well as recommendations.

### 1-1.5 Responsibility of the Governing Body.

It is the responsibility of the governing body of the health care facility to provide its staff, patients, and visitors with an environment that is reasonably safe from the shock and burn hazards associated with the use of high-frequency electricity. In order to discharge this obligation, the governing body is permitted to delegate appropriate authority to its medical staff, consultants, architects, engineers, and others. *(See Section 1-5 for further information.)*

## 1-1.6  Interpretations.

The National Fire Protection Association does not approve, inspect, or certify any installation, procedure, equipment, or material. With respect to this annex, its role is limited solely to an advisory capacity. The acceptability of a particular piece of equipment, installation, or procedure is a matter between the health care facility and the authority having jurisdiction. However, in order to assist in the determination of such acceptability, the National Fire Protection Association has established interpretation procedures. These procedures are outlined in the NFPA *Regulations Governing Committee Projects*.

## 1-1.7  General Introduction.

The flow of electric energy at conventional power frequencies is generally understood and predictable. As the frequency is increased to the radio-frequency range, that is, above 100 kHz (100,000 cyc/sec), the electric current might not be restricted to obvious conductive paths and consequently can have effects not generally appreciated.

High-frequency power-generating equipment can present a hazard to the patient or to the operator by the nature of its use, or by its electrical interference with other apparatus in contact with or implanted within the patient. Since the equipment usually requires direct connections to the patient, it can also present a current path through the body tissues for electrical faults occurring within it or in other equipment.

It should be kept in mind that this annex is intended for use by operating personnel practicing the electrical or the medical arts, as well as apparatus designers. Some of the comments might appear overly simple, since it was considered desirable to err on the side of clarity rather than conciseness.

Some statements in this annex concerning waveforms, frequency, and so on, refer to specific designs of apparatus that are in common use. These are cited for illustrative purposes only. Other techniques for accomplishing the same medical purposes have been developed. This annex is not intended to assess the relative merits of any of these techniques, but rather to provide guidelines for the safe use of any type of high-frequency, power-generating, medical equipment.

This annex indicates circumstances and procedures that can produce hazards during the use of high-frequency electrosurgical or diathermy equipment, and it suggests protective measures against such hazards. This annex is concerned specifically with electrical effects and safety. The high-frequency power generated by these devices can interfere with the operation of other apparatus such as physiological monitors or pacemakers. The mechanisms of heat generation in body tissues by high-frequency energy needs to be understood and controlled to be effective therapeutically, while avoiding unwanted burning. The arc that is likely to occur when an energized high-frequency electrode contacts tissues can be an ignition source for flammable vapors and gases. Although referenced in this annex, full recommendations for safety from explosion hazards in the presence of flammable anesthetic agents are given in Annex 2 of this standard and should be consulted for detailed specifications. Surgical effects of electrosurgery are described in Section 1-6 of this annex. A recommendation for the clinical use of electrosurgical equipment is outlined in Section 1-7 of this annex.

These sections are included because there is little available in the medical literature on the effective and safe use of these powerful electrical therapeutic instruments.

The waveforms, energies, and so forth, commonly used were arrived at largely through experience. Research has been conducted on mechanisms for therapeutic action, but no optimum design has been developed (some question whether there is an optimum design). Therefore, technical descriptions have been kept general with the understanding that a variety of devices could achieve equivalent therapeutic results.

## 1-2 High-Frequency Equipment

### 1-2.1 Types of Apparatus.

#### 1-2.1.1 Electrosurgery.

**1-2.1.1.1 General.** Electrosurgical techniques utilize the heating effect of high-frequency current passing through tissues to desiccate, fulgurate, coagulate, or cut tissues. A very small active electrode concentrates the current with resulting rapid heating at the point of application. A larger dispersive electrode providing broad coupling with the skin is used to minimize the current density and heating at the other end of the body circuit.

**1-2.1.1.2 Electrocoagulation and Fulguration.** Coagulation and fulguration procedures generally employ a damped sine waveform or a train of low duty-cycle pulses. The frequency is in the 0.1- to 5-MHz (million cycles per second) region, but a wide spectrum of high frequencies also could be generated.

**1-2.1.1.3 Electrocutting.** High-frequency cutting of tissue is more effective with an undamped sinusoidal current or continuous pulse train. Most electrosurgical equipment provides a selection of coagulating current, cutting current, or a blended output.

**1-2.1.1.4 Electrosurgical Oscillators.** Electrosurgical oscillators operate in the general range of 0.5 MHz to 5.0 MHz with average output power capabilities as high as 500 watts. The actual amount of power required depends on the type of electrode used, the modality (cutting or coagulating), the operative procedure, and the conditions surrounding the operating field. In open-air cutting or coagulating, the power will generally range from 50 to 100 watts. In a transurethral resection, higher power might be required because of the bypassing effect of the irrigating fluid around the electrode. An electrosurgical unit must have a relatively low output impedance (typically 100 to 1000 ohms) in order to match the tissue electrical load and to limit open-circuit peak voltage with its attendant danger of insulation failure of electrodes, surgical handles, and so on.

NOTE: Most older instruments used a spark gap oscillator to generate highly damped radio-frequency sine waveforms, often modulated at 120 Hz, characterized by high peak voltages and low duty cycle, for coagulating purposes. Newer instruments use solid-state circuits to generate complex pulse trains with similar characteristics. Limited studies indicate that the frequency range is not very critical, but that the low duty cycle train is the key to the coagulating process. A continuous, unmodulated sine waveform or pulse train, delivering a high average power generated by a vacuum tube or solid state oscillator, is used for free cutting with little or no hemostasis. Higher-duty-cycle, moderately damped waveforms are used when a greater degree of hemostasis is desired while cutting. *(See Section 1-6 of this annex.)*

The frequency used for electrosurgery is not critical. The frequency range indicated, 0.1 MHz to 5.0 MHz, is well above the possibility of electrically stimulating nerve or muscle, but not so high that there is excessive radiation of power from leads or electrodes. See Exhibit A1.1.

Although the high-frequency energy would not directly stimulate nerve or muscle, the modulation of the signal can produce stimulating effects. A good discussion on electrical stimulation can be found in Bruner and Leonard, "Electricity, Safety, and the Patient" [1].

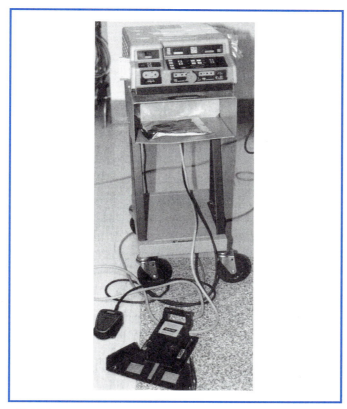

**Exhibit A1.1** *Typical electrosurgical unit used in surgery today.*

**1-2.1.2 Electrocautery.** Electrocautery is a surgical technique that utilizes a heated electrode or glowing wire to conduct heat to the tissue. It usually uses power frequency (60 Hz) current at low voltage to heat the electrode and hence is not a high-frequency device. It is described here because of possible confusion in terminology. In electrocautery there is no intentional passage of current through the tissues. While the voltage and frequency are low, these are patient-connected devices using electrical power, and appropriate precautions should be used. *(See Chapter 7, Electrical Equipment, in the requirements portion of this document.)*

> Hazards of patient-care-related electrical appliances, particularly with respect to power-line operation, are addressed in Chapter 7 of NFPA 99. Readers are urged to review that chapter because even in the standby state these appliances present power-line frequency hazards.

**1-2.1.3 Neurosurgical Lesion Generator.** Specialized instruments with lower power, 1 to 30 watts, are used in neurosurgery to make carefully delineated lesions in neural tissue. They employ continuous waveform radio-frequency power. Some designs use stereotactic instruments or neural signals for position control, and temperature measurement for size control. The temperature rise is limited to achieve tissue protein denaturation but not gross tissue destruction.

> Other types of high-frequency devices are used for special purposes, such as dental work, cardiac lesions, and so forth. The same general safety principles apply for all types.

**1-2.1.4 Radio-Frequency Diathermy.**

**1-2.1.4.1 General.** Diathermy utilizes the heating effect of the passage of a high-frequency current or an electromagnetic field in body tissues. In contrast to electrosurgery, it applies a relatively even heat distribution within the tissue well below a temperature that would cause tissue destruction. Diathermy equipment operates at 27.12 MHz, with some older units at 13.56 MHz. These frequencies are assigned for this purpose by the Federal Communications Commission with rigid regulations regarding frequency control, harmonics, or spurious radiation. *(See Section 1-9, Informatory and Referenced Publications and Articles, in this annex.)*

> Radio-frequency fields (both magnetic and electric) can have undesirable effects (such as heating of tissues, cataracts in the eye, and neurological disturbances) on general nonpatient populations and are regulated by safety rules generally based on ANSI Standard C95.1 [2]. These regulations apply to medical staff and visitors who are at risk of exposure to radio-frequency fields. Patients who are exposed to radio-frequency fields for therapeutic reasons are, generally, exempt from these regulations. Exposure time for these patients is relatively short, and the medical benefits far outweigh the risks. In addition to ANSI C95.1, a valuable source of information on radio-frequency fields is NCRP

Report No. 67, *Radio-Frequency Electromagnetic Fields, Properties, Quantities and Units, Biophysical Interaction and Measurements* [3].

**1-2.1.4.2 Dielectric or Spaced-Plate Diathermy.** With spaced-plate applicators, heating is the result of alternating current in the tissues caused by the high potential difference between the electrodes. This alternating electric field permeates the interposed tissues, which act as lossy dielectrics between capacitor plates.

**1-2.1.4.3 Inductive Diathermy.** The high-frequency current of inductive diathermy is passed through a coil or coils to produce rapidly reversing magnetic fields through the tissue. Heating is caused by eddy currents set up by the alternating magnetic field.

**1-2.1.5 Microwave Diathermy.** Microwave energy is radiated from a reflector, usually parabolic, air-spaced from the tissue. The energy is "beamed" like light to the intended area. The depth of penetration and intensity of heating are determined by the spacing and energy output of the microwave source. The assigned medical frequency is 2450 MHz. Electromagnetic energy at this frequency has an appropriate combination of penetration and absorption in tissue.

**1-2.1.6 Ultrasonic Diathermy.** Ultrasonic energy in the high-frequency range (approximately 0.05 MHz to 5 MHz) is also used for therapeutic heating and for making lesions. It should be noted that the energy modality is mechanical (acoustic) and not electrical, and hence some of the hazards described herein do not apply. However, these are patient-connected devices employing substantial electrical power, and appropriate precautions must be used.

**1-2.1.7 Hyperthermia.** Heating, controlled in spatial distribution and temperature, can be applied to tumors as a therapeutic adjunct to other therapeutic techniques. Techniques similar to diathermy can be used, often with implanted antennas or coupling devices.

In this technique, high-level fields, usually at microwave frequencies, are used since fields at this frequency will raise the temperature of tissue. In the procedure, the temperature of tissue surrounding a tumor is raised almost to the point of irreversible damage. The electrical safety concerns of hyperthermia should be carefully considered because this technique often uses experimental systems and is applied while the patient is isolated in an ionizing radiation chamber.

**1-2.1.8 Medical Lasers.** The spatial and frequency coherence properties of laser-generated radiation allow the localized deposition of large amounts of energy in tissue. This can be used for cutting, coagulation, or photochemoactivation. This apparatus per se is an electrical device, subject to the requirements of Chapter 7, Electrical Equipment (in the requirements portion of this document), but the peculiar hazard is the result of the unusual optical properties of this radiation.

Light amplification by stimulated emission of radiation (laser) technology is well established, although it has only been used in surgery for the last 15 years or so. While not a high-frequency device in the same sense as other types listed in 1-2.1

of this annex, laser technology does have properties that present unique hazards, as well as hazards similar to high-frequency devices.

Medical lasers use electromagnetic radiation in the infrared and visible spectrums. This is not usually considered high-frequency electricity in the radio-frequency sense of the term. However, in medical use, these devices apply thermal energy to cause cutting and coagulation of tissue analogous to electrosurgery.

Although both modalities are thermal in effect, electrosurgery involves direct contact with a flow of current, while lasers use a radiated beam of energy without the need for direct contact with the intended target (i.e., location on body). The laser beam can be focused, reflected or piped, and pointed at intended or unintended targets.

Many of the risks from thermal hazards in electrosurgery apply to lasers—for example, burns in unintended places—and to ignition of drapes and flammable liquids. Lasers present added hazards as well. Laser beams that operate in the invisible radiation spectrum can be reflected from surgical tools, and so forth, that in visible light appear dull and nonreflective. Such reflection can cause unintended injury to the patient or attendant staff who are hit by the misdirected laser beam. Surgeons need to receive specific training in the use of lasers.

Lasers are also used as spatial localizing beams. While they are usually very low power, prolonged exposure to such beams by the patient or staff should be avoided. The eye is a particularly sensitive target because the lens can focus a beam on the retina.

See 1-3.8.2 and accompanying commentary in this annex for further information and guidance. See also NFPA 115, *Recommended Practice on Laser Fire Protection* [4], for more general laser safety guidance.

## 1-2.2 Properties of High-Frequency Circuits.

**1-2.2.1 General.** In low-frequency apparatus, the circuit elements are usually discrete components, physically obvious, interconnected by wires or other conductors. At higher frequencies, distributive elements and less obvious forms of coupling (capacitive, inductive, and radiative) become increasingly important. Since these properties might not be fully appreciated by personnel using high-frequency medical equipment, this section reviews some aspects of them.

### 1-2.2.2 Nonconductive Coupling.

**1-2.2.2.1 Capacitive.** Any two conductors separated by a dielectric constitute a capacitor through which alternating current will pass. This capacitor has a reactance that varies inversely with frequency. Thus, when a conductive material is placed near a conductor carrying high-frequency current, some of the high-frequency energy can be transferred to this material. This coupling might exist, for example, between an electrosurgical power cable and an adjacent input lead of an electrocardiograph. Similarly, a low-impedance ground path might be presented by the capacitance between an electrode lead and its grounded metal shield.

Capacitive coupling exists at all frequencies but is relatively more significant at higher frequencies.

**1-2.2.2.2 Inductive.** Energy might also be transferred without an obvious interconnection by the magnetic field that surrounds all current paths. This effect is used in the familiar transformer but could also produce coupling between two adventitiously placed adjacent wires. If a large conductor is placed in a magnetic field, the coupling could induce circulating current in the conductor. These "eddy currents" generate heat as would any other current in the conductor. Inductive coupling could be affected relatively little by shielding intended to inhibit capacitive coupling.

**1-2.2.3 Skin Effect.** Because of self-induced eddy currents, high-frequency current could be confined to the surface of metal conductors. This "skin effect" can cause a simple conductor to have a much higher effective impedance at high frequencies than it would have at low frequencies.

Skin effect should not be confused with the change of impedance of a patient's skin. Living tissue is a complex electrical system of ionic conductors and capacitors. The skin contact impedance shows a marked decrease at higher frequencies largely because of capacitive coupling through the poorly conductive outer skin layers.

**1-2.2.4 Modulation and Detection.** The high-frequency currents present in medical apparatus often have complex waveforms. The frequency and amplitude of the oscillations can vary. The peaks of successive oscillations form an "envelope" of the signal, or modulation. Thus a 1-MHz radio-frequency waveform might be modulated by a 120-Hz signal. When such a waveform passes through a nonlinear circuit element, other frequency waveforms are produced, including some at the modulating frequency (here 120 Hz). Since the contact between an electrode and tissue, and the tissue itself, contain nonlinear elements, low-frequency currents could be present when high-frequency currents pass through the body.

**1-2.2.5 Electromagnetic Radiation.**

**1-2.2.5.1 General.** In the radio-frequency region, energy is also propagated by direct radiation through air or other media. This is the basis of radio communication and microwave diathermy, and can produce undesired effects in other high-frequency apparatus.

(a) *Long Wires and Antennas.* At sufficiently high frequencies, a conductor such as a simple wire can become "electrically long" and constitute a complex circuit element. In free space this length is governed by the relation

$$\lambda f = 300$$

where $\lambda$ is the wavelength, in meters, $f$ is the frequency, in megahertz, and 300 is the velocity of light, in meters per microsecond. The velocity is less in other media. If the conductor is an appreciable fraction of a wavelength, it is no longer a simple resistive conductor. It could have a large impedance and become an effective antenna. If the length approaches $\frac{1}{4}\lambda$ (or more), it could be part of the resonant output system of the apparatus.

**1-2.2.5.2 Sources of High-Frequency Radiation.**

(a) *Electrosurgical Equipment Radiation.* Such radiation derives from the following:

1. The active cable
2. The dispersive return cable
3. Electrical power lines (minimized by filtering)
4. Direct radiation from components, especially the spark gap and associated wiring (minimized by proper cabinet design)
5. Radio-frequency current paths through the patient and from the patient to ground via alternative paths, such as capacitive coupling to the table

Since the operating frequency is relatively low and the leads in the output circuit are electrically short, radiation from them is at a low level. Generally, interference with other equipment is caused by the conduction of high-frequency energy through common power lines or by capacitive and inductive coupling. Interference can be minimized by proper shielding and filtering.

(b) *Diathermy Equipment Radiation.* Such radiation derives from the following:

1. Electromagnetic radiation from the applicators and their connecting cables. The amount of radiation is dependent on the treatment level and on the orientation of the drum or spaced plates and can be influenced by the placement of the leads.
2. At 27.12 MHz, a quarter wavelength ($\frac{1}{4} > 1$) is 2.76 m (about 10.9 ft). The "ground" wire in the supply cable might be low impedance only at a low frequency, so that the cabinet of the diathermy acts as the "ground" plane for the unit and under unusual conditions might be at appreciable high-frequency voltage above power supply ground.
3. A patient under treatment with spaced plates is in a strong electric field and is a conductor at some voltage above ground, as evidenced by the fact that he or she can receive a burn by touching a bare metal part of the cabinet. Since diathermy equipment is used to produce heat in tissues without direct contact with the body, the energy transferred must be by means of induction from resonant electrodes or applicators. This energy can be picked up by adjacent equipment, such as remote monitoring systems or by power lines, and can be difficult to control. Physical separation is the best solution since the signals attenuate rapidly with distance and interposed walls and building structures. The construction of shielded rooms might be necessary if the radiation problem is serious. The radiation from components and supply cable must be kept low to meet Federal Communications Commission requirements.

(c) *Microwave Therapy Radiation.* Such radiation is at extremely high frequency and short wavelength. A quarter wavelength in tissue is about 3 cm (1.18 in.). The electrical properties of tissue at these high frequencies are complex and need to be investigated further.

Only a limited statement on microwave therapy radiation is included here. The subject is complex and requires further investigation.

The use of microwave radiation as a source of energy for hyperthermia in cancer therapy is expanding. Care must be taken when microwave radiation is used for this purpose to avoid injuries.

See also commentary under 1-2.1.7 in this annex.

# 1-3 The Hazard

## 1-3.1 Hazards Covered.

This annex is concerned with the hazards that can exist during the use of high-frequency power equipment in the health care facility. The danger can be to the patient, the operating personnel, or to other equipment. Some of these problems are common to all electrical apparatus and are the subject of other manuals and codes. These are appropriately referenced. The following kinds of hazards are considered:

(a) Radio-frequency interference. *(See 1-3.2.)*
(b) High-frequency burns. *(See 1-3.3.)*
(c) Low-frequency electrical shock. *(See 1-3.4.)*
(d) Explosions and fire. *(See 1-3.5.)*
(e) Complications of the use of the apparatus. *(See 1-3.6.)*
(f) Direct current burns. *(See 1-3.7.)*
(g) Nonionizing radiation burns and ignition. *(See 1-3.8.)*

## 1-3.2 Radio-Frequency Interference.

**1-3.2.1 General.** The high-frequency output of therapeutic equipment can propagate by radiation or other coupling through air, tissue, or current conductors to affect the operation of other equipment, that is, by distorting or obscuring displayed data, blocking normal operation, or causing damage through thermal or electrical breakdown. The extent of the effect will depend upon operating frequency, power level, intercoupling of circuits, distance, and the sensitivity and selectivity of the affected apparatus. This could be of particular concern if the affected apparatus is computer-based since some digital circuits are very sensitive to interference.

The hazards of radio-frequency interference (RFI) have become a subject of increasing concern in recent years because of the proliferation of diagnostic and monitoring devices based on digital circuitry. Some of these devices are extremely sensitive to RFI but can exhibit this sensitivity in ways that are not immediately obvious, such as in random malfunctions or the production of erroneous data. If such devices are to be used in conjunction with high-frequency apparatus, or will be in close proximity to such apparatus, the entire system should be checked for compatibility. These concerns apply not only to electrosurgical apparatus, but also to diathermy, hyperthermia, or other techniques that may radiate or conduct significant high-frequency energy. See Exhibit A1.2.

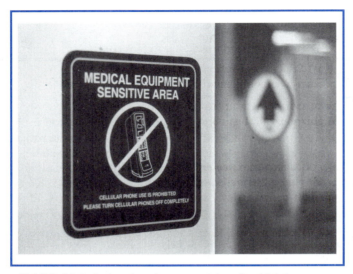

***Exhibit A1.2*** *A sign denoting an area housing high-frequency medical equipment. Cellular phones have been reported to interfere with medical monitoring equipment and fire alarm systems. As a result, some facilities have restricted their use in certain locations. The Center for Devices and Radiological Health (CDRH) of the Food and Drug Administration has conducted research in this area.*

**1-3.2.2 Equipment in Contact with Patient.** High-frequency currents flowing through body tissues can be conducted directly to equipment having input electrodes on or in the patient, or can be capacitively or inductively coupled to implanted sensors, to affect their operation. The performance of implanted pacemakers can be disrupted, particularly those having sensing circuits. The pacemaker manufacturer's literature should be consulted before using high-frequency equipment on a patient with a pacemaker.

**1-3.2.3 Equipment in Patient Area—No Direct Contact.** Telemetering and similar equipment in the immediate vicinity of the patient can be affected by energy radiated from high-frequency sources. The degree of interference depends on the strength of the interfering radiation and on the sensitivity of the affected equipment to the interfering signal. Before new configurations of equipment are utilized, they should be checked to ensure that no unacceptable interference could occur.

**1-3.2.4 Equipment in Remote Areas.** Equipment in remote areas can be affected by radiated energy or by energy conducted through power lines. Intensive care areas adjacent to treatment or operating areas are examples. In extreme cases shielding might be necessary, but spatial separation is usually adequate. If such interference occurs, the equipment should be modified or locations changed to reduce the interference to an acceptable level.

### 1-3.3  High-Frequency Burns.

**1-3.3.1  Electrosurgical Equipment.**  When electricity flows in a conductor, heat is generated at a rate proportional to the product of the resistance and the square of the current. This thermal effect is the basis of function for electrosurgical and dielectric diathermy equipment. In the case of electrosurgical equipment, the cutting electrode is made very small to produce a high current density and consequently a very rapid temperature rise at the point of contact with tissue. The high-frequency current is intended to flow through the patient to the dispersive electrode. The dispersive electrode provides a large contact with skin to minimize the current density at that end of the patient circuit. However, when the resistance between the body and the dispersive electrode is excessive, significant current can flow via alternative paths. The relative areas are indicated in Figure 1-3.3.1. If the dispersive electrode presents too small a contact area, deep tissue burns can result not only at the dispersive electrode but also at other sites. *(See also Section 1-6 of this annex.)*

The issue of the contact size of the dispersive electrode becomes more complex as the number of devices connected to the patient increases (i.e., as the number of possible alternative paths for current to flow increases). Techniques such as thermography have been used to quantitatively study skin temperature rise at the dispersive electrode and other sites. These studies indicate that maximum heating takes place along the edges of the electrode, particularly the edge of the dispersive electrode closest to the active electrode.

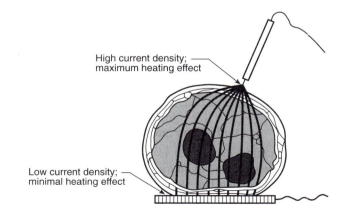

High current density; maximum heating effect

Low current density; minimal heating effect

*Figure 1-3.3.1* *Relative current densities at contact with patient.*

NOTE: The optimum characteristics and area of tissue contact for a dispersive electrode are matters of controversy. Factors pertinent to tissue injury include adequacy of gel, anatomic placement and orientation of the electrode, edge phenomena, and principles of fabrication (such as proprietary pregelled pads as opposed to metal foil or plate). Additional considerations are the manner of use of the ESU and the adequacy of skin perfusion (related to body temperature, circulatory integrity, and pressure points).

Thermal probes, monitoring electrodes, intravascular wires, or incidental contacts with metal furniture such as operating tables, IV poles, or instrument trays could provide better opportunities for return paths for current, particularly if the preferred path is inadequate.

Historical experience suggests that 1 cm$^2$ for each 1.5 watts of applied power appears to offer a generous margin of safety for most applications using gelled metal plates. Continuing research might establish confidence in the utilization of less generous contact areas in view of modern practices and equipment.

**1-3.3.1.1 Burns from Inadequate Dispersive Electrode Contact.** Inadequate contact with a dispersive electrode can result from the following:

(a) Electrode area too small for application
(b) Electrode not in adequate contact with tissue
(c) Electrode insulated from the skin by interposition of bedding, clothing, or other unintended material

With the advent of a multitude of configurations and designs (e.g., pregelled, electrically conductive adhesive, capacitively coupled, and combinations), and since each type presents application requirements peculiar to its design, the manufacturers' instructions should be carefully read and followed.

When electrosurgical equipment is brought into use after the start of an operating procedure and after the patient has been draped, extreme care is necessary in the placement and attachment of the dispersive electrode to be sure that proper contact is made directly with the skin and that there is no intervening insulating material. Electrode paste is useful to reduce the impedance of the contact between the electrode and the patient's skin. In a prolonged procedure, this should be checked periodically to ensure that the paste has not dried up.

It should be recognized that while a dispersive electrode might be making proper and sufficient contact with a patient at the beginning of an operation, conditions requiring repositioning of the patient can arise. This repositioning might reduce or completely eliminate contact with the electrode, and burns might result. Electrode placement must be checked whenever the patient is moved.

Electrode paste reduces impedance of the contact but by itself does not ensure good contact. Care should be used when electrodes are first applied. They should also be checked periodically during long procedures.

A variety of pregelled electrodes are now widely used. However, if they are opened and exposed to the air for too long before they are used, or if insufficient gel is supplied by the manufacturer, or if the gel is removed by careless handling, their advantage of ease is lost. Pregelled electrodes often have minimally adequate surface area. Care needs to be taken, therefore, that all available surface area is used.

Capacitively coupled electrodes do not use conductive gel. However, instructions need to be followed carefully to ensure good electrical contact.

**1-3.3.1.2 Burns from Uneven Electrode Contact.** Pressure points caused by bony protuberances or irregularities in electrode surface can concentrate current flow with resulting excessive temperature rise. Loose skin overhanging the edges of the electrode, or areas pinched by sliding a plate beneath the patient without lifting the patient sufficiently contribute to the burn hazard. *(See Figure 1-3.3.1.2.)*

Some heat is generated at the dispersive electrode contact, but it normally is carried away by the circulation of blood under the skin, so that the temperature rise is small. However, at pressure points or after prolonged pressure, the blood flow could be impeded, so that adequate cooling is not obtained. Skin and subcutaneous tissue blood flow could be altered by body temperature, anesthetic agents, and other drugs used during surgery. The effect could vary with the patient's age and clinical condition. The significance of these factors is not always fully appreciated.

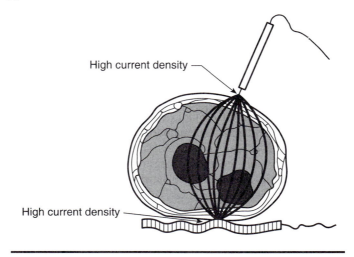

High current density

High current density

**Figure 1-3.3.1.2** *High current density at irregularity of electrode.*

**1-3.3.1.3 Burns at Unintended Current Paths with Various Types of Electrosurgical Units.** Normally, the current from the active electrode flows through the patient to the dispersive electrode and then back to the generator via the dispersive cable as shown in Figure 1-3.3.1.3. If other paths are available, the current will divide among the several paths.

The effect of alternate paths will vary depending on the type of electrosurgical unit employed.

(a) *Electrosurgical Unit with a Grounded Dispersive Electrode and No Dispersive Cable Continuity Monitor.* Normally the high-frequency current will flow as shown in Figure 1-3.3.1.3. If the dispersive cable is broken and the unit is activated, then the current could flow through unintended ground paths as shown in Figures 1-3.3.1.3(a)(1) and (2).

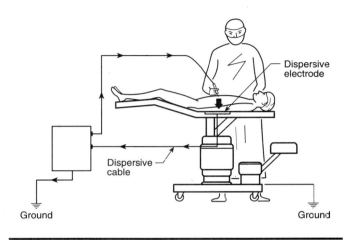

**Figure 1-3.3.1.3** *Correct flow of high-frequency current from electrosurgery through tissue to dispersive electrode and patient cord back to generator.*

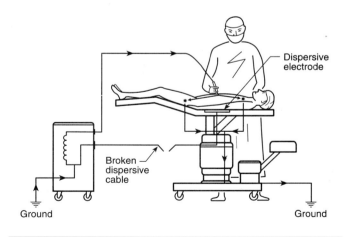

**Figure 1-3.3.1.3(a)(1)** *Alternate return paths to ground when normal return path through patient cord is broken.*

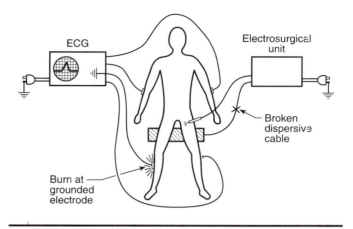

*ECG*

*Electrosurgical unit*

*Broken dispersive cable*

*Burn at grounded electrode*

***Figure 1-3.3.1.3(a)(2)*** *Alternate return path to ground through grounded electrode of ECG.*

(b) *Electrosurgical Unit with a Grounded Dispersive Electrode and a Dispersive Cable Continuity Monitor.* If an electrosurgical unit has a dispersive cable monitor, the break in the dispersive cable shown in Figure 1-3.3.1.3(a)(1) can be detected, and the machine inactivated.

Care should be taken not to activate these types of ESUs until the active electrode is about to contact the patient. Conversely, activation should be terminated as soon as possible after removing the active electrode.

This problem is of particular concern when finger-operated pencil electrodes are used because it is very easy to activate the electrode before it is in contact with the patient.

In Chapter 7, 7-6.2.3 contains requirements for the use of electrosurgical units to avoid fires. Electrodes that are resting in the surgical field or that are allowed to dangle in the drapes when contaminated can be particularly dangerous if inadvertently activated.

(c) *Electrosurgical Unit with an RF Isolated Output Circuit (Floating Output).*Because RF isolation is inherently imperfect, stray RF currents (leakage currents) can flow from the electrodes to any grounded conductor contacting the patient as shown in Figure 1-3.3.1.3(c). This stray RF current is greatest when the unit is activated with the active electrode not in contact with the patient.

**1-3.3.1.4 Dispersive Cable Monitoring Circuits.** The incorporation of a monitoring circuit will warn of a broken dispersive electrode cable. However, the monitoring circuit does not ensure that the dispersive electrode contact with the body is adequate and might lead to a false sense of security on the part of the surgeon or attendant.

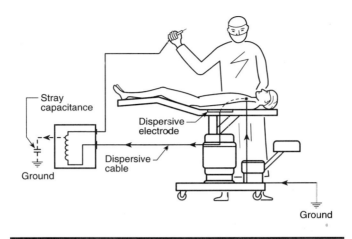

*Figure 1-3.3.1.3(c)  Stray current flow from an RF isolated electrosurgical unit.*

To ensure alarm with broken cable but with alternate ground paths as shown in Figure 1-3.3.1.3(a)(1), the dispersive cable monitor should alarm if the series resistance [R in Figure 1-3.3.1.4(a)] exceeds 150 ohms.

NOTE:  The monitoring current might produce interference on an ECG display.

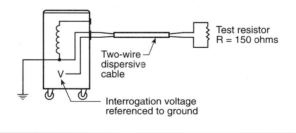

*Figure 1-3.3.1.4(a)  Trip-out resistance R.*

If an electrosurgical unit has its dispersive cable connected as shown in Figure 1-3.3.1.4(b), with a capacitor between it and ground, the dispersive cable monitor circuit might not respond to an alternate ground path.

Whether or not a monitoring circuit is provided, the method of attachment of the dispersive electrode should be such that the cable connector cannot be readily disconnected accidentally. A clip-on type of connection can be used only if it meets this criterion.

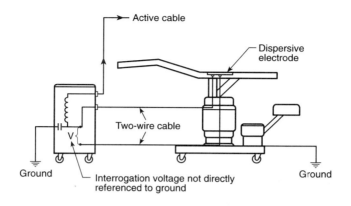

*Figure 1-3.3.1.4(b)*  *Electrosurgical unit with a DC isolated patient plate.*

**1-3.3.1.5 Other Causes of Burns at Unintended Current Paths.** These can be caused by the following:

(a) Other electrodes providing direct or capacitance-coupled ground returns. Needle electrodes are often used for ECG or other physiological monitoring procedures. The subcutaneous application of these needles provides good connection to the patient, but their small surfaces could produce high-current densities, especially if they are near the operating site. They should be used with great care when electrosurgery is employed. *(See Section 1-7 of this annex.)*

(b) Proximity of high-frequency leads to other wires, causing capacitive or inductive coupling, with resultant current in electrodes attached to the patient

**1-3.3.2 Diathermy.** Radio-frequency diathermy can induce currents that cause excessive heating in metal devices in the dielectric field (e.g., bone pins, dental fillings, metal sutures, implanted electrodes and leads), producing burns in the adjacent tissue and jeopardizing the tolerance of the metal in the tissues. The magnetic field of inductive diathermy can cause eddy currents that produce a similar effect in implanted metals.

## 1-3.4 Low-Frequency Shocks (60 Hz).

**1-3.4.1 General.** Depending on the type of electrosurgical unit employed, the dispersive electrode can present a direct or low-impedance ground path for a fault current emanating from other equipment connected to the patient. The dispersive electrode can be connected in either of two ways:

(a) An electrosurgical unit with a grounded dispersive electrode that provides a direct path for low-frequency current. *[See Figure 1-3.3.1.4(a).]*

(b) An RF grounded (low-frequency isolated) electrosurgical unit with capacitance between the electrodes and ground will provide isolation from low-frequency currents inversely proportional to the value of the capacitor (i.e., the smaller the capacitor, the better the low-frequency isolation). *[See Figure 1-3.3.1.4(b).]*

**1-3.4.2 Equipment Faults.** Insulation failure or loose wiring in power-operated devices used for surgery, such as bone saws and dye injectors, or monitoring equipment such as an ECG, can result in high voltage being applied to the patient through contact with the device.

**1-3.4.3 Equipment Not Isolated from Power Lines.** Low-voltage power sources of older design, which use an autotransformer, do not provide isolation from the main power lines. Contact of the patient with the frame or other exposed conductive surfaces of the device could apply full-line voltage to a grounded patient. This is often true of power sources for resectoscope lights, electrocautery units, stimulators, and other low-voltage devices commonly used in conjunction with electrosurgery, particularly in urology. Such low-voltage equipment should not be used unless provided with an isolated power supply.

**1-3.4.4 Rectified Modulation.** A peculiar hazard exists in electrosurgical equipment where the high-frequency energy is modulated at low frequencies, as in the coagulating mode. The contact between the active electrode and the tissue can demodulate the high-frequency current, generating power frequency components. If a low-impedance path is present through the apparatus and ground back to the patient, hazardous current levels might be generated. Thus, the application of what is believed to be solely high-frequency current might also be the application of dangerous low-frequency currents.

## 1-3.5 Explosion and Fire.

**1-3.5.1 General.** Since electrosurgery operates on the basis of tissue destruction by high-frequency arcs, it must be used with great caution when flammable anesthetic, disinfecting, or cleaning agents are employed. If the medical procedure requires the simultaneous use of electrosurgery and flammable agents, the responsible surgeon must be fully aware of the risks he or she is taking. *(See Section 2-6 in Annex 2.)*

The same caution applies to the use of surgical lasers or other appliances that apply localized high energy.

**1-3.5.2 Explosions in Hollow Organs.** The intestines, especially the colon, can contain flammable mixtures of hydrogen, hydrogen sulfide, methane, and oxygen. These gases are readily ignited and can burn explosively and disrupt organs. Hence, special precautions are necessary in surgery on the colon and paracolonic tissue. During laparoscopy, the abdominal cavity should be filled with a nonflammable gas, such as $CO_2$. When fulguration is done through a sigmoidoscope, an indwelling suction device is used to remove flammable gases. Explosive mixtures of hydrogen and oxygen form by electrolysis of electrolyte solutions used to distend the bladder during fulguration or resection. Isomolar solutions of crystalloids are used to avoid this complication.

In a large portion of the U.S. population, methane is a normal constituent of flatulent gas. It is prudent to assume that methane is present in all cases, and appropriate measures must be taken before the use of electrosurgery. Measures include evacuation, filling the colon with nonflammable gas, or clamping.

**1-3.5.3 Explosions during Operations on Head, Neck, Oropharynx, and in Body Cavities.** Flammable mixtures of anesthetic agents can persist in the exhaled air of patients for long periods, and such mixtures can persist in hollow viscera and body cavities. Electrosurgical equipment should not be used for operations on the head, neck, oropharynx, or body cavities during or following the administration of a flammable anesthetizing agent.

**1-3.5.4 Ignition of Combustibles in Mouth or Oropharynx during Oxygen Administration.** A hot needle or blade can ignite combustibles such as dry sponges, lubricants on endotracheal tubes, or the endotracheal tube itself. In the presence of an oxygen-enriched atmosphere, a major conflagration can occur, resulting in severe burns to the mouth, oropharynx, or the respiratory tract. Wet sponges are employed when electrosurgery is contemplated in the mouth or oropharynx. It is necessary to exercise care to ensure that the blade, needle, or hot metal particles do not contact the endotracheal tube. It is not advisable to use lubricants in these circumstances. *(See NFPA 53, Recommended Practice on Materials, Equipment, and Systems Used in Oxygen-Enriched Atmospheres, for details.)*

NOTE: Nitrous oxide will dissociate with heat to produce an oxygen-enriched atmosphere that readily supports combustion.

**1-3.5.5 Fire from Flammable Germicides and Defatting Agents.** The vapors from flammable solutions of disinfecting agents, or fat solvents left on the skin or saturating the drapes, can persist for long periods and be ignited by the arc that occurs when a high-frequency electrode contacts tissue. Nonflammable germicides or detergents should be used when the use of electrosurgery is contemplated.

**1-3.5.6 Fires from Microwave Heating.** Microwave ovens are frequently used in health care facilities to dry towels or linens, or to heat compresses or applicators. Although they are intended to heat at relatively low temperatures, they can cause fires by a kind of spontaneous combustion. A thick, tight cloth pack, particularly if there is metal or greasy material in the interior, can have a significant internal temperature rise and smolder. On opening and exposing this heated material to air, the cloth may spontaneously begin to burn.

Care should be taken to ensure that metal or other foreign materials are not left in such packs.

## 1-3.6 Complications of Electrosurgery.

**1-3.6.1 General.** Electrosurgery provides a method of cutting and hemostasis. It is an adjunct rather than a substitute for the scalpel, scissors, and hemostatic ligature. It always results in some tissue destruction and affects cells beyond the point of contact. Unless precautions are taken, electrosurgery could be followed by the complications of impaired tissue healing, enhanced risk of infection, surface burns, and explosion. It is effective in cutting muscle and in obtaining hemostasis of small or moderately sized blood vessels. It is also effective in excising and dissecting malignant lesions when primary healing is not important.

**1-3.6.2  Tissue Damage.** Electrosurgery always destroys tissue. The damage extends radially from the needle or blade electrode. Too much power, especially damped sinusoidal coagulating currents, results in excessive destruction of tissue. When organs or tissues are isolated, as when on a stretched pedicle, current and heat concentrate in the pedicle and could destroy the circulation. Skin flaps and fascia could be overheated. Contact of the high-frequency electrode with instruments or retractors in the wound could result in accidental burns. Defective or extra-thin gloves can result in burns to the surgeon's fingers.

**1-3.6.3  Special Electrosurgical Instruments.** Some surgical techniques require special instrumentation such as a resectoscope for transurethral resections or a laparoscope for tubal ligations. Since it is desired to keep the size of these instruments to a minimum, electrical distances are also minimal. To allow minimal separation, electrical insulation is used to provide isolation between various portions of these instruments. Complications during surgery can occur for the following reasons:

(a)  The instrument has an insufficient amount of insulating material.
(b)  The insulation has cracks.
(c)  The instrument has a poor grade of insulating material.
(d)  The insulation gets wet.
(e)  More than normal power settings are required of the electrosurgical unit.

With all electrosurgical instruments the manufacturer's recommendations should be followed. *(See Section 1-7 in this annex.)*

These types of devices, as well as those discussed in 1-3.6.4, should be especially examined for signs of insulation breakdown before each use.

**1-3.6.4  Use of Surgical Instruments to Deliver Electrosurgical Current.** When electrosurgical current is intentionally delivered through a surgical instrument, insulation might be needed so that only the desired portion of the instrument is exposed. This will preclude undesired contact with the patient or operator.

**1-3.6.5  Use of Hand Controls.** The use of pencil-type electrodes that include hand controls, particularly multiple electrodes on the same electrosurgical unit, or contact-activated electrodes presents special problems because of ease of misuse and inadvertent activation. Appropriate holsters should be provided to house electrodes in the sterile field when not in use.

There have been reports of fires, as well as patient burns and injuries, associated with these types of hand controls. They operate differently from older, simpler controls and offer more opportunity to be used incorrectly because of the mechanism of activation (i.e., a slight touch of a finger). Although manufacturers have designed these devices with ease of use in mind, it is the user (e.g., the surgeon) who must study the operating characteristics of these controls and learn how to use them as intended. See also 7-6.2.3 in Chapter 7 and the commentary after it.

## 1-3.7 Direct Current Burns.

Some electrosurgical devices utilize low direct currents to interrogate the continuity of leads in the dispersive electrode cable. The interruption of current can then be used to inhibit the operation of the machine. An alarm system is sometimes activated as well. *(See 1-3.3.1.4.)*

Where the dc voltage is referenced to ground, an inadvertent ground could provide a pathway for small direct currents to flow from the interrogation circuitry through the patient to ground.

The burns that can be produced due to the application of dc voltage are generally not thermal burns, as high-frequency ones are. Rather, they are electrochemical ones, caused by the production of caustic agents at the cathode site and chlorine gas at the anode.

The threshold level of voltage required to support electrolytic burning is close to 3 volts dc. The active electrolytic threshold depends in a complex way on many factors, some of which are electrode material, viscosity of electrolytic medium, and the chemical composition of electrolytic medium.

The amount of caustic and acidic products formed depends on the cumulative amount of current that flows through the electrolytic medium. The longer the current flows, the greater the quantity produced. Tissue fluids are converted chiefly to sodium and potassium hydroxides, and chlorine gas. Saline-soaked pads, jellies, and so on, could thus be rendered caustic.

## 1-3.8 Nonionizing Radiation Burns and Ignition.

**1-3.8.1 Radio-Frequency Devices.** In electrosurgery or diathermy it is intended to apply significant energy to the tissue of a patient for a desired therapeutic effect. However, the attendant staff are also subjected to some level of radiant energy. While this hazard is usually insignificant, peculiar circumstances might warrant closer attention. The nature of radio-frequency hazard and recommended levels are addressed in ANSI Standard C95.1, *Safety Levels of Electromagnetic Radiation with Respect to Personnel.*

**1-3.8.2 Medical Laser Devices.** Laser radiation does not present the same type of hazard as lower-frequency electromagnetic energy, nor does it have the ionizing effects of X-rays and radioisotopes. However, the concentration of energy in a narrow beam is high enough to destroy tissue or to ignite combustible materials in its path. These issues are addressed in ANSI Z136.1, *Safe Use of Lasers*, and in ANSI/Z136.3, *Safe Use of Lasers in Health Care Facilities*. The former (Z136.1) addresses general safety aspects of lasers; the latter (Z136.3) provides guidance for lasers specifically for use in health care facilities.

Laser systems have rapidly become a valuable tool in the therapeutic and diagnostic medical appliances field. These systems are now being utilized in various medical applications ranging from surgical instruments to pattern refractometers and teletherapy alignment scanning devices used for patient positioning.

Laser systems differ from one another in regards to their names, active laser mediums, wavelengths generated, power outputs, operating modes, and clinical applications. The beam generated by a laser system is very powerful because it possesses the unique characteristics of being monochromatic and coherent. Hazards from the use of laser systems include optical radiation (hazards to the eye and skin), fire hazards (especially in an oxygen-enriched environment), chemical hazards, and RF emission hazards that could affect other systems placed in close proximity to the laser system. Laser systems are classified in four control groups according to their output power and risk.

Electrical accidents (without injury), accidental shock of personnel, and electrocutions and fires in operating rooms all have been reported as a result of the use of lasers. It is important to permit only trained professionals to use and maintain laser systems. The extremely high energies and voltages present in the power supplies of many lasers require institutions to establish hazard-control policies and procedures. All precautionary labels should be visible, and warning devices should be operational.

Suggested safety measures for laser systems used in the operating theater include the following:

(a) An institutional Laser Safety Committee should be established to help develop, monitor, and evaluate policies and procedures relating to the safe use of medical lasers.

(b) Laser systems should be properly registered and calibrated before their first use. It is important to plan for their incorporation into a maintenance program.

(c) Surgeons and other operating room (OR) personnel should be trained in, and be familiar with, the guidelines of laser radiation safety as outlined by respective state agencies.

(d) Lighted or clearly marked signs should be posted on OR door(s) indicating when lasers are in use in the room. No one should enter or exit an OR when a laser is actually being used.

(e) OR personnel should be aware that the laser beam, though invisible for most systems, can ignite flammable or combustible materials, inflict third-degree burns, and be reflected off shining or even dull light metal or invisible glass surfaces, causing severe eye injuries.

(f) OR personnel should be aware that the visible He-Ne laser system aiming beam can also cause eye injuries.

(g) Appropriate safety glasses need to be worn by everyone in the OR. The glasses can be plastic or glass and should have sideguards.

(h) The patient's eyes need to be covered with moist eye pads or protected with proper goggles.

(i)  A laser surgeon and his or her assistant need to have attended a laser training course prior to attempting laser surgery. In addition, the surgeon should have satisfied all the requirements for laser surgery privileges as set out by the Laser Safety Committee of the particular institution.

(j)  Lasers should not be used with or around alcohol preps, ether, and other flammable anesthetic gases.

(k)  Laser systems should be locked when not in use. Access keys should be kept by one person, preferably an OR nurse specifically in charge of the OR where the laser system is used.

(l)  An in-house qualified person should be trained to troubleshoot minor problems with laser systems, for example, problems involving gas flow gauges, water temperature, mirror adjustments, or the microscope and the microsled. The laser system needs to be maintained in accordance with the manufacturer's guidelines and checked prior to each operation. Cooling fan(s) and radiator(s) should be cleaned periodically.

(m)  Ideally, only one footpedal should be used for a laser system.

(n)  Nonreflective or blackened retractors and other instruments have to be used during laser surgery since the laser beam can reflect off shiny instruments.

(o)  The laser system needs to be put on standby whenever the surgeon is performing a nonlaser maneuver (such as suturing). After all laser procedures are accomplished for an individual case, the laser system should be turned off immediately. (The surgeon should make this determination.)

(p)  Flame-retardant drapes and surgical gowns need to be used. In addition, portions of the patient's skin that are not involved with surgery must be protected, such as by saline-soaked gauze or towels.

(q)  The patient's breathing circuit and oxygen hoses should be well protected. One method of protection is to cover the hoses with aluminum foil and towels.

Site preparation for laser system installation is critical because most laser systems require special utilities. For example, electrical specifications might require a 3-phase, 208-VAC, 50-ampere service. For systems that use water, requirements might include a minimum flow rate of 4 gal/min at 50 psi (17.6 L/min at 345 kPa), with an input temperature of not higher than 60°F (15°C) and water conductivity of less than 100 micro-ohms. Because of spillage problems, water systems might require an area to be designated as a wet location, which means a GFCI or isolated power system would be necessary.

Since a loss of circulating water can cause system overheating problems, it is a good practice to connect the water pump to a circuit on the essential electrical system. This will enable the pump to continue operating if normal power is interrupted. If the emergency power fails, or the pump itself fails, the laser system should also have sensors to detect loss of pumping action and shut the system down before overheating occurs. If the laser is self-contained, the coolant level and filtering system, including hoses, need to be inspected routinely.

A sample site installation is pictured in Exhibit A1.3.

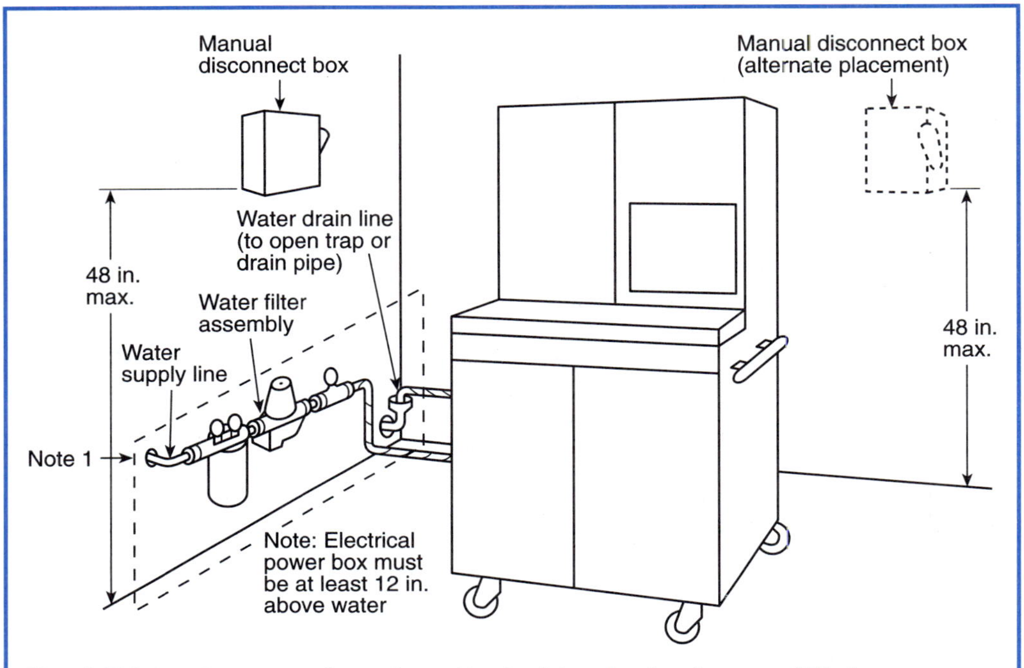

*Exhibit A1.3* One type of installation for a laser system.

In summary, practitioners who use laser systems should be aware of laser technology and its limitations, they should have a good working knowledge of the equipment, and they should be specially trained in its proper use. They should also be aware of two unique safety-related laser issues.

(a) Laser energy can travel over distances and can interact with flammable material (i.e., ignite them).

(b) The effect of laser radiation on tissue ranges from absorption, coagulation, and vaporization in the short term to photochemical effects in the long term. It is thus important for staff to control not only the area immediately around the laser instrument itself, but also the total environment in which the system is being used. If both fire hazard and optical radiation are closely controlled, the medical community can take full advantage of the benefits of laser systems without unnecessary risks. A sample procedure for approval of new lasers is shown in Exhibit A1.4.

For more information and material on lasers, readers can contact the Laser Institute of America, 12424 Research Parkway, Suite 125, Orlando, FL 32826. [5]

Publications on laser safety include *Guide for Control of Laser Hazards* [6]; ANSI Z136, *Standards for the Safe Use of Lasers* [7]; and ANSI Z136.3, *Safe Use of Lasers in Health Care Facilities* [8]. See the sample inspection checklist in Exhibit A1.5 and the sample user application for new lasers in Exhibit A1.6.

---

**PROCEDURE FOR APPROVAL OF NEW LASERS AT _____ HOSPITAL**

1. The Chief of the Service or his or her designee shall submit an application requesting approval of new lasers to the Laser Committee.

2. The Laser Committee shall meet to discuss and decide on the application. The committee may invite the Chief of the Service or his or her designee to make a presentation.

**PROCEDURE FOR GRANTING LASER PRIVILEGES AT _____ HOSPITAL**

1. Candidate applies to Chief of Service and submits documentation of having received hands-on instruction in the use of a particular laser.

2. Chief of Service approves and authorizes members of his or her staff for laser privileges. (Note: Chief of Service should have the Laser Committee's approval of the guidelines that are used to grant laser privileges to physicians.)

3. Chief of Service is responsible for sending copies of the approval of such physicians to the Medical Staff Office with the request to distribute to the following staff:
   - Chairperson of Laser Committee
   - Laser Safety Officer
   - Operating Room Supervisor(s)

4. Annually, Chief of Service is responsible for sending the list of residents who have been approved to use lasers only under direct supervision of approved physicians to the following staff:
   - Chairperson of Laser Committee
   - Chief Operating Room Nurse
   - Office of Medical Staff Affairs

---

**Exhibit A1.4** *Sample procedure for approval of new lasers.*

---

# 1-4 Equipment Safety Measures

## 1-4.1 General.

**1-4.1.1 Equipment Requirements.** Special requirements for anesthetizing locations are discussed in Section 12-4.1, Anesthetizing Locations, in the requirements portion of this standard. Additional considerations outlined in this section are primarily performance recom-

## SEMI-ANNUAL LASER INSPECTION CHECK LIST

Laser: _____

Serial Number: _____

| | | | | | | | |
|---|---|---|---|---|---|---|---|
| Date | | | | | | | |
| Location | | | | | | | |
| Laser Classification (labeled on unit) | | | | | | | |
| Area: Laser operation must take place in controlled area posted with suitable warning signs | | | | | | | |
| Warning Signs: Warning logo on laser must state maximum output, pulse duration, and laser median or emitted wavelength | | | | | | | |
| Housing: No modifications in manufacturer's design | | | | | | | |
| Date of Last Calibration | | | | | | | |
| Safety Glasses: Available and appropriate for laser type | | | | | | | |
| Date of Last Inspection | | | | | | | |
| Completed by: | _____ | _____ | _____ | _____ | _____ | _____ | _____ |

**Exhibit A1.5**  *Laser inspection check list.*

## SAMPLE USER APPLICATION FOR NEW LASER

*Application for User of New Laser at* _____ *Hospital*

### I. APPLICANT

Name _____     Title _____

Department _____     Tel. No. _____

### II. PROJECT

Description of laser use _____

_____

_____

Guidelines for laser use [safety measures (attach literature and manuals)].

Is this use investigational?  ❑ Yes  ❑ No

If yes, attach a copy of the Institutional Review Board application and Board approval (if available).

Anticipated duration of the project _____

### III. LASER

Manufacturer _____

Model No. _____     Serial No. _____

Description (Ar, Kr, $CO_2$, etc.) _____     Class _____

Emission levels _____     Continuous power _____

Pulsed

   Pulse width _____     Pulse rate _____     Pulse power _____

Emission wavelength _____     Fixed or mobile _____

Special accessories or preparation for installation needed _____

_____

Aiming laser (if used) _____

   Emission level _____     Emission wavelength _____

### IV. OPERATIONAL SAFEGUARDS

Has this system been registered by the Laser Safety Office with the State's Department of Health, Bureau of Radiation Control?  ❑ Yes  ❑ No

Will an in-service education program on this laser be provided to appropriate hospital staff?  ❑ Yes  ❑ No

When? _____     By whom? _____

How often, by whom, and by what method will the output of the laser be calibrated? _____

_____

Are adequate safety glasses supplied or available for personnel when this laser is used?  ❑ Yes  ❑ No

I am familiar with the "Regulations for the Control of Laser Radiation Hazards" and the administrative procedures established by this hospital's Laser Safety Committee and will abide by them.

_____     _____

Laser applicant     Date

**Exhibit A1.6** *Sample user application for new laser.*

mendations, which should be implemented in the manner indicated or by other equivalent methods.

> The general electrical safety requirements of Chapter 7 apply to high-frequency equipment. In particular, high-frequency equipment, when not activated, must meet the patient lead leakage current requirements. In large, high-power equipment, it can be difficult to meet the chassis leakage current limits, and isolation transformers, redundant grounds, or other special techniques might be necessary.

**1-4.1.2 Applicability.** These recommendations apply to the high-frequency equipment itself to reduce its potential as a source of radio-frequency interference, burns, shock, and explosion. Recommendations are also made relating to other associated electrical appliances to make them less susceptible to malfunction in the presence of the high-frequency apparatus.

## 1-4.2 High-Frequency Apparatus.

**1-4.2.1 Input Power Circuits.** Input power circuits should be provided with low-pass filters, electrostatically shielded isolation transformers, or other means for preventing the injection of high-frequency energy into the power lines. The use of a simple capacitive low-pass filter might introduce excessive line-to-ground leakage, which should be taken into account.

**1-4.2.2 Output Circuits.** High-frequency output circuits should be provided with isolation, high-pass filters, or other means to isolate these circuits from low-frequency voltages and rectified currents that could be produced in the patient circuit.

*Exception: Specialized low-power equipment such as a neurosurgical lesion generator, where precise control is important, might have the return (dispersive) electrode directly connected to ground.*

> While precise RF control can be achieved in several ways, direct connection to ground has many operational advantages. Since the devices identified in the exception are used only briefly during an operation, and when the electrosurgical unit is not in use, the committee considered this exception acceptable.

Isolated outputs are desirable practice for protection against 60-Hz electric shock. In some circumstances, however, the effective operation of devices individually or in combination might dictate connection, by the user, of a dispersive electrode to an equipment grounding conductor or to another grounding point. Such grounding will defeat any radio-frequency isolation existing in the electrosurgical unit.

NOTE: In electrosurgery, low-frequency or faradic currents can result from a rectification phenomenon occurring between the active electrode and body tissue during arcing. These low-frequency currents could constitute an electric shock hazard to the patient, as discussed in 1-3.4.

### 1-4.2.3  Dispersive Cable Continuity Monitor.

**1-4.2.3.1** In electrosurgical apparatus, a monitor circuit can be incorporated to indicate that the connection to the dispersive electrode is intact. This monitor should not utilize currents that could be a shock or burn hazard to the patient or that could interfere with other instruments.

**1-4.2.3.2** It is preferable that the dispersive cable continuity monitor also indicate that the plate is in contact with the patient, but this should not result in increased hazard to the patient or surgeon.

**1-4.2.3.3** There should be a suitable caution notice against defeat of the dispersive cable continuity-monitoring circuit. This could take the form of a label on the apparatus itself and explanatory material in the operating manual.

### 1-4.2.4  Foot Switches.

**1-4.2.4.1** Electrically powered foot switches for use in flammable anesthetizing locations are to be explosionproof or approved as intrinsically safe, as described by Section 2-6 in Annex 2.

**1-4.2.4.2** All foot switches should be provided with features to prevent accidental operation to a degree consistent with the need for facility of operation.

### 1-4.2.5  Power-Supply Cord.

**1-4.2.5.1** The power-supply cord for high-frequency equipment should incorporate a separate grounding conductor connected to the grounding contact in the attachment cap (plug).

**1-4.2.5.2** Where a detachable power supply cord set is used, the design of the connectors at the instrument end should prevent accidental disconnection.

### 1-4.2.6  FCC Regulations.

**1-4.2.6.1** Shortwave diathermy should meet all requirements of Part 18, *Industrial, Scientific and Medical Service*, of the Rules and Regulations of the Federal Communications Commission. *(See Section 1-9, Informatory and Referenced Publications and Articles, in this annex.)*

**1-4.2.6.2** The power line filter must prevent the 13.56-MHz or 27.12-MHz energy from feeding back into the power line.

## 1-4.3  Protection of Associated Apparatus.

**1-4.3.1  Input Power Circuits.** The introduction of high-frequency energy into patient monitors or other apparatus by inductive coupling or radiation to the power supply cord, or by conduction on the power supply lines, should be minimized. Low-pass filters or shielding in the power input circuits of equipment could introduce excessive leakage paths from line to ground, in which case they should not be used.

**1-4.3.2  Signal Input Circuits.**

**1-4.3.2.1** Low-pass filters can be incorporated in the signal input circuits of patient monitoring equipment to limit the flow of high-frequency currents from body electrodes to the equipment.

Since the attenuation of the higher frequencies can be achieved by providing a low-impedance path to ground, such filters can increase the possibility of burns where small electrodes are used.

**1-4.3.2.2** Isolation of input circuits from high-frequency signals can be accomplished by automatically disconnecting the input terminals when the high-frequency device is energized.

**1-4.3.2.3** Short-circuiting of input terminals might be effective in protecting signal input circuits but care should be taken that a low-resistance path is not provided for the high-frequency currents.

### 1-4.3.3 Patient Monitoring Electrodes.

**1-4.3.3.1** High-frequency current densities at a monitoring, electrode-to-skin interface can be reduced by the use of a large surfaced electrode. Needle electrodes normally should not be employed during an electrosurgical procedure, but if this mode of monitoring is judged necessary it should be done with extreme care.

**1-4.3.3.2** In the application of inductive diathermy, remote placement of patient monitoring electrodes might eliminate high-frequency burns.

**1-4.3.3.3** Where possible, all physiological monitoring circuits with conductive contacts of small surface area on or in the body should present a high impedance to the passage of high-frequency current between the contacts and ground.

**1-4.3.4  Cardiac Pacemakers.** Cardiac pacemakers, particularly external pacemakers of the demand type, can be susceptible to interference. Their input circuits require careful design to minimize these effects.

### 1-4.3.5  Low-Voltage Electrical Devices.

**1-4.3.5.1** Low-voltage power sources for endoscopy illuminators and other devices should incorporate transformers with isolated secondary circuits so that there is no possibility of patient contact with the primary power source.

**1-4.3.5.2** Exposed metal parts of line-operated low-voltage sources should be kept to a minimum. The chassis and exposed metal parts likely to become energized, if any, should be connected to ground through a third wire in the power supply cord or protected by double insulation when no grounding conductor is used. Low-voltage sources for devices that should have this protection include resectoscopes, stimulators, pumps, and photographic equipment. Small exposed surfaces not likely to come energized, particularly those that contact the patient, should not be grounded.

**1-4.3.5.3** A particular problem exists with resectoscopes used in conjunction with electrosurgical apparatus for urological procedures. These devices often have small clearances and insulation resulting in capacitively coupled RF currents. Repeated use could damage the insulation and expose the operator and patient to high-frequency burns. These devices should be designed to withstand high RF voltages in addition to low voltages used for illumination.

The patient is not the only one who can receive a burn from defective equipment or changes that occur in the active or dispersive electrode during an operation. The surgeon can be burned as well.

Care of the apparatus should be of particular concern because more operative procedures are being performed in walk-in clinics without full support from an operating room ancillary staff.

## 1-5 Administration and Maintenance

### 1-5.1 Responsibility.

**1-5.1.1 Administration.** Responsibility for the maintenance of safe conditions surrounding the use of high-frequency equipment falls mutually upon the governing body of the health care facility, the administration, the physicians using the equipment, and all personnel concerned with the application of the equipment to the patient.

Given the litigious climate that exists in the United States today and the hazards surrounding the use of high-frequency equipment, everyone associated with these appliances shares the responsibility for their safe use. Burns and other problems allegedly associated with the use of high-frequency apparatus are common reasons for liability litigation.

**1-5.1.2 Medical Staff.** It is important that the organized medical staff of the health care facility adopt regulations and practices with respect to the use of anesthetics and electrical devices in the presence of high-frequency energy, and jointly with the facility authorities set up requirements for training physicians, nurses, and other personnel who might be involved in the procurement, application, use, or maintenance of equipment used in conjunction with high-frequency equipment.

**1-5.1.3 Qualifications for Use of Electrosurgery.** No physician should attempt electrosurgery unless he or she is first adept with the scalpel and hemostat. Except for endoscopic surgery or when excising malignancy, sharp dissection provides safer surgery with more predictable wound healing.

The physician who chooses electrosurgery should know how to adjust the electrosurgical unit at his or her disposal. The physician is responsible for the proper placement of the dispersive electrode and the selection of the mode of attaching other electronic equipment to the patient.

### 1-5.2 Personnel, Training, and Clearance.

**1-5.2.1 Qualifications for Use of High-Frequency Equipment.** All personnel concerned with the application of high-frequency equipment, including surgeons, nurses, operating room technicians, and orderlies, should be fully cognizant of the potential hazards associated with its use, as outlined in Section 1-3 of this annex.

Surgical lasers, as an example, can be very hazardous if misused. Personnel must be specifically qualified in the use of these devices. These devices are also sensitive to mechanical disturbances, such as misalignment of the aiming and power beams, and ancillary staff must be instructed in their safe handling. The recommendations contained in this section for electrosurgical devices apply to laser systems where relevant.

**1-5.2.2 Instruction Manuals.** A complete instruction manual for each model of apparatus should be conveniently available for reference at the location of use *(see 1-5.3.2 in this annex).*

**1-5.2.3 Operating Instructions on Apparatus.** Information necessary for the safe use of the apparatus, in the form of condensed operating instructions, should be visibly and permanently displayed on, or attached to, the appliance itself.

**1-5.2.4 Qualifications for Use of Monitoring Equipment in Presence of High-Frequency Currents.** All personnel concerned with the application of monitoring or auxiliary apparatus that might be used in the same area as the high-frequency apparatus, or that might be in contact with the patient to whom high-frequency power is applied, should be fully cognizant of the hazards presented by that equipment in the presence of high-frequency energy.

**1-5.2.5 In-Service Training.** The health care facility administration should institute an obligatory in-service training program for the surgical staff and others involved in the use of high-frequency energy sources. With the current rapid changes in medical device technology, many techniques that were appropriate a short time in the past are no longer so. There is a great potential for patient injury and fire ignition if these high-powered energy devices are improperly used. Education and retraining are essential to avoid these hazards.

This section, added in 1993, is included to remind those responsible for the safety of patients and staff of the need for training and appropriate periodic retraining on the use of high-frequency, high-energy medical devices. New equipment should never be used until it has been inspected for safety and proper operation and appropriate training has been conducted.

## 1-5.3 Maintenance.

**1-5.3.1 Periodic Maintenance.** For the continued safe operation of high-frequency apparatus, a schedule of periodic preventive maintenance should be established. It is the responsibility of the health care facility to see that this program is effective. Because of the complex nature of this apparatus and associated electrical equipment, repairs should be made by qualified service personnel. Service could be provided by a competent internal engineering group, the manufacturer, or other reliable agency.

**1-5.3.2 Instruction Manuals.** Proper maintenance, as well as safe use, requires that the manufacturer provide operator's or user's manuals with all units. These manuals should include operating instructions, maintenance details, and calibration and testing procedures. The manuals should include the following:

> Manufacturers usually provide one copy of an operator and service manual with delivery of a device but might charge for additional copies. It can well be worth the investment to have a second copy retained in the biomedical engineering department (or its equivalent).

(a) Illustrations showing location of controls
(b) Explanation of the function of each control
(c) Illustrations of proper connection to the patient and to other equipment
(d) Step-by-step procedures for proper use of the apparatus
(e) Safety considerations in application and in servicing
(f) Effects of probable malfunction on safety
(g) Difficulties that might be encountered, and cautions to be observed, if the apparatus is used on a patient simultaneously with other electrical appliances
(h) Principles of operation
(i) Functional description of the circuitry
(j) Schematics, wiring diagrams, mechanical layouts, and parts list for the specific unit as shipped
(k) Power requirements, heat dissipation, weight, dimensions, output current, output voltage, and other pertinent data

The instruction manual can be in two parts: one, primarily operating instructions, addressed to medical personnel; the other, detailed maintenance and repair instructions addressed to technical personnel, except that the separate maintenance manual should include essentially all the information included in the operating manual.

**1-5.3.3 Physical Inspection.**

**1-5.3.3.1 Cables and Electrodes.** Connectors, cables, and electrodes should be inspected for damage before each use of the apparatus.

**1-5.3.3.2 Mechanical Damage.** The apparatus should not be used if examination of the cabinet indicates that it has suffered mechanical damage. Dial markings should be clean and legible. At all times there should be evidence that the apparatus has been protected from liquid and electrolyte contamination.

**1-5.3.3.3 Inspection.** The governing body should provide training for user personnel and other appropriate personnel to detect externally evident damage. The apparatus should not be used if inspection of the cord, cabinet, switches, knobs, or dials discloses hazardous mechanical damage.

Specific procedures should be developed for reporting and repair of equipment found to be damaged.

**1-5.3.3.4 Electrical Inspection.**

**1-5.3.3.4.1 Dispersive Cable Monitor.** If the apparatus includes a continuity monitor for the dispersive cable, it should be checked for proper operation before each use of the apparatus.

**1-5.3.3.4.2 Output Power.** Provision for periodic measurement of the output power of the apparatus is essential. *(See Section 1-8 in this annex.)*

# 1-6 The Effects of Electrosurgery on Tissue

## 1-6.1 Waveforms.

High-frequency electricity applied to tissue through a suitable electrode results in an arc that produces three different effects: dehydration, coagulation, or dissolution (cutting). Pulsed sine waveforms [Figures 1-6.1(a) and 1-6.1(b)] with a low duty cycle are commonly used for dehydration and coagulation; for cutting, continuous undamped sine waveforms [Figure 1-6.1(c)] are used. If additional hemostasis is required while cutting, modulated [Figure 1-6.1(d)] pulsed sine waveforms are used with a high duty cycle [Figures 1-6.1(e) and 1-6.1(f)]. Some instruments use other related waveforms.

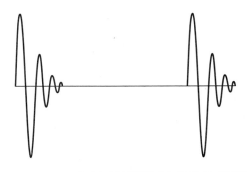

*Figure 1-6.1(a) Typical spark-gap waveform with a low duty cycle.*

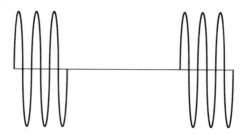

**Figure 1-6.1(b)** *Typical solid-state waveform with a low duty cycle.*

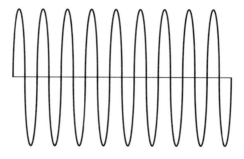

**Figure 1-6.1(c)** *Continuous undamped sine waveform.*

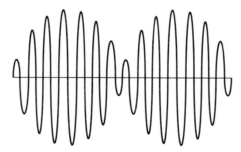

**Figure 1-6.1(d)** *120-Hz modulated sine waveform, also referred to as a fully rectified waveform.*

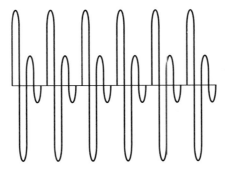

*Figure 1-6.1(e)* Typical spark-gap waveform with a high duty cycle.

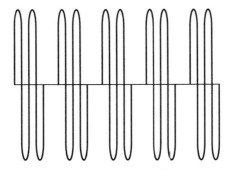

*Figure 1-6.1(f)* Typical solid-state waveform with a high duty cycle.

## 1-6.2 Fulguration.

This is a technique used for superficial dehydration or coagulation of the tissue. The electrode is held a short distance away and sparks jump to the tissue as shown in Figure 1-6.2.

## 1-6.3 Desiccation.

This is a technique used for dehydration and deliberate destruction of tissue. The electrode is placed in contact with the tissue and left in to char the tissue as shown in Figure 1-6.3.

## 1-6.4 Coagulation.

This is the sealing of small blood vessels. The electrode is left in contact with the tissue for a period of time until a deep white coagulum is formed *(see Figure 1-6.4).* Time is an

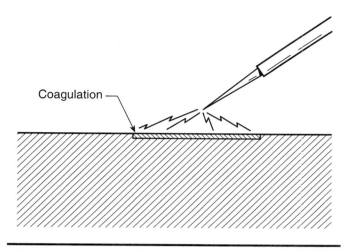

***Figure 1-6.2*** *Fulguration.*

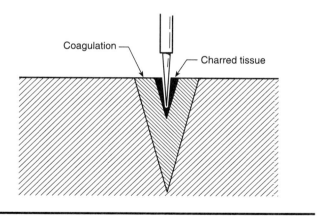

***Figure 1-6.3*** *Desiccation.*

important parameter for proper coagulation. Excessive power is of questionable advantage, since it may actually cause the tissue to dissolve.

## 1-6.5 Cutting.

Dissolution (cutting) occurs when power is increased until arcing persists as the electrode is moved through the tissue. Dissolution of the molecular structure of tissue cells in the path of the arc makes it appear that the tissue is falling apart.

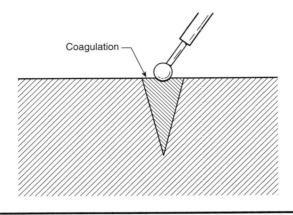

*Figure 1-6.4  Coagulation.*

## 1-6.6  Hemostatic Cutting.

Although the preceding effects of high-frequency current are quite different, they are interrelated. The success of electrosurgery results from an appropriate combination of the pulsed and continuous modes to achieve the desirable degree of cutting and hemostasis. Maximal hemostasis is generally accompanied by complete coagulation of tissue. The depth of coagulation is dependent upon the kind of tissue, the power, the waveforms, the type of electrode, and the cutting speed.

## 1-6.7  Procedures.

**1-6.7.1  Cutting.** When primary healing is desired, a small flat blade or needle electrode is used to cut with sufficient power to part tissues cleanly with little hemostasis of small vessels. A wire loop is also used to skive tissue; it is the electrode commonly used in the resectoscope. When cutting with the resectoscope more hemostasis is usually required, and a hemostatic cutting waveform would normally be required. The effect on tissue of electrosurgery is a function of waveform, time, and energy. Energy transfer and necrosis extend radially from the electrode. Greater power leads to greater energy release and wider areas of cell death. Hence, power should be maintained at the lowest level that achieves the desired results. A large dispersive electrode is essential.

**1-6.7.2  Monoterminal Technique.** Small or shallow surface growths are often desiccated with a monoterminal technique. A fine needle is inserted into the growth and current is applied for several seconds until a mild blanching of tissue occurs. When small lesions are to be destroyed the capacitance of the body suffices for coupling to ground, and the use of a dispersive electrode is unnecessary.

**1-6.7.3  Bipolar Technique.** Both conductors of the high-frequency electrical circuit are applied to the tissue by paired electrodes so that the energy is dissipated between and around them. Tissue destruction is restricted to a controllable volume. The depth is controlled by the distance to which the electrodes are inserted into the tissue; the breadth by the space between the two active electrodes. This modality is used for coagulation of larger lesions. Tissue destruction extends beyond the ends of the electrodes to about the same extent as is visible around the electrodes. Bipolar current is also used to coagulate blood vessels. The bleeder is grasped in the forceps and current is applied momentarily to congeal the vessel. A dispersive electrode need not be used with bipolar electrodes.

### 1-6.8 Spark-Gap versus Solid-State Coagulation.

The principal clinical differences between spark-gap and solid-state coagulation lie in the ability of a spark-gap generator to develop higher peak powers, which results in a lower duty cycle for the same average power. This lower-duty-cycle waveform results in less cutting or dissolution in the coagulation mode. In addition, spark-gap generators are able to produce higher open-circuit voltages, which results in a better ability to fulgurate.

### 1-6.9 Demonstration of Effect on Tissue.

The effects of the various modalities can be differentiated by holding a warm, moist, lean piece of beef in the hand while applying high-frequency current in various ways and strengths. The tester's body provides capacitance comparable to that of the patient at low powers. The meat should be placed on the dispersive electrode for higher power. The meat can be cut to reveal the extent of blanching that results from heating by the high-frequency current. Also, the amount of cutting in the coagulation mode between various units can be checked.

## 1-7 The Care and Use of Electrosurgery

### 1-7.1 General.

This section is for the indoctrination of operating room nurses, aides, and technicians in the care and use of electrosurgical equipment.

### 1-7.2 Purpose and Scope.

The indications for the use of high-frequency electrosurgery are described elsewhere in this annex. The purpose of this section is to promote safety for the patient and personnel and efficient operation of the unit. The steps detailed below for operating room personnel to follow for preparation, operation, and storage of the electrosurgical unit are designed to meet those ends.

### 1-7.3 Setting Up the Electrosurgical Unit.

The following procedures should be followed:

(a) Prior to the use of the electrosurgical unit, verify with anesthesia personnel the type of anesthetic to be used. Check Section 12-4.1, Anesthetizing Locations, in the requirements portion of this standard and the operating suite fire safety regulations as necessary.

(b) Prior to sterilization, inspect patient leads and fulgurating and coagulating tips for integrity and cleanliness and bits of tissue or carbon that would interfere with proper function. Test them for electrical continuity. Similarly, check when these leads and tips are removed from the sterile package by the instrument nurse.

(c) Make certain that the electrosurgical unit, together with its dispersive electrode and cable, foot switch and cable, and line cord, is free of dust and "operating room clean."

(d) Locate the electrosurgical unit on the operator's side of the table as far as possible from the anesthesia machine and monitoring equipment. Locate where the power cables, and the active electrode and dispersive electrode leads hang naturally and are not stretched across traffic lanes.

(e) Position the leads and electrodes for physiological monitoring equipment as far as possible from the active cable and active electrode when it is in use.

(f) Utilize as large a dispersive electrode as practical, commensurate with the site of the operation and position and size of the patient. Locate electrode as close as possible to the operative site. If a plate is used, exercise care so that the patient's skin is not traumatized or folded. Provide contact with as great an area of skin as is possible.

NOTE: If contact jelly is used on the dispersive electrode, use the correct type and spread uniformly over the electrode.

(g) Place the dispersive electrode against as large an area of soft tissue of the patient as practical. Avoid direct contact with bony prominences such as those of the scapula, sacrum, ilium, or patella. Check for continued contact during a long procedure, or when changes in patient's position are necessary.

With many medical procedures lasting several hours, checking the placement and conditions of electrodes becomes very important not only to avoid thermal burns, but to avoid chemical burns from the pooling of liquids, ischemic necrosis, and other effects that simulate thermal burns. It is common to describe these other lesions as thermal burns.

(h) Attach the dispersive electrode securely to its cable, and check its mechanical and electrical integrity prior to preparing the operative site and draping the patient.

NOTE 1: On an electrosurgical unit with a dispersive cable continuity alarm and automatic cutoff switch, follow the manufacturer's directions for preoperative testing.

NOTE 2: On electrosurgical units without a continuity alarm, the hospital should provide an external means for periodically testing the integrity of the dispersive cable.

(i) Do not employ electrosurgery without use of the dispersive electrode, unless the operator specifically orders monoterminal or bipolar techniques and directs the omission of the dispersive electrode.

## 1-7.4 Operation of the Electrosurgical Unit.

**1-7.4.1** It is important that personnel adjusting the electrosurgical unit during the operative procedure be aware that if the surgeon needs currents in excess of those usually required for a comparable procedure, a fault might have developed in the active electrode or dispersive electrode cables.

**1-7.4.2** If a flammable anesthetic agent has been employed for induction of inhalation anesthesia, even if followed by a nonflammable agent for maintenance, the electrosurgical unit should not be used on the neck, nasopharynx, and adjacent areas.

## 1-7.5 Electrosurgery with the Resectoscope.

The resectoscope should be maintained in top working order by periodical inspection and factory service. Discard loop electrodes, sheaths, and cords that show breaks, holes, or other evidence of deterioration.

Safe, effective use of electrosurgery for transurethral resections requires:

(a) The prevention of injury to the patient
(b) The prevention of injury to the user
(c) Minimizing electrical damage to equipment

**1-7.5.1 Patient Burns.** To minimize burns to the patient:

(a) Make sure the conductive surface of the dispersive electrode is in good contact with the skin.
(b) Do not make a large increase in power setting for an unexpected weak surgical effect.
(c) Keep metal parts of the resectoscope from contact with the patient.

**1-7.5.2 Operator Burns.** To minimize burns to the operator:

(a) Check to see that the control dials are set at the operator's minimum preferred settings.
(b) If the operator's hand touches some metal part of the resectoscope, as it often does, it should be with a firm, positive contact. Pinpoint contacts lead to burns even with low currents.
(c) Use only telescopes with fully insulated, nonmetal eyepieces.
(d) Avoid the use of eyeglasses with metal frames.

**1-7.5.3 Telescope Use.** To minimize damage to the telescope:

(a) Check to see that the loop is not bent. Guard against it touching or coming too close to the telescope.
(b) Avoid activating the electrosurgical unit when the electrode is not touching tissue.
(c) Use the minimum required power.
(d) Start each procedure with a new loop.
(e) Retract the telescope as far as possible to the point where the sheath is just visible under water to maximize the distance between the telescope and loop.
(f) Follow manufacturer's recommendations when using attached lenses.

### 1-7.6 Putaway and Storage.

After using an electrosurgical unit:

(a)  Clean cutting and fulgurating tips of all blood, debris, carbon, and tissue prior to storage.

When sterilizing electrodes, tips, wires, and so forth, after use, manufacturer's recommendations should be followed to ensure that there is no mechanical or electrical damage, particularly so that insulation is not compromised.

(b)  Clean all electrical contacts.

Dirt on electrical contacts can increase their resistance. As a consequence of dirt buildup, more power than normal will be necessary when the ESU is used. Because the resistance of dirty contacts can change with current flow, the operation of the device might become erratic.

(c)  Coil lead cables neatly and store in appropriate locations.
(d)  If the electrosurgical unit is stored other than in an operating room, select a dust-free location within the operating suite.

### 1-7.7 Repair of the Electrosurgical Unit.

**1-7.7.1**  The electrosurgical apparatus contains complex circuits that can develop malfunction after a period of operation. Prominently tag any item of electrosurgical equipment that is known or suspected to be defective and do not use again until it has been inspected and repaired by competent personnel.

# 1-8 Determination of Output Power

## 1-8.1 Output Power.

An approximate determination of output power of the electrosurgical device can be made using a radio-frequency ammeter of suitable range in series with a resistance. A simplified schema is shown in Figure 1-8.1. Maintain spacing and insulation appropriate to the high frequency and high voltage involved. The power, $P$, in watts can be calculated by:

$$P = I^2 \times 500$$

where $I$ is the rms current in amperes.

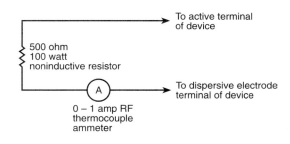

**Figure 1-8.1** *Simplified apparatus to measure power output of electrosurgical unit.*

## 1-9 Informatory and Referenced Publications and Articles

### 1-9.1 NFPA Publication.

National Fire Protection Association, 1 Batterymarch Park, P.O. Box 9101, Quincy, MA 02269-9101.

NFPA 53, *Recommended Practice on Materials, Equipment, and Systems Used in Oxygen-Enriched Atmospheres*, 1999 edition.

### 1-9.2 ANSI Publications.

American National Standards Institute, 11 West 42nd Street, New York, Ny 10036.

ANSI C95.1-1991, *Safety Levels of Electromagnetic Radiation with Respect to Personnel.*
ANSI Z136.1-1993, *Safe Use of Lasers.*
ANSI/Z136.3-1988, *Safe Use of Lasers in Health Care Facilities.*
ANSI/AAMI HF 18-1993, *Electrosurgical Devices.*

### 1-9.3 IEC Publication.

(Available in U.S. through American National Standards Institute, 11 West 42nd Street, New York, NY 10036.)

IEC 601-2-2, *Medical Electrical Equipment, Part 2: Particular Requirements for the Safety of High Frequency Surgical Equipment.*

### 1-9.4 U.S. Government Publications.

U.S. Government Printing Office, Superintendent of Documents, Washington, DC 20402.

Federal Communication Rules and Regulations, Part 18, *Industrial, Scientific and Medical Service.*
Food and Drug Administration, *Regulations for the Administration and Enforcement of the Radiation Control for Health and Safety Act of 1968.*

## 1-9.5  Articles on the Subject of High-Frequency Electricity.

Battig, Charles G., M.D. Electrosurgical burn injuries and their prevention. *JAMA*, Vol. 204, No. 12, 17 June 1968.

Billin, A. G. *Electrosurgery in the Operating Room.* Ritter Company, Inc., 400 West Avenue, Rochester, NY 14611.

Bruner, J., and Leonard, P., "Electricity, Safety, and the Patient," Year Book Medical Publishers, Inc., 1989.

Chapter 8 of the Bruner and Leonard book [1] covers electrosurgery from its inception, including safety measures.

Conolly, W. B., Hunt, T. K., and Dunphy, J. E. The place of electrosurgery in abdominal operations. *Amer. J. of Surgery*, 118:422-426 (Sept.), 1969.

Dobbie, A. K. The electrical aspects of surgical diathermy. *Biomedical Engineering*, pp. 206–216, May 1969.

Fein, Richard L. Transurethral electrocautery procedures in patients with cardiac pacemakers. *JAMA*, Vol. 202, No. 2, pp. 101-103, 2 October 1967.

Hussey, John L., and Pois, Allen J. Bowel gas explosion. *Amer. J. of Surgery*, 120:103, 1970.

Leeming, M. N. Low voltage direct current burns. *JAMA*, 214:1681-1684, 1970.

Mitchell, J. P., and Lomb, G. N. *A Handbook of Surgical Diathermy.* John Wright and Sons Ltd., Bristol, 1966.

Pearce, J. A., PhD, *Electrosurgery.* John Wiley & Sons, New York, 1986.

### References Cited in Commentary

1. J. Bruner and P. Leonard, "Electricity, Safety, and the Patient," Year Book Medical Publishers, Inc., Chicago, 1989, pp. 62–63, 231–232.
2. ANSI/IEEE C95.1 (R1997), *Safety Levels with Respect to Human Exposure to Radio Frequency Electromagnetic Fields, 3 kHz to 300 GHz,* 1991.
3. NCRP Report No. 67, *Radio-Frequency Electromagnetic Fields, Properties, Quantities and Units, Biophysical Interaction and Measurements,* March 1, 1981, National Council on Radiation Protection and Measurements, 7910 Woodmont Ave. NW, Washington, DC 20014.
4. NFPA 115, *Recommended Practice on Laser Fire Protection,* 1999 edition.
5. *Laser Safety Guide,* Laser Institute of America, 1993.
6. *Guide for Control of Laser Hazards,* 1990, American Conference of Governmental Industrial Hygienists, 1330 Kemper Meadow Drive, Suite 600, Cincinnati, OH 45240.
7. ANSI Z136.1, *Safe Use of Lasers,* 1993 American National Standards Institute, 11 West 42nd Street, New York, NY 10036.
8. ANSI Z136.3, *Safe Use of Lasers in Health Care Facilities,* 1996, American National Standards Institute, 11 West 42nd Street, New York, NY 10036

# ANNEX 2

# Flammable Anesthetizing Locations

NOTE 1: This annex is not a part of the requirements of this NFPA document but is included for informational purposes only.

NOTE 2: The text of this annex is a compilation of requirements included in previous editions of NFPA 99 on safety practices for facilities that used flammable inhalation anesthetics. This material is being retained in this annex by the Technical Committee on Anesthesia Services for the following reasons: (1) the Committee is aware that some countries outside the United States still use this type of anesthetics and rely on the safety measures herein; and (2) while the Committee is unaware of any medical schools in the U.S. still teaching the proper use of flammable anesthetics or any health care facilities in the U.S. using flammable anesthetics, retaining this material will serve as a reminder of the precautions that would be necessary should the use of this type of anesthetics be re-instituted.

This annex applies only to anesthetizing locations where flammable anesthetics are still used. Facilities that no longer use flammable anesthetics will find requirements for nonflammable anesthetizing locations in 12-4.1 of Chapter 12, including those facilities where conductive floors are still present. Institutions that prohibit the use of flammable anesthetics in anesthetizing locations need not follow the requirements in this annex.

As discussed in the commentary at the beginning of 12-4.1, the use of flammable anesthetics as general anesthesia in the United States has, for all practical purposes, ceased. (See "The Case for Abandonment of Explosive Anesthetic Agents" [1] and "Flammable Anesthetics Are Nearing Extinction" [2]. These papers remain the defining body of work on this subject.)

There are several reasons for the almost exclusive use of nonflammable anesthetics, the most obvious one being the elimination of the explosion hazard. This switchover became possible when nonflammable anesthetizing agents became

751

acceptable alternatives to the various flammable agents previously in use. The switch has also created a debate in the U.S. medical community over whether to ban the use of flammable anesthetics. Until the NFPA committee responsible for anesthesia safety or some authority having jurisdiction prohibits the use of flammable anesthetics in U.S. operating rooms, a set of procedures for the safe use of flammable anesthetics is necessary. In fact, the infrequent use of flammable anesthetics has been cited as a strong reason for the continued need for the requirements in this annex. Unfamiliarity with flammable anesthetics can be hazardous in and of itself. Because some countries still make use of flammable anesthetics, the guidance imparted in the code and this handbook is beneficial to those health care providers who still employ these anesthetics.

## 2-1 Definitions

### 2-1.1 Antistatic.

That class of materials that includes conductive materials and, also, those materials that throughout their stated life meet the requirements of 2-6.3.8(f)(3) and (4) of this annex. (AS)

### 2-1.2 Conductive.

Not only those materials, such as metals, that are commonly considered electrically conductive, but also that class of materials that, when tested in accordance with this document, have a resistance not exceeding 1,000,000 ohms. Such materials are required where electrostatic interconnection is necessary. (AS)

### 2-1.3 Flammable Anesthetizing Location.

Any area of a facility that has been designated to be used for the administration of any flammable inhalation anesthetic agents in the normal course of examination or treatment. (AS)

### 2-1.4 Hazardous Area in a Flammable Anesthetizing Location.

The space extending 152 cm (5 ft) above the floor in a flammable anesthetizing location. *(See 2-6.3 in this annex.)* (AS)

NOTE: The definition in this annex is based on the following considerations:

(a) Available data and recent investigations indicate that under customary operating procedures, flammable anesthetic mixtures are diluted by air in the anesthetizing area to a nonflammable range before reaching a vertical height of about 1 ft (30 cm) from any source of leakage or spillage involving quantities of anesthetics used in anesthesia procedures. These findings corroborate the premises on which safeguards required in this standard were originally based and do not negate the need for any of the protective measures required; however, they do provide a sound basis for the statement that recirculation of air in ventilating systems serving anesthetizing locations does not increase the hazards of fire and explosions from flammable anesthetic vapors.

References to investigations are those by M. D. Vickers in "Explosion Hazards in Anesthesia." [3]

(b) The mobile character of the operating table and portable equipment and the variety of the surgeon's techniques and surgical positions that will alter the physical relationship of the anesthesia gas machine, the surgeon, the anesthetist, and the patient's head, and all of these with respect to their relative location within the room, must be considered in the determination of the electrical safeguards to be provided.

(c) The portion of the flammable anesthetizing location extending 5 ft (152 cm) above the floor as defined in Chapter 2 constitutes a "hazardous area." Because persons entering such anesthetizing locations may have accumulated electrostatic charges, the floors of corridors and rooms contiguous to the flammable inhalation anesthetizing location must be conductive and at the same potential as the floor in the flammable anesthetizing location. Patients should not be transported while flammable anesthetics are being administered. Rooms such as sterilizing rooms directly communicating with flammable anesthetizing locations are required by 2-6.3.1(c) in this annex to be provided with conductive floors to equalize static charges. Such rooms, if not used as flammable anesthetizing locations, are not required to be served by explosionproof wiring specified in 2-2.1 in this annex. Where flammable anesthetizing locations open directly onto a passageway not a part of an operating room or delivery room, the conductive floor should extend 3 m (9.84 ft) from either side of the door frame and out from the frame (into the passageway) for 3 m (9.84 ft). It is desirable to demarcate the hazardous location of such a corridor by a physical barrier (doors) and cautionary signs to check smoking, use of open flame, wearing of improper clothing and shoes, and the application of insulating floor wax.

(d) Designated areas in which the use and handling of flammable anesthetic agents are prohibited by hospital regulations, such as corridors in the surgical suite, rooms adjacent to flammable anesthetizing locations, and nonflammable anesthetizing locations, should be indicated by prominent signs permanently installed.

(e) Postoperative recovery units that are not immediately adjacent to flammable anesthetizing locations and in which the use of flammable anesthetic agents is prohibited are not considered to involve explosion hazards and therefore do not require the installation of static-dissipation systems nor explosionproof equipment required for explosive atmospheres. Prohibition of the use of flammable anesthetic agents by hospital regulation and the proper indication of such prohibition by prominent signs, as recommended in subsection (c) above, is recommended.

In the 1980s, the boundaries for the hazardous area in a flammable anesthetizing location were heavily criticized by a portion of the health care community. Much was written about changing the boundary, for example, to "2 ft from anesthetizing circuits." The following, taken from the newsletter of NFPA's Health Care Section *Code Red* ! [4] is a summary of the position of the then Committee on Anesthesia Agents (now incorporated into the Committee on Gas Delivery Equipment), which is responsible for the definition.

> Anesthesia personnel have a multiplicity of responsibilities in the operating room, many of which must be carried out simultaneously, or almost so. Included are administering the anesthetic, monitoring the vital signs of the patient, administering blood, fluids, and medications other than anesthetic agents, and recording all of these events in a fairly detailed manner. It would be literally impossible to add to this burden the task of monitoring and policing a movable zone of risk, especially since the area in the vicinity of the head of the operating room table and gas anesthesia apparatus is one that visitors to the operating room frequently, but inappropriately, use to be able to look over the ether screen to view the site of the operation.
>
> The concept of a moving hazard makes accidental violation of safe practice more likely than when a fixed hazardous area is defined. For example, in the usual operation of some gas scavenging systems, and in a failure mode of some others, anesthetic gases are discharged through tubing that vents near the floor. If an explosive agent is being scavenged with such a device, a nonexplosionproof foot switch could easily be bumped into the zone of discharge of an explosive mixture.
>
> By retaining the *5-foot level,* one is able to keep flammable agents in the gaseous, vaporous, or liquid state well away from sources of ignition. The fact that the gas anesthesia apparatus can be moved widely around the operating room to accommodate operative requirements would make the role of a fire or building safety inspector infinitely complicated in any attempt to police a *zone of risks.* With the present 5-foot level, hospital inspectors are afforded a standard that is readily subject to inspection. Costs are not increased, since nonexplosionproof electrical outlets can be installed above the 5-foot level. Finally, anesthesia personnel who utilize flammable agents are afforded much peace of mind.

Arguments were submitted again during the 1984 revision of NFPA 99 to change the 5-ft (1.5-m) level requirement. The committee, however, still considered the current requirement necessary. In addition to the preceding arguments, the committee noted that the current requirements were necessary in light of the infrequency of use of flammable anesthetics and the concomitant decrease of familiarity with safety requirements involved in such use. The committee also cited the following: (1) The lack of control studies for a 2-ft (.61-m) zone, (2) the litigious climate prevailing in the United States today, and (3) the cessation of teaching the use of flammable inhalation anesthetics in medical schools.

Clearly, the use of flammable inhalation anesthetics has fallen off to the vanishing point in the United States in a little more than the last decade. However, the use of flammable anesthetic agents may be continuing in other parts of the world. Facilities elsewhere may be built partly with U.S. funds, sponsorship, or architectural guidance and are, by implication, subject to U.S. standards of safety and liability. In Annex 2, 2-6.3 provides a guide to prudent construction and conduct.

What was at issue in the 1980s was the necessity of some of the criteria developed for flammable anesthetizing locations, particularly the 5-ft (1.5-m) level.

### 2-1.5 Hazardous Location.

An anesthetizing location or any location where flammable agents are used or stored. (AS)

### 2-1.6 Mixed Facility.

A facility wherein flammable anesthetizing locations and nonflammable anesthetizing locations coexist within the same building, allowing interchange of personnel or equipment between flammable and nonflammable anesthetizing locations. (AS)

### 2-1.7 Storage Location for Flammable Inhalation Anesthetics.

Any room within a consuming facility used for the storage of flammable anesthetic or flammable disinfecting agents *(see NFPA 30, Flammable and Combustible Liquids Code),* or inhalation anesthetic apparatus to which cylinders of flammable gases are attached.

NOTE: Such a storage location is considered a hazardous area throughout the location. (AS)

## 2-2 Electrical System Criteria

**2-2.1** Electric wiring installed in the hazardous area of a flammable inhalation anesthetizing location shall comply with the requirements of NFPA 70, *National Electrical Code*, Article 501, Class I, Division 1. Equipment installed therein shall be approved for use in Class I, Group C, Division 1 hazardous areas.

**2-2.2** Wiring for low-voltage control systems and nonemergency communications and signaling systems shall be installed in metal raceways unless located outside or above the hazardous area in the flammable anesthetizing location.

**2-2.3** Electric switches installed in hazardous areas of flammable anesthetizing locations shall comply with the requirements of Section 501-6(a) of NFPA 70, *National Electrical Code*.

**2-2.4** Receptacles in hazardous areas shall comply with the requirements of Section 501-12 of NFPA 70, *National Electrical Code*. They shall be a part of an approved unit device with an interlocking switch arranged so that the plug cannot be withdrawn or inserted when the switch is in the "on" position.

NOTE: It should be recognized that any interruption of the circuit, even of circuits as low as 8 volts, either by any switch or by loose or defective connections anywhere in the circuit, might produce a spark sufficient to ignite a flammable anesthetic agent.

This requirement for explosionproof receptacles was applicable only up to the 5-ft (1.5-m) level. Above that height, normal straight-blade receptacles were acceptable because the hazardous area in a flammable anesthetizing location extended only up to 5 ft (1.5 m) above the floor. (See 2-1.4 in this annex.)

# 2-3 Ventilation—Flammable Anesthetizing Locations

**2-3.1** Relative humidity of not less than 50 percent, at a temperature range of 64.4°F (18°C) to 80.6°F (27°C), shall be maintained in flammable inhalation anesthetizing locations.

See commentary on 12-4.1 of Chapter 12 for a discussion of the relative humidity requirements in anesthetizing locations.

**2-3.2** Requirements for ventilation and cooling set forth in 5-4.1.2 through 5-4.1.6 of Chapter 5 of NFPA 99 shall apply.

## 2-3.3 Ductwork for Air Handling.

It is not required that ductwork be fabricated of nonsparking material.

In the past, critical interpreters of requirements for flammable anesthetizing locations thought that the ductwork in such locations, perhaps because of the presence of some flammable vapors, needed to be constructed of nonsparking material (e.g., made out of stainless steel). This paragraph is included to prevent further misinterpretation of this section.

The divider in a through-the-wall air conditioner that is designed to separate indoors from outdoors should always be gasketed to prevent direct outdoor leakage. The room is at a higher pressure than outdoors to maintain sepsis and thus cannot tolerate leaks. A divider without gasketing could not be depended on after many years to remain free of leaks.

**2-3.4** If a window-type temperature regulating unit (air conditioner) is installed so that any part is less than 5 ft (152 cm) from the floor of a flammable anesthetizing location, such unit shall comply with the requirements set forth in 2-3.5 below.

**2-3.5** Such a window-type temperature regulating unit shall be provided with a vertical divider that effectively prevents airflow from the room side to the outside side, and all electric equipment on the room side of this divider shall meet the requirements of 2-2.1 of this annex. The installed unit shall tightly fit the opening in the window or wall. Openings in the divider for shafts of fans, other moving parts, or wiring shall be gasketed unless the local air pressure on the room side of the opening when the unit is in operation is less than that on the outdoor side. A fresh-air port is permitted in the divider if it is automatically closed when the unit is not in operation. The rotating parts of fans on the room side of the divider shall not cause percussion sparks if they accidentally contact surrounding objects.

NOTE:  Ventilation of Anesthetizing Locations. Mechanical ventilation is required as a means of diluting flammable gases and maintaining the proper humidity. It is also the most effective and aseptic method of maintaining a uniform humidity within the area.

*General.* Anesthetizing locations used solely for the induction of anesthesia need only be ventilated at a rate sufficient to maintain the proper humidity.

Anesthetizing locations in which clinical procedures are performed, such as operating rooms, delivery rooms, and certain treatment rooms, require special ventilation as described below. This special ventilation serves not only to maintain humidity but also to reduce the hazard of infection, which is accomplished by dilution and removal of airborne microbial contamination and dilution of flammable gases. It also contributes to odor control and comfort of personnel.

The Committee on Anesthesia Services recognizes that a hazard can be created by the chronic exposure of anesthesia and other operating room personnel to low concentrations of vapors or commonly employed volatile liquid inhalation anesthetic agents. For further information see:

(a)  Cohen, E. N., et al. Anesthesia, pregnancy and miscarriage; A study of operating room nurses and anesthetists. *Anesthesiology* 35:343, 1971.
(b)  Whitcher, C. E., et al. Chronic exposure to anesthetic gas in the operating room. *Anesthesiology* 35:348, 1971.
(c)  Yanagida, H., et al. Nitrous oxide content in the operating suite. *Anesth. and Analg.* 53:347, 1974.
(d)  Frey, R., et al. How strong is the influence of chronic exposure to inhalation anesthetics on personnel working in operating theatres? W.F.S.A. *Newsletter* No. 10, June 1974.

*The Health Hazard*

(a)  Cohen, E. N., et al. Occupational disease among operating room personnel—a national study. *Anesthesiology* 41:321-340, 1974.
(b)  Spence, A. A., et al. Occupational hazards for operating room-based physicians. *JAMA* 238:955-959, 1977.
(c)  Cohen, E. N., et al. A survey of anesthetic health hazards among dentists. J. *Am. Dent. Assoc.* 90:1291-1296, 1975.

(d) Greene, N., Report on American Cancer Society study of causes of death amongst anesthetists. Annual Meeting, American Society of Anesthesiologists, New Orleans, Louisiana, 18 October 1977.

(e) Hazleton Laboratories America, Inc. Final Reports, CDC-99-74-46, National Institute for Occupational Safety and Health, 1014 Broadway, Cincinnati, Ohio. Long-term inhalation reproductive and teratogenic toxicity evaluation of nitrous oxide plus halothane. 14 November 1975. Cytogenic evaluation of spermatogonial cells in the rat following long-term inhalation exposure to nitrous oxide plus halothane. 17 November 1976.

(f) Chang, W. C., et al. Ultrastructural changes in the nervous system after chronic exposure to halothane. *Exp. Neurol.* 45:209-219, 1974.

(g) Quimby, K. L., et al. Behavioral consequences in rats from chronic exposure to 10 ppm halothane during early development. *Anesth. and Analg.* 54:628-633, 1975.

(h) Kripke, B. J., et al. Testicular reaction to prolonged exposure to nitrous oxide. *Anesthesiology* 44:104-113, 1976.

(i) Fink, B. R., ed. *Toxicity of Anesthetics.* Part Four, "Teratogenic Effects." Baltimore, Williams & Wilkins Co., 308-323, 1968.

(j) Bruce, D. L., et al. Trace anesthetic effects on perceptual, cognitive and motor skills. *Anesthesiology* 40:453-458, 1973.

(k) Bruce, D. L., and Bach, M. J. Psychological studies of human performance as affected by traces of enflurane and nitrous oxide. *Anesthesiology* 42:194-196, 1975.

(l) Smith, G., and Shirley, A. W. Failure to demonstrate effects of low concentrations of nitrous oxide and halothane on psychomotor performance. *Br. J. Anaesth.* 48:274, 1976.

(m) Davison, L. A., et al. Psychological effects of halothane and isoflurane anesthesia. *Anesthesiology* 43:313-324, 1975.

(n) Walts, L. F., et al. Critique: Occupational disease among operating room personnel. *Anesthesiology* 42:608-611, 1975.

(o) Cohen, E. W., and Brown, B. W. Comment on the critique. *Anesthesiology* 42:765-766, 1975.

(p) Fink, B. R., and Cullen, B. F. Anesthetic pollution: What is happening to us? *Anesthesiology* 45:79-83, 1976.

(q) Lecky, J. H. Chronic exposure to anesthetic trace levels. *Complications in Anesthesia,* edited by L. H. Cooperman and F. K. Orkin. J. B. Lippincott Co., Phila. In press.

*Reduction and Control Methods*

(a) Pisiali, R. L., et al. Distribution of waste anesthetic gases in the operating room air. *Anesthesiology* 45:487-494, 1976.

(b) Whitcher, C. E., et al. Control of occupational exposure to nitrous oxide in the dental operatory. *J. Am. Dent. Assoc.* 95:763-766, 1977.

(c) Muravchick, S. Scavenging enflurance from extracorporeal pump oxygenators. *Anesthesiology* 47:468-471, 1977.

(d) Whitcher, C. E., et al. Development and evaluation of methods for the elimination of waste anesthetic gases and vapors in hospitals. HEW Publication No. (NIOSH) 75-137, GPO stock no. 1733-0071. Supt. of Documents, Govt. Print. Off., 1975.

(e) Whitcher, C. E., et al. Control of occupational exposure to $N_2O$ in the dental operatory. HEW Publication No. (NIOSH) 77-171. Cincinnati, U.S. Department of Health, Education and Welfare, Public Health Services Center for Disease Control, National Institute for Occupational Safety and Health.
(f) Lecky, J. H., et al. In-house manual for the control of anesthetic gas contamination in the operating room. University of Pennsylvania Hospital publication.
(g) Lecky, J. H. The mechanical aspects of anesthetic pollution control. *Anesth. and Analg.* 56:769, 1977.

*Dealing with Personnel*

(a) Lecky, J. H. Notice to employees on the potential health hazards associated with occupational exposure to anesthetics. University of Pennsylvania Hospital publication.

*NIOSH—OSHA*

(a) Criteria for a recommended standard: Occupation exposure to waste anesthetic gases and vapors. HEW Publication No. (NIOSH) 77-140. Cincinnati, U.S. Department of Health, Education and Welfare, Public Health Service Center for Disease Control, National Institute for Occupational Safety and Health.

*ANSI Z79*

(a) American National Standards Institute, Committee Z79, SC-4 *Anesthesia Gas Scavenging Devices and Disposal Systems*, J. H. Lecky, M.D., Chairman, ANSI/Z79.11-1982.

A prudent course of action pending further data on this topic lies in the installation of a gas scavenging system for use when inhalation anesthetic techniques are employed with gas flows in excess of metabolic and anesthetic requirements. Care must be taken in the selection and application of any such system to a gas anesthesia apparatus or anesthesia ventilator to avoid exposing the breathing circuit to any pressure less than atmospheric, and also to avoid the dumping of any flammable vapors into a central suction system not designed for such operation.

*Operating Rooms, Delivery Rooms, and Special Procedure Rooms.* Ventilation air should be supplied from several outlets located on the ceiling or high on the walls of the location. Air should be exhausted by several inlets located near the floor on opposite walls. The air distribution pattern should move air down and through the location with a minimum of draft to the floor for exhaust.

Studies indicate that an air change rate equivalent to 25 room volumes of air per hour dilutes bacteria dispersed into the room by human activity. When properly filtered, 80 percent can be recirculated with no more microbial contamination than 100 percent outdoor air filtered in the same manner. *(See ASHRAE Handbook—1982 Applications, Chapter 7, "Table on Pressure Relationships and Ventilation of Certain Hospital Areas.")* A positive air pressure relative to the air pressure of adjoining areas should be maintained in the anesthetizing location. This is accomplished by supplying more air to the location than is exhausted from it. Such pressurization will eliminate the infiltration of contaminated air around perimeter openings of door closures or other wall openings during clinical procedures.

Ventilation systems should incorporate air filters with an efficiency of not less than 90 percent when tested in accordance with ASHRAE Standard 52-76, *Method of Testing Air Cleaning Devices Used in General Ventilation for Removing Particulate Matter.* (Summarized in ASHRAE *Handbook*—1983 Equipment, Chapter 10.)

*Humidity Control.* The ventilation system must incorporate humidity equipment and controls to maintain a relative humidity of at least 50 percent or as provided in 5-4.2.1. Although the high level of humidity is not sufficiently reliable for complete dissipation of electrostatic charges, this humidity does reduce the hazard of electrostatic spark discharges under many conditions. The control of airborne bacteria is facilitated in this range of humidity.

*Temperature.* The temperature to be maintained in operating rooms should be chosen on the basis of the well-being of patient and operating teams. It is recommended that the equipment provide for a room temperature in a range of 20°C (68°F) to 24°C (75°F) with controls for selecting any desired temperature within this range.

## 2-4  Electrical Equipment Criteria

### 2-4.1  Wiring.

Wiring for fixed equipment installed outside the hazardous area of a flammable inhalation anesthetizing location shall comply with 3-3.2.1.2(a)5 in NFPA 99.

### 2-4.2  Installation.

All service equipment, switchboards, or panelboards shall be installed outside hazardous areas.

### 2-4.3  Control Devices.

Devices or apparatus such as motor controllers, thermal cutouts, switches, relays, the switches and contactors of autotransformer starters, and resistance and impedance devices, which tend to create arcs, sparks, or high temperatures, shall not be installed in hazardous areas unless devices or apparatus are of a type approved for use in Class I, Group C atmospheres in accordance with Sections 501-6(a), 501-7(a), or Sections 501-6(b) and 501-7(b) of NFPA 70, *National Electrical Code.*

NOTE:  It is recommended that control devices for such purposes be installed in a nonhazardous area and actuated by some suitable mechanical, hydraulic, or other nonelectric remote-control device that can be operated from any desired location. This recommendation applies particularly to foot and other switches that must be operated from a location at or near the floor.

## 2-4.4 Location.

Equipment in storage locations for flammable anesthetic locations shall comply with 2-6.5(f) in this annex.

## 2-4.5 Line Voltage Equipment—All Anesthetizing Locations.

(a) Portable equipment shall be provided with a storage device for its flexible cord.

(b) Flexible cord for portable lamps or portable electric appliances operating at more than 12 volts between conductors, intended for use in all anesthetizing locations, shall be continuous and without switches from the appliance to the attachment plug and of a type designated for extra-hard usage in accordance with Section 501-11 of NFPA 70, *National Electrical Code.* Such flexible cord shall contain one extra insulated conductor to form a grounding connection between the ground terminal of the polarized plug and metal lamp guards, motor frames, and all other exposed metal portions of portable lamps and appliances. Cords shall be protected at the entrance to equipment by a suitable insulating grommet. The flexible cord shall be of sufficient length to reach any position in which the portable device is to be used, and the attachment plug shall be inserted only in a fixed, approved receptacle. For correct use and maintenance of adapters, the provisions of 7-6.2.1.5 shall apply.

*Exception No. 1: Foot-treadle-operated controllers are permitted in any anesthetizing location if appended to portable electric appliances in an approved manner or if integral with the supply cord and equipped with a connector containing a flammable anesthetizing location receptacle approved for use in Class I, Group C, Division 1 hazardous locations into which the equipment plug [see 2-2.4 and 2-4.3 in this annex] may be inserted. Foot-treadle-operated controllers and their connector shall be splashproof.*

*Exception No. 2: Listed double-insulated appliances with two-wire cords shall be permitted.*

*Exception No. 3: Small metal parts not likely to become energized (e.g., nameplates, screws) shall not be required to be grounded.*

*Exception No. 4: Two or more power receptacles supplied by a flexible cord are permitted to be used to supply power to plug-connected components of a movable equipment assembly that is rack-, table-, or pedestal-mounted in a nonflammable anesthetizing location provided:*

*(a) The receptacles are an integral part of the equipment assembly, permanently attached; and*

*(b) The sum of the ampacity of all appliances connected to the receptacles shall not exceed 75 percent of the ampacity of the flexible cord supplying the receptacles; and*

NOTE: Whole-body hyperthermia/hypothermia units should be powered from a separate branch circuit.

*(c) The ampacity of the flexible cord is suitable and in accordance with the current edition of NFPA 70; and*

*(d) The electrical and mechanical integrity of the assembly is regularly verified and documented through an ongoing maintenance program.*

NOTE: See 3-3.2.1.2(d)4 for criteria of receptacles.

*Exception No. 5: Overhead power receptacles, not in a hazardous location, are permitted to be supplied by a flexible cord (ceiling drop) that is connected at a ceiling-mounted junction box either:*

*(a) Permanently; or*

*(b) Utilizing a locking-type plug cap and receptacle combination, or other method of retention. In either connection mode, suitable strain relief shall be provided.*

NOTE 1: The disconnection means is permitted only to facilitate replacement; as such, ceiling drop cords may not be disconnected for alternative usage.

NOTE 2: See 3-3.2.1.2(d)4 for criteria of receptacles.

## 2-4.6 Line Voltage Equipment—Flammable Anesthetizing Locations.

(a) All equipment intended for use in anesthetizing locations shall be labeled by the manufacturer to indicate whether it is permitted to be used in a flammable anesthetizing location. Electric equipment presently in use shall be so labeled by the user. Labeling shall be permanent, conspicuous, and legible when the equipment is in the normal operating position *[see 2-4.6(f) in this annex]*.

(b) Suction, pressure, or insufflation equipment, involving electric elements and located within the hazardous area, shall be of a type approved for use in Class I, Group C, Division 1 hazardous areas. Means shall be provided for liberating the exhaust gases from such apparatus in such a manner that gases will be effectively dispersed without making contact with any possible source of ignition.

NOTE: Suction of pressure apparatus serving flammable anesthetizing locations but located outside such flammable anesthetizing locations need not be approved for Class I, Group C, Division 1 hazardous areas, providing the discharge from suction machines is kept away from sources of ignition.

(c) Portable X-ray equipment intended for use in flammable anesthetizing locations shall be approved for use in Class I, Group C, Division 1 hazardous areas and shall be permitted to be provided with an approved positive-pressure system for the tube head and cables within the hazardous area *[see 2-4.6(f)(2) in this annex].* All devices and switches for X-ray equipment within the hazardous area shall conform to requirements of 2-4.2 and 2-6.3.5(f) and (h) in this annex. X-ray equipment shall be provided with an approved method of eliminating electrostatic accumulation *[see 12-4.1.2.6(c) in Chapter 12 of NFPA 99 and 2-6.3.5(f)].*

(d) High-frequency equipment intended for use in flammable anesthetizing locations shall be approved for use in Class I, Group C, Division 1 hazardous areas.

NOTE 1: Remote-control switches are recommended *[see 2-4.3 and 2-6.3.9(c) in this annex].*

NOTE 2: For recommendations in connection with the use of cautery and high-frequency equipment in flammable anesthetizing locations, see 2-6.3.8(j), 2-7 and 2-8 in this annex; and Annex 1, "Safe Use of High-Frequency Electricity in Health Care Facilities."

(e) Portable electric equipment, such as incubators, lamps, heaters, motors, and generators, used in flammable anesthetizing locations in which anesthesia equipment is present or in operating condition, shall comply with the requirements of Articles 500, 501, and 517 of NFPA 70, *National Electrical Code,* for Class I, Division 1 locations and shall be approved for Class I, Group C, Division 1 hazardous areas except as permitted in 2-4.3(f) in this annex.

NOTE: The resistance and capacitive reactance between the conductors and the noncurrent-carrying metallic parts must be high enough to permit the use of the equipment on an ungrounded distribution system having a line isolation monitor specified in 3-3.2.2.3.

(f) The following shall be considered exceptions to 2-4.6(a) and (e) in this annex.

1. Equipment designed to operate on circuits of 10 volts or less. (Reserved)
2. Portable electric or electronic equipment mounted within an enclosure and protected by an approved positive-pressure ventilating system that conforms with the following requirements shall otherwise comply with the standards of NFPA 70, *National Electrical Code,* for ordinary locations. The enclosure of such a system shall be supplied with air taken from a nonhazardous area and circulated to maintain within the enclosure a pressure of at least 1 in. (2.5 cm) of water above that of the hazardous area, and shall be provided with means to deenergize the equipment if the air temperature exceeds 140°F (60°C) or if the pressure differential drops below 1 in. (2.5 cm) of water. The positive pressure shall be continuously maintained whether or not the equipment is in use, or means shall be provided to ensure that there are at least ten changes of air within the enclosure before any electric equipment within the enclosure that does not comply with the requirements of 2-4.4 in this annex is energized. The enclosure with its equipment shall be approved for use in Class I, Group C, Division 1 hazardous areas.
3. Portable electric or electronic equipment, if it is mounted on a floor-borne movable assembly that will not overturn either when it is tilted through an angle of 20 degrees

or when in a normal operating position a horizontal force of 25 lb (11.3 kg) is applied at a height of 5 ft (152 cm) above the floor; and if the equipment, together with its enclosure, cannot be lowered within 5 ft (152 cm) of the floor without tilting the assembly, need not be approved for use in Class I, Group C, Division 1 hazardous areas, but shall comply with the requirements of 2-4.6(e) in this annex. The entire assembly shall be approved for use in flammable anesthetizing locations as defined in 2-1.3 of this annex.

4.  Intrinsically safe electric or electronic equipment, which is incapable of releasing sufficient electric energy under normal or abnormal conditions to cause ignition of flammable anesthetic mixtures.

(g) Photographic lighting equipment used in flammable anesthetizing locations shall comply with the provisions of 2-4.6 of this Annex to prevent ignition of flammable gases. Lamps used above the hazardous area shall be suitably enclosed to prevent sparks and hot particles falling into the hazardous area. Photoflash and photoflood lamps that are not suitably enclosed shall not be used within an anesthetizing location. Neither flash tubes nor their auxiliary equipment shall be used within the hazardous area.

NOTE: Flash tube operation can be accompanied by sparking at switches, relays, and socket contacts, and by corona discharge of flashovers from high-voltage circuits.

(h) The exposed metal parts of photographic lighting equipment shall be grounded as specified in 7-5.1.2.2 of Chapter 7 of NFPA 99.

### 2-4.7 Low-Voltage Equipment—Flammable Anesthetizing Locations.

[Specifications for portable equipment operating on low-voltage power supplies are stated in 2-4.6(f)(1) and 2-6.3 of this annex.]

## 2-5 Gas Equipment Criteria

**2-5.1** Equipment capable of producing surface temperatures sufficient to cause chemical breakdown of the atmosphere within a patient enclosure shall not be permitted therein.

(a) Where diethyl ether vapor is involved, surface temperatures shall not exceed 248°F (120°C).

NOTE 1: Such a potentially hazardous atmosphere can be created by the placement in an incubator of a recently anesthetized infant or one whose mother received an inhalation anesthetic during delivery.

NOTE 2: Diethyl ether vapor can produce formaldehyde upon contact with a heating element.

This requirement was necessary when flammable anesthetics were used for expectant mothers during delivery. Flammable gases found their way into the fetus' lungs through the mother's blood. This requirement also dates from the time when flammable anesthetics were used during surgery on infants.

A study [5], unrelated to medicine, on the thermal decomposition of ether was conducted by M. K. Menderhall in the late 1950s.

## 2-6 Additional Criteria and Guidance

NOTE 1: When this material was first published in 1941 as a separate document, the majority of inhalation anesthetics were administered with flammable agents, and fires and explosions in operating rooms occurred with disturbing frequency. Promulgation of this material by NFPA and the use of this material by hospitals has lowered the incidence of such tragedies significantly.

Since 1950, nonflammable inhalation anesthetics possessing relatively safe properties have been developed. The increasing use of these agents has curtailed, and in most institutions completely eliminated, the use of flammable agents. This change in anesthetic practice has made it desirable to delineate standards of construction and operation in facilities where flammable agents will never be used. It must be emphasized that many safety recommendations pertain to hazards other than those related to fires and explosions, e.g., electric shock. It must also be recognized that these agents might possess toxicologic hazards to patients and personnel.

One report from 1950, when flammable inhalation anesthetics were still used exclusively, listed 67 operating room explosions with a mortality rate of about 50 percent in U.S. hospitals.

This material has been formulated in the belief that, although materials and mechanical equipment must be relied upon to the fullest possible extent for the mitigation of fire, explosion, and electric shock hazards, such physical safeguards are most effective only when augmented by safety precautions conscientiously applied by operating room and supporting personnel. This section emphatically calls attention to the need for constant human diligence in the maintenance of safe practices because of the peculiar intermixing of flammable anesthetic hazards and electric shock hazards, together with the mental strain in the environment of surgical operations.

Studies of these operating room hazards by many investigators over more than 30 years have pointed to the conclusion that the greatest degree of safety possible within the limitations of our present knowledge is secured only through a completely coordinated program rather than by the application of individual and unrelated safeguards. Compliance with certain requirements of this section will be effective, or even permissible, only when accompanied by compliance with the full program of precautionary measures.

It is necessary that all personnel having any responsibility for safety in anesthesia collaborate in the precautionary program. In the case of hospitals, this will apply to members of the governing body, physicians, administrative personnel, nursing staff, and maintenance staff. Not only must such personnel achieve an understanding of the hazards involved, but, in addition, they must be reminded periodically of the dangers posed by electric shock, compressed gases and their cylinders, the explosive nature of all flammable agents, and the hazards created by oxygen-enriched atmospheres. *(See NFPA 53, Recommended Practice on Materials, Equipment, and Systems Used in Oxygen-Enriched Atmospheres.)*

*For further discussion on the nature of the hazards, see Appendix C-12.1 in NFPA 99.*

NOTE 2: This section recognizes that some hospitals contain operating and delivery rooms designed and maintained for the use of flammable anesthetic agents. It also recognizes that there are some operating rooms and even entire operating suites designed for the exclusive use of nonflammable agents. A particular hazard exists where personnel elect to employ a flammable agent in a room not designed for it, or where a flammable agent is employed in a nonflammable anesthetizing location without taking the proper administrative steps.

Although the use of flammable anesthetics has been almost entirely eliminated in the United States, the first sentence of Note 2 acknowledges that flammable anesthetics are still used in other parts of the world. This guidance could be required for foreign facilities, built with U.S. funds, that still use flammable anesthetic agents. An inquiry from India in 1993 confirmed that flammable anesthetics were still being used and that reference to NFPA 99 was still being made.

NOTE 3: Sections 2-7 and 2-8 contain proposed regulations applying to specific types of inhalation anesthetizing locations.

Section 2-7 contains regulations for flammable anesthetizing locations that can be adopted by hospitals for all anesthetizing locations designed for the safe administration of flammable inhalation anesthetic agents.

Section 2-8 contains regulations for mixed facilities that can be adopted by hospitals in which flammable anesthetizing locations and nonflammable anesthetizing locations coexist within the same building, allowing interchange of personnel and equipment between flammable and nonflammable anesthetizing locations.

## 2-6.1 Identifying Flammable Anesthetizing Locations.

Anesthetizing locations shall be identified as listed in 2-6.4.5 of this annex.

## 2-6.2 Equipment Labeling.

All pieces of equipment used in flammable anesthetizing locations shall be labeled to indicate that they comply with applicable safety regulations.

NOTE: A generally recognized mark or symbol will meet the intent of this requirement.

### 2-6.3 Requirements for Flammable Anesthetizing Locations.

#### 2-6.3.1 Areas Adjoining Flammable Inhalation Anesthetizing Locations and Flammable Anesthetizing Storage Locations.

(a) An adjoining area connected by a closable doorway, such as a corridor, sterilizing room, scrub room, X-ray control room, or monitoring room, where it is not intended to store or administer flammable inhalation anesthetics, is not considered a hazardous area.

(b) Areas described in 2-6.3.1(a) above shall be permitted to be ventilated in accordance with the applicable sections of NFPA 70, *National Electrical Code*, for ordinary locations.

(c) Conductive flooring is required in these adjoining areas to remove static charges from personnel or objects before they enter the flammable inhalation anesthetizing location or agent storage location *[see 2-6.3.8(b)]*.

(d) Postanesthesia recovery rooms are not considered to be hazardous areas unless specifically intended for the induction of inhalation anesthesia with flammable anesthetic agents *[see 2-6.3.9(b)]*.

(e) All doorways leading to flammable inhalation anesthetic agent storage locations shall be identified with NFPA 704, *Standard System for the Identification of the Fire Hazards of Materials*, symbols as appropriate.

#### 2-6.3.2 Isolated Power Systems. A local ungrounded electric system shall be provided.

The installation of isolated power systems in anesthetizing locations was one of several measures instituted in 1941 to reduce the spark hazard in operating rooms. At that time, flammable inhalation anesthetics were generally used and electrical equipment was beginning to be used more frequently. Because these protective measures are believed to have reduced the number of incidents, they have been retained in flammable anesthetizing locations.

For further discussion, see commentary under the definition of *isolated power system* in Chapter 2.

For performance criteria for isolated power systems, see 3-3.2.2 in Chapter 3.

NOTE 1: The isolated system reduces the ignition hazard from arcs and sparks between a live conductor and grounded metal and mitigates the hazard of shock or burn from electric current flowing through the body to ground. The latter hazard usually follows inadvertent contact with one live conductor or results from unrecognized failure of insulation.

NOTE 2: Such a system provides protection from spark and electric shock hazards due to the most common types of insulation failure. It does not, however, prevent all electric sparks or completely eliminate the possibility of electric shock from insulation failure. Patients and personnel often are wet with prepping solutions, blood, urine, and other conductive fluids that greatly reduce resistance to the passage of unintended electrical current. More than ordinary care is crucially necessary in the use and maintenance of all electric systems and equipment.

NOTE 3: The ungrounded electrical distribution system specified in this annex is intended to reduce the possibility of electric shocks and recurring arcs and sparks in the event of insulation failure of the electrical wiring system in anesthetizing locations. Because of the difficulty in achieving a sufficiently high level of insulation to permit operation of a line isolation monitor, and in recognition of evolving capabilities in medical care, an exception has been made so that permanently installed equipment as well as nonadjustable lighting fixtures in specified locations need not be supplied by the ungrounded system. *(See 2-6.3.3 and 2-6.3.4.)*

Note 3 refers to material in 2-6.3.3 and 2-6.3.4 in this annex on fixed equipment and lighting. Prior to the 1984 edition of NFPA 99, only permanently installed X-ray equipment could be supplied by grounded power.

---

**Formal Interpretation**

Reference: 2-6.3.2 in Annex 2 of NFPA 99

*Background:* Paragraph 2-6.3.2 requires the use of an isolated power system in flammable anesthetizing locations. In neither case is any specific mention made of isolated power systems being required in any facility constructed prior to the first mention of such systems (1941).

*Question:* Is it the intent that the requirements of 2-6.3, such as 2-6.3.2, be applied retroactively?

*Answer:* No. Paragraph 2-6.3 may be enforced only upon adoption by the authority having jurisdiction over the hospital in question. Only this authority has the right to demand retroactivity. Since the Committee accepts the possibility that such a demand may be made, it has provided for such an eventuality in several places, such as in 2-6.3.2(a). But such alternatives do not imply that the Committee wishes to see its standard applied retroactively. It must emphatically state that such a determination must be made only by the authority having jurisdiction.

*Issue Edition:* 1973 of NFPA 56A

*Reference:* 1215, 3311

*Date:* July 1976

---

(a) Hospitals complying with NFPA 56A, *Standard for the Use of Inhalation Anesthetics*, prior to 1970 shall not be required to change ground fault detectors to a line isolation monitor.

The committee has taken into consideration existing conditions by precluding the retroactive application of revised requirements on this subject that occurred subsequent to the 1970 edition of NFPA 56A.

(b) The isolated electric system shall be required to be explosionproof only if installed in the hazardous areas of a flammable inhalation anesthetizing location.

It is not required or necessary that the isolated power system be installed in the hazardous area of the flammable anesthetizing location.

**2-6.3.3 Power for Fixed Equipment.** Approved, fixed, therapeutic, and diagnostic equipment, permanently installed outside the hazardous area of a flammable anesthetizing location, is permitted to be supplied by a grounded single- or three-phase system of less than 600 V provided (a) the equipment complies with 7-5.1.1.1 in Chapter 7 of NFPA 99; (b) cord-connected accessories (such as positioning controls, aiming lights and fiberoptic light sources, slaved monitors, motorized cameras and video cameras, dosimeters, and exposure triggers) likely to come in contact with patients or personnel are supplied by isolated power at line voltage, or operate at 24 V or less, supplied by an isolating transformer; and (c) wiring is installed in accordance with NFPA 70, *National Electrical Code*, Section 517-61.

NOTE: It is intended that this section apply to positioning motors for patient tables associated with radiographic and other imaging equipment and to sometimes massive equipment for radiotherapy or for the delivery of other forms of energy.

Prior to 1978, only fixed lighting fixtures and permanently installed X-ray equipment were exempted from the requirement that electrical equipment in anesthetizing locations be supplied by an isolated power source. Certain fixed-type equipment was added to the exemption (originally TIA 56A-78-2) because of the difficulty in achieving a sufficiently high level of insulation to permit operation of line isolation monitors and because of the massive size of the line isolation transformers that would be required. In addition, allowance for three-phase power was made (only single-phase power had previously been allowed in anesthetizing locations), with the committee noting (in TIA 56A-78-2) that conditions and state-of-the-art technology no longer warranted this exclusion.

**2-6.3.4 Fixed Lighting.** Branch circuits supplying only fixed lighting shall be permitted to be supplied by a conventional grounded system provided (a) such fixtures are located at least 2.4 m (8 ft) above the floor; (b) switches for the grounded circuits are wall-mounted and installed in accordance with NFPA 70, *National Electrical Code*, Article 517, Part D; and (c) wiring for grounded and ungrounded circuits is installed in accordance with NFPA 70, *National Electrical Code*, Article 517, Part D.

NOTE: Wall-mounted remote-control stations for lighting control switches operating at 24 V or less can be installed in any anesthetizing location.

### 2-6.3.5 Ceiling-Suspended Fixtures.

(a) Ceiling-suspended surgical lighting fixtures shall be supplied from an ungrounded electric distribution system *(see 2-6.3.2 in this annex),* which shall be monitored by a line isolation monitor as required by 3-3.2.2.3(a) in Chapter 3 of NFPA 99. Switching or dimmer devices shall control secondary circuit conductors only.

*Exception No. 1: Where interruption of illumination is acceptable, as with single-filament lights, ceiling-suspended surgical lighting fixtures shall be permitted to be connected to a grounded source of supply, protected by approved individual ground fault circuit interrupters.*

*Exception No. 2: The secondary circuit of the ceiling-mounted surgical lighting fixture supplied by a step-down isolation transformer need not be equipped with a line isolation monitor provided that the step-down transformer is located in the same enclosure as the lamp fixture, or that the conductors carrying the current from the transformer to the lamp fixture are contained in metallic conduit that forms an integral electrical (ground) pathway between the transformer enclosure and the lamp fixture, and provided that the voltage in the secondary (lamp) circuit is not greater than 30 V.*

Exception No. 2 was added because some ceiling-mounted surgical fixtures include a step-down transformer mounted externally to the lighting fixture itself. The question arose whether this would constitute an isolated power system and thus require a line isolation monitor. The committee deemed it reasonable to address this configuration as similar to low-voltage signal and control circuits and as isolation transformers that are an integral part of an assembly of components. Although technically isolated, such secondary circuits are not required to be monitored.

(b) The light source of ceiling-suspended surgical lighting fixtures installed above hazardous areas shall not enter the hazardous area, and, if in an enclosure, the enclosure shall not enter the hazardous area in its lowest position, unless it was approved for hazardous areas.

(c) If installed above a hazardous area, fixtures with sliding contacts or arcing or sparking parts shall be installed so that in any position of use, no sliding contacts or arcing or sparking parts shall extend within the hazardous area.

(d) Integral or appended switches, if installed on ceiling-suspended surgical lighting fixtures, shall be approved for use in Class I, Group C, Division 1 hazardous areas if a switch is installed in, or can be lowered into, the hazardous area.

(e) Lamps installed in fixed position in hazardous areas shall be enclosed in a manner approved for use in Class I, Group C, Division 1 hazardous areas and shall be properly protected by substantial metal guards or other means where exposed to breakage. Lamps shall not be of the pendant type unless supported by and supplied through hangers of rigid conduit or flexible connectors approved for use in Class I, Group C, Division 1 hazardous areas in accordance with Section 501-9(a) or Section 501-9(b) of NFPA 70, *National Electrical Code.*

(f) Tube heads and cable of permanently installed X-ray equipment in flammable anesthetizing locations shall be approved for use in Class I, Group C atmospheres.

(g) Film viewing boxes in hazardous areas shall either comply with the requirements of Section 501-9(a) of NFPA 70, *National Electrical Code*, or they shall be of a type that excludes the atmosphere of the room. If located above the 5-ft (152-cm) level in a flammable anesthetizing location or mixed facility, or in a nonflammable anesthetizing location, the film viewing box shall be permitted to be of the totally enclosed type or so constructed as to prevent the escape of sparks or hot metal. Such viewing boxes shall be permitted to be connected to a conventional grounded supply circuit if the device is protected by an approved system of double insulation. Where such an approved system is employed, the equipment shall be distinctly marked.

(h) Control units and other electric apparatus installed or intended for use in a flammable anesthetizing location shall comply with the requirements of 7-5.1.1 in Chapter 7 of NFPA 99 and 2-4 of this annex [*see also 2-6.3.5(d) and 2-6.4.6 in this annex*].

**2-6.3.6 Signaling and Communications Systems.** All equipment of signaling and communications systems in hazardous areas, irrespective of voltage, shall be of a type approved for use in Class I, Group C, Division 1 hazardous areas in accordance with Section 501-14(a) or Section 501-14(b) of NFPA 70, *National Electrical Code*.

**2-6.3.7 Piping.** This section (2-6.3) prohibits the piping of flammable anesthetic gases [*see 4-3.5.2.3(a)*].

**2-6.3.8 Reduction in Electrostatic Hazard.**

(a) *Purpose.*

1. The requirements of this section have been promulgated to reduce the possibility of electrostatic spark discharges, with consequent ignition of flammable gases *(see C-12.1.3.1 in Appendix C of NFPA 99).*
2. The prevention of the accumulation of static charges revolves about a number of safeguards that shall be complied with in flammable anesthetizing locations; in corridors and passageways adjacent thereto; in rooms connecting directly to anesthetizing locations, such as scrub rooms and sterilizing rooms; and in storage locations for flammable anesthetics located in an operating suite.
3. The methods employed to prevent such accumulation include the installation of conductive flooring [*see 2-6.3.8(b) in this annex*], the maintenance of the relative humidity at 50 percent at least, and the use of certain items of conductive equipment, accessories, and wearing apparel.

(b) *Conductive Flooring.*

NOTE: A conductive floor serves as a convenient means of electrically connecting persons and objects together to prevent the accumulation of electrostatic charges.

A resistance not exceeding 50 megohms between objects or persons is generally sufficient to prevent accumulation of dangerous voltages. The upper limit of 1,000,000 ohms for the resistance of the floor has been chosen as meeting this requirement with a reasonable factor of safety and with reasonable provision for other resistances in the conductive path.

The resistance of some flooring materials changes with age. Floors of such materials should have an initial resistance that permits changes in resistance with age without exceeding the limits prescribed in 2-6.3.8(b)3 and 4 of this annex.

*Conductive flooring is just one of the safety precautions used to reduce the risk of electrostatic hazards when flammable anesthetics are used.*

1. Conductive flooring shall be installed in those areas specified in 2-6.3.8(a)2 in this annex. Conductive flooring installed in corridors or passageways in compliance with 2-6.3.8(a)2 in this annex shall extend the width of the corridor and along the corridor a minimum of 9.84 ft (3 m) on each side of door frames.

2. A conductive floor shall meet the resistance provisions through its inherent conductive properties. The surface of the floor in the locations specified by 2-6.3.8(a)2 and (b)1 in this annex shall provide a patch of moderate electric conductivity between all persons and equipment making contact with the floor to prevent the accumulation of dangerous electrostatic charges. No point on a nonconductive element in the surface of the floor shall be more than ¼ in. (6.4 mm) from a conductive element of the surface, except for insulated floor drains.

3. The resistance of the conductive floor shall be less than an average of 1,000,000 ohms, as measured in accordance with 2-6.3.8(b)7 in this annex.

*This upper value (1,000,000 ohms) for conductive floors in flammable anesthetizing locations was selected for several reasons. Part of the reasoning included the balancing of the need to dissipate static electricity (lowering floor resistance) with the protection against grounding personnel (raising floor resistance). Values of 20,000,000 ohms or more are technically acceptable to discharge static electricity [see note under 2-6.3.8(b) for further information]. However, other factors influenced the committee to reduce that value. These factors included the long-term characteristics of conductive floors, the need for some safety factor, and the maintenance necessary to reduce resistance buildup due to dirt.*

4. The resistance of the floor shall be more than an average of 25,000 ohms, as measured in accordance with 2-6.3.8(b)7 in this annex.

*A lower limit of 25,000 ohms is necessary to limit the current flow that could occur under fault conditions.*

5. A deliberate connection of the conductive floor to the room ground shall not be required.

*The purpose of the conductive floor is to interconnect equipment and personnel in order to equalize static potentials. Connection is achieved whether or not the conductive floor is connected to the room ground.*

6. The resistance of conductive floors shall be initially tested prior to use. Thereafter measurements shall be taken at intervals of not more than one month. A permanent record of the readings shall be kept.

7. The following test method shall be used *(see 2-6.3.12 in this annex)*.

   a. The floor shall be clean and dry, and the room shall be free of flammable gas mixtures.

   b. Each electrode shall weigh 5 lb (2.268 kg) and shall have a dry, flat, circular contact area 2½ in. (6.35 cm) in diameter, which shall comprise a surface of aluminum or tin foil 0.0005 in. (0.013 mm) to 0.001 in. (0.025 mm) thick, backed by a layer of rubber ¼ in. (6.4 mm) thick and measuring between 40 and 60 durometer hardness as determined with a Shore Type A durometer (ASTM D2240-91).

   c. Resistance shall be measured by a suitably calibrated ohmmeter that shall have a nominal open circuit output voltage of 500 V dc and a nominal internal resistance of not less than 100,000 ohms, with tolerance defined as follows:
   (i) Short-circuit current of from 2.5 mA to 5 mA.
   (ii) At any value of connected resistance, $Rx$, the terminal voltage, V, shall be

   $$\frac{Rx}{Rx + \text{internal resistance}} \times 500 \text{ V} \pm 15\%$$

   Revision for the 1978 edition of NFPA 56A took into account those existing test instruments that had output resistance of approximately 200,000 ohms and a short-circuit current of 2.5 milliamperes.

   d. Measurements shall be made between five or more pairs of points in each room and the results averaged. For compliance with 2-6.3.8(b)3 in this annex, the average shall be within the limits specified and no individual measurement value shall be greater than 5 megohms, as measured between two electrodes placed 3 ft (91 cm) apart at any points on the floor. For compliance with 2-6.3.8(b)4 in this annex, the average value shall be no less than 25,000 ohms with no individual measurement's value less than 10,000 ohms as measured between a ground connection and an electrode placed at any point on the floor, and also as measured between two electrodes placed 3 ft (91 cm) apart at any points on the floor. There is no upper limit of resistance for a measurement between a ground connection and an electrode placed on the conductive floor.

   Although 2-6.3.8(b)5 does not require a deliberate connection between the conductive floor and room ground, if such a connection is made, the resistance value between the two electrodes on the floor still has to meet both parts of the third sentence—25,000 ohms (average) with no value less than 10,000 ohms.

NOTE: If the resistance changes appreciably with time during a measurement, the value observed after the voltage has been applied for about 5 seconds can be considered to be the measured value.

Initial decay is generally quite fast. Settling out usually occurs within 5 seconds.

(c) *Accessories.* Coverings of operating tables, stretcher pads, pillows and cushions, etc., shall be fabricated from conductive materials throughout. Conductive sheeting shall be tested on a nonconductive surface. The resistance between two electrodes placed 3 ft (91 cm) apart, or as close to this distance as the size of the material will permit, on the same surface, and between two electrodes placed in the middle of opposite surfaces, shall not exceed 1 megohm. Individual items covered with conductive sheeting shall be tested on a metal surface. The resistance between an electrode placed on the upper surface of the covered item and another electrode placed on the metal surface shall not exceed one megohm. The electrodes and ohmmeter used for these tests shall be of the type specified in 2-6.3.8(b)7b. and c. in this annex, respectively.

(d) *Interconnecting Conductive Accessories.*

1. All accessories that are required to be resilient or flexible on the anesthesia machine, and that form part of an interconnecting electrically conductive pathway, such as tubing, inhalers, rebreathing bags, headstraps, retainers, face masks, handbulbs, and similar items, shall be of conductive material throughout. Electric resistance of such accessories shall be not greater than 1 megohm when tested as specified in 2-6.3.8(e)1 in this annex.

High-pressure flexible tubing used to interconnect the gas anesthesia apparatus with the central piping station outlets shall be antistatic and shall be conductive throughout with a maximum resistance of 100,000 ohms per linear foot during the specified life of the material.

NOTE: When a nonconductive endotracheal catheter is in use, the conductive path from the patient to the anesthesia machine should be maintained by the use of a conductive headstrap.

2. Tubing and connectors used for suctioning shall provide a continuous electrically conductive pathway to the vacuum bottle and to the vacuum outlet. The materials used shall be conductive throughout or, where it is necessary for visual monitoring, shall be permitted to be of antistatic material with antistatic properties good for the specified life of the material provided the tubing or connector embodies a continuous integral conductive pathway designed so that in normal use the conductive pathway shall make and maintain conductive contact with conducting materials. Electric resistance of such tubing and connectors shall be not greater than 1 megohm when tested as specified in 2-6.3.8(e) in this annex.

NOTE: Specified life refers to the permanence of the antistatic property with respect to the stated life of the material, including storage, and is of particular importance if the material is expected to be used and cleaned (e.g., washed) several times.

> The configuration for suctioning tubing shown in Exhibit A2.1 was interpreted in July 1976 by the committee responsible for NFPA 56A as meeting the intent of "conductive throughout." The committee indicated, however, that the configuration was **not** acceptable for use elsewhere (e.g., on anesthesia machines).

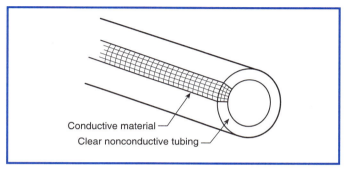

Conductive material
Clear nonconductive tubing

**Exhibit A2.1** *Suctioning tubing.*

---

**Formal Interpretation**

Reference: 2-6.3.8(d)2 in NFPA 99

*Background:* Paragraph 2-6.3.8(d)2 describes the requirements for conductive tubing used on suctioning apparatus operating from a vacuum outlet.

*Question:* Is it the intent of 2-6.3.8(d)2 to permit the use of transparent tubing having a conductive strip in lieu of a tube that is everywhere conductive throughout its body but perhaps not transparent, provided such transparent tubing is not used elsewhere (such as on an anesthesia machine)?

*Answer:* Yes.

*Issue Edition:* 1973 of NFPA 56A

*Reference:* 4642

*Date:* July 1976

---

3. All belting used in connection with rotating machinery shall have incorporated in it sufficient material to prevent the development of electrostatic charges. A conductive pulley shall be used.

NOTE: The conductivity of the path from the pulley to the ground should be considered. If ball bearings are used, the contact between the balls and the races will probably be sufficient when bearings are lubricated with graphitized oil or grease. If sleeve bearings are used, some means of conducting the charge from the pulley should be provided.

4. Wherever possible, items that are not parts of a machine shall be of conductive materials throughout, particularly where the item is depended on to provide a conductive pathway between other conductive items and/or the patient *[see Note after 2-6.3.8(d)(1) in this annex]*.

NOTE: For essential elements in surgery, such as prosthetic and therapeutic devices, bacterial barriers, instruments, gloves (thermoplastic: for example, PVC), or biomechanical equipment, antistatic materials should be used if conductive materials are not available or are impractical. Any material can be employed if clearly nonhazardous owing to improbability of acquiring and holding a significant charge, e.g., suction catheter, endotracheal tube, plastic inserts in joint prostheses.

5. Nonconductive, nonantistatic parts shall be used where necessary as electricinsulators or heat-insulating handles on approved devices. Where exposed metal parts of machines of necessity are insulated from each other by other nonconductive parts, they shall be electrically interconnected. The resistance of the grounding path between these metal parts shall not exceed 0.1 ohm.

6. Antistatic materials are not acceptable where they are relied upon to provide an interconnecting electrically conductive pathway.

(e) *Testing for Conductivity.*

1. An ohmmeter of the type specified in 2-6.3.8(b)7c in this annex shall be used for testing. Where possible, electrodes shall be of the type to make contact with metal positions across which it is desired to ensure a conductive pathway provided by the accessory, but care must be taken to ensure that the placing of the electrodes has not inadvertently provided an alternate conductive path to that under test; or, electrodes shall be of the type specified in 2-6.3.8(b)7b in this annex, where applicable; or, equivalent electrode contact shall be employed as practical. All items that are parts of a machine such as tubing, bags, face masks, etc., shall be tested either in place or detached from the machine in accordance with one of the methods listed under 2-6.3.8(e)2 through 8 in this annex.

2. When tested in place on the machine, it is first necessary to purge the entire system of flammable or explosive gases. The anesthesia jar and cylinders of flammable gases shall be removed from the machine and all the remaining parts purged by flowing air through them in sufficient quantity to assure that all residual anesthetic gases have been removed. All parts shall be tested and each part shall be tested separately.

3. For interconnecting parts that are to be classed as conductive throughout, one electrode shall be attached in a satisfactory manner to the metal frame of the machine, and the conductivity shall be determined by measuring the resistance between this first electrode

and a second electrode consisting of a metal band snugly fitted around the midpart of the item being tested, or, for face masks and similar objects, between the first electrode and a second electrode *[see 2-6.3.8(b)7b in this annex]* resting on the item.

4.  For interconnecting parts that are to be classed as antistatic with a continuous integral conductive pathway, the conductivity test shall be performed as given in 2-6.3.8(e)1 in this annex above except that, in place of the metal band electrode or the standard electrode of 2-6.3.8(b)7b in this annex, there shall be a suitable second electrode making contact with the part in a manner that simulates the actual second contact area made when the part is connected for use.

5.  Metal parts of machines that are required to be apparently insulated from each other by other nonconductive parts shall be suitably tested for electric interconnection; this shall be permitted to be an ohmmeter test. The resistance of the grounding path between these metal parts shall not exceed 0.1 ohm.

6.  When tubing and other accessories are tested for conductivity while detached from a machine, each part shall be fitted with a clean brass nipple of the same outside diameter as the connector by which the part is normally connected to the machine. A nipple shall be inserted into each such opening of the part. When two or more nipples are involved, satisfactory conductivity shall be determined by measuring the resistance between nipples. If only one nipple is involved, as in the case of a face mask or breathing bag, the resistance shall be measured between the nipple and another electrode suitably connected elsewhere (e.g., a standard electrode resting on the part).

7.  While the above are given as standard test methods, where these methods cannot be applied, an equivalent test method is permitted to be used. Interconnecting conductivity is acceptable if the measured resistance is not greater than one megohm.

8.  Conductive items containing antistatic material shall have the antistatic properties tested as described in 2-6.3.8(f)3 and 4 in this annex.

(f) *Antistatic Accessories and Testing.*

1.  For conductive accessories containing antistatic material see 2-5.3.8(d)1 and 2 in this annex; the antistatic material of these accessories shall be tested as given in 2-6.3.8(f)3 and 4 in this annex. For other individual items that are permitted to be of antistatic material, see 2-6.3.8(d)4 in this annex.

2.  Plastic sheeting, film, and other nontextile, nonmetal materials, if not required to form a conductive interconnecting pathway between machines, objects, and persons, need not be conductive but shall be of antistatic material except as given in 2-6.3.8(d)4 in this annex. They shall be of antistatic material throughout their specified life when tested as described in 2-6.3.8(f)3 and 4 in this annex.

3.  Antistatic sheeting, film, and textiles shall meet the specified requirements of at least one of the following test methods when preconditioned at 50 percent ± 2 percent RH

at $23° \pm 1°C$ for 25 hours or until equilibrium is reached, and tested at 50 percent $\pm$ 2 percent RH at $23° \pm 1°C$.

a. Method 4046 of Federal Test Method Standard 101B. After the specimen has received its maximum charge from the application of 5000 V, the time for the indicated specimen potential to drop to 10 percent of its maximum value shall not exceed ½ second.

NOTE: The static detector head should be of a type that is adequately shielded to minimize responses to potentials on the electrodes, and other stray pickup. The sample is held between electrically interconnected electrodes. The 5000 V are applied to the electrodes for 10 seconds after the indicated potential of the sample reaches equilibrium before the charge decay rate is measured.

b. Method 76 of the AATCC. Applied voltage should be 102 V per in. (40 V per cm) of interelectrode spacing. The measured resistivity shall be less than $1 \times 10^{11}$ ohms per unit square of material.

A Formal Interpretation to NFPA 56A was issued in July 1976 to reaffirm the requirement that sheeting, film, and textiles needed to meet one of the two test methods listed, but not necessarily both.

Another Formal Interpretation was issued in January 1978 regarding a test specimen that could not be charged to the 5000 V prescribed by the Federal Test Method (FTM) Standard. If the specimen decayed as prescribed in the FTM Standard after being charged as high as possible, the specimen could be considered to have met the intent of the FTM Standard.

Another Formal Interpretation issued in January 1978 regarded the American Association of Textile Chemists and Colorists (AATCC) test method. The current method [AATCC Test Method 76 Electrical Resistivity of Fabrics (current test dated 1995)] requires that the resistivity of the material be less than 10 ohms per unit square of material and that for textiles the measurement be made in several different directions parallel to the textile's yarn or thread. The Interpretation Committee affirmed that the less than 10-ohm value has to be met regardless of direction or side.

This testing is applicable only to manufacturers, as noted in 2-6.3.8(f)5.

---

**Formal Interpretation**

Reference: 2-6.3.8(f)3 in NFPA 99

*Background:* Paragraph 2-6.3.8(f)3 lists two test methods for determining the antistatic properties of sheeting, film, and textiles used in flammable anesthetizing locations.

---

*Question:* Is it the intent of 2-6.3.8(f)3 to require antistatic sheeting, film, and textiles to meet the requirements of either (but not necessarily both) of the tests described in 2-6.3.8(f)3a and 2-6.3.8(f)3b?

*Answer:* Yes.

*Issue Edition:* 1973 of NFPA 56A

*Reference:* 4663

*Date:* July 1976

**Formal Interpretation**

Reference: 2-6.3.8(f)3a in NFPA 99

*Background:* Paragraph 2-6.3.8(f)3a describes one of the two test procedures for determining the antistatic properties of sheeting, film, and textiles used in flammable anesthetizing locations. The procedure (Method 4046 of Federal Test Method Standard 101B) requires the specimen under test be charged to 5 kilovolts with respect to ground and the rate at which this charge decays be measured. Occasionally a test specimen will stably change only to a voltage less than 5 kilovolts. An alternative test method (measurement of resistance) is given in 2-6.3.8(f)3b. In a previous Formal Interpretation it was ruled that a material under test must meet the requirements of either 2-6.3.8(f)3a or 2-6.3.8(f)3b, but was not required to meet both.

*Question:* Does a test specimen which cannot be charged to a full 5 kilovolts, but whose charge does otherwise decay in the fashion prescribed in 2-6.3.8(f)3a meet the intent of 2-6.3.8(f)3?

*Answer:* Yes.

*Issue Edition:* 1973 of NFPA 56A

*Reference:* 4663(a)

*Date:* January 1978

**Formal Interpretation**

Reference: 2-6.3.8(f)3b in NFPA 99

*Background:* Paragraph 2-6.3.8(f)3b describes one of the two test procedures for determining the antistatic properties of sheeting, film, and textiles used in flammable anesthetizing

*(continues)*

locations. The test (American Association of Textile Chemists and Colorists Method 76-1972) requires the resistivity of the material to be less than $10^{11}$ ohms per unit square of the material and requires that for textiles the measurement be made in several different directions parallel to the textile's yarn or thread. It also notes that it may be necessary to differentiate between the two sides of the material.

*Question:* Assuming that measurements are made in the directions specified, is it the intent of 2-6.3.8(f)3b that all measurements made on textiles in accordance with AATCC Method 76-1972 be less than $10^{11}$ ohms regardless of direction or side?

*Answer:* Yes.

*Issue Edition:* 1973 of NFPA 56A

*Reference:* 4663(b)

*Date:* January 1978

4. Antistatic items other than sheeting, film, and textiles shall be tested in a manner as closely as possible equivalent to that given in 2-6.3.8(f)3 in this annex.
5. The supplier of conductive and antistatic accessories shall certify that the item or items supplied meet the requirements of one of the tests specified in 2-6.3.8(f)3 in this annex. The supplier shall certify the conditions of storage, shelf life, and, in the case of reusable items, the methods of repreparation necessary to allow the product or device to return to its antistatic or conductive properties.

(g) *Conductive Footwear.*

1. The resistance of any static conductive footwear or any equivalent static conductive device used in conjunction with nonconductive footwear shall have a value before the item is first put in use not exceeding 500,000 ohms when tested in the following manner. The static conductive shoe or any equivalent static conductive device attached to a nonconductive shoe shall have clean contact surfaces. It shall be placed on a nonoxidizing metal plate wetted with water. A brass electrode having a contact area of 1 sq in. (6.5 sq cm) shall be placed on the inside of the sole or heel of the shoe after the surface under the electrode has been wetted by water. The resistance shall be measured between the plate and the electrode using a dc ohmmeter supplying a potential in excess of 100 V *[e.g., see 2-6.3.8(b)7c in this annex]*.
2. In the case of static conductive booties, the test shall be made as follows: The bootie shall be laid flat on an insulating surface. Two brass electrodes, each 1.5 in. (3.8 cm) long, having a contact area of 1 sq in. (6.5 sq cm), shall be used. One electrode shall be placed on the bootie near the toe and on the part of the bootie that normally comes in contact with the floor. The other electrodes shall be placed on the ankle section. The booties shall be wetted under the electrodes only.

3. If the tests as here described are not technically feasible for the device under consideration, an alternative equivalent means of testing shall be used. The static conductive footwear and any static conductive device used with nonconductive footwear shall also meet, during use, the requirements of 2-6.3.10(a), (b), and (c) and 2-6.3.13(c) in this annex.

4. For protection of personnel against electric shock and high-frequency burns, static conductive footwear and equivalent static conductive devices shall not have any metal parts (nails, etc.) that normally come in contact with the floor.

(h) *Textiles. [See also 2-6.3.10(d), (e), and (f) in this annex.]*

1. Silk, wool, synthetic textile materials, blends of synthetic textile materials with unmodified cotton or rayon, or nonwoven materials shall not be permitted in hazardous locations as outer garments or for nonapparel purposes, unless such materials have been tested and found to be antistatic by meeting the requirements of 2-6.3.8(f)3 in this annex.

In the case of reusable materials, the manufacturer shall certify that the antistatic properties shall be maintained through 50 wash-autoclave cycles or throughout the useful life of the material, whichever is greater.

In the case of nonreusable materials, the manufacturer shall certify that the antistatic properties shall be maintained throughout the useful life of the material.

NOTE: It is preferable to use only one textile material because static electricity is more readily generated by contact between articles of different materials than by contact between articles of the same material.

(i) *Furniture.*

NOTE: In its requirement for furniture in a flammable anesthetizing location to be constructed of conductive materials, the Subcommittee on Anesthesia Services specifically intends that any shelves within such furniture as well as the top also be conductive. Furniture is intended to include movable and permanently installed objects in the room, such as stools, tables, and cabinets. Wooden racks, however, are permitted for storage of cylinders of flammable as well as nonflammable gases.

1. If the furniture is conductive but not made of metal, then it shall have casters, tires, or legs of metal, conductive rubber, or equivalent conductive material with a floor contact surface having one dimension of at least ⅝ in. (1.58 cm). Approved equivalent means of making conductive contact between the piece of furniture and the floor is acceptable, provided the contact device is securely bonded to the piece of furniture and is of material that will not oxidize under conditions of normal use (so as to decrease the conductivity of the circuit), and that uninterrupted contact with the floor is at least ⅝ in. (1.6 cm) in one dimension *[see also 2-6.3.13(d) in this annex]*.

2. Surfaces on which movable objects are placed shall be without insulating paint, lacquer, or other nonconductive finish.

NOTE: An economical way to make painted furniture conform to this requirement is to attach unpainted sheet metal to the furniture's shelf or top with screws, rivets, or similar fasteners that provide electrical continuity to the frame and casters of the furniture.

3. The resistance between the conductive frame of the furniture referred to in 2-6.3.8(i)2 in this annex and a metal plate placed under one supporting member but insulated from the floor shall not exceed 250,000 ohms, measured with an ohmmeter of the type described in 2-6.3.8(b)7c in this annex.

The following two-part Formal Interpretation was issued on NFPA 56A in July 1976 relative to furniture used in flammable anesthetizing locations. The first part ruled that using insulating or nonconductive materials in furniture in such locations was permitted, provided the furniture's conductive frame met the requirements of 2-6.3.8(i). The second part ruled that a vertical surface bulletin board did not constitute a surface on which movable objects could be placed such that 2-6.3.8(i)2 would apply. In either case, the Interpretation Committee emphasized that these interpretations were **not** to be construed as allowing the use of nonconductive seats or cushions on stools and chairs in flammable anesthetizing locations.

---

**Formal Interpretation**

Reference: 2-6.3.8(i) in NFPA 99

*Background:* Paragraph 2-6.3.8(i) describes the requirements for furniture used in a flammable anesthetizing location.

*Question:* 1. Does 2-6.3.8(i) rule out the use of insulating or nonconductive materials in furniture used in flammable anesthetizing locations provided it has a conductive frame that meets the requirements of 2-6.3.8(i)1 through 3, and 2. Does a vertical surface bulletin board constitute a surface on which movable objects may be placed such that 2-6.3.8(i)3 applies?

*Answer:* No to both parts of the question. However, the Committee emphasizes that this interpretation should not be construed as allowing nonconductive seats or cushions on stools and chairs in flammable anesthetizing locations.

*Issue Edition:* 1973 of NFPA 56A

*Reference:* 469

*Date:* July 1976

---

(j) *High-Frequency Equipment.* Potential sources of ignition, such as electrosurgical units, shall be prohibited during the administration of flammable anesthetizing agents.

The allowance of electrosurgical units (ESUs) in flammable locations under certain circumstances became a controversial issue in the 1980s. As a result of public comments in 1983, the former Committee on Anesthetizing Agents (now a part of the Committee on Gas Delivery Equipment) removed even the limited use of ESUs in flammable anesthetizing locations because of the lack of knowledge and training in the safe use of flammable anesthetic agents by operating room personnel due to the infrequent use of such agents.

### 2-6.3.9 General Requirements for Flammable Anesthetizing Locations.

(a) Hospital authorities in consultation with others as noted in 6-2.2.1 shall adopt regulations to control apparel and footwear allowed, the periodic inspection of conductive materials, the control of purchase of static-conductive and antistatic materials, and the testing of conductive floors.

(b) All required precautions shall apply to all anesthetizing locations in which flammable inhalation anesthetics are used.

(c) Hospital regulations shall be established and enforced to control the use of electronic equipment such as television equipment, diathermy equipment, public address systems, monitoring equipment, and similar electronic and high-frequency apparatus in the presence of flammable inhalation anesthetic agents.

(d) Hospital regulations shall prohibit the use of X-ray equipment in flammable anesthetizing locations if such equipment is not approved for operation in hazardous locations *[see 2-6.3.5(f) and (g) and 2-4.6(c) in this annex]*.

(e) Covers of fabric or of any form of sheeting shall not be used on anesthesia equipment capable of utilizing flammable anesthetizing agents because a cover will confine gas that could leak from a cylinder.

NOTE: When the cover is removed from the anesthesia machine under such conditions, a static charge might be created that could ignite the gas confined beneath the cover.

(f) The use of rebreathing techniques in administering flammable anesthetic agents at all times is highly desirable. Through the use of these techniques, the escape of flammable mixtures is substantially limited.

(g) Residual ether remaining in ether vaporizers at the end of each day shall be returned to its original containers for disposal or laboratory use only. The ether vaporizer, container, and such shall be thoroughly washed and dried before being returned to use *(see C-12.1.3 in NFPA 99)*.

(h) Waste liquid ether and other flammable volatile liquid inhalation anesthetic agents shall be disposed of outside of the hospital building according to the recommendations of the authority having jurisdiction. One method is to allow the agent to evaporate in a shallow pan, well removed from possible sources of ignition under supervision.

While it is acceptable to use the evaporative technique, it is very important that constant supervision be maintained when allowing the ether to evaporate in a shallow pan.

(i) Members of the professional staff shall be required to submit for inspection and approval any special equipment they wish to introduce into flammable anesthetizing locations *[see 12-4.1.2.4(f) in Chapter 12 of NFPA 99]*. Such equipment shall be approved for use in Class I, Group C, Division 1 hazardous areas or comply with 2-4.6(e) in this annex. It shall be equipped with approved cords and attachment plugs *[see 7-5.1.2.5(a) and (b) in Chapter 7 of NFPA 99 and 2-2.4 in this annex]*.

(j) High-frequency electric and electronic equipment, such as electrosurgery amplifiers, monitors, recorders, television cameras, portable electrical tools, maintenance equipment, and certain sterilizing equipment that does not comply with the provisions of 2-4.6(e) in this annex shall not be used when flammable inhalation anesthetic agents are being administered.

Cautery and electric surgical equipment shall not be used during procedures involving flammable inhalation anesthetic agents unless the equipment complies with the requirements of 2-4.6(d) in this annex.

NOTE:  See Annex 1, The Safe Use of High-Frequency Electricity in Health Care Facilities.

**2-6.3.10  Electrostatic Safeguards.**

Readers are reminded that this section is applicable only to flammable anesthetizing locations.

NOTE: Section 2-6.3.8 in this annex deals with the elements required to be incorporated into the structure and equipment to reduce the possibility of electrostatic spark discharges, which are a frequent source of the ignition of flammable anesthetic agents. The elimination of static charges is dependent on the vigilance of administrative activities in material selection, maintenance supervision, and periodic inspection and testing. It cannot be too strongly emphasized that an incomplete chain of precautions will generally increase the electrostatic hazard. For example, conductive flooring *[see 2-6.3.8(b) in this annex]* can contribute to the hazard unless all personnel wear conductive shoes and unless all objects in the room are electrically continuous with the floor.

(a) All personnel entering flammable anesthetizing locations, mixed facilities, or storage locations for flammable anesthetics located in the surgical suite shall be in electrical contact with the conductive floor through the wearing of conductive footwear or an alternative method of providing a path of conductivity. The provision of conductive floors in corridors and rooms directly communicating with flammable anesthetizing locations *[see 2-6.3.8(b) in this annex]* will minimize the possibility of static discharge from patients or personnel entering such anesthetizing locations.

NOTE: One method for electrically connecting all persons to conductive floors is through the wearing of shoes conforming to the following specifications:

Each shoe having a sole and heel of conductive rubber, conductive leather, or equivalent material should be so fabricated that the resistance between a metal electrode placed inside the shoe and making contact with the inner sole equivalent in pressure and area to normal contact with the foot, and a metal plate making contact with the bottom of the shoe, equivalent in pressure and area to normal contact with the floor, be not more than 250,000 ohms.

(b) Electric connection of the patient to the operating table shall be ensured by the provision of a high-impedance strap in contact with the patient's skin, with one end of the strap fastened to the metal frame of an operating table.

The term *high-impedance strap* is a misnomer in the sense that the strap has a high impedance compared to electric wire, but it actually has some conductive properties impregnated into it. A high-impedance strap could also be termed a *conductive strap.*

(c) Because of the possibility of percussion sparks, shoes having ferrous nails that make contact with the floor shall not be permitted in flammable anesthetizing locations or mixed facilities or in storage locations for flammable anesthetic agents in the surgical suite.

(d) Silk, wool, or synthetic textile materials, except rayon, shall not be permitted in flammable anesthetizing locations or mixed facilities as outer garments or for nonapparel purposes, unless these materials have been approved as antistatic in accordance with the requirements of 2-6.3.8(f)3 and 4 in this annex.

NOTE: Rayon refers to regenerated cellulose, not cellulose acetate. Cotton and rayon must be unmodified; i.e., must not be glazed, permanently starched, acetylated, or otherwise treated to reduce their natural hygroscopic quality. Fabrics of intimate blends of unmodified cotton or rayon with other textile materials are not acceptable unless tested and found to be antistatic.

(e) Hosiery and underclothing in which the entire garment is in close contact with the skin shall be permitted to be of silk, wool, or synthetic material.

(f) Undergarments with free-hanging skirts, such as slips or petticoats, shall be of cotton, rayon, or other materials demonstrated to be antistatic by the requirements of 2-6.3.8(f)3 and 4 in this annex.

(g) Antistatic materials for use in flammable anesthetizing locations shall be handled and used in the following manner:

1. Antistatic materials shall be stored at the temperature and humidity required for flammable anesthetizing locations or they shall be allowed to equilibrate to the humidity and temperature of the flammable anesthetizing location prior to use.
2. Antistatic materials shall be stored in such a manner that will ensure that the oldest stocks will be used first.
3. Controls shall be established to ensure that manufacturers' recommendations as to use are followed in the case of antistatic materials.

(h) All antistatic accessories intended for replacement, including belting, rubber accessories, plastics, sheeting, and the like, shall meet pertinent requirements for conductivity as specified in 2-6.3.8(f) in this annex.

### 2-6.3.11  Discretionary Use of Nonconforming Materials.

(a) Suture material, alloplastic or therapeutic devices, bacterial barriers, instruments, gloves (thermoplastic), surgical dressings, and biologic interfaces of these otherwise prohibited materials shall be permitted to be used at the discretion of the surgeon.

(b) Disposable supplies that contribute to the electrostatic hazard shall be so labeled on the unit package.

### 2-6.3.12  Maintenance of Conductive Floors.

(a) The surface of conductive floors shall not be insulated by a film of oil or wax. Any waxes, polishes, or dressings used for maintenance of conductive floors shall not adversely affect the conductivity of the floor.

(b) Floors that depend upon applications of water, salt solutions, or other treatment of a nonpermanent nature for their conductivity are not acceptable.

*Exception: Treatment of the floor to modify conductivity shall be considered permanent provided the floor meets the requirements of this section (2-6.3) for a period of not less than 2 years, during which no change or modification beyond normal washing is performed.*

(c) Cleaning procedures for conductive floors shall be established, then carefully followed to assure that conductivity characteristics of the floor are not adversely affected by such treatment.

(d) Conductive floors shall be tested as specified in 2-6.3.8(b) in this annex.

A Formal Interpretation was issued on NFPA 56A in August 1977 that ruled that sealers or dressings intended to adjust the resistivity of a floor are acceptable. The only criterion for such items was that they not adversely affect the conductivity of the floor. A second question in the Formal Interpretation, on the permanence of sealers or dressings, subsequently resulted in an exception being formally adopted for the 1978 edition of NFPA 56A, which is now the exception to 2-6.3.12(b) in this annex.

### 2-6.3.13  Other Conductive Equipment.

(a) The resistance of conductive accessories shall be tested prior to use as described in 2-6.3.8(c) or (d) in this annex. Thereafter, measurements shall be taken at intervals of not more than 1 month. A permanent record of the readings shall be kept.

(b) Antistatic plastics shall meet the requirements of 2-6.3.8(f)2 in this annex. It shall be the responsibility of the hospital to ensure that antistatic sheeting, etc., is used in accordance with the manufacturer's instructions. Failure to do so could in some cases lead to loss of antistatic properties. Antistatic materials that are reused [e.g., antistatic tubing incorporating a continuous conductive pathway as described in 2-6.3.8(d)1 in this annex] shall be tested *[see 2-6.3.8(f)1 in this annex]* periodically to ensure retention of conductive properties.

(c) Conductive footwear and other personnel-to-floor connective devices shall be tested on the wearer each time they are worn. An approved resistance-measuring device having a short-circuit current not exceeding 0.5 mA shall be used.

NOTE: The reading may be taken between two insulated, nonoxidizing, metal plates so located that the wearer can stand in a normal manner with a foot on each, in which case the indicated resistance shall not exceed 1,000,000 ohms (1 megohm). *[See also Note under 2-6.3.10(a) in this annex.]*

(d) The resistance of furniture *[see 2-6.3.8(i) and Note thereunder]* and equipment shall be tested prior to use as described in 2-6.3.8(i)3 in this annex. Thereafter, measurements shall be taken at intervals of not more than 1 month. A permanent record of the readings shall be kept. The monthly tests can conveniently consist of measurements of the resistance between an electrode placed on the floor and an electrode placed successively on each article of furniture in the room. Additional tests of any individual item shall be made if the measured resistance exceeds 5 megohms.

(e) Periodic inspection shall be made of leg tips, tires, casters, or other conductive devices on furniture and equipment to ensure that they are maintained free of wax, lint, or other extraneous material that insulates them and defeats the purpose for which they are used, and also to avoid transporting to conductive floors such materials from other areas.

(f) Excess lubrication of casters shall be avoided to prevent accumulation of oil on conductive caster wheels and sides. Dry graphite or graphitized oil are preferable lubricants.

## 2-6.4 Requirements for Mixed Facilities.

NOTE: A serious behavioral hazard exists in a "mixed facility," i.e., where there are some rooms where flammable agents are prohibited. In the latter situation, inadvertent use of a flammable agent in the "nonflammable" room could be disastrous. It is important to understand the regulations recommended in Section 2-7 of this annex.

The term *mixed facilities* was introduced by the committee for two reasons: (1) While the use of flammable anesthetics diminished, many institutions wanted to retain some locations suitable for the use of such anesthetics; and (2) even if only a few locations were being maintained for flammable anesthetics, many enforcing authorities were requiring all anesthetizing locations in a facility to meet flammable requirements.

A mixed facility places an added burden on anesthesiologists and nurse anesthetists because these staff members usually are responsible for enforcing requirements for mixed facilities. Fixed equipment doesn't present a problem to the staff. However, movable items such as portable equipment, furniture, and supplies can be moved from nonflammable locations to flammable locations. Some items are not permitted to be moved in that direction. Although procedures can be established and followed under normal conditions, in an intense, life-threatening situation there is no guarantee that safety procedures will always be followed.

Items acceptable for use in flammable anesthetizing locations can safely be used in nonflammable anesthetizing locations, but the opposite is not always true. While a facility could elect to make all movable items suitable for both locations, 2-6.4 allows the two types of locations to exist independently in the same facility, as long as requirements peculiar to each location are observed.

**2-6.4.1 General.** The mixed facility is defined in 2-1.6 in this annex.

**2-6.4.2 Construction of Anesthetizing Locations and Storage Locations.**

(a) Flammable anesthetizing locations shall be designed, constructed, and equipped as stated in 12-4.1.2 in Chapter 12 of NFPA 99 and 2-6.3 of this annex.

(b) Nonflammable anesthetizing locations shall be designed, constructed, and equipped as stated in 12-4.1.2 in Chapter 12 of NFPA 99.

(c) Storage locations for flammable anesthetics shall be constructed as provided in 2-6.5 of this annex. Storage locations for nonflammable medical gas cylinders shall be constructed as provided in 4-3.1.1.2(a).

**2-6.4.3 Conductive Flooring in Posted Nonflammable Anesthetizing Locations Within a Mixed Facility.** (Reserved)

**2-6.4.4 Provision for Connection of Patient to Operating Table.** Electric connection of the patient to the operating table shall be ensured by the provision of a high-resistance (conductive) strap in contact with the patient's skin, with one end of the strap fastened to the metal frame of an operating table.

Conductive straps are an example of an item that can be moved between any type of anesthetizing location since they are suitable for both flammable and nonflammable anesthetizing locations. Only one type of strap needs to be maintained. [See also commentary on conductive straps under 2-6.3.10(b).] An item suitable only for *nonflammable* anesthetizing locations, however, would not be acceptable in flammable anesthetizing locations.

**2-6.4.5 Precautionary Signs.**

(a) The entrances to all anesthetizing locations shall be identified by prominently posted signs denoting individually whether the anesthetizing location is designed for flammable inhalation anesthetic agents or for nonflammable anesthetic agents.

NOTE: Suggested explanatory texts of such signs are as follows:

SUITABLE FOR USE WITH
FLAMMABLE INHALATION ANESTHETIC AGENTS

or

RESTRICTED TO NONFLAMMABLE INHALATION ANESTHETIC AGENTS

(b) In addition, a removable sign shall be posted to all entrances to the anesthetizing location indicating whether a flammable inhalation anesthetic agent is being employed.

NOTE: Suggested explanatory text of such a sign is as follows:

**CAUTION:** FLAMMABLE INHALATION ANESTHETIC IN USE
OBSERVE AND OBEY ALL SAFETY REGULATIONS

It shall be the responsibility of the anesthesiologist or nurse anesthetist to ensure that the room is suitably designated for use of the particular agent, whether flammable or nonflammable.

(c) Regulations for the conduct of personnel, administration, and maintenance in mixed facilities shall be posted in at least one prominent location within the operating and, if applicable, delivery suite *[see Note 2 under Section 2-6 in this annex]*. Suggested text of such regulations is contained in Section 2-8 of this annex.

### 2-6.4.6 Movable Equipment and Furniture.

(a) All equipment intended for use in both flammable and nonflammable anesthetizing locations shall meet the antistatic requirements of 2-6.3.8 of this annex.

(b) Equipment intended for use only in nonflammable anesthetizing locations shall be labeled in accordance with 2-4.6(a) in this annex, and shall not be introduced into flammable anesthetizing locations. This equipment is not required to meet the antistatic requirements of 2-6.3.8 in this annex.

(c) No portable equipment, including X-ray equipment, shall be introduced into mixed facilities unless it complies with the requirements of 2-4.6(c) in this annex and is approved for use in Class I, Group C, Division 1 hazardous areas, or unless it is prominently labeled for use only in the presence of nonflammable anesthetic agents and then restricted to such use.

(d) Portable electric equipment, such as incubators, lamps, heaters, motors, and generators used in mixed facilities in which flammable anesthetics are being employed shall comply with the requirements of Articles 500, 501, and 517 of NFPA 70, *National Electrical Code*, for Class I, Division 1 locations and shall be approved for Class I, Group C, Division 1 hazardous areas, except as permitted in 2-4.6(f) of this annex.

NOTE: The resistance and capacitive reactance between the conductors and the noncurrent-carrying metallic parts must be high enough to permit the use of the equipment on an ungrounded distribution system having a line isolation monitor specified in 3-3.2.2.3 of Chapter 3 in NFPA 99.

(e) Furniture intended for use in both flammable and nonflammable anesthetizing locations of mixed facilities shall meet the antistatic requirements of 2-6.3.8(i) of this annex.

(f) Furniture intended for use only in nonflammable anesthetizing locations of mixed facilities shall comply with 2-6.3.8(i) of this annex or shall be conspicuously labeled and not be introduced into flammable anesthetizing locations.

## 2-6.5 Storage Locations for Flammable Anesthetic Agents (Any Quantity).

(a) Enclosures in which flammable inhalation anesthetic agents are stored shall be individually and continuously ventilated by gravity or by mechanical means at a rate of not less than eight air changes per hour. The fresh-air inlet and the exhaust-air outlet within the enclosure shall be located as far apart as feasible consistent with the enclosure layout. The fresh-air inlet shall be located at or near the ceiling, and the bottom of the exhaust-air outlet shall be located 3 in. (7.6 cm) above the floor. The fresh-air supply shall be permitted to be heated. Exhaust air shall be discharged to the exterior of the building at least 12 ft (3.6 m) above grade in a manner to prevent its reentry into the building.

(b) Exhaust fans shall have nonsparking blades. The fan motor shall be connected into the equipment system (either automatic or delayed restoration) *(see Chapter 3, "Electrical Systems")*. All electric installations shall conform to NFPA 70, *National Electrical Code*, and, when inside the storage area or exhaust duct, shall be approved for use in Class I, Division 2, Group C locations. A visual signal that indicates failure of the exhaust system shall be installed at the entrance to the storage area.

NOTE: Exhaust fans in all new installations, and whenever possible in existing installations, should be located at the discharge end of the exhaust duct.

(c) Approved fire dampers shall be installed in openings through the required fire partition in accordance with the requirements of NFPA 90A, *Standard for the Installation of Air Conditioning and Ventilating Systems*.

(d) Enclosures shall not be used for purposes other than storage of flammable inhalation anesthetic agents.

(e) Flooring shall comply with 2-6.3.8(b)1 in this annex.

(f) Electric wiring and equipment in storage locations for flammable inhalation anesthetic agents shall comply with the requirements of NFPA 70, *National Electrical Code*, Article 500, Class I, Division 2, and equipment used therein shall be approved for use in Class I, Division 1, Group C hazardous areas *(see 3-3.3.2 in NFPA 99 for grounding requirements)*.

(g) The provisions of 2-6.3.2 in this annex for ungrounded electric distribution systems do not apply to storage locations for flammable agents.

(h) Storage locations for flammable anesthetics shall meet the construction requirements stated in 4-3.1.1.2(a)2 and 3 of NFPA 99 and shall be ventilated as provided in 2-6.5 of this annex.

(i) Flammable inhalation anesthetizing agents shall be stored only in such locations. Flammable inhalation anesthetizing agents shall not be stored in anesthetizing locations, except for cylinders of flammable anesthetic agents connected to a gas anesthesia apparatus.

(j) Cylinders containing flammable gases (e.g., ethylene and cyclopropane) and containers of flammable liquids (e.g., diethyl ether, divinyl ether, ethyl chloride) shall be kept out of proximity to cylinders containing oxidizing gases (e.g., oxygen or nitrous oxide) through the use of separate rooms.

(k) Storage locations for flammable inhalation agents shall be kept free of cylinders of nitrous oxide, compressed air, oxygen, and mixtures of oxygen.

(l) Sources of illumination and ventilation equipment in storage locations for flammable inhalation anesthetic agents, wherever located, and especially in storage locations that are remote from the operative suite, shall be inspected and tested on a regular schedule. Such procedures shall determine that adequate ventilation is maintained under supervision.

## 2-7 Sample of Regulations for Flammable Anesthetizing Locations

### REGULATIONS FOR SAFE PRACTICE IN FLAMMABLE ANESTHETIZING LOCATIONS

The following rules and regulations have been adopted by the medical staff and by the administration. Annex 2, Flammable Anesthetizing Locations, of NFPA 99-1999 shall apply in all inhalation anesthetizing locations.

| | |
|---|---|
| (Insert Date) | (Insert Name of Hospital Authority) |

By reason of their chemical compositions, the following flammable anesthetic agents present a hazard of explosion in anesthetizing locations:

cyclopropoane     ethyl chloride
ethyl              etherethylene

### REGULATIONS

1. Flammable Anesthetizing Location.

    (a) *Definition.*The term flammable anesthetizing location shall mean any area of the hospital designated for the use of flammable anesthetizing agents.

2. Equipment.

    (a) No electrical equipment except that judged by the Engineering Department of _____ Hospital as being in compliance with Annex 2, "Flammable Anesthetizing Locations," of NFPA 99-1999 shall be used in any flammable anesthetizing location.

    (b) When a physician wishes to use his or her personal electrical equipment, it shall first be inspected by the Engineering Department and, if judged to comply with Annex 2, Flammable Anesthetizing Locations, of NFPA 99-1999, it shall be so labeled.

(c) Portable X-ray equipment used in flammable anesthetizing locations shall be approved for use in hazardous areas.

(d) Only approved photographic lighting equipment shall be used in flammable anesthetizing locations. Because of occasional bursting of bulbs, suitable enclosures shall be used to prevent sparks and hot particles from falling into the hazardous area.

(e) Covers shall not be used on anesthesia machines designed for flammable anesthetic agents.

3. Personnel.

(a) Outer garments worn by the operating room personnel and visitors shall not include fabrics of silk, wool, or synthetic textile materials such as nylon, polyester, acrylic, or acetate unless such fabrics have been tested and found to be antistatic in accordance with the requirements of Annex 2, Flammable Anesthetizing Locations, of NFPA 99-1999.

(b) Silk, wool, or synthetic textile materials, except untreated rayon, shall not be permitted in anesthetizing locations as outer garments, or for nonapparel purposes, unless such fabrics have been tested and found to be antistatic in accordance with the requirements of Annex 2, Flammable Anesthetizing Locations, of NFPA 99-1999. Hosiery and underclothing in which the entire garment is in close contact with the skin shall be permitted to be of silk, wool, or synthetic material.

(c) All personnel and visitors entering flammable anesthetizing locations shall wear conductive footwear or other floor-contacting devices, that shall have been tested on the wearer and found to be satisfactorily conductive.

(d) It shall be the responsibility of each individual entering a flammable anesthetizing location to determine at least once daily that he is in electrical contact with the conductive floor. Apparatus for testing shall be available.

(e) Moving of patients from one area to another while a flammable anesthetic is being administered shall be prohibited.

(f) Smoking shall be limited to dressing rooms and lounges with the doors leading to the corridor closed.

4. Practice.

(a) Flammable anesthetic agents shall be employed only in flammable anesthetizing locations.

(b) Woolen and synthetic blankets shall not be permitted in flammable anesthetizing locations.

(c) Electrical connection of the patient to the conductive floor shall be ensured by a high-impedance (conductive) strap in contact with the patient's skin with one end of the strap fastened to the metal frame of an operating table or shall be electrically interconnected by other means.

(d) If cautery, electrosurgery, or electrical equipment employing an open spark is to be used during an operation, flammable anesthetics shall not be used. Flammable germicides or flammable fat solvents shall not be applied for the preoperative preparation of the field.

(e) A visual (lighted red lamp) or audible warning signal from the line isolation monitor serving an anesthetizing location indicates that the total hazard current has exceeded allowable limits. This suggests that one or more electrical devices is contributing an excessively low impedance to ground, which might constitute a fault that would expose the patient or hospital personnel to an unsafe condition should an additional fault occur. Briefly and sequentially unplugging the power cord of each electrical device in the location will usually cause the green signal lamp to light, showing that the system has been adequately isolated from ground, when the potentially defective device has been unplugged. The continuing use of such a device, so identified, should be questioned, but not necessarily abandoned. At the earliest opportunity the device should be inspected by the hospital engineer or other qualified personnel and, if necessary, repaired or replaced.

5. Enforcement.

It shall be the responsibility of _____
(name)
(an anesthesiologist or other qualified person appointed by the hospital authority to act in that capacity) to enforce the above regulations.

## 2-8 Sample of Regulations for Mixed Facilities

### REGULATIONS FOR SAFE PRACTICE IN MIXED FACILITIES

The following rules and regulations have been adopted by the medical staff and by the administration. NFPA 99-1999, Annex 2, Flammable Anesthetizing Locations, shall apply in all inhalation anesthetizing locations. This hospital is a mixed facility. Personnel are cautioned as to the existence of both flammable and nonflammable inhalation anesthetizing locations within the hospital building and the different practices that apply to each location.

(Insert Date)                    (Insert Name of Hospital Authority)

By reason of their chemical compositions, the following flammable anesthetic agents present a hazard of explosion in anesthetizing locations:

cyclopropoane     ethyl chloride
ethyl             etherethylene

REGULATIONS

1. Mixed Facility

(a) *Definition.* The term mixed facility shall mean a hospital wherein flammable anesthetizing locations and nonflammable anesthetizing locations coexist within the same building, allowing interchange of personnel and equipment between flammable and nonflammable anesthetizing locations.

(b) *Definition.* Flammable anesthetizing location shall mean any area of the hospital designated for the administration of flammable anesthetic agents.

(c) *Definition.* Nonflammable anesthetizing location shall mean any anesthetizing location permanently designated for the exclusive use of nonflammable anesthetizing agents.

2. Equipment.

(a) No electrical equipment except that judged by the Engineering Department of _____ Hospital as being in compliance with NFPA 99-1999, Annex 2, Flammable Anesthetizing Locations, shall be used in any flammable anesthetizing location.

(b) When a physician wishes to use his or her personal electrical equipment, it shall first be inspected by the Engineering Department and, if judged to comply with NFPA 99-1999, Annex 2, Flammable Anesthetizing Locations, it shall be so labeled.

(c) Portable X-ray equipment used in flammable anesthetizing locations shall be approved for use in hazardous areas.

(d) Only approved photographic lighting equipment shall be used in flammable anesthetizing locations. Because of occasional bursting of bulbs, suitable enclosures shall be used to prevent sparks and hot particles from falling into the hazardous area.

(e) Covers shall not be used on anesthesia machines designed for flammable anesthetic agents.

(f) All portable electrical equipment shall meet the requirements for flammable anesthetizing locations.

3. Personnel.

(a) Outer garments worn by the operating room personnel and visitors in mixed facilities shall not include fabrics of silk, wool, or synthetic textile materials such as nylon, polyester, acrylic, or acetate, unless such fabrics have been tested and found to be antistatic in accordance with the requirements of NFPA 99-1999, Annex 2, Flammable Anesthetizing Locations.

(b) Silk, wool, or synthetic textile materials, except untreated rayon, shall not be permitted in mixed facilities as outer garments, or for nonapparel purposes, unless such fabrics have been tested and found to be antistatic in accordance with the requirements of NFPA 99-1999, Annex 2, Flammable Anesthetizing Locations. Hosiery and underclothing in which the entire garment is in close contact with the skin shall be permitted to be made of silk, wool, or synthetic material.

(c) All personnel and visitors entering all anesthetizing locations in mixed facilities shall wear conductive footwear or other floor-contacting devices that shall have been tested on the wearer and found to be satisfactorily conductive.

(d) It will be the responsibility of each individual entering an anesthetizing location of a mixed facility to determine at least once daily that he is in electrical contact with the conductive floor. Apparatus for testing shall be available.

(e) Moving of patients from one area to another while a flammable anesthetic is being administered shall be prohibited.

(f) Smoking shall be limited to dressing rooms and lounges with the doors leading to the corridor closed.

4. Practice.

(a) Flammable anesthetic agents shall be employed only in flammable anesthetizing locations.

(b) The administration or the intended administration of a flammable anesthetic agent shall be brought to the attention of all personnel within the flammable anesthetizing location by verbal communication by the anesthesiologist and by posting prominent signs in the operating room and at all entrances to the operating room stating that a flammable anesthetic agent is in use.

(c) Woolen and synthetic blankets shall not be permitted in anesthetizing locations.

(d) Electrical connection of the patient to the conductive floor in a flammable anesthetizing location shall be assured by a high-impedance conductive strap in contact with the patient's skin with one end of the strap fastened to the metal frame of an operating table or shall be electrically interconnected by other means.

(e) If cautery, electrosurgery, or electrical equipment employing an open spark is to be used during an operation, flammable anesthetics shall not be used. Flammable germicides and flammable fat solvents shall not be applied for the preoperative preparation of the field.

(f) If, in the combined judgment of the anesthesiologist responsible for the administration of the anesthetic and the surgeon performing the operation, the life of the patient would be jeopardized by not administering a flammable anesthetic agent in a nonflammable anesthetizing location, the following steps shall be taken:

1. Both surgeon and anesthesiologist involved in the case shall attest to the reason for administering a flammable anesthetic in a nonflammable anesthetizing location on the patient's record and in the operating room register.
2. The hazard of static sparks shall be reduced by electrically connecting the patient, operating room table, anesthesia gas machine, and anesthesiologist by wet sheets or other conductive materials. Conductive accessories shall be used for the electrically conductive pathways from the anesthesia gas machine to the patient.

(g) A visual (lighted red lamp) or audible warning signal from the line isolation monitor serving an anesthetizing location indicates that the total hazard current has exceeded allowable limits. This suggests that one or more electrical device is contributing an excessively low impedance to ground, which might constitute a fault that would expose the patient or hospital personnel to an unsafe condition should an additional fault occur. Briefly and sequentially unplugging the power cord of each electrical device in the location will usually cause the green signal lamp to light, showing that the system has been adequately isolated from ground, when the potentially defective device has been unplugged. The continuing use of such a device, so identified, should be questioned, but not necessarily abandoned. At the earliest opportunity the device should be inspected by the hospital engineer or other qualified personnel and, if necessary, repaired or replaced.

(h) Interchange of personnel and portable equipment between flammable and nonflammable anesthetizing locations shall be strictly controlled.

(i) Transportation of patients while an inhalation anesthetic is being administered by means of a mobile anesthesia machine shall be prohibited, unless deemed essential for the benefit of the patient in the combined judgment of the surgeon and anesthetist.

5. Enforcement.

It shall be the responsibility of _____
                                                                    (name)
(an anesthesiologist or other qualified person appointed by the hospital authority to act in that capacity) to enforce the above regulations.

## References Cited in Commentary

1. H. V. Fineberg et al., "The Case for Abandonment of Explosive Anesthetic Agents," *New England Journal of Medicine,* September 11, 1980.
2. Deryck Duncalf, M.D., "Flammable Anesthetics Are Nearing Extinction," *Anesthesiology,* vol. 56, no. 3, March 1982.
3. M. D. Vickers, "Explosion Hazards in Anesthesia," *Anesthesia,* 1970, vol. 25, pp. 482–492.
4. *Code Red!* April 1979 (newsletter of NFPA's Health Care Section).
5. M. K. Menderhall, Paper on the study on thermal decomposition of ether, *Journal of the American Medical Association* 173:123, 1960.

# PART 2

# Supplements

For the first time, the *Health Care Facilities Handbook* also includes supplements. Part 2 is devoted to supplements that explore in detail the background of four selected topics related to NFPA 99. Supplements are not part of the standard but are included as additional information for handbook users.

**1** Codes and Standards in the Health Care Environment: Their Use, Application, and Impact

**2** User's Guide to Inspecting, Testing, and Maintaining Emergency Power Supply Systems in Health Care Facilities

**3** Conducting Emergency Drills at Health Care Facilities

**4** Regulatory Issues Affecting the Safety of Clinical Hyperbaric Medicine Facilities

Part 1 of this handbook includes the complete text and illustrations of the 1999 edition of NFPA 99, *Standard for Health Care Facilities,* as well as Formal Interpretations and commentary that provide the history and other background information as well as practical applications for specific paragraphs in the standard.

# SUPPLEMENT 1

# Codes and Standards in the Health Care Environment: Their Use, Application, and Impact

## Robert E. Solomon, P.E.

*Robert E. Solomon is chief building fire protection engineer at the NFPA in Quincy, Massachusetts.*

## INTRODUCTION

The regulatory structure of nearly every aspect of a health care facility is a complex matter in which patient care is the ultimate responsibility. The general public is primarily focused on the level of medical care being provided, the abilities of the medical staff, and the use of state-of-the-art equipment and procedures. A number of features go into making the facility safe from the effects of fire. Documents such as NFPA 99 address the operational aspects of many of the pieces of specialized equipment that go into the facility. In addition to the integration of items such as medical gas piping, electrical systems, and specialized treatment equipment, a number of other provisions also work in conjunction with NFPA 99 to keep the occupants safe from the effects of an unwanted fire.

The regulation of the built environment of the health care facility is sometimes as complex as the overall operation of the facility itself. The requirements to maintain a state-of-the-art facility, to keep it functional, and to keep it safe are high-priority items for any facility administrator. A variety of agencies and organizations contribute in one way or another to maintain patient safety and a safe facility.

## HISTORY AND BACKGROUND

Regulation of the physical environment in a health care facility is no accident, nor is it taken for granted. Nearly all of the regulatory impact stems from some form of federal government supervision and intervention. Although the level of this oversight and regulation is more noticeable in the health care field, it is by no means unique. In addition to providing a standardized or minimum level of medical care to patients, the need to ensure that patient safety is maintained for other reasons is also of vital importance. Reimbursement for Medicaid/Medicare charges and reimbursement for private health care insurance, as well as the need to defend the typically vulnerable occupants from fire, are pressing issues that must be evaluated by any health care facility.

Fundamental and formalized regulation of such facilities dates back to 1970 when the U.S. Department of Health and Human Services mandated that compliance with NFPA *101®, Code for Safety to Life from Fire in Buildings and Structures (Life Safety Code®)*, would be used as the basis for part of the conditions of participation (COP) for the physical environment. This change, implemented through the Hill–Burton Act of 1970, has served the health care industry well. More importantly, given the excellent fire loss record that this particular category of occupancy has enjoyed, this particular approach to health care fire safety has served the public justly. This rule, which has been updated on several occasions, stipulates that health care facilities, including nursing homes, intermediate care facilities, ambulatory surgical centers, and hospices, are obligated to meet the requirements of NFPA *101* in order to be eligible for Medicare and Medicaid funding reimbursement.

The *U.S. Code of Federal Regulations (CFR)* accomplishes these mandates through a series of regulations as well as statutory requirements that give the secretary of Health and Human Services (HHS) broad-based power to impose fire protection and fire safety provisions on provider facilities. The authority for monitoring and enforcing these regulations resides within HHS through the Health Care Financing Administration (HCFA). HCFA then works with various state administrative agencies to ensure that adherence to NFPA *101* is implemented and carried out by the facility.

As previously mentioned, a level of complexity surrounds enforcement of the health care environment. Although federal regulation sets the minimum level of fire protection, a state or even a local authority having jurisdiction can supplement certain parts of the federal rules. This is not always an easy task and in many cases will still require a ruling from HCFA. Such rulings are usually used to evaluate the impact of imposing a change—either financial or operational—along with making a determination that the change will in no way lower the level of life safety and fire protection that is afforded to the patients, visitors, and staff who are in the facility at any given time. The Joint Commission on Accreditation of Health Care Organizations (JCAHO) also evaluates the overall level of care being provided including adherence to NFPA *101*. While JCAHO is charged with addressing a host of other items relating to the operation of the health care facility, it also conducts a survey to determine compliance with NFPA *101* as well as other NFPA codes and standards and those of other organizations. The impact of this level of scrutiny is that not only is the federal government involved, but the additional surveillance from state agencies, local fire department or fire marshal offices, local building departments, and JCAHO puts multiple sets of eyes on the lookout for the myriad fire protection issues that reside in a health care facility. The overlap in these responsibilities, however, is largely uniform because in the majority of situations, it is the NFPA code or standard that is being used as the basis to evaluate the facility.

As with any regulated industry, the health care industry itself is a vital key to cooperation and adherence to ensure that their constituent facilities comply with the letter of the federal rules and that their facilities are deemed to be safe from the impact of fire. Among industry groups that participate in this endeavor are the American Hospital Association (AHA) and the American Healthcare Association (AHCA). Both groups participate fully in the development of the NFPA codes and standards that most affect the built environment for the health care industry. AHA representation is normally made by the American Society for Healthcare Engineering (ASHE), a subsidiary organization of AHA. ASHE staff or their members represent the society on the various NFPA Committees that maintain NFPA documents such as NFPA 99 and NFPA *101*.

Both AHA and AHCA also maintain representation on the JCAHO Committee on Healthcare Safety (CHS). The CHS group meets on a semi-annual basis to discuss issues surrounding the safety concerns of the patient. Although the CHS group considers a wide range of issues—everything from infection control to physical security—much of their deliberation is based on the fire protection needs of the facility. The CHS group meets to debate the requirements being imposed, the intent of some of the requirements, and potential impacts when newer rules or regulations are proposed. This gives another opportunity to debate the merits and impacts of a proposed change or to implement new or more current regulations or procedures.

## CODES AND STANDARDS

In this category are numerous documents used to construct, maintain, and operate a health care facility. Just within the NFPA system of codes and standards are several documents that relate specifically to the health care atmosphere. Beyond NFPA requirements, there are also related documents from JCAHO via the Environment of Care (EC) standards as well as the regional building official codes used in the United States. This supplement will review those documents that have the largest impact on health care facilities.

### NFPA *101, Life Safety Code*

NFPA *101* was previously mentioned as the basic document that the *Code of Federal Regulations* invokes as providing the prescribed level of safety. The current edition of NFPA *101* is the 1997 edition. Unique among codes, NFPA *101* provides requirements for both new construction as well as existing construction. Chapter 12 of the *Code* addresses requirements for new health care occupancies, and Chapter 13 addresses the requirements for existing construction. This theme is consistent with how the *Code* manages to treat other occupancies that it governs. Unlike a regional building officials code that accepts a level of safety that was acceptable when the building was built, NFPA *101* establishes a minimum level of protection not only for newly constructed buildings, but also for existing buildings.

The *Code* provides a delineated progression to the level of protection afforded by means of the total concept approach. The total concept is utilized given the special nature of the facility, namely that the occupants (the patients) are mostly incapable of self-preservation. The total concept approach has three separate and distinct parts centering on the physical structure, the staff, and the operating and procedural protocol. They are (1) design, construction, and compartmentation; (2) provision for detection, alarm, and extinguishment; and (3) fire prevention and the planning, training, and drilling in programs that relate to isolation of the fire, transfer of occupants to areas of refuge, or the evacuation of occupants from the building.

In the total concept philosophy, NFPA *101* is developed around the goal that the last part of item (3) above will not occur. The total concept approach allows occupants to be defended in place through a variety of means including limiting the allowable types of construction, installing complete automatic sprinkler protection throughout all new construction, subdividing patient sleeping floors into two or more barriered smoke compartments, carefully regulating interior furnishings and contents, and involving staff in their critical roles of rescuing patients and working to relocate patients should either become necessary.

NFPA *101* recognizes that the vulnerability of the building occupants, whether they be immobilized or unaware of their surroundings, places them in a high-risk category. Whereas occupants in other types of buildings and environments are given numerous safeguards to protect them from fire, patients in a health care atmosphere do not normally have the ability to self-preserve. Thus, the role of the health care facility staff becomes critically important.

NFPA *101* is the centerpiece in terms of providing the necessary level of protection for occupants. By way of mandatory reference, NFPA *101* assures that the installed systems will meet the highest levels of reliability by requiring systems to be installed in accordance with the appropriate installation documents. These would include NFPA 10, *Standard for Portable Fire Extinguishers;* NFPA 13, *Standard for the Installation of Sprinkler Systems;* NFPA 14, *Standard for the Installation of Standpipe and Hose Systems;* NFPA 72, *National Fire Alarm Code®;* and NFPA 221, *Standard for Fire Walls and Fire Barrier Walls.* In addition, the continual and ongoing inspection, testing, and maintenance requirements of those documents must also be followed. Water-based fire protection systems must comply with NFPA 25, *Standard for the Inspection, Testing, and Maintenance of Water-Based Fire Protection Systems.*

NFPA *101* also requires compliance with other NFPA codes and standards such as NFPA 99. The specific reference to NFPA 99 is for the power supply arrangement for emergency lighting circuits and exit signs, laboratories, anesthetizing locations, and medical gas storage and administration areas. As previously described in the earlier parts of this handbook, NFPA 99 provides extensive coverage with respect to the many facets of equipment found in the facility.

Beyond the regulation of these types of systems and subsystems, the *Life Safety Code* also specifies the number, type, and arrangement of exits required for a health care facility. Common features include minimum corridor widths of 8 ft (2.4 m) for new construction. This unusually wide width recognizes that there might be instances when multiple patient beds must be in the corridor during a relocation procedure due to a fire. In reality, however, this width also is very practicable for the daily operational concerns associated with the routine use of the facility.

Stairs and doors, including the minimum width for both components, are governed to ensure that they are usable by the ambulatory occupants. Such measures are necessary if the need arises to relocate to another area or floor. Exit stairs in the health care environment, as in nearly all other types of occupancies, are designed to be a "safe haven" once an occupant reaches the interior of the stair. Construction of the stair includes everything from the geometry of the treads and the risers, to the allowable type of handrail, to the construction of the walls in the stair to keep it safe from the effects of a fire.

The design of smoke barrier walls is intended to provide for a point of horizontal refuge on any given floor. A standard procedure in the event of a fire would include immediate removal of a patient from a room of fire origin. If the fire is not immediately controlled, all of the patients in the barriered compartment of origin may have to be relocated to the opposite side of a smoke barrier wall. This precaution not only moves the occupant to a safer position, it also allows an emergency response team or fire brigade to have more room in which to maneuver or work on the incident. NFPA *101*, therefore, provides very specific requirements on not only the design of such walls, but also on the available space needed in each smoke compartment in order to accommodate bed-borne occupants.

Additional information on this subject can be found in the *Life Safety Code Handbook*, seventh edition.

## NFPA 13, *Standard for the Installation of Sprinkler Systems*

As mentioned under the discussion on NFPA *101*, all new health care facilities are required to be protected with an automatic sprinkler system. Also of importance is the fact that many types of renovation and modernization to existing health care facilities will trigger a requirement to retrofit an automatic sprinkler system. NFPA 13, which was the first document ever developed by NFPA in 1896, provides the requirements for "how to" install a sprinkler system. This standard is used to define acceptable materials, minimum water supply requirements, acceptable design methods, and proper installation techniques to ensure that a reliable system is provided.

NFPA 13 addresses the system design parameters for all types of sprinkler systems.

Common types of systems found in a health care facility would include a wet-pipe system in most areas; preaction systems in areas containing sensitive electronic equipment; and dry-pipe systems in areas subject to freezing such as outside loading docks, ambulance receiving areas, and walk-in refrigeration units.

Additional information on this subject can be found in the *Automatic Sprinkler Systems Handbook*, seventh edition.

## NFPA 72, *National Fire Alarm Code*

Just as NFPA 13 provides the various details that go into the design of an automatic sprinkler system, NFPA 72 does the same for the required fire alarm system. NFPA *101* mandates that a fire alarm system be provided to allow for prompt notification of the occupants as well as the fire department. Activation of this required alarm system is to be achieved through the activation of water flow switches, manual fire alarm stations, or any of the required detection systems.

The details governed by NFPA 72 include the types of manual fire alarm stations that are permitted, the mounting height of such devices, and the location of the devices with respect to exits and travel distance. NFPA 72 contains design requirements for location and position of detection devices for a variety of circumstances. The use of smoke detectors in a health care occupancy is minimized to a large extent, in part due to the presence of trained staff, the presence of residential or quick-response sprinklers in all new construction, and the regulation of various other construction features associated with the facility.

Reliability for the circuitry (type of conductors, arrangements of circuits, monitoring of circuits) is achieved by requiring certain levels of supervision of the circuits. Such measures help to ensure that the system is functional, or at a minimum, that some form of notification is provided should some type of system fault occur. Annunciating devices are also regulated by NFPA 72. These devices are normally a combination of an audible as well as a visual device. Because the sounding portion of the alarm is quite loud (90 dB minimum), both NFPA *101* and NFPA 72 allow the use of visual-only alarms in critical care areas.

In some circumstances described in the *Life Safety Code*, the building fire alarm system is also required to perform supplemental duties, such as closing smoke barrier doors or activating smoke control systems. The requirements for utilization of the fire alarm system for this purpose are also detailed in NFPA 72.

In addition to describing the design and installation parameters for new fire alarm systems, NFPA 72 has a chapter that deals with the required inspection, testing, and maintenance of the fire alarm system. System integrity and reliability is maintained through a periodic and systematic approach for verifying that the system components work as intended and that they are able to carry out all of their required functions.

Additional information on this subject can be found in the *National Fire Alarm Code® Handbook*, third edition.

## NFPA 25, *Standard for the Inspection, Testing, and Maintenance of Water-Based Fire Protection Systems*

NFPA *101* places a very high reliance on the proper performance of the automatic sprinkler system. Consequently, the suitable treatment of that system is of paramount importance. NFPA 25 is typically used by the hospital engineer to derive the frequency of the items to be checked and to determine which items are to be evaluated and what corrective actions are to be taken should a system component fail to perform as intended. In addition, NFPA 25 specifies a very detailed procedure for the shutdown of the various fire protection systems. Additional fire protection systems, such as standpipe systems and fire pumps that are usually found in high-rise health care facilities, are also regulated by NFPA 25. The proper maintenance of any required fire protection system is crucial to ensure that they operate and perform as intended.

## NFPA 110, *Standard on Emergency and Standby Power Systems*

The health care environment is unique, given the inability to readily ask occupants to leave the building in the event of an emergency, or withstand—even for a short time—what would be deemed an inconvenience in other buildings in the event of a loss of electrical power. NFPA 110 mandates the level of reliability and redundancy, the types of prime movers that are acceptable, and the arrangement of the power transfer switch equipment. Chapter 3 of NFPA 99 also regulates certain aspects of the emergency power supply.

## Regional Building Official Codes

There are three regional building official codes in the United States at the present time that also play a role in the local and state regulation of the health care environment. These codes are important in developing requirements for the structural provisions for the facility and for establishing other construction provisions. These codes would typically include accessibility features, fundamental lighting and ventilation levels, acceptable roofing methods, and features and requirements for glass and glazing used in various parts of a health care facility.

These regional codes are used in select geographic regions of the United States and are usually updated every three years. The three codes in use in the United States are the *Uniform Building Code*, the *National Building Code,* and the *Standard Building Code*. Each code governs identical subject matter but might have slightly different requirements. Many of these differences have been narrowed thanks in part to the regional code organization participation in the Board for the Coordination of Model Codes (BCMC).

Detailed information on any of these codes can be found by contacting the individual organization.

**Uniform Building Code**

International Conference of Building Officials
5360 Workman Mill Road
Whittier, CA 90601
(562) 699-0541

**National Building Code**

Building Officials and Code Administrators International, Inc.
4051 West Flossmoor Road
Country Club Hills, IL 60478
(708) 799-2300

**Standard Building Code**

Southern Building Code Congress International, Inc.
900 Montclair Road
Birmingham, AL 35213
(205) 591-1853

## JCAHO Management of the Environment of Care (EC) Standards

The EC standards are used by JCAHO to provide specific guidance to hospital facilities in terms of JCAHO expectations for measuring compliance with any number of applicable codes and standards. The ultimate goal of the EC standards is to provide a safe and effective environment for patient care. The physical plant characteristics of the facility are centered on standard EC.1, *Design*. This standard establishes the expected levels of safety, accessibility, effectiveness, efficiency, mission and service, and compliance with legal and regulatory provisions.

The life safety aspect of the regulated design utilizes the 1997 edition of NFPA *101* to measure this level of performance. The building space design aspect is compared against the requirements of the 1993 edition of the *Guidelines for Construction and Equipment of Hospitals and Medical Facilities*. These guidelines are published by the American Institute of Architects:

American Institute of Architects
1735 New York Avenue
Washington, DC 20006
(202) 626-7448

Once the level of compliance (or noncompliance) with any one of the EC standards is determined, through a survey or through a review of the Statement of Conditions (SOC), the facility can then develop a plan for improvement to correct any identified deficiencies. Depending on the severity of the violation or on the amount of work needed to correct a situation, the facility normally is given a time frame for correcting a physical plant problem or for establishing a potential solution through an application for equivalency.

More information on the various health care programs with which JCAHO is involved can be found by contacting the organization:

Joint Commission on Accreditation of Healthcare Organizations
One Renaissance Boulevard
Oakbrook Terrace, IL 60181
(708) 916-5800

## CONCLUSIONS

Although occupants in health care facilities are in an extremely vulnerable state, usually as the result of not being capable of self-preservation in the event of a fire, they are one of the most protected segments of the population due to the numerous codes and standards in existence today. These documents, some of which have been described in this supplement, work in harmony when properly implemented and enforced to make the health care environment very safe from the effects of unwanted fire. Since the Cleveland Clinic fire in 1929 that resulted in the loss of 125 lives, those groups involved with health care fire safety issues have worked to prevent any such reoccurrence.

In fact, according to the NFPA Fire Analysis and Research Division, the annual average civilian loss of life in health care facilities was four deaths per year for the period of 1991 through 1995. The average number of civilian injuries per year during this same time frame was 107 per year. These numbers, which ideally should be zero but which realistically may never reach that point due to any number of factors, help to show the level of safety provided by the facility, the staff, and the various authorities having jurisdiction, whether they be local, state, federal, or private sector. Anyone who has anything to do with the health care industry has a tremendous responsibility for supervision and conformance to the numerous codes and standards that regulate the fire protection and fire safety issues in the health care environment.

# SUPPLEMENT 2

# User's Guide to Inspecting, Testing, and Maintaining Emergency Power Supply Systems in Health Care Facilities

### A. Dan Chisholm
### *Healthcare Circuit News*

*Dan Chisholm of Winter Park, Florida, is the editor and publisher of* Healthcare Circuit News, *a publication devoted to the electrical distribution systems of health care facilities. In addition, he is a member of NFPA 99 Technical Committee (Chapter 3); NFPA 110,* Standard for Emergency and Standby Power Systems; *and NFPA 111,* Standard on Stored Electrical Energy Emergency and Standby Power Systems. *Mr. Chisholm also serves as the chair for the health care Energy Initiative Network, an American Society for Healthcare Engineering project for showcasing health care electric and gas profiles to interested utilities.*

## OVERVIEW

Paragraphs 3-4.1.1.2 and 3-4.1.1.3 of NFPA 99, *Health Care Faciiities,* describe situations that require emergency power supply systems in health care facilities. The fundamental reason for requiring such systems is relatively simple: Hospitals have been constructed to "defend in place," and the emergency power supply systems must therefore be independent of an electric utility in case of a disaster.

The failure of both the normal "essential" power sources and the emergency power supply systems (EPSS) would result in a lack of electricity for multiple essential loads. The lack of electricity could cause multiple sentinel events that are unexpected occurrences involving death or serious physical or psychological injury. Both staff and patients could be affected during the time of a total power outage.

**Exhibit S2.1**  *Parallel gear and monitoring center for emergency power supply system.*

The sheer number of EPSS components is daunting. Multiplying the estimated 6400 active acute care facilities in the United States by the average 3.3 diesel generators in each, 9.7 transfer switches, 9.7 EPSS feeder breakers, and 1 day tank per diesel generator produces the total 169,100, which roughly represents the number of main components in the country that could potentially fail.[1] Actual statistics from maintenance records indicate one tenth of one percent of these components will not function properly at any given time—a number large enough to prevent power from being available at the output terminals of over 169 transfer switches during an extended power outage at any moment.

The loads powered by the EPSS range from egress lighting and hospital communications to ICU ventilating equipment and other life support systems. Loss of these systems in the time of a natural disaster could produce internal disasters only limited by the imagination. Having high testing standards and eliminating shortcuts are two approaches that could aid in eliminating the total blackout that could result from EPSS failure. Increasing manufacturing standards would do little, if anything, to improve reliability.

## HIGHER TESTING STANDARDS

The goal of the emergency power testing program should be to comply with regulatory requirements without adversely affecting the operation of the hospital or the well-being of the patient.[2]

To many, complying with published standards sounds both reasonable and adequate. Yet arguably, using regulatory requirements by themselves to define a testing program destines it to inherent flaws. Although the process of maintaining the reliability of the EPSS components is included in the "regulatory requirements," such requirements fall short of ensuring a testing protocol that encompasses the EPSS as a whole. Why is that? The regulator's most commonly used standards or requirements are NFPA 70, *National Electrical Code®*, 517-30(a),(b); NFPA 99, *Health Care Facilities,* 3-4.4.1.1(b)(1); NFPA *101®*, *Life Safety Code®*, 5-9.3, 7.13; and JCAHO, 2.14. These standards are unified in that they are rooted in NFPA 110, *Standard for Emergency and Standby Power Systems,* which in turn refers ultimately to manufacturer's suggestions (see 6-1.1 of NFPA 110).

Herein lies the problem. Taking each manufacturer's recommendations for testing each EPSS component and stringing them all together does not necessarily result in a procedure that guarantees the functionality of the EPSS as a whole. This is a case where the whole is greater than the sum of its parts, and different component manufacturer's standards are component specific and not necessarily written with the other EPSS components in mind—nor the specific installation details of an individual facility's EPSS. To yield adequate information about how the system is performing, *one* EPSS testing protocol must test *one* specific site. It should attempt to replicate *real life scenarios* as opposed to the *minimum requirements* set forth in NFPA 110 and the manufacturer's recommendations. If all real power outages were limited to 30 minutes, our lives obviously would be simpler—but such is not the case. So how long *should* the EPSS be run to assure its reliability?

An EPSS testing program that includes testing the entire EPSS annually for a minimum 24-hour consecutive full-load run is recommended. (This type of testing more closely resembles the acceptance testing standards of most professional engineers and the standards found in Section 5-13 of NFPA 110.) That first 24-hour test period will likely be quite an eye opener—especially because a large percentage of the problems will be with personnel dealing with no power at the normal receptacles—if you interrupt normal power to these circuits as well. Practice *defending in place* for one full day to see whether you, the staff, and the EPSS can come through with a passing grade. Testing under controlled long-term outages rather than during a real outage is the objective.

In defense of this proposal for a test of such long duration, at least two other well-known agencies have more stringent EPSS testing standards than the NFPA: the Canadian Standards Association (CSA) for office buildings and the Federal Aviation Administration (FAA) for flight control centers. In fact, waste water treatment facilities in Florida, with their required 4-hour monthly tests, have more demanding standards than do health care facilities.

As deregulation and utility company incentives become more widespread, the debate surrounding how the EPSS is tested will become a moot point. Generators will serve dual purposes—as alternative sources of power and as active tools to cut costs.

Administration will understand that in order to obtain the greatest dollar benefit from its investment, the EPSS must be able to operate at or close to its nameplate rating for extended periods of time. In this new environment, testing the EPSS under load will be accomplished almost without notice as it serves its other purpose, as stated in the exception to 6-4.1 in NFPA 110: "If the generator set is used for standby power or for peak load shaving, such use shall be recorded and shall be permitted to be substituted for scheduled operations and testing of the generator set, provided the appropriate data are recorded."

## ELIMINATING SHORTCUTS THAT COULD "SHORT CIRCUIT" SUCCESS OF PERFORMANCE-BASED STANDARDS

Many people in the health care industry welcome the trend of standards evolving from prescriptive- to performance-based. In fact, the trend toward performance-based standards will give facilities more "rights" in designing policies and procedures with respect to preventive maintenance and testing. Unfortunately, there is a downside. As with any change involving greater freedom, there is a corresponding requirement to assume greater responsibility. Swept up in the euphoria of financial savings, it's easy to become lax in the documentation and establishment of benchmarks, the backbone of performance-based standards. Unless proper care is taken, all gains can be lost.

Is there any basis for taking such a pessimistic outlook? Deregulation of the airline industry (much like the trend toward performance-based standards in health care) gave the airlines greater control over many aspects of their business. However, the transition to deregulation was not completely smooth. What has evolved in the airline industry could also happen in the health care industry with the current move away from regulatory/prescription-based standards.

With the decrease in full-time employees, it will be necessary to automate the reading and documentation of real time data from EPSS components during monthly tests. Just as a pilot cannot arrive at a destination without first knowing the plane's location, performance-based preventive maintenance standards cannot be effective without the aid of accurate benchmarks. Benchmarks include laboratory analysis of the engine coolant and lubricating oil, and comparing the exhaust temperatures of each cylinder at rated load with manufacturers' standards.

## CONCLUSIONS

The following techniques can be instituted to ensure the EPSS failure rate does not increase:

- Improve educational programs of essential electrical contractors and staff.
- Refer to all applicable NFPA standards in maintenance agreements with contractors, to add emphasis to compliance and legal issues.

- Test according to worst-case scenarios.
- Test the entire EPSS for 24 continuous hours annually, at a minimum.
- Automate reporting and documentation procedures.

A feedback loop is mandatory and one of the greatest benefits of a performance-based plan. It provides the basic framework with which to obtain key information to fine-tune the EPSS — and actually *improve* upon the statistics of reliability.

## REFERENCES

1. Motor and Generator Institute and *Healthcare Circuit News®*, PO 2474, Winter Park, FL 32790.
2. David L. Stymiest, P.E., "Managing the Impact and Cost of Emergency Power Testing on Hospital Operations," 35th Annual ASHE Conference, Denver, 1998.

# Conducting Emergency Drills at Health Care Facilities

## Russell Phillips
## Russell Phillips and Associates, Inc.

*Russell Phillips is president of Russell Phillips and Associates, Inc. (a MEDSAFE company) of Rochester, New York. His articles have appeared in such publications as* Code Red, Health Facilities Management, *and* Nursing Home Long Term Care Management. *A member of the NFPA Health Care Section, Mr. Phillips serves on the Education and Codes/Standards Committees and chairs the NFPA Technical Committee on Emergency Prepardeness Disaster Planning.*

## INTRODUCTION

Health care professionals are responsible for the medical needs and physical safety of patients who have been entrusted to their care. In addition to day-to-day safety, health care facilities must also plan and practice for safety during emergencies. Once procedures are written and staff/residents (where applicable) are trained for fires and other types of disasters, emergency preparedness drills must be conducted.

The necessity of drills for fires and other disasters is based on two reasons: (1) They are required by authorities having jurisdiction who regulate and inspect the health care industry, and more importantly, (2) they can ensure the effectiveness of the emergency preparedness plan (EPP) within particular facilities, as well as serve as one method of continuing the staff's knowledge of the EPP throughout the year.

This supplement addresses drills for all types of disasters and gives a brief overview of code requirements.

## OBJECTIVES OF AN EMERGENCY PREPAREDNESS PLAN

If a facility has clear, concise objectives for fire drills, staff members are much more likely to support and fully participate in the exercise. The following objectives are suggested.

## Evaluate

The drill should seek to evaluate the staff's knowledge and understanding of the present emergency preparedness procedures. In this way, the effectiveness of a procedure can be evaluated. An example of effectiveness can be seen by examining a particular facility's (hypothetical) fire drills. The fire drill reports in this facility indicate that staff constantly re-entered the room of fire origin, after the fire had been discovered, the room evacuated, and the door closed by the discovering staff member. Although the action of re-opening the door was wrong, it was a procedural problem. This inappropriate re-entering of the fire room stopped once the fire procedures were modified to state that a person who discovers a fire and carries out the critical procedures of rescue, door closure, and alarm activation must stay near the fire room to advise responding staff members of the fire location. The procedures were subsequently updated further to add a door marking system whereby staff would be able to easily recognize the fire room door.

This process of evaluation and review by the appropriate committee, which resulted in a procedural change, is a good example of a "performance measure" requirement by the Joint Commission on Accreditation of Healthcare Organizations (JCAHO).

An effective fire drill evaluation also serves to identify additional or specific staff training needs, based on staff actions during drills.

## Practice

During orientation sessions and actual in-service programs, staff learn the facility's emergency preparedness procedures. However, they frequently do not have a chance to use this information at the time of the training session. Therefore, emergency preparedness drills enable staff to carry out their procedures in an actual "hands-on" scenario.

Investigations of health care fires and other types of disasters indicate that staff react much more appropriately if they have had a chance to actually carry out their procedures in a practice session than if they have seen the procedures carried out on a video or have read about the actions to take in a policy manual.

Practical examples of hands-on scenarios include the following:

- Disconnecting medical equipment, as necessary, to remove a resident from the fire room.
- Practicing the proper technique for removal of a nonambulatory resident from bed.

NOTE: These scenarios can be done most effectively by placing a staff member or Resusci® Anne in bed, posing as a resident.

The following are some practical guidelines for making emergency preparedness drills as realistic as possible to enable staff to truly "practice" their procedures.

# HOW TO SET UP A FIRE DRILL

As indicated in the objectives of an emergency preparedness drill, health care facilities safety managers need to prepare staff to carry out their procedures in the event of an actual fire or other disaster. The drill, therefore, must be as realistic as possible. Consider the following options.

## Notification

The Health Care Finance Administration (HCFA) has stated that, in general, staff should not be prenotified of a drill. In fact, HCFA requires fire drills to be held at varying times and under varying simulated conditions. However, certain people and organizations need to know of a drill in advance.

## Fire Department and Fire Alarm Monitoring Company

If allowed by the fire department, it is recommended that the fire alarm system be allowed to transmit the alarm signal through to the fire alarm monitoring company without prior notification. The fire department receives two telephone calls in a drill set up in this fashion. One call originates from the monitoring company, advising they have received an alarm. The second call originates from a position in the facility that has been assigned the responsibility of making a backup phone call to the fire department. The fire department *should not respond* to this drill, as they will have been prenotified. This procedure allows the facility to thoroughly check its fire alarm connection to the monitoring company, the procedures of the monitoring company, and the procedures of the staff person responsible for the backup phone call to the fire department.

NOTE: Some fire departments will allow this situation to occur only if someone from the facility remains on-line with the fire department throughout the drill so that, should an actual fire occur, they can be advised to respond. In some small communities, fire departments do not have the personnel to allow this type of test to occur. Thus, the person responsible for making the back-up phone call and the fire alarm monitoring company would have to be prenotified of the drill.

## Need-to-Know Staff

The "need-to-know" group includes such people as surgical staff. In some facilities, surgical cases that have not yet started would not be started in the event of a fire alarm. Cases in progress would be reviewed for "quick closure" if the need became apparent. If this is the policy of a facility, it is best for the surgery department to be notified if a drill that *does not apply* to their unit is scheduled to take place. In this way, the surgical schedule can continue. However, any fire alarm should alert the surgical staff to review the procedures to take if their unit were affected by a fire. Surgical staff should also be made aware that in the absence of a phone call advising of a drill not affecting the surgical department, they should take the appropriate actions at the sound of alarm.

### Person in Charge of the Area of Drill Origin

People in charge of the area of drill origin should be made aware of drills scheduled in their areas so they can closely watch and evaluate their staff's actions throughout the entire drill. This will be discussed further under Observation of Drills.

### Location

Locations in which to originate fire drills should be rotated so that, eventually, all areas of the facility will have participated in a drill. If a particular area of the facility is not the origin of the fire drill, few steps are to be taken by area staff. In general, patients should be protected in place (close doors), and some staff, depending on the fire procedures, can be required to respond to the fire area to assist. All of the critical steps of rescue, alarm activation, closing of doors, and evacuation or fire extinguishment are to be completed by staff in the area of origin.

To make the drill as realistic as possible, a staff member can pose as a patient in the room of fire origin. In this way, staff must physically remove a person from the fire room, as they would during a fire situation. This exercise will enable safety staff to evaluate staff knowledge of techniques to be used when removing a nonambulatory patient from the room. It will also help prepare nonnursing staff for the fact that they might discover a fire in a patient care area, at which point they would have to rescue a patient from the fire room instead of leaving the patient in danger while they summon the assistance of a nurse. This situation could occur in the event of an electrical fire in a bed motor with a nonambulatory patient in the bed.

The hypothetical patient should have medical equipment typically found in medical or surgical areas. An IV pump or feeding pump could be outwardly attached to a staff member posing as a patient, forcing the discovering staff member to properly break down this equipment in order to rescue the patient.

In special care areas of intensive care, surgery, sub-acute nursing areas, and so on, medical staffing is much higher than in a general area. In these specialized areas, fires tend to be discovered by knowledgeable medical staff, and critical patients are evacuated by the physicians and nurses who are immediately available.

### Fire Indicator

There are numerous ways to alert staff to the fact that they have discovered a fire in a fire drill scenario. These methods include the following:

- Place a sign or picture of a fire in the area of fire origin. Staff members who see the sign/picture are expected to carry out the fire procedures. At times, very large signs are used to indicate a fire. If the person conducting the drill is seen carrying this large sign through the corridor, everyone knows that a fire drill is going to take place. Because this destroys the "surprise" factor, it is suggested that a small sign be used or another method, such as one listed below, be used.
- Hand a note to the staff explaining that they have just discovered a fire in a room, asking them to carry out the fire procedures.
- Activate the alarm and have staff respond appropriately.
- Activate a patient call-light to summon a staff member to the room.

It is important to use a variety of techniques, not always the same method, to indicate that a fire drill is going to occur.

## Start and Finish of Drills

**Start of the Fire Drill.** Using methods just outlined, initiate the drill. Regardless of the method chosen to initiate the drill, it is imperative for staff to be well aware of the actions to be taken upon discovery of a specific fire. For example, if the hypothetical situation is a large fire in a room, the proper response is to close the door and activate the alarm. However, the hypothetical situation can be a fire in the television in a patient room, with substantial smoke development and a nonambulatory patient in bed. In that situation, the staff member should respond by immediately removing the patient from danger and closing the door to contain the fire and smoke to the room, while simultaneously calling out the facility's code word for assistance of nearby staff.

Actual fires are discovered in two ways: (1) The fire may be detected by the fire alarm/detection system, or (2) a staff member may be the first to observe the smoke or flame. More and more health care facilities in the United States place smoke detectors in patient rooms. For facilities with smoke detectors in patient rooms, a fire in a patient's room will most likely be discovered by the smoke detector before staff are aware of the situation. To provide the most realistic scenario, fire drills originating in patient care areas (without room smoke detection) should begin with staff discovery of the situation. If room smoke detection is available, the drill should commence with alarm activation. Whichever way the drill is started, it should vary from time to time so as not to "program" staff that a fire will always occur in the same fashion.

When fire alarm systems are the means of fire discovery, staff often spend time carrying out the latter part of the procedures such as clearing halls and shutting doors. They fail to quickly find the area of alarm origin and rescue any patients in immediate danger. This must be closely supervised and discussed in the fire drill critique.

**Extent of Drill.** The fire drill starts with the discovery of a fire, either by the fire alarm system or a member of the staff, and ends with the simulated evacuation of the fire compartment. Partial and full building evacuations are part of the full EPP.

The length of time it takes staff to accomplish their actions is not as important as the fact that all of the procedures must be carried out effectively. Later in this supplement, the important components of a fire drill that must be evaluated will be covered.

### Observations of Drills

A dangerous situation can exist when the person who guides and directs staff through a fire drill is someone other than the regular leader or person who will most likely be there at the time of a fire. Therefore, instructions to staff during a drill should originate from the charge person of the area at the time. If this charge person is not present, a senior staff person must step forward to take the lead. If guidance during drills comes from the person who conducts and critiques the drill, it is quite probable that this person will not be present during an actual fire. In this situation, staff may become nervous and frightened if their "fire drill leader" is not present. For this reason, the charge person should be prenotified for a fire drill originating in his or her area and be present to observe and guide staff through the drill.

The Joint Commission's Environment of Care Standards include very strict requirements on observation of staff actions throughout the facility during drills. One option is to have an observer in *every* smoke compartment during fire drills. In recognition of the impracticality of this requirement, the 20 percent Rule has come to mean that trained observers (persons who know the fire procedures well, such as members of the Safety Committee) are to observe fire drills from the following locations:

- The area of fire drill origin
- A smoke compartment above or below the fire area (if an occupied compartment exists)
- A smoke compartment on one or the other side of the fire compartment (if an occupied compartment exists)
- In 20 percent of the total number of smoke compartments that are occupied

NOTE: 10 percent of the smoke compartments may be observed if fire drill reports have indicated to the Safety Committee or Emergency Preparedness Committee that there are effective drills and knowledgeable staff. This requirement could change if and when the Joint Commission's Committee on Health Care Safety so chooses.

## EVALUATION OF DRILLS

To properly evaluate fire procedures and staff knowledge of these procedures, it is important to consider the following critical components of the fire procedures. Using trained observers is one way to accomplish this.

## Crucial Actions

Crucial actions that must be carried out after the discovery of a fire are summarized by the acronym RACE.

**R**emove anyone in immediate danger and close the door to contain the fire, while calling out the facility's code word for assistance.

**A**ctivate the fire alarm.

**C**lose all other doors and windows (if applicable) in the area.

**E**vacuate the smoke compartment, as directed by the person in charge at the time of the fire.

NOTE: If the fire has not spread from the point or origin (e.g., the fire remains contained in a wastebasket or is confined to a smoldering appliance) and the staff is *sure* the fire can be extinguished safely, they should do so.

**Response of Staff to Alarm Activation.** Appropriate staff are to respond to the area of fire alarm origin. Others respond according to the facility's procedures.

**Internal Control and Overall Building Command.** Appropriate staff should set up a control station, linked to a command post that is part of the fire department's incident command post, in the area of the fire.

**Extended Evacuation.** Appropriate staff must decide to which area the fire area should evacuate for the safety of patients and to obtain a head count of staff and patients.

NOTE: Further floor or full building evacuation will be considered at this time by the command post.

It is important to question staff during drills at the various positions, rather than allow staff to stand in a group and discuss their actions. Consider the following examples.

- On an evening shift, the nursing supervisor at the control station of the fire area might be questioned about where to obtain extra personnel for evacuation of patients. If the nursing supervisor or the person at the inside control station needs to communicate with the administrator and fire chief at the command post, where would they be located and how would this communication take place? How would the person who is responsible for meeting the fire department direct fire fighters to enter the building so as not to have them penetrate smoke-barrier doors, beyond which patients and staff are being gathered?
- Surveyors (from health departments and the Joint Commission) often ask staff members what they would do if they discovered a fire. This is generally followed

by questions such as, "Where is the fire alarm pull station for the area?" "Where is the nearest fire extinguisher?" and "If you had to evacuate, where would you go?"

**Non-Fire Areas.** As mentioned earlier, there are few steps to be taken by staff members in areas outside the area of fire alarm origin. However, because normal activity other than in critical areas should cease, the downtime provides an excellent time for a "mini-review" session. The person in charge should conduct this short review with staff members once their fire procedures have been completed. Typically fire procedures involve clearing the halls, closing doors, and reassuring patients. The following questions might be asked during such a verbal review:

- What would you do if the fire had originated in this area?
- If we have to evacuate patients, where would we go?
- What would you do if the fire had originated in a smoke compartment immediately adjacent to our area?

The location and operating techniques of fire alarm pull stations, fire extinguishers, and so forth as well as the method to be used to identify the fire room door should be reviewed.

## REVIEW/CRITIQUE OF DRILLS WITH STAFF

The drill should be reviewed from start to finish to determine which areas went smoothly and correctly and which areas were improperly carried out. It is helpful to allow staff members to tell the observers what their actions were upon discovery of the fire and to critique their own actions.

Following the drill it is important to determine corrective actions and to report to the safety committee or emergency preparedness committee (a performance measure for the JCAHO) for follow-up, which may possibly result in additional educational programs, procedural changes, and so forth.

## REPORTS

Reports should be generated from the fire area as well as other areas. Observers should complete their reports and return them to the person responsible for the facility's fire drill system. This person would then analyze the comments and write one overall fire drill report. The fire drill report should address the critical parts of the fire procedures.

Exhibit S3-1 is a checklist of what observers should look for during a fire drill and include in the drill report. Exhibit S3-2 presents what observers should look for in non-fire areas during a drill.

# FIRE DRILL EVALUATION FORM
## FIRE AREAS

Facility _____

Date _____  Location _____

Time _____  Observer _____

| **At discovery of fire:** Please check one | YES | NO | N/A* |
|---|:---:|:---:|:---:|
| 1. Was CODE WORD called out? | ☐ | ☐ | ☐ |
| 2. Was fire room evacuated? | ☐ | ☐ | ☐ |
| a. Was room checked thoroughly, including bathrooms, alcoves, small work stations, etc.? | ☐ | ☐ | ☐ |
| b. Was staff member familiar with handling technique for patient medical equipment? | ☐ | ☐ | ☐ |
| 3. Were all doors to fire room closed? | ☐ | ☐ | ☐ |
| a. Was door marked to indicate evacuated room? | ☐ | ☐ | ☐ |
| 4. Was fire alarm activated (or simulated)? | ☐ | ☐ | ☐ |
| 5. Was call placed to switchboard operator? | ☐ | ☐ | ☐ |
| a. Was proper extension used? | ☐ | ☐ | ☐ |
| b. Was proper information given? | ☐ | ☐ | ☐ |

**At the sound of alarm:**

| | YES | NO | N/A* |
|---|:---:|:---:|:---:|
| 1. Was overhead page announcement of fire location made? | ☐ | ☐ | ☐ |
| 2. Was back-up call made (simulated) to fire department? | ☐ | ☐ | ☐ |
| 3. Were all doors in fire area closed? | ☐ | ☐ | ☐ |
| a. Were patients in corridors placed in rooms? | ☐ | ☐ | ☐ |
| b. Was equipment cleared from corridor? | ☐ | ☐ | ☐ |
| 4. Were elevators recalled and locked? | ☐ | ☐ | ☐ |
| 5. Did staff in immediate area respond to fire scene? | ☐ | ☐ | ☐ |
| 6. Did proper staff from other areas respond to fire area? | ☐ | ☐ | ☐ |
| 7. Was Control Station established in vicinity of fire area? | ☐ | ☐ | ☐ |
| 8. Was proper decision made regarding evacuation of the fire/smoke compartment? | ☐ | ☐ | ☐ |
| 9. Were staff familiar with proper evacuation destination for the fire area? | ☐ | ☐ | ☐ |
| 10. Were staff familiar with the method to indicate evacuated rooms? | ☐ | ☐ | ☐ |
| 11. Did individual in charge of the fire area provide adequate leadership to staff? | ☐ | ☐ | ☐ |
| 12. Was staff member in place to meet the fire department? | ☐ | ☐ | ☐ |
| a. Was staff member aware of fire location and appropriate building entry point for fire department use? | ☐ | ☐ | ☐ |

* N/A indicates the action is not applicable to the drill.

Additional comments:

**Exhibit S3-1**  *Fire drill evaluation form.*

## OBSERVER FIRE DRILL FORM
### NON-FIRE AREAS

Facility _____

Date _____   Area Observed _____

Time _____   Observer _____

NOTE: Observers are to complete the portions of this form that apply to the area for which they are responsible.

| | **Please check one** | **YES** | **NO** | **N/A\*** |
|---|---|---|---|---|
| 1. Was fire alarm loud enough to be heard by all in this area? | | ☐ | ☐ | ☐ |
| 2. Was overhead page announcement of fire location made? | | ☐ | ☐ | ☐ |
| 3. Could the page be heard from your location? | | ☐ | ☐ | ☐ |
| 4. Was the back-up phone call made (simulated) to the fire department? | | ☐ | ☐ | ☐ |
| 5. Were the strobe lights flashing? | | ☐ | ☐ | ☐ |
| 6. Did the smoke doors close? | | ☐ | ☐ | ☐ |
| 7. Were all doors in the area closed? | | ☐ | ☐ | ☐ |
| 8. Were patients in corridors placed into rooms? | | ☐ | ☐ | ☐ |
| 9. Was equipment cleared from the corridor? | | ☐ | ☐ | ☐ |
| 10. Were elevators recalled and locked? | | ☐ | ☐ | ☐ |
| 11. Did staff, assigned to respond to the fire scene, do so immediately? | | ☐ | ☐ | ☐ |
| 12. Were other staff standing by for further instructions? | | ☐ | ☐ | ☐ |
| 13. Were patients in rooms being checked on by the staff? | | ☐ | ☐ | ☐ |
| 14. Did person in charge of area provide adequate leadership to staff? | | ☐ | ☐ | ☐ |
| 15. Were staff members prepared to receive evacuated patients? | | ☐ | ☐ | ☐ |
| 16. Was staff member in place to meet the fire department? | | ☐ | ☐ | ☐ |
|    a. Was staff member aware of fire location and appropriate building entry point for fire department use? | | ☐ | ☐ | ☐ |
| 17. Was a copy of the current fire procedures available in this area? | | ☐ | ☐ | ☐ |
| 18. Did the person in charge of this area conduct a "mini-review" of fire procedures with his/her staff? | | ☐ | ☐ | ☐ |
| 19. Did the locked doors in the means of egress unlock at sound of alarm? | | ☐ | ☐ | ☐ |
| 20. Were the exit signs illuminated? | | ☐ | ☐ | ☐ |

\* N/A indicates the action is not applicable to the drill.

Additional comments:

**Exhibit S3-2** *Observer fire drill form (non-fire areas).*

# EMERGENCY PREPAREDNESS DRILLS FOR DISASTERS OTHER THAN FIRE

There are key components to an emergency preparedness manual that should be practiced.

## Emergency Preparedness Plan Infrastructure

The infrastructure consists of those components of the plan that would be applicable to any type of disaster. Considerations include the following components:

- Chain of command followed in any disaster: This indicates the position in charge, regardless of the time of day. The chain of command should be set up in an incident command system format, listing specific functions of various positions at the command post and providing job action sheets.
- Command post and communication system: This command post would be the same in any disaster, except a fire. In a fire, the command post would be set up with the fire department's incident command post.
- Building security issues.
- Staff callback plan.
- Procedures for hosting news media, families, and responsible parties.
- Full building evacuation plans: These plans should be used if any disaster forced the facility to evacuate the entire building.

NOTE: More details on the preceding plans can be found in Chapter 11.

## Suggested Disaster Drill for the Infrastructure Section of the Plan

In conjunction with other health care facilities that have agreed to accept your patients in the event of a disaster forcing evacuation of the facility, as well as other local authorities such as the fire department and representatives of the Office of Emergency Preparedness, a live drill could be conducted. A multi-organizational drill allows all involved to practice many parts of the Emergency Preparedness Procedures. A typical scenario could be as follows — participating facilities send several staff members to the host site (facility of disaster origin) to pose as patients, placing them in various areas of the building. In this way each unit could practice, to some degree, a portion of its evacuation plan. The actual disaster that forces the building evacuation is somewhat incidental, as this drill is meant to activate the infrastructure of the plan.

"Patients" should be "packaged" with appropriate medical records, medications, and so forth, and evacuated from various areas of the facility to a discharge area. The command post forms and goes through its assigned functions. The "patients" should be transported to various receiving facilities (those facilities from which these staff members originated). Once arriving at the receiving facilities, "patients" are triaged and housed appropriately. This allows the receiving facilities to practice their "influx of patients" plan. Communication taken place between the receiving facilities and the sending facility, confirming arrival of the patients, adequacy of the medical records, and so forth. The receiving facilities will want to activate support plans to check and confirm the availability of extra staff and supplies to care for the additional patients.

## Specific Disasters

**Technological Disasters.** Technological disasters include bomb threats and contamination of inside or outside air. A suggested drill for a bomb threat assumes that a phone call has been received warning of a bomb placed somewhere in the facility. Prior to this call, a "suspicious" box should be placed in the building for the staff to locate during their search. Staff should then be asked to carry out their procedures to locate the suspicious item or situation, after which the police would take over.

**Natural Disasters.** Natural disasters include earthquakes and weather-related disasters such as high winds and winter storms. A suggested scenario includes a "tornado watch" (threat of a tornado). Staff should be asked to follow their specific disaster procedures which could include such activities as bringing people who are outside the building inside and securing any items outside that could be blown into windows. The drill would carry through to the "tornado warning" (imminent strike), during which time staff would carry out that portion of the procedures (e.g., move a sample of patients to hallways or into rooms without windows) as well. Prior to the drill, staff members should review the tornado disaster procedures.

**Loss of Central Services.** This type of non-fire disaster includes loss of water, gas, electric, elevator service, cooking ability, HVAC systems, sewage service, or telephone service. A scenario could assume that the building has lost all power. At the start of this drill a command post is set up and all department heads summoned. A brief explanation of the scenario is offered. Maintenance must be prepared to advise which building services are still available and to discuss the actions they will take if the generator is not operational over an extended period of time or if the facility does not have a generator. After being briefed at their command posts, department heads return to their respective departments to cover operational guidelines with staff members. These guidelines will follow the departmental disaster procedure for loss of power. For example:

Nursing staff covers the following:

- How to handle emergency bedside suctioning
- Light sources to be used at night
- Medications that must be refrigerated
- If there are locked exit doors that release upon loss of power, how nursing would provide for resident safety

Laundry staff covers the following:

- Whether washers and dryers are functional
- How to provide linens for up to three days
- Whether it would be valuable to design a linen-reduction plan in advance of such an emergency

Dietary personnel cover the following:

- Whether cooking and dishwashing abilities will be lost
- How staff will prepare and deliver meals for the next three days
- Determining which plan is in place to prevent food spoilage
- Determining how meals will be delivered to floors if elevators are not operational

Department heads reconvene to review the effectiveness of written procedures for loss of power, based on the drill.

**Other Types of Disasters.** This category includes a missing patient, low staffing, or an influx of patients (other than mass casualty incidents). Most facilities often practice the mass casualty portions of their procedures.

## EMERGENCY PREPAREDNESS DRILL REQUIREMENTS

HCFA and the JCAHO require hospitals and nursing homes to conduct one fire drill per shift per quarter. When there are special shifts, such as personnel who *only* work weekend shifts, fire drills should also be required once per shift per quarter on the weekends.

The Joint Commission makes an exception to the number of fire drills required for clinics and medical office buildings (each freestanding building classified as a business occupancy) where the ability of patients to evacuate is not compromised. In these situations, only one drill is required per shift per year. The Joint Commission reports that a study of fire statistics has shown that there is no need for more drills.

Several other items are important to note when planning fire drill programs:

(a) JCAHO will allow false alarms to take the place of 50 percent of the fire drills. If false alarms are allowed to count for a fire drill, it is recommended that staff members carry out the full procedures during the fire alarm activation.

(b) Audible alarms are required in fire drills, except from 9:00 p.m. to 6:00 a.m. During these hours, a coded announcement can be used so as not to disturb patients. When using this exception to audible alarms during drills, it is important to note the following three things:

1. The requirement for monthly fire alarm system tests would have to be accomplished at another time, other than fire drills, when that particular monthly drill is held between 9:00 p.m. and 6:00 a.m.

2. If the night shift (11:00 p.m. to 7:00 a.m.) never uses fire alarms, staff might not be familiar with the sound of the fire alarm indicating devices and might not take appropriate actions.
3. JCAHO requires a second fire drill, once per shift per quarter, if there is a *Life Safety Code* deficiency. The Joint Commission further requires that the second drill originate in the area of the deficiency.

NOTE:  Check with local authorities having jurisdiction for additional fire drill requirements.

## DRILLS FOR DISASTERS, OTHER THAN FIRE

Staff should practice responding to two disasters other than fire each year. In hospitals or nursing homes that have agreed to receive patients from another facility, one of these drills must be a mass casualty incident / influx of patients drill.

Many facilities conduct a fire drill that results in a practiced evacuation of more than the area of fire origin, and they attempt to qualify this as a disaster drill. The two disaster drills should not involve fire scenarios in any way.

For more guidance, review Chapter 11. In addition to practicing two disaster drills per year other than fire, this standard requires that, at the time of hiring, staff must receive an overview of all disaster procedures. Annually, specific responsibilities in disaster drills should be covered within individual departments.

In the *Environment of Care Standard* 2.9, the Joint Commission requires that disaster drill exercises are conducted at least four months apart and no more than eight months apart. In addition, tabletop exercises that could be useful in training are not acceptable as substitutes for a drill. However, drills that involve packages of information, and simulate patients, families, and visitors, are acceptable. In other words, instead of moving an actual body through the drill, the staff can move a package representing an individual.

## CONCLUSION

This supplement offers an overview of effective and practical guidelines for conducting emergency preparedness drills. With this information, the "dreaded drill" can be turned into a positive and effective educational tool that will enable the evaluation and practice of sound emergency preparedness procedures.

# Regulatory Issues Affecting the Safety of Clinical Hyperbaric Medicine Facilities

## W. T. Workman
## Workman Hyperbaric Services, Inc.

*Wilbur T. Workman, M.S., CHT, is president of Workman Hyperbaric Services, Inc., in San Antonio, Texas. He has served on the NFPA Technical Committee on Hyperbaric and Hypobaric Facilities since 1984 and has been chairman since 1996. Mr. Workman specialized in Aerospace and Hyperbaric Physiology throughout his 23-year career in the United States Air Force. He holds dual board certifications in Aerospace Physiology and Hyperbaric Technology and now specializes in hyperbaric facility planning, staff training, operational safety, and regulatory compliance.*

## INTRODUCTION

The application of high atmospheric (or other gas) pressure for medical purposes dates back to 1650 when von Guericke developed the first practical air pump. It was not until nearly 180 years later, however, that this technology was used to provide compressed air for manned caisson work in the construction of bridges and underwater tunnels. Workers who spent long periods of time under increased pressure would often experience excruciating joint pain when returning to the surface (or decompressing). At the time, this condition was called "compressed-air illness" or "caisson's disease." It is now referred to as decompression sickness.

The technology and practical application of high pressure for medical purposes (through the use of hyperbaric chambers) continued to flourish throughout Europe in the 1800s. In 1854, Pol and Watelle reported what is thought to be the first account of the use of recompression to relieve the pain of compressed-air illness. This technique was endorsed by the renowned French physiologist Paul Bert who, in 1878, stated that a combination of oxygen and recompression was a treatment for the illness. It was not until 1912, however, that a study of a large series of caisson's disease cases clearly established the benefits of recompression therapy. Twelve years later, the U.S. Navy published its first standardized compressed air treatment schedules for decompression sickness.

The use of hyperbaric facilities to treat a variety of other medical conditions began in the late 1950s and early 1960s with the work of Dr. Borema and his colleagues in Amsterdam, the Netherlands, treating gas gangrene with high-pressure oxygen. Subsequently, high-pressure oxygen was found to be effective in the treatment of carbon monoxide poisoning, air embolism, and a variety of other conditions. Treatment was conducted in single-patient or multi-patient hyperbaric chambers; some were even designed with operating room capability to allow surgical procedures to be performed on patients who would otherwise not receive enough oxygen if operated on at ambient atmospheric pressure.

Along with the treatment benefits hyperbaric facilities brought to the medical community came a host of new safety concerns. The very nature of a hyperbaric chamber, a device where a patient is confined in an enclosure that contains an atmosphere where the burning rate of materials is, generally, markedly enhanced and the ease of their ignition greatly increased, created the urgent need for safety requirements governing their use. In 1964, a Subcommittee on Hyperbaric and Hypobaric Facilities was appointed by NFPA to address the subject. The subcommittee membership included representatives from chamber and component manufacturers, chamber operators, fire service personnel, government personnel from the National Aeronautics and Space Administration and the military services, and others interested in hyperbaric chamber safety.

A significant, but unfortunate, impetus for the development of the standard from which Chapter 19 derived occurred on January 23, 1967. A fire erupted in the Apollo 1 Command Module while on its launch pad at Cape Canaveral, Florida, killing all three astronauts inside. The fire, believed to be of electrical origin, broke out during a test in which the module was pressurized with 100 percent oxygen at 20 psia. A few days later another fire, proven to be of electrical origin, occurred in an Air Force hypobaric (altitude) chamber in San Antonio, Texas. The chamber contained pure oxygen at one-fifth of an atmosphere pressure. Two airmen were in the chamber at the time of the fire and both died of massive burns. These two tragic events spurred the development and adoption of NFPA 56D. Adopted as a tentative standard in 1968 and a full standard in 1970, NFPA 56D was incorporated into NFPA 99 in 1984. During this entire period, the document and its subject have undergone a process of continuous use, careful scrutiny, and regular review and revision.

The major changes of Chapter 19 in the last few revision cycles of NFPA 99 were a direct result of the continual input from both military and civilian representatives on the Technical Committee (TC) on Hyperbaric and Hypobaric Facilities. In preparation for the 1999 edition, membership of the TC was expanded to include representation from the Food and Drug Administration (FDA) and those with special expertise from the active fire research, fire sprinkler, and forensic communities. Their input proved invaluable to better understand the issues in support of the changes made to Chapter 19 for the 1999 edition. The most significant changes adopted for this 1999 edition are in the area of electrical requirements for Class A (multiplace) chambers. Support for these changes culminate many years of dedicated effort by committee members to update this portion of the standard and reflect an awareness of the technology now available to hyperbaric chamber designers that perhaps did not exist when the initial requirements were put into place. A better understanding of what constitutes an oxygen-enriched environment, the effects of hyperbaric conditions on the burning rate of materials, and the role that static electricity may play has also contributed to the ongoing revision process. It has been the committee's desire to reflect advances in technology and the ever-increasing understanding of the design and operation of hyperbaric facilities without compromising safety.

It is unfortunate that the majority of the accidents involving hyperbaric facilities that have occurred within the last 10 to 15 years have been the result of human error. Two TC members, Dr. Paul Sheffield and David Desautels, recently reported information on 77 fatalities in 35 hyperbaric chamber fires from 1923 to 1996.[1] These mishaps occurred in Asia, Europe, and North America. Information on mishaps from other regions was not reported. Of the 77 fatalities cited, none occurred in North American *clinical* hyperbaric chambers. Prior to 1980, the primary cause of hyperbaric chamber fires was electrical. After 1980, the vast majority were attributed to either prohibited materials allowed in the chamber or operator error. Careful analysis of these data clearly points to the success of engineering and fire safety codes and standards as applied in North America to clinical hyperbaric medicine facilities. Because of recent tragic accidents in other countries, there is a growing recognition of the need for comprehensive fire safety standards in developing countries. Also, setting minimum training standards on the safe operation of hyperbaric systems will have a positive effect on maintaining hyperbaric safety standards throughout the world.

Although it is not the purpose of this supplement to describe the detailed requirements of organizations such as the American Society of Mechanical Engineers' Committee on Pressure Vessels for Human Occupancy (ASME-PVHO), the FDA, and others related to hyperbaric facility safety, a short overview of the more prominent organizations is warranted. A comprehensive appreciation of how collateral hyperbaric safety requirements are woven together with NFPA 99 will help maintain the highest level of hyperbaric safety possible.

## ORGANIZATIONAL INFORMATION

### The American Society of Mechanical Engineers—Committee on Pressure Vessels for Human Occupancy

The ASME-PVHO *Safety Standard for Pressure Vessels for Human Occupancy* defines the engineering parameters for the safe design, fabrication, testing, and installation of manned hyperbaric systems. Components covered are the actual pressure vessel, acrylic viewports, and relating piping systems. In response to the growing need for educating the engineering community on the design requirements for clinical hyperbaric systems, the ASME-PVHO established the Medical Systems Subcommittee in 1991. The purpose of the subcommittee is to define the minimum design considerations that should be evaluated by engineers when designing a hyperbaric system intended for clinical use. Guidance developed by the subcommittee is to be integrated into the standard as a separate chapter. Input to this document has been provided by a cross section of experienced hyperbaric systems designers, clinical hyperbaric medicine physicians, and technical personnel. Chapter 19 invokes compliance with ASME-PVHO for all hyperbaric chambers used in health care facilities.

See contact information at the conclusion of this supplement.

## The Food and Drug Administration

The Medical Device Amendments of 1976 (Public Law 91-295)[2] established a comprehensive system for the regulation of medical devices intended for human use. Specifically, it mandated that the FDA classify all medical devices into three categories: Class I, General Controls; Class II, Performance Standards; and, Class III, Pre-Market Approval. Devices in commercial distribution prior to May 28, 1976, are not required to comply with this law and are "grandfathered" as preamendment devices. However, devices developed after this date are required to establish either validated performance or substantial equivalency to devices already in commercial distribution.

The FDA Anesthesiology Panel categorizes hyperbaric chambers as Class II medical devices. As such, before being placed into commercial sales, the manufacturer must submit a 510(k) Pre-Market Notification request. This application can be based on an entirely new design or by establishing substantial equivalency. The majority of clinical hyperbaric chamber manufacturers are in compliance with this requirement; however, there are some that are not. Efforts are underway to ensure compliance by all manufacturers.

In addition to being defined as a Class II medical device, clinical hyperbaric chambers are also considered as "Prescription Devices" by the FDA. A "Prescription Device" is one that requires a physician to issue a prescription for the use of high-pressure oxygen and to be involved in its procurement.

The manufacture, packaging, storage, and installation of hyperbaric chambers are to be in compliance with the Quality Systems Regulations (QSRs) as described by the FDA. Failure to comply with any of the requirements of the QSR directives renders the device adulterated. Such a device, as well as the person responsible for the failure to comply, is subject to regulatory action. Any written or oral complaint under the FDA's mandatory Medical Device Reporting program or its voluntary MedWatch program concerning a hyperbaric chamber relative to its quality, reliability, safety, effectiveness, or performance shall be reviewed, evaluated, and documented. This includes taking action on a hyperbaric chamber manufacturer for promotion and advertisement of their chamber for medical conditions that are not recognized as approved indications by the Undersea and Hyperbaric Medical Society (UHMS). Failure to comply with these requirements can result in the hyperbaric chamber being withdrawn from commercial distribution.

See contact information at the conclusion of this supplement.

### The Joint Commission on Accreditation of Healthcare Organizations

The Joint Commission on Accreditation of Healthcare Organizations (JCAHO) is the organization that provides accreditation for all U.S. hospitals. Even though the earlier editions of the NFPA standard stipulated that accreditation agencies such as JCAHO "establish and enforce appropriate programs to fulfill the provisions of this chapter," this requirement is not being universally applied. There is a broad educational effort underway to ensure that licensing and accrediting agencies are fully aware of their responsibilities.

See contact information at the conclusion of this supplement.

### The Occupational Safety and Health Administration

The Occupational Safety and Health Administration (OSHA) is the agency of the U.S. Department of Labor that promotes safe and healthful working conditions. Their chief responsibility is to develop and enforce job safety and health regulations. OSHA regulations deal with fire prevention, protective garments and railings, and many other safety matters. They have no direct program or regulations that deal specifically with hyperbaric facilities.

### The Uniform Boiler and Pressure Vessel Laws Society

The Uniform Boiler and Pressure Vessel Laws Society is the organization that promotes legislative adoption of pressure vessel rules for design, fabrication, testing, and installation. ASME-PVHO is currently mandated by public law in only eleven states, five Canadian provinces, and three U.S. cities. Education efforts are aggressively underway to educate the remaining state pressure vessel inspectors and fire marshals as to their responsibilities regarding hyperbaric facilities in hopes of achieving national adoption of PVHO requirements. As cited earlier, Chapter 19 invokes compliance with ASME-PVHO for all hyperbaric chambers used in health care facilities.

See contact information at the conclusion of this supplement.

### The Undersea and Hyperbaric Medical Society

The Undersea and Hyperbaric Medical Society is an international medical society whose purpose is to provide a forum for professional scientific communication among individuals and groups involved in basic and applied studies concerned with life sciences and human factors aspects of the undersea environment and hyperbaric medicine; to promote cooperation between the life sciences and other disciplines with undersea activity and hyperbaric medicine; and to develop and promote educational activities and other programs which improve the scientific knowledge of matters related to undersea and hyperbaric environments and the accepted indications of hyperbaric oxygen therapy for the membership, as well as physicians and allied health professionals, divers, diver technicians, and the public at large.

In support of the society objectives, the Hyperbaric Safety Committee of the UHMS has been very active in establishing a leading role in promoting hyperbaric facility safety. Practical guidelines on both monoplace and multiplace hyperbaric facility operations have been published and widely distributed. These common sense documents should be required for every hyperbaric facility.

Recognizing the need for a comprehensive set of standards of practice for use throughout the U.S. hyperbaric medicine community, the UHMS recently established a special committee tasked to develop consensus criteria on minimum training, staffing, skills verification for each specialty level, and for overall facility safety. Adoption of these standards will, for the first time, provide a national set of guidelines for the appropriate and safe application of hyperbaric medicine.

See contact information at the conclusion of this supplement.

## The American College of Hyperbaric Medicine

Unlike the UHMS with its broad-based membership, the American College of Hyperbaric Medicine (ACHM) is specifically for hyperbaric physicians. The college promotes and develops liaison with individuals and groups with similar interests in the field of hyperbaric medicine. A primary goal of the college is to enhance the exchange of scientific and therapeutic information related to the specialty of hyperbaric medicine in a manner that will encourage national and international goodwill and social and cultural exchanges.

The ACHM has been very active in the effort to develop a specific credentialling policy for physicians. The ACHM recommends that physicians hold an unrestricted medical license as an MD or DO; demonstrate completion of at least two hyperbaric training courses, sponsored or presented by different organizations, for a total training time in excess of 60 hours, or the equivalent (i.e., full fellowship training in hyperbaric medicine); be physically able to meet the tasks of a hyperbaric physician at the facility where he or she practices; be familiar with the operation of the equipment of that facility; obtain probationary privileges with formal chart review after six months of practice in the facility; and again at one year for full hyperbaric privileges (the reviewer must be a qualified hyperbaric physician, and may be from another facility if no local hyperbaric physician is available); and become certified by the American Board of Hyperbaric Medicine within two years of eligibility.

Recredentialling is achieved by active practice and compliance with the ACHM membership continuing hyperbaric education requirement. This requirement is to take effect in 1999 and can be met by obtaining 16 hours of hyperbaric specific continuing medical education requirements every two years.

See contact information at the conclusion of this supplement.

## CONCLUSION

While organizations such as the NFPA, ASME, FDA, and so forth, have done a superb job in ensuring that hyperbaric pressure vessels and related systems are safely designed, manufactured, and installed, it is up to the operator to ensure that the equipment is properly used and maintained. All personnel involved in hyperbaric medicine need to have a complete understanding of the safety requirements in NFPA 99 and other standards. There must be an active, ongoing safety awareness and training program that involves the entire hyperbaric staff and local fire personnel. Prevention and training are key elements to any effective safety program. There is much work needed to ensure that all jurisdictional agencies fully understand how hyperbaric facilities are currently used, appreciate their rate of growth, and exercise their enforcement role as it exists today. Standards need to be uniformly applied across all venues to ensure that we continue to enjoy our safety record.

Today, hyperbaric medicine stands on the threshold of a major international expansion. Under the guidance of the Undersea and Hyperbaric Medical Society, the American College of Hyperbaric Medicine, the European Committee on Clinical Hyperbaric Medicine, the Japanese Hyperbaric Medicine Society, the British Hyperbaric Association, and a growing number of other international professional organizations, hyperbaric medicine practitioners throughout the world now use this powerful therapy for a growing number of conditions. A few medical conditions from this growing list are decompression sickness, problem wounds, air or gas embolism, carbon monoxide poisoning and smoke inhalation, gas gangrene, crush injury and other acute traumatic ischemias, necrotizing soft tissue infections, osteomyelitis, osteoradionecrosis of the mandible, nonhealing diabetic wounds, failing skin flaps, and selected burns. Exciting research into new applications for hyperbaric medicine will help foster further expansion.

However, the optimism for the future of clinical hyperbaric medicine must be tempered with a few words of caution. As with any rapidly growing specialty, there will be those who will try to cut corners by purchasing hyperbaric equipment that has not gone through the rigors of regulatory review, install the equipment in nontraditional health care locations (such as regular business occupancies where NFPA 99 may not necessarily be applied), fail to receive adequate training in the safe and appropriate use of the equipment, and then use the equipment to treat medical conditions not recognized as appropriate. There is a growing concern, due to these shortcomings, that the likelihood of a major hyperbaric accident occurring in North America is much greater. A mishap occurring in any type of hyperbaric facility will affect the entire community. Authorities having jurisdiction are encouraged to become more proactive in learning more of how these systems are being used and how existing safety standards can be appropriately applied.

## CONTACT INFORMATION

American College of Hyperbaric Medicine
PO Box 25914-130
Houston, TX 77265
(713) 528-5931

American Society of Mechanical Engineers International
Three Park Avenue
New York, NY 10016-5990
(212) 591-8537

Baromedical Nurses Association
PO Box 24113
Halethorpe, MD 21227
(410) 789-5690

Food and Drug Administration
Center for Devices and Radiological Health
Office of Device Evaluation
9200 Corporate Boulevard (HFZ-450)
Rockville, MD 20850
(301) 443-8609

The Joint Commission for Accreditation of Health Care Organizations
One Renaissance Boulevard
Oakbrook Terrace, IL 60181
(630) 792-5000

The Undersea and Hyperbaric Medical Society
10531 Metropolitan Avenue
Kensington, MD 20895-2627
(301) 942-2980

The Uniform Boiler and Pressure Vessel Laws Society
308 North Evergreen Road, Suite 240
Louisville, KY 40243
(502) 244-6029

# REFERENCES

1. P. J. Sheffield and D. A. Desautels, "Hyperbaric and Hypobaric Chamber Fires: A 73-Year Analysis," *Undersea & Hyperbaric Medicine,* 1997; 24(3): 153–164.
2. *Federal Register,* Vol. 44, No. 214, November 2, 1979.

# Index

© 1999 National Fire Protection Association. All Rights Reserved.

The copyright in this index is separate and distinct from the copyright in the document that it indexes. The licensing provisions set forth for the document are not applicable to this index. This index may not be reproduced in whole or in part by any means without the express written permission of the National Fire Protection Association, Inc.

## -A-

**Absolute atmosphere,** *see* Atmosphere, absolute
**Absolute pressure,** *see* Pressure, absolute
**AC current method,** A-7-5.1.3.2
**Acetylene,** 4-6.1.2.4
**ACFM (actual cubic feet per minute)**
 Definition, 2-2
**Active electrode,** *see* Electrode, active
**Actuator (vacuum) switch,** 4-3.2.2.8(b),
 4-3.2.2.9(d) to (e), A-4-3.2.2.9(d)
**Adapters,** 7-5.1.2.6, 7-6.2.1.5, A-7-5.1.2.6
**Adiabatic heating,** C-19.1.2.4.1, C-19.1.3.4.4
 Definition, 2-2
**Aerosols,** 12-4.1.2.2(c), A-12-4.1.2.2(c),
 C-12.1.3.2
 Definition, 2-2
**Aftercoolers,** 4-3.1.1.9(g), 4-4.1
**Air**
 Medical, *see* Medical air
 Monitoring, hyperbaric chamber, 19-2.8.7,
 A-19-2.8.7
 Recirculation of, 5-3.1
**Air compressors**
 Level 3, 4-5.1.1.4, 4-5.4.2, A-4-5.1.1.4
 Definition, 2-2

Medical, 4-3.1.1.2(a)(10)(d), 4-4.1
 Accessories, 4-3.1.1.9(g), A-4-3.1.1.9(g)
 Activibration considerations, 4-3.1.1.9(j)
 Component material, 4-3.1.1.9(l)
 Definition, 2-2
 Electrical power and control, 4-3.1.1.9(d)
 Intake, 4-3.1.1.9(b)
 Monitors and alarms,
 4-3.1.1.9(d)(1),4-3.1.1.9(e), 4-3.1.1.9(i),
 4-5.1.3.4, A-4-3.1.1.9(e), A-4-3.1.1.9(h)
 Multiple, 4-3.1.1.9(c)
 Pressures, different, 4-3.1.1.9(k)
 Receivers, 4-3.1.1.9(f)
 Supply system, 4-3.1.1.9, A-4-3.1.1.9
 Testing, 4-3.4.1.3(j), 4-3.4.1.4(b)
 Patient gas supply systems, 4-5.1.1.3(a)
**Air conditioners, anesthetizing locations,**
 5-4.1.5
**Air supply, closing off,** C-12.4.3
**Alarm annunciator,** 3-4.1.1.15
**Alarm panels,** 4-3.2.2.8(c) to (d), 4-3.2.2.9(c),
 13-3.4.1
**Alarm systems**
 Actuator switch, 4-3.2.2.8(b), 4-3.2.2.9(d) to
 (e), A-4-3.2.2.9(d)

**Surface-mounted medical gas rail systems,** 4-3.1.2.5, A-4-3.1.2.2(c)
Definition, 2-2, A-2-2
**Surgeons, discretionary use of nonconforming materials,** 19-3.1.5.4(c)
**Switches,** *see also* specific types of switches such as Transfer switches
Anesthetizing locations, 3-3.2.1.2(c), (Annex 2)2-2.3
Essential electrical systems, 3-4.2.1, 3-4.2.2.4(c), 3-5.3.2
Hyperbaric facilities, 19-2.7.3.6, A-19-2.7.3.6
Isolation switch, bypass, 3-4.2.1.7, A-3-4.2.1.7(c)
Test, 3-4.2.1.4(g), A-3-4.2.1.4(g)
**Synthetic materials,** *see* Textiles

**-T-**

**Task illumination (definition),** 2-2
**Telephones,** 9-2.1.10.1
**Temperature**
Anesthetizing locations, 5-4.1.5, 19-2.4.1, A-5-4.1, A-19-2.4.1.1
Cylinders or compressed gases, 4-3.1.1.2(a)(1)
Generator sets and, 3-4.1.1.9
Hazardous, 7-5.2.2.2(b)
Hyperbaric chambers, 19-2.4.1, 19-2.7.3.7, 19-3.2.1.4, A-19-2.4.1.1, A-19-2.7.3.7
**Terminals**
Definition, 2-2, A-2-2
Inlets, *see* Station inlets
**Test equipment,** 3-3.3.2.5
**Test logs,** 7-6.3.1.3
**Test switches,** 3-4.2.1.4(g), A-3-4.2.1.4(g)
**Textiles, electrostatic hazard,** 2-6.3.10(d), 19-3.1.5.4, 19-3.6.1.2, (Annex 2)2-6.3.8(h)
**Thermal standards,** 9-2.1.6.1
**Thorax (definition),** C-8.2
**Tissue processors,** 10-4.2.1, A-10-4.2.1
**Total hazard current,** *see* Hazard current, total
**Toxicity**
Anesthetizing locations, C-12.1.2.2
Electrical equipment, surfaces of, 9-2.1.6.2
Oxygen, *see* Oxygen, toxicity
Products of combustion, 6-2.3
Respiratory therapy, 8-2.2.1

**Trachea (definition),** C-8.2
**Tracheotomy tube,** C-8.1.3
Definition, 2-2, A-2-2
**Training, employee**
Anesthetizing locations, 12-4.1.2.10(d), C-12.4.6
Disasters, 11-5.3.3
Electrical equipment, 7-6.5
Gas equipment, 8-6.5
High frequency equipment, use of, (Annex 1)1-5.2
Hyperbaric facilities, 19-3.1.4.3
Laboratories, 10-2.1.4, 10-8.1.2, A-10-2.1.4.3, A-10-8.1.2
Respiratory therapy, C-8.3.6
**Transfer switches,** 3-4.2.1, 3-5.2.2.1, A-3-4.2.1.4, A-3-5.2.2.1
*see also* Switches
Automatic, 3-3.2.1.2(a)(1), 3-4.2.1.3 to 3-4.2.1.4, A-3-4.2.1.4
Load interruption, A-3-4.2.1.7(c)
New construction, 3-5.2.2.1, A-3-4.2.2.1, A-3-5.2.2.1
Nonautomatic, 3-4.2.1.5 to 3-4.2.1.6, 3-4.3.2.7, 3-5.3.2.7
Performance criteria and testing, 3-4.3.2, 3-5.3.2, 3-5.4.1.1, 3-6.3.2 to 3-6.3.3, 3-6.4.1.1
**Transformer, isolation,** *see* Isolation transformer
**Transportation of cylinders,** 4-3.5.5, 4-5.5.5
**Transurethral resection,** 1-7.5, (Annex 1)1-2.1.1.4
**Trap bottles,** C-8.1.4.5
**Trichloroethylene,** C-12.1.3.1.2
**Tube,** *see* Endotracheal tube; Tracheotomy tube
**Two-wire resistance technique,** A-7-5.1.3.2

**-U-**

**Ultrasonic diathermy,** (Annex 1)1-2.1.6
**Ultrasonic nebulizer (definition),** C-8.2
**Unattended laboratory operation,** 10-2.1.1.3, 10-4.2.2, A-10-2.1.1.3, A-10-4.2.2
Definition, 2-2
**Use point (definition),** 2-2
**Utility center (J box), (definition),** 2-2, A-2-2

**Voltages**
 Abnormal, 3-4.1.1.1(a)
 Grounding, A-3-3.3.2.3
 Measuring, 3-3.3.2.3, A-3-3.3.2.3

**-W-**

**Warning signs,** *see* Labeling
**Warning systems,** *see* Alarm systems
**Waste anesthetic gas disposal (WAGD) systems**
 Alarms, 4-3.3.2.4
 Anesthetizing locations, 5-4.1.6
 Definition, 2-2
 Designation colors, Table 4-3.1.2.4
 Distribution, Level 1, 4-3.3.2
 Hazards of, 4-2.4
 Hospitals, 12-3.4.5
 Inlets, 4-3.3.2.3
 Installation, 4-3.3.2.5
 Interface (definition), 2-2, A-2-2
 Level 1, 4-3.3
  Dedicated vacuum producers, 4-3.3.1.2
  Source, 4-3.3.1
 Level 2, 4-4.3, 4-4.4.3, 4-4.4.5.4
 Maintenance, 4-3.5.9.1
 Operating pressures, Table 4-3.1.2.4
 Other health care facilities, 13-3.4.7
 Performance criteria and testing, 4-3.4.3,
  4-3.5.9.2, 4-4.4.3

 Policies, 4-3.5.9
 Source, A-4-3.3.1
 Valves and dampers, 4-3.3.2.2
 Venturi-driven, 4-3.3.1.4
**Waste disposal**
 Anesthetic gas, 5-4.1.6
  *see also* Waste anesthetic gas disposal
  (WAGD) systems
 Hazardous materials, A-10-7.5, A-10-8.1.5
 Nonflammable gases in Level 3 system,
  4-5.2.2.2
**Water as extinguishing agent,** C-8.3.4,
  C-12.4.4.1, C-12-4.4.3
**Water handlines,** *see* Handlines, water
**Wet locations,** 3-3 2.1.2(f), 12-2.6(c),
  A-3-3.2.1.2(f)(1)
 Definition, 2-2
**Wiring,** *see* Electrical wiring
**Work space or room (generators),** 3-4.1.1.6
**Working pressure,** *see* Pressure, working
**Working supplies**
 Flammable and combustible liquids, 10-7.2.2,
  A-10-7.2.2
 Laboratory gases, 4-3.5.2.1(e)(2) to (3)

**-X-**

**X-ray equipment,** 12-4.1.2.6(b)
 Anesthetizing locations, (Annex 2)2-4.6(c)
 Hyperbaric facilities, 19-3.2.1.1